FISHES OF THE WORLD

G. U. Lindberg

FISHES OF THE WORLD

A KEY TO FAMILIES AND A CHECKLIST

Chief Editor B.E. Bykhovskii
Editor A.P. Andriyashev

Translated from Russian by Hilary Hardin

A HALSTED PRESS BOOK

JOHN WILEY & SONS
New York · Toronto

ISRAEL PROGRAM FOR SCIENTIFIC TRANSLATIONS
Jerusalem · London

Sole distributors for the Western Hemisphere and Japan

HALSTED PRESS, a division of
JOHN WILEY & SONS, INC., NEW YORK

Library of Congress Cataloging in Publication Data

Lindberg, Georgiĭ Ustinovich.
Fishes of the world.

Translation of *Opredelitel' i kharakteristika semeĭstv ryb mirovoĭ fauny.*
"A Halsted Press book."
Bibliography: p.
1. Fishes – Classification. I. Title.
QL618.L5513 597'.001'2 73-16382
ISBN 0-470-53565-2

Distributors for the U.K., Europe, Africa and the Middle East

JOHN WILEY & SONS, LTD., CHICHESTER

Distributed in the rest of the world by
KETER PUBLISHING HOUSE JERUSALEM LTD.
ISBN 0 7065 1345 2
IPST 22062

This book is a translation from Russian of
OPREDELITEL' I KHARAKTERISTIKA SEMEISTV RYB MIROVOI FAUNY
Izdatel'stvo "Nauka"
Leningrad, 1971

Printed in Israel

CONTENTS

INTRODUCTION

The admirable work by the late Academician Lev Semenovich Berg "Sistema ryboobraznykh i ryb, nyne zhivushchikh i iskopaemykh" (Classification of Fishes Both Recent and Fossil), which was published in 1940 and appeared in a second edition in 1955, after the author's death, gives a complete picture of the diversity of the fish fauna and of the relationships between fishes. It presents an exhaustive description of the large systematic units: orders, suborders, and superfamilies, but in most cases descriptions of families are absent or very brief, containing, as a rule, data on anatomy, especially with regard to the skull and other parts of the skeleton that are very important for determining group affiliation but are very hard to use for rapid and large-scale determinations, particularly for the one who is not a specialist. It thus did not dispense with the need for a handbook that would be suitable for a wide circle of readers, one that would not only encompass the whole spectrum of this fauna in general terms but would also enable one to determine, primarily according to the gross morphology, to which, out of the 550 extant families of fish, including about 5000 genera and from 20,000 to 22,000 species, a particular fish belongs (Add. II — Cohen, 1970).

In view of this, the author decided to compile a work which would acquaint the general reader with all the marine, brackish-water, and freshwater families of fish. The present book is thus intended as a practical manual for ichthyologists, students at fishery institutes and technical colleges, fishermen, and workers in the fish-processing industry, in particular for master crews of exploratory and fishing vessels operating long distance, and also for university students of biology. However, the nature lover may also find it of value, since it gives indexes of common names in several languages and includes some 1000 drawings which depict all the multiformity of the fish fauna in the seas and oceans, rivers and lakes of all the continents.

The keys to the orders are based mainly on Berg's work (1940), with the addition of data taken from Norman (1958), Matsubara (1955), and other authors. The same works and many others were used in drawing up the keys to the families. The information given in the keys is primarily on gross morphological characters, so as to permit determination without dissection as far as possible.

The basic principle to which the author adhered in making the keys was that of gradually excluding from the overall composition of the families of a particular order those families which differ markedly from fish belonging to other families in the form of the body, habitus, or structural features of different organs. However, in several cases it was possible to avoid including certain anatomical characters, such as the presence or absence of mesacoracoid, the Weberian apparatus, etc. In such cases, for dissection to be avoided, the determination must be made with the arbitrary assumption that the fish shows this character; if the determination in fact turns out to be a family the illustration of which does not resemble the fish under investigation, the determination must be repeated with the assumption that the fish does not have this character.

A few words on the technique of determination. In the keys the serial number of the thesis is followed by the number of the antithesis in parentheses, e.g., 1(4). Determination involves comparing the data given in thesis 1 and antithesis 4 and then deciding which fits the particular fish. If the antithesis gives the appropriate description, and the name of the family is not found there, the serial number of the thesis following it, 5(10), must be read and the content compared with that of its antithesis. If the thesis or antithesis leads to the name of a family, the determination is almost definitive. It remains to compare the fish with the drawing of the representative of this family, locate its description according to its number, and see whether the mode of life and distribution are appropriate. If they are, the determination is definite.

At this point it must be noted that the keys, based on gross morphological characters, are rather artificial. The characters of some rare genera and species may not find a place in the descriptions given in the theses. However, a check of these keys against actual material showed that the bulk of genera correspond to the characterization given. A full idea of a family may be obtained by integrating the content of all the theses adopted.

The order of determination is as follows. First the order is determined. Then, using the key of the order, the appropriate family is established. In the order Perciformes, which includes a very large number of families, the appropriate suborder (out of the 16) must first be determined, and then the family. In the suborder Percoidei, the correct superfamily out of the 13 is determined before the family.

The figures clarify the text of the keys.* However, they give only a very approximate notion of the family, as the modern systematics of orders, and often also of families, is built up mainly on the internal anatomy, and the gross morphological characters used here are highly variable not only within orders but also within families and subfamilies. Hence our use of the expressions "mostly," "as a rule," etc. Nevertheless, despite their incompleteness, they keys will, in the author's opinion, be of use as a preliminary guide to the composition of a catch and will help the reader to find his way among the astounding diversity of the world's fish fauna.

In the section "Checklist of families" the following information is given for each family: its scientific name, page references to both editions of Berg's work, the thesis of the key, and the number of the figure. Latin synonyms are given in parentheses with the sign =, while names of families which are not accepted as valid families in this work are given with the sign + in parentheses. Then follow common names in various languages.

In a new paragraph references are given to published sources which will broaden the reader's acquaintanceship with either the world literature on a given family or works on specific countries or seas. These are strictly

* For convenience of determination some figures are repeated in the key to the orders and in those to the suborders and families.

In the figure legends the names of several authors who are the sources are given in abbreviated form: B. and S. — Bigelow and Schroeder; J. and E. — Jordan and Evermann; L. and L. — Lindberg and Legeza; M. — Matsubara; W. and B. — Weber and Beaufort; GRWM — Greenwood et al.; MA — McAllister.

selected references, in view of the fact that the literature is now so voluminous that it is very difficult to make use of all of it. At any rate, the lists mention works that contain keys to the genera and species of the relevant family or that will provide additional general information. In several cases, surveys or monographs on a group of families are given in lists of works under the headings of superfamilies, suborders, and orders. Works published before 1917 are mentioned only in part, as an excellent bibliographic index is available (Dean, 1923).

In the following paragraph data are given on the distribution of the family in broad terms; for the Atlantic and Pacific oceans, the region of habitat is frequently specified (northern, eastern, southern or western), as some families occurring in the eastern Atlantic are absent in its western part, and what is more frequently the case, the reverse. As a rule, families absent in the eastern Pacific occur in the Indian Ocean and belong to the Indo-West Pacific group. Where the ranges of certain families are very narrow, the distribution is described in greater detail.

After the distribution, the composition of the family is mentioned, i. e., the number of genera and species. The numbers given are approximate since different authors disagree as to the generic and specific composition of the families. The number of genera is written as a figure, while the specific abundance is generally described in a phrase:

small number: 1—5	considerable number: 20—50
a few: 1—10	many: 50—100
several: 5—15	very many: 100—200
quite a large number: 10—20	extremely large number: 200—500.

A similar but abbreviated description is given for the systematic categories above the family; the number of smaller systematic groups entering this category is mentioned, and their serial number in parentheses.

The author did not aim to present a critical review of Berg's system. He has merely mentioned in footnotes or parentheses new ideas that have been put forward since 1940 on the validity of some orders accepted by Berg or on the validity of other orders that Berg considered suborders or superfamilies. Our main deviation from his system is our elimination of the order Thunniformes and the isolation of the suborder Cottoidei of the order Perciformes into an independent order Scorpaeniformes. Apart from this, the author considers that a greater number of groups are valid families, not subfamilies as held by Berg and some American authors (Greenwood, Rosen, Weitzman, and Myers, 1966—GRWM), this because such families are sufficiently different externally from related families and are therefore easy to determine. On the other hand, for many collective families, keys are given to the subfamilies and drawings of their representatives are provided.

The alphabetized list of publications on systematics makes it possible to interpret references to authors given in the descriptions of individual orders and families. It is to be noted that the works are arranged according to the name of the first author and in chronological order, while for the same year the order is taken from the number of a particular journal in which the work was published. In addition to this list, a list is given of works of more general interest and of monographs on different seas and countries, published since 1920.

In the indexes to scientific and common names, references are not to page numbers but to the number of the family, which can be found from the list of families. The position in the list of names of systematic categories higher than family is indicated by the number of the family before which it occurs, printed in italics. If the name of a family is set in light type, this means that it is a synonym or is not considered a valid family. For each family accepted as valid, its own number is supplemented with an index (the number of the order and of the thesis in the key) and with a figure reference.

Such is the content of this work in brief. It was initially proposed that only keys be published, but when they had been drafted out, the author decided to append a list of families with mention of synonyms. When this was completed, the work by the four American authors (GRWM) was published. Without entering into an examination of their system for the Teleostei, and diverging basically from Berg's system, it was found necessary to introduce the views of these authors into our own list of families. Apart from this, it was decided not to write the names of families in the form accepted by Berg, a view which this author shared (Lindberg, 1963), but to write them with strict observance of the rule of priority, as stipulated by the International Code of Zoological Nomenclature, adopted at the XV International Zoological Congress in London in July 1958. The first edition of this code appeared in 1961 and the second in 1964, from which the Russian translation was prepared, published in 1966. In conformity with the code, Berg's -oidae ending for superfamilies was changed to -oidea. Names of superfamilies that are found in the literature with the former ending and also names of orders with the ending - da (Stenzel) instead of -formes are not given in the synonymy.

In completing the work it was decided to supplement the data given in descriptions of families with a few references to the literature, so as to help the reader to orient himself in the systematics, understand the biology and ecology of different species, and perceive their importance for man, and, finally, to get an idea of the composition of the fish fauna of different countries and seas. The bibliographic references are by no means exhaustive, and the author will be very grateful to receive notice of works he has omitted and to be informed, or even better, to be sent, works that have appeared recently.

In conclusion, the author wishes to express his sincere gratitude to A. P. Andriyashev for undertaking the editing of this book and for his advice at the time it was being written, to T. S. Rass for his help with the Russian common names, and also to V. M. Makushok, A. V. Neelov, Z. V. Krasyukova, N. G. Popova, and other colleagues of the ichthyological laboratory for consultations and technical assistance, and to the artist M. M. Zharenkov for making most of the drawings.

Special thanks go to the management of the Zoological Institute of the Academy of Sciences of the USSR for the interest shown and help given in bringing this work to completion.

The author earnestly requests ichthyologists, systematists, and faunists to report to him on published summaries on systematics and the titles of review on the fish fauna of different seas and countries which have been omitted from the references given here, if possible, by way of an exchange. Any critical comments on the keys will also be gratefully received.

SYSTEMATIC LIST OF FAMILIES

The list gives: 1) the serial number of the order, suborder, superfamily, and family in front of the name; 2) the thesis under which the family is to be found in the keys; 3) the number (N) or numbers (NN) of the figures giving an idea of the appearance of representatives of the family.

1. **Branchiostomatiformes** 0—1

1. Branchiostomatidae 1—0; N 176

2. **Petromyzoniformes** 0—4

2. Petromyzonidae 2—0; NN 177, 178

3. **Myxiniformes** 0—5

3. Myxinidae 3—1; N 179
4. Eptatretidae 3—4; N 181
5. Paramyxinidae 3—3; N 180

4. **Heterodontiformes** 0—12

6. Heterodontidae 4—0; N 182

5. **Hexanchiformes** 0—10

7. Hexanchidae 5—2; N 184
8. Chlamydoselachidae 5—1; N 183

6. **Lamniformes** 0—13

9. Orectolobidae 6—4; N 186
10. Rhincodontidae 6—2; N 185
11. Odontaspididae 6—19; N 197
12. Scapanorhynchidae 6—20; N 198
13. Lamnidae 6—10; N 189
13a. Lamiostomatidae 6—10 fn.* N 189A
14. Cetorhinidae 6—11; N 190
15. Alopiidae 6—15; N 192
16. Scyliorhinidae 6—5; N 187
17. Pseudotriakidae 6—13; N 191
18. Carcharhinidae 6—17; NN 193—196
19. Sphyrnidae 6—7; N 188

7. **Squaliformes** 0—15

20. Squalidae 7—2; N 199
21. Dalatiidae 7—4; N 200
22. Echinorhinidae 7—5; N 201
23. Squatinidae 7—6; N 202

8. **Pristiophoriformes** 0—16

24. Pristiophoridae 8—0; N 203

9. **Rajiformes** 0—18

25. Rhinobatidae 9—6; N 206
25a. Gurgesiellidae 9—0 fn.
26. Rhynchobatidae 9—4; N 205
27. Pristidae 9—1; N 204
28. Platyrhinidae 9—7; N 207
29. Rajidae 9—10; N 209
30. Arhynchobatidae 9—12; N 210
31. Anacanthobatidae 9—14; N 211
32. Pseudorajidae 9—15; N 212
33. Dasyatidae 9—21; N 215
34. Urolophidae 9—17; N 214
35. Gymnuridae 9—23; N 217
36. Potamotrygonidae 9—22; N 216
37. Myliobatidae 9—25; N 218
38. Mobulidae 9—26; N 219

10. **Torpediniformes** 0—19

39. Torpedinidae 10—1; N 220
40. Narkidae 10—3; N 221
41. Temeridae 10—4

11. **Chimaeriformes** 0—21

42. Chimaeridae 11—2; N 222
43. Rhinochimaeridae 11—3; N 223
44. Callorhynchidae 11—4; N 224

12. **Ceratodiformes** 0—24

45. Ceratodidae 12—0; N 225

13. **Lepidosireniformes** 0—25

46. Lepidosirenidae 13—1; N 226
47. Protopteridae 13—2; N 227

14. **Coelacanthiformes** 0—27

48. Latimeriidae 14—0; N 228

15. **Polypteriformes** 0—29

49. Polypteridae 15—0; N 229

* [fn. — footnote.]

16. **Acipenseriformes** 0—31

50. Acipenseridae 16—1; NN 230, 231
51. Polyodontidae 16—2; NN 232, 233

17. **Amiiformes** 0—34

52. Amiidae 17—0; N 234

18. **Lepisosteiformes** 0—35

53. Lepisosteidae 18—0; N 235

19. **Clupeiformes** 0—79

54. Elopidae 19—45; N 266
55. Megalopidae 19—46; N 267
56. Albulidae 19—49; N 268
57. Pterothrissidae 19—50; N 269
58. Clupeidae 19—52; NN 271, 273, 275
58a. Dorosomatidae 19—52.8; N 274
58b. Dussumieridae 19—52.10; N 276
58c. Congothrissidae 19—52.0 fn.
59. Engraulidae 19—53; NN 277, 278
60. Alepocephalidae 19—40; N 263
60a. Leptochilichthyidae 19—40 fn.
60b. Bathyprionidae 19—40 fn.; N 263A
61. Searsiidae 19—39; NN 260—262
62. Dolichopterygidae 19—37, 67, 74; NN 259, 283, 287
63. Macristiidae 19—42; 264
64. Chirocentridae 19—22; N 248
65. Chanidae 19—15; N 243
66. Kneriidae 19—18; N 244
67. Phractolaemidae 19—19; N 245
68. Cromeriidae 19—20; N 246
69. Salmonidae 19—79; N 288
70. Thymallidae 19—80; N 289
71. Plecoglossidae 19—81; N 290
72. Osmeridae 19—83; N 291
73. Salangidae 19—86; N 293
74. Retropinnidae 19—87; N 294
75. Aplochitonidae 19—84; N 292
76. Dalliidae 19—5; N 237
77. Umbridae 19—6; N 238
78. Esocidae 19—3; N 236
79. Gonostomatidae 19—91; NN 295, 296
80. Sternoptychidae 19—92; N 297
81. Stomiatidae 19—95; N 299
82. Chauliodontidae 19—94; N 298
83. Astronesthidae 19—98; N 300
84. Melanostomiatidae 19—101; N 302
85. Malacosteidae 19—102; N 303
86. Idiacanthidae 19—99; N 301
87. Argentinidae 19—70; N 284
88. Bathylagidae 19—73; N 286
89. Microstomatidae 19—71; N 285
90. Xenophthalmichthyidae 19—66; N 282 A
91. Opisthoproctidae 19—61; N 281
92. Macropinnidae 19—64; N 282
93. Gonorynchidae 19—12; N 242
94. Hiodontidae 19—10; N 241
95. Notopteridae 19—9; N 240
96. Arapaimidae 19—30; N 254
97. Osteoglossidae 19—29; NN 252, 253
98. Heterotidae 19—27; N 251
99. Denticipitidae 19—25; NN 249, 250
100. Pantodontidae 19—32; N 255
101. Anotopteridae 19—55; N 279; supp.* 23—27; N 310
102. Rosauridae 19—57; N 280
103. Bathylaconidae 19—34; N 256

20. **Miripinniformes** 0—45

104. Miripinnidae 20—1; NN 304, 305
104a. Kasidoridae 20—0 fn.; N 303A
104b. Megalomycteridae 20—0 fn.; N 35
105. Eutaeniophoridae 20—2; NN 306, 307

21. **Bathyclupeiformes** 0—78

106. Bathyclupeidae 21—0; N 308

22. **Galaxiiformes** 0—83

107. Galaxiidae 22—0; N 309

23. **Myctophiformes** 0—81

108. Synodontidae 23—21; N 320; supp. 23—6
108a. Harpadontidae 23—23; N 321
108b. Bathysauridae supp. 23—7
109. Aulopodidae 23—17; N 318; supp. 23—1
110. Scopelarchidae 23—24; N 322; supp. 23—30
111. Evermannellidae 23—12; N 316; supp. 23—29
112. Paralepididae 23—7; NN 313, 314; supp. 23—23
113. Chlorophthalmidae 23—6; N 312; supp. 23—14
114. Bathypteroidae 23—25; NN 323; supp. 23—11
114a. Ipnopidae 23—19; N 319; supp. 23—12
115. Scopelosauridae 23—10; N 315; supp. 23—19
116. Omosudidae 23—13; N 317; supp. 23—24
117. Alepisauridae 23—3; N 311; supp. 23—26
118. Myctophidae 23—27; N 324; supp. 23—16
118a. Neoscopelidae 23—28; N 325; supp. 23—17

24. **Cetomimiformes** 0—81 fn.

119. Cetomimidae 24—1; N 326
120. Rondeletiidae 24—4; N 328; 43—5
121. Barbourisiidae 24—3; N 327

* [supp. — supplement.]

25. **Ateleopodiformes** 0—85

122. Ateleopodidae 25—0; N 329

26. **Giganturiformes** 0—47

123. Giganturidae 26—0; N 330

27. **Saccopharyngiformes** 0—63

124. Saccopharyngidae 27—1; N 333
125. Eurypharyngidae 27—2; N 334

28. **Monognathiformes** 0—61

126. Monognathidae 28—0; N 335

29. **Mormyriformes** 0—76

127. Gymnarchidae 29—1; N 336
128. Mormyridae 29—2; N 337

30. **Cypriniformes** 0—73

129. Characidae 30—3 fn.; N 338
129a. Erythrinidae 30—3 fn.; N 339
129b. Hepsetidae 30—3 fn.; N 340
129c. Cynodontidae 30—3 fn.; N 341
129d. Lebiasinidae 30—3 fn.; N 342
130. Gasteropelecidae 30—3 fn.; N 343
131. Ctenoluciidae 30—3 fn.; N 344
132. Anostomidae 30—3 fn.; N 345
132a. Prochilodontidae 30—3 fn.; N 346
132b. Curimatidae 30—3 fn.; N 347
132c. Chilodontidae 30—3 fn.; N 348
133. Hemiodontidae 30—3 fn.; N 349
133a. Parodontidae 30—3 fn.; N 350
134. Citharinidae 30—3 fn.; N 351
134a. Distichodontidae 30—3 fn.; N 352
134b. Ichthyboridae 30—3 fn.; N 353
135. Rhamphichthyidae 30—6; N 354
136. Apteronotidae 30—7; N 355
137. Gymnotidae 30—9; N 356
138. Electrophoridae 30—10; N 357
139. Catostomidae 30—14; N 359, 360
140. Cyprinidae 30—15; NN 362—371, 374, 375
140a. Psilorhynchidae 30—15 fn.; NN 372, 373
141. Gyrinocheilidae 30—19; N 380
142. Homalopteridae 30—18; NN 377, 378
142a. Gastromyzonidae 30—18 fn.; N 379
143. Cobitidae 30—17; N 376
144. Diplomystidae 30—63; N 404
145. Ariidae 30—43, 56, 60, 66; NN 393, 400, 402, 405
146. Doradidae 30—83; N 416
147. Auchenipteridae 30—74; N 409
148. Ageneiosidae 30—75; N 410
149. Plotosidae 30—30; N 384
150. Siluridae 30—25; N 381
151. Bagridae 30—38, 57; NN 389, 401
151a. Cranoglanididae 30—38 fn.; N 390
152. Doiichthyidae 30—33 fn.; N 387
153. Ictaluridae 30—61; N 403
154. Amblycipitidae 30—36; N 388
155. Akysidae 30—44; N 394
156. Sisoridae 30—42; N 392
157. Amphiliidae 30—52; N 398
158. Chacidae 30—31; N 385
159. Schilbeidae 30—47; N 395
159a. Pangasiidae 30—33; N 386
160. Heteropneustidae 30—26; N 382
161. Clariidae 30—27, 48; NN 383, 396
162. Olyridae 30—39; N 391
163. Mochokidae 30—54; N 399
164. Malapteruridae 30—50; N 397
165. Pimelodidae 30—72; N 406
166. Callophysidae 30—73
167. Helogeneidae 30—72 fn.; N 407
168. Hypophthalmidae 30—72 fn.; N 408
169. Trichomycteridae 30—80; NN 413, 414
170. Cetopsidae 30—79; N 412
171. Aspredinidae 30—78; N 411
172. Callichthyidae 30—82; N 415
173. Loricariidae 30—86; N 419
174. Astroblepidae 30—85; N 418

31. **Anguilliformes** 0—49

175. Derichthyidae 31—10; N 427
176. Anguillidae 31—21; N 431
177. Simenchelyidae 31—22; N 432
178. Xenocongridae 31—15; N 429
179. Myrocongridae 31—19
180. Muraenidae 31—13; N 428
181. Heterenchelyidae 31—16; N 430
182. Moringuidae 31—23; N 433
183. Muraenesocidae 31—28; N 434
184. Neenchelyidae 31—29; N 435
185. Nettastomatidae 31—31; N 436
186. Nessorhamphidae 31—32; N 437
187. Congridae 31—34; N 438
187a. Todaridae 31—34 fn.
188. Echelidae 31—36; N 439
189. Ophichthidae 31—37; N 440
190. Ilyophidae 31—40; N 441
191. Dysommidae 31—41; N 442
191a. Dysomminidae 31—41 fn.; N 443
192. Synaphobranchidae 31—42; N 444
193. Serrivomeridae 31—2; N 422
194. Nemichthyidae 31—6; N 424
195. Cyemidae 31—4; N 423
196. Avocettinopsidae 31—7; N 425
197. Macrocephenchelyidae 31—0 fn.; N 420
198. Aoteidae 31—0 fn.; N 421

32. **Halosauriformes** 0—55

199. Halosauridae 32—0; N 445

33. **Notacanthiformes** 0—56

200. Lipogenyidae 33—1; N 446
201. Notacanthidae 33—2; NN 447, 448

34. **Beloniformes** 0—101

202. Belonidae 34—2; N 450
203. Scomberesocidae 34—3; N 451
204. Hemiramphidae 34—5; N 453
205. Exocoetidae 34—8; N 457
206. Oxyporhamphidae 34—7; N 456

35. **Gadiformes** 0—159

207. Muraenolepididae 35—6; N 464
208. Moridae 35—2; N 459
208a. Melanonidae 35—2 fn.
209. Bregmacerotidae 35—4; N 460
210. Gadidae 35—5; N 461, 463
210a. Merlucciidae 35—5 fn.; N 462

36. **Macrouriformes** 0—160, 165

211. Macrouridae 36—1; NN 465—467
212. Macrouroididae 36—2; N 468

37. **Gasterosteiformes** 0—108

213. Gasterosteidae 37—1; N 469
214. Aulorhynchidae 37—2; N 470

38. **Syngnathiformes** 0—69

215. Indostomidae 38—10; N 478
216. Aulostomidae 38—3; N 473
217. Fistulariidae 38—4; NN 474, 475
218. Macrorhamphosidae 38—6; N 476
219. Centriscidae 38—7; N 477
220. Solenostomidae 38—11; N 479
221. Syngnathidae 38—12; NN 480—485

39. **Lampridiformes** 0—93, 137

222. Lampridae 39—2; N 486
223. Veliferidae 39—3; N 487
224. Lophotidae 39—7; N 490
225. Regalecidae 39—9; N 491
226. Trachipteridae 39—10; N 492
227. Stylephoridae 39—5; NN 488, 489

40. **Cyprinodontiformes** 0—102, 157

228. Amblyopsidae 40—1; NN 493, 494
229. Cyprinodontidae 40—6; NN 497—499
229a. Oryziatidae 40—6 fn.; N 496
230. Horaichthyidae 40—8; N 500
231. Tomeuridae 40—9; NN 501, 502
232. Adrianichthyidae 40—4; N 495
233. Goodeidae 40—15; N 505
234. Jenynsiidae 40—13; N 504
235. Anablepidae 40—11; N 503
236. Poeciliidae 40—16; NN 506, 507

41. **Phallostethiformes** 0—43

237. Phallostethidae 41—0; N 508
237a. Neostethidae 41—0 fn.; N 509

42. **Percopsiformes** 0—99, 104, 162

238. Percopsidae 42—1; N 510
239. Aphredoderidae 42—2; N 511

43. **Stephanoberyciformes** 0—95, 164

240. Stephanoberycidae 43—3; N 512
241. Rondeletiidae 43—5; 24—4; N 514
242. Anoplogasteridae 43—7; N 515
243. Korsogasteridae 43—8; N 516
244. Melamphaeidae 43—4; N 513

44. **Beryciformes** 0—106, 126, 138, 140, 142, 144, 147, 148, 149

245. Polymixiidae 44—1; N 517
246. Berycidae 44—13; N 523
247. Diretmidae 44—7; N 520
247a. Paradiretmidae 44—7 fn.; N 520A
248. Caristiidae 44—16; 50.1.1—45; NN 525, 624
249. Trachichthyidae 44—12; N 522
250. Monocentridae 44—3; N 518
251—252. Anomalopidae 44—5; N 519
253. Holocentridae 44—9; N 521
254. Sorosichthyidae 44—9 fn.
255. Gibberichthyidae 44—15; N 524

45. **Zeiformes** 0—167

256. Zeidae 45—1; NN 527
256a. Parazenidae 45—1 fn.; N 528
256b. Macrurocyttidae 45—1 fn.; N 529
256c. Oreosomatidae 45—1 fn.; N 530
257. Grammicolepididae 45—2; N 531

46. **Mugiliformes** 0—128

258. Sphyraenidae 46—1; N 532
259. Mugilidae 46—3; NN 533—535
260. Atherinidae 46—4; NN 536
260a. Melanotaeniidae 46—4 fn.; N 537
260b. Isonidae 46—4 fn.; N 538

47. **Polynemiformes** 0—71

261. Polynemidae 47—0; N 539

48. **Channiformes** 0—88

262. Channidae 48—0; N 540

49. **Synbranchiformes** 0—52

263. Alabetidae 49—1; N 541
264. Synbranchidae 49—3; NN 542, 543
265. Amphipnoidae 49—4; N 544

50. **Perciformes** 0—90, 129, 170

50.1. P e r c o i d e i 50.0—30

50.1.1. Percoidea 50.1.0—24

266. Centropomidae 50.1.1—85, 123; NN 648, 675—677
267. Serranidae 50.1.1—148, 164; NN 705
267a. Grammistidae 50.1.1—164 fn.; N 706
267b. Percichthyidae 50.1.1—164 fn.
268. Pseudochromidae 50.1.1—72; N 641
269. Pseudogrammidae 50.1.1—74; N 642
270. Grammidae 50.1.1—63, 75; NN 636, 643
271. Glaucosomidae 50.1.1—153; N 699
272. Theraponidae 50.1.1—163; N 704
273. Banjosidae 50.1.1—102; N 657
274. Pseudoplesiopidae 50.1.1—56; N 631
275. Anisochromidae 50.1.1—57; N 632
276. Plesiopidae 50.1.1—70, 161; NN 640, 703
277. Acanthoclinidae 50.1.1—6; N 595
278. Kuhliidae 50.1.1—159; N 702
279. Centrarchidae 50.1.1—157; N 701
280. Priacanthidae 50.1.1—152, 155; NN 698, 700
281. Apogonidae 50.1.1—94; NN 652,653
281a. Henichthyidae 50.1.1—94 fn.
282. Acropomatidae 50.1.1—90; N 650
283. Percidae 50.1.1—95, 149; NN 654, 697
284. Sillaginidae 50.1.1—80, 146; NN 646, 696
285. Branchiostegidae 50.1.1—60, 144; NN 634, 695
286. Malacanthidae 50.1.1—59; N 633
287. Labracoglossidae 50.1.1—141; N 694
288. Lactariidae 50.1.1—78; N 645
289. Pomatomidae 50.1.1—82; N 647
290. Scombropidae 50.1.1—92; N 651
291. Rachycentridae 50.1.1—11; N 598
292. Carangidae 50.1.1—13; NN 600—604
293. Nematistiidae 50.1.1—15; N 605
294. Formionidae 50.1.1—40; N 621
295. Menidae 50.1.1—43; N 623
296. Bramidae 50.1.1—48; NN 625, 626
297. Pteraclidae 50.1.1—49; N 627
298. Coryphaenidae 50.1.1—52; N 630
299. Arripidae 50.1.1—124; N 678
300. Emmelichthyidae 50.1.1—87, 109; NN 649, 662
301. Inermiidae 50.1.1—88
302. Lutjanidae 50.1.1—128; NN 679—681
303. Aphareidae 50.1.1—62; N 635
304. Caesionidae 50.1.1—138; N 689
305. Nemipteridae 50.1.1—130; N 683
306. Lobotidae 50.1.1—107, 132; NN 661, 684
307. Leiognathidae 50.1.1—111; N 663
308. Gerridae 50.1.1—112; N 664
309. Pomadasyidae 50.1.1—139; NN 690—693
310. Sciaenidae 50.1.1—100; N 656
311. Lethrinidae 50.1.1—134; N 686
312. Pentapodidae 50.1.1—136; NN 687, 688
313. Sparidae 50.1.1—114; NN 665—668
314. Centracanthidae 50.1.1—105; NN 659, 660
315. Mullidae 50.1.1—9; N 597
316. Monodactylidae 50.1.1—24; N 610
317. Pempheridae 50.1.1—50; NN 628
317a. Leptobramidae 50.1.1—50.2 fn.; N 629
318. Toxotidae 50.1.1—17; N 606
319. Scorpididae 50.1.1—129; N 682
320. Coracinidae 50.1.1—119; N 672
321. Kyphosidae 50.1.1—120; N 674
322. Girellidae 50.1.1—117; N 671
323. Ephippidae 50.1.1—22, 32; N N609, 616
324. Rhinoprenidae 50.1.1—32 fn.; N 616A
325. Platacidae 50.1.1—25; N 612
326. Drepanidae 50.1.1—34; N 617
327. Scatophagidae 50.1.1—31; N 615
328. Chaetodontidae 50.1.1—36, 98; NN 618, 619, 655
329. Caproidae 50.1.1—37; N 620
330. Enoplosidae 50.1.1—21; N 608
331. Pentacerotidae 50.1.1—28; N 613
332. Pristolepididae 50.1.1—67; N 638
333. Nandidae 50.1.1—68; N 639
333a, 417d. Badidae 50.1.1—68; N 848A
334. Polycentridae 50.1.1—7; N 596
335. Oplegnathidae 50.1.1—3; N 593, 594
336. Cichlidae 50.1.1—1; N 592

50.1.2. Cepoloidea 50.1.0—5

337. Cepolidae 50.1.2—0; N 707

50.1.3. Embiotocoidea 50.1.0—20

338. Embiotocidae 50.1.3—0; N 708

50.1.4. Pomacentroidea 50.1.0—17

339. Pomacentridae 50.1.4—0; NN 709—712

50.1.5. Labroidea 50.1.0—21

340. Labridae 50.1.5—1; NN 713—720
341. Odacidae 50.1.5—3; N 721
342. Scaridae 50.1.5—4; NN 723, 724

50.1.6. Gadopsoidea 50.1.0—3

343. Gadopsidae 50.1.6—0; N 725

50.1.7. Cirrhitoidea 50.1.0—13

344. Cirrhitidae 50.1.7—2; N 726
345. Chironemidae 50.1.7—5, N 728
346. Aplodactylidae 50.1.7—4; N 727
347. Cheilodactylidae 50.1.7—7; N 729
347a. Gregoryinidae 50.1.7—7 fn.; N 730
348. Latridae 50.1.7—8; N 731

50.1.8. Trichodontoidea 50.1.0—9

349. Trichodontidae 50.1.8—0; N 732

50.1.9. Trachinoidea 50.1.0—23

350. Opisthognathidae 50.1.9—25; N 745
351. Owstoniidae 50.1.9—24; N 744
352. Bathymasteridae 50.1.9—26; N 746
353. Mugiloididae 50.1.9—9; N 736
354. Cheimarrichthyidae 50.1.9—13; N 738
355. Trachinidae 50.1.9—6; N 735
356. Percophididae 50.1.9—5; N 734
357. Bembropsidae 50.1.9—4; N 733
358. Hemerocoetidae 50.1.9—10; N 737
359. Trichonotidae 50.1.9—15; N 739
360. Creediidae 50.1.9—19; N 742
361. Kraemeriidae 50.1.9—16; 50.16—7; NN 740, 862
362. Limnichthyidae 50.1.9—18; N 741
363. Oxudercidae 50.1.9—21; N 743

50.1.10. Uranoscopoidea 50.1.0—1

364. Leptoscopidae 50.1.10—3; N 748
365. Dactyloscopidae 50.1.10—4; N 749
366. Uranoscopidae 50.1.10—2; N 747

50.1.11. Champsodontoidea 50.1.0—11

367. Champsodontidae 50.1.11—0; N 750

50.1.12. Chiasmodontoidea 50.1.0—8

368. Chiasmodontidae 50.1.12—0; N 751

50.1.13. Notothenioidea 50.1.0—16

369. Bovichthyidae 50.1.13—1; N 752
370. Nototheniidae 50.1.13—5; N 753
371. Harpagiferidae 50.1.13—6; N 754
372. Bathydraconidae 50.1.13—7; N 755
373. Channicthyidae 50.1.13—8; N 756

50.2. Blennioidei 50.0—27

374. Blenniidae 50.2—14; NN 770, 771
374a. Chaenopsidae 50.2—14.1; N 769
375. Anarhichadidae 50.2—1; N 762
376. Xenocephalidae 50.2—0 fn.; 50.0—27 fn.
377. Congrogadidae 50.2—27; N 792
378. Haliophidae 50.2—21; N 789
379. Notograptidae 50.2—0 fn.; 50.0—27 fn.; N 757
380. Peronedysidae 50.2—0 fn.; 50.0—27 fn.; N 758
381. Ophiclinidae 50.2—0 fn.; 50.0—27 fn.; N 759
382. Clinidae 50.2—13; NN 767, 768
383. Tripterygiidae 50.2—11; N 766
384. Stichaeidae 50.2—17; NN 779—786
385. Cryptacanthodidae 50.2—6; N 764
386. Pholididae 50.2—16; NN 776, 777
387. Ptilichthyidae 50.2—3; N 763
388. Zoarcidae 50.2—28; NN 793—804
389. Lycodapodidae 50.2—19; N 787
390. Derepodichthyidae 50.2—25; N 791
391. Scytalinidae 50.2—23; N 790
392. Schindleriidae 50.2—0 fn.; 50.0—27 fn.; N 760
393. Zaproridae 50.2—8; N 765

50.3. Ophidioidei 50.0—23

394. Brotulidae 50.3—2; NN 805—808
394a. Aphyonidae see Add. II
395. Ophidiidae 50.3—3; NN 809, 810
396. Carapidae 50.3—4; N 811
396a. Pyramodontidae 50.3—4 fn.; N 813
397. Disparichthyidae 50.3—4 fn.; N 812

50.4. Ammodytoidei 50.0—25

398. Ammodytidae 50.4—3; N 815
399. Bleekeriidae 50.4—2; N 814
400. Hypoptychidae 50.4—4; N 816

50.5. Callionymoidei 50.0—13

401. Callionymidae 50.5—2; N 818
402. Draconettidae 50.5—1; N 817

50.6. Siganoidei 50.0—3

403. Siganidae 50.6—0; N 819

50.7. Acanthuroidei 50.0—29

404. Zanclidae 50.7—2; N 821
405. Acanthuridae 50.7—1; N 820

50.8. Trichiuroidei 50.0—19

406. Gempylidae 50.8—1; N 822
406a. Scombrolabracidae 50.8—1 fn.; N 882A
407. Trichiuridae 50.8—4; N 824
408. Lepidopidae 50.8—3; N 823

50.9. Scombroidei 50.0—18

409. Scombridae 50.9—1; NN 825—829

410. Istiophoridae 50.9—3; N 830
411. Xiphiidae 50.9—4; N 831

50.10. Luvaroidei 50.0—16

412. Luvaridae 50.10—0; N 832

50.11. Tetragonuroidei 50.0—9

413. Tetragonuridae 50.11—0; N 833; supp. 50.12—5

50.12. Stromateoidei 50.0—11

414. Stromateidae 50.12—2; N 834; supp. 50.12—8
414a. Centrolophidae 50.12—2 fn.; N 837; supp. 50.12—7
415. Pampidae 50.12—4; N 842; supp. 50.12—8
416. Nomeidae 50.12—3; N 838; supp. 50.12—3.
416a. Ariommidae supp. 50.12—4; N 844A
416b. Amarsipidae 50.12—3 fn.

50.13. Anabantoidei 50.0—6

417. Anabantidae 50.13—3; N 846
417a. Belontiidae 50.13—1; N 845
417b. Helostomatidae 50.13—6; N 848
417c. Osphronemidae 50.13—5; N 847
417d, 333a. Badidae 50.13—0 fn.; N 848A

50.14. Luciocephaloidei 50.0—7

418. Luciocephalidae 50.14—0; N 849

50.15. Kurtoidei 50.0—1

419. Kurtidae 50.15—0; N 850

50.16. Gobioidei 50.0—21

420. Eleotridae 50.16—3.1; NN 852
420a. Rhyacichthyidae 50.16—3.2; N 854
421. Gobiidae 50.16—5; NN 855—860
421a. Trypauchenidae 50.16—10; N 863
422. Gobioididae 50.16—11; N 864
423. Periophthalmidae 50.16—6; N 861
424. Microdesmidae 50.16—12; 50.0—21 fn.; 50.2—0 fn.; NN 761, 865

51. **Scorpaeniformes** 0—111, 114, 116, 117, 119, 121, 123, 124, 133

425. Scorpaenidae 51—49, 55; NN 916, 919
426. Triglidae 51—30; N 906
427. Peristediidae 51—31; N 907
428. Caracanthidae 51—51; N 917
429. Aploactinidae 51—48; N 915
430. Synancejidae 51—54; N 918
431. Pataecidae 51—45; N 914
432. Gnathanacanthidae 51—46
433. Hexagrammidae 51—58; NN 921, 922
433a. Zaniolepididae 51—58 fn.; N 923
434. Anoplopomatidae 51—57; N 920
435. Platycephalidae 51—38; N 910
436. Parabembridae 51—35; N 908
437. Bembridae 51—37; N 909
438. Hoplichthyidae 51—39; N 911
439. Congiopodidae 51—41; NN 912, 913
440. Cottidae 51—27; NN 891—904
441. Scorpaenichthyidae 51—1; N 866
442. Synchiridae 51—14; N 884
443. Rhamphocottidae 51—16; N 885
444. Ereuniidae 51—19; N 886
445. Marukawichthyidae 51—20; N 887
446. Hemitripteridae 51—23; N 888
447. Blepsiidae 51—24; N 889
448. Ascelichthyidae 51—26; N 890
449. Comephoridae 51—10; N 880
450. Normanichthyidae 51—3 fn.; N 867
451. Psychrolutidae 51—12; NN 881, 883
451a. Cottunculidae 51—12 fn.; N 882
452. Agonidae 51—8; NN 872—879
453. Cyclopteridae 51—5; N 868
454. Liparidae 51—6; N 869
455. Eutelichthyidae 51—6 CH.; N 870

52. **Dactylopteriformes** 0—132

456. Dactylopteridae 52—0; N 924

53. **Pleuronectiformes** 0—37

457. Psettodidae 53—1; N 925
458. Bothidae 53—6; NN 928, 931
458a. Scophthalmidae 53—6,4; N 932
459. Citharidae 53—4; NN 926, 927
460. Pleuronectidae 53—7; NN 935, 937, 939—941
461. Soleidae 53—9; NN 942—947
462. Cynoglossidae 53—10; NN 948, 949

54. **Icosteiformes** 0—97, 156

463. Icosteidae 54—0; N 950

55. **Chaudhuriiformes** 0—59

464. Chaudhuriidae 55—0; N 951

56. **Mastacembeliformes** 0—58

465. Mastacembelidae 56—0; N 952

57. **Echeneiformes** 0—65

466. Echeneidae 57—0; N 953

58. **Tetraodontiformes** 0—151

467. Triacanthidae 58—4; N 955
468. Triacanthodidae 58—3; N 954
469. Balistidae 58—8; N 956
470. Aluteridae 58—9; N 957
471. Psilocephalidae 58—6
472. Ostraciontidae 58—13; N 959
473. Aracanidae 58—12; N 958
474. Triodontidae 58—17; N 960
475. Tetraodontidae 58—18; NN 961, 962
476. Diodontidae 58—19; N 963
477. Molidae 58—20; N 964

59. **Gobiesociformes** 0—41

478. Gobiesocidae 59—0; NN 965, 966

60. **Batrachoidiformes** 0—169

479. Batrachoididae 60—0; N 967

61. **Lophiiformes** 0—67

480. Lophiidae 61—2; N 968
480a. Galatheathaumatidae 480 fn.
481. Antennariidae 61—6; N 970
482. Brachionichthyidae 61—5; N 969
483. Chaunacidae 61—8; N 971
484. Ogcocephalidae 61—9; N 972
485. Melanocetidae 61—15; N 975
486. Diceratiidae 61—19; N 977
487. Himantolophidae 61—27; N 981
488. Oneirodidae 61—26; 61—30; NN 980, 984
489. Centrophrynidae 61—24; N 979
490. Gigantactinidae 61—21; N 978
491. Neoceratiidae 61—11; N 973
492. Ceratiidae 61—17; N 976
493. Caulophrynidae 61—13; N 974
494. Linophrynidae 61—29; NN 982, 983

62. **Pegasiformes** 0—39

495. Pegasidae 62—0; N 985

KEYS

Procedure and order of determination

Procedure. The serial number of the thesis is followed by the number of the antithesis in parentheses, e.g., 1 (4). The descriptions found under thesis 1 and antithesis 4 are compared to decide which of them fits the characteristics of the fish in question. If the thesis or antithesis is appropriate but does not give the name of the family, the following thesis must be read, 5 (10), and its content compared with that of its antithesis, 10. If, on the other hand, the selected thesis or antithesis does lead to the family name, the determination is almost definitive. It remains to compare the given fish with the figure of the representative of the family, given nearby, and then locate this family according to its number in the fourth section, "Checklist of families" to see whether the fish corresponds to this family in mode of life and distribution. If it does, the determination is definitive.

Order of determination. The order to which the fish belongs is first found by consulting the key of 62 orders with the index 0. Then, using the number of the order, the key to the families of this order is sought and the family is determined. In the order Perciformes, which includes 16 suborders, the correct suborder must first be found from the key with the index 50.0, and in the largest suborder, the Percoidei, the appropriate superfamily must be found out of the 13 superfamilies in the key with the index 50.1.0. Determination of families is done by using the keys with the indexes of the suborders from 50.1.1 to 50.1.13.

The indexes of orders, suborders, and superfamilies are printed in Italicized figures in the bottom corner of the page.

0 — key to orders
1 — 49 and 51 — 62 — keys to families included in a given order
50.0 — keys to suborders of the order Perciformes (order 50)
50.1.0 — key to superfamilies of the suborder Percoidei of the order Perciformes
50.1.1 — 50.1.13 — keys to families included in the superfamily Percoidea of the suborder Percoidei
50.2—50.16 — keys to the families of the other 15 suborders of the order Perciformes

The names of orders, suborders, superfamilies, and families are preceded by a serial number by which they are designated in the section "Checklist of families." In the case of subfamilies, the serial number of the subfamily is given after the number of the family, from which it is separated by a period. The names of the orders, suborders, and superfamilies are followed by the index to the key and the numbers of the theses.

Text given in square brackets is intended for ichthyological specialists.

Glossary of terms

Explanation of some terms used in the keys, with reference to figures in the text.

Accessory fins — numbering 4 to 10 and situated behind the dorsal and anal fins (Figure 825).

Adipose fin — a median fin without rays, situated behind the dorsal fin (Figure 288). Usually small, but occasionally long in the Siluridae (Figure 399).

Alae — scalelike appendages at the base of the caudal fin (Figure 243).

Ascending process of premaxillary bone — see Figure 659, in which the anterior end of the ascending process is shown by a dotted line.

Axillary lobe — enlarged scale at the base of the ventral fin (Figures 660, 664).

Bony plates — rhomboid plates arranged in rows on the body of Acipenseridae (Figure 21).

Branchiostegal membrane — covers the gill opening during the swallowing of water.

Branchiostegal rays — serve to hold the branchiostegal membrane spread out.

Caudal fin — median fin at the end of the caudal part of the body; it may be rounded (Figure 614), truncate (Figure 606), with a notch (Figure 607), with a deep incision (Figure 599), forked (Figure 604), or it may be of a different form.

Caudal peduncle — the part of the body behind the anal fin.

Chin — area between the lower jaw and the point of attachment of the branchiostegal membranes.

Claspers — modified ventral fins in male sharks and rays adapted for internal fertilization (Figures 209, 215).

Ctenoid scales — scales which, unlike the cycloid type, have spines or cilia.

Cycloid scales — resembling a thin, smooth plate of oval form, streaked with oval and radial striae. The scales are as a rule arranged in oblique rows, superimposed tilelike on each other.

Fin rays — **unbranched** and **branched** (Figure 773, center); unbranched rays classed as **jointed** (Figure 773, at the sides) and **unjointed** (Figure 778, top); the latter may be soft or hard, generally spiny, sometimes markedly enlarged and thickened.

Fins — median (D — dorsal, A — anal, C — caudal, and adipose) or paired (P — pectoral, V — ventral).

Ganoid scales — scales covered on the outside with a layer of ganoin, having the form of rhombic plates. An example is L e p i s o s t e u s (Figure 235). In the Acipenseridae these scales are rudimentary and occur on the upper caudal lobe in the form of fulcra (Figure 232).

Genipores — very small pores on the head of Gobiidae and some other fishes.

Gill cover — covers the branchial cavity and as a rule consists of 4 bones: operculum, suboperculum, preoperculum, and interoperculum (Figure 105).

Gill opening — in teleosts, a slit of various size through which water issues from the gill cavity to the outside when it is propelled through the gills during respiration.

Gill rakers — situated on the inside of the gill arch, of diverse form, from long, thin plates, serving to filter plankton, to tubercles and even teeth.

Gular plate — see Figure 265.

Hairlike teeth — teeth resembling the hairs of a clothes brush; if short, the bands and oval aggregations look like strips of velvet; if the teeth are somewhat thickened, they give the impression of the surface of a bristle brush.

Hyoid barbels — barbels attached in the interbranchial space in the region of the hyoid arches (Figure 100). Not to be confused with the barbels on the symphysis (Figure 101).

Infrapharyngeal bones — situated below the entrance to the esophagus, lying under the suprapharyngeal bones, and sometimes bearing teeth (Figure 455, bottom).

Interbranchial space — the part dividing the gill cavities into left and right.

Lateral line — a sense organ, seen as a row of openings in the scales (Figure 908), skin (Figure 891), or plates (Figure 873); the openings are arranged in one row (Figure 937), several rows (Figure 786), without interruption (Figures 641, 643).

Lower jaw — consists of three bones: dentale, articulare, and angulare (Figure 105).

Maxillary bone — one of the upper jaw bones; usually surrounds the mouth together with the premaxillary (Clupeiformes) (Figure 238) and has teeth, but is often shifted higher up and the mouth is surrounded by the premaxillary (Figures 105, 659, 665, 669). In the Perciformes (Figure 105) it is moved away from the premaxillary and bears no teeth; in the Clupeiformes the mouth is bordered by both the premaxillary and the maxillary (Figure 249). The premaxillaries are often small and entirely shifted forward, and one maxillary surrounds the upper margin of the mouth (Figure 257).

Median notch — see Figure 272.

Mesethmoid — see Figure 63.

Mouth — variously shaped. **Inferior** — when the upper jaw is much longer than the lower (Figure 85); subterminal, when the upper jaw is only slightly longer than the lower (Figures 377, 378); **superior**, when the upper jaw is shorter and the oral slit is almost vertical (Figures 66, 90); **half-superior**, when the lower jaw protrudes just slightly forward, and the oral slit is oblique (Figure 84); **terminal**, when the two jaws are equal and the oral slit is horizontal or slightly slanted (Figure 91).

Opercular bone — see Gill cover.

Orbitosphenoid — see Figure 117.

Paired fins — see Fins.

Palate — upper fornix of the oral cavity.

Palatine bones — arranged on the sides of the upper part of the oral cavity, near the maxillaries.

Palatine membrane — a dermal fold in the anterior part of the palate.

Parasphenoid — an elongate bone lying at the base of the skull (Figure 116).

Periorbital bones — ossicles situated around the eye; the anterior, the **preorbital**, is usually enlarged; the smaller ones under the eye are generally called **suborbital** (Figure 670).

Pharyngeal teeth — situated in the pharynx and serving for grinding food. Divided into suprapharyngeal and infrapharyngeal. Especially strongly developed in the Cyprinidae (Figure 361) and Catostomidae (Figure 358).

Photophore — luminescent organ in deepwater fish (Figures 75, 140).

Placoid scales — consisting of a basal plate and a tooth. These scales occur in sharks and more rarely in rays, and they are arranged in diagonal rows, making the skin very rough.

Protrusible mouth — occurs in fish in which the premaxillary and often also the maxillary bones are free and capable of moving forward (Figure 659).

Pseudobranch — rudiments of a gill situated on the inside of the gill cover.

Snout — the part of the head in front of the eye.

Spiracle — an opening situated behind the eye in sharks (Figure 199) and rays (Figure 215) which leads into the oral cavity.

Suborbital bones — see Periorbital bones.

Suborbital process — a process or processes of the suborbital bones, directed inward and supporting the eyeball (Figure 670, cf. Figure 673).

Suborbital stay — a bony crosspiece crossing the cheek from the suborbital bones to the preoperculum (Figure 105).

Supramaxillary bone, or accessory maxillary — a small bone which is contiguous with the upper margin of the maxillary in its posterior part. There are sometimes two of these accessory bones (Figures 270, 271).

Suprapharyngeal bones — bones situated above the entrance to the esophagus, sometimes supplied with teeth (Figure 455, top, 2 pairs).

Symphysis — site of union of the left and right lower jaw bones.

Teeth on the jaws — for holding the prey and for swallowing. This is aided by the folding teeth, present in some predatory fish (Figure 316, 317), which push the food down toward the throat but prevent its moving in the opposite direction. The teeth vary widely in form depending on the type of food. They may be **hairlike, velutinous, setiform, pectinate, caninelike** (Figures 23, 105), **dagger-shaped** (Figure 311), **needlelike** (Figure 973), **scalpriform, faced, or molar** (Figure 665).

Throat — area on the ventral side of the body between the base of the pectoral fins and the point of attachment of the branchiostegal membranes.

Vent — anal opening, in which the intestine terminates; it is situated in front of the anal fin (Figure 637).

Ventral fins — paired fins, situated as a rule on the abdomen (Figure 362) but often shifted forward under the base of the pectorals (Figure 697), more rarely attached in front of these on the throat (Figure 698) or on the chin (Figures 808—810). They are sometimes transformed into a sucker (Figures 28—30) and frequently are absent.

Vomer — an unpaired bone in the anterior part of the lower base of the skull, distinguishable in the front part of the palate.

Weberian apparatus — see Figure 59.

KEYS TO ORDERS AND FAMILIES

Key to orders (1–62)

1 (2). Skull absent. [Peribranchial cavity as a rule present.] Blood colorless. (Subphylum Acrania, class I. Amphioxi—lancelets.) (Figure 1). . . . . 1. **Branchiostomatiformes**

2 (1). Skull present. [Peribranchial cavity absent.] Blood red.[1] (Subphylum Craniata.)

3 (6). Jaws absent. Paired fins absent. No gill covers. One unpaired nasal (naso-hypophysial) opening. Body vermiform, bare.

4 (5). Dorsal fins present (usually two, rarely one). Eyes normal in adults. Mouth apparatus of the sucking type. [Naso-hypophysial cavity not communicating with pharynx.] Seven outer gill openings situated on each side in the anterior part of the body directly behind the head. Snout without barbels. Nasal opening on dorsal side of head. (Class II. Petromyzones—lampreys.) (Figure 2). . . . . 2. **Petromyzoniformes**

5 (4). Dorsal fins absent. Eyes degenerate, not distinguishable externally. [No orbital muscles or the corresponding nerves.] Mouth apparatus not of the sucking but of the crushing type. [Naso-hypophysial cavity communicating with pharyngeal cavity.] One or 6—15 openings on each side of the body, situated far from the head. Snout with barbels. Nasal opening on tip of snout. (Class III. Myxini—hagfish.) (Figure 3) .3. **Myxiniformes**

6 (3). Jaws present. Paired fins generally present; if absent, inner gill slits covered by gill cover. Nasal openings paired.

7 (20). 5—7 outer gill openings on each side of the head; no gill cover or skin fold covering the gill slits. Males usually with claspers. (Class IV. Elasmobranchii—Selachii.)

8 (17). Gill slits situated on sides of body, if only partially (Figure 4). Anterior margin of pectorals free, not united with the sides of the body or head, in front of the gill openings. Upper margin of orbit free of the eyeball (eyelid free). (Superorder A—sharks.)

9 (14). Anal fin present.

10 (11). 6—7 gill slits. One dorsal fin, without a spine. (Figure 5). . . . . 5. **Hexanchiformes**

11 (10). Five gill slits. Two dorsal fins.[2]

12 (13). Both dorsal fins with a spine (Figure 6). [Palatoquadratum articulates with preorbital region of skull. Rostral cartilages absent.] Anterior teeth on jaws markedly different from the posterior teeth . . . . 4. **Heterodontiformes**

[1] The blood is white in the Antarctic family 373. Channichthyidae (Perciformes).

[2] The first dorsal fin is sometimes absent in the genus Pentarchus = Apristurus of family 16. Scyliorhinidae.

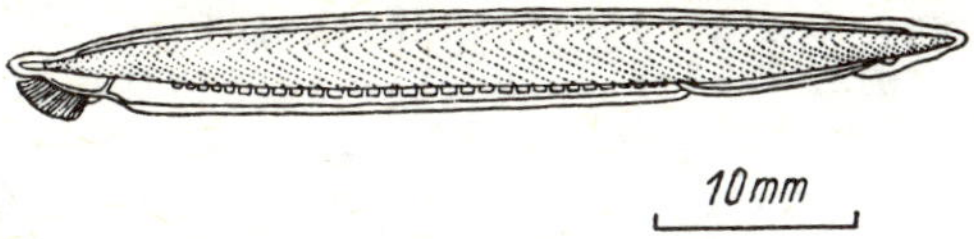

FIGURE 1. Branchiostomatiformes — *Branchiostoma belcheri* (L. and L., 1959, fig. 4)

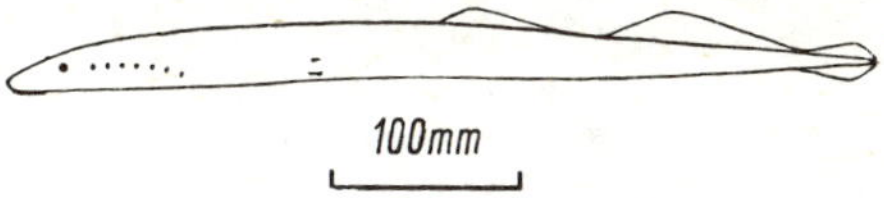

FIGURE 2. Petromyzoniformes — *Lampetra japonica* (L. and L., 1959, fig. 5)

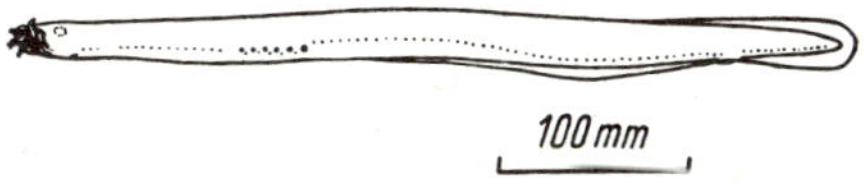

FIGURE 3. Myxiniformes — *Heptatretus burgeri* (L. and L., 1959, fig. 11)

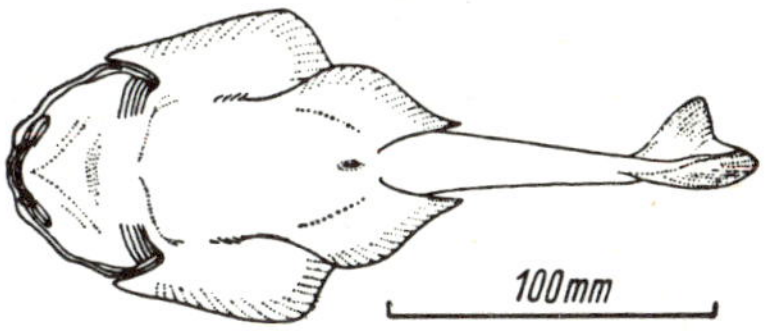

FIGURE 4. Arrangement of gill slits in *Squatina* (L. and L., 1959, fig. 62)

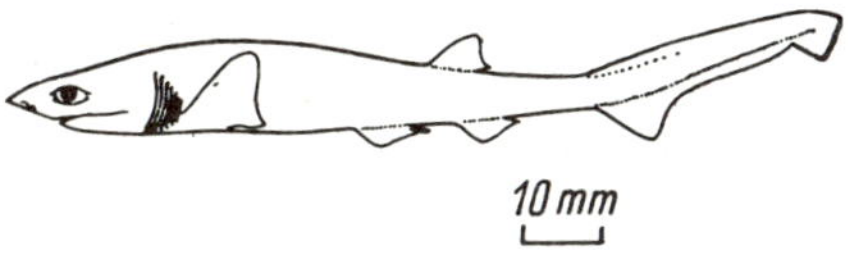

FIGURE 5. Hexanchiformes — *Heptranchias perlo* (M., 1955, III, fig. 6, diagr.)

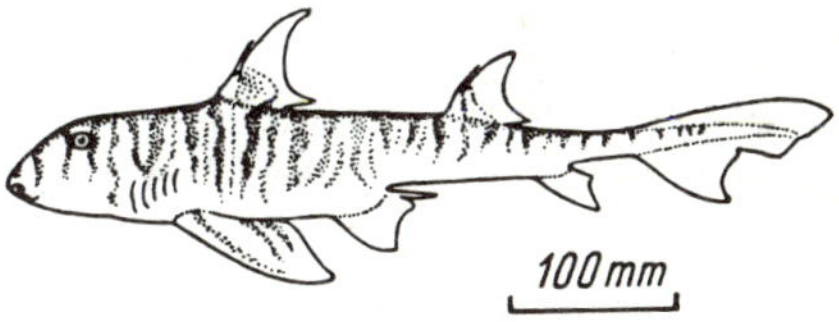

FIGURE 6. Heterodontiformes — *Heterodontus zebra* (M., 1955, III, fig. 5)

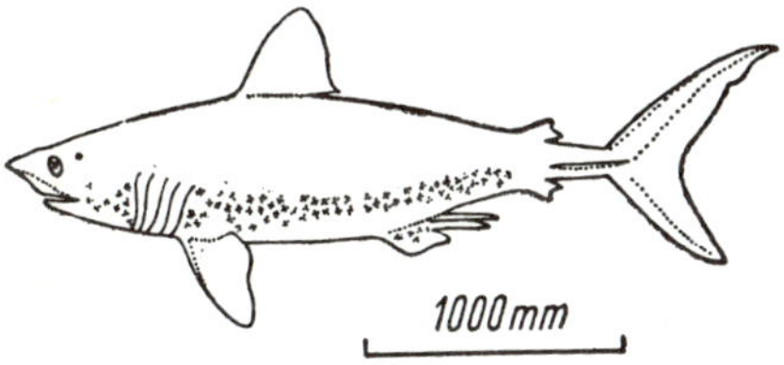

FIGURE 7. Lamniformes - *Lamna ditropis* (M., 1955, III, fig. 12, diagr.)

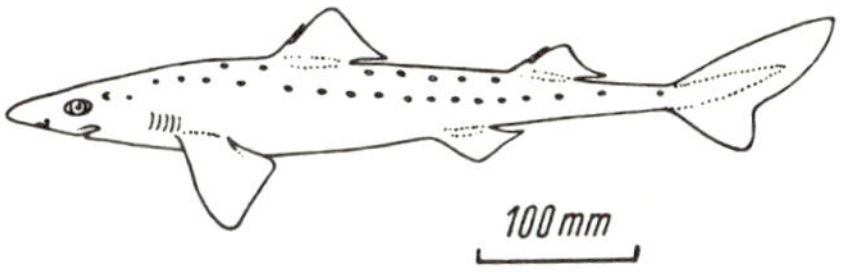

FIGURE 8. Squaliformes — *Squalus acanthias* (L. and L., 1959, fig. 57)

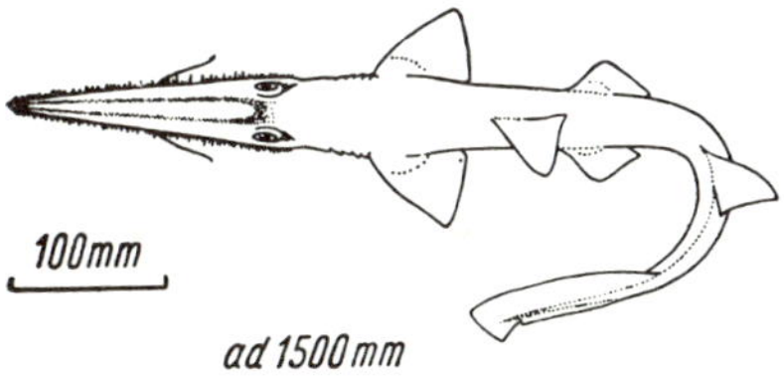

FIGURE 9. Pristiophoriformes — *Pristiophorus japonicus* (L. and L., 1959, fig. 63, diagr.)

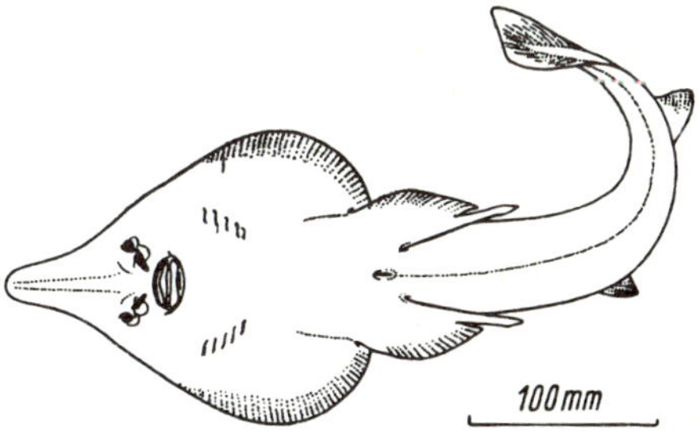

FIGURE 10. Arrangement of gill slits in *Rhinobatis hynnicephalus* (L. and L., 1959, fig. 69)

13 (12). Both dorsal fins without a spine (Figure 7). [Palatoquadratum not articulated or weakly articulated with skull. Rostral cartilages present, as a rule of 3 elements.] Anterior and posterior teeth on jaws similar . . . . 6. Lamniformes

14 (9). Anal fin absent. 5—6 gill openings. Two dorsal fins with or without spines.

15 (16). Snout of moderate length, not drawn out into a plate and bearing neither lateral teeth nor barbels (Figure 8) . . . . 7. Squaliformes

16 (15). Snout drawn out into a long plate which bears sharp toothlike appendages on the sides giving the snout the appearance of a saw. A pair of long, fleshy barbels is present near the middle of the produced snout, in front of the mouth (Figure 9) . . . . 8. Pristiophoriformes

17 (8). Gill slits situated on ventral side of body (Figure 10). Anterior margin of pectoral fins united with sides of body or head in front of of the gill openings (Figure 11). Upper margin of orbit not free of the eyeball (free eyelid absent). Anal fin absent. (Superorder B—skates.)

18 (19). [No electrical organs between head and pectorals. Preorbital cartilages not enlarged.] Disk of rhombic, more rarely of triangular, form; the snout forms a protuberance, albeit a small one (Figure 12) . . . . 9. Rajiformes

19 (18). [A large electrical organ present on each side of the body between head and pectoral fins. Preorbital cartilages markedly enlarged.] Disk oval; snout rounded, without protuberance (Figure 13) . . . . 10. Torpediniformes

20 (*7*). One outer gill opening on each side of the head; gill cover or skin fold present covering the gill slits.

21 (22). Inner gill slits (4) covered from above by a skin fold which has no bony skeleton (Figure 14). Claspers present in males. (Class V. Holocephali) . . . . 11. Chimaeriformes

22 (21). Inner gill slits (4—5) covered by gill cover which has a special bony skeleton.[3] Claspers never present.

23 (26). [Skull autostylic (palatoquadrate cartilage fused with the skull).] Jaws not covered with bones; special tooth plates present (Figure 15). [Paired fins of the archipterygial type (Figure 16).] Dorsal and anal fins fused with the caudal. [Internal nares present. Swim bladder opening ventrally, serving as lungs; corresponding pulmonary circulation present.] (Class VI. Dipnoi.)

24 (25). [Swim bladder unpaired. Endocranium cartilaginous.] Paired fins well developed. (Figure 17). . . . . 12. Ceratodiformes

25 (24). [Swim bladder paired. Endocranium strongly membranous.] Humeral girdle and paired fins reduced. (Figure 18). . . . . 13. Lepidosireniformes

26 (23). [Skull hyostylic (palatoquadrate cartilage not fused with the skull and not articulated with it directly, but united by means of ligaments; attachment of jaw apparatus to skull achieved by a stay (hyomandibulare), sometimes amphistylic (palatoquadrate cartilage

[3] An opercular skeleton is absent in fish of order 27. Saccopharyngiformes (Teleostomi) (cf. Figure 48).

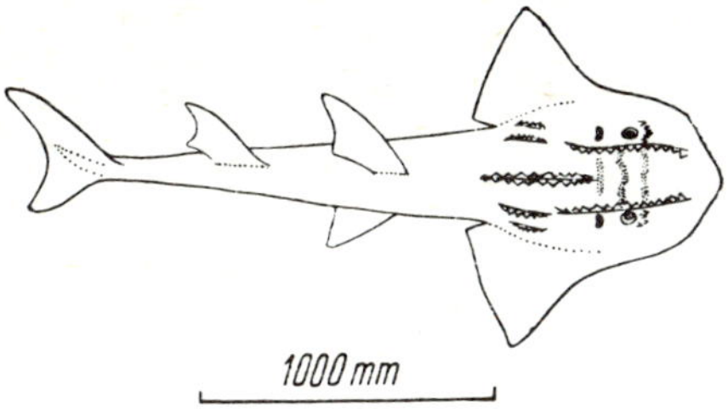

FIGURE 11. Rhina ancylostoma (Wang, 1958, fig. 35, diagr.)

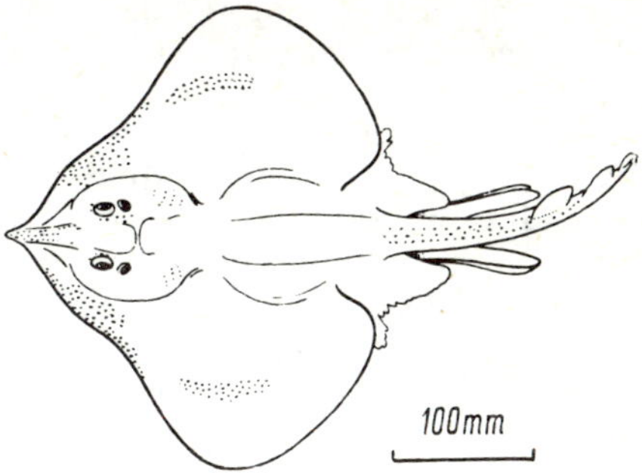

FIGURE 12. Rajiformes — Raja porosa (L. and L., 1959, fig. 70, diagr.)

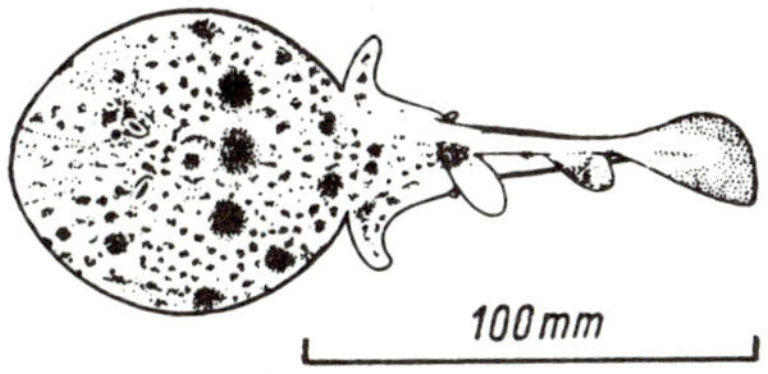

FIGURE 13. Torpediniformes — Narcine lingula (L. and L., 1959, fig. 103, diagr.)

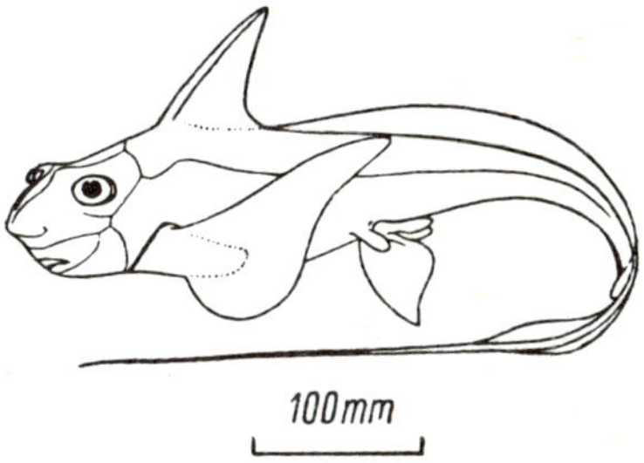

FIGURE 14. Chimaeriformes — Phasmichthys mitsukurii (L. and L., 1959, fig. 107)

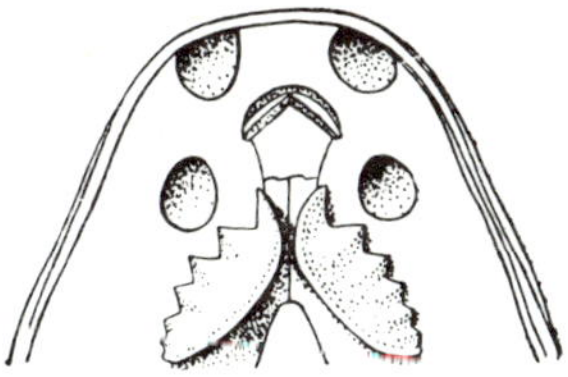

FIGURE 15. Tooth plates of the upper jaw in Neoceratodus forsteri (Traité, 1958, III, fig. 1808a, diagr.)

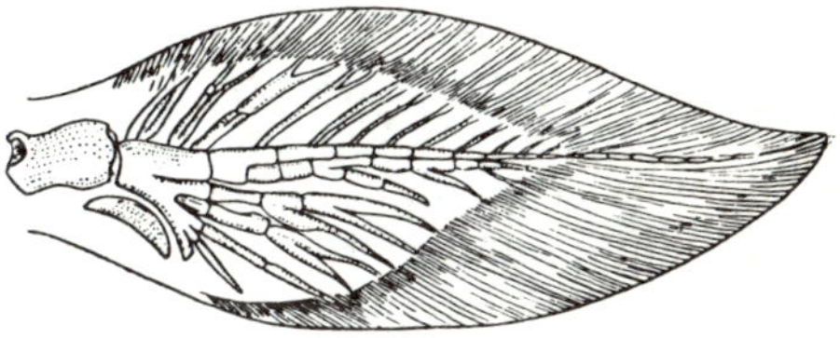

FIGURE 16. Pectoral fin of Neoceratodus forsteri (Jordan, 1925, fig. 174, diagr.)

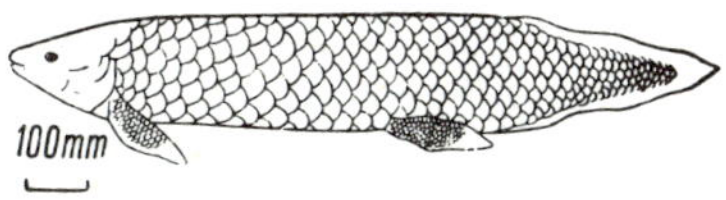

FIGURE 17. Ceratodiformes — Neoceratodus forsteri (Jordan, 1925, fig. 173, diagr.)

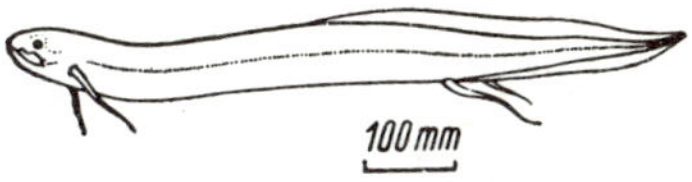

FIGURE 18. Lepidosireniformes — Lepidosiren paradoxa (Traité, 1958, III, fig. 1811, diagr.)

articulated with the skull by processes, without appreciable aid from the hyomandibulare) in orders 48. Channiformes and 49. Synbranchiformes.] Both jaws covered with bones; jaw bones with teeth. (Class VII. Teleostomi—higher fishes.)

27 (28). [Paired fins with a fleshy, scale-covered lobe which projects into the fin and includes radials. Pectoral fins constructed according to the archipterygial type (Figure 16).] Two dorsal fins. Caudal fin diphycercal, consisting of three lobes. (Figure 19.) (Subclass Crossopterygii). . . . . 14. **Coelacanthiformes**

28 (27). [Paired fins supported by a skeleton not of the archipterygial type.] Caudal fin of a different form. (Subclass Actinopterygii.)

29 (30). [Pectoral fins with a small fleshy lobe; fin rays situated on numerous radials, which are attached to a cartilaginous plate and to two elongate bones situated on the ossified scapula and coracoid.] Dorsal fin consisting of many distinctive finlets; each finlet, consisting of several rays, is supported by one radial. (Figure 20) . . . . 15. **Polypteriformes**

30 (29). [Pectoral fins with a different structure; radials situated, if only in part (Amia), directly on the humeral girdle (on the scapular-coracoid cartilage or on the scapula and coracoid).] Dorsal fin of another structure; no separate finlets consisting of several rays supported by one radial.

31 (32). Body covered with 5 rows of large bony scutes of rhombic form (Figure 21) or else bare, but in any case the upper lobe of the caudal fin is always covered with rhombic scales—fulcra (Figure 22). Mouth inferior, protrusible, snout more or less elongate. [The number of rays in the relatively short dorsal and anal fins is much greater than the number of unossified radials.] . . . . 16. **Acipenseriformes**

32 (31). Body not covered with 5 rows of large bony scutes, but if it is bare, the upper lobe of the [heterocercal] tail is not covered with fulcra.

33 (36). Lower jaw of complex structure; inner surface of lower jaw with 3 dermal bones which bear teeth (Figure 23).

34 (35). Snout not elongate. Scales cycloid, thin, rounded, with tilelike arrangement. (Figure 24). . . . . 17. **Amiiformes**

35 (34). Snout markedly elongate. Scales ganoid, rhombic, bearing denticles resembling dermal teeth. (Figure 25) . . . . 18. **Lepisosteiformes**

36 (33). Lower jaw without complex structure, consisting of only 3 bones: dentale, articulare, and angulare; no dermal bones on inner surface of lower jaw.

37 (38). Skull asymmetrical; both eyes on one (right or left) side of the head, which is the dorsal side of the body (Figure 26). Dorsal and anal fins with numerous rays. Body markedly laterally compressed, deep, oval. The fish swim and lie on the bottom on their side . . . . 53. **Pleuronectiformes**

38 (37). Skull symmetrical; eyes situated on both sides of the longitudinal plane of the head. The fish usually swim with their back, or occasionally with the head or belly, up; lying on the bottom, they swim on their belly, not on the side.

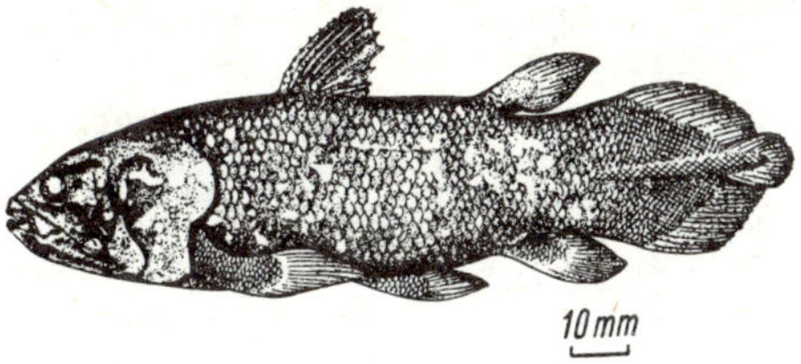

FIGURE 19. Coelacanthiformes — *Latimeria chalumnae* (Traité, 1958, III: 2554, pl. V)

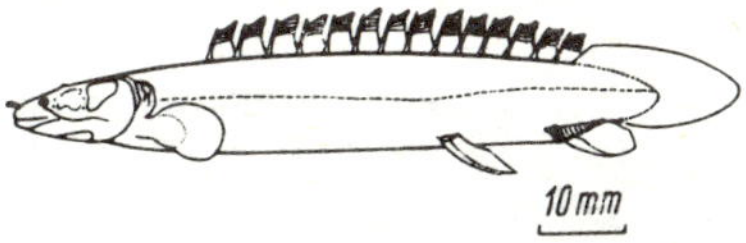

FIGURE 20. Polypteriformes — *Polypterus congicus* (Poll, 1957, fig. 76, diagr.)

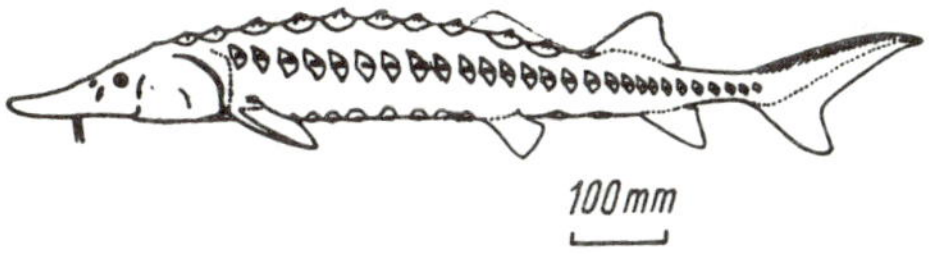

FIGURE 21. Acipenseriformes — *Acipenser medirostris* (Berg, 1948, fig. 76, diagr.)

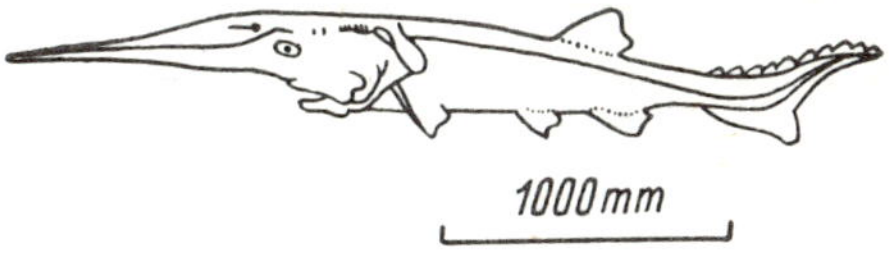

FIGURE 22. Acipenseriformes — *Psephurus gladius* (L. and L., 1965, fig. 2)

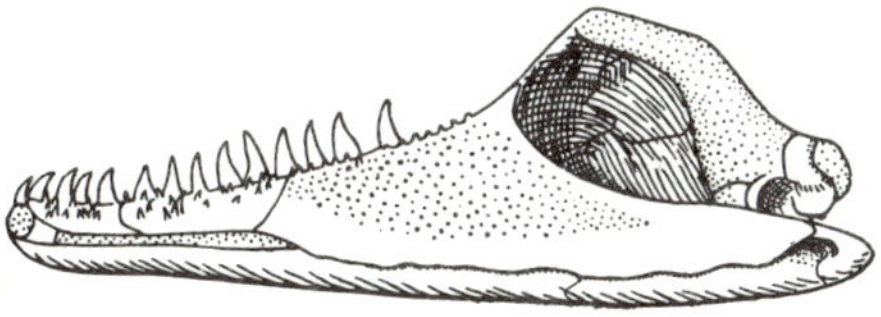

FIGURE 23. Dermal bones of the lower jaw in *Amia calva* (Berg, 1940, fig. 86)

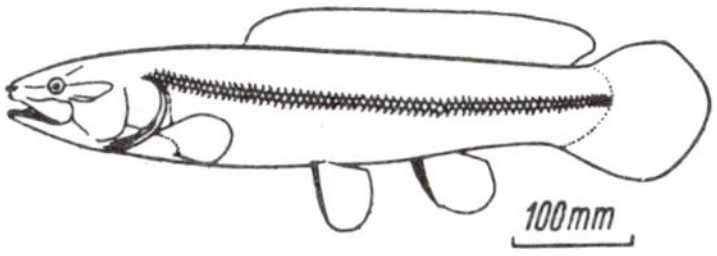

FIGURE 24. Amiiformes — *Amia calva* (Jordan, 1925, fig. 198, diagr.)

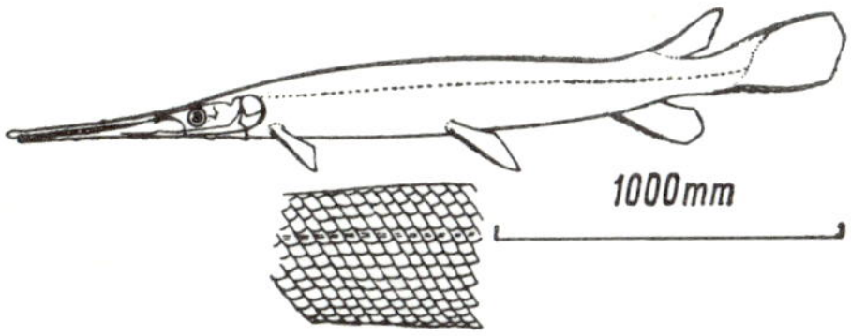

FIGURE 25. Lepisosteiformes — *Lepisosteus osseus* (Traité, 1958, III, fig. 1548, diagr.)

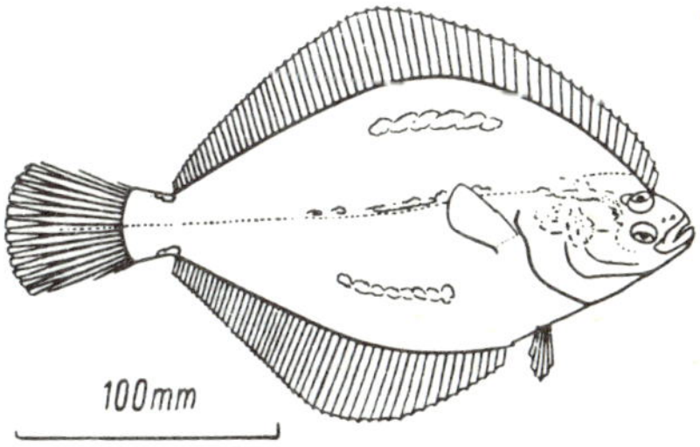

FIGURE 26. Pleuronectiformes — *Kareius variegatus* (L. and L., 1965, fig. 3)

39 (40). Body strongly flattened from top to bottom, enclosed in an armor of bony plates. Pectoral fins very large, with 10 – 18 unbranched rays which are hard, in the form of spines, at the base, and soft, jointed, at the end. The pectorals are distributed horizontally, which underlines the markedly flattened form of the body.[4] Dorsal fin single, short; like the anal, it contains 5 soft, unbranched rays. Ventral fins markedly behind the base of the pectorals, on the belly, each with one spiny and 1–3 branched rays. Caudal fin with 8 rays. Snout elongate, often awl-shaped, crenate. Mouth inferior, toothless. [Suborbital bones united with preoperculum. Swim bladder absent.] (Figure 27) . . . . 62. Pegasiformes

40 (39). Body, head, and fins not as in Figure 27.

41 (42). Semicircular sucking disk present on the thorax (Figure 28).[5] [It is formed by the widely separated ventral fins and a skin fold which is supported in front by the cleithra and behind by the postcleithra; each ventral fin has 1 concealed spiny and 4 unbranched rays.] One dorsal fin, situated in the posterior part of the body above the anal; fins without spiny rays. Skin bare. [Swim bladder absent.] (Figure 31) . . . . 59. Gobiesociformes

42 (41). There is no such sucking disk on the thorax.

43 (44). A special copulatory organ (priapium) is present in males under the head (Figure 32, 1). Vent under pectoral fins or anterior to them. Ventral fins absent or rudimentary . . . . 41. Phallostethiformes

44 (43). This organ absent in males.

45 (46). Basal ossicles of ventral fins, if these fins are present, united with each other and not connected to pectoral girdle, protruding above the surface of the body almost their whole length (Figure 306); a peculiar "hair cover" is sometimes present (Figures 33, 34); olfactory organs sometimes exceedingly enlarged, so that the diameter of the posterior naris is equal to or exceeds the diameter of the eye (Figure 35) in the Megalomycteroidei.[6] . . . . 20. Miripinniformes

46 (45). Basal ossicles of ventral fins not protruding above surface of body and there is no "hair cover" as in Figure 34. No excessive enlargement of posterior naris as in Figure 35.

47 (48). Caudal fin as long as or longer than the body (Figure 36). Ventral fins absent. [Operculum, suboperculum, and interoperculum not ossified. Posttemporale and supracleithrum absent.] Eyes telescopic. Deepwater fishes. The large mouth and short dorsal fin differentiate them from fish of family 227. Stylephoridae (order 39. Lampridiformes) (see Figures 134, 135) . . . . 26. Giganturiformes

[4] In some fish with a similar form belonging to family 452. Agonidae the pectoral fins have vertical bases (cf. Figures 872 – 879).

[5] Not to be confused with the ventral disk in the Gobioidei (Figure 29) of order 50. Perciformes and family 453. Cyclopteridae (Figure 30) of order 51. Scorpaeniformes. (See also Figure 566.)

[6] This suborder, with the sole family 104c. Megalomycteridae, and also the entire order 20. Miripinniformes, is considered as a suborder and included in order 24. Cetomimiformes (Myers and Freihofer, 1966 : 193 – 206). See footnote to thesis 0-81.

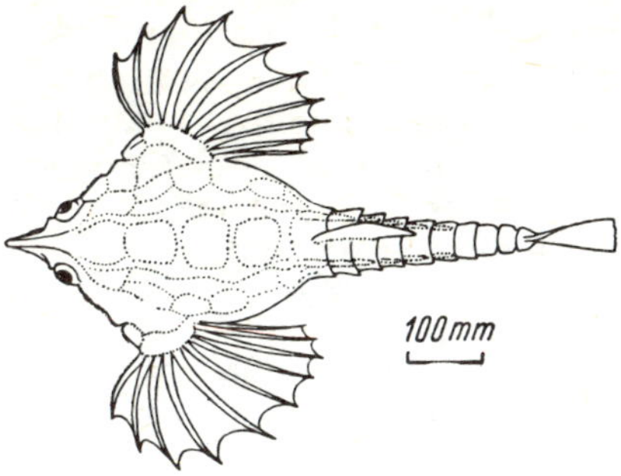

FIGURE 27. Pegasiformes — *Pegasus volitans* (L. and L., 1956, fig. 4)

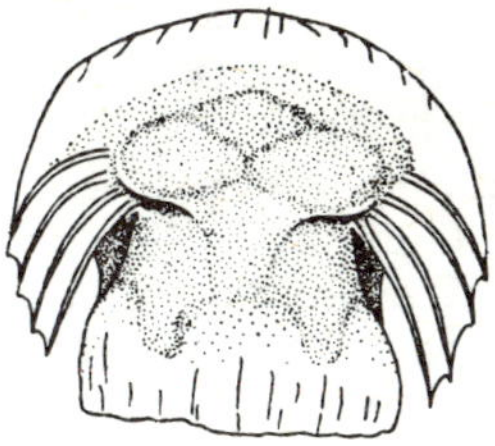

FIGURE 28. Sucking disk in the Gobiesociformes (L. and L., 1965, fig. 5)

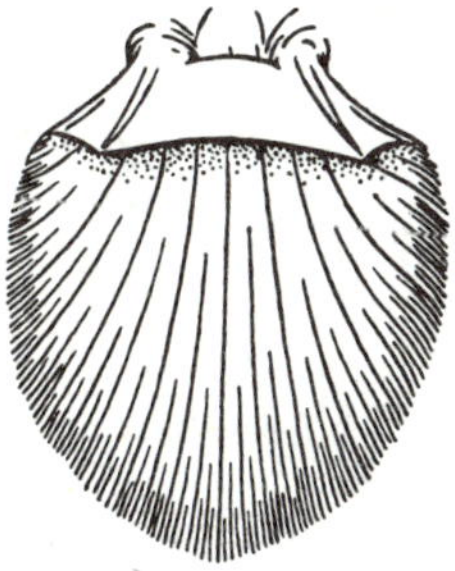

FIGURE 29. Disk in the Gobiidae (L. and L., 1965, fig. 6)

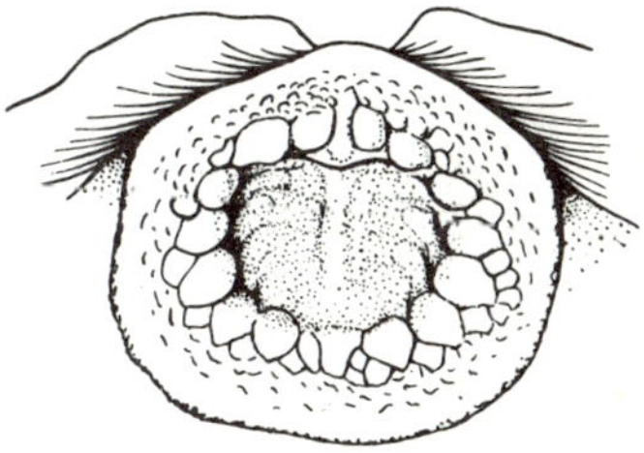

FIGURE 30. Disk in the Cyclopteridae (L. and L., 1965, fig. 7)

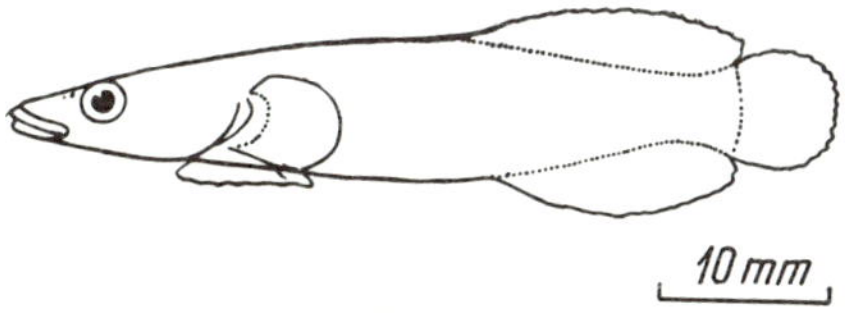

FIGURE 31. Gobiesociformes — *Aspasma misakia* (L. and L., 1965, fig. 8)

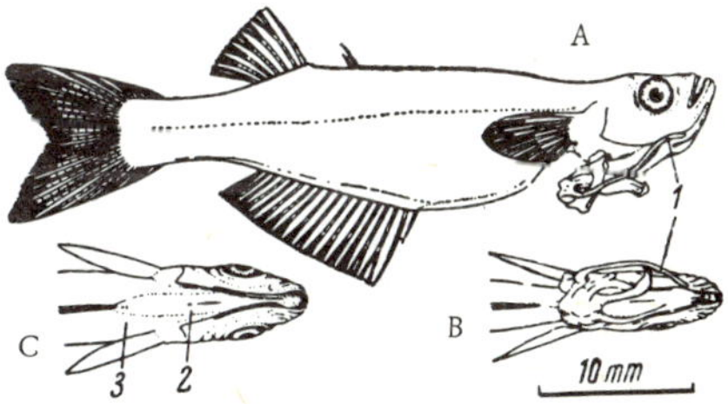

FIGURE 32. Phallostethiformes — *Galophallus eximius* (M., 1955, I, fig. 126):

A — male, lateral; B — head of male, ventral; C — head of female, ventral. 1) priapium; 2) vent; 3) genital opening.

48 (47). Caudal fin much shorter than the body.[7]

49 (50). Body eel-like, long,[8] round in section. Ventral fins absent. Dorsal and anal fins with a long base, connected to or fused with the caudal; if caudal fin absent, end of caudal part of body bare. No spiny rays in the fins. Gill slits small, narrow, situated on the sides of the head in front of the pectoral fins, if these are present. Branchiostegal rays long; they support the skin covering the very large gill cavity. Vertebrae numerous — up to 260. [Premaxillary bones not separate, fused with the mesethmoid and often also with the vomer; dorsal margin of mouth bordered both by these bones and by the maxillaries. Swim bladder, if present, united with the intestine by means of a duct (physostomous forms).] (Figure 38) . . . . 31. Anguilliformes

50 (49). Body not eel-like, but if it does have an eel-like form, then either the gill openings are not separated from each other, as they are in the true eels, but are fused and form one small slit on the ventral side of the body near the throat (Figure 39), or there are ventral fins or spiny rays in the dorsal and anal fins, or else the gill cavity is not enlarged.

51 (60). Form of body resembling that of an eel.[9]

52 (53). Gill openings fused into one small slit situated in the throat region. Pectoral and generally ventral fins absent in adults (present in fish of family 263. Alabetidae), but pectorals still present in larvae of 15 mm. Rays absent or present (in the Alabetidae) in dorsal and anal fins. [No swim bladder. Premaxillaries not fused with mesethmoid; they almost or completely shift the maxillaries away from the upper margin of the mouth.] Form of body definitely eel-like. (Figure 39) . . . . 49. Synbranchiformes

53 (52). Gill openings not fused into one small slit in the throat region. Pectorals present. Physoclistous forms.

54 (57). Ventral fins present, situated on the abdomen, with 8 — 10 rays.

55 (56). Fins without spiny rays. [Mouth bordered by premaxillaries and maxillaries.] Preoperculum rudimentary. Some forms with well developed photophores on ventral margin of body. (Figure 40). . . . . 32. Halosauriformes

56 (55). Fins with spiny rays: one outer ray of ventral fin; several (more than 30) rays in front of anal fin; several (more than 3) rays anterior to dorsal, which has a short base; otherwise dorsal fin represented just by a few spines. [Mouth bordered only by premaxillaries.] Preoperculum normally developed, not rudimentary. Photophores absent. (Figure 41) . . . . 33. Notacanthiformes

57 (54). Ventral fins absent.

[7] Except in family 227. Stylephoridae of order 39. Lampridiformes (see thesis 0—137 and Figures 134, 135).

[8] As an exception, in family 195. Cyemidae the body is short, and the caudal part is shorter than the trunk and head together (Figure 37).

[9] See thesis 0—76. In order 29. Mormyriformes, fishes of family 127. Gymnarchidae have an eel-like shape (see Figure 336).

0

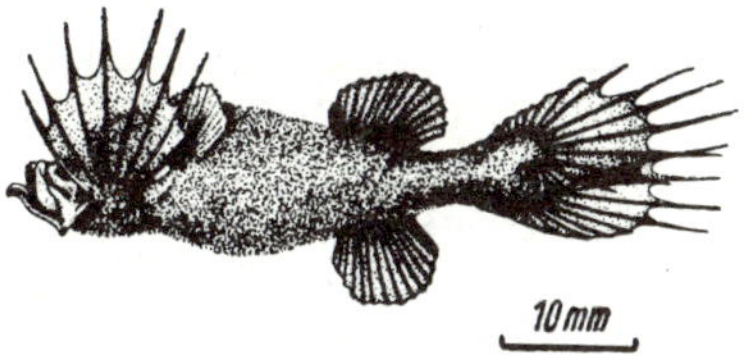

FIGURE 33. Miripinniformes — *Miripinna esau* (Bertelsen and Marshall, 1956, fig. 1A)

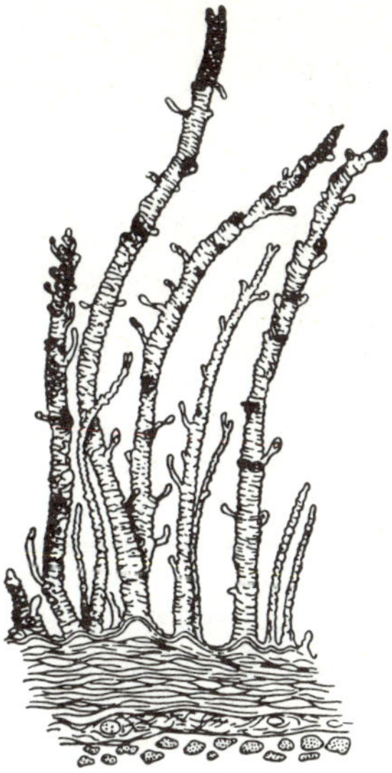

FIGURE 34. "Hair cover" in *Miripinna esau* (Bertelsen and Marshall, 1956, fig. 1B) (high magnification)

FIGURE 35. Miripinniformes — *Ataxolepis apus* (Myers and Freihofer, 1966, fig. 2)

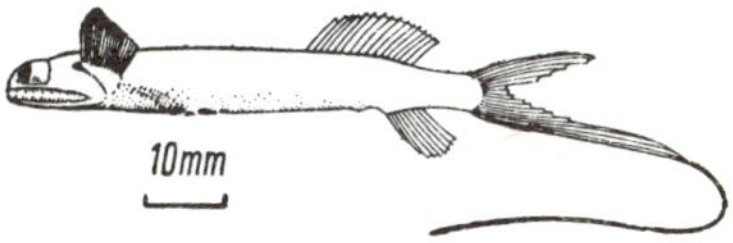

FIGURE 36. Giganturiformes -- *Gigantura vorax* (Traité, 1958, III, fig. 1669)

Lower ray of caudal fin straight, firm; it is bent in the figure.

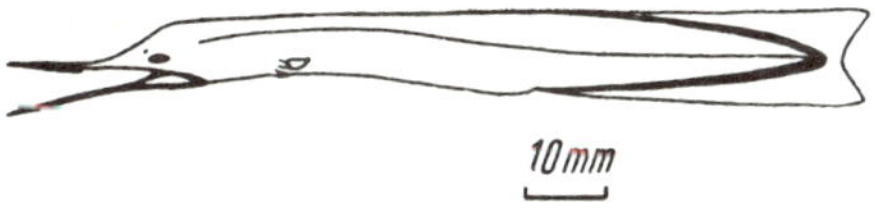

FIGURE 37. *Cyema atrum* (Anguilliformes) (Fowler, 1936, fig. 136, diagr.)

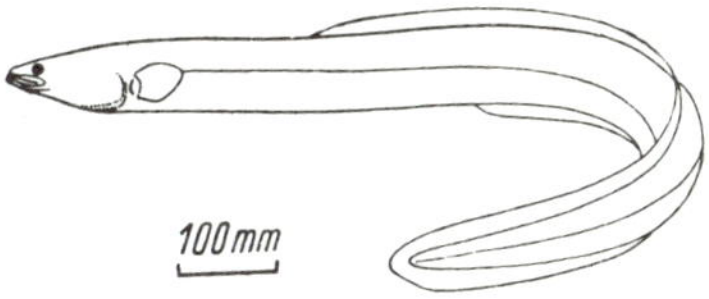

FIGURE 38. Anguilliformes — *Anguilla japonica* (L. and L., 1965, fig. 9)

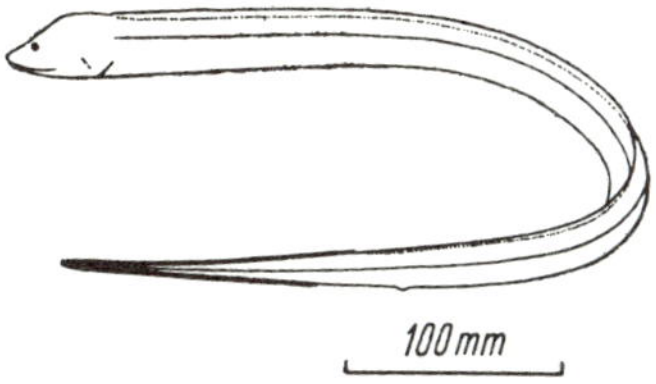

FIGURE 39. Synbranchiformes — *Monopterus albus* (L. and L., 1965, fig. 10)

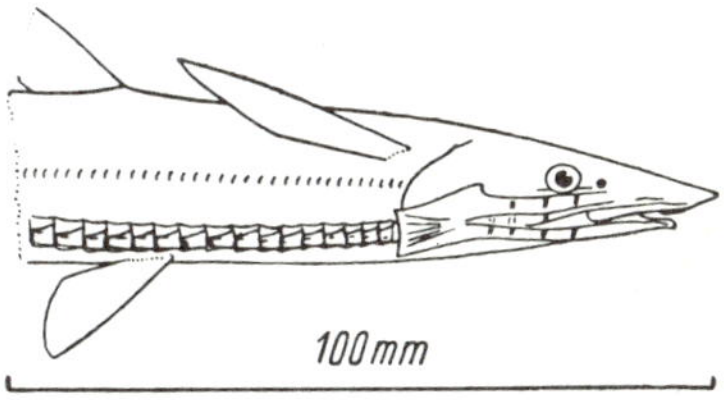

FIGURE 40. Halosauriformes — *Halosauropsis affinis* (L. and L., 1965, fig. 12)

58 (59). Dorsal and anal fused with caudal, if this fin is present, or else with each other. Numerous spiny rays, some free, others interconnected, anterior to dorsal fin. Three spiny rays in front of anal fin. Gill openings small, opening on ventral side of body. Anterior nares tubular, opening on barbels situated on each side of the snout on a fleshy appendage. (Figure 42) . . . . 56. Mastacembeliformes

59 (58). Dorsal and anal not fused with caudal, in which there are 7 unbranched rays. Spiny rays absent in fins. No fleshy appendage on the snout. Body bare. [Humeral girdle degenerate and represented by a single plate.] Branchiostegal rays extending to dorsal end of margin of pectoral, not concealed under the gill cover but distinctly protruding to the outside on the sides of the head. Length to 50 mm (Figure 43). [Allied to the Mastacembeliformes in the anatomical respect] . . . . 55. Chaudhuriiformes

60 (51). Form of body not eel-like, but if it is, the fish differ in all other characters from the descriptions given in theses 52—59.

61 (62). Upper jaw absent; mouth very large. [Quadrate bone very long, as long as the lower jaw, which protrudes far forward.] (Figure 44) . . . . 28. Monognathiformes

62 (61). Upper jaw present; if absent (very rarely) (Figure 45), the mouth is very small (family 91. Opisthoproctidae, Clupeiformes).

63 (64). Jaws [and also the hyomandibular and quadrate bones] very long, extending far posteriorly and exceeding the length of the cranium several (7—9) times (Figure 46). Mouth enormous, pharynx huge, extensible.[10] Opercular bones absent. Ventral and caudal fins absent, or caudal rudimentary. No spiny rays in the fins. Gill openings in the form of oval slits on the abdomen. Luminescent organs present in the form of furrows along the base of the dorsal fin. [Swim bladder absent.] (Figure 48) . . . . 27. Saccopharyngiformes

64 (63). Jaws of normal length in relation to skull, but if enlarged, they protrude forward, not backward. Pharynx not huge and not extensible.

65 (66). First dorsal fin transformed into a sucking organ. (Figures 49, 50) . . . . 57. Echeneiformes

66 (65). First dorsal fin normal, not transformed into a sucking organ.

67 (68). Gill openings situated under or behind pectoral fins, but not in front of them, or only partly in front, small, of oval form. Ventral fins, if present, on the throat, with one spiny and 5 branched rays. First dorsal, if present, modified, its first ray transformed into an illicium. (Figure 51) . . . . 61. Lophiiformes

68 (67). Gill openings distributed wholly in front of pectoral fins.

69 (70). Snout markedly elongate, in the form of a tube at the end of which the small mouth is situated. [Quadrate and preopercular bones markedly elongate (Figure 52).] Ventral fins, if present, situated

[10] Representatives of family 368. Chiasmodontidae (Figure 47) or 119. Cetomimidae (Figure 69) have a large mouth as compared with other families, but their mouth is still negligibly small as compared with the mouth and pharynx in order 27. Saccopharyngiformes.

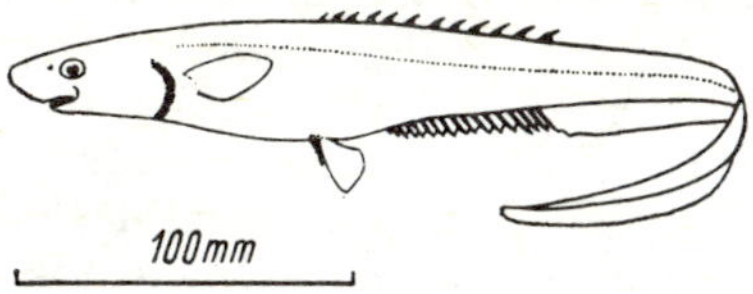

FIGURE 41. Notacanthiformes — *Notacanthus macrorhynchus* (L. and L., 1965, fig. 11)

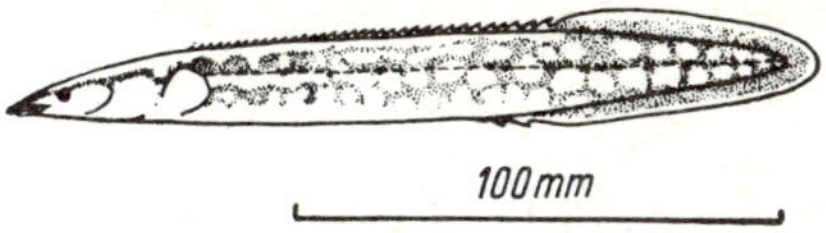

FIGURE 42. Mastacembeliformes — *Mastacembelus armatus* (Wang, 1958, fig. 588, diagr.)

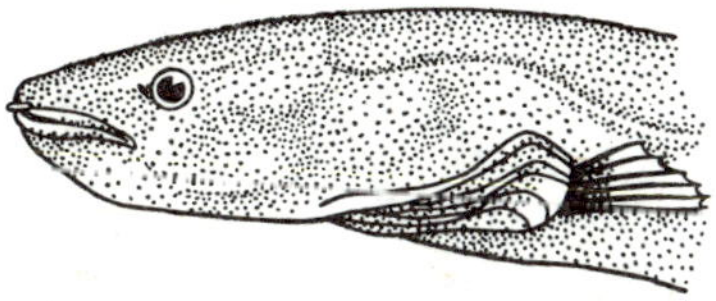

FIGURE 43. Chaudhuriiformes — *Chaudhuria caudata* M., 1955, II, fig. 510)

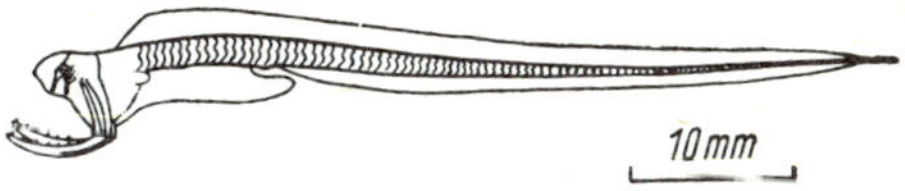

FIGURE 44. Monognathiformes — *Monognathus taeningi* (Traité, 1958, III, fig. 1674, diagr.)

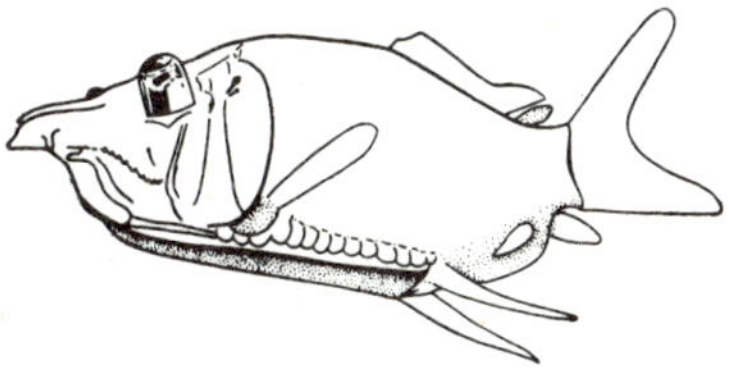

FIGURE 45. Opisthoproctidae (Clupeiformes) (Traité, 1958, III: 1900, pl. IV, fig. 2, diagr.)

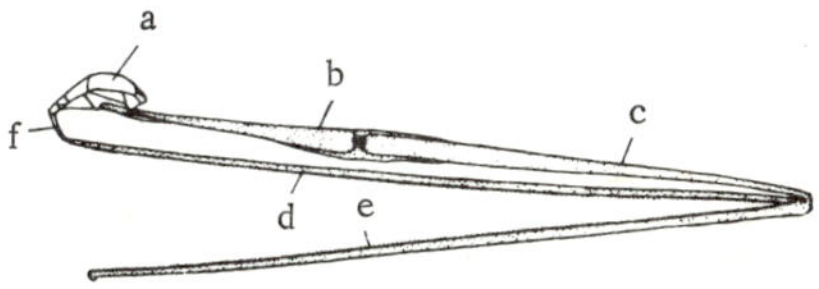

FIGURE 46. Jaws of *Eurypharynx pelecanoides* (Saccopharyngiformes) (L. and L., 1965, fig. 13):

a — cranium; b — hyomandibulare; c — quadrate bone; d — maxillary; e — mandibular bone; f — ligament.

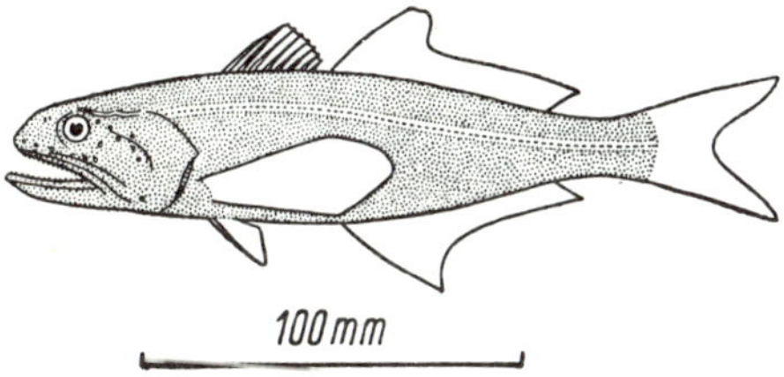

FIGURE 47. *Pseudoscopelus scriptus sagamiensis* (Chiasmodontidae, Perciformes) (Abe, 1958, fig. 437, diagr.)

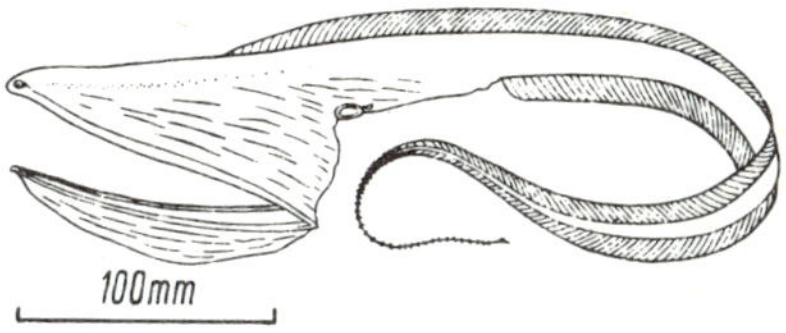

FIGURE 48. Saccopharyngiformes — *Eurypharynx pelecanoides* (L. and L., 1965, fig. 14)

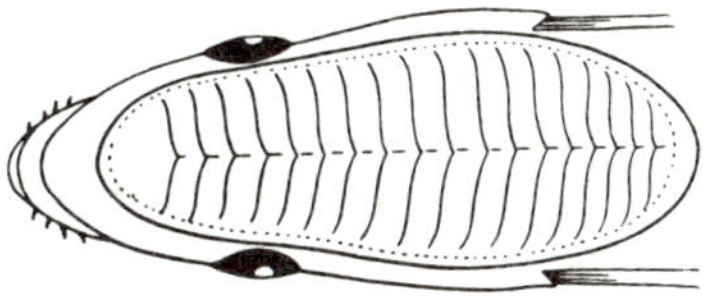

FIGURE 49. Sucking organ of *Remora remora* (Echeneiformes) (Traité, 1958, III, fig. 1764)

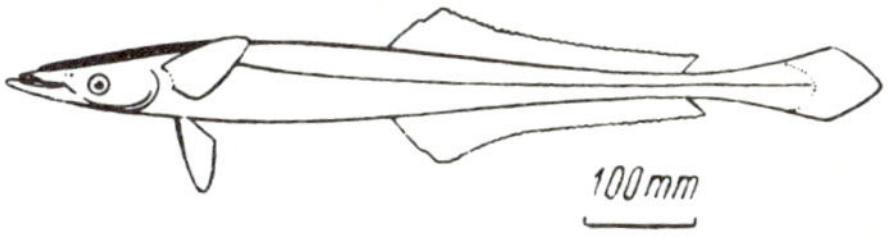

FIGURE 50. Echeneiformes — *Echeneis naucratus* (L. and L., 1965, fig. 15)

on the abdomen or at any rate markedly behind the pectorals,[11] without spiny rays, just 3—7 soft rays. One dorsal fin, also without spiny rays (Figures 54, 55), but if there are two dorsal fins, the first usually does have spiny rays (Figure 56). Body generally markedly elongate . . . . 38. **Syngnathiformes**

70 (69). Snout not in the form of a tube, but if it does resemble a tube, the ventral fins are placed under or not far behind the pectorals and as as a rule have a strong spine.

71 (72). Pectoral fin with two bases[12] (Figure 57) [upper part of fin attached to upper two radials; the lower part, consisting of several free filaments, is attached to the fourth (lower) radial; the intermediate third radial does not bear fin rays]. Ventral fins situated under pectorals, slightly behind their base (Figure 58) . . . . 47. **Polynemiformes**

72 (71). Pectoral fin with one base. [All the radials bear rays; the lower rays are sometimes markedly modified as compared with the upper, but there is no considerable interval between the bases of the two groups of rays.]

73 (74). Weberian apparatus present (Figure 59). Ventral fins, if present, behind the pectorals on the belly. Fins without spines (Figure 60), or there may be one spine each in the dorsal (Figure 61), more rarely in the anal (see Figure 362), or pectoral (Figure 62), sometimes two spines in the dorsal. Adipose fin occasionally present (Figure 62). [Swim bladder as a rule connected with the intestine by a duct (physostomous forms)] . . . . 30. **Cypriniformes**

74 (73). Weberian apparatus absent.

75 (80). Mesocoracoid (Figure 63) generally present. [It is absent only in the suborders Esocoidei (Figures 236—238) and Bathylaconoidei (Figure 256), and also in family 89. Microstomatidae of the suborder Opisthoproctoidei (Figure 285).]

76 (77). Cerebellum enormously developed, reaching the forebrain (Figure 64). Gill cover covered with skin (Figure 65). Electrical organs present (see also Figures 336 and 337) . . . . 29. **Mormyriformes**

77 (76). Cerebellum developed normally, small, ending far before the forebrain.

78 (79). Ventral fins situated in front of pectorals, with 1 spiny and 5 soft rays. Anal fin with a spine anteriorly (Figure 66). . . . . 21. **Bathyclupeiformes**

79 (78). Ventral fins, if present, situated on the belly (Figure 67). Pectorals set low near the abdominal margin of the body. True spiny rays absent in the fins.[13] One dorsal fin; an adipose fin commonly present (Figure 68). Oral slit as a rule bordered above by pre-

[11] In family 215. Indostomidae (Figure 53), hypothetically included by Berg in order 37. Gasterosteiformes, the ventrals are situated under the pectorals, but markedly behind their base; the body is covered with bony annuli, as in fish of order 38. Syngnathiformes. In this book this family is included in the order Syngnathiformes.

[12] There are two bases in the genus Rhodichthys and in some species of the genus Paraliparis (family 54. Liparidae).

[13] In some cases the unbranched soft rays at the beginning of the fins may be mistaken for a spine, e.g., in family 57. Pterothrissidae.

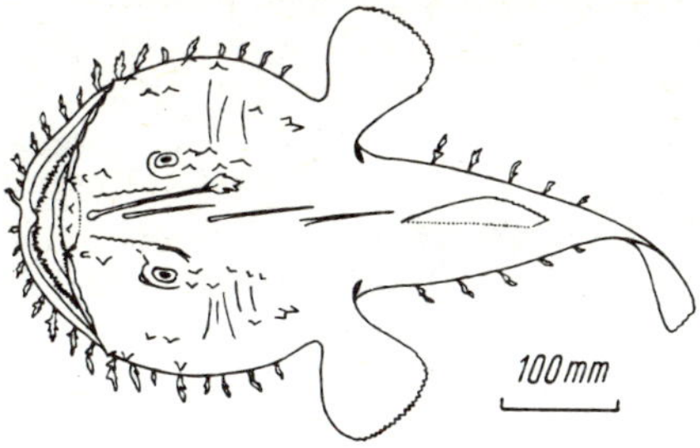

FIGURE 51. Lophiiformes — Lophiomus setigerus (L. and L., 1965, fig. 16)

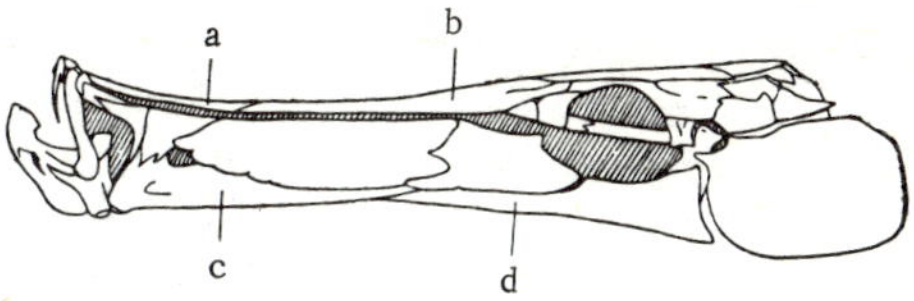

FIGURE 52. Skull of Syngnathus typhle (Syngnathiformes) (L. and L., 1965, fig. 15):

a — vomer; b — mesethmoid; c — quadrate bone; d — preoperculum.

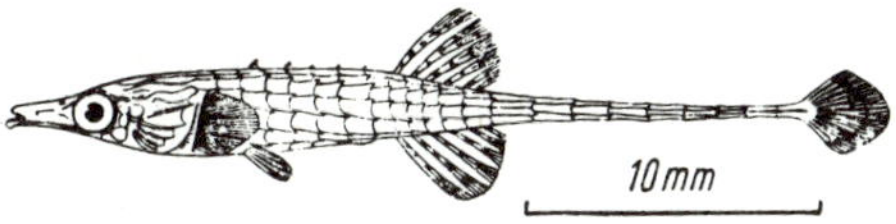

FIGURE 53. Indostomus paradoxus (Syngnathiformes) (Berg, 1940, fig. 170, diagr.)

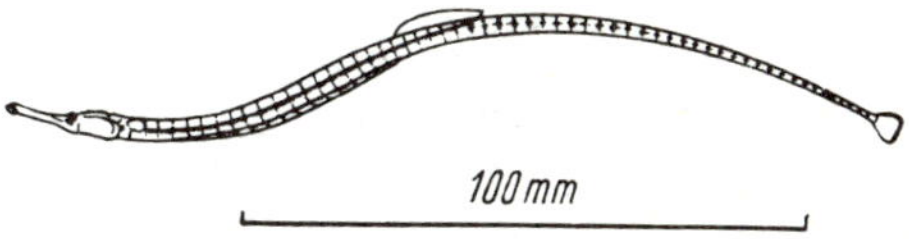

FIGURE 54. Syngnathiformes — Syngnathus schlegeli (Okada, 1955, fig. 100, diagr.)

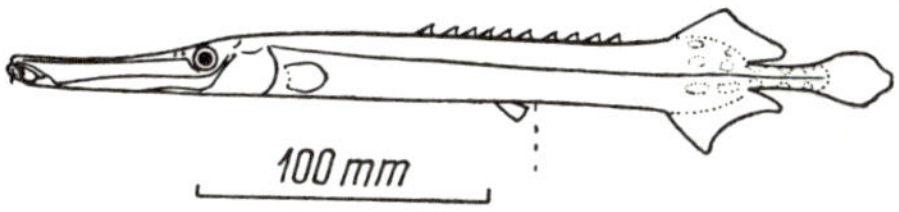

FIGURE 56. Syngnathiformes — Aulostomus valentini (L. and L., 1965, fig. 250)

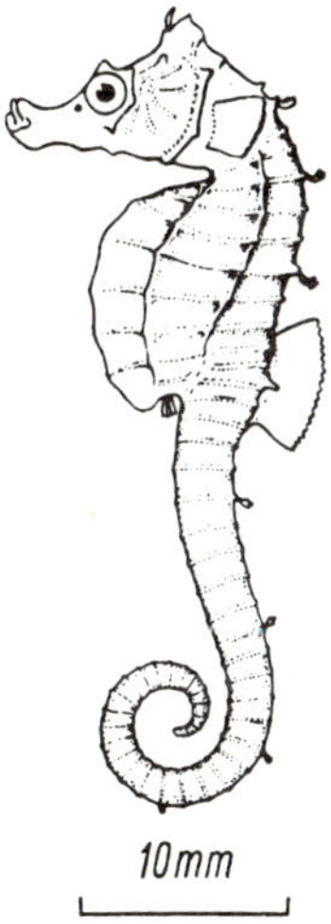

FIGURE 55. Syngnathiformes — Hippocampus japonicus (Okada, 1955, fig. 101, diagr.)

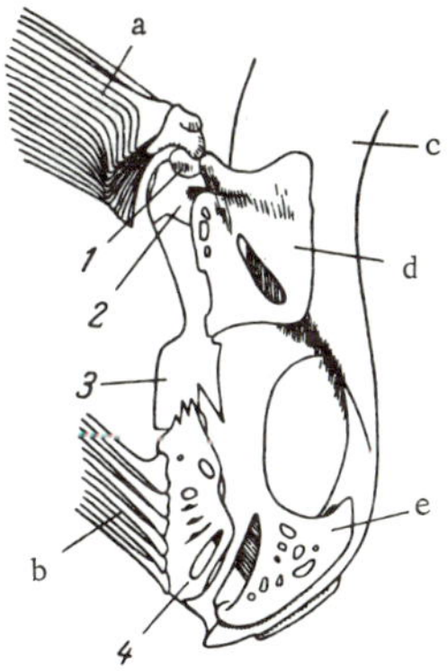

FIGURE 57. Humeral girdle of Polynemus approximans (Polynemiformes) (L. and L., 1965, fig. 18):

1—4) radials of pectoral fin; a — upper part of pectoral; b — free filamentous rays of pectoral; c — cleithrum; d — scapula; e — coracoid.

maxillaries and maxillaries (only by premaxillaries in families 56. Albulidae and 65. Chanidae). Scales generally cycloid. Swim bladder usually with a duct (physostomous forms) . . . . 19. **Clupeiformes**

80 (75). Mesocoracoid absent.

81 (82). Adipose fin generally present.[14] [This order is similar to the suborder Stomiatoidei (order 19. Clupeiformes), from which it differs, apart from in the absence of a mesocoracoid, in that the mouth is bordered only by the premaxillaries (Figure 71).[15]] Ventral fins with 6—13 rays arranged behind the pectoral fins (Figure 73) or under them (Figure 74). [But the pelvic bones are not united with the cleithrum.] Luminescent organs present (Figure 75). [Swim bladder absent or else with a duct (physostomous forms). Radials of pectoral fin ossified.] Caudal fin well developed, not fused with anal . . . . 23. **Myctophiformes**

82 (81). Adipose fin absent.[16]

83 (84). [Olfactory bulbs situated in the region of the nares, and the olfactory nerves, properly the tractus olfactorii, do not pass through the cavity of the orbit (just as in families 140. Cyprinidae and 210. Gadidae).] These characters, like the absence of a mesocoracoid and adipose fin, distinguish these catadromous fish (Figure 77) of the southern hemisphere from the ecologically similar salmonids of the northern hemisphere belonging to order 19. Clupeiformes (Salmonoidei)[17] . . . . 22. **Galaxiiformes**

84 (83). [Olfactory bulbs and olfactory nerves with a different arrangement.]

[14] An adipose fin is absent in fishes that may be isolated from order 20. Myctophiformes and placed in a special order 24. Cetomimiformes. This order is weakly characterized osteologically. These fish differ from the Myctophiformes in the bare, scale-free body, which is sometimes thickly covered with small spines. The mouth is very large; the upper jaw passes beyond the anterior margin of the eye and even far behind the eyes. Eyes small, often very small, or absent. Dorsal fin shifted posteriorly, situated above the anal. Ventral fins absent or small, set on the belly far behind the pectorals. Lateral line canals extremely well developed, represented externally by a few large pores (Figure 69), but if the pores are small, the spaces between them are filled with vertical rows of pores, 5—10 pores per row (Figure 70). Except for family 121. Barbourisiidae, the fishes of this order are included in order 43. Stephanoberyciformes (Bertin and Arambourg, 1958: 2376). Myers and Freihofer (1966: 193—206) recently increased the scope of order 24. Cetomimiformes considerably, including three suborders: Cetomimoidei (families 119. Cetomimidae, 121. Barbourisiidae, and 120. Rondeletiidae), Miripinnoidei (104. Miripinnidae, 105. Eutaeniophoridae, and 104a. Kasidoridae Robins and Silva, 1965), and Megalomycteroidei (104b. Megalomycteridae Myers and Freihofer, 1966—4 genera: Megalomycter M. and F., Ataxolepix M. and F., Cetomimoides Koefoed, 1955, and Vitiaziella Rass, 1955) (see footnote to 0—45). The last suborder differs from the other two above all in the markedly enlarged nasal openings and very strongly developed olfactory organs, which occupy almost the entire area from the apex of the snout to the anterior margin of the eye; the body is covered with a mosaic pattern of scales of various size or else it is bare; ventral fins present or absent. (See Figure 35.) Another two suborders are included in the Cetomimiformes (GRWM, 1966:395): Ateleopodoidei and Giganturoidei, which Berg considered as independent orders (see theses 0—85 and 0—47).

[15] The suborder Bathylaconoidei (order 19. Clupeiformes), which also lacks a mesocoracoid, differs from order 23. Myctophiformes in that the mouth is bordered by the maxillaries, while the small premaxillaries are shifted anteriorly, toward the symphysis (Figure 72).

[16] This fin is sometimes present as an exception in a small family (2 genera and 2 species) of North American freshwater fishes, 238. Percopsidae (Figure 76) of order 42. Percopsiformes (Salmopercae), which is related to order 50. Perciformes.

[17] Unlike the salmonids, which have anadromous migrations, in order 22. Galaxiiformes, migrations are catadromous, that is, spawning is in the sea.

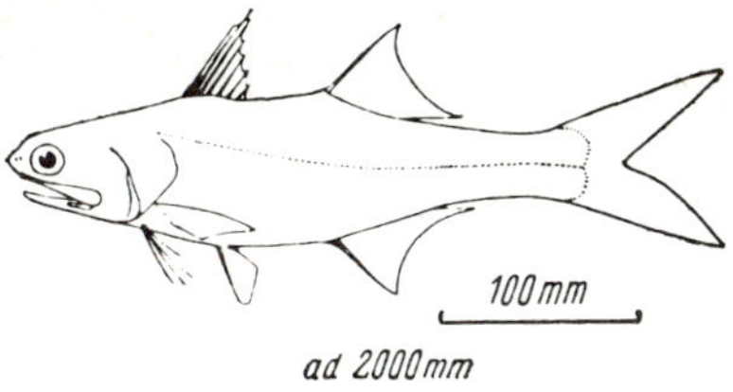

FIGURE 58. Polynemiformes — Eleutheronema tetradactylum (L. and L., 1965, fig. 323)

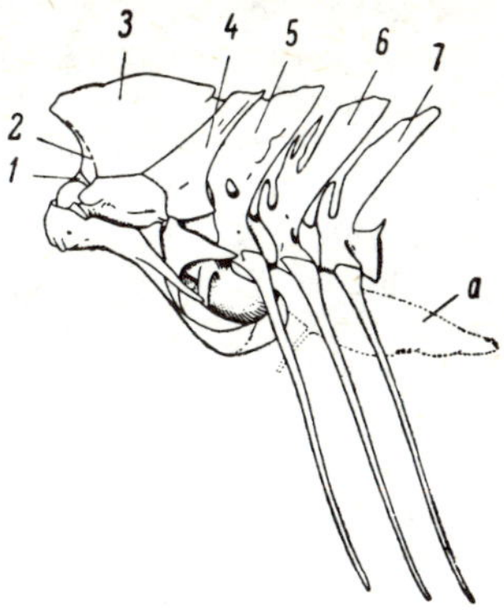

FIGURE 59. Weberian apparatus in Leptobotia mantschurica (Cypriniformes) (L. and L., 1965, fig. 19):

1—7) neutral processes of vertebrae I—VII; a—swim bladder.

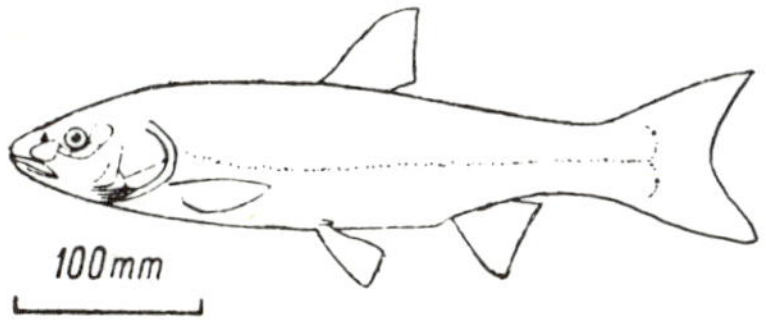

FIGURE 60. Cypriniformes — Leuciscus brandti (L. and L., 1965, fig. 20)

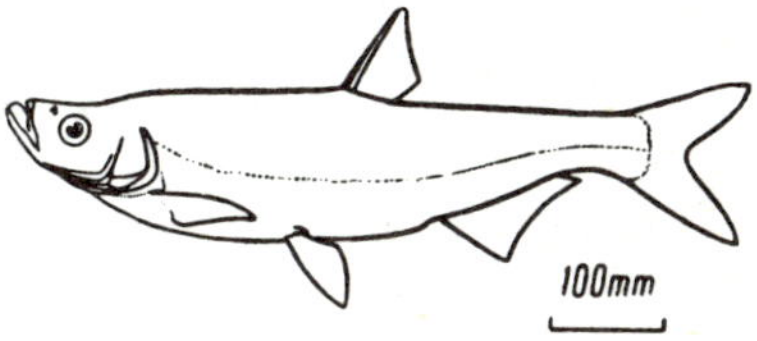

FIGURE 61. Cypriniformes — Erythroculter erythropterus (Berg, 1948, fig. 550, diagr.)

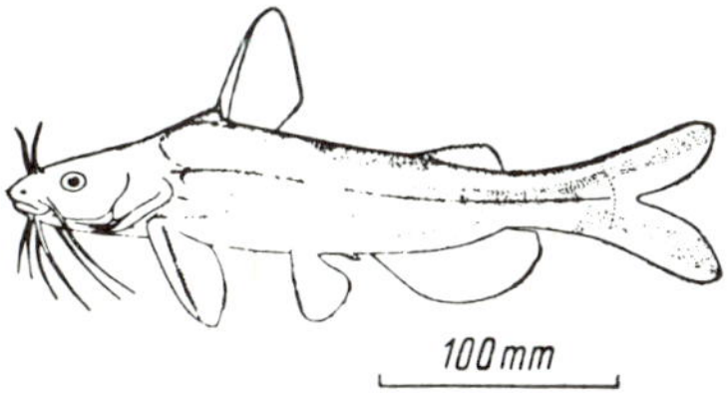

FIGURE 62. Cypriniformes — Pseudobagrus fulvidraco (Berg, 1948, fig. 659, diagr.)

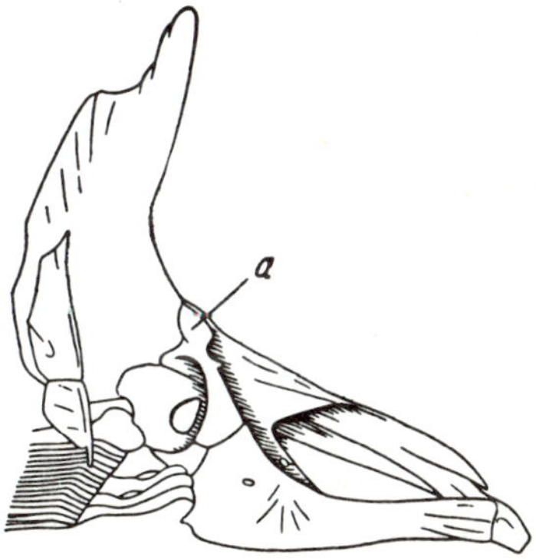

FIGURE 63. Humeral girdle of Stenodus leucichthys nelma (Clupeiformes) (L. and L., 1965, fig. 21):

a — mescoracoid.

85 (86). Caudal fin reduced and fused with the long anal (Figure 78)[18]; dorsal fin with very short base, high, situated almost above base of pectoral. Ventral fins in front of pectorals, each consisting of 1—2 rays. [Closely related to order 23. Myctophiformes, but radials of pectoral fin represented by a single cartilaginous . . . . plate] . . . . 25. Ateleopodiformes

86 (85). Caudal fin, if present, well expressed, but if fused, then to the same extent with the anal as with the dorsal.

87 (130). Ventral fins present[19] and inserted normally on the belly[20] or not far behind the pectorals, or, finally, under the pectorals, but more or less markedly behind the vertical of the posterior margin of the base of the pectorals[21]; they are sometimes very small and widely separated from each other.

88 (89). Suprabranchial nonlabyrinthine organ (Figure 86) present . . . . . . (Figure 87) . . . . 48. Channiformes

89 (88). Suprabranchial nonlabyrinthine organ absent.

90 (91). Distinctive rhombic scales with keels present (Figure 88), arranged in oblique transverse rows. The scales of each row are united with each other. Anterior part of dorsal fin spiny (Figure 89). . . . . 50. Perciformes (Family 413. Tetragonuridae)

91 (90). Such scales absent.

92 (103). True spiny rays not present in any fin.[22] Suborbital stay also absent (see Figure 105).

93 (94). Ventral fins with 15—17 rays; fins long, similar in form and size to pectorals. Body deep, laterally compressed. Anterior part of dorsal fin high, sickle-shaped (Figure 91) . . . . 39. Lampridiformes (Family 222. Lampridae)

[18] This type of caudal region is typical for fish of family 95. Notopteridae of order 19. Clupeiformes (Figure 79), but only in these fish is the caudal not reduced but well expressed, while the dorsal is situated not near the occiput above the base of the pectoral, but roughly in the middle of the body. An even greater external similarity is seen in family 150. Siluridae (order 30. Cypriniformes), but here the caudal fin is distinctly developed (Figure 80), and, the main feature, a Weberian apparatus is present. A similar type of caudal region occurs in fish of order 33. Notacanthiformes (Figure 81), but in these fishes the dorsal fin consists of several low spines separated from each other and the anal has spiny rays anteriorly. In addition, in all these families the ventral fins are situated not in front of the pectorals but on the belly.

[19] As an exception the ventrals are absent in the genus Eumethichthys of family 224. Lophotidae (order 39. Lampridiformes), but typical for these fish is a forehead that protrudes forward, sometimes very far; on the anterior margin of the forehead originates the long dorsal fin which extends to the caudal fin; anal with a very short base, very small, almost imperceptible, situated not far from the posterior end of the ribbonlike body (Figures 82, 83), or absent. Ventrals absent also in Trachipterus ishikawi of family 226. Trachipteridae (Lampridiformes), but they may be meager and therefore not noticeable; the body is again ribbonlike (see Figure 133).

[20] Ventral fins, situated on the belly, are present as an exception in order 45. Zeiformes in Parazen pacificus of family 256. Zeidae (Figure 84).

[21] The ventral fins are as an exception set markedly behind the base of the pectorals in the genus Lyconodes Gilchrist, 1922 and in some species of the genus Coelorhynchus Giorna, 1805 (Figure 85) (family 211. Macrouridae, order 36. Macrouriformes).

[22] In the genus Dermogenys Van Hasselt, 1823 (family 224. Hemiramphidae, order 34. Beloniformes) (Figure 90) the anal fin has 3 weak spiny rays which are somewhat separate from the fin (Fowler, 1933 (1934):326, Figure 80).

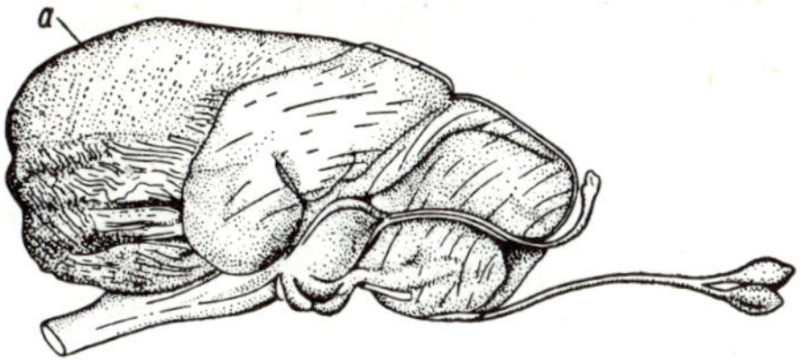

FIGURE 64. Brain of the Mormyriformes (Traité, 1958, III, fig. 1575):

a — cerebellum.

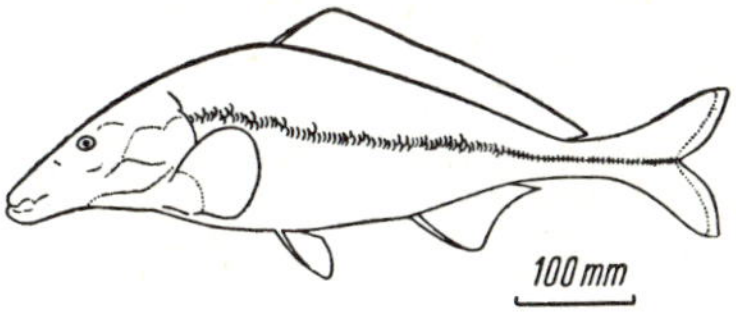

FIGURE 65. Mormyriformes — Mormyrus caballus (Poll, 1957, fig. 93, diagr.)

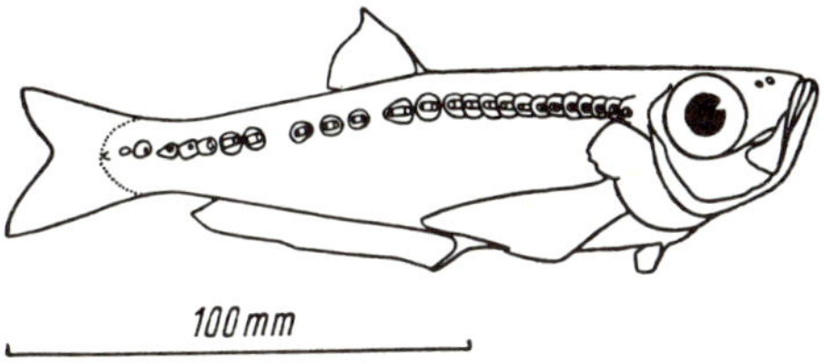

FIGURE 66. Bathyclupeiformes — Bathyclupea malayama (Berg, 1940, fig. 147, diagr.)

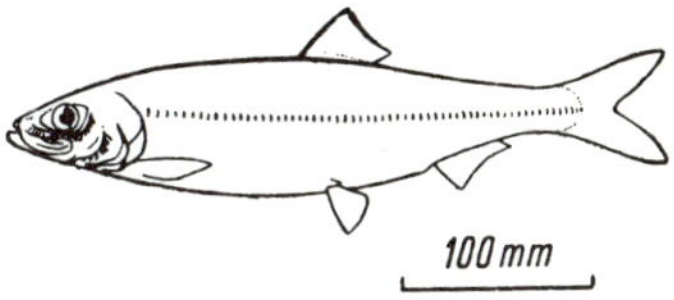

FIGURE 67. Clupeiformes — Clupea harengus pallasi (Svetovidov, 1952, pl. 3, fig. 2, diagr.)

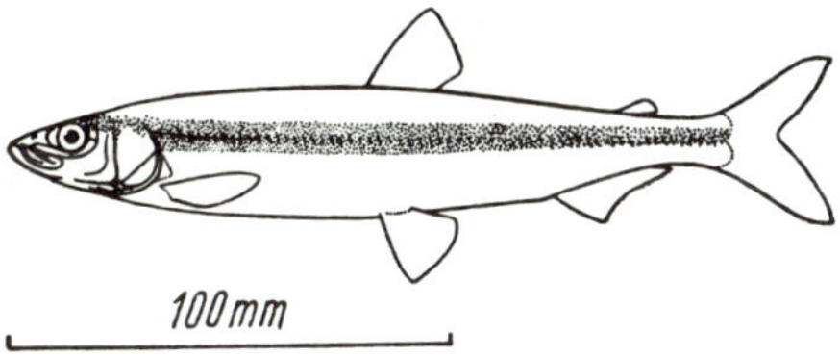

FIGURE 68. Clupeiformes — Hypomesus pretiosus (Berg, 1948, fig. 271, diagr.)

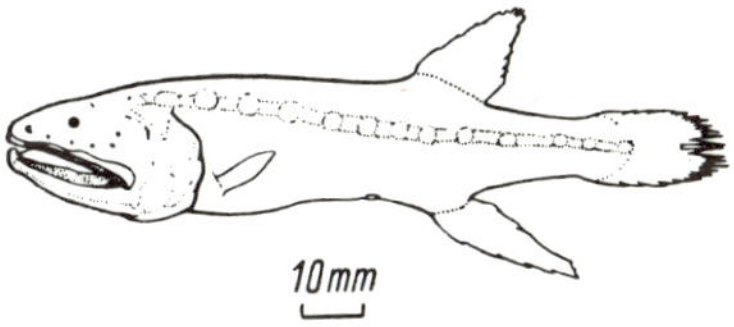

FIGURE 69. Cetomimiformes — Cetomimus indagator (Rofen, 1957—59, fig. 1, diagr.)

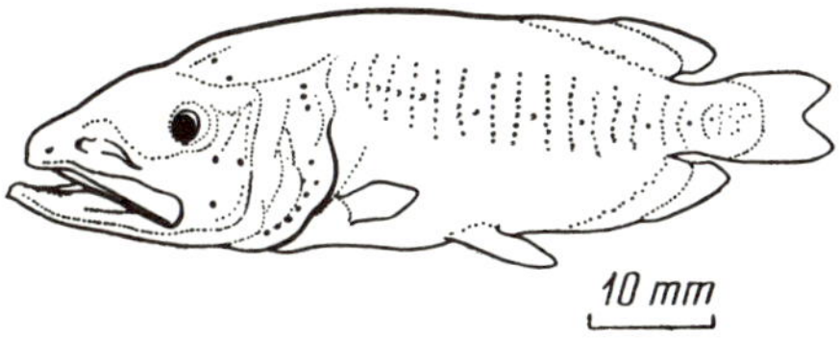

FIGURE 70. Cetomimiformes — Rondeletia bicolor (Rofen, 1957—59, fig. 4, diagr.)

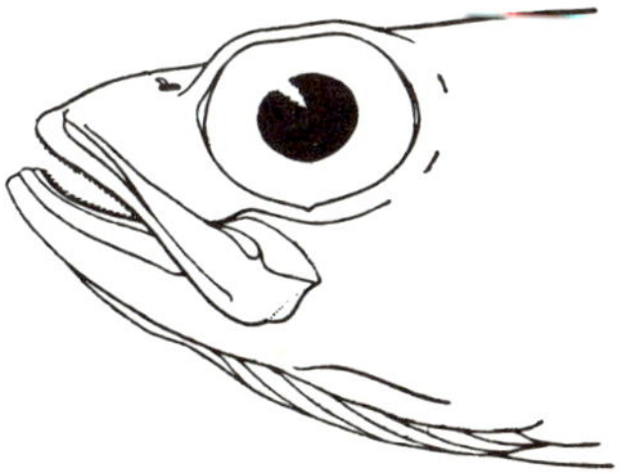

FIGURE 71. Myctophiformes — Hime japonica (head)

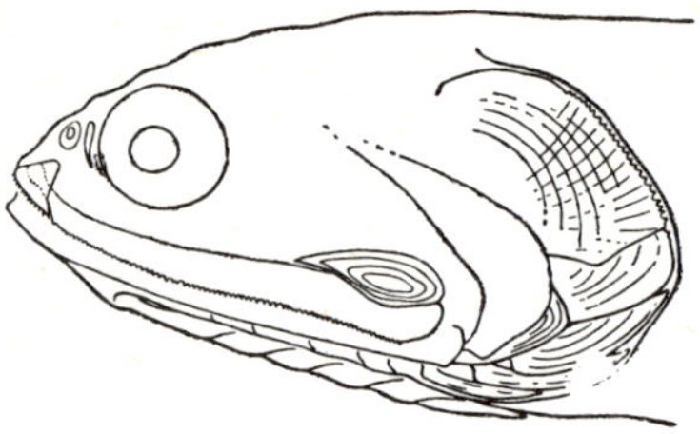

FIGURE 72. *Bathylaco nigricans* (Clupeiformes) (Parr, 1948, fig. 2, diagr.)

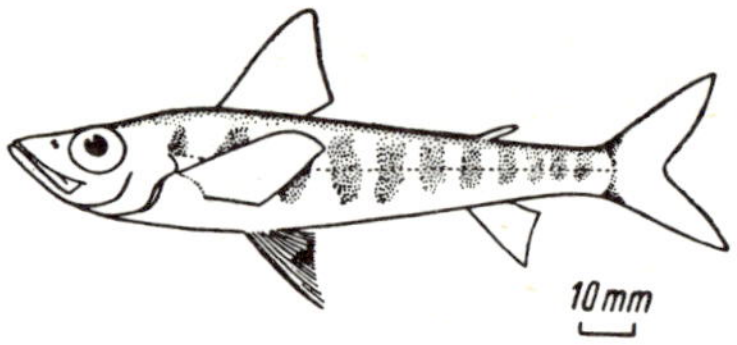

FIGURE 73. Myctophiformes — *Chlorophthalmus albatrossis* (Abe, 1958, fig. 806, diagr.)

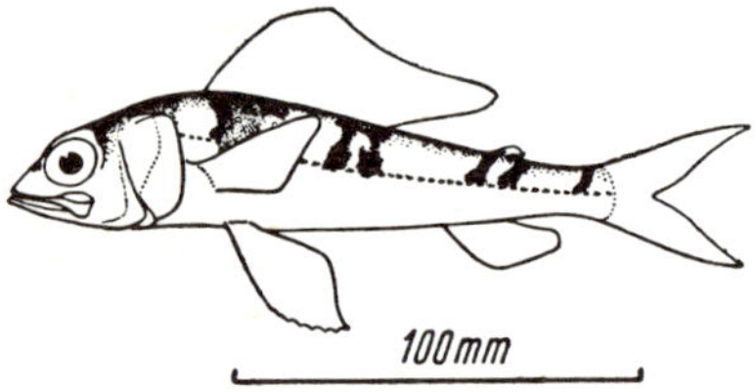

FIGURE 74. Myctophiformes — *Hime japonica* (L. and L., 1965, fig. 23)

FIGURE 75. Myctophiformes — luminescent organs of the Myctophidae (L. and L., 1965, fig. 24)

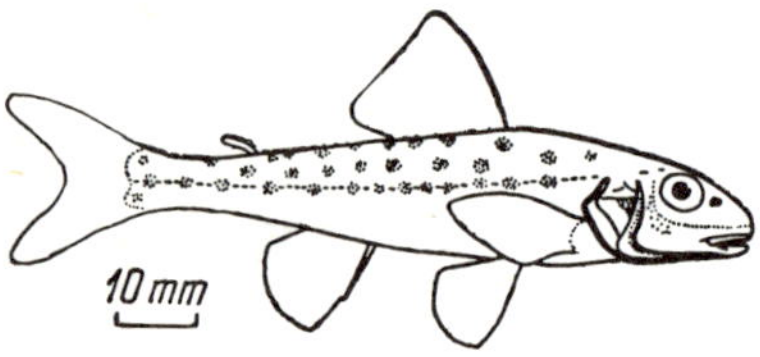

FIGURE 76. *Percopsis omiscomaycus* (Percopsiformes) (Jordan, 1925, fig. 360, diagr.)

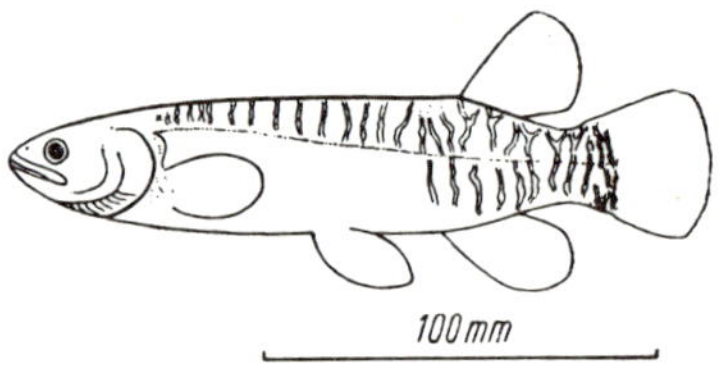

FIGURE 77. Galaxiiformes — *Galaxias fasciatus* (Fowler, 1940, fig. 15, diagr.)

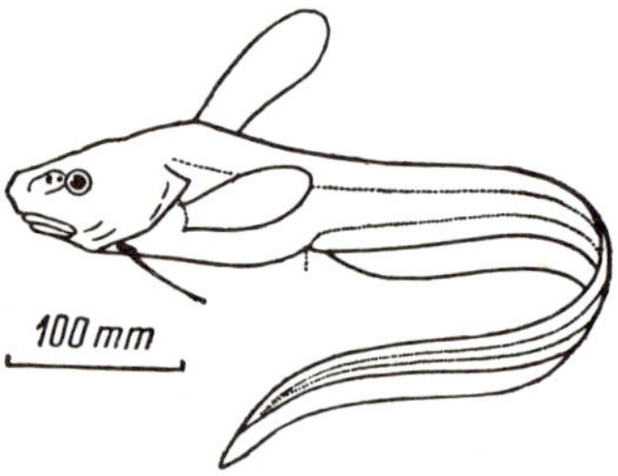

FIGURE 78. Ateleopodiformes — *Ateleopus japonicus* (L. and L., 1965, fig. 25)

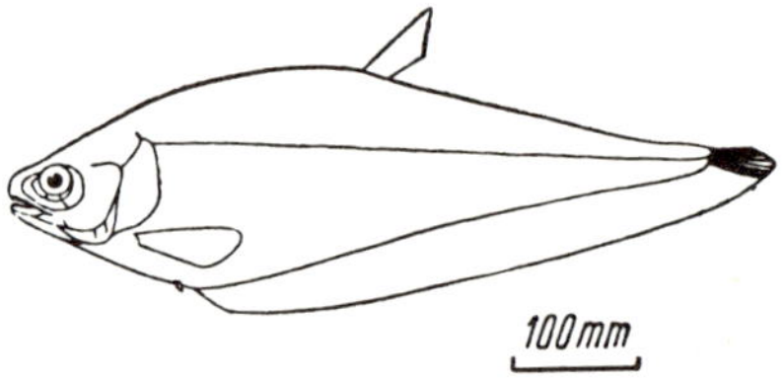

FIGURE 79. *Notopterus notopterus* (Clupeiformes (Day, 1878, pl. 159, fig. 4, diagr.)

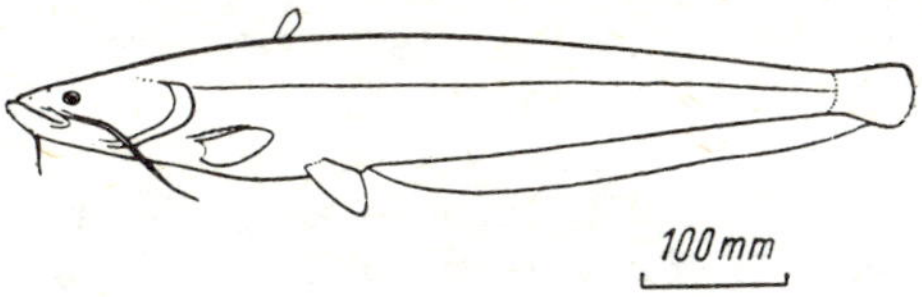

FIGURE 80. Parasilurus asotus (Cypriniformes) (Berg, 1948, fig. 658, diagr.)

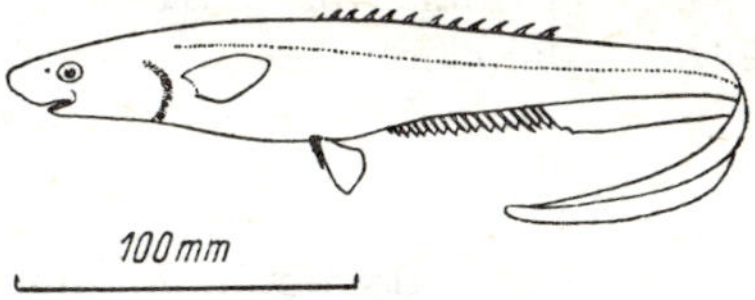

FIGURE 81. Notacanthus macrorhynchus (L. and L., 1965, fig. 11)

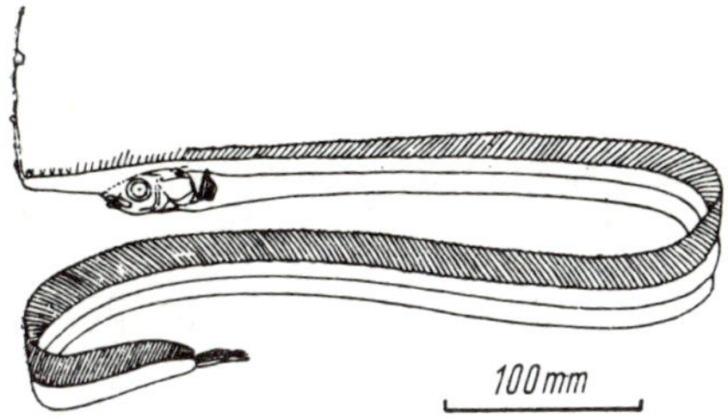

FIGURE 82. Eumetichthys fiski (Lampridiformes) (L. and L., 1965, fig. 26)

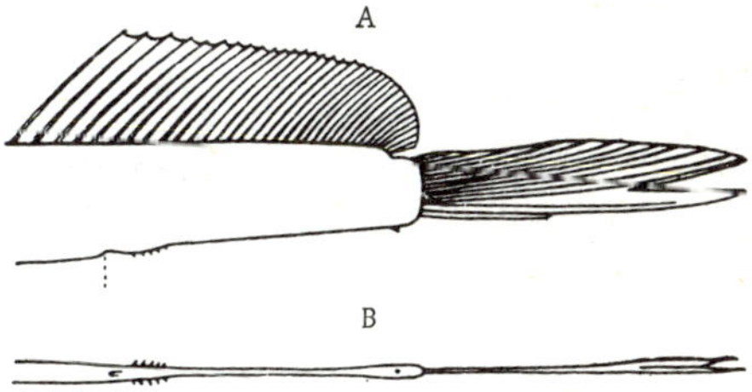

FIGURE 83. Eumetichthys fiski (Lampridiformes) (L. and L., 1965, fig. 278).

Caudal region: A—lateral; B—ventral.

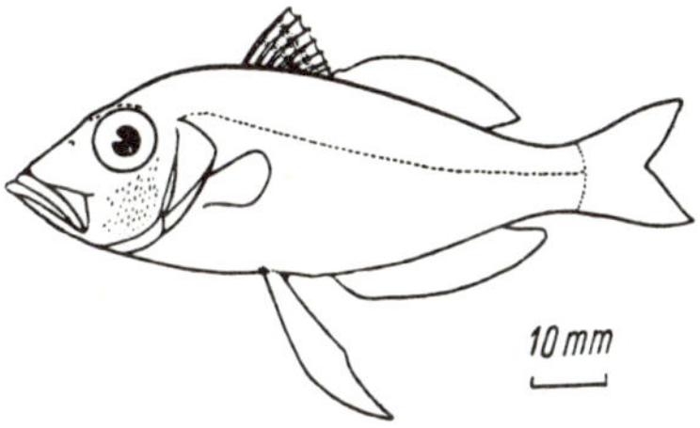

FIGURE 84. Parazen pacificus (Zeiformes) (L. and L., 1965, fig. 49)

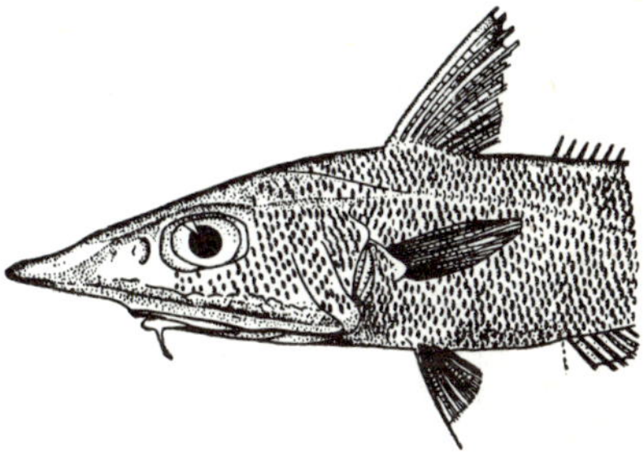

FIGURE 85. Coelorhynchus (Macrouriformes) (L. and L., 1965, fig. 237a)

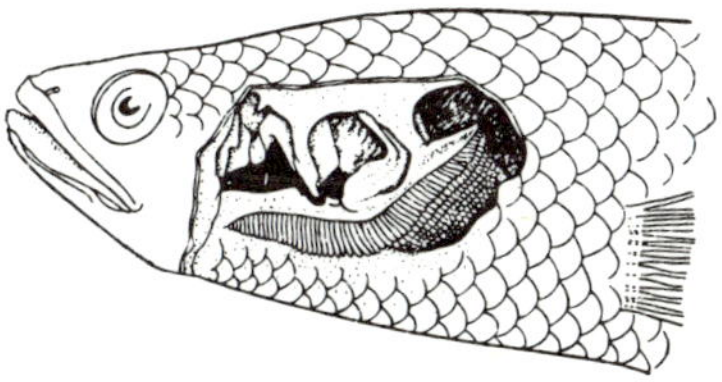

FIGURE 86. Suprabranchial apparatus in Channa (Channiformes) (Traité, 1958, III, fig. 988)

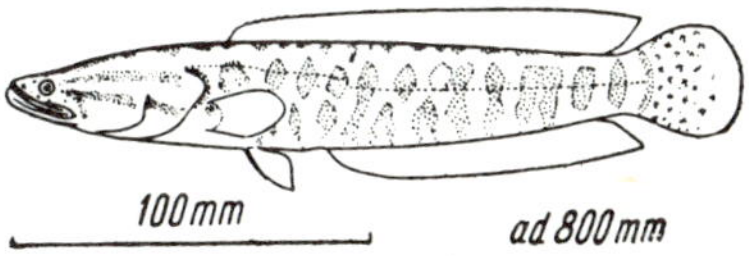

FIGURE 87. Channiformes — Channa argus warpachowskii (Berg, 1948, fig. 740, diagr.)

94 (93). No more than 8 rays in ventral fins.

95 (96). Maxillary usually extending far behind the eye, its length more than half that of the head. Vent on the belly. [Orbitosphenoid absent. Physostomous, or else swim bladder absent.] (Figure 92) . . . . 43. **Stephanoberyciformes**

96 (95). Maxillary not extending beyond eye; if it does, though (in Amblyopsis) (see Figure 493), it is only 1/3 as long as the head and the vent is on the throat.

97 (98). Dorsal and anal with a long base; dorsal beginning on the occiput, anal almost on the vertical of the end of the pectoral. Body quite deep, laterally compressed. Caudal peduncle relatively long, low, almost round in section. (Figure 93) . . . . 54. **Icosteiformes** (Genus Icosteus)

98 (97). Dorsal and anal fins with a short base; accessory fins sometimes present behind them. Body cylindrical. Caudal peduncle not round in section.

99 (100). Adipose fin present. Lateral line passing along middle of sides of body. Ventral fins with 7—8 rays. (Figure 94) . . . . 42. **Percopsiformes** (Family 238. **Percopsidae**)

100 (99). Adipose fin absent. Lateral line passing along underside of body, or else absent.

101 (102). Lateral line present, passing along lower margin of body. Caudal fin with a fairly deep notch (Figure 95). [Infrapharyngeal bones completely fused] . . . . 34. **Beloniformes**

102 (101). Lateral line absent (Figure 96), but if traces are present in the form of seismosensory pores (Gambusia), they are distributed on the sides of the body (Figure 97). [Infrapharyngeal bones not fused.] Caudal fin rounded, truncate, or with a weak notch . . . . .40. **Cyprinodontiformes**

103 (92). Spiny rays present if only in one fin,[23] but if they are weakly expressed, a suborbital stay is present (see Figure 105).

104 (105). Vent situated on the throat, in front of ventral fins. Ventrals with 7—8 rays. (Figure 99) . . . . 42. **Percopsiformes** (Family 239. Aphredoderidae)

105 (104). Vent behind ventral fins.

106 (107). Hyoid barbels present (Figure 100).[24] [Orbitosphenoid present.] Dorsal fin single, with a long base. Ventral fins with 7—8 rays. . . . . 44. **Beryciformes** Family 245. Polymixiidae)

107 (106). Hyoid barbels absent.

[23] Spiny rays are absent in adult specimens of family 295. Menidae (Perciformes) (Figure 98).

[24] Fishes of family 315. Mullidae (Perciformes) also have barbels, but not hyoid barbels; they are situated directly behind the symphysis of the lower jaw (Figure 101); in addition, in the Mullidae the dorsal fin has two bases, and the ventrals are inserted under the base of the pectorals [and there is no orbitosphenoid].

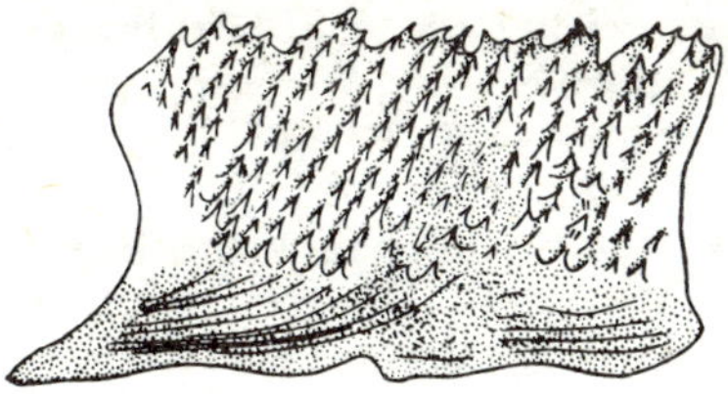

FIGURE 88. Scales in *Tetragonurus cuvieri* (Perciformes) (L. and L., 1965, fig. 28)

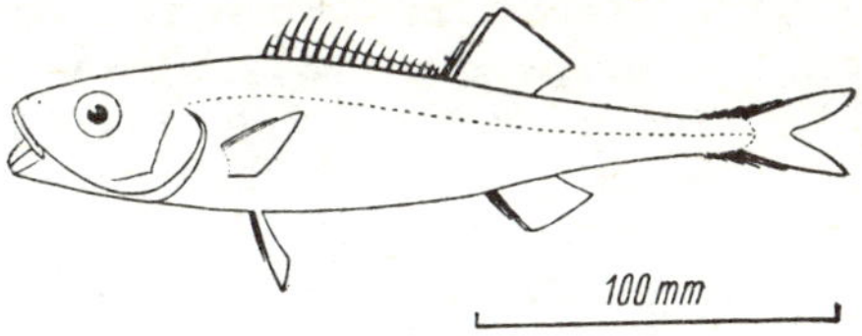

FIGURE 89. Perciformes — *Tetragonurus cuvieri* (L. and L., 1965, fig. 29)

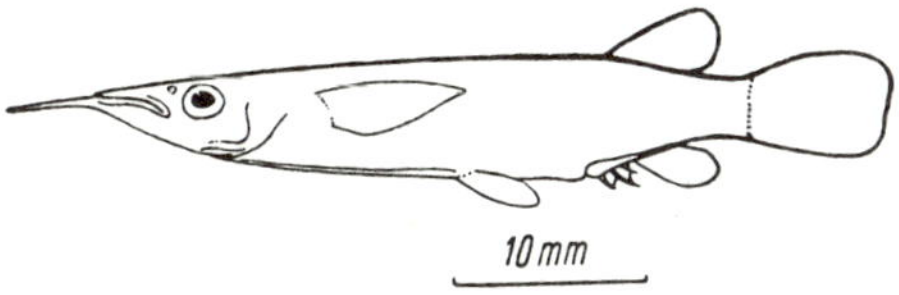

FIGURE 90. *Dermogenys pectoralis* (Beloniformes) (Fowler, 1933—34, fig. 80, diagr.)

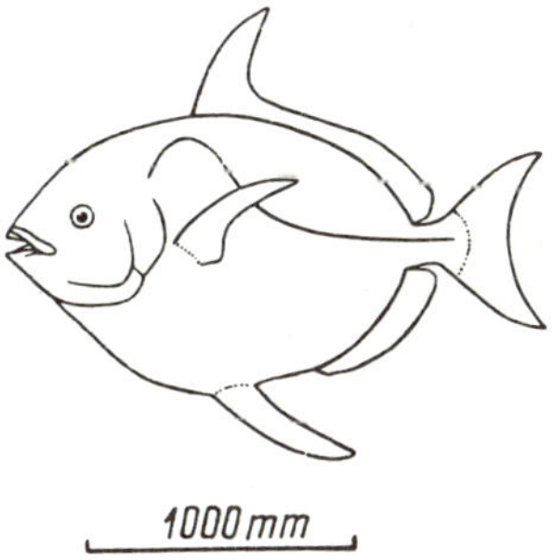

FIGURE 91. Lampridiformes — *Lampris regius* (L. and L., 1965, fig. 31)

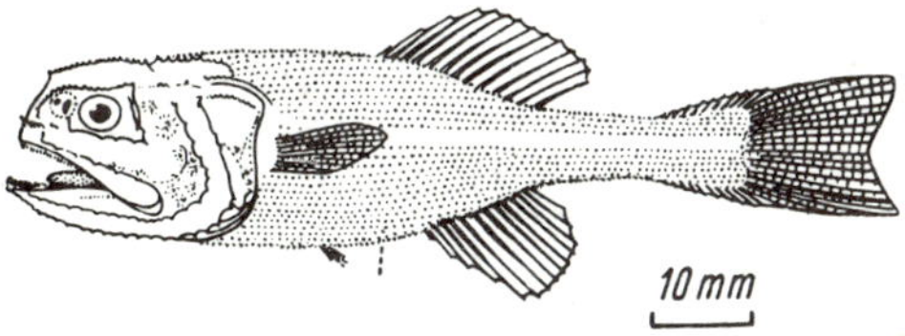

FIGURE 92. Stephanoberyciformes — *Stephanoberyx monae* (Goode and Bean, 1896, pl. 55, fig. 205)

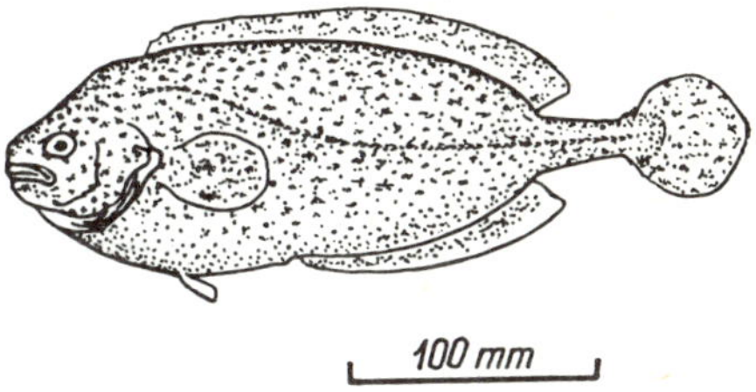

FIGURE 93. Icosteiformes — *Icosteus aenigmaticus*, juv. (M., 1955, II, fig. 509)

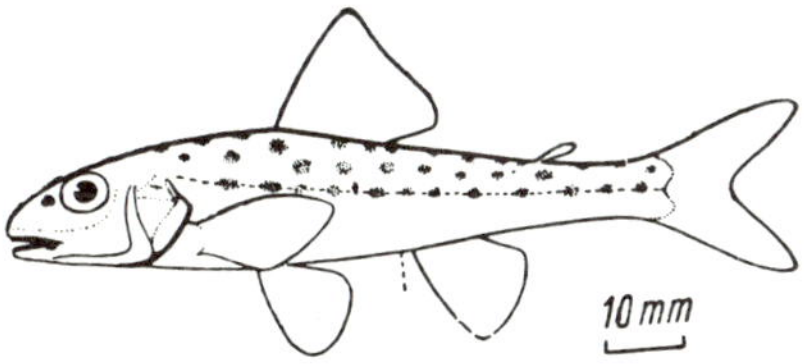

FIGURE 94. Percopsiformes — *Percopsis guttatus* (J. and E., 1900, fig. 329, diagr.)

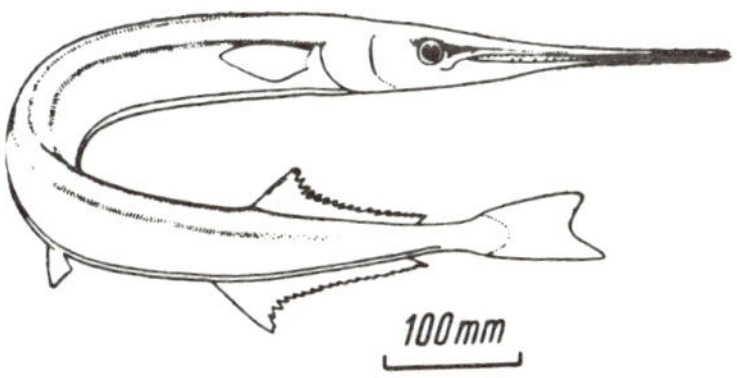

FIGURE 95. Beloniformes — *Tylosurus anastomella* (L. and L., 1965, fig. 200)

108 (109). Ventral fins situated very close behind the pectorals, with a strong spine and 0—4 soft rays (Figure 102).[25] At least two free spines, not connected by a membrane, in front of the dorsal fin. Body spindle-shaped, bare, or with a row of plates along the sides. [Pelvic bones not directly articulating with cleithrum] . . . . 37. Gasterosteiformes

109 (108). Spiny ray in ventral fins not as above, and there are usually in addition at least 5 branched rays.

110 (125). Suborbital stay present (Figure 105); this is a process of the suborbital bone which is intergrown with the preoperculum; it can be probed with a needle under the skin of the cheek.

111 (112). Pectoral fin with 3 radials (Figure 106) . . . . 51. Scorpaeniformes (Family 441. Scorpaenichthyidae)

112 (111). Pectoral fin with 4 radials.

113 (118). Skin not covered with normal scales, bare or with spines, tubercles, or scalelike formations which are reminiscent of strongly developed ctenoid scales. Spiny rays of dorsal fin generally weak.

114 (115). Head enormous, about half as long as the body (without C) (Figure 107). Body and head laterally compressed . . . . 51. Scorpaeniformes (Family 443. Rhamphocottidae)

115 (114). Head much shorter than half the body length. Body spindle-shaped.

116 (117). Ventral fins with 1 concealed spine and 5 soft rays.(Figure 108). . . . . .51. Scorpaeniformes (Family 440. Cottidae, genus J o r d a n i a)

117 (116). Ventral fins with 1 concealed spine and 3 soft rays. (Figure 109) . . . . 51. Scorpaeniformes (Family 440. Cottidae, genus O l i g o c o t t u s)

118 (113). Skin covered with normal scales, but if bare, there are true hard rays in the dorsal fin.

119 (120). Body and head distinctly flattened vertically (Figure 110) . . . . 51. Scorpaeniformes (Family 435. Platycephalidae)

120 (119). Body and head laterally compressed.

121 (122). One pair of nares, one naris on each side. Gill openings sometimes markedly shortened. Rays of first dorsal fin strong (Figures 111, 112). . . . . 51. Scorpaeniformes (Family 439. Congiopodidae)

122 (121). Two pairs of nares, 2 nares on each side; if the second pair is weakly developed, the rays of the first dorsal fin are weak (Figure 114). Gill openings not shortened.

[25] A strong spine in the ventral fins with less than 5 branched rays is present in fishes of family 250. Monocentridae (Beryciformes), in which the whole body is encased in an armor of large bony plates (Figure 103) [and the orbitosphenoid is present]. A strong spine is present also in families 468. Triacanthodidae and 467. Triacanthidae (Tetraodontiformes) [in these fish the pelvic bones are attached directly to the cleithrum], for which a very small mouth and intergrown or united maxillaries and premaxillaries are typical (Figure 104).

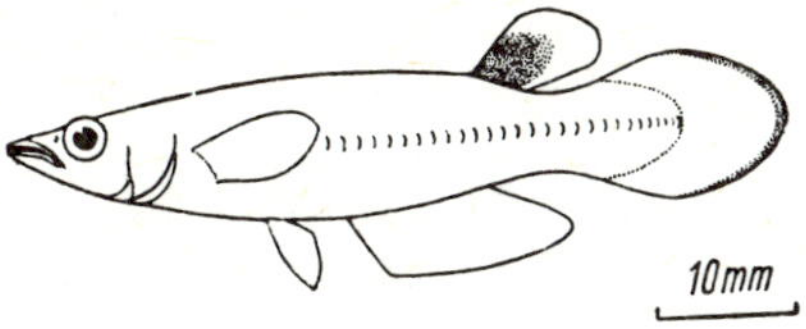

FIGURE 96. Cyprinodontiformes—*Aplochelius panchax* (H. Smith, 1945, fig. 4, diagr.)

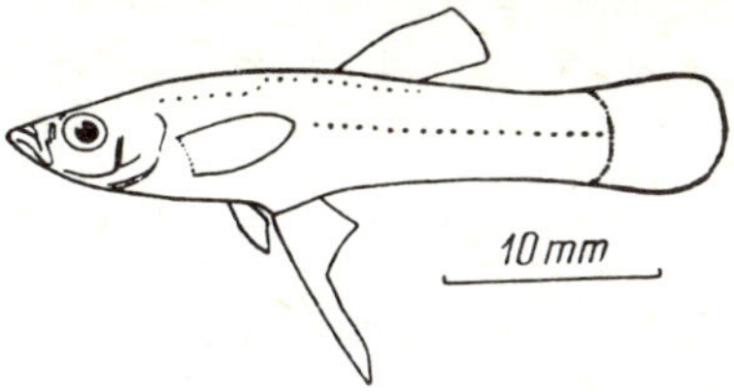

FIGURE 97. Cyprinodontiformes—*Gambusia affinis* (L. and L. , 1965, fig. 285)

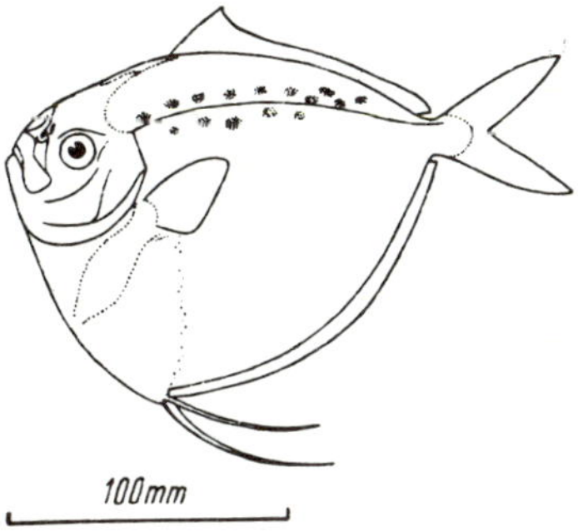

FIGURE 98. *Mene maculata* (Perciformes) (Okada, 1955, fig. 161, diagr.)

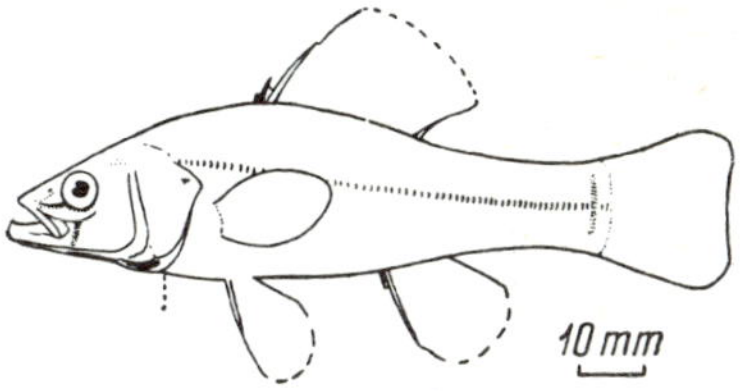

FIGURE 99. Percopsiformes—*Aphredoderus sayanus* (Jordan, 1925, fig. 337, diagr.)

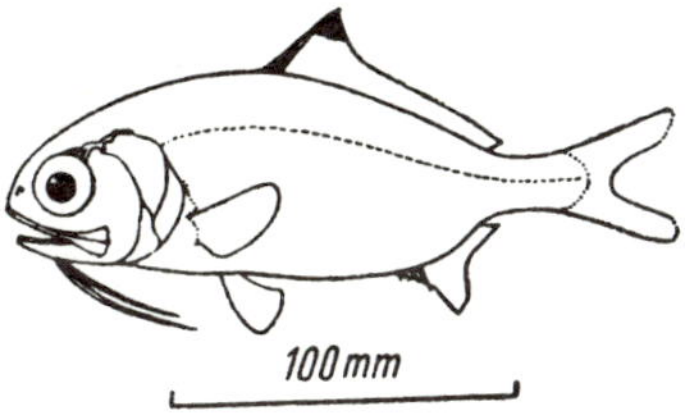

FIGURE 100. Beryciformes—*Polymixia japonica* (L. and L., 1965, fig. 32)

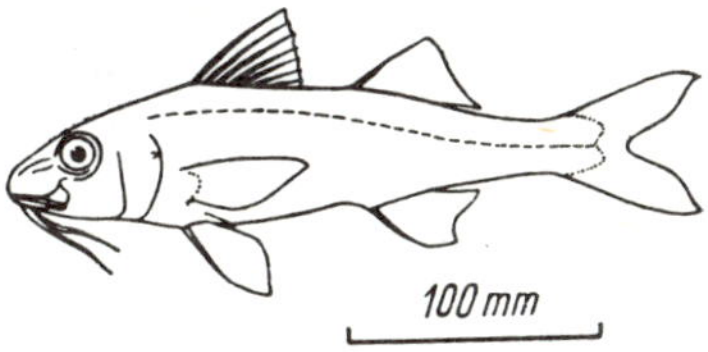

FIGURE 101. *Upeneoides bensasi* (Perciformes) (L. and L., 1965, fig. 33)

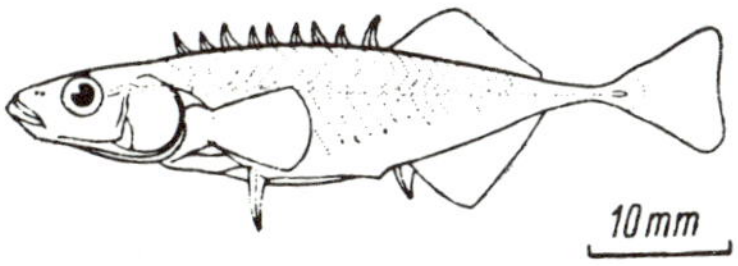

FIGURE 102. Gasterosteiformes—*Pungitius sinensis* (Berg, 1948, fig. 696, diagr.)

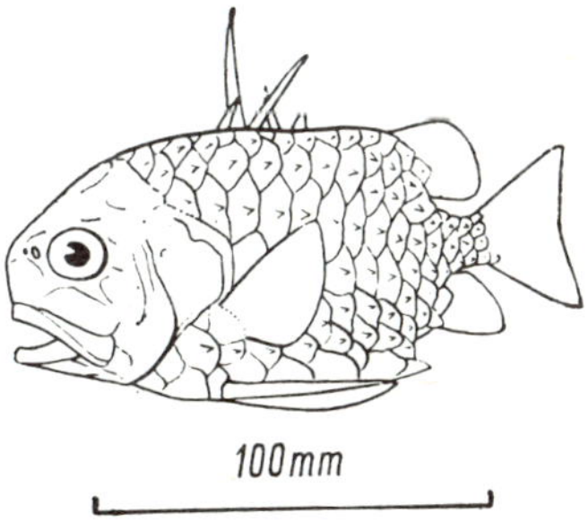

FIGURE 103. *Monocentris japonicus* (Beryciformes) (L. and L., 1965, fig. 35)

123 (124). Keel-shaped protuberances and spines on the head. Spiny rays of dorsal fin strong. [Less than 30, rarely 31, vertebrae.] . . . Figure 113 . . . . 51. Scorpaeniformes (Family 425. Scorpaenidae)

124 (123). No keel-shaped protuberances and spines on the head. Dermal processes (lobes) present. Spiny rays of dorsal fin rather weak. Second pair of nares sometimes weakly developed and not noticeable (Figures 114, 115) . . . . .51. Scorpaeniformes (Family 433. Hexagrammidae)

125 (110). Suborbital stay absent.

126 (127). Orbitosphenoid present (Figure 116). Ventral fins with 5 soft rays. Body low. Anterior rays of dorsal fin short, in the form of spines. (Figure 117) . . . . 44. Beryciformes (Family 255. Gibberichthyidae)

127 (126). Orbitosphenoid absent.

128 (129). Dorsal fins widely separated from each other (Figure 118). Ventral fins situated on the belly or under the spectorals, but markedly behind their base. [Pelvic bones joined to pectoral girdle (with the cleithra or postcleithra), not directly but by a ligament] . . . . 46. Mugiliformes[26]

129 (128). Dorsal fins with contiguous bases (Figure 119), but if (more rarely) the fins are separate, the separation is negligible and the ventral fins are situated not on the belly but near the base of the pectorals (Figure 120). [Pelvic bones united with pectoral girdle by direct attachment to the cleithra (Figure 121).] . . . . 51. Perciformes (Percoidei)

130 (87). Ventral fins absent, but if present, inserted under base of pectorals, or in front of them on the throat, or even on the chin.

[26] Gosline (1962) includes in the order Mugiliformes apart from the Sphyraenidae, Mugilidae, and Atherinidae also the Polynemidae and Phallostethoidei. Rosen (1964) considers, on the other hand, that the families Mugilidae and Sphyraenidae of the order Mugiliformes and the order Polynemiformes should be included in the order Perciformes, thus depriving these orders of their validity, as he created a new order, Atheriniformes, on the basis of the family Atherinidae. He includes here the following orders in our key: Beloniformes (34), Cyprinodontiformes (40), Phallostethiformes (41), and from the Mugiliformes (46) the family Atherinidae. He distinguishes three suborders in the new order: I – Atherinoidei with 2 superfamilies: Atherinoidea (3 families – 260. Atherinidae, the newly established 26b. Isonidae, and 260a. Melanotaeniidae) and Phallostethoidea (2 families – 237a. Neostethidae and 237. Phallostethidae); II – Cyprinodontoidei with 2 superfamilies: Cyprinodontoidea (5 families – 229. Cyprinodontidae, 233. Goodeidae, 234. Jenynsiidae, 235. Anablepidae, and 236. Poeciliidae) and Adrianichthyoidea (3 families – 232. Adrianichthyidae, the newly established 229a. Oryziatidae, and 230. Horaichthyidae); III – Exocoetoidei with 2 superfamilies: Exocoetoidea (2 families – 204. Hemiramphidae and 205. Exocoetidae) and Scomberesocoidea (2 families – 202. Belonidae and 203. Scomberesocidae). The characterization of the order Atheriniformes is built primarily on the skeletal features, and therefore it is difficult to use when determining families according to external characters. While noting Rosen's very interesting anatomical theories on the phylogenetic kinship and integrity of his group, but not pursuing the aim of making a critical analysis of the system, we have not introduced changes in Berg's system and have not used Rosen's data in this work, since our main task is to facilitate the determination of families primarily according to gross morphological characters.

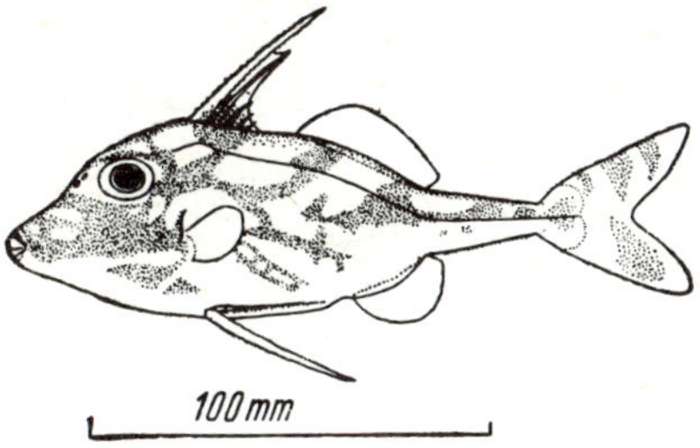

FIGURE 104. Triacanthus strigillifer (Tetraodontiformes) (Fowler, 1937, fig. 289)

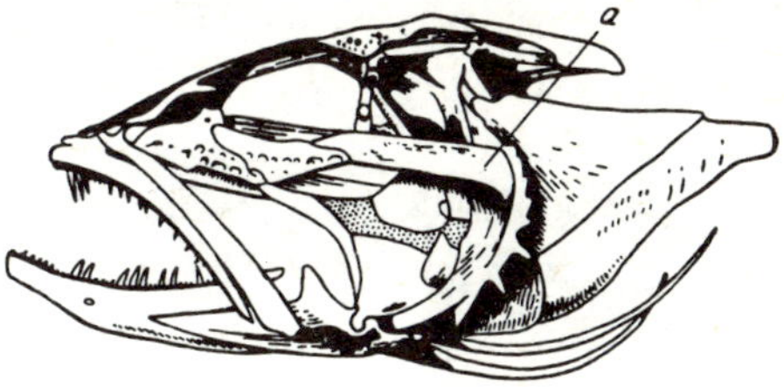

FIGURE 105. Skull of Ophiodon elongatus (Scorpaeniformes) (L. and L., 1965, fig. 53):

a—suborbital stay.

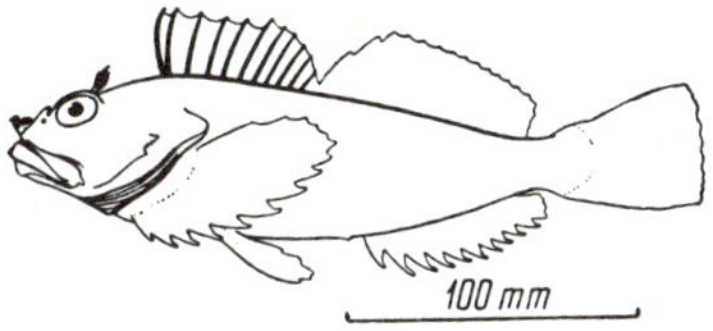

FIGURE 106. Scorpaeniformes—Scorpaenichthys marmoratus (Bolin, 1944, fig. 1, diagr.)

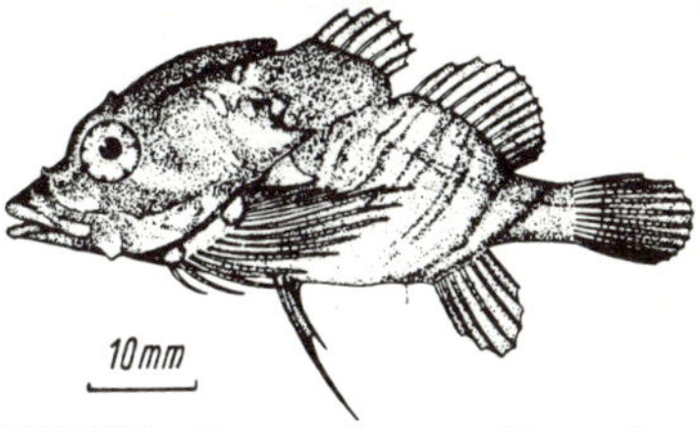

FIGURE 107. Scorpaeniformes—Rhamphocottus richardsoni (J. and E., 1900, fig. 742)

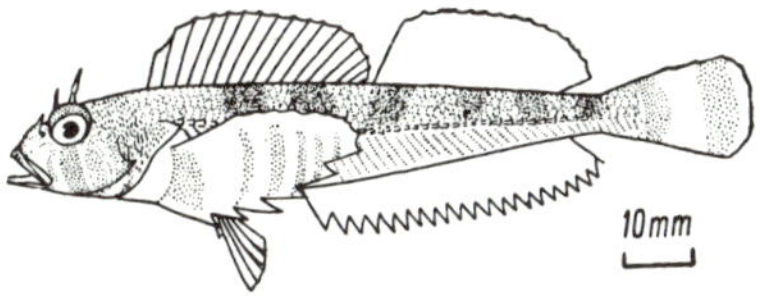

FIGURE 108. Scorpaeniformes—Jordania zanope (J. and E., 1900, fig. 684, diagr.)

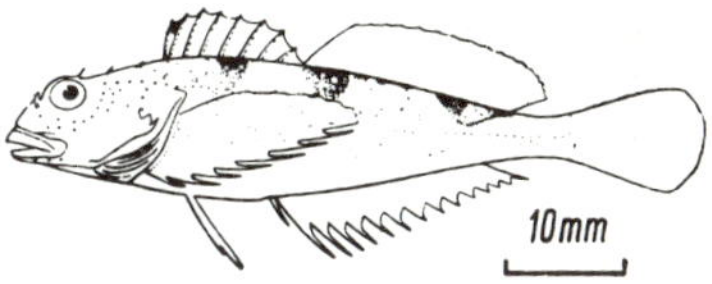

FIGURE 109. Scorpaeniformes—Oligocottus maculosus (J. and E., 1900, fig. 734, diagr.)

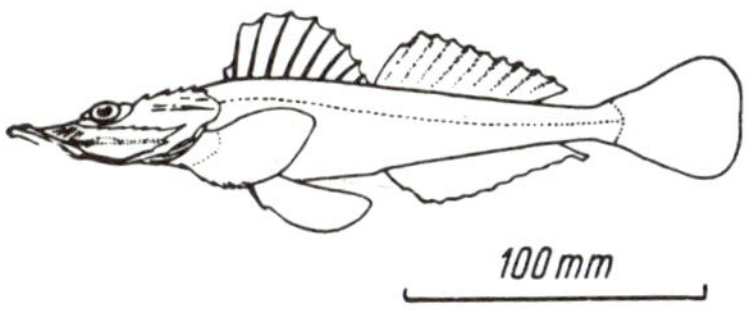

FIGURE 110. Scorpaeniformes—Suggrundes meerdervoorti (Okada, 1955, fig. 313, diagr.)

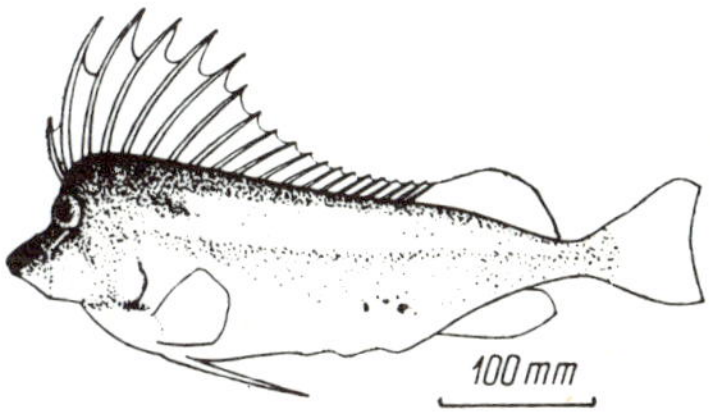

FIGURE 111. Scorpaeniformes—Congiopodus torvus (Smith, 1950, pl. 84, fig. 1060, diagr.)

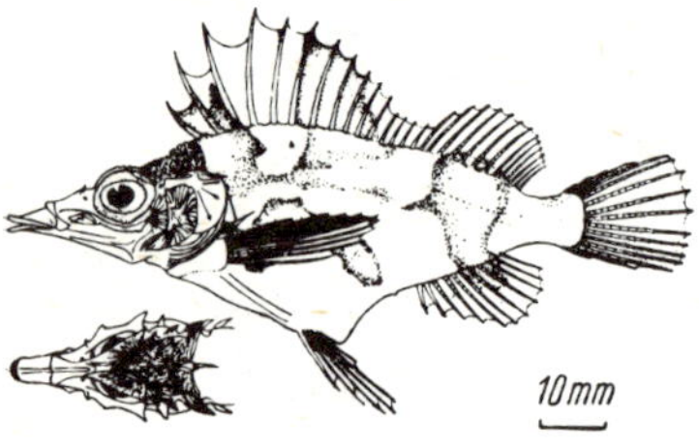

FIGURE 112. Scorpaeniformes—Alertichthys blacki (Moreland, 1960, figs, 1, 2)

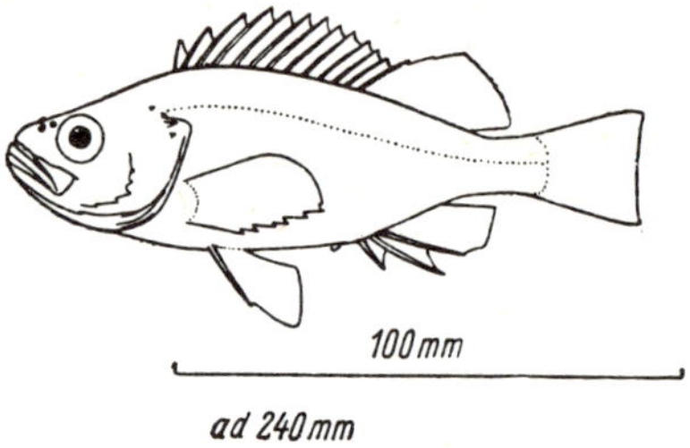

FIGURE 113. Scorpaeniformes—Sebastes steindachneri

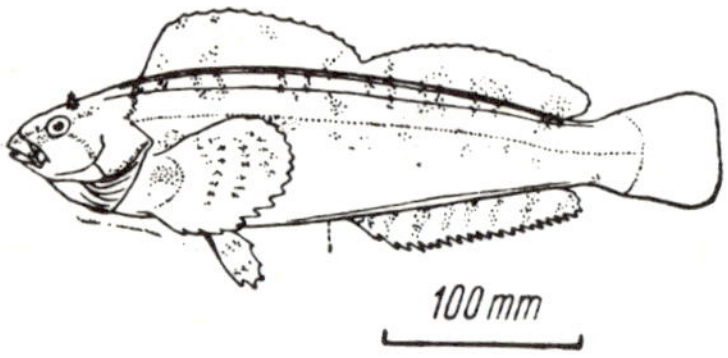

FIGURE 114. Scorpaeniformes—Hexagrammos octogrammus (M., 1955, III, fig. 420, diagr.)

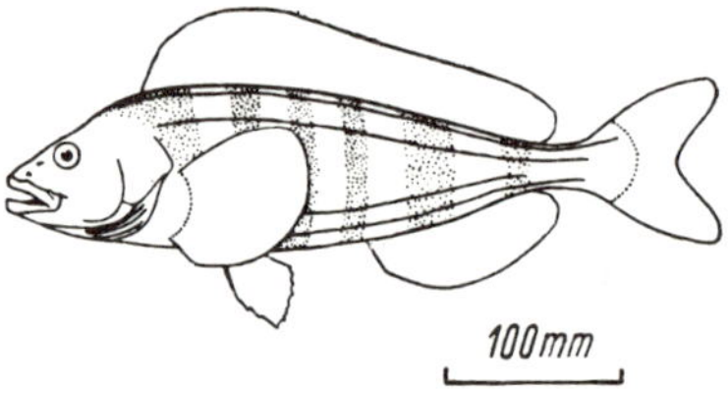

FIGURE 115. Scorpaeniformes—Pleurogrammus monopterygius (J. and E., 1900, fig. 676, diagr.)

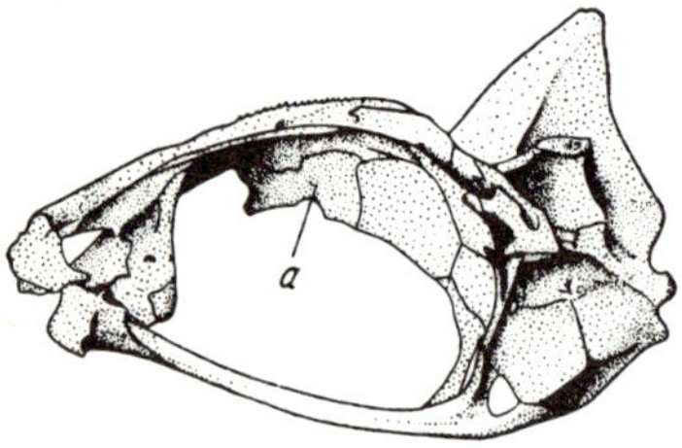

FIGURE 116. Skull of Beryx splendens (L. and L., 1965, fig. 42):

a—orbitosphenoid.

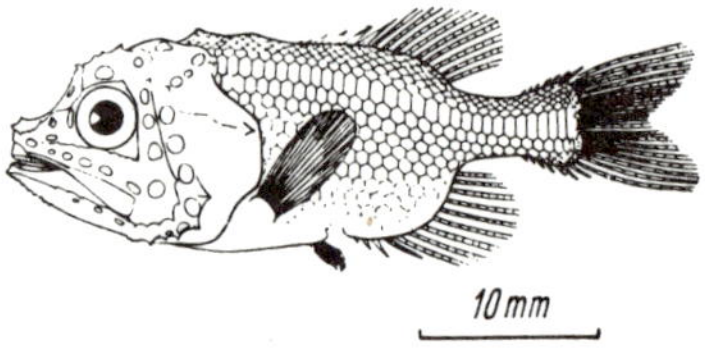

FIGURE 117. Beryciformes—Gibberichthys pumilus (Parr, 1933, fig. 1)

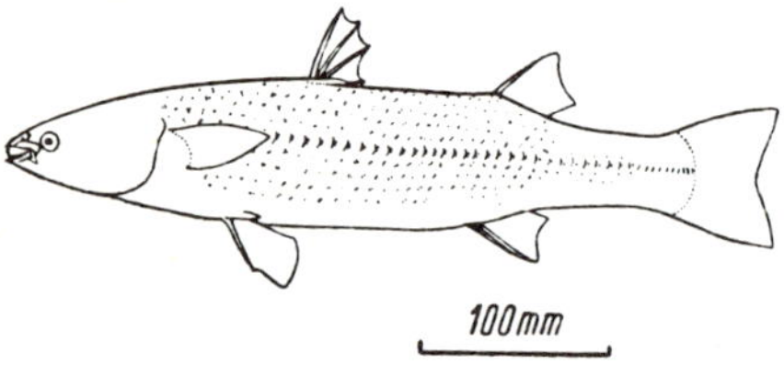

FIGURE 118. Mugiliformes—Mugil so-iuy (L. and L., 1965, fig. 40)

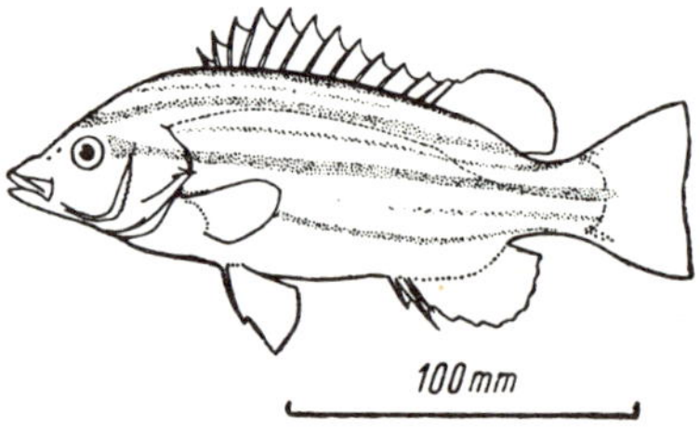

FIGURE 119. Perciformes—Therapon oxyrhynchus (Okada, 1955, fig. 205, diagr.)

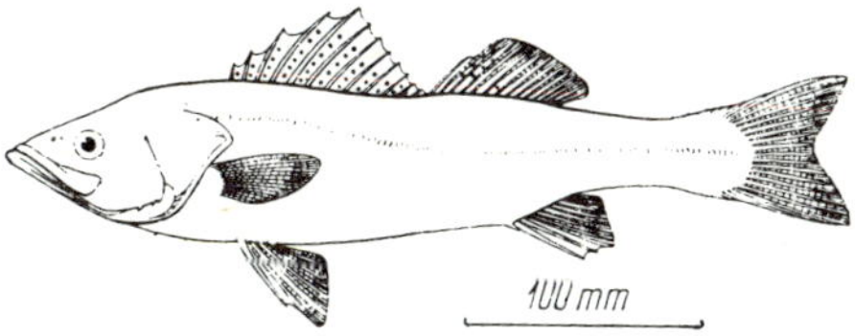

FIGURE 120. Perciformes—*Lateolabrax japonicus* (Lindberg and Krasyukova, 1969, fig. 124)

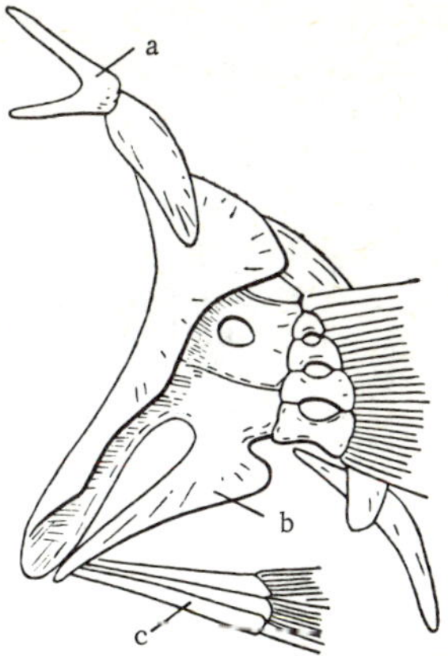

FIGURE 121. Pectoral girdle in *Serranus cabrilla* (Perciformes) (W. and B., 1931, 6, fig. 80):

a—posttemporal bone; b—cleithrum; c—pelvic bones.

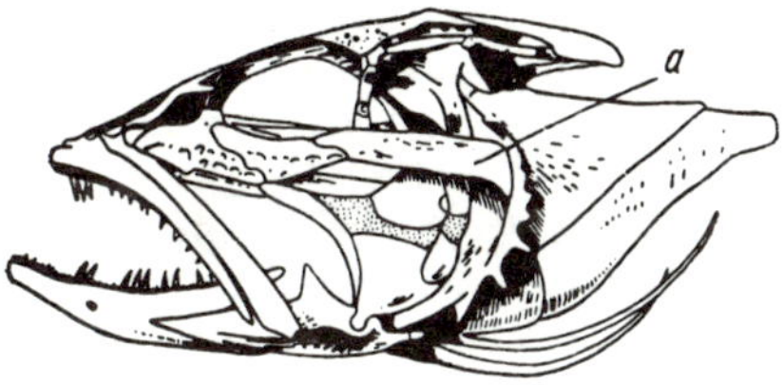

FIGURE 122. Suborbital stay (a) (*Ophiodon elongatus*) (L. and L., 1965, fig. 53)

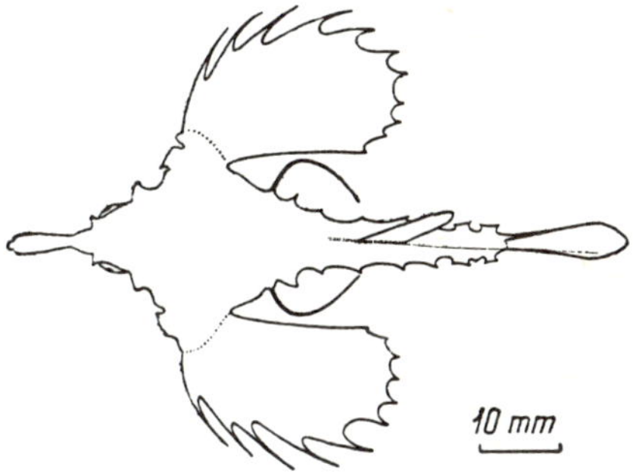

FIGURE 123. *Pegasus papilio* (Pegasidae) (Gosline and Brock, 1960, fig. 92)

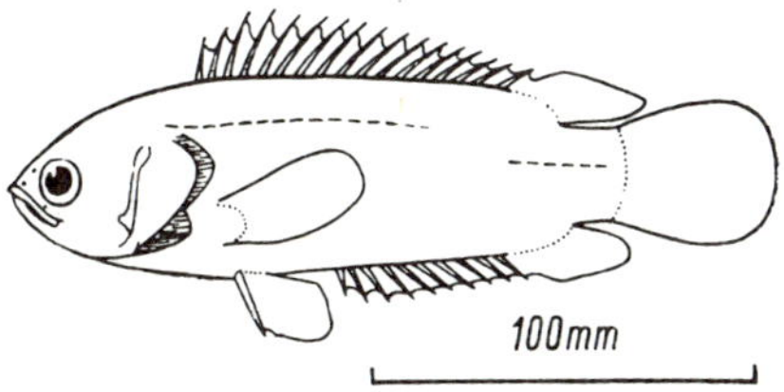

FIGURE 124. *Anabas testudineus* (Perciformes) (Wang, 1958, fig. 469, diagr.)

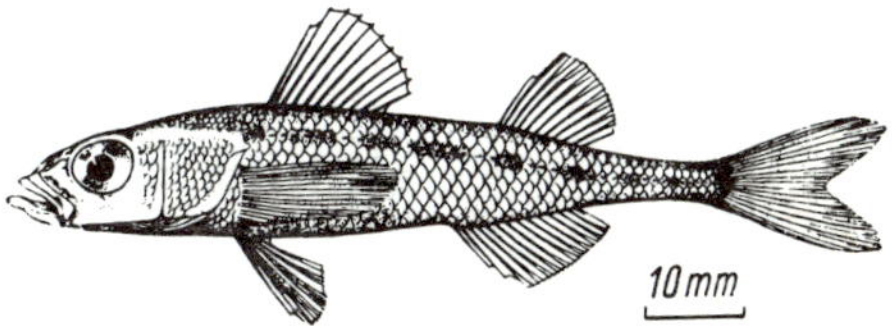

FIGURE 125. *Normanichthys crockeri* (Scorpaeniformes) (Norman, 1938, fig.)

131 (134). Suborbital stay present (Figure 122)[27] — suborbital bones firmly connected with preoperculum by their posterior process; this process is probed by a needle under the skin of the cheek.

132 (133). [Nasals fused, forming a single unpaired bone. Behind the supraoccipital and parietal bones there are two pairs of tabularia, the posterior pair of which is very large (Figure 126). The first suborbital is united with the preoperculum.] Pectorals reaching the base of the caudal fin. (Figure 127) . . . . 52. Dactylopteriformes

133 (132). [Nasals not fused. Two pairs of tabularia absent behind the supraoccipital and parietal bones. Second suborbital united with preoperculum.] Pectorals much shorter. (Figures 128 — 130) . . . . 51. Scorpaeniformes

134 (131). Suborbital stay absent.

135 (150). [Orbitosphenoid present (Figure 131).] See theses 0—136—149, and if they do not fit, continue to thesis 0 — 150.

136 (139). Spiny rays absent both in dorsal and in anal fin.

137 (138). Ventral fins absent, but if present, without spiny ray. Body either markedly elongate, often ribbonlike, with the dorsal fin beginning in front of the eyes (Figure 132), sometimes with an upward bent (Figure 133) or elongate caudal fin (Figures 134, 135), but frequently with long rays of the dorsal fin on the head (Figure 136), or, finally, if the body is deep, the dorsal and anal fins are high, exceeding the length of the head, and the ventrals are well developed (Figure 237). . . . . 39. Lampridiformes (Families 223 — 227, see thesis 0—93)

138 (137). Ventral fins present, each with one spiny flattened ray in the form of a plate and 6 branched rays. Body not elongate. Lateral line absent. (Figure 138) . . . . 44. Beryciformes (Family 247. Diretmidae)

139 (136). Spiny rays present in both dorsal and anal. Body not elongate.

140 (141). Body with distinctive armor of large hard scales. One large thick spine and 3 small soft rays in the ventral fin. First dorsal separated from second by a considerable space and consisting of 5 — 6 long, thick, strong spines that are not connected by a membrane and that are similar to the spine in the ventral fins. Mouth and gill openings not decreased in size. (Figure 139) . . . . 44. Beryciformes (Family 250. Monocentridae)

141 (140). No such armor present and no large separate spines as described in thesis 140.

142 (143). A large luminescent organ under the eye. Dorsal fin with one or two bases; dorsal fin with 4 — 5 spiny rays, anal with 2. (Figure 140) . . . . 44. Beryciformes (Families 251—252. Anomalopidae)

[27] A suborbital process is present also in order 62. Pegasiformes (Figure 123) and in the genus A n a b a s sensu stricto (Figure 124). (Berg, 1940: 328). On the other hand, in the genus N o r m a n i c h t h y s (Figure 125) of order 51. Scorpaeniformes, although the second suborbital bone does have a process, it is attached to the preopercular bone by muscles, since it is relatively short, as it is in the genus C o m e p h o r u s as well. Both in outer appearance and in the well developed normal scales, the genus N o r m a n i c h t h y s differs from members of the Cottoidei, although it is still included in this suborder.

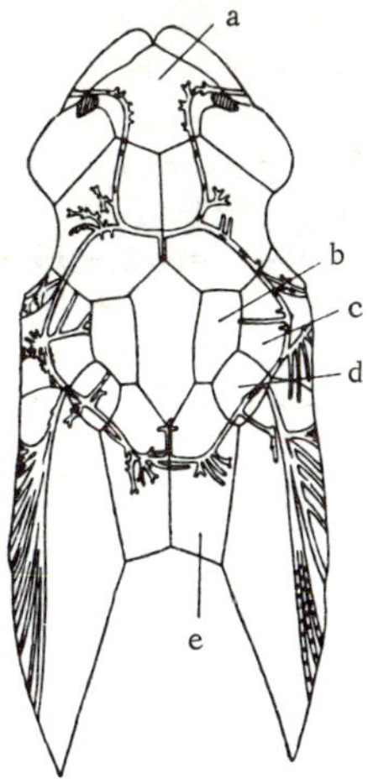

FIGURE 126. Skull of *Dactylopterus volitans* (Dactylopteriformes) (L. and L., 1965, fig. 54):

a—nasal bone; b—supraoccipital bone; c—parietal bone; d—tabularia I; e—tabularia II.

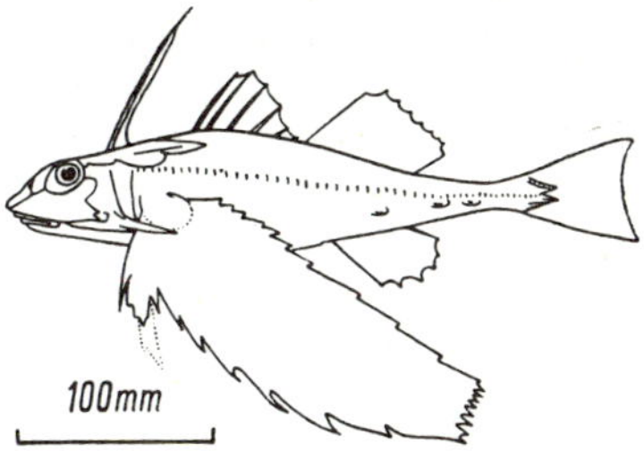

FIGURE 127. Dactylopteriformes—*Daicocus peterseni* (L. and L., 1965, fig. 55)

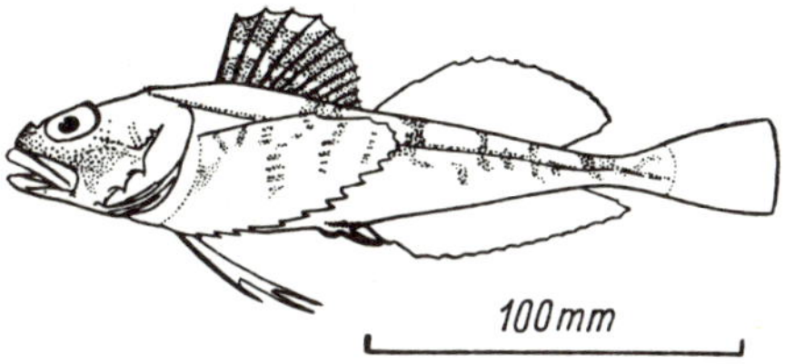

FIGURE 128. Scorpaeniformes—*Gymnocanthus pistilliger* (J. and E., 1900, fig. 730, diagr.)

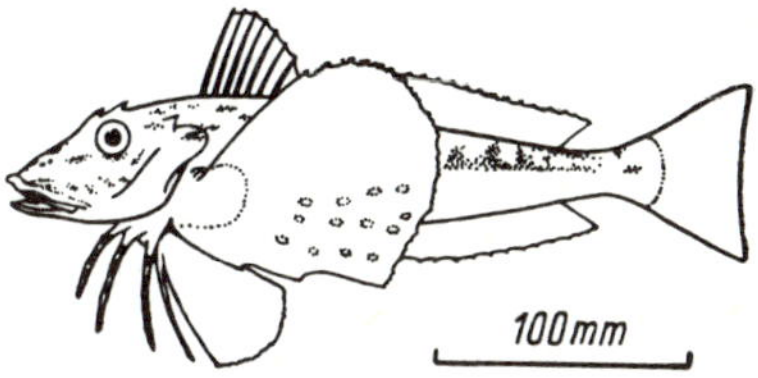

FIGURE 129. Scorpaeniformes—*Chelidonichthys kumu* (Okada, 1955, fig. 315, diagr.)

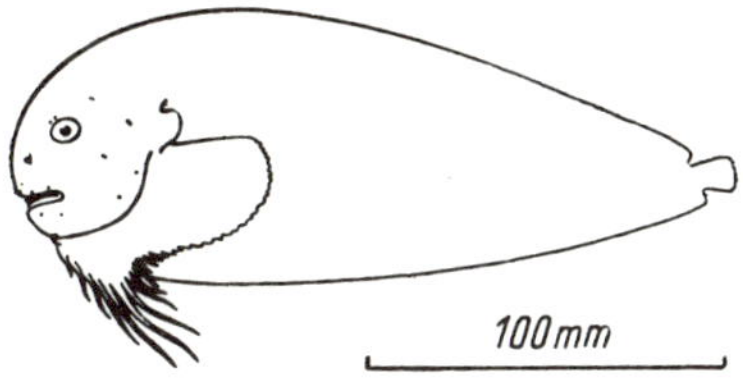

FIGURE 130. Scorpaeniformes—*Careproctus rastrinus* (Okada and Matsubara, 1938, pl. 85, fig. 2, diagr.)

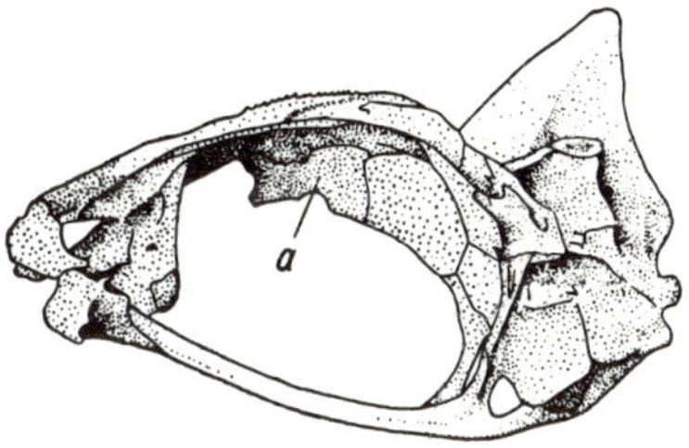

FIGURE 131. Skull of *Beryx splendens* (L. and L., 1965, fig. 42):

a—orbitosphenoid.

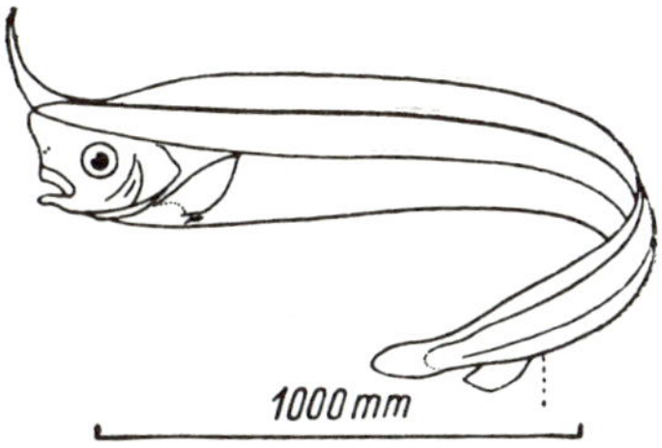

FIGURE 132. Lampridiformes—*Lophotus capellei* (L. and L., 1965, fig. 277)

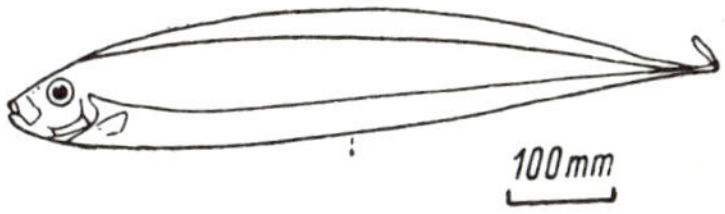

FIGURE 133. Lampridiformes—*Trachipterus ishikawai* (L. and L., 1965, fig. 27)

143 (142). Luminescent organ under eye absent

144 (145). Dorsal fin deeply incised. Opercular bones strongly serrate. Scales distinctly ctenoid, coarse, hard. Dorsal fin with 10—13, more rarely 7, well developed rays connected by a membrane; anal with 4, less often 3, rays. One spiny and 7 branched rays in ventrals. (Figure 141) . . . . 44. **Beryciformes**
(Family 253. Holocentridae)

145 (144). Dorsal fin without deep incision.

146 (149). More than 5 soft rays in ventral fin. Height of dorsal fin less than maximum depth of body.

147 (148). Ventral fin with 6, rarely 7 soft rays; anal with 1—2, more rarely 3 spiny rays. Base of anal smaller than base of dorsal. Abdomen usually serrate, with a median row of keel-like scales (Figure 142) . . . . 44. **Beryciformes**
(Family 249. Trachichthyidae)

148 (147). Ventral fin with from 7 (rarely) to 13 (rarely), usually about 10 soft rays; anal fin with 4 spiny rays. Base of anal larger than base of dorsal. Belly not serrate (Figure 143)
. . . . 44. **Beryciformes**
(Family 246. Berycidae)

149 (146). Ventral fin with 5 soft rays, but since they are split near the base they may be considered as 10 rays. Height of dorsal fin far exceeding maximum depth of body. Ventral fins much larger than pectorals (Figure 144). . . . . 44. **Beryciformes**
(Family 248. Caristiidae, see theses 44—16 and 50.1. 1—45)

150 (135). Orbitosphenoid absent.

151 (152). Mouth very small. Maxillaries generally closely united with premaxillaries, sometimes even fused with them. Teeth sometimes clearly distinguishable, but often fused and forming a beak. Gill openings small (Figure 145). Ventral fins, if present, in the form of strong spines (Figure 146), if absent and 2 dorsal fins present, the first dorsal has spines (Figure 147). If there is only one dorsal, it does not have spiny rays. Body sometimes encased in armor (Figure 148) . . . .
. . . . 58. **Tetraodontiformes**

152 (151). Mouth not so small. If maxillaries fused with premaxillaries, or mouth relatively small, then gill openings as a rule of normal size.

153 (166). [Pelvic bones attached to pectoral girdle by a ligament, not directly to the cleithrum.] See theses 0—154—165, and if they do not fit, continue to thesis 0—166.

154 (161). Dorsal and anal fins without spiny rays.

155 (158). Ventral fins absent.

156 (157). Body deep, laterally compressed. Base of dorsal and anal fins long (Figure 149) . . . . 54. **Icosteiformes**
(Genus Acrotus = Icosteus Clemens and Wilby, 1961 : 235)

157 (156). Body cylindrical. Base of dorsal and anal fins short (Figures 150, 151). . . . . 40. **Cyprinodontiformes**
(Genera Chologaster, Empetrichthys)

158 (155). Ventral fins present.

0

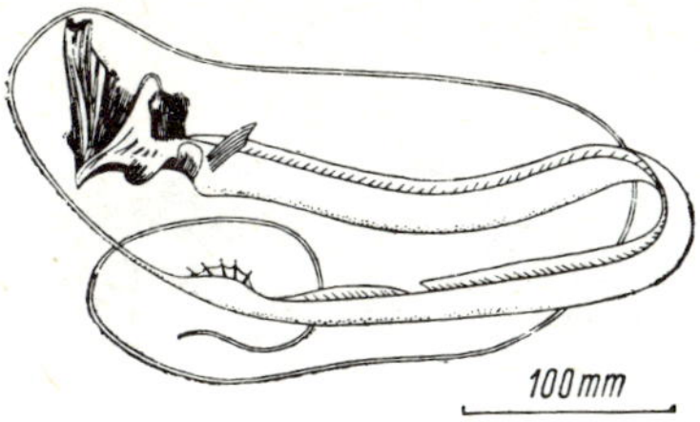

FIGURE 134. Lampridiformes—*Stylephorus chordatus*, adult (Goode and Bean, 1896, pl.94, fig. 394)

FIGURE 135. Lampridiformes—*Stylephorus chordatus*, juvenile (Norman, 1930, fig. 36)

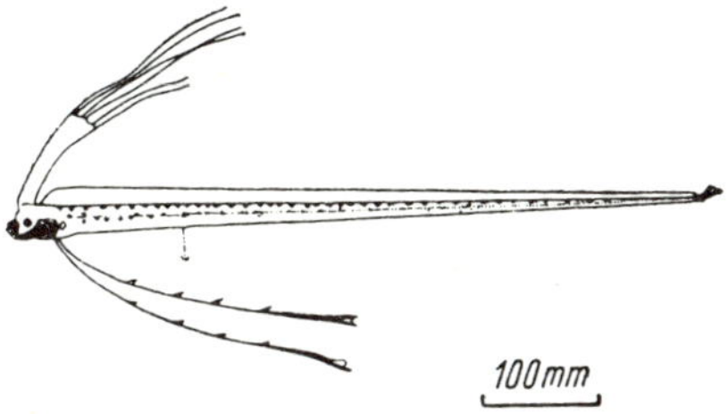

FIGURE 136. Lampridiformes—*Regalecus russelli* (L. and L., 1965, fig. 41)

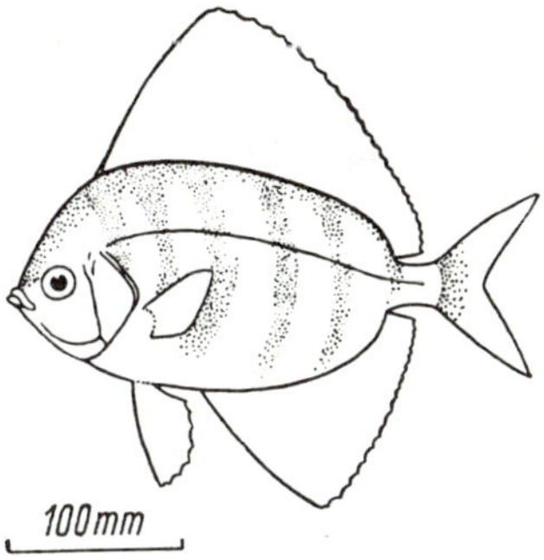

FIGURE 137. Lampridiformes—*Velifer hypselopterus* (L. and L., 1965, fig. 30)

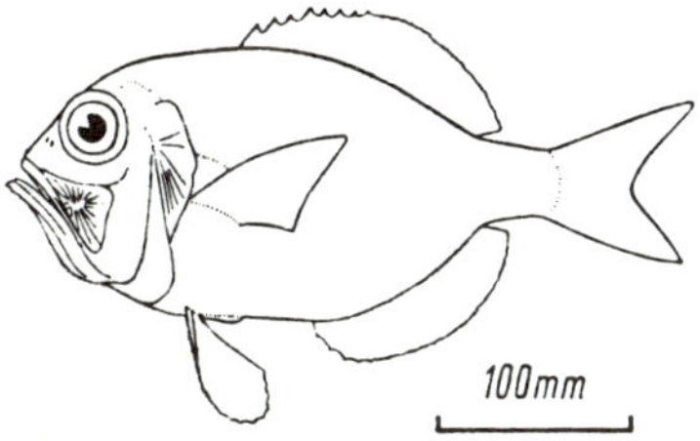

FIGURE 138. Beryciformes—*Diretmus argenteus* (L. and L., 1965, fig. 45)

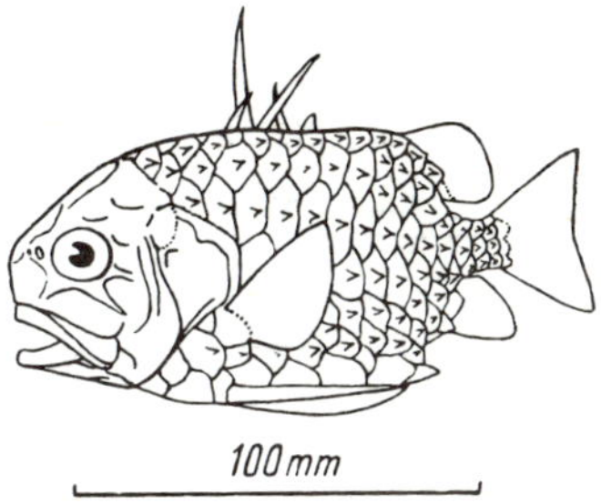

FIGURE 139. Beryciformes—*Monocentris japonicus* (L. and L., 1965, fig. 35)

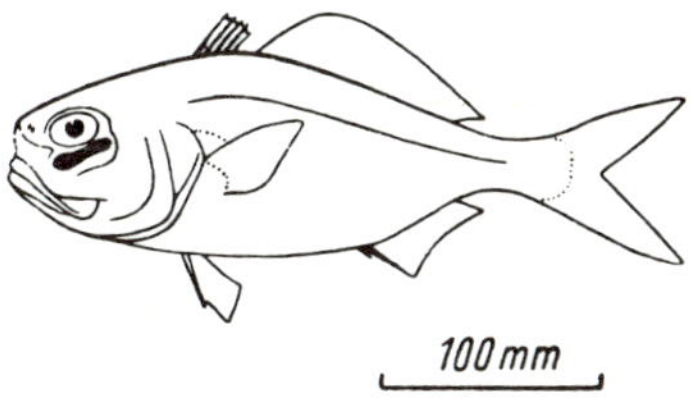

FIGURE 140. Beryciformes—*Anomalops katoptron* (L. and L., 1965, fig. 52)

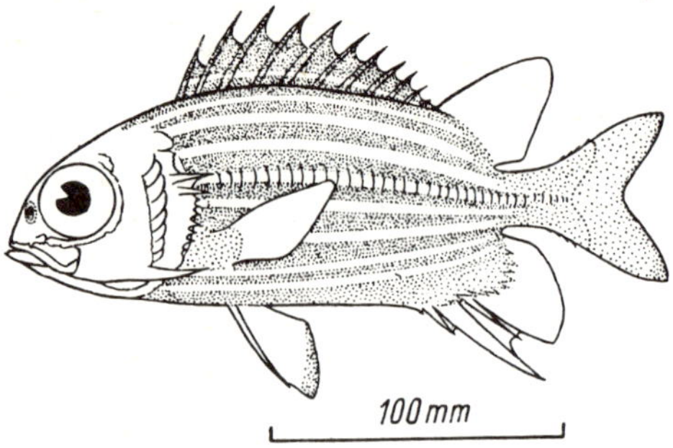

FIGURE 141. Beryciformes—Holocentrus ruber (L. and L., 1965, fig. 47)

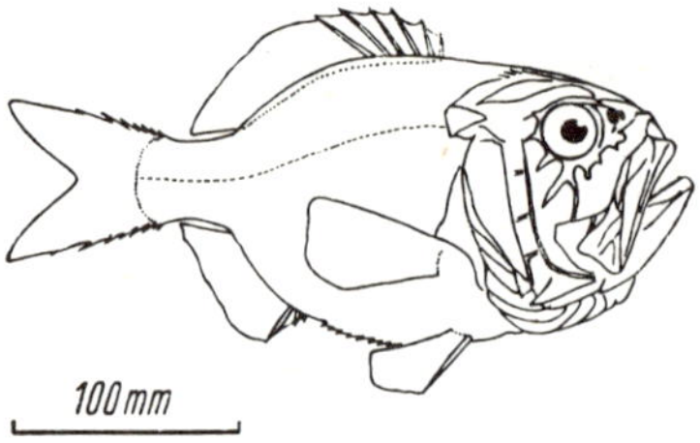

FIGURE 142. Beryciformes—Hoplostethus mediterraneus (L. and L., 1965, fig. 41)

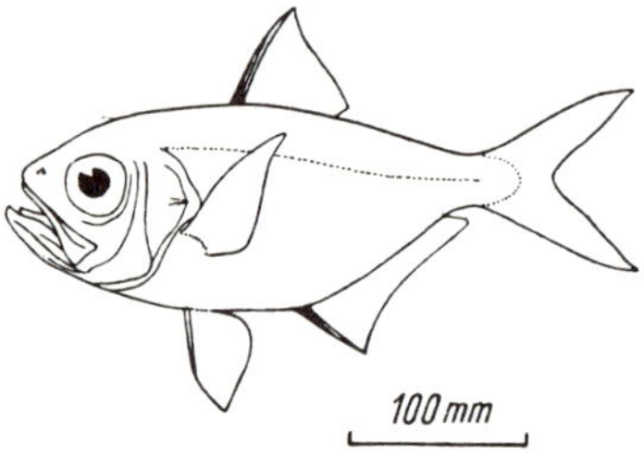

FIGURE 143. Beryciformes—Beryx splendens (L. and L., 1965, fig. 50)

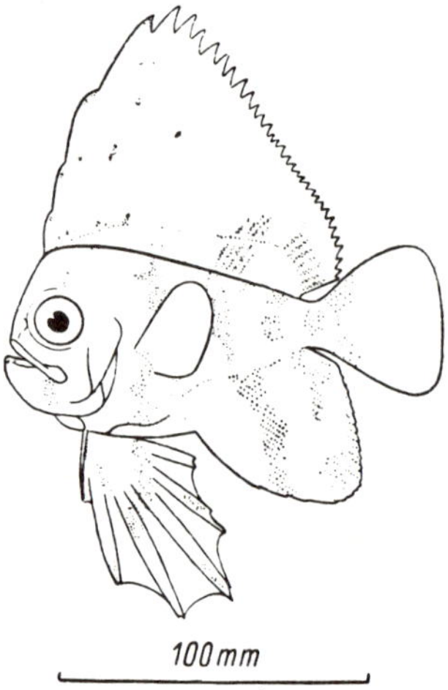

FIGURE 144. Beryciformes—Caristius macropus (L. and L., 1965, fig. 46)

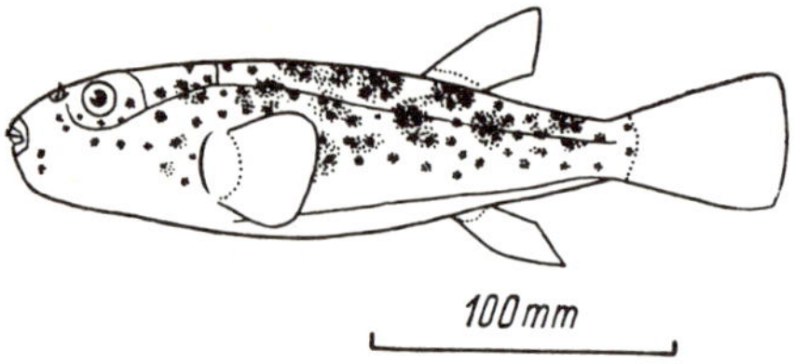

FIGURE 145. Tetraodontiformes—Fugu pardalis (Okada, 1955, fig. 270, diagr.)

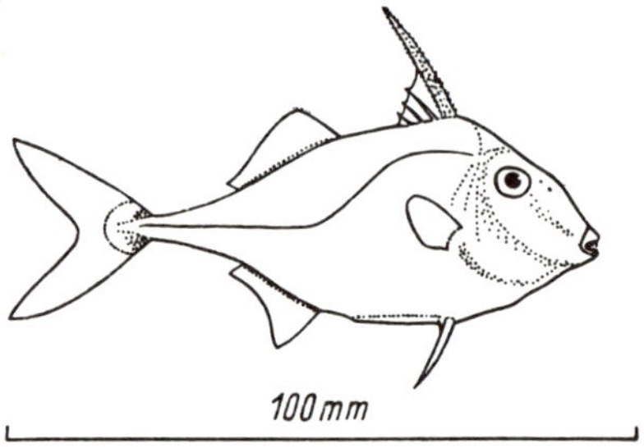

FIGURE 146. Tetraodontiformes—Triacanthus brevirostris (Okada, 1955, fig. 265, diagr.)

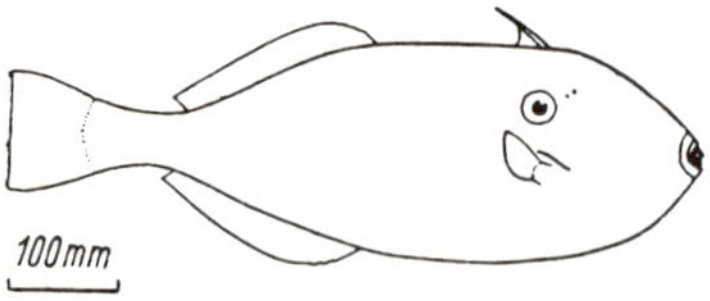

FIGURE 147. Tetraodontiformes—Aluterus monoceros (Wang, 1958, fig. 608, diagr.)

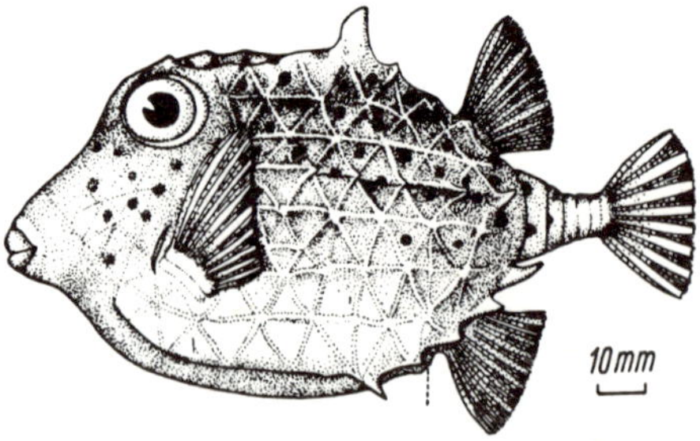

FIGURE 148. Tetraodontiformes—Kentrocarpos aculeatus (M., 1955, III, fig. 356)

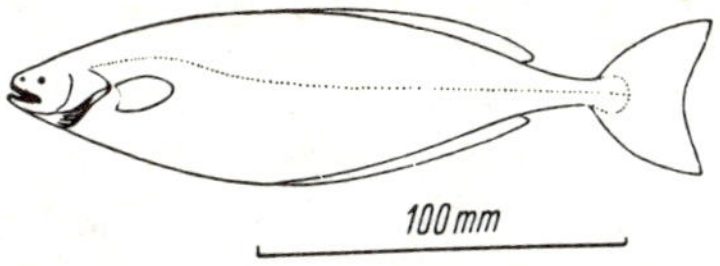

FIGURE 149. Icosteiformes—Acrotus willoughbyi = Icosteus aenigmaticus, ad.

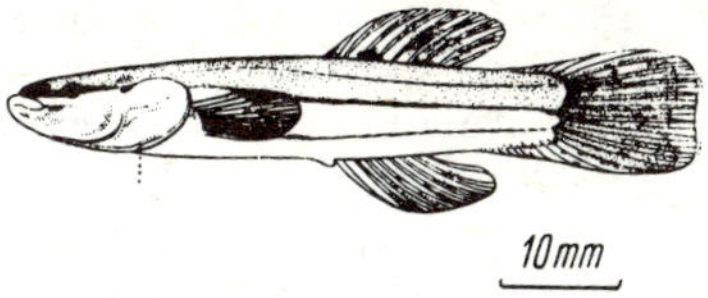

FIGURE 150. Cyprinodontiformes—Chologaster cornutus (Fowler, 1935, fig. 31)

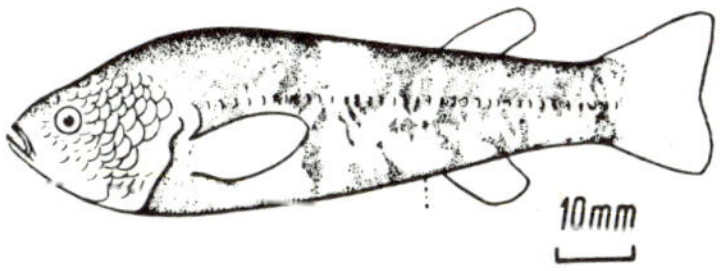

FIGURE 151. Cyprinodontiformes—Empetrichthys merriami (Jordan, 1925, fig. 328, diagr.)

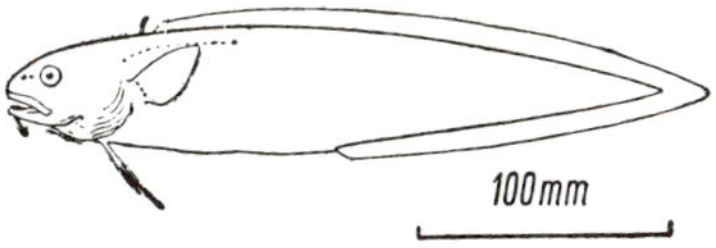

FIGURE 152. Gadiformes—Muraenolepis microps (Norman, 1938, fig. 2, diagr.)

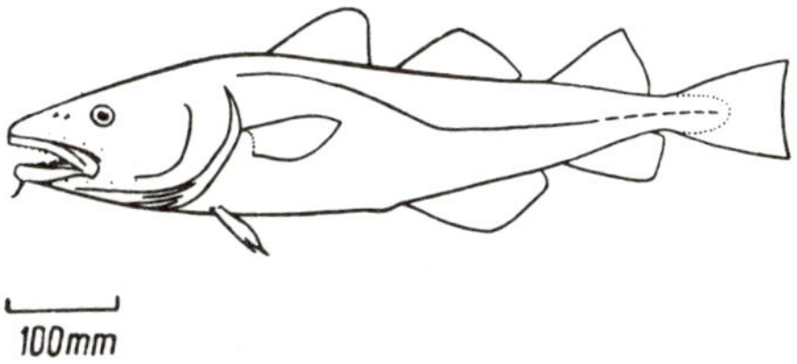

FIGURE 153. Gadiformes—Gadus morhua macrocephalus (L. and L., 1965, fig. 43)

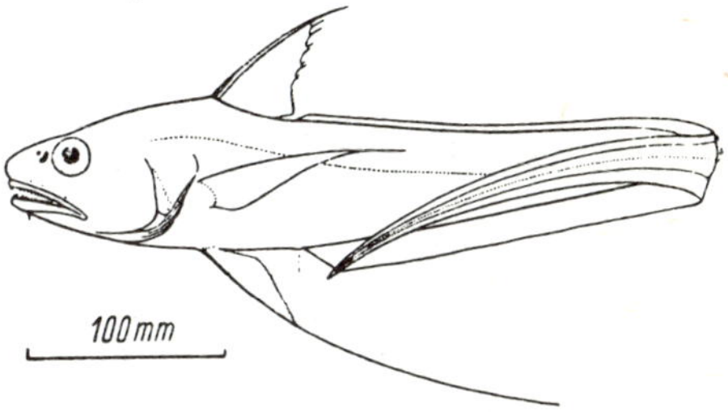

FIGURE 154. Macrouriformes—Macrourus longifilis (Günther, 1897:151, pl. 35)

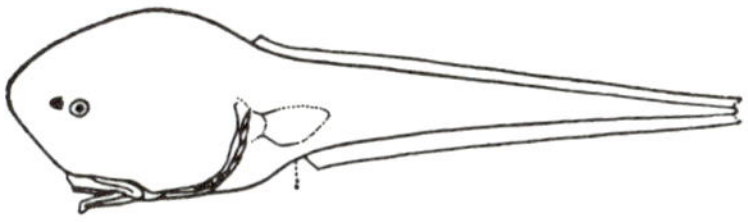

FIGURE 155. Macrouriformes—Macrouroides inflaticeps (Smith and Radcliffe, 1912, pl. 31, fig. 2, diagr.)

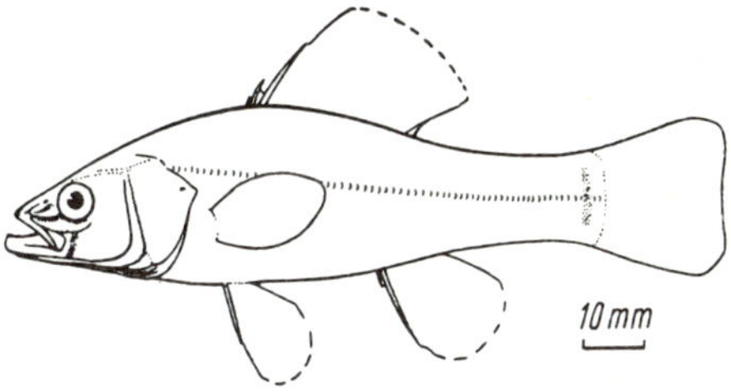

FIGURE 156. Percopsiformes—Aphredoderus sayanus (Jordan, 1925, fig. 397, diagr.)

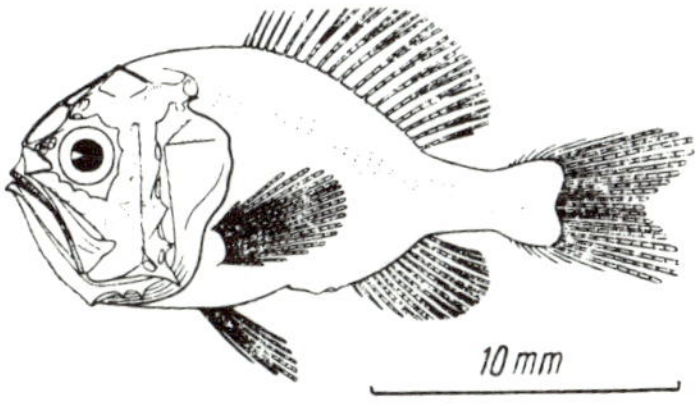

FIGURE 157. Stephanoberyciformes—Korsogaster nanus (Parr, 1933, fig. 3)

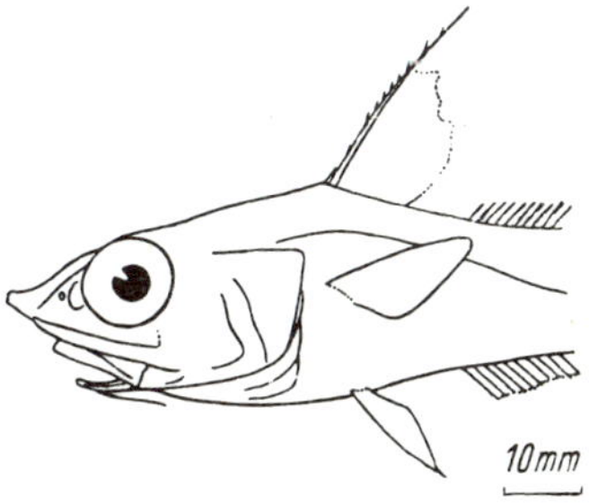

FIGURE 158. Macrouriformes—Hemimacrurus macrolepis (L. and L., 1965, fig. 44)

159 (160). Caudal fin present, well expressed.[28] One, 2 or 3 dorsal fins, 1 or 2 anals. [Olfactory nerves situated in a canal above the interorbital septum and continuing far forward, ending in olfactory lobes near the nasal capsules.] (Figure 153) .... 35. **Gadiformes**

160 (159). Caudal fin absent or weakly expressed. Body becoming markedly thinner posteriorly, often passing into a filament. Dorsal and anal fins fused with the caudal or with each other (Figures 154, 466). Head sometimes massive and, like the body, soft. (Figure 155) .... **36. Macrouriformes** (in part)

161 (154). Dorsal fin, and sometimes anal, with spiny rays.

162 (163). Vent situated in front of ventral fins. (Figure 156)......... .... 42. **Percopsiformes** (Family 239. Aphredoderidae, see theses 0—93 and 0—104)

163 (162). Vent situated normally behind ventral fins.

164 (165). Caudal fin well developed, distinctly expressed, not fused with dorsal and anal. (Figure 157) ..... 43. **Stephanoberyciformes** (Family 243. Korsogesteridae)

165 (164). Caudal fin small, weakly developed or absent, as the dorsal and anal fins are fused with the caudal or with each other. (Figures 154, 158) ....36. **Macrouriformes** (in part)

166 (153). [Pelvic bones attached to pectoral girdle directly to cleithrum, not by a ligament.]

167 (168). Anterior part of anal fin usually with 1—5 strong spiny rays which are set somewhat forward and stand out as an independent fin (Figure 160).[29] Ventral fins with 1 spiny and 6—9 branched rays. Caudal 1+10—13+1. [Posttemporal bone not furcate] .... 45. **Zeiformes**

168 (167). Anal fin without independent separate spiny part anteriorly.

169 (170). [Posttemporal bone not furcate, connected with the skull by a suture.] Mouth bordered by both premaxillaries and maxillaries, the latter without teeth. Ventral fins situated on the throat, with 1 spiny and 2—3 soft rays. [Pectorals with 4—5 radials; lower radial enlarged and widened at distal end.] (Figures 161, 162)................. 60. **Batrachoidiformes**

170 (169). [Posttemporal bone usually furcate (Figure 163).] Maxillaries generally not bordering the mouth. Ventral fins usually present, with 1 spiny and as a rule 5 soft rays, more rarely fewer, and not more than 6. Ventrals sometimes absent (Figures 164—166). Ventral fins situated primarily under base of pectorals, but often in front of these fins, on the throat, and even near the chin. [Lower radial of pectoral fin not widened at distal end.] Sometimes 2, even 3, dorsal fins, more commonly 1, generally with spiny rays in the anterior part (Figures 167, 168), although in several cases the spiny rays are weak (Figure 169, 170) or absent in the dorsal fin, or else also in the anal (Figures 171, 172), and occasionally also in the ventral (Figures 173—175). .... 50. **Perciformes** (in part)

[28] As an exception the caudal fin is fused with the dorsal and anal in Muraenolepis (Gadiformes) (Figure 152).

[29] The genus Parazen Kamohara, 1935 (Zeiformes) has no strong spiny rays in either the ventral (which has 7 branched rays) or the anal fin, and the ventrals are situated on the belly (Figure 159).

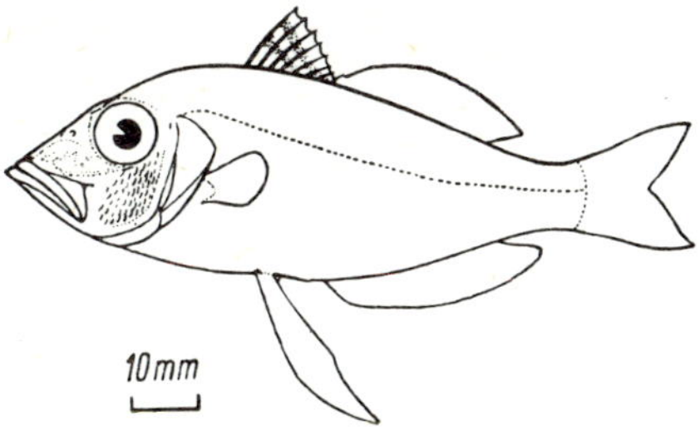

FIGURE 159. Parazen pacificus (Zeiformes (L. and L., 1965, fig. 49)

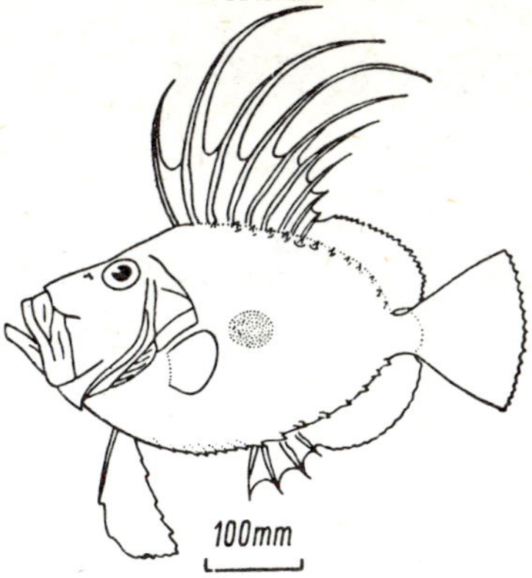

FIGURE 160. Zeiformes — Zeus japonicus (L. and L., 1965, fig. 48)

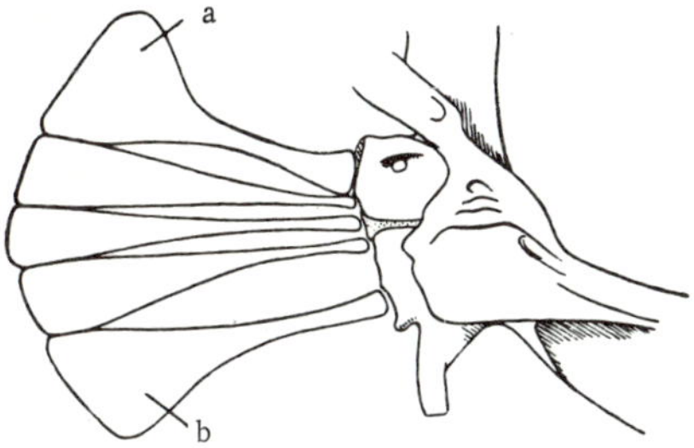

FIGURE 161. Pectoral girdle in Porichthys notatus (Batrachoidiformes) (Berg, 1940, fig. 190):

a — first radial; b — fifth radial.

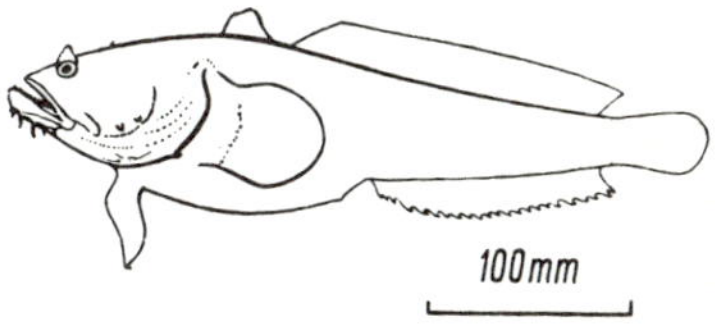

FIGURE 162. Batrachoidiformes — Opsanus pardus (Jordan, 1925, fig. 648)

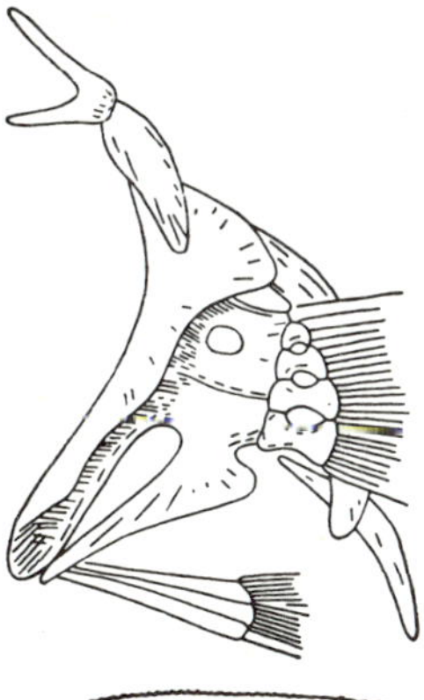

FIGURE 163. Pectoral girdle in Serranus cabrilla (Perciformes) (W. and B., 1931, 6, fig. 80). (See Figure 121.)

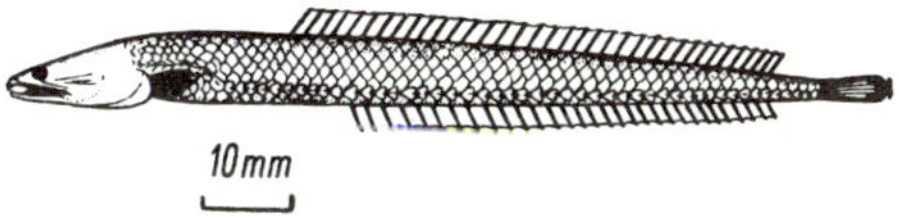

FIGURE 164. Perciformes — Apodocreedia vanderhorsti (Smith, 1950, fig. 375)

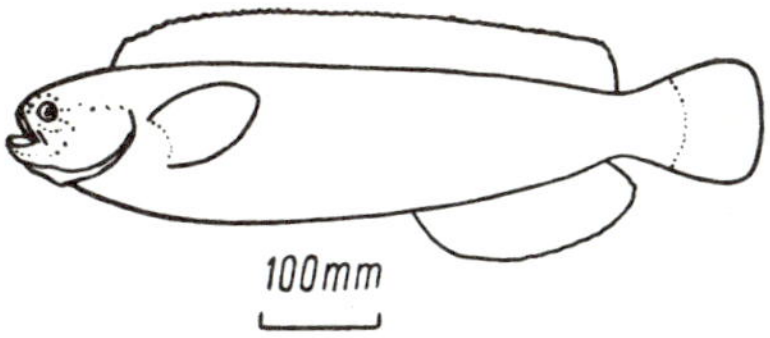

FIGURE 165. Perciformes — Zaprora silenus (M., 1955, III, fig. 273, diagr.)

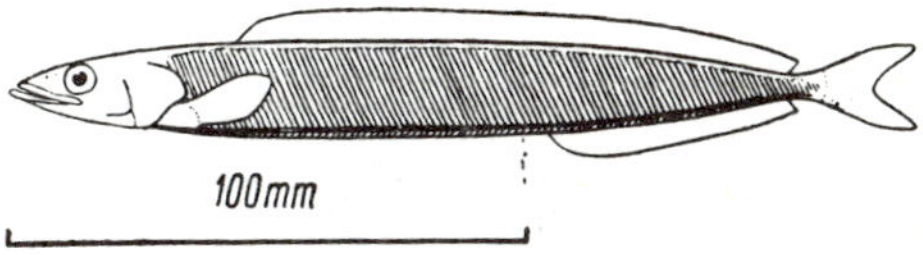

FIGURE 166. Perciformes — Ammodytes personatus (Wang, 1958, fig. 443, diagr.)

Keys to families (1–495)

Order 1. BRANCHIOSTOMATIFORMES (thesis 0—1)

1 family: 1. Branchiostomatidae.

3 subfamilies:

1 (4). Mouth almost median in position, surrounded by barbels. [Peribranchial cavity with an opening (atriopore) in front of the vent.] Two rows of gill slits along the sides of the body.
2 (3). [Two rows of gonads, one on each side of the body; both metapleura terminating immediately behind the atriopore.] (Figure 176) . . . . . . subfamily 1.1. Branchiostomatinae
3 (2). [One row of gonads on right side of body; right metapleuron fused with abdominal fin, left metapleuron terminating behind the atriopore.] . . . . subfamily 1.2. Epigonichthyinae
4 (1). Mouth situated on left side, not surrounded by barbels. [Peribranchial cavity absent.] One row of gill slits distributed along the abdominal side of the body . . . . subfamily 1.3. Amphioxidinae

Order 2. PETROMYZONIFORMES (thesis 0—4)

1 family: 2. Petromyzonidae

2 subfamilies.

1 (2). [Maxillary teeth arranged on one plate. Margins of oral disk with velutinous lobes.] (Figure 177). . . . . .subfamily 2.1. Petromyzoninae
2 (1). [Maxillary teeth arranged on two plates. Margins of oral disk without velutinous lobes.] (Figure 178). . . . . subfamily 2.2. Mordacilinae

Order 3. MYXINIFORMES (thesis 0—5)

3 families (3—5):

1 (2). Only 1 gill opening on each side of the body (Figure 179). . . . . 3. Myxinidae
2 (1). At least 5 gill openings on each side of the body.
3 (4). Six pairs of gill openings; they are small, situated close together, their diameter greater than or the same as the space between them. Distance between first and last gill openings smaller than the depth of the body. (Figure 180). . . . . 5. Paramyxinidae

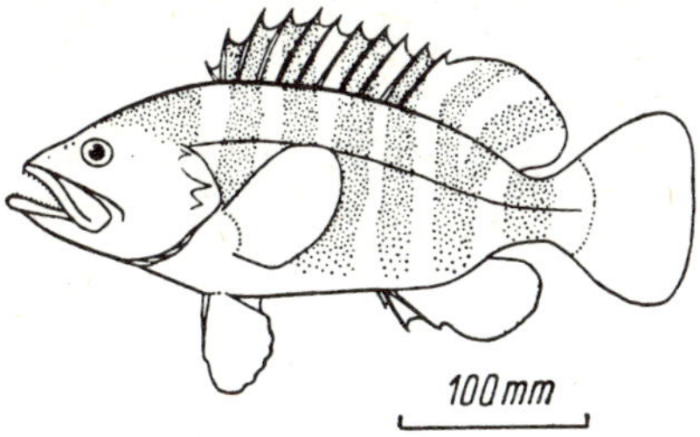

FIGURE 167. Perciformes—*Epinephelus septemfasciatus* (Okada, 1955, fig. 183, diagr.)

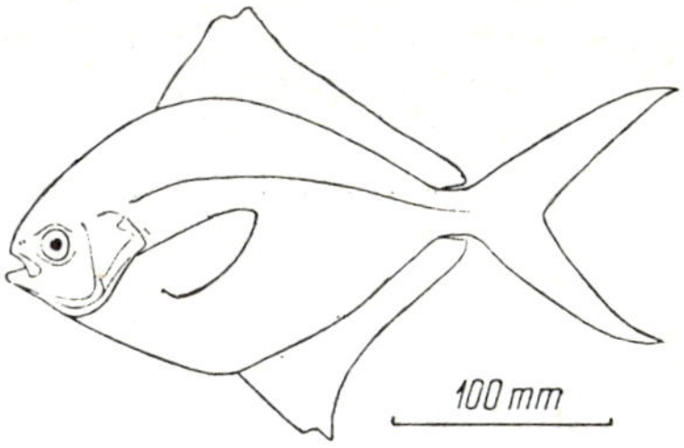

FIGURE 168. Perciformes—*Stromateus fiatola* (Haedrich, 1967, fig. 39)

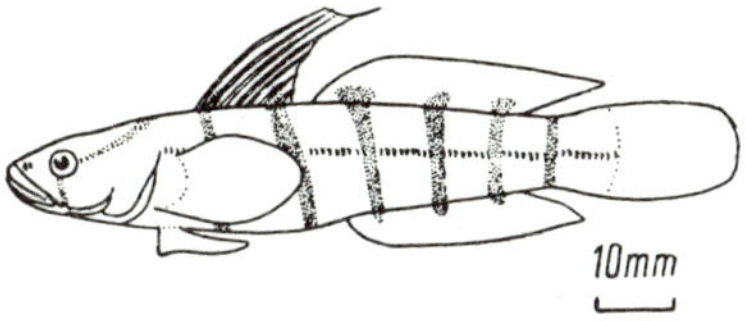

FIGURE 169. Perciformes—*Pterogobius elapoides* (Okada, 1955, fig. 334, diagr.)

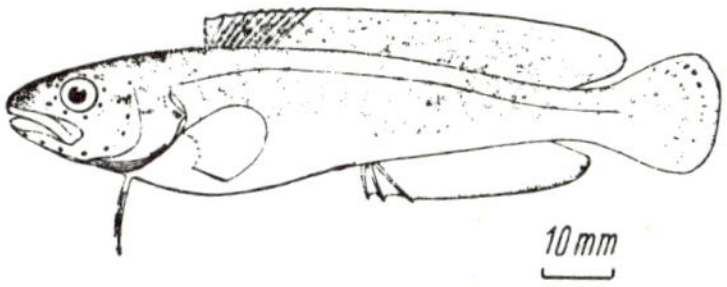

FIGURE 170. Perciformes—*Gadopsis marmoratus* (Richardson, 1844, pl. 59, fig. 6)

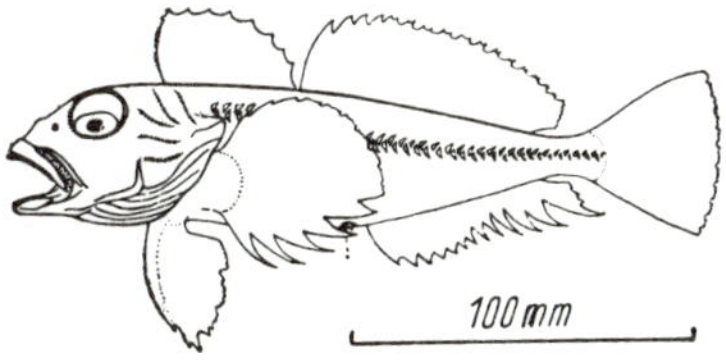

FIGURE 171. Perciformes—*Bovichthys variegatus* (Richardson, 1844, pl. 34, figs. 1–4, diagr.)

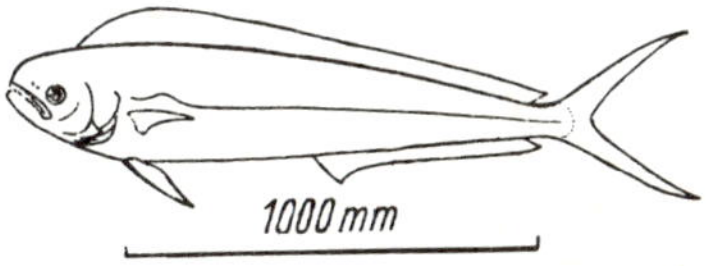

FIGURE 172. Perciformes—*Coryphaena hippurus* (Okada, 1955, fig. 141, diagr.)

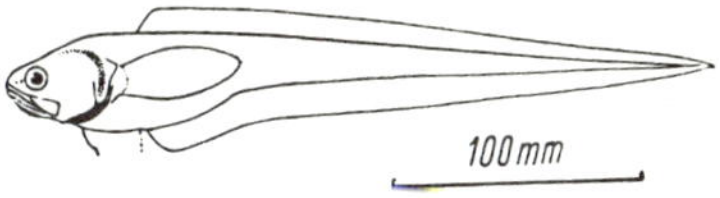

FIGURE 173. Perciformes—*Pyramodon ventralis* (M., 1955, III, fig. 303, diagr.)

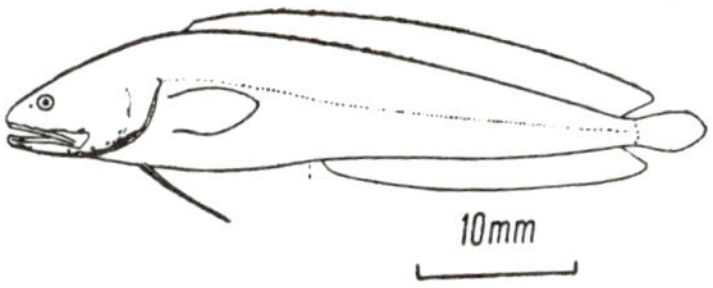

FIGURE 174. Perciformes—*Ogilbia cayorum* (J. and E., 1900, fig. 873, diagr.)

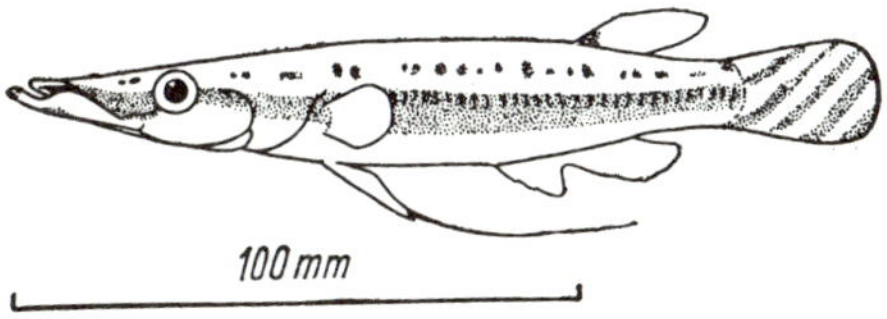

FIGURE 175. Perciformes—*Luciocephalus pulcher* (W. and B., 4, 1922, fig. 94, diagr.)

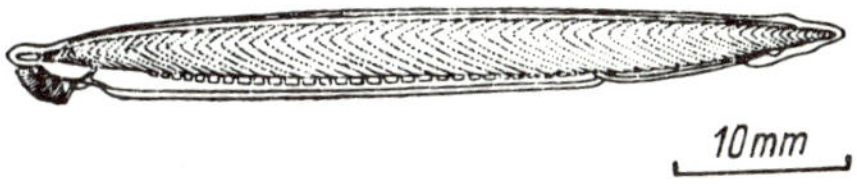

FIGURE 176. Branchiostomatidae (Branchiostomatinae) *Branchiostoma belcheri* (L. and L., 1965, fig. 4)

4 (3). From 5 to 15 pairs of gill openings; they are large, spaced far apart, their diameter about half as large as the space between them. Distance between first and last much greater than the depth of the body. (Figure 181) . . . . 4. Eptatretidae

Order 4. HETERODONTIFORMES (thesis 0—12)

1 family: 6. **Heterodontidae** (Figure 182), 2 genera.

Order 5. HEXANCHIFORMES (thesis 0—10)

2 families (7, 8):

1 (2). Body markedly elongate, almost eel-like. Mouth almost terminal; teeth on both jaws identical in both the anterior and the posterior part. Membranes of first gill slit connected with each other below on the throat. Dorsal, anal, and ventral fins situated near each other in the posterior part of the body. [Palatoquadratum articulated in one place, only with the anterior part of the skull, by means of an orbital process.] (Figure 183) . . . . 8. **Chlamydoselachidae**

2 (1). Body moderately elongate, not eel-like. Mouth inferior, lower jaw much shorter than upper; teeth in anterior part of upper jaw very different from anterior teeth in lower jaw. Membranes of first gill slit not connected on the throat. [Palatoquadratum articulated with the skull in two places.] (Figure 184). . . . . 7. **Hexanchidae**

Order 6. LAMNIFORMES (thesis 0—13)

11 families (9—19):

1 (6). Base of first dorsal fin situated distinctly behind vertical of origin of ventrals, but if above this, as in family 10. Rhincodontidae (Figure 185), gill slits are present also above the base of the pectorals.

2 (3). Axis of caudal fin turned steeply upward; fin large, in the shape of a half-moon. Gill arches connected with each other by spongy tissue which has a sievelike structure. (Figure 185) . . . . .10. **Rhincodontidae**

3 (2). Axis of caudal fin situated almost horizontally, not directed upward. Gill arches not connected by spongy tissue.

4 (5). Nares connected with the mouth by a deep furrow; a well developed barbel present on their anterior margin. (Figure 186) . . . . 9. **Orectolobidae**

5 (4). Nares not connected with mouth by a deep furrow, but if connected, there is no well developed barbel on their anterior margin. (Figure 187). . . . . 16. **Scyliorhinidae**

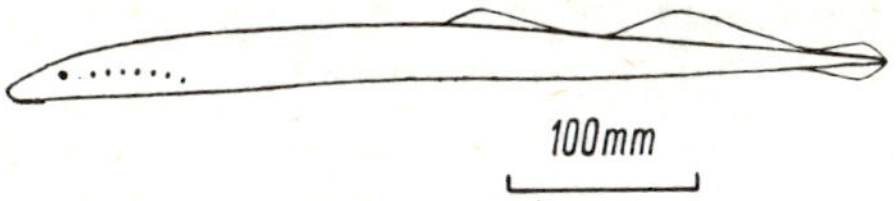

FIGURE 177. Petromyzonidae (Petromyzoninae) — Lampetra japonica (L. and L., 1965, fig. 5)

FIGURE 178. Petromyzonidae (Mordaciinae) — Mordacia mordax (Traité, 1958, III, fig. 106, diagr.)

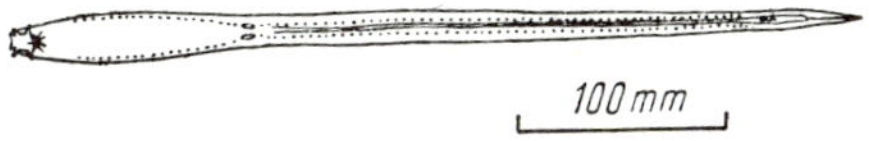

FIGURE 179. Myxinidae — Myxine paucidens (Nikol'skii, 1954, fig. 10, 4)

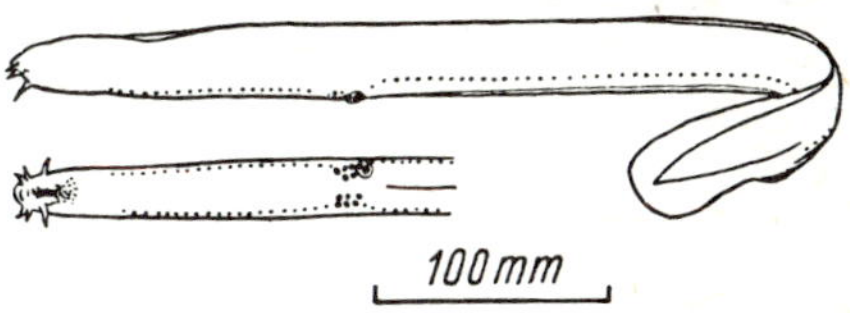

FIGURE 180. Paramyxinidae — Paramyxine atami (M., 1955, III, fig. 2)

FIGURE 181. Eptatredidae — Eptatretus burgeri (L. and L., 1959, fig. 11)

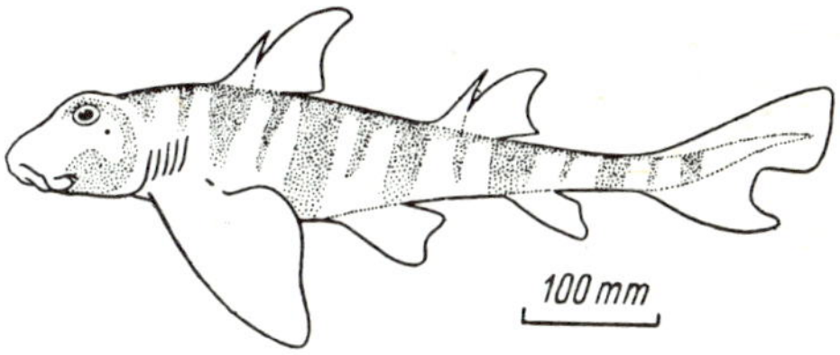

FIGURE 182. Heterodontidae — Heterodontus japonicus (L. and L., 1959, fig. 18)

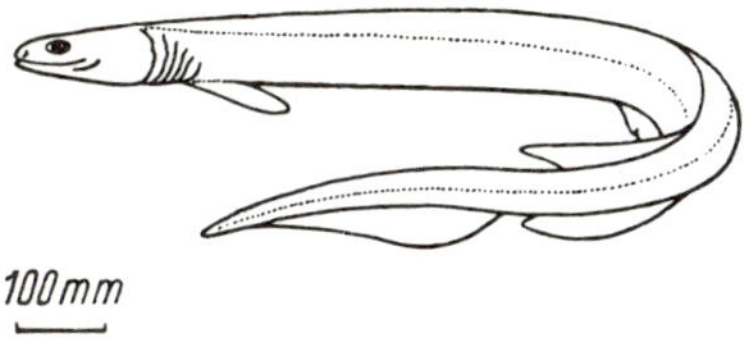

FIGURE 183. Chlamydoselachidae — Chlamydoselachus anguineus (Okada, 1955, fig. 5, diagr.)

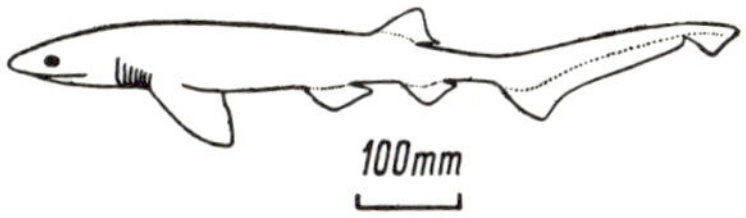

FIGURE 184. Hexanchidae — Notorhynchus platycephalus (Fang and Wang, 1932, fig. 1, diagr.)

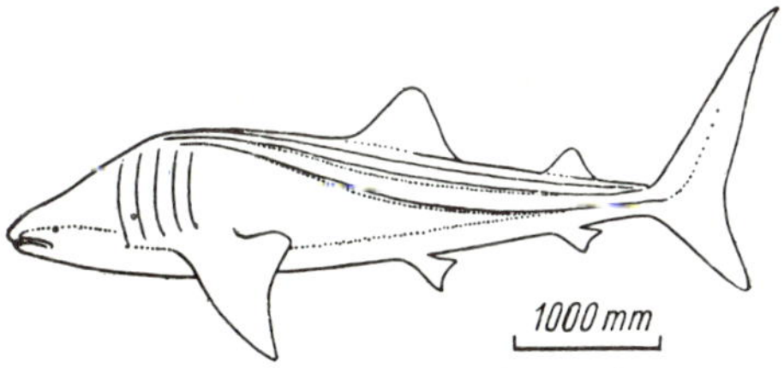

FIGURE 185. Rhincodontidae — Rhincodon typus (L. and L., 1959, fig. 19, 1)

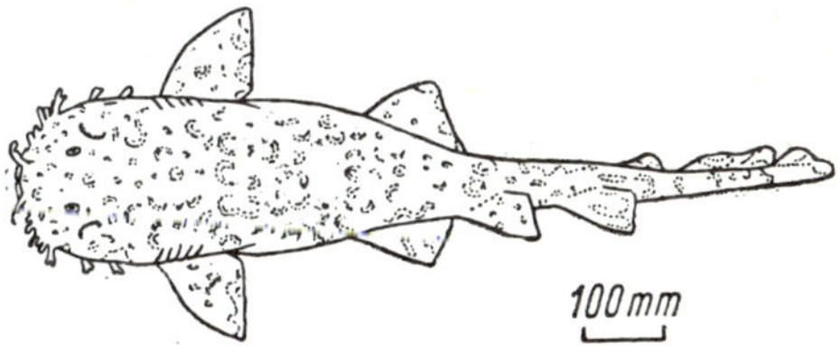

FIGURE 186. Orectolobidae — Orectolobus japonicus (L. and L., 1959, fig. 20)

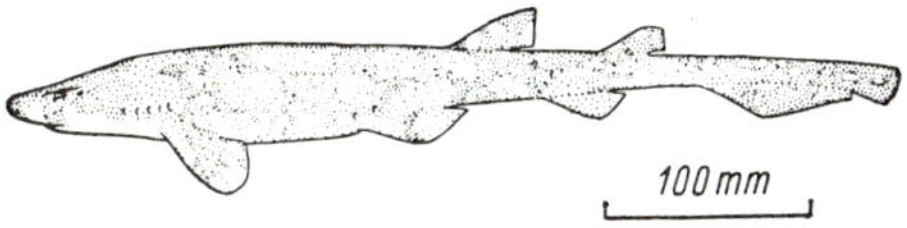

FIGURE 187. Scyliorhinidae — Scyliorhinus torazame (L. and L., 1959, fig. 25)

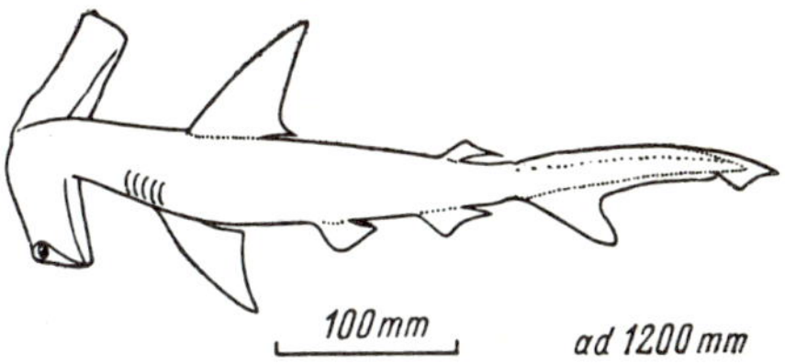

FIGURE 188. Sphyrnidae — Sphyrna blochi (Day, 1875–1878, pl. 184, fig. 1, diagr.)

6 (1). Base of first dorsal fin situated distinctly in front of vertical of origin of ventrals, but if above this, as in family 11. Odontaspidae (Figure 197), gill slits are present only in front of pectoral fin, absent above the base of the fin.

7 (8). Head with the shape of a hammer. (Figure 188). . . . . 19. Sphyrnidae

8 (7). Head of normal shape.

9 (12). Caudal fin in the shape of a half-moon; its axis is very steeply turned upward and the posterior end of both lobes of the fin is situated approximately on one vertical.

10 (11). Teeth sparse, large, no more than 30 on each side of upper and lower jaw. Gill slits of moderate size, distributed on the sides of the body and not extending onto the belly. [Gill arches without rakers.] (Figure 189) . . . . 13. Lamnidae[30]

11 (10). Teeth very numerous, small, conical, with one apex. Gill slits markedly enlarged, continuing up to the back and down to the belly. [Gill arches bearing long, well developed rakers, resembling the gill rakers of bony fishes.] (Figure 190) . . . . 14. Cetorhinidae

12 (9). Caudal fin not in the form of a half-moon.

13 (14). Length of base of first dorsal fin equal to or even greater than length of caudal fin (Figure 191) . . . . 17. Pseudotriakidae

14 (13). Length of base of first dorsal fin smaller than length of caudal fin.

15 (16). Caudal fin half as long as the body, or even longer (Figure 192) . . . . 15. Alopiidae

16 (15). Caudal fin not half as long as the body but longer than the base of the first dorsal fin.

17 (18). Last (fifth) gill slit situated on the vertical of the origin of the pectoral fin or behind this. Eyes with more or less well developed nictitating membrane or lower eyelid with longitudinal fold . . . . .18. Carcharhinidae

4 subfamilies:

1 (4). One row of teeth normally functioning.

2 (3). Spiracles very small or absent, precaudal fossa present, well expressed. (Figure 193). . subfamily 18. 1. Carcharhininae

3 (2). Spiracles small, but present; precaudal fossa absent both above and below. (Figure 194) . . . subfamily 18. 2. Galeorhininae

4 (1). More than 1 row of teeth normally functioning, the teeth arranged in the form of bands or similar to paving stones.

5 (6). Anterior nasal ridge short, well separated from the mouth. (Figure 195) . . . . subfamily 18. 3. Mustelinae

6 (5). Anterior nasal ridge reaching the mouth, which is connected with the nares via a groove. (Figure 196) . . . . subfamily 18. 4. Scylliogaleinae

[30] Glikman (1964:105) isolated a separate family, 13a. Lamiostomatidae (Figure 189A). Garrick (1967) does not recognize this family.

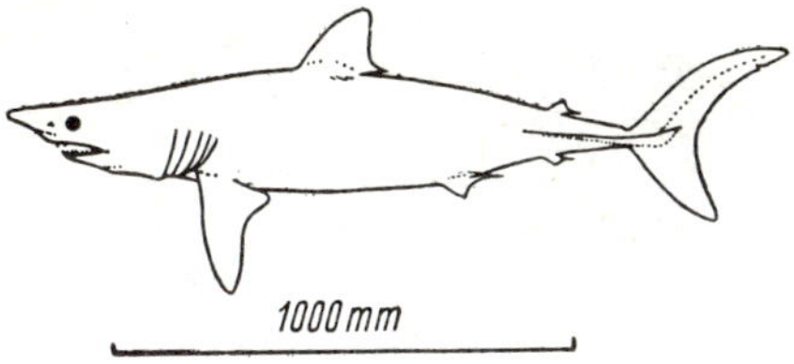

FIGURE 189. Lamnidae — *Isurus glaucus* (L. and L., 1959, fig. 34)

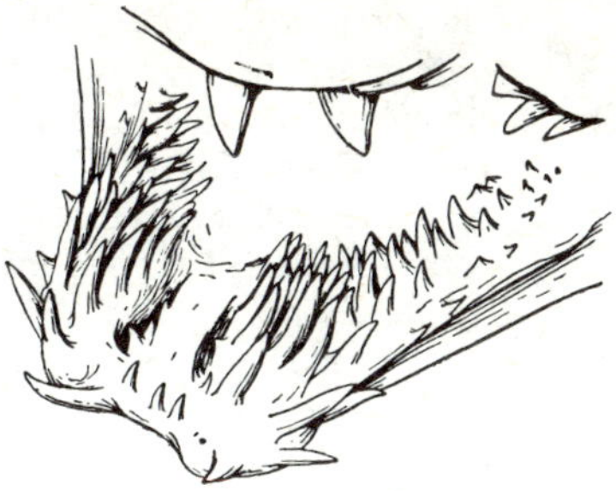

FIGURE 189A. Lamiostomatidae — *Lamiostoma belyaevi* (Glikman, 1964, fig. 31)

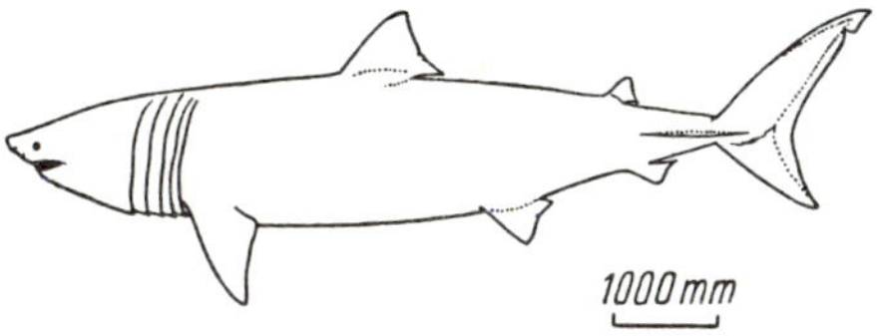

FIGURE 190. Cetorhinidae — *Cetorhinus maximus* (L. and L., 1959, fig. 36)

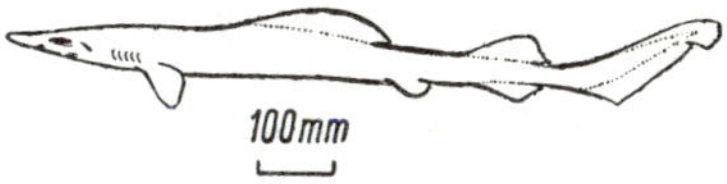

FIGURE 191. Pseudotriakidae — *Pseudotriakis microdon* (B. and S., 1948, fig. 40)

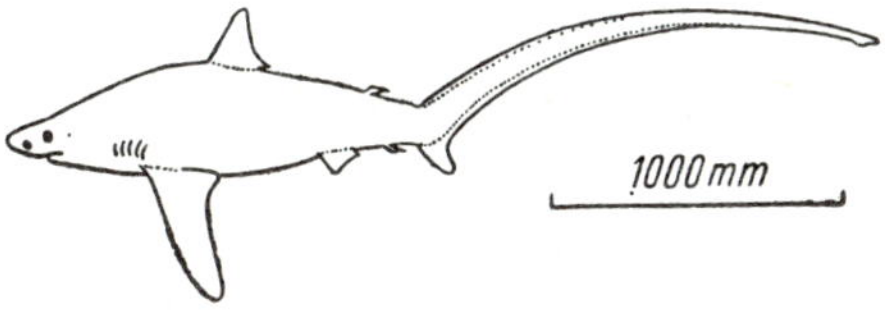

FIGURE 192. Alopiidae — *Alopias pelagicus* (L. and L., 1959, fig. 37)

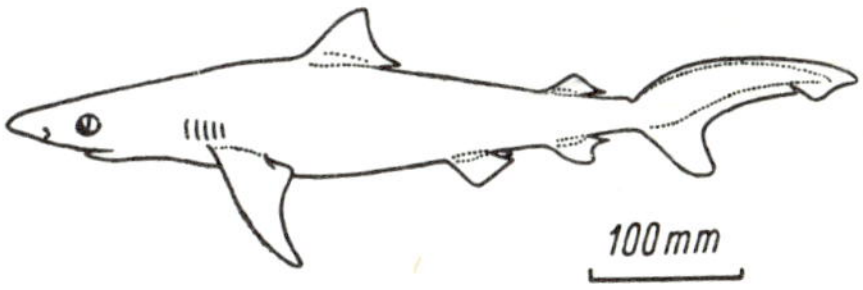

FIGURE 193. Carcharhinidae (Carcharhininae) — *Carcharinus brachyurus* (L. and L., 1959, fig. 52)

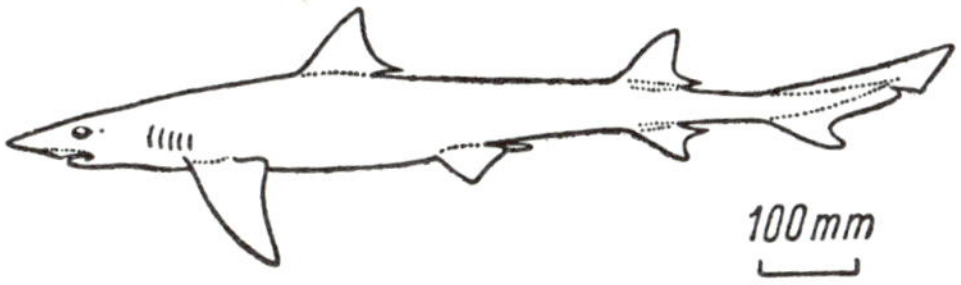

FIGURE 194. Carcharhinidae (Galeorhininae) — *Galeorhinus japonicus* (L. and L., 1959, fig. 48)

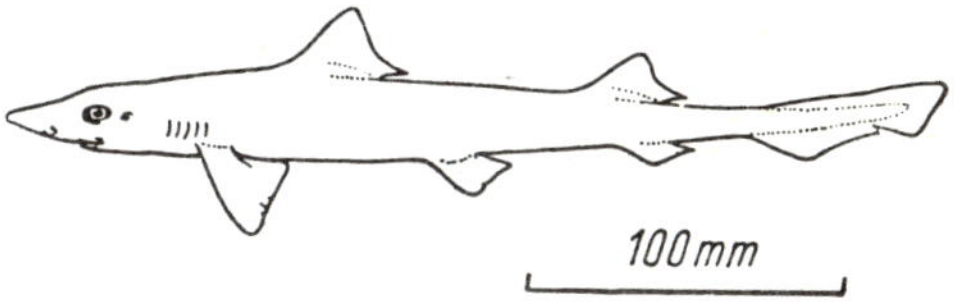

FIGURE 195. Carcharhinidae (Mustelinae) — *Mustelus griseus* (L. and L., 1959, fig.41)

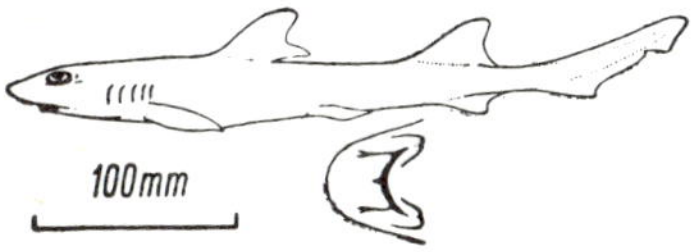

FIGURE 196. Carcharhinidae (Scylliogaleinae) — *Scylliogaleus queketti* (Smith, 1950, fig. 16, diagr.)

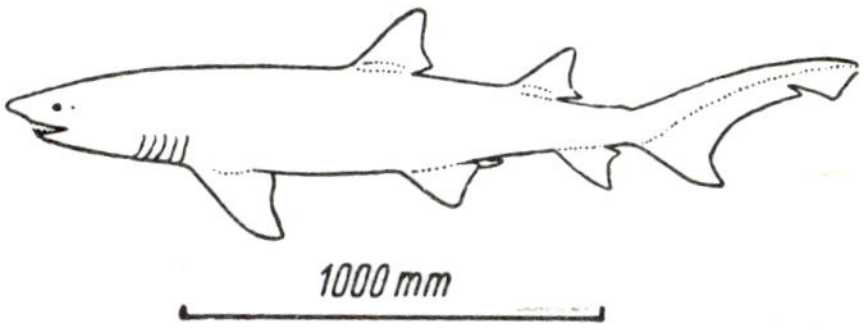

FIGURE 197. Odontaspidae — *Odontaspis tricuspidatus* (Fang and Wang, 1932), fig. 12, diagr.)

18 (17). Last (fifth) gill slit situated markedly in front of origin of pectoral fin. Eyes without nictitating membrane or fold.

19 (20). Snout of normal length and form; jaws not shifted far forward. Dorsal, ventral, and anal fins of about the same size; upper precaudal fossa clearly distinguishable; anterior part of lower lobe of caudal fin forming a distinct protuberance (Figure 197) . . . . 11. Odontaspidae

20 (19). Snout markedly elongate and in the form of a sharp protuberance when seen in profile; jaws shifted markedly forward in the form of a beak. Dorsal fins much smaller than ventrals and anal; upper precaudal fossa not distinguishable; anterior part of lower caudal lobe not forming a protuberance. (Figure 198) . . . . 12. Scapanorhynchidae

Order 7. SQUALIFORMES (thesis 0—15)

4 families (20—23):

1 (6). Body spindle-shaped, sharklike. Eyes on sides of head. Anterior margin of pectoral fins set behind gill openings.

2 (3). A long or short, sometimes concealed but readily felt prickly spine in front of both dorsal fins (Figure 199) . . . 20. Squalidae

3 (2). No prickly spine present in front of second dorsal or, usually, of first dorsal.

3 (5). Teeth with one apex; teeth of upper jaw different from those on lower jaw; upper teeth narrow, conical, lower teeth wide and flat, forming a cutting edge. (Figure 200) . . . . 21. Dalatiidae

5 (4). Teeth with several apexes, similar on both jaws, forming cutting edges. (Figure 201) . . . . 22. Echinorhinidae

6 (1). Body flattened, skatelike. Eyes on dorsal side of head. Anterior margin of pectoral fins set far forward from gill openings, but the base of the pectorals is behind the first gill slit (Figure 202) . . . . 23. Squatinidae

Order 8. PRISTIOPHORIFORMES (thesis 0—16)

1 family: 24. Pristiophoridae (Figure 203).

Order 9. RAJIFORMES[31] (thesis 0—18)

14 families (25—38):

1 (2). Snout markedly elongate, transformed into a narrow, flat plate

[31] A new family has been described, 25a. Curgesiellidae (Buen, 1959: 171—201) but it has not been included in the key, as this work was not available to the author.

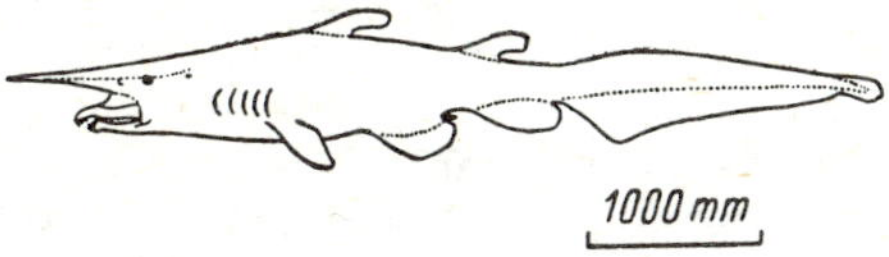

FIGURE 198. Scapanorhynchidae — Mitsukurina jordani (Jordan, Tanaka, and Snyder, 1913, fig. 7, diagr.)

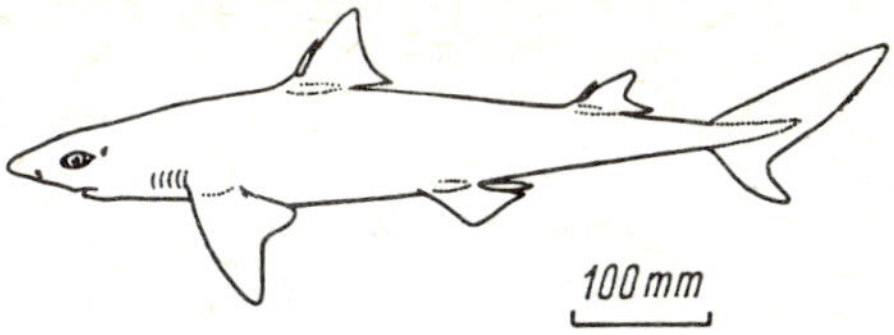

FIGURE 199. Squalidae — Squalus brevirostris (L. and L., 1959, fig. 59)

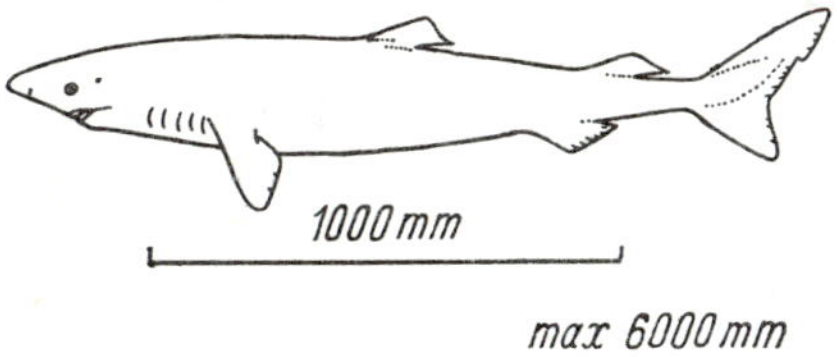

FIGURE 200. Dalatiidae — Somniosus pacificus (M., 1955, III, fig. 17, diagr.)

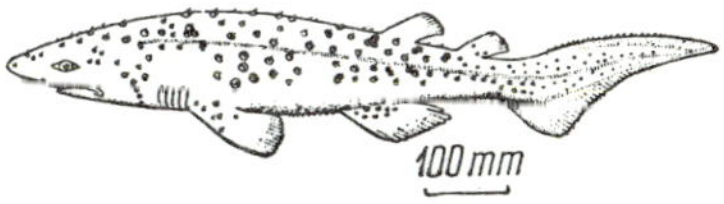

FIGURE 201. Echinorhinidae — Echinorhinus brucus (M., 1955, III, fig. 18)

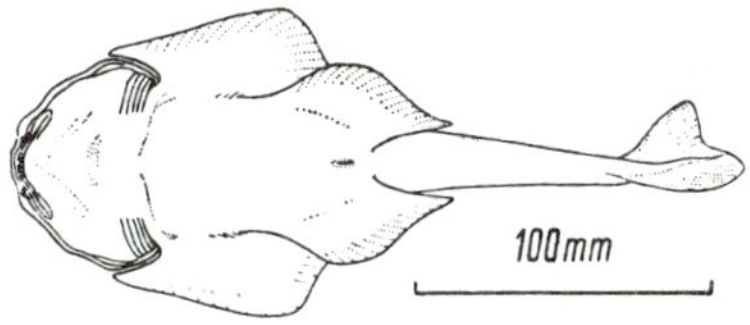

FIGURE 202. Squatinidae — Squatina japonica (L. and L., 1959, fig. 62). Ventral.

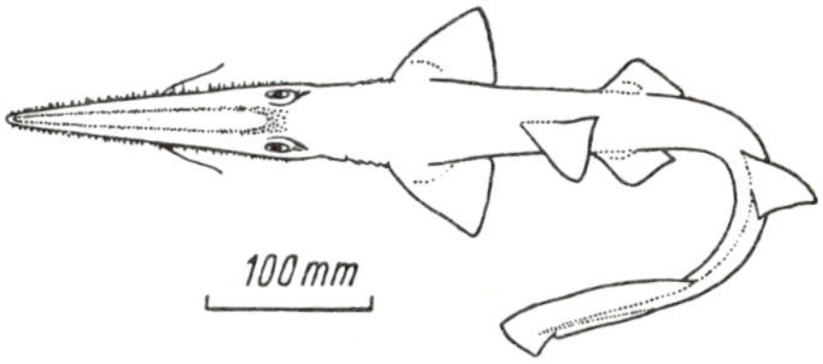

FIGURE 203. Pristiophoridae — Pristiophorus japonicus (L. and L., 1959, fig. 63, diagr.)

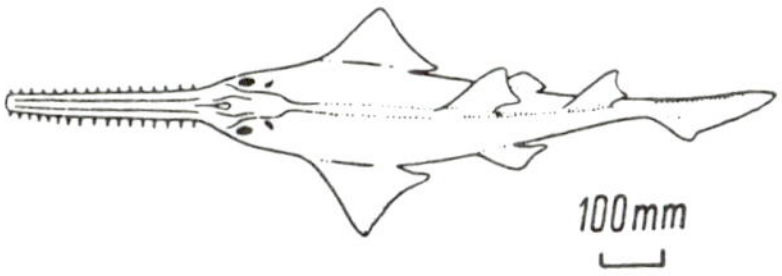

FIGURE 204. Pristidae — Pristis microdon (Day, 1878, pl. 191, fig. 1, diagr.)

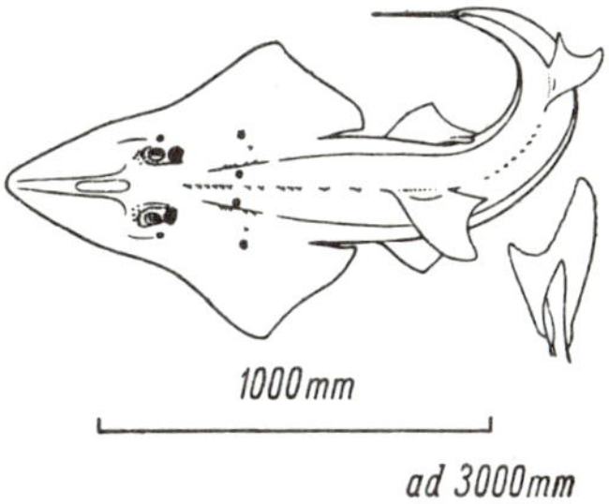

FIGURE 205. Rhynchobatidae — Rhynchobatus djiddensis (L. and L., 1959, fig. 67, diagr.)

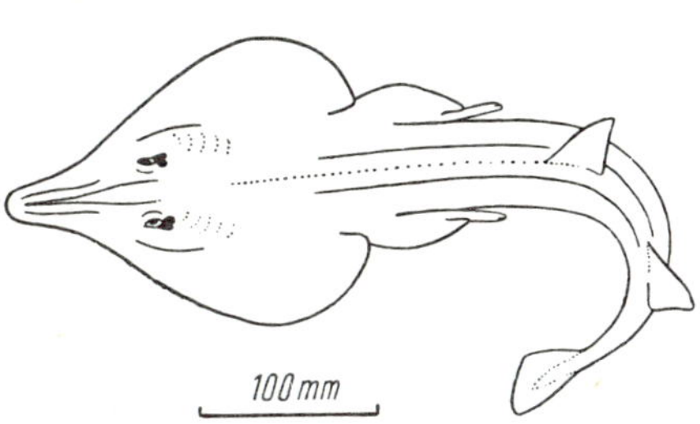

FIGURE 206. Rhinobatidae — Rhinobatos hynnycephalus (L. and L., 1959, fig. 69)

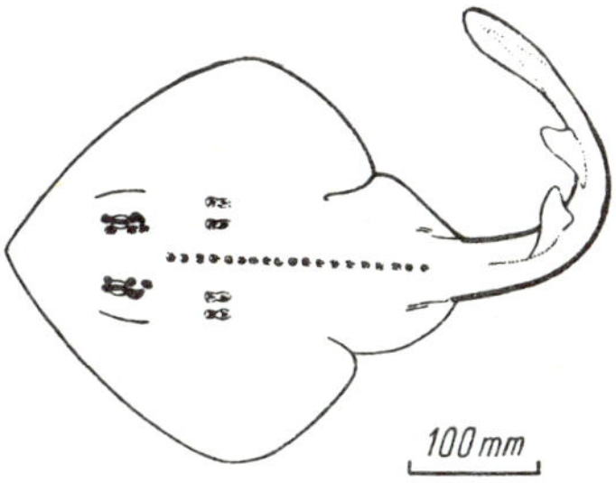

FIGURE 207. Platyrhinidae — Platyrhina sinensis (L. and L., 1959, fig. 70)

bearing a row of large toothlike processes on each margin (Figure 204) . . . . **27. Pristidae**[32]

2 (1). Snout not elongate, but if slightly elongate, not transformed into a narrow plate and not bearing toothlike processes on the sides.

3 (8). Caudal part of body so massive that it is completely fused with the anterior part of the body and cannot be demarcated from it; if a dividing line can be drawn, however (Figure 207), the origin of the first dorsal fin is much closer to the posterior end of the ventral fins then to the apex of the caudal. Dorsal and caudal fins well developed, supported by horny rays at the apex.

4 (5). Caudal fin distinctly bilobed, more or less in the shape of a half-moon, both lobes pointed. Axis of caudal fin moderately curved upward. Posterior margin of pectorals ending far short of origin of ventrals. Origin of first dorsal above or somewhat in front of base of ventrals. (Figure 205) . . . . 26. Rhynchobatidae

5 (4). Caudal fin not bilobed and not in the shape of a half-moon; its axis is curved upward very slightly if at all. Posterior margin of pectorals reaching origin of ventrals or even passing beyond this. Origin of first dorsal considerably behind ends of rays of ventral fins.

6 (7). Rostral cartilage well developed and stretching forward to the anterior projection of the snout. Snout narrow, bluntly pointed. Pectoral fins ending far short of the snout and widely separated from each other. (Figure 206). . . . . 25. Rhinobatidae

7 (6). Rostral cartilage reduced, not reaching anterior projection of snout. Snout broad, almost rounded. Pectoral fins extending forward and almost touching the tip of the snout. (Figure 207). . . . . .28. Platyrhinidae

8 (3). Caudal part of body not massive, narrow, thin, in many cases extremely thin, but if thicker, at any rate distinctly demarcated from the anterior part of the body, and the origin of the first dorsal fin is much closer to the apex of the caudal than to the posterior end of the ventrals. Dorsal and caudal fins, if present, not supported by horny rays at the apex.

9 (16). Outer margin of ventrals with a well expressed notch [absent only in family 32. Pseudorajidae, but here, as in all Rajidae (sensu lato), the axial cartilage of the abdominal girdle is straight, set horizontally, and has a forward-projecting (directed toward the head) pointed excrescence on each of the outer ends (Figure 208)].

10 (11). Two dorsal fins (Figure 209) . . . . 29. Rajidae

11 (10). Only one dorsal fin or none.

12 (13). One dorsal fin. Surface of disk with spines. Inner margin of ventral fins separated from caudal part of body, not fused with it. (Figure 210). . . . . 30. Arhynchobatidae

13 (12). No dorsal fin.

14 (15). A wide leathery outgrowth present on the tip of the snout. Caudal part of body not thickened anteriorly. Ventral fins with a deep notch. (Figure 211) . . . . 31. Anacanthobatidae

[32] Not to be confused with family 24. Pristiophoridae, in which there is a pair of long fleshy barbels near the middle of the drawn-out snout and the gill slits are distributed on the sides of the body, not on the belly (see Figure 203).

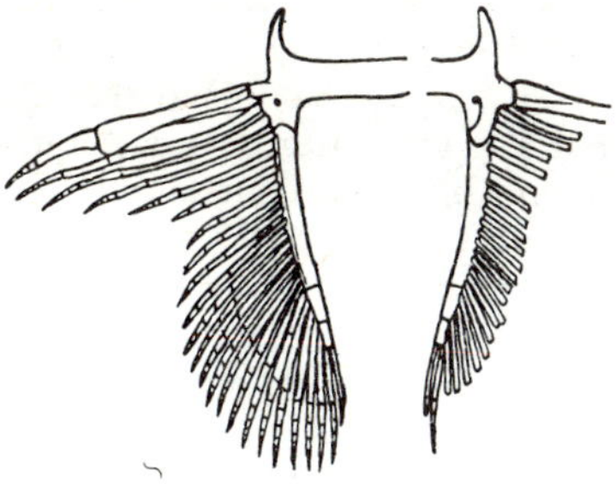

FIGURE 208. Axial cartilage of abdominal girdle of the type in the Rajidae (L. and L., 1959, fig. 64)

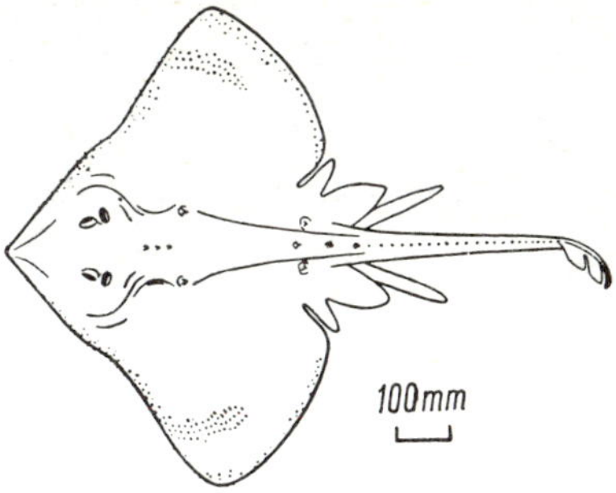

FIGURE 209. Rajidae — Breviraja smirnovi (L. and L., 1959, fig. 85)

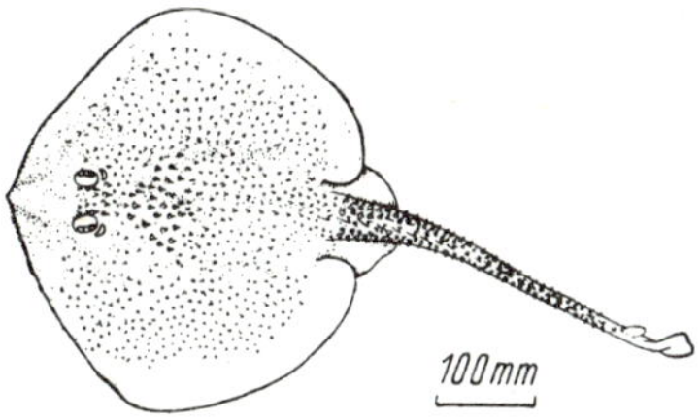

FIGURE 210. Arhynchobatidae — Arhynchobatus asperrimus (Waite, 1909, pl. 20)

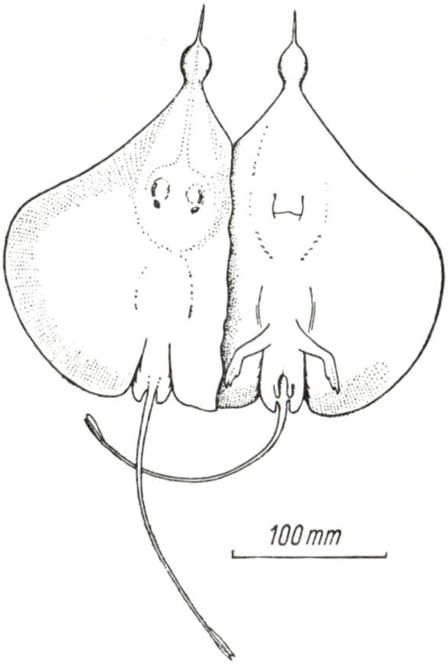

FIGURE 211. Anacanthobatidae — Springeria folirostris (B. and S., 1953, fig. 78a, diag.)

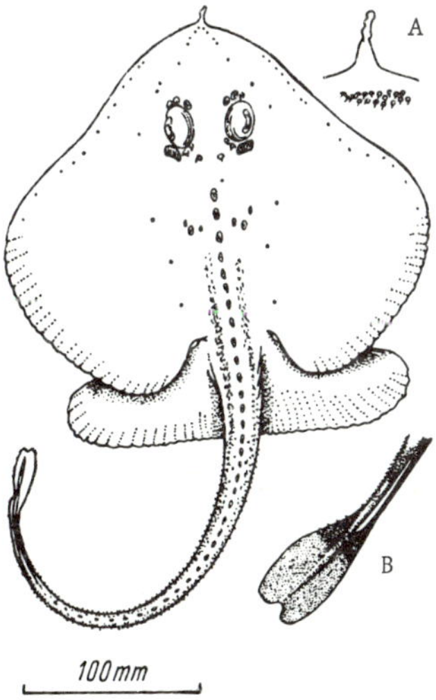

FIGURE 212. Pseudorajidae — Pseudoraja fischeri (B. and S., 1954, fig. 1):

A — rostral protuberance; B — caudal fin.

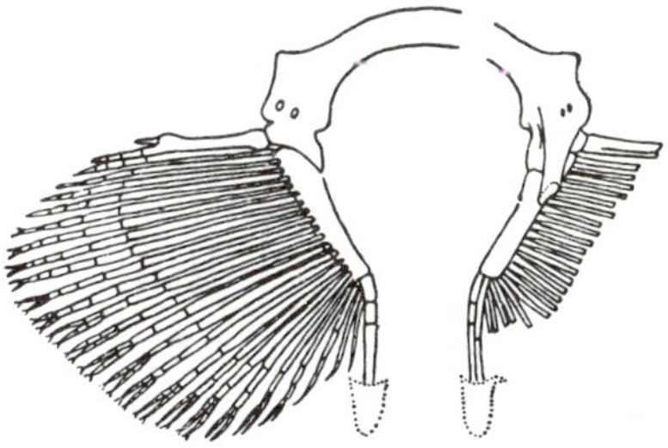

FIGURE 213. Axial cartilage of abdominal girdle of the type in the Dasyatidae (L. and L., 1959, fig. 65)

15 (14). No such leathery outgrowth on tip of snout. Caudal part of body thickened anteriorly (Figure 212). Ventral fins large, without a notch (but axial cartilage of abdominal girdle of the type in the Rajidae). (Figure 208) . . . . 32. **Pseudorajidae**

16 (9). Outer margin of ventral fins without a notch, straight or rounded. (Axial cartilage of abdominal girdle not straight, but curved and without excrescences on the outer ends (Figure 213).]

17 (18). Caudal fin well developed, supported by cartilaginous radials (Figure 214) . . . . 34. **Urolophidae**

18 (17). Caudal fin absent.

19 (24). Outer anterior margin of pectorals encircling side of head without interruption, not forming separate cephalic fins or rostral projections. Eyes and spiracles on top of head.

20 (23). Disk not more than 1.3 times as wide as long; length of tail, measured from center of cloaca to end of tail, about equal to or greater than width of disk. No distinctly expressed dorsal fin. Transverse valve on palate with festooned margins; lower surface of oral cavity with several fleshy papillae.

21 (22). [Anterior margin of abdominal girdle rounded, without a long process projecting forward in the middle part.] Marine and brackish-water species. (Figure 215) . . . . 33. **Dasyatidae**

22 (21). [Anterior margin of abdominal girdle with a long, thin, pointed process in the middle part which projects forward along the midline of the abdomen.] Exclusively freshwater species. (Figure 216) . . . . 36. **Potamotrygonidae**

23 (20). Disk more than 1.5 times as wide as long; length of tail, measured from center of cloaca to end of tail, much smaller than width of disk. A small dorsal fin is sometimes present near the middle of the tail. Transverse valve on palate with a smooth margin; lower surface of oral cavity without fleshy papillae. (Figure 217) . . . . 35. **Gymnuridae**

24 (19). Outer anterior margin of pectorals deeply incised or anterior part of fins completely separated from posterior part immediately behind the eye, so that the front part of the head is sharply distinguished from the remaining part of the disk; anterior part of pectoral fins forming a separate protuberance. Eyes and spiracles on side of head.

25 (26). Anterior protuberances of pectoral fins forming one soft fleshy lobe protruding markedly forward under the head and resembling a duck's beak. Teeth large, platelike, arranged in a few rows (1—7). (Figure 218) . . . . 37. **Myliobatidae**

26 (25). Anterior protuberances of pectoral fins in the form of two thin, narrow formations similar to fins, standing broadly away from each other and resembling ears (Figure 219). Teeth small, arranged in numerous rows. . . . . 38. **Mobulidae**

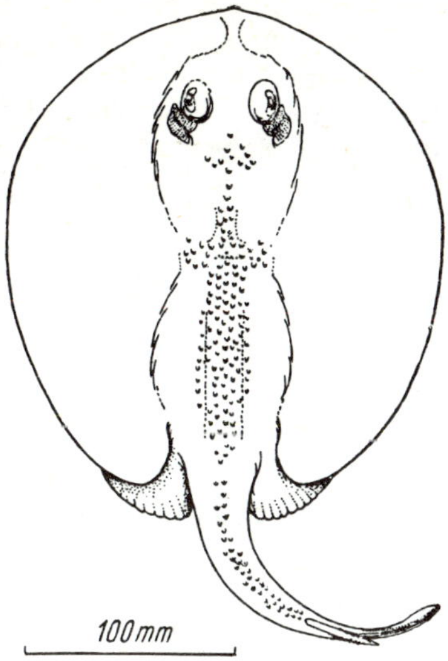

FIGURE 214. Urolophidae — Urolophus jamaicensis (B. and S., 1953, fig. 99)

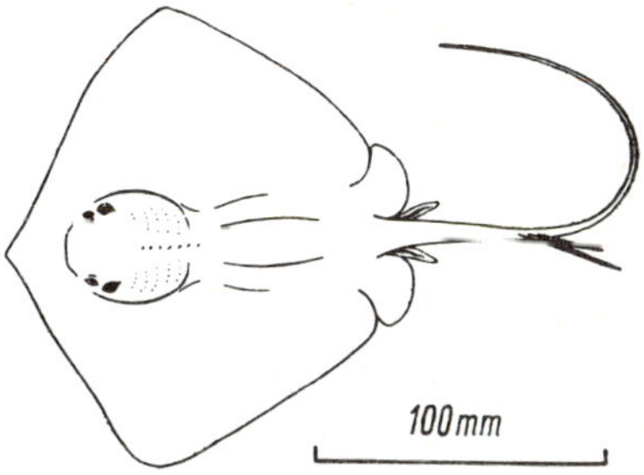

FIGURE 215. Dasyatidae — Dasyatis akajei (L. and L., 1959, fig. 94)

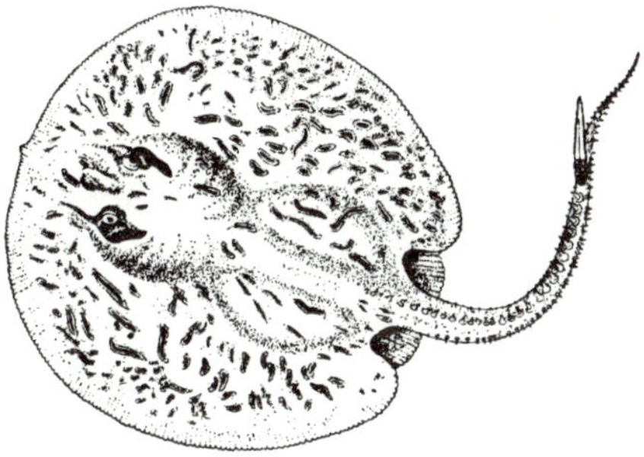

FIGURE 216. Potamotrygonidae — Potamotrygon histris (Orbigny, 1835, pl. 13)

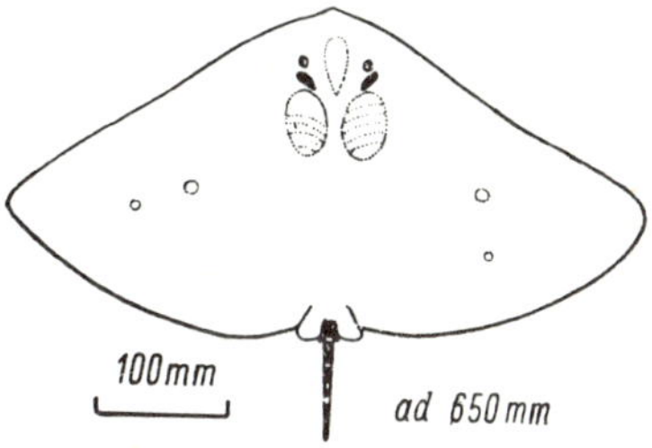

FIGURE 217. Gymnuridae — Gymnura japonica (L. and L., 1959, fig. 96)

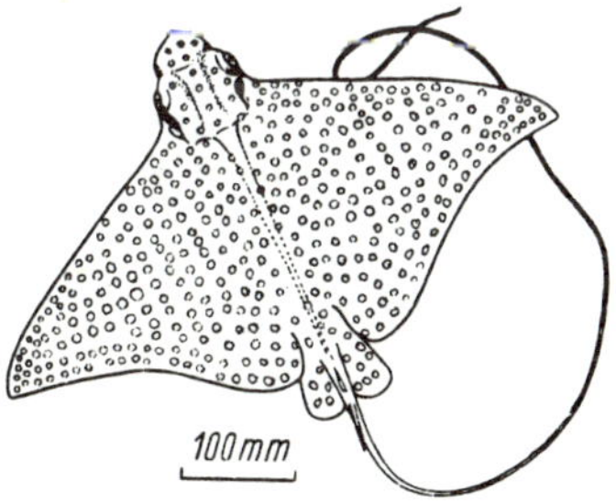

FIGURE 218. Myliobatidae — Aetobatus narinari (L. and L., 1959, fig. 98, 1)

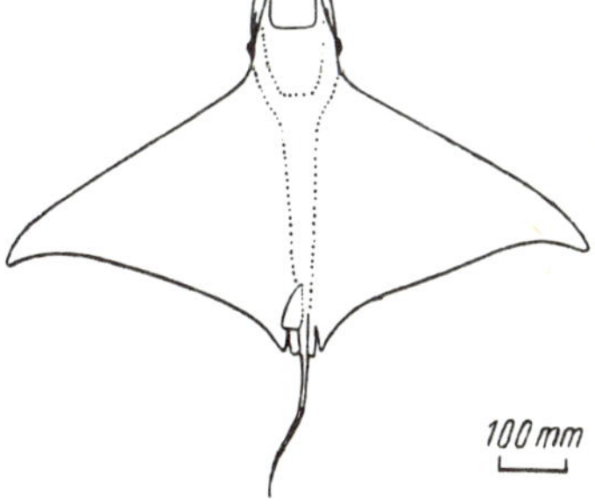

FIGURE 219. Mobulidae — Mobula eregoodootenkee (Day, 1875—1878, pl. 193, fig. 1, diagr.)

Order 10. TORPEDINIFORMES (thesis 0–19)

3 families (39–41):

1 (2). Two dorsal fins. (Figure 220) . . . . 39. **Torpedinidae**
2 (1). One or no dorsal fin.
3 (4). One dorsal fin. (Figure 221) . . . . 40. **Narkidae**
4 (3). No dorsal fin . . . . 41. **Temeridae**

Order 11. CHIMAERIFORMES (thesis 0–21)

3 families (42–44):

1 (4). No leathery spadelike appendage on end of snout. Caudal part of body long, often terminating in a filament.
2 (3). Snout not drawn out at the end. Claspers split into 2–3 branches. (Figure 222) . . . . 42. **Chimaeridae**
3 (2). Snout markedly drawn out and pointed at the end. Claspers simple, not split into branches (Figure 223) . . . . 43. **Rhinochimaeridae**
4 (1). End of slightly elongate snout bearing a leathery appendage in the form of a spade (Figure 224, A). Caudal part of body moderately long, not terminating in a filament (Figure 224, B) . . . . 44. **Callorhynchidae**

Order 12. CERATODIFORMES (thesis 0–24)

1 family: 45. **Ceratodidae** (Figure 225).

Order 13. LEPIDOSIRENIFORMES (thesis 0–25)

2 families (46, 47):

1 (2). Five gill arches and 4 gill slits. Freshwater fishes of South America (Figure 226) . . . . 46. **Lepidosirenidae**
2 (1). Six gill arches and 5 gill slits. Freshwater fishes of tropical Africa. (Figure 227) . . . . 47. **Protopteridae**

Order 14. COELACANTHIFORMES (thesis 0–27)

1 family: 48. **Latimeriidae** (Figure 228).

Order 15. POLYPTERIFORMES (thesis 0–29)

1 family: 49. **Polypteridae** (Figure 229).

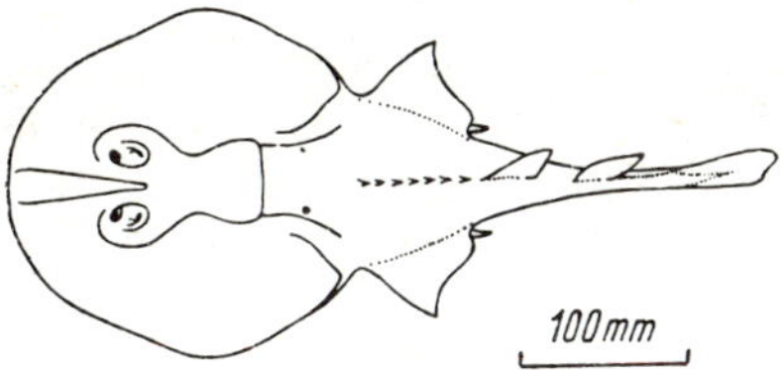

FIGURE 220. Torpedinidae — Narcine timlei (Day, 1875—1878, pl. 192, fig. 3, diagr.)

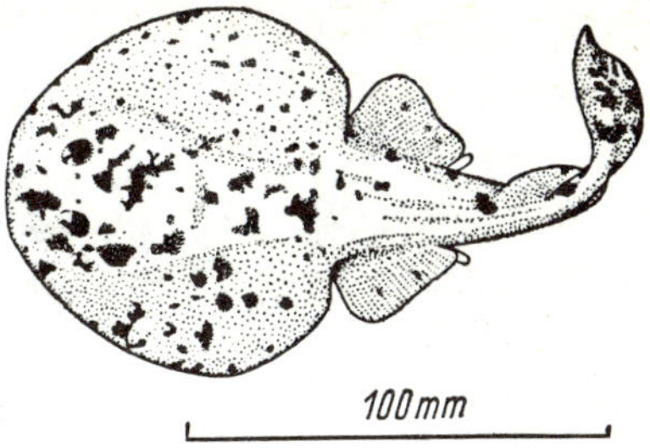

FIGURE 221. Narkidae — Narke japonica (Okada, 1955, fig. 30)

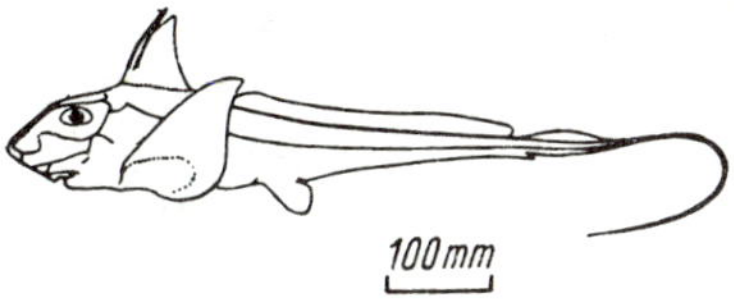

FIGURE 222. Chimaeridae — Chimaera phantasma (M., 1955, III, fig. 31, diagr.)

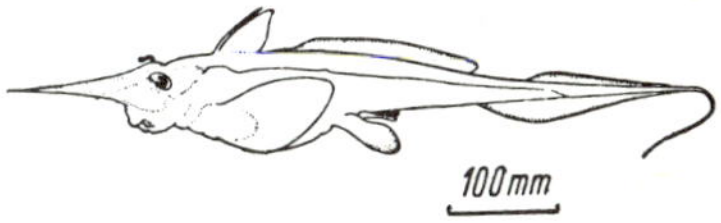

FIGURE 223. Rhinochimaeridae — Harriota raleighana (M., 1955, III, fig. 33, diagr.)

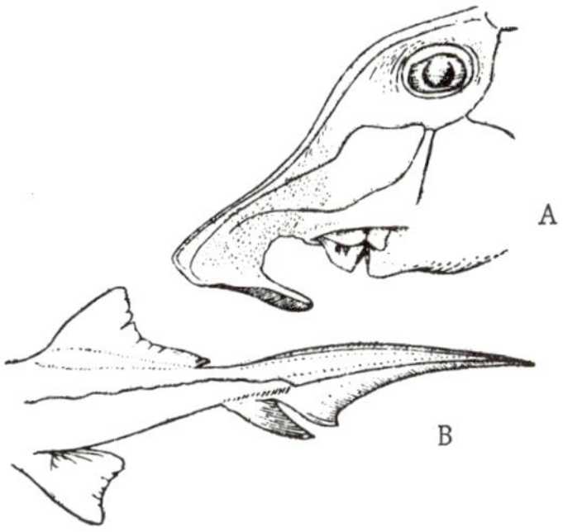

FIGURE 224. Callorhynchidae — Callorhynchus milii (B. and S., 1953, fig. 1, fig. 127, A, C):

A — head; B — caudal part.

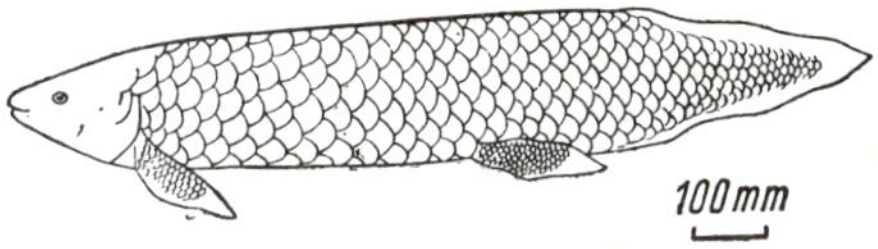

FIGURE 225. Ceratodidae — Neoceratodus forsteri (Jordan, 1925, fig. 173, diagr.)

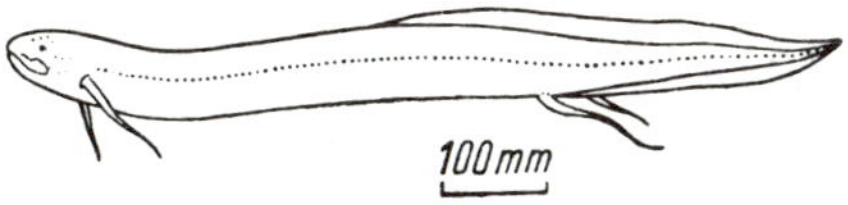

FIGURE 226. Lepidosirenidae — Lepidosiren paradoxa (Traité, 1958, III, fig. 1811, diagr.)

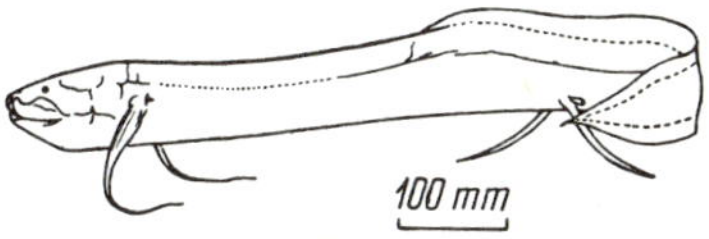

FIGURE 227. Protopteridae — Protopterus dulloi (Poll, 1957, fig. 70)

Order 16. ACIPENSERIFORMES (thesis 0—31)

2 families (50, 51):

1 (2). Body with 5 rows of bony scutes. Mouth small (A c i p e n s e r), but if large (H u s o), then strongly protrusible. Four barbels in front of mouth, arranged in one transverse row parallel to the oral slit . . . . 50. **Acipenseridae**

2 subfamilies:

1 (2). Spiracle present; snout pointed, conical. (Figure 230). . . . . subfamily 50.1. A c i p e n s e r i n a e

2 (1). Spiracle absent; snout very broad and flat. (Figure 231) . . . . subfamily 50.2. S c a p h i r h y n c h i n a e

2 (1). Body without rows of bony scutes. Mouth large, but weakly protrusible. No barbels in front of the mouth. Snout in the form of a flat, swordlike protrusion (P s e p h u r u s, Figure 232) or an oar (P o l y o d o n, Figure 233) . . . . 51. **Polyodontidae**

Order 17. AMIIFORMES (thesis 0—34)

1 family: 52. **Amiidae** (Figure 234).

Order 18. LEPISOSTEIFORMES (thesis 0—35)

1 family: 53. **Lepisosteidae** (Figure 235).

Order 19. CLUPEIFORMES (thesis 0—79)

15 suborders and 50 families (54—103):

1 (54). No adipose fin and no photophores—luminescent organs arranged in 2 rows on the belly, but sometimes present on the head and body.

2 (7). Dorsal fin shifted to the posterior half of the body and completely or partly above the short anal fin the length of whose base is equal to or smaller than the base of the dorsal and considerably smaller than the length of the head. In fishes with a notched caudal fin the length of the snout is about the same as the postorbital section of the head. Eyes not telescopic. There are no markedly elongate rays unconnected by a membrane in

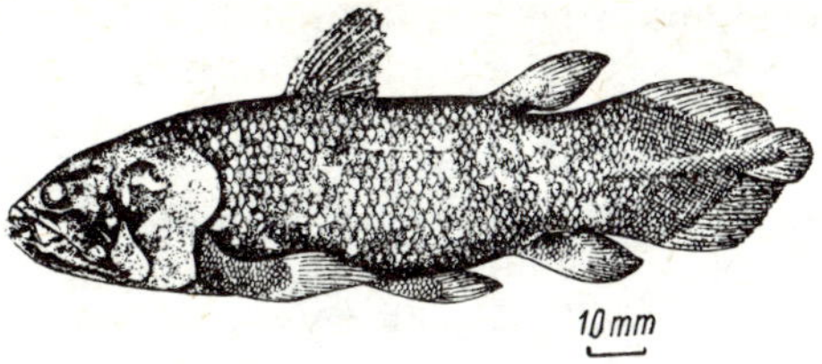

FIGURE 228. Latimeriidae — *Latimeria chalumnae* (Traité, 1958, III: 2554, pl. V)

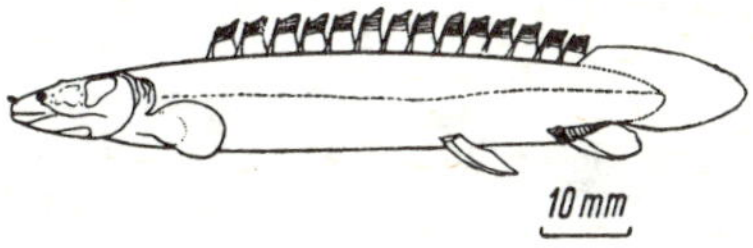

FIGURE 229. Polypteridae — *Polypterus congicus* (Poll, 1957, fig. 76, diagr.)

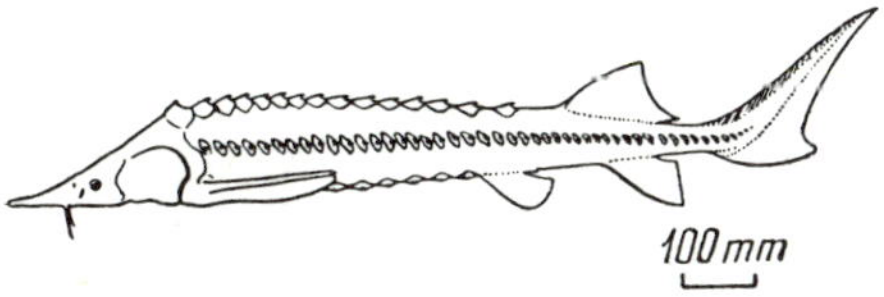

FIGURE 230. Acipenseridae (Acipenserinae) — *Acipenser schrencki* (Berg, 1948, fig. 73, diagr.)

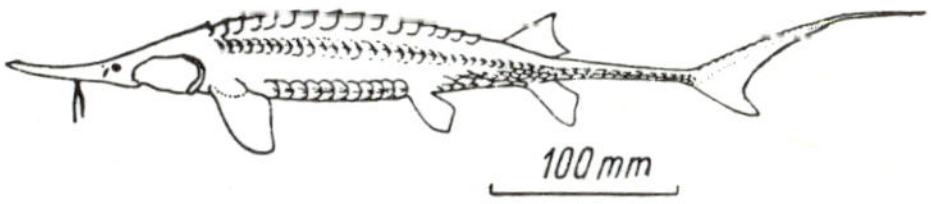

FIGURE 231. Acipenseridae (Scaphirhynchinae) — *Scaphirhynchus platyrhynchus* (J. and E., 1900, fig. 48, diagr.)

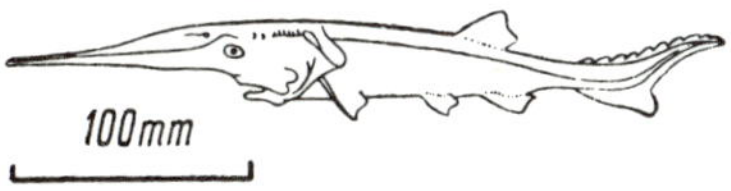

FIGURE 232. Polyodontidae — *Psephurus gladius* (L. and L., 1965, fig. 2)

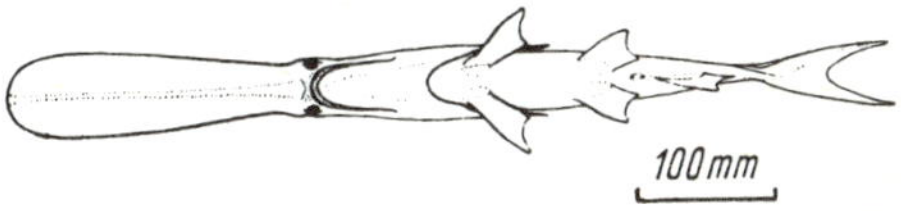

FIGURE 233. Polyodontidae — *Polyodon spatula* (Jordan, 1925, fig. 193, diagr.)

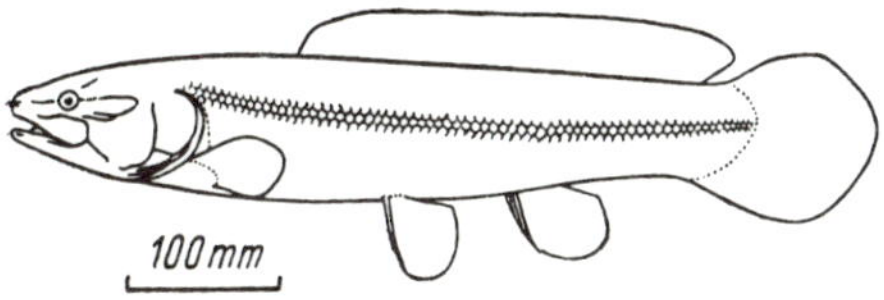

FIGURE 234. Amiidae — *Amia calva* (Jordan, 1925, fig. 138, diagr.)

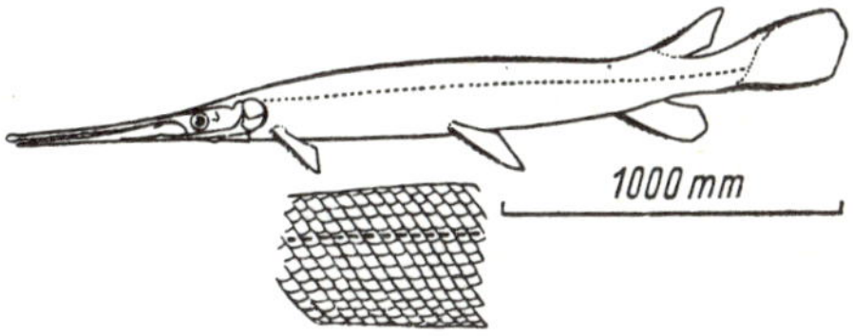

FIGURE 235. Lepisosteidae — *Lepisosteus osseus* (Traité, 1958, III, fig. 1548, diagr.)

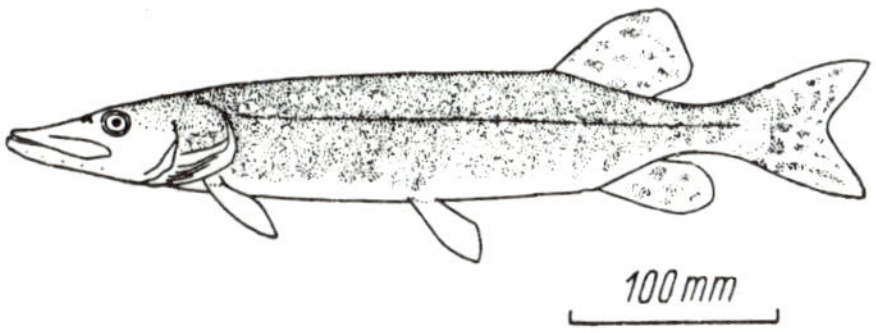

FIGURE 236. Esocidae — *Esox lucius* (Berg, 1948, fig. 278, diagr.)

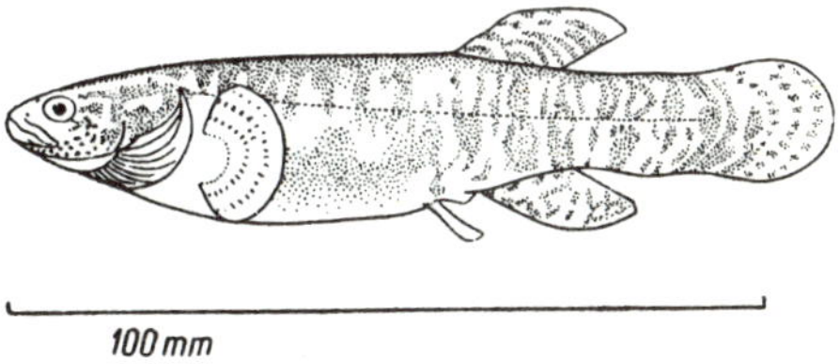

FIGURE 237. Dalliidae — *Dallia pectoralis* (Berg, 1948, fig. 273, diagr.)

the ventral fins [Mesocoracoid absent.[33] Mesethmoid ("proethmoid") paired.] (Suborder 19.7. **Esocoidei**, families 76—78.)

3 (4). Head large, with greatly drawn out and flattened snout. Mouth large, articulation of forward-projecting lower jaw behind vertical of posterior margin of eye; teeth large, pointed, canine-like. Ventral fins with 1—2 spiny and 7—12 soft rays. Caudal fin with a notch. (Figure 236). . . . . 78. **Esocidae**

4 (3). Head of moderate size. Snout not drawn out. Mouth not as large as in the pike; articulation of lower jaw in front of vertical of posterior margin of eye. Teeth weak, no canines. Caudal fin rounded.

5 (6). Pectoral fin fanlike, with 33—37 rays; ventral fins with 3 rays. Base of dorsal about the same size as base of anal. (Figure 237) . . . . 76. **Dalliidae**

6 (5). Pectoral fin with 12—23 rays; ventral with 6—7 rays. Base of dorsal markedly larger than base of anal. . . . . 77. **Umbridae**

2 subfamilies:

1 (2). Pectoral fin with fewer than 15 rays (12); 3 radials. Supramaxillary bone present. (Figure 238) . . . . subfamily 77.1. Umbrinae

2 (1). Pectoral fin with 18—23 rays; 4 radials. Supramaxillary bone absent. . . . . subfamily 77.2. Novumbrinae

7 (2). Dorsal fin not shifted to posterior half of body, but if it is, the base of the anal fin is as long as or longer than the base of the dorsal and as long as or longer than the head, or else the ventral fins have markedly elongate rays unconnected by a membrane, or else the length of snout in fishes with a notched caudal fin is considerably smaller than the postorbital section of the head, or, finally, the eyes are telescopic. [Mesocoracoid present (Figure 239), but if absent (occasionally—family 103. Bathylaconidae, thesis 19—34), photophores are present on the head. Mesethmoid not paired (as an exception paired in some members of family 72. Osmeridae).]

8 (11). [Oviducts absent.] Body fairly deep, strongly laterally compressed. Freshwater fishes of North America, tropical Africa, India, and the Indo-Malay Archipelago. (Suborder 19.11. **Notopteroidei**, families 94, 95.)

9 (10). Anal fin very long, fused with the caudal, which, however, is clearly expressed. Dorsal fin with a very short base, situated in the middle part of the body. (Figure 240). . . . . 95. **Notopteridae**

10 (9). Anal fin of moderate length, not fused with the caudal, which is normally developed and has a deep notch. (Figure 241) . . . . 94. **Hiodontidae**

11 (8). [Oviducts normally developed.]

[33] [The mesocoracoid is also absent in family 103. Bathylaconidae, but these fishes do have photophores (thesis 19—34).] (See Figure 256.)

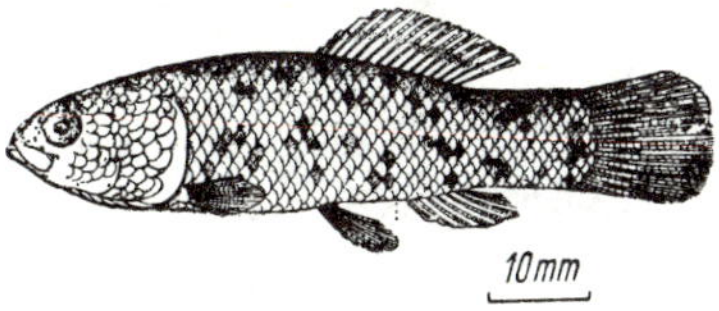

FIGURE 238. Umbridae (Umbrinae) — Umbra krameri

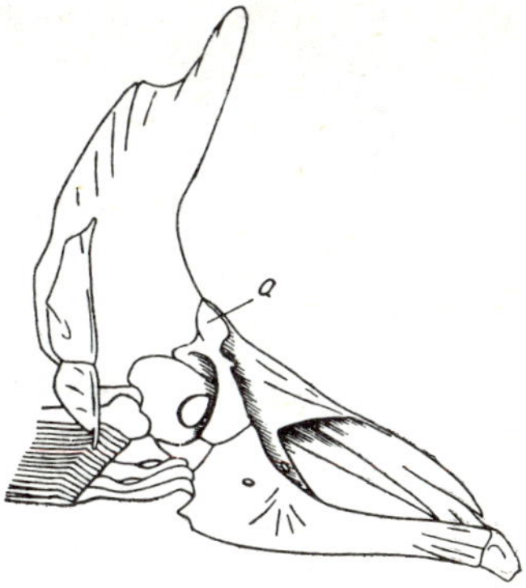

FIGURE 239. Humeral girdle in Stenodus leucichthys nelma (Salmonidae) (L. and L., 1965, fig. 21):

a — mesocoracoid.

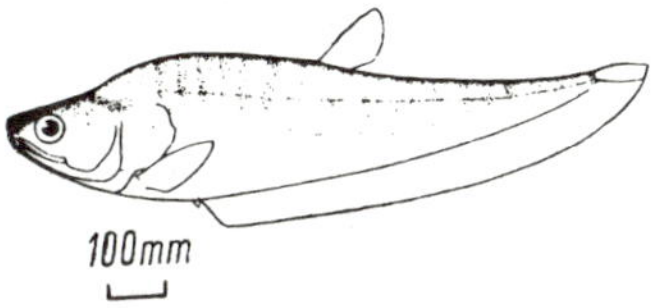

FIGURE 240. Notopteridae — Notopterus chitala (H. Smith, 1945, fig. 1, diagr.)

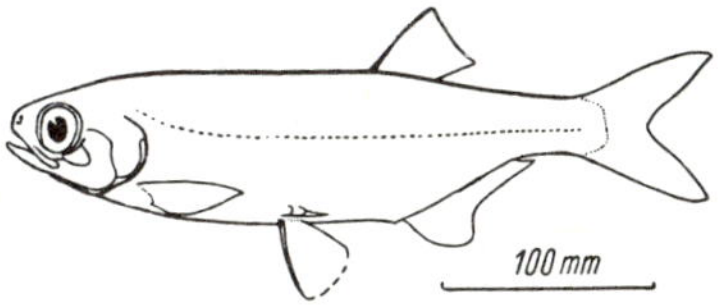

FIGURE 241. Hiodontidae — Hiodon selenops (J. and E., 1900, fig. 181, diagr.)

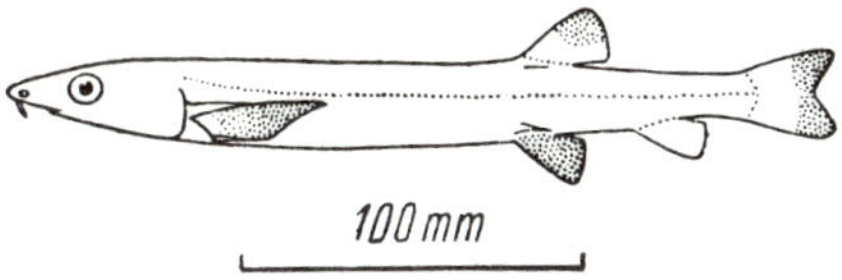

FIGURE 242. Gonorynchidae — Gonorynchys abbreviatus (M., 1955, III, fig. 45, diagr.)

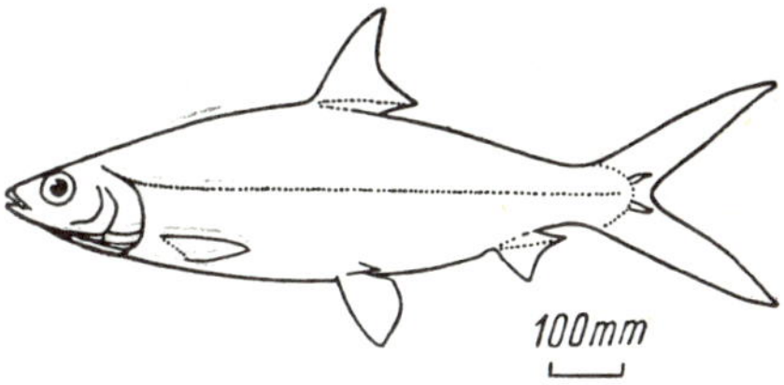

FIGURE 243. Chanidae — Chanos chanos (M., 1955, III, fig. 44, diagr.)

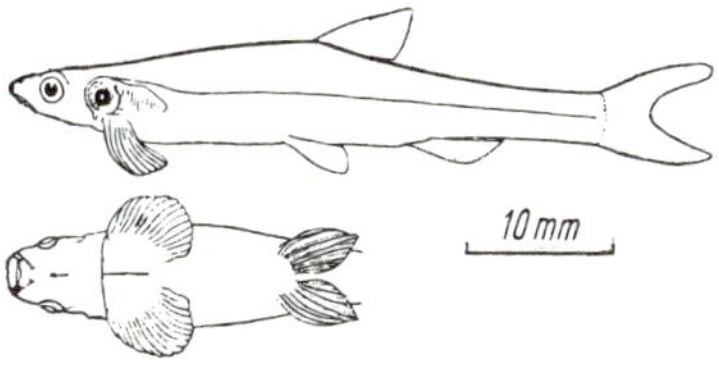

FIGURE 244. Kneriidae — Kneria auriculata (Poll, 1957, figs. 37, 38, diagr.)

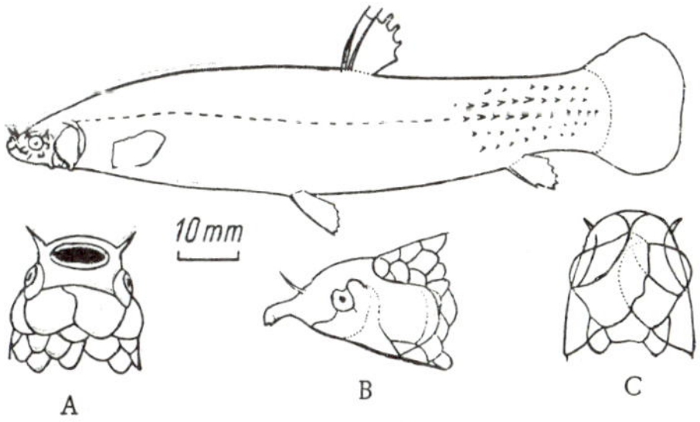

FIGURE 245. Pharactolaemidae — Phractolaemus ansorgii (Poll, 1957, fig. 30, diagr.):

Head: A — ventral; B — lateral; C — dorsal.

12 (13). Scales ctenoid, small, covering the head as well as the body. Snout with barbels. Body cylindrical. Mouth inferior, toothless; margin of upper jaw formed by premaxillaries. [Swim bladder absent. Suprabranchial organ present.] (Suborder 19.10. **Gonorhynchoidei**, family 93.) (Figure 242) . . . . 93. **Gonorhynchidae**

13 (12). Scales cycloid, covering only the body, leaving the head bare. Snout without barbels.

14 (21). At most 3 or 4 branchiostegal rays.[34]

15 (16). Gill openings wide. Ventral fins with 11–12 rays. Mouth small, toothless; margin of mouth formed by premaxillaries. Dorsal fin situated in the middle of the back. [Swim bladder present, but not connected with auditory capsule. Suprabranchial organ present.] Four branchiostegal rays. Body quite deep. (Suborder 19.3. **Chanoidei**, families 65, 66) (Figure 243) . . . . 65. **Chanidae**

16 (15). Gill openings narrow. Ventral fins with 6–9 rays. Body low.

17 (20). Body covered with scales.

18 (19). Mouth inferior, not protrusible. Lower part of preoperculum not enlarged. Three branchiostegal rays (Chanoidei ?). . . . . . (Figure 244) . . . . 66. **Kneriidae**

19 (18). Mouth superior, strongly protrusible, bordered above by both premaxillaries and maxillaries; lower part of preoperculum (interoperculum absent) very large, its lower margin contiguous under the head with the lower margin of the preoperculum of the other side. Three branchiostegal rays. (Suborder 19.4. **Phractolaemoidei**, family 67.) (Figure 245) . . . . 67. **Phractolaemidae**

20 (17). Body bare; mouth inferior, not protrusible. Mouth bordered by both premaxillaries and maxillaries. Three branchiostegal rays. (Suborder 19.5. **Cromeriodei**, family 68.) (Figure 246). . . . . 68. **Cromeriidae**

21 (14). Five or more branchiostegal rays.

22 (23). A long bony appendage at the base of the pectoral fin (Figure 247). The short dorsal fin is situated in the posterior part of the body above the slightly longer anal fin. Lateral line absent. Mouth of moderate size, superior; lower jaw produced forward; teeth large, caninelike anteriorly. [Pseudobranch absent. Intestine with a spiral valve in adults.] Scales very small. (Suborder 19.2. **Chirocentroidei**, family 64.) (Figure 248) . . . . 64. **Chirocentridae**

23 (22). Base of pectoral fin without long bony appendage.

24 (31). Dorsal fin always situated in posterior part of body. Caudal peduncle very short, its length contained at least twice in that of the base of the anal fin and often of the dorsal as well. [Swim bladder present.] Lateral line clearly expressed, complete. Dermal bones of the top of the skull with sculptured ornamentation or else almost all the bones of the head are covered with numerous dermal teeth. Freshwater tropical fishes. (Suborder 19.12. **Osteoglossoidei**, families 96–99).

[34] The presence of 4 branchiostegal rays is indicated for the new family 58c. **Congothrissidae**, particularly from the family Clupeidae, in which we have placed it provisionally (see thesis 19–52). (Poll, 1964:1–40).

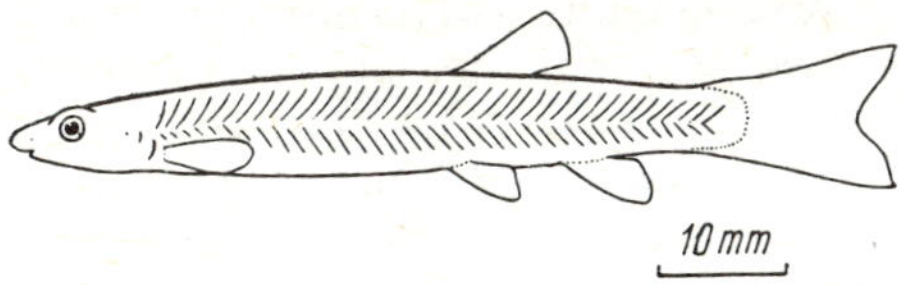

FIGURE 246. Cromeriidae — Cromeria nilotica (Poll, 1957, fig. 40, diagr.)

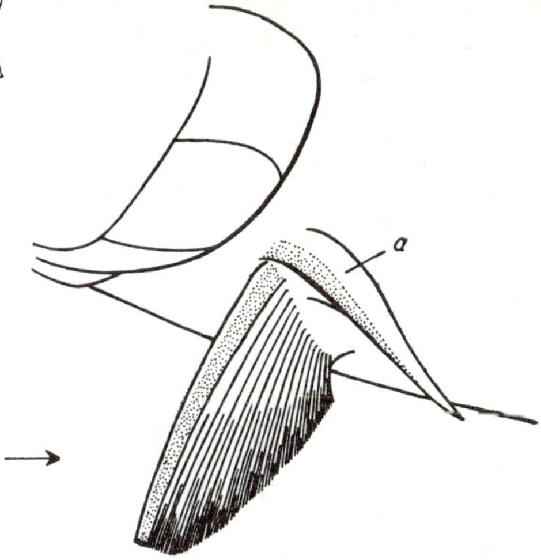

FIGURE 247. Chirocentridae — Chirocentrus dorab (L. and L., 1965, fig. 96):

a — bony appendage at base of pectoral fin.

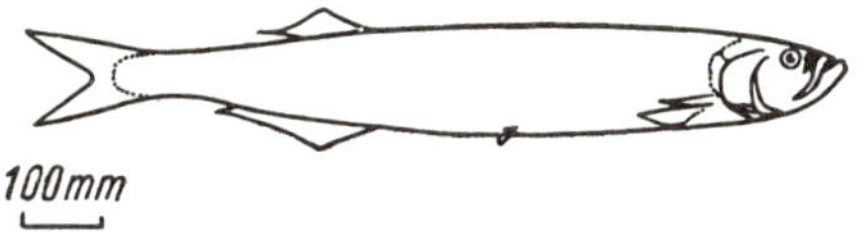

FIGURE 248. Chirocentridae — Chirocentrus dorab (L. and L., 1965, fig. 97)

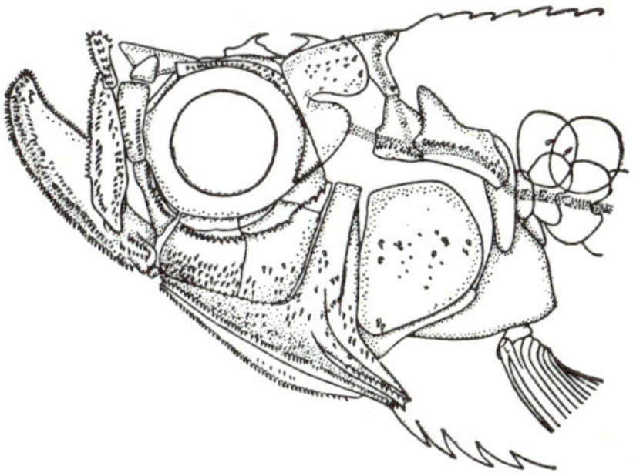

FIGURE 249. Dermal teeth on the bones of the head in Denticeps (Clausen, 1959, pl. 1, fig. 1)

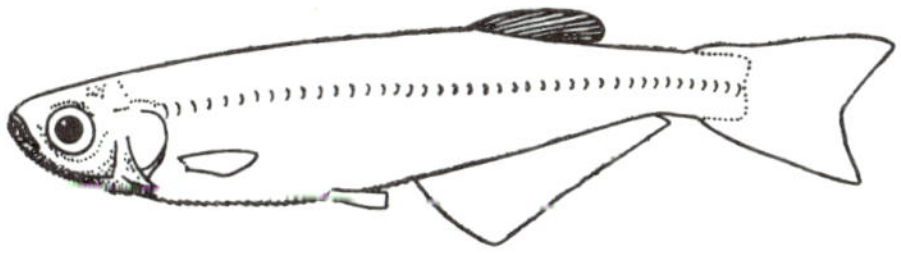

FIGURE 250. Denticipetidae — Denticeps clupeoides (Clausen, 1959, pl. 1, fig. 2, diagr.)

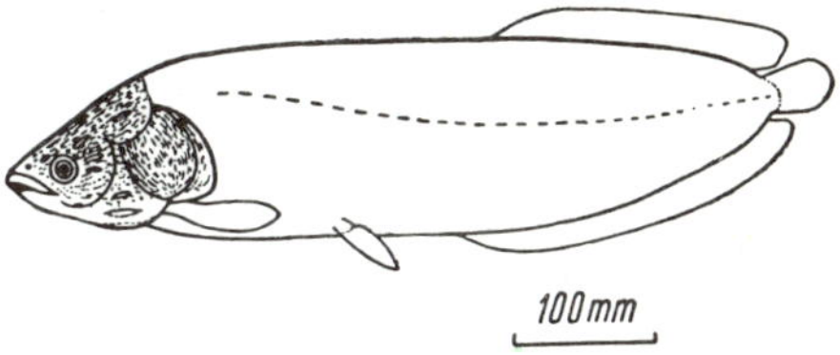

FIGURE 251. Heterotidae — Heterotis niloticus (Traité, 1958, III, fig. 1370 A, diagr.)

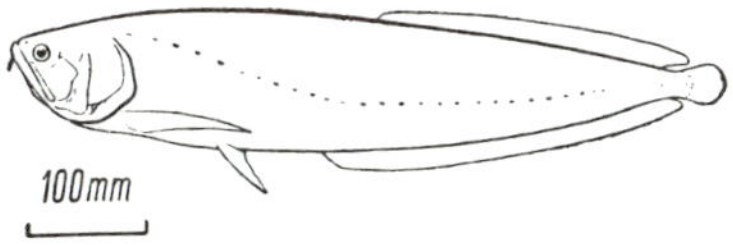

FIGURE 252. Osteoglossidae — Osteoglossum bicirrhosum (Suvorov, 1948, fig. 243 B, diagr.)

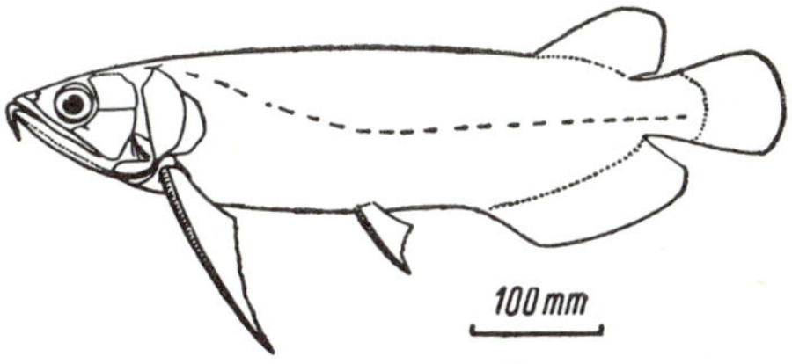

FIGURE 253. Osteoglossidae — Scleropages formosus (Traité, 1958, III, fig. 1570 B, diagr.)

25 (26). Dermal bones of head thickly covered with small dermal teeth (Figure 249). Preopercular bone with a strong spine which is crenate on the lower margin. [Supra- and infrapharyngeal teeth present.] Five branchiostegal rays. (Figure 250) . . . . 99. **Denticipitidae**

26 (25). Dermal bones of head not bearing dermal teeth; dermal bones of top of skull with sculptured ornamentation. Preopercular bone without a spine. (Supra- and infrapharyngeal teeth absent.] 7—17 branchiostegal rays.

27 (28). Mouth of moderate size; lower jaw not protruding forward, without barbels. Seven branchiostegal rays. Vomer and palatines without teeth. (Figure 251) . . . . 98. **Heterotidae**

28 (27). Mouth large; lower jaw more or less protruding forward, with or without barbels. 10—17 branchiostegal rays. Teeth present on vomer, palatines, pterygoids, and tongue.

29 (30). Barbels present on lower jaw. Body laterally compressed, with a tapering belly. [Coracoid bones forming an abdominal keel.] (Figures 252, 253). . . . . .97. **Osteoglossidae**

30 (29). Barbels absent on lower jaw. Belly rounded. [Coracoid bones not forming an abdominal keel.] (Figure 254) . . . . 96. **Arapaimidae**

31 (24). Dorsal fin situated in the middle or anterior part of the back, but if in the posterior part, the caudal peduncle is quite large, well expressed; it is almost as long as or even longer than the base of the anal fin.

32 (33). Dorsal fin very high in comparison with the length of its base, which is only 1/5—1/6 as long as the height of the fin. [Suboperculum and interoperculum absent. Parapophyses intergrown with the bodies of the vertebrae.] (Suborder 19.3. **Pantodontoidei**, family 100.) (Figure 255) . . . . .100. **Pantodontidae**

33 (32). Dorsal fin not very high, and without a shortened base, its height almost the same as or smaller than the length of its base. [Suboperculum and interoperculum present.]

34 (35). First (upper) branchiostegal ray markedly shortened, flattened and, situated under the suboperculum and interoperculum, takes part in the formation of the gill cover (Figure 256). [Mesocoracoid absent.] A large photophore in front of the eye and small ones on the head. (Suborder 19.15. **Bathylaconoidei**, family 103) . . . . .103. **Bathylaconidae**[35]

35 (34). First (upper) branchiostegal ray normal and not taking part in formation of gill cover. [Mesocoracoid present.] Photophores as a rule absent, but there may be some on the head and body; however, they do not form two rows on the belly (see thesis 19—1). (Suborder 19.1. **Clupoidei**, families 54—63).

[35] Family 103. Bathylaconidae (suborder Bathylaconoidei Bertin and Arambourg, Traité, 1958: 2259) occupies an intermediate position between the Esocoidei and the Stomiatoidei. It resembles the former in the absence of a mesocoracoid and the latter in the maxillary bone, which borders the mouth along almost its whole length (Figure 257, b).

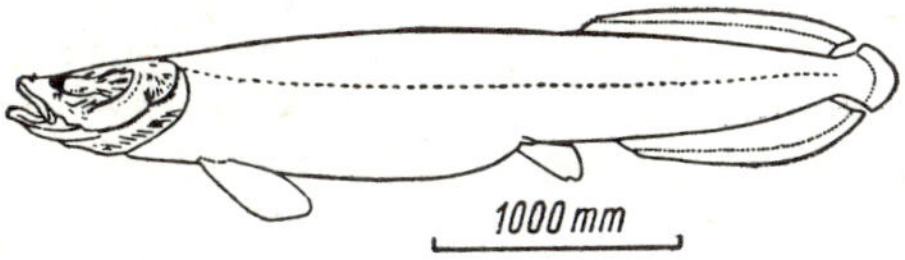

FIGURE 254. Arapaimidae — *Arapaima gigas* (Traité, 1958, III, fig. 1572, diagr.)

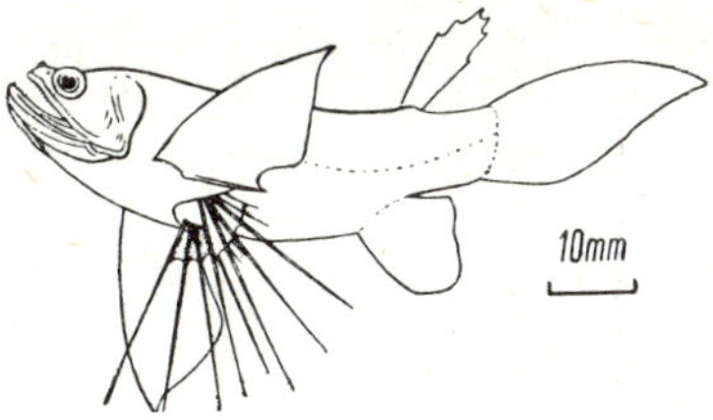

FIGURE 255. Pantodontidae — *Pantodon buchholzi* (Poll, 1957, fig. 68, diagr.)

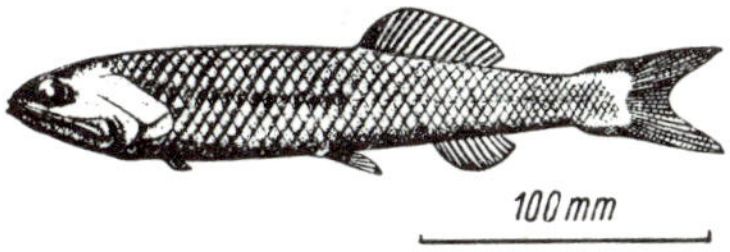

FIGURE 256. Bathylaconidae — *Bathylaco nigricans* (Parr, 1948, fig. 1)

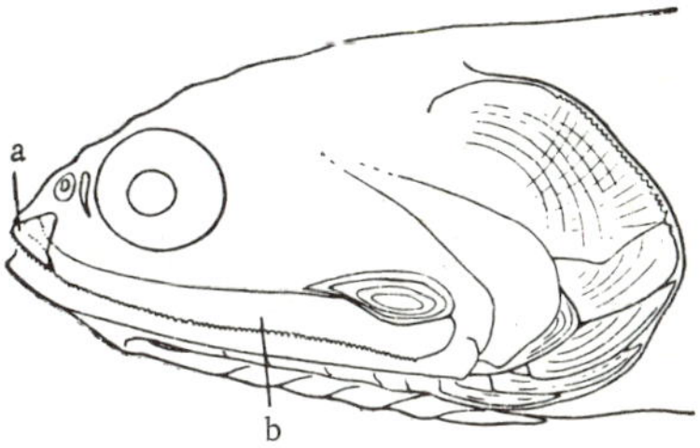

FIGURE 257. Head of *Bathylaco nigricans* (Parr, 1948, fig. 2A):

a — premaxillary; b — maxillary.

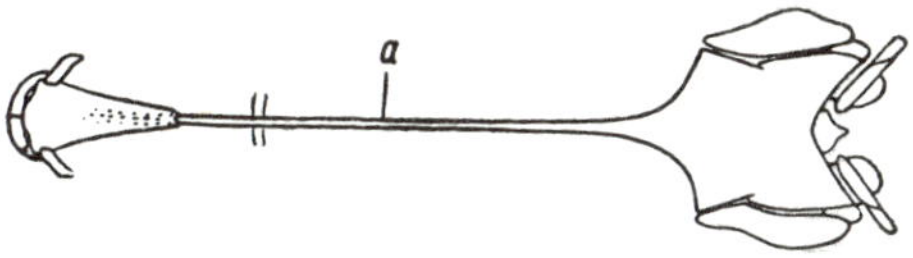

FIGURE 258. Skull of *Dolichopteryx binocularis* (Berg, 1940, fig. 117):

Dorsal, a — frontal bones.

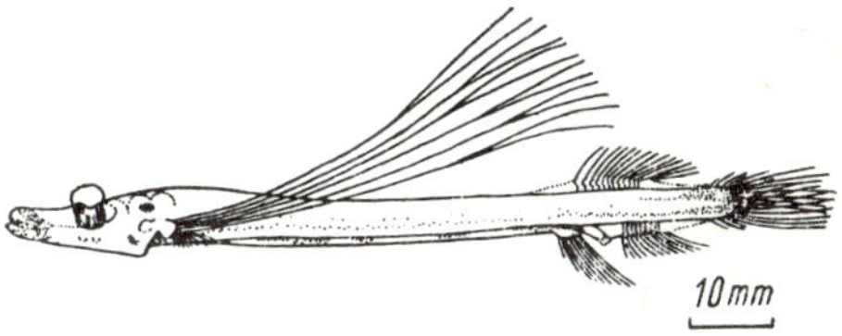

FIGURE 259. Dolichopterygidae — *Dolichopteryx binocularis* (Beebe, 1933, fig. 16)

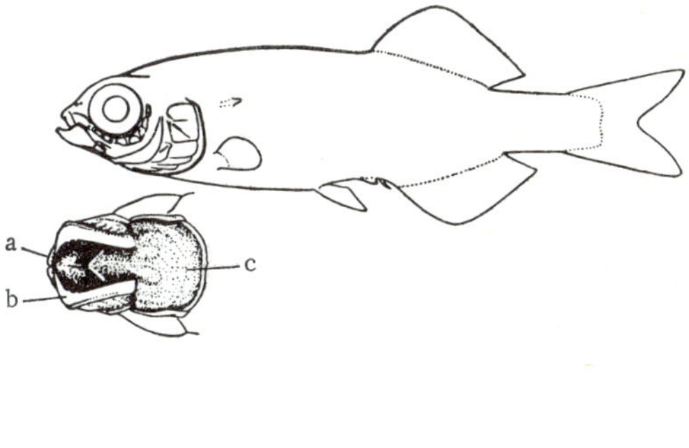

FIGURE 260. Searsiidae (Mirorictinae) — *Mirorictus taeningi* (Parr, 1960, figs. 18E and 19, diagr.):

a — premaxillary; b — maxillary; c — lower jaw, recurved.

36 (41). Dorsal fin shifted posteriorly, above the anal fin or, rarely, slightly in front of it. Marine deepwater fishes.

37 (38). [Frontal bones markedly elongate and fused, resulting in considerable elongation of the orbital and preorbital part of the head (Figure 258).] Eyes telescopic or strongly convex. Ventral fins inserted far behind midlength of body, near the anal fin. Pectorals, if not broken off, very long, filamentous. Jaws small. Luminescent organs present. (Figure 259) .... 62. **Dolichopterygidae**

38 (37). [Frontal bones normally developed.] Eyes not telescopic. Ventral fins, if present, inserted in the middle of the body, on the belly. Pectorals not elongate. Luminescent organs present or absent.

39 (40). There is a large subcutaneous sac—"humeral organ"—in which a luminescent mucus is produced; the sac ends in an efferent tubule, with an opening at the end, which protrudes from under the skin to the outside, slightly behind the upper part of the cleithrum, nearer to the lateral line than to the base of the pectoral fins .... 61. Searsiidae

3 subfamilies:

1 (2). Upper jaw partly forming the roof of the oral cavity (Figure 260); 1 supramaxillary bone; the posterior, larger, part of the upper jaw is concealed under the upward- and outward-projecting process of the lower jaw ..... subfamily 61.1. Mirorictinae

2 (1). Jaws normal. Upper jaw forming the outer margin and lateral parts of the oral cavity; 2 supramaxillaries; posterior part of upper jaw not covered by lower jaw.

3 (4). Body leaflike (flounderlike) owing to the fleshy, flat hump in front of the dorsal fin which resembles the fleshy keel in front of the anal. (Figure 261) .. subfamily 61.2. Platytroctinae

4 (3). Body not leaflike (flounderlike). No fleshy hump in front of dorsal fin or similar keel in front of anal. (Figure 262) .... subfamily 61.3. Searsiinae

40 (39). "Humeral" organ producing luminescent mucus absent. Color generally dark blue, purple, or black. (Figure 263) .... 60. Alepocephalidae[36]

41 (36). Dorsal fin not shifted posteriorly. Marine, more rarely brackish-water, fishes living at moderate depths.

42 (43). Dorsal fin with a long base, the larger part of the fin situated in the anterior half of the back. Ventral fins inserted almost under base of pectorals, long, extending beyond the origin of the anal fin. (Figure 264) .... 63. **Macristiidae**

[36] Marshall (1942, 1966) isolates 2 independent families: 60a. Leptochilichthyidae and 60b. Bathyprionidae, which differ from family 60. Alepocephalidae in the long maxillary bones, which extend far beyond the eye, and in the larger number of branchiostegal rays (12—13 instead of 4—8). Family 60b. Bathyprionidae (Figure 263A) differs from family 60a. Leptochilichthyidae in the well developed teeth on the premaxillaries and maxillaries, which are absent in Leptochilichthys.

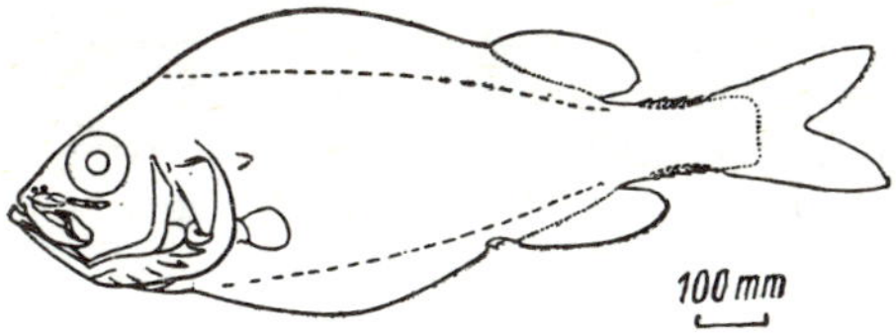

FIGURE 261. Searsiidae (Platytroctinae) — Platytroctes apus (Parr, 1960, fig. 23, diagr.)

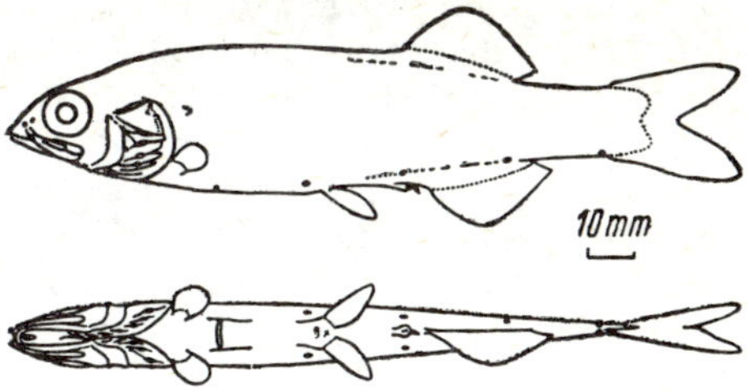

FIGURE 262. Searsiidae (Searsiinae) — Searsia koefoedi (Parr, 1960, fig. 38, diagr.)

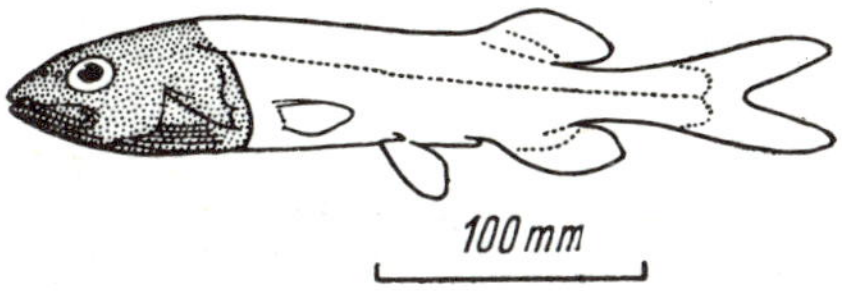

FIGURE 263. Alepocephalidae — Alepocephalus umbriceps (M., 1955, III, fig. 42, diagr.)

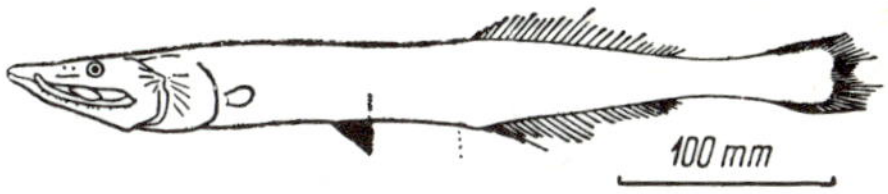

FIGURE 263 A. Bathyprionidae — Bathyprion danae (Marshall, 1966, fig. 1, diagr.)

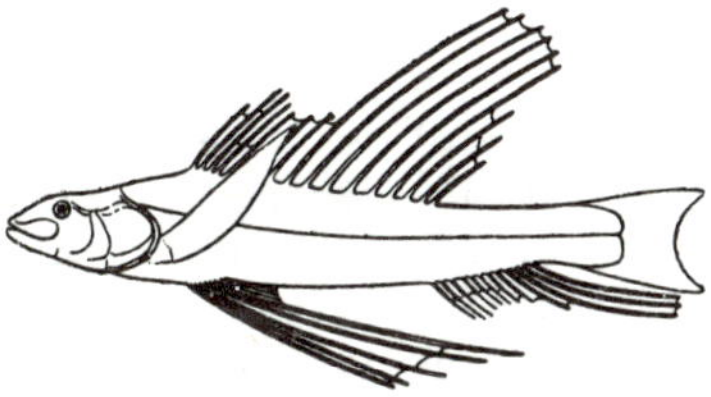

FIGURE 264. Macristiidae — Macristium chavesi (Regan, 1911 : 204, fig.)

FIGURE 265. Head of Elops saurus, ventral (L. and L., 1965, fig. 59):

a — gular plate.

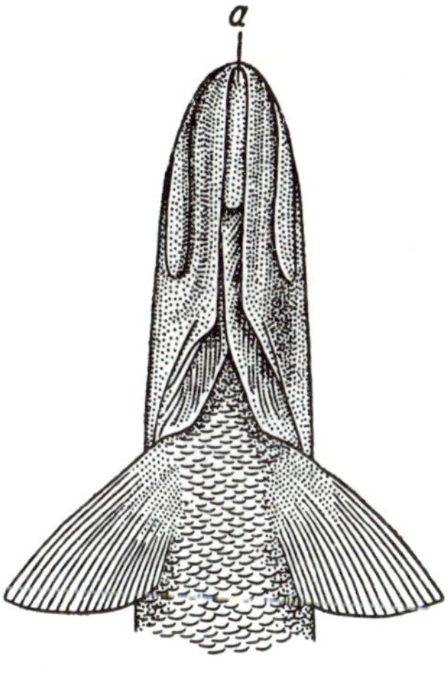

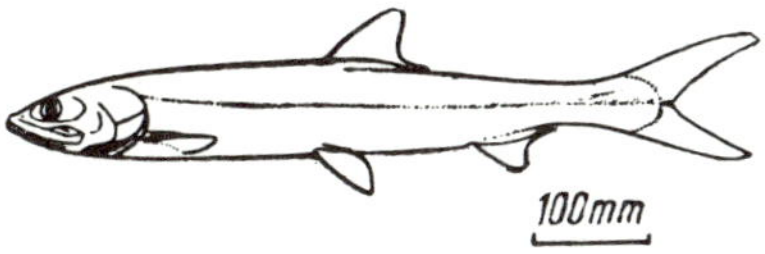

FIGURE 266. Elopidae — Elops saurus (Okada, 1955, fig. 37, diagr.)

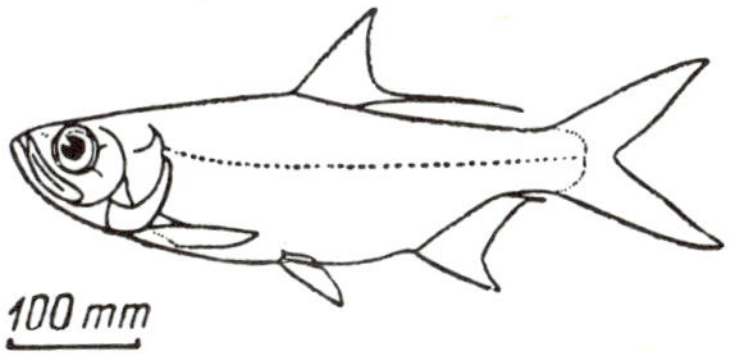

FIGURE 267. Megalopidae — Megalops cyprinoides (M., 1955, III, fig. 37, diagr.)

43 (42). Dorsal fin situated in the middle of the back or along almost the whole back, but if in the anterior part, the base is short. Ventrals inserted far behind the base of the pectorals, on the belly; they are small and do not reach the origin of the anal fin.
44 (47). Gular plate behind symphysis of lower jaw (Figure 265).
45 (46). Mouth terminal; upper jaw passing far beyond posterior margin of eye. Scales small, about 100 pores in lateral line. Dorsal fin a little larger than anal, its last ray not produced into a filament. Pseudobranchs well developed. (Figure 266) . . . . 54. Elopidae
46 (45). Mouth half-superior, upper jaw not reaching posterior margin of eye. Scales large, about 40 pores in lateral line. Dorsal fin slightly smaller than anal, its last ray produced into a filament. Pseudobranchs absent. (Figure 267). . . . . 55. **Megalopidae**
47 (44). Gular plate absent behind symphysis of lower jaw.
48 (51). Lateral line well developed.
49 (50). Dorsal fin short, with 15 rays. (Figure 268) . . . . 56. **Albulidae**
50 (49). Dorsal fin very long, with 55—65 rays. (Figure 269) . . . . 57. **Pterothrissidae**
51 (48). Lateral line rudimentary, consisting of 2—5 perforated scales behind the head.
52 (53). Snout not protruding forward; mouth terminal or half-superior, of moderate size . . . . 58. **Clupeidae**[37]

6 subfamilies:

1 (10). Abdominal keeled scales present, usually well developed. Abdomen markedly laterally compressed, but sometimes rounded.
2 (9). Anal fin with fewer than 25 rays. Ventral fins well developed.
3 (6). Upper jaw without marked median notch.
4 (5). Two supramaxillary (accessory) bones. (Figure 270) . . . . (subfamily 58.1. Clupeinae
5 (4). One supramaxillary (accessory) bone. (Figure 271) . . . . subfamily 58.2. Pellonulinae
6 (3). Upper jaw with a median notch. (Figure 272).
7 (8). Last ray of dorsal fin not produced into a filament. Caudal fin with an elongate scale (ala) at the base of each lobe; this is absent in the genera Hilsa and Gudusia. (Figure 273) . . . . subfamily 58.3. Alosinae
8 (7). Last ray of dorsal fin produced into a long filament; this is absent in Gonialosa and Anodontostoma, but these genera do not have an ala. Body, except in Clupanodon, deep, mouth small, slightly subterminal, anal fin long, making the fish look similar to bream. (Figure 274) . . . . subfamily 58.4. Dorosomatinae[38]

[37] Poll (1964:1—40) described the new family 58c. **Congothrissidae, which differs from the other Clupeoidei,** particularly from the Clupeidae, in the presence of only 4 branchiostegal rays (McAllister, 1968:42).

[38] Family 58a. **Dorosomatidae** is isolated as a separate family (MA:41).

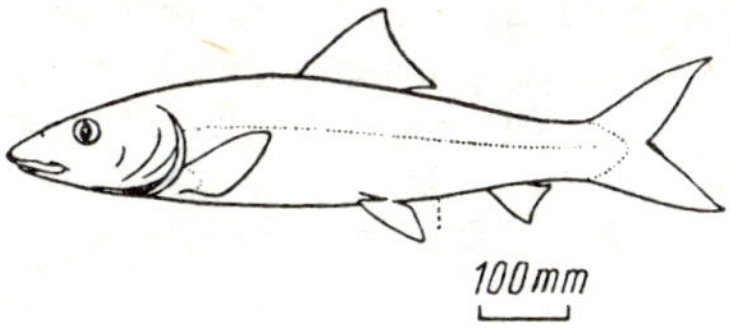

FIGURE 268. Albulidae — Albula vulpes (M., 1955, III, fig. 39, diagr.)

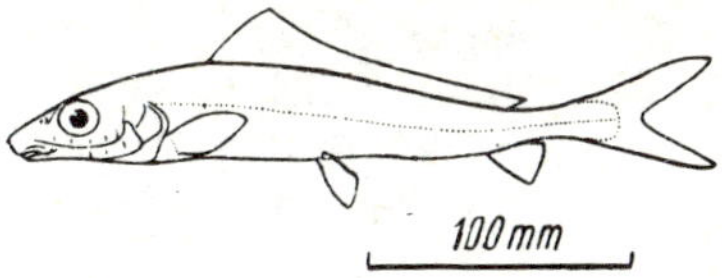

FIGURE 269. Pterothrissidae — Pterothrissus gissu (Okada, 1955, fig. 36, diagr.)

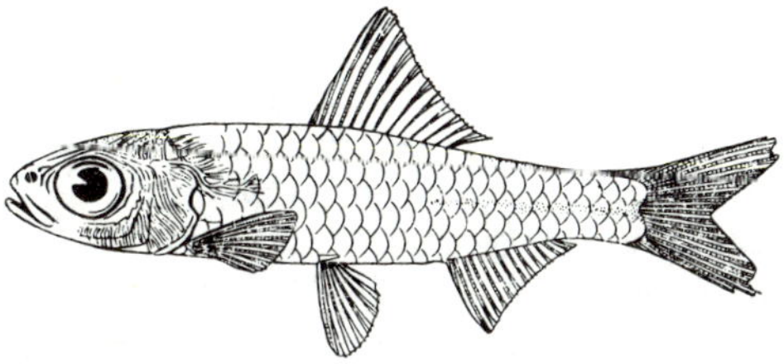

FIGURE 269A. Congothrissidae — Congothrissa gossei (Poll, 1964, fig. 1)

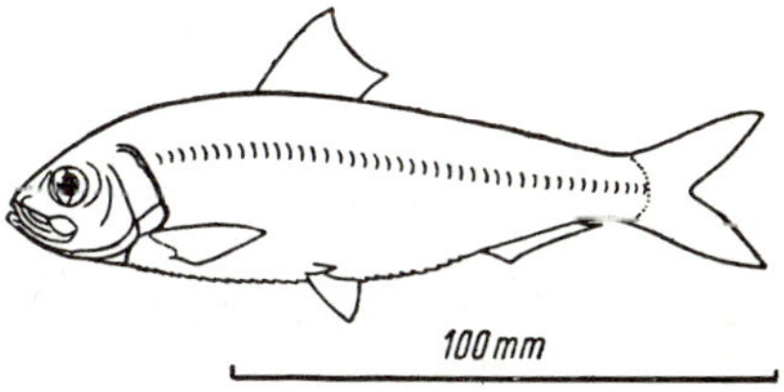

FIGURE 270. Clupeidae (Clupeinae) — Harengula zunasi (Svetovidov, 1952, pl. 5, fig. 1, diagr.)

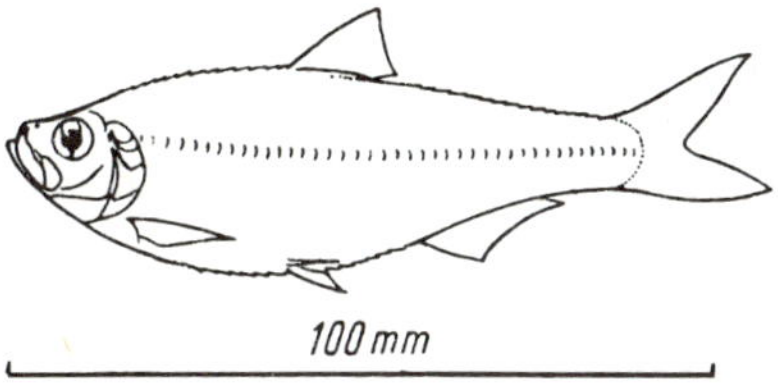

FIGURE 271. Clupeidae (Pellonulinae) — Clupeoides lile (W. and B., 1913, 2, fig. 22, diagr.)

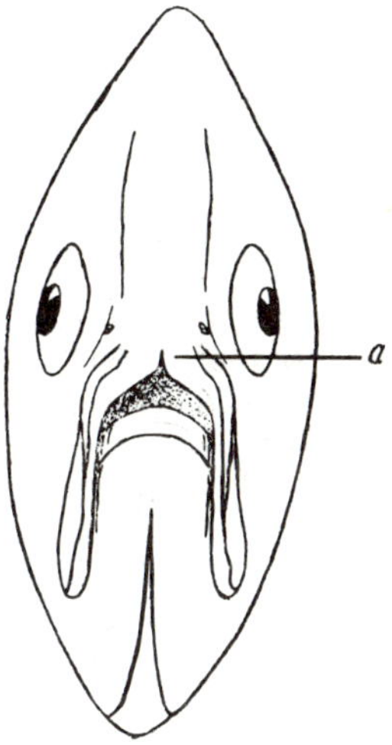

FIGURE 272. Head of Alosa sp. (Alosinae), from the front:

a — median notch.

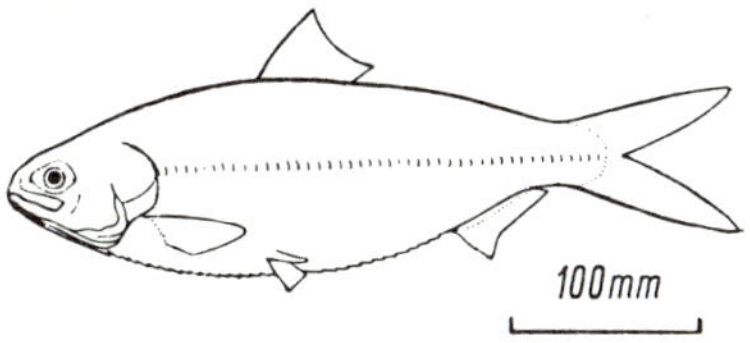

FIGURE 273. Clupeidae (Alosinae). Hilsa reevesi (Wang, 1958, fig. 76, diagr.)

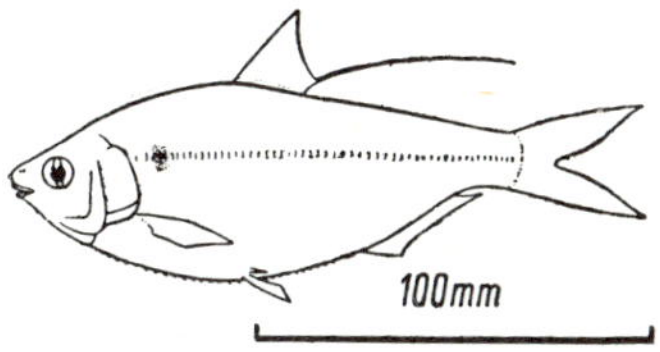

FIGURE 274. Clupeidae (Dorosomatinae) — Nematalosa nasus (Chevey, 1932, pl. 2, diagr.)

9 (2). More than 30 rays in anal fin. Ventrals small or absent. (Figure 275) . . . . subfamily 58.5. Pristigasterinae

10 (1). Abdominal keeled scales absent. Belly distinctly rounded. One supramaxillary bone. Upper jaw without an incision. No ala. (Figure 276) . . . . subfamily 58.6. Dussumieriinae[39]

53 (52). Snout protruding markedly in front of lower jaw; mouth distinctly subterminal or inferior, very large . . . . 59. **Engraulidae**

2 subfamilies:

1 (2). Body moderately elongate. Anal fin not fused with the caudal, which has a deep notch. Upper rays of pectoral fin, except sometimes for the uppermost ray, not passing into long, thin filaments. (Figure 277) . . . . subfamily 59.1. Engraulinae

2 (1). Body very elongate. Anal fin long, fused with the lower caudal lobe. Several (4—6) upper rays of pectoral fin passing into long, thin filaments. (Figure 278) . . . . subfamily 59.2. Coiliinae

54 (1). There is an adipose fin, or photophores present, arranged in 2 rows on the belly or in another place.

55 (56). No dorsal fin, only an adipose fin. Ventral fins present but very small and hard to distinguish. Luminescent organs absent. [81 vertebra.] Suborder 19.4. **Anotopteroidei**, families 101, 102.) (Figure 279) . . . . .101. **Anotopteridae**[40]

56 (55). Dorsal fin present in addition to adipose fin.

57 (58). Opercular bones strongly reduced, function of gill cover fulfilled by the markedly enlarged branchiostegal membranes, each of which is supported by 10 long rays. Premaxillaries small, equipped with strong teeth and with long ascending processes. Truncal part of body enlarged and thickened, caudal part shortened and thinner. Eyes not telescopic.(Figure 280). . . . . .102. **Rosauridae**[41]

58 (57). Opercular bones normally developed.

59 (88). Photophores absent; adipose fin present.[42] [Oviducts absent or incompletely developed and represented by folds of the abdomen and an unpaired peritoneal oviduct.]

[39] Family 58b. **Dussumieriidae** is isolated as a separate family (MA : 40)

[40] Matsubara (1955 : 262) includes this family in the suborder Alepisauroidei of order 23. Myctophiformes. It is presented in both orders in this work (see thesis 23—1).

[41] According to GRWM, 1966 : 395, these are apparently the young of family 123. Giganthuridae.

[42] There is no adipose fin in the genus Dolichopteryx (Figure 283).

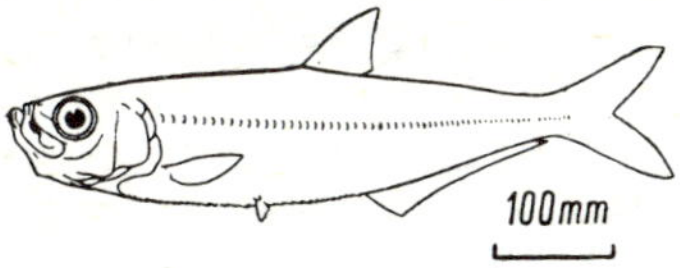

FIGURE 275. Clupeidae (Pristigasterinae) — *Ilisha elongata* (Svetovidov, 1952, pl. 26, fig. 2, diagr.)

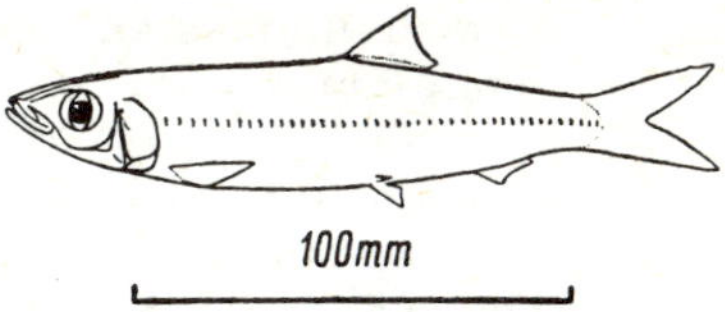

FIGURE 276. Clupeidae (Dussumieriinae) — *Dussumieria acuta* (W. and B., 1913, 2, fig.13, diagr.)

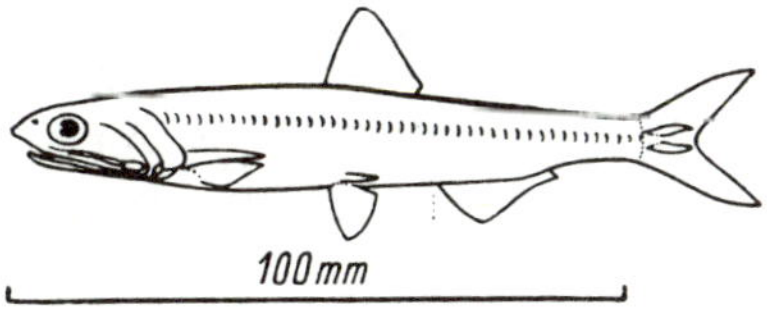

FIGURE 277. Engraulidae (Engraulinae) — *Eugraulis japonicus* (Okada, 1955, fig. 45, diagr.)

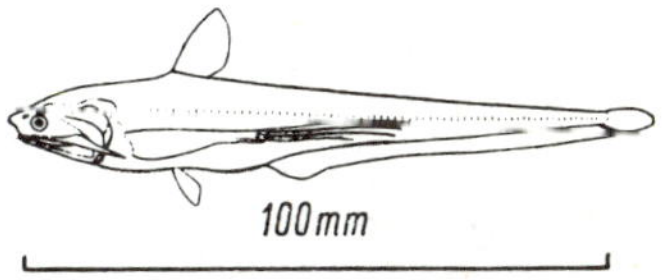

FIGURE 278. Engraulidae (Coiliinae) — *Coilia ectenes* (Jordan and Seale, 1906, fig. 1, diagr.)

FIGURE 279. Anototopteridae — *Anotopterus pharao* (M., 1955, III, fig. 89, diagr.)

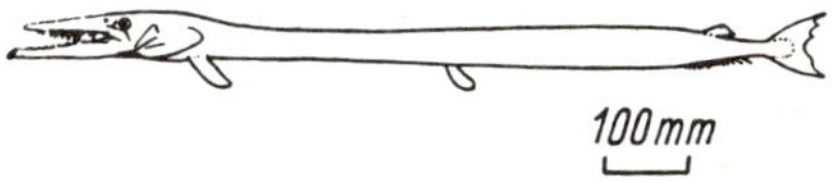

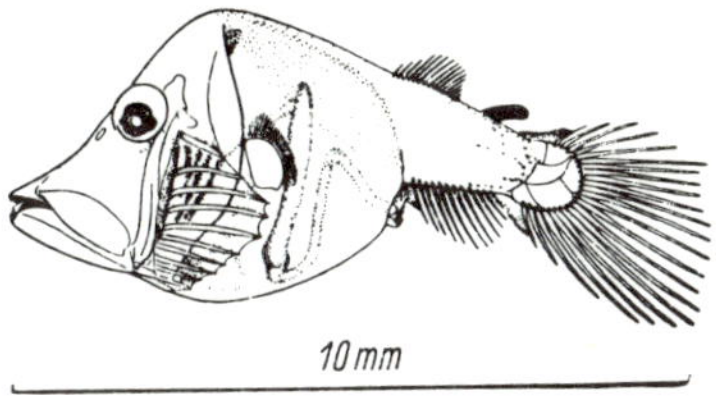

FIGURE 280. Rosauridae — *Rosaura rotunda* (Tucker, 1954, fig. 1)

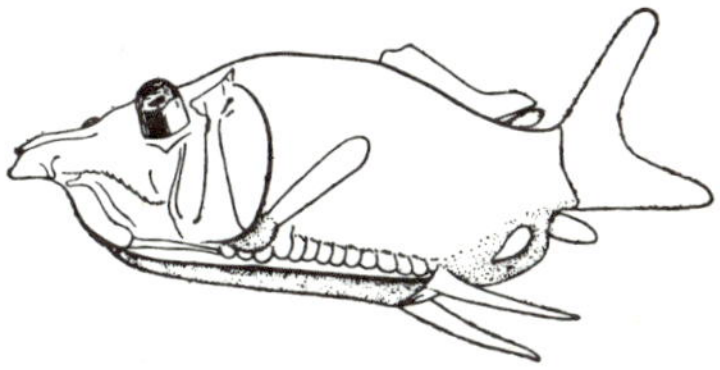

FIGURE 281. Opisthoproctidae — *Opistoproctus* sp. (Traité, 1958, III: 1900, pl. IV, fig. 2, diagr.)

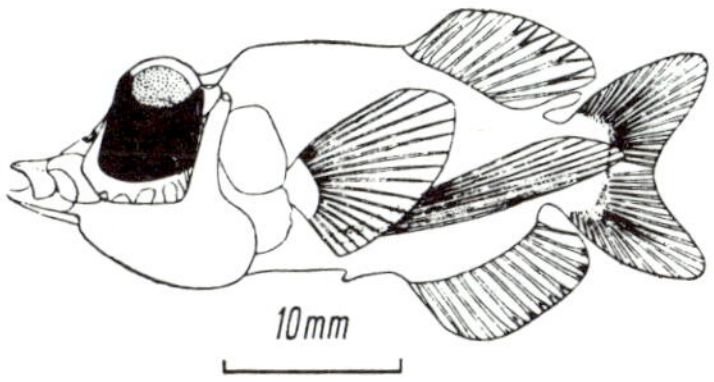

FIGURE 282. Macropinnidae — *Macropinna microstoma* (Chapman, 1939, fig. 59)

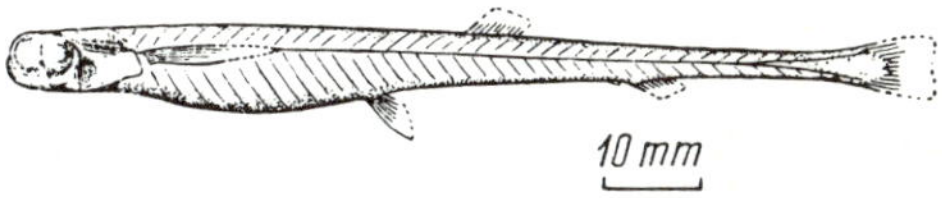

FIGURE 282A. Xenophthalmichthyidae — *Xenophthalmichthys danae* (*Protoscope stilbia*) (Rass, 1961, fig. 1)

60 (75). Premaxillaries and sometimes also maxillaries absent, or the maxillaries are very small and without a supramaxillary (accessory) bone. Mouth very small, without teeth. Eyes telescopic or, in fishes with the dorsal fin situated above the ventrals, they are large, about 1/3 as long as the head, and protrude from the orbit [Physoclistous forms, or swim bladder absent.] (Suborder 19.9. Opisthoproctoidei,[43] families 87—92.)

61 (62). Maxillary bones absent (Berg, 1940: 249, figs. 144, 145). On the belly there is a formation resembling the sole of a boot, to which the lower surface of the large swim bladder is attached from the inside. Anal fin very small in comparison with the dorsal (which is situated in the posterior part of the body), the same size as the adipose fin. Eyes telescopic. (Figure 281). . . . . 91. Opisthoproctidae

62 (61). Maxillaries present. No "sole" on the abdomen. Anal fin about the same size as the dorsal. Eyes convex or telescopic.

63 (68). Eyes telescopic.

64 (65). Body short, its depth contained 2.5—3 times in the length of the body without the caudal fin. Ventral fins long, in juveniles passing beyond origin of anal, in older fishes reaching the caudal fin. (Figure 282). . . . . 92. Macropinnidae[44]

65 (64). Body long, its depth contained 10—14 times in the length without the caudal fin.

66 (67). Dorsal and ventral fins situated in about the middle of the body. Pectorals short. Snout short. (Figure 282A). . . . . 90. Xenophthalmichthyidae[45]

67 (66). Dorsal and ventral fins situated in the posterior part of the body. Pectorals very long, but possibly truncated. Snout not shortened, its length more or less equal to that of the postorbital space. (Figure 283). (Suborder Clupeoidei) . . . . .62. Dolichopterygidae[46] (Genus Dolichopteryx)

68 (63). Eyes convex, but not telescopic.

69 (72). Swim bladder and orbitosphenoid present.

70 (71). Branchiostegal rays numbering 6—7. Teeth on the tongue. Mesocoracoid present. 54 vertebrae. (Figure 284). . . . . 87. Argentinidae

[43] [Recently (Cohen, 1964: 1—70) the name of the suborder Opisthoproctoidei was changed to Argentinoidei, at the genus Argentina is better known and more representative. In addition, families 92. Macropinnidae (thesis 19—64) and 62. Dolichopterygidae (theses 19—67 and 19—74) have been dissolved and their genera included in family 91. Opisthoproctidae, which has the following genera: Opisthoproctus (syn. Grimaldia and Monacoa), Rhynchohyalus (syn. Hyalorhynchus and Ophthalmopelton), and Winteria. Family 89. Microstomatidae (thesis 19—71) has been included in family 87. Argentinidae as the subfamily Microstomatinae, in which is also placed the genus Xenophthalmichthys, which was until now considered a separate family (thesis 19—66). Since this author's classification is based on differences in the position of the parietal bones and on the presence or absence of the postcleithrum, characters which are difficult to use when carrying out a determination on board ship, and since it is not our aim to make a critical review of the system, we have confined ourselves to this footnote and have not entered changes in the key.]

[44] Included in family 91. Opisthoproctidae (Cohen, 1964).

[45] Included in the subfamily Microstomatinae of family 97. Argentinidae (Cohen, 1964).

[46] Included in family 91. Opisthoproctidae (Cohen, 1964).

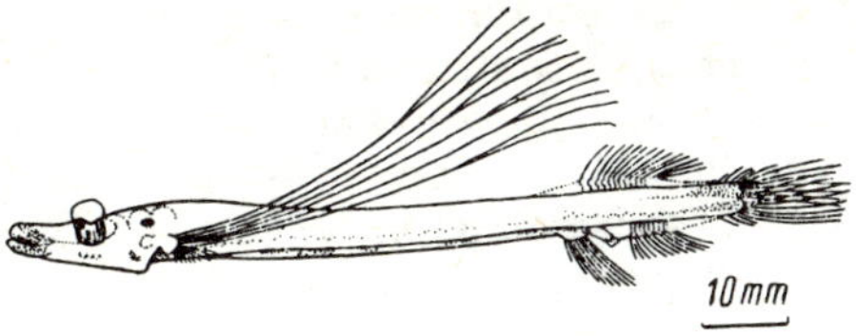

FIGURE 283. Dolichopterygidae (Alepocephaloidei). — Dolichopteryx binoculatus (Beebe, 1933, fig. 16)

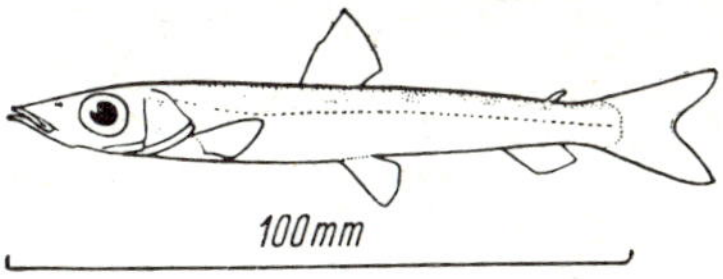

FIGURE 284. Argentinidae — Argentina semifasciata (M., 1955, III, fig. 55, diagr.)

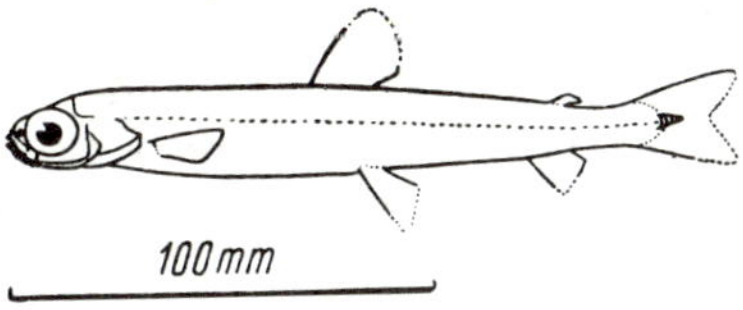

FIGURE 285. Microstomatidae — Nansenia ardesiaca (M., 1955, III, fig. 56, diagr.)

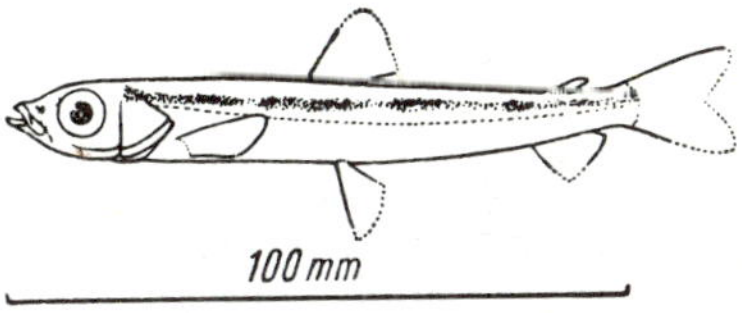

FIGURE 286. Bathylagidae — Leuroglossus lineatus (M., 1955, III, fig. 57, diagr.)

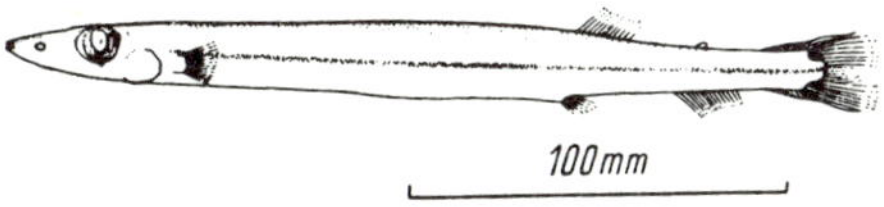

FIGURE 287. Dolichopterygidae (Alepocephaloidei). — Bathylychnops exilis (Cohen, 1958, fig. 1)

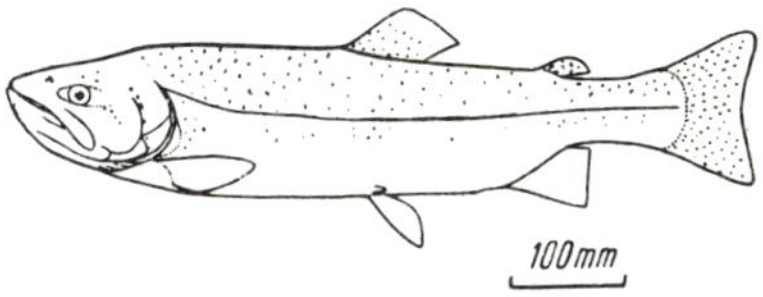

FIGURE 288. Salmonidae — Salmo mykiss (Soldatov and Lindberg, 1930, pl. 4, diagr.)

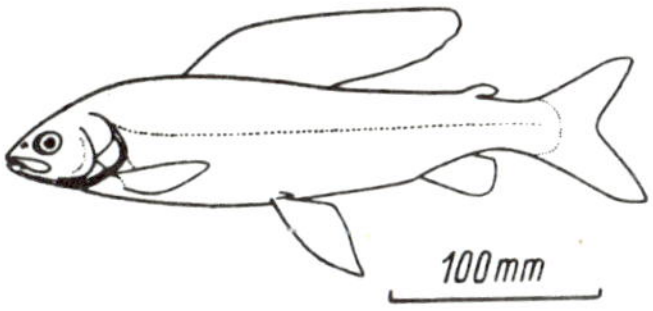

FIGURE 289. Thymallidae — Thymallus arcticus grubei (Berg, 1948, fig. 259, diagr.)

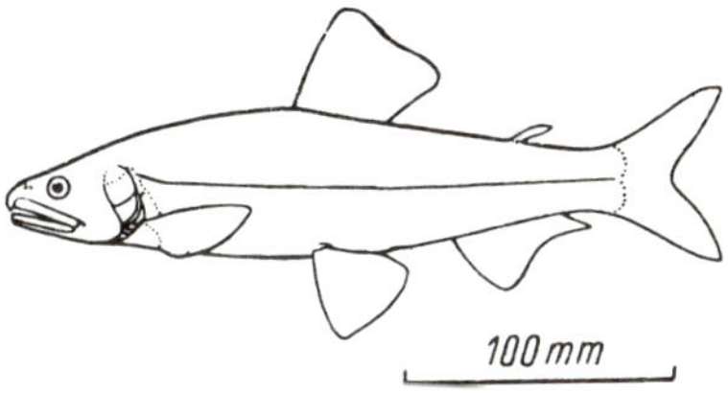

FIGURE 290. Plecoglossidae — Plecoglossus altivelis (Okada, 1955, fig. 53, diagr.)

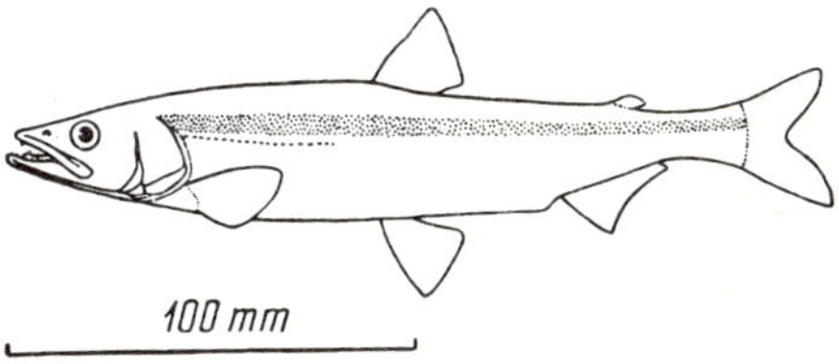

FIGURE 291. Osmeridae — Osmerus mordax dentex (Berg, 1948, fig. 266, diagr.)

71 (7). Branchiostegal rays numbering 3–4. No teeth on the tongue. Mesocoracoid absent. 43 – 47 vertebrae. (Figure 285) . . . . 89. **Microstomatidae**

72 (69). No swim bladder and no orbitosphenoid.

73 (74). Dorsal and ventral fins situated in the middle of the body. Snout shorter than postorbital space. (Figure 286) . . . . 88. **Bathylagidae**

74 (73). Dorsal and ventral fins situated in the posterior part of the body. Snout longer than postorbital space. (Figure 287). (Suborder Clupeoidei) . . . . 62. **Dolichopterygidae**[46] (Genus Bathylychnops)

75 (60). Well developed premaxillaries and maxillaries present. Supramaxillary (accessory) bone usually present (absent in family 71. Plecoglossidae). Mouth large, length of oral slit markedly greater than diameter of eye. Eyes not telescopic, not enlarged (less than 1/4 the length of the head), and not protruding from orbit, but if slightly enlarged, the dorsal fin is situated not above the ventrals but above the anal. [Physostomous forms.] (Suborder 19.6. **Salmonoidei**, families 69 – 75.[47])

76 (85). Dorsal fin situated above ventrals. At least 6 branchiostegal rays, more rarely 5 or even 4. Anal fin with fewer than 20 rays.

77 (82). Scales firmly set, small (more than 100 in lateral line); lateral line complete. Manubrium of vomer with teeth. 10 – 20 branchiostegal rays (6 in the Plecoglossidae).

78 (81). Teeth, if present, large and of conical form on the jaws, vomer, palatines, and tongue; no flat, wide teeth.

79 (80). Dorsal fin short, with no more than 16 rays (counting the branched and unbranched rays together). (Figure 288). . . . . 69. **Salmonidae**

80 (79). Dorsal fin long, with at least 17 rays. (Figure 289) . . . . .70. **Thymallidae**

81 (78). A few conical teeth present on the premaxillaries and very small ones on the tongue; teeth on maxillaries and on lower jaw flat, wide, serrate, sparse, arranged in one row and mobile, as they sit on the skin and are not attached to the jaw bones. (Figure 290) . . . . .71. **Plecoglossidae**

82 (77). Scales readily deciduous, of medium size, number of transverse rows of scales (squ.) 50 – 70; if the scales are very small (squ. 170 – 220), they are distributed in males in one row above the lateral line and also on each side on the belly, enlarged, and hairlike during spawning (Mallotus). Lateral line rudimentary or incomplete, although in Mallotus it reaches the vertical of the posterior margin of the anal fin. Manubrium of vomer without teeth. 6 – 7 branchiostegal rays.

83 (84). Maxillary covered with teeth and forming the margin of the upper jaw. (Figure 291) . . . . 72. **Osmeridae**

[46] Included in family **91.** Opisthoproctidae (Cohen, 1964).

[47] A characterization is given in this thesis which differentiates suborder **19.6.** Salmonoidei from families 87. Argentinidae; 88. Bathylagidae, 89. Microstomatidae, and 90. Xenophthalmichthyidae, included by Berg in this suborder but in this work referred to suborder 19. 9. Opisthoproctoidei (see thesis 19 – 60).

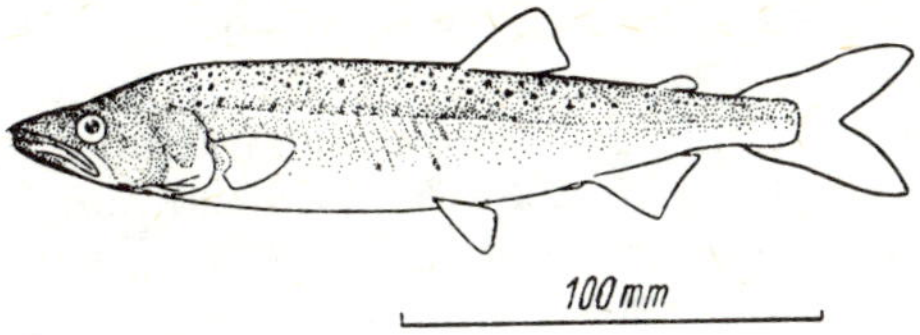

FIGURE 292. Aplochitonidae – Aplochiton marinus (Eigenmann, 1928, pl. 11, fig. 5, diagr.)

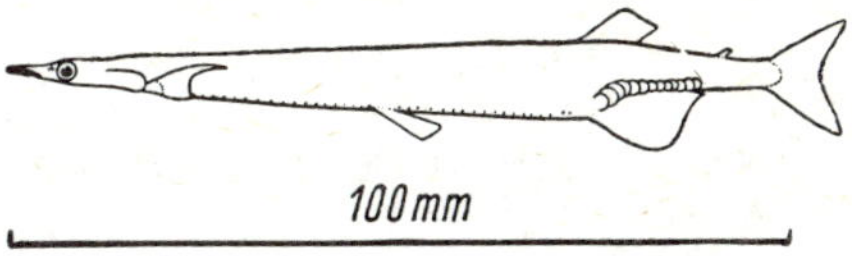

FIGURE 293. Salangidae – Salanx acuticeps (Wakiya and Takahasi, 1937, pl. 19, fig. 20, diagr.)

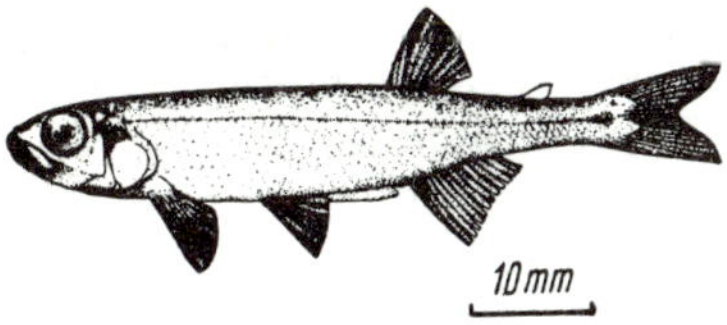

FIGURE 294. Retropinnidae – Retropinna semoni (Waite, 1921, fig. 62)

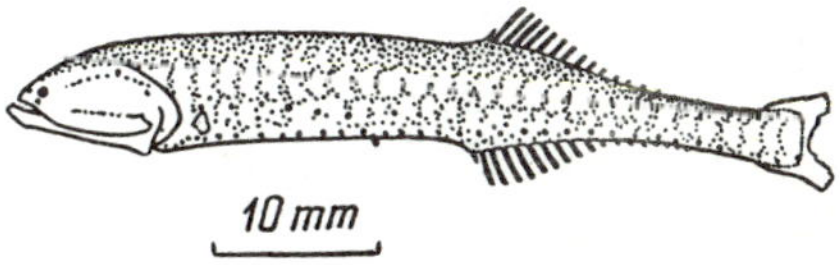

FIGURE 295. Gonostomatidae (Gonostomatinae) – Cyclothone microdon (M., 1955, III, fig. 58)

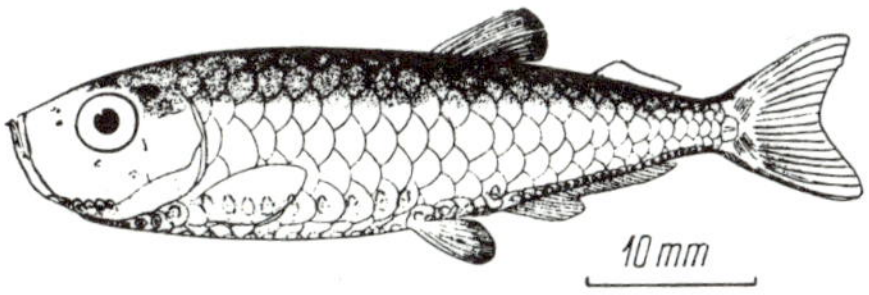

FIGURE 296. Gonostomatidae (Maurolicinae) – Maurolicus muelleri (Ishikawa, 1915, pl. 12, fig. 1)

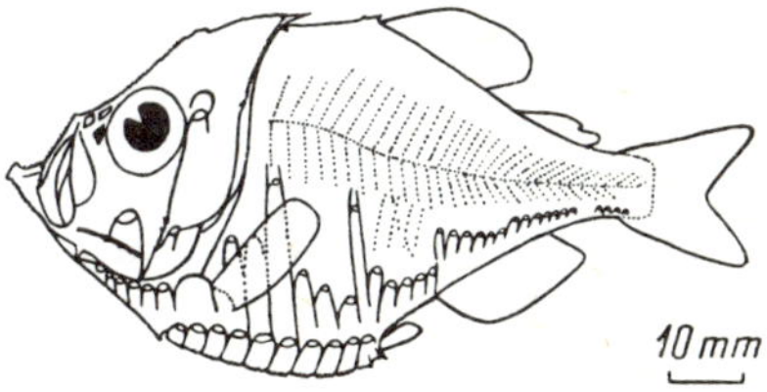

FIGURE 297. Sternoptychidae – Polypnus spinosus (W. and B., 1913, 2, fig. 47, diagr.)

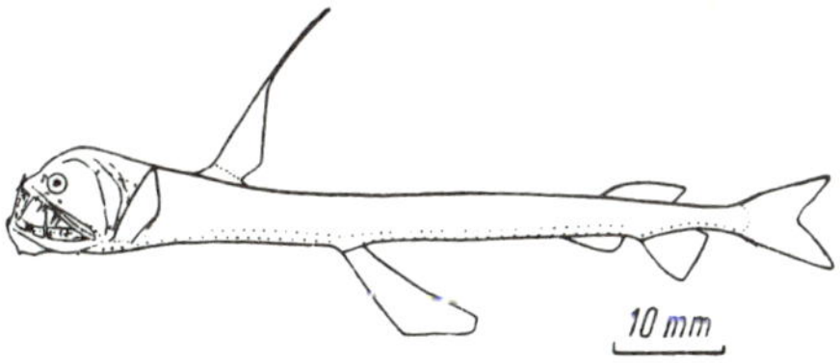

FIGURE 298. Chauliodontidae – Chauliodus sloani (L. and L., 1965, fig. 22 D)

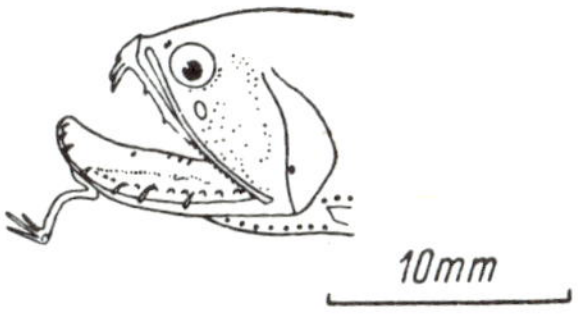

FIGURE 299. Stomiatidae – Stomias affinis (M., 1955, III, fig. 67)

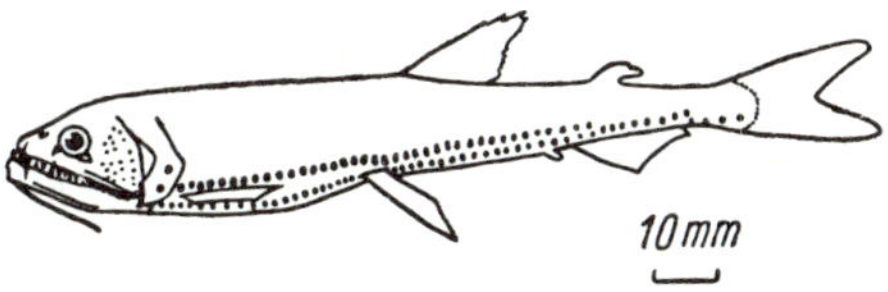

FIGURE 300. Astronesthidae – Astronesthes lucifer (W. and B., 1913, 2, fig. 42, diagr.)

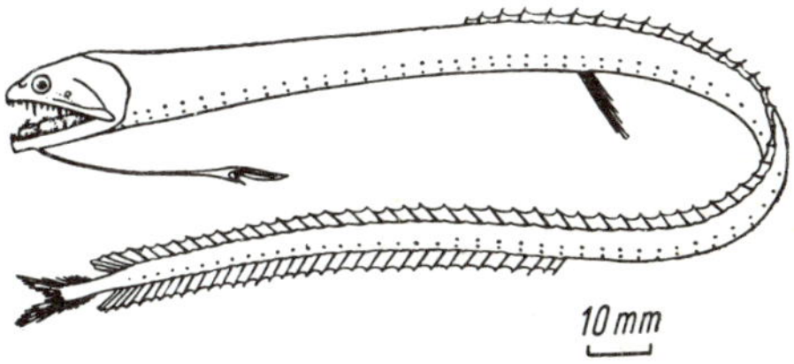

FIGURE 301. Idiacanthidae – Idiacanthus sp. (Traité, 1958, III, fig. 1598E)

84 (83). Maxillary without teeth and not forming margin of upper jaw. Premaxillary very strongly developed, almost extending beyond posterior margin of maxillary and moving it away from the margin of the mouth. (Figure 292)........75. **Aplochitonidae**

85 (76). Dorsal fin situated considerably behind ventrals, partly above the anal. Four branchiostegal rays. More than 20 rays in anal fin.

86 (87). Head flattened. [Mesopterygoid absent. Ribs not ossified.] (Figure 293) .... 73. **Salangidae**

87 (86). Head not flattened, but laterally compressed. [Mesopterygoid well developed. Ribs ossified.] (Figure 294)............ .... 74. **Retropinnidae**

88 (59). Photophores present, generally in 2 rows on the belly; there are additional rows of photophores on the sides of the body and isolated photophores and groups of them on the branchiostegal membrane and under the eyes. Adipose fin may be present. [Oviducts present, normally developed.] Body laterally compressed, bare or covered with large, thin, readily deciduous scales. (Suborder 19.8. **Stomiatoidei**, families 79—86.)

89 (96). Body covered with large, readily deciduous scales, traces of which are preserved in the form of scaly pockets.

90 (93). Lower jaw without a barbel. Photophores various. No backward-directed ascending process on the anterior margin of the premaxillary bone. Two supramaxillary (accessory) bones present. Gill arch bearing true rakers.

91 (92). Body elongate. Oral slit horizontal or oblique, almost vertical. No keel in front of dorsal fin .... 79. **Gonostomatidae**

2 subfamilies:

1 (2). Serial photophores relatively small, arranged in continuous rows on the body, not interrupted by longitudinal rows. Pseudobranchs absent or weakly developed. (Figure 295) .... subfamily 79.1. Gonostomatinae

2 (1). Serial photophores relatively large, not arranged in continuous rows but divided more or less distinctly into separate groups. Pseudobranchs present. (Figure 296) .... subfamily 79.2. Maurolicinae

92 (91). Body markedly deep. Oral slit distinctly vertical. A peculiarly developed keel, formed by the projecting upper (neural) awned processes, is present on the back in front of the dorsal fin. (Figure 297) .... 80. **Sternoptychidae**

93 (90). Lower jaw with a barbel, which is sometimes very small. Photophores small. Backward-directed ascending process present on anterior margin of premaxillary. Maxillaries without supramaxillary (accessory) bones or with only one. Gill arch without rakers, or else there are teeth instead of these.

94 (95). Dorsal fin situated markedly in front of ventrals. First ray of dorsal filamentous. One adipose fin behind the dorsal and another one in front of the anal. Barbels on lower jaw very small. Teeth on both jaws caninelike. (Figure 298) . . . . 82. Chauliodontidae

95 (94). Dorsal fin situated almost in the caudal part of the body, opposite the anal fin. Adipose fins absent. Barbels on lower jaw well developed. Teeth on both jaws not caninelike but pointed. (Figure 299) . . . . 81. Stomiatidae

96 (89). Body black, bare, not even with scaly pockets. Barbels on lower jaw usually well developed. Photophores very small. Ascending process on anterior margin of premaxillary. Maxillary with or without an accessory bone. Gill arch with teeth instead of rakers.

97 (100). Dorsal fin situated wholly, or originating, in middle of body, far in front of origin of anal.

98 (99). Base of dorsal fin short, its posterior end situated above or in front of vertical of origin of base of anal. Small prickly spines absent on sides of base of dorsal and anal fins. Adipose fins present behind dorsal and another, very small one, in front of the vent (Figure 300). D 9—20 . . . . 83. Astronesthidae

99 (98). Base of dorsal fairly long and terminating on vertical of posterior end of base of anal. Small prickly spines present along sides of base of dorsal and anal fins (Figure 301). Adipose fin absent. D 54—75 . . . . 86. Idiacanthidae

100 (97). Dorsal fin markedly shifted posteriorly, opposite the anal. No prickly spines along the sides of the base of the dorsal and anal fins. Adipose fins absent.[48]

101 (102). First vertebra ossified, and the head is immobile. [There is a membrane connecting the lower jaw with the hyoid arch.] (Figure 302) . . . . 84. Melanostomiatidae

102 (101). First vertebra not ossified, and the head may turn through 90°, so that the oral slit assumes a vertical position. [No membrane connecting the lower jaw with the hyoid arch.] (Figure 303) . . . . 85. Malacosteidae

Order 20. MIRIPINNIFORMES[49] (thesis 0—45)

2 families (104, 105):

1 (2). Whole surface of body with a peculiar hair cover (Figure 304). Lower rays of upper caudal lobe lying over upper rays of lower lobe. (Figure 305). . . . . 104. Miripinnidae

[48] There is one small adipose fin in Chirostomias (Regan and Trewavas, 1930. Dana Rep., 6:53).

[49] Two more families in this order have recently been described: 104a. **Kasidoridae** (=Kasidoroidae) (Figure 303 A) and 104b. **Megalomycteridae** (see Figure 35 and theses 0—45 and 0—81, footnote).

2 (1). Surface of body bare and smooth. No such superposition of rays in caudal fin, but in young and not fully mature specimens the middle rays of the caudal are markedly elongate and form a wimplelike outgrowth up to three times as long as the body. (Figures 306, 307) . . . . .105. **Eutaeniophoridae**

Order 21. BATHYCLUPEIFORMES (thesis 0—78)

1 family: 106. **Bathyclupeidae** (Figure 308).

Order 22. GALAXIIFORMES (thesis 0—83)

1 family: 107. **Galaxiidae** (Figure 309).

Order 23. MYCTOPHIFORMES (thesis 0—81)

12 families (108—118):

1 (2). Dorsal fin absent; only one adipose fin present. (Figure 310) . . . . 101. **Anotopteridae** (see footnote to thesis 19—65)

2 (1). Dorsal fin present in addition to adipose fin.

3 (4). Base of dorsal fin very long and extending from the occiput to the vertical of the origin of the anal fin or even beyond this, its height far exceeding the length of the head. (Figure 311) . . . . 117. **Alepisauridae**

4 (3). Base of dorsal fin short, but if long, it does not reach the vertical of the origin of the anal; height of dorsal much smaller or barely equal to length of head.

5 (8). Oral slit not passing beyond vertical of middle of eye.

6 (7). Dorsal and ventral fins situated in anterior half of body (without C). (Figure 312) . . . . 113. **Chlorophthalmidae**

7 (6). Dorsal and ventral fins situated in posterior half of body (without C) . . . . 112. **Paralepididae**

2 subfamilies:

1 (2). Teeth on lower jaw narrow, not with serrate margins. Anterior nares large. Outer rays of ventral fins shorter than or of the same length as inner rays. Pectorals small in fish of all ages. [There is an opening in the premaxillary bone.] (Figure 313) . . . . subfamily 112.1. Paralepidinae

2 (1). Teeth on lower jaw wide and with serrate margins. Anterior nares reduced to small pores. Outer rays of ventral fins longer than inner rays. Pectorals markedly elongate in fishes in the early postembryonic state. [No opening in premaxillary.] (Figure 314) . . . . subfamily 112.2. Sudinae

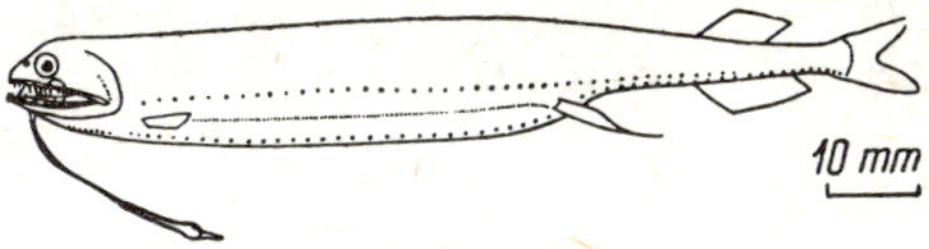

FIGURE 302. Melanostomiatidae – Melanostomias pauciradius (M., 1955, III, fig. 72, diagr.)

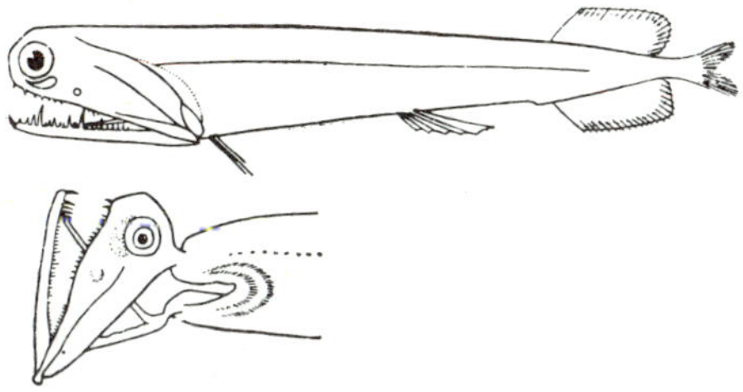

FIGURE 303. Malacosteidae – Malacosteus sp. (Traité, 1958, III, figs. 1598, 1602)

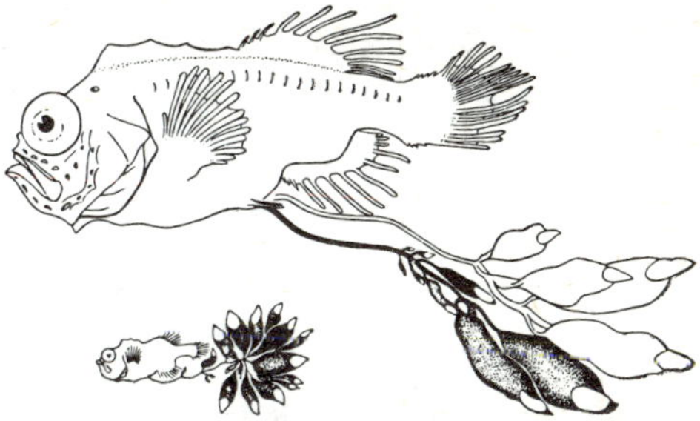

FIGURE 303 A. Kasidoridae – Kasidoron edom (Robins and Sylva, 1965, fig. 1, diagr.)

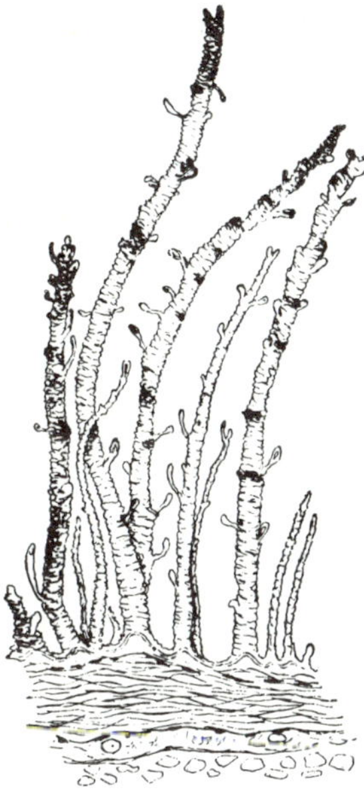

FIGURE 304. "Hair cover" of Miripinna esau, high magnification (Bertelsen and Marshall, 1956, pl. 1, fig. B)

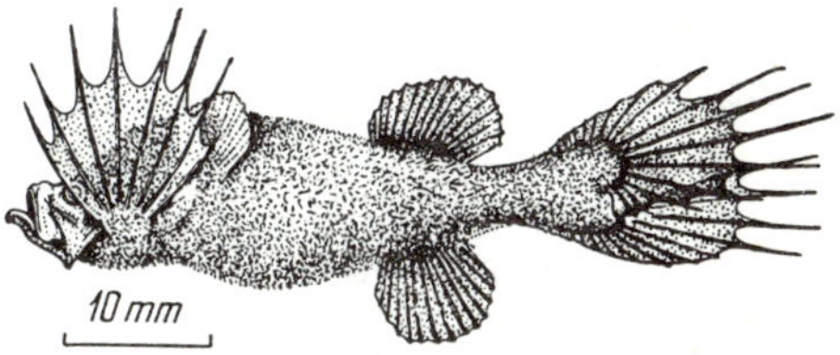

FIGURE 305. Miripinnidae – Miripinna esau (Bertelsen and Marshall, 1956, fig. 1)

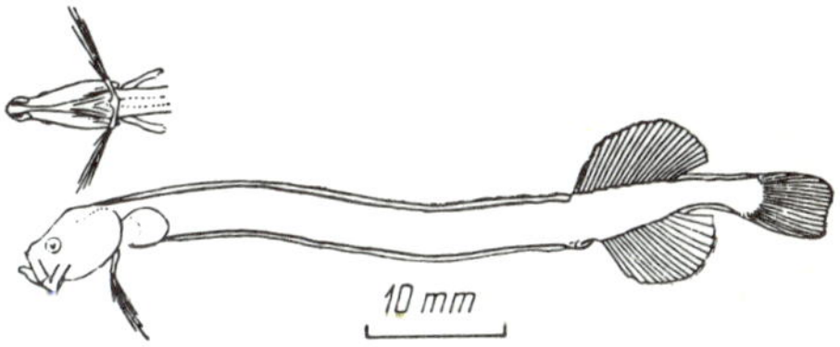

FIGURE 306. Eutaeniophoridae – Eutaeniophorus festivus (Bertelsen and Marshall, 1956, fig. 4)

FIGURE 307. Eutaeniophoridae – Eutaeniophorus festivus, juv. (Bertelsen and Marshall, 1956, fig. 8)

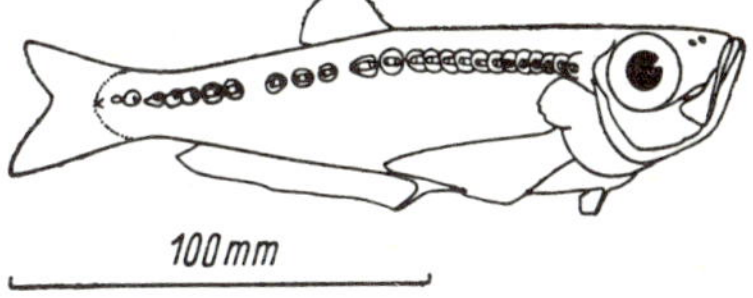

FIGURE 308. Bathyclupeidae – Bathyclupea malayana (Berg, 1940, fig. 147, diagr.)

8 (5). Oral slit passing beyond vertical of middle of eye and generally much farther.

9 (14). Origin of dorsal situated in posterior half of body (without C) or about midway along, but whatever the case the body is without photophores.

10 (11). Ventral fins inserted markedly in front of vertical of origin of dorsal fin. Pectorals long, reaching the ventrals. Origin of dorsal in posterior half of body (without C), origin of ventrals in the middle of this length. (Figure 315) . . . . 115. Scopelosauridae

11 (10). Ventrals inserted on vertical of origin of dorsal. Pectorals short, falling far short of ventrals.

12 (13). Origin of dorsal and ventrals situated roughly in the middle of the body (without C). Ventrals well developed. (Figure 316) . . . . 111. Evermannellidae

13 (12). Origin of dorsal and ventrals situated in posterior half of body (without C). Ventrals rudimentary. (Figure 317) . . . . 116. Omosudidae

14 (9). Origin of dorsal situated in anterior half of body (without C).

15 (26). Photophores absent on body.

16 (25). Pectoral fin normal, not divided into 2 parts and without elongate rays in the upper part.

17 (18). Maxillary bone markedly widened posteriorly (Figure 318) . . . . 109. Aulopodidae

18 (17). Maxillary bone, if present, not widened posteriorly.

19 (20). Eyes poorly distinguishable. (Figure 319). . . . 114a. Ipnopidae

20 (19). Eyes clearly distinguishable.

21 (22). Scales well developed, firmly set. Teeth on jaws arranged in bands in several rows (more than 3 rows). Eyes normal. Pectoral and ventral fins small (Figure 320) . . . . 108. Synodontidae

22 (21) Scales weakly developed, readily deciduous. Teeth on jaws arranged in rows, of which there are not more than 3.

23 (24). Eyes small. Pectoral and ventral fins long, passing beyond the origin of the dorsal and anal fins, respectively. (Figure 321) . . . . 108a. Harpadontidae[50]

24 (23). Eyes enlarged and in many forms directed anteriorly. Pectoral and ventral fins short. (Figure 322) . . . . . 110. Scopelarchidae

25 (16). Pectoral fin distinctly divided into 2 parts; lower part normal, upper part with very elongate rays stretching beyond the dorsal fin. (Figure 323). . . . . 114. Bathypteroidae

26 (15). Photophores present on body.

27 (28). Photophores distributed in 1 row which passes along the lower margin of the abdomen; there are isolated photophores above this row, but they are not arranged in a row parallel to the one below. (Figure 324). . . . . 118. Myctophidae

28 (27). Photophores distributed in 2 rows: along the lower margin of the abdomen and in the lower half of the sides of the body, parallel to the lower row. (Figure 325) . . . . . 118a. Neoscopelidae

[50] Isolated as a separate family 108a. Harpadontidae (GRWM:395).

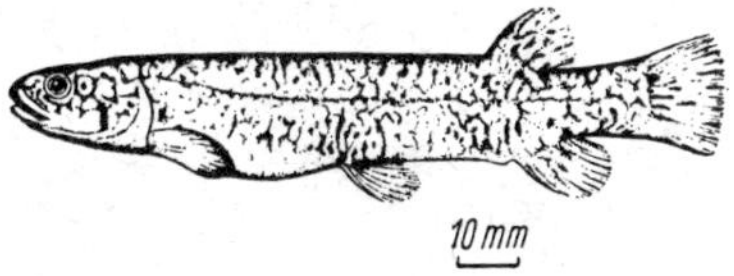

FIGURE 309. Galaxiidae — Galaxias brevispinnis (Nikol'skii, 1954, fig. 124)

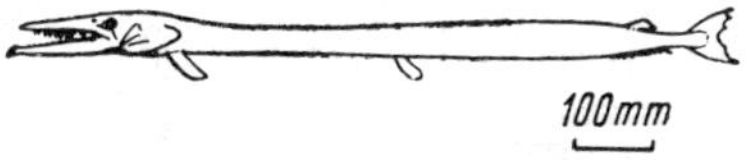

FIGURE 310. Anotopteridae — Anotopterus pharao (M., 1955, III, fig. 89)

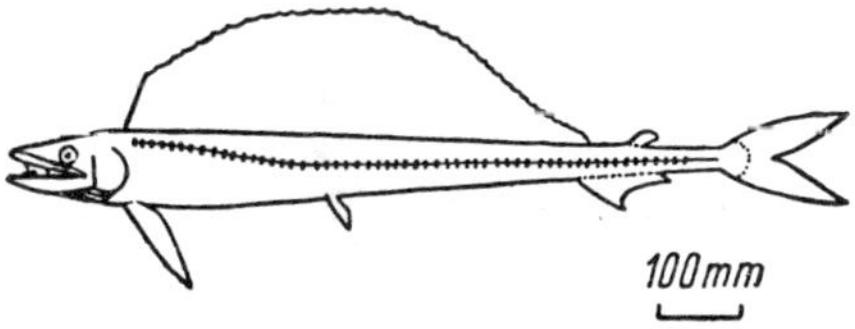

FIGURE 311. Alepisauridae — Alepisaurus borealis (M., 1955, III, fig. 90, diagr.)

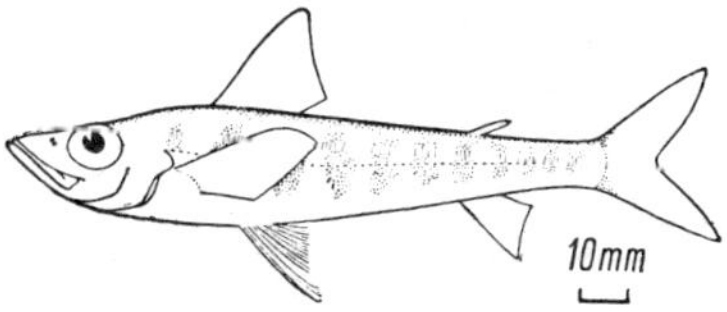

FIGURE 312. Chlorophthalmidae — Chlorophthalmus albatrossis (Abe, 1958, fig. 806, diagr.)

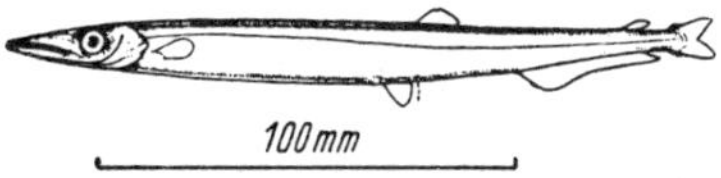

FIGURE 313. Paralepididae (Paralepidinae) — Lestidium prolixum (M., 1955, III, fig. 88, diagr.)

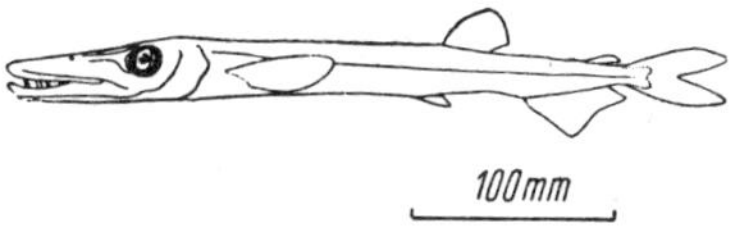

FIGURE 314. Paralepididae (Sudinae) — Sudis hyalina (Harry, 1953, fig. 21, diagr.)

FIGURE 315. Scopelosauridae — Notosudis lepida (Kreft and Maul, 1955, fig. 1)

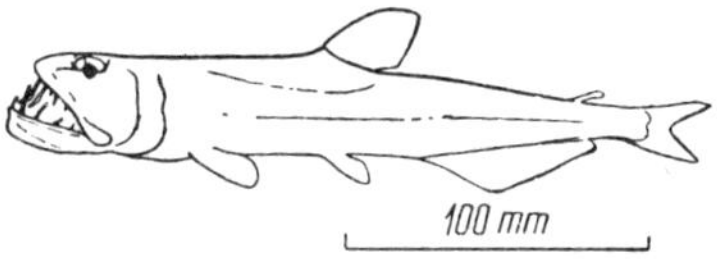

FIGURE 316. Evermannellidae — Evermannella balbo (Günther)

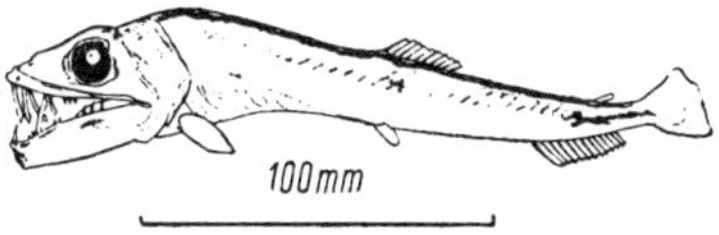

FIGURE 317. Omosudidae — Omosudis funchali (Traité, 1958, III, fig. 1610)

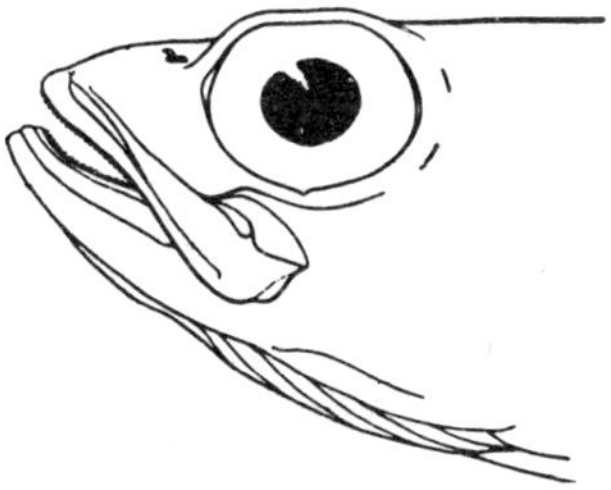

FIGURE 318. Aulopodidae — Hime japonica

[Supplementary key to families of the order Myctophiformes, Iniomi[51]*]*

1 (2). Well developed horizontally arranged bony plates (fulcra) present in the flesh of the caudal peduncle, immediately behind the last spiny ray of the caudal fin, both above and below. Posttemporal fossa present in posterior part of skull. There are two accessory maxillary bones (Figure 318) . . . . 109. **Aulopodidae**

2 (1). Such plates absent. No posttemporal fossa. One accessory maxillary bone or none.

3 (18). Premaxillary teeth arranged in several rows or in the form of a band of varying width, except in Parasudis and Trachinocephalus.

4 (1). Teeth and gill rakers needlelike or lanceolate. Maxillary bone absent or reduced, not widened and not flattened at the posterior end; postorbital bone widened, serving as a support for the upper jaw.

5 (8). Head and body covered with scales.

6 (7). Scales of lateral line not enlarged (Figure 320) . . . . 108. **Synodontidae**

7 (6). Scales of lateral line enlarged (Figure 320 A) . . . . 108b. **Bathysauridae**[52]

8 (5). Head and body bare or with one row of scales along the lateral line and on the tail . . . . 108a. **Harpadontidae**

9 (4). Teeth not needlelike or lanceolate. Gill rakers of usual form. Maxillary bone not reduced, normal in outward appearance and its posterior end widened and flattened as a rule or in the extreme case club-shaped externally. Postorbital bone not forming a support for the upper jaw. Eyes very small and apparently without function, probably sometimes absent.

10 (13). Lower jaw sensory canal concealed in the dentale its whole length except for the large pores outside; outer surface of dentale either convex or flat in cross section in the middle of the bone.

11 (12). Pectoral fin divided into 2 separate parts. Eyes very small, arranged on sides of head just above the upper jaw. Gill rakers of usual form (Figure 323). . . . . 114. **Bathypteroidae**

12 (11). Pectoral fin not divided into 2 parts. Eyes very small, arranged on the sides of the head just above the upper jaw or absent in this place and the photoreceptors are represented by a pair of large, wide plates which are yellow during life and are covered by the frontal bones. Gill rakers of usual form, either absent altogether or represented by a single raker in the corner of the arch (Figure 319). 114a. **Ipnopidae**

13 (10). Lower jaw sensory canal concealed in the dentale for more than half its length; outer surface of dentale more or less concave in cross section in the middle of the bone (except in Parasudis).

[51] This key for the determination of families, compiled as a result of a monographic treatment of the fishes belonging to this order (Gosline, Marshall, and Mead, 1966: 1–18, 15–17), allows for the results of determinations made according to the first key to be checked more precisely.

[52] GRWM: 395 include family 108b. **Bathysauridae** in family 108. Synodontidae, but from family Synondontidae they isolate a separate family, 108a. Harpadontidae.

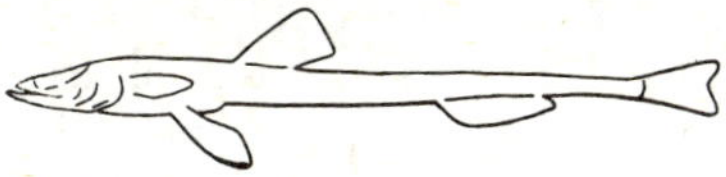

FIGURE 319. Ipnopidae (GRWM, 1966: 409, fig.)

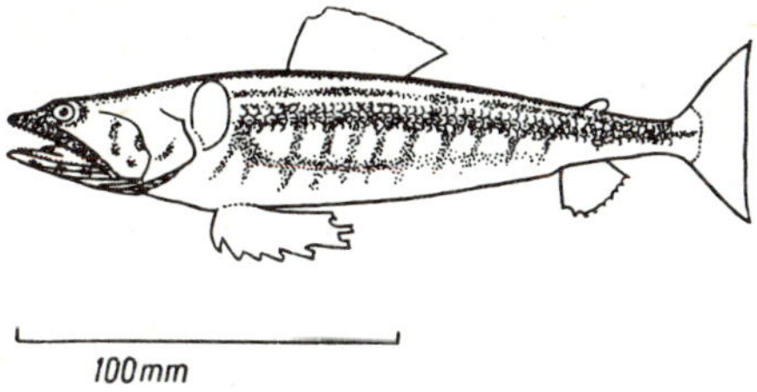

FIGURE 320. Synodontidae — *Synodus variegatus* (Okada, 1955, fig. 60, diagr.)

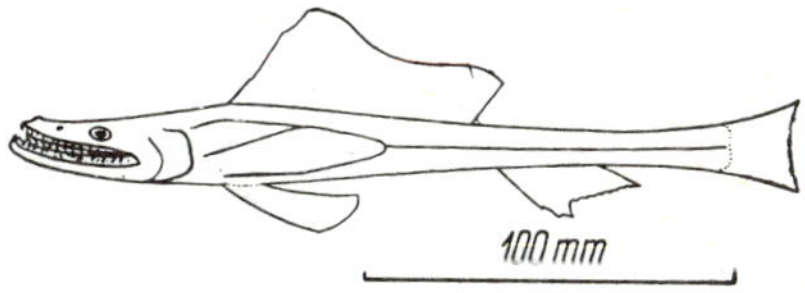

FIGURE 320 A. Bathysauridae — *Bathysaurus ferox* (Smith, 1950, fig. 179)

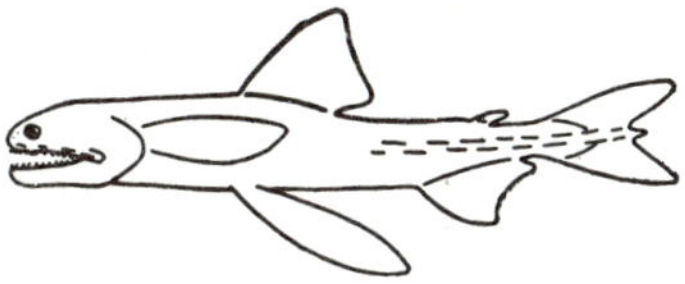

FIGURE 321. Harpadontidae (GRWM, 1966: 408, fig.)

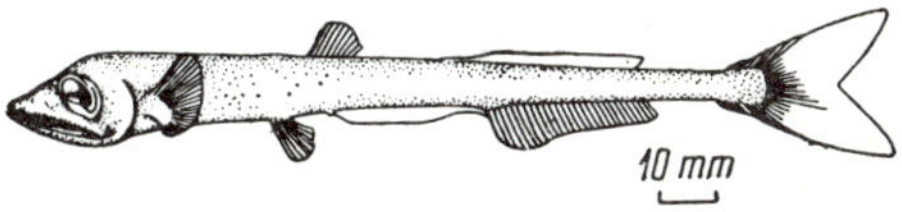

FIGURE 322. Scopelarchidae — *Scopelarchus linguidens* (M., 1955, III, fig. 87)

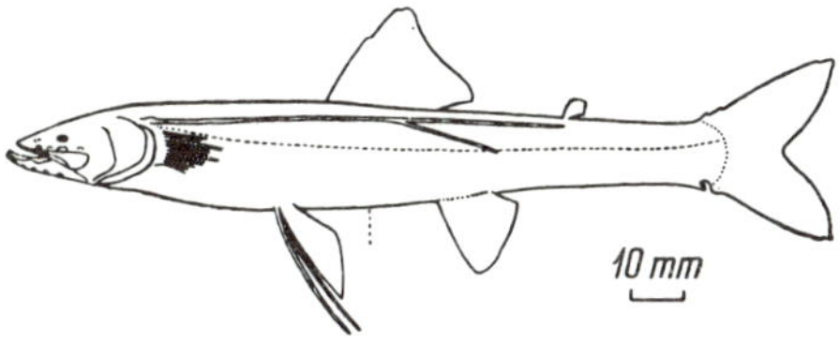

FIGURE 323. Bathypteroidae — *Bathypterois atricolor* (M., 1955, III, fig. 79, diagr.)

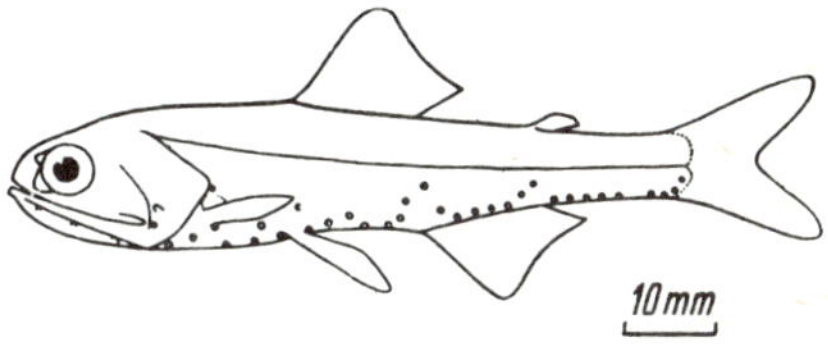

FIGURE 324. Myctophidae — *Diaphus coeruleus* (L. and L., 1965, fig. 24, diagr.)

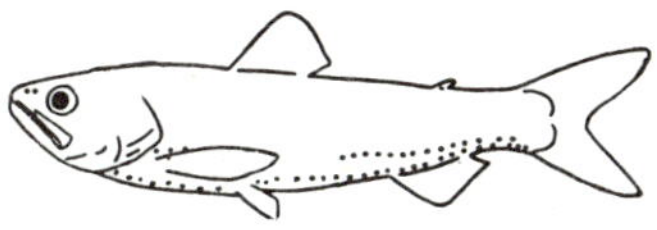

FIGURE 325. Neoscopelidae (GRWM, 1966 : 409, fig.)

14 (15). Snout flattened. No luminescent organs. Swim bladder absent. (Figure 312) . . . . 13. Chlorophthalmidae
15 (14). Snout laterally compressed. Luminescent organs generally present, as also swim bladder.
16 (17). Accessory maxillary absent (Figure 324) . . . .118. Myctophidae
17 (16). Accessory maxillary present (Figures 23—28) . . . . 118a. Neoscopelidae
18 (3). Teeth on premaxillaries arranged in a single row.
19 (20). Gill rakers of usual form (Figure 315). . . 115. Scopelosauridae
20 (19). Gill rakers reduced to toothlike formations or spines.
21 (28). Eyes of normal form, not tubular. Parietal bones not fused with frontals; vent nearer to point of insertion of ventral fins than to origin of anal fin.
22 (25). Dorsal fin present, its base shorter than half the length of the fish.
23 (24). Disproportionately enlarged canine absent on lower jaw. Head and body covered with scales or bare, but always with one row of ossified scutes along the lateral line (Figures 313, 314). . . . . 112. Paralepididae
24 (23). One disproportionately enlarged canine on each side of lower jaw; enlarged canines also present on palatines. Head and body bare, without scales (Figure 317) . . . . . . 116. Omosudidae
25 (22). Dorsal fin absent, but if present, its base is more than half as long as the fish.
26 (27). Dorsal fin present, high, sail-shaped; its base extends for almost 2/3 of the length of the fish (Figure 311) . . . . .117. Alepisauridae
27 (26). Dorsal fin absent (Figure 310) . . . . .101. Anotopteridae
28 (21). Eyes tubular and directed upward (except in *Evermanella normalops* Parr), parietal bones fused with frontals; vent near origin of base of anal fin or in the middle between the ventral and anal fins.
29 (30). Tongue without teeth (Figure 316) . . . . . .111. Evermannellidae
30 (29). Tongue with teeth (Figure 322) . . . . 110. Scopelarchidae

Order 24. CETOMIMIFORMES (thesis 0—81, footnote)

3 families (119—121):

1 (2). Ventral fins absent. Gill rakers club-shaped or lamellar. Eyes small, set roughly in the middle between the upper jaw and the dorsal surface of the head, or closer to the upper jaw; they are sometimes rudimentary or even absent. (Figure 326) . . . . 119. Cetomimidae
2 (1). Ventral fins present, small, but well developed, situated on the belly far behind the pectorals. Gill rakers long and thin. Eyes small, set closer to the dorsal surface of the head than to the upper jaw, or in the middle between them.

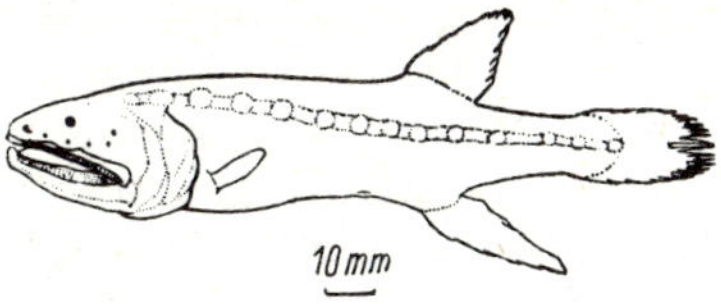

FIGURE 326. Cetomimidae — Cetomimus indagator (Rofen, 1957—59, fig. 1, diagr.)

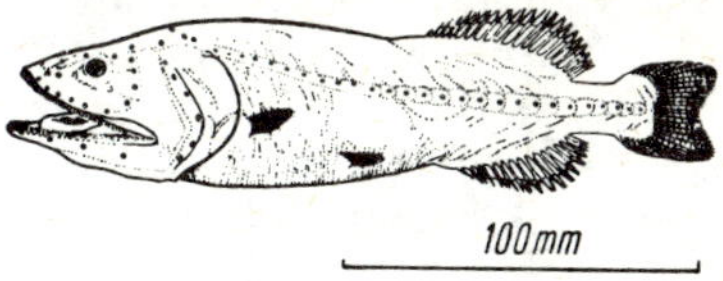

FIGURE 327. Barbourisiidae — Barbourisia rufa (Parr, 1945, fig. 1)

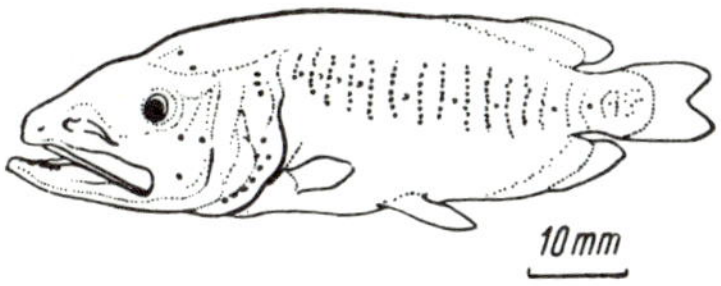

FIGURE 328. Rondeletiidae — Rondeletia bicolor (Rofen, 1957—59, fig. 4 (Goode and Bean, 1895, fig. 77, diagr.)

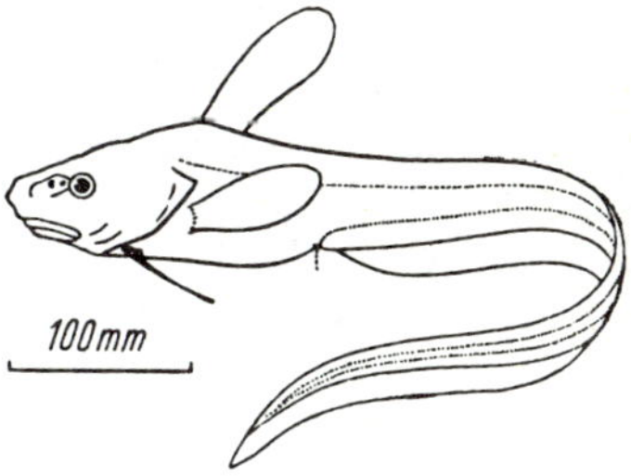

FIGURE 329. Ateleopodidae — Ateleopus japonicus (Okada and Matsubara, 1938, pl. 9, fig. 3, diagr.)

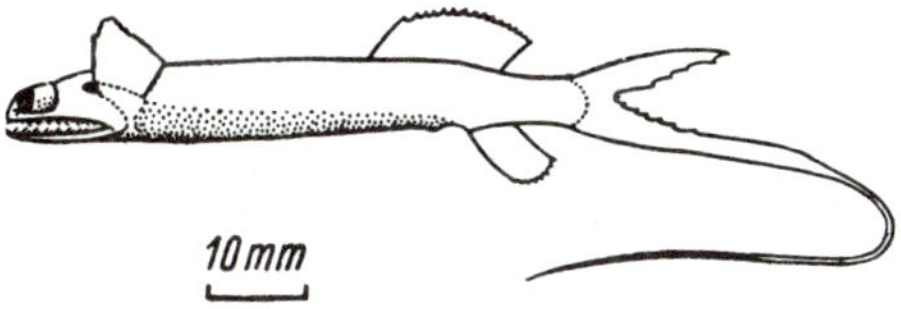

FIGURE 330. Giganturidae — Gigantura vorax (Traité, 1958, III, fig. 1669, diagr., modified; tail straight)

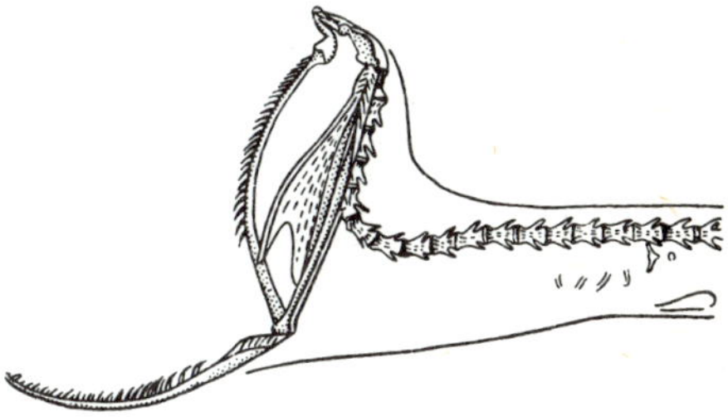

FIGURE 331. Anterior part of the body of Saccopharynx ampullaceus (M. 1955, I, fig. 77B)

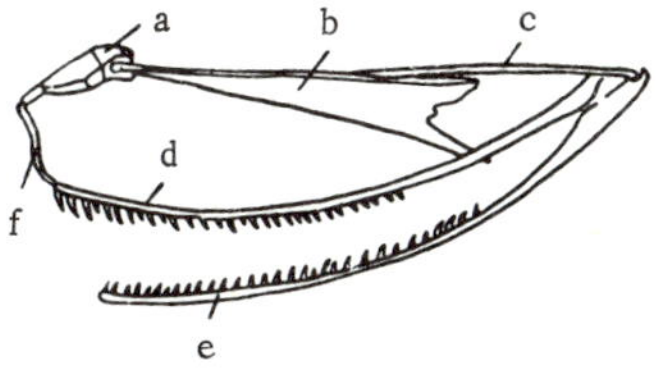

FIGURE 332. Head of Saccopharynx sp. (M., 1955, I, fig. 78A, copy):

a — cranium; b — hyomandibulare; c — quadrate bone; d — maxillary; e — dentary; f — ligament.

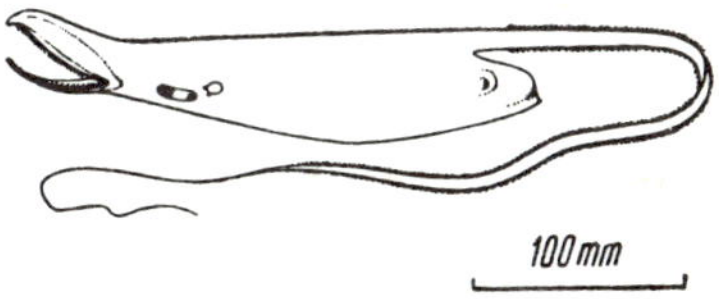

FIGURE 333. Saccopharyngidae — Saccopharynx flagellum (Goode and Bean, 1896, pl. 48, fig. 178, diagr.)

3 (4). Skin on the body thickly covered with small spines. Lateral line without transverse rows of pores in the spaces between the pores of the horizontal row. Upper jaw passing markedly beyond the eyes (Figure 327) . . . . .12. **Barbourisiidae**

4 (3). Skin completely bare. Lateral line on body with transverse rows of pores in the spaces between the pores of the horizontal row. Upper jaw reaching only to the vertical of the eye. (Figure 328) . . . . 120 (241). **Rondeletiidae** (See thesis 43—5)

Order 25. ATELEOPODIFORMES (thesis 0—85)

1 family: 122. **Ateleopodidae** (Figure 329).

Order 26. GIGANTURIFORMES (thesis 0—47)

1 family: 123. **Giganturidae** (Figure 330).

Order 27. SACCOPHARYNGIFORMES (thesis 0—63)

2 families: (124, 125):

1 (2). Gill opening situated much closer to apex of snout than to vent. Mouth very large, but not enormous. Length of oral slit about 1/10 of length of body. Jaws with fine, curved, sharp teeth. Pectoral fins quite well developed (Figures 331—333) . . . . 124. **Saccopharyngidae**

2 (1). Gill opening situated closer to vent than to apex of snout. Mouth enormous. Length of oral slit about 1/5 of length of body. Jaws with small teeth; there is sometimes a pair of symphysial canines on the lower jaw. Pectoral fins small, hard to make out (Figure 334) . . . . 125. **Eupharyngidae**

Order 28. MONOGNATHIFORMES (thesis 0—61)

1 family: 126. **Monognathidae** (Figure 335).

Order 29. MORMYRIFORMES (thesis 0—76)

2 families (127, 128):

1 (2). Anal, caudal, and ventral fins absent. No teeth on tongue or

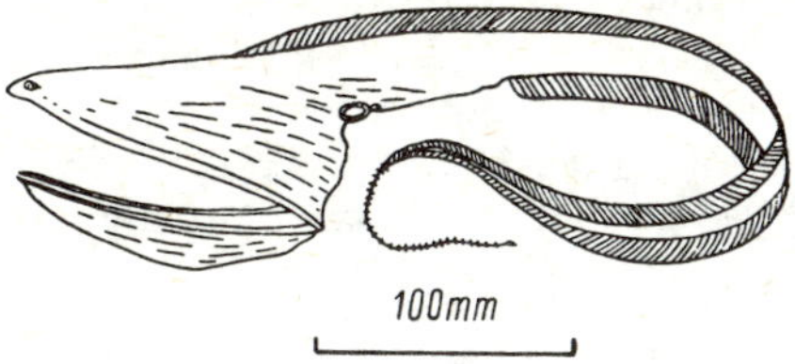

FIGURE 334. Eurypharyngidae – *Eurypharynx pelecanoides* (L. and L., 1965, fig. 14)

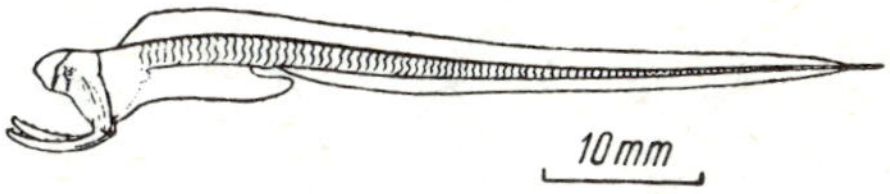

FIGURE 335. Monognathidae – *Monognathus taeningi* (Traité, 1958, III, fig. 1674, diagr.)

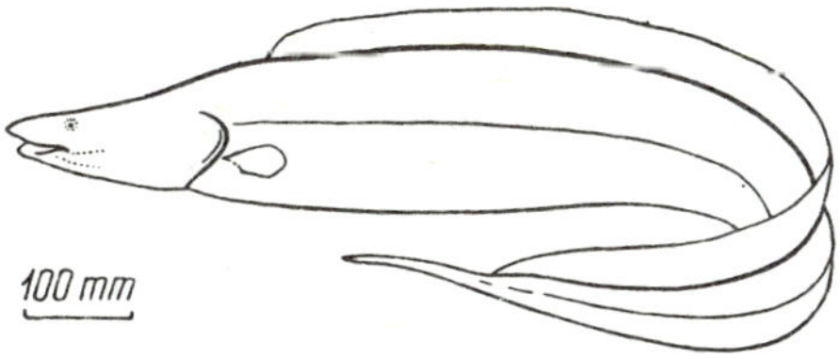

FIGURE 336. Gymnarchidae – *Gymnarchus niloticus* (Poll, 1957, fig. 42, diagr.)

FIGURE 337. Mormyridae – *Gnathonemus numenius* (Poll, 1957, fig. 111, diagr.)

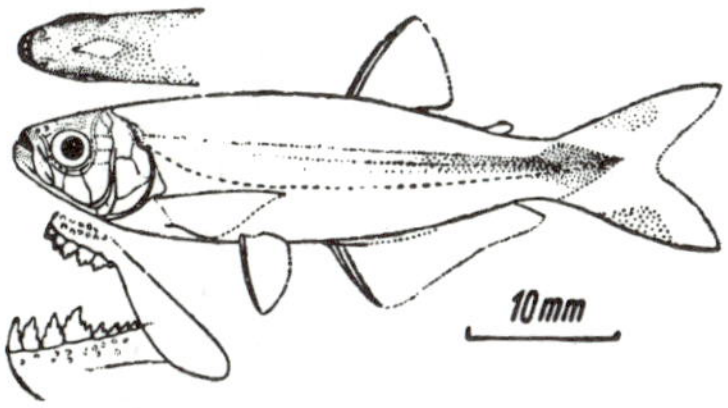

FIGURE 338. Characinidae (Characininae) – *Gephyrocharax chaporae* (Fowler, 1940, figs. 25, 26, 27, diagr.)

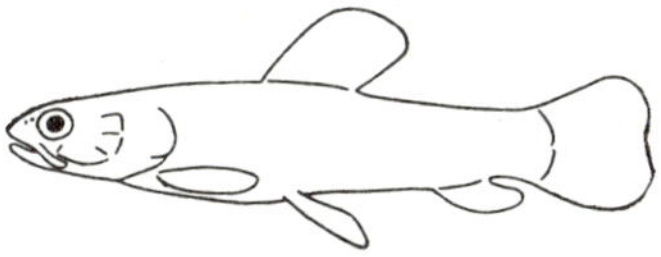

FIGURE 339. Erythrinidae (GRWM, 1966: 410, fig.)

FIGURE 340. Hepsetidae (GRWM, 1966: 410, fig.)

FIGURE 341. Cynodontidae (GRWM, 1966: 410, fig.)

FIGURE 342. Lebiasinidae (GRWM, 1966: 410, fig.)

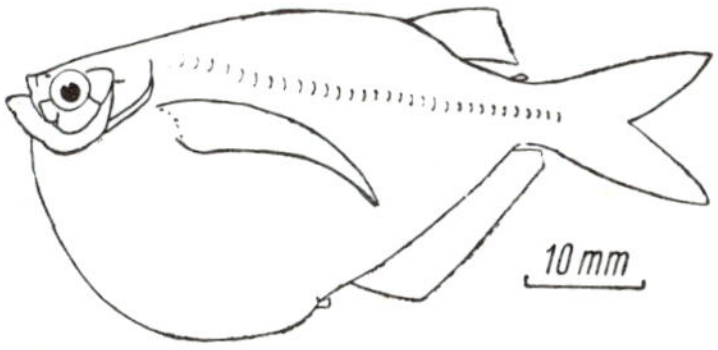

FIGURE 343. Gasteropelecidae – *Thoracocharax magdolenae* (Eigenmann, 1922, pl. 24, fig. 4, diagr.)

parasphenoid. Form of body somewhat eel-like. (Figure 336) ....127. Gymnarchidae

2 (1). Anal, caudal, and ventral fins present. Teeth on tongue and parasphenoid. Body not eel-like (Figure 337) .... 128. Mormyridae

Order 30. CYPRINIFORMES (thesis 0–73)

4 suborders, 46 families (129–174):

1 (20). Body and head never covered with bony plates; body generally covered with scales, more rarely bare, but in all cases the suboperculum [and also the parietalia and symplecticum] is present. [Third vertebra not fused with fourth.] (Cyprini.)

2 (11). Mouth not protrusible, usually with teeth. Infrapharyngeal bones not enlarged and not sickle-shaped, covered with very small teeth. Barbels generally absent.

3 (4). Dorsal fin present, well developed, not transformed into a threadlike fleshy fin; there is usually an adipose fin behind the dorsal. Ventral fins present. Caudal fin well developed. Anal fin not very long, but if long, not more than half as long as the head. Vent situated on the belly behind pectoral fins, not under the head. Barbels generally absent. Scales present (except in the Erythrininae). Jaws with teeth. Body not eel-like. (Suborder 30.1. **Characoidei**,[53] families 129–134).

4 (3). Dorsal fin absent or transformed into a threadlike, fleshy appendage. Ventrals absent. Caudal absent or weakly developed. Anal fin very long, often originating in front of the pectorals. Vent generally situated on ventral side of body or on the throat. Jaws usually with teeth. Body elongate, often eel-like. Suborder 30.2. **Gymnotoidei**, families 135–138).

[53] In the last few years the system of the suborder Characoidei has been changed considerably and at present, instead of the 6 families (129–134) accepted by Regan (1911) and later by Berg (1950 : 263), 16 separate families have been isolated (GRWM: 395). A list and drawings of these are given below instead of keys. Family 129. **Characidae** (Figure 338) has more than 150 genera in Africa and South America; 4 independent families have been isolated from it: 129a. **Erythrinidae** (Figure 339), 129b. **Hepsetidae** (Figure 340), 129c. **Cynodontidae** (Figure 341), and 129d. **Lebiasinidae** (Figure 342). Family 130. **Gasteropelecidae** (Figure 343), 3 genera in South America. Family 131. **Ctenoluciidae** (Figure 344), 2–3 genera in South America. Family 132. **Anostomidae** (Figure 345), about 40 genera in South America; 3 independent families have been isolated from it: 132a. **Prochilodontidae** (Figure 346), 132b. **Curimatidae** (Figure 347), and 132c. **Chilodontidae** (Figure 348). Family 133. **Hemiodontidae** (Figure 349), more than 10 genera in South America; one family has been isolated: 133a. **Parodontidae** (Figure 350). Family 134. **Citharinidae** (Figure 351), about 20 genera; 2 families have been isolated: 134a. **Distichodontidae**, 134b. **Ichthyboridae** (Figure 353).
It should be noted that Weitzman (1962), on the other hand, includes these five families (130. Gasteropelecidae, 131. Xiphiostomatidae, 132. Anostomidae, 133. Hemiodontidae, and 134. Citharinidae) in family 129. Characidae.

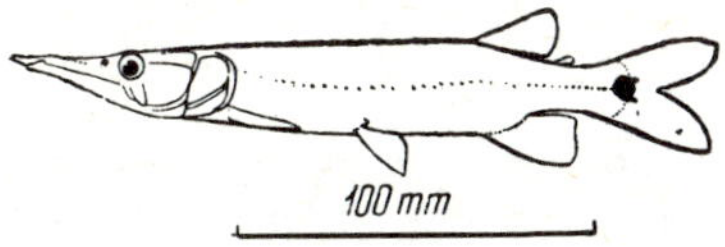

FIGURE 344. Ctenoluciidae — *Ctenolucius beani* (Eigenmann, 1922, pl. 26, fig. 4, diagr.)

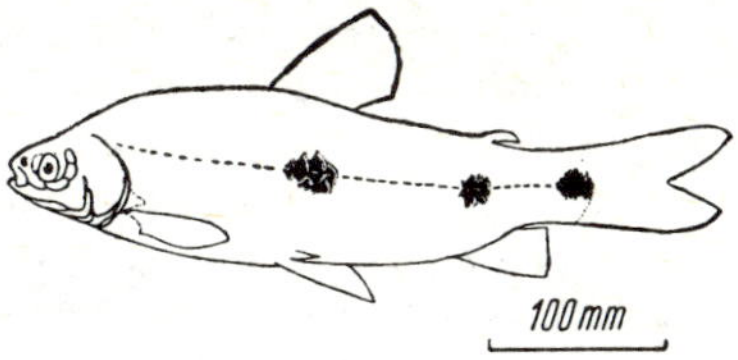

FIGURE 345. Anostomidae — *Leporinus ecuadoriensis* (Eigenmann, 1922, pl. 20, fig. 6, diagr.)

FIGURE 346. Prochilodontidae (GRWM, 1966: 411, fig.)

FIGURE 347. Curimatidae (GRWM, 1966: 411, fig.)

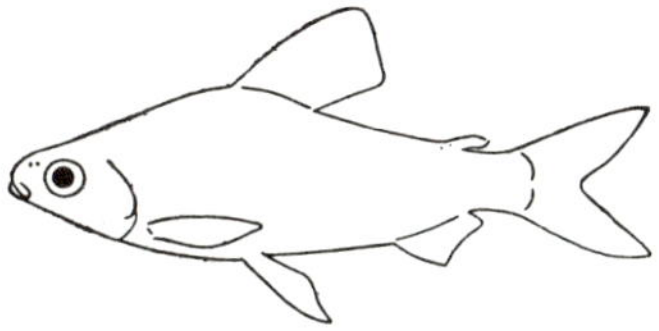

FIGURE 348. Chilodontidae (GRWM, 1966: 411, fig.)

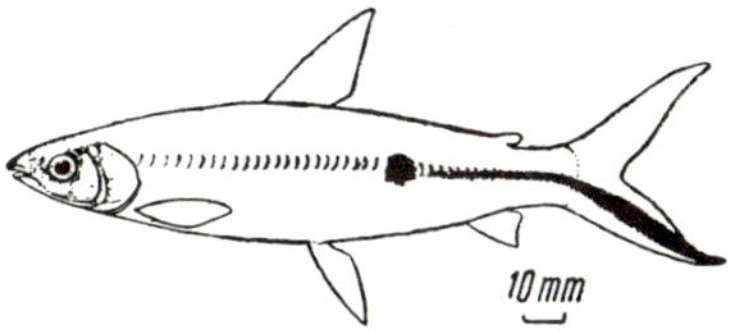

FIGURE 349. Hemiodontidae — *Hemiodus semitaeniatus* (Sterba, 1959, fig. 284, diagr.)

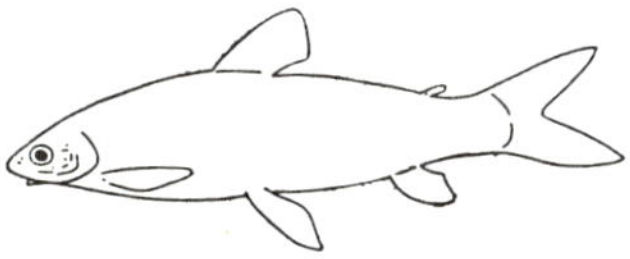

FIGURE 350. Parodontidae (GRWM, 1966: 410, fig.)

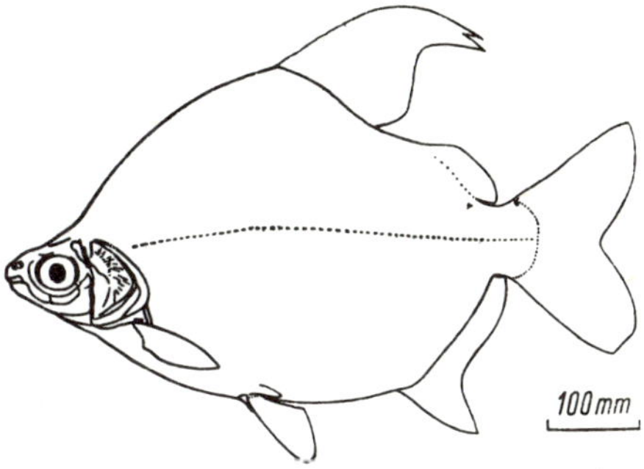

FIGURE 351. Citharinidae — *Citharinus gibbosus* (Poll, 1957, fig. 152, diagr.)

FIGURE 352. Distichodontidae (GRWM, 1966: 411, fig.)

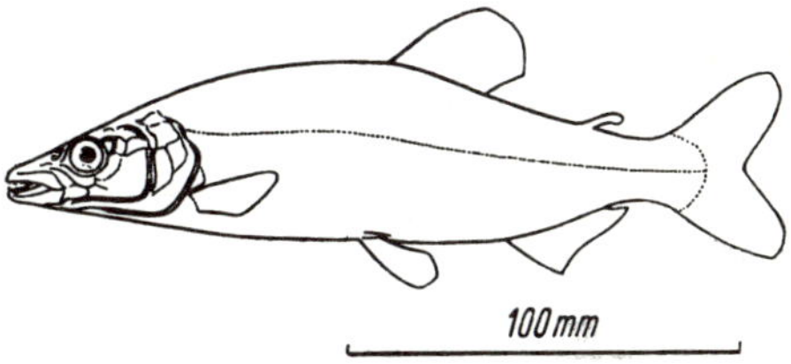

FIGURE 353. Ichthyboridae — *Ichthyborus besse congolensis* (Poll, 1957, fig. 138, diagr.)

5 (8). Maxillary well developed, larger than premaxillary. Anterior naris set high, considerably above the lip. Vent situated under the head. Body laterally compressed, covered with scales. Electrical organs absent.

6 (7). Anal fin originating in front of gill opening. Vent situated under the eye or in front of it. Snout drawn out into a tube. Caudal fin fin absent. No dorsal threadlike fin. [Mesocoracoid well developed.] (Figure 354). . . . . 135. **Rhamphichthyidae**

7 (6). Anal fin originating not in front of gill opening but under or behind it. Vent situated considerably behind vertical of eye. Snout not drawn out into a tube. Caudal fin present. Dorsal threadlike fin usually present. [Mesocoracoid absent.] (Figure 355) . . . . 136. **Apteronotidae**

8 (5). Maxillaries very small. Anterior naris set low, in the region of the lip. Vent situated on the throat.

9 (10). Body covered with scales, laterally compressed, moderately elongate. About 120 vertebrae. Electrical organs absent. [Pectoral fin with 4 radials.] (Figure 356). . . 137. **Gymnotidae**

10 (9). Body bare, not laterally compressed, sometimes very elongate. About 250 vertebrae. There is a large electrical organ in the caudal part of the body. [Pectoral fin with 7—8 radials.] (Figure 357) . . . . 138. **Electrophoridae**

11 (2). Mouth more or less protrusible, always toothless. Infrapharyngeal bones greatly enlarged, sickle-shaped, usually with 1—3 rows of teeth (teeth are absent in family 141. Gyrinocheilidae). Dorsal fin present, of normal appearance. No adipose fin behind dorsal fin. Vent not situated on the throat. Jaws without teeth. (Suborder 30.3. **Cyprinoidei**, families 139—143).

12 (19). Gill opening not divided into two parts. Infrapharyngeal bones always bearing teeth.

13 (16). Barbels absent or not more than 2 pairs (as an exception the genus Gobiobotia (see Figure 375) of family 140. Cyprinoidei, has 4 pairs of barbels but one pair is in the angles of the mouth and the other three on the ventral surface of the head, behind the mouth). [Swim bladder large, free, not contained in a bony capsule.]

14 (15). Mouth bordered by both premaxillaries and maxillaries. Pharyngeal teeth in a single row, generally crestlike (Figure 358), numerous, more than 16 in the row. Gastrolith absent. Barbels absent. (Figures 359, 360). . . . . 139. **Catostomidae**

15 (14). Mouth bordered only by premaxillaries. Pharyngeal teeth arranged in 1, 2, or even 3 rows, sparse, not more than 8 in the long row (Figure 361). Gastrolith present. Barbels present or absent. (Figures 362—375). . . . . 140. **Cyprinidae**[54]

16 (13). Barbels always present, but not more than 3 pairs, and there is never a pair on the ventral surface of the head, behind the mouth. [Swim bladder contained, wholly or just the anterior part, in a bony capsule.]

[54] Because there is no generally accepted system of the subfamilies of the Cyprinidae, we found it necessary to give drawings of the most important representatives of this extremely large family. A separate family has been isolated, 140a. **Psilorhynchidae** (GRWM; 115) (Figure 372).

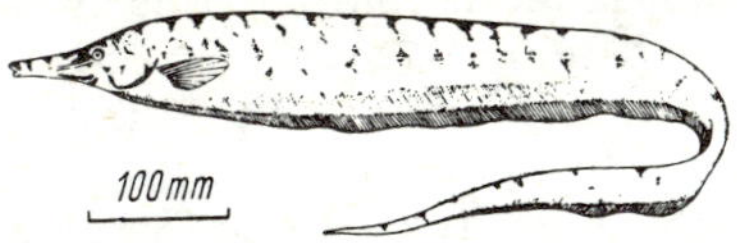

FIGURE 354. Rhamphichthyidae — Rhamphichthys rostratus (Sterba, 1959, fig. 503, diagr.)

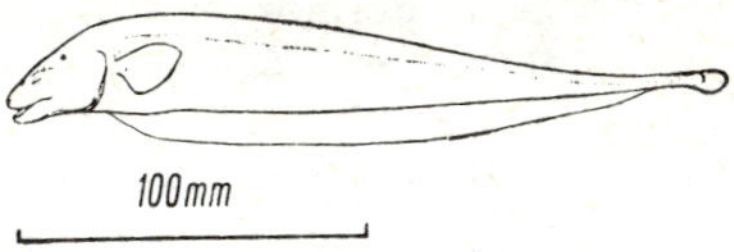

FIGURE 355. Apteronotidae — Sternarchus rostratus (Eigenmann, 1922, pl. 34, fig. 6, diagr.)

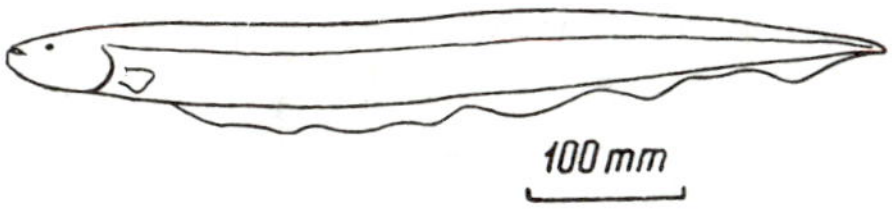

FIGURE 356. Gymnotidae — Gymnotus carapo (Sterba, 1959, fig. 456, diagr.)

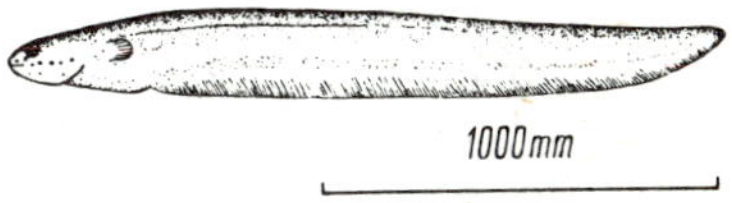

FIGURE 357. Electrophoridae — Electrophorus electricus (M., 1955, I, fig. 92A)

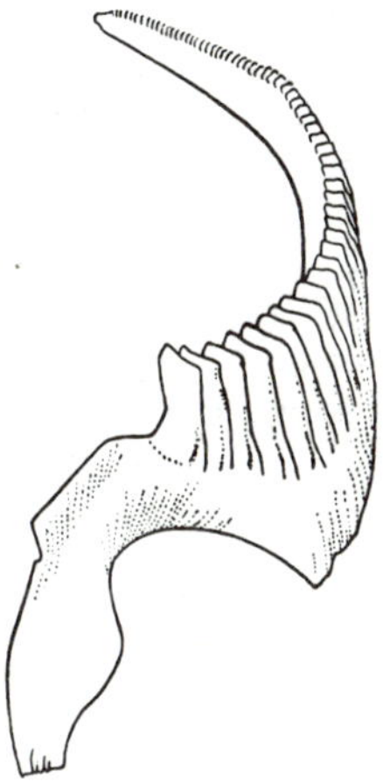

FIGURE 358. Pharyngeal teeth in Catostomus sp. (Traité, 1958, III, fig. 1637)

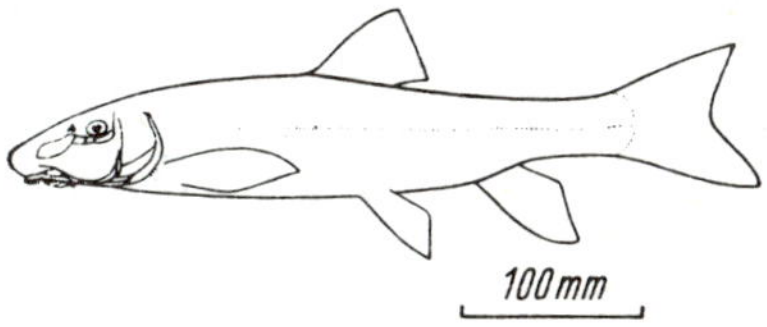

FIGURE 359. Catostomidae — Catostomus catostomus (Berg, 1948, fig. 288, diagr.)

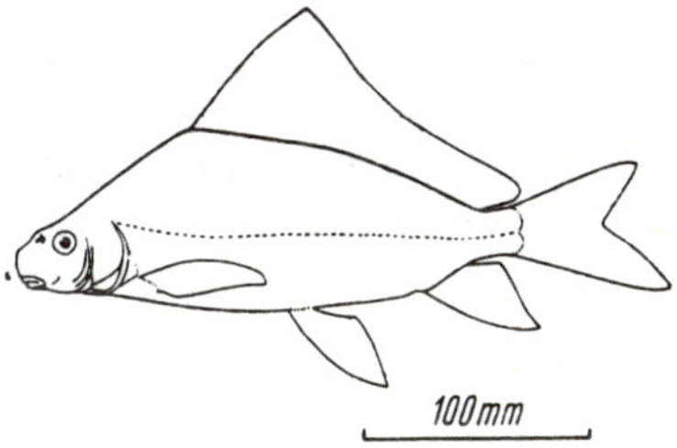

FIGURE 360. Catostomidae — Myxocyprinus asiaticus chinensis (Nichols, 1943, fig. 15, diagr.)

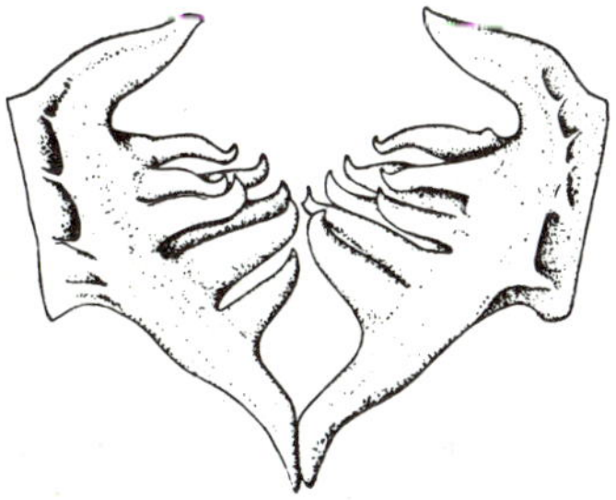

FIGURE 361. Pharyngeal bones in the Cyprinidae (Berg, 1949, fig. 323)

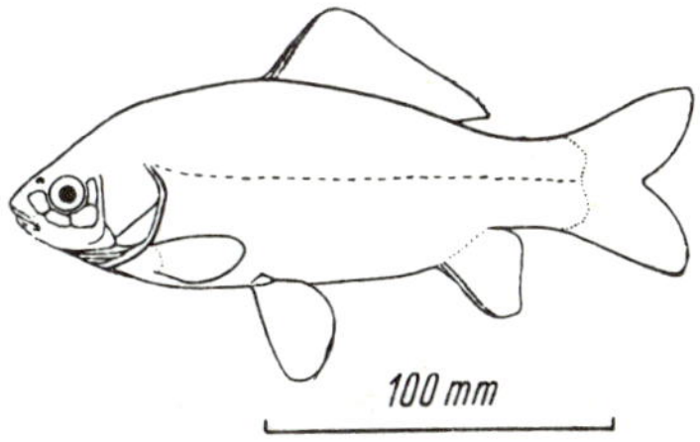

FIGURE 362. Cyprinidae — Carassius auratus (Wang, 1958, fig. 107, diagr.)

17 (18). Body cylindrical or laterally compressed but not vertically flattened. 3—6 pairs of barbels. (Figure 376)..143. **Cobitidae**

18 (17). Body strongly vertically flattened. 3—4 pairs of barbels. (Figures 377—379)............... 142. **Homalopteridae**[55]

19 (12). Gill opening divided into 2 parts, lower and upper. Teeth absent on pharyngeal bones; no barbels and no gastrolith. (Figure 380) .... 141. **Gyrinocheilidae**

20 (1). Body or head covered with bony plates or spines, or bare, but in all cases suboperculum [and also parietalia and symplecticum] absent. [Second, third, and fourth, and sometimes also the fifth, vertebrae intergrown.] Infrapharyngeal bones not sickle-shaped; jaws with teeth. Mouth not protrusible. (Siluri.)
(Suborder 30.4. **Siluroidei**, families 144—174.)

21 (58). Catfishes of the countries of the Old World.

22 (45). Catfishes of Eurasia.

23 (28). Dorsal fin absent, but if present, it is without spiny rays. No adipose fin.

24 (27). Dorsal fin, if present, rudimentary, with few rays.

25 (26). Two or three pairs of barbels. [Respiratory apparatus of the type usual for fish.] (Figure 381) ....150. **Siluridae**

26 (25). Four pairs of barbels (nasal, supra- and infrapharyngeal, and chin). [Respiratory apparatus markedly modified; there is a pair of cylindrical air sacs extending from the gill cavity through the back muscles to the tail.] (Figure 382) .... 160. **Heteropneustidae**

27 (24). Dorsal fin well developed, with a very large number of rays, stretching along almost the whole back. Four pairs of barbels. [There is a supplementary branching respiratory organ in the upper part of each gill cavity.] (Figure 383). . . .161. **Clariidae**

28 (23). Dorsal fin always present, with a spiny ray.

29 (32). No adipose fin on the back. Second dorsal fin, and sometimes also the anal, fused with the caudal.

30 (31). Branchiostegal membrane not attached to interbranchial space. (Figure 384) ....149. **Plotosidae**

31 (30). Branchiostegal membrane attached to interbranchial space. (Figure 385) ....158. **Chacidae**

32 (29). Adipose fin present. No second dorsal fin. Caudal fin well differentiated.

33 (34). Anal fin long, with 28—40 rays. Adipose fin small. Branchiostegal membrane free of the interbranchial space. (Figure 386) .... 159a. **Pangasiidae**[56]

34 (33). Anal fin relatively short, with 8—22 rays. Adipose fin large, well developed.

[55] A separate family is isolated 142a. **Gastromyzonidae** (MA : 71).

[56] Family 152. **Doiichthyidae** (Figure 387), represented in fresh and brackish waters of New Guinea by one genus and species *Doiichthys novaeguineae* Weber, 1913, also with a long anal fin, differs from the family Pangasiidae in the large oral slit, the strong development of the adipose fin, and in the presence of nasal barbels. GRWM place this family in the synonymy of family 145. **Ariidae**, whereas McAllister (MA : 75) accepts family 159a. **Pangasiidae** as a separate family.

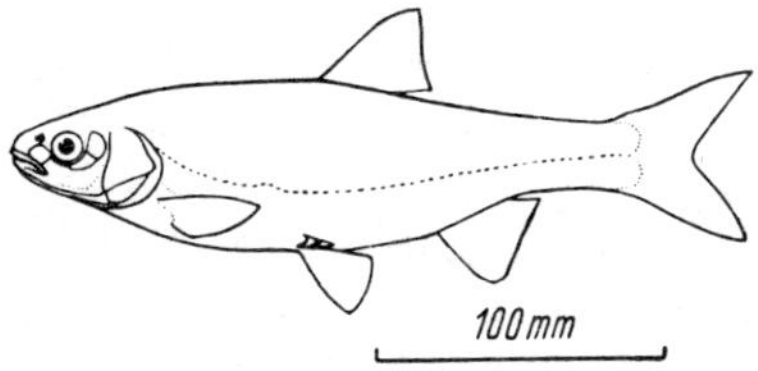

FIGURE 363. Cyprinidae — Leuciscus waleckii (Berg, 1949, fig. 332, diagr.)

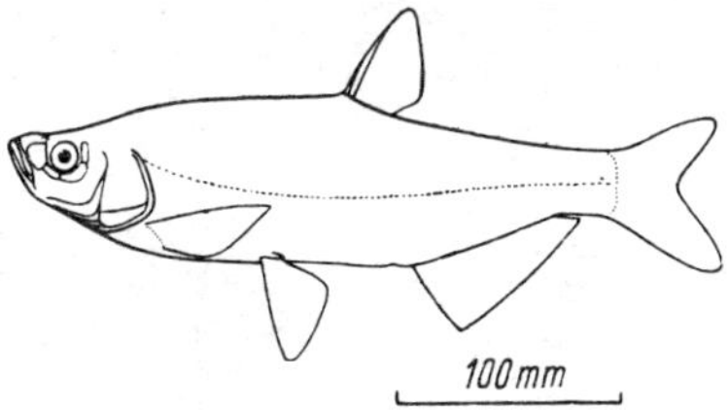

FIGURE 364. Cyprinidae — Culter alburnus (Berg, 1949, fig. 552, diagr.)

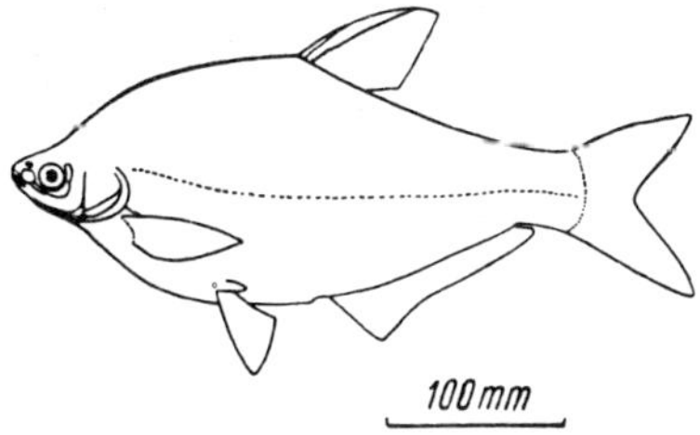

FIGURE 365. Cyprinidae — Parabramis pekinensis (Berg, 1949, fig. 549, diagr.)

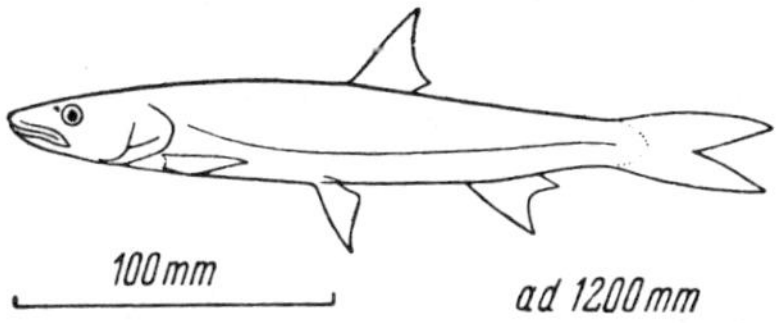

FIGURE 366. Cyprinidae — Elopichthys bambusa (Nichols, 1943, fig. 29, diagr.)

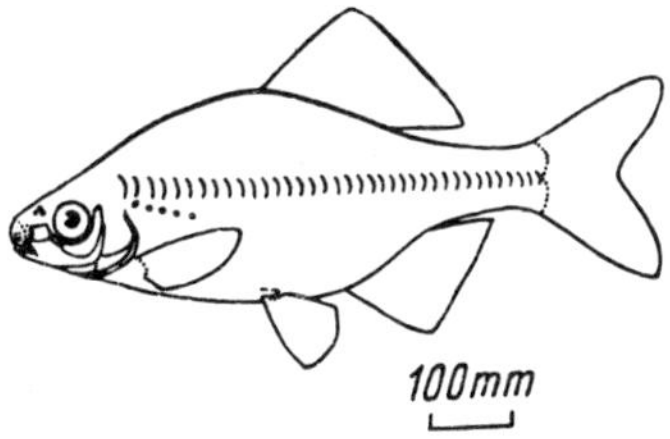

FIGURE 367. Cyprinidae — Rhodeus sericeus (Berg, 1949, fig. 559, diagr.)

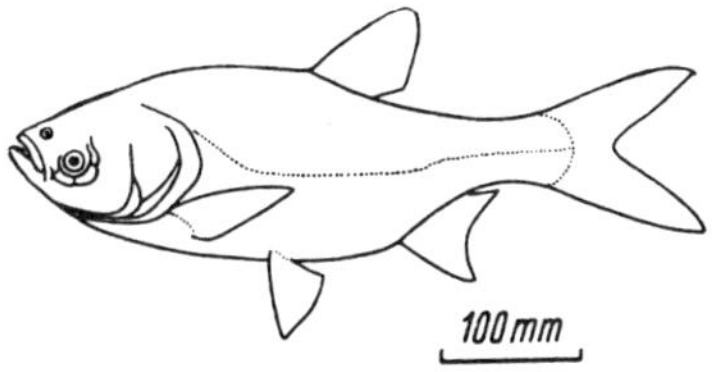

FIGURE 368. Cyprinidae — Hypophthalmichthys harmandi (Sauvage, 1884, pl. 7, fig. 1, diagr.)

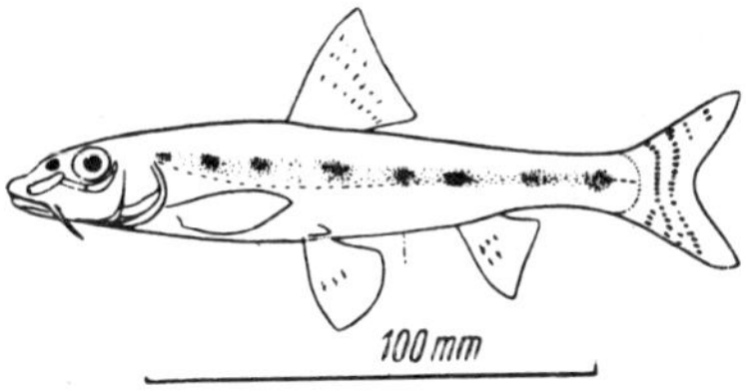

FIGURE 369. Cyprinidae — Gobio gobio cynocephalus (Berg, 1949, fig. 394, diagr.)

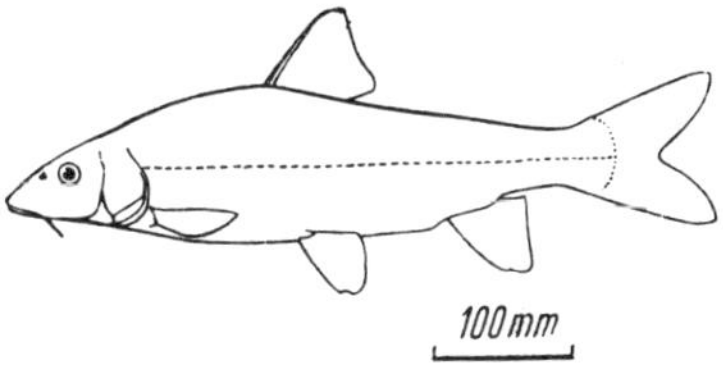

FIGURE 370. Cyprinidae — Hemibarbus barbus (Okada, 1955, fig. 80, diagr.)

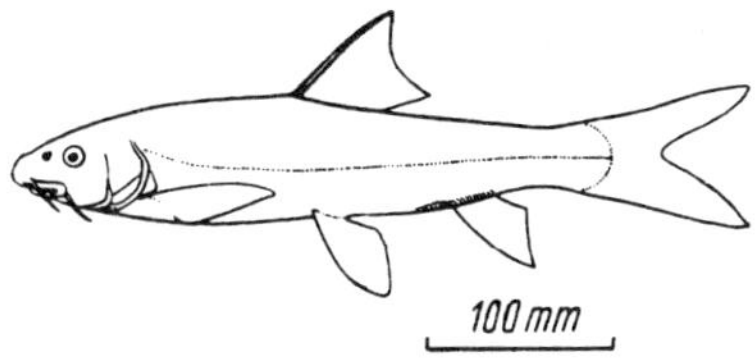

FIGURE 371. Cyprinidae — Schizothorax sinensis (Tchang, 1959, fig. 69, diagr.)

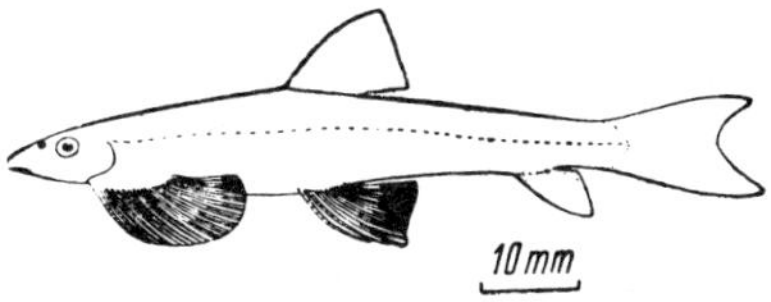

FIGURE 372. Cyprinidae — Psilorhynchus homaloptera (Hora and Mukerji, 1935, pl. 7, fig. 1, diagr.)

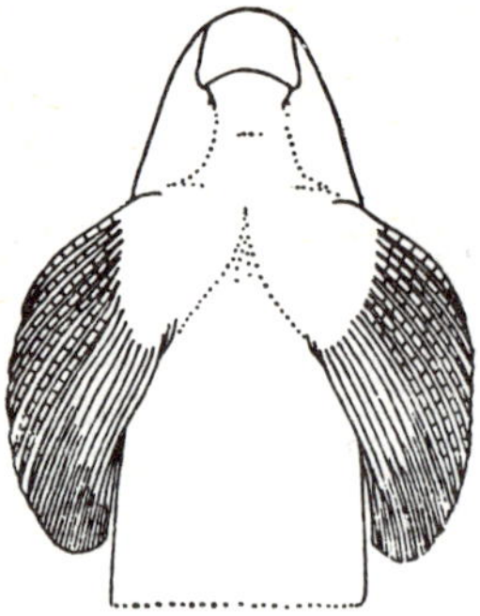

FIGURE 373. Cyprinidae — Psilorhynchus homaloptera (Hora and Mukerji, 1935, pl. 7, fig. 3, diagr.):

Anterior part of body, ventral.

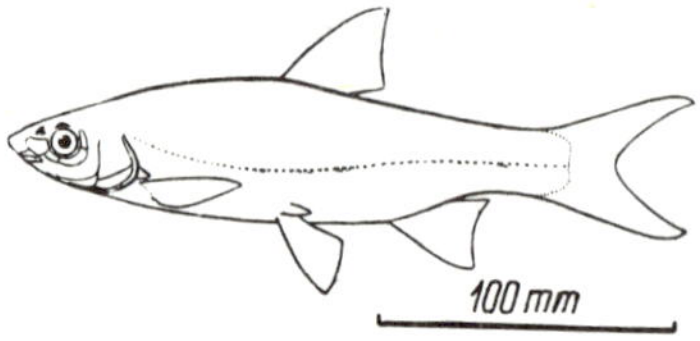

FIGURE 374. Cyprinidae — Chondrostoma nasus nasus natio borysthenicum (Berg, 1949, fig. 370, diagr.)

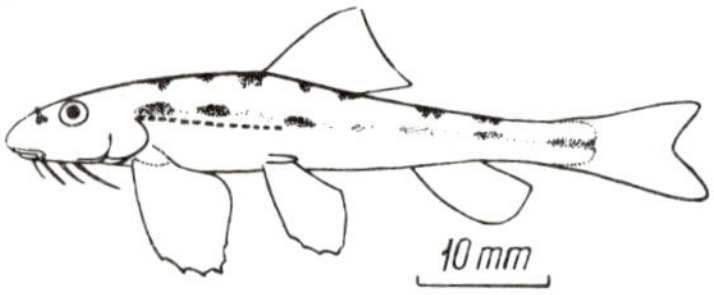

FIGURE 375. Cyprinidae — Gobiobotia pappenheimi (Berg, 1949, fig. 428, diagr.)

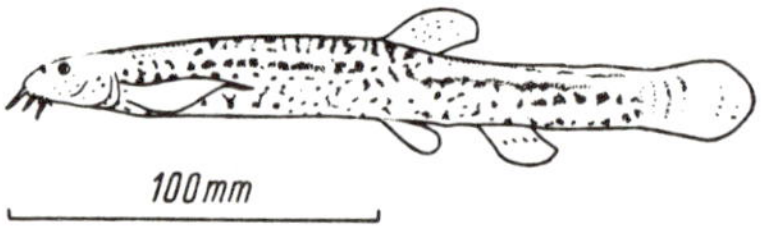

FIGURE 376. Cobitidae — Misgurnus anguillicaudatus (Berg, 1949, fig. 654, diagr.)

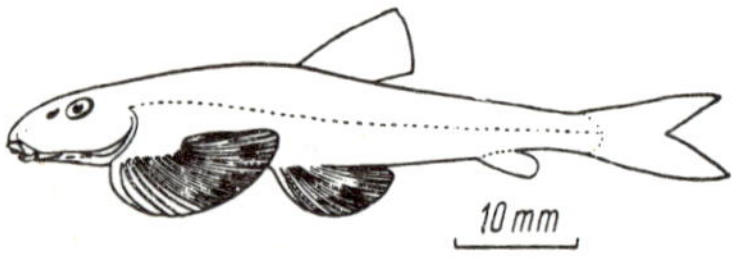

FIGURE 377. Homalopteridae (Homalopterinae) — Homaloptera stephensoni (Hora, 1932, pl. 11, fig. 1, diagr.)

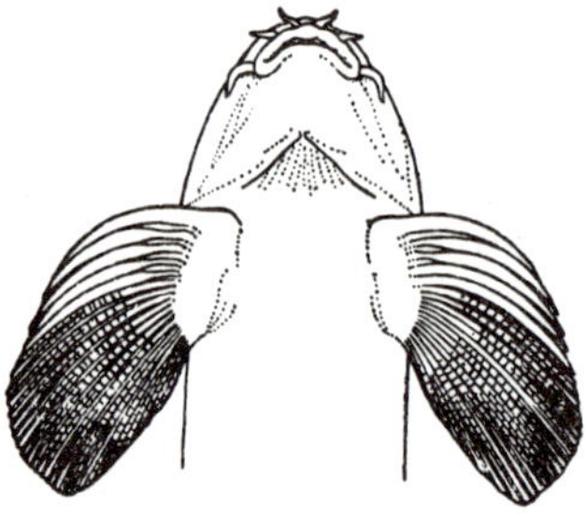

FIGURE 378. Homalopteridae (Homalopterinae) — Homaloptera stephensoni amphisquamata (Hora, 1935, pl. 10, fig. 4):

Anterior part of body, ventral.

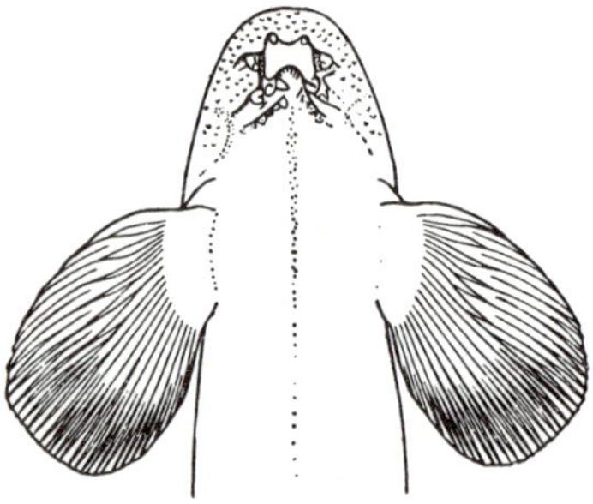

FIGURE 379. Homalopetridae (Gastromyzoninae) — Parhomaloptera microstoma (Hora, 1935, pl. 12, fig. 7):

Anterior part of body, ventral.

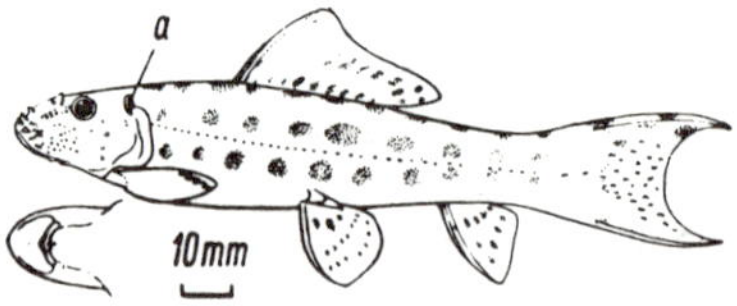

FIGURE 380. Gyrinocheilidae — Gyrinocheilops pennocki (Fowler, 1937, figs. 98, 99, diagr.):

a — upper gill opening.

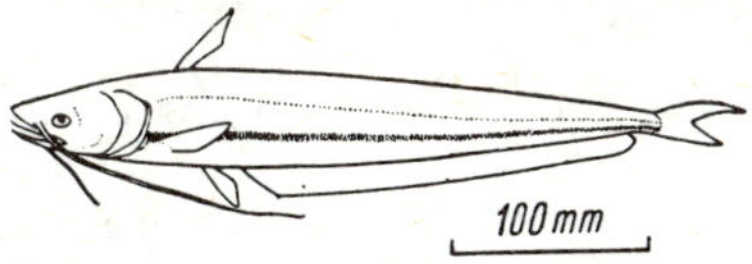

FIGURE 381. Siluridae — Wallago attu (Tchang, 1960, fig. 5, diagr.)

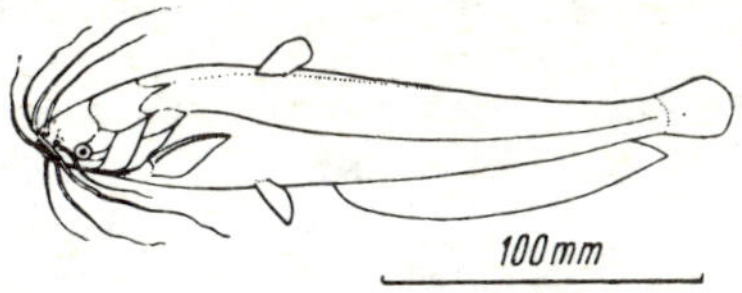

FIGURE 382. Heteropneustidae — Saccobranchus fossilis (Bloch, 1797, pl. 370, fig. 2, diagr.)

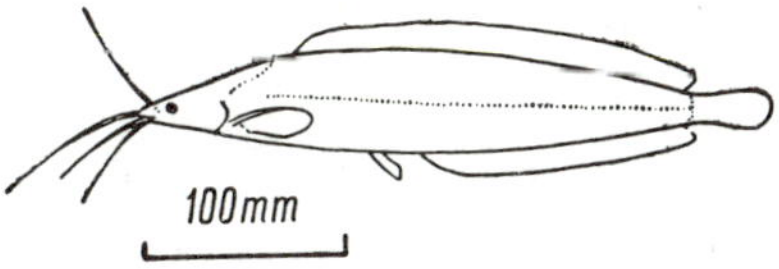

FIGURE 383. Clariidae — Clarias leiocanthus (H. Smith, 1945, fig. 79, diagr.)

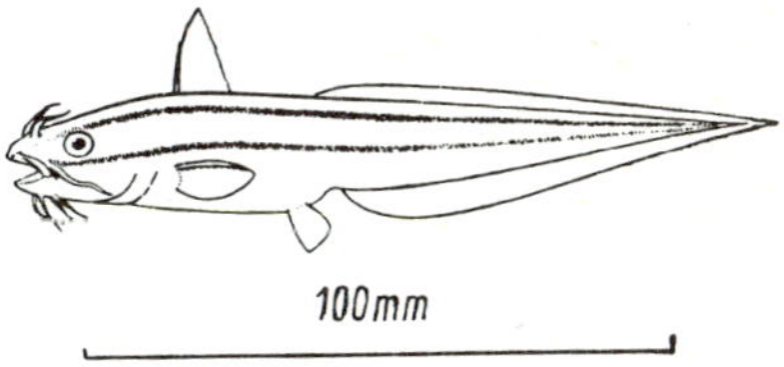

FIGURE 384. Plotosidae — Plotosus anguillaris (L. and L., 1965, fig. 160)

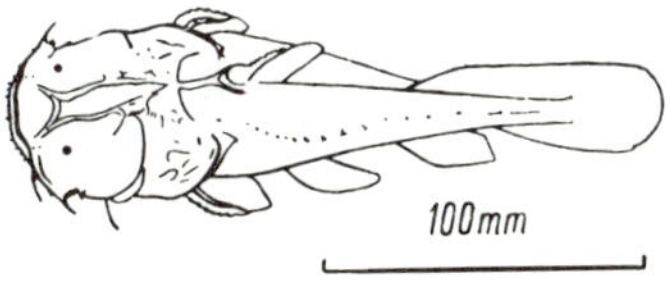

FIGURE 385. Chacidae — Chaca chaca (Day, 1878, pl. 112, fig. 2, diagr.)

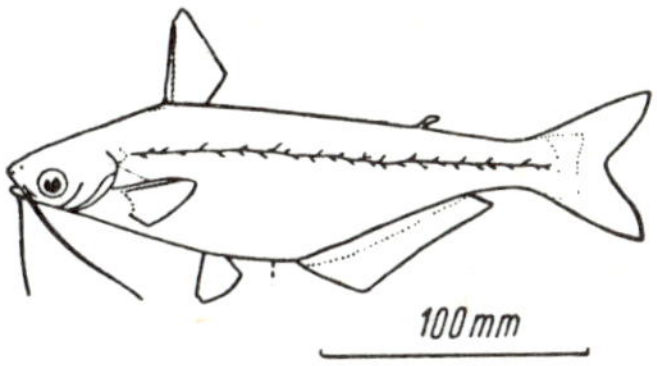

FIGURE 386. Pangasiidae — Pangasius macronema (Bleeker, 1862—1878, pl. 75, fig. 3, diagr.)

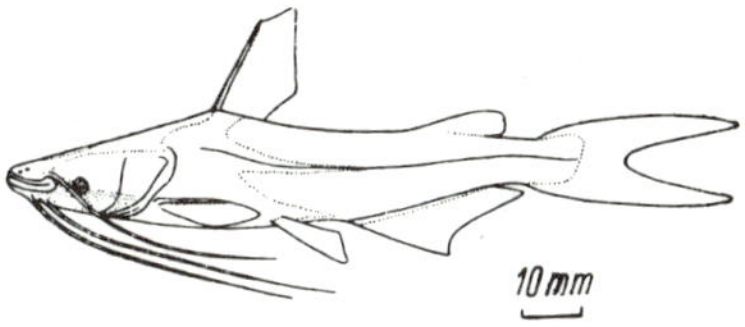

FIGURE 387. Doiichthyidae — Doiichthys novaeguineae (W. and B. 1913, 2, fig. 144, diagr.)

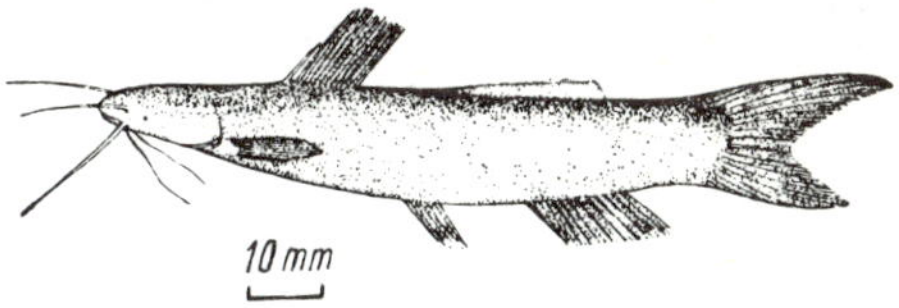

FIGURE 388. Amblycipitidae — Amblyceps mangois (Day, 1878, pl. 102, fig. 6)

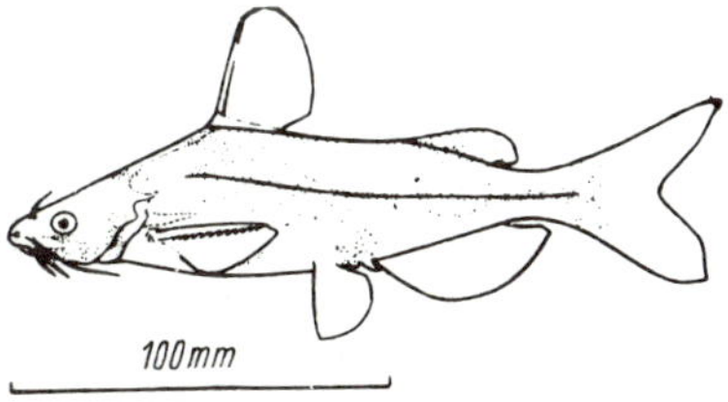

FIGURE 389. Bagridae — Leiocassis braschnikowi (Berg, 1949, fig. 668, diagr.)

FIGURE 390. Cranoglanididae (GRWM, 1966: 412, fig.)

35 (40). Branchiostegal membranes united, but free of the interbranchial space.

36 (37). Nares situated close together. Spiny ray of dorsal and pectoral fins weak. (Figure 388) . . . . 154. **Amblycipitidae**

37 (36). Nares widely separated. Spiny ray of dorsal and pectoral fins strong.

38 (39). Palatines with teeth. (Figures 389, 390). . . . . . 151. **Bagridae**[57]

39 (38). Palatines without teeth (Figure 393) . . . . 162. **Olyridae**

40 (35). Branchiostegal membranes attached to interbranchial space.

41 (44). Nares close together.

42 (43). Barbel present between the nares. (Figure 392) . . . . 156. **Sisoridae**

43 (42). Vale present between the nares. (Figure 393) . . . . 145. **Ariidae**

44 (41). Nares well separated; posterior naris with barbel. (Figure 394) . . . . 155. **Akysidae**

45 (22). Catfishes of Africa.

46 (49). Anal fin long, about 1/2—1/3 as long as the body without the caudal fin.

47 (48). Dorsal fin with a short base, or fin absent. Body more or less laterally compressed. (Figure 395) . . . . 159. **Schilbeidae**

48 (47). Dorsal fin with a long base. Body flattened or of cylindrical form. (Figure 396) . . . . 161. **Clariidae**

49 (46). Anal fin short, at any rate much less than 1/3 as long as the body without the caudal fin.

50 (51). Dorsal fin with rays absent; there is only an adipose fin situated in the posterior part of the body above the anal. A subcutaneous electrical organ is present, stretching along the whole upper part of the body. (Figure 397) . . . . 164. **Malapteruridae**

51 (50). Dorsal fin with clearly expressed rays present. No electrical organ.

52 (53). No strong spiny ray in the anterior part of the dorsal fin. (Figure 398) . . . . 157. **Amphiliidae**

53 (52). A strong spiny ray is present in the anterior part of the dorsal fin.

54 (55). Gill openings well separated; branchiostegal membranes always intergrown with the skin of the interbranchial space, not forming a fold. Lower jaw barbels with numerous branches (Figure 399) or the mouth has a thickened lip of semicircular form, forming a sucker . . . . 163. **Mochokidae**

55 (54). Gill openings close together; branchiostegal membranes free of the interbranchial space or only lightly attached to it. Lower jaw barbels without branchings and lip not forming sucker.

56 (57). Nares close together, not bearing barbels. Brachiostegal membranes united, but forming a fold across the interbranchial space. (Figure 400). . . . . 145. **Ariidae**

57 (56). Nares widely separated; posterior nares usually with a barbel. Branchiostegal membranes separated or deeply incised, free of the interbranchial space or forming a free fold across it. (Figure 401) . . . . 151. **Bagridae**

[57] Family 151a. Cranoglanididae has been isolated as a separate family (GRWM: 396; MA: 74).

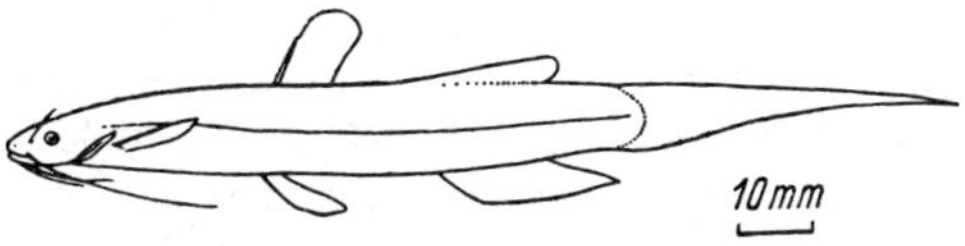

FIGURE 391. Olyridae — Olyra burmanica (Day, 1878, pl. III, fig. 5, diagr.)

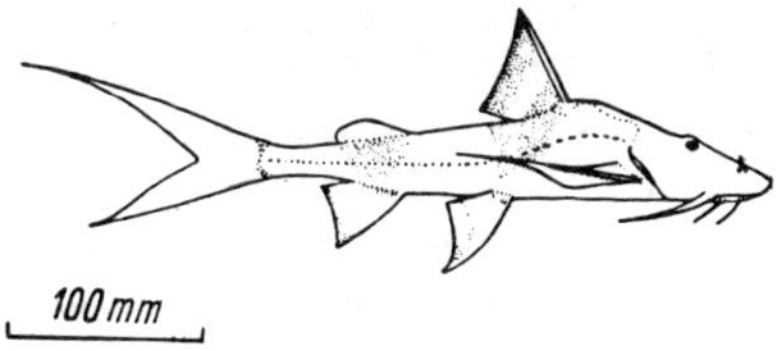

FIGURE 392. Sisoridae — Bagarius bagarius (W. and B., 1913, 2, fig. 105, diagr.)

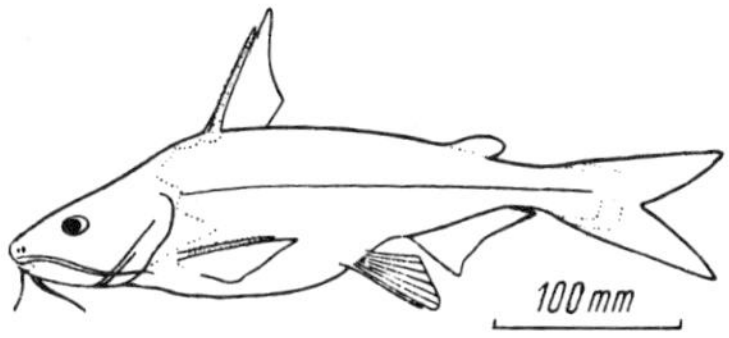

FIGURE 393. Ariidae — Arius falcarius (Wang, 1958, fig. 213, diagr.)

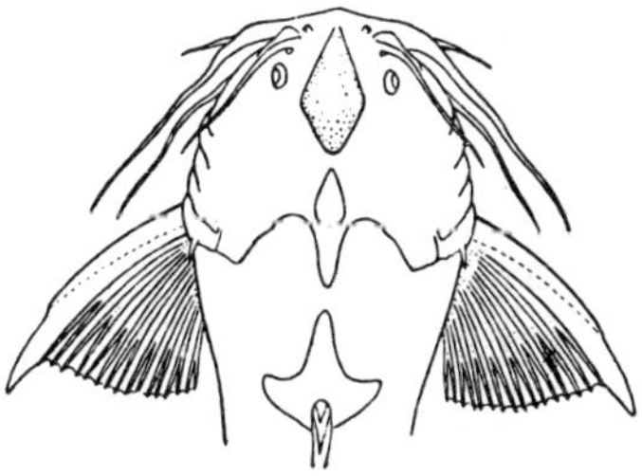

FIGURE 394. Akysidae — Akysis prashadi (Hora, 1936, fig. 1, diagr.)

FIGURE 395. Schilbeidae (GRWM, 1966:412, fig.)

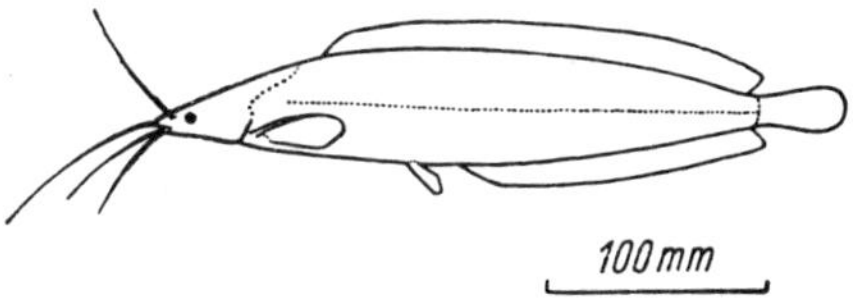

FIGURE 396. Clariidae — Clarius liocanthus (H. Smith, 1945, fig. 79, diagr.)

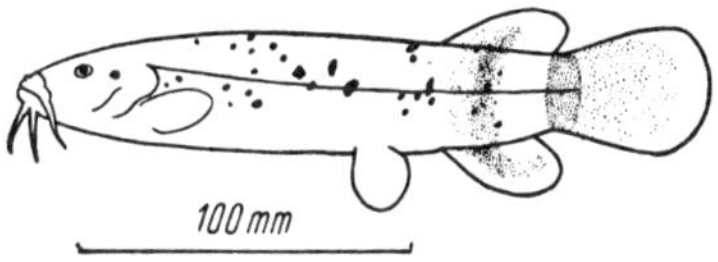

FIGURE 397. Malapteruridae — Malapterurus electricus (Fowler, 1936, fig. 113, diagr.)

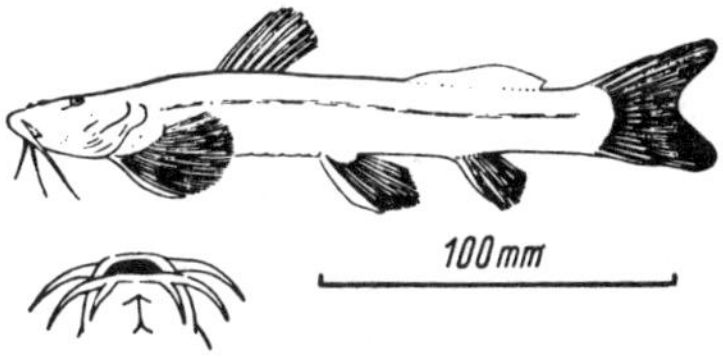

FIGURE 398. Amphiliidae — Amphilius platychir (Poll, 1957, figs. 243, 244)

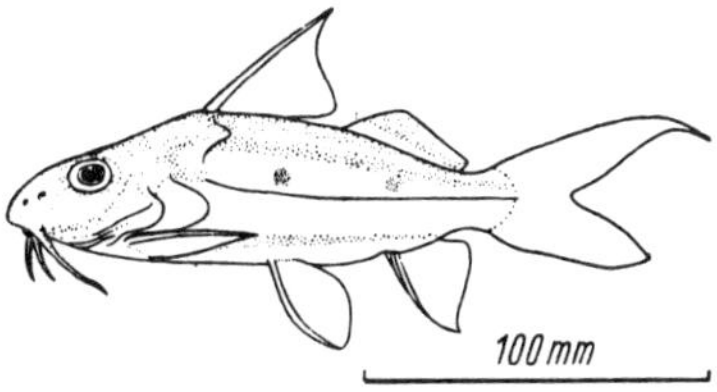

FIGURE 399. Mochokidae — Mochokus (Synodontis) nummifer (Fowler, 1936, fig. 101, diagr.)

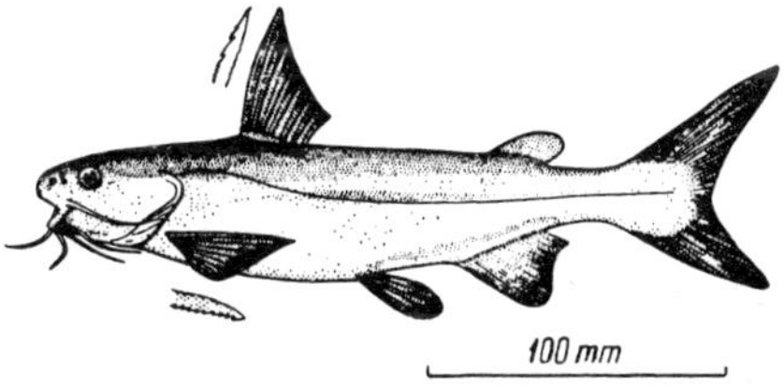

FIGURE 400. Ariidae — Tachysurus feliceps (Smith, 1950, fig. 165)

58 (21). Catfishes of the countries of the New World.
59 (62). Catfishes of North America.
60 (61). Nares close together, not bearing barbels. Each ventral fin with 6 rays. Marine fishes. (Figure 402) . . . . . 145. **Ariidae**
61 (60). Nares widely separated; posterior nares usually with a barbel. Each ventral fin with 8—9 rays. Freshwater fishes. (Figure 403) . . . . 153. **Ictaluridae**
62 (59). Catfishes of Central and South America.
63 (64). Maxillary bones well developed, with teeth. [Fifth vertebra not connected by a suture with the modified anterior vertebrae.] (Figure 404) . . . . 144. **Diplomystidae**
64 (63). Maxillary bones rudimentary, without teeth. [Fifth vertebra connected by a suture or intergrown with the modified anterior vertebrae.]
65 (84). Mouth terminal, but if inferior, the lower lip is not turned back and does not form a disklike mouth (see Figure 417).
66 (67). Anterior and posterior nasal openings usually very close together; posterior opening covered by a valve, but it does not have a barbel. Skin bare, plates absent. Two pairs of chin barbels, one pair of maxillary barbels. Ventral fins inserted behind the base of the dorsal fin. Adipose fin present, its base shortened. 13—15 branched rays in caudal fin. Marine fishes. (Figure 405) . . . . 145. **Ariidae**
67 (66). Anterior and posterior nasal openings usually widely separated and distinctly marked off by the skin covering the head, but if close together, the body is not bare but covered with bony plates.
68 (81). Skin rare or, occasionally, with scattered small bony verrucas; no large polygonal bony plates with backward-directed prickly spines distributed along the lateral line.
69 (76). Adipose fin present, long or short, but with a clearly expressed posterior end protruding outward (see Figures 406, 409, 410).
70 (75). Four chin barbels, generally arranged in 2 pairs. [Swim bladder well developed.]
71 (74). Branchiostegal membranes not united and gill openings stretching far forward ventrally.
72 (73). Teeth in the form of velutinous bands. Ventral fins usually inserted under the posterior end of the base of the dorsal. Base of adipose fin short or moderately long, shorter than the head. (Figure 406) . . . . 165. **Pimelodidae**[58]

[58] The following 2 monotypic families of South American catfishes occupy a rather indeterminate systematic position, being at the same time related to the family Pimelodidae. One of them, family 167. **Helogeneidae** (Figure 407), distributed in the eastern part of the Amazon basin and in the rivers of Guiana, differs from the Pimelodidae in the absence of a spine in the short dorsal fin, which is situated in the middle of the back, and in the small adipose fin, which lies above the long anal fin which has 42 rays. One genus and species: Helogenes marmoratus Günther, 1863, length up to 100 mm. The other family, 168. **Hypophthalmidae** (Figure 408), differs from the Pimelodidae in the position of the ventral fins in front of the dorsal, the low-set eyes, the swim bladder, which is contained in a capsule, the toothless mouth, the very long anal fin, and the Y-shaped form of the infrapharyngeal bones (Regan, 1911 : 573). There is a small adipose fin. The dorsal fin is situated above the anal. One genus.

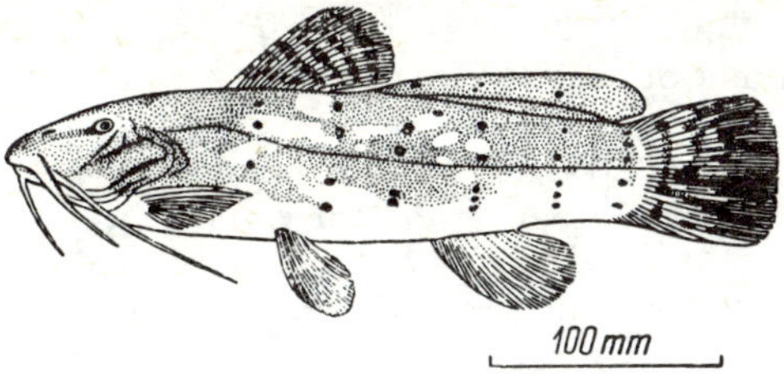

FIGURE 401. Bagridae — Auchenoglanis iturii (Fowler, 1936, fig. 84)

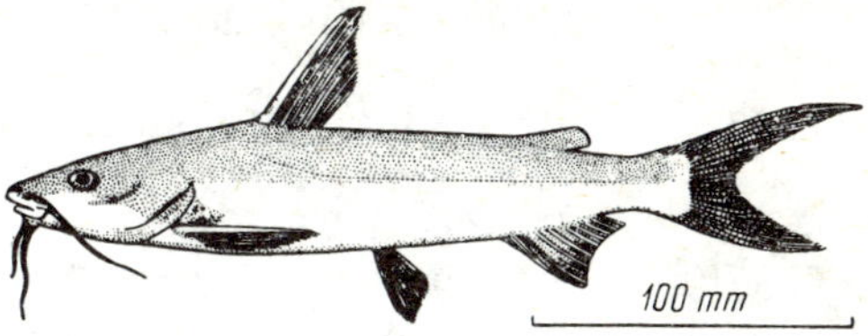

FIGURE 402. Ariidae — Galeichthys felis (J. and E., 1900, fig. 53)

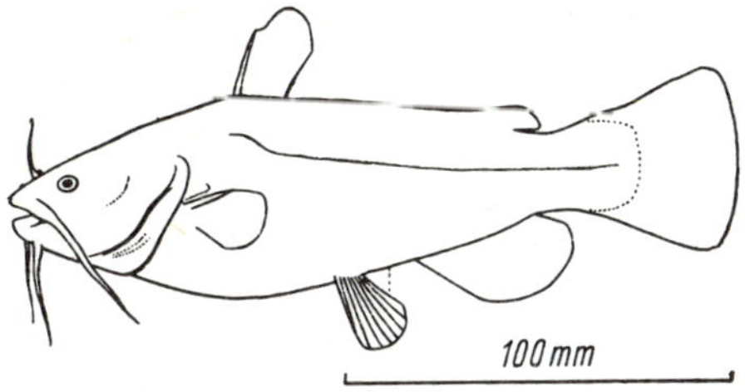

FIGURE 403. Ictaluridae — Ictalurus (Amiurus) melas (J. and E., 1900, fig. 60, diagr.)

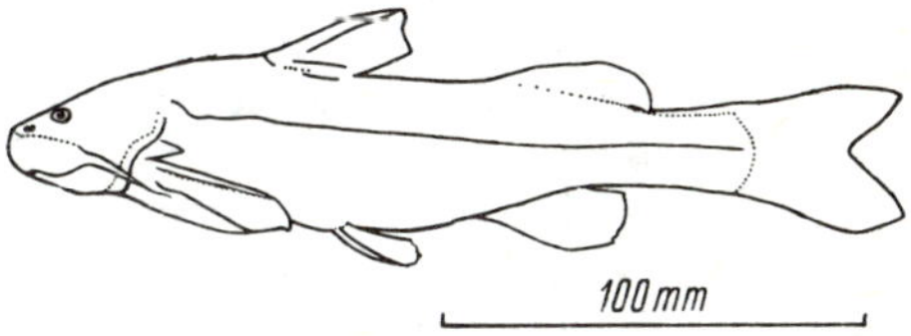

FIGURE 404. Diplomystidae — Dyplomyste chilensis (Eigenmann, 1928, pl. 7, fig. 1, diagr.)

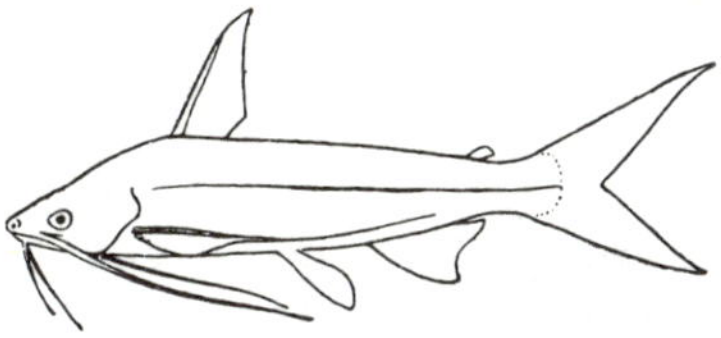

FIGURE 405. Ariidae — Aelurichthys scuttatus (Regan, 1906—08, pl. 15, fig. 2)

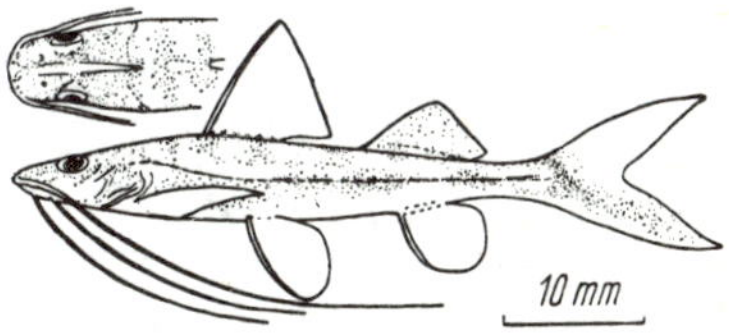

FIGURE 406. Pimelodidae — Nannorhambia stictonotus (Fowler, 1940, figs. 21, 22, diagr.)

FIGURE 407. Helogeneidae (GRWM, 1966:414, fig., amended)

FIGURE 408. Hypophthalmidae (GRWM, 1966:414, fig.)

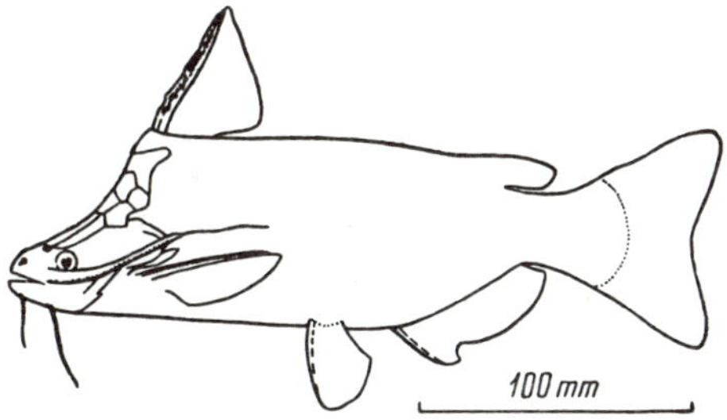

FIGURE 409. Auchenipteridae — Trachycorystes fisheri (Eigenmann, 1922, pl. 5, fig. 1, diagr.)

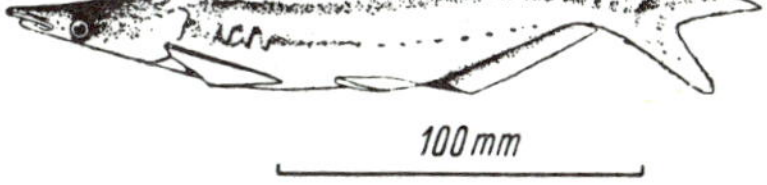

FIGURE 410. Ageneiosidae — Ageneiosus freiei (Schultz, 1944, pl. 4, fig. B, diagr.)

73 (72). Teeth arranged in one row. Ventral fins inserted slightly behind base of dorsal fin. Base of adipose fin very long . . . . .166. **Callophysidae**

74 (71). Branchiostegal membranes united, attached to interbranchial space, and gill openings not extending below and forward. (Figure 409) . . . . 147. **Auchenipteridae**

75 (70). Chin barbels absent. Swim bladder markedly reduced, concealed in a bony capsule (Figure 410) . . . . 148. **Ageneiosidae**

76 (69). Adipose fin absent; in its place there is sometimes a shallow fold of skin the posterior end of which, however, does not protrude but fuses imperceptibly with the upper margin of the caudal fin (Figure 412).

77 (80). Dorsal fin situated in the middle or the anterior part of the body. Two pairs of chin barbels; one pair of maxillary barbels. Opercular and interopercular bones not bearing bundles of prickly spines. Ventral fins inserted under or behind dorsal fin.

78 (79). There are 6 — 8 branched rays in the caudal fin, but if all the rays are unbranched, there are 6 — 10; anal fin always with fewer than 11 rays. Skin of head and body with small, bony verrucas scattered over it or arranged in rows, with spaces of bare skin between the verrucas. Opercular bone very weakly developed. Spines of pectoral fins with large, strong teeth. Body flattened anteriorly, especially in the head region. Eyes small. (Figure 411) . . . . 171. **Aspredinidae**

79 (78). Usually 15 branched rays in caudal fin, more rarely 14 or 16; 20 — 29 in anal fin. Skin of head and body bare. Opercular bone well developed. Spines of pectoral fins without large teeth. Body not flattened. Eyes small, almost concealed in the skin, their margins merging with the skin. (Figure 412) . . . . 170. **Cetopsidae**

80 (77). Dorsal fin situated in the posterior part of the body, usually in the posterior half of the standard body length (i. e., measured to the base of the caudal fin). Chin barbels absent; usually one conjugate barbel in each angle of the mouth. Opercular and interopercular bones with bundles of prickly spines. Ventral fins inserted under or in front of dorsal fin. Caudal fin with 10—12 branched rays. (Figures 413, 414) . . . . 169. **Trichomycteridae**

81 (68). Skin of sides of body with a continuous cover of polygonal bony plates, or more rarely these plates form a continuous row along the lateral line, in the posterior part of which the plates bear backward-directed prickly spines.

82 (83). Plates in 2 rows completely cover the sides of the body. Adipose fin, if present, represented by a membrane which begins behind the slightly raised bony dorsal shield. Generally 12 branched rays in caudal fin, occasionally 11; 7—12 rays in dorsal fin. Nares not fused, but very close together, separated by only a very short distance (see theses 30 — 66 and 67). (Figure 415) . . . . 172. **Callichthyidae**

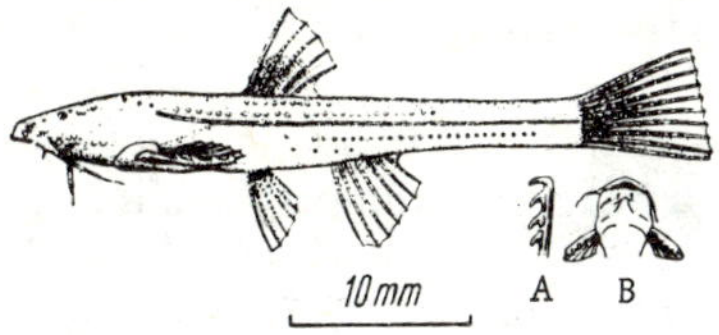

FIGURE 411. Aspredinidae — Xiliphius magdalenae (Eigenmann, 1922, pl. 1, figs. 1, 1a, 1b):

A — ray of pectoral fin; B — head, ventral.

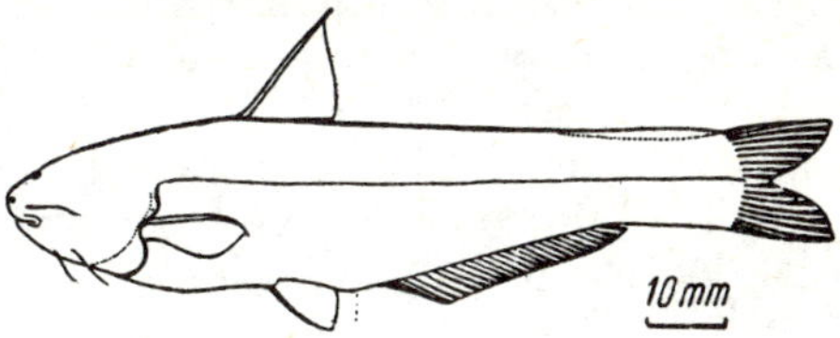

FIGURE 412. Cetopsidae — Pseudocetopsis plumbeus orinoco (Schultz, 1944, pl. 5, fig. A, diagr.)

FIGURE 413. Trichomycteridae — Pygidium chiltoni (Eigenmann, 1928, pl. 8, fig. 1, diagr.)

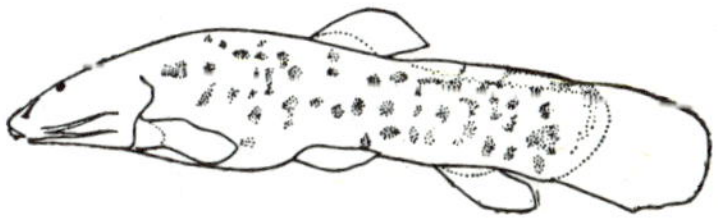

FIGURE 414. Trichomycteridae — Nemotogenys inermis (Eigenmann, 1928, pl. 7, fig. 4, diagr.)

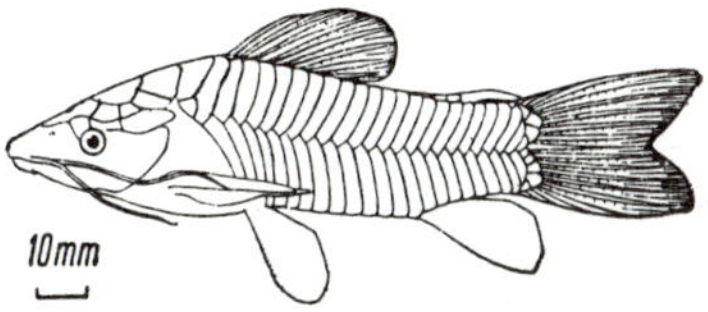

FIGURE 415. Callichthyidae — Hoplosternum magdalenae (Eigenmann, 1922, pl. 8, fig. 3, diagr.)

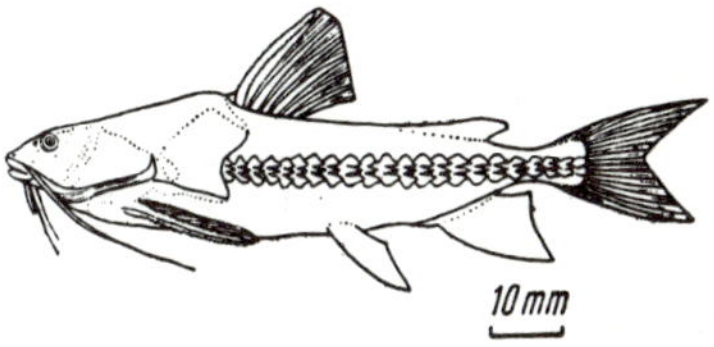

FIGURE 416. Doradidae — Doras maculatus (d'Orbigny, 1835, pl. 5, fig. 3, diagr.)

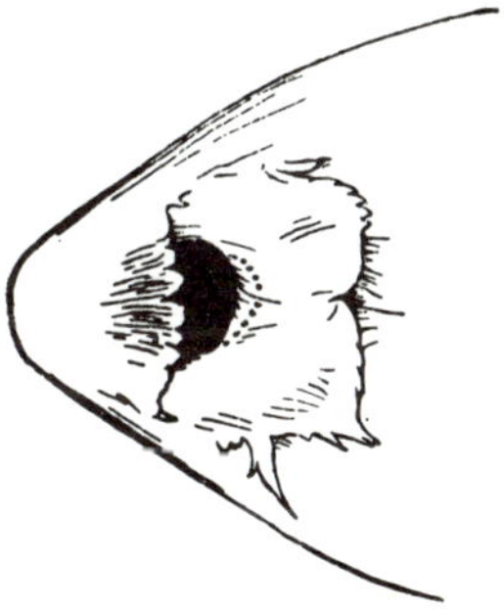

FIGURE 417. Disklike mouth of Loricaria seminuda (Eigenmann, 1922, pl. 14, fig. 2)

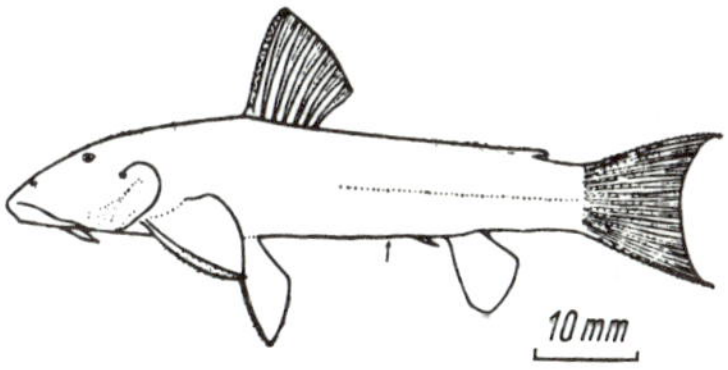

FIGURE 418. Astroblepidae — Astroblepis latidens (Eigenmann, 1922, pl. 6, fig. 3, diagr.)

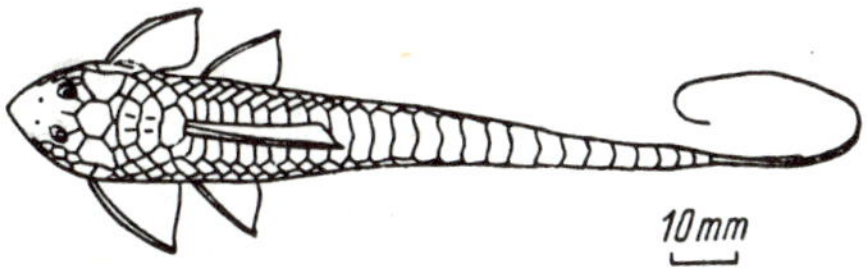

FIGURE 419. Loricariidae — Loricaria seminuda (Eigenmann, 1922, pl. 14, fig. 1, diagr.)

83 (82). One row of plates along the sides of the body, with backward-directed prickly spines, at any rate in the posterior part of the r row. Adipose fin present. Generally 15 branched rays in caudal fin; dorsal fin with 1 spiny and 4—6 branched rays. Dorsal and pectoral spines with a hinge mechanism. (Figure 416) . . . . 146. **Doradidae**

84 (65). Mouth inferior; lower lip turned back and together with the upper lip forming a disklike mouth (Figure 417). Branchiostegal membranes broadly united with the interbranchial space. Nasal openings very close together. Chin barbels absent; maxillary barbel more or less fused with the lip by its base, taking part in the formation of the disklike mouth. Adipose fin, if present, represented by a projection of a bony plate and a membrane.

85 (86). Body bare, only occasionally covered with plates. Generally 11 branched rays in caudal fin. (Figure 418) . . . . 174. Astroblepidae

86 (85). Body with a continuous cover of polygonal bony plates arranged in rows. Ten or about 14 branched rays in caudal fin. (Figure 419) . . . . 173. **Loricariidae**

Order 31. ANGUILLIFORMES[59] (thesis 0—49)

2 suborders, 22 families (175—198):

1 (8). There is no ossified supraoccipital bone (suborder 31.2. **Nemichthyoidei**, families 193—198). If theses 2—7 do not fit, continue to thesis 8.

2 (3). Full set of gill cover bones. Lateral line absent. Dorsal fin originating far behind vertical of base of pectoral. Vent situated far behind pectorals. (Figure 422) . . . . . .193. Serrivomeridae

3 (2). Set of gill cover bones not full—preoperculum and suboperculum absent.

4 (5). Caudal part of body shorter than trunk and head together. Dorsal and anal fins stretching to the end of the body, where they form a pair of widening lobes (Figure 423) . . . . 195. Cyemidae

5 (4). Caudal part of body appreciably longer than trunk and head. Dorsal and anal fins not widening out at the end of the body and not forming lobes. Origin of dorsal in front of pectorals.

6 (7). Jaws markedly elongate, thin (Figure 424); there are small teeth, arranged in checkerboard fashion . . . 194. Nemichthyidae

7 (6). Jaws not elongate, without teeth. (Figure 425) . . . . .196. Avocettinopsidae[60]

[59] They key does not include family 197. **Macrocephenchelidae**—one genus (Figure 420) and family 198. **Aoteidae** —one genus (Figure 421), the systematic position of which is still not clear.

[60] The genus Avocettinops Roule and Bertin is hypothetically regarded as a neotenic form from fish which are similar to Avocettina Jordan and Davis (Böhlke and Cliff, 1956 : 99) of the Nemichthyidae.

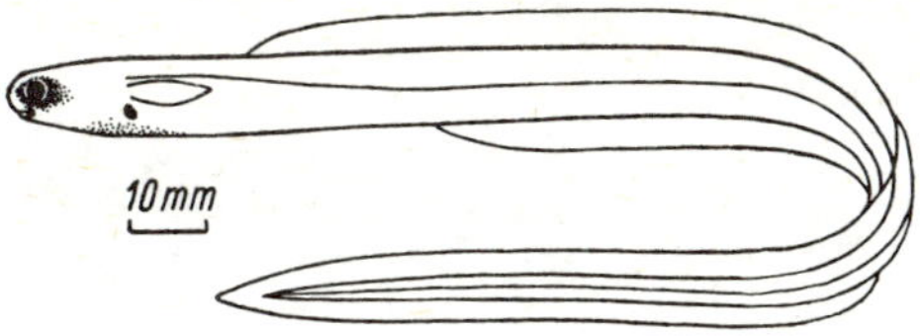

FIGURE 420. Macrocephenchelidae — Macrocephenchelys brachialis (Fowler, 1933, fig. 36, diagr.)

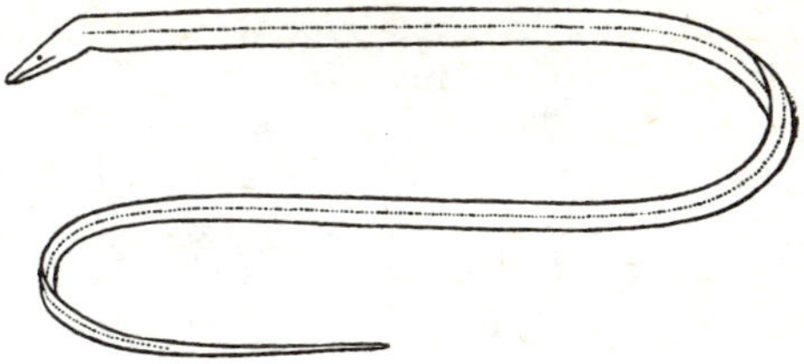

FIGURE 421. Aoteidae — Aotea acus (Phillips, 1926, pl. 90, diagr.)

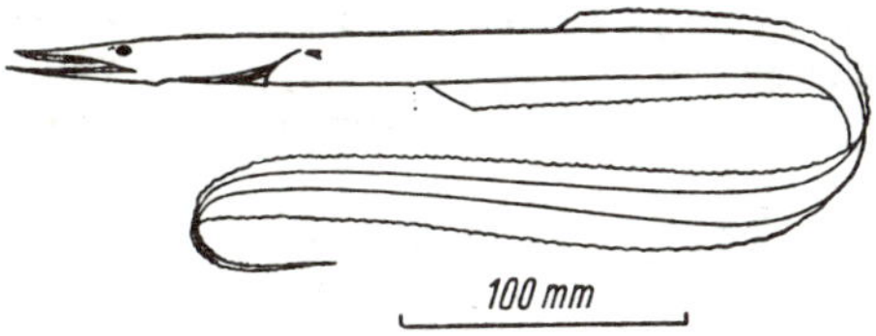

FIGURE 422. Serrivomeridae — Serrivomer beani (J. and E., 1900, fig. 153, diagr.)

FIGURE 423. Cyemidae — Cyema atrum (Fowler, 1936, fig. 136, diagr.)

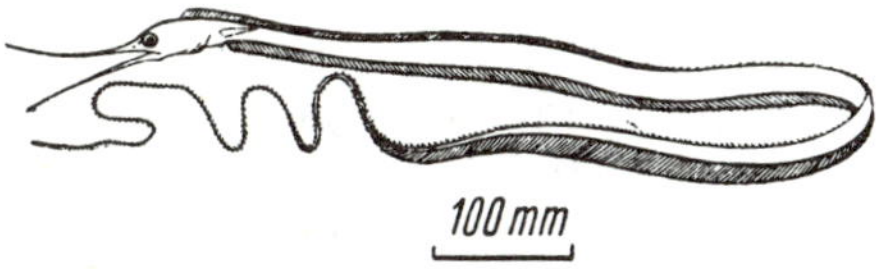

FIGURE 424. Nemichthyidae — Nemichthys scolopaceus (Roule and Bertin, 1929, pl. 1, fig. 5, diagr.)

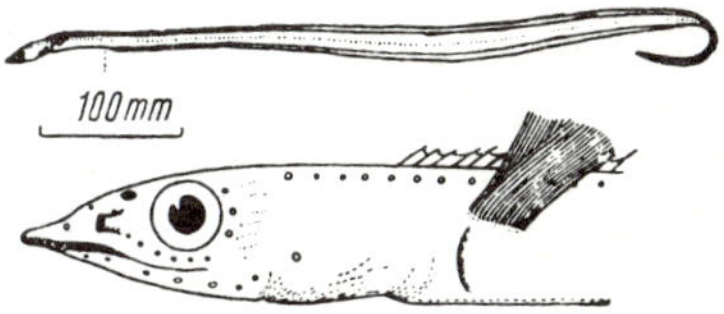

FIGURE 425. Avocettinopsidae — Avocettinops schmidti (Roule and Bertin, 1929, pl. 1, fig. 1)

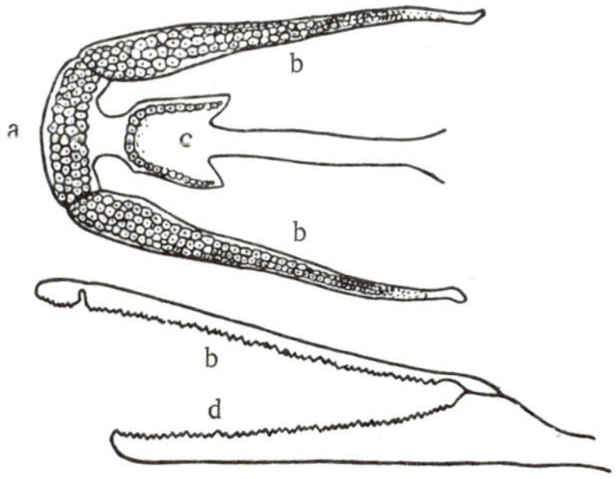

FIGURE 426. Jaws and vomer of Derichthys serpentinus (Beebe, 1935, fig. 5):

a — "prevomer"; b — maxillaries; c — vomer; d — lower jaw.

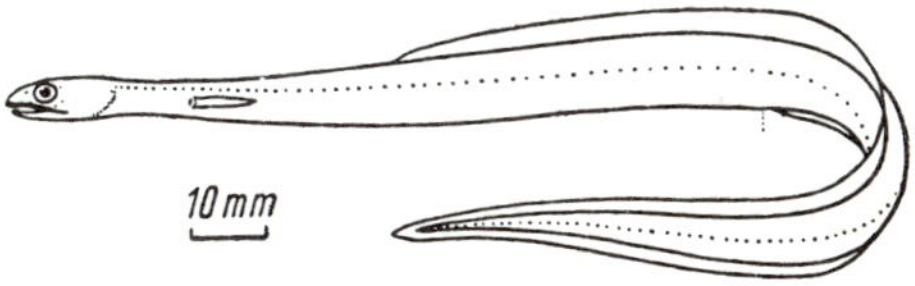

FIGURE 427. Derichthyidae — Derichthys serpentinus (J. and E., 1900, fig. 142, diagr.)

8 (1). Ossified supraoccipital bone present (suborder 31.1. **Anguilloidei** families 175—192).

9 (24). "Prevomer" (Figure 426) present.

10 (11). "Prevomer" separated from vomer by a ligament. (Figure 427) . . . . 175. **Derichthyidae**

11 (10). "Prevomer" fused with the vomer.

12 (17). Pectoral fins present or absent.[61]

13 (14). Dorsal fin originating in front of gill opening. (Figure 428). . . . . 180. Muraenidae

14 (13). Dorsal fin originating behind gill opening.

15 (16). Origin of dorsal fin less than a head's length away from the vertical passing through the gill opening. (Figure 429) . . . . 178. Xenocongridae

16 (15). Origin of dorsal fin considerably more than a head's length away from the vertical passing through the gill opening. (Figure 430) . . . . 181. **Heterenchelyidae**

17 (12). Pectoral fins present.

18 (23). Pectoral fins well developed, at least 1/3 as long as the head.

19 (20). Dorsal fin originating in front of gill opening. There are no scales on the body but the skin on the throat and thorax show traces of large scale pockets the size of the eye . . . . 179. **Myrocongridae**

20 (19). Dorsal fin originating far behind gill opening. Scales present on body, strongly grown into the skin.

21 (22). Gill openings distributed on the sides of the head and having the appearance of vertical slits. Lips present. Snout slightly pointed. Oral slit longitudinal (Figure 431) . . . 176. **Anguillidae**

22 (21). Gill openings situated under the head and having the appearance of horizontal slits. No lips. Snout blunt. Oral slit transverse. (Figure 432) . . . . 177. **Simenchelyidae**

23 (18). Pectoral fins weakly developed, small, less than 1/4 as long as the head, or else absent. (Figure 433) . . . . . . 182. **Moringuidae**

24 (9). "Prevomer" absent.

25 (38). Jaws thickened, strong. [Hyomandibulare vertical or directed obliquely forward.]

26 (33). Caudal vertebrae without transverse processes above the hemal arches. If theses 27—32 do not fit, continue to thesis 33.

27 (30). Maxillary bones articulating with ethmoid markedly behind apex of snout.

28 (29). Pharyngeal openings of gill slits wide. Jugostegals absent. (Figure 434) . . . . 183. **Muraenosocidae**

29 (28). Pharyngeal openings of gill slits narrow. Jugostegals present. (Figure 435) . . . . .184. **Neenchelyidae**

30 (27). Maxillary bones articulating with ethmoid near apex of snout.

31 (32). Pectoral fins small or absent. (Figure 436). . . . . 185. **Nettastomatidae**

32 (31). Pectoral fins well developed. (Figure 437) . . . . 186. **Nessorhamphidae**

[61] Pectorals are present in some genera of family 178. Xenocongridae which were earlier placed in family 189. Ophichthyidae.

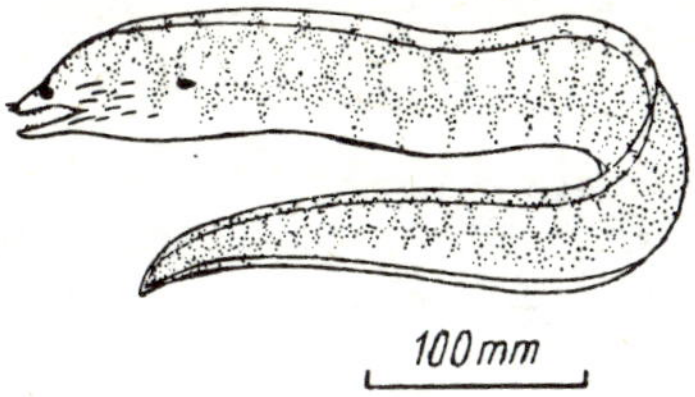

FIGURE 428. Muraenidae – *Gymnothorax kidako* (Okada, 1955, fig. 93, diagr.)

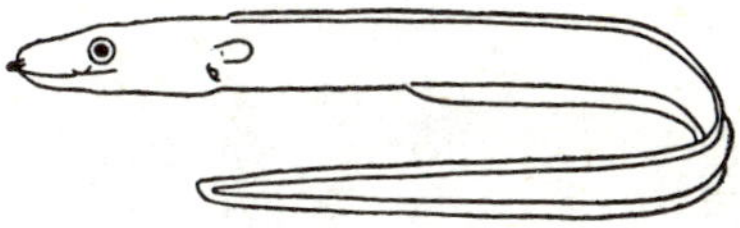

FIGURE 429. Xenocongridae (GRWM, 1966: 404, fig.)

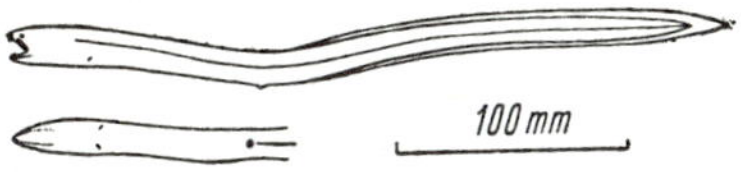

FIGURE 430. Heterenchelyidae – *Heterenchelys microphthalmus* (Fowler, 1936, fig. 144, diagr.)

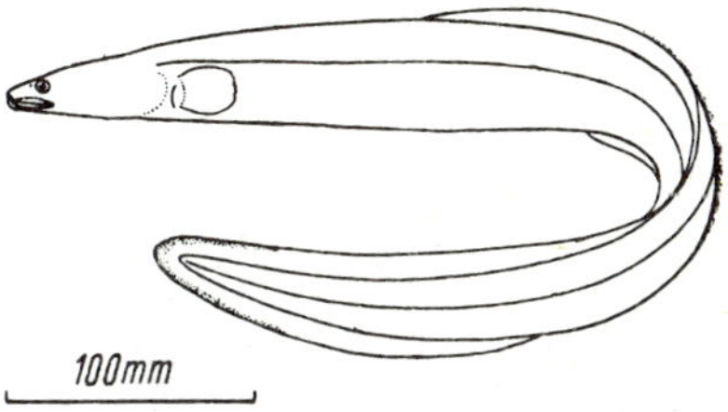

FIGURE 431. Anguillidae – *Anguilla sinensis* (Nichols, 1943, fig. 4, diagr.)

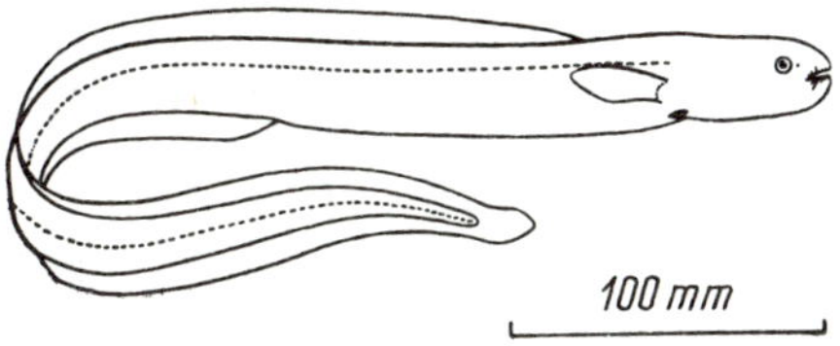

FIGURE 432. Simenchelyidae – *Simenchelys dofleini* (Franz, 1910, pl. III, fig. 1, diagr.)

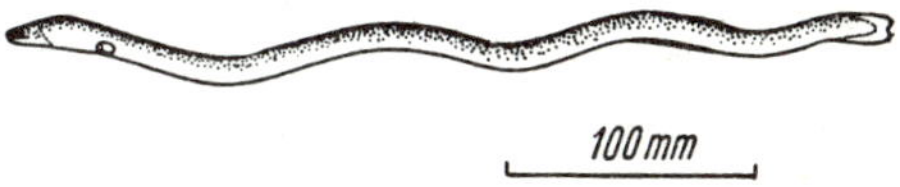

FIGURE 433. Moringuidae – *Moringua macrochir* (Chu et al., 1962, fig. 149)

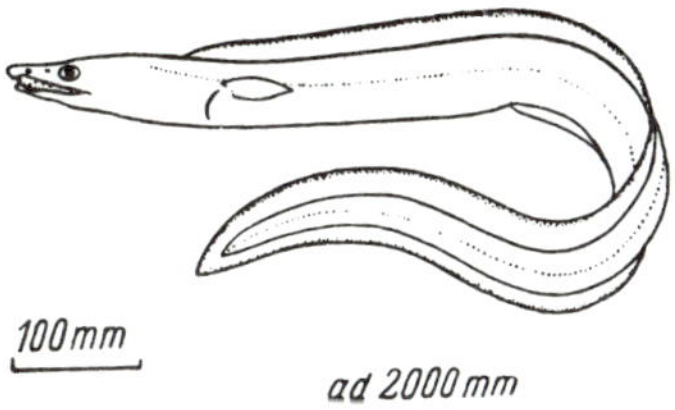

FIGURE 434. Muraenesocidae – *Muraenesox cinereus* (Okada, 1955, fig. 92, diagr.)

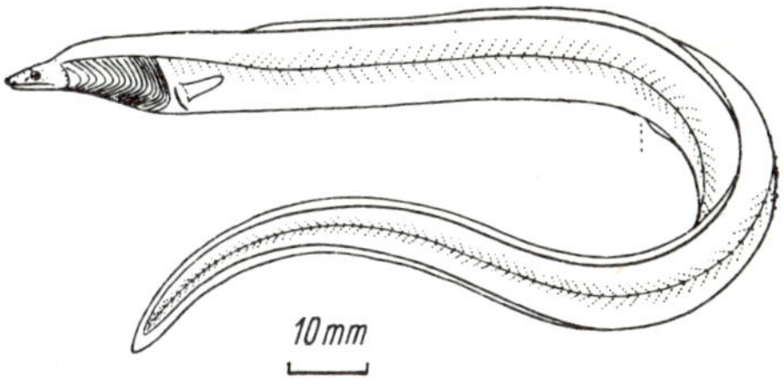

FIGURE 435. Neenchelyidae – *Neenchelys buitendijui* (W. and B. 1916, 3, fig. 116, diagr.)

FIGURE 436. Nettastomatidae – *Metopomycter parviceps* (M., 1955, III, fig. 119, diagr.)

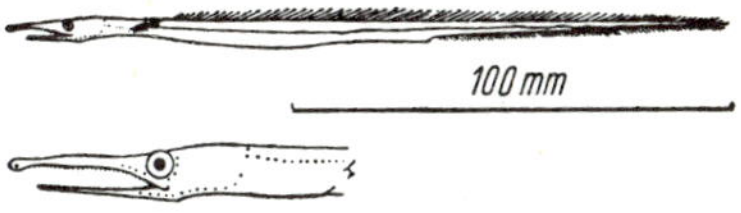

FIGURE 437. Nessorhamphidae – *Nesoramphus ingolfianus* (Beebe, 1935, figs. 10H, 11E)

33 (26). Caudal vertebrae with transverse processes above the hemal arches. Maxillaries articulating with ethmoid near apex of snout.

34 (35). Position of nares not labial but dorsal or lateral. (Figure 438) . . . . 187. **Congridae**[62]

35 (34). Position of nares labial (posterior nares sometimes lateral).

36 (37). Caudal fin present, fused with dorsal and anal. (Figure 439) . . . . 188. **Echelidae**

37 (36). Caudal fin absent; end of caudal part of body unadorned, as neither the dorsal nor the anal fin passes into it. (Figure 440) . . . . 189. **Ophichthidae**

38 (25). Jaws thin, weak. [Hyomandibulare directed obliquely backward.]

39 (42). Gill openings well separated.

40 (41). Vent situated very far from the head. (Figure 441) . . . . 190. **Hyophiidae**

41 (40). Vent situated near the head in the region of the pectoral fins, not far from the gill openings. (Figure 442) . . . . 191. **Dysommidae**[63]

42 (39). Gill openings fused, forming a single slit on the throat. (Figure 444) . . . . 192. **Synaphobranchidae**

Order 32. HALOSAURIFORMES (thesis 0—55)

1 family: 199. **Halosauridae** (Figure 445).

Order 33. NOTACANTHIFORMES (thesis 0—56)

2 families (200, 201):

1 (2). Mouth small, toothless, with thick lips. Dorsal fin with a short base; anterior rays of fin spiny, posterior rays not. (Figure 446) . . . . 200. **Lipogenyidae**

2 (1). Mouth of moderate size; lips not thickened; premaxillaries, bordering upper margin of mouth, bearing teeth. Dorsal fin with a long base, but represented by a large number of isolated spiny rays. (Figures 447, 448) . . . . .201. **Notacanthidae**

[62] A separate family is isolated, 187a. **Todaridae** (GRWM: 393)

[63] Dysommina rugosa Ginsburg, 1951 (Figure 443) externally resembles the species of family 191. Dysommidae but differs in the position of the origin of the anal and dorsal fins and in the position of the vent, all of which are shifted markedly back from the gill slit (cf. Figure 442); however, where anatomical characters are concerned (the presence of paired frontal bones and a different structure of the auditory apparatus) the difference is considerable and served as the basis for establishing a separate family, 191a. 191a. **Dysomminidae** (Bohlke and Hubbs, 1951).

32, 33

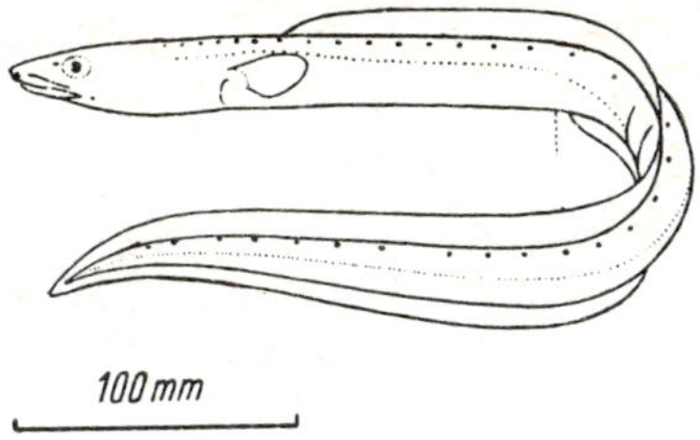

FIGURE 438. Congridae — Astroconger myriaster (M., 1955, III, fig. 109, diagr.)

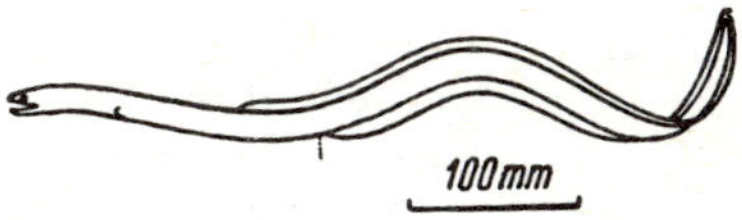

FIGURE 439. Echelidae — Muraenichthys gymnopterus (Bleeker, 1862—1878, 4, pl. 6, fig. 1, diagr.)

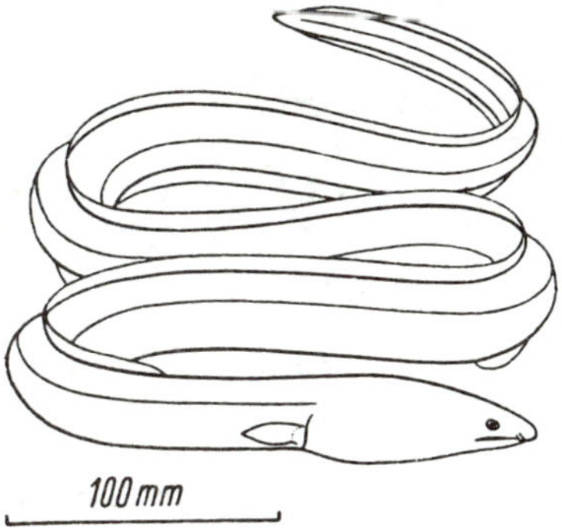

FIGURE 440. Ophichthidae — Pisoodonophis boro (Wang, 1958, fig. 229, diagr.)

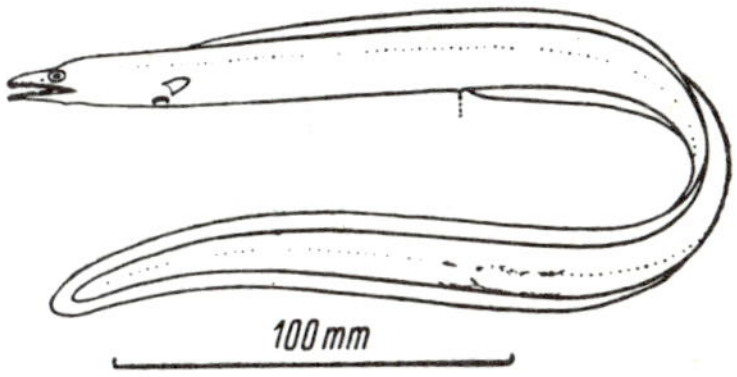

FIGURE 441. Ilyophidae — Ilyophis brunneus (J. and E., 1900, fig. 145, diagr.)

FIGURE 442. Dysommidae — Dysomma anguillare (M., 1955, III, fig. 129, diagr.)

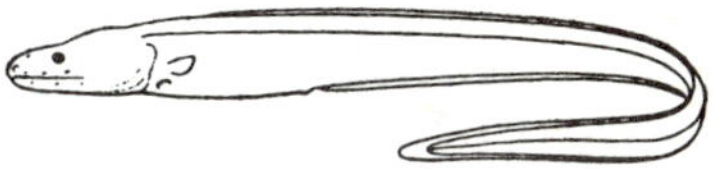

FIGURE 443. Dysomminidae (GRWM, 1966: 405, fig.)

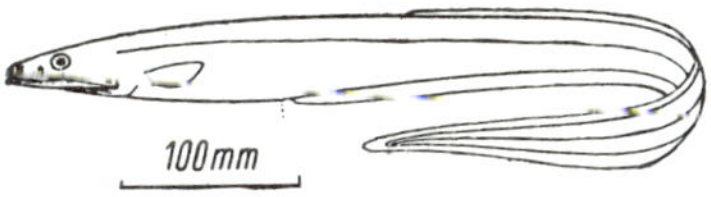

FIGURE 444. Synaphobranchidae — Synaphobranchus pinnatus (J. and E., 1900, fig. 146, diag.)

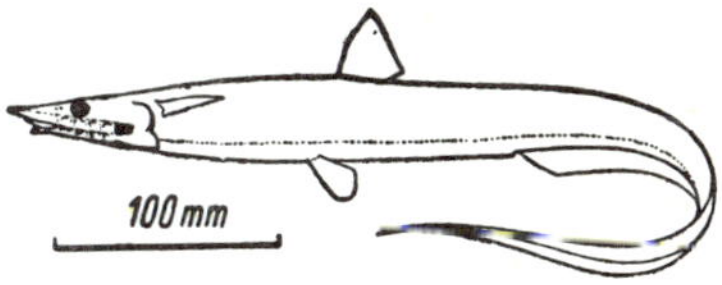

FIGURE 445. Halosauridae — Halosaurus oweni (Goode and Bean, 1895, pl. 15, fig. 152, diagr.)

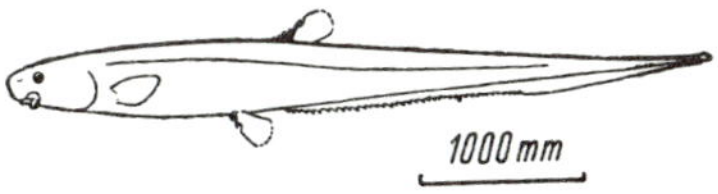

FIGURE 446. Lipogenyidae — Lipogenys gilli (Goode and Bean, 1895, pl. 51, fig. 190, diagr.)

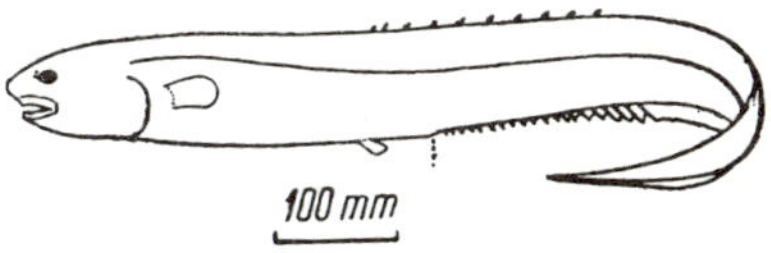

FIGURE 447. Notacanthidae — Notacanthus phasganorus (Jordan, 1925, fig. 287)

Order 34. BELONIFORMES (thesis 0—101)

2 suborders, 5 families (202—206):

1 (4). Mouth as a rule large, but if small, there are small accessory fins behind the dorsal and anal fins; both jaws (in adults) usually project markedly forward and are narrowed in the anterior part. Scales small, generally many more than 100 in the longitudinal row. [Nasal bones large, lying directly on the dorsal side of the cartilaginous skull and united by a suture (Berg, 1940: 282). Suprapharyngeal bones (third pair) moderately elongate, distinctly divided into right and left, fourth pair usually long and narrow (Figure 449).] (Suborder 34.1. **Scomberesocoidei**, families 202, 203).

2 (3). No small accessory fins behind the relatively long bases of the dorsal and anal fins. Both jaws markedly elongate, drawn out anteriorly and forming (in adults) a long beak (in juveniles the upper jaw is shortened). The jaws bear, apart from bands with small teeth, a row of enlarged, conical, pointed teeth. (Figure 405) . . . . .202. **Belonidae**

3 (2). Small accessory fins present behind the relatively short bases of the dorsal and anal fins. Both jaws more or less projecting forward, but the beak thus formed is not long. Teeth on jaws very small. (Figure 451). . . . . 203. **Scomberesocidae**

4 (1). Mouth small; only the lower jaw sometimes projects forward. No accessory fins. Scales of moderate size, usually not more than 110 in longitudinal row. [No large nasal bones lying directly on the dorsal side of the cartilaginous skull and united by a suture. Right and left suprapharyngeal bones (third pair) fused or closely contiguous with each other, but possibly disjunct; fourth pair absent. Infrapharyngeal bone of triangular form, with a wide base, the upper surface concave (Figure 452).] (Suborder 34.2. **Exocoetoidei**, families 204—206.)

5 (6). Premaxillaries forming anteriorly a flat triangular projection which protrudes with the apex forward. Lower jaw in adults markedly protruding forward, forming a long excrescence (Figure 453). Pectoral fins short or of moderate length. [Suprapharyngeal bones (third pair) fused (Figure 454)] . . . . .204. **Hemiramphidae**

6 (5). Premaxillaries with a straight transverse anterior margin. Lower jaw in adults not projecting forward and not forming a long beak. Pectoral fins elongate and usually serving as an organ of flight. [Suprapharyngeal bones (third pair) closely continguous with each other, but possibly disjunct (Figure 455).]

7 (8). Pectoral fins relatively short, at best just reaching the ventral fins. Lower jaw beaklike in juveniles. (Figure 456) . . . . 206. **Oxyporhamphidae**

8 (7). Pectoral fins very long, stretching beyond ventral fins and even farther than origin of dorsal. Lower jaw not protruding beaklike in juveniles (except in the genus *Fodiator*). (Figure 457). . . . . 205. Exocoetidae

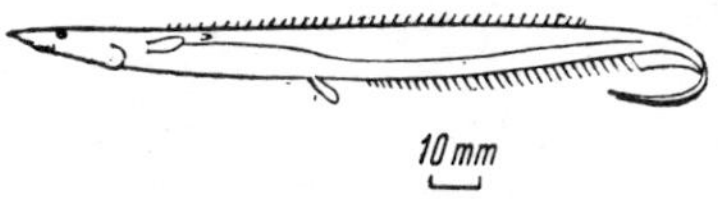

FIGURE 448. Notacanthidae — Polyacanthonotus rissoanus (Goode and Bean, 1895, pl. 51, fig. 188, diagr.)

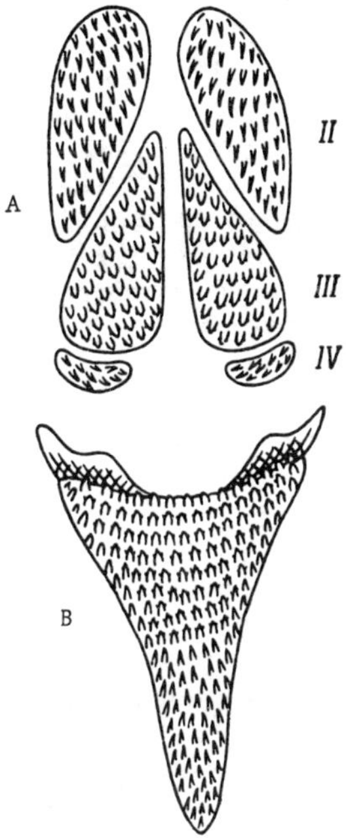

FIGURE 449. Pharyngeal bones of Belone belone (L. and L., 1965, fig. 196):

A — suprapharyngeal bones, pairs II—IV; B — infrapharyngeal bone.

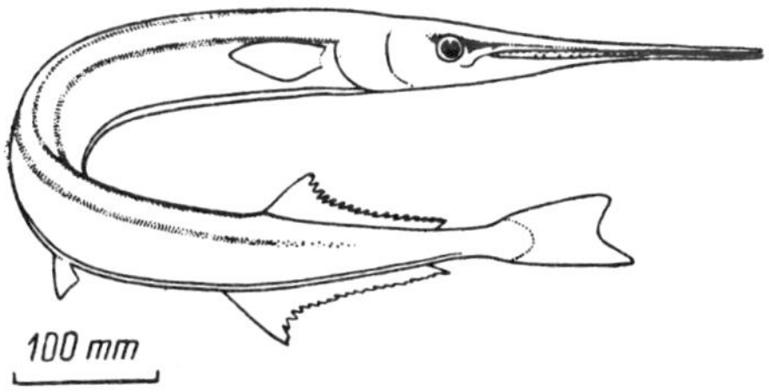

FIGURE 450. Belonidae — Tylosurus anastomella (L. and L., 1965, fig. 200)

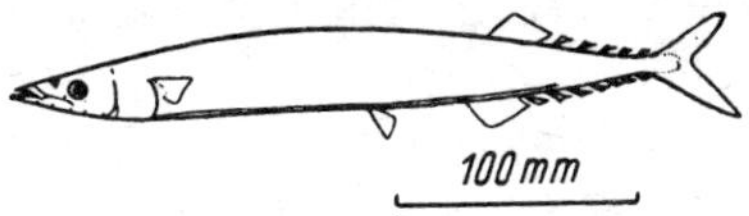

FIGURE 451. Scomberesocidae — Cololabis saira (Okada, 1955, fig. 109, diagr.)

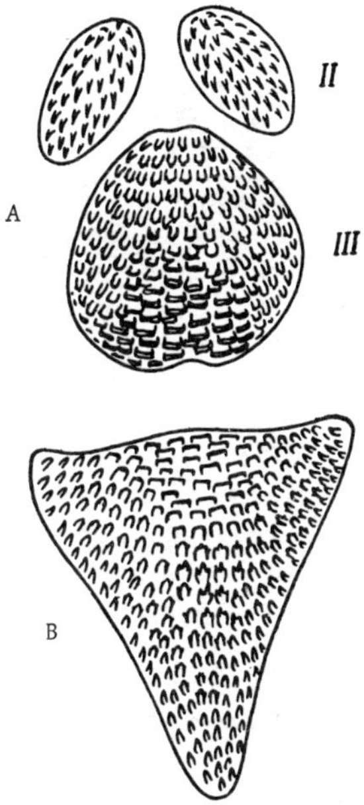

FIGURE 452. Pharyngeal bones of Exocoetus lineatus (L. and L., 1965, fig. 198):

A — suprapharyngeal bones, pairs II and III; B — infrapharyngeal bone.

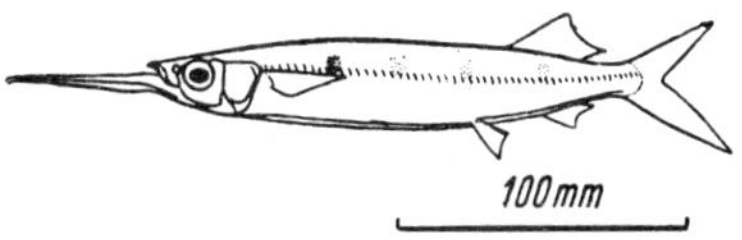

FIGURE 453. Hemiramphidae — Hemiramphus far (Wang, 1958, fig. 234, diagr.)

Order 35. GADIFORMES (thesis 0–159)

2 suborders, 4 families (207–210):

1 (6). Caudal fin not fused with dorsal and anal. Scales, if present, not markedly elongate and not set at an angle to each other as in the eel *Anguilla*. [Markedly fewer than 10 radials in pectoral fins.] (Suborder 35.2. **Gadoidei**, families 208–210).

2 (3). Swim bladder in contact with auditory capsules via fontanelles in in the occipitalia lateralia at the back of the skull.[64] [Neurocranium almost closed anteriorly, canal of olfactory nerves and partly interorbital septum bony.] Capitulum of vomer often without teeth. Deepwater fishes. (Figure 459) . . . . 208. **Moridae**[65]

3 (2). Fontanelles absent at the back of the skull in the occipitalia lateralia and the swim bladder is not in contact with the auditory capsules. [Neurocranium broadly open anteriorly, interorbital septum and canal of olfactory nerves membranous below.] Capitulum of vomer always with teeth. Generally inhabitants of moderate depths.

4 (5). First dorsal fin situated on the occiput or above the base of the pectoral fins, reduced and consisting of a single elongate ray, behind which there is no row of very short leathery rays set in a dorsal groove. Second dorsal with a very deep and broad notch, giving the impression of two fins. Snout without barbels. Vent situated roughly under vertical of origin of second dorsal fin or in front of this. (Figure 460) . . . . 209. **Bregmacerotidae**

5 (4). First dorsal fin generally situated behind the head and with a normal structure (Figure 461, 462), but if, occasionally, situated on the occiput and modified, it consists of one elongate ray and a row of very short leathery rays set behind it in a deep dorsal groove; moreover, the second dorsal is without a notch, the snout has barbels, and the vent is situated markedly behind the vertical of the origin of the second dorsal fin. (Figure 463) . . . . 210. **Gadidae**[66]

6 (1). Caudal fin completely fused with dorsal and anal. Scales of the type in *Anguilla*. [At least 10 (10–13) radials in pectoral fins.] (Suborder 35.1. **Muraenolepoidei**, family 207.) (Figure 464) . . . . 207. **Muraenolepididae**

[64] This can be discovered, as Svetovidov notes (1948:66), by raising the gill cover and making a longitudinal section above the gills along the base of the skull. In fishes of family 208. Moridae, a hornlike process of the swim bladder is visible, and if this is raised, the fontanelle also (Figure 458).

[65] A separate family is isolated, 208a. **Melanonidae** (Marshall, 1964).

[66] A separate family is isolated, 210a. **Merlucciidae** (GRWM:397) (Figure 462).

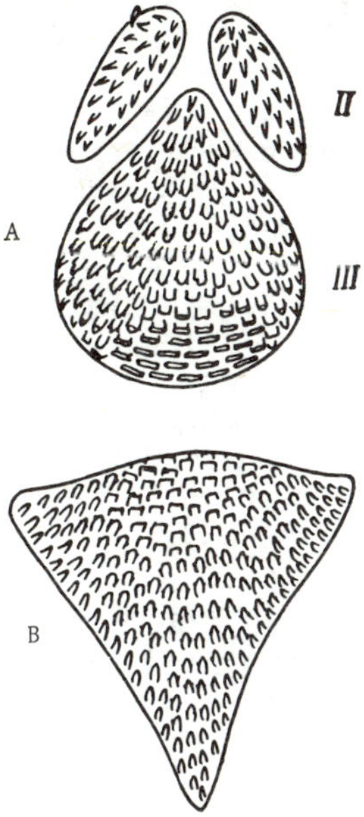

FIGURE 454. Pharyngeal teeth of *Hemiramphus intermedius* (L. and L., 1965, fig. 197):

A — suprapharyngeal bones, pairs II and III;
B — infrapharyngeal bone.

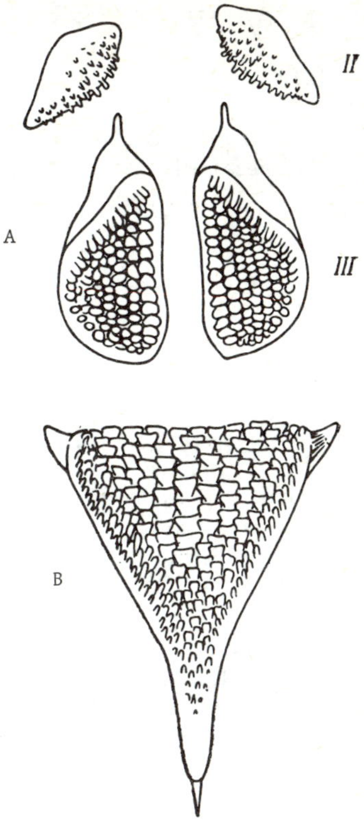

FIGURE 455. Pharyngeal bones of *Hirundichthys speculiger* (L. and L., 1965, fig. 199):

A — suprapharyngeal bones, pairs II and III;
B — infrapharyngeal bone.

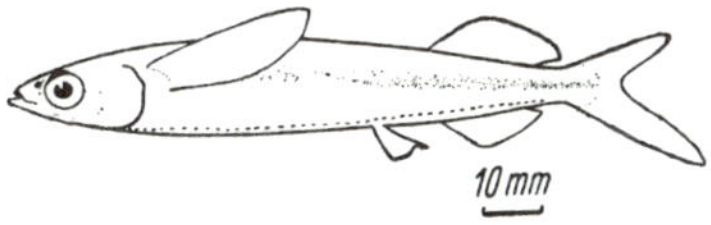

FIGURE 456. Oxyporhamphidae — *Oxyporhamphus micropterus* (Abe, 1956, pl. 221, fig. 572, diagr.)

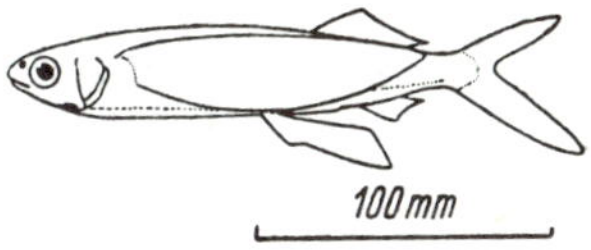

FIGURE 457. Exocoetidae — *Cypselurus agoo* (L. and L., 1965, fig. 38)

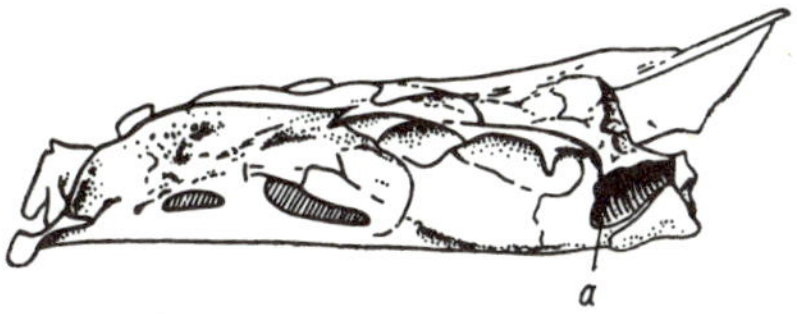

FIGURE 458. Skull of *Physiculus japonicus* (L. and L., 1965, fig. 222):

a — fontanelle, stretched by a membrane.

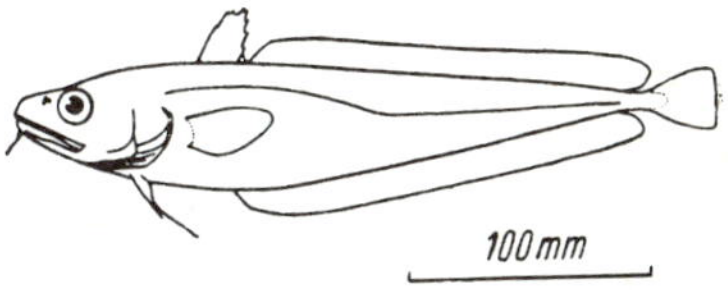

FIGURE 459. Moridae — *Lotella maximoviczi* (L. and L., 1965, fig. 225)

Order 36. MACROURIFORMES (theses 0—160, 165)

2 families (211, 212):

1 (2). Head of normal size and firmness, but if enlarged and soft, there are two dorsal fins. Ventral fins well developed . . . . 211. **Macrouridae**

3 subfamilies:

1 (4). First gill arch free anteriorly and first gill slit not reduced in size. Second ray of dorsal fin not resembling a spine.

2 (3). Two dorsal fins separated from each other by a deep notch. No teeth on the vomer. (Figure 465) . . . . subfamily 211.1. Bathygadinae

3 (2). A single dorsal fin. Vomer bearing teeth. (Figure 466) . . . . subfamily 211.2. Lyconinae

4 (1). First gill arch intergrown anteriorly with a membrane which reduces the size of the first gill slit. Second ray of dorsal fin resembling a spine, not jointed and sometimes serrate. . . . . . . (Figure 467) . . . . subfamily 211.3. Macrourinae

2 (1). Head very massive and soft. Dorsal fin single, united with the anal. Eyes small. Mouth inferior, situated under the vertical through the middle of the eye or behind this. Ventral fins markedly reduced or absent. (Figure 468) . . . . 212. **Macrouroididae**

Order 37. GASTEROSTEIFORMES (thesis 0—108)

2 families (213, 214):

1 (2). Three branchiostegal rays. Snout cone-shaped or only slightly tubular. [Ribs of the normal type, free.] (Figure 469) . . . . 213. **Gasterosteidae**

2 (1). Four branchiostegal rays. Snout distinctly tubular. [Ribs fused with the lateral bony plates.] (Figure 470) . . . . 214. **Aulorhynchidae**

Order 38. SYNGNATHIFORMES (thesis 0—69)

2 suborders, 7 families (215—221):

1 (8). Gills pectinate, as in most fish. [First 4—6 vertebrae elongate and modified (Figure 471); vertebrae with articular processes. Postcleithrum (Figure 472) and metapterygoid present.] Mucous canals present. (Suborder 38.1. **Aulostomoidei**, families 216—219.)

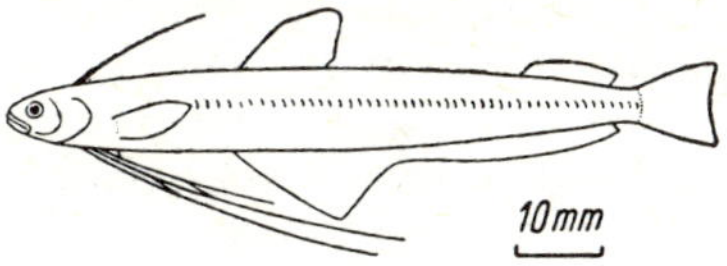

FIGURE 460. Bregmacerotidae — Bregmaceros japonicus (L. and L., 1965, fig. 228)

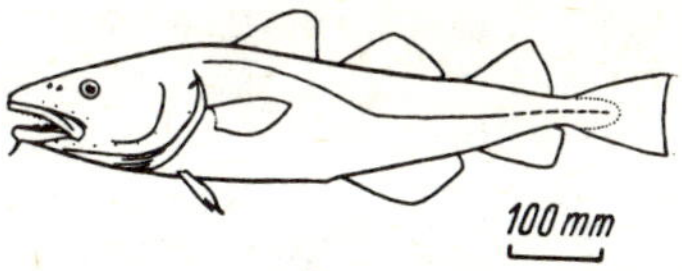

FIGURE 461. Gadidae — Gadus morhua macrocephalus (L. and L., 1965, fig. 230)

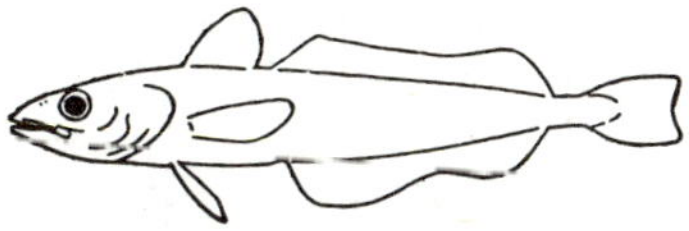

FIGURE 462. Merlucciidae (GRWM, 1966: 417, fig.)

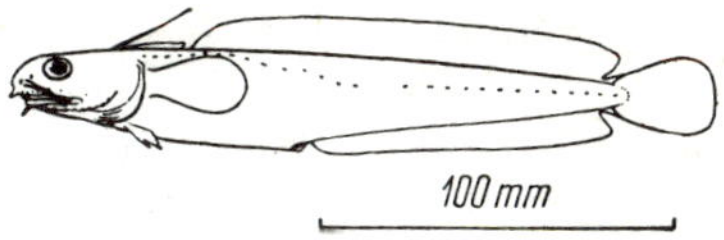

FIGURE 463. Gadidae — Enchelyopus cimbrius (Svetovidov, 1948, pl. 2, fig. 2, diagr.)

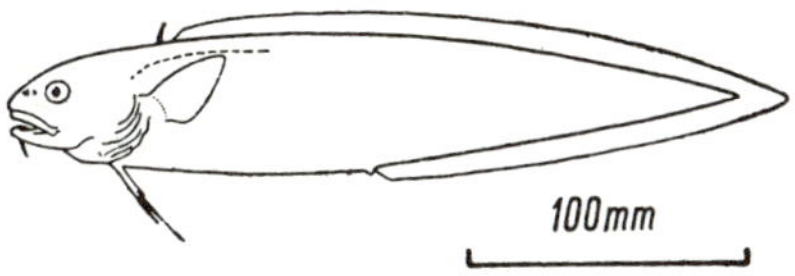

FIGURE 464. Muraenolepididae — Muraenolepis microps (Norman, 1938, fig. 2, diagr.)

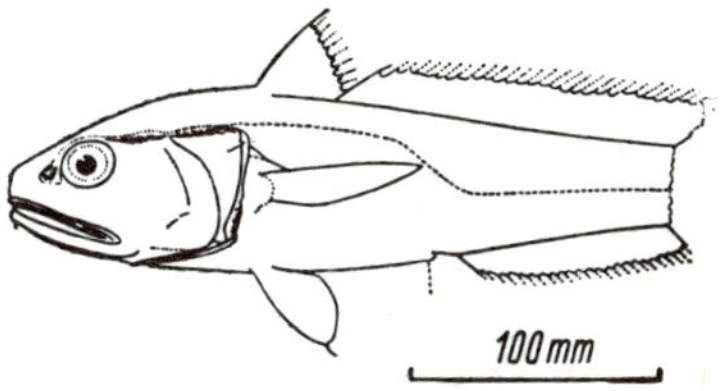

FIGURE 465. Macrouridae (Bathygadinae) — Bathygadus garretti (Gilbert and Hubbs, 1916, pl. 8, fig. 1, diagr.)

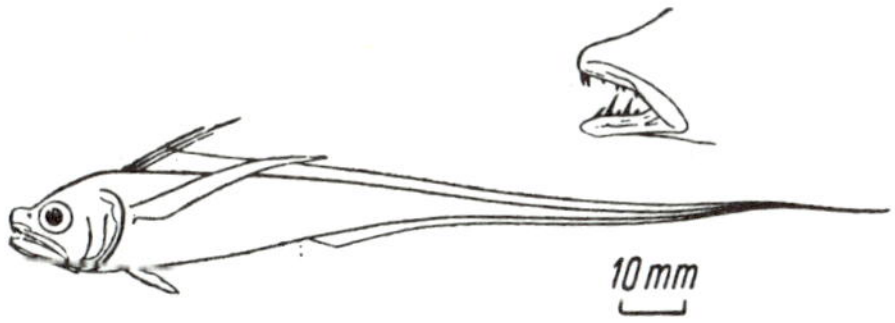

FIGURE 466. Macrouridae (Lyconinae) — Lyconus pinnatus (Günther, 1897, pl. 42, fig. C, diagr.)

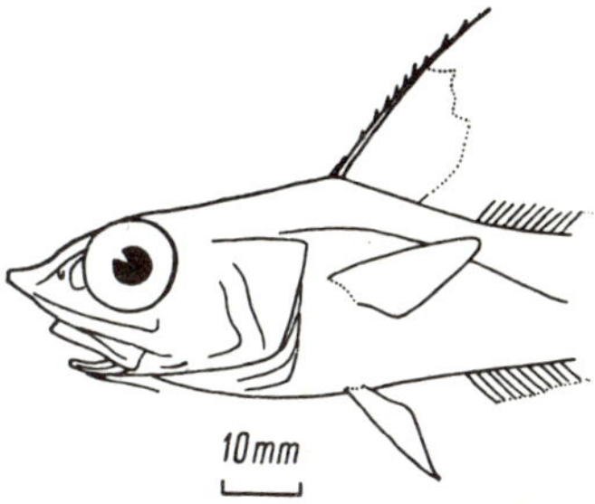

FIGURE 467. Macrouridae (Macrourinae) — Hemimacrurus acrolepis (L. and L., 1965, fig. 44).

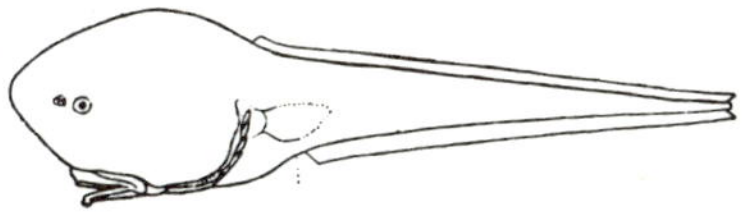

FIGURE 468. Macrouroididae — Macrouroides inflaticeps (Smith and Radcliffe, 1913, pl. 31, fig. 2, diagr.)

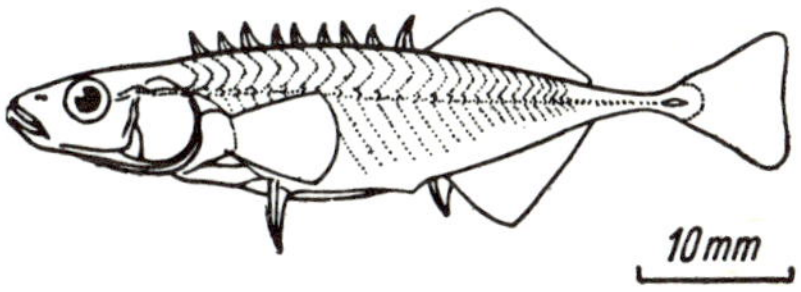

FIGURE 469. Gasterosteidae — Pungitius pungitius sinensis (Berg, 1949, fig. 696, diagr.)

2 (5). Mouth small, with teeth that are more easily distinguishable on the lower jaw. Upper jaw equal to or longer than longitudinal diameter of eye. Body greatly elongate. Lateral line present, complete. [First 4—6 vertebrae elongate, immovably connected; their transverse processes form an uninterrupted process (Figure 471). Nasal and preorbital bones absent or rudimentary.]

3 (4). Body laterally compressed, covered with ctenoid scales. First dorsal fin represented by a few isolated, thin, rather weak spiny rays. Premaxillaries not bearing teeth. Vent immediately behind the ventral fins. A barbel at the symphysis of the lower jaw. Caudal fin without a notch. (Figure 473). . .216. **Aulostomidae**

4 (3). Body vertically flattened, bare or with one row of scales along the midlines of the back (Figure 474) and belly. No isolated spiny rays at the site of the first dorsal fin, which has one base and consists only of soft rays. Premaxillaries bearing teeth. Vent situated far behind ventral fins, in front of the origin of the anal. No barbel at symphysis of lower jaw. Posterior margin of caudal fin concave; the two middle rays of the fin are elongate in the form of filaments. (Figure 475) . . . . 217. **Fistulariidae**

5 (2). Mouth very small, without teeth. Upper jaw much smaller than longitudinal diameter of eye. Body deep or moderately elongate. Lateral line absent. [First 5—6 vertebrae elongate, but their transverse processes are usually separated from each other. Nasal and preorbital bones well developed.]

6 (7). Body laterally compressed, but not very strongly, covered with bony plates and rough scales. Caudal fin situated normally, at the end of the body. (Figure 476) . . . 218. **Macrorhamphosidae**

7 (6). Body very strongly laterally compressed, as if pressed and squeezed into thin, transparent, bony shields. Caudal fin and soft dorsal situated on the ventral margin of the body; at the end of the body projects not the caudal, but the spiny dorsal fin (Figure 477) . . . . 219. **Centriscidae**

8 (1). Gills more or less fascicular. [First 3 vertebrae not elongate, united by sutures; the vertebrae do not have articular processes. Postcleithrum and metapterygoid absent.] No mucous canals. . . . . (Suborder 38.2. **Syngnathoidei**, families 215, 220, 221.)

9 (12). Two dorsal fins. Ventral fins developed. One nasal opening on each side of the head.

10 (11). First dorsal fin consisting of five isolated spines. Body covered with bony rings, as in the Syngnathidae. (Figure 748). .215. **Indostomidae**

11 (10). First dorsal fin without spiny rays, high. Body covered with individual star-shaped ossified plates. (Figure 479) . . . . 220. **Solenostomidae**

12 (9). Dorsal fin single or absent; if present, without spiny rays. Ventral fins absent. Two nasal openings on each side of the head. Body with a continuous cover of bony scutes in the form of spines . . . . 221. **Syngnathidae**

6 subfamilies:

1 (6). Males with a brood pouch under the belly.

2 (5). Eggs not covered by lateral skin folds or bony plates.

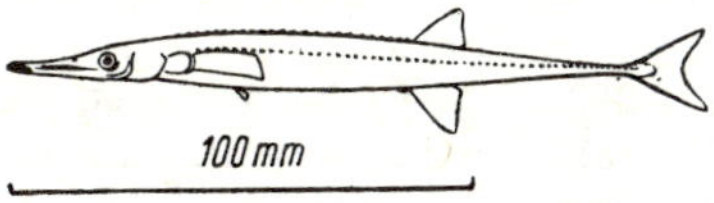

FIGURE 470. Aulorhynchidae – Aulichthys japonicus (Abe, 1958, fig. 713, diagr.)

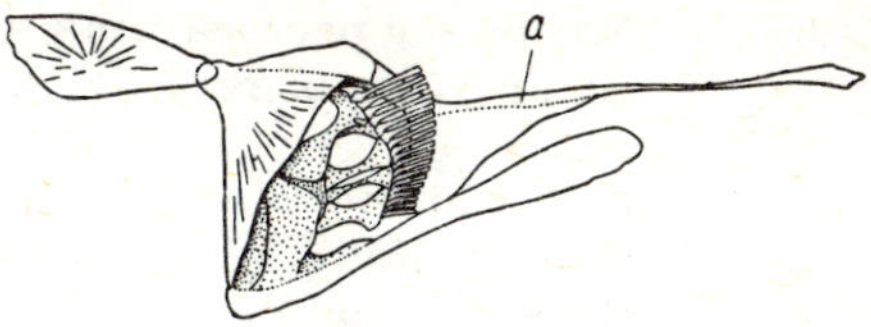

FIGURE 472. Humeral girdle of Aulostomus valentini (L. and L., 1965, fig. 249):

a – elongate postcleithrum.

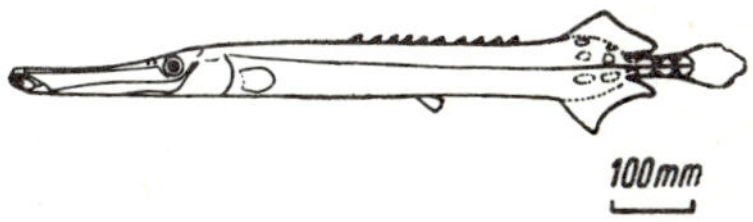

FIGURE 473. Aulostomidae – Aulostomus chinensis (L. and L., fig. 250)

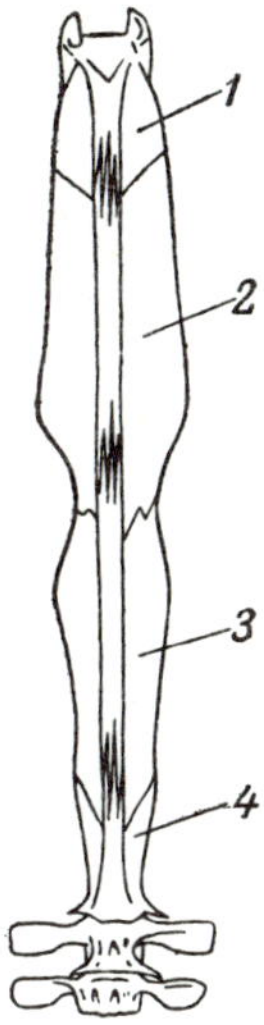

FIGURE 471. Anterior vertebrae of Fistularia petimba (L. and L., 1965, fig. 248):

1–4 – consecutive vertebrae.

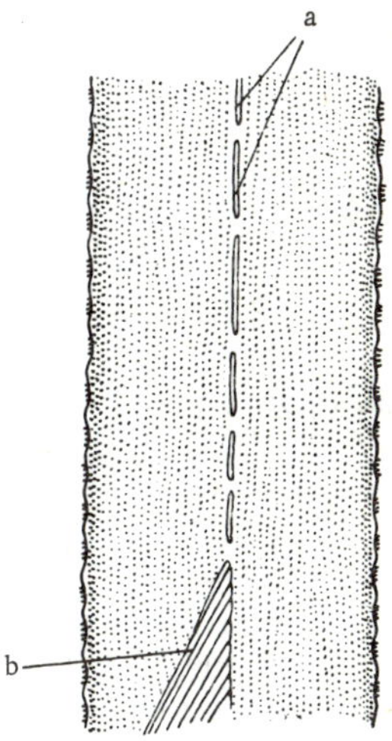

FIGURE 474. Middle dorsal row of scales in Fistularia villosa (L. and L., 1965, fig. 251, diagr.):

a – scales; b – dorsal fin.

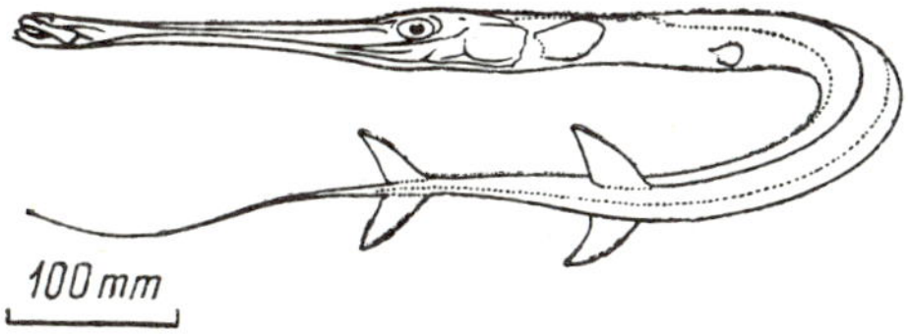

FIGURE 475. Fistulariidae – Fistularia petimba (L. and L., 1965, fig. 256)

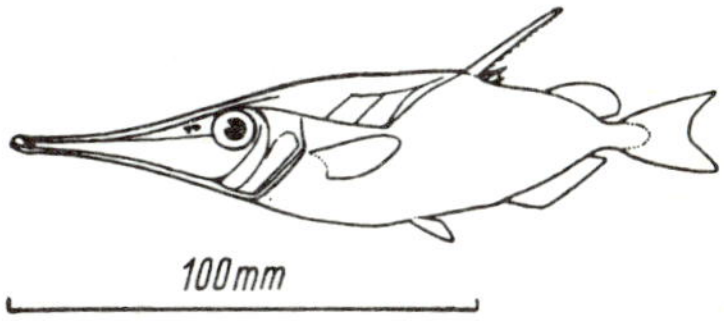

FIGURE 476. Macrorhamphosidae – Macrorhamphosus japonicus (Okada, 1955, fig. 99, diagr.)

3 (4). No anal or pectoral fins (except in very young specimens). Lateral line present. (Figure 480) . . . . subfamily 221.1. Nerophinae

4 (3). Anal and pectoral fins present. Lateral line absent. (Figure 481) . . . . subfamily 221.2. Syngnathoidinae

5 (2). Eggs covered by bony plates or lateral skin folds which intergrow at the time of spawning. Anal and pectoral fins present. Lateral line present. (Figure 482) . . . . subfamily 221.3. Doryrhamphinae

6 (1). Males with a brood pouch under the caudal part of the body.

7 (10). Brood pouch not permanently closed. Axis of head roughly coinciding with axis of body.

8 (9). Eggs not covered by bony plates or lateral skin folds. Caudal fin absent. No lateral line. (Figure 483) . . . . subfamily 221.4. Solenognathinae

9 (8). Eggs covered by lateral skin folds which grow together at the time of spawning. (Figure 484) . . . . subfamily 221.5. Syngnathinae

10 (7). Brood pouch permanently closed; there is an anterior opening which is closed by a circular muscle. Caudal part of body twisted. Axis of head at a wide angle, often a right angle, to axis of body. (Figure 485) . . . . subfamily 221.6. Hippocampinae

Order 39. LAMPRIDIFORMES (theses 0—93, 137)

6 families (222—227):

1 (4). Body very deep, laterally compressed, Soft rays of fins jointed.. [Fewer than 50 vertebrae. Ribs well developed. Posttemporale furcate.]

2 (3). Dorsal fin with a deep notch, its anterior part high, the posterior low; anal fin low, without a notch. Ventral fin with 15—17 soft rays. None of the fins has rays resembling spines. [About 46 vertebrae; vertebrae without transverse processes.] (Figure 486) . . . . 222. **Lampridae**

3 (2). Dorsal and anal fins without a notch, both fins very high. Ventral fin with 8—9 soft rays. Rays in fins faintly resembling spines. [33—34 vertebrae; vertebrae with transverse processes, directed downward.] (Figure 487) . . . . 223. **Veliferidae**

4 (1). Body not very deep, markedly thin, moderately laterally compressed, often greatly elongate. Soft rays of fins not jointed. [Far more than 50 vertebrae (90—93). Ribs absent. Posttemporale not furcate.]

5 (6). Lower ray of caudal fin strongly elongate and transformed into a threadlike appendage which is much longer than the body (in adults almost twice as long) (Figures 488, 489). Eyes telescopic. Mouth very strongly protrusible; lower jaw very long, stretching very far beyond the eyes; premaxillaries and maxillaries very short.. 227. **Stylophoridae**

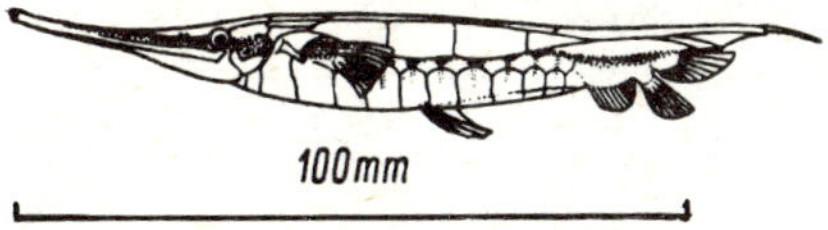

FIGURE 477. Centriscidae – Aeoliscus striagatus (Abe, 1958, fig. 709, diagr.)

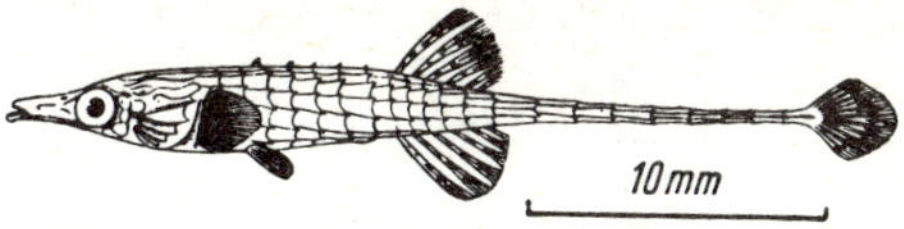

FIGURE 478. Indostomidae – Indostomus paradoxus (Berg, 1940, fig. 170)

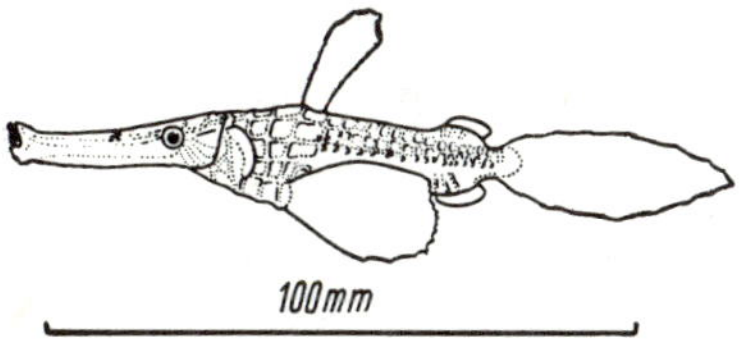

FIGURE 479. Solenostomidae – Solenostomus cyanopterus (L. and L., 1965, fig. 253)

FIGURE 480. Syngnathidae (Nerophinae) – Entelurus aequoreus (Andriyashev, 1954, fig. 100)

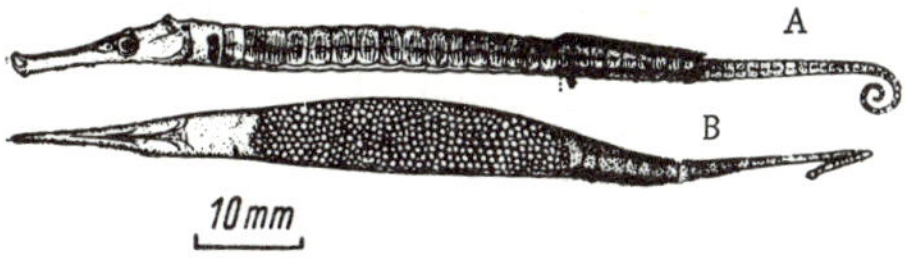

FIGURE 481. Syngnathidae (Syngnathoidinae) – Syngnathoides biaculeatus (W. and B. 1922, 4, fig. 18):

A – female; B – male with eggs in brood pouch.

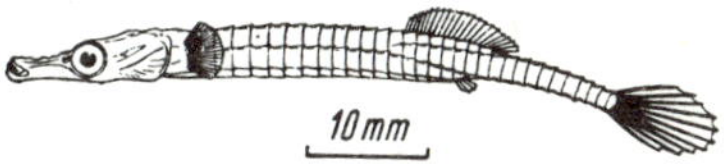

FIGURE 482. Syngnathidae (Doryrhamphinae) – Doryrhamphus melanopleura (W. and B., 1922, 4, fig. 27)

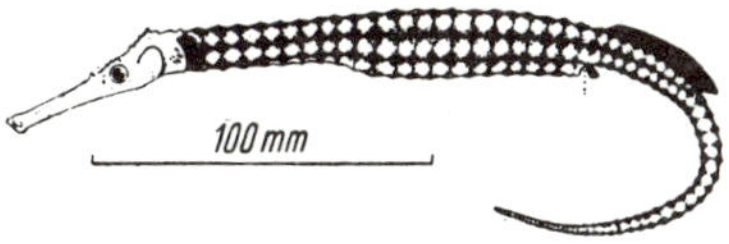

FIGURE 483. Syngnathidae (Solenognathinae) – Solenognathus lettiensis (W. and B., 1922, 4, fig. 28)

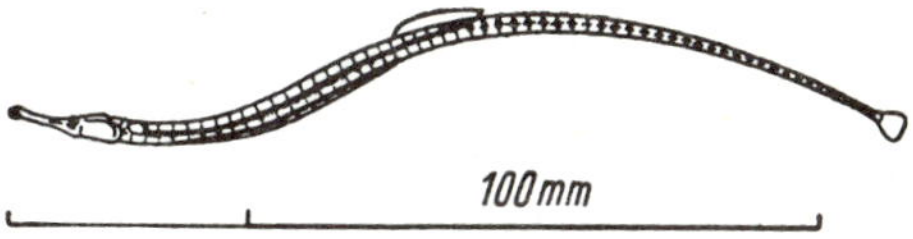

FIGURE 484. Syngnathidae (Syngnathinae) – Syngnathus schlegeli (Okada, 1955, fig. 100, diagr.)

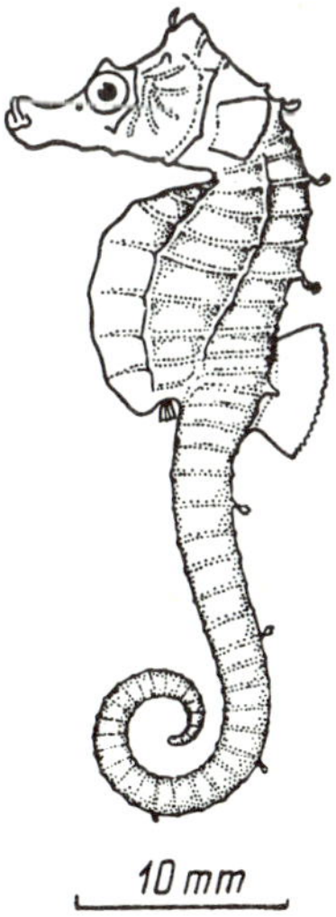

FIGURE 485. Syngnathidae (Hippocampinae) – Hippocampus japonicus (Okada, 1955, fig. 101, diagr.)

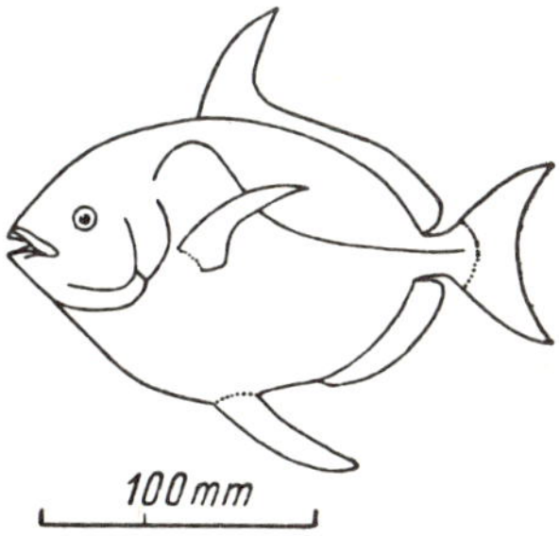

FIGURE 486. Lampridae – Lampris regius (L. and L., 1965, fig. 31)

6 (5). Caudal fin, if present, without an elongate lower ray. Eyes not telescopic. Mouth weakly protrusible, if at all; lower jaw not extending beyond the eye, its length comparable with that of the premaxillary and maxillary bones.

7 (8). Anal fin present, but short, and if poorly distinguishable, the vent is situated in the posterior part of the body, near the caudal fin. Ventral fins, if present, situated directly under the pectorals, very small, widely separated from each other and consisting of 5—6 soft rays. Anterior part of head considerably raised and projecting slightly or appreciably in front of the mouth. (Figure 490) . . . . 224. **Lophotidae**

8 (7). Anal fin absent. Vent situated in the middle part of the body. Ventral fins, if present, touching with their bases and each consisting of 1—9 soft rays. Anterior part of head not projecting in front of the mouth.

9 (10). Ventral fins modified, each transformed into a long, thin, filamentous ray (Figure 491). . . . . .225. **Regalecidae**

10 (9). Ventral fins either well developed or absent, but not transformed into long filamentous rays (Figure 492) . . .226. **Trachipteridae**

Order 40. CYPRINODONTIFORMES (theses 0—102, 157)

2 suborders, 9 families (228—236):

1(2). Vent shifted far forward and situated on the throat in adults, but occupying an intermediate position in the young. Premaxillaries almost straight, not protrusible. Scales small, deeply grown into the skin. Sensory papillae present. Blind or semiblind fishes of grottoes in the central and eastern parts of the USA. (Figures 493, 494). (Suborder 40.1. **Amblyopsoidei**, family 228) . . . . 228. **Amblyopsidae**[67]

2 (1). Vent occupying the normal position adjacent to the origin of the anal fin. Premaxillaries usually strongly curved, protrusible. Scales large, not grown deeply into the skin. No sensory papillae. (Suborder 40.2. **Cyprinodontoidei**, families 229—236.)

3 (10). Egg-laying forms.

4 (5). Premaxillaries and maxillaries fused, and snout resembling a duck's beak. Sulawesi Island. (Figure 495) . . . . 232. **Adrianichthyidae**

5 (4). Premaxillaries and maxillaries not fused, and snout not resembling a duck's beak.

6 (7). Gonopodium absent. (Figures 496—499). . . . . .229. **Cyprinodontidae**[68]

7 (6). Gonopodium present.

8 (9). Brackish waters of India. (Figure 500) . . . 230. **Horaichthyidae**

[67] Sometimes isolated into an independent order, Amblyopsiformes.

[68] A separate family is isolated, 229a. Oryziatidae (GRWM: 397; MA: 127).

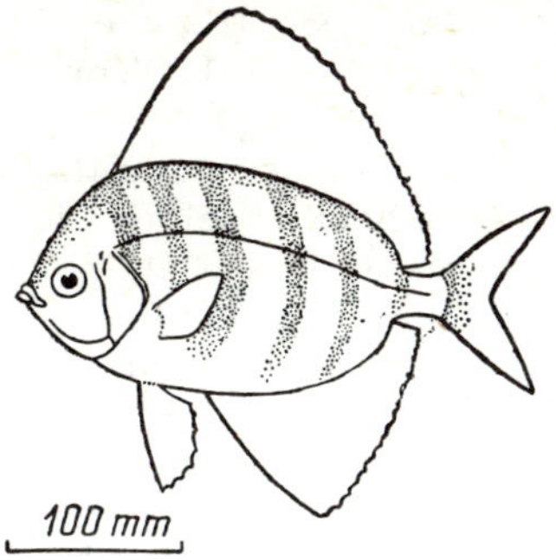

FIGURE 487. Veliferidae – Velifer hypselopterus (L. and L., 1965, fig. 30)

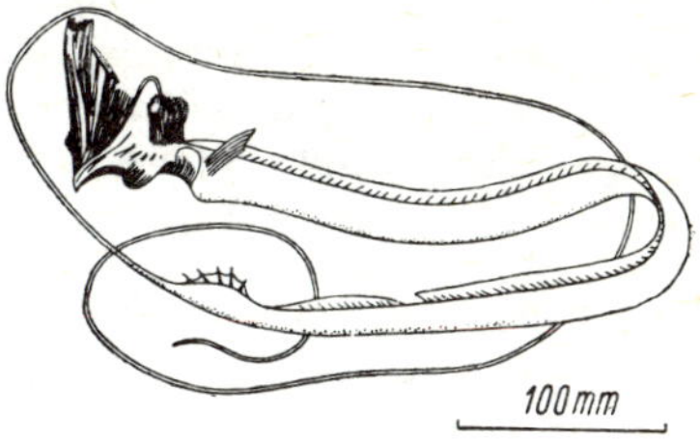

FIGURE 488. Stylephoridae – Stylephorus chordatus, ad. (Goode and Bean, 1895, pl. 94, fig. 394)

FIGURE 489. Stylephoridae – Stylephorus chordatus, juv. (Norman, 1930, fig. 36)

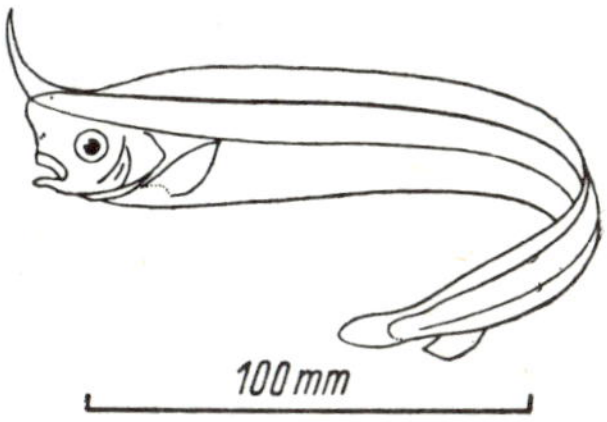

FIGURE 490. Lophotidae – Lophotus capellei (L. and L., 1965, fig. 277)

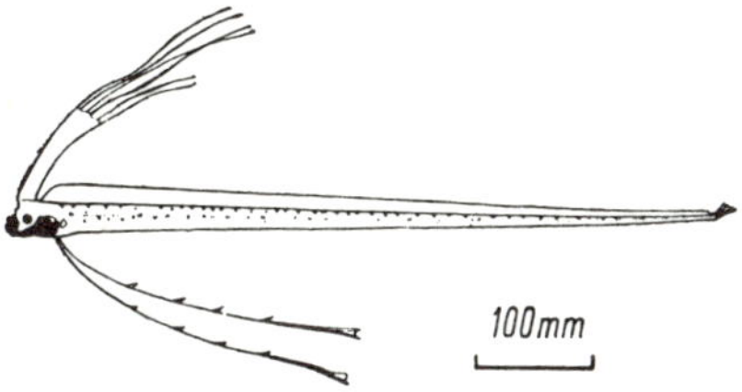

FIGURE 491. Regalecidae – Regalecus russelli (L. and L., 1965, fig. 279)

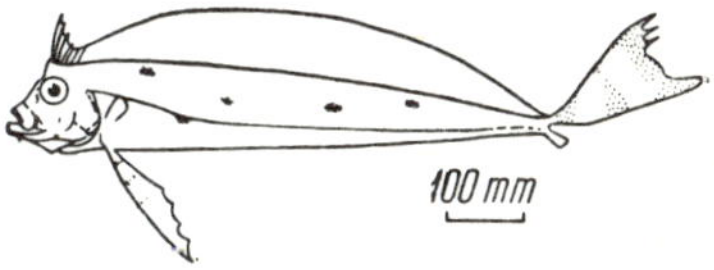

FIGURE 492. Trachipteridae – Trachipterus iris (L. and L., 1965, fig. 283)

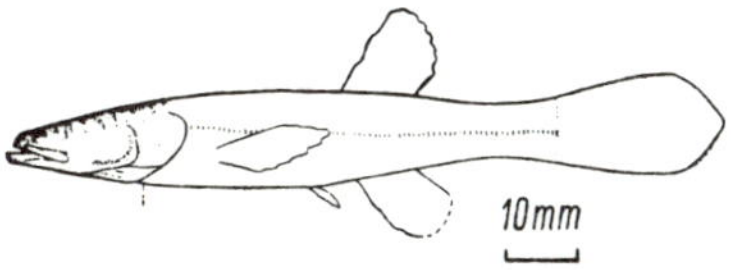

FIGURE 493. Amblyopsidae – Amblyopsis spelaeus (Jordan, 1925, fig. 332, diagr.)

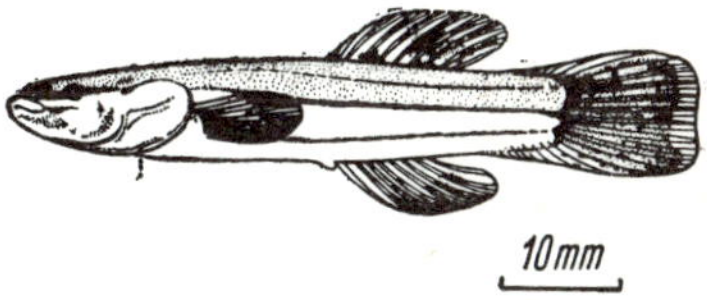

FIGURE 494. Amblyopsidae – Cholagaster cornutus (Fowler, 1935, fig. 31)

9 (8). Fresh and brackish waters of South America. (Figures 501, 502) . . . . 231. **Tomeuridae**[69]

10 (3). Viviparous forms.

11 (12). Eyes with a transverse partition; they protrude from the orbit and are raised above the surface of the head; each eye is divided across into two parts: an upper, which sticks out above the water, and a lower, which remains under the water (four-eye). Gonopodium tubular, in the form of a papilla, covered outside with scales. (Figure 503) . . . . 235. **Anablepidae**

12 (11). Eyes normal, without transverse partition.

13 (14). Males with a tubular gonopodium not covered by scales, formed by an elongate urinogenital papilla which is supported by the first ray of the anal fin; the other rays of this fin are not modified. Fresh waters of South America. (Figure 504) . . . . 234. **Jenynsiidae**

14 (13). Males without tubular gonopodium formed by a urinogenital papilla. Gonopodium either absent or formed from the first rays of the anal fin.

15 (16). Anterior (5—6) rays of anal fin rigid, separated from the other rays by a notch and much shorter than the long rays of the posterior part of the anal (Lerma River basin in Mexico). (Figure 505) . . . . 233. **Goodeidae**

16 (15). Anterior rays of anal fin much longer than the rays in the posterior part of the fin, strongly modified and transformed into a gonopodium. (Figures 506, 507) . . . . . .236. **Poeciliidae**[70]

Order 41. PHALLOSTETHIFORMES (thesis 0—43)

1 family: 237. **Phallostethidae**[71] (Figures 508, 509).

Order 42. PERCOPSIFORMES (theses 0—99, 104, 162)

2 suborders, 2 families (238, 239):

1 (2). Adipose fin present. Vent situated normally, immediately in front of the anal fin. Palatines without teeth. Caudal fin with 19 main rays (17 of them branched). Ventral fins with 8 rays. (Figure 510.) (Suborder 42.1. **Percopsidoidei**) . . . . .238. **Percopsidae**

[69] The sole species Tomeurus gracilis Eigenmann, 1909 is considered a representative not of an independent family but only of the subfamily Tomeurinae of family 236. Poeciliidae (Rosen and Bailey, 1963:35).

[70] Rosen and Bailey (1963) recognize 3 subfamilies, of which the Tomeurinae and Xenodexiinae are each represented by only one species.

[71] Family 237a. **Neostethidae** is recognized as valid (Berg, 1940: 298; GRWM:398) but MA:127 includes it in the synonymy of family 237. Phallostethidae.

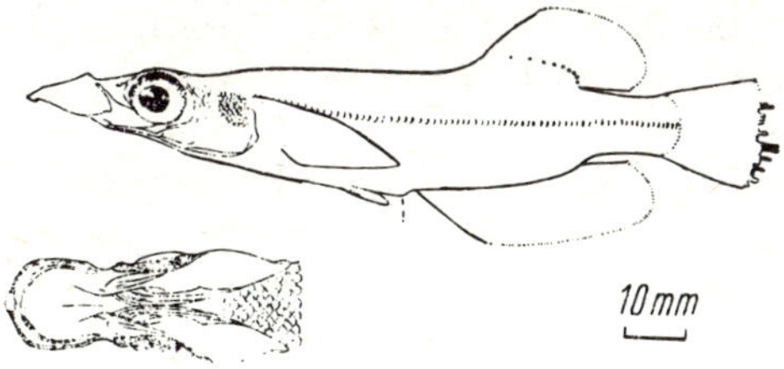

FIGURE 495. Adrianichthyidae — Adrianichthys kruyti (W. and B., 1922, 4, fig. 101, diagr.)

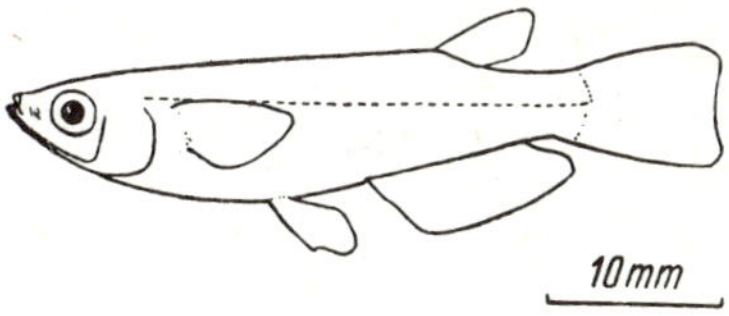

FIGURE 496. Cyprinodontidae — Oryzias latipes (L. and L., 1965, fig. 284)

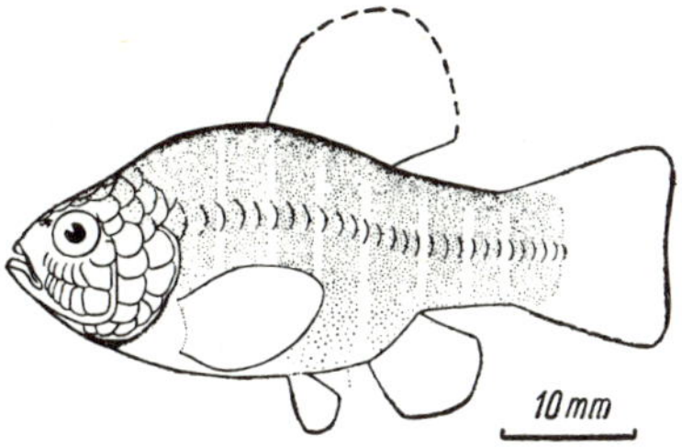

FIGURE 497. Cyprinodontidae — Cyprinodon variegatus (Jordan, 1925, fig. 323, diagr.)

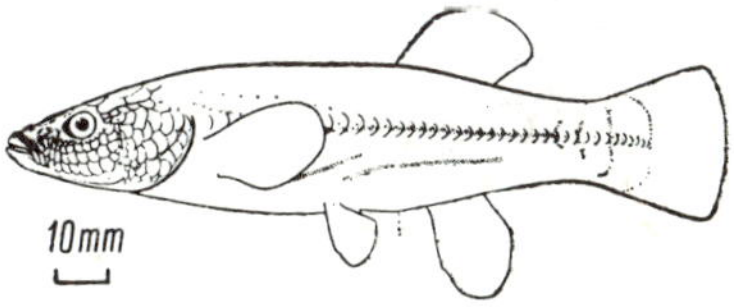

FIGURE 498. Cyprinodontidae — Fundulus majalis (Jordan, 1925, fig. 325, diagr.)

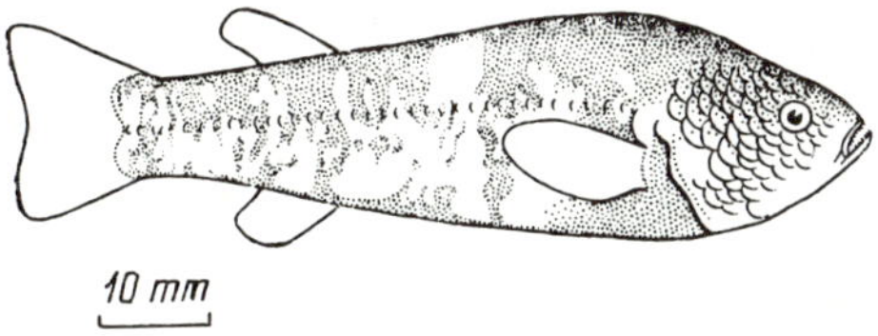

FIGURE 499. Cyprinodontidae — Empetrichthys merriami (Jordan, 1925, fig. 328, diagr.)

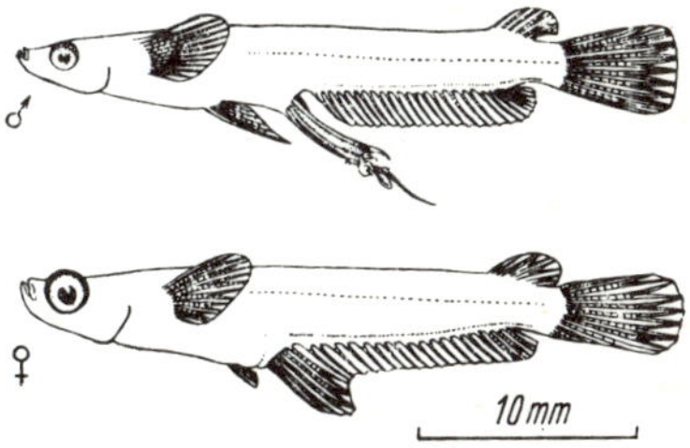

FIGURE 500. Horaichthyidae — Horaichthys setnai (Nikol'skii, 1954, fig. 184)

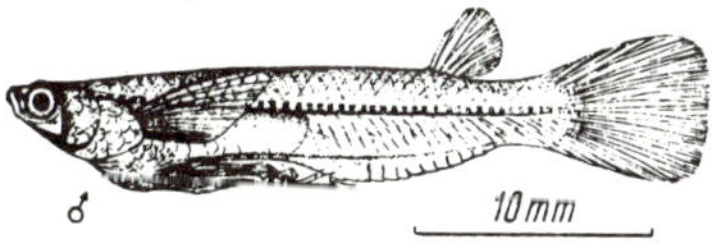

FIGURE 501. Tomeuridae — Tomeurus gracilis (Rosen and Bailey, 1963, fig. 7, a)

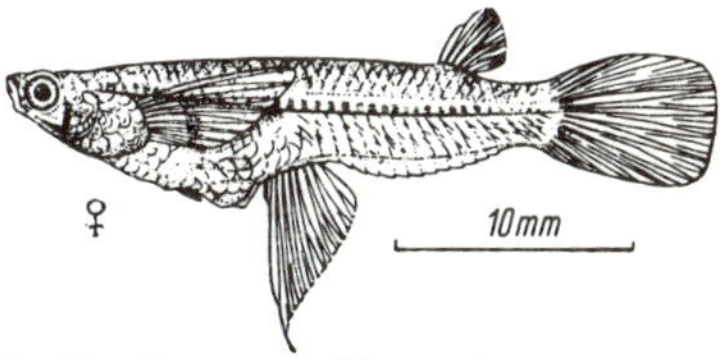

FIGURE 502. Tomeuridae — Tomeurus gracilis (Rosen and Bailey, 1963, fig. 7, b)

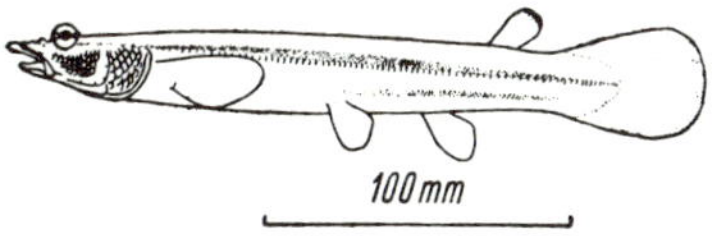

FIGURE 503. Anablepidae — Anableps dovii (Jordan, 1925, fig. 322, diagr.)

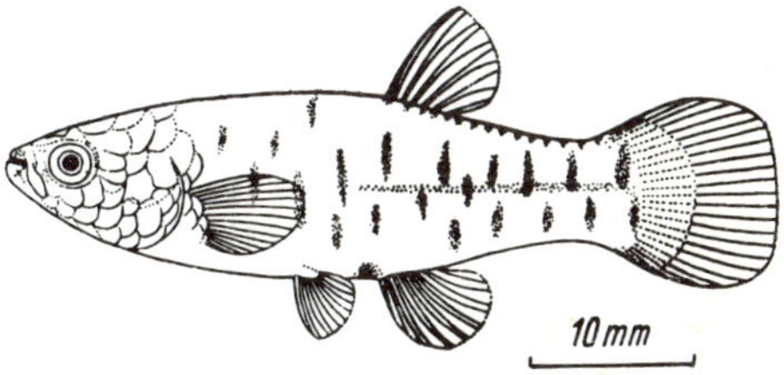

FIGURE 504. Jenynsiidae — Fitzroyia alternimaculata (Fowler, 1940, fig. 12)

2 (1). Adipose fin absent. Vent on the throat (in adults). Palatines and vomer with teeth. Caudal fin with 18 main rays (16 of which are branched). Ventral fins with 7 rays. (Figure 511) (Suborder 42.2. **Aphredoderoidei**) . . . . . 239. **Aphrederodidae**

Order 43. STEPHANOBERYCIFORMES (theses 0—95, 164)

5 families (240—244):

1 (6). Body oblong, its depth less than the length of the head. Lateral line absent.
2 (5). Body covered with scales. Origin of anal fin always behind vertical of origin of dorsal fin. Head of moderate size, usually with ridges and projections. Ventral fins inserted under pectorals.
3 (4). Shortened rays of caudal fin numerous, passing far in front of the base of the caudal fin, almost reaching the middle of the caudal peduncle and projecting outward in the form of individual spines (Figure 512). . . . . .240. **Stephanoberycidae**
4 (3). Shortened rays of caudal fin not numerous, not passing in front of base of caudal fin, but if projecting outward, then they do have the character of spines. (Figure 513) . . . .244. **Melamphaeidae**
5 (2). Body bare. Origin of anal fin on the vertical of the origin of the dorsal fin. Head markedly enlarged, without ridges and projections. Ventral fins inserted behind pectorals. (Figure 514) . . . . 241 (120). **Rondeletiidae** (see thesis 24—4)
6 (1). Body short and deep, its depth exceeding the length of the head. Lateral line present.
7 (8). Base of pectoral fins horizontal. Ventral fins inserted behind base of pectorals. (Figure 515) . . . . . . 242. **Anoplogasteridae**
8 (7). Base of pectoral fins vertical. Ventral fins inserted under the base of the pectorals. (Figure 516) . . . . 243. **Korsogasteridae**

Order 44. BERYCIFORMES (theses 0—106, 126, 138, 140, 142, 144, 147, 148, 149)

11 families (245—255):

1 (2). There is a pair of hyoid barbels behind the symphysis of the lower jaw. First ray of ventral fins soft, jointed; only 7—8 rays in the ventrals. (Figure 517). . . . . 245. **Polymyxiidae**
2 (1). No hyoid barbels. First ray of ventral fins spiny.
3 (4). Body with a distinctive armor of large, hard scales. Ventral fins with one large, thick, strong spine and 3 small, soft rays; first dorsal fin separated from second and represented by 5—6 long, thick, strong spines that are not connected by a membrane and resemble the spine in the ventral fins. (Figure 518) . . . . 250. Monocentridae

43, 44

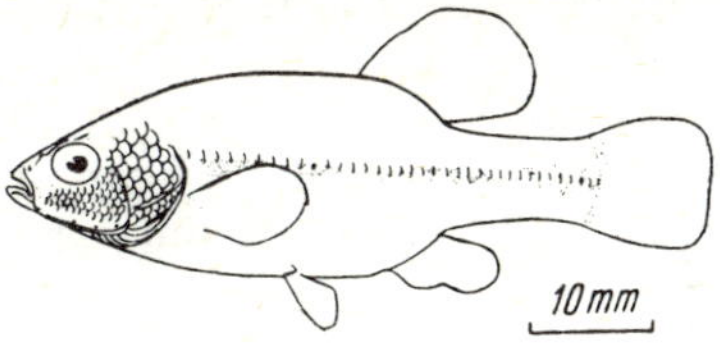

FIGURE 505. Goodeidae – Characodon variatus (J. and E., 1900, fig. 295, diagr.)

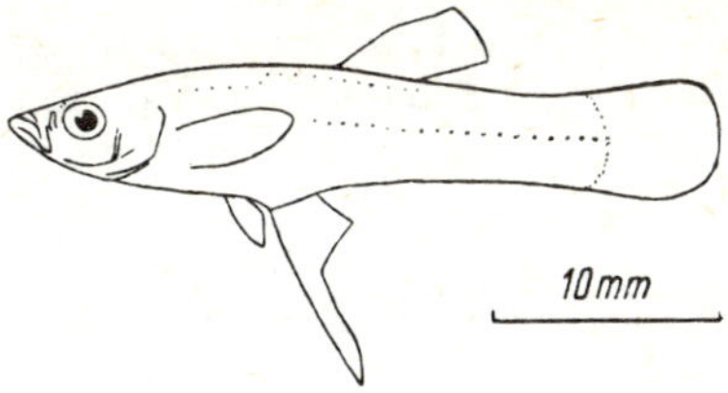

FIGURE 506. Poeciliidae – Gambusia affinis (L. and L., 1965, fig. 285)

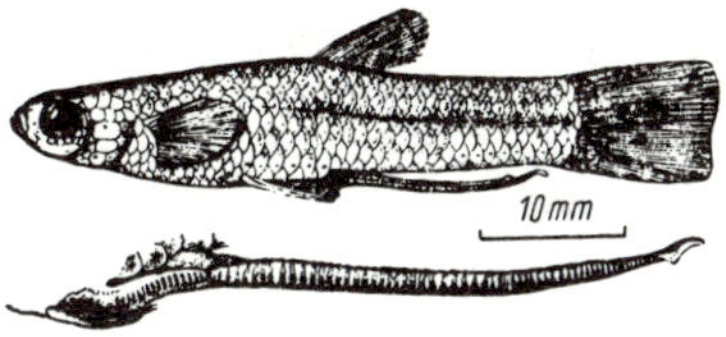

FIGURE 507. Poeciliidae – Xenodexia ctenolepis (Hubbs, 1950, pl. 1, figs. 1, 2)

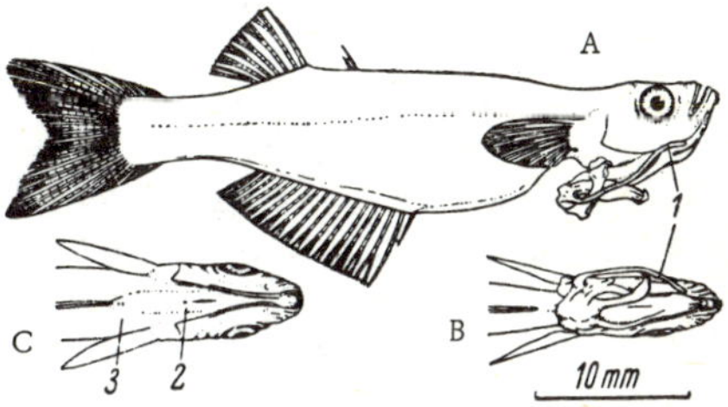

FIGURE 508. Phallostethidae – Gulophallus eximius (M., 1955, 1, fig. 126):

A – male, from the side; B – head of male, ventral; C – head of female, ventral.
1 – priapium; 2 – vent; 3 – genital opening.

FIGURE 509. Neostethidae (GRWM, 1966:418, fig.)

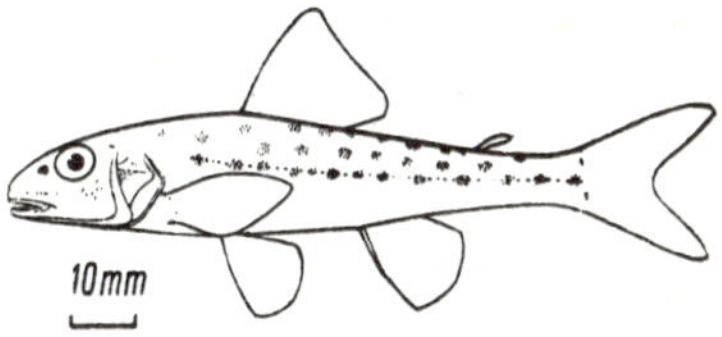

FIGURE 510. Percopsidae – Percopsis omiscomaycus (Jordan, 1925, fig. 360, diagr.)

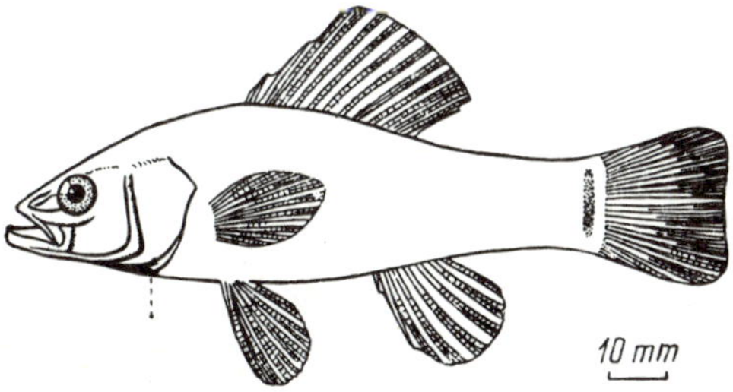

FIGURE 511. Aphredoderidae – Aphredoderus sayanus (Jordan, 1925, fig. 337)

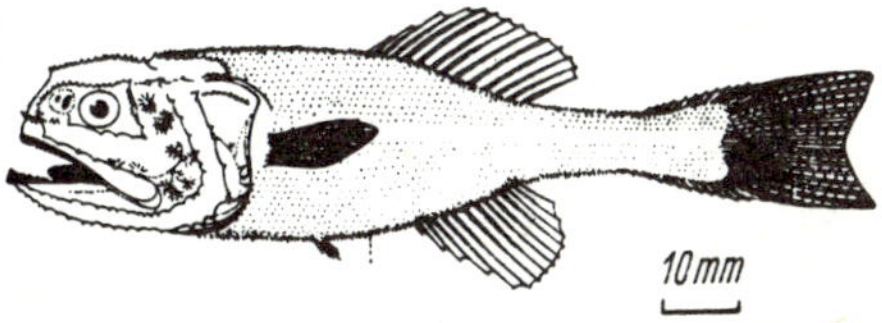

FIGURE 512. Stephanoberycidae – Stephanoberyx monae (Goode and Bean. 1895, pl. 55, fig. 206)

4 (3). No armor on the body and no individual spines in the first dorsal and in the ventral fins.

5 (6). A large luminescent organ under the eye. Dorsal fin with 1 or 2 bases; 4—5 spiny rays in dorsal fin, 2 in the anal (Figure 519) . . . . 251—252. **Anomalopidae**[72]

6 (5). No luminescent organ under the eye.

7 (8). Spiny ray of ventral fins flattened and looking like a plate. Spiny rays absent in dorsal and anal fins. (Figure 520) . . . . 247. **Diretmidae**[73]

8 (7). Spiny ray of ventral fins not flattened. Spiny rays present in dorsal and anal fins.

9 (10). Dorsal fin with a deep incision. Opercular bones strongly serrate. Scales distinctly ctenoid, coarse, hard. Dorsal fin with 10—13, less often 7 well developed spiny rays; anal with 4, more rarely 3. Ventral fins with 1 spiny and 7 branched rays (Figure 521). 253. **Holocentridae**[74]

10 (9). Dorsal fin without an incision.

11 (14). More than 5 soft rays in ventral fins.

12 (13). Abdomen generally with a row of keeled or serrate scales in the middle. Base of anal fin smaller than base of dorsal. Ventral fins with 1 spiny and 6, less often 7 soft rays. Anal fin with 1—2, more rarely 3 spiny rays. (Figure 522) . . . . 249. **Trachichthyidae**

13 (12). Abdomen not serrate. Base of anal fin larger than base of dorsal. Ventral fins with 1 spiny and from 7 (rarely) to 13 (rarely), usually about 10 soft rays. Anal fin with 4 spiny rays. (Figure 523) . . . . 246. **Berycidae**

14 (11). Ventral fins with 5 soft rays which if split near their base may be taken for 10 rays.

15 (16). Body low. Ventral fins much smaller than pectorals, their rays not split. Anterior rays of dorsal fin not elongate. (Figure 524) . . . . 255. **Gibberichthyidae**

16 (15). Body deep. Ventral fins much larger than pectorals, their rays split near the base so that the impression is gained of there being 10 rays. Anterior rays of dorsal fin strongly elongate. (Figure 525) . . . . 248. **Caristiidae**

(see thesis 50.1.1—45)

[72] The genus Trachyberyx Roule has been isolated into a separate family, Trachyberycidae (see Golvan, 1962: 88), but GRWM include this family in the synonymy of family 296. Bramidae.

[73] A separate family has been isolated, 247a. **Paradiretmidae** (Whitley, 1951), with spiny rays in the dorsal and anal fins.

[74] The genus Sorosichthys Whitley, 1945 is isolated into a separate family, 254. **Sorosichthyidae** (see Golvan, 1962: 89) but GRWM (1966: 398) include the genus in the synonymy of family 249. **Trachichthyidae**, even though it differs in the long base of the spiny dorsal fin.

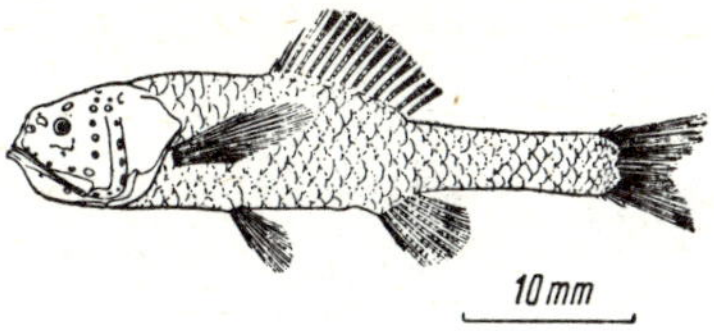

FIGURE 513. Melamphaeidae—*Melamphaes opisthopterus* (Parr, 1933, fig. 7)

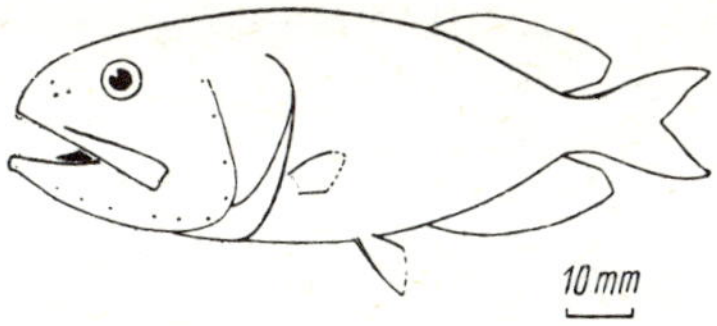

FIGURE 514. Rondeletiidae – *Rondeletia bicolor* (Goode and Bean, 1895, fig. 77, diagr.)

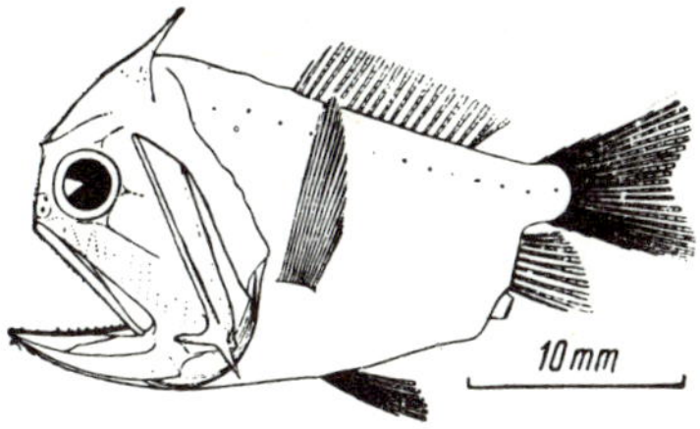

FIGURE 515. Anoplogasteridae – *Anoplogaster cornutus* (Parr, 1933, fig. 5)

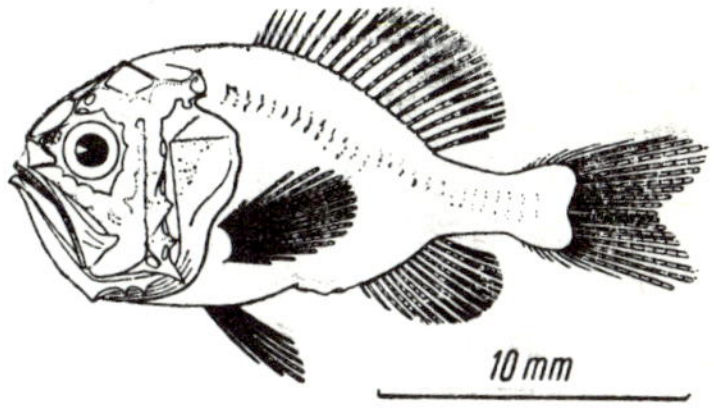

FIGURE 516. Korsogasteridae – *Korsogaster nanus* (Parr, 1933, fig. 3)

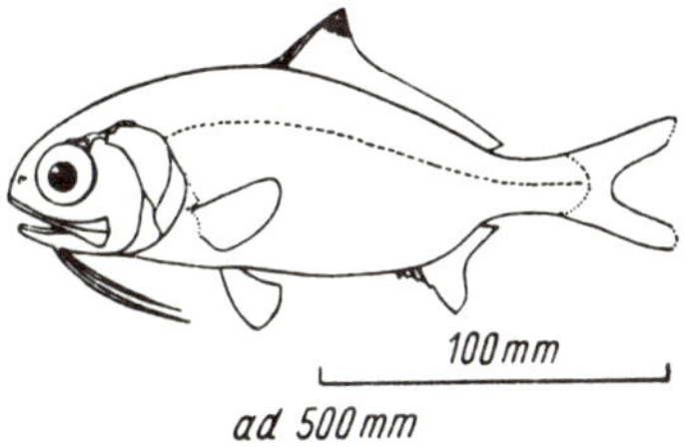

FIGURE 517. Polymixiidae – *Polymixia japonica* (L. and L., 1965, fig. 286)

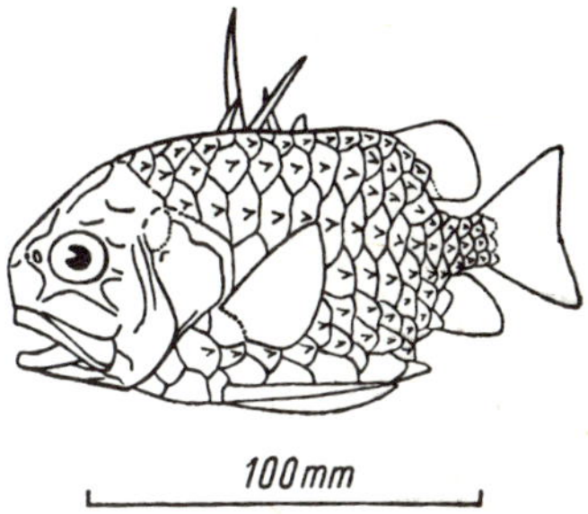

FIGURE 518. Monocentridae – *Monocentris japonicus* (L. and L., 1965, fig. 35)

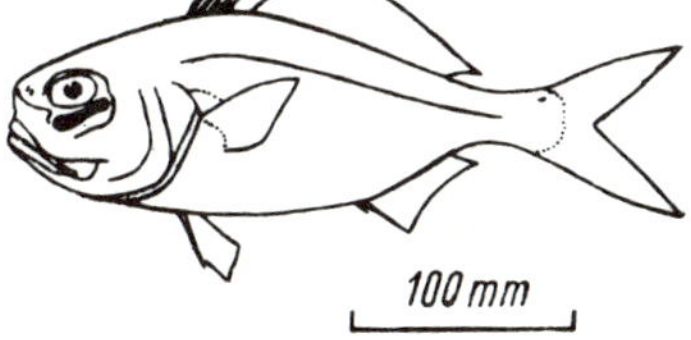

FIGURE 519. Anomalopidae – *Anomalops katoptron* (L. and L., 1965, fig. 52)

Order 45. ZEIFORMES[75] (thesis 0—167)

2 families (256, 257):

1 (2). Scales either absent or relatively large, ctenoid, but if small and cycloid, they are not arranged in vertically drawn-out rows. Mouth relatively large, oblique, sometimes almost superior. Maxillary bone generally large. Four gills. (Figures 527—530) . . . . 256. Zeidae[76]

2 (1). Scales small, vertically elongate, arranged in vertically drawn-out rows. Mouth small, superior, almost vertical. Maxillary bone very short. $3\,^1/_2$ gills. [46 vertebrae.] (Figure 531) . . . . 257. Grammicolepididae

Order 46. MUGILIFORMES (thesis 0—128)

2 suborders, 3 families (258—260):

1 (2). Lateral line well developed. Mouth very large. Teeth strong, pointed, set in deep alveoli. Maxillary with an accessory small bone. Gill rakers atrophied. Head long, tapering. Pectoral fins set quite low. There are 24 vertebrae. (Figure 532.) (Suborder 46.1. **Sphyraenoidei,** family 258) . . . . 258. **Sphyraenidae**

2 (1). Lateral line absent or rudimentary. Mouth small or of moderate size. Teeth absent or very small and not always set in deep alveoli. Maxillary without an accessory bone. Gill rakers long and thin. (Suborder 46.1. **Mugiloidei,** families 259—260.)

3 (4). Head flattened, short and wide. Fewer than 30 vertebrae (24—26). [Stomach croplike, intestine long; silt-eaters.] (Figures 533—535) . . . . 259. **Mugilidae**

4 (3). Head more or less elongate. More than 30 vertebrae (32—60). [Stomach not croplike; carnivorous forms.] (Figures 536—538). . . . . 260. Atherinidae

Order 47. POLYNEMIFORMES (thesis 0—71)

1 family: 262. Polynemidae (Figure 539).

[75] Family 329. Caproidae (Antigoniidae) (Figure 526) is treated in the order Perciformes (see thesis 50.1.1—37).

[76] Three separate families are isolated: 256a. Parasenidae (Figure 528), 256b. Macrurocyttidae (Figure 529), and 256c. Oreosomatidae (Figure 530).

[77] Two separate families have been isolated: 26a. Melanotaeniidae and 260b. Isonidae (Rosen, 1964: 217—268). See footnote to thesis 0—128.

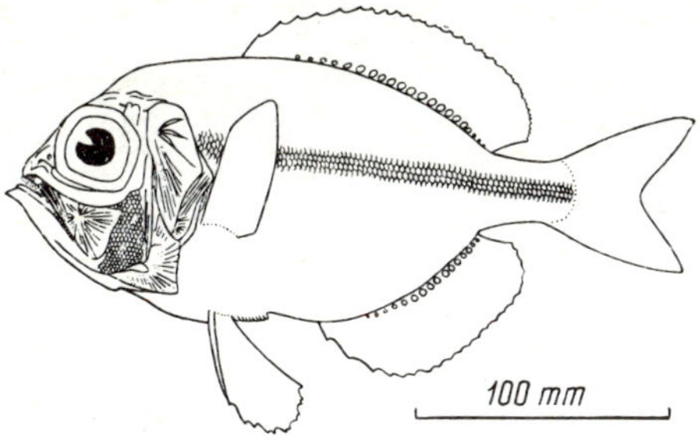

FIGURE 520. Diretmidae – Diretmus argenteus (M., 1955, III, fig. 145, diagr.)

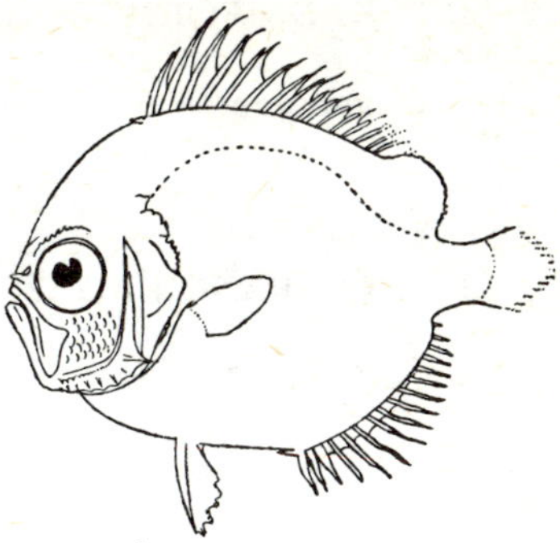

FIGURE 520A. Paradiretmidae – Paradiretmus circularis (Whitley, 1948, fig. 6)

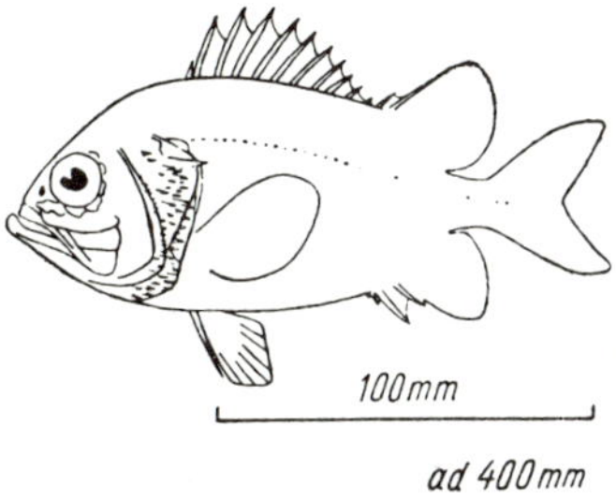

IGURE 521. Holocentridae – Ostichthys japoicus (L. and L., 1965, fig. 294)

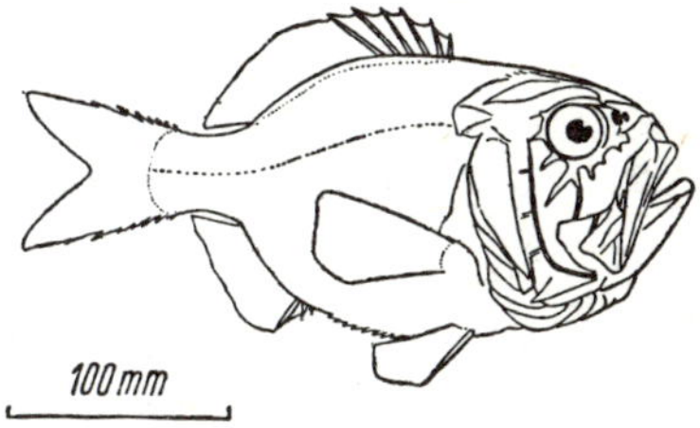

FIGURE 522. Trachichthyidae – Hoplostethus mediterraneus (L. and L., 1965, fig. 51)

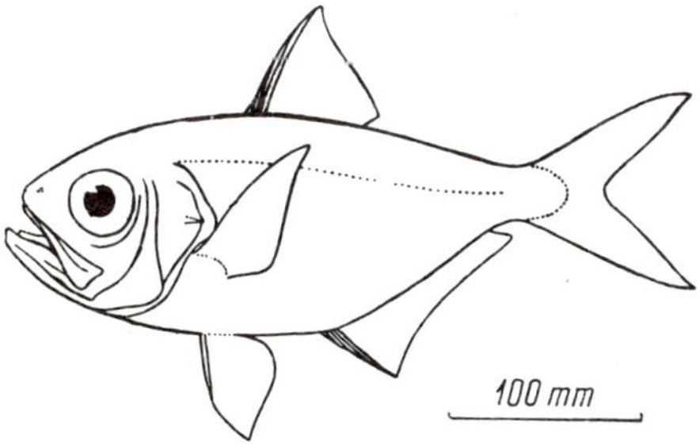

[GURE 523. Berycidae – Beryx splendens
. and L., 1965, fig. 50)

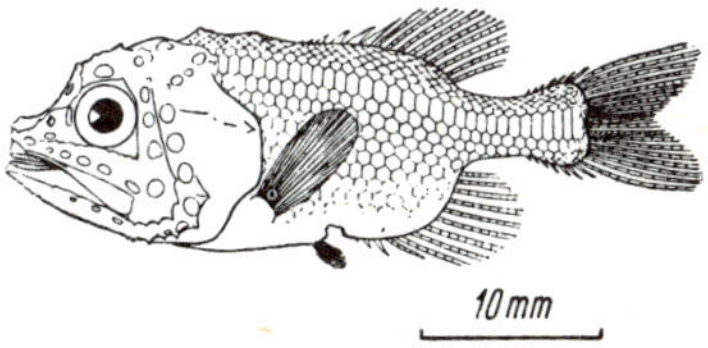

FIGURE 524. Gibberichthyidae – Gibberichthys pumilus (Parr, 1933, fig. 1)

Order 48. CHANNIFORMES (thesis 0—88)

1 family: **Channidae** (Figure 540).

Order 49. SYNBRANCHIFORMES (thesis 0—52)

2 suborders, 3 families (263—265):

1 (2). Dorsal and anal fins well developed and supported by rays. Ventral fins present but very small (consisting only of 2 rays), situated on the throat immediately behind the gill opening. Mouth small. [Parasphenoid not united with frontals. 75 vertebrae.] (Suborder 49.1. **Alabetoidei**, family 263.) (Figure 541) . . . . 263. **Alabetidae**[78]

2 (1). Dorsal and anal fins represented by skin folds without rays. Ventral fins absent. Mouth of moderate size. [Parasphenoid united with frontals by a suture. 100—188 vertebrae.] (Suborder 49.2. **Synbranchoidei**, families 264, 265.)

3 (4). Body bare. [No air sacs resembling lungs.] . . . . 264. **Synbranchidae**

3 subfamilies:

1 (2). Gills well developed, 4 pairs. (Figure 542). . . . . subfamily 264.1. Synbranchinae

2 (1). Gills rudimentary or absent.

3 (4). Gills rudimentary, 3 pairs. (Figure 543) . . . . subfamily 264.2. Monopterinae

4 (3). Gills absent on three anterior gill arches. Eyes absent. No caudal fin . . . . . . subfamily 264.3. Typhlosynbranchinae

4 (3). Body covered with scales. [There is a pair of air sacs resembling lungs and communicating with the gill cavity.] (Figure 544) . . . . 265. **Amphipnoidae**

Order 50. PERCIFORMES (theses 0—90, 129, 170)

Key to suborders of the order Perciformes (50.1—50.16)

1 (2). Supraoccipital bone in males with a peculiar serrate crest and a hooklike appendage which supports the ligament of the developing eggs (Figure 545). [Swim bladder contained in a bony tube in the formation of which participate the enlarged and superimposed ribs (pairs V—X).] (Figure 546) . . . . suborder 50.15. **Kurtoidei**

[78] Sometimes isolated into a separate order, Alabiformes (Golvan, 1962 : 72).

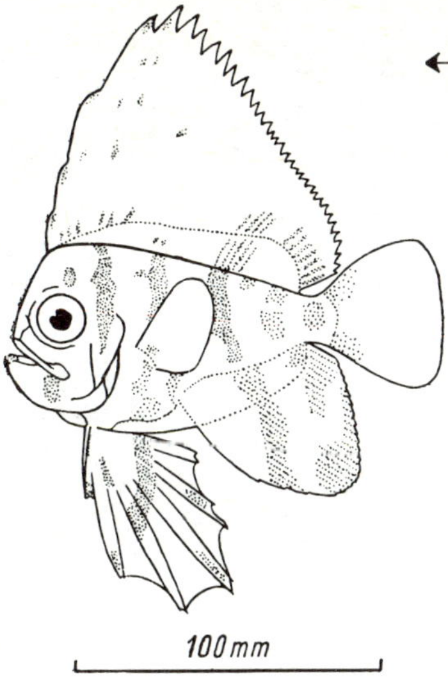

FIGURE 525. Caristiidae – *Caristius macropus* (L. and L., 1965, fig. 46)

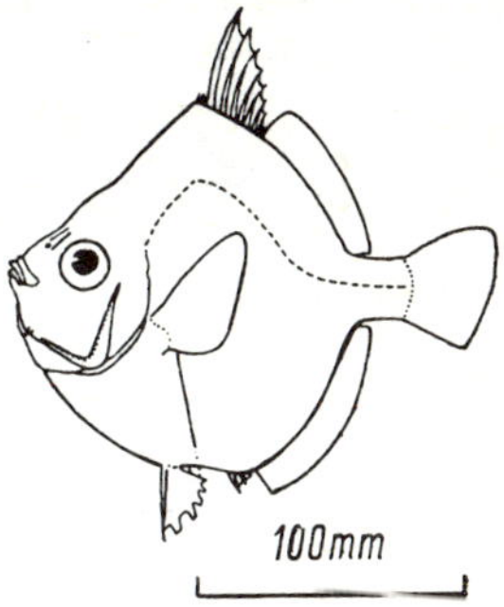

FIGURE 526. Caproidae (Antigoniidae) – *Antigonia rubescens* (L. and L., 1965, fig. 296)

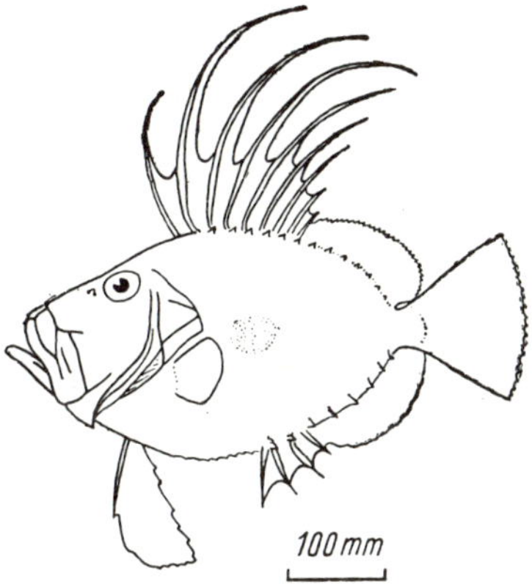

FIGURE 527. Zeidae – *Zeus japonicus* (L. (L. and L., 1965, fig. 48)

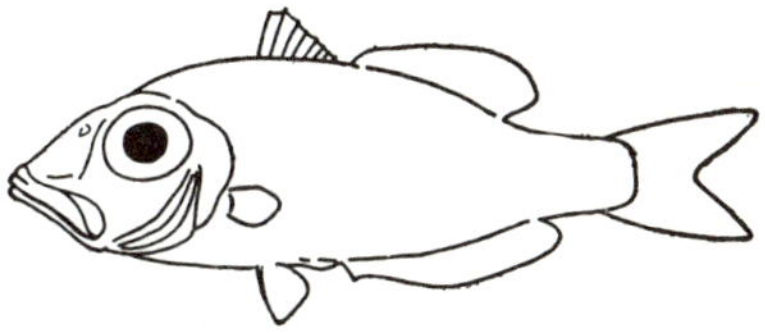

FIGURE 528. Parazenidae (GRWM, 1966:419, fig.)

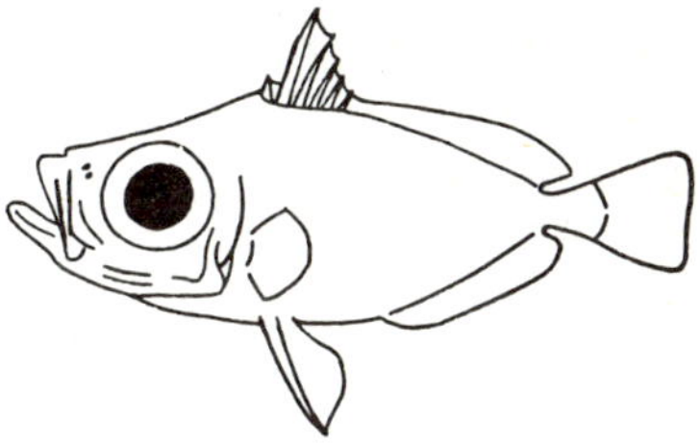

FIGURE 529. Macrurocyttidae (GRWM, 1966:419, fig.)

FIGURE 530. Oreosomatidae (GRWM, 1966:419, fig.)

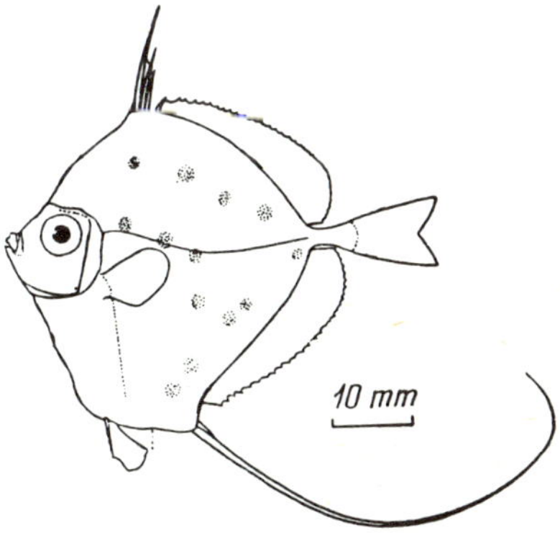

FIGURE 531. Grammicolepididae – *Xenolepedichthys dalgleishi* (L. and L., 1965, fig. 297)

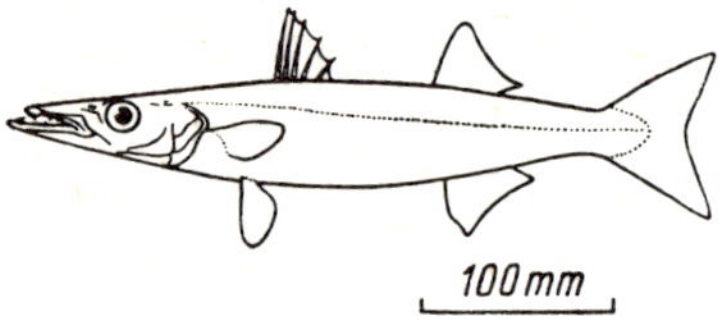

FIGURE 532. Sphyraenidae — Sphyraena pinguis (Okada, 1955, fig. 110, diagr.)

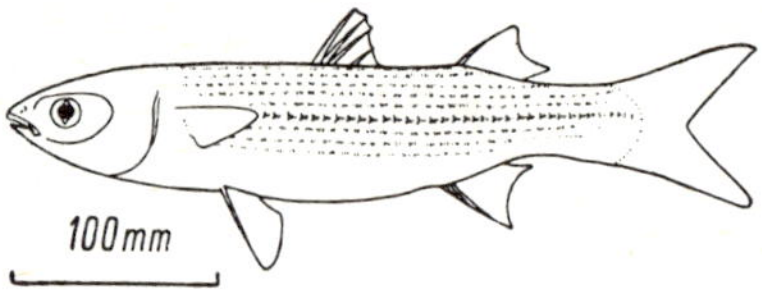

FIGURE 533. Mugilidae — Mugil cephalus (Berg, 1949, fig. 724, diagr.)

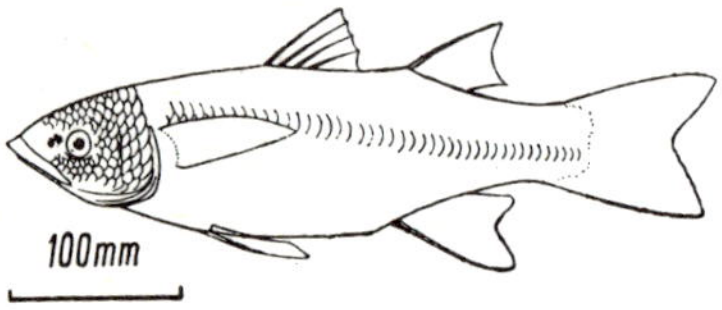

FIGURE 534. Mugilidae — Cestraeus goldiei (W. and B., 1922, 4, fig. 68, diagr.)

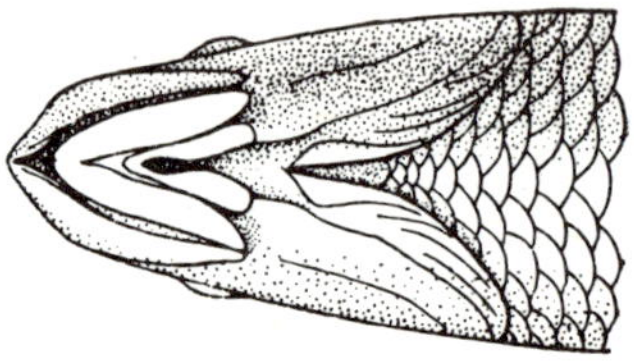

FIGURE 535. Mugilidae — Cestraeus goldiei (W. and B., 1922, 4, fig. 69).

Head, ventral.

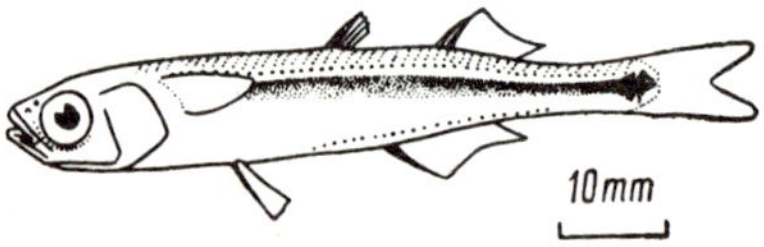

FIGURE 536. Atherinidae — Atherion elymus (Okada, 1955, fig. 112, diagr.)

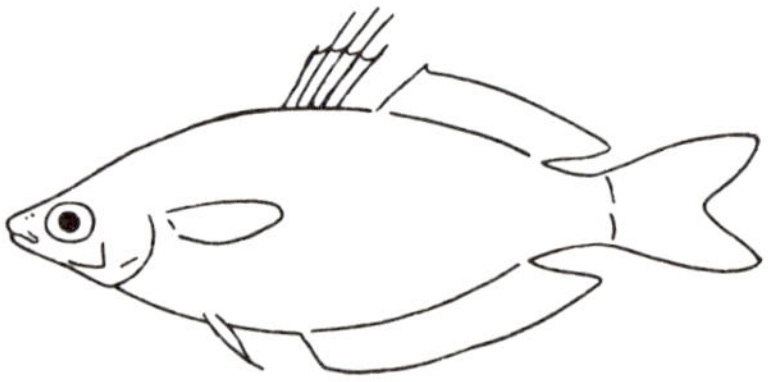

FIGURE 537. Melanotaeniidae (GRWM, 1966:418, fig.)

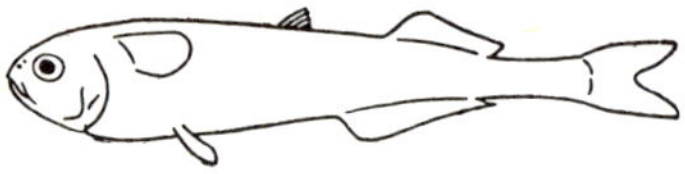

FIGURE 538. Isonidae (GRWM, 1966:418, fig.)

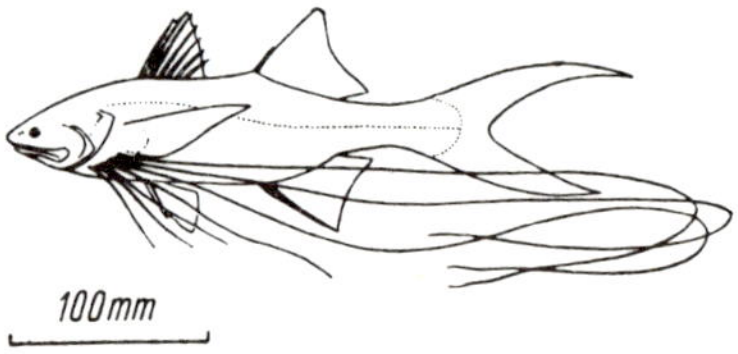

FIGURE 539. Polynemidae — Polynemus paradiseus (Fowler, 1937, fig. 216, diagr.)

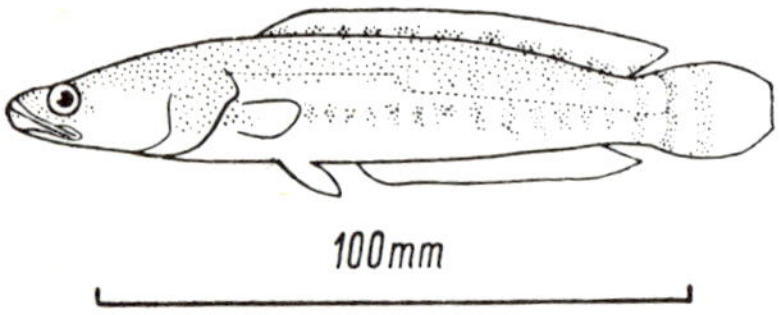

FIGURE 540. Channidae — Channa (Ophicephalus) maculatus (Nichols, 1943, fig. 127, diagr.)

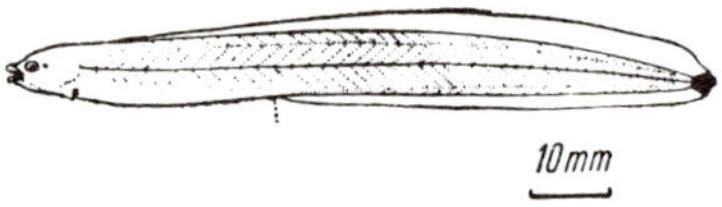

FIGURE 541. Alabetidae — Cheilobranchus dorsalis (Richardson, 1844, pl. 30, fig. 1, diagr.)

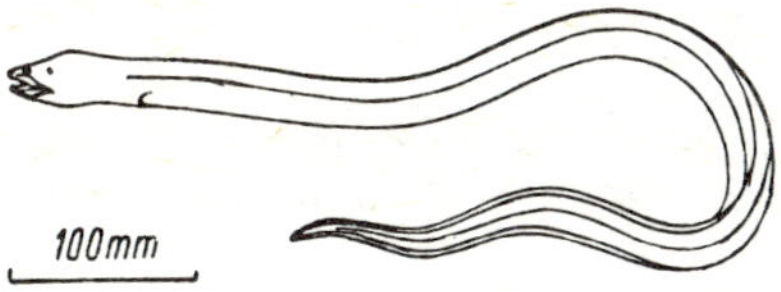

FIGURE 542. Synbranchidae (Synbranchinae) – *Synbranchus bengalensis* (Chevey, 1935, fig. 14, diagr.)

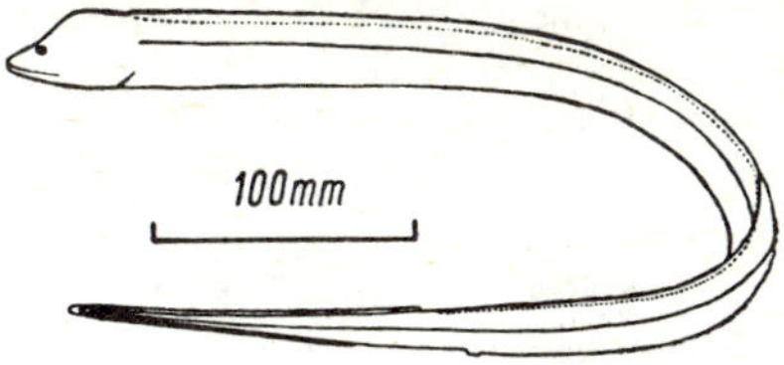

FIGURE 543. Synbranchidae (Monopterinae) – *Fluta alba* (L. and L., 1965, fig. 10)

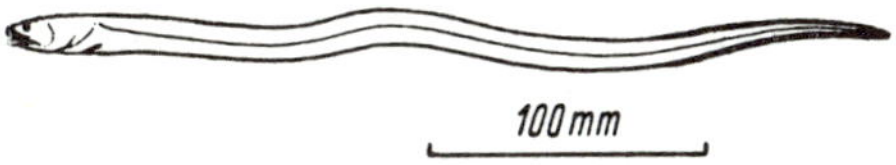

FIGURE 544. Amphipnoidae – *Amphipnous cuchia* (Day, 1878, pl. 167, fig. 1, diagr.)

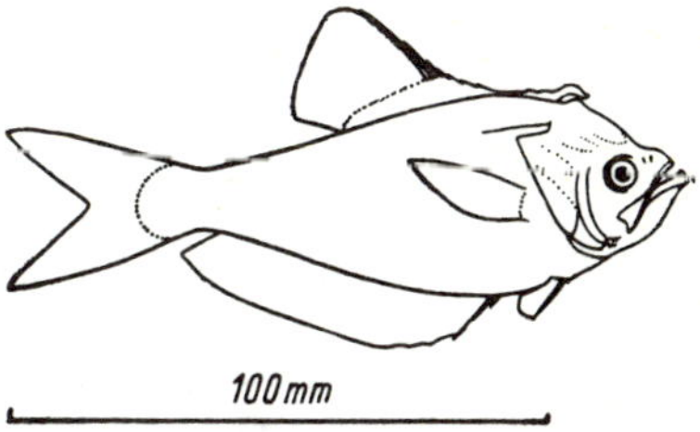

FIGURE 545. Kurtoidei – *Kurtus indicus* (Kurtidae) (Wang, 1958, fig. 472, diagr.)

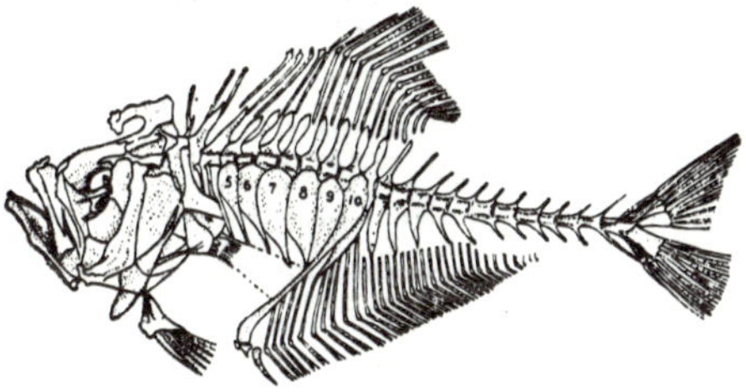

FIGURE 546. Kurtoidei – *Kurtus* sp. – skeleton (Kurtidae) (Traité, 1958, III, fig. 1758)

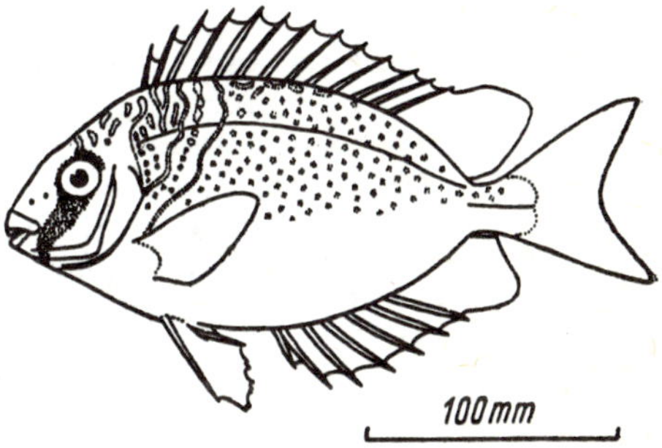

FIGURE 547. Siganoidei – *Siganus virgatus* (Siganidae) (Day, 1878, pl. 40, fig. 3, diagr.)

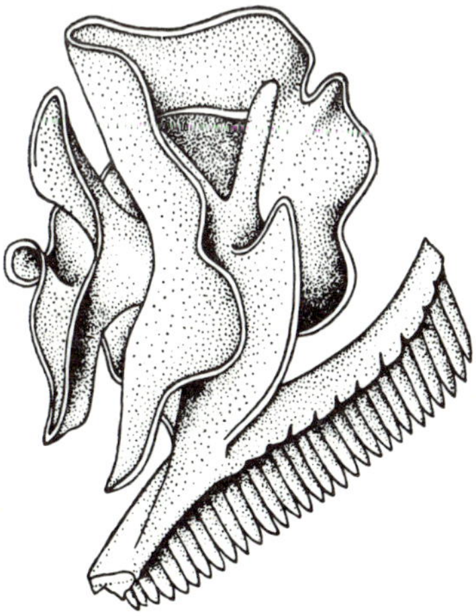

FIGURE 548. Anabantoidei –labyrinthine organ in *Anabas* (Anabantidae) (Traité, 1958, III, fig. 982)

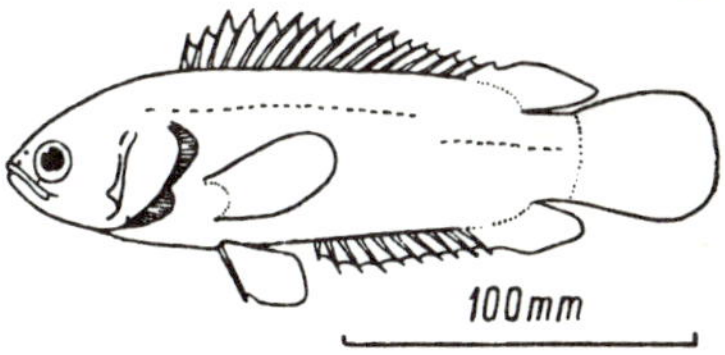

FIGURE 549. Anabantoidei – *Anabas testudineus* (Anabantidae) (Wang, 1958, fig. 469, diagr.)

2 (1). Supraoccipital bone (in males) and ribs normal.

3 (4). Ventral fins with 2 spiny and 3 soft branched rays; spiny rays distributed one on the outside and one on the inside of each fin. Anal fin with 7–9 spiny rays. (Figure 547) . . . . suborder 50.6. **Siganoidei**

4 (3). Ventral fins, if present, with a maximum of 1 spiny ray or with no spiny rays.

5 (8). Suprabranchial organ present.

6 (7). Suprabranchial organ labyrinthine (Figure 548). Dorsal and anal fin usually with spines. Caudal fin with 14 branched rays. Mouth moderately protrusible. Gill openings narrow; branchiostegal membranes broadly united, covered with scales. (Figure 549) . . . . suborder 50.13. **Anabantoidei**

7 (6). Suprabranchial organ not labyrinthine,[79] its stem lamellar, giving rise to only one secondary lamella. Dorsal and anal fins with a short base and without spines. Caudal fin with 10 branched rays. Mouth strongly protrusible; premaxillaries with long ascending processes which reach the posterior margin of the eye. Gill openings wide. Branchiostegal membranes not connected and not covered with scales (Figure 551) . . . . suborder 50.14. **Luciocephaloidei**

8 (5). Suprabranchial organ absent.

9 (10). Peculiar scales of rhomboid form present, overlapping one another and forming sharp ridges or keels arranged obliquely and across the sides of the body (Figure 522). There are two small keels at the base of the caudal fin on each side (Figure 553). Both jaws with well developed teeth that resemble the teeth of a rake. [Pelvic bones not united with humeral girdle. Lateral sacs of esophagus present (Figure 554), but the esophageal teeth do not have roots and their bases are embedded in the tissue of the walls of the esophagus (Figure 555)] . . . . suborder 50.11. **Tetragonuroidei**

10 (9). Such scales absent.

11 (12). Anterior part of esophagus immediately behind the pharynx with lateral sacs (Figure 556) which are supplied inside with papillae or longitudinal folds bearing teeth with roots (Figure 557). Scales small or medium-sized, cycloid, readily deciduous, arranged normally. No keels at the base of the caudal fin. Teeth on jaws very small, bearing no resemblance to the teeth of a rake. [Pelvic bones united with humeral girdle, although weakly.] (Figure 558) . . . . suborder 50.12. **Stromateoidei**[80]

[79] A suprabranchial organ that is not labyrinthine is present in family 262. Channidae (order 48. Channiformes) (Figure 550). These fishes differ from those of the suborder Luciocephaloidei in the long bases of the dorsal and anal fins and from those of the suborder Anabantoidei in the absence of spiny rays in the fins.

[80] Following the work of several investigators (Abe, Barnard, Matsubara), the suborder Stromateoidei underwent detailed study, which led to considerable changes in the systematics (Matsubara, 1955: 572, text-figs. 241–244). A detailed summary was published in 1967 (Haedrich).

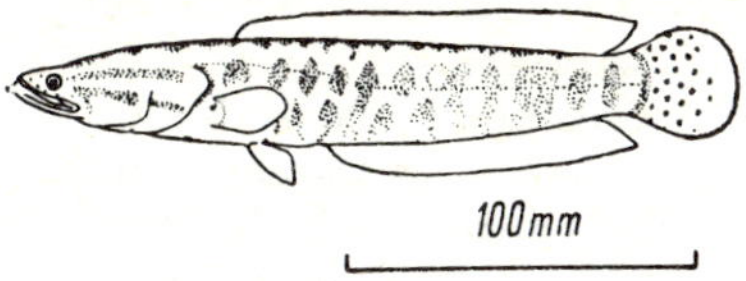

FIGURE 550. Channa (Ophicephalus) argus warpachowskii (Channiformes) (Berg, 1949, fig. 740, diagr.)

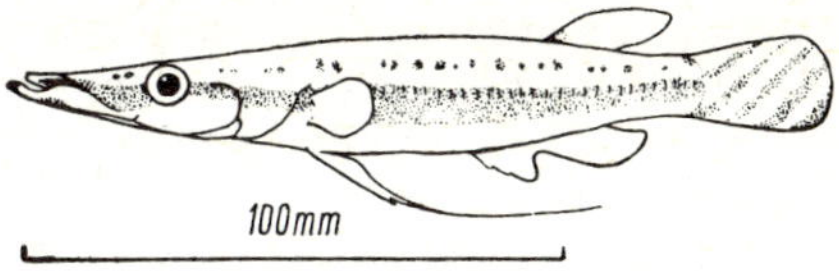

FIGURE 551. Luciocephaloidei – Luciocephalus pulcher (Luciocephalidae) (W. and B., 1922, 4, fig. 94, diagr.)

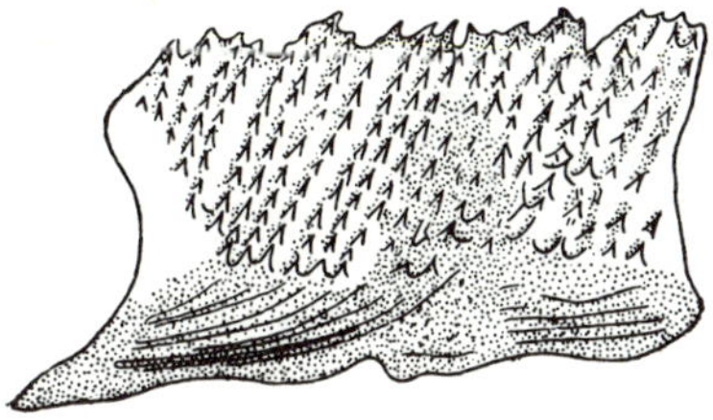

FIGURE 552. Tetragonuroidei – scales in Tetragonurus (Tetragonuridae) (L. and L., 1965, fig. 28)

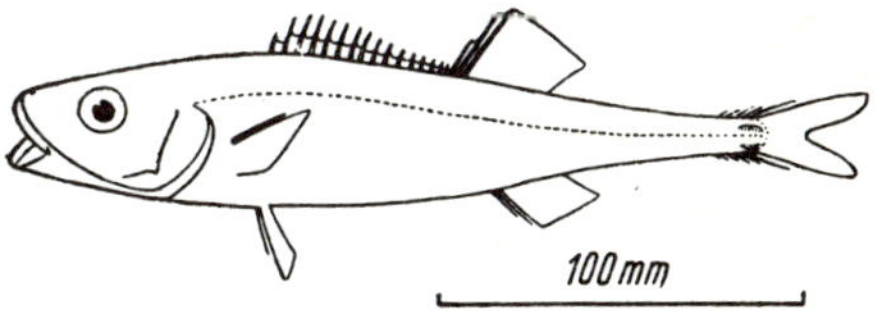

FIGURE 553. Tetragonuroidei – Tetragonurus cuvieri (Tetragonuridae) (Abe, 1958, fig. 601)

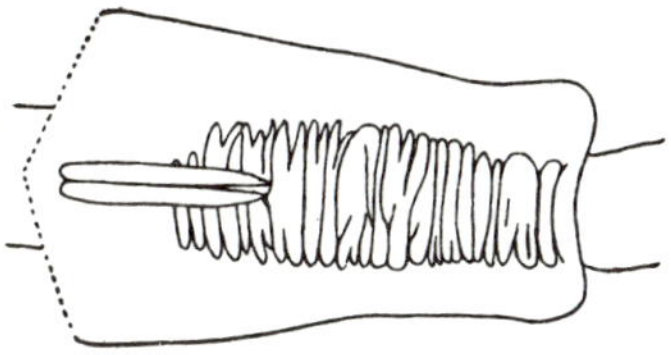

FIGURE 554. Tetragonuroidei – lateral sacs of esophagus in Tetragonurus (Tetragonuridae) (M., 1955, I, fig. 241A)

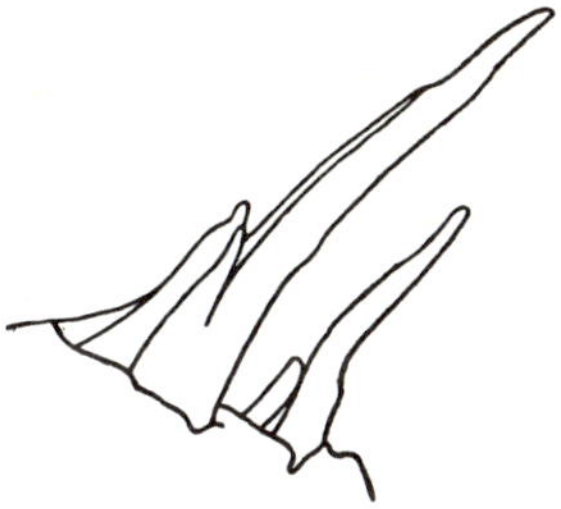

FIGURE 555. Tetragonuroidei – teeth without roots in Tetragonurus (Tetragonuridae) (M., 1955, I, fig. 242, A)

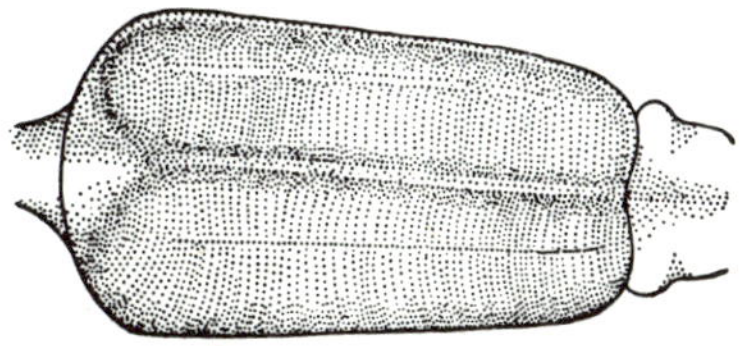

FIGURE 556. Stromateoidei – lateral sacs of esophagus in Pampus (Pampidae) (M., 1955, I, fig. 241, B)

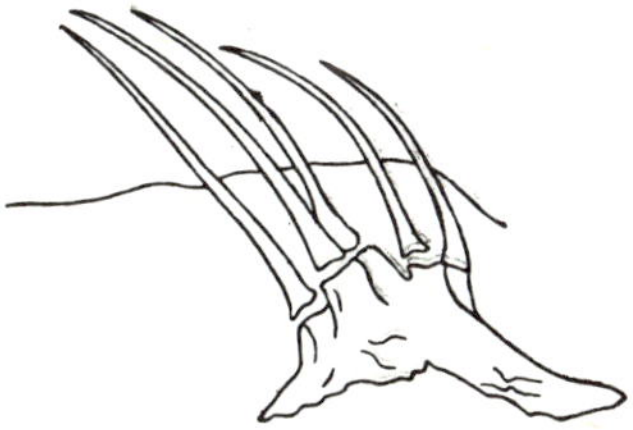

FIGURE 557. Stromateoidei – teeth with roots in Psenopsis (Stromateidae) (M., 1955, I, fig. 242, F)

12 (11). Anterior part of esophagus immediately behind pharynx without saclike widenings bearing teeth on the sides.

13 (14). Form of head and body, and also character of fins and their arrangement, reminiscent of some representatives of family 440. Cottidae (order 51. Scorpaeniformes); a difference is the absence of a suborbital stay (Figure 559). [Mesethmoid large, forming the interorbital septum and replacing the orbitosphenoid (Figure 560). Ribs absent.] Body and wide head strongly flattened. Ventral fins in front of pectorals, with 1 spiny and 5 soft rays. No scales on the body. (Figure 561) . . . . suborder 50.5. **Callionymoidei**

14 (13). Form of head and body, and also character of fins and their arrangement, not reminiscent of some representatives of family 440. Cottidae (order 51. Scorpaeniformes). [Mesethmoid not replacing orbitosphenoid. Ribs present.[81]]

15 (20). Maxillary bones very firmly attached to the nonprotrusible premaxillaries,[82] which often form a more or less long, forward-projecting swordlike process. Mouth not protrusible.

16 (17). Branchiostegal membranes broadly intergrown with the interbranchial space. Dorsal fin originating in the middle of the back. Mouth small, terminal. Snout shortened, blunt. Premaxillaries not transformed into a swordlike process. (Figure 562) . . . . suborder 50.10. **Luvaroidei**

17 (16). Branchiostegal membranes free of the interbranchial space.

18 (19). Caudal fin always present, well developed, in the shape of a half-moon or strongly notched, with hard rays; [the bases of its rays fully embrace the hypurals.] Body spindle-shaped, length of head almost equal to maximum depth of body, but if longer, then not more than 1.5 times as long, and if the body is drawn out, it has a forward-projecting swordlike process. Caudal peduncle strong, with 1—2 keels on the sides. (Figure 563) . . . . suborder 50.9. **Scombroidei**[83]

19 (18). Caudal fin often absent, but if present, then not large, although it sometimes has a deep notch, but it is not shaped like a half-moon, is only slightly furcate, and its rays are not hard; [the base of its rays do not fully embrace the hypurals.] Body ribbonlike, but if moderately drawn out, the length of the head considerably exceeds the maximum depth of the body (about twice this value) and the snout does not have a strongly elongate projection formed by the maxillary bones. Caudal peduncle usually without keels. (Figure 564) . . . . suborder 50.8. **Trichiuroidei**

20 (15). Maxillaries not very firmly attached to premaxillaries, which are hence free to move forward.

[81] [There are no ribs in family 386. Pholididae (Blennioidei).]

[82] The maxillaries are firmly connected to the premaxillaries in family 342. Scaridae and family 335. Oplegnathidae from the suborder Percoidei, but in these fishes both the jaws and the teeth are fused.

[83] The family Thunnidae, which Berg (1940 : 333) made into a separate order, Thunniformes, is very closely related to the family Cybiidae of the Scombroidei. Japanese workers (Matsubara, 1955 : 506) discovered several gradual morphological transitions between representatives of the families Scombridae, Cybiidae, and Thunnidae and regard them merely as subfamilies of family 409. Scombridae, which is definitely correct.

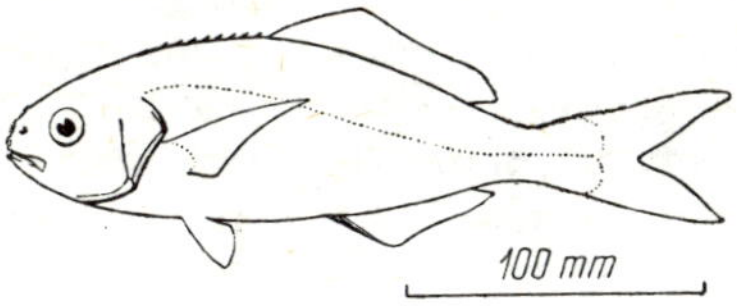

FIGURE 558. Stromateoidei – Ocycrius japonicus (Stromateidae) (Okada, 1955, fig. 146, diagr.)

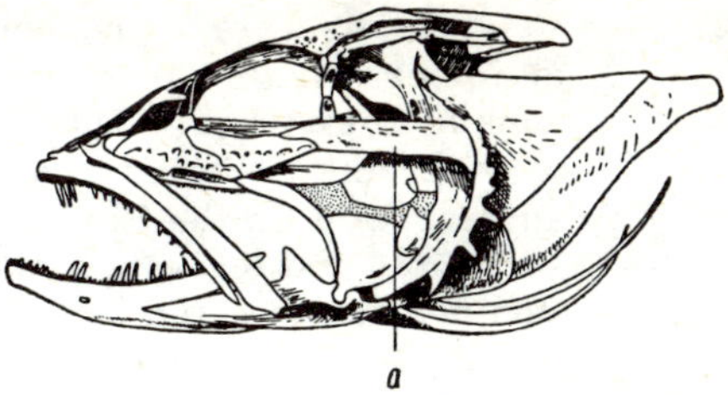

FIGURE 559. Suborbital stay (a) in Ophiodon elongatus (Scorpaeniformes) (Boulenger, 1904, fig. 422)

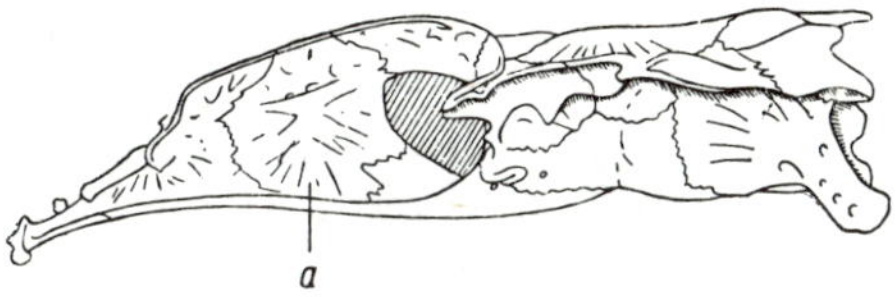

FIGURE 560. Callionymoidei – skull of Callionymus (Callionymidae) (Berg, 1940, fig. 181).

Lateral: a – mesethmoid.

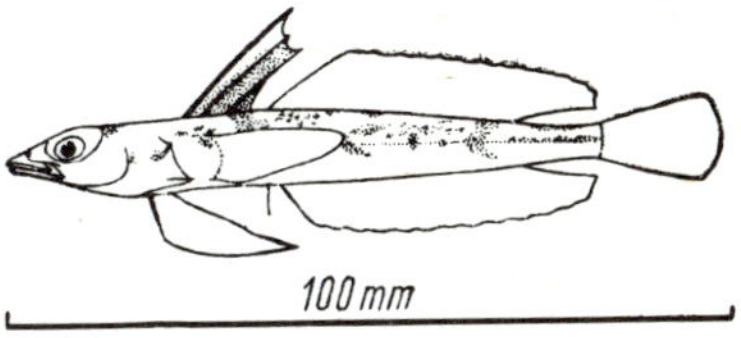

FIGURE 561. Callionymoidei – Draconetta xenica (Draconettidae) (M., 1955, III, fig. 260, diagr.)

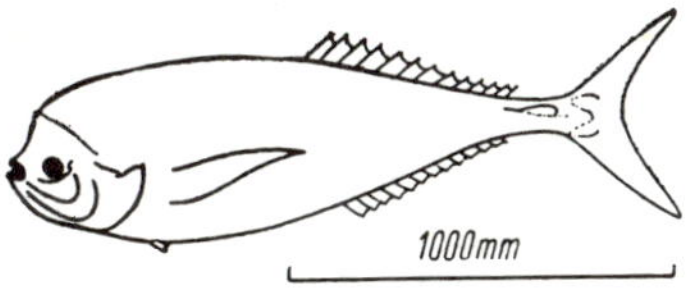

FIGURE 562. Luvaroidei – Luvarus imperialis (Luvaridae) (Jordan, 1925, fig. 396, diagr.)

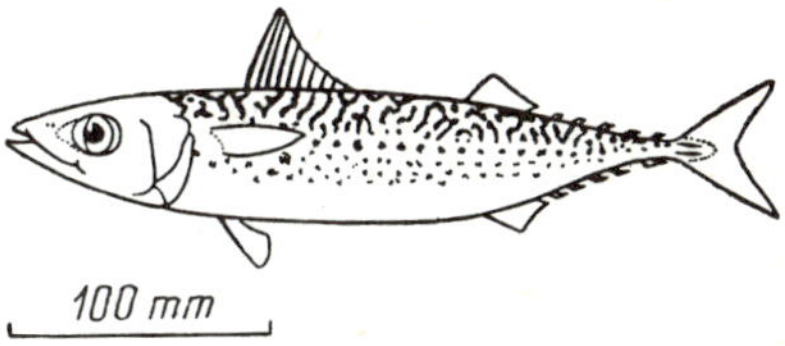

FIGURE 563. Scombroidei – Scomber tapeinocephalus (Scombridae) (Okada, 1955, fig. 125, diagr.)

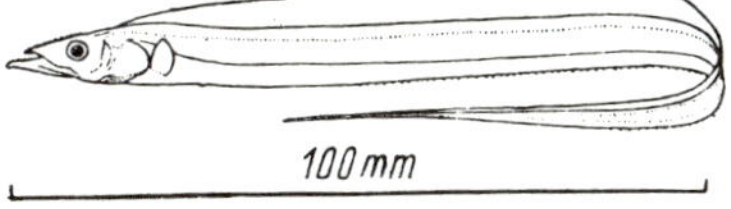

FIGURE 564. Trichiuroidei – Trichiurus muticus (Trichiuridae) (Fowler, 1937, fig. 217, diagr.)

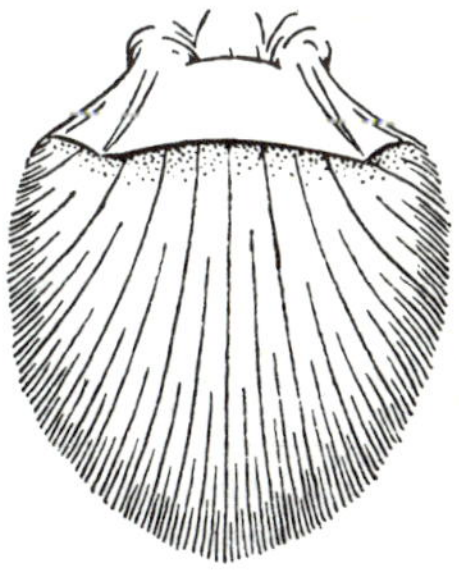

FIGURE 565. Gobioidei – ventral fins in the Gobiidae

21 (22). Ventral fins always present, serving as an organ of attachment or for crawling; they are generally grown together and form a sucking disk (Figure 565), but sometimes they are not grown together, but their bases are close together and contiguous; as an exception (in the Rhyacichthyinae) the bases are widely separated and there is a sucker between them (Figure 566). Ventral fins situated under the pectorals, or a little in front of them; they have 1 spiny and 4—5 soft rays.[84] As a rule there are two separate dorsal fins; the first, occasionally absent, is short, consisting of 1—8 flexible spiny rays; more rarely the dorsal, caudal, and anal fins are fused. No lateral line in the form of perforated scales. Gill openings only on the sides of the head. Branchiostegal membranes fused and attached to the interbranchial space. [Parietal absent. Opisthoticum large, reaching the basioccipitale. Periorbital ring not ossified, or absent.] (Figure 568). . . . . suborder 50.16. **Gobioidei**

22 (21). Ventral fins sometimes absent, but if present, they do not serve as an organ of attachment or for crawling; they are never grown together and do not form a sucking disk; their bases do not touch.

23 (24). [Number of rays in dorsal and anal fins greater than number of corresponding neural and hemal processes of the vertebrae.] Spiny rays not developed at all in all fins, including the ventrals, which (if present) are inserted on the throat or on the chin, are not rudimentary, but well expressed in the form of 1—2 long, threadlike or cirriform rays. If the ventrals are absent, and the body is markedly elongate, the vent is situated on the throat, near the base of the pectoral fins. Caudal fin more or less distinguishable, but with a tendency to fuse with the dorsal and anal; it is never forked. Body oblong or elongate. Operculum with spines. (Figure 569) . . . . suborder 50.3. **Ophidioidei**

24 (23). [Number of rays in dorsal and anal fins equal to number of corresponding neural and hemal processes of the vertebrae.] Spiny rays as a rule developed in at least one of the fins. But if there are no spiny rays at all, the ventral fins (if present) are short, rudimentary, sometimes hard to distinguish, situated on the throat, near the base of the pectoral fins and as an exception on the vertical of the eye—family 390. Derepodichthyidae. If the ventrals are absent, the vent is situated far behind the pectoral

[84] Ventral fins with 1 spiny and 1—2 soft rays are present in family 424. **Microdesmidae** (Cerdalidae) (2 genera, several species), which Gosline (1955, Pac. Sci. 9, 2:158—170, figs. 1—7) places in the suborder Gobioidei. This family occurs in the central part of the Pacific, off the Pacific and Atlantic coasts of Central America, and off the west coast of Africa. The body is typically elongate, laterally compressed, covered with small scales, and with a small head (Figure 567). No lateral line. Gill openings reduced to small, more or less horizontally distributed gill slits. Dorsal fin very long, low, consisting of thin spiny rays which pass gradually into soft rays. Ventral fins arranged under the base of the pectorals. Caudal fin with 15 main rays which are linked to the rays of the dorsal and anal fins. A detailed description of family 424. Microdesmidae is given by Schultz (in Schultz, Woods, and Lachner, 1966:1—13, figs. 133—135). In the ventral fins this author mentions 3—5 soft rays, the longest being the middle one, which he considers an important character for the whole suborder Gobioidei, in which he places this family. It should be noted, however, that as an exception in Ctenotrypauchen microcephalus (Bleeker) and Trypauchenichthys typus (Bleeker) (Herre, 1927:337, fig. 6) the inner rays of the ventral fins are shorter than the outer rays.

fins, or the caudal fin is forked, or else the body is deep, markedly laterally compressed.

25 (26). In fishes with an elongate body the dorsal and anal fins do not have spiny rays, even thin and flexible ones. Caudal fin forked and clearly separated from dorsal and anal. Ventral fins, if present, with 1 spiny and 3 soft rays, situated on the throat. Body oblong; vent situated behind the middle of the body. Snout slightly elongate, pointed, lower jaw projecting markedly forward. Lateral line present. Gill opening normal, not reduced. Scales if present, cycloid. (Figure 570). . . .suborder 50.4. **Ammodytoidei**

26 (25). Spiny rays generally present, even if thin and flexible, in dorsal fin (if more than one dorsal fin, then in the first); if there are no spiny rays at all in the dorsal fin, and the body is oblong, the caudal fin is of any form except furcate.

27 (28). Ventral fins quite frequently absent, but if present, then generally poorly developed; either there is no spiny ray at all or it is small and hardly distinguishable; 2—4, less often 1, jointed, generally unbranched soft rays (Figure 571). If, however, the ventral fins are relatively developed and have 1 spiny and 3—4 double- or triple-branched rays, they are much less than half as long as the pectoral fin, except in the genus Leptoclinus (Figure 572), in which they are more than half as long. Ventral fins situated on the chin or throat, but always somewhat in front of the base of the pectoral fins. Body never deep; it is oblong or else moderately or even markedly elongate
. . . . suborder 50.2. **Blennioidei**[85]

28 (27). Ventral fins nearly always present, well developed, with 1 well expressed spiny ray and, generally, 5 soft branched rays, occasionally fewer; ventral fins markedly more than half as long as pectorals, distributed as a rule under these but sometimes on the throat and as an exception on the chin. If the ventrals are absent, which is very rare, the body is deep, with strong lateral compression.

[85] Four endemic families are known in the southern part of the Pacific Ocean which can hypothetically be placed in the suborder Blennioidei. One of these, family 376. Xenocephalidae, with one genus, Xenocephalus Kaup, 1858 and one species, is known off the shores of New Guinea; it has been described very incompletely and has not been found by anyone since; the other 3 families are distributed around Australia. Owing to the lack of material on these families, their systematic position cannot be defined accurately, and so they have not been included in the general key. Differences between the three Australian families are presented below.

1 (2). Pectoral fins absent. Three lateral lines, passing under the dorsal and above the anal and along the midline of the body. (Figure 573) . . . . 380. Peronedysidae

2 (1). Pectoral fins present. Lateral line single, passing under the dorsal fin.

3 (4). Mouth superior or half-superior. (Figure 574) . . . . 381. Ophiclinidae

4 (3). Mouth terminal or subterminal. (Figure 575) . . . . 379. Notograptidae

Berg (1940:317, fig. 179) places in the same suborder also family 392. Schindleriidae, known from the region of the Hawaiian Islands (Gosline and Brock, 1960:273, figure 137) and around New Guinea. One genus, Schindleria Giltay, 1934 (Figure 576). These fishes were at first taken to be larval stages of the genus Hemiramphus of family 204. Hemiramphidae.

29 (30). Sides of caudal peduncle showing prickly spines or lanceolate outgrowths (Figure 577) or the scales covering the body are very small, scarcely visible to the naked eye, but lending a marked roughness to the skin, giving the impression of a short bristle . . . . suborder 50.7. **Acanthuroidei**

30 (29). No prickly spines or lanceolate outgrowths on sides of caudal peduncle; nor are there scales making the skin bristly. [Pelvic bones attached directly to cleithra.] Ventral fins with a well developed spiny ray; the fins are as a rule situated under the pectorals, rarely in front of them; as an exception they are absent in fishes with deep, laterally compressed body. Dorsal and anal fins generally with well developed spiny rays, but these are sometimes weakly expressed in the dorsal, which has one base, more rarely in the anal. (Figure 578) . . . . suborder 50.1. **Percoidei**

Suborder 50.1. **Percoidei** (thesis 50.0-30)

Key to superfamilies of the suborder Percoidei of the order Perciformes (50.1.1—50.1.13)

1 (2). Eyes situated on top of the head, looking upward. Ventral fins inserted well in front of the base of the large pectorals or even on the throat. Mouth very oblique, almost vertical, small. (Figure 579) . . . . superfamily 50.1.10. **Uranoscopoidea**

2 (1). Eyes situated on the sides of the head, looking to the side. Ventral fins, if present, inserted under the base of the pectoral fins, behind this, or occasionally in front. Mouth not oblique, but if it is, and if sometimes the eyes are also displaced upward, then either the pectorals are small, much shorter than the head, or the ventrals are inserted under the base of the pectorals.

3 (4). Ventral fins with one weakly expressed and one long soft ray, split into two. The ventrals are situated slightly in front of the base of the pectorals. Body oblong. Anal fin with 3 spiny rays. (Figure 580) . . . . superfamily 50.1.6. **Gadopsoidea**

4 (3). Ventral fins with 1 spiny and 2 or more soft rays, but sometimes these fins are absent.[86]

5 (6). Dorsal and anal fins fused with the well expressed caudal fin. Body elongate. Bases of vertical fins very long; dorsal originating on the occiput or slightly behind it, anal originating under the pectorals or a little behind them. Vent shifted forward almost under the vertical of the base of the pectoral. Ventral fins somewhat in front of base of pectorals. Palatines without teeth. Color of body red. (Figure 581) . . . . superfamily 50.1.2. **Cepoloidea**

6 (5). Dorsal and anal fins not fused with the caudal.

[86] See families 360. Creediidae and 363. Oxudercidae in superfamily 8. Trichodontoidea, theses 50.1.9—19 and 50.1.9—21.

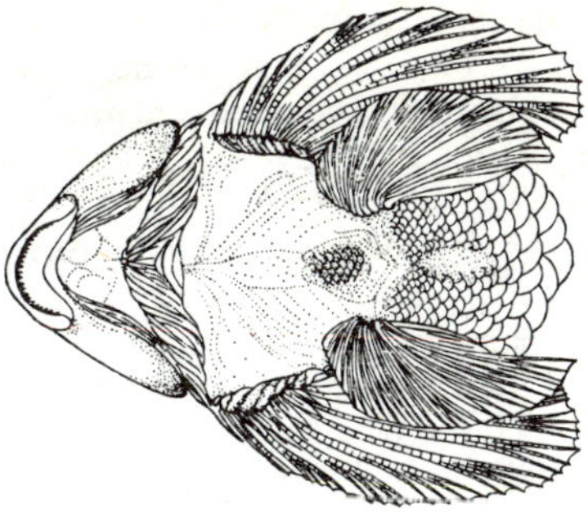

FIGURE 566. Gobioidei – ventral fins of Rhyacichthys (Eleotridae) (Herre, 1927, pl. 1, fig. 1)

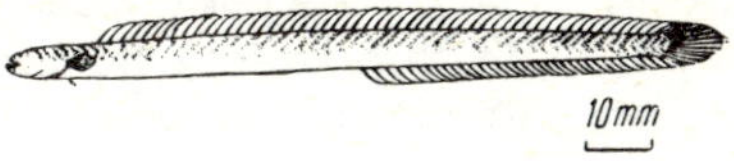

FIGURE 567. Gobioidei – Microdesmus dipus (Microdesmidae) (Günther, 1864, pl. 3, fig. 2)

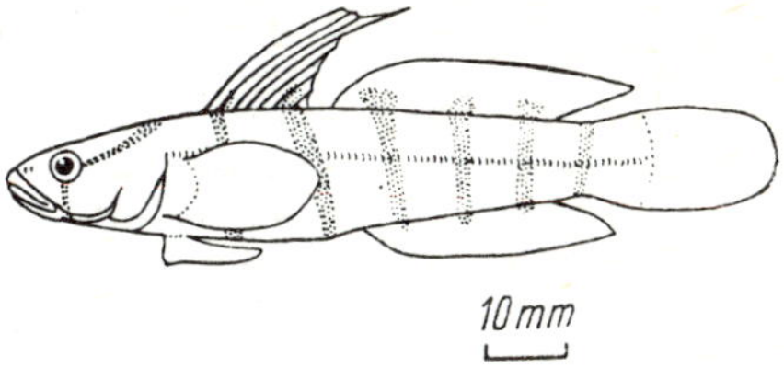

FIGURE 568. Gobioidei – Pterogobius elapoides (Gobiidae) (Okada, 1955, fig. 334, diagr.)

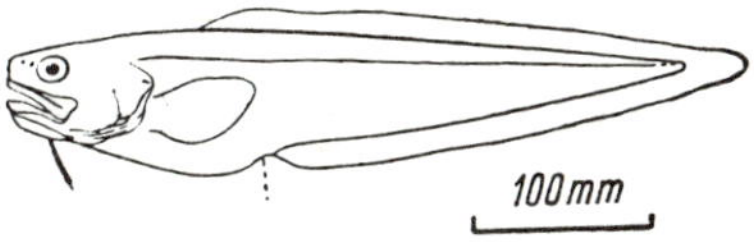

FIGURE 569. Ophidioidei – Haplobrotula armata (Brotulidae) (Okada, 1955, fig. 382, diagr.)

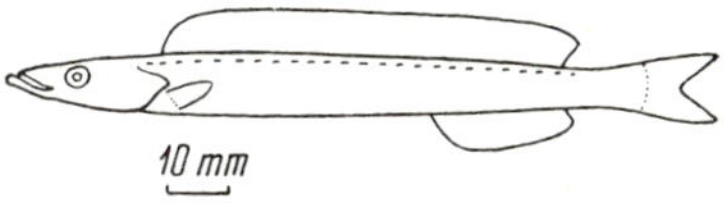

FIGURE 570. Ammodytoidei – Bleekeria gilli (Ammodytidae) (Gosline and Brock, 1960, fig. 146)

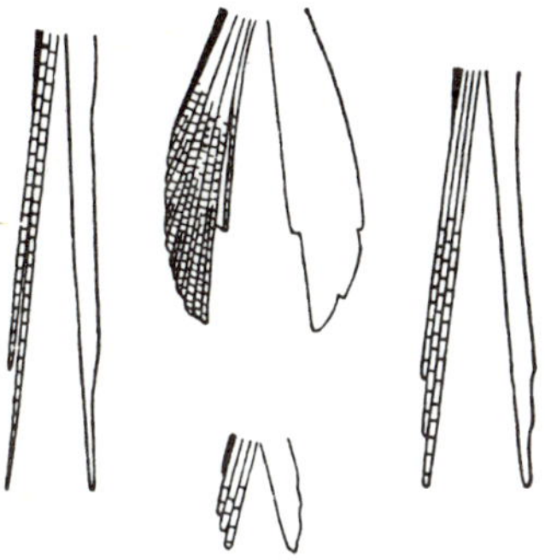

FIGURE 571. Blennioidei – types of ventral fins (Makushok, 1958, fig. 26)

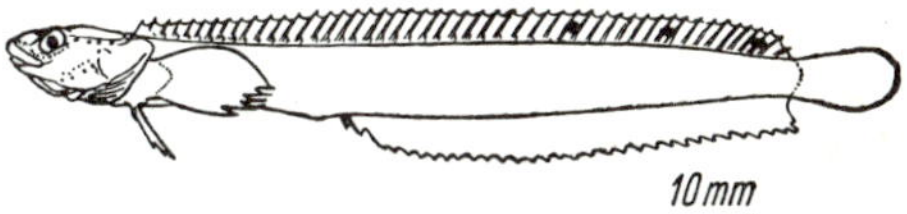

FIGURE 572. Blennioidei – Leptoclinus sp. (Stichaeidae) (M., 1955, III, fig. 283, A, diagr.)

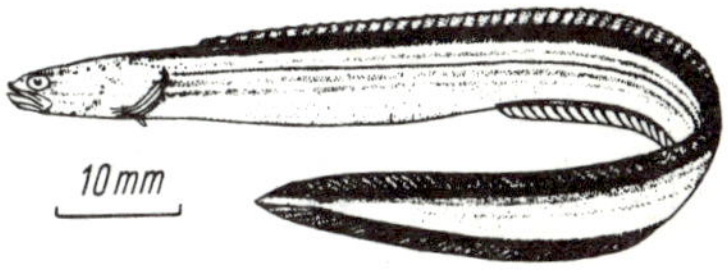

FIGURE 573. Blennioidei – Peronedys anguillaris (Peronedysidae) (Waite, 1921, fig. 240)

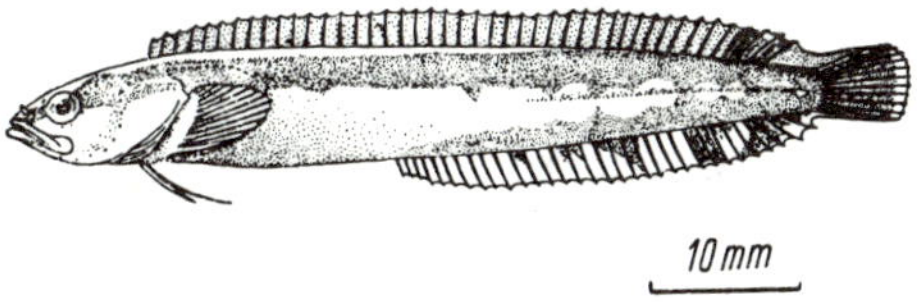

FIGURE 574. Blennioidei – Ophiclinus gracilis (Ophiclinidae) (Waite, 1921, fig. 243)

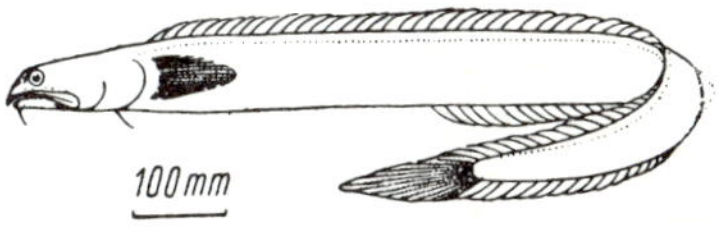

FIGURE 575. Blennioidei – Notograptus guttatus (Notograptidae) (W. and B., 1951, 9, fig. 57, diagr.)

7 (10). Body bare, not covered with scales.

8 (9). Mouth terminal, horizontal, very large. End of oral slit passing far beyond the eyes. Color of body uniformly black. (Figure 582) . . . . superfamily 50.1.12. **Chiasmodontoidea**

9 (8). Mouth half-superior or superior, oblique or vertical, of moderate size. End of oral slit not passing beyond the eyes. Body variegated. (Figure 583) . . . . superfamily 50.1.8. **Trichodontoidea**

10 (7). Body as a rule covered with scales.[87]

11 (12). Corner of preoperculum with a strong ring-shaped spine. Scales barleylike, coarse, ctenoid. Two dorsal fins, with well defined bases. Mouth large, slit oblique. There are keels that can be folded in like the blade of a penknife. Two lateral lines and a large number of short vertical lines on each side of the body. (Figure 584) . . . . superfamily 50.1.11. **Champsodontoidea**

12 (11). Corner of preoperculum without a ring-shaped spine. Scales, when present, of normal appearance, cycloid or ctenoid, but not barleylike.

13 (14). Lower 5—8 rays of pectoral fins simple, not branched, generally slightly thickened, and some of them often ending in a free, threadlike tip. Ventral fins situated slightly behind the base of the pectorals. (Figure 585). . . . . superfamily 50.1.7. **Cirrhitoidea**

14 (13). Lower rays of pectoral fins branched, no different from the upper rays; they are not lengthened or thickened.

15 (18). On pair of nasal openings, 1 naris on each side of the head.[88]

16 (17). Vertical fins without spiny rays. (Figure 586) . . . . superfamily 50.1.13. **Notothenioidea**

17 (16). Vertical fins with spiny rays. Usually 2, rarely 3, spiny rays in anal. Gills 3 ½. No opening, or a small one, behind fourth gill arch. Vertebrae 25—27. (Figure 587) . . . . superfamily 50.1.4. **Pomacentroidea**

18 (15). Two pairs of nasal openings, 2 nares on each side of the head.

19 (22). Infrapharyngeal bones fused into one and forming an oval, triangular, Y-shaped, or T-shaped plate which bears strong molars of the cobblestone type, more rarely conical.

20 (21). Viviparous forms. Four gills. Caudal fin distinctly forked. [Suborbital process present.] (Figure 588) . . . . superfamily 50.1.3. **Embiotocoidea**

21 (20). Egg-laying forms. 3 ½ gills. Caudal fin rounded, truncate, or with a slight notch, but not forked. [No suborbital process.] (Figure 589) . . . . superfamily 50.1.5. **Labroidea**

22 (19). Infrapharyngeal bones not fused into one bone.

23 (24). Body as a rule elongate, its maximum depth contained from 6 to 13 times in the whole length, but if oblong (about 5 times), then the lateral line is shorter and passes under the base of the dorsal fin (families 350. Opisthognathidae, see Figure 745;

[87] The body is bare in family 371. Harpagiferidae (Notothenioidea) (see Figure 754).

[88] There is one pair of nares in family 336. Cichlidae of the superfamily Percoidea.

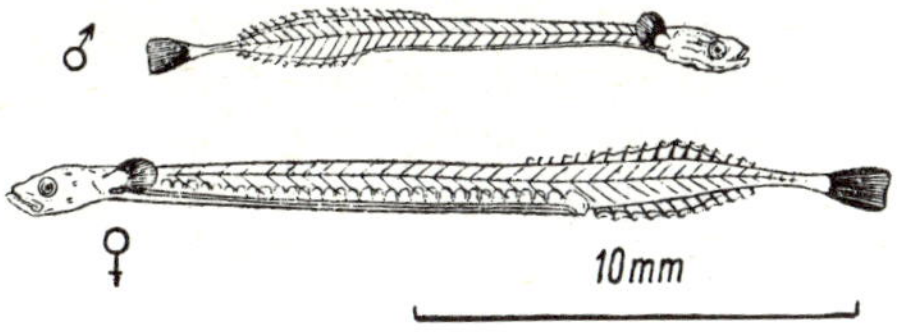

FIGURE 576. Blennioidei – Schindleria praematura (Schindleriidae) (Berg, 1940, fig. 179, 1, 2)

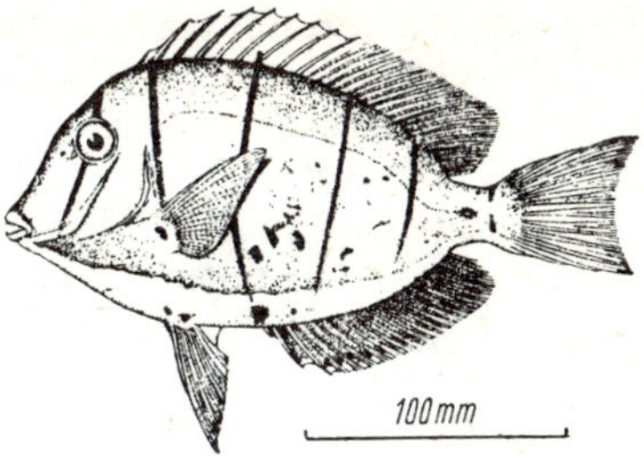

FIGURE 577. Acanthuroidei – Acanthurus triostegus (Acanthuridae) (M., 1955, III, fig. 347)

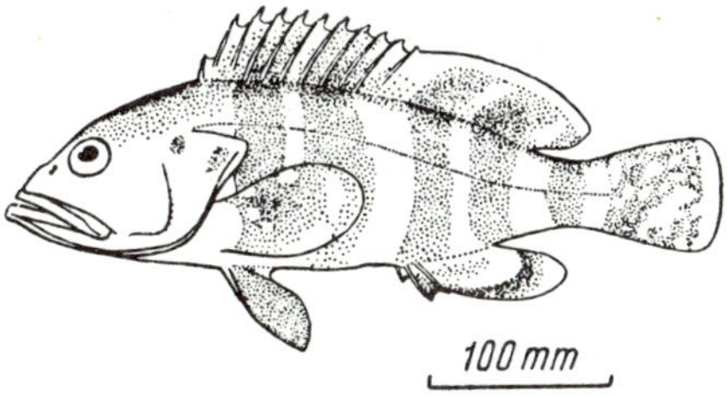

FIGURE 578. Percoidei – Epinephelus awoara (Matsubara, 1955, III, fig. 211, diagr.)

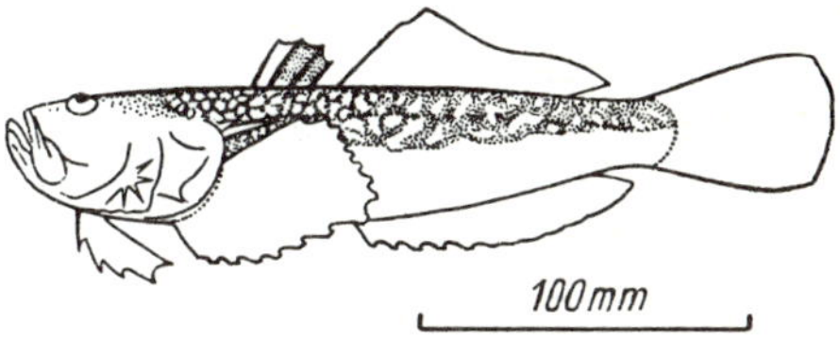

FIGURE 579. Uranoscopoidea – Uranoscopus japonicus (Uranoscopidae) (Okada, 1955, fig. 359, diagr.)

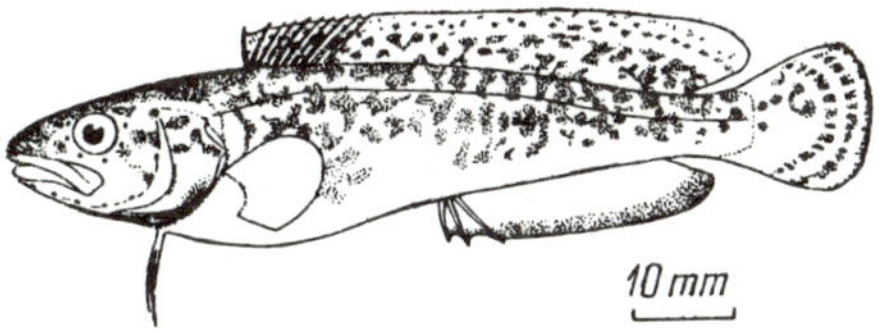

FIGURE 580. Gadopsoidea – Gadopsis marmoratus (Gadopsidae) (Richardson, 1844, pl. 59, fig. 6, diagr.)

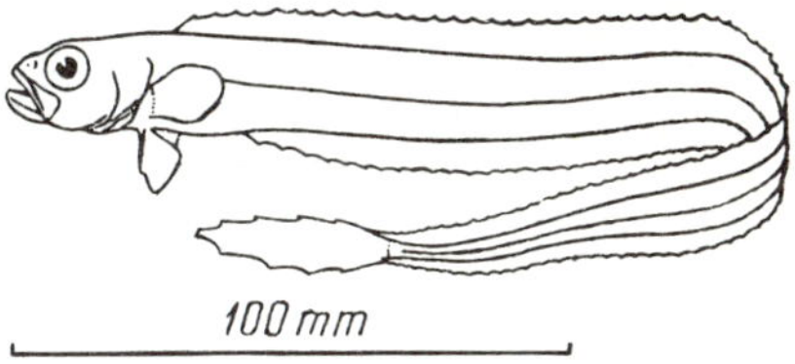

FIGURE 581. Cepoloidea – Cepola schlegeli (Cepolidae) (Okada, 1955, fig. 237, diagr.)

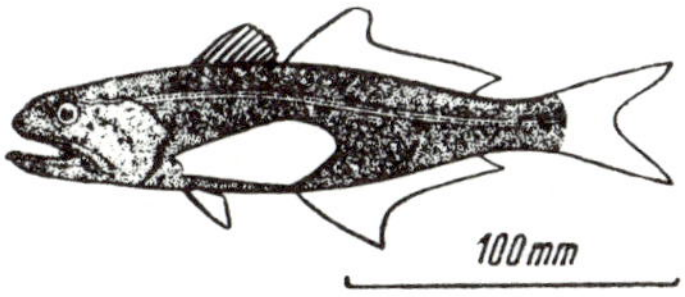

FIGURE 582. Chiasmodontoidea – Pseudoscopelus scriptus (Chiasmodontidae) (Abe, 1958, fig. 437, diagr.)

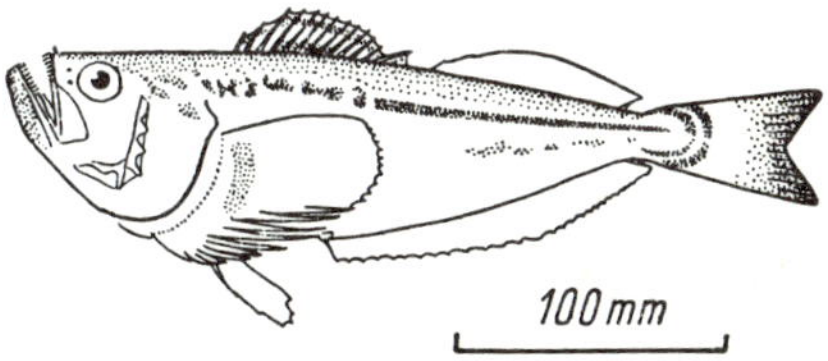

FIGURE 583. Trichodontoidea – Trichodon trichodon (Trichodontidae) (M., 1955, III, fig. 190, diagr.)

351. Owstoniidae, see Figure 744; 352. Bathymasteridae, see Figure 746) or the ventral fins are inserted markedly in front of the base of the pectorals (families 353. Mugiloididae, see Figure 736, and 355. Trachinidae, see Figure 735). Anal fin with a long base, markedly more than half as long as the ba base of the soft dorsal, and with 1—2 weak spiny rays. Mouth of moderate size or even quite large; upper jaw reaching anterior margin of eye, often far beyond this and even beyond the eye. Caudal fin rounded or truncate, but not forked, but if there is a weak notch (family 354. Cheimarrichthyidae, Figure 738), the ventral fins are inserted far in front of the base of the pectorals. (Figure 590) . . . . superfamily 50.1.9. **Trachinoidea**

24 (23). Body as a rule deep, its maximum depth contained less than 6 times in the whole body length, but if oblong, then the lateral line is not shortened and passes in the middle of the sides of the body (family 285. Branchiostegidae, Figure 634) or the ventral fins are inserted approximately under the base of the pectorals (many families), or the anal fin has a shortened base which is much less than half as long as the base of the soft dorsal (family 310. Sciaenidae, Figure 656), or the upper jaw is short, ending far short of the eye (family 284. Sillaginidae, Figure 646). or, finally, the caudal fin is forked (families 291. Rachycentridae, Figure 598; 292. Carangidae, Figure 601; 298. Coryphaenidae, Figure 630; 304. Caesionidae, Figure 689). The spiny dorsal fin is generally well developed, but when it has one base, the spiny rays may be weakly developed (and sometimes hard to distinguish from the soft unbranched rays) or they may be absent. Ventral fins well developed, with few exceptions (they are small in family 316. Mondactylidae, Figure 610, and in the genus Bentenia of family 297. Pteraclididae, Figure 627, and they are absent in family 294. Formionidae, Figure 621); they are situated roughly under the base of the pectoral fins, occasionally slightly in front of this, or behind in families 319. Scorpididae (Figure 682) and 272. Theraponidae (Figure 704); each of them has a well developed spiny ray and 4—5 soft rays. [Pelvic bones attached directly to cleithra.] Mouth usually protrusible; premaxillaries with more or less developed anterior ascending processes (pedicels) and almost always free of the maxillaries. [Posttemporale furcate.] (Figure 591, see Figures 392—706). . . . . superfamily 50.1.1. Percoidea

Superfamily 50.1.1. *Percoidea* (thesis 50.1.0—24)

111 families (266—336):

1 (2). One pair of nares, one naris on each side. Freshwater tropical fishes (Figure 592). . . . . 336. **Cichlidae**

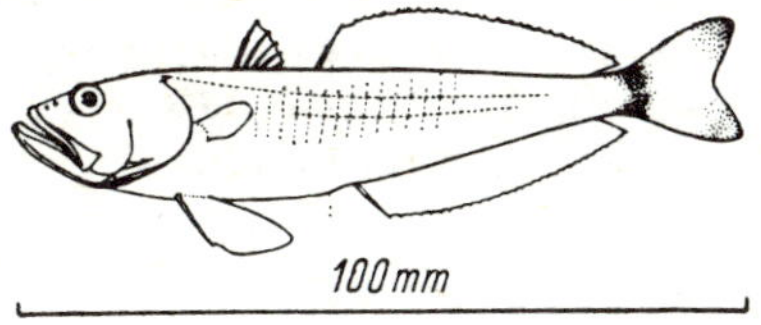

FIGURE 584. Champsodontoidea – *Champsodon snyderi* (Champsodontidae) (M., 1955, III, fig. 259, diagr.)

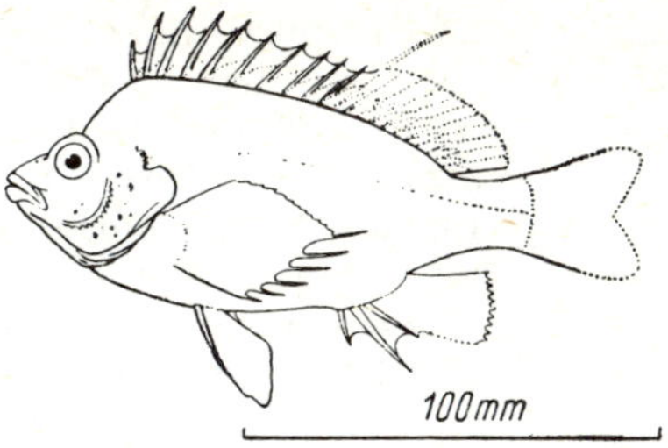

FIGURE 585. Cirrhitoidea – *Cirrhitichthys aureus* (Cirrhitidae) (M., 1955, III, fig. 246, diagr.)

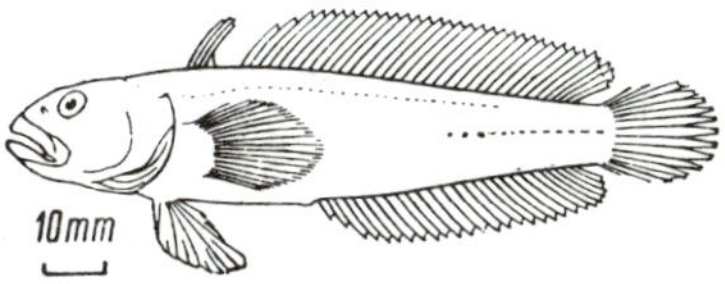

FIGURE 586. Notothenioidea – *Notothenia cyanobrancha* (Nototheniidae) (Norman, 1938, fig. 11, diagr.)

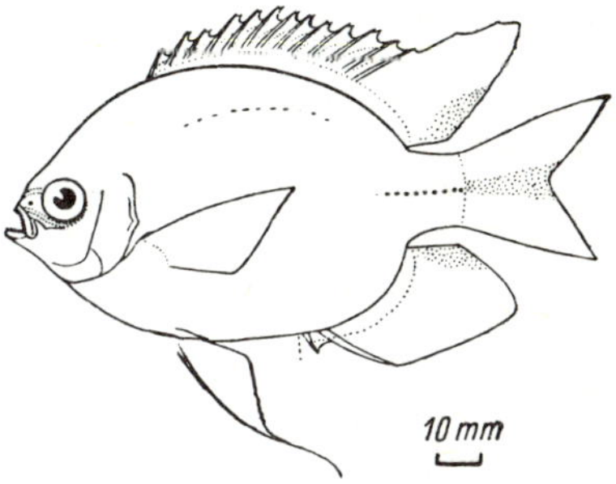

FIGURE 587. Pomacentroidea – *Abudefduf aureus* (Pomacentridae) (Bleeker, 1878, pl. 405, fig. 4, diagr.)

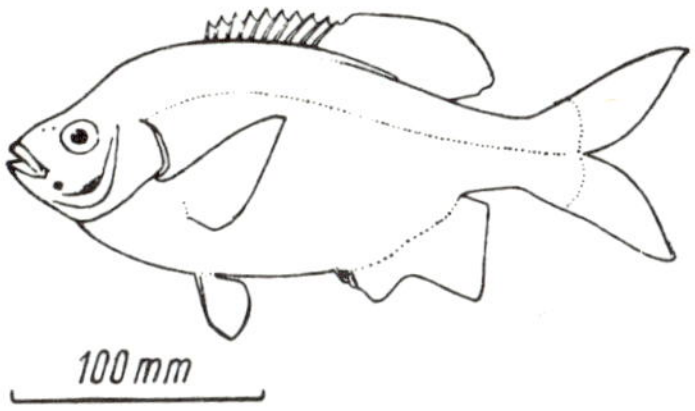

FIGURE 588. Embiotocoidea – *Ditrema temmincki* (Embiotocidae). (Okada, 1955, fig. 240, diagr.)

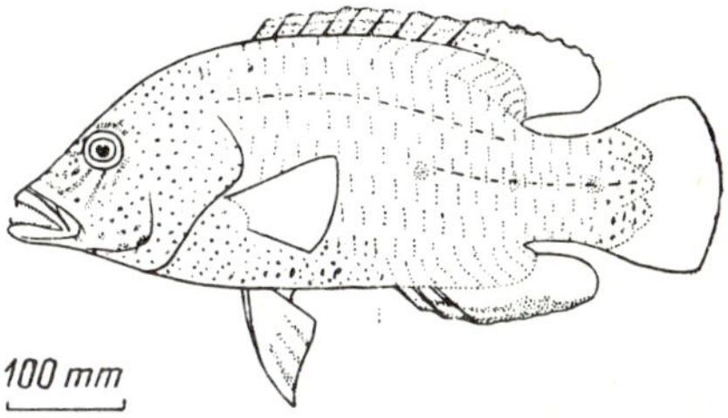

FIGURE 589. Labroidea – *Cheilinus trilobatus* (Labridae) (Bleeker, 1862, pl. 27, fig. 2, diagr.)

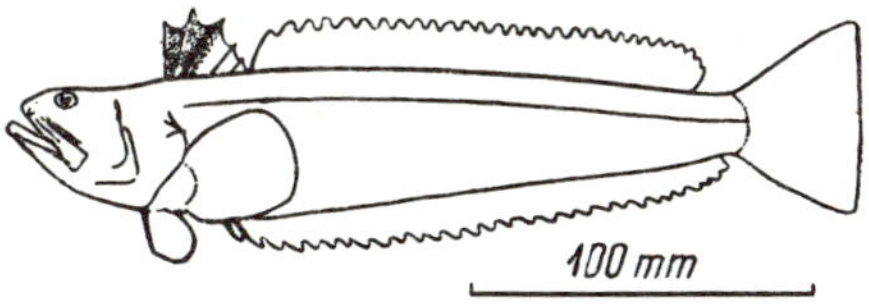

FIGURE 590. Trachinoidea – *Trachinus draco* (Trachinidae) (Fowler, 1936, fig. 422, diagr.)

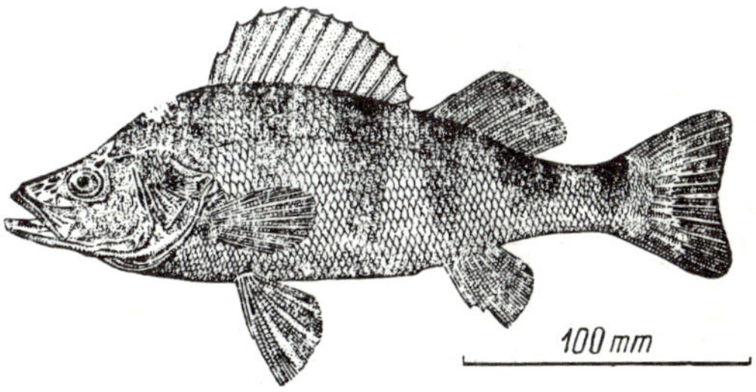

FIGURE 591. Percoidea – *Perca flavescens* (Percidae) (Jordan, 1925, fig. 409)

2 (1). Two pairs of nares, two nares on each side.

3 (4). Teeth on jaw fused among themselves and with the jaw; spaces between teeth filled and cemented by a substance containing lime; a strong, hard beak is formed as a result of the growing together (Figure 393). Mouth not protrusible. Maxillaries weakly united with premaxillaries. Ventral fins with an axillary lobe (Figure 594) . . . . 335. **Oplegnathidae**

4 (3). Teeth not fused among themselves or with the jaw; spaces between teeth not cemented; no beak as in Figure 593.

5 (8). At least 8 (8—15) spiny rays in anal fin.

6 (7). Ventral fins with 2—3 soft rays. Body relatively elongate. Three lateral lines (Figure 595) . . . . .277. **Acanthoclinidae**

7 (6). Ventral fins with 5—6 soft rays. Body relatively deep. One very short lateral line. (Figure 596) . . . . . 334. **Polycentridae**

8 (5). Not more than 6 spiny rays in anal fin.

9 (10). Two long barbels directly behind symphysis of lower jaw. Two dorsal fins, widely separated from each other; base of second dorsal relatively short, more or less equal to base of anal (Figure 597) . . . . 315. **Mullidae**

10 (9). Barbels absent directly behind symphysis of lower jaw.

11 (12). In front of the soft dorsal fin there are several (7—9) free, low spiny rays which are well developed and considerably separated from each other not joined up by a membrane; each spiny ray may be concealed independently in its own depression. No separate spiny rays in front of anal fin. Body drawn out, spindle-shaped, its anterior part slightly flattened. Length of head far exceeding depth of body.[89] Soft dorsal and the anal with long bases. Scales small. No suborbital process. (Figure 598) . . . . 291. **Rachycentridae**

12 (11). There are no free spiny rays not connected by a membrane in front of the soft dorsal fin, but if there are, then fewer than 7.

13 (14). In adults there are in front of the anal fin 2 spiny rays which are independent of the fin; these disappear or are hard to distinguish in old fish, while in very young forms they are connected to the fin by a membrane. First dorsal fin quite short with thin (but if thickened, then short), sometimes free spiny rays. Caudal peduncle markedly tapering. Caudal fin widely forked (see Figures 600—604) . . . . . . 292. **Carangidae**

5 subfamilies:

1 (2). Premaxillaries not protrusible (except in the very young). Scales small, elongate, more or less grown into the skin. Lateral line without scutes. No accessory maxillary bone. Pectoral fins short, not sickle-shaped. Posterior rays of soft dorsal and of anal fin connected by a membrane, but with the tips protruding from it, so that they look like the free rays that are typical for many genera of this family. (Figure 600) . . . . subfamily 292.1. Chorinemìnae

[89] The similarly shaped fish Ocycrius japonicus (Döderlein) of family 414. Stromateidae differs externally in that the head is not as long as the body is deep (Figure 599).

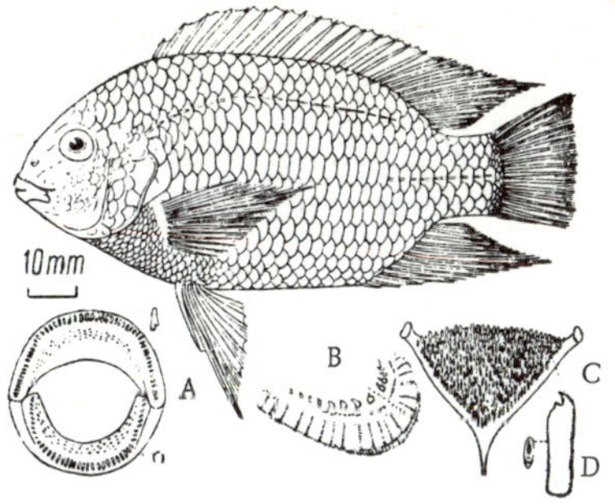

FIGURE 592. Cichlidae – Tilapia melanopleura (Poll, 1957, fig. 320, 1–3):

A – arrangement of teeth on the jaws; B – gill arch; C – pharyngeal teeth; D – form of teeth.

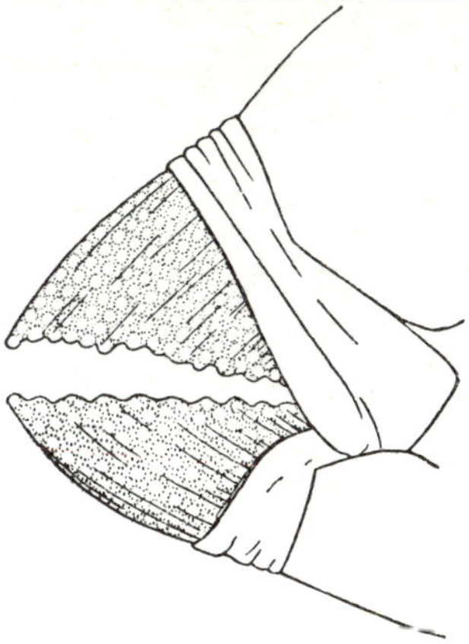

FIGURE 593. Beak of Oplegnathus fasciatus (Oplegnathidae)

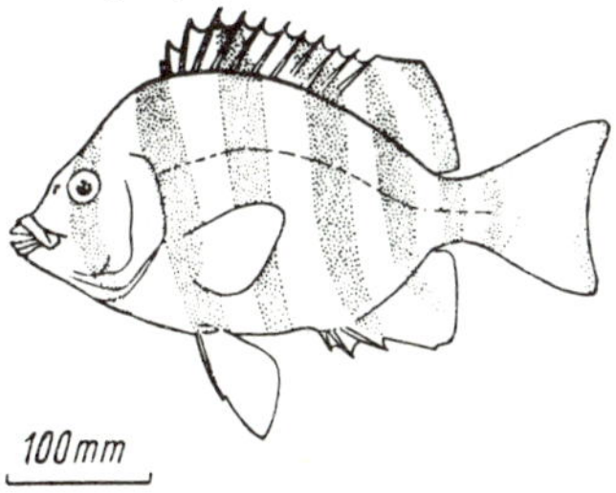

FIGURE 594. Oplegnathidae – Oplegnathus fasciatus (Okada, 1955, fig. 227, diagr.)

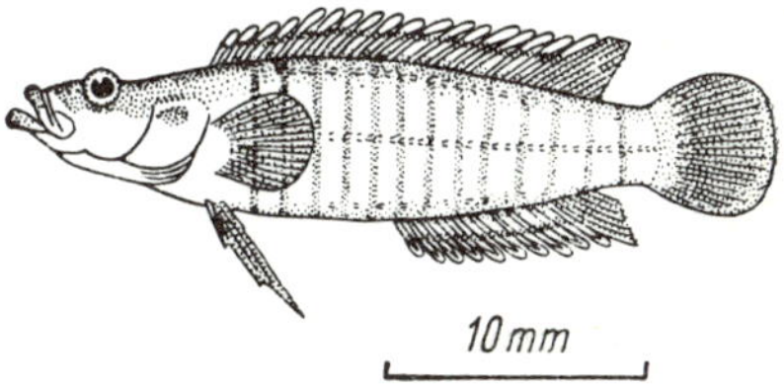

FIGURE 595. Acanthoclinidae – Ernogrammoides fasciatus (M., 1955, III, fig. 224)

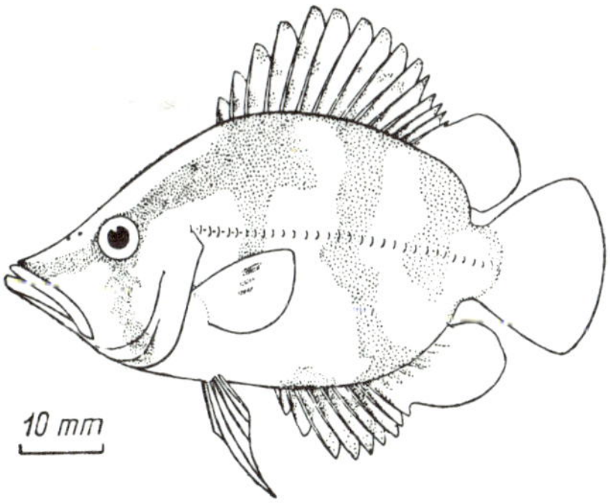

FIGURE 596. Polycentridae – Polycentropsis abbreviata (Sterba, 1959, fig. 1037, diagr.)

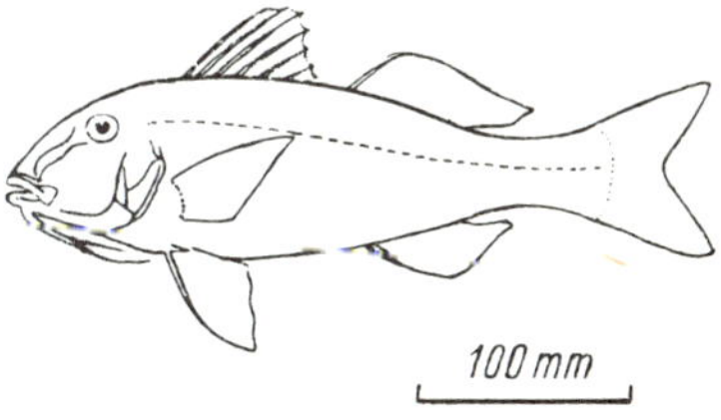

FIGURE 597. Mullidae – Pseudupeneus chrysopleuron (Okada, 1955, fig. 233, diagr.)

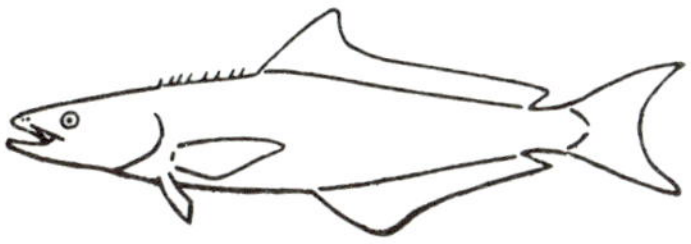

FIGURE 598. Rachycentridae (GRWM, 1966: 425, fig.)

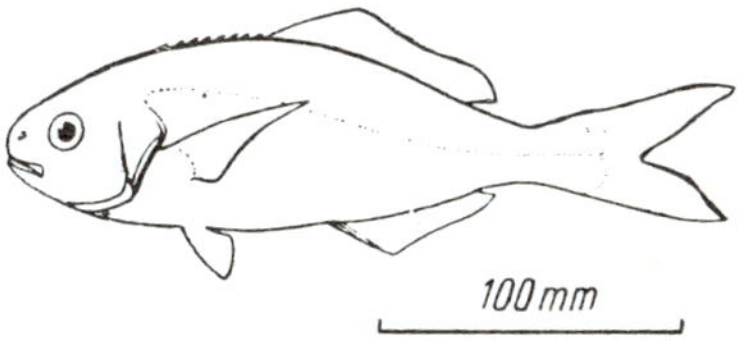

FIGURE 599. Ocycrius japonicus (Stromateidae) (Okada, 1955, fig. 146, diagr.)

2 (1). Premaxillaries protrusible.

3 (4). Base of anal fin much shorter than base of soft dorsal and not longer than the distance from the base of the ventrals to the origin of the anal. Pectoral fins usually short, not sickle-shaped. There is a clearly defined accessory maxillary bone. (Figure 601) . . . . subfamily 292.2. Seriolinae

4 (3). Base of anal fin together with the separate spiny rays and accessory fins, if these present, about the same length as the base of the soft dorsal and longer than the distance from the base of the ventrals to the origin of the anal fin.

5 (8). Lateral line generally with well developed scutes, at any rate in the posterior part; if the scutes are weakly developed, the pectoral fins are long and sickle-shaped.

6 (7). Scutes of lateral line distinctly defined. (Figure 602) . . . . subfamily 292.3. Caranginae

7 (6). Scutes of lateral line weakly expressed and hard to distinguish. Dorsal profile of body curved slightly less than ventral profile. Body strongly laterally compressed, with somewhat tapering margins. Pectoral fins sickle-shaped. (Figure 603) . . . . subfamily 292.4. Chloroscombrinae

8 (5). Lateral line without scutes. Pectoral fins short, not sickle-shaped. Scales small, round, or pointed. (Figure 604) . . . . subfamily 292.5. Trachinotinae

14 (13). Two spiny rays in front of anal fin, separated from it, absent in adults.

15 (16). All spiny rays of dorsal fin with long, threadlike tips. Ventral fins with 6 branched rays. (Figure 605). . . .293. Nematistiidae

16 (15). Spiny rays of dorsal fin without long, threadlike tips, but if these do occur exceptionally, then there are fewer than 6 branched rays in the ventral fins.

17 (18). Dorsal fin shifted to posterior half of body and situated above anal fin, the base of which is about as long as the dorsal fin. Dorsal with 4—6 strong spiny rays. Head tapering. Lower jaw protruding forward; mouth half-superior, strongly protrusible. Ventral fins well developed. Scales large. Lateral line with 20—40 perforated scales. (Figure 606) . . . . 318. Toxotidae

18 (17). Dorsal fin not shifted posteriorly; it occupies both the posterior and part of the anterior half of the back, but if it is shifted,[90] the spiny rays are very weak.

19 (26). Anterior rays of soft dorsal and of anal markedly elongate and giving both fins a sickle shape.[91]

20 (23). Dorsal fin with two separate bases.

[90] In the genus Leptobrama of family 317. Pempheridae the dorsal is shifted somewhat back, but its spiny rays are weak and the base of the fin is much shorter than the long base of the anal fin (Figure 607).

[91] The dorsal and anal fins are sickle-shaped in the genus Taractichthys of family 296. Bramidae, but here the dorsal has one base and no spiny rays, the ventral fins are not sickle-shaped, and the lower jaw protrudes far in front of the upper.

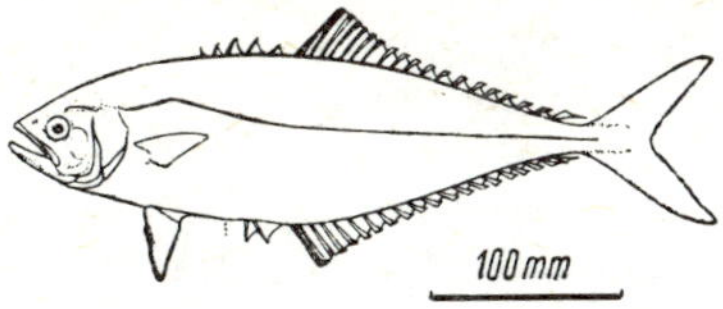

FIGURE 600. Carangidae (Chorineminae) – *Oligoplites saurus* (J. and E., 1900, fig. 378, diagr.)

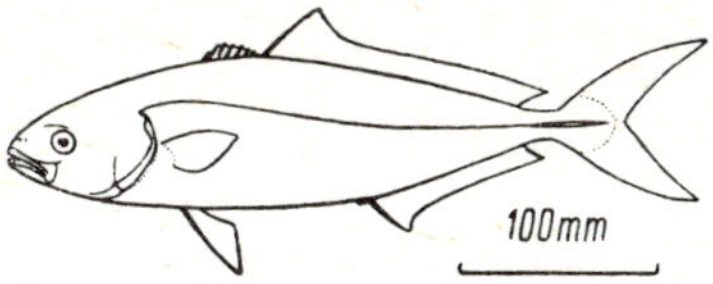

FIGURE 601. Carangidae (Seriolinae) – *Seriola aureovittata* (Okada, 1955, fig. 152, diagr.)

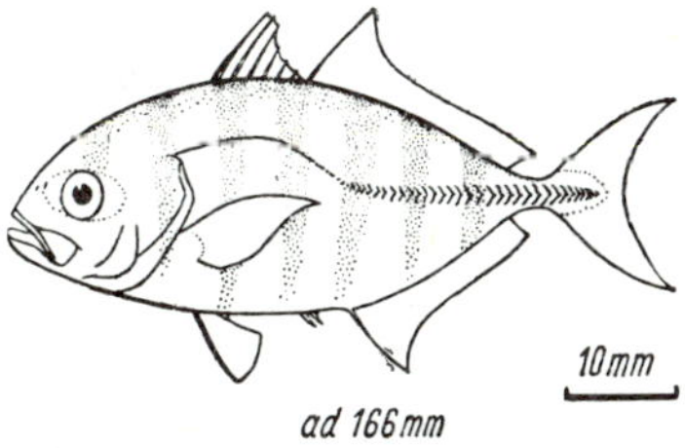

FIGURE 602. Carangidae (Caranginae) – *Caranx sexfasciatus* (Quoy and Gaimard, 1824, pl. 65, fig. 4, diagr.)

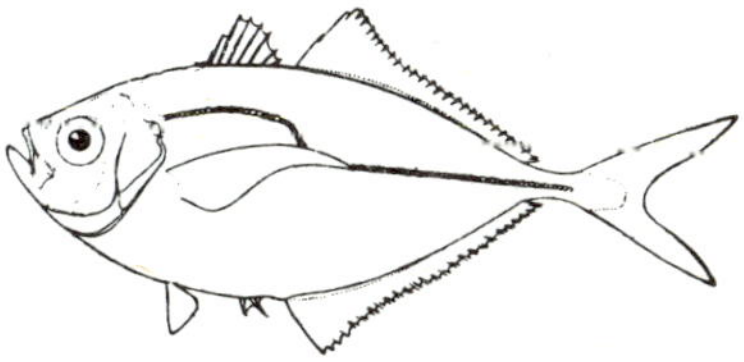

FIGURE 603. Carangidae (Chloroscombrinae) – *Chloroscombrus chrysurus* (J. and E., 1900, fig. 394, diagr.)

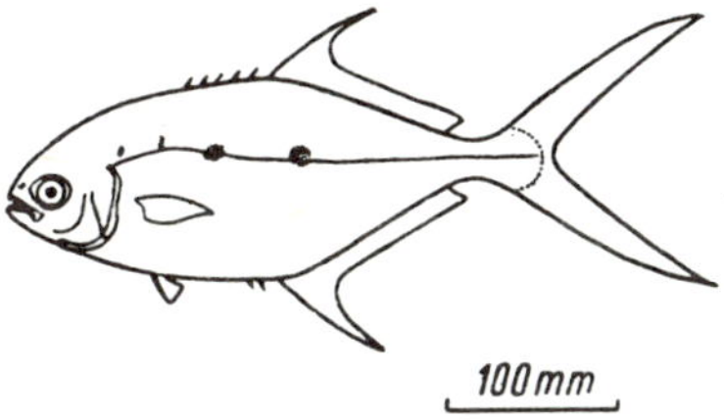

FIGURE 604. Carangidae (Trachinotinae) – *Trachinotus jordani* (Okada, 1955, fig. 160, diagr.)

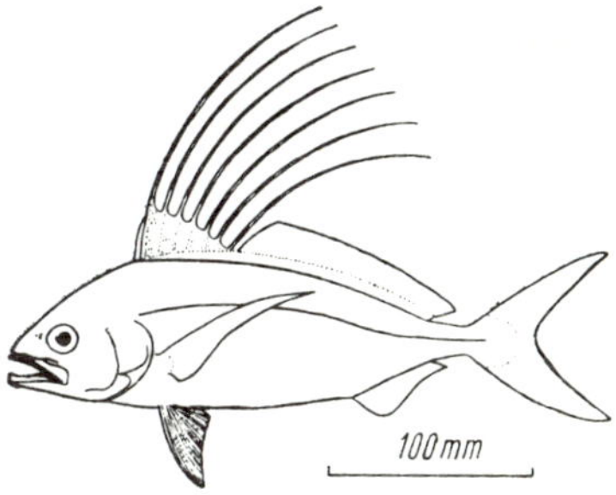

FIGURE 605. Nematistiidae – *Nematistius pectoralis* (J. and E., 1900, fig. 377, diagr.)

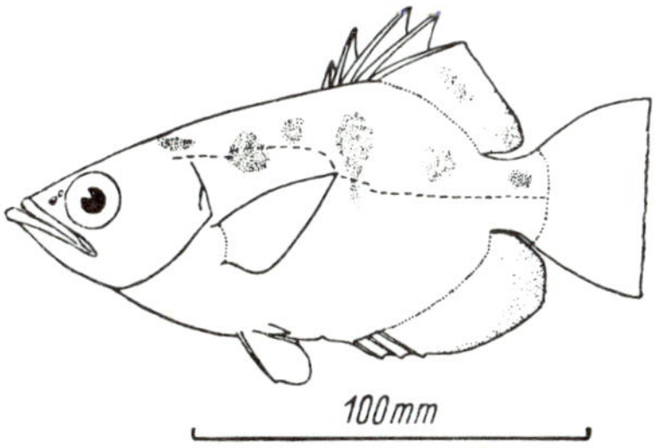

FIGURE 606. Toxotidae – *Toxotes chatareus* (W. and B., 1936, 7, fig. 53, A, diagr.)

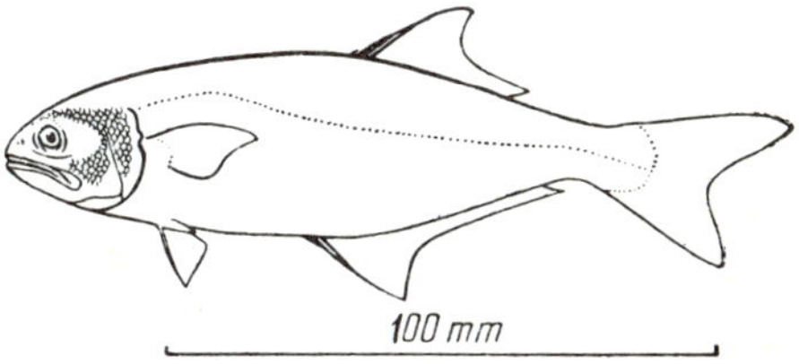

FIGURE 607. *Leptobrama muelleri* (Leptobramidae) (W. and B., 1936, 7, fig. 57, diagr.)

21 (22). Ventral fins broadly attached to the body, large, and bearing quite a long, thick spiny ray. Snout pointed; palatines with teeth. (Figure 608) . . . . 330. Enoplosidae

22 (21). Ventral fins narrowly attached to body, of moderate size, with a thin spiny ray. Snout blunt; palatines without teeth. (Figure 609) . . . . .323. Ephippidae . . . . (Ex parte—Chaetodipterus)

23 (20). Dorsal fin with one base.

24 (25). Ventral fins either small and scarcely distinguishable (Figure 610), or if of normal size, not sickle-shaped. Branchiostegal membranes free of the interbranchial space. Palatines with teeth . . . . 316. Monodactylidae[92]

25 (24). Ventral fins long, sickle-shaped (Figure 612). Branchiostegal membranes broadly attached to the interbranchial space. Palatines without teeth. . . . . 325. Platacidae

26 (19). Anterior rays of soft dorsal and of anal fin not elongate, but if they are, they do not make either fin sickle-shaped.

27 (38). Body as a rule very deep, its maximum depth more than 1/2 the entire length of the body, but if slightly less than this, then there are 4—6 spiny rays in the anal fin or one long, barbel-like ray in the first dorsal, pectoral, and ventral fins (see thesis 50.1.1—32, footnote). Dorsal fin with one base, but its spiny rays are clearly expressed.

28 (29). Ventral fins large, with a long (2/3 as long as the fin), thick spine; they are inserted under or a little behind the base of the pectorals. From 4 to 14 spiny rays in dorsal fin, 3—6 in anal (Figure 613). [Preorbital bone shifted forward and not taking part in formation of margin of orbit.] Bones of head rough, not covered with skin . . . . 331. Pentacerotidae

29 (28). Ventral fins of moderate size or small; if enlarged, the spiny ray is not large, less than 2/3 as long as the fin, and not thick.

30 (33). First spiny ray of dorsal fin directed forward, projecting markedly from under the skin and clearly distinguishable. Second spiny ray of anal fin not greatly enlarged.[93]

31 (32). Anal fin with 4 spiny rays (Figure 615). Branchiostegal membranes narrowly attached to interbranchial space, forming a fold across it. . . . . 327. Scatophagidae

32 (31). Anal fin with 3 spiny rays (Figure 616). Branchiostegal membranes broadly attached to interbranchial space . . . . 323. Ephippidae[94]

[92] In the outwardly similar form Pampus argenteus of family 415. Pampidae (Figure 611) ventral fins are absent, the gill openings are shortened, and the pharyngeal sacs bear teeth.

[93] In the genus Hapalogenys of family 309. Pomadasyidae and in representatives of some other families, but less distinctly, the first spiny ray of the dorsal fin is also directed forward (Figure 614) but the second spiny ray of the anal fin is greatly enlarged.

[94] The species Rhinoprenes pentanemus, which Munro (1964) described and took as the type of a new family, 324. Rhinoprenidae, is characterized by the presence, in the first dorsal and in the pectoral and ventral fins, of one long, barbel-like ray which reaches or even passes beyond the base of the caudal fin, 3-apexed teeth on the lower jaw, a peculiar structure of the nares, and also by the insertion of the ventral fins almost under the eye (Figure 616 A).

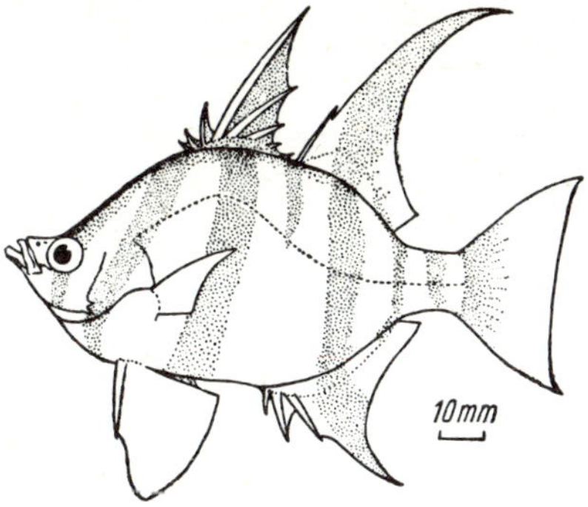

FIGURE 608. Enoplosidae – *Enoplosus armatus* (Waite, 1921, fig. 178, diagr.)

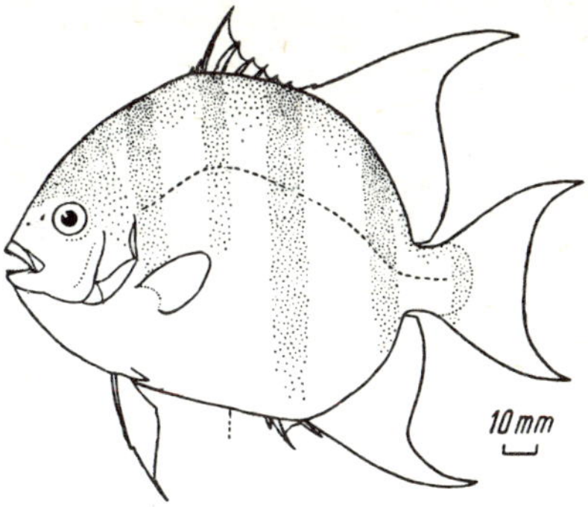

FIGURE 609. Ephippidae – *Chaetodipterus faber* (Jordan, 1925, fig. 506, diagr.)

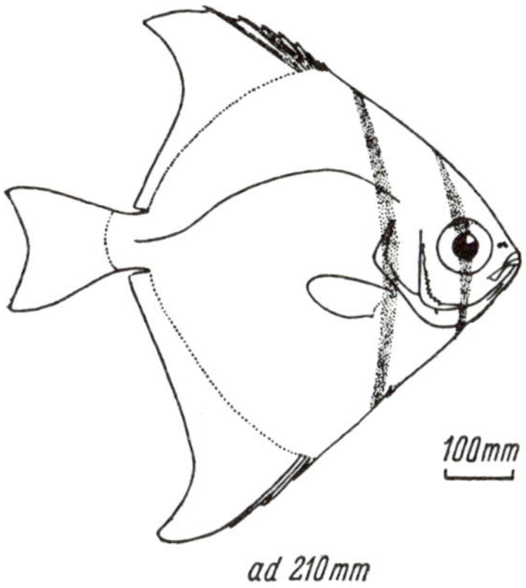

FIGURE 610. Monodactylidae – *Monodactylus (Psettus) argenteus* (W. and B., 1936, 7, fig. 54, diagr.)

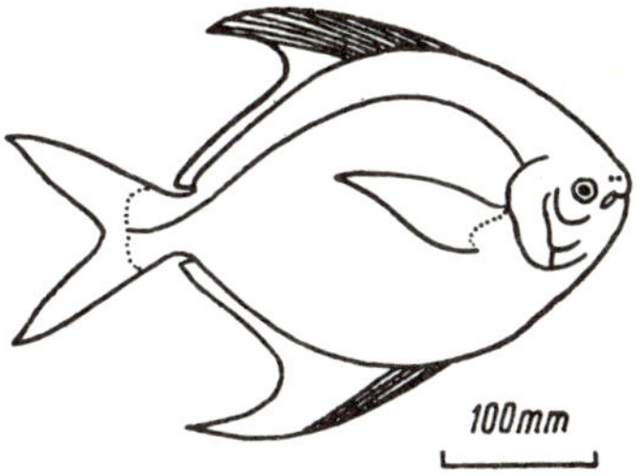

FIGURE 611. *Pampus argenteus* (Pampidae) (Okada, 1955, fig. 145, diagr.)

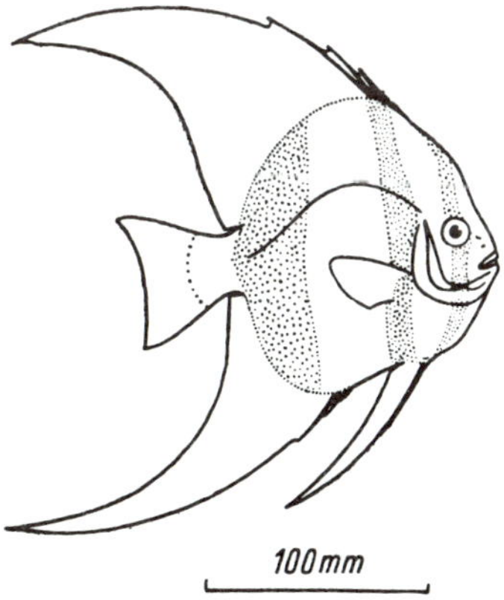

FIGURE 612. Platacidae – *Platax orbicularis* (Okada, 1955, fig. 259, diagr.)

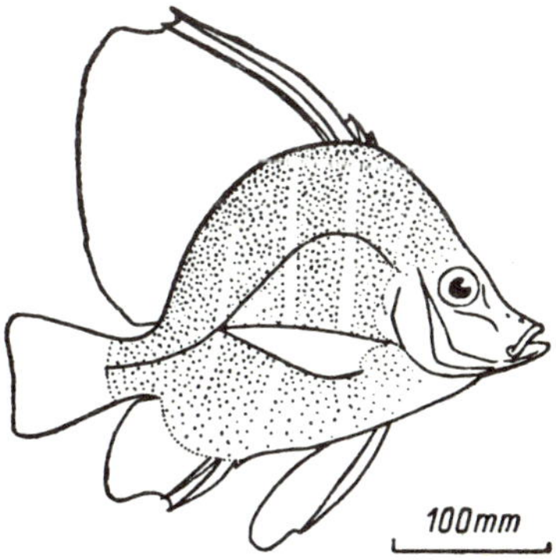

FIGURE 613. Pentacerotidae – *Histiopterus typus* (Okada, 1955, fig. 229, diagr.)

33 (30). First spiny ray of dorsal fin not directed forward but normally, like all the other rays, upward, but if it is directed forward, this can be discerned only on X-ray photographs.

34 (35). Pectoral fin sickle-shaped, very long, much longer than the head. Scales cycloid. Lateral line complete, with about 50 perforated scales. Branchiostegal membranes narrowly attached to interbranchial space. (Figure 617) . . . . 326. **Drepanidae**

35 (34). Pectoral fins not sickle-shaped, of moderate size, not longer than the head.

36 (37). Lateral line not complete, not reaching to the base of the caudal fin. Small fishes of coral islands, brightly colored . . . . 328. Chaetodontidae (Ex parte, see thesis 50.1.1—98)

2 subfamilies:

1 (2). Margin of preoperculum sometimes serrate, but there is no strong spine in the corner in adults (Figure 618) . . . . subfamily 328.1. Chaetodontinae

2 (1). Margin of preoperculum often serrate and there is always a strong spine in the corner (Figure 619) . . . . subfamily 328.2. Pomacanthinae

37 (36). Lateral line complete, reaching to the base of the caudal fin. The spiny dorsal fin has a very short base and is similar to the ventrals in size and form. (Figure 620) . . . . 329. **Caproidae**

38 (27). Body as a rule oblong or moderately deep, its maximum depth less than 1/2 the entire length of the body; no long, barbel-like rays in the first dorsal or in the pectoral and ventral fins; if the body is deep, and the dorsal fin has one base, then the spiny rays of the dorsal are hard to distinguish from the soft rays, or there are no spiny rays.

39 (64). No spiny rays in the dorsal fin, which has one base, or else they are difficult to distinguish from the soft rays, or, finally, they are thin and flexible and similar to unbranched soft rays.

40 (41). Ventral fins absent. Body deep, with strong lateral compression. A clearly expressed keel on each side of the dorsal peduncle (Figure 621). [Posterior part of pharynx without lateral expansions (sacs) supplied with teeth[95]] . . . . 294. **Formionidae**

41 (40). Ventral fins present.

42 (51). Body deep, with strong lateral compression; depth of body greater than length of head, but sometimes the impression of the body's being deep is produced by the very long rays of the vertical fins.

43 (44). Form of body almost triangular; abdominal part with a much larger area than the dorsal part, strongly flattened and bearing the character of a keel. First ray of ventral fins elongate in adults. (Figure 623) . . . . 295. **Menidae**

[95] [Lateral expansion (sacs) in the posterior part of the pharynx, supplied with teeth, are present in members of suborder 50.12. Stromateoidei (Perciformes), which are outwardly very similar to the fish of family 294. Formionidae, but they do not have keels on the sides of the caudal peduncle (Figure 622).]

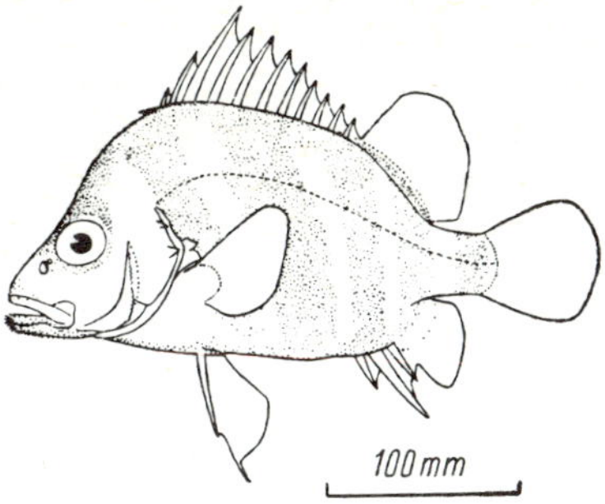

FIGURE 614. Hapalogenys mucronatus (Pomadasyidae) (M., 1955, III, fig. 244, diagr.)

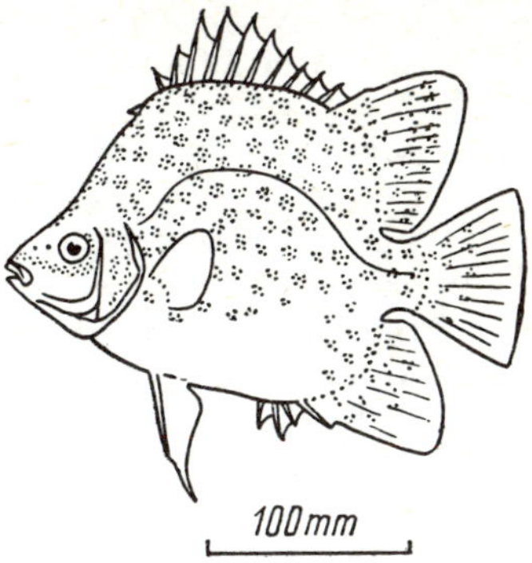

FIGURE 615. Scatophagidae – Scatophagus argus (M., 1955, III, fig. 346, diagr.)

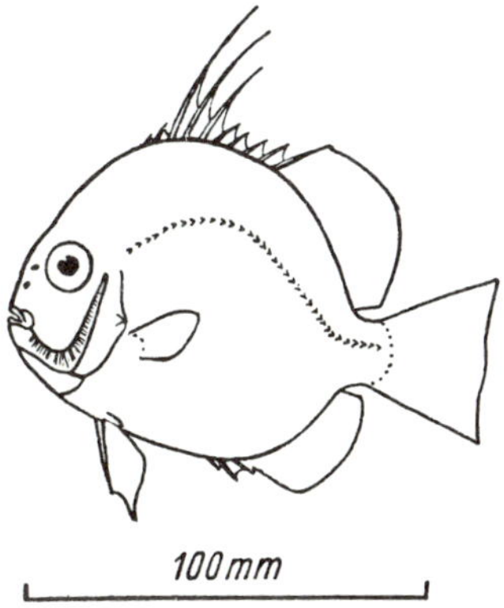

FIGURE 616. Ephippidae – Ephippus orbis (M., 1955, III, fig. 338, diagr.)

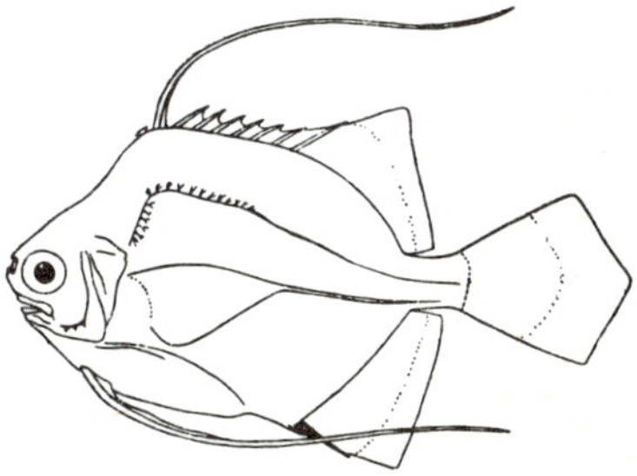

FIGURE 616A. Rhinoprenidae – Rhinoprenes pentanemus (Munro, 1964, fig. 19)

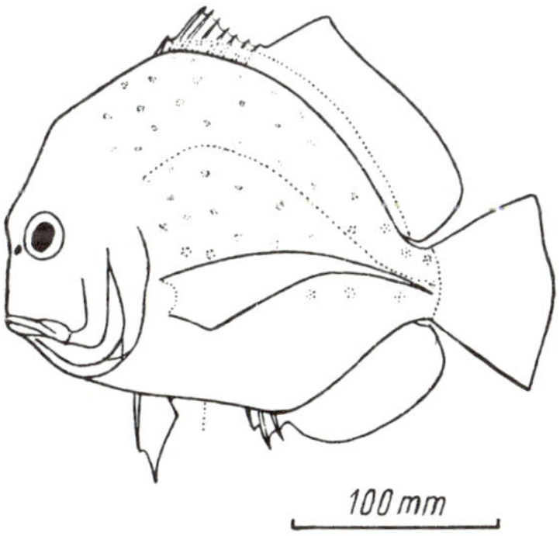

FIGURE 617. Drepanidae – Drepana punctata (Chevey, 1932, fig. 37, diagr.)

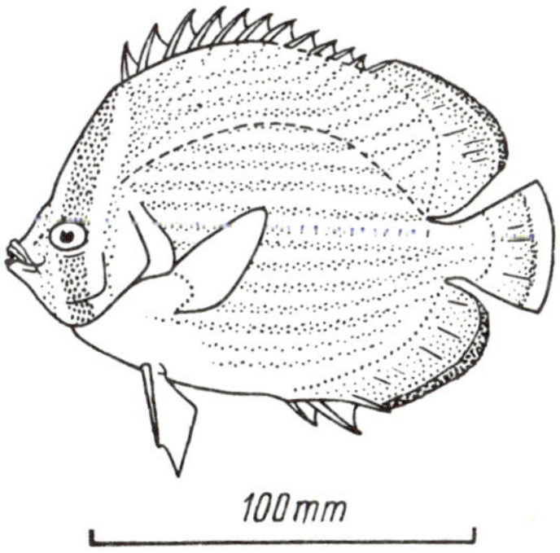

FIGURE 618. Chaetodontidae (Chaetodontinae) – Chaetodon collaris (Okada, 1955, fig. 255, diagr.)

44 (43). Form of body not triangular; abdominal and dorsal parts about the same in area. First ray of ventral fins not elongate.

45 (46). Ventral fins large and long, more than twice as long as the pectorals and about as long as the trunk. (Figure 624) . . . . 248. **Caristiidae**[96]

46 (45). Ventral fins small or of moderate size, shorter than the pectorals.

47 (50). Base of dorsal fin longer than base of anal.

48 (49). Ventral fins inserted on the thorax under the base of the pectoral fins or somewhat in front of them (Taractes).[97] Most rays of dorsal and anal fins jointed and branched. Fins covered with scales which, however, do not form a sheath for the rays. (Figure 625) . . . . 296. **Bramidae**

49 (48). Ventral fins inserted considerably in front of base of pectorals, more or less on the throat. All rays of dorsal and anal fins unjointed and simple, not branched. Fins very high, not covered with scales, but there is a sheath of scales for the bases of the rays (Figure 627). . . . . 297. **Pteraclidae**

50 (47). Base of dorsal fin much shorter than base of anal . . . . 317. **Pempheridae**

2 subfamilies:

1 (2). Dorsal fin in front of the vertical passing through the middle of the length of the body (without C). Eyes large, without an adipose eyelid. Maxillary bone strongly widened posteriorly, but relatively short, not passing beyond the vertical of the posterior margin of the pupil. (Figure 628) . . . . subfamily 317.1. Pempherinae

2 (1). Dorsal fin behind the vertical passing through the middle of the length of the body (without C). Eyes small, with a well developed adipose eyelid. Maxillary bone not strongly widened posteriorly, relatively long, passing beyond the vertical of the posterior margin of the pupil (Figure 629) . . . . subfamily 317.2. Leptobraminae[98]

51 (42). Body oblong or elongate, with moderate lateral compression; depth of body approximately equal to or smaller than length of head.

52 (53). Dorsal fin originating on the head directly behind the eyes, long; it has 57—64 soft rays; no spiny rays. Snout markedly rounded, blunt, its anterior margin with a very steep profile. Body elongate, scales small. Pseudobranch absent. (Figure 630) . . . . 298. **Coryphaenidae**

[96] Berg (1940) included family 248. Caristiidae in order 44. Beryciformes (see theses 0—149 and 44—16), but here it is treated at the same time in the Perciformes.

[97] [The genus Steingeria Jordan and Evermann, 1886 (Figure 626), a synonym of the genus Taractes Lowe, 1843 and hypothetically placed by Norman (1958:271) in family 297. Pteraclidae, is referred, like the Trachyberycidae (Maul, 1954), to family 296. Bramidae (G. W. Mead and G. E. Maul, Bull. Mus. Comp. Zool., Harvard Coll., Cambridge, Mass., USA, 119, 6, 1958:393—418, figs.).]

[98] Isolated as a separate family, 317a. Leptobramidae (Tominaga, 1965:33—56, 1968:43—95).

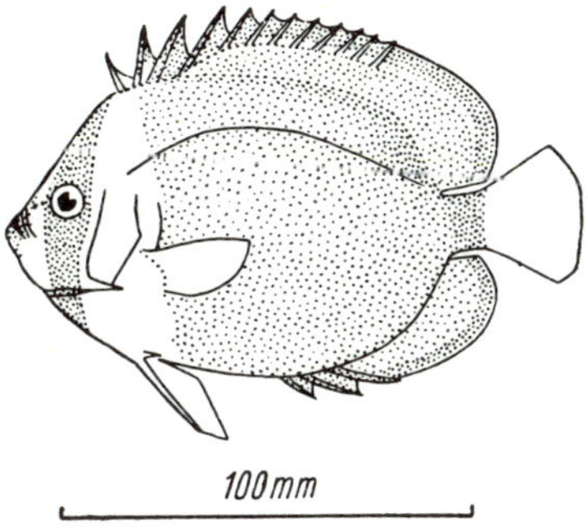

FIGURE 619. Chaetodontidae (Pomacanthinae) – *Holacanthus mesoleucus* (W. and B., 1936, 7, fig. 31)

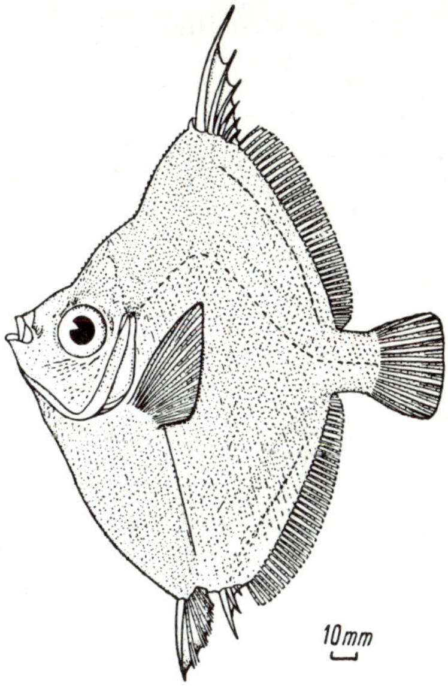

FIGURE 620. Caproidae – *Antigonia capros* (M., 1955, III, fig. 339)

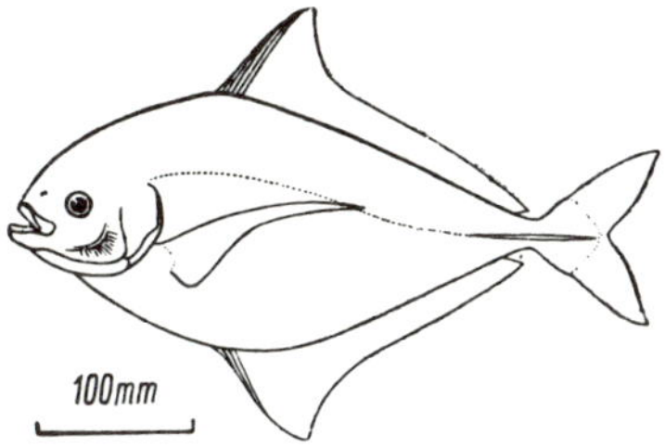

FIGURE 621. Formionidae – *Formio niger* (M., 1955, III, fig. 181, diagr.)

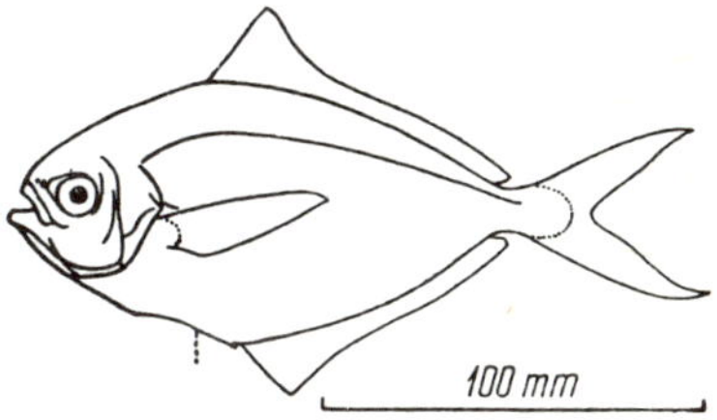

FIGURE 622. *Perpilus triacanthus* (Stromateidae) (Haedrich, 1967, fig. 40, diagr.)

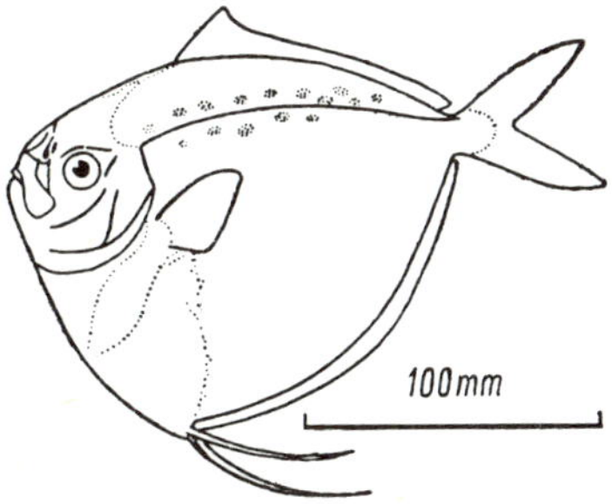

FIGURE 623. Menidae – *Mene maculata* (Okada, 1955, fig. 161, diagr.)

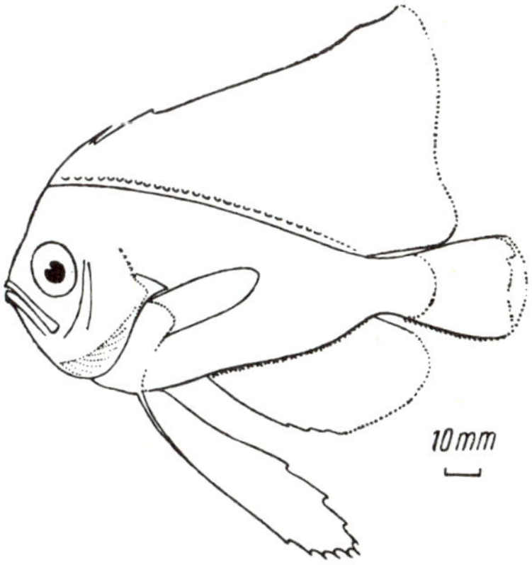

FIGURE 624. Caristiidae – *Elephenor macropus* (M., 1955, III, fig. 173, diagr.)

53 (52). Dorsal fin originating behind the head; several of its anterior rays are unjointed and resemble very thin spiny rays.

54 (61). Anal fin with 1 — 2 weak spiny rays or with none. Last soft rays of dorsal and anal fins shortened.

55 (58). Lateral line incomplete, passing near the base of the dorsal fin. Ventral fins with 1 spiny and 4 soft rays. Not more than 3 unbranched rays in dorsal fin.

56 (57). Head covered with scales. [Vertebrae 11 + 16.] (Figure 631) . . . . 274. **Pseudoplesiopidae**

57 (56). Head bare. [Vertebrae 11 + 22.] (Figure 632) . . . . 275. **Anisochromidae**

58 (55). Lateral line complete, passing along the sides of the body. Ventral fins with 1 spiny and 5 soft rays. Often more than 3 unbranched rays or weak spiny rays in dorsal fin.

59 (60). At least 40 rays in each of the soft dorsal and the anal fin. Body markedly thin. Margin of preoperculum not serrate. (Figure 633) . . . . 286. **Malacanthidae**

60 (59). Less than 30 rays in each of the soft dorsal and the anal fin. Body not very thin. Margin of preoperculum more or less serrate. (Figure 634) . . . . 285. **Branchiostegidae**

61 (54). Anal fin with 3 weak spiny rays.

62 (63). Last soft rays of dorsal and anal fins markedly elongate. Pectoral fin with a deep notch. Lateral line present. Both jaws thick, lower jaw projecting forward. Snout longer than diameter of eye. (Figure 635) . . . . .303. **Aphareidae**

63 (62). Last soft rays of dorsal and anal fins not elongate. Pectoral fin without a notch. Lateral line absent. Jaws not thickened. Snout shorter than diameter of eye. (Figure 636). . . . . 270. **Grammidae** (Ex parte — *Lipogramma*)

64 (39). Dorsal fin with one base, bearing spiny rays which are well developed and are clearly expressed, or else dorsal fin absent.

65 (76). Two lateral lines,[99] both incomplete, the upper one in the anterior part of the body above the midline, the lower one in the posterior part along the middle of the sides.

66 (69). Teeth present on parasphenoid. Anal fin with 3 — 4 spiny rays. Freshwater fishes of West Africa and Southeast Asia.

67 (68). Mouth small, moderately protrusible, ascending processes of premaxillaries not reaching the frontal bones. Branchiostegal membranes united (Figure 638) . . . . 382. **Pristolepididae**

68 (67). Mouth large, strongly protrusible, ascending processes of premaxillaries long, not just reaching but even passing beyond the frontal bones and situated in furrows formed by bifurcation of the occipital crest. Branchiostegal membranes not united. (Figure 639) . . . . 333. **Nandidae**[100]

[99] There are also two lateral lines in the genus *Gymnapogon* of family 281. Apogonidae but here in addition there are numerous vertical lines of pores and the body is bare (Figure 637).

[100] A separate family is isolated, 33a. Badidae, with the genus *Badis* Bleeker (Barlow, Liem, and Wickler, 1968).

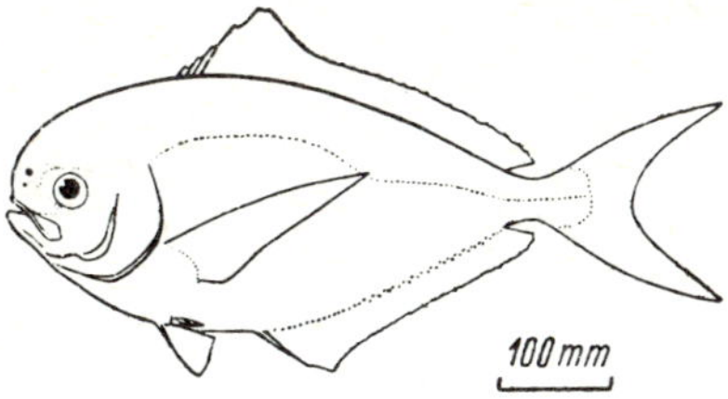

FIGURE 625. Bramidae – Brama brama (Okada, 1955, fig.163, diagr.)

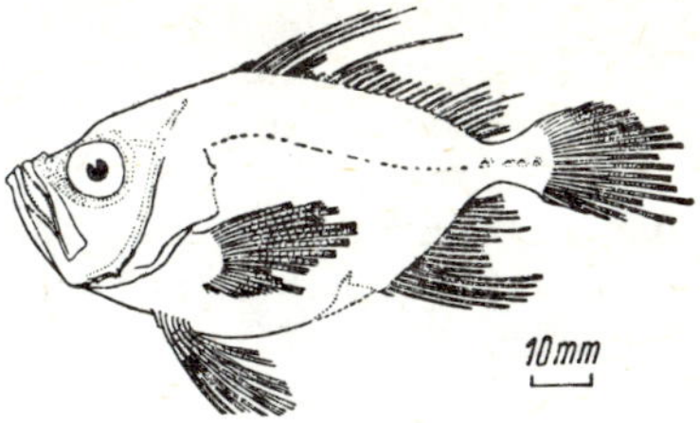

FIGURE 626. Steinegeria rubescens Taractes rubescens (Bramidae) (Mead and Maul, 1958, fig. 3, diagr.)

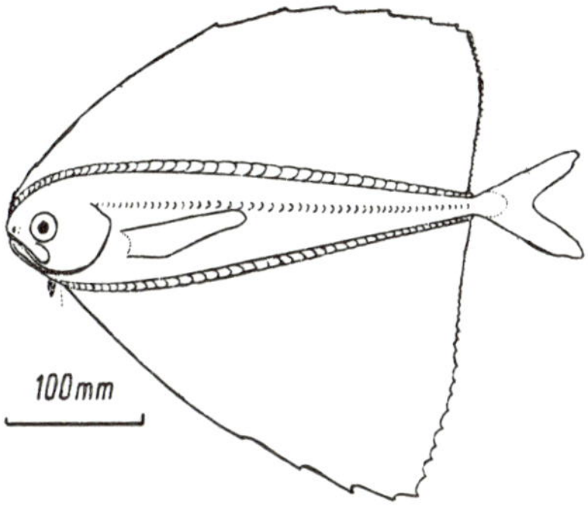

FIGURE 627. Pteraclidae – Bentenia aesticola (M., 1955, III, fig. 171, diagr.)

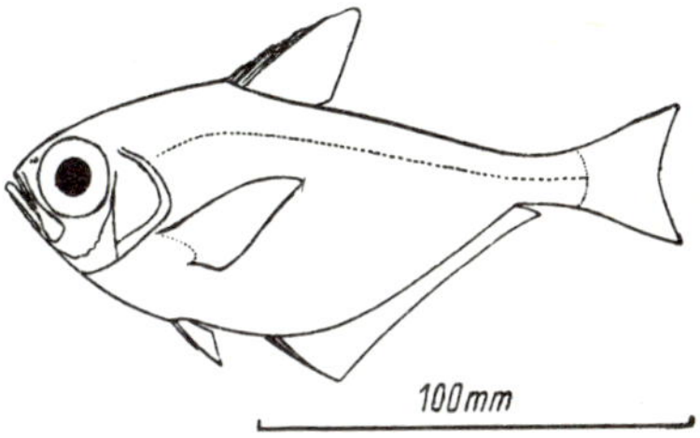

FIGURE 628. Pempheridae (Pempherinae) – Pempheris moluca (Chu et al., 1962, fig. 466, diagr.)

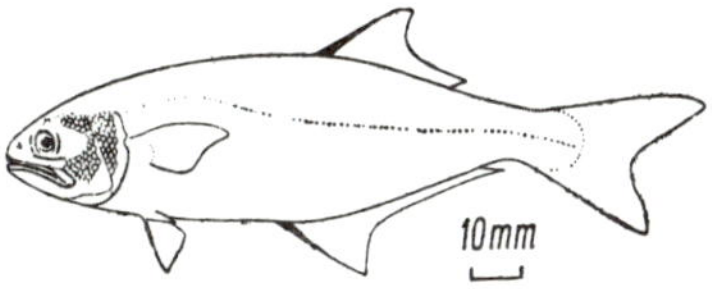

FIGURE 629. Leptobramidae – Leptobrama muelleri (W. and B., 1936, 7, fig. 57, diagr.)

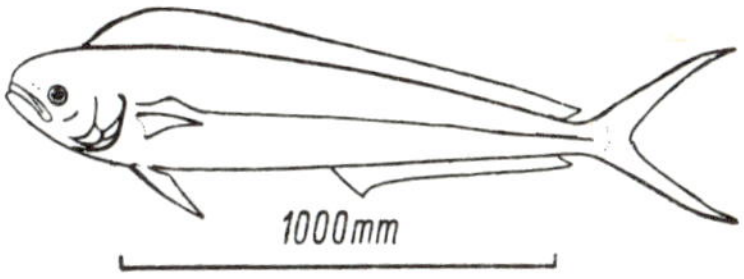

FIGURE 630. Coryphaenidae – Coryphaena hippurus (Okada, 1955, fig. 141, diagr.)

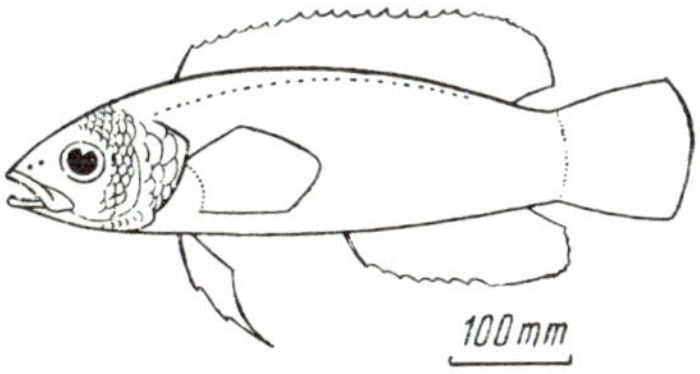

FIGURE 631. Pseudoplesiopidae – Pseudoplesiops typus (W. and B., 1929, 5, fig. 92)

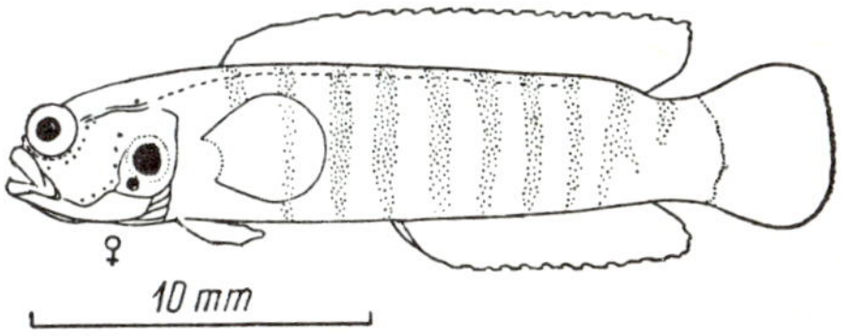

FIGURE 632. Anisochromidae – Anisochromis kenyae (H. Smith, 1954, fig. 1, diagr.)

69 (66). Teeth absent on parasphenoid.

70 (71). Ventral fins with 1 concealed spiny and 4 soft rays the first of which is thickened and bifurcate. Dorsal fin with 11–14 spiny rays. (Figure 640) . . . . 276. **Plesiopidae**

71 (70). Ventral fins with 1 spiny and 5 soft rays.

72 (73). No more than 3 spiny rays in dorsal fin. (Figure 641) . . . . 268. **Pseudochromidae**

73 (72). More than 3 spiny rays in dorsal fin.

74 (75). Dorsal fin with 6–7 spiny rays. (Figure 642). . . . . 269. **Pseudogrammidae**

75 (74). Dorsal fin with 11–13 spiny rays. (Figure 643)[101] . . . . 270. **Grammidae** (Ex parte—without L i p o g r a m m a)

76 (65). One lateral line.

77 (96). Two dorsal fins, their bases well separated, but if close together, then not joined by a membrane.[102]

78 (79). Base of anal fin considerably longer than the base of the soft dorsal. Height of first dorsal greater than the length of its base. (Figure 645). . . . . 288. **Lactariidae**

79 (78). Base of anal fin as long as or shorter than the base of the soft dorsal. Height of first dorsal smaller than the length of its base, more rarely the same as this.

80 (81). Oral slit small; maxillary bone very short, ending far short of the eye and even before the nares. Body shallow, almost cylindrical, with slight lateral compression. Length of base of soft dorsal more or less similar to that of anal. (Figure 646) . . . . 284. **Sillaginidae** (see thesis 146)

81 (80). Oral slit of moderate size or large; maxillary bone reaching the nares, but often passing beyond the anterior margin of the eye or even farther.

82 (83). Spiny dorsal fin very low, about twice as low as the soft dorsal which is long (about 25 rays) and is similar in size and form to the anal fin; both these fins are covered with scales. First spiny ray of anal fin small, often overgrown. (Figure 647) . . . . 289. **Pomatomidae**

83 (82). Spiny dorsal fin not low, the same height or a little lower or higher than the soft dorsal.

84 (89). There is an axillary lobe[103] at the base of the ventral fin.

85 (86). Preopercular bone with two serrate ridges on the margins. (Figure 648) . . . . 266. **Centropomidae** (Ex parte—266.1. Centropominae, see thesis 50.1.1—123)

86 (85). Preopercular bone with smooth margins.

[101] There is no lateral line in the genus L i p o g r a m m a (see Figure 636).

[102] Such fins are present in the genus O s t r a c o b e r y x Fowler, 1934, placed by Berg (1940 : 301) as the independent family Ostracoberycidae in the order Beryciformes, but included by other authors either in family 267. Serranidae (Matsubara, 1955 : 631) or in family 289. Pomatomidae (Norman, 1958 : 260) (Figure 644). In this work the genus is placed in the Serranidae.

[103] A long scaly appendage at the base of the ventral fin, represented by several elongate overlapping scales.

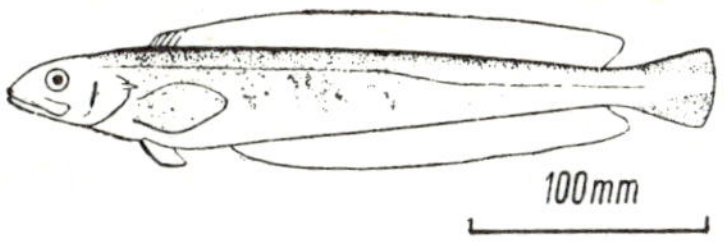

FIGURE 633. Malacanthidae – *Malacanthus parvipinnis* (J. and E., 1903 (1905), fig. 118, diagr.)

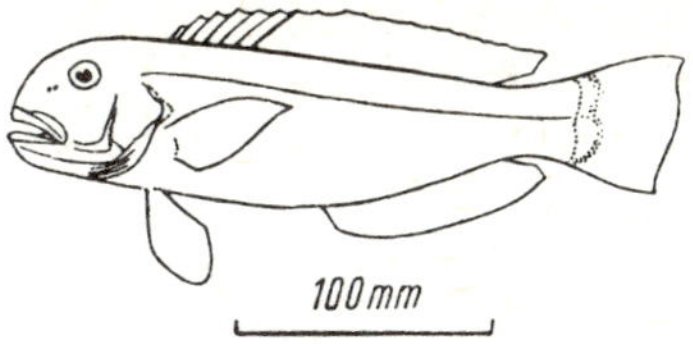

FIGURE 634. Branchiostegidae – *Branchiostegus (Latilus) japonicus* (Okada, 1955, fig. 238, diagr.)

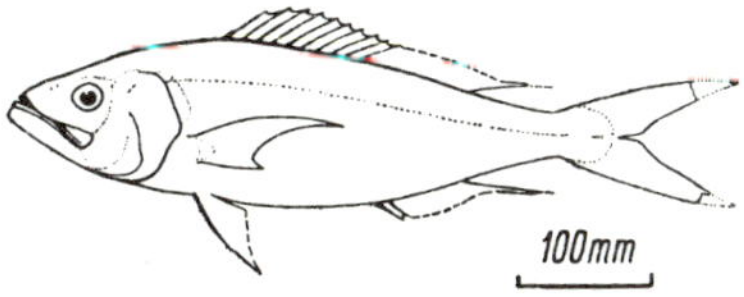

FIGURE 635. Aphareidae – *Aphareus furcatus* (M., 1955, III, fig. 239, diagr.)

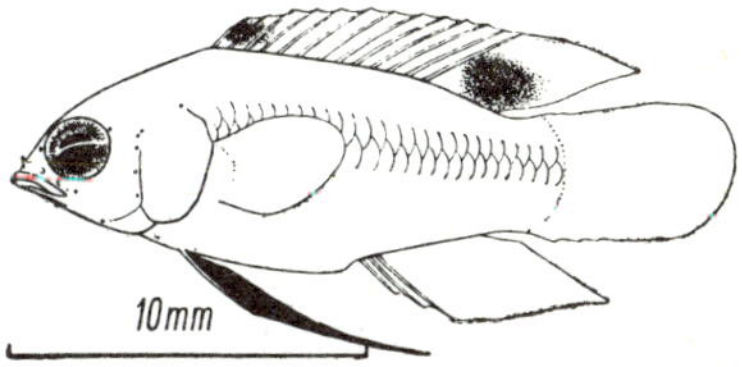

FIGURE 636. Grammidae – *Lipogramma anabantoides* (Böhlke, 1960, fig. 1, diagr.)

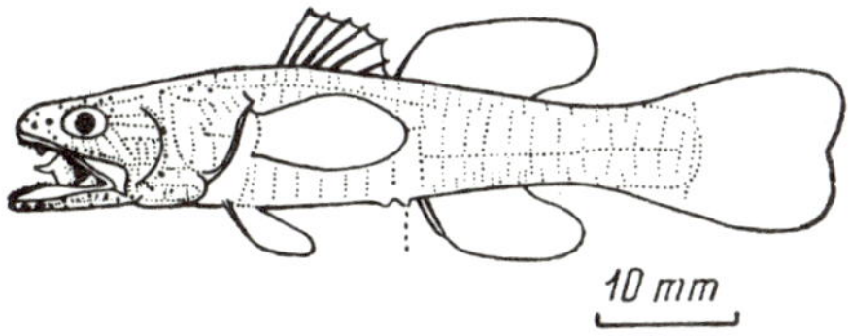

FIGURE 637. *Gymnapogon japonicus* (Apogonidae) (M., 1955, III, fig. 198, diagr.)

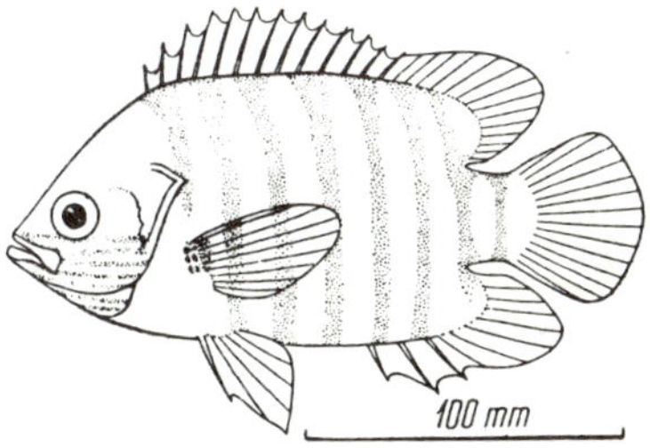

FIGURE 638. Pristolepididae – *Pristolepis fasciatus* (Sterba, 1959, fig. 1038)

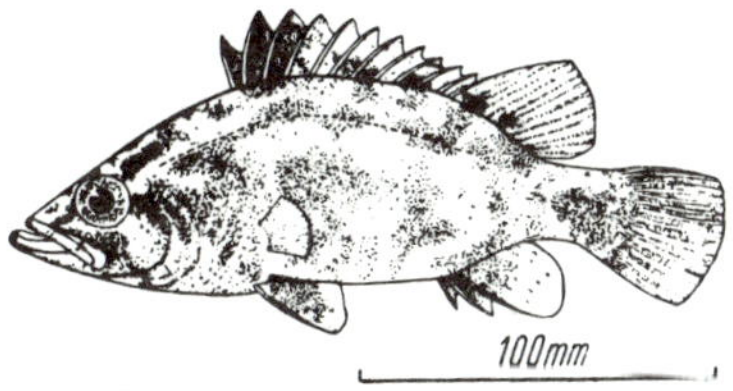

FIGURE 639. Nandidae – *Nandus nandus* (Sterba, 1959, fig. 845, diagr.)

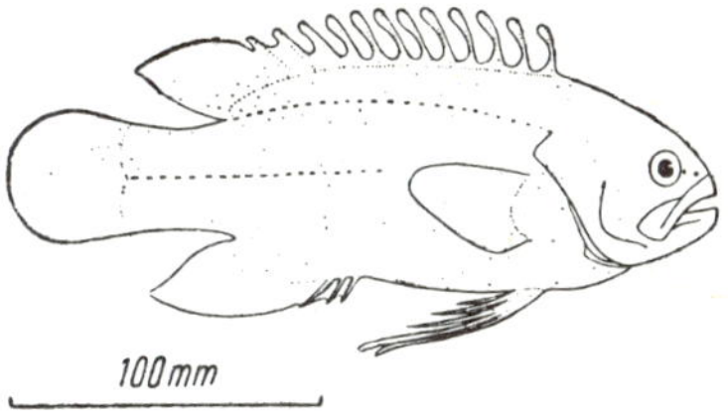

FIGURE 640. Plesiopidae – *Plesiops nigricans* (Wang, 1958, fig. 297, diagr.)

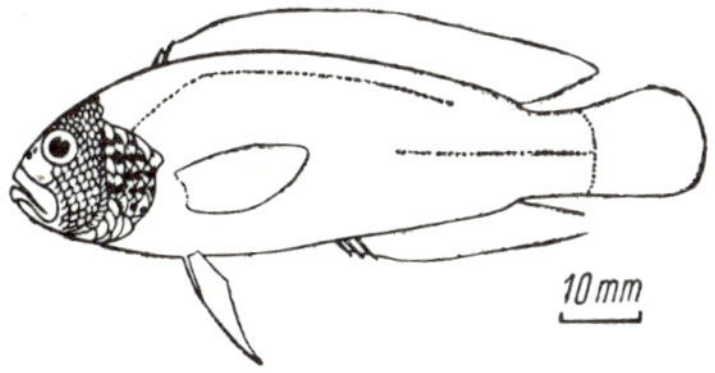

FIGURE 641. Pseudochromidae – *Dampieria spilopterus* (W. and B., 1931, 6, fig. 22, diagr.)

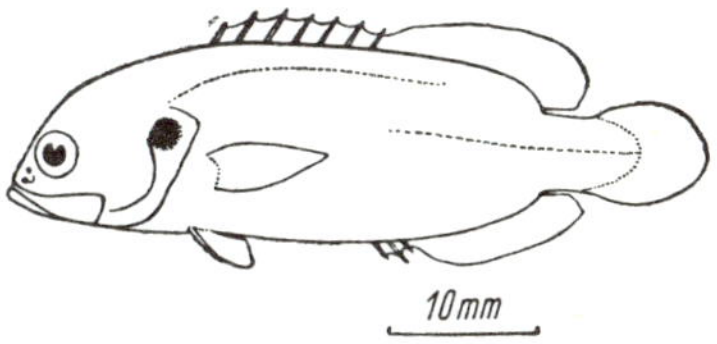

FIGURE 642. Pseudogrammidae – *Pseudogramma polyacanthus* (W. and B., 1931, 6, fig. 21, diagr.)

87 (88). Maxillary bone wide, not concealed under the preorbital (Figure 649) . . . . 300. **Emmelichthyidae** (see thesis 50.1.1—109)

88 (87). Maxillary narrow, completely concealed under the preorbital. (No figure) . . . . .301. **Inermiidae**

89 (84). No axillary lobe at the base of the ventral fin.

90 (91). Vent situated closer to base of ventral fins than to base of anal.[104] Anal fin with 3 spiny rays. Teeth velutinous. Vertebrae 31—35. (Figure 650). . . . . .202. **Acropomatidae**

91 (90). Vent situated closer to base of anal fin than to base of ventrals.

92 (93). Soft dorsal and the anal fin covered with scales; neither fin has more than 13 soft rays.[105] Anal fin with 3 spiny rays. (Figure 651) . . . . 290. **Scombropidae**

93 (92). Soft dorsal and the anal fin not covered with scales. Anal fin with 1—2 spiny rays.

94 (95). Dorsal fin with 5—6, more rarely 8—9 spiny rays; anal with 2 spiny rays. [Vertebrae 24—27.] Marine fishes . . . . 281. **Apogonidae**[106]

2 subfamilies:

1 (2). Body covered with scales. Lateral line generally complete. (Figure 652) . . . . subfamily 281.1. Apogoninae

2 (1). Body bare, not covered with scales. Lateral line interrupted; short vertical rows of pores on the body. (Figure 653) . . . . subfamily 281.2. Gymnapogoninae

95 (94). Dorsal fin as a rule with 8—19 spiny rays; anal with 1—2. [Vertebrae 30—48.] Freshwater fishes. (Figure 654) . . . . 283. **Percidae** (see thesis 50.1.1—149)

96 (77). Dorsal fins with one base; there is sometimes a more or less deep notch between the spiny and the soft part of the fin, but in this case, the membrane joining the two parts of the fin is always preserved.

97 (140). Axillary lobe usually present.

98 (99). Setiform teeth present, but canines absent, both anteriorly and on the outside of the sides of the jaws. (Figure 655) . . . . 328. **Chaetodontidae** (Ex parte, see thesis 50.1.1—36)

99 (98). Setiform teeth absent, but if sometimes present, then caninelike teeth are also present.

100 (101). Anal fin with 1—2 spiny rays. (Figure 656). . . . 310. **Sciaenidae**

101 (100). Anal fin with 3 spiny rays.

104 The same applies to fish of the genus Desmoamia of family 281. Apogonidae, but in these the anal fin has 2 spiny rays and there are small, sparse canines in the anterior part of the jaws.

105 Matsubara (1955:612) includes the genus Scombrops Temminck and Schlegel, 1845 in family 289. Pomatomidae (see Figure 647), in the representatives of which there are about 25 rays in the soft dorsal and in the anal fin.

106 A separate family is isolated, 281a. **Henichthyidae** (MA:138).

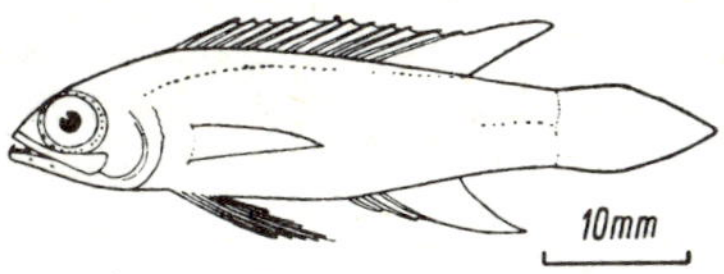

FIGURE 643. Grammidae – Gramma loreta (J. and E., 1900, fig. 508, diagr.)

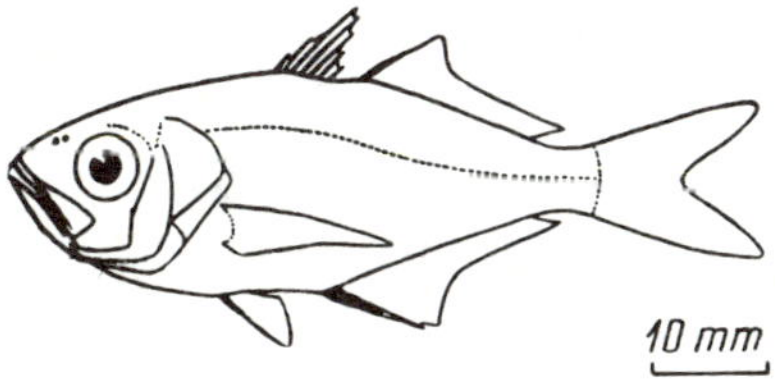

FIGURE 645. Lactariidae – Lactarius lactarius (W. and B., 1931, 6, fig. 65, diagr.)

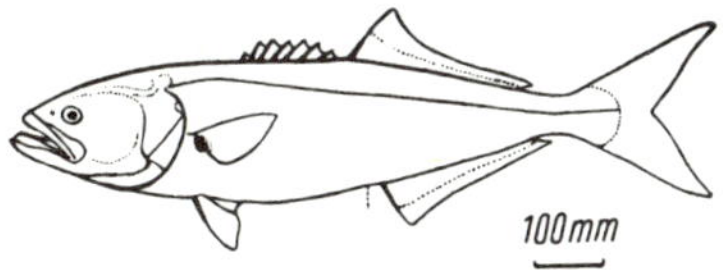

FIGURE 647. Pomatomidae – Pomatomus saltatrix (J. and E., 1900, fig. 400, diagr.)

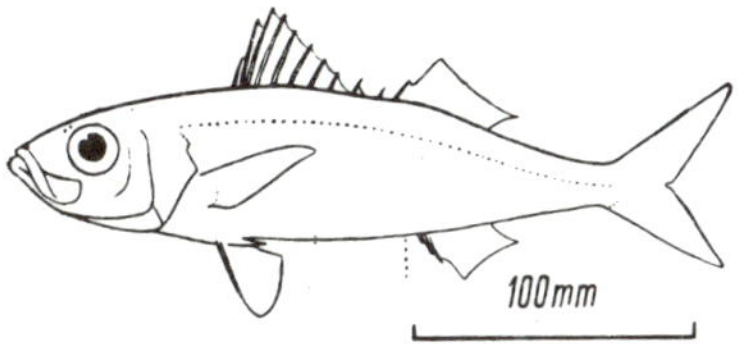

FIGURE 649. Emmelichthyidae – Erythrocles schlegeli (Wang, 1958, fig. 306, diagr.)

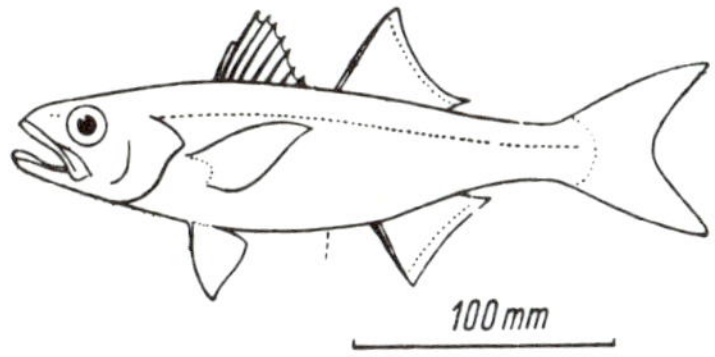

FIGURE 651. Scombropidae – Scombrops boops (Okada, 1955, fig. 173, diagr.)

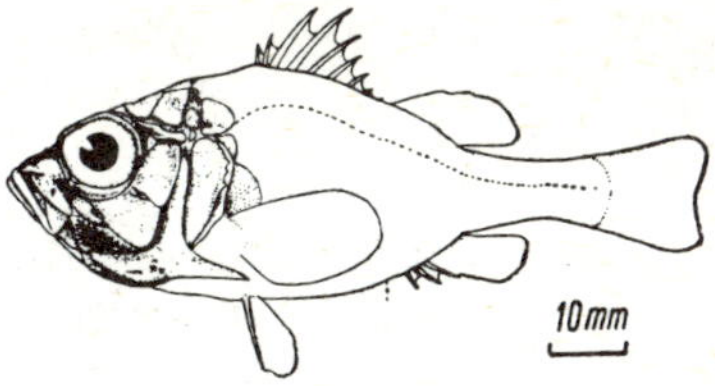

FIGURE 644. Ostracoberyx sp. (Serranidae) (M., 1955, III, fig. 216, diagr.)

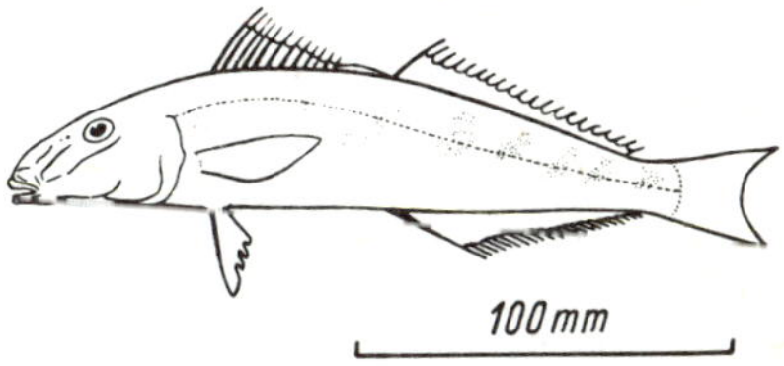

FIGURE 646. Sillaginidae – Sillago maculata (Quoy and Gaimard, 1824, pl. 5, fig. 2, diagr.)

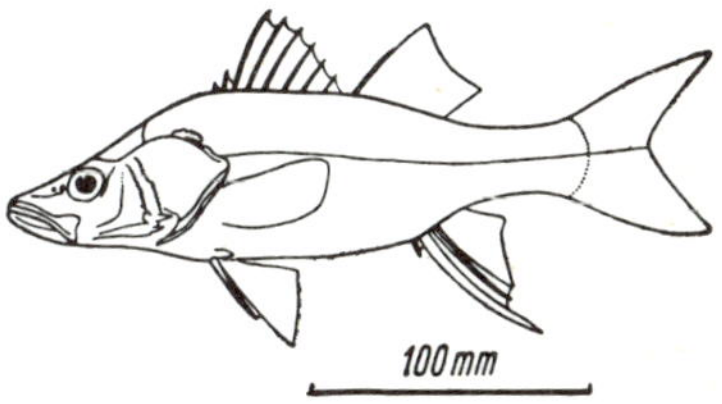

FIGURE 648. Centropomidae – Centropomus ensiferus (Fowler, 1936, fig. 548, diagr.)

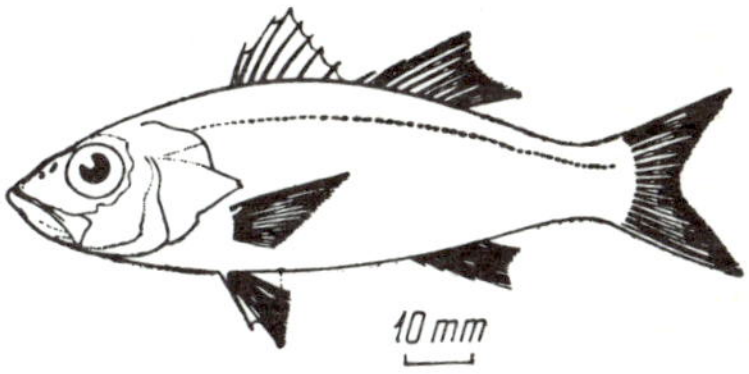

FIGURE 650. Acropomatidae – Acropoma japonicum (Temm. and Schl., 1842, pl. 12, fig. 2, diagr.)

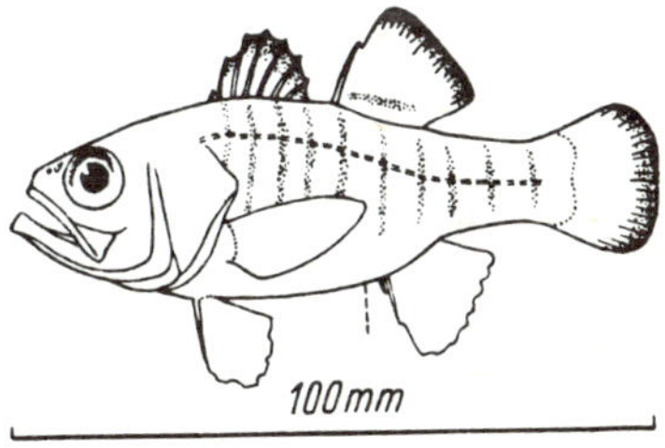

FIGURE 652. Apogonidae (Apogoninae) – Apogon lineatus (M., 1955, III, fig. 196, diagr.)

102 (103). Spiny rays of dorsal fin strongly flattened and high; height of third ray of fin greater than the length of the base of the soft dorsal. Second spiny ray of anal fin very strongly elongate, twice as large as the third, and strongly thickened. Caudal fin with a small notch. (Figure 657) . . . . 273. **Banjosidae**[107]

103 (102). Spiny rays of dorsal fin not flattened, of moderate height; height of third fin ray smaller than the length of the base of the soft dorsal. Second spiny ray of anal fin of normal size, but if sometimes elongate, then less than twice as much as the third, or the caudal fin is rounded.

104 (113). Mouth very strongly protrusible, ascending processes of premaxillaries passing, if only partly, onto the frontal bones.

105 (106). Maxillaries contiguous anteriorly and forming a semioval notch (Figure 659) on the anterior end of the snout, into which the premaxillaries enter when the mouth is shut. Ascending processes of premaxillaries extending to the occiput. (Figure 660) . . . . 314. **Centracanthidae**

106 (105). Maxillaries not forming a notch on the anterior end of the snout into which the premaxillaries might enter.

107 (108). Caudal fin rounded. Ventral fins situated far behind the base of the pectorals. (Figure 661) . . . . .306. **Lobotidae** (Ex parte, genus Datnioides)

108 (107). Caudal fin forked or with a notch in adults, less often rounded, but in any case the ventrals are inserted under the base of the pectorals.

109 (110). Pseudobranchs present. Maxillary bone wide, with an accessory small bone which departs under the preorbital. Dorsal and anal fins without a scaly sheath. (Figure 662). . . . . 300. **Emmelichthyidae**

110 (109). Pseudobranchs absent. Maxillary bone S-shaped, its end not hidden under the preorbital; no accessory supramaxillary bone. Dorsal and anal fins with a scaly sheath. Maxillaries very mobile, moving up, forward, and down.

111 (112). Scales small. Branchiostegal membranes attached to interbranchial space. Dorsal surface of head with bony ridges and occipital spines. Dorsal fin with 7—8 spiny and 16—17 soft rays. (Figure 663) . . . . 307. **Leiognathidae**

112 (111). Scales of moderate size or large. Branchiostegal membranes free of the interbranchial space. Dorsal surface of head smooth, without occipital spines. Dorsal fin with 9—10 spiny and 10—15 soft rays. (Figure 664) . . . . 308. **Gerridae**

113 (104). Mouth moderately protrusible; ascending processes of premaxillaries not reaching the frontal bones. Maxillary bone immovable.

114 (115). Premaxillaries overlying the posterior widened part of the maxillary. (Figure 665) . . . . 313. **Sparidae**

[107] Very similar to Banjos banjos is Hapalogenys mucrognathus (of family 309. Pomadasyidae, see thesis 139) but in this species the spiny rays of the dorsal fin are not flattened and the caudal fin is rounded (Figure 658).

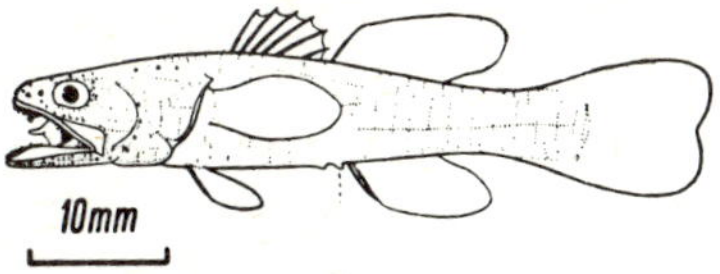

FIGURE 653. Apogonidae (Gymnapogoninae) – *Gymnapogon japonicus* (M., 1955, III, fig. 198, diagr.)

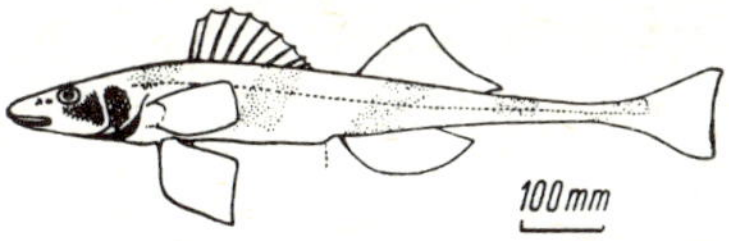

FIGURE 654. Percidae – *Aspro streber* (Berg, 1949, fig. 766, diagr.)

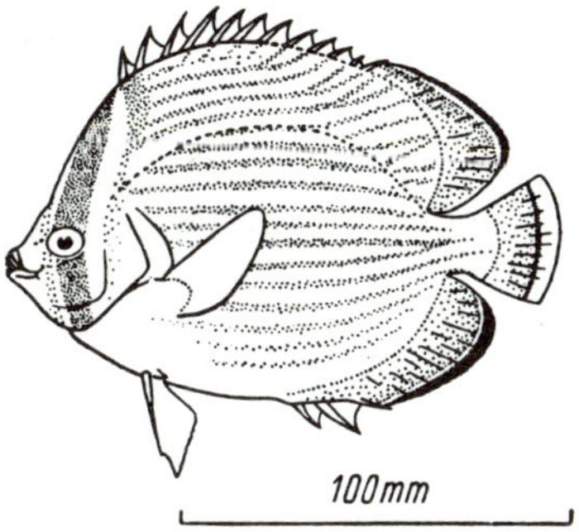

FIGURE 655. Chaetodontidae – *Chaetodon collaris* (Okada, 1955, fig. 255, diagr.)

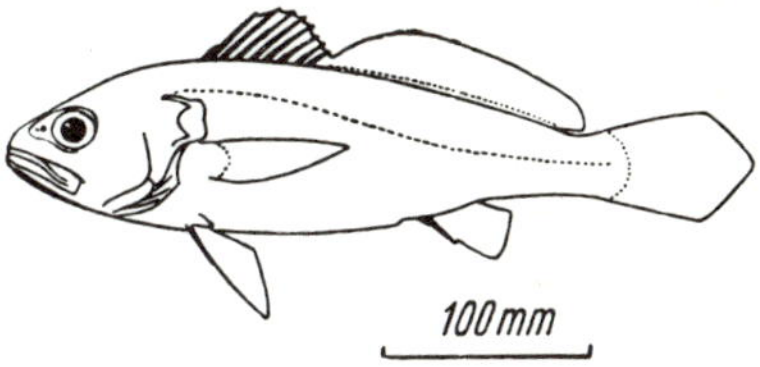

FIGURE 656. Sciaenidae – *Argyrosomus nibe* (Wang, 1958, fig. 335, diagr.)

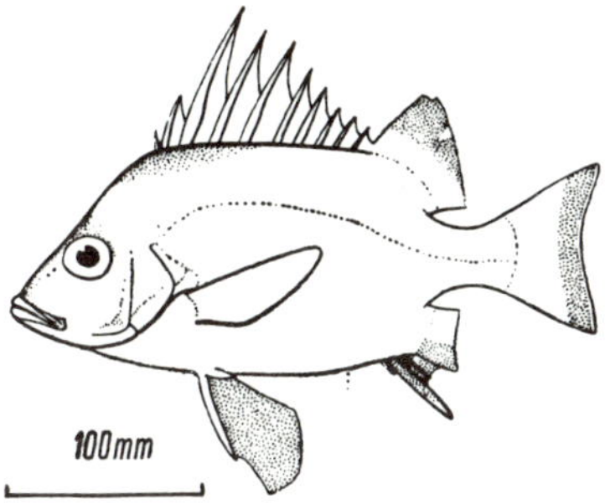

FIGURE 657. Banjosidae – *Banjos banjos* (Jordan and Thompson, 1912, fig. 2, diagr.)

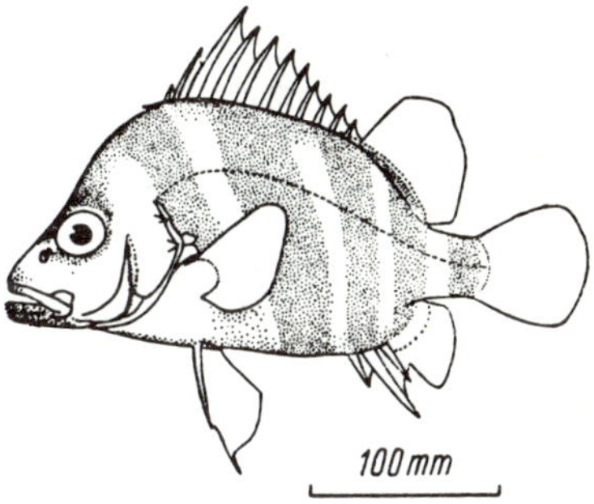

FIGURE 658. *Hapalogenys mucronathus* (Pomadasyidae) (M., 1955, III, fig. 244, diagr.)

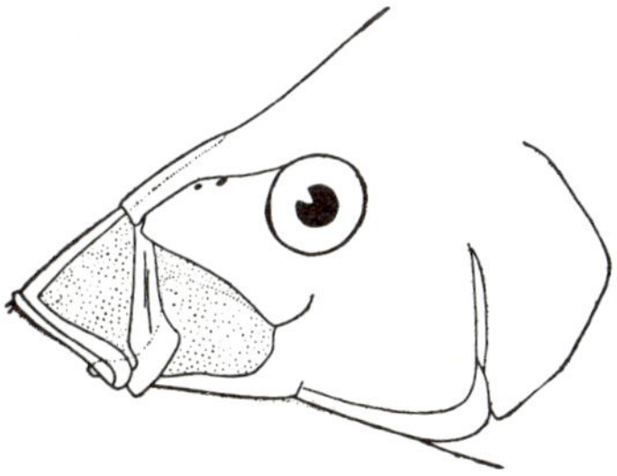

FIGURE 659. Jaw bones of *Spicara maena* (Centracanthidae)

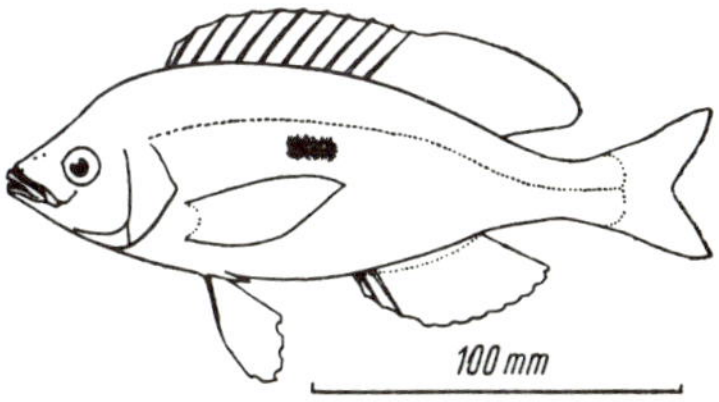

FIGURE 660. *Spicara maena* (Svetovidov, 1964, fig. 89, diagr.)

3 subfamilies:

1 (2). No teeth of molar or scalpriform type. All teeth conical, the anterior ones caninelike. Premaxillaries quite thin and narrow, markedly longer than their ascending processes. [Precaudal vertebrae with parapophyses only beginning with the third.] (Figure 666) . . . . subfamily 313.1. Denticinae

2 (1). Teeth of molar or scalpriform type present. Premaxillaries not thin, quite wide, especially in the posterior part, and not longer, or just slightly longer, than their ascending processes. [All precaudal vertebrae with parapophyses.]

3 (4). No canines even in anterior part of mouth, and no transverse row of a few enlarged anterior scalpriform teeth. Various teeth at the sides of the mouth, including sometimes those of the molar type. (Figure 667). . .subfamily 313.2. Pagellinae

4 (3). Canines present in the anterior part of the mouth or instead of them a few enlarged scalpriform teeth, arranged in a transverse row. Teeth of the molar type always present at the sides of the mouth. (Figure 668) . . . . subfamily 313.3. Sparinae

115 (114). Premaxillary not overlying the posterior widened part of the maxillary. (Figure 669).

116 (121). Typical scalpriform teeth present.

117 (118). Maxillary concealed under the preorbital and first suborbital. [There is a suborbital process.] (Figure 670). Soft dorsal and anal fins not covered or only partly covered with scales. (Figure 671) . . . . 322. Girellidae

118 (117). Maxillary more or less protruding from under the preorbital.

119 (120). [Suborbital process strong (Figure 670).] Outer row of scalpriform teeth without horizontal roots; similar teeth, but considerably smaller, behind this row. [Ribs sessile, except for the last three pairs.] (Figure 672) . . . . . 320. Coracinidae

120 (119). [Suborbital process absent (Figure 673).] Outer row of scalpriform teeth with horizontal roots; a band of small velutinous teeth behind this row. [Ribs sessile, except for the last pair.] (Figure 674) . . . . 321. Kyphosidae

121 (116). Typical scalpriform teeth absent.

122 (125). Dorsal fin as a rule with a deep notch, giving the impression of two fins, but the fins are still joined by a membrane.[108]

123 (124). Base of anal fin together with its spiny rays longer, the same length as, or a little shorter than the base of the soft dorsal. Lateral line distinctly expressed, passing onto the caudal fin . . . . 266. Centropomidae

(Ex parte, Chandinae and Latinae, see thesis 50.1.1—85)

[108] A deep incision in the dorsal is seen also in subfamilies 309.1. Xenichthyinae and 309.2. Pomadasyinae of family 309. Pomadasyidae (see Figures 690, 691). On the other hand, the notch is not deep in some representatives of 262.2. Chandinae and 299. Arripidae (see Figures 676, 678).

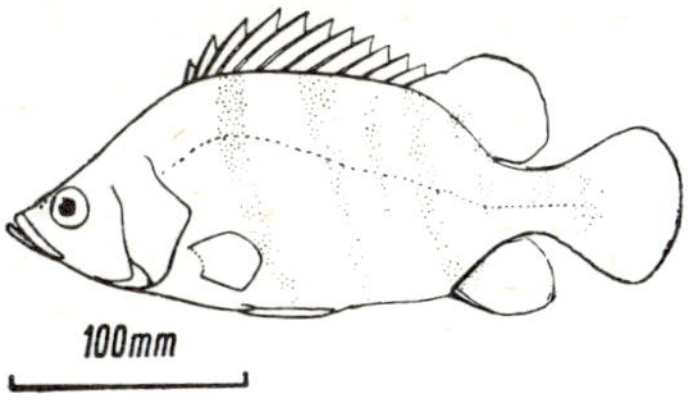

FIGURE 661. Lobotidae – Datnioides quadrifasciatus (Sterba, 1959, fig. 823, diagr.)

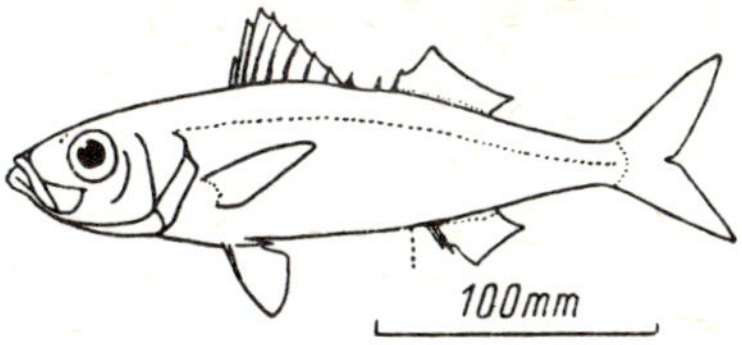

FIGURE 662. Emmelichthyidae – Erythrocles schlegeli (Wang, 1958, fig. 306, diagr.)

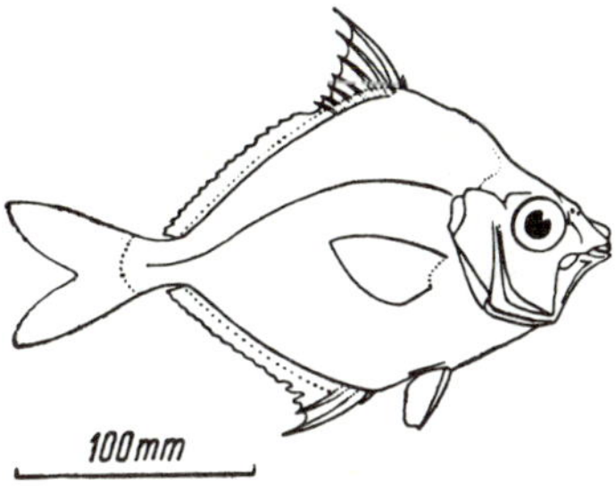

FIGURE 663. Leiognathidae – Leiognathus equulus (Wang, 1958, fig. 365, diagr.)

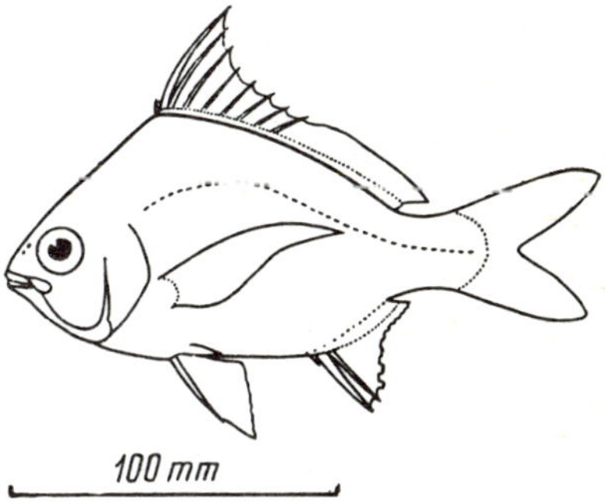

FIGURE 664. Gerridae – Gerres abbreviatus (Day, 1878, pl. 25, fig. 6, diagr.)

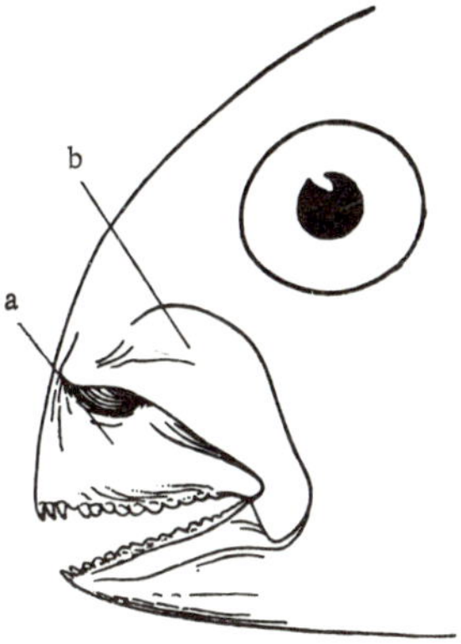

FIGURE 665. Jaw bones of Sparus aries (Sparidae):

a – premaxillary; b – maxillary.

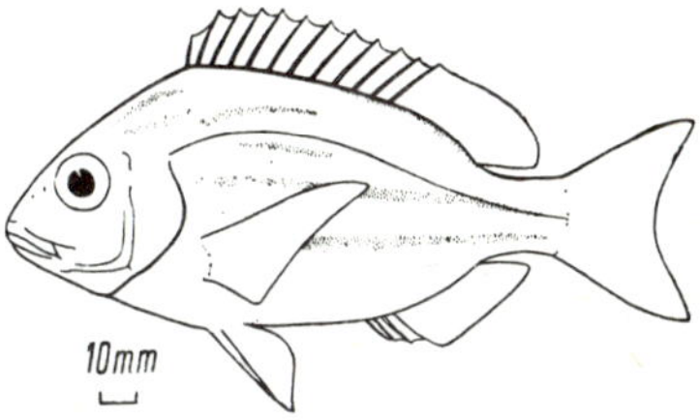

FIGURE 666. Sparidae (Denticinae) – Dentex maroccanus (Fowler, 1936, fig. 353, diagr.)

FIGURE 667. Sparidae (Pagellinae) – Pagellus erythrinus (Fowler, 1936, fig. 359, diagr.)

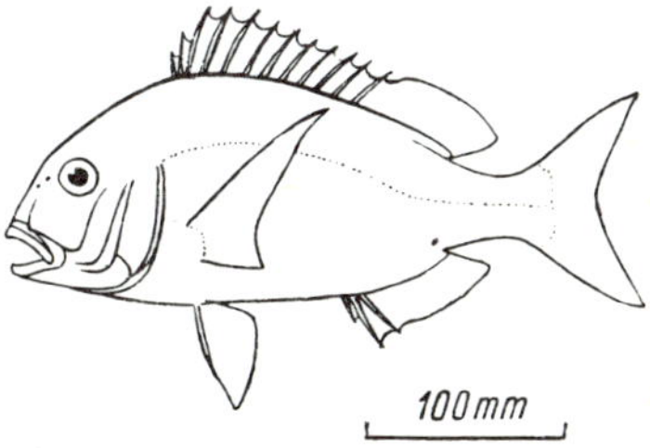

FIGURE 668. Sparidae (Sparinae) – Chrysophrys major (Wang, 1958, fig. 325, diagr.)

3 subfamilies:

1 (2). Opercular bone with a flat spine; preoperculum not having two crests. Accessory maxillary bone present. Dorsal fins with one base. Scales ctenoid. [Vertebrae 25.] Caudal fin rounded. (Figure 675) . . . . subfamily 266.1. Latinae

2 (1). Opercular bone without a spine; preoperculum with two crests. [Vertebrae 24.]

3 (4). Dorsal fin with one base. No accessory maxillary bone. Scales cycloid. Axillary lobe poorly developed. (Figure 676) . . . . subfamily 266.2. Chandinae

4 (3). Dorsal fin with two separate bases. Accessory maxillary bone present. Scales ctenoid. Axillary lobe well developed. (Figure 677) . . . . subfamily 266.3. Centropominae

(See thesis 50.1.1—81)

124 (123). Base of anal fin together with its spiny rays much shorter than base of soft dorsal. Lateral line not distinctly expressed and reaching only to the base of the caudal fin, not passing onto the fin. (Figure 678) . . . . 299. Arripidae

125 (122). Dorsal fin without a notch or with a weak one.[109]

126 (131). Suborbital process well developed.

127 (130). Palatines and vomer generally with teeth. [Anterior 2—6 vertebrae without parapophyses; sessile ribs.]

128 (129). Ventral fins inserted under the base of the pectorals or just slightly behind them. [First pairs of ribs (1st to 4th) sessile] . . . . .302. **Lutjanidae**

3 subfamilies:

1 (4). Dorsal and anal fins generally more or less covered with scales. Interorbital space not flat, not separated from the occipital region by a transverse groove; occipital and parietal crests extending forward into the frontal region.

2 (3). Nares close together, situated immediately in front of the eyes; anterior naris never tubular. All teeth on jaws pointed; vomerine teeth, if present, small, in the form of velutinous bands. (Figure 679) . . . . subfamily 302.1. Lutjaninae

3 (2). Nares widely separated; anterior naris tubular, situated near the tip of the snout. Teeth on jaws large and blunt; lateral teeth of the molar type; vomerine teeth also large, of the molar type. (Figure 680) . . . . . . subfamily 302.2. Hoplopagrinae

4 (1). Dorsal and anal fins not covered with scales. Interorbital space flat, separated from the occipital region by a transverse dividing line in the form of a groove; occipital and parietal crests not extending forward into the frontal region. (Figure 681) . . . . subfamily 302.3. Etelinae

[109] The dorsal notch is deep in fishes of subfamilies 309.1. Xenichthyinae and 309. 2. Pomadasyinae of family 309. Pomadasyidae (see Figures 690, 691).

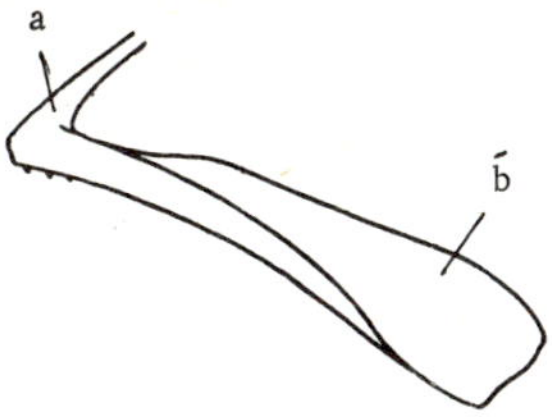

FIGURE 669. Jaw bones of Serranus acutirostris:

a – premaxillary; b – maxillary.

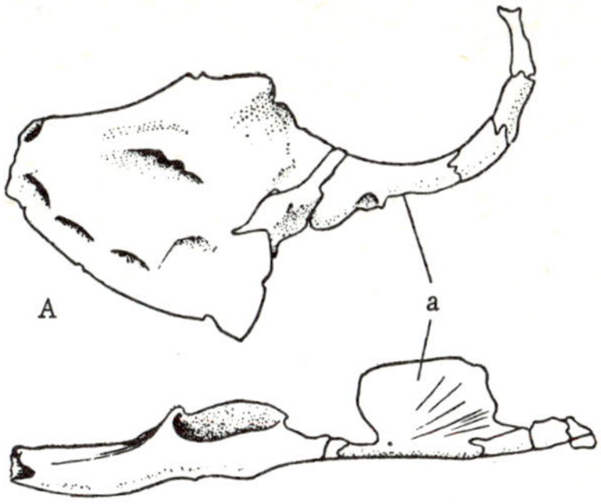

FIGURE 670. Suborbital bones with well developed suborbital process (a) (C. Smith and Bailey, 1962, pl.3, fig. P, diagr.):

A – lateral; B – dorsal.

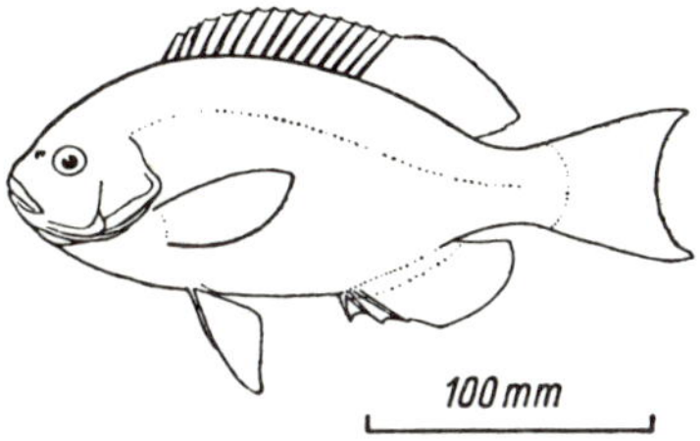

FIGURE 671. Girellidae – Girella punctata (Okada, 1955, fig. 222, diagr.)

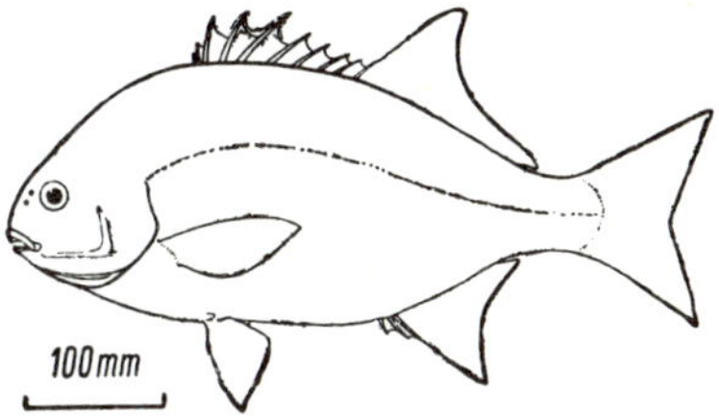

FIGURE 672. Coracinidae – Coracinus capensis (Smith, 1950, fig. 644, diagr.)

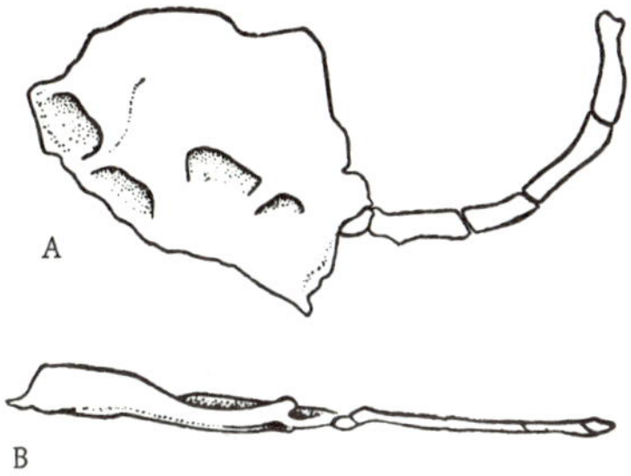

FIGURE 673. Suborbital bones without suborbital process (C. Smith and Bailey, 1962, pl.3, fig. 0, diagr.):

A – lateral; B – dorsal. Cf. Figure 670.

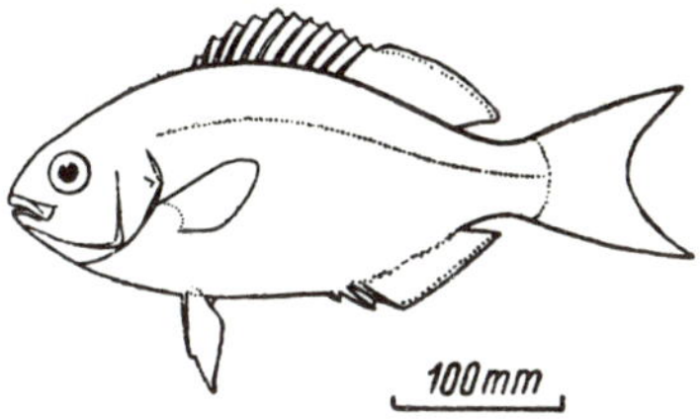

FIGURE 674. Kyphosidae – Kyphosus lembus (M., 1955, III, fig. 233, diagr.)

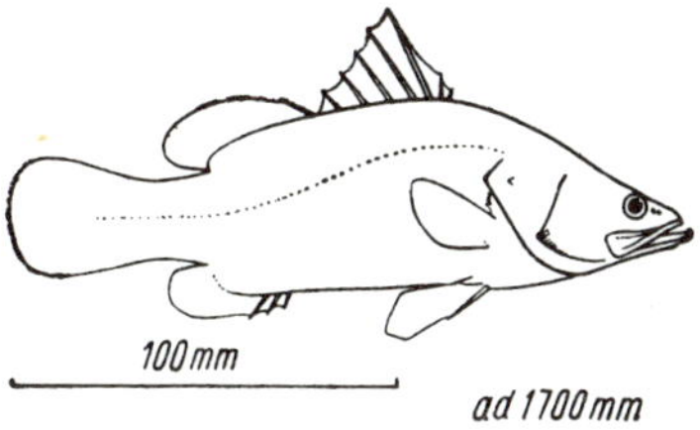

FIGURE 675. Centropomidae (Latinae) – Lates calcarifer (W. and B., 1929, 5, fig. 96, diagr.)

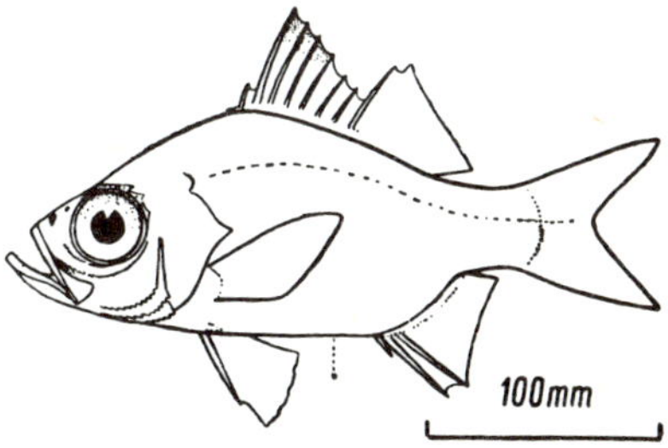

FIGURE 676. Centropomidae (Chandinae) – Ambassis kopsi (Bleeker, 1862–1878, pl.384, fig. 1, diagr.)

129 (128). Ventral fins inserted markedly behind base of pectorals. [Ribs, apart from last pair, not on parapophyses.] (Figure 682) . . . . 319. **Scorpididae**

130 (127). Palatines always without teeth; small teeth sometimes present on vomer. [All precaudal vertebrae with parapophyses and all ribs attached to them.] (Figure 683) . . . . . 305. **Nemipteridae**

131 (126). Suborbital process either absent or weakly developed; just from second suborbital bone there is a triangular process which projects forward.

132 (133). Caudal fin rounded.[110] (Figure 684) . . . . 306. **Lobotidae** (Ex parte, see thesis 50.1.1—107)

133 (132). Caudal fin with a notch (sometimes weak), but not rounded.

134 (135). Cheeks bare, without scales. (Figure 686). . . . 311. **Lethrinidae**

135 (134). Cheeks covered with scales.

136 (137). Well expressed canines in the anterior part of the jaws. (Figures 687, 688) . . . . 312. **Pentapodidae**

137 (136). Well expressed canines absent.

138 (139). Posterior margin of preoperculum not serrate. Spiny rays weak. There is a weak suborbital process. (Figure 689) . . . . 304. **Caesionidae**

139 (138). Posterior margin of preoperculum serrate. Spiny rays strong . . . . 309. **Pomadasyidae**

4 subfamilies:

1 (2). Teeth present on vomer, usually small. (Figure 690) . . . . subfamily 309.1. Xenichthyinae

2 (1). No teeth on vomer.

3 (4). Behind the symphysis on the chin there is a pit (Figure 690 A) which passes along the midline. Bases of soft dorsal and of anal fin situated in a scaly sheath. Spiny rays of anal powerful, especially the second ray. Dorsal fin with 12—18 soft rays. (Figure 691) . . . . subfamily 309.2. Pomadasyinae

4 (3). No such pit behind the symphysis on the chin.

5 (6). Spines absent under the eyes. Bases of soft dorsal and of anal fin situated in a scaly sheath. Scales small, from 50 to 150 perforated scales in lateral line. Dorsal fin with 15—23 soft rays. (Figure 692) . . . . subfamily 309.3. Plectorhynchinae

6 (5). There is a spine under the eye which is usually directed backward. No scaly sheath. Scales large, 35—50 perforated scales. Dorsal fin with 9—11 soft rays. (Figure 693). . . . . subfamily 309.4. Scolopsinae[111]

140 (97). Axillary lobe absent.

141 (142). Soft dorsal and anal fin with a continuous cover of elongate, readily deciduous scales arranged in longitudinal rows. Dorsal fin with a weak notch. Oral slit slightly oblique; lower jaw coming up to upper jaw. No accessory maxillary bone. Canine-like teeth absent. (Figure 694) . . . . . . 287. **Labracoglossidae**

[110] The caudal fin is rounded in the genus Hapalogenys of family 309. Pomadasyidae (Figure 685) but here the second spiny ray of the anal fin is strongly enlarged.

[111] GRWM (1966 : 400) include subfamily 309.4. Scolopsinae in the synonymy of family 305. Nemipteridae.

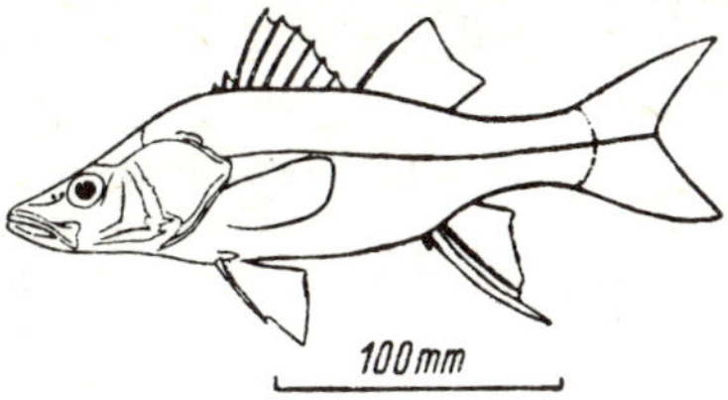

FIGURE 677. Centropomidae (Centropominae) – *Centropomus ensiferus* (Fowler, 1936, fig. 548, diagr.)

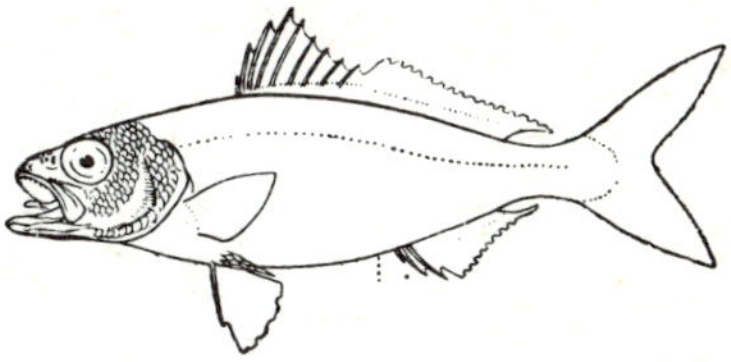

FIGURE 678. Arripidae – *Arripes georgianus* (Richardson, 1844–1848, pl. 54, fig. 3, diagr.)

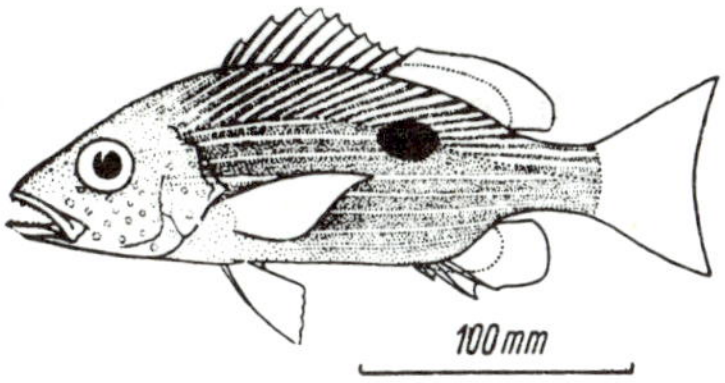

FIGURE 679. Lutjanidae (Lutjaninae) – *Lutjanus fulviflamma* (Fowler, 1937, fig. 232, diagr.)

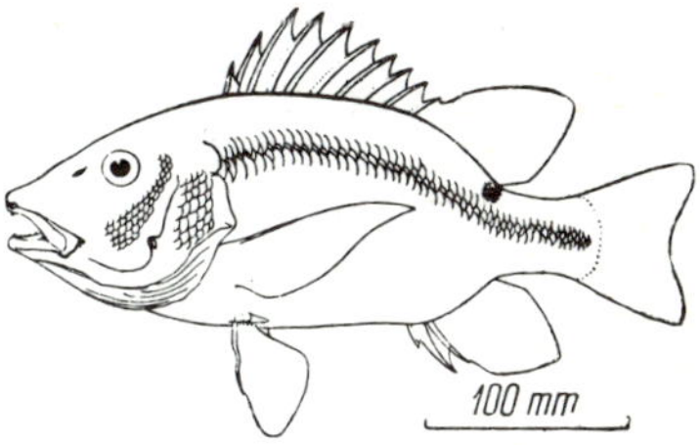

FIGURE 680. Lutjanidae (Haplopagrinae) – *Haplopagrus guentheri* (J. and E., 1900, fig. 513, diagr.)

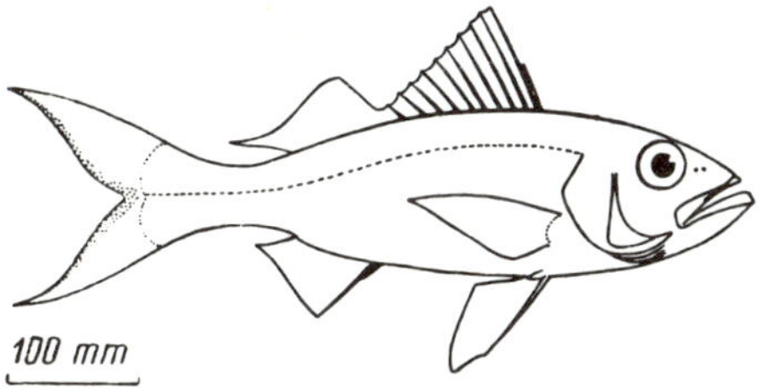

FIGURE 681. Lutjanidae (Etelinae) – *Etelis carbunculus* (Wang, 1958, fig. 307, diagr.)

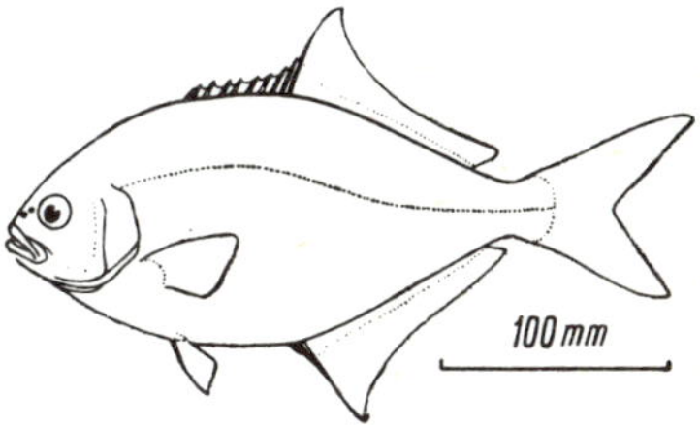

FIGURE 682. Scorpididae – *Scorpis aequipinnis* (Waite, 1921, fig. 172, diagr.)

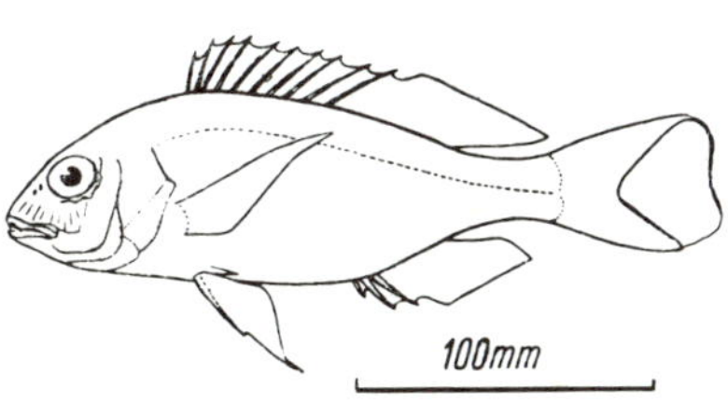

FIGURE 683. Nemipteridae – *Nemipterus japonicus* (Day, 1878, pl. 24, fig. 2, diagr.)

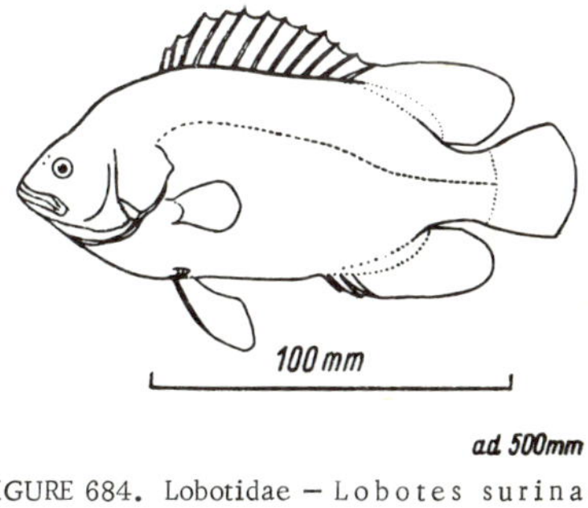

FIGURE 684. Lobotidae – *Lobotes surinamensis* (Wang, 1958, fig. 313, diagr.)

142 (141). Soft dorsal and anal fin not covered with scales.
143 (150). Anal fin with 1—2 spiny rays.
144 (145). Dorsal fin with one base and without an incision. (Figure 695) . . . . 285. **Branchiostegidae** (see thesis 60)
145 (144). Two dorsal fins, but if the base is single, there is a deep incision.
146 (147). Maxillary concealed under preorbital. (Figure 696). . . . . 284. **Sillaginidae** (see thesis 80)
147 (146). Maxillary not concealed under orbital.
148 (149). Head markedly flattened. Four weak spiny rays in dorsal fin. Bones of gill cover, except opercular, with strong spines . . . . 267. **Serranidae** (Ex parte, Rainfordiinae)[112]
149 (148). Head not markedly flattened. Dorsal fin with 6 — 15 strong spiny rays. Opercular with 1—2 weak flat spines. [Vertebrae 30 — 48.] (Figure 697) . . . . 283. **Percidae** (see thesis 50.1.1—95)
150 (143). Anal fin with 3 spiny rays.
151 (154). Last spiny ray of dorsal fin, which has one base, considerably longer than the spiny rays distributed in front of the fin, but much shorter (1.5 — 2 times) than the soft rays.
152 (153). Ventrals inserted before base of pectorals. (Figure 698) . . . . .280. **Priacanthidae** (see thesis 155)
153 (152). Ventrals inserted before base of pectorals. (Figure 698) . . . . 271. **Glaucosomidae**
154 (151). Last spiny ray of dorsal fin, which has one base, shorter than or the same length as, but not longer than spiny rays in front of the fin.
155 (156). Scales small, but very rough. Mouth very oblique. Caudal fin with 16 main rays, 14 branched. (Figure 700) . . . 280. **Priacanthidae** (see thesis 152)
156 (155). Scales not very small and not very rought to the touch. Mouth rarely oblique. Caudal fin with 17 main rays of which 15 branched.
157 (158). Pseudobranchs absent or rudimentary. No suborbital process. (Figure 701) . . . . 279. **Centrarchidae**
158 (157). Pseudobranchs generally well developed.
159 (160). Dorsal and anal fins set in a scaly sheath. Suborbital process absent. (Figure 702) . . . . 278. **Kuhliidae**
160 (159). Dorsal and anal fins without a scaly sheath. Suborbital process present.
161 (162). Ventral fins with 1 spiny and 4 sort rays, the first split, so that there seem to be 5 soft rays. Spiny rays of dorsal with deeply incised membranes. (Figure 703). . . . . 276. **Plesiopidae** (see thesis 50.1.1—70)
162 (161). Ventral fins with 1 spiny and 5 soft rays.
163 (164). Ventral fins inserted distinctly behind base of pectorals. Teeth on vomer and palatines, if present, usually deciduous (milk teeth). (Figure 704) . . . . 272. **Theraponidae**

[112] The subfamily Rainfordiinae occurs in Australian waters.

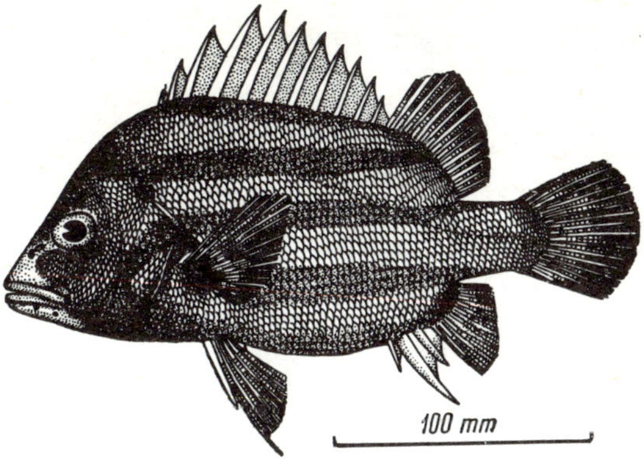

FIGURE 685. Hapalogenys kishinouyi (Pomadasyidae) (M., 1955, III, fig. 242)

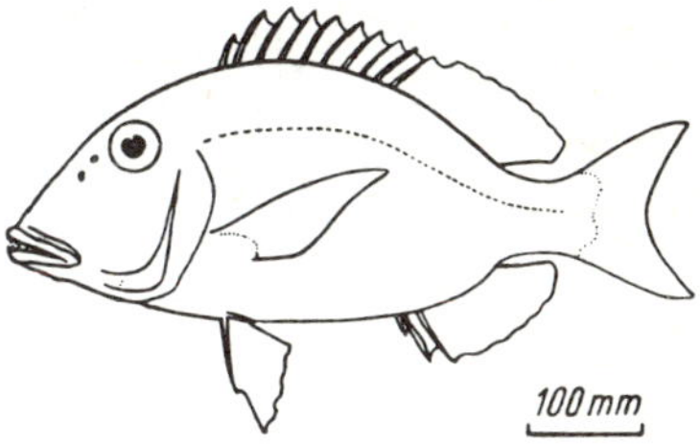

FIGURE 686. Lethrinidae — Lethrinus haematopterus (M., 1955, III, fig. 236, diagr.)

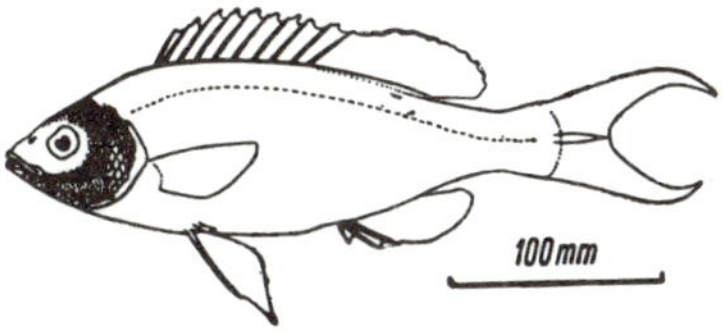

FIGURE 687. Pentapodidae — Pentapodus macrurus (M., 1955, III, fig. 240, diagr.)

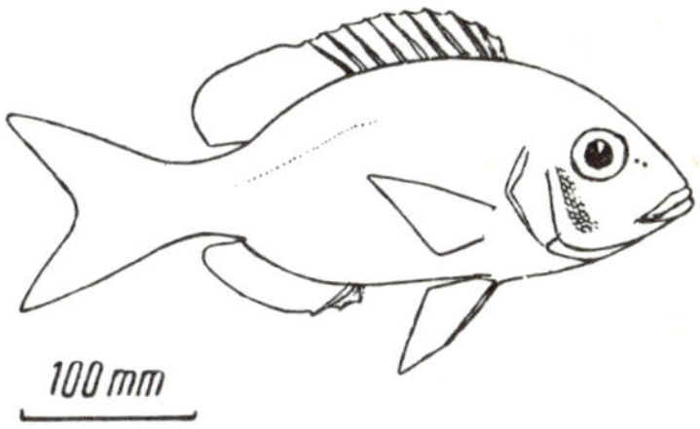

FIGURE 688. Pentapodidae — Gymnocranius griseus (W. and B., 1936, 7, fig. 76, diagr.)

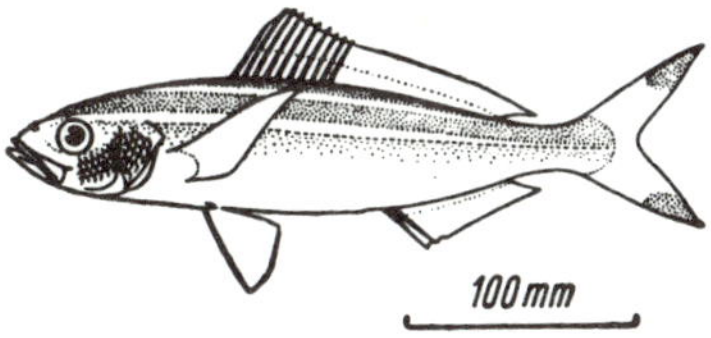

FIGURE 689. Caesionidae — Caesio chrysozoma (Abe, 1958, fig. 510, diagr.)

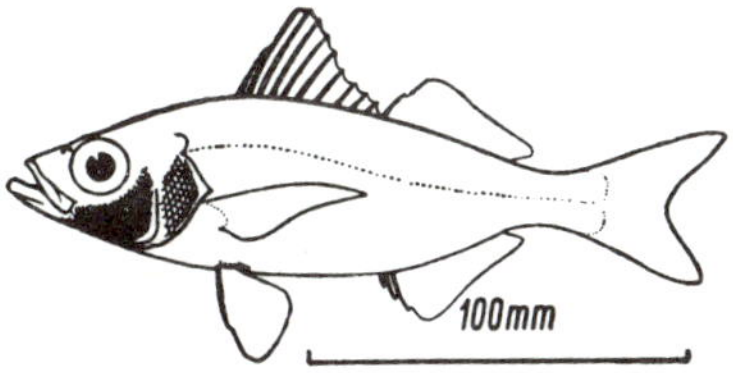

FIGURE 690. Pomadasyidae (Xenichthyinae) — Xenichthys agassizi (J. and E., 1900, fig. 527, diagr.)

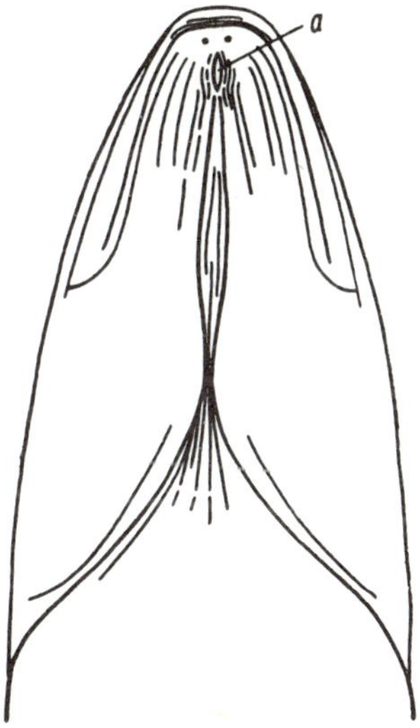

FIGURE 690A. Head of Pomadasys hasta (Pomadasyidae) (Lindberg and Krasyukova, 1969, fig. 273):

Ventral: a — pit on chin behind symphysis of lower jaw.

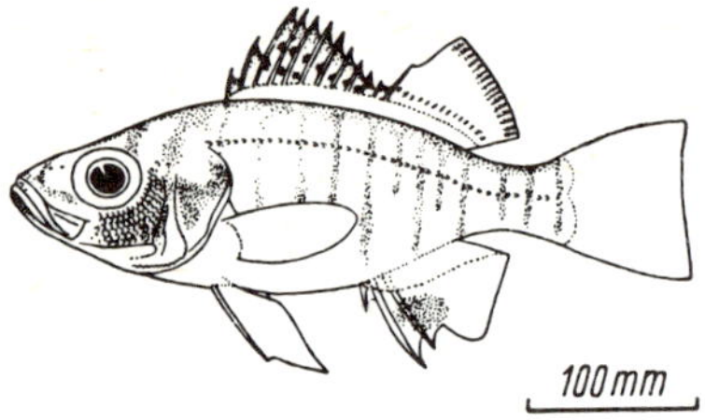

FIGURE 691. Pomadasyidae (Pomadasyinae) — Pomadasys hasta (Fowler, 1937, fig. 233, diagr.)

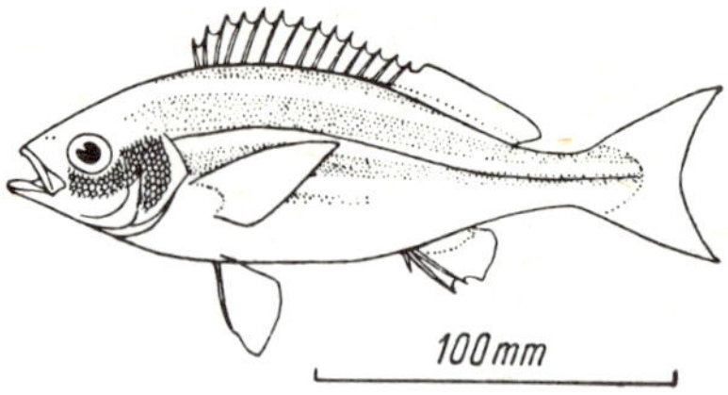

FIGURE 692. Pomadasyidae (Plectorhynchinae) — Parapristipoma trilineatum (Abe, 1958, fig. 518, diagr.)

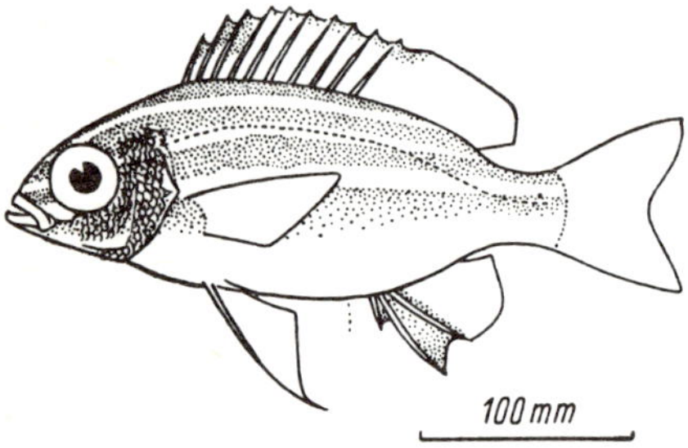

FIGURE 693. Pomadasyidae (Scolopsinae) — Scolopsis bilineatus (Bleeker, 1876—8:342, fig. 1, diagr.)

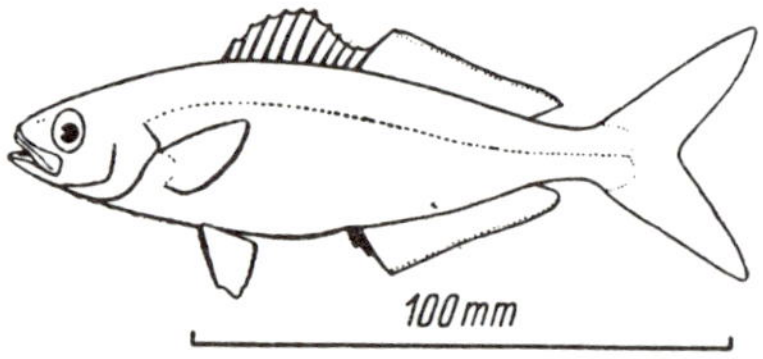

FIGURE 694. Labracoglossidae — Labracoglossus argentiventris (Okada, 1955, fig. 147, diagr.)

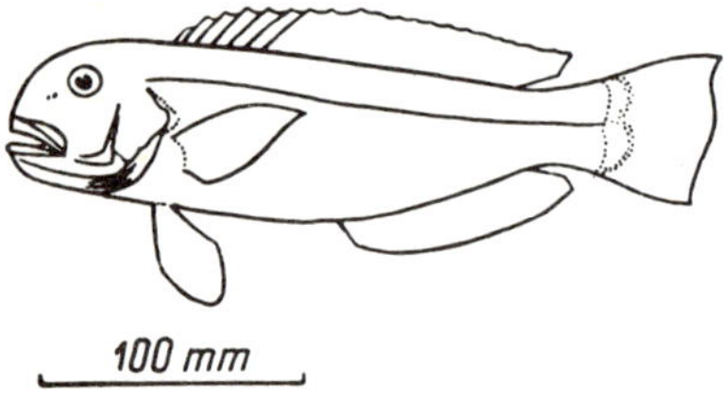

FIGURE 695. Branchiostegidae — Branchiostegus (Latilus) japonicus (Wang, 1958, fig. 305, diagr.)

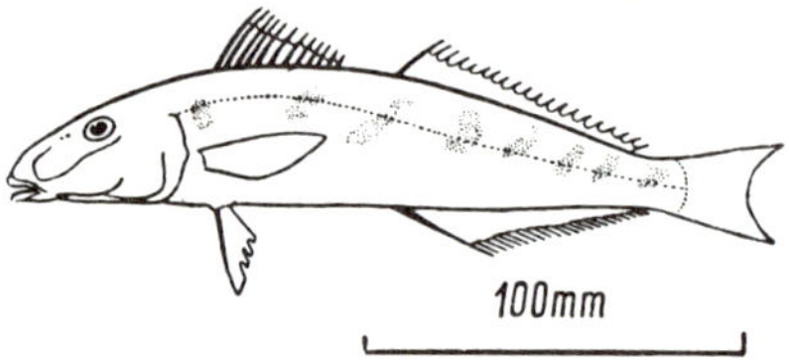

FIGURE 696. Sillaginidae — Sillago maculata (Quoy and Gaimard, 1824, pl. 5, fig. 2, diagr.)

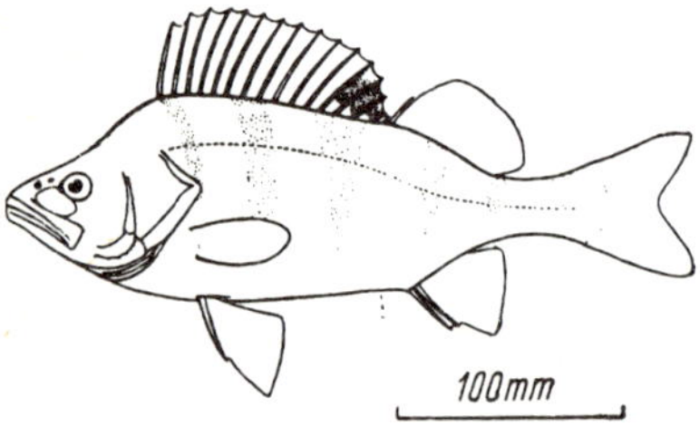

FIGURE 697. Percidae — Perca fluviatilis (Berg, 1949, fig. 756, diagr.)

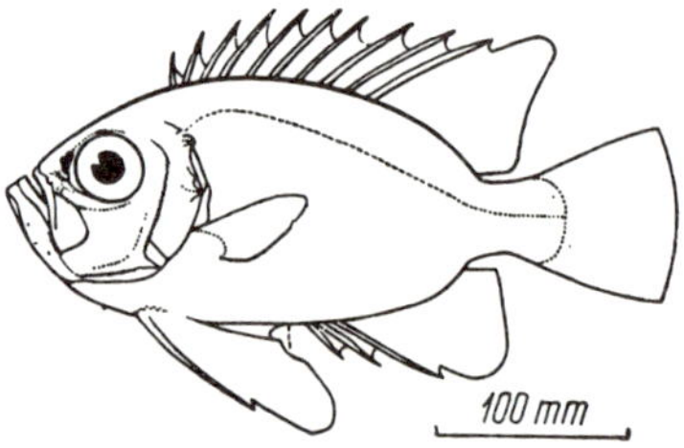

FIGURE 698. Priacanthidae — Priacanthus boops (M., 1955, III, fig. 199)

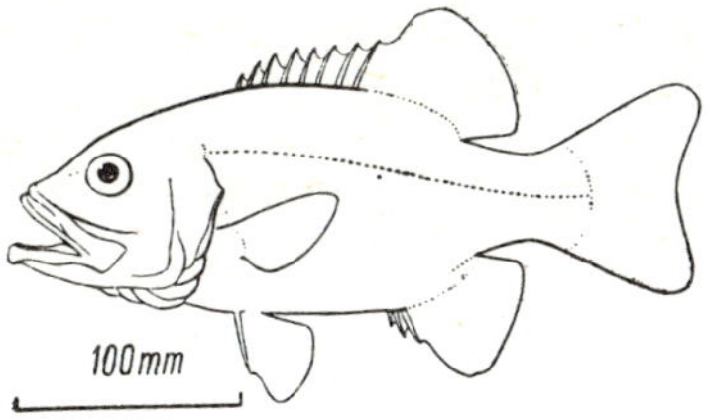

FIGURE 699. Glaucosomidae — *Glaucosoma hebraicum* (M., 1955, III, fig. 209, diagr.)

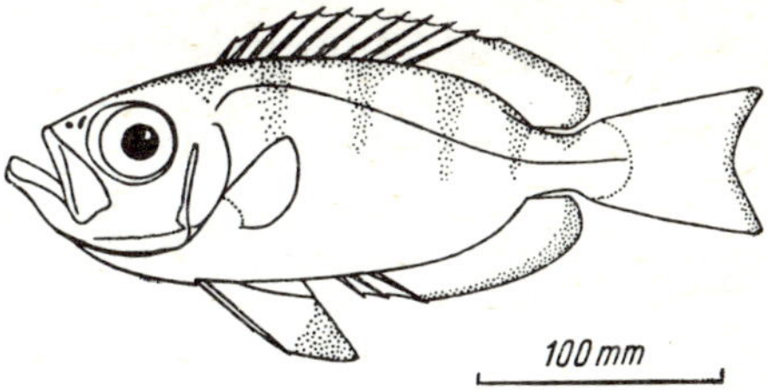

FIGURE 700. Priacanthidae — *Priacanthus hamrur* (W. and B., 1929, 5, fig. 93, diagr.)

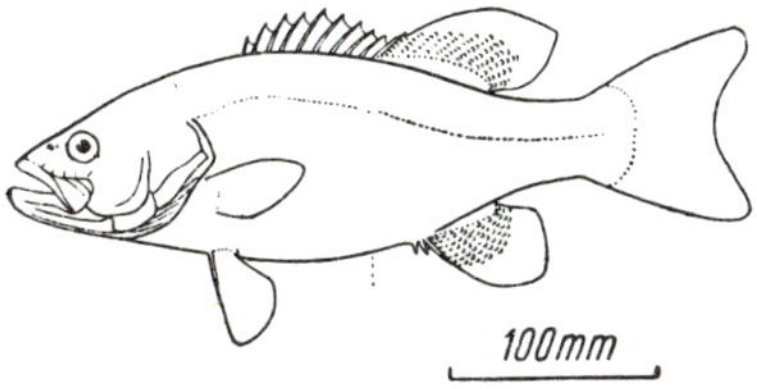

FIGURE 701. Centrarchidae — *Micropterus dolomieu* (J. and E., 1900, fig. 430, diagr.)

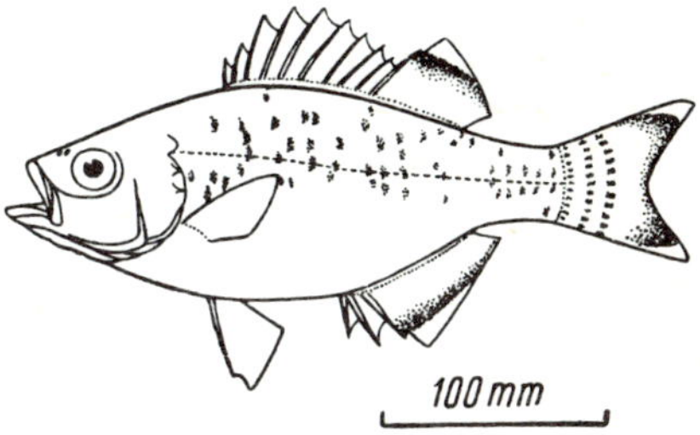

FIGURE 702. Kuhliidae—*Kuhlia marginata* (M., 1955, III, fig. 202, diagr.)

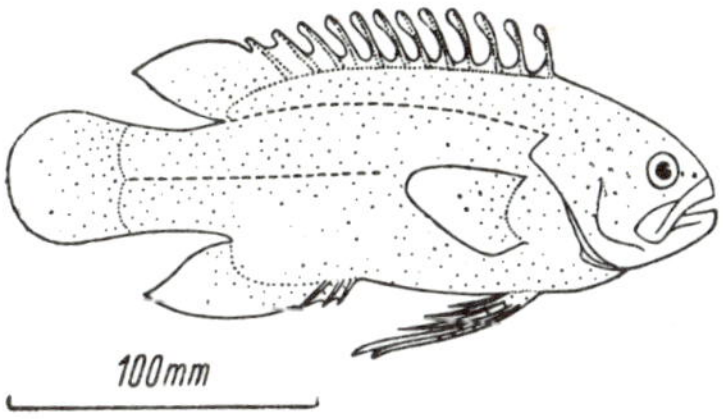

FIGURE 703. Plesiopidae — *Plesiops nigricans* (Wang, 1958, fig. 207, diagr.)

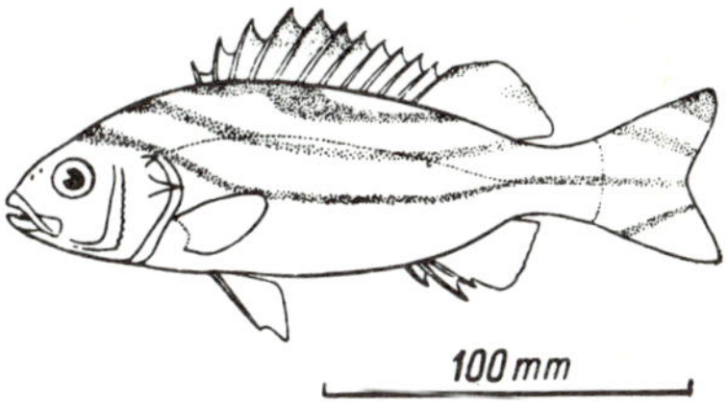

FIGURE 704. Theraponidae — *Therapon jarbua* (Okada, 1955, fig. 206, diagr.)

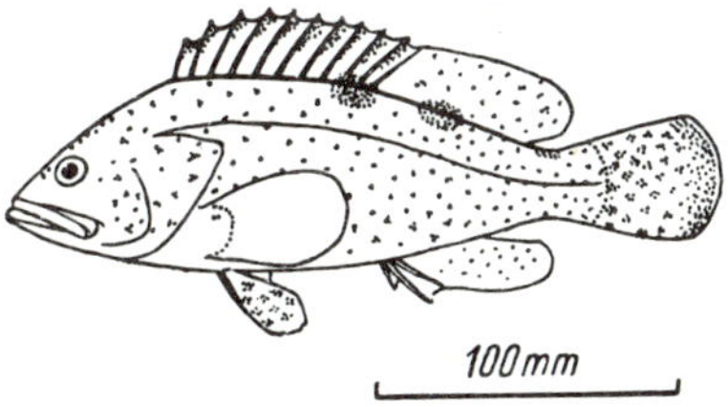

FIGURE 705. Serranidae — *Epinephelus fario* (Fowler, 1937, fig. 229, diagr.)

FIGURE 706. Grammistidae (GRWM, 1966:424, fig.)

164 (163). Ventral fins inserted a little in front of, under, or a little behind the base of the pectorals. Teeth almost always present on vomer and palatines. (Figures 705, 706) . . . . 267. **Serranidae**[113] (see thesis 50.1.1—148)

Superfamily 50.1.2. *Cepoloidea* (thesis 50.1.0—5)

1 family: 337. **Cepolidae** (Figure 707) (see thesis 50.1.9—22).

Superfamily 50.1.3. *Embiotocoidea* (thesis 50.1.0—20)

1 family: 338. **Embiotocidae**[114] (Figure 708).

Superfamily 50.1.4. *Pomacentroidea* (thesis 50.1.0—17)

1 family: 339. **Pomacentridae.**

4 subfamilies:

1 (6). Teeth conical or of cylindrical form, or else setiform, but never laterally compressed.
2 (5). Scales rather small, generally more than 50 scales in longitudinal row. Bases of spiny and soft parts of dorsal fin usually about the same length. All bones of gill cover serrate.
3 (4). Preorbital bone without a strong spine. (Figure 709). . . . . .subfamily 339.1. Amphiprioninae
4 (3). Preorbital bone terminating in a strong spine (Figure 710) . . . . subfamily 339.2. Premninae
5 (2). Scales large or of medium size, fewer than 50 in longitudinal row. Base of spiny part of dorsal fin much longer than base of soft part of fin. (Figure 711) . . .subfamily 339.3. Chrominae
6 (1). Teeth more or less laterally compressed, at any rate anteriorly. Scales large or of moderate size. (Figure 712) . . . . subfamily 339.4. Pomacentrinae

Superfamily 50.1.5. *Labroidea* (thesis 50.1.1—21)

3 families (340—342):

1 (2). Mouth protrusible. Teeth on jaws not fused among themselves and as a rule not forming plates with the sharp margin; there are spaces between them, but occasionally (Pseudodax) they are close together on the sides of the jaws and form plates . . . . 340. **Labridae**

[113] Two separate families are recognized, 267a. **Grammistidae** (GRWM: 399) and 267b. **Percichthyidae** (Gosline, 1966: 99—112).

[114] This includes 2 subfamilies which are hard to distinguish according to external characters.

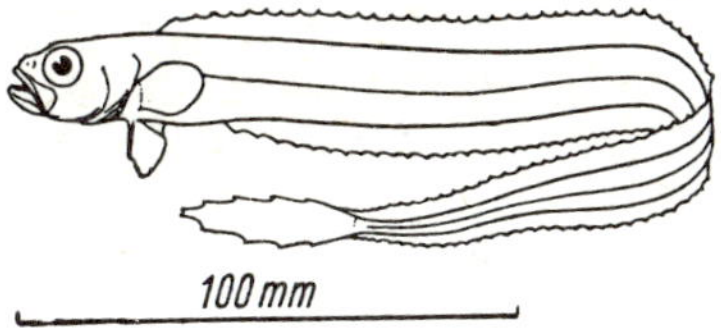

FIGURE 707. Cepolidae — Cepola schlegeli (Okada, 1955, fig. 237, diagr.)

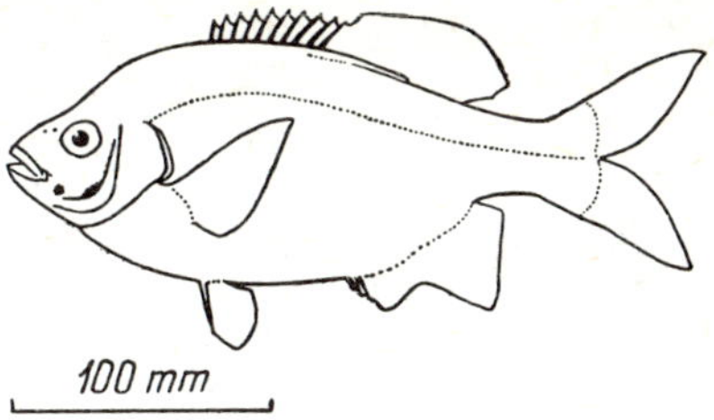

FIGURE 708. Embiotocidae — Ditrema temmincki (Okada, 1955, fig. 240, diagr.)

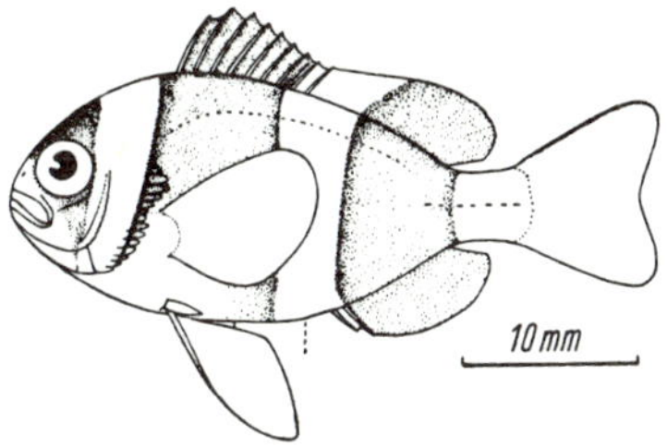

FIGURE 709. Pomacentridae (Amphiprioninae) — Amphiprion sebae (Okada and Ikeda, 1939, fig. 27, diagr.)

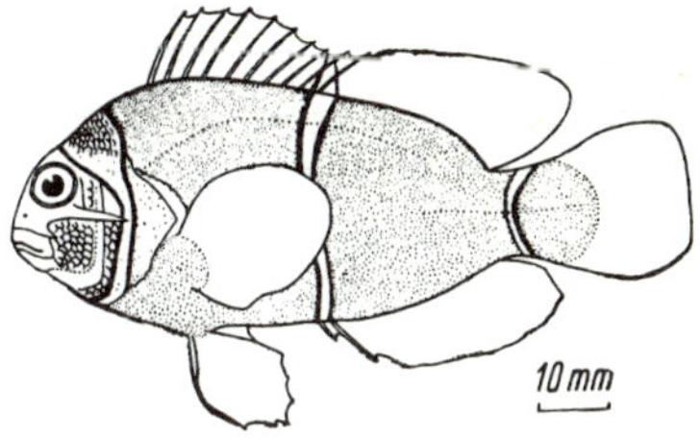

FIGURE 710. Pomacentridae (Premninae) — Premnas biaculeatus (W. and B., 1940, 8, fig. 41, diagr.)

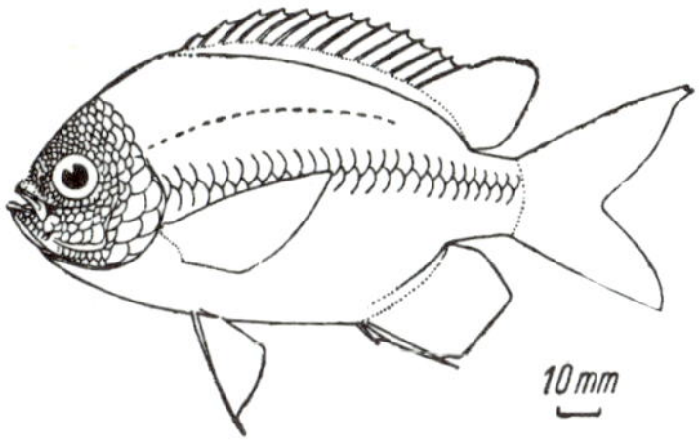

FIGURE 711. Pomacentridae (Chrominae) — Chromis albomaculatus (Kamohara, 1960, fig. 1, diagr.)

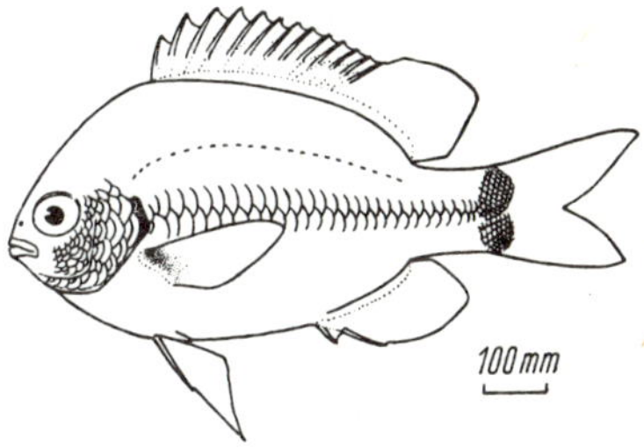

FIGURE 712. Pomacentridae (Pomacentrinae) — Abudefduf notatus (M., 1955, III, fig. 332, diagr.)

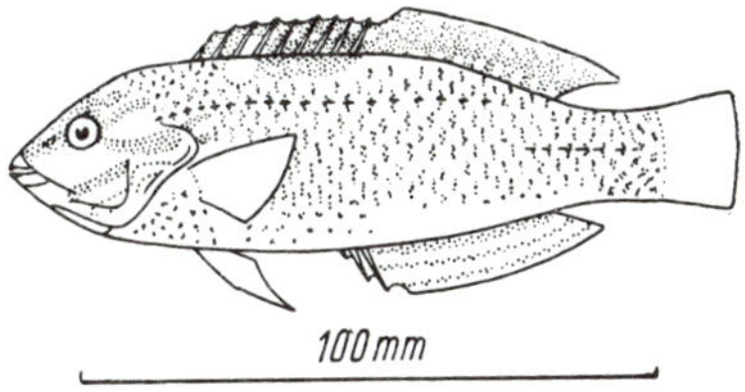

FIGURE 713. Labridae (Julidinae) — Halichoeres centiquadra (Wang, 1958, fig. 414, diagr.)

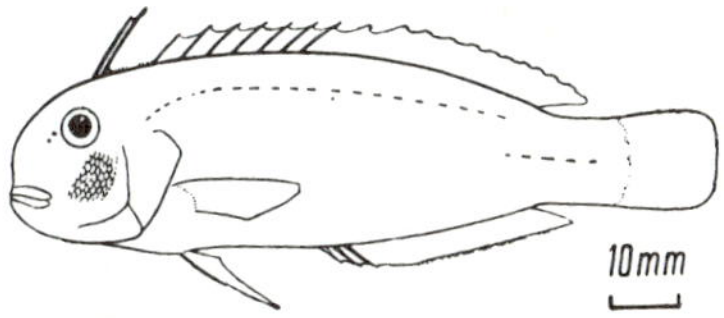

FIGURE 714. Labridae (Hemipteronotinae) — Hemipteronotus pentadactylus (W. and B., 1940, 8, fig. 12, diagr.)

9 subfamilies:

1 (16). Anal fin with 7—14 soft rays.
2 (15). Dorsal fin with 8—14 spiny rays. [Vertebrae 23—30.]
3 (14). Teeth on sides of jaws more or less separate from each other, not fused and not forming a single plate.
4 (11). Infrapharyngeal plate with conical or blunted teeth; the plate is of triangular form or Y- or T-shaped.
5 (10). Mouth moderately protrusible; jaws normal. [All ribs attached to parapophyses.]
6 (7). Frontal bones anteriorly with excavate canals into which the ascending processes of the premaxillaries move. (Figure 713). . . . . subfamily 340.1. Julidinae
7 (6). Frontal bones without such canals anteriorly.
8 (9). Parietal crests rudimentary or absent. Infrapharyngeal plate triangular or Y-shaped. Dorsal fin with 9 spiny and 12 soft rays; the two anterior spiny rays are flexible and often form what appears to be a separate fin. Anal fin with 3 spiny and 12 soft rays. [Vertebrae 25.] (Figure 714) . . . . subfamily 340.2. Hemipteronotinae
9 (8). Occipital and parietal crests strong, reaching anteriorly to the vertical of the anterior margin of the orbit. Infrapharyngeal plate T-shaped. Dorsal fin with 9—11 spiny and 9—11 soft rays, anal with 3 spiny and 8—9 soft rays. (Figure 715) . . . . subfamily 340.3. Cheilininae
10 (5). Mouth very protrusible and forming a long membranous tube; ascending processes of premaxillaries reaching to the occiput and the flattened occipital crest when the mouth is shut. [First 3 ribs sessile.] Dorsal fin with 9 spiny and 10—11 soft rays. Anal with 3 spiny and 8—9 soft rays. (Figure 716) . . . . subfamily 340.4. Epibulinae
11 (4). Infrapharyngeal plate bearing very blunt teeth, making the surface of the plate look like cobblestones, or teeth which are fused and form vertical plates with serrate margins.
12 (13). Mouth small, strongly protrusible, with weakly developed teeth. Infrapharyngeal plate small, Y-shaped; teeth on supra- and infrapharyngeal bones fused and forming vertical plates with serrate margins. Dorsal fin with 12 spiny and 10 soft rays, and anal with 3 spiny and 12 soft rays. (Figure 717) . . . . subfamily 340.5. Clepticinae
13 (12). Mouth fairly large, usually with well developed conical teeth in one row the anterior teeth of which have the form of canines. Infrapharyngeal plate somewhat triangular or T-shaped, wider than long, covered with blunt teeth that give a cobblestone effect. Dorsal fin with 11—14 spiny and 7—11 soft rays, anal with 3 spiny and 9—14 soft rays. (Figure 718) . . . . subfamily 340.6. Bodianinae

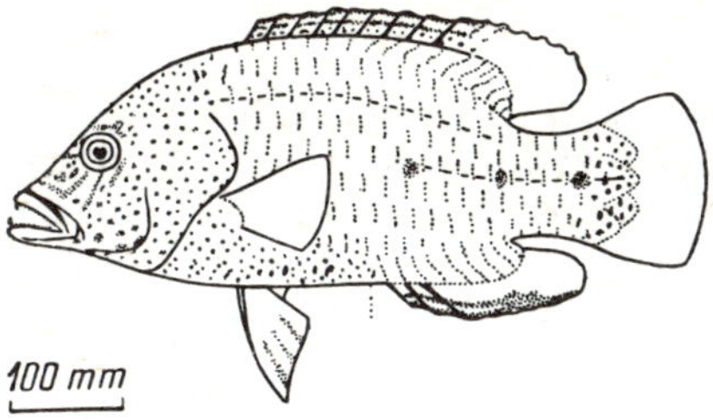

FIGURE 715. Labridae (Cheilininae) — Cheilinus trilobatus (Bleeker, 1862, pl. 27, fig. 2, diagr.)

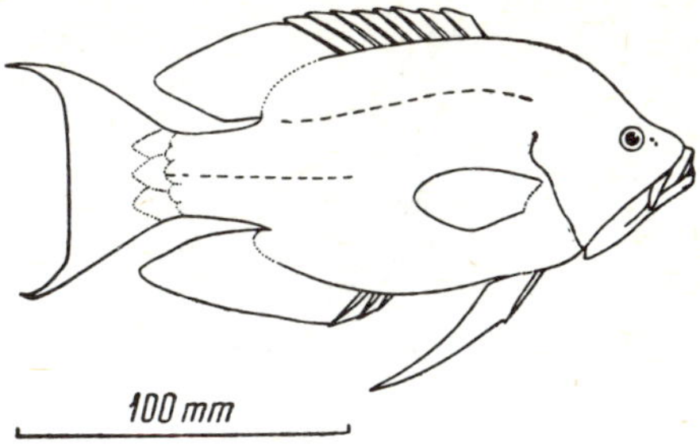

FIGURE 716. Labridae (Epibulinae) — Epibulus insidiator (Wang, 1958, fig. 403, diagr.)

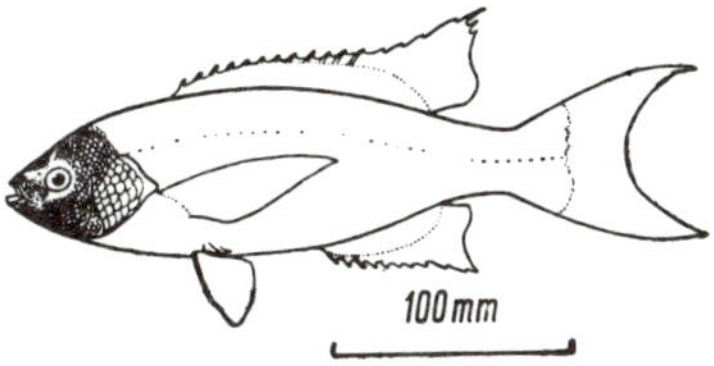

FIGURE 717. Labridae (Clepticinae) — Clepticus porrae (J. and E., 1900, fig. 599, diagr.)

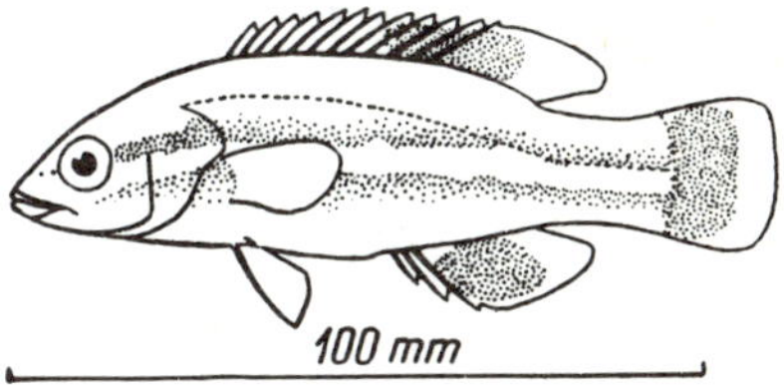

FIGURE 718. Labridae (Bodianinae) — Semicossyphus reticulatus (Okada, 1958, fig. 246, diagr.)

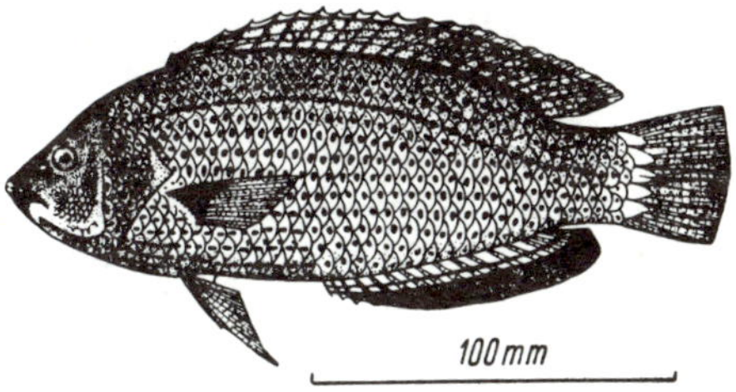

FIGURE 719. Labridae (Pseudodacinae) — Pseudodax moluccanus (W. and B., 1940, 8, fig. 6)

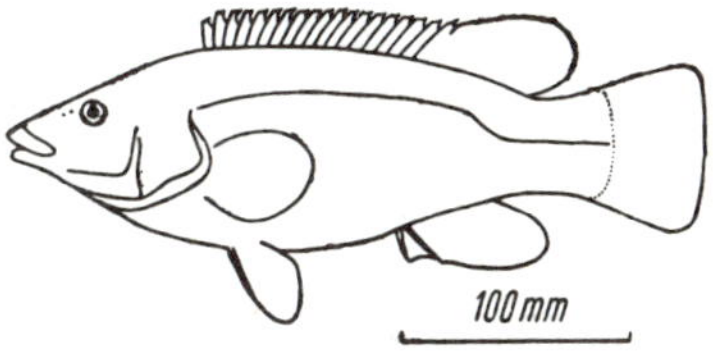

FIGURE 720. Labridae (Labrinae) — Labrus berggylta (Fowler, 1936, fig. 398, diagr.)

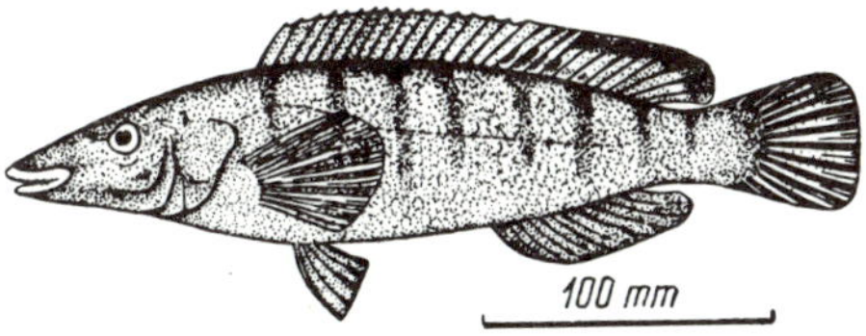

FIGURE 721. Odacidae — Odax richardsoni (Waite, 1921, fig. 206)

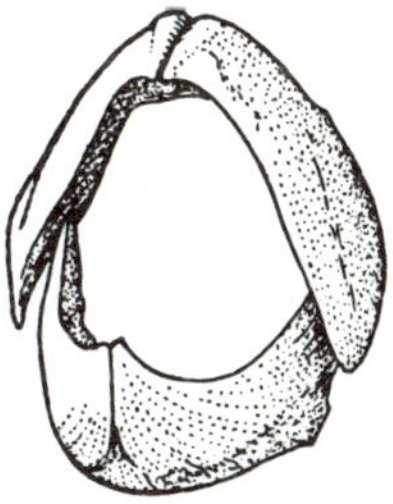

FIGURE 722. "Parrot's beak" in the Scaridae (J. and E., 1900, fig. 613)

14 (3). Teeth on sides of jaws fused and forming a plate with sharp margins. Anterior part of jaws bearing 2 pairs of wide scalpriform teeth. Infrapharyngeal bone of oval form with concave upper surface; plate longer than wide, covered with several rows of blunt teeth giving a cobblestone effect; there is a short anterior process bearing a single row of 3 conical teeth. Dorsal fin with 11 spiny and 12 soft rays, anal with 3 spiny and 14 soft rays. (Figure 719) . . . . subfamily 340.7. Pseudodacinae

15 (2). Dorsal fin with 13—21 sharp spiny rays. [Vertebrae 31—41.] Teeth on sides of jaws separate from one another, not fused. Infrapharyngeal plate somewhat triangular, bearing pointed or blunt-conical teeth. [All ribs attached to parapophyses.] Frontal bones anteriorly with excavate canals into which the ascending processes of the maxillaries move. Occipital and parietal crests well developed. (Figure 720) . . . . subfamily 340.8. Labrinae

16 (1). Anal fin with 18 soft rays. Dorsal with 18 spiny and 14 soft rays. Teeth on jaws conical, in one row. Anterior teeth enlarged . . . . subfamily 340.9. Neolabrinae[115]

2 (1). Mouth not protrusible. Teeth on jaws more or less fused with each other and forming plates with sharp margins which are sometimes very similar to a parrot's beak.

3 (4). Dorsal fin with 14—24 flexible spiny rays. Ventral fins, if present, with 1 spiny and 4 soft rays. Scales small or of moderate size; lateral line straight, complete. Tooth plates bearing no resemblance to a parrot's beak. [Vertebrae 36—53.] (Figure 721) . . . . 341. **Odacidae**

4 (3). Dorsal fin with 9 spiny rays. Ventrals with 1 spiny and 5 soft rays. Scales large, about 25 in longitudinal row. Lateral line bent in posterior part or interrupted and represented by two short parts. Tooth plates forming a "parrot's beak" (Figure 722). [Vertebrae 25] . . . . 342. **Scaridae**

2 subfamilies:

1 (2). Branchiostegal membranes broadly attached to interbranchial space, not forming a fold across it. Infrapharyngeal plate wider than long. (Figure 723) . . . . subfamily 342.1. Sparisomatinae

2 (1). Branchiostegal membranes forming a wide fold across the interbranchial space. Infrapharyngeal plate considerably longer than wide, spoon-shaped. (Figure 724) . . . . subfamily 342.2. Scarinae

[115] Subfamily 340.9. Neolabrinae occurs off the Juan Fernández Islands.

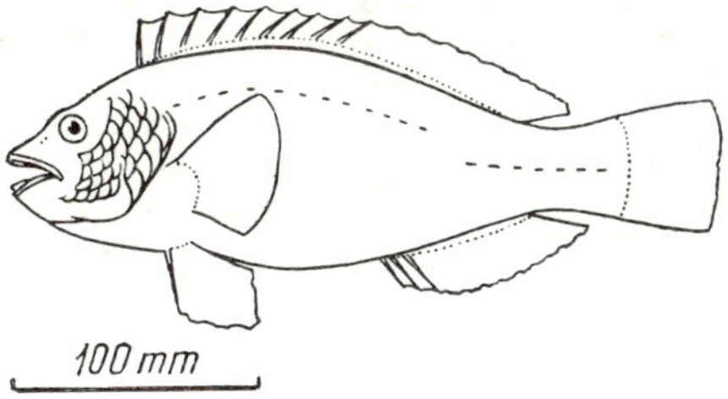

FIGURE 723. Scaridae (Sparisomatinae) — *Leptoscarus japonicus* (Okada, 1955, fig. 254, diagr.)

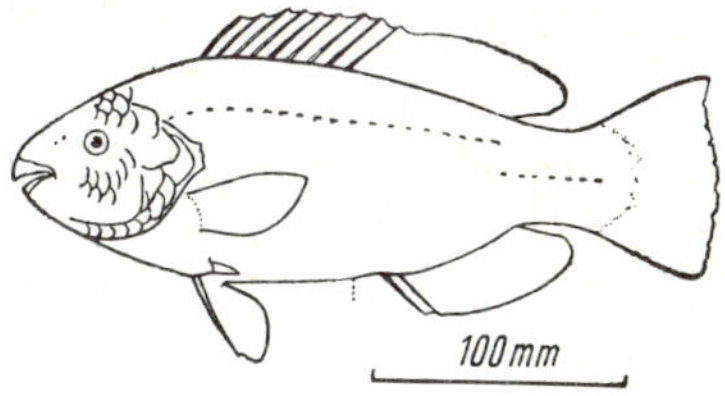

FIGURE 724. Scaridae (Scarinae) — *Pseudoscarus guacamaia* (J. and E., 1900, fig. 617, diagr.)

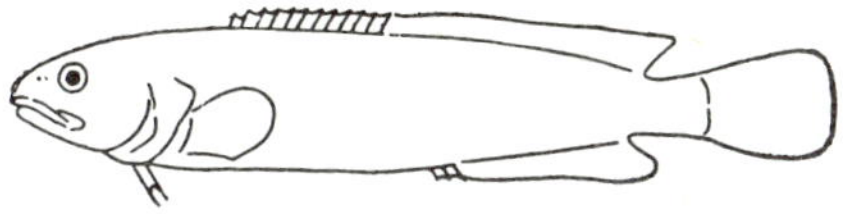

FIGURE 725. Gadopsidae (GRWM, 1966: 428. fig.)

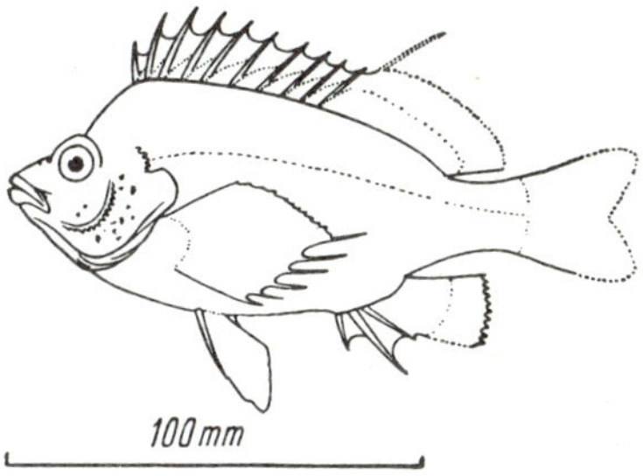

FIGURE 726. Cirrhitidae - *Cirrhitichthys aureus* (Wang, 1958, fig. 420, diagr.)

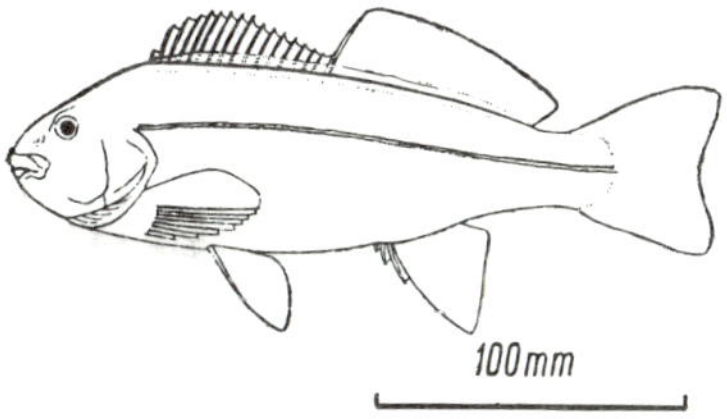

FIGURE 727. Aplodactylidae — *Aplodactylus punctatus* (Fowler, 1940, fig. 60, diagr.)

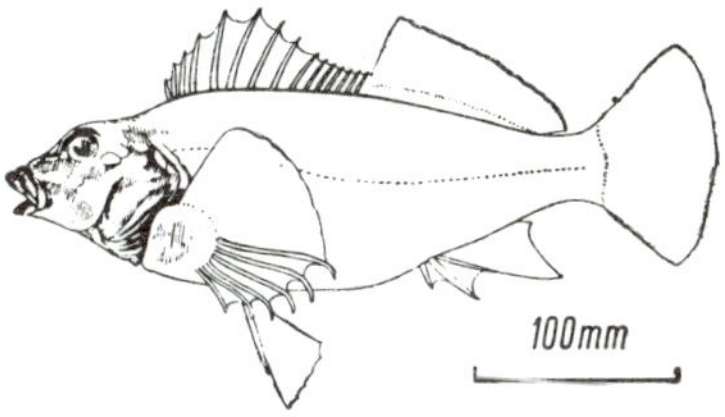

FIGURE 728. Chironemidae — *Chironemus marmoratus* (Ogilby, 1893, pl. 17, diagr.)

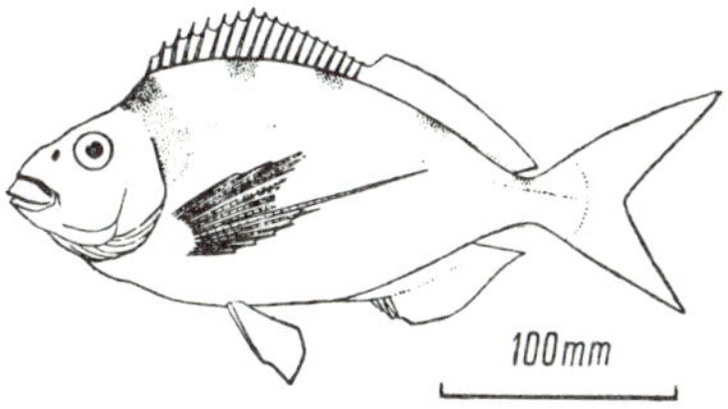

FIGURE 729. Cheilodactylidae — *Cheilodactylus macropterus* (Waite, 1911, pl. 95, diagr.)

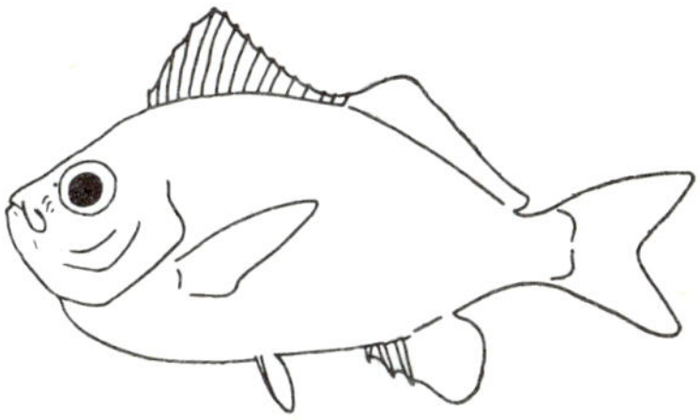

FIGURE 730. Gregoryinidae (GRWM, 1966: 425, fig.)

Superfamily 50.1.6. *Gadopsoidea* (thesis 50.1.0–3)

1 family: 343. **Gadopsidae** (Figure 725).

Superfamily 50.1.7. *Cirrhitoidea* (thesis 50.1.0–13)

5 families (344–348):

1 (6). Dorsal fin with 11–21 soft rays.
2 (3). Dorsal fin with 10–12 spiny rays. Base of spiny part of fin longer than base of soft part. [Vertebrae 10+16. Suborbital process present.] (Figure 726) . . . . 344. **Cirrhitidae**
3 (2). Dorsal fin with 14 or more spiny rays. Base of spiny part of fin almost the same length as base of soft part. [Suborbital process absent.]
4 (5). Teeth on jaws scalpriform or lanceolate, or with 3 apexes. [Vertebrae 35 (16+19). All precaudal vertebrae with parapophyses.] (Figure 727) . . . . 346. **Aplodactylidae**
5 (4). Teeth on jaws setiform or conical. [Vertebrae 33 (13+20). Precaudal vertebrae with parapophyses beginning from the 4th or 5th.] (Figure 728) . . . . 345. **Chironemidae**
6 (1). Dorsal fin with 23–39 soft rays.
7 (8). Anal fin with 7–19 soft rays. Unbranched rays of pectoral fin more or less thickened and elongate. [Suborbital process well developed.] (Figure 729) . . . . .347. **Cheilodactylidae**[116]
8 (7). Anal fin with 18–32 soft rays. Unbranched rays of pectoral fin not thickened and not elongate. [Suborbital process absent.] (Figure 731) . . . . 348. **Latridae**

Superfamily 50.1.8. *Trichodontoidea* (thesis 50.1.0–9)

1 family: 349. **Trichodontidae** (Figure 732).

Superfamily 50.1.9. *Trachinoidea* (thesis 50.1.0–23)

14 families (350–363):

1 (20). Lateral line situated on sides of body, passing along the midline (a little above or below it), complete, reaching the base of the caudal fin.
2 (7). Two dorsal fins, both well developed; their bases are clearly disjunct, but if they touch, there is a very deep notch.
3 (6). Bases of dorsal fins markedly disjunct.

[116] Family 347a. Gregoryinidae (Figure 730) has recently been established upon the suggestion of GRWM (1966: 400, 425), described from a young specimen from family 347. Cheilodactylidae.

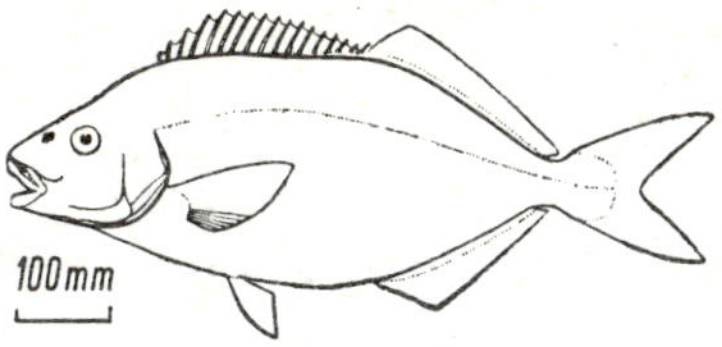

FIGURE 731. Latridae — *Latridopsis forsteri* (Waite, 1921, fig. 190, diagr.)

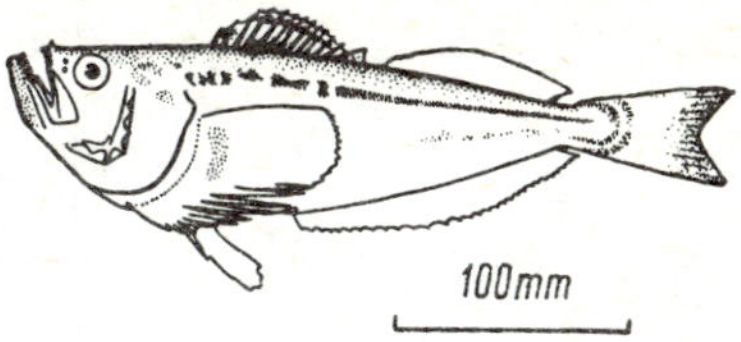

FIGURE 732. Trichodontidae — *Trichodon trichodon* (M., 1955, III, fig. 190, diagr.)

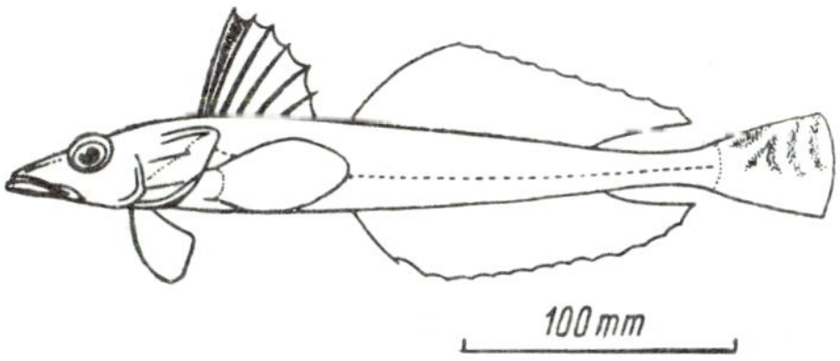

FIGURE 733. Bembropsidae — *Bembrops caudimaculata* (Abe, 1958, fig. 349, diagr.)

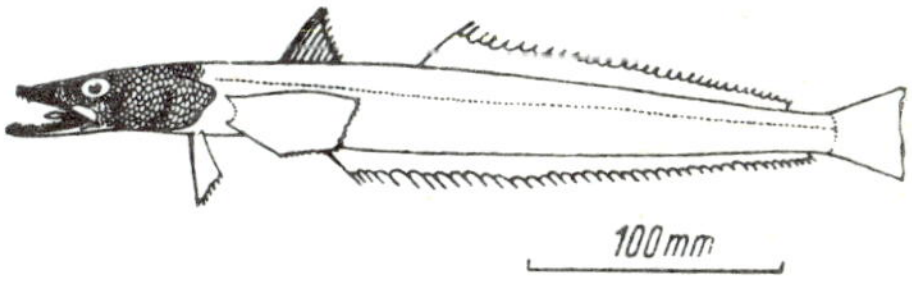

FIGURE 734. Percophididae — *Percophis fabre* (Quoy and Gaimard, 1824, pl. 53, fig. 1, diagr.)

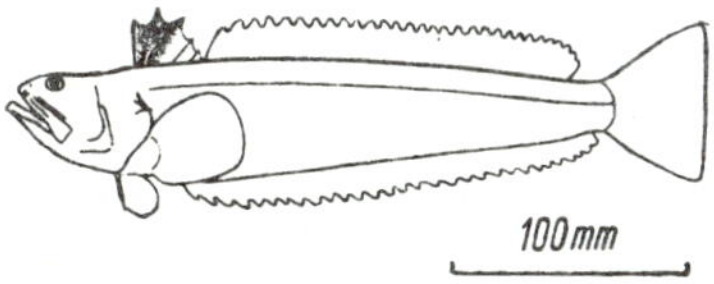

FIGURE 735. Trachinidae — *Trachinus draco* (Fowler, 1936, fig. 422, diagr.)

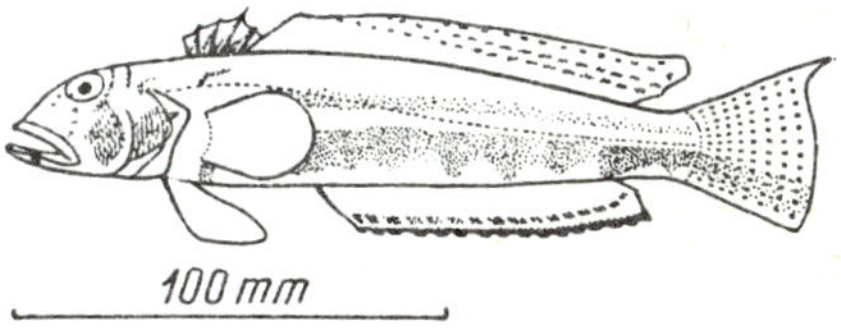

FIGURE 736. Mugiloididae — *Parapercis pulchella* (Wang, 1958, fig. 423, diagr.)

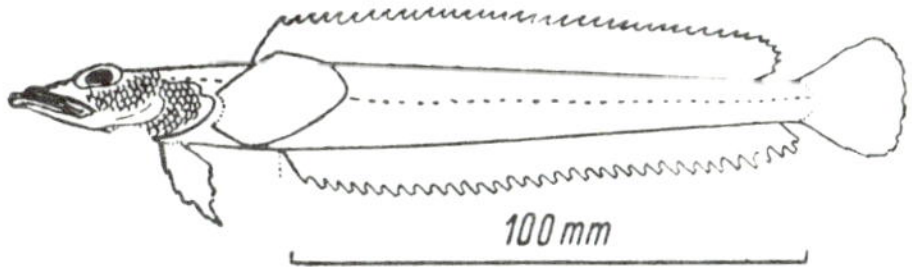

FIGURE 737. Hemerocoetidae — *Hemerocoetes acanthorhynchus* (Richardson, 1844–1848, pl. 54, fig. 7, diagr.)

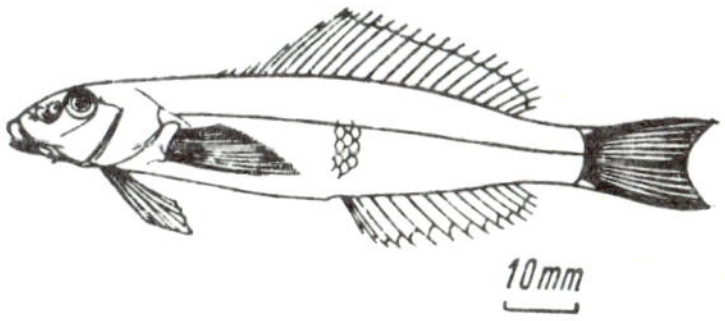

FIGURE 738. Cheimarrhichthyidae — *Cheimarrhichthys forsteri* (Haast, 1873 (74), pl. 18, fig. 38a)

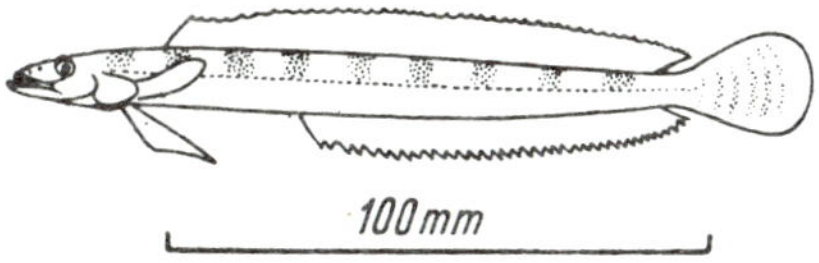

FIGURE 739. Trachinotidae — *Trachinotus setigerus* (M., 1955, III, fig. 250)

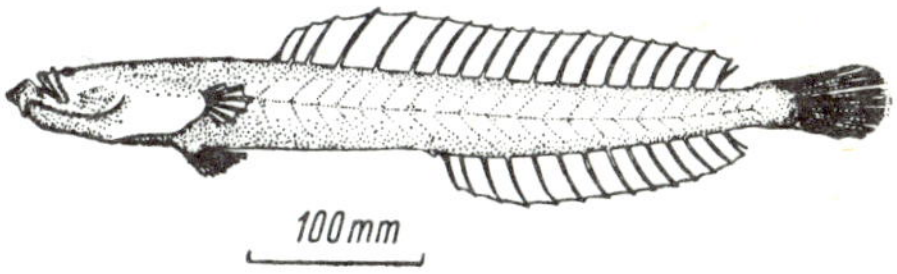

FIGURE 740. Kraemeriidae — *Kraemeria sexradiata* (Matsubara and Iwai, 1959, fig. 1)

4 (5). Anal fin without spiny, only with 15 soft rays; caudal fin with 10—11 branched rays. (Figure 733) . . . . . .357. **Bembropsidae**

5 (4). Anal fin with 1 spiny and 42 soft rays; caudal fin with 13 branched rays. (Figure 734) . . . . 356. **Percophididae**

6 (3). Bases of dorsal fins touching, but the fins are separated by a deep notch and are not connected by a membrane. Oral slit oblique, but not vertical, maxillary bone passing far beyond the eyes; eyes on the sides, not on top, of the head. (Figure 735); in this differing from fishes of the superfamily Uranoscopoidea (see Figures 747—749) and from family 353. Mugiloididae in the presence of a suborbital process and the larger number of rays (D VI 30, A II 30). (Figure 736) . . . . . . 355. **Trachinidae**

7 (2). One dorsal fin; if it has spiny rays, these are not separated by a deep notch from the soft rays, or else they are represented by 3—4 low barbs that are not connected by a membrane.

8 (11). Sides of head covered with scales.

9 (10). Dorsal fin with fewer than 30 rays, anal with fewer than 20. Ventral fins inserted approximately under base of pectorals or a little way in front. (Figure 736) . . . . 353. **Mugiloididae**

10 (9). Dorsal fin with more than 35 rays; anal with more than 25. Ventral fins inserted markedly in front of base of pectorals. (Figure 737) . . . . 358. **Hemerocoetidae**

11 (8). Sides of head not covered with scales.

12 (17). Lateral line running along the middle of the sides of the body.

13 (14). Lower jaw shorter than upper. Mouth subterminal. Anterior rays of dorsal fin low, in the form of 3—4 unconnected small barbs. Ventral fins inserted markedly in front of base of pectorals. (Figure 738). . . . . 354. **Cheimarrhichthyidae**

14 (13). Lower jaw longer than upper jaw. Mouth half-superior. Anterior rays of dorsal fin scarcely shortened. Ventral fins inserted under base of pectorals, or just in front of them.

15 (16). Eyes of normal size, at least 1/10 as long as the head. Dorsal fin with 46 rays, anal with 36. (Figure 739) . . . . 359. **Trichonotidae**

16 (15). Eyes very small, at most 1/20 as long as the head. Dorsal fin with 22 rays, anal with 14. (Figure 740) . . 361. **Kraemeriidae**[117]

17 (12). Lateral line passing markedly below the midline of the sides of the body, at least in its posterior part.

18 (19). Mouth subterminal. Ventral fins present. Teeth on jaws and palatines setiform. (Figure 741) . . . . . . .362. **Limnichthyidae**

19 (18). Mouth terminal. Ventral fins as a rule absent. Teeth only on lower jaw, small, pointed. (Figure 742) . . . . . 360. **Creediidae**

20 (1). Lateral line situated near base of dorsal fin, but if slightly lower, on the back, then incomplete, not reaching the base of the caudal fin, or else absent.

21 (22). Lateral line absent. No ventral fins. (Figure 743) . . . . 363. **Oxudercidae**

22 (21). Lateral line present. Ventral fins also present.

[117] Berg (1940 : 328), following Regan (1911 : 733), included this family in the suborder Gobioidei, but hypothetically (see also thesis 50.16—12).

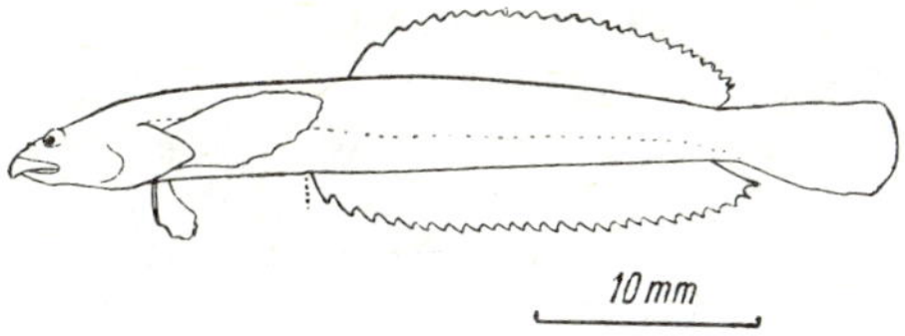

FIGURE 741. Limnichthyidae — Limnichthys fasciatus (M., 1955, III, fig. 252, diagr.)

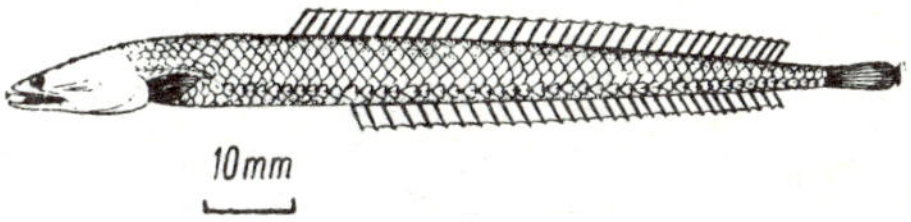

FIGURE 742. Creediidae — Apodocreedia vanderhorsti (Smith, 1950, fig. 375)

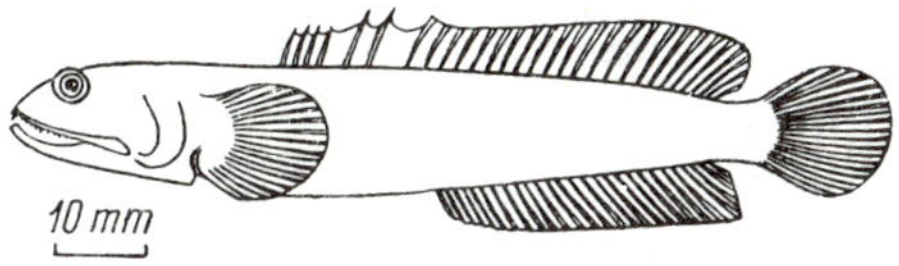

FIGURE 743. Oxudercidae — Oxuderces dentatus (Fowler, 1937—1957, fig. 61, diagr.)

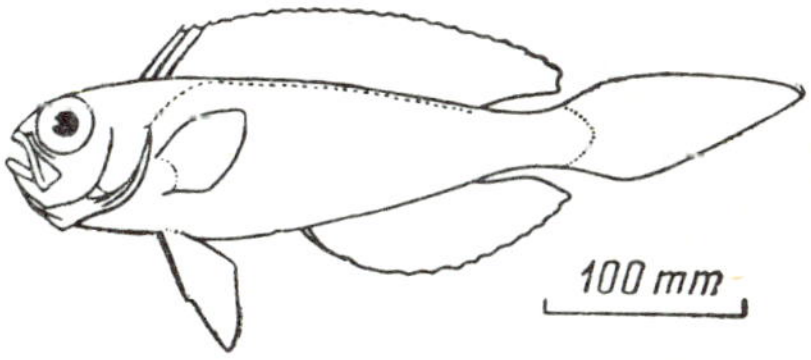

FIGURE 744. Owstoniidae — Owstonia totomiensis (M., 1955, III, fig. 253, diagr.)

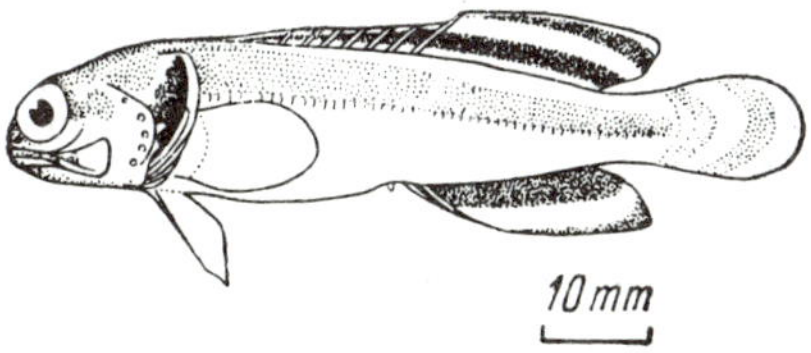

FIGURE 745. Opisthognathidae — Stalix histrio (M., 1955, III, fig. 254, diagr.)

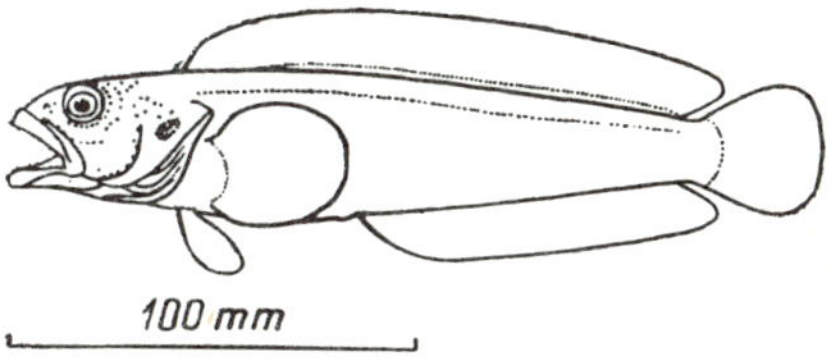

FIGURE 746. Bathymasteridae — Bathymaster derjugini (M., 1955, III, fig. 258, diagr.)

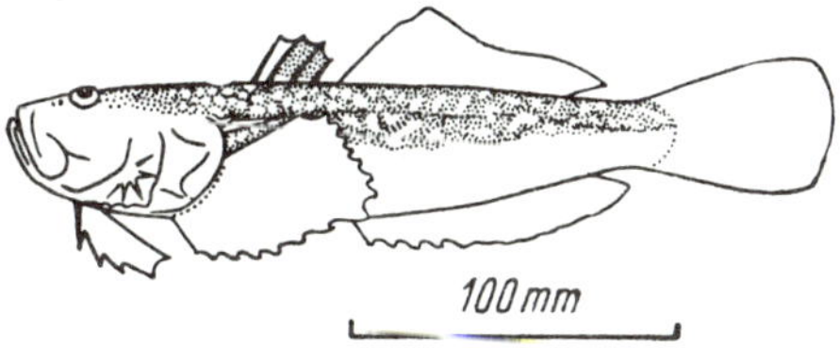

FIGURE 747. Uranoscopidae — Uranoscopus japonicus (Okada, 1955, fig. 359, diagr.)

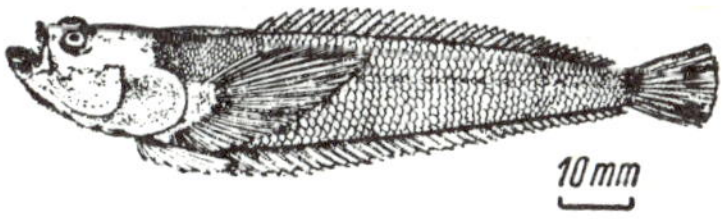

FIGURE 748. Leptoscopidae — Crapatulus novaezealandiae (Günther, 1861, pl. 10, fig. A)

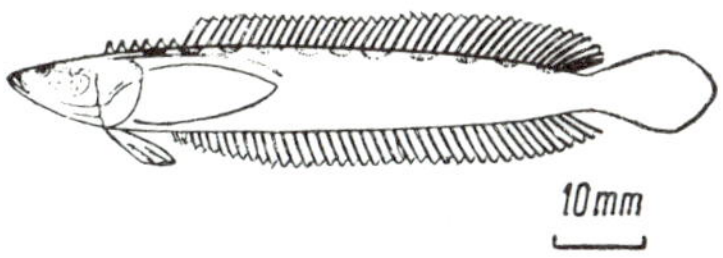

FIGURE 749. Dactyloscopidae — Gillellus australis (Fowler, 1940, fig. 68, diagr.)

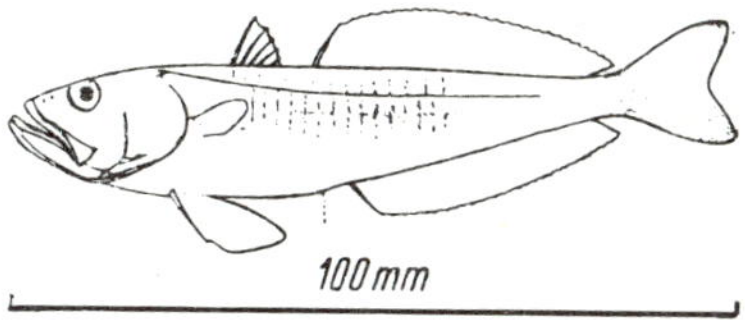

FIGURE 750. Champsodontidae — Champsodon snyderi (M., 1955, III, fig. 259, diagr.)

23 (26). Scales cycloid. Posterior part of maxillary bone greatly widened; a supramaxillary accessory bone is present. Outer branched rays of ventral fin longer than middle rays. [Fewer than 30 vertebrae (about 27).]

24 (25). Mouth small, oral slit oblique. Only the anterior 3 rays of the dorsal fin are in the form of weak spiny rays. Lower margin of preoperculum serrate. Lateral line reaching the end of the base of the dorsal fin. (Figure 744) . . . . . 351. **Owstoniidae**[118]

25 (24). Mouth large, oral slit horizontal. Spiny rays present in the whole anterior part of the dorsal fin. No serration on lower margin of preoperculum. Lateral line reaching only to the middle of the dorsal fin. (Figure 745) . . . . 350. **Opisthognathidae**

26 (23). Scales ctenoid. Posterior part of maxillary not widened at all or weakly widened; no accessory bone. Outer branched rays of ventral fin shorter than middle rays. [About 50 vertebrae.] (Figure 746) . . . . 352. **Bathymasteridae**

Superfamily 50.1.10. *Uranoscopoidea* (thesis 50.1.0—1)

3 families (364—366):

1 (4). Ventral fins with 1 spiny and 5 soft rays.

2 (3). Lateral line passing markedly above the midline of the sides of the body. One or two dorsal fins. Ventral fins close together. (Figure 747) . . . . 366. Uranoscopidae[119]

3 (2). Lateral line passing along the middle of the sides of the body. Dorsal fin, with one base, and anal fins longer than in 366. Uranoscopidae, reaching anteriorly almost to base of pectoral. Ventral fins clearly separated from each other. (Figure 748) . . . . 364. Leptoscopidae

4 (1). Ventral fins with 1 spiny and 3 soft rays. (Figure 749) . . . . 365. Dactyloscopidae

Superfamily 50.1.11. *Champsodontoidea* (thesis 50.1.0—11)

1 family: 367. Champsodontidae (Figure 750).

[118] The Japanese authors Okada and Suzuki (1956: 194) determined a close resemblance of osteological characters in representatives of families 351. Owstoniidae and 337. Cepolidae, due to which they concluded that the family Owstoniidae should be included in the Cepolidae (see thesis 50.1.2—1).

[119] The outwardly extremely similar family 335. Trachinidae (thesis 50.1.9—6) of the superfamily Trachinoidea (Figure 735) differs from the Uranoscopidae in that the ventral fins are situated not on the throat but just slightly in front of the base of the pectorals and in that the eyes are set on the sides, not on top, of the head.

Superfamily 50.1.12. *Chiasmodontoidea* (thesis 50.1.0—8)

1 family: 368. Chiasmodontidae (Figure 751).

Superfamily 50.1.13. *Notothenioidea* (thesis 50.1.0—16)

5 families (369—373):

1 (2). Branchiostegal membranes not united, free of the interbranchial space. Palatines and vomer with teeth. Snout not elongate. First dorsal fin almost separated from the second; its rays are not spiny but soft, unbranched. (Figure 752) . . . . 369. **Bovichthyidae**

2 (1). Branchiostegal membranes united, free of or attached to the interbranchial space, usually forming a fold across it. Palatines without teeth.

3 (8). Snout relatively short; eyes not less than half its length; the snout is not flattened and not similar to the snout of pike (Esox). Palatine bones normally developed. [Ribs well ossified.]

4 (7). First dorsal fin present. Mouth protrusible.

5 (6). Body covered with scales. Opercular bone rounded, without spines in the upper corner. Branchiostegal membranes forming a fold across the interbranchial space. (Figure 753) . . . . 370. **Nototheniidae**

6 (5). Body bare. Opercular bone with a hooklike process in the upper corner; its upper margin is strongly concave. Branchiostegal membranes broadly united with the interbranchial space. (Figure 754) . . . . 371. **Harpagiferidae**

7 (4). First dorsal fin absent. Mouth generally not protrusible. (Figure 755) . . . . 372. **Bathydraconidae**

8 (3). Snout markedly drawn out, flattened and resembling that of pike; eyes usually less than half its length. Greater part of palatine bones having the form of a ligament. [Ribs not ossified.] (Figure 756) . . . . 373. **Channichthyidae**

Suborder 50.2. **Blennioidei**[120] (thesis 50.0—27)

20 families (374—393):

1 (2). Teeth on vomer, palatines, and on sides of lower jaw well developed, large, and massive; strong conical canines on

[120] Families 376. Xenocephalidae, 379. Notograptidae (Figure 757), 380. Peronedysidae (Figure 758), 381. Ophiclinidae (Figure 759), and 392. Schindleriidae (Figure 760) are not included in the key to families of the suborder Blennioidei as they have been incompletely described. For more details on them see the footnote to thesis 50.0—27 in the key to the suborders of the Perciformes. The families Xiphisteridae (Figure 786), Pholididae (ex parte Chirolophidinae) (Figure 782), and Lumpenidae (Figure 783) are included in family 384. Stichaeidae (thesis 50.2—17). Family 424. Microdesmidae (Figure 761) has been transferred to suborder 50.16. Gobioidei; for more details see footnote to thesis 50.0—21 and thesis 50.16—12.

anterior part of lower jaw and on premaxillaries. Dorsal fin consisting of flexible spiny rays, at least in anterior part; posterior rays thicker and harder. Scales very small, grown into the skin. Branchiostegal membranes broadly intergrown with the interbranchial space. Ventral fins absent.[121] Body moderately elongate; fewer than 100 rays in dorsal and anal fins. (Figure 762). As an exception the body may be elongate, eel-like, and the number of rays in the fins much greater, over 200 (genus Anarhichthys) . . . . 375. **Anarhichadidae**

2 (1). Such teeth absent.

3 (4). Dorsal fin with very many spiny and soft rays, more than 200 (90 spiny, not connected by a membrane, and 145 soft). A leathery outgrowth on the chin. No ventral fins. Body greatly elongate. [More than 200 vertebrae.] Caudal fin fused with dorsal and anal. (Figure 763) . . . . 387. **Ptilichthyidae**

4 (3). If spiny rays present in dorsal fin, they number considerably fewer than 200 together with the soft rays.

5 (18). Considerably more spiny than soft rays as a rule in dorsal fin; soft rays often absent, but if present, then caudal fin more or less defined, not fused wholly with dorsal and anal.

6 (7). Mouth superior; oral slit almost vertical. Dorsal fin with a long base, of moderate height, consisting only of spiny rays. Ventral fins absent. Scales as a rule absent.[122] Gill openings small. Branchiostegal membranes grown together, united with the interbranchial space. Teeth quite strong. (Figure 764) . . . . 385. **Cryptacanthodidae**

7 (6). Mouth not superior; oral slit horizontal or oblique, but not vertical.

8 (9). Caudal peduncle short but well expressed; dorsal and anal fins not connected with caudal. Base of anal short, much less than half as long as the base of the dorsal. Lower jaw thickened, slightly protruding in front of the upper jaw. No ventral fins. Small scales present not only on the body but also on the fins. (Figure 765) . . . . 393. **Zaproridae**

9 (8). Caudal peduncle weakly expressed or absent, but if present, base of anal fin long, considerably more than half as long as the base of the dorsal; dorsal and anal usually united or fused with the caudal. Lower jaw not thickened.

10 (15). Tropical warmth-loving blennies. Soft (jointed) rays in ventral, dorsal, and anal fins as a rule simple, unbranched. Ventral fins long,[123] more than half as long as the pectorals, with a weakly developed spiny ray and 1—3 soft, unbranched, clearly defined rays which are rarely rudimentary. Lateral line, if present, always single, passing above the pectoral fins. Rays in caudal

[121] In the genus Andamia (Salariinae, family 374. Blenniidae) the ventral fins are short, less than half as long as the pectorals, but they are adapted for creeping over rocks; apparently serving the same purpose is the sucker on the lower lip.

[122] There are small scales in Cryptacanthodes giganteus.

[123] Relatively long ventral fins (more than half as long as the pectorals) are known for the genus Leptoclinus of family 384. Stichaeidae.

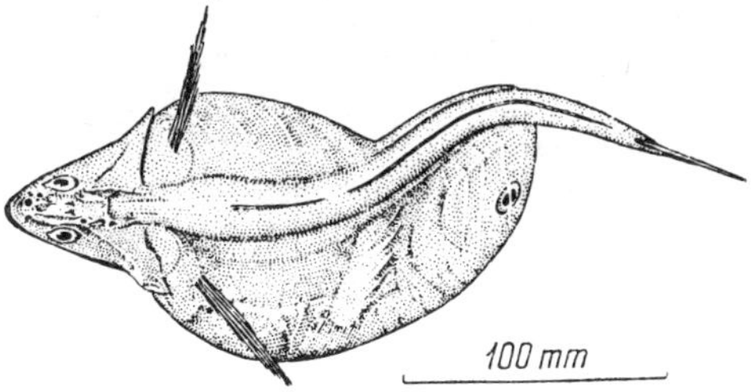

FIGURE 751. Chiasmodontidae — Chiasmodon niger (Jordan, 1925, fig. 469)

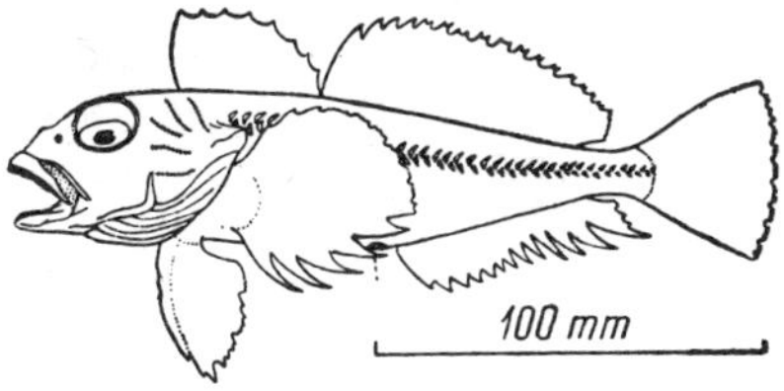

FIGURE 752. Bovichthyidae — Bovichthys variegatus (Richardson, 1844, pl. 34, figs. 1–4, diagr.)

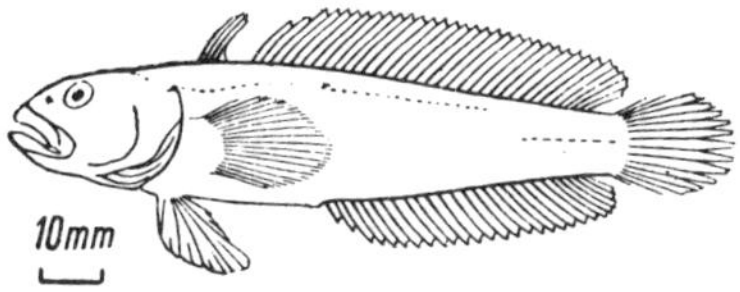

FIGURE 753. Nototheniidae — Notothenia cyanobrancha (Norman, 1938, fig. 11, diagr.)

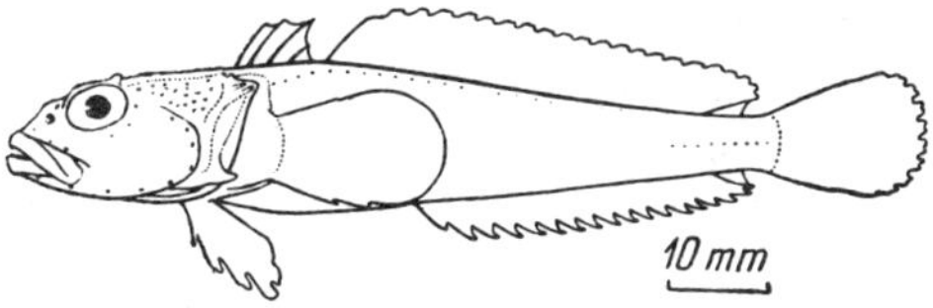

FIGURE 754. Harpagiferidae — Harpagifer georgianus kerguelensis (Orig., A.N. Andriyashev)

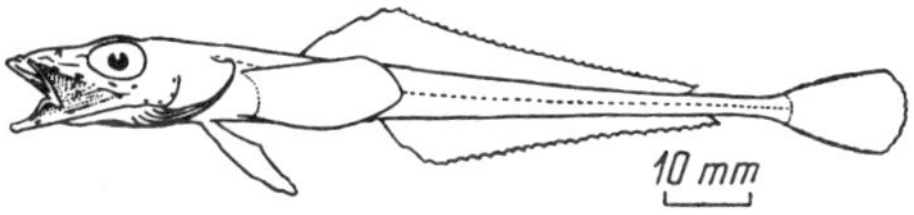

FIGURE 755. Bathydraconidae — Bathydraco marri (Norman, 1938, fig. 33, diagr.)

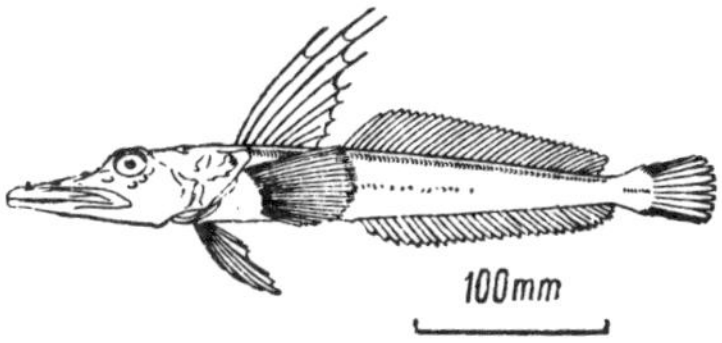

FIGURE 756. Channicthyidae — Channicthys rhinoceratus (Norman, 1938, fig. 47)

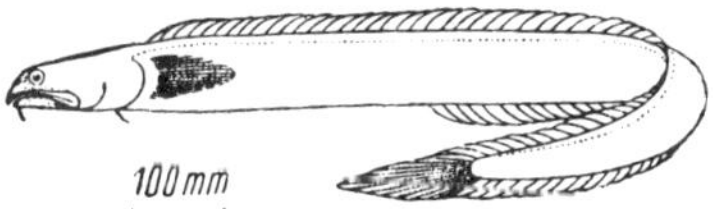

FIGURE 757. Notograptidae — Notograptus guttatus (W. and B., 1951, 9, fig. 57, diagr.)

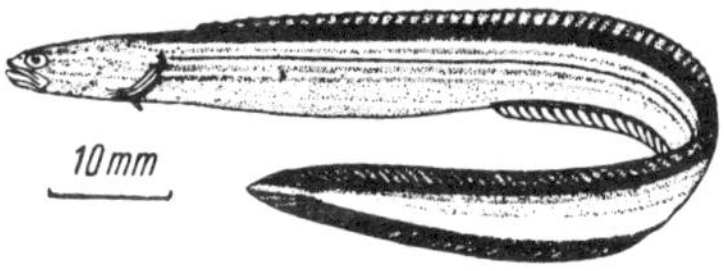

FIGURE 758. Peronedysidae — Peronedys anguillaris (Waite, 1921, fig. 240)

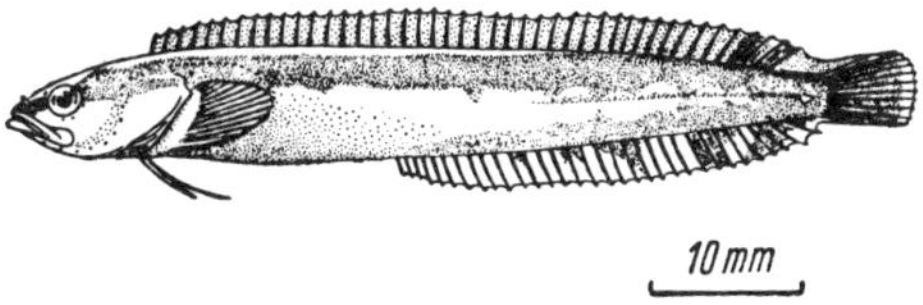

FIGURE 759. Ophiclinidae — Ophiclinus gracilis (Waite, 1921, fig. 243)

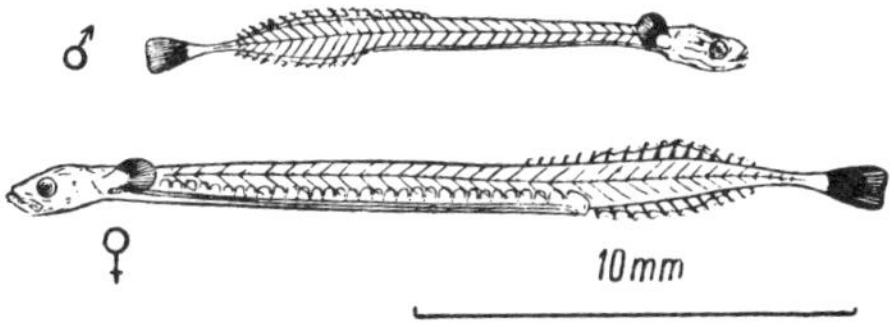

FIGURE 760. Schindleriidae — Schindleria praematura (Berg, 1940, fig. 179, 1, 2)

fin 13 or fewer. [Four suborbital bones (counting the preorbital). Ascending wings of parasphenoid not overlapping descending wings of frontal bones.] Two nasal openings on each side of the snout.

11 (12). As a rule, 3 clearly defined dorsal fins. [Lateral line canals on suborbital ring and preoperculum not covered by bone.] Barbel-like appendages absent on occiput. Scales generally ctenoid. Rays of pectoral fin usually branched; rays of caudal almost always branched. [First gill arch united with opercular bone by a membrane and interbranchial slit diminished in size.] (Figure 766) . . . . 383. Tripterygiidae

12 (11). One or two dorsal fins. [Lateral line canals on suborbital ring and preoperculum covered by bone.] Barbel-like appendages usually present both above the eyes and on the occiput. Scales, if present, not ctenoid. Rays of pectoral fin never branched; rays of caudal more often than not unbranched. [First gill arch not united with opercular bone by a membrane and interbranchial slit normal, not diminished in size.]

13 (14). First dorsal fin short.[124] [Suborbital bony ring weak and flexible; lachrymal (preorbital) bone widened anteriorly, not reaching the vertical of the middle of the eye posteriorly; other 3 bones also weakly developed, higher than wide.] Scales present, tilelike or of another character . . . . 382. Clinidae

2 subfamilies:

1 (2). [No hooklike process on anterior margin of pectoral girdle.] Scales with radial striation only on the anterior margin. The scales are never small and grown into the skin. (Figure 767) . . . . subfamily 382.1. Labrisomatinae

2 (1). [A small, clearly expressed process on the anterior margin of the pectoral girdle.] Scales with radial striation along the whole margin, anteriorly, laterally, and posteriorly. Scales usually small and grown into the skin. (Figure 768) . . . . subfamily 382.2. Clininae

14 (13). First dorsal fin long. [Suborbital bony ring firm; lachrymal (preorbital) bone reaching the vertical of the middle of the eye or farther posteriorly; other 3 bones also firm, well developed wider than high.] Scales absent, except in Neoclinus (Figure 769), which has small scales that do not have a tilelike arrangement . . . . 374. Blenniidae

[124] The base of the first dorsal may be separated by a space from the base of the rest of the fin or, if there is a single base, there is a more or less deep notch, or, finally, the space between the bases of the rays is larger. Exceptions are members of the tribe Clinini, in which the first dorsal fin is uninterrupted and long.

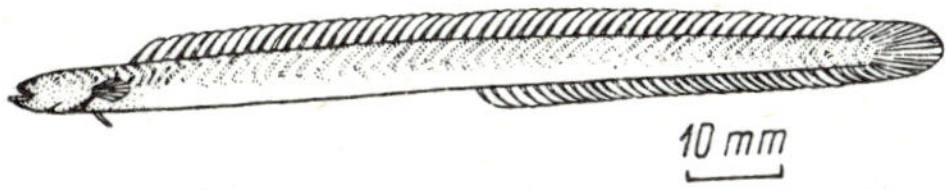

FIGURE 761. Microdesmidae (Gobioidei) — Microdesmus dipus (Günther, 1864, pl. 3, fig. 2)

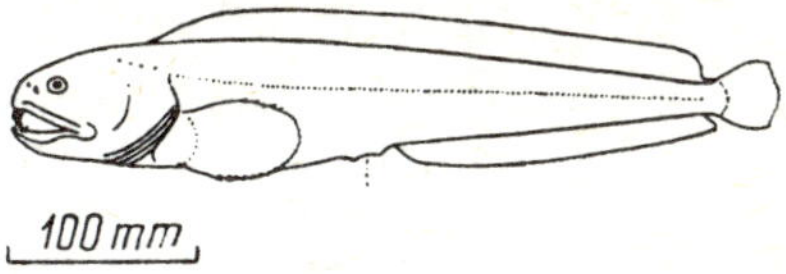

FIGURE 762. Anarhichadidae — Anarhichas orientalis (M., 1955, III, fig. 271, diagr.)

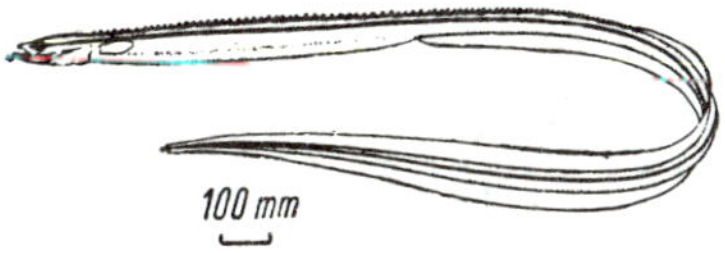

FIGURE 763. Ptilichthyidae — Ptilichthys goodei (Jordan, 1925, fig. 630, diagr.)

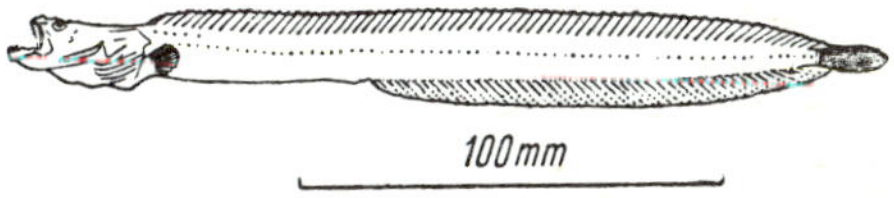

FIGURE 764. Cryptacanthodidae — Cryptacanthoides bergi (Soldatov and Lindberg, 1930, fig. 66, diagr.)

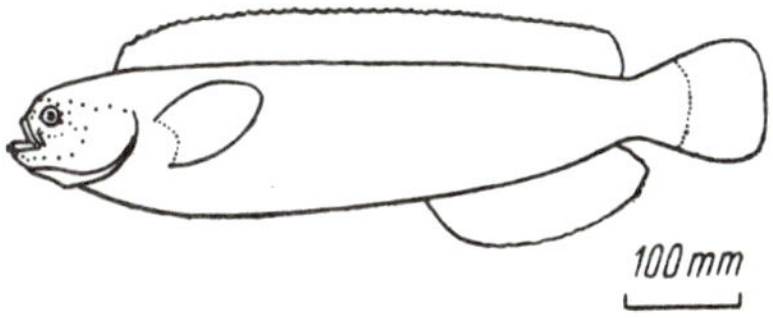

FIGURE 765. Zaproridae — Zaprora silenus (M., 1955, III, fig. 273, diagr.)

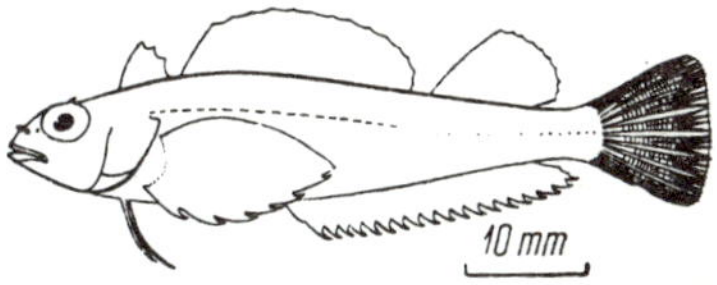

FIGURE 766. Tripterygiidae — Tripterygion etheostoma (M., 1955, III, fig. 263, diagr.)

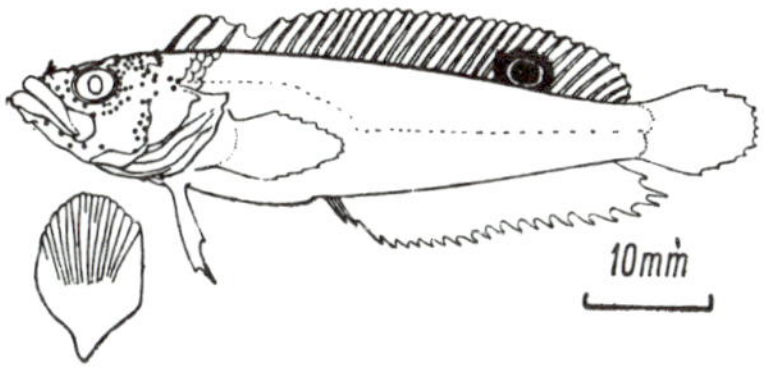

FIGURE 767. Clinidae (Labrisomatinae) — Paraclinus walkeri (Clark Hubbs, 1952, fig. 24, diagr.)

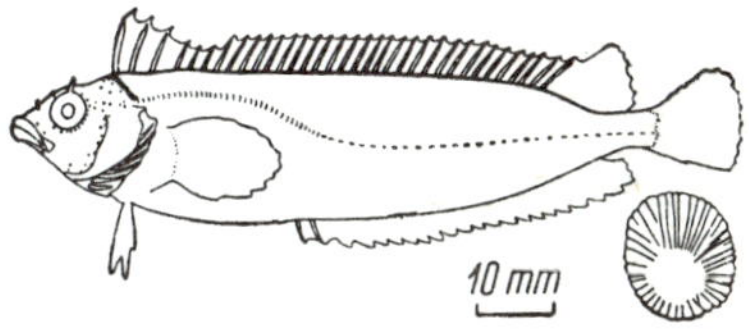

FIGURE 768. Clinidae (Clininae) — Gibbonsia elegans (Clark Hubbs, 1952, fig. 61, diagr.)

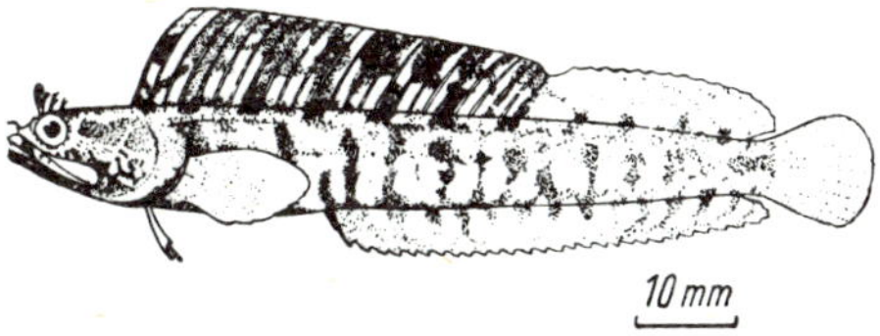

FIGURE 769. Blenniidae (Chaenopsinae) — Neoclinus bryope (M., 1955, III, fig. 265, diagr.)

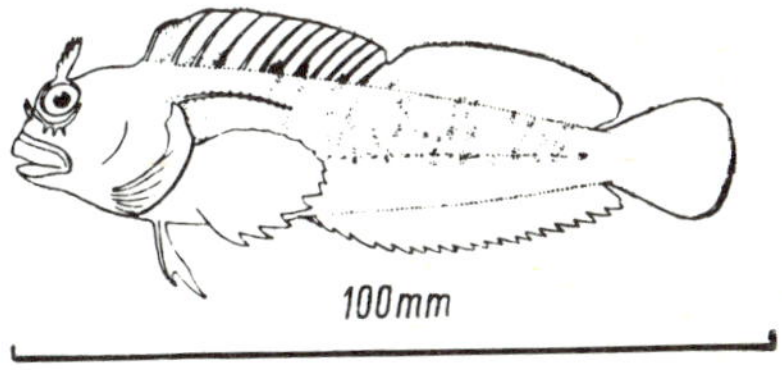

FIGURE 770. Blenniidae (Blenniinae) — Blennius yatabei (M., 1955, III, fig. 266, diagr.)

3 subfamilies:

1 (2). Anterior teeth on jaws often scalpriform, but never enlarged, pectinate. Teeth of jaws usually conical, some of them possibly enlarged and curved. Mouth large. Upper jaw as a rule extending markedly beyond the eyes. [First suborbital bone long, supporting the whole lower margin of the eye.] Body generally eel-like. (Figure 769) . . .subfamily 374.1. Chaenopsinae[125]

2 (1). Anterior teeth on jaws rakelike; one or more canines as a rule developed on each side behind these. Mouth comparatively small; upper jaw generally not extending beyond the eyes. [First suborbital bone not so long.] Body not eel-like, except in the genus Xiphasia.

3 (4). Teeth on both jaws large or of medium size, immovable, firmly set in alveoli of the jaw bones. (Figure 770) . . . . .subfamily 374.2. Blenniinae

4 (3). Teeth on both jaws small, extremely mobile, set not in alveoli of the jaw bones but in the skin of the lips. (Figure 771). . . . . subfamily 374.3. Salariinae

15 (10). Northern, cold-loving blennies. Soft (branched) rays in the ventral (if these fins are present), dorsal, and anal fins as a rule branched; if the rays in the ventrals are not branched, they are so markedly reduced that the number of joints in the ray next to the spiny ray does not exceed 5, being more numerous only in the genus Leptoclinus of family 384. Stichaeidae (Figure 772). Ventral fins short (again except in Leptoclinus), less than half as long as the pectorals, with one weakly developed spiny ray and 2—4 branched (Figure 571) or rudimentary, unbranched rays, overgrown with skin and hard to distinguish. Lateral line, if present, as a rule not simple: it often branches or is made complex by supplementary lines; the dorsal branch passes onto the pectoral fin, not descending behind it and not running into the line passing along the middle of the sides of the body, but if continuous, then without an arc. [Suborbital bones numbering 5—6 or more, counting the preorbital. Ascending wings of parasphenoid overlapping descending wings of frontals.] One nasal opening on each side of the snout.

16 (17). Both the main rays and the nearest marginal rays branched in the caudal fin (Figure 773). Ventral fins, if present, rudimentary, with 1 short spiny and 1 small unbranched ray (Figure 774). [Ribs absent. Parapophyses of truncal vertebrae transformed into hemonephrapophyses (Figure 775). Two tabularia supraoccipitalia] . . . . 386. **Pholididae**

2 subfamilies:

1 (2). Two spines at origin of anal fin. Ventral fins present. [Not more than 47 truncal vertebrae.] (Figure 776) . . . . subfamily 386.1. Pholidinae

[125] Isolated into a separate family, 374a. Chaenopsidae (GRWM: 401, 431; MA: 145).

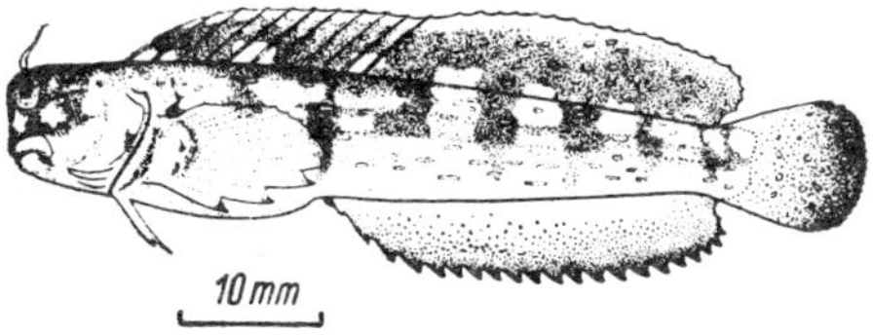

FIGURE 771. Blenniidae (Salariinae) — Rhabdoblennius ellipes (M., 1955, III, fig. 268, diagr.)

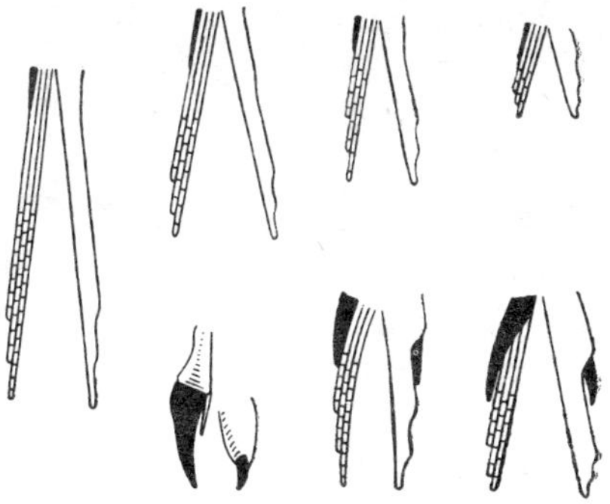

FIGURE 772. Ventral fins of northern blennies (Leptoclinus — long ones, left) (Makushok, 1958, fig. 26)

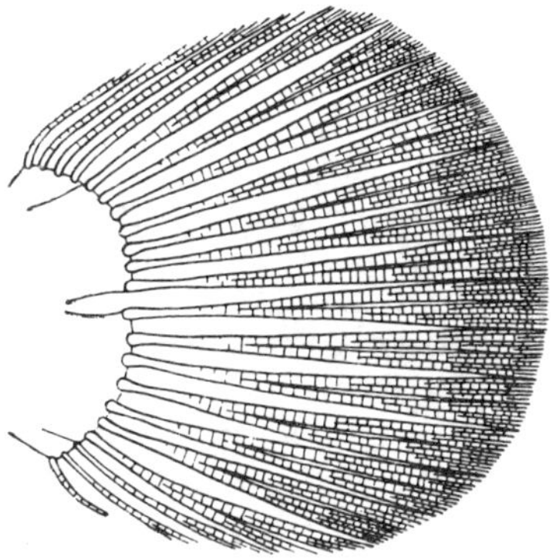

FIGURE 773. Caudal fin of Enedrias nebulosus (Pholididae)

FIGURE 774. Ventral fins of Pholis pictus (Pholididae) (Makushok, 1958, fig. 26K):

left — without skin cover; spines shaded in.

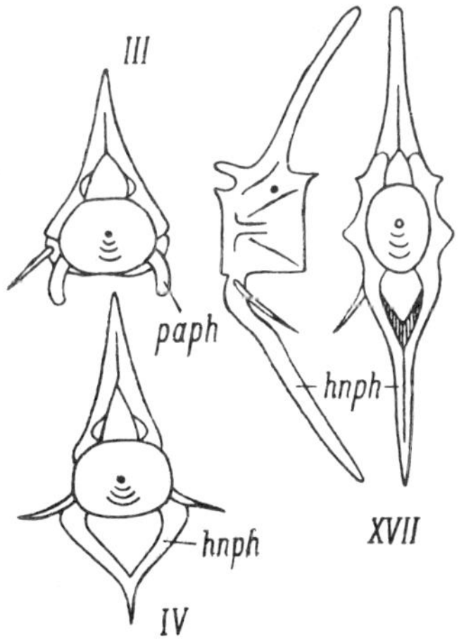

FIGURE 775. Hemonephrapophyses of Pholis gunnellus (Makushok, 1958, fig. 14):

paph — parapophysis; hnph — hemonephrapophysis; Roman numbers — serial numbers of vertebrae.

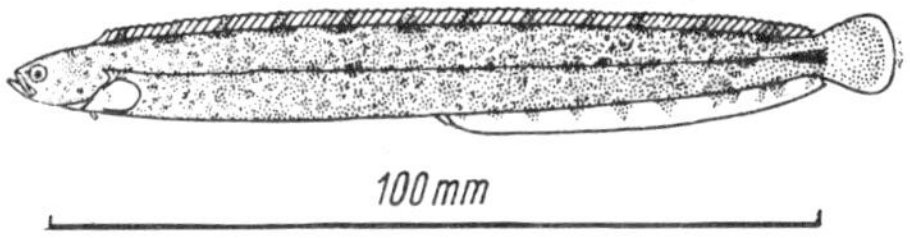

FIGURE 776. Pholididae (Pholidinae) — Enedrias nebulosus (Okada, 1955, fig. 374, diagr.)

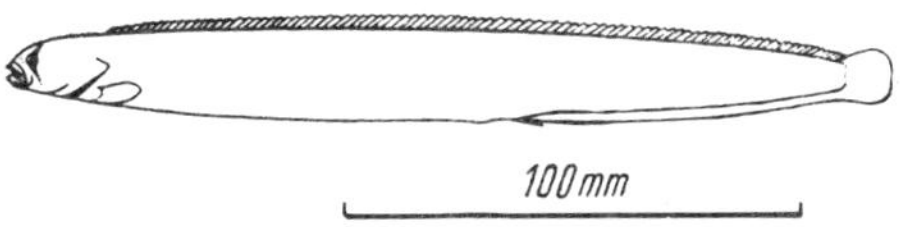

FIGURE 777. Pholididae (Apodichthyinae) — Apodichthys flavidus (J. and E., 1900, fig. 830, diagr.)

2 (1). One spine at origin of anal fin. Ventral fins absent. [Not less than 50 truncal vertebrae.] (Figure 777) . . . . subfamily 386.2. Apodichthyinae

17 (16). Only the main rays are branched in the caudal fin (Figure 778). Ventral fins, if present, more or less developed, with 1 spiny and 2–4 soft rays. [Ribs present. Parapophyses of truncal vertebrae not transformed into hemonephrapophyses. One tabulare supraoccipitale or none] . . . . 384. Stichaeidae

8 subfamilies:

1 (2). Pectoral fins absent; [radials of humeral girdle also absent.] Ventral fins also absent. (Figure 779). . . . . subfamily 384.1. Azygopterinae

2 (1). Pectoral fins present.

3 (4). [Not less than 130 vertebrae.] Caudal fin completely fused with dorsal and anal, with at most 10 rays, this apparently also including the marginal rays. (Figure 780) . . . . subfamily 384.2. Eulophiinae

4 (3). [Not more than 134 vertebrae.] Caudal fin more or less separate, with at least 12 (12–15) main rays.

5 (6). Seismosensory canals on trunk well developed; ventral fins present. (Figure 781) . . . . . subfamily 384.3. Stichaeinae

6 (5). Seismosensory canals absent on trunk, but if well developed, ventral fins are absent. The canals are sometimes weakly developed, in the form of a short canal, but in this case ventral fins are present.

7 (8). Head covered with numerous leathery appendages in the form of barbels and lobes. (Figure 782) . . . . subfamily 384.4. Chirolophinae

8 (7). Head without leathery appendages in the form of barbels and lobes, but there may be a leathery rostral-occipital crest (in *Alectrias cirratus*).

9 (12). Pectoral fins large (more than half as long as the head), with at least 12 (12–21) rays. Ventral fins as a rule present (absent in *Kasatkia* and *Opisthocentrus*).

10 (11). Gill openings protracted downward and forward; branchiostegal membranes separated and attached to the anterior part of the interbranchial space. Postorbital, occipital, and suborbital seismosensory canals of the head completely reduced. Not more than 2 dentary pores. (Figure 783). . . . . subfamily 384.5. Lumpeninae

11 (10). Gill openings not protracted downward and forward; branchiostegal membranes broadly intergrown and free of the interbranchial space. Postorbital and occipital canals of the head normally developed, while if the suborbital is reduced, it is only partly so. At least 3 dentary pores. (Figure 784) . . . . subfamily 384.6. Opisthocentrinae

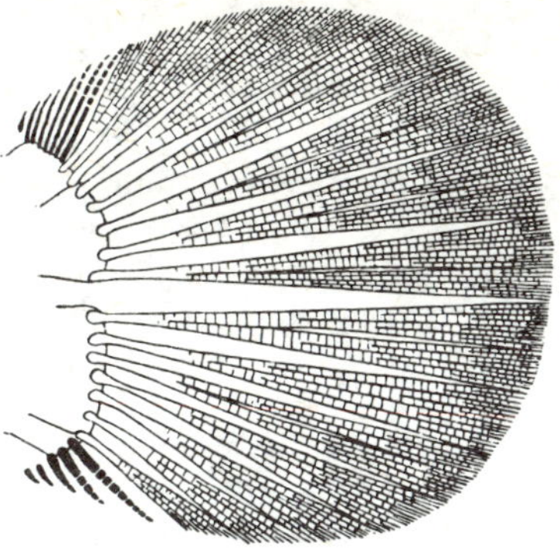

FIGURE 778. Caudal fin of *Opisthocentrus dybowskii* (Stichaeidae) (Makushok, 1958, fig. 3)

FIGURE 779. Stichaeidae (Azygopterinae) — *Azygopterus corallinus* (Andriyashev and Makushok, 1955, fig., diagr.)

FIGURE 780. Stichaeidae (Eulophiinae) — *Eulophias tanneri* (Jordan, Tanaka, and Snyder, 1913, fig. 359)

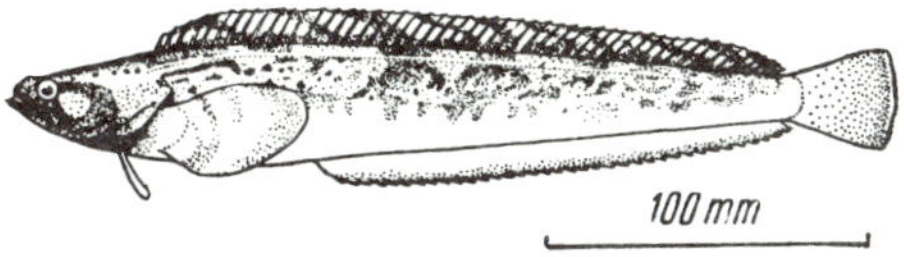

FIGURE 781. Stichaeidae (Stichaeinae) — *Stichaeus nozawae* (Jordan, Tanaka, and Snyder, 1913, fig. 368, digr.)

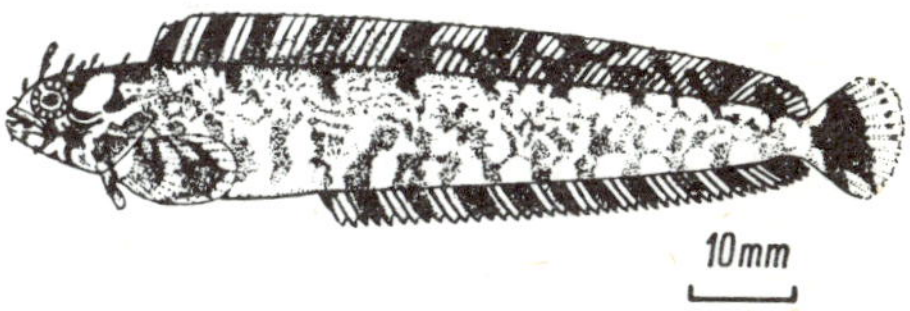

FIGURE 782. Stichaeidae (Chirolophinae) — *Chirolophus japonicus* (Jordan, Tanaka, and Snyder, 1913, fig. 353)

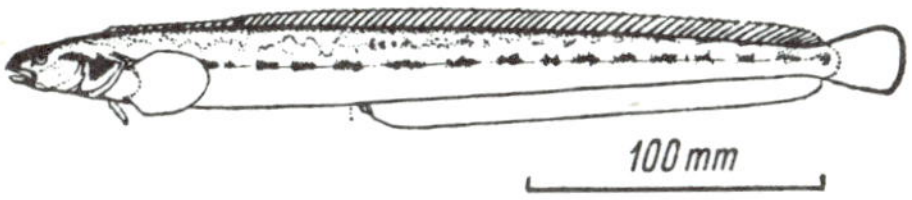

FIGURE 783. Stichaeidae (Lumpeninae) *Lumpenus fowleri* (Jordan, Tanaka, and Snyder, 1913, fig. 370, diagr.)

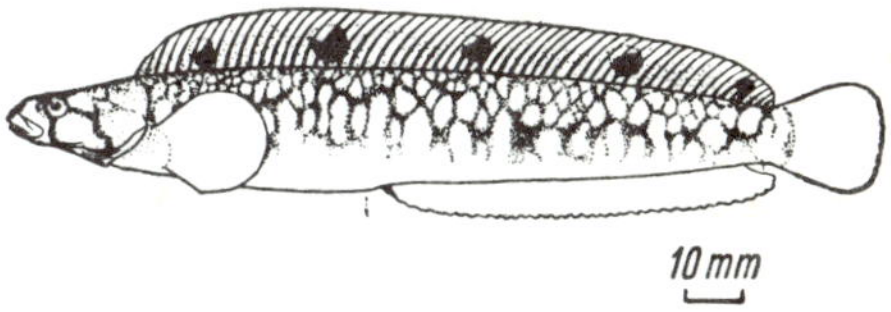

FIGURE 784. Stichaeidae (Opisthocentrinae) — *Opisthocentrus ocellatus* (M., 1955, III, fig. 279, diagr.)

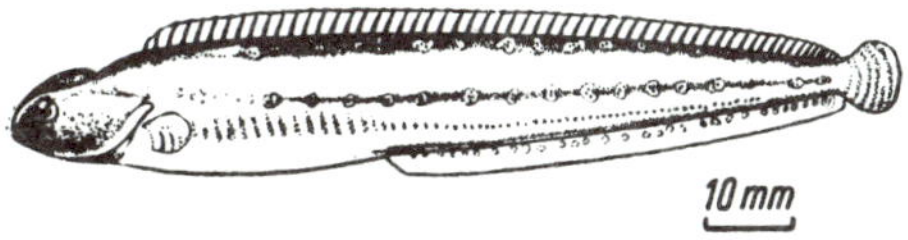

FIGURE 785. Stichaeidae (Alectriinae) — *Alectrias alectrolophus benjamini* (M., 1955, III, fig. 282, diagr.)

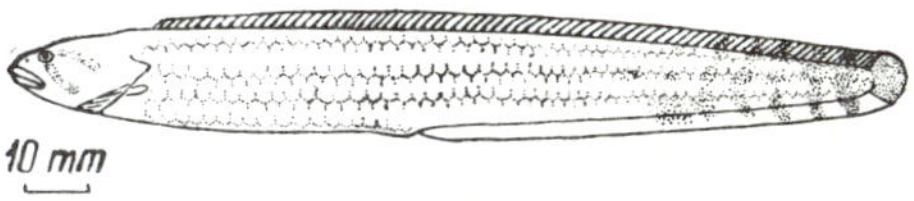

FIGURE 786. Stichaeidae (Xiphisterinae) — *Xiphister mucosus* (Makushok, 1961, fig. 257, diagr.)

12 (9). Pectoral fins small (less than half as long as the head) or markedly reduced, with at most 12 (8—12) rays. Ventrals absent.

13 (14). Truncal seismosensory canals absent (seismosensory buds lying open in the form of a middle and an upper branch). Five branchiostegal rays. Scales covering only the posterior half of the body or absent altogether. Spines in anterior part of dorsal fin thin and flexible, posteriorly gradually becoming thicker and hard. (Figure 785) . . . . subfamily 384.7. Alectriinae

14 (13). Truncal seismosensory canals present. Six branchiostegal rays. Scales covering the whole body apart from the head. Spines in dorsal fin of even thickness, not flexible. (Figure 786) . . . . subfamily 348.8. Xiphisterinae

18 (5). Spiny rays as a rule absent in dorsal fin, but if present, they are much fewer than the soft rays and in addition, the caudal fin is this case clearly fused with the dorsal and anal fins (Zoarces, Krusensterniella, Zoarchias, Neozoarces); if the caudal fin is separate, only the first dorsal ray is spiny and there is a space between it and the fin (in family 378. Haliophidae, Figure 789).

19 (20). Gill openings large, continuing far down and forward. Branchiostegal membranes well separated and barely, very narrowly, united anteriorly, where they are lightly attached to the interbranchial space or are free of this.[126] Scales absent. Vent considerably, even far, behind base of pectoral fins, in contrast to the case in family 396. Carapidae (Ophidioidei, Figure 811). Ventral fins present or absent. (Figure 787). . . . . 389. **Lycodapodidae**

20 (19). Gill openings small or of moderate size, not continuing far down and forward.[127] Branchiostegal membrane broadly united and sometimes forming a fold across the interbranchial space.

21 (22). Caudal fin clearly distinguishable, although lightly connected with dorsal and anal. There is a small, curved spiny ray in front of the dorsal fin and separate from it. Ventral fins absent, but if present, with a small spine. [Opercular bone triangular, with a long spine forming the upper margin of the bone. Interoperculum long, articulating with the angulare.] Mouth of moderate size; oral slit not extending beyond the eyes. Teeth present on vomer. (Figure 789) . . . . 378. **Haliophidae**[128]

[126] The genus Lycogramma shows a similar character of the gill openings and branchiostegal membranes (family 388. Zoarcidae, Figure 788), but here scales are present. Shmidt (1950 : 108) treats family 389. Lycodapodidae as a subfamily of the Zoarcidae.

[127] Except in Lycogramma (Zoarcidae) (see previous footnote).

[128] J. Smith (1952 : 87) considers the family which he established, 378. Haliophidae (Halidesmidae), as a specialized group of the Percoidei, gravitating toward families 302. Lutjanidae and 313. Sparidae; it should apparently even be isolated into a separate order. The family is subdivided into 3 subfamilies.

22 (21). Caudal fin fully fused with dorsal and anal, and hard or impossible to distinguish. No single spiny ray set at an interval in front of the dorsal fin.

23 (24). Caudal part of body widened, laterally compressed, and ending in the wide caudal fin, which is rounded at the end but is fused with the dorsal and anal. Dorsal fin originating far behind pectorals, approximately in the middle of the body. Pectorals small. Ventral fins absent. Eyes very small. (Figure 790) . . . . 391. **Scytalinidae**

24 (23). Caudal part of body not widened but tapering; if it does not taper markedly, the caudal fin is pointed, and the dorsal originates in the anterior half of the body, roughly above the pectoral fins.

25 (26). Ventral fins very small and situated far in front of pectorals, more or less on the vertical through the eyes. Gill openings in the form of very small vertical slits, situated in front of the base of the pectoral fins. Caudal part of body markedly thinner. (Figure 791) . . . . 390. **Derepodichthyidae**

26 (25). Ventral fins often absent, but if present, then situated on the thorax, not shifted far forward to the vertical of the eye.

27 (28). Branchiostegal membranes free of the interbranchial space.[129] Ventral fins absent. Pectorals small, much less than half as long as the head. Dorsal and anal fins without spiny rays. Lower jaw protruding slightly in front of upper jaw. (Figure 792) . . . . 377. **Congrogadidae**[130]

28 (27). Branchiostegal membranes attached to interbranchial space (see footnote to thesis 27). Ventral fins, if present, situated on the thorax. Pectorals large, at least half as long as the head, but if somewhat smaller, the dorsal fin has spiny rays or the gill opening is very small, the same size as the pupil . . . . 388. Zoarcidae

10 subfamilies:

1 (16). Northern subfamilies.

2 (3). Branchiostegal membranes broadly grown together and forming a wide fold across the interbranchial space. Ventral fins present. Vomer and palatines with teeth. (Figure 793) . . . . subfamily 388.1. L y c o z o a r c i n a e

3 (2). Branchiostegal membranes more or less attached to the interbranchial space, but not forming a free fold across it.

4 (7). Dorsal fin with spiny rays.

5 (6). Short spiny rays situated in posterior part of dorsal fin. (Figure 794) . . . . subfamily 388.2. Z o a r c i n a e

6 (5). Short spiny rays situated in anterior part of dorsal fin. (Figure 795) . . . . subfamily 383.3. N e o z o a r c i n a e

[129] The branchiostegal membranes are not attached to the interbranchial space in the genus L y c o z o a r c e s (family 388. Zoarcidae, Figure 793), but here ventral fins are present.

[130] J. Smith (1952: 86) considers this family as monotypic.

7 (4). No spiny rays in dorsal fin.
8 (11). Ventral fins present, but very small, in adults.
9 (10). Chin bearing a pair of crests each of which has one row of large pores or mucous cavities. (Figure 796) . . . . subfamily 388.4. Lycodinae
10 (9). Chin not bearing a pair of crests, nor are there pores or mucous cavities on the ventral surface of the head. (Figure 797) . . . . subfamily 388.5. Hadropareinae
11 (8). Ventral fins absent.
12 (13). Gill slit very small, situated above the upper margin of the base of the pectoral fin. Body bare. (Figure 798) . . . . subfamily 388.6. Melanostigminae
13 (12). Gill slit not so small, extending down past the upper margin of the base of the pectoral fin.
14 (15). Palatine membrane well developed. Gill slit reaching below upper margin of base of pectoral fin but not extending beyond the lower margin of its base. (Figure 799) . . . . subfamily 388.7. Gymnelinae
15 (14). Palatine membrane absent or rudimentary. Gill slit large, reaching beyond the lower margin of the base of the pectoral fin. (Figure 800). . . . . .subfamily 388.8. Lycogramminae
16 (1). Southern subfamilies.
17 (20). Ventral fins present.
18 (19). Snout and lower jaw without dermal appendages in the form of a fimbria. (Figure 801) . . . . . . subfamily 388.4. Lycodinae
19 (18). Snout and lower jaw with a dermal fimbria. (Figure 802) . . . . subfamily 388.9. Plateinae
20 (17). Ventral fins absent.
21 (22). Gill slit very small, situated above the upper margin of the base of the pectoral fin. Body bare. Head without dermal appendages. (Figure 803) . . . . subfamily 388.6. Melanostigminae
22 (21). Gill slit not so small, reaching below to the middle of the base of the pectoral fin. Body bare or covered with small scales grown into the skin. Head with or without dermal appendages. (Figure 804) . . . . subfamily 388.10. Mayneinae

Suborder 50.3. Ophidioidei (thesis 50.0—23)

4 families (394—397):

1 (4). Vent situated normally, on the belly. Scales usually present, and ventral fins generally developed. Mouth usually protrusible.
2 (3). Ventral fins, if present, inserted on the throat, more rarely under the eye, but in any case the pectoral fins almost reach the vent. Arrangement of scales normal, not at right angles to one another. Branchiostegal membranes usually separated and free of the interbranchial space . . . . 394. Brotulidae

FIGURE 787. Lycodapodidae — *Lycodapus mandibularis* (Clemens and Wilby, 1961, fig. 273, diagr.)

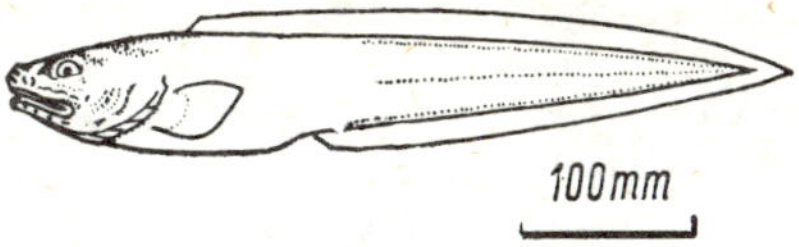

FIGURE 788. *Lycogramma zesta* (Zoarcidae) (M., 1955, III, fig. 301, diagr.)

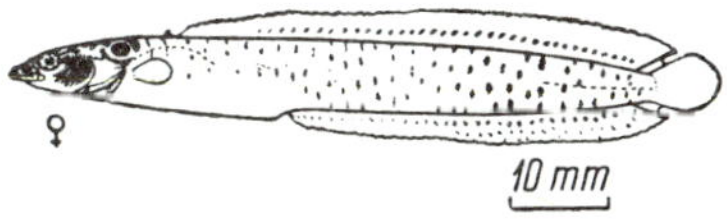

FIGURE 789. Haliophidae — *Haliophis guttatus* (Smith, 1952, fig. 1, diagr.)

FIGURE 790. Scytalinidae — *Scytalina cerdale* (Clemens and Wilby, 1961, fig. 256, diagr.)

FIGURE 791. Derepodichthyidae — *Derepodichthys alepidotus* (Clemens and Wilby, 1961, fig. 274, diagr.)

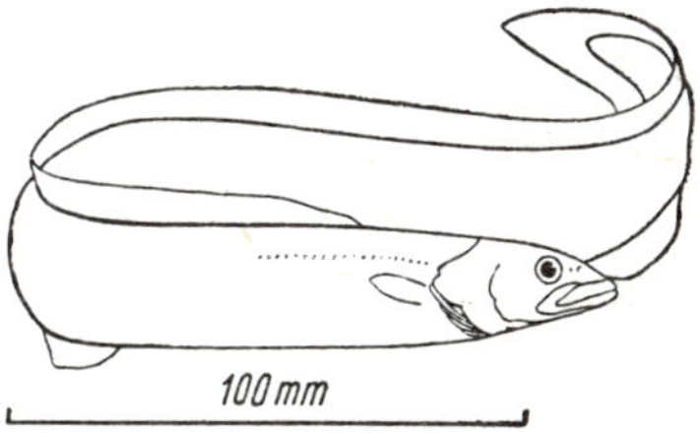

FIGURE 792. Congrogadidae — *Congrogadus subducens* (W. and B., 1951, 9, fig. 55)

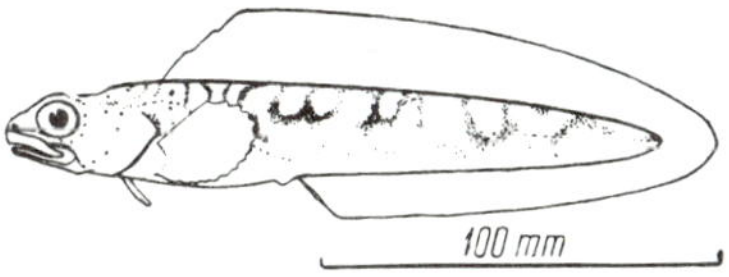

FIGURE 793. Zoarcidae (Lycozoarcinae) — *Lycozoarces hubbsi* (Shmidt, 1950, pl. 10, fig. 2, diagr.)

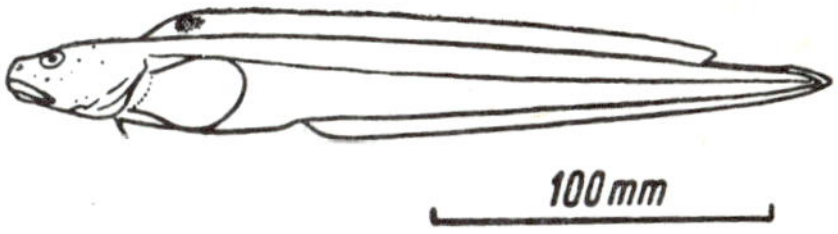

FIGURE 794. Zoarcidae (Zoarcinae) — *Zoarces elongatus* (Kner, 1868, pl. 7, fig. 2, diagr.)

FIGURE 795. Zoarcidae (Neozoarcinae) — *Zoarchias veneficus* (Jordan, Tanaka, and Snyder, 1913, fig. 361, diagr.)

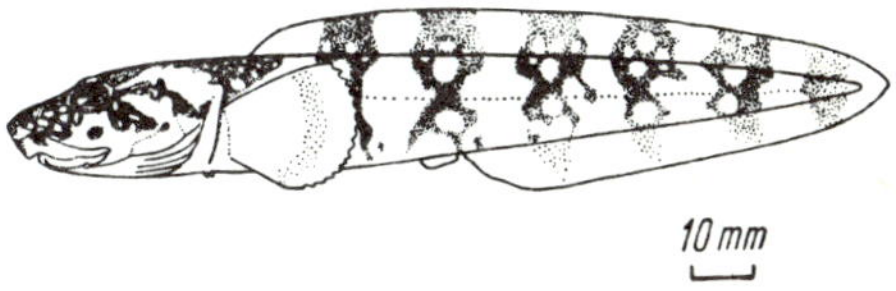

FIGURE 796. Zoarcidae (Lycodinae) — *Lycodes heinemanni* (Soldatov and Lindberg, 1930, fig. 70, diagr.)

4 subfamilies:

1 (2). Caudal fin defined, more or less separate from the dorsal and anal. Head almost bare, except for small areas of scales on the cheeks and sometimes on the operculum. Eyes, if present, small. [Two blind pyloric ceca.] Gill rakers reduced. (Figure 805) . . . . subfamily 394.1. Bromophycinae

2 (1). Caudal fin not defined, but if marked, fused with dorsal and anal. Head as a rule with scales all over, but bare in some oceanic genera. If eyes present, they are either slightly enlarged or small. [A few finger-shaped pyloric ceca are usually present.]

3 (6). Ventral fins generally inserted behind the vertical of the eye. [Cleithra not strongly projecting forward, their symphysis usually behind the eyes.]

4 (5). Snout and lower jaw without barbels. (Figure 806) . . . . subfamily 394.2. Bythitinae

5 (4). Snout and lower jaw with well developed barbels. (Figure 807) . . . . subfamily 394.3. Brotulinae

6 (3). Ventral fins inserted on the vertical of the eye. Pectorals almost reaching the vent. [Cleithra strongly shifted forward, their symphysis under the eyes.] (Figure 808) . . . . subfamily 394.4. Sirembinae

3 (2). Ventral fins inserted under the anterior margin of the eye, almost on the chin between the right and left halves of the lower jaw and bearing a resemblance to chin barbels. Pectoral fins short, not more than 1/2 the distance to the vent. Distribution of scales sometimes unusual — scales arranged at right angles to each other, as in river eels of the genus Anguilla. Branchiostegal membranes almost separate, lightly attached to the interbranchial space . . . . 395. Ophidiidae

2 subfamilies:

1 (2). Scales on body elongate, arranged more or less at right angles to to each other. [Pyloric ceca absent.] (Figure 809) . . . . subfamily 395.1. Ophidiinae

2 (1). Scales on body oval, normally distributed; scales sometimes not tilelike, but grown into the skin. [Pyloric ceca present.] (Figure 810) . . . . subfamily 395.2. Lepophidiinae

4 (1). Vent situated on the throat near the base of the pectoral fins. No scales, and ventral fins not developed. Mouth not protrusible. (Figure 811) . . . . 396. Carapidae[131]

[131] Family 397. Disparichthyidae, one genus and one species (Herre, 1935; 383, fig. 31) (Figure 812), referred by Herre and also by Schultz (1938:492) to order 31. Anguilliformes, cannot, according to Berg (1940:281), belong to this order. Fowler (1938:150, 151, and 302, figs. 29, 30) includes the genus Disparichthys in the Fierasferidae (family 396. Carapidae). In the related family 396a. Pyramodontidae, in contrast to 396. Carapidae, the dorsal fin originates on the vertical of the gill opening, and the pectoral fins are well developed, 3/4 as long as the head (Figure 813).

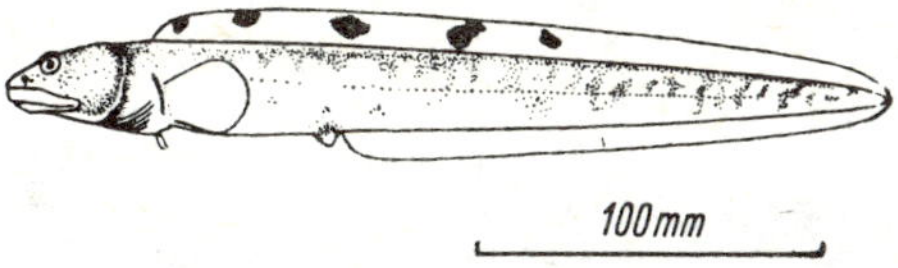

FIGURE 797. Zoarcidae (Hadropareinae) — *Hadropareia middendorffi* (Soldatov and Lindberg, 1930, fig. 69, diagr.)

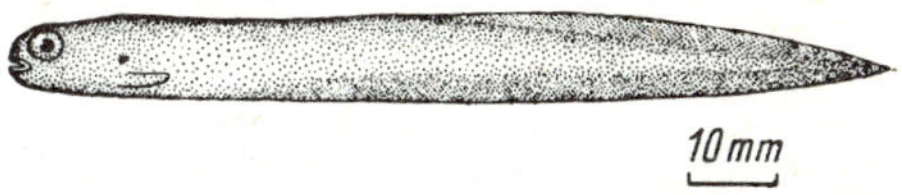

FIGURE 798. Zoarcidae (Melanostigminae) — *Melanostigma pamellas* (J. and E., 1900, fig. 865)

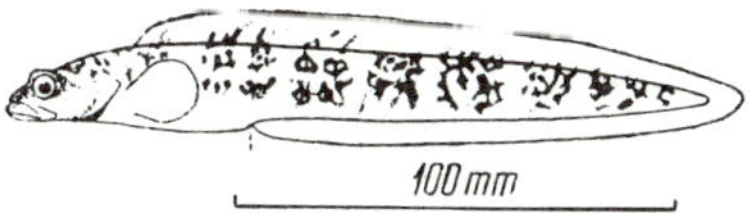

FIGURE 799. Zoarcidae (Gymnelinae) — *Gymnelis bilabrus* (Andriyashev, 1954, fig. 140, diagr.)

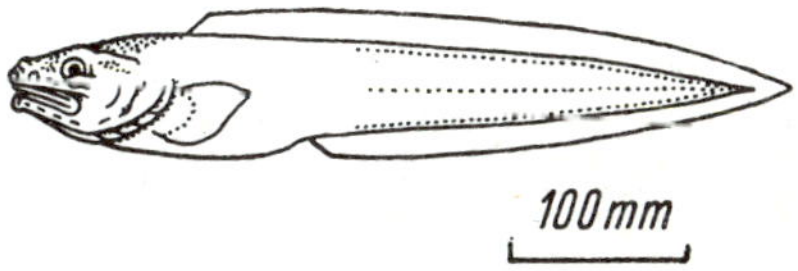

FIGURE 800. Zoarcidae (Lycogramminae) — *Lycogramma zesta* (M., 1955, III, fig. 301, diagr.)

FIGURE 801. Zoarcidae (Lycodinae) — *Lycodichthys antarcticus* (Andriashev, 1965, fig. 9, diagr.)

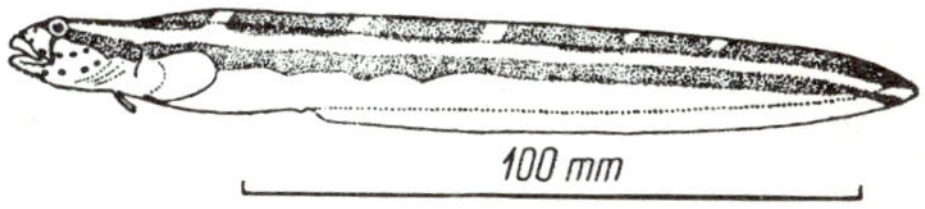

FIGURE 802. Zoarcidae (Plateinae) — *Pogonolicus elegans* (Norman, 1937, fig. 55, diagr.)

FIGURE 803. Zoarcidae (Melanostigminae) — *Melanostigma gelatinosus* (McAllister and Rees, 1964, fig. 1, 2A, diagr.)

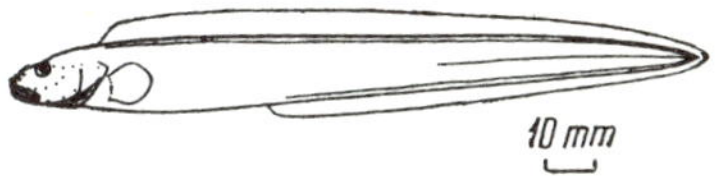

FIGURE 804. Zoarcidae (Mayneinae) — *Maynea patagonica* (Günther, 1881, pl. 2, figs. C, D, diagr.)

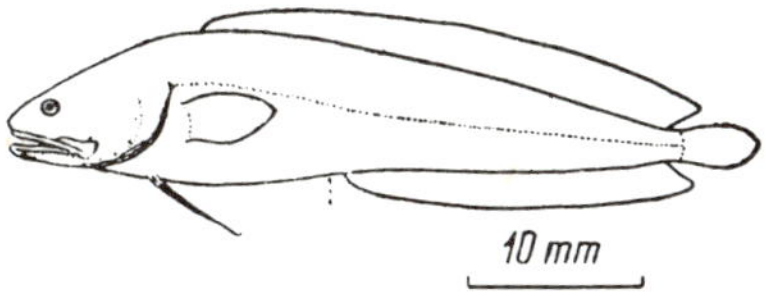

FIGURE 805. Brotulidae (Brosmophycinae) — *Ogilbia cayorum* (J. and E., 1900, fig. 873, diagr.)

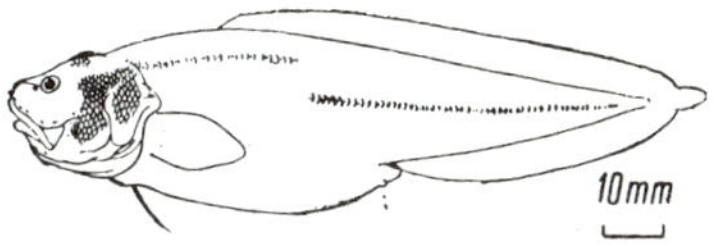

FIGURE 806. Brotulidae (Bythitinae) — *Bythites lepidogenys* (M., 1955, III, fig. 311, diagr.)

Suborder 50.4. **Ammodytoidei** (thesis 50.0—25)

3 families (398—400):

1 (4). Base of dorsal fin markedly longer than base of anal. Body covered with scales. Lateral line passing along the back. Branchiostegal membranes separated from each other.

2 (3). About 40 rays in dorsal fin. Dermal processes (keels) absent on both sides of abdomen. No obliquely arranged skin folds on the sides of the body. (Figure 814) . . . . .399. **Bleekeriidae**

3 (2). About 60 rays in dorsal fin. Dermal processes (keels) present on sides of abdomen. Oblique skin folds on sides of body. (Figure 815) . . . . 398. **Ammodytidae**

4 (1). Bases of dorsal and anal fin equal in length. Branchiostegal membranes united but free of the interbranchial space. (Figure 816) . . . . .400. **Hypoptychidae**

Suborder 50.5. **Callionymoidei** (thesis 50.0—13)

2 families (401, 402):

1 (2). Preoperculum without spines; operculum and suboperculum poorly developed; each with one straight, strong spine. Lateral line absent. Gill openings of average size. (Figure 817) . . . . 402. **Draconettidae**

2 (1). Preoperculum with one long, prickly spine; operculum and suboperculum without spines. Lateral line present. Gill openings extremely small. (Figure 818) . . .401. **Callionymidae**

Suborder 50.6. **Siganoidei** (thesis 50.0—3)

1 family: 403. **Siganidae** (Figure 819).

Suborder 50.7. **Acanthuroidei** (thesis 50.0—29)

2 families (404, 405):

1 (2). Sides of caudal peduncle usually bearing prickly spines or lanceolate processes, tubercles, and plates. Teeth scalpriform, arranged in one row. Scales small, setiform. (Figure 820). Spiny rays of dorsal fin without threadlike tips . . . . 405. Acanthuridae

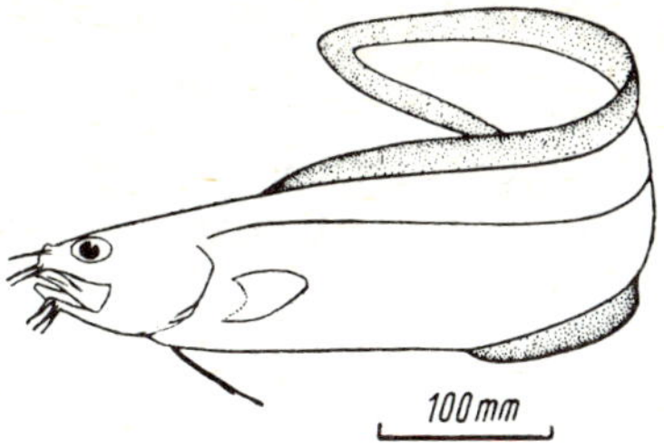

FIGURE 807. Brotulidae (Brotulinae) — Brotula multibarbata (Okada, 1955, fig. 381, diagr.)

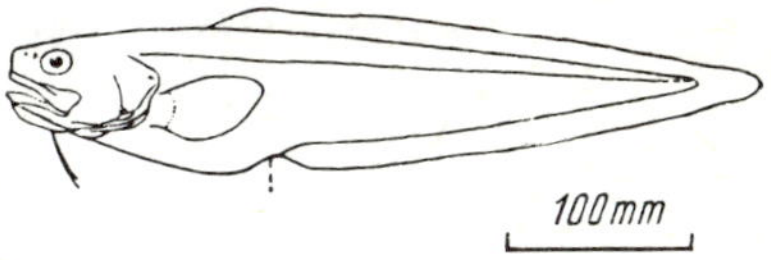

FIGURE 808. Brotulidae (Sirembinae) — Hoplobrotula armata (Okada, 1955, fig. 382, diagr.)

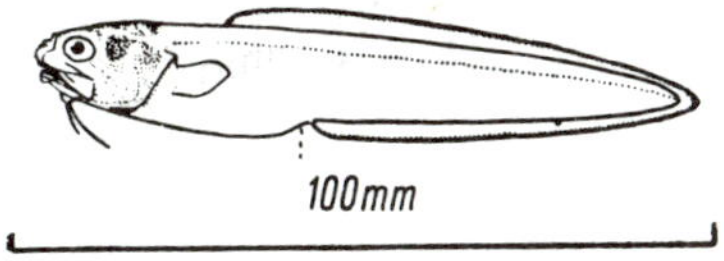

FIGURE 809. Ophidiidae (Ophidiinae) — Otophidium asiro (M., 1955, III, fig. 313)

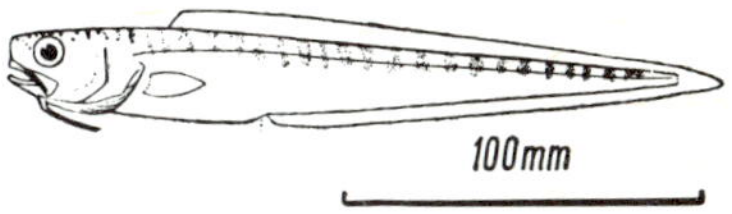

FIGURE 810. Ophidiidae (Lepophidiinae) — Lepophidium marmoratum (J. and E., 1900, fig. 866, diagr.)

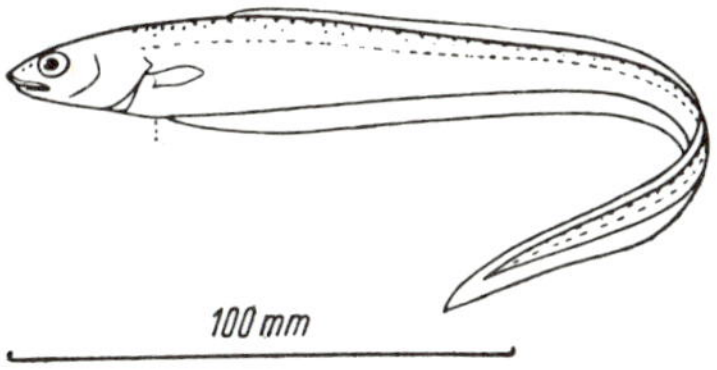

FIGURE 811. Carapidae — Jordanicus sagamianus (Abe, 1958, fig. 459, diagr.)

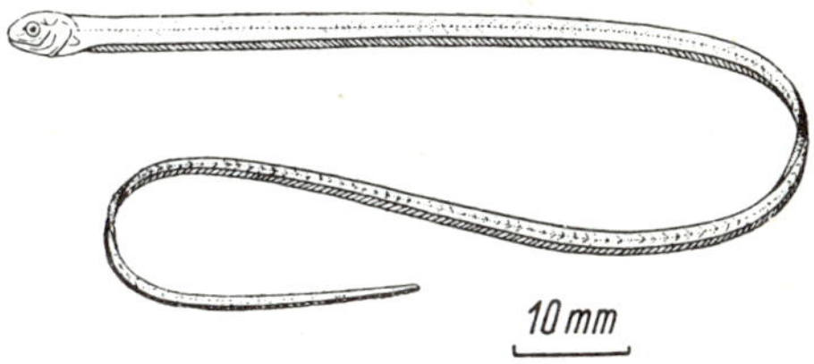

FIGURE 812. Disparichthyidae — Disparichthys lucillae (Fowler, 1938, pl. 12, fig. 30)

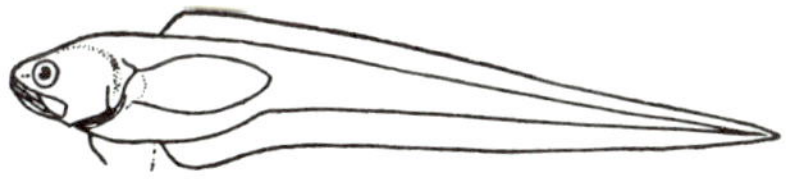

FIGURE 813. Pyramodontidae — Pyramodon ventralis (M., 1955, III, fig. 303, diagr.)

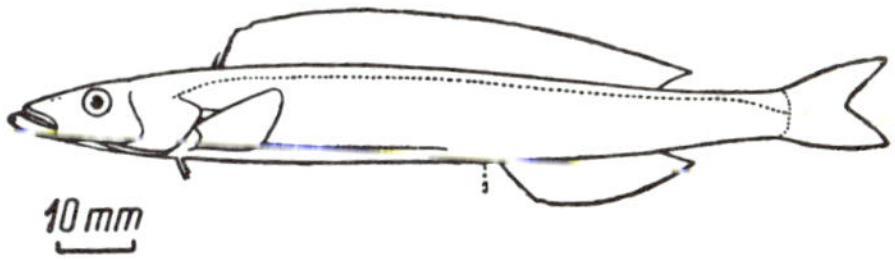

FIGURE 814. Bleekeriidae — Embolichthys mitsukurii (M., 1955, III, fig. 261, diagr.)

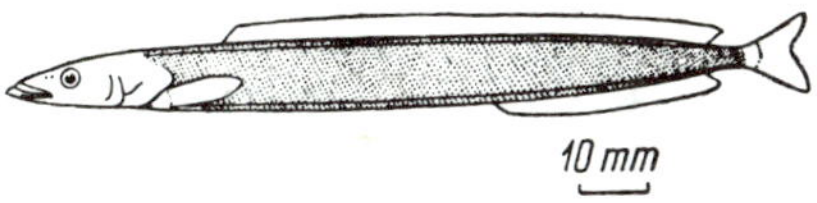

FIGURE 815. Ammodytidae — Ammodytes personatus (Wang, 1958, fig. 443, diagr.)

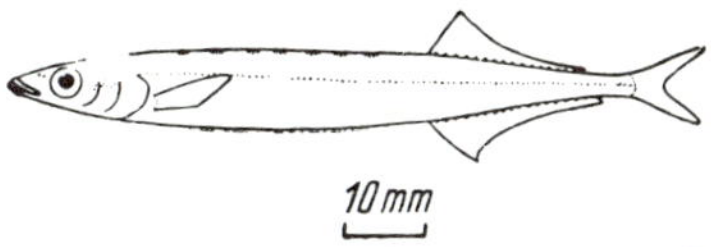

FIGURE 816. Hypoptychidae — Hypotychus dybowskii (Abe, 1958, fig. 466, diagr.)

2 (1). Sides of caudal peduncle not bearing prickly spines or lanceolate processes, tubercles, and plates. Teeth setiform, elongate, markedly protruding forward. Scales very small, setiform. Some spiny rays of dorsal fin strongly produced and with long, threadlike tips. (Figure 821). . . . . 404. **Zanclidae**

Suborder 50.8. Trichiuroidei (thesis 50.0—19)

3 families (406—408):

1 (2). Body drawn out but not ribbonlike. Caudal peduncle and fin well developed. Boundary between spiny and soft rays of dorsal fin clearly defined. Ventral fins, sometimes absent, with 1 spiny and 5 (or fewer) soft rays. [Fewer than 50 vertebrae.] (Figure 822). . . . . .406. **Gempylidae**[132]

2 (1). Body ribbonlike. Caudal peduncle weakly developed, delicate, caudal fin rudimentary, forked, or absent altogether. Boundary between spiny and soft rays in dorsal fin imperceptible or hard to discern. Ventral fins rudimentary or absent. [Vertebrae 100—160.]

3 (4). A rudimentary forked caudal fin present.[133] Base of anal fin relatively short; fin rays not shortened, similar to rays of dorsal fin. (Figure 823) . . . . 408. **Lepidopidae**

4 (3). Caudal fin absent; posterior part of tail filamentous. Base of anal fin long; fin rays very low, much shorter than those of the dorsal fin. (Figure 824) . . . . 407. **Trichiuridae**

Suborder 50.9. Scombroidei[134] (thesis 50.0—18)

3 families (409—411):

1 (2). Snout not protruding forward in the form of a long projection or swordlike process. Pectoral fins usually set high. Ventral fins with 1 spiny and 5 soft rays . . . . 409. **Scombridae**

4 subfamilies:

1 (6). Belly without a depression in the form of a groove for the concealment of the folded ventral fins.

[132] A separate family is isolated, 406a. Scombrolabracidae (Gosline, 1968:31—38) (Figure 822 A).

[133] D. W. Tucker (1956. Bull. Brit. Mus. Nat. Hist., Zool., 4, 3:73—130, 23 figs., 1 pl.) includes the genera Eupleurogrammus and Tentoriceps in the Lepidopinae; these forms do not have a split caudal fin but they do have ventral fins, in this differing from the Trichiurinae.

[134] The family Thunnidae, isolated by Berg (1940:333) in the order Thunniformes, is related to the family Cybiidae of the Scombroidei. Japanese workers (Matsubara, 1955) discovered several gradual morphological transitions between the members of the families Scombridae, Cybiidae, and Thunnidae and consider them merely as subfamilies of family 409. Scombridae (Gasterochisminae, Scombrinae, Acanthocybiinae, and Sardinae), which is definitely correct.

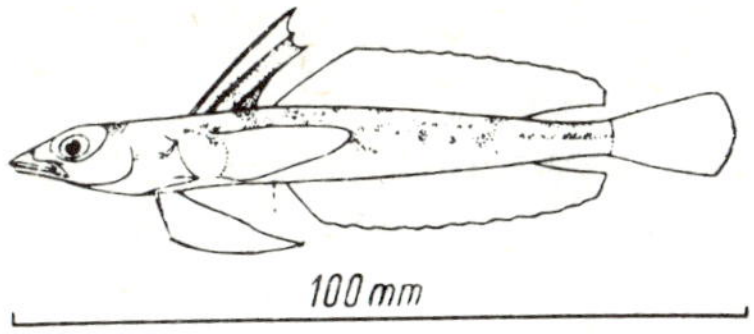

FIGURE 817. Draconettidae — *Draconetta xenica* (M., 1955, III, fig. 260, diagr.)

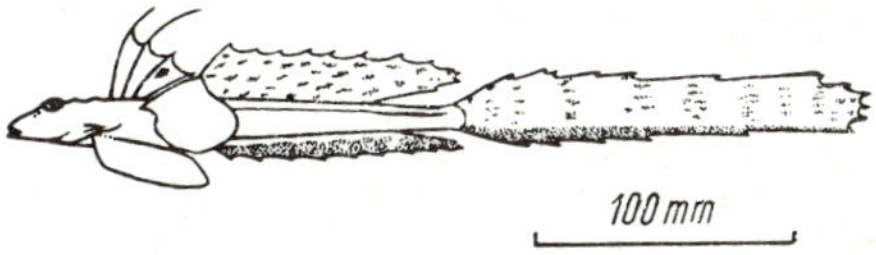

FIGURE 818. Callionymidae — *Calliurichthys japonicus* (Jordan, Tanaka, and Snyder, 1913, fig. 330, diagr.)

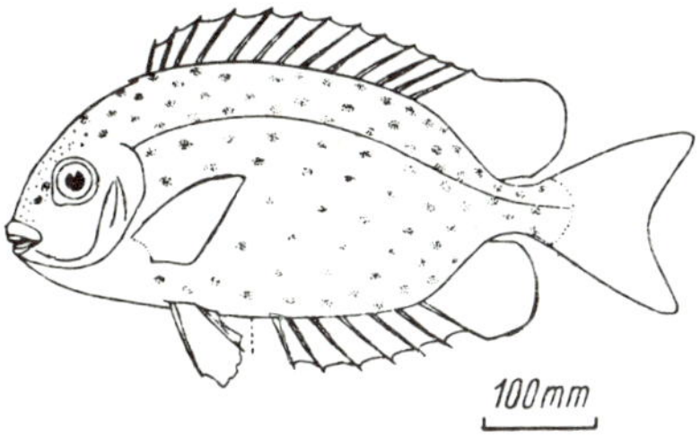

FIGURE 819. Siganidae — *Siganus concatenatus* (Chevey, 1932, pl. 38, diagr.)

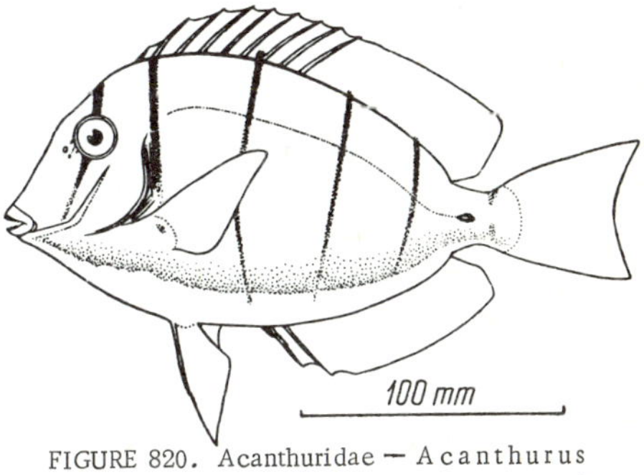

FIGURE 820. Acanthuridae — *Acanthurus triostegus* (M., 1955, III, fig. 347, diagr.)

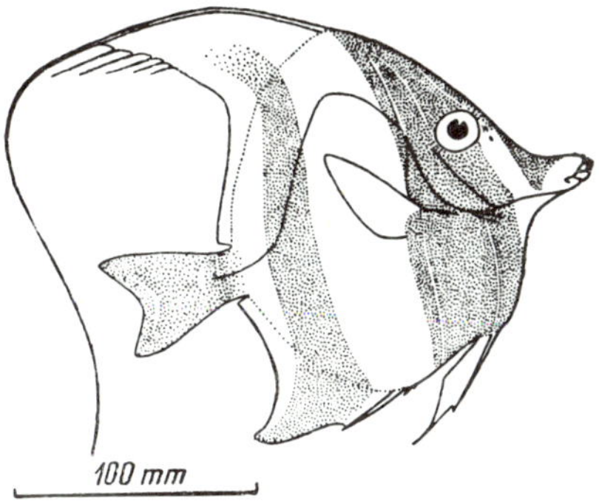

FIGURE 821. Zanclidae — *Zanclus cornutus* (Day, 1878, pl. 28, fig. 4, diagr.)

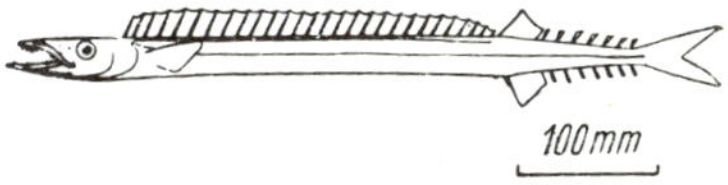

FIGURE 822. Gempylidae — *Acinacea notha* (M., 1955, III, fig. 165, diagr.)

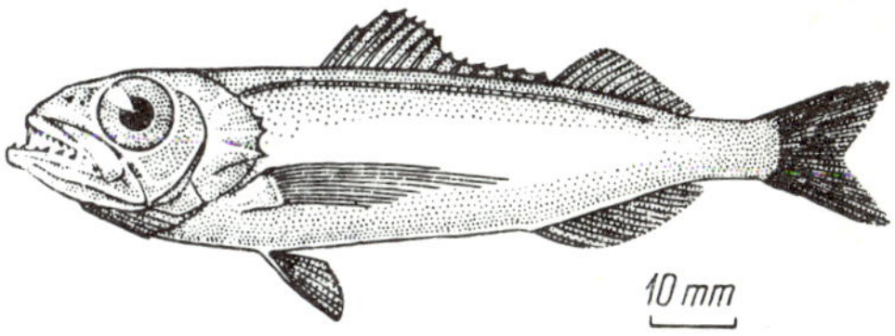

FIGURE 822A. Scombrolabracidae — *Scombrolabrax heterolepis* (Gosline, 1968, fig. 6)

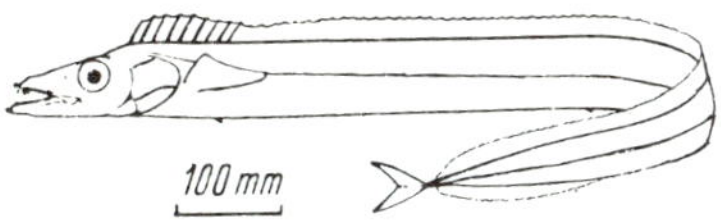

FIGURE 823. Lepidopidae — *Lepidopus caudatus* (Tucker, 1956, fig. 10, diagr.)

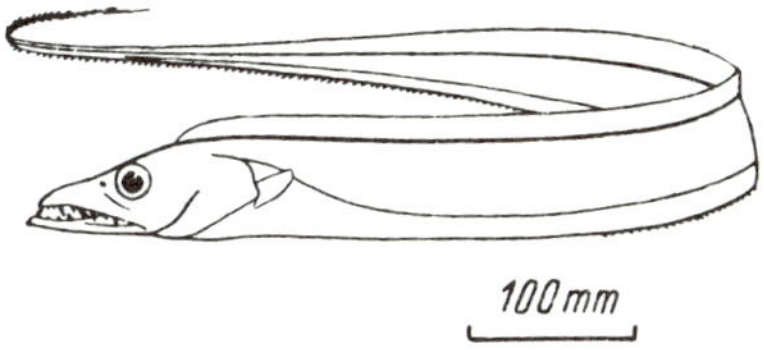

FIGURE 824. Trichiuridae — *Trichiurus haumela* (W. and B., 1951, 9, fig. 31, diagr.)

2 (3). Caudal peduncle with 2 small keels on each side, but without a median keel. [Generally 31 vertebrae.] Dorsal fins set far from each other; first dorsal with 9—13 spiny rays. (Figure 825) . . . . subfamily 409.1. Scombrinae

3 (2). Caudal peduncle bearing one median keel on each side and usually with a small keel above and below the median keel. [More than 35 vertebrae.]

4 (5). Gill leaflets not reticular; gill rakers generally present. [Fewer than 50 vertebrae.] Body spindle-shaped, not very elongate or thin. (Figures 826, 827) . . . . subfamily 409.2. Sardinae

5 (4). Gill leaflets reticular; no gill rakers. [More than 50 vertebrae.] Body markedly elongate and thin. (Figure 828) . . . . subfamily 409.3. Acanthocybiinae

6 (1). Belly with a depression in the form of a groove for the concealment of the folded ventral fins. Caudal peduncle with 2 small keels on each side, but without a median keel. [About 44 vertebrae.] (Figure 829). . . . . subfamily 409.4. Gasterochisminae

2 (1). Snout protruding forward in the form of an elongate projection or swordlike process formed by the premaxillaries and nasal bones. Pectoral fins set low. Ventral fins, if present, with 3 rays.

3 (4). Body markedly elongate, laterally compressed, covered with scales. Teeth small, but retained throughout life. Ventral fins present. Two keels on each side of the caudal peduncle. Base of first dorsal fin long, markedly more than half as long as the trunk, and close to the base of the second dorsal. Snout in the form of an elongate process, almost round in section. (Figure 830) . . . . 410. Istiophoridae

4 (3). Body less elongate, somewhat spindle-shaped, not covered with scales. Teeth not preserved in adults. Ventral fins absent. One keel on each side of the caudal peduncle. Base of first dorsal fin short, markedly less than half as long as the trunk, situated far from the base of the second dorsal. Snout long, shaped like a sword with sharp margins; snout not round but flattened in section. (Figure 831). . . . . 411. Xiphiidae

Suborder. 50.10. Luvaroidei (thesis 50.0—16)

1 family: 412. Luvaridae (Figure 832).

50.10

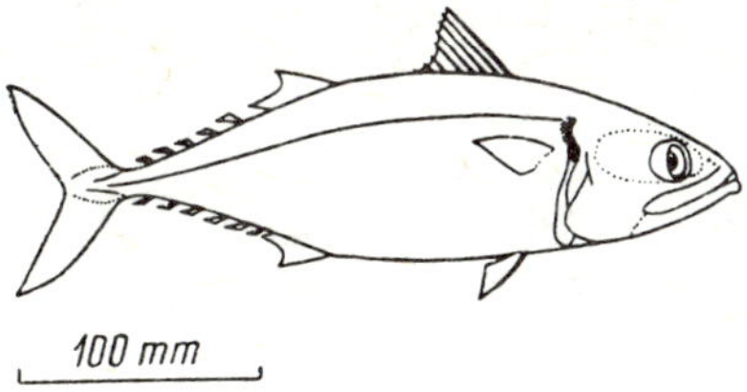

FIGURE 825. Scombridae (Scombrinae) — Rastrelliger kanagurta (W. and B., 1951, 9, fig. 36, diagr.)

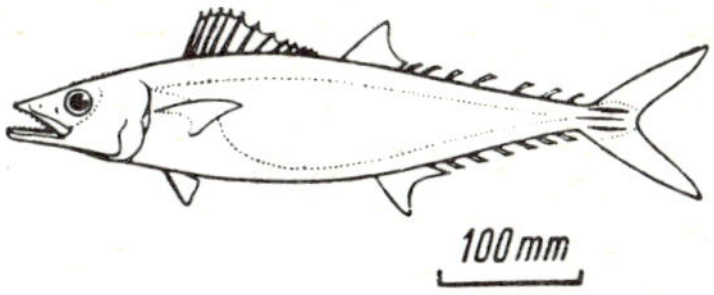

FIGURE 826. Scombridae (Sardinae)—Grammothorcinus bicarinatus (W. and B. 1951, 9, fig. 37, diagr.)

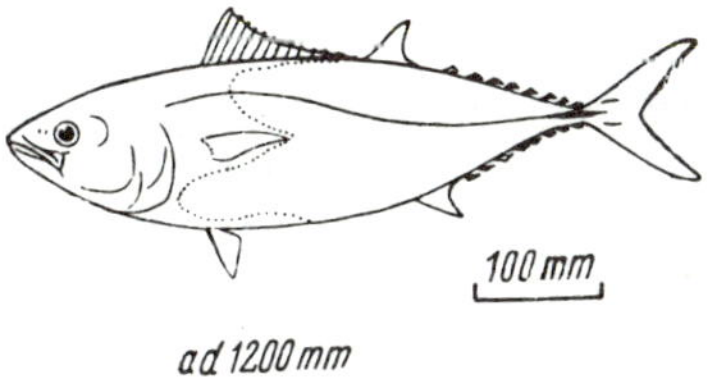

FIGURE 827. Scombridae (Sardinae)—Thunnus thynnus (Okada, 1955, fig. 129, diagr.)

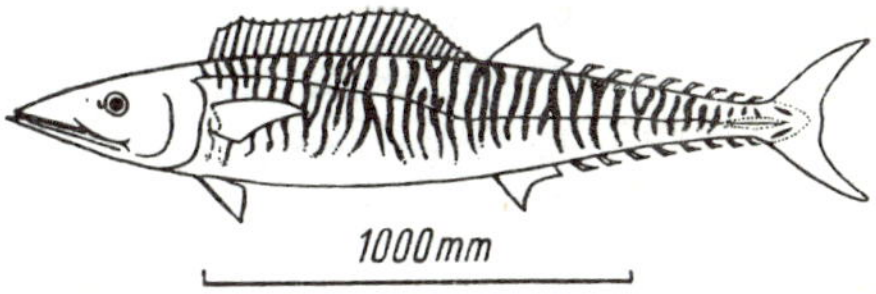

FIGURE 828. Scombridae (Acanthocybiinae)—Acanthocybium solandri (Wang, 1958, fig. 456, diagr.)

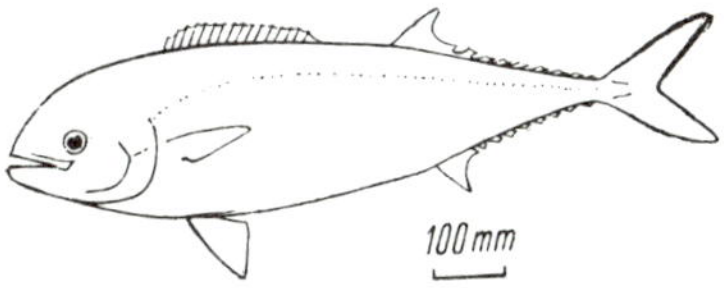

FIGURE 829. Scombridae (Gasterochisminae) — Gasterochisma melampus (Fraser-Brunner, 1950, fig. 3, diagr.)

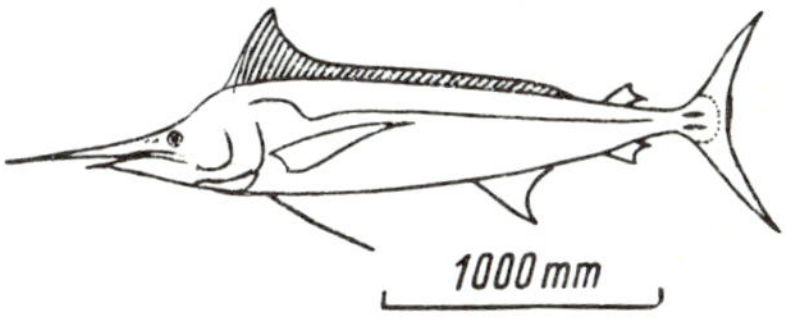

FIGURE 830. Istiophoridae — Makaira mazara (Okada, 1955, fig. 138, diagr.)

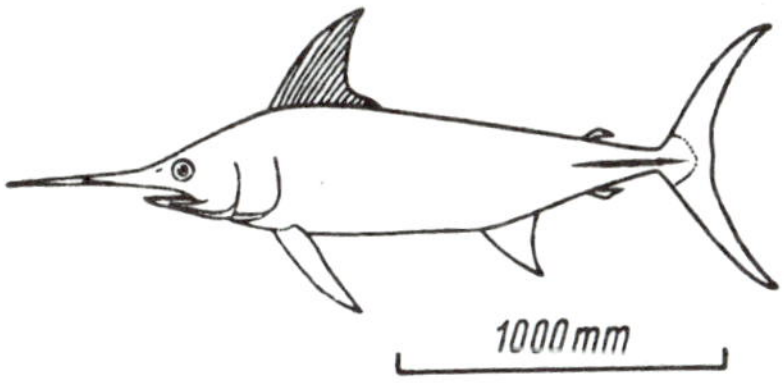

FIGURE 831. Xiphiidae — Xiphias gladius (Okada, 1955, fig. 140, diagr.)

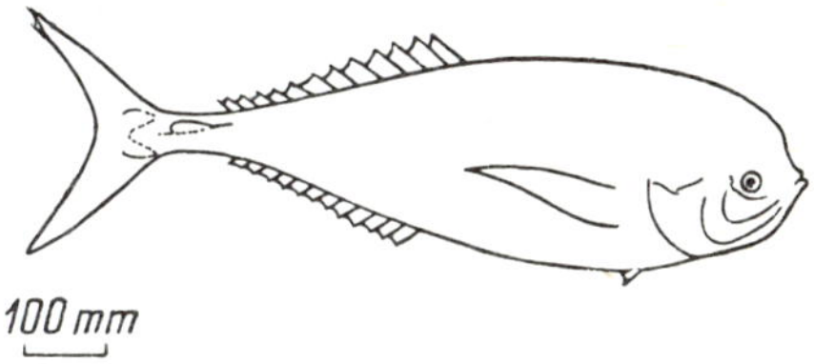

FIGURE 832. Luvaridae — Luvarus imperialis (Jordan, 1925, fig. 396, diagr.)

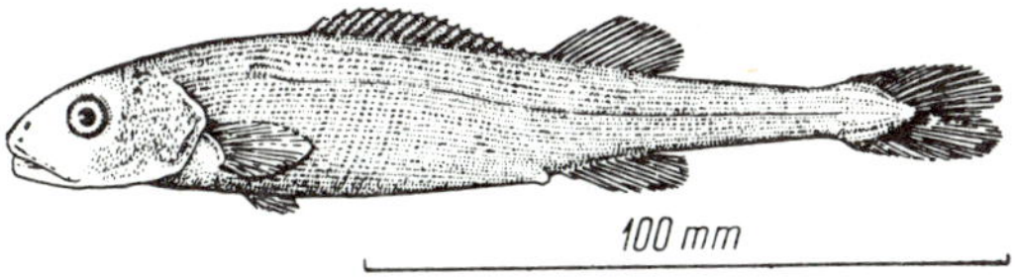

FIGURE 833. Tetragonuridae — Tetragonurus cuvieri (Haedrich, 1967, fig. 38)

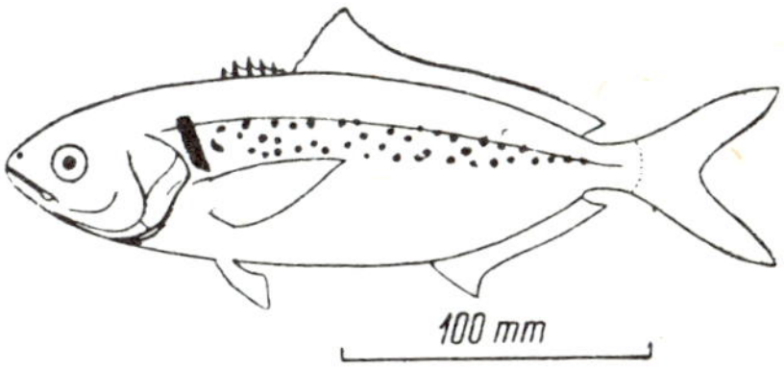

FIGURE 833A. Centrolophidae — Seriolella punctata (Haedrich, 1967, fig. 18)

Suborder 50.11. **Tetragonuroidei** (thesis 50.0—9)

1 family: 413. **Tetragonuridae**[135] (Figure 833).

Suborder 50.12. **Stromateoidei**[136] (thesis 50.0—11)

3 families: (414—416):

1 (4). Ventral fins present in adults. Gill openings large and wide; branchiostegal membranes not attached to the interbranchial space.

2 (3). Dorsal fin with one base; its spiny rays poorly developed; no notch separating the spiny from the soft rays. (Figure 834). [Lateral sacs of esophagus (Figure 835) with papillae inside; esophageal teeth with roots which, however, do not have a star-shaped arrangement.] (Figure 836). . . . . . 414. **Stromateidae**[137]

3 (2). Dorsal fin with two bases; spiny dorsal fin clearly expressed (Figure 838). [Lateral sacs of esophagus (Figure 839) with longitudinal folds inside; teeth of esophageal folds (Figure 840) with roots having a star-shaped arrangement (5—10 roots radiating from the center in all directions).] (Figure 841) . . . . 416. **Nomeidae**[138]

4 (1). Ventral fins absent in adults. Gill openings small and narrow; branchiostegal membranes broadly attached to the interbranchial space. Dorsal fin with one base; rudimentary spiny rays more or less concealed in the skin in the anterior part of the fin (Figure 842). [Saclike widening of esophagus of elliptical form (Figure 843), inside this expansion teeth with 4—7 roots having a star-shaped arrangement.] (Figure 844) . . . . 415. **Pampidae**

[135] Some authors (Haedrich, 1967) include family 413. Tetragonuridae in the suborder Stromateoidei.

[136] The key has been compiled after Matsubara (1955 : 575). On p. 216 a key is given to the families of this suborder according to data of the latest revision of the Stromateoidei (Haedrich, 1967). *Seriolella punctata*, (Bloch and Schneider), a fish of the Stromateoidei, resembles the members of family 292. Carangidae in the presence of two small spiny rays slightly separated from the anal fin but it differs in that the widened part of the esophagus bears teeth (Haedrich, 1967 : 69, fig. 18); see family 414a. Centrolophidae, Figure 833A.

[137] Members of family 414a. Centrolophidae (Figure 837), which is accepted as valid (GRWM, 1966 : 402, 433), have, just like those of family 414. Stromateidae (Figure 834), one uninterrupted dorsal fin, but unlike in the Stromateidae, the origin of the fin is shifted markedly forward. In addition, in the Centrolophidae the depth of the body is slightly greater than the length of the head, whereas in the Stromateidae it is about twice this value (Figure 837).

[138] A new family has been described, 416b. Amarsipidae (Haedrich, 1967, fig. 7) which resembles family 416. Nomeidae, but differs substantially from it in anatomical characters: the total absence of a saclike widening of the esophagus (pharyngeal sac), although the teeth on the pharyngeal bones are extremely developed and have the form of long, sharp canines (Haedrich, 1969, fig. 6), and the presence in the skeleton of the caudal fin of 6 hypurals instead of 4, and 2 epurals instead of 3 in the Nomeidae (Haedrich, 1969, fig. 5).

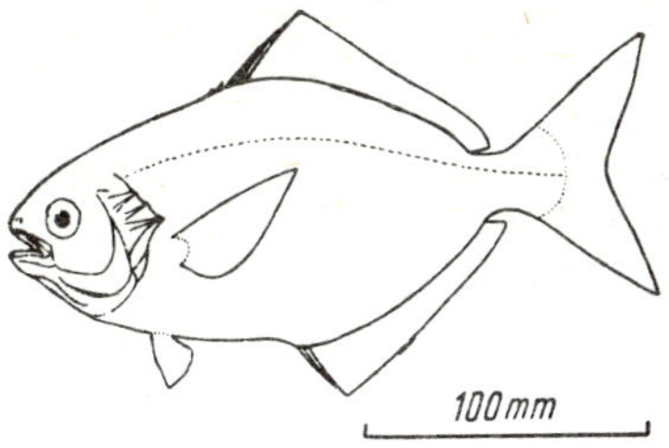

FIGURE 834. Stromateidae — Psenopsis anomala (Okada, 1955, fig. 143, diagr.)

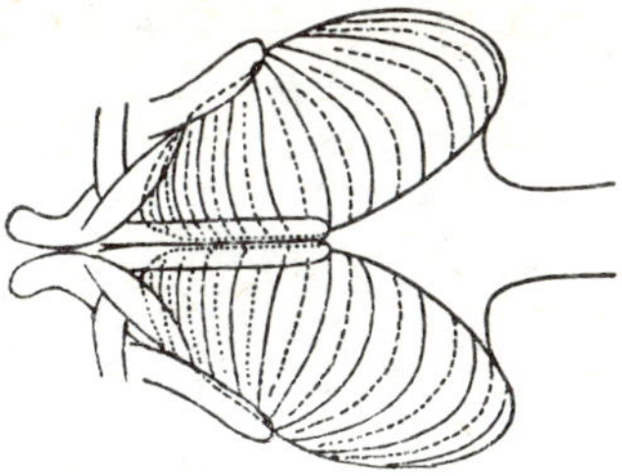

FIGURE 835. Lateral sacs of esophagus in the Stromateidae (M., 1955, I, fig. 241, D)

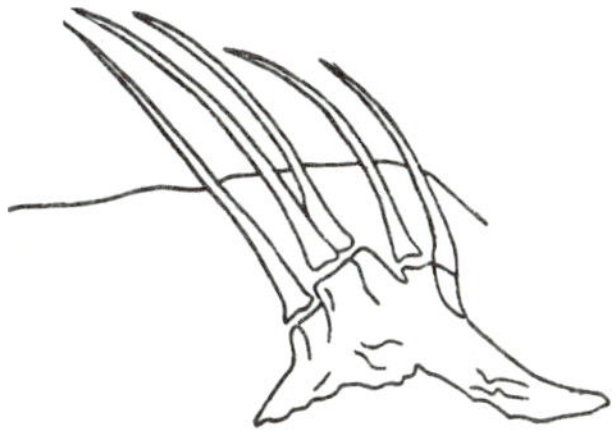

FIGURE 836. Teeth of lateral sacs of esophagus in the Stromateidae (M., 1955, I, fig. 242, F)

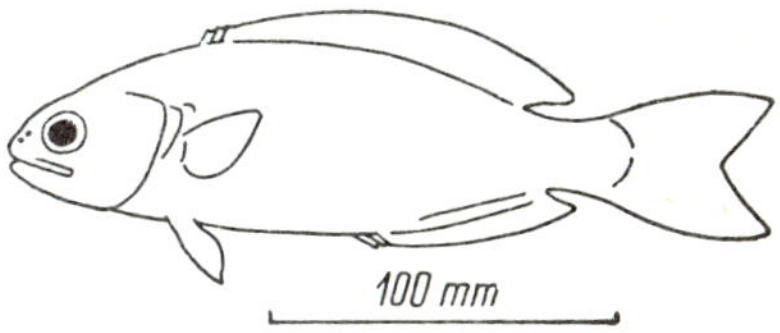

FIGURE 837. Centrolophidae (GRWM, 1966: 433, fig.)

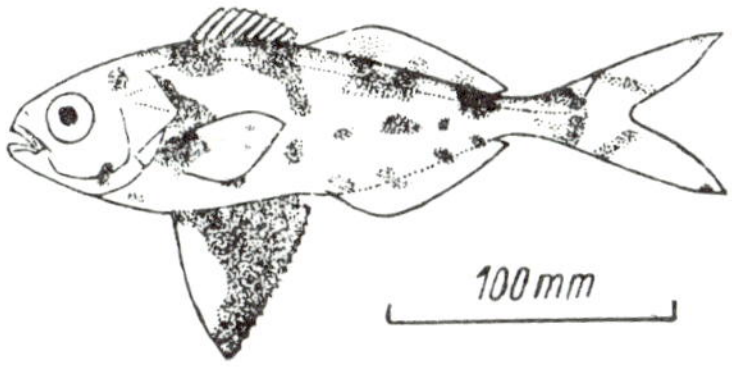

FIGURE 838. Nomeidae — Nomeus albula (M., 1955, III, fig. 186, diagr.)

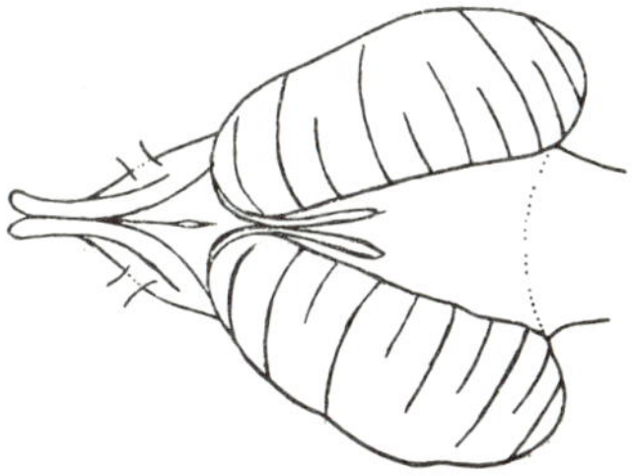

FIGURE 839. Lateral sacs of esophagus in the Nomeidae (M., 1955, I, fig. 241, C)

FIGURE 840. Teeth of esophageal folds in the Nomeidae projecting onto the surface of the mucous membrane (M., 1955, I, fig. 243)

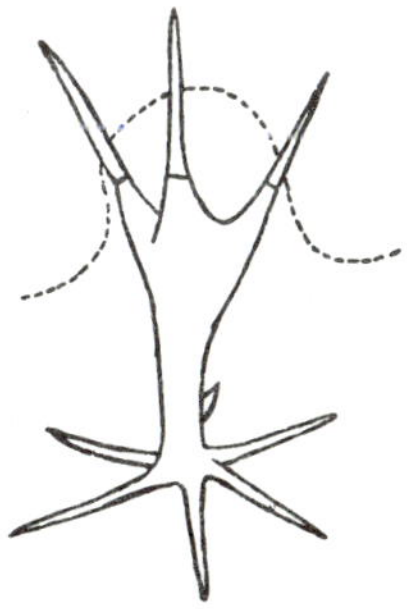

FIGURE 841. Teeth and radially diverging roots embedded in the tissue of the esophageal folds in the Nomeidae (M., 1955, I, fig. 242, C)

Supplementary key to families of the suborder Stromateoidei, taken from the latest revision of the suborder (Haedrich, 1967)

1 (6). Two distinctly expressed dorsal fins, but their bases are contiguous. First dorsal usually with 10—12 spiny rays, but if fewer than 10, the longest ray is equal to the longest soft ray. Ventral fins always present.

2 (5). Scales normal, cycloid, thin, readily deciduous. Keels absent or only weakly developed at the base of the caudal fin. Vertebrae 29—42. Longest spiny ray of first dorsal fin almost as long as or longer than the longest soft ray of the second dorsal.

3 (4). Generally more than 15 (14—32) soft rays in the second dorsal and the anal fin. Keels absent at base of caudal. Caudal peduncle laterally compressed, its minimum height more than 5% of the length of the body (without C). Vomer and palatines with small, scarcely distinguishable teeth. . . . . 416. Nomeidae

4 (3). Generally not more than 15 (13—16) soft rays in the second dorsal and the anal fin. Two weakly developed, low lateral keels on each side of the base of the caudal fin. Caudal peduncle square in cross section, its minimum height less than 5% of the length of the body (without C). Vomer and palatines without teeth. (Figure 844 A) . . . . 416a. Ariommidae

5 (2). Scales distinctive, rhombic, overlapping and forming sharp ridges or keels arranged obliquely and across the sides of the body (see Figure 552). Two distinctly expressed keels on each side at the base of the caudal fin. Vertebrae 43—58. Longest spiny ray of first dorsal fin half as long as longest soft ray of second dorsal . . . . 413. Tetragonuridae

6 (1). One dorsal fin, but if two, they are not distinctly expressed; however, if they are, the first has up to 10 spiny rays (5—10); if spiny rays are present, the longest is less than half as long as the longest soft ray. Ventral fins present or absent.

7 (8). Ventral fins always present. Spiny rays in dorsal fin either absent or numbering from 1 to 5 weak ones or from 5 to 10 strong ones, distributed markedly in front of the soft rays. Anal fin with 15—30 rays. Vertical fins never sickle-shaped, and their bases are rarely of the same length. All teeth on jaws conical, simple, with one apex. Accessory maxillary bone generally present, but sometimes difficult to discern. Seven branchiostegal rays. [Vertebrae 25—30 or 50—60.] . . . . 414a. Centrolophidae

8 (7). Ventral fins never present in adults and rarely in the young. No true large spiny rays present in front of the soft rays in the dorsal fin, but in some species there are 5—10 small spiny rays resembling outward-projecting tips of interneural processes. Anal fin with 30—50 rays. Vertical fins sickle-shaped, their bases of about the same length. Teeth on jaws laterally compressed, each with 3 apexes. No accessory maxillary bone. 5—6 branchiostegal rays. [Vertebrae 30—48] . . . . 414 (=415). Stromateidae

50.12, supp.

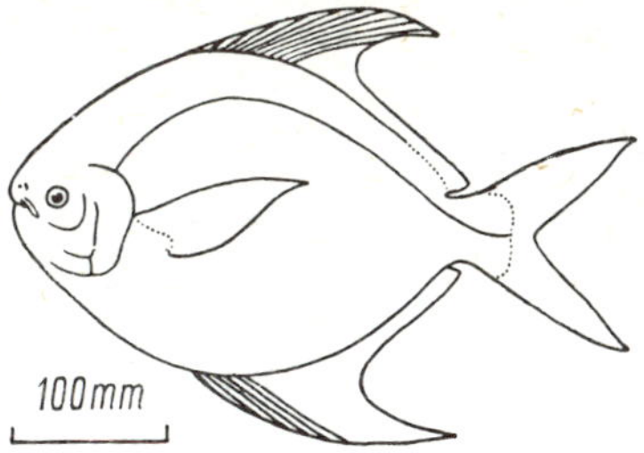

FIGURE 842. Pampidae — Pampus argenteus (Okada, 1955, fig. 145, diagr.)

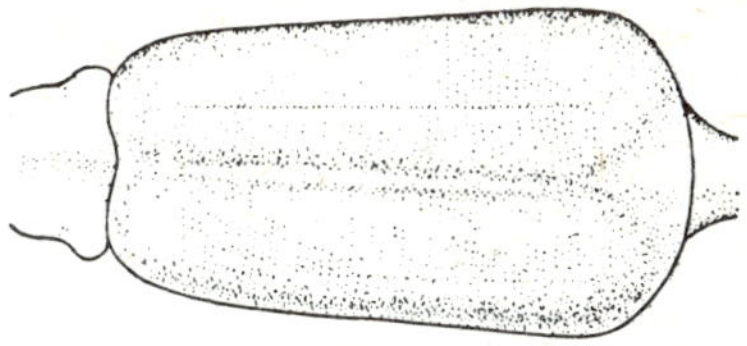

FIGURE 843. Lateral sacs of esophagus in the Pampidae (M., 1955, I, fig. 241,B)

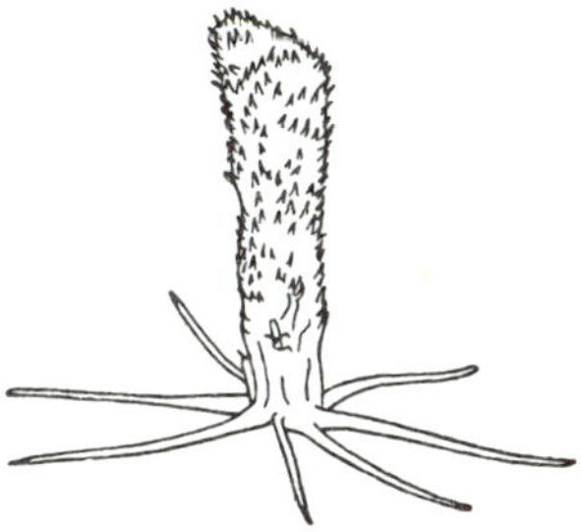

FIGURE 844. Esophageal teeth in the Pampidae, with star-shaped roots (M., 1955, I, fig. 242, B)

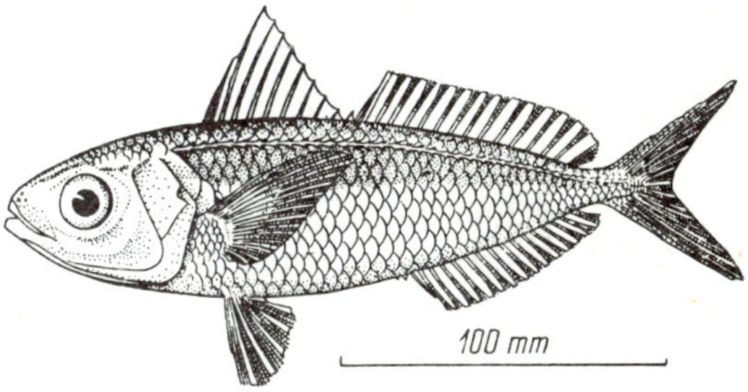

FIGURE 844A. Ariommidae — Ariomma ledanoisi (Haedrich, 1967, fig. 34)

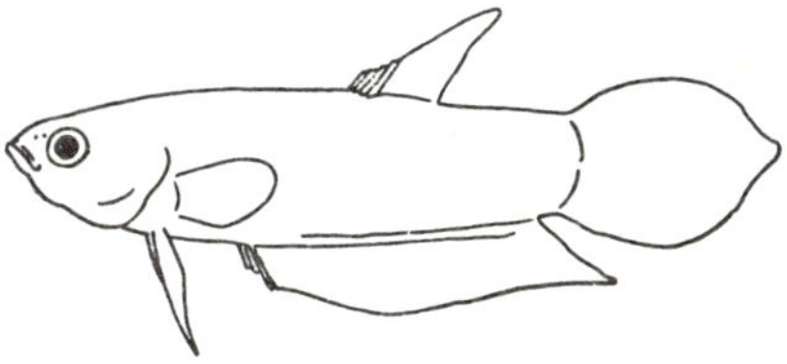

FIGURE 845. Belontiidae (GRWM, 1966: 433, fig.)

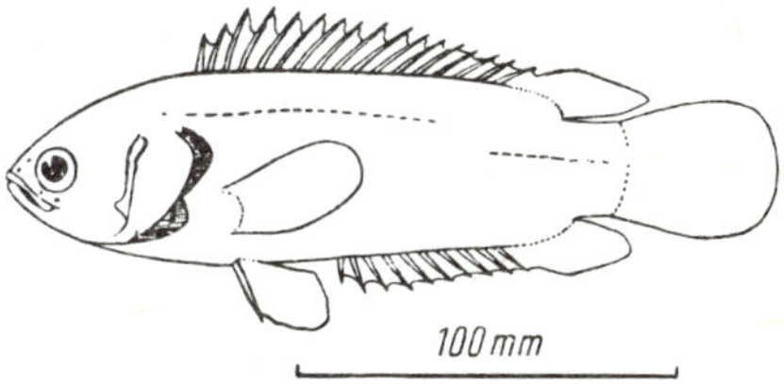

FIGURE 846. Anabantidae (GRWM, 1966: 433, fig.)

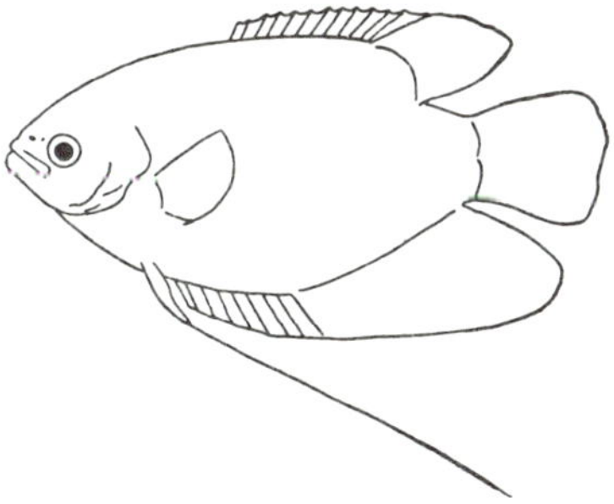

FIGURE 847. Osphronemidae (GRWM, 1966: 433, fig.)

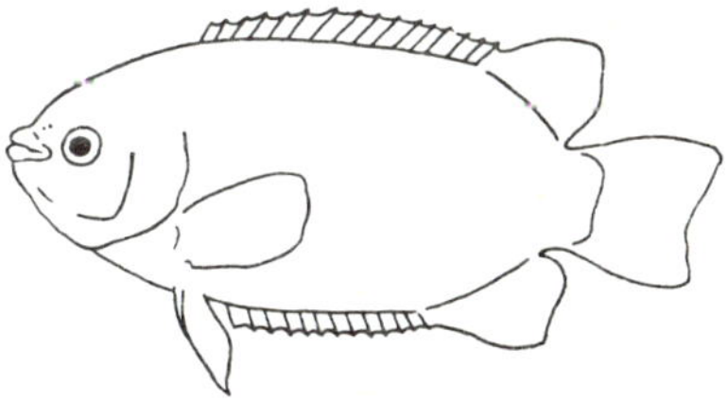

FIGURE 848. Helostomatidae (GRWM, 1966: 433, fig.)

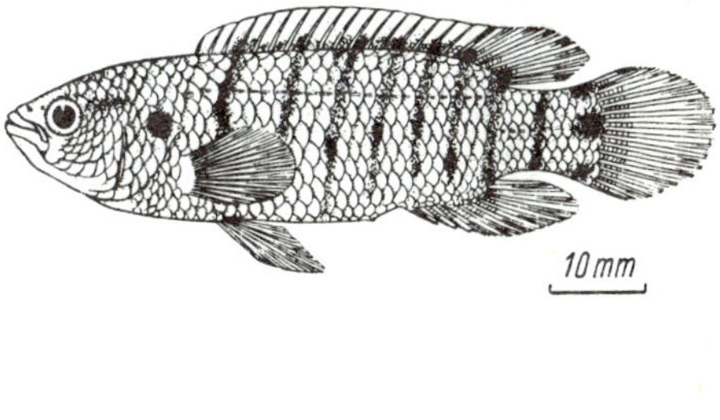

FIGURE 848A. Badidae — Badis badis (Horn, and Mukerji, 1938, pl. 14, fig. 15)

Suborder 50.13. Anabantoidei[139] (thesis 50.0—6)

4 families (417, 417a—c):

1 (2). Base of dorsal fin just over 1/3 as long as base of anal. (Figure 845) . . . . 417a. Belontiidae

2 (1). Base of dorsal fin larger, as long as the anal, but if shorter, then only by about 1 ½ times.

3 (4). Base of dorsal fin considerably longer than base of anal; origin of anal fin roughly on the vertical of the tip of the pectoral fin. (Figure 846) . . . . 417. Anabantidae

4 (3). Base of dorsal fin about as long as or shorter than base of anal; origin of anal fin almost on the vertical of the base of the pectoral.

5 (6). Ventral fins with a filamentous ray; origin of dorsal fin on the vertical of the tip of the pectoral fin. (Figure 847) . . . . 417c. Osphronemidae

6 (5). Ventral fins without filamentous ray; origin of dorsal fin on the vertical of the base of the pectoral fin. (Figure 848) . . . . 417b. Helostomatidae

Suborder 50.14. Luciocephaloidei (thesis 50.0—7)

1 family: 418. Luciocephalidae (Figure 849).

Suborder 50.15. Kurtoidei (thesis 50.0—1)

1 family: 419. Kurtidae (Figure 850).

Suborder 50.16. Gobioidei (thesis 50.0—21)

5 families (420—424):

1 (8). Dorsal and anal fins not concrescent with caudal, except in Caragobius.

2 (7). Dorsal fins separate or with a deep notch.

3 (4). Ventral fins separate, close together, even touching, but not concrescent and not forming a sucker . . . . 420. Eleotridae

[139] A new family has been described, 417d. Badidae (Barlow, Liem, and Wickler, 1968: 415—447), which in behavior resembles family 333. Nandidae and family 417. Anabantidae, but is more closely related to the latter with regard to reproduction habits. This relation is confirmed osteologically, as the Badidae (Figure 848 A) are adapted for air respiration. With respect to the nature of the eggs and larvae, the species Badis badis is unique among the bony fishes.

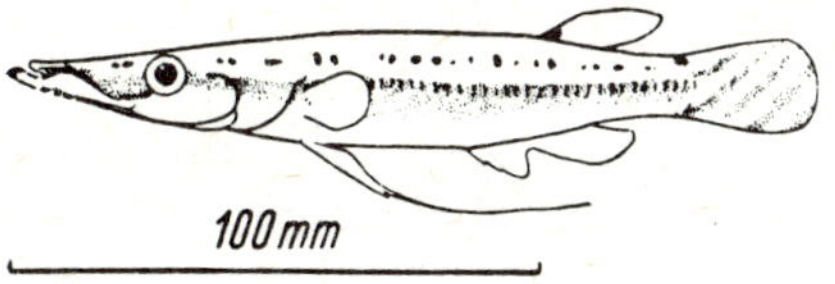

FIGURE 849. Luciocephalidae — *Luciocephalus pulcher* (W. and B., 1922, 4, fig. 94)

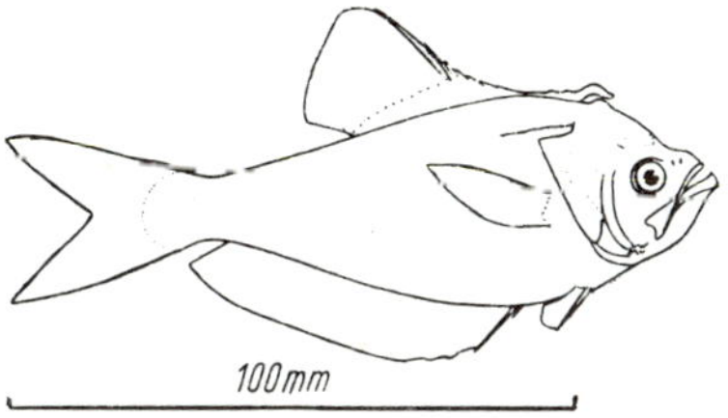

FIGURE 850. Kurtidae — *Kurtus indicus* (Wang, 1958, fig. 472, diagr.)

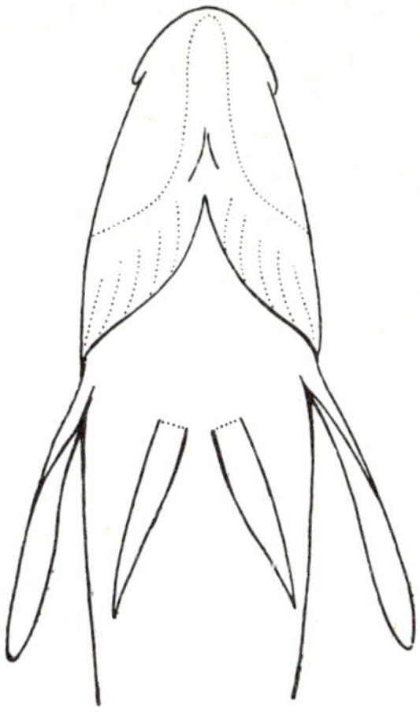

FIGURE 851. Form and arrangement of the ventral fins in the Eleotridae

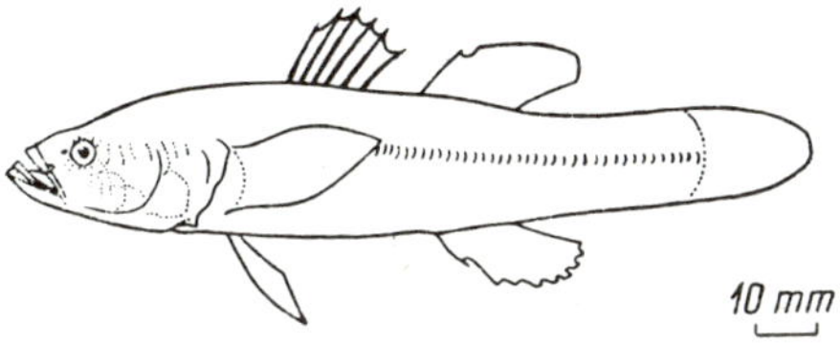

FIGURE 852. Eleotridae — *Eleotris melanosoma* (Chevey and Lemasson, 1937, pl. 42, fig. 91)

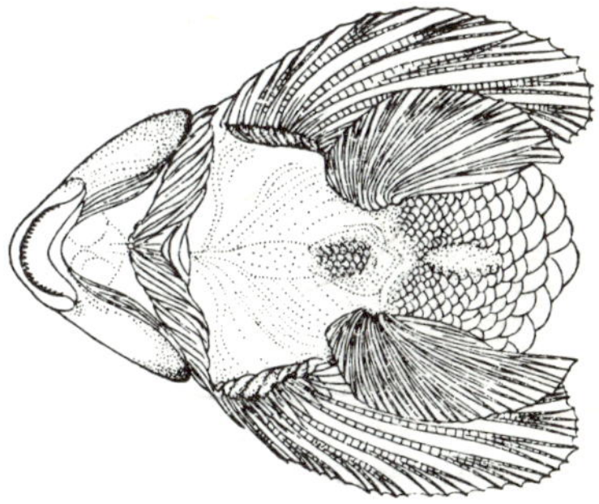

FIGURE 853. Form and arrangement of the ventral fins in *Rhyacichthys* (Herre, 1927, pl. 1, fig. 1)

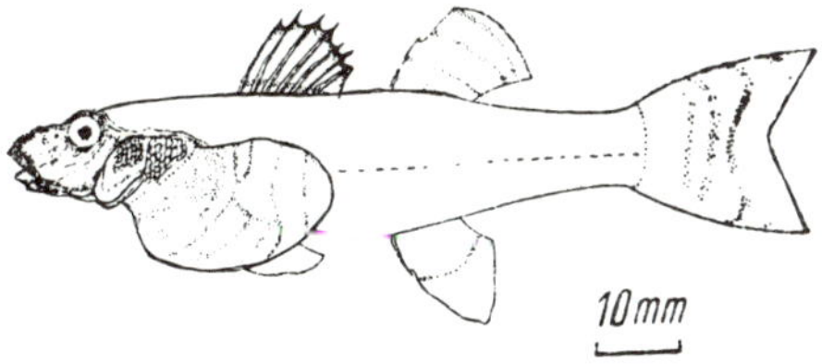

FIGURE 854. Eleotridae (Rhyacichthyinae) — *Rhyacichthys aspro* (Herre, 1927, pl. 1, fig. 1)

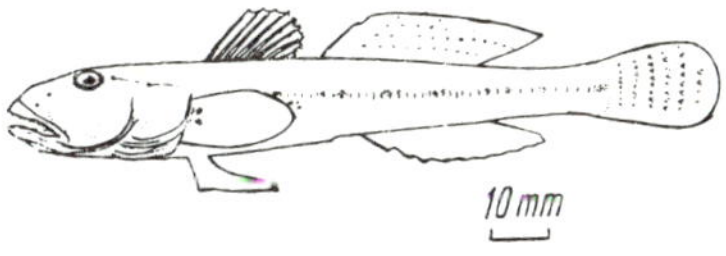

FIGURE 855. Gobiidae (Gobiinae) — *Acanthogobius flavimanus* (Berg, 1949, fig. 808, diagr.)

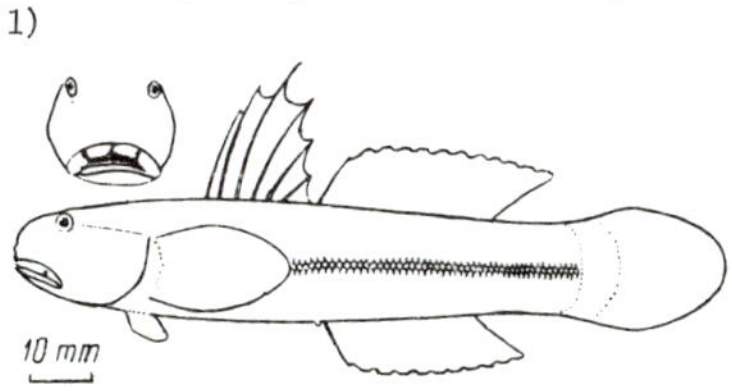

FIGURE 856. Gobiidae (Sicydiaphiinae) — *Sicyopterus crassus* (Herre, 1927, pl. 24, fig. 2, diagr.)

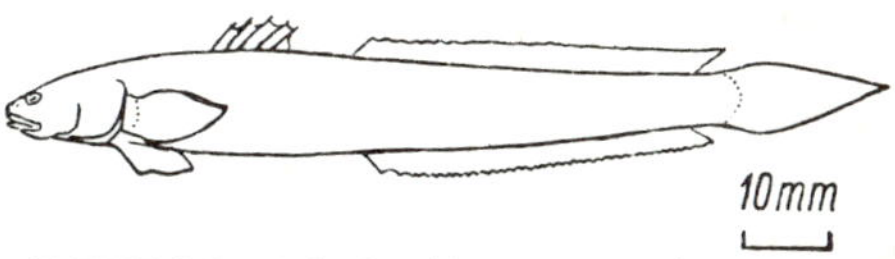

FIGURE 857. Gobiidae (Apocrypteinae) — *Pseudapocryptes lanceolatus* (Day, 1878, pl. 64, fig. 5, diagr.)

2 subfamilies:

1 (2). Ventral fins fused at the base but if disjunct, the space between them is small and narrow (Figure 851); pectoral fins never markedly widened; ventral surface of head and anterior part of body clearly not flattened. Mouth never inferior. (Figure 852) . . . . subfamily 420.1. Eleotrinae

2 (1). Ventral fins widely disjunct; pectorals strongly widened; ventral surface of head and anterior part of body forming, together with the ventral and pectoral fins, a flattened sucking disk (Figure 853). Mouth inferior. (Figure 854) . . . . .subfamily 420.2. Rhyacichthyinae[140]

4 (3). Ventral fins concrescent, as a rule forming a sucker.

5 (6). Eyes not protrusible, but if they are, the bases of the pectoral fins are normal, not thickened and not strongly muscular, and the fins themselves do not serve for creeping . . . 421. **Gobiidae**

6 subfamilies:

1 (10). Scales, if developed, cycloid or normally ctenoid.

2 (9). Body more or less elongate, sometimes markedly so.

3 (8). Teeth generally simple, at least on the lower jaw.

4 (5). Teeth on lower jaw arranged in more than one row. (Figure 855) . . . . subfamily 421.1. Gobiinae

5 (4). Teeth on lower jaw arranged in one row.

6 (7). Base of second dorsal fin not elongate, less than half as long as the trunk (without the head and the caudal fin). (Figure 856) . . . . subfamily 421.2. Sicydiaphiinae

7 (6). Base of second dorsal fin elongate, more than half as long as the trunk (without the head and the caudal fin). Teeth on lower jaw distributed almost horizontally. One upright canine on each side of symphysis of lower jaw. Scales cycloid. (Figure 857). . . . . subfamily 421.3. Arocrypteinae

8 (3). Teeth in outer row on both jaws with 3 apexes. (Figure 858). . . . . subfamily 421.4. Tridentigerinae

9 (2). Body oval or elongate-oval, laterally compressed. Teeth simple, arranged in several rows on each jaw. Dorsal fins close together and more or less fused with each other. (Figure 859) . . . . subfamily 421.5. Gobiodontinae

10 (1). Scales not cycloid, but differing from the normally ctenoid type in that the spinules on their margins are considerably longer than those in the middle of the scales, or else the scales are in the form of spiny bony tubercles. (Figure 860) . . . . subfamily 421.6. Benthophilinae

6 (5). Eyes protrusible. Bases of dorsal fins strongly muscular and the fins serve for creeping. (Figure 861) . . . . .423. **Periophthalmidae**

[140] A separate family is isolated, 420a. Rhyacichthyidae (GRWM:402; MA:147).

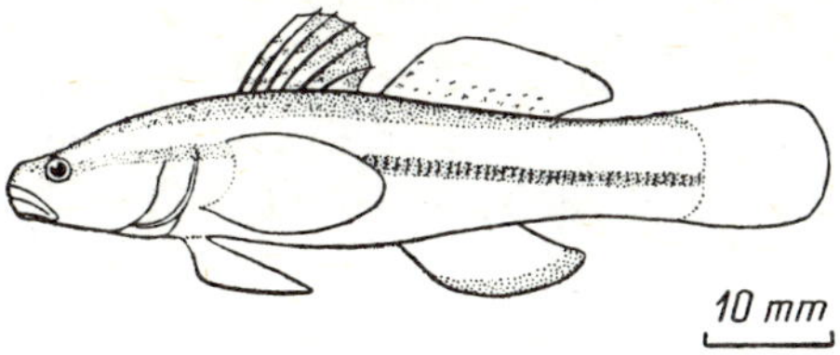

FIGURE 858. Gobiidae (Tridentigerinae) — *Tridentiger trigonocephalus*) (M., 1955, III, fig. 318, diagr.)

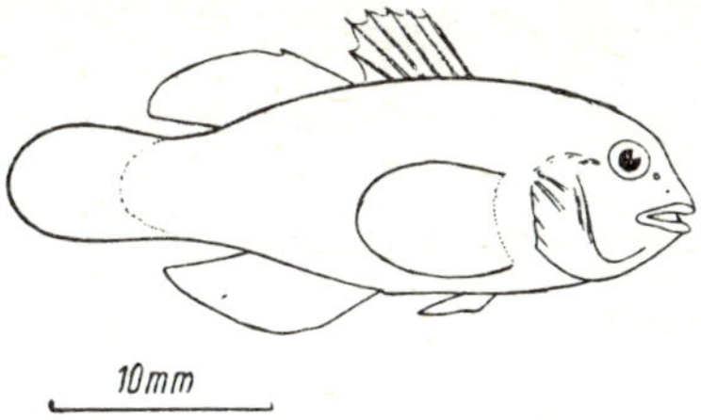

FIGURE 859. Gobiidae (Gobiodontinae) — *Gobiodon quinquestrigatus* (Wang, 1938, fig. 480, diagr.)

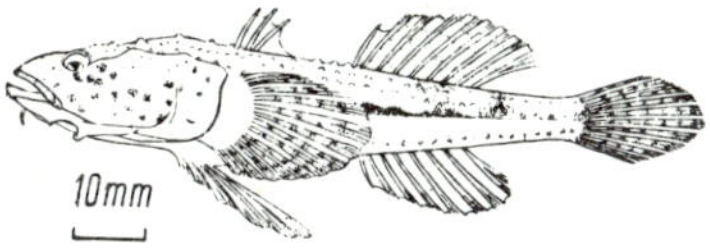

FIGURE 860. Gobiidae (Benthophilinae) — *Benthophilus stellatus* (Berg, 1949, fig. 856)

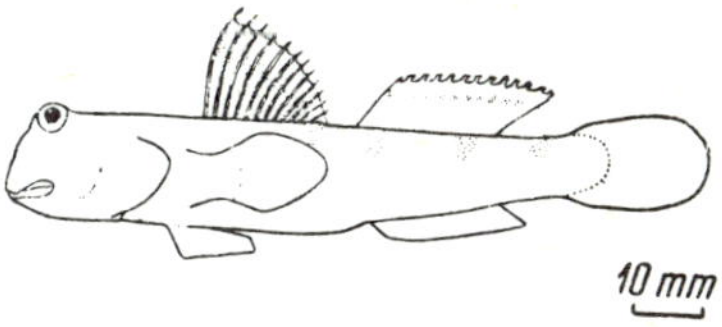

FIGURE 861. Periophthalmidae — *Periophthalmus cantonensis* (Wang, 1958, fig. 510, diagr.)

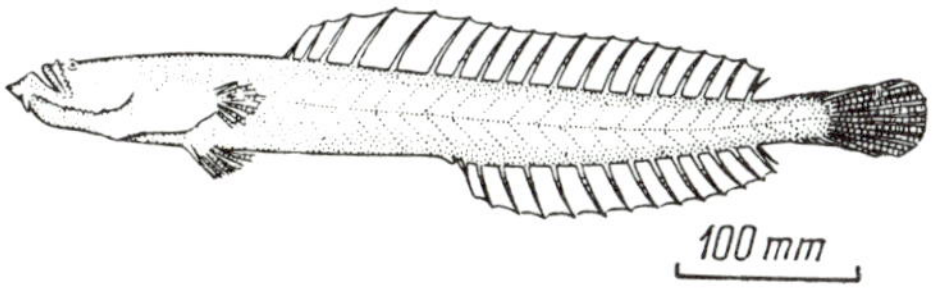

FIGURE 862. Kraemeriidae — *Kraemeria sexradiata* (Matsubara and Iwai, 1959, fig. 1)

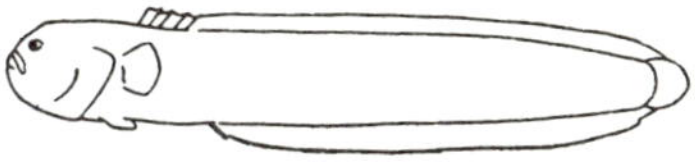

FIGURE 863. Trypauchenidae (GRWM, 1966: 432, fig.)

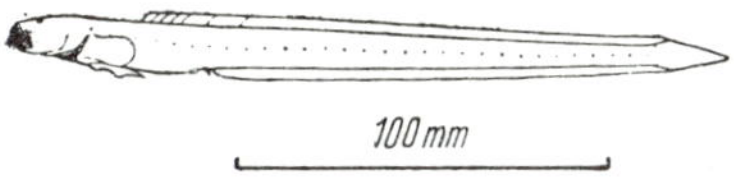

FIGURE 864. Gobioididae — *Taenioides gracilis* (Herre, 1927, pl. 26, fig. 1, diagr.)

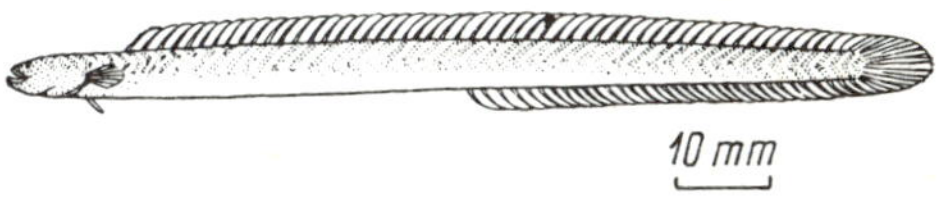

FIGURE 865. Microdesmidae — *Microdesmus* sp. (Günther, 1864, pl. 3, fig. 2)

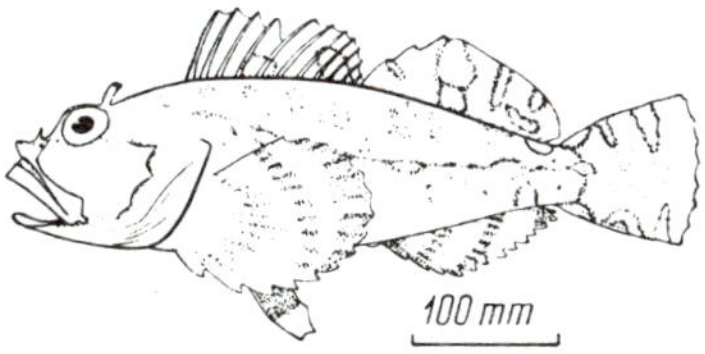

FIGURE 866. Scorpaenichthyidae — *Scorpaenichthys marmoratus* (Clemens and Wilby, 1961, fig. 173, diagr.)

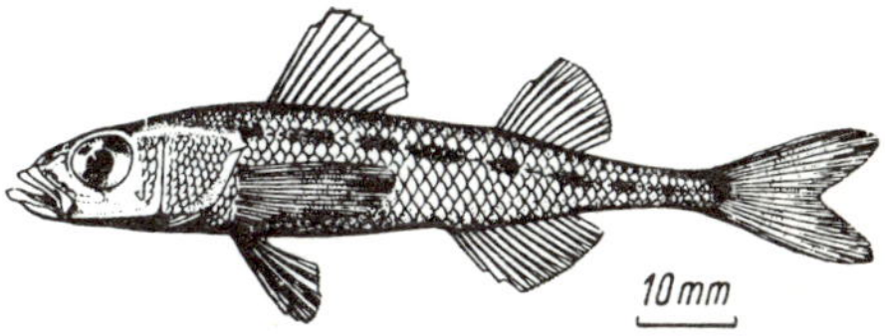

FIGURE 867. Normanichthyidae — *Normanichthys crockeri* (Norman, 1938, fig.)

7 (2). Dorsal fins fused, without a notch. Lower jaw jutting strongly forward. Chin inflated, constituting part of the dorsal profile of the head. Dorsal fin with at most 34 rays. (Figure 862) . . . . 361. **Kraemeriidae**[141]

8 (1). Dorsal and anal fins concrescent with the caudal; dorsal fins fused, without a notch.

9 (12). Origin of anal fin in anterior third of body.

10 (11). Top of opercular bone with an incision which leads into a deep cavity situated above the gill cavity. Body shortened. (Figure 863) .421a. **Trypauchenidae**

11 (10). Opercular bone without an incision leading into a suprabranchial cavity. Body elongate. (Figure 864) . . . . . . 422. **Gobioididae**

12 (9). Origin of anal fin on the vertical of the middle of the body length. (Figure 865) . . . . 424. **Microdesmidae**

Order 51. SCORPAENIFORMES (thesis 0—138)

6 suborders, 31 families (425—455):

1 (2). [Three radials in pectoral fin.] (Figure 866) . . . . 441. Scorpaenichthyidae[142]

2 (1). [Four radials in pectoral fin.]

3 (28). Skin not covered normally with scales, bare, or with spinules, tubercles, scalelike formations of the type of strongly ctenoid scales,[143] or else covered with large plates that encase the body in armor and lend it an octagonal shape. True hard spiny rays in dorsal fin absent. (Suborder 51.6. **Cottoidei.**)[144]

4 (7). Sucking disk (see Figure 30) present on belly or throat, formed from the modified ventral fins; the disk is sometimes very small or absent, but in this case the body is typically as if filled with fluid, very soft, with very mobile, soft, slippery skin. [Myodome absent.]

[141] Family 361. Kraemeriidae is placed at the same time in the superfamily Trachinoidea, suborder Percoidei (see thesis 50.1.9—16).

[142] The presence of 3 radials in the pectoral fin (Starks, 1895) clearly distinguishes this family, as Taranets (1941 : 428) points out, from all the Scleroparei; this group gravitates to the Notothenioidea and merits consideration as a separate family.

[143] This mention by Taranets (1941 : 440) apparently refers also to the genera Ricuzenius Jordan and Starks, 1904 and Daruma Jordan and Starks, 1904, for which scales on the body are indicated. An exception is the genus Normanichthys Clark, 1937 (Figure 867, family 450. **Normanichthyidae**), in which, in contrast to all the families of the Cottoidea, there are uniform, normal scales evenly covering the whole body and a large part of the head. This genus occurs around Chile (Norman, Copeia, 1938, 1 : 29). [The process of the second suborbital bone just fails to reach the preoperculum, as in Comephorus.]

[144] Hard spiny rays in the first dorsal are present as an exception in the subfamily Percidinae of family 452. Agonidae, (Percis, Agonomalus, partly Hypsagonus) and in the subfamily Hemilepidotinae of family 440. Cottidae (Hemilepidotus), but they are not the true spiny rays that are typical for the representatives of the suborder Percoidei, order Perciformes.

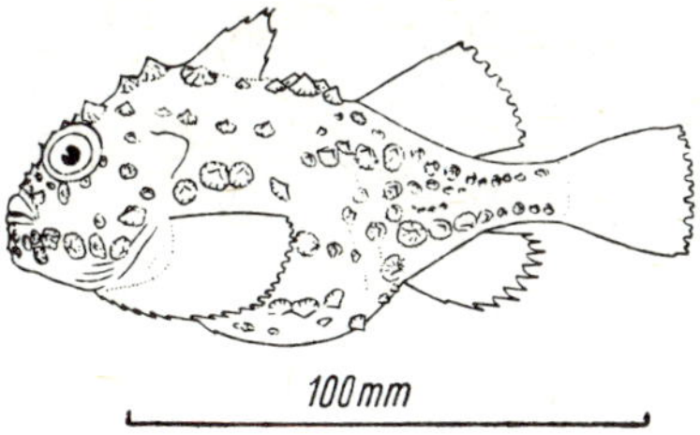

FIGURE 868. Cyclopteridae — *Eumicrotremus soldatovi* (Okada and Matsubara, 1938, pl. 83, fig. 2, diagr.)

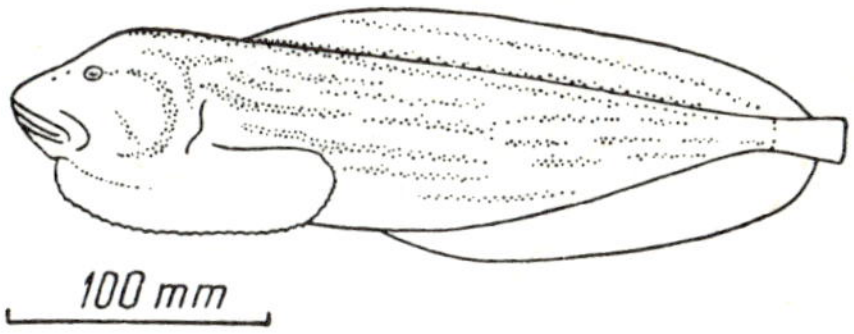

FIGURE 869. Liparidae — *Liparis tanakae* (Okada, 1955, fig. 320, diagr.)

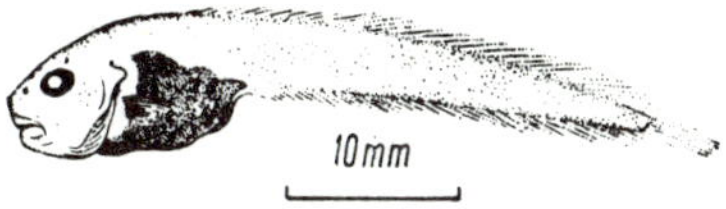

FIGURE 870. Eutelichthyidae — *Eutelichthys leptochirus* (Tortonese, 1960, fig. 1)

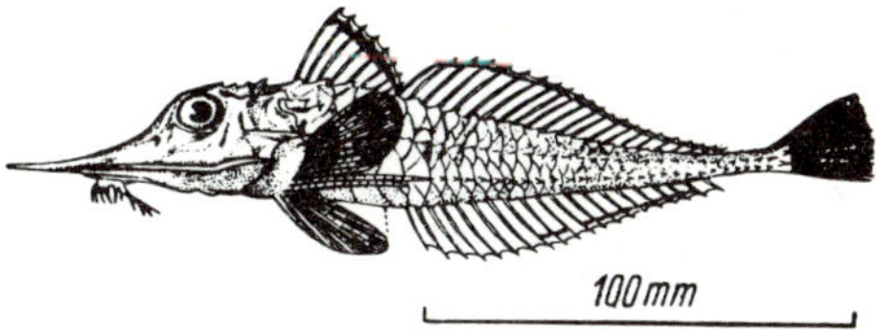

FIGURE 871. *Peristedion nierstraszi* (Peristediidae) (M., 1955, III, fig. 441)

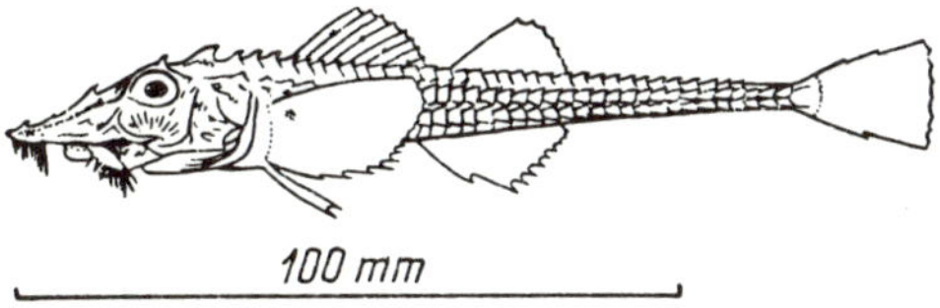

FIGURE 872. Agonidae — *Podothecus gilberti*

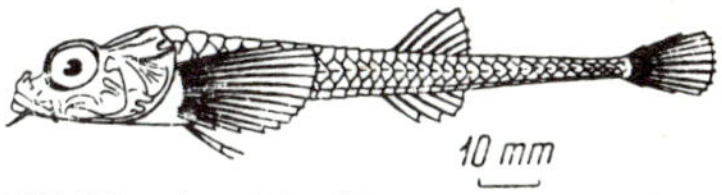

FIGURE 873. Agonidae (Aspidophoroidinae) — *Aspidophoroides otrikii*

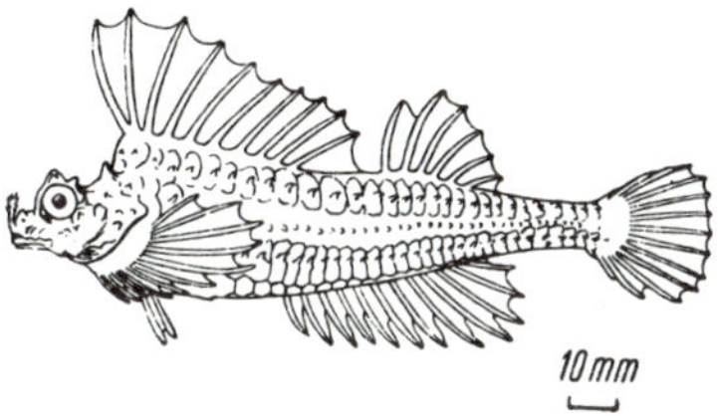

FIGURE 874. Agonidae (Percidinae) — *Agonomatus proboscidalis*

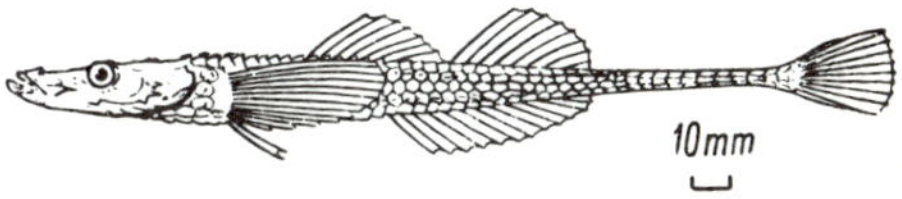

FIGURE 875. Agonidae (Brachyopsinae) — *Brachyopsis rostratus*

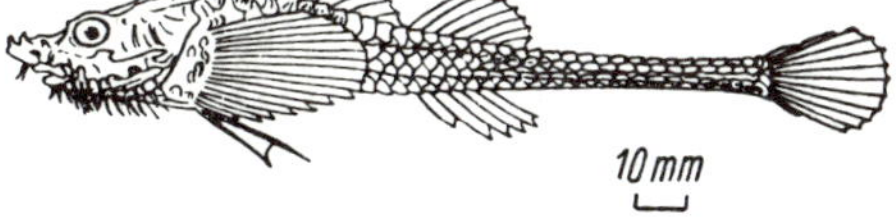

FIGURE 876. Agonidae (Agoninae) — *Agonus cataphractus*

FIGURE 877. Agonidae — *Bothragonus swanii*:

a – rostral plate.

5 (6). Trunk more or less spherical, about as long as the caudal part of the body. Anal fin with at most 20 soft rays. Body usually covered with bony plates or tubercles, rarely bare. (Figure 868) . . . . 453. **Cyclopteridae**

6 (5). Trunk not spherical, and considerably shorter than caudal part of body. Anal fin with more than 20 soft rays. Body generally bare, rarely covered with spinules or tubercles. . . . . 454. **Liparidae**[145]

7 (4). No sucking disk, either on belly or on throat. Body compact, with very rare exceptions, and the skin as a rule is little mobile. [Myodome more or less developed.]

8 (9). Vent shifted forward under the base of the pectoral fins and usually very close to the base of the ventrals. Body angular, ribbed, covered with eight longitudinal rows of bony plates.[146] (Figure 872) . . . . 452. **Agonidae**

6 subfamilies:

1 (2). One dorsal fin (Figure 873) . . . . subfamily 452.1. A s p i d o p h o r o i d i n a e

2 (1). Two dorsal fins.

3 (6). Branchiostegal membranes free of the interbranchial space.

4 (5). Body laterally compressed. Mouth terminal, jaws equal. First dorsal fin originating immediately behind the occiput; its rays are thickened and sometimes have the form of spines. (Figure 874) . . . . subfamily 452.2. P e r c i d i n a e

5 (4). Body elongate, not laterally compressed. Mouth superior; lower jaw markedly jutting forward. First dorsal fin originating markedly behind occiput; its rays are not thickened and are not transformed into spines. (Figure 875) . . . . subfamily 452.3. B r a c h y o p s i n a e

6 (3). Branchiostegal membranes attached to the interbranchial space.

7 (8). Mouth inferior; lower jaw markedly shorter than upper. [Unpaired rostral plate absent.] (Figure 876) . . . . subfamily 452.4. A g o n i n a e

8 (7). Mouth terminal or half-superior; jaws equal or lower jaw longer. [Unpaired rostral plate present.] (Figure 877).

9 (10). Body elongate, not laterally compressed. Dorsal and anal fins well developed. (Figure 878) . . . . subfamily 425.5. B a t h y a g o n i n a e

[145] A new family, 445. Eutelichthyidae (Tortonese, 1959 : 226, fig. 1), has recently been described which is related to family 454. Liparidae, differing in the narrow bases of the pectoral fins, the posterior position of the vent, and the absence of an abdominal sucker (Figure 870). One genus.

It has recently been established (Cohen, 1968 : 384—388) that the genus E u t e l i c h t h y s is a synonym of the genus P a r a l i p a r i s, as the narrow base of the pectoral fin is the result of the reduction of the fin, and the indication of the posterior position of the vent proved erroneous. In fact, the vent is situated markedly in front of the anal fin between the bases of the pectorals. The absence of an abdominal sucker is known in several species of the genus P a r a l i p a r i s (Liparidae).

[146] Fish of family 427. Peristediidae have similar plates on the body but the vent is here situated on the belly, and there are also other differences (Figure 871).

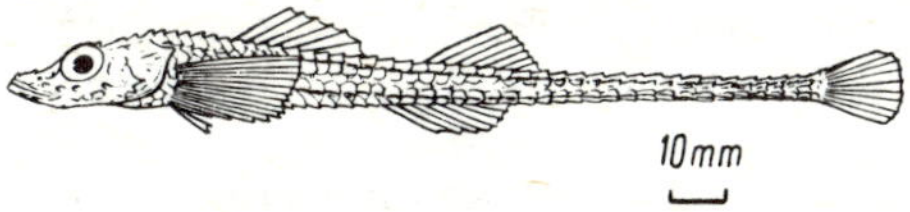

FIGURE 878. Agonidae (Bathyagoninae) — Bathyagonus nigripinnis

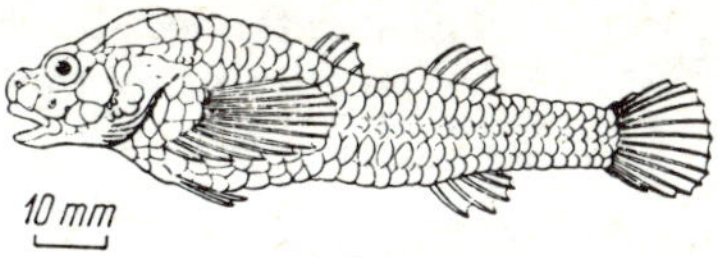

FIGURE 879. Agonidae (Bothragoninae) — Bothragonus swanii

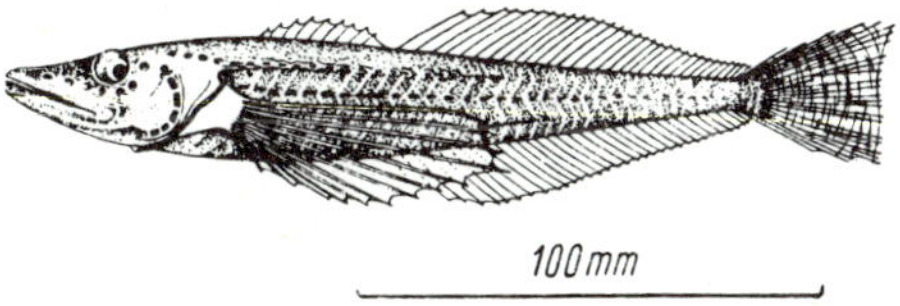

FIGURE 880. Comephoridae — Comephorus baicalensis (Berg, 1949, fig. 936)

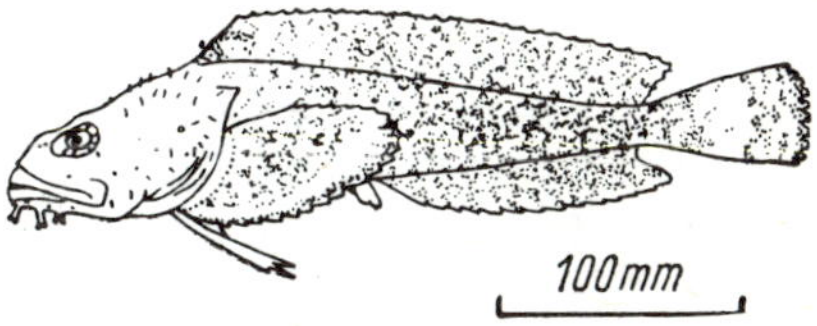

FIGURE 881. Psychrolutidae — Eurymen gyrinus (M., 1955, III, fig. 436, diagr.)

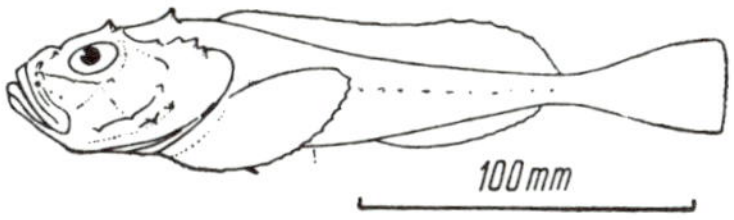

FIGURE 882. Psychrolutidae — Cottunculus thompsoni (Günther, 1887, pl. 9, B, diagr.)

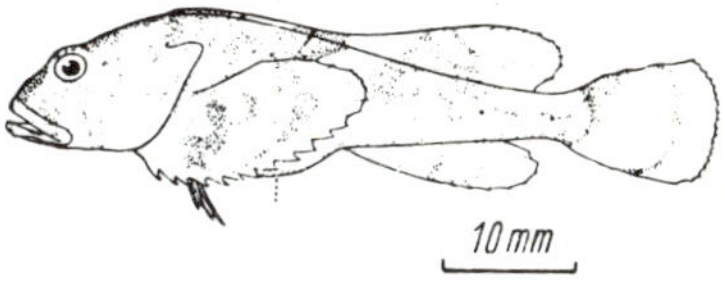

FIGURE 883. Psychrolutidae — Psychrolutes paradoxus (J. and E., 1900, fig. 740, diagr.)

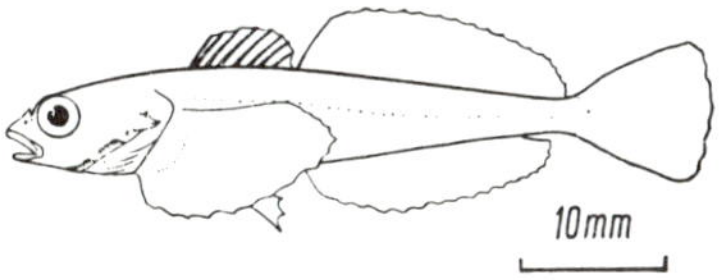

FIGURE 884. Synchiridae — Synchirus gilli (Clemens and Wilby, 1961, fig. 207, diagr.)

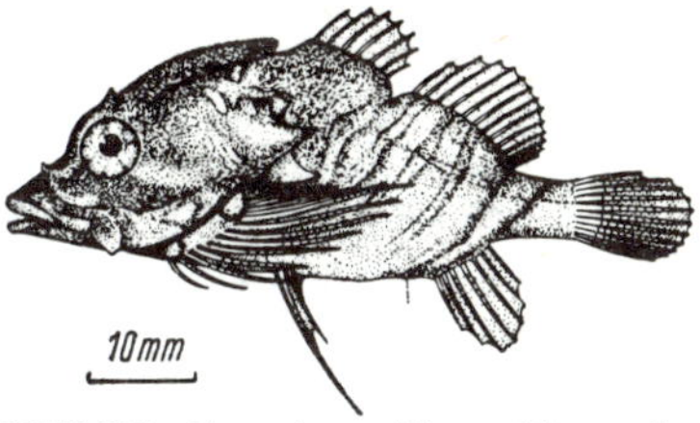

FIGURE 885. Rhamphocottidae — Rhamphocottus richardsoni (J. and E., 1900, fig.742)

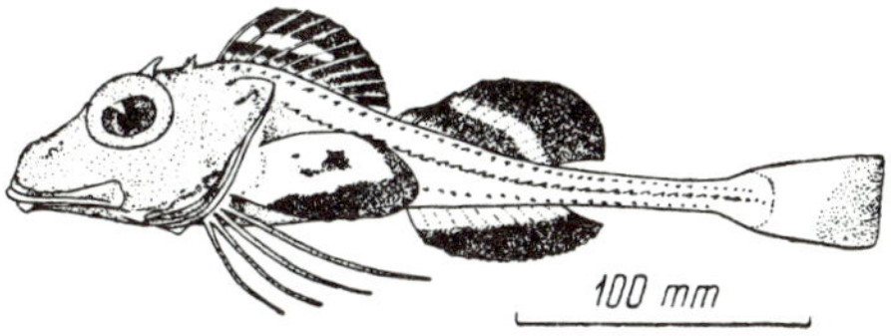

FIGURE 886. Ereuniidae — Ereunias grallator (M., 1955, III, fig. 429, diagr.)

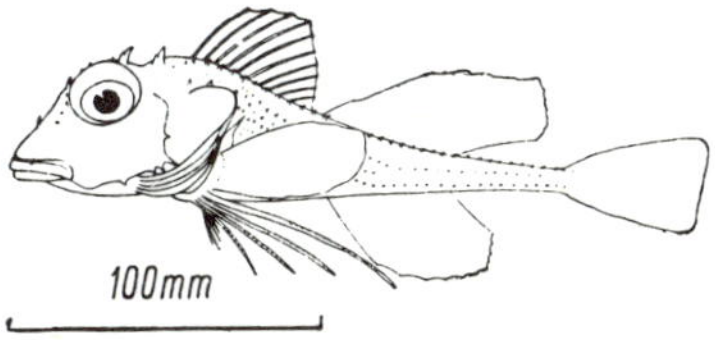

FIGURE 887. Marukawichthyidae — Marukawichthys ambulator (M., 1955, III, fig. 428, diagr.)

10 (9). Body shortened, laterally compressed. Dorsal and anal fins very weakly developed. (Figure 879) . . . . subfamily 425.6. Bothragoninae

9 (8). Vent situated on the belly. Body not angular and not ribbed, as it is covered with longitudinal rows of bony plates.[147]

10 (11). Suborbital and preopercular bones and also lower jaw cavernous; bones thin. [Process of second suborbital just failing to reach the preoperculum.] No ventral fins. Two dorsals. Pectorals large. Viviparous fishes of Lake Baikal. (Figure 880) . . . . 449. Comephoridae

11 (10). Suborbital and other bones of the head normally developed [and second suborbital, as in other families of the order, united with the preoperculum.]

12 (13). Seven branchiostegal rays. Lateral line strongly reduced, represented by one row of very scattered pores, of which there are no more than 20 (usually at most 17). Skin mobile in most genera. (Figures 881—883) . . . . . 451. Psychrolutidae[148]

13 (12). Always 6 branchiostegal rays,[149] except in very rare, abnormal forms. Lateral line (except in some representatives of the Artediellini in which the number of pores is reduced to 17) well developed, in several cases extremely strongly. Skin as a rule quite compact, often covered with various scalelike formations.

14 (15). Pectoral fins joined on the thorax. (Figure 884) . . . . 442. Synchiridae

15 (14). Pectoral fins separated by a considerable space.

16 (17). Head enormous, constituting almost half the length of the body (without C). (Figure 885) . . . . 443. Rhamphocottidae

17 (16). Head of normal size, much less than half the length of the body.

18 (21). Lower 4 rays of pectoral fin separated from rest of fin and greatly enlarged.[150]

19 (20). Ventral fins absent. (Figure 886) . . . . 444. Ereuniidae

20 (19). Ventral fins present. (Figure 887) . . . 445. Marukawichthyidae

21 (18). Lower 4 rays of pectoral fin not separated from rest of fin and not enlarged, but if they are separated, they are fewer than 4 and are soft, and the head is flattened.

22 (25). Rays of caudal fin always unbranched.

23 (24). At least 13 rays in first dorsal fin; base of fin greatly elongate, much larger than the base of the second dorsal. Head markedly flattened. Unjointed ray of ventral fin closely adjacent to first jointed ray. (Figure 888) . . . . 446. Hemitripteridae

[147] Except in family 427. Peristediidae (see thesis 51—31).

[148] A separate family is isolated, 451a. Cottunculidae (GRWM:399; MA:142) (Figure 882).

[149] Family 440. Cottidae is said to have (5) 6—7 branchiostegal rays (Gosline, 1968:148).

[150] Such pectoral rays are present in family 438. Hoplichthyidae (see thesis 51—39), but in these fish the head is strongly flattened and the ventral fins are situated markedly in front of the base of the pectorals (see Figure 911).

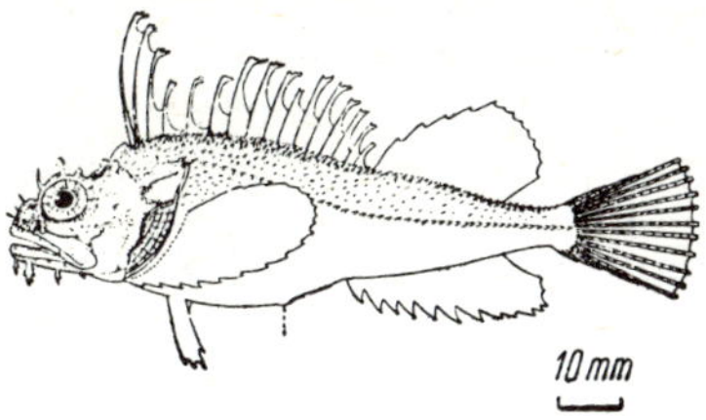

FIGURE 888. Hemitripteridae — Hemitripterus americanus (J. and E., 1900, fig. 738, diagr.)

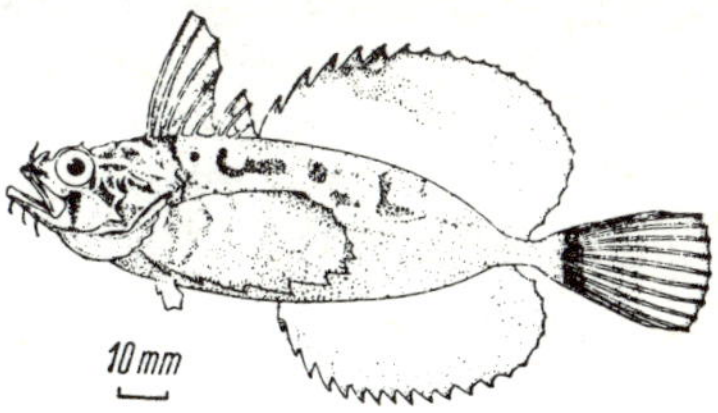

FIGURE 889. Blepsiidae — Blepsias cirrhosus (J. and E., 1900, fig. 737, diagr.)

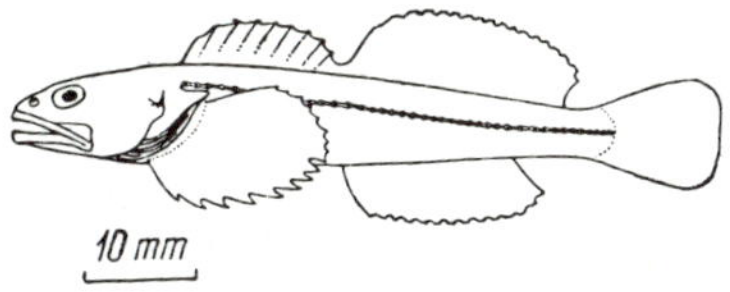

FIGURE 890. Ascelichthyidae — Ascelichthys rhodorus (J. and E., 1900, fig. 739, diagr.)

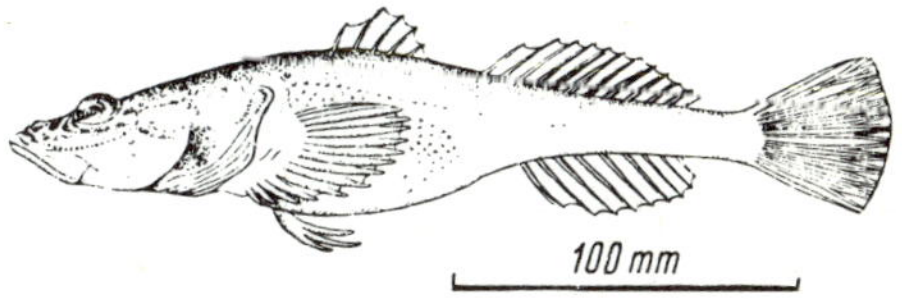

FIGURE 891. Cottidae (Cottocomephorinae) — Limnocottus bergianus (Berg, 1949, fig.920)

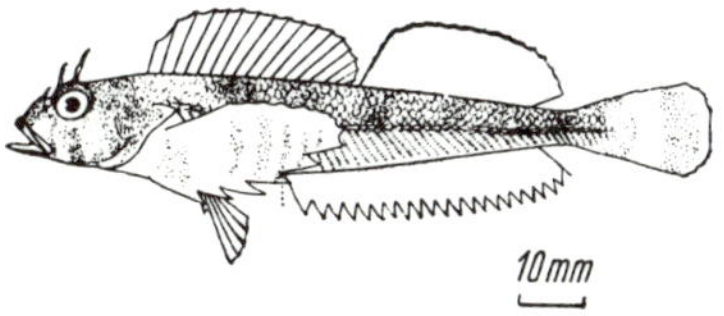

FIGURE 892. Cottidae (Jordaniinae) — Jordania zonope (J. and E., 1900, fig. 684, diagr.)

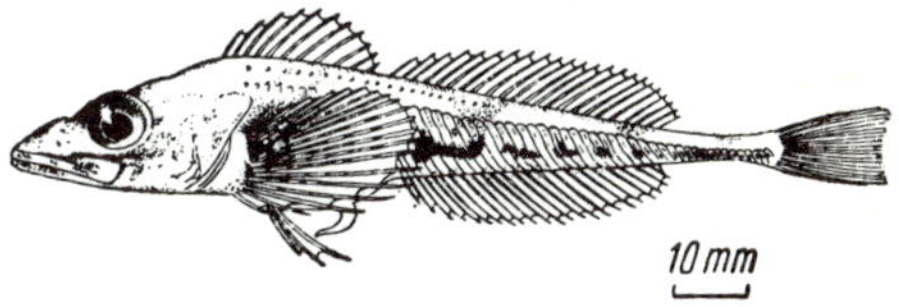

FIGURE 893. Cottidae (Triglopinae) — Triglops pingeli (Andriyashev, 1954, fig. 196)

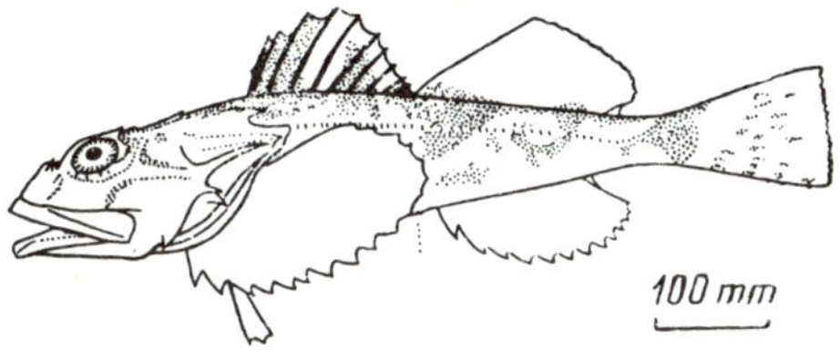

FIGURE 894. Cottidae (Myoxocephalinae) — Myoxocephalus polyacanthocephalus (J. and E., 1900, fig. 719, diagr.)

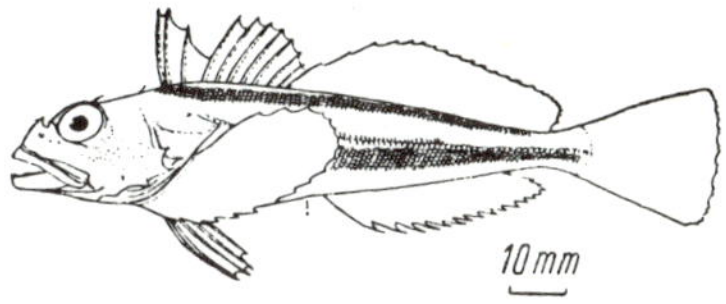

FIGURE 895. Cottidae (Hemilepidotinae) — Hemilepidotus jordani (J. and E., 1900, fig. 704, diagr.)

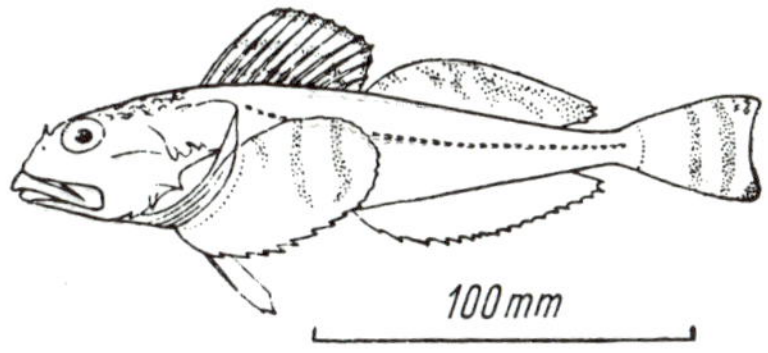

FIGURE 896. Cottidae (Gymnocanthinae) — Gymnocanthus herzensteini (Okada, 1955, fig. 304, diagr.)

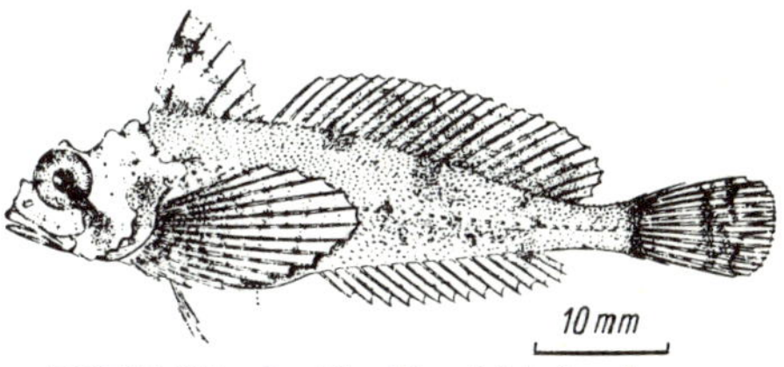

FIGURE 897. Cottidae (Nautichthyinae) — Nautichthys pribilovius (Jordan and Starks, 1904, fig. 229)

24 (23). At most 9 rays in first dorsal fin; base of fin not elongate. Head laterally compressed. Unjointed ray of ventral fin separated from first jointed ray by a space, connected to it by a membrane. (Figure 889) . . . . 447. **Blepsiidae**

25 (22). Rays of caudal fin always branched.

26 (27). Ventral fins absent. (Figure 890) . . . . . . .448. **Ascelichthyidae**

27 (26). Ventral fins present . . . . 440. **Cottidae**

14 subfamilies:

1 (2). Postorbital bones absent. Fishes of Lake Baikal. (Figure 891) . . . . subfamily 440.1. Cottocomephorinae

2 (1). Postorbital bones well developed, numbering 2—3.

3 (4). Ventral fins with 1 concealed spiny and 5 soft rays. (Figure 292) . . . . subfamily 440.2. Jordaniinae

4 (3). Fewer than 5 soft rays in ventral fins.

5 (6). Numerous transverse folds of skin with serrate margins below the lateral line. (Figure 893) . . . . subfamily 440.3. Triglopsinae

6 (5). Numerous transverse folds of skin with serrate margins absent below the lateral line.

7 (8). Two postorbital bones. (Figure 894) . . . . subfamily 440.4. Myoxocephalinae

8 (7). Three postorbital bones.

9 (10). Dorsal preopercular spine not the longest in comparison with the lower spines. Slit present behind the last gill. Four soft rays in ventral fins. (Figure 895) . . . . subfamily 440.5. Hemilepidotinae

10 (9). Dorsal preopercular spine always the longest.

11 (12). Top of head bearing large, very rough bony plates. Dorsal preopercular spine with strong hornlike processes. (Figure 896) . . . . .subfamily 440.6. Gymnocanthinae

12 (11). Top of head not bearing large rough bony plates.

13 (14). Occiput deeply indented behind the eyes; orbits raised above dorsal profile of head. (Figure 897) . . . . subfamily 440.7. Nauthichthyinae

14 (13). Occiput slightly flattened but not indented behind the eyes.

15 (16). Body and often also the head with a continuous or partial cover of fairly large, uniform scalelike plates distributed in straight rows. Dorsal preopercular spine without hornlike processes. (Figure 898) . . . . subfamily 440.8. Ricuzeniinae

16 (15). Body, and especially the head, not covered with such scalelike plates, but if partially covered, the dorsal preopercular spine has hornlike processes.

17 (20). Plates of lateral line considerably enlarged or strongly serrate.

18 (19). Dorsal preopercular spine with hornlike processes. (Figure 899) . . . . subfamily 440.9. Stlenginae

19 (18). Dorsal preopercular spine without processes. (Figure 900) . . . . subfamily 440.10. Radulininae

20 (17). Plates of lateral line not enlarged, but if slightly enlarged, then not serrate and the dorsal preopercular spine does not have hornlike processes.

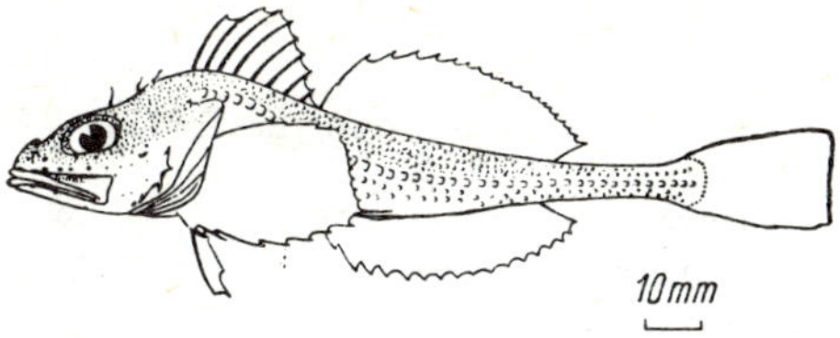

FIGURE 898. Cottidae (Ricuzeniinae) — Ricuzenius toyamensis (M., 1955, III, fig. 431, diagr.)

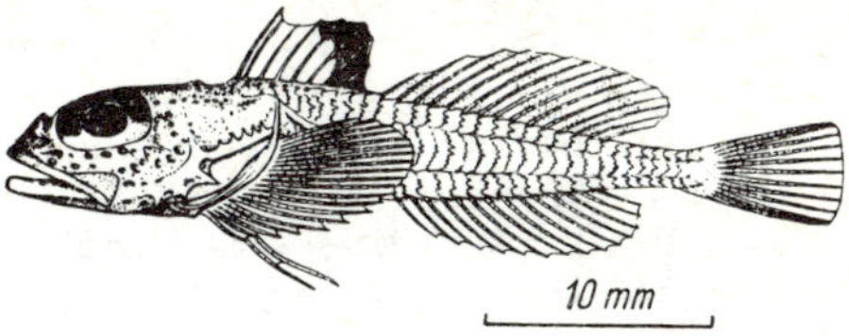

FIGURE 899. Cottidae (Stlenginae) — Stlengis osensis (Jordan, Tanaka, and Snyder, 1913, fig. 189)

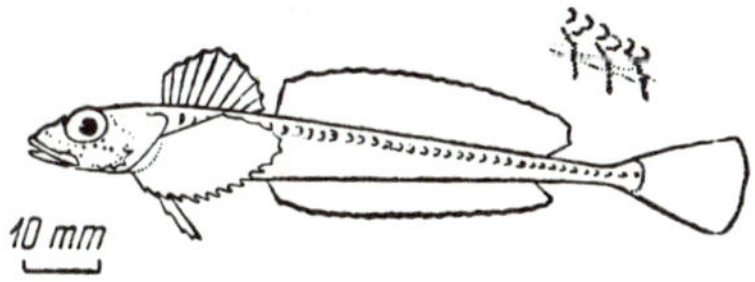

FIGURE 900. Cottidae (Radulininae) — Radulinus asprellus (J. and E., 1900, fig. 696, diagr.)

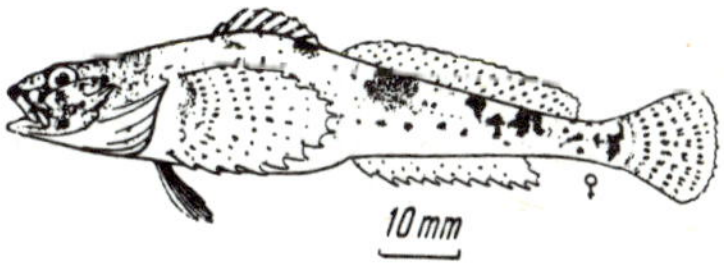

FIGURE 901. Cottidae (Cottinae) — Cottus gobio (Berg, 1949, fig. 896, diagr.)

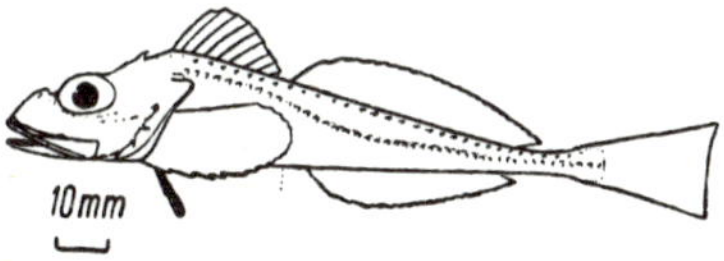

FIGURE 902. Cottidae (Icelinae) — Icelus spiniger (J. and E., 1900, fig. 693, diagr.)

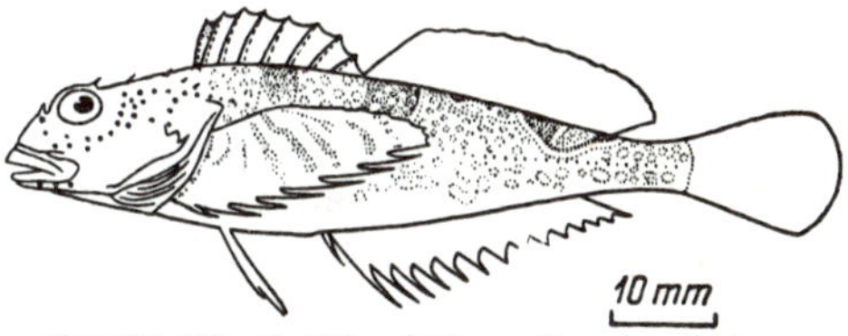

FIGURE 903. Cottidae (Oligocottinae) — Oligocottus maculosus (J. and E., 1900, fig. 734, diagr.)

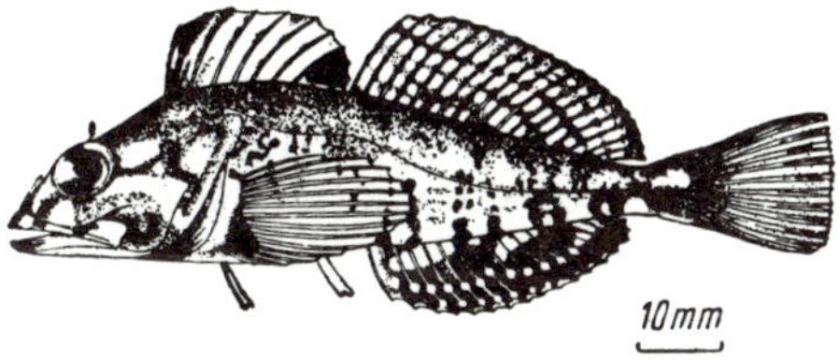

FIGURE 904. Cottidae (Pseudoblenniinae) — Pseudoblennius zonostigma (Jordan, Tanaka, and Snyder, 1913, fig. 223)

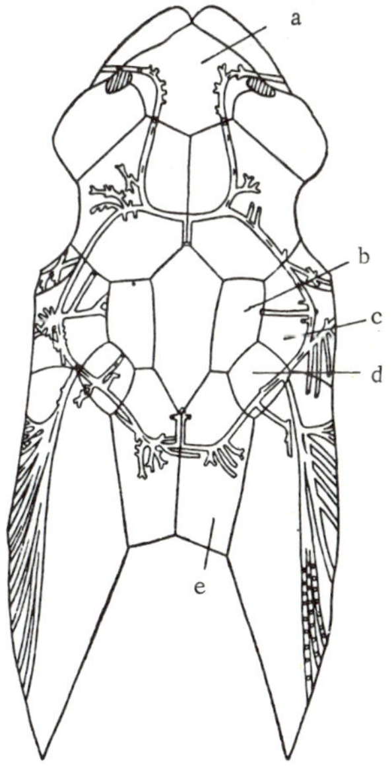

FIGURE 905. Skull of Dactylopterus volitans (Dactylopteriformes) (L. and L., 1965, fig. 54, diagr.):

a — nasal; b — supraoccipital; c — parietal; d — tabularia I; e — tabularia II.

21 (22). Branchiostegal membranes not forming a fold across the interbranchial space. (Figure 901) . . . . subfamily 440.11. Cottinae

22 (21). Branchiostegal membranes forming a fold across the interbranchial space.

23 (26). Ventral fins with 1 indistinct spiny and 3 soft rays.

24 (25). [Suprapharyngeal teeth in the form of one aggregation on each side of the pharynx.] Bony plates as a rule distributed in 2 rows on the body: one row along the lateral line and the other along the base of the dorsal fins; there are sometimes numerous smaller accessory plates. (Figure 902) . . . . subfamily 440.12. Icelinae

25 (24). [Suprapharyngeal teeth in the form of two aggregations on each side of the pharynx.] Usually no bony plates along and above the lateral line. (Figure 903) . . . . subfamily 440.13. Oligocottinae

26 (23). Ventral fins with 1 indistinct spiny and 2 soft rays. [Suprapharyngeal teeth in the form of two aggregations on each side of the pharynx.] (Figure 904) . . . . .subfamily 440.14. Pseudobleniinae

28 (3). Skin covered with normal scales, but if bare, then true hard spiny rays are present in the dorsal fin; if the body is covered with bony plates, the head is fully encased in armor and the vent is on the belly, not shifted forward under the base of the pectoral fins.

29 (32). Head fully encased in bony armor.[151] End of snout bearing spiny, forward-directed processes. (Suborder 51.1. **Scorpaenoidei**, Trigloidea.)

30 (31). Lower 3 rays of pectoral fin separated from the fin and from each other. Both jaws with teeth. Scales normal, not resembling bony plates. No barbels on lower jaw. (Figure 906) . . . . 426. **Triglidae**

31 (30). Lower 2 rays of pectoral fin separated from the fin and from each other. Teeth absent on lower jaw. Scales in the form of bony plates, resembling the skin cover in the Agonidae. Barbels present on lower jaw. (Figure 907) . . . . . . 427. **Peristediidae**

32 (29). Head not encased in bony armor, or only partially covered. End of snout usually not bearing forward-directed spiny processes.

33 (40). Head and body showing marked vertical flattening.

34 (39). Skin covered with tilelike scales. Lower rays of pectoral fin not separated from the fin. Spiny rays of dorsal fin fairly strong. Rays of soft dorsal fin in males not having filamentous tips. [Interoperculum present.] (Suborder 51.3. **Platycephaloidei**.)

35 (36). Anal fin with 3 spiny and 5 soft rays. (Figure 908) . . . . 436. **Parabembridae**

[151] [Similar armor on the head is present in family 456. Dactylopteridae (order 52. Dactylopteriformes, see Figure 924 and thesis 52—1) but in these fishes there is one unpaired nasal bone and 2 pairs of tabularia the posterior of which is very large (Figure 905).]

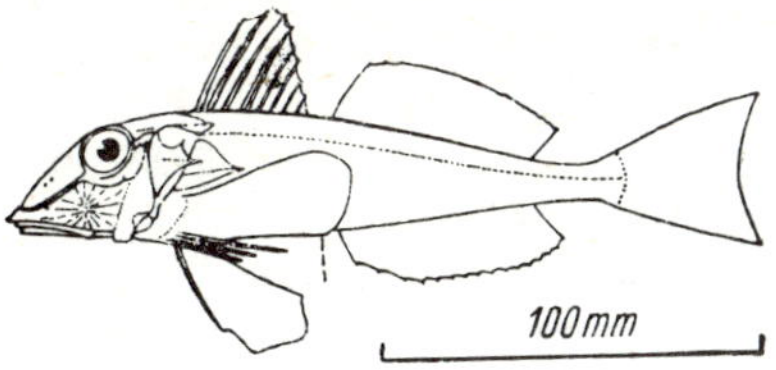

FIGURE 906. Triglidae — Trigla microptera (Okada, 1955, fig. 314, diagr.)

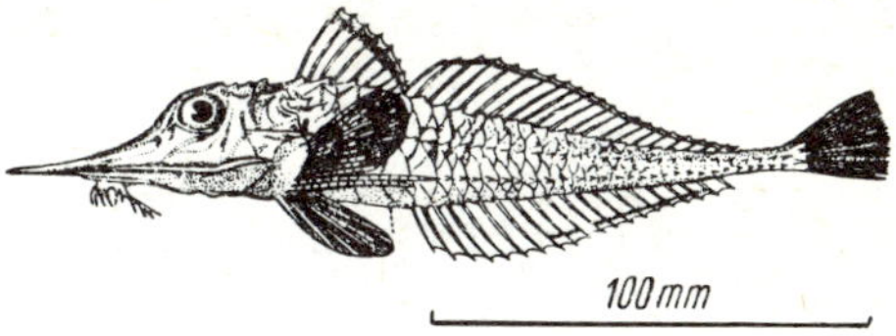

FIGURE 907. Peristediidae — Peristedion nierstraszi (M., 1955, III, fig. 441)

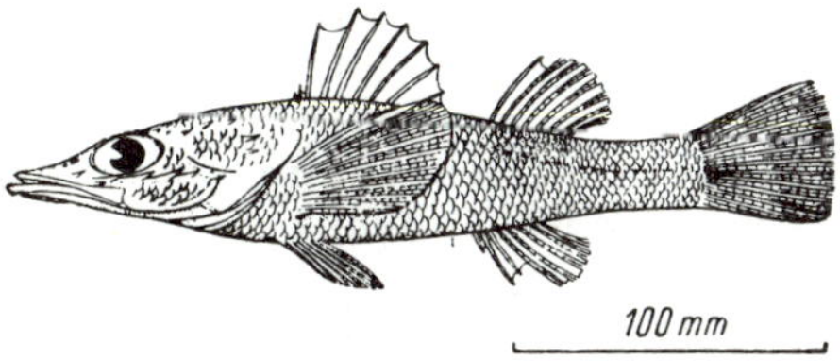

FIGURE 908. Parabembridae — Parabembras curtus (M., 1955, III, fig. 421)

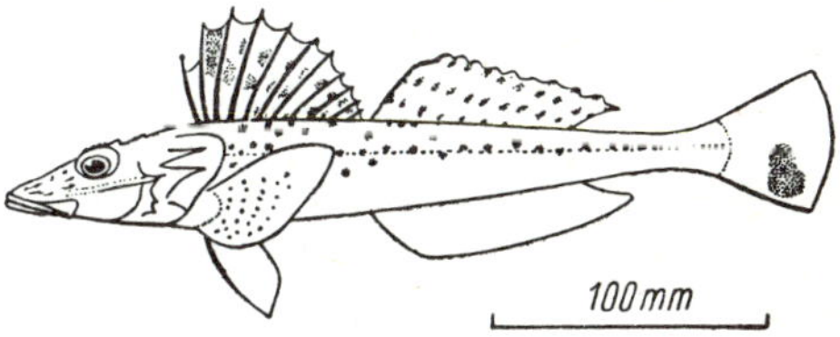

FIGURE 909. Bembridae — Bembras japonicus (Abe, 1958, fig. 197, diagr.)

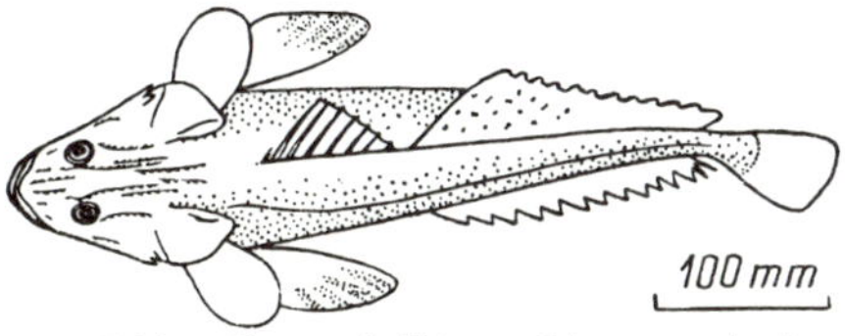

FIGURE 910. Platycephalidae — Platycephalus indicus (Okada, 1955, fig. 311, diagr.)

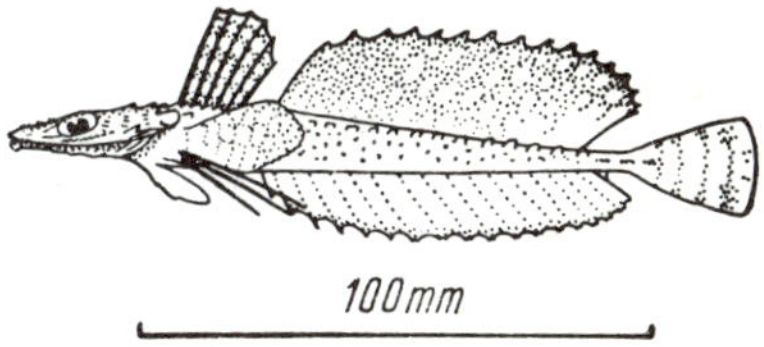

FIGURE 911. Hoplichthyidae — Hoplichthys regani (Jordan, Tanaka, and Snyder, 1913, fig. 237, diagr.)

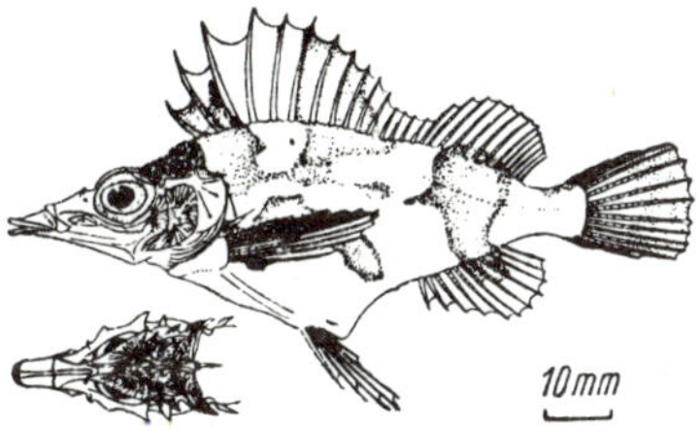

FIGURE 912. Congiopodidae — Alertichthys blacki (Moreland, 1960, figs. 1, 2)

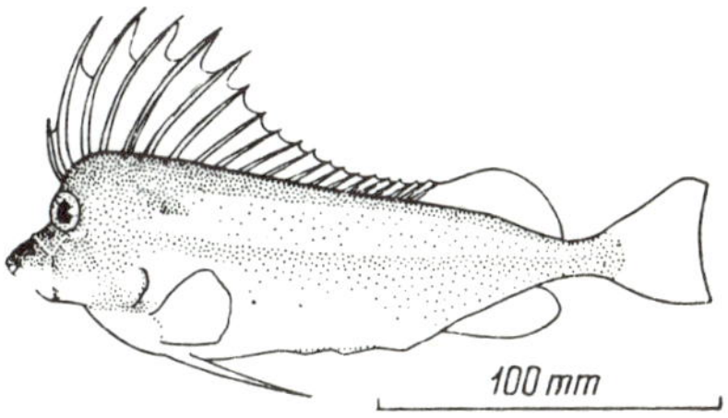

FIGURE 913. Congiopodidae — Congiopodus torvus (Smith, 1950, fig. 1060, diagr.)

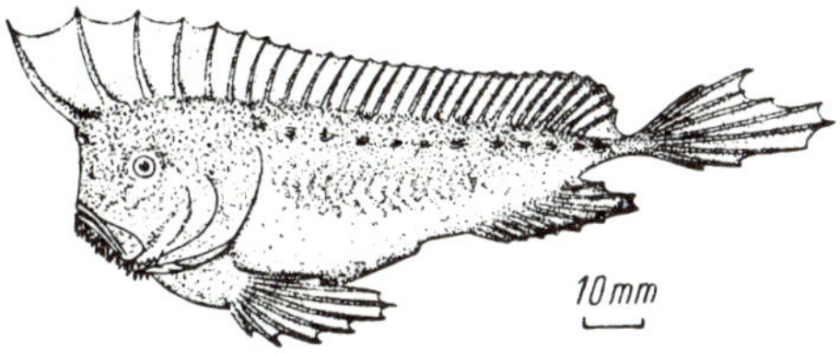

FIGURE 914. Pataecidae — Neopataecus waterhousi (Waite, 1921, fig. 278)

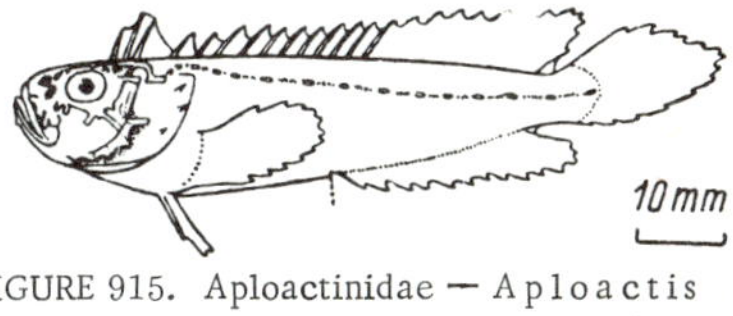

FIGURE 915. Aploactinidae — Aploactis aspera (M., 1955, III, fig. 417, diagr.)

36 (35). Spiny rays absent in anal fin.

37 (38). Ventral fins inserted in front of, more rarely under, the base of the pectorals. [Pelvic bones united with each other all along, small.] (Figure 909) . . . . 437. **Bembridae**

38 (37). Ventral fins inserted markedly behind the base of the pectorals. [Pelvic bones united anteriorly and posteriorly but not in the middle, where an oval bone-free area is formed.] (Figure 910) . . . . 435. **Platycephalidae**

39 (34). Skin, apart from the lateral line, bare. Lower 3—4 soft rays of pectoral fin separated from the fin and from each other. Spiny rays of dorsal fin rather weak. The rays of the soft dorsal fin have threadlike tips in the males. [Interoperculum absent.] (Figure 911). Suborder 51.4. **Hoplichthyoidei**) . . . . .438. **Hoplichthyidae**

40 (33). Body and head generally laterally compressed, more rarely slightly flattened.

41 (42). One pair of nares, one naris on each side. Gill openings markedly shortened. Head with spinelike outgrowths (Figure 912), or the dorsal fin originates above the eyes (Figure 913). Snout long and pointed, with a small protrusible mouth. Ventral fins situated behind the base of the pectorals, sometimes at a considerable distance, distinctly on the belly. (Suborder 51.5. **Congiopodidoidei**) . . . . 439. **Congiopodidae**

42 (41). Two pairs of nares, but if the posterior pair is weakly expressed or absent, the gill openings are not shortened, the head has no spinelike outgrowths, or the dorsal fin originates in front of the eyes.

43 (50). Dorsal fin originating on the throat [basal elements of first rays united with the skull]. (Suborder 51.1. **Scorpaenoidei.**)

44 (47). Suborbital bones very thin or even membranous. [One pair of suprapharyngeal bones with teeth.]

45 (46). Snout very blunt; dorsal fin originating on the vertical of the tip of the snout, markedly in front of the eyes; its first rays do not form an independent lobe. Ventral fins absent. [Vertebrae 35.] (Figure 914) . . . . 431. **Pataecidae**

46 (45). Snout tapering; dorsal fin originating above the eye or slightly behind; its first rays form an independent lobe consisting of 7 rays which is separated from the posterior part of the fin by a deep incision. Ventral fins present. [Vertebrae 29] . . . . 432. **Gnathanacanthidae**

47 (44). Suborbital bones well ossified. Dorsal fin originating behind, above, or even slightly in front of the eyes, but not considerably in front, not on the level of the tip of the snout. Ventral fins present.

48 (49). Anal fin with 1—2 flexible spiny rays. [One pair of suprapharyngeal bones with teeth. Ribs absent.] (Figure 915) . . . . 429. **Aploactinidae**

49 (48). Anal fin with 3 large, strong spiny rays. [Three pairs of suprapharyngeal bones with teeth. Ribs present.] Caudal fin never forked. (Figure 916). . . . . .425. **Scorpaenidae**
(Ex parte, Tetraroge and related genera)

50 (43). Dorsal fin originating behind the head [basal elements of its first rays not united with the skull].

51 (52). Ventral fins rudimentary, very small, hard to discern, with 1 spiny and 3 soft rays. Body of oval form, deep, its depth more than half the length of the body without C, with strong lateral compression. Gill openings small; branchiostegal membranes intergrown with the interbranchial space for a large distance. First dorsal fin with a short base, semicircular, similar in size and form to the soft dorsal, which is separated from the spiny fin by a deep notch. [Ribs absent.] (Figure 917) . . . . 428. **Caracanthidae**

52 (51). Ventral fins normally developed, not shortened. Gill openings wide. First dorsal fin not shortened. [Ribs present.]

53 (56). Keel-shaped processes and barbs generally developed on the head. [Fewer than 30 vertebrae, rarely 31.]

54 (55). Body not covered with scales. Branchiostegal membrane attached to the interbranchial space. [Posttemporale curved but not furcate, fused with the skull.] Ventral fins with 1 spiny and 4–5 soft rays. (Figure 918) . . . . 430. **Synancejidae**

55 (54). Body covered with scales. Branchiostegal membrane free of the interbranchial space. [Posttemporale furcate, not fused with the skull.] Ventral fins with 1 spiny and 5 soft rays. (Figure 919) . . . . 425. **Scorpaenidae**

56 (53). Head not bearing keel-shaped processes, crests, barbs or spines. [More than 40 vertebrae.] (Suborder 51.2. **Hexagrammoidei.**)

57 (58). Head not bearing leathery processes. Two distinct pairs of nares. One lateral line. Two dorsal fins, their bases well separated. (Figure 920) . . . . 434. **Anoplopomatidae**

58 (57). Leathery processes present on the head. Anterior pair of anal openings well developed; posterior pair, if present, small, difficult to perceive. There are generally several lateral lines, more rarely one. Dorsal fin with one base, usually with a notch. (Figures 921–923). . . . . 433. **Hexagrammidae**[152]

Order 52. DACTYLOPTERIFORMES (thesis 0–132)

1 family: 456. Dactylopteridae (Figure 924).

Order 53. PLEURONECTIFORMES (thesis 0–37)

2 suborders, 6 families (457–462):

1 (2). Dorsal fin not passing forward onto the head, originating considerably behind the upper eye, its first rays spiny. Palatines

[152] A separate family is isolated, 433a. **Zaniolepididae** (GRWM: 399, 422) (Figure 923).

with teeth. [Vertebrae 24—25.] Ventral fins with 1 spiny and 5 soft rays. Maxillary with an accessory bone. (Suborder 53.1. **Psettodoidei.**) (Figure 925) . . . . 457. **Psettodidae**

2 (1). Dorsal fin passing forward onto the head behind the eyes and situated, at least partially, above the eye; spiny rays absent. Palatines without teeth. [Usually more than 27 vertebrae, rarely 24 in some Achirinae.] (Suborder 53.2. **Pleuronectoidei.**)

3 (8). The skin covering the margin of the lower jaw and the interoperculum on both sides of the head does not continue onto the chin, so that the interbranchial space and the branchiostegal rays, and generally also the margins of the preoperculum, are not concealed and are more or less distinctly discernible. Eyes as a rule large or of moderate size. [Monomorphic type of chiasma (in right-sided species the left optic nerve is on top, in left-sided species the right).] Vertical through center of upper eye passing usually behind, more rarely in front of, vertical through center of lower eye. [Postcleithrum and ribs present.] (Pleuronectoidea.)

4 (5). Ventral fins with 1 slightly flexible spiny ray and 5 soft rays. Vomer with teeth. Branchiostegal membranes broadly disjunct and free of the interbranchial space.[153] Maxillary with an accessory bone . . . . 459. **Citharidae**

2 subfamilies:

1 (2). Eyes on the left side. [Right optic nerve on top.] All the rays of the dorsal and anal fins and all the soft rays of the ventrals are branched. Clearly expressed dark patches are present on the caudal peduncle at the base of the last rays of the dorsal and anal fins. (Figure 926) . . . subfamily 459.1. C i t h a r i n a e

2 (1). Eyes on the right side. [Left optic nerve on top.] Only the posterior rays of the dorsal and anal fins are branched; at least the first soft ray of the ventrals is unbranched. No patches on the body at the base of the dorsal and anal fins. (Figure 927). . . . . subfamily 459.2. B r a c h y p l e u r i n a e

5 (4). Spiny ray absent in ventral fin. Vomer usually without teeth. Branchiostegal membranes united and attached to the interbranchial space. Maxillary without an accessory bone.

6 (7). Eyes on the left side (except in a few specimens). [Nerves of right eye always on top in the chiasma.] Yolk of eggs with an oil droplet . . . . 458. **Bothidae**

3 subfamilies:

1 (2). Bases of ventral fins usually narrow, but if the base is slightly widened on the seeing side, the origin of the fin is very slightly in front of the origin of the base of the fin on the blind side, the

[153] The branchiostegal membranes are disjunct in the Scophthalminae (family 458. Bothidae), but unlike the Citharidae, these fish have ventral fins with a wide (not narrow) base.

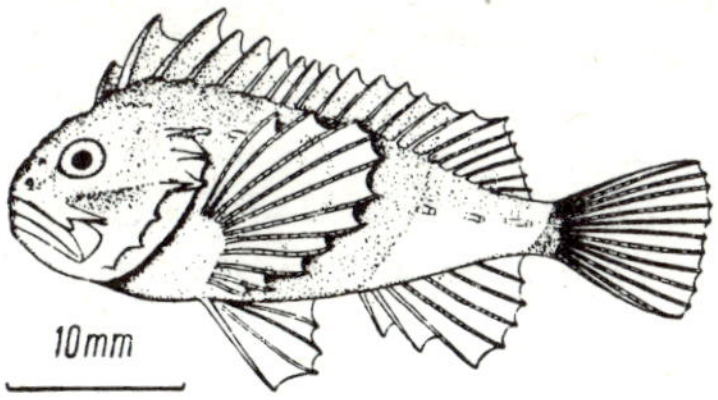

FIGURE 916. Scorpaenidae — *Coccotropsis gymnoderma* (Smith, 1950, fig. 1031)

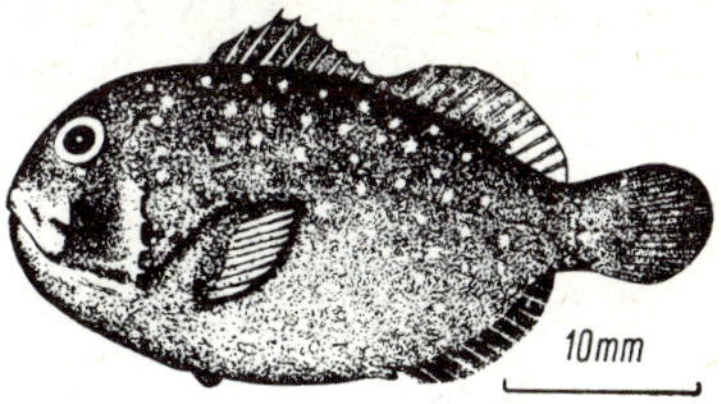

FIGURE 917. Caracanthidae — *Caracanthus maculatus* (Fowler, 1900, pl. 20, fig. 5)

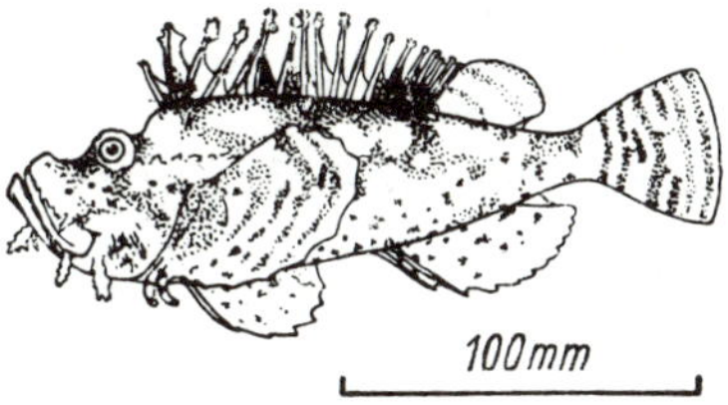

FIGURE 918. Synancejidae — *Inimicus japonicus* (Abe, 1958, fig. 213, diagr.)

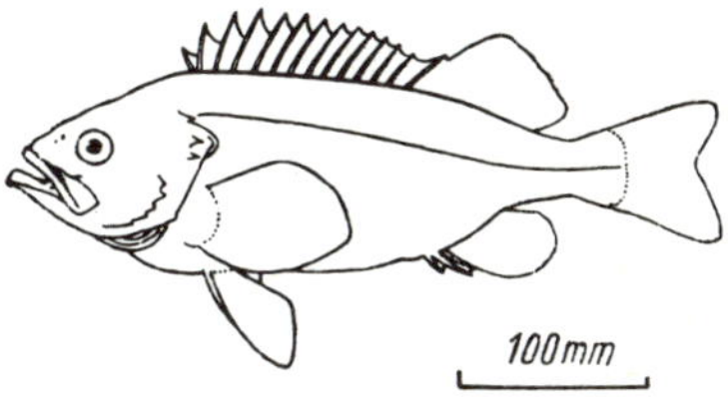

FIGURE 919. Scorpaenidae — *Sebastes glaucus* (M., 1955, III, fig. 363, diagr.)

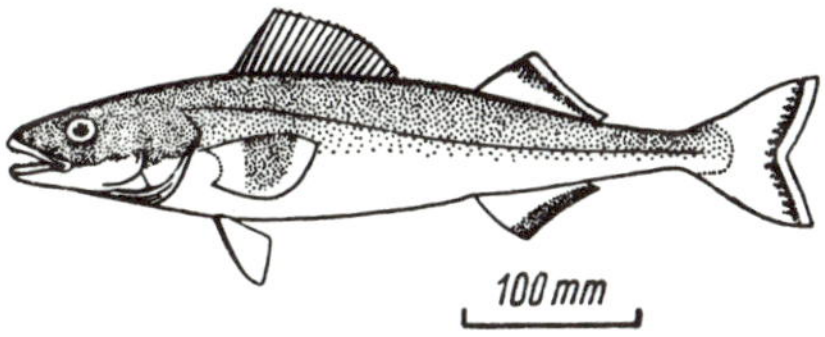

FIGURE 920. Anoplopomatidae — *Anoplopoma fimbria* (J. and E., 1900, fig. 675, diagr.)

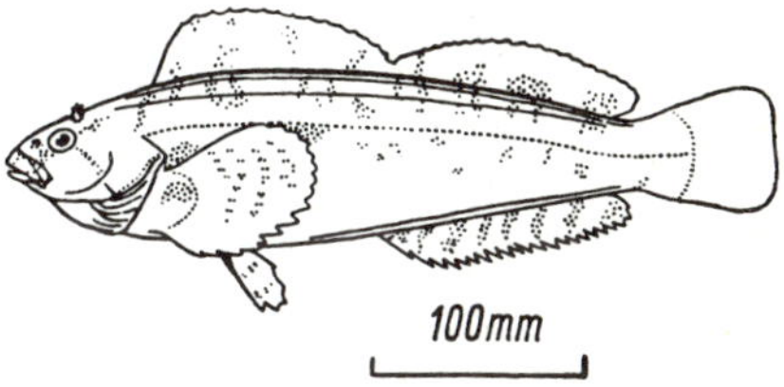

FIGURE 921. Hexagrammidae — *Hexagrammus octogrammus* (M., 1955, III, fig. 420, diagr.)

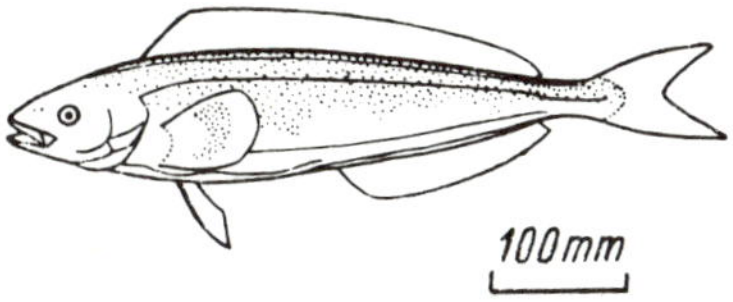

FIGURE 922. Hexagrammidae — *Pleurogrammus azonus* (Abe, 1958, fig. 206, diagr.)

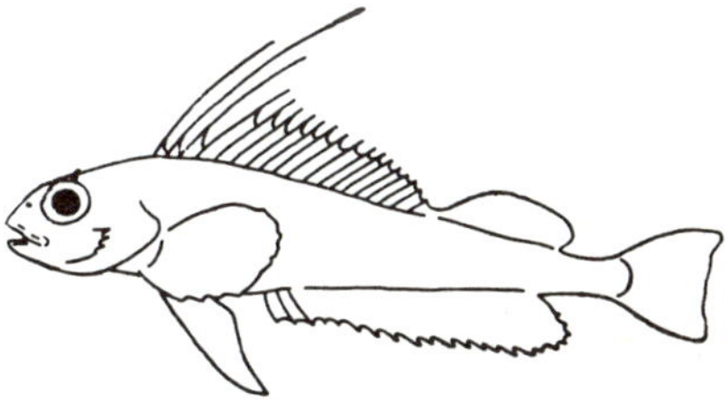

FIGURE 923. Zaniolepididae (GRWM, 1966: 422, fig.)

interval roughly equaling the space between the first and second ray. [Ventral fins supported by pelvic bones situated behind the cleithra, not having cartilaginous plates projecting in front of the cleithra.] (Figures 928, 929) . . . . subfamily 458.1. Paralichthyinae

2 (1). Base of both ventral fins, or only of that on the seeing side, widened, shifted markedly forward toward the hyoid bone and extending well forward beyond the cleithrum [the rays are supported by cartilaginous plates of the pelvic bones]. (Figure 930).

3 (4). Base of ventral fin on the blind side narrow; first fin ray considerably behind the first ray of the fin on the seeing side. (Figure 931) . . . . subfamily 458.2. Bothinae

4 (3). Bases of both ventral fins widened. (Figure 932) . . . . subfamily 458.3. Scophthalminae[154]

7 (6). Eyes on the right side (except in a few specimens). [Nerve of left eye always on top in the chiasma.] Eggs without an oil droplet . . . . 460. Pleuronectidae

5 subfamilies:

1 (8). Ventral fin on seeing side usually with a narrow base; [pelvic bones without a cartilaginous plate, and situated either behind or under the cleithrum but not in front of it.] The fins are arranged symmetrically, or the fin on the seeing side has the base set along the midline of the abdomen and shifted slightly forward from the origin of the fin on the blind side. [Radials present in pectoral fins.]

2 (5). Dorsal fin originating above the eye, behind the olfactory organ on the blind side.[155]

3 (4). Lateral line well developed on both sides of the body. Plates of olfactory organ almost always (except in Atherestes — Figure 934) parallel, without a median axis. (Figure 935) . . . . subfamily 460.1. Pleuronectinae

4 (3). Lateral line on blind side of body rudimentary and difficult to find. Plates of olfactory organ radiating from a short median axis. (Figures 936, 937) . . . . subfamily 460.2. Poecilopsettinae

5 (2). Dorsal fin originating in front of the eyes; the fin extends onto the snout anteriorly and down along the midline of the head approximately to the level of the olfactory organ on the blind side.

6 (7). Origin of dorsal fin above the level of the olfactory organ. Plates of olfactory organ arranged at an angle to the median axis (Figure 938). Lateral lines well developed on both sides of the body. Fin rays of normal length. (Figure 939) . . . . subfamily 460.3. Paralichthodinae

[154] A separate family is isolated, 458a. Scophthalmidae (GRWM:402, 434)

[155] In the genus Pleuronichthys (Pleuronectinae) the dorsal fin originates on the blind side, below the level of the angle of the oral slit (Figure 933).

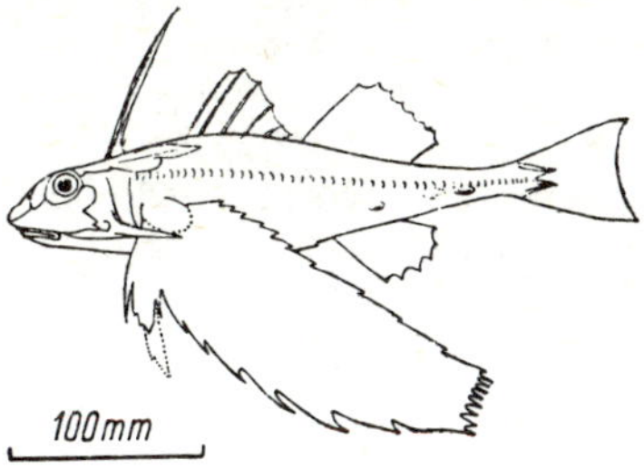

FIGURE 924. Dactylopteridae — Daicocus peterseni (L. and L., 1965, fig. 55)

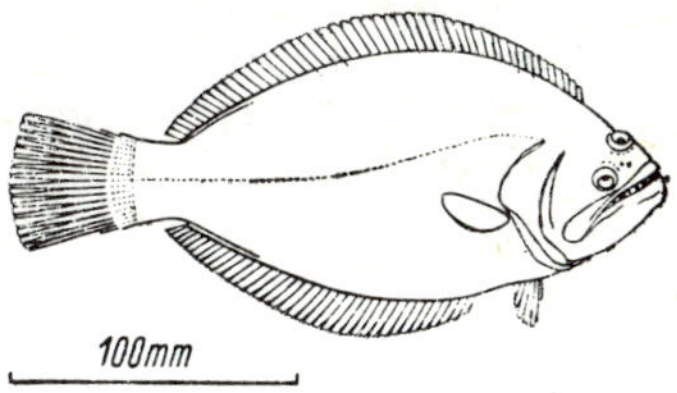

FIGURE 925. Psettodidae — Psettodus erumei (Norman, 1934, fig. 30)

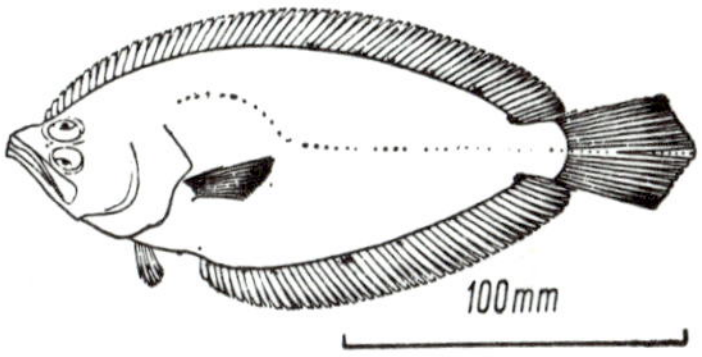

FIGURE 926. Citharidae (Citharinae) — Eucitharus linguatula (Norman, 1934, fig. 121)

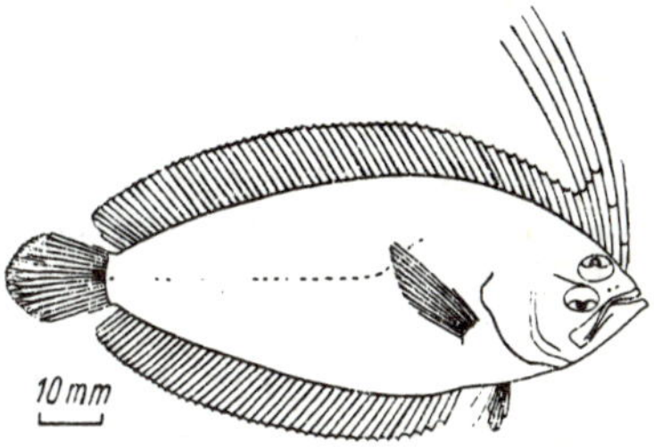

FIGURE 927. Citharidae (Brachypleurinae) — Brachypleura novae-zealandiae (Norman, 1934, fig. 289)

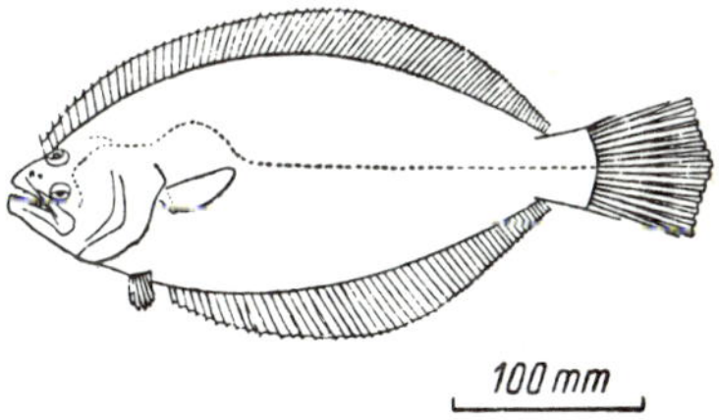

FIGURE 928. Bothidae (Paralichthyinae) — Paralichthys olivaceus (Norman, 1934, fig. 50)

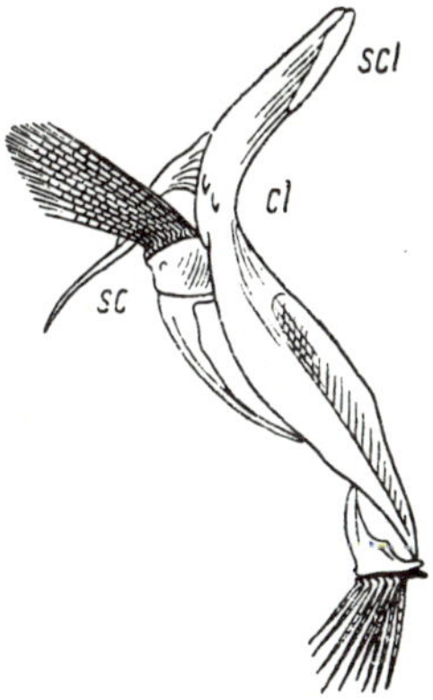

FIGURE 929. Humeral girdle and pelvic bones of Pseudorhombus arsius (Paralichthyidae) (Norman, 1934, fig. 24 A):

cl — cleithrum; sc — hypercoracoid (scapula); scl — supracleithrum.

7 (6). Origin of dorsal fin below the level of the olfactory organ on the blind side. Plates of weakly developed olfactory organ slightly curved, parallel, without a median axis. Lateral line on blind side rudimentary and difficult to find. Rays of pectoral fin markedly elongate; the 5—6 posterior rays of the dorsal and anal fins are shortened. (Figure 940) . . . . subfamily 460.4. Samarinae

8 (1). Ventral fin on seeing side with a wide base. [Pelvic bones with a cartilaginous plate protruding far in front of the cleithrum.] Fins arranged extremely asymmetrically: the base of the fin on the seeing side, which is often concrescent with the anal, is distributed along the midline of the abdomen and is shifted markedly forward from the origin of the base of the fin on the blind side, which is sometimes absent. [Radials absent in pectoral fins; the rays are attached to the hypercoracoid.] Dorsal fin as a rule originating in front of the eyes, immediately behind the olfactory organ on the blind side, or on the snout, at the level of this organ. Lateral lines uniformly developed on both sides of the body. (Figure 941) . . . . subfamily 460.5. Rhombosoleinae

8 (3). The skin covering the margin of the lower jaw and the interoperculum continues onto the chin, so that the interbranchial space and branchiostegal rays, and generally also the margins of the preoperculum, are indiscernible. Eyes usually small. [Dimorphic type of chiasma (the right or left optic nerve is on top irrespective of whether the specimens are right- or left-sided).] Vertical through center of upper eye usually passing in front of vertical through center of lower eye. [Postcleithrum and ribs absent.] (Soleoidea.)

9 (10). Eyes on the right side . . . . 461. Soleidae

5 subfamilies:

1 (2). Margin of preoperculum distinguishable, represented as a shallow groove of skin that is not covered by scales. No pharyngeal slit behind the last gill arch. (Atlantic Ocean.) (Figure 942) . . . . subfamily 461.1. Achirinae

2 (1). Margin of preoperculum not distinguishable, fully concealed under scales. There is a small pharyngeal slit behind the last gill arch.

3 (4). Snout in the form of a hook; its anterior end is dropped well below the posterior end of the oral slit, which is thus strongly curved. Ventral fin on seeing side fused with the anal. (Figure 943) . . . . . . subfamily 461.2. Heteromycterinae

4 (3). Snout not in the form of a hook; its anterior margin is almost on the same level as the posterior end of the oral slit, which is thus almost straight, horizontal, more rarely arcuate. Ventral fin on seeing side with a short base, not fused with the anal.

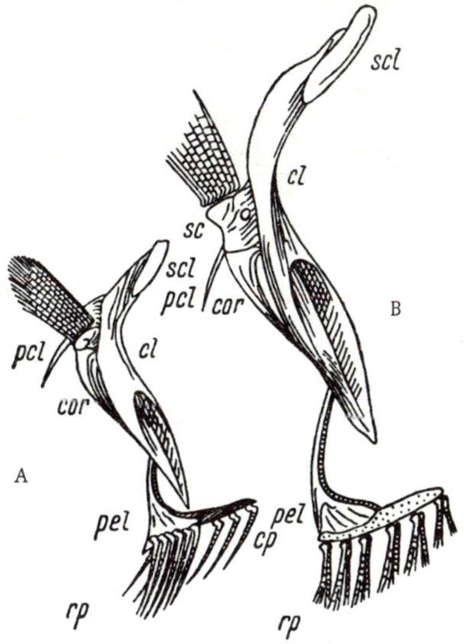

FIGURE 930. Humeral girdle and pelvic bones (A) of Arnoglossus imperialis (Bothinae) (A) and Scophthalmus maximus (Scophthalminae) (B) (Norman, 1934, fig. 24,B, C):

cl — cleithrum; cor — hypocoracoid; pcl — postcleithrum; pel — pelvic bones; rp — right ventral (pelvic) fin; sc — hypercoracoid (scapula); scl — supracleithrum.

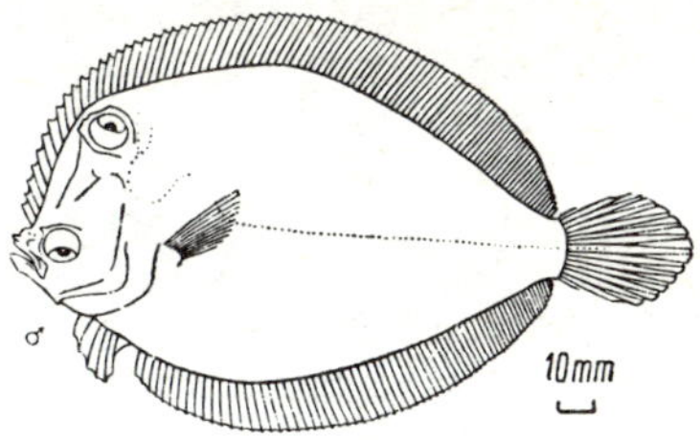

FIGURE 931. Bothidae (Bothinae) — Bothus podas (Norman, 1934, fig. 169)

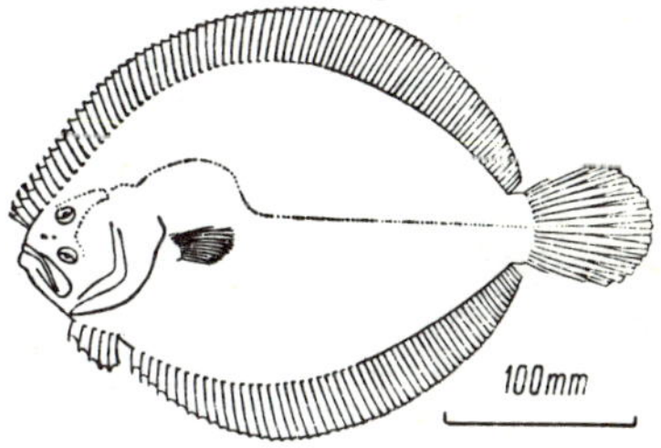

FIGURE 932. Bothidae (Scophthalminae) Scophthalmus rhombus (Norman, 1934, fig. 207)

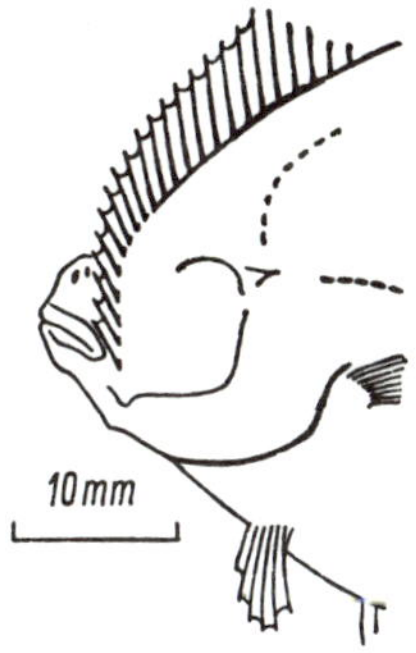

FIGURE 933. Pleuronichthys decurrens (Pleuronectinae) (Norman, 1934, fig. 235).

Blind side of head.

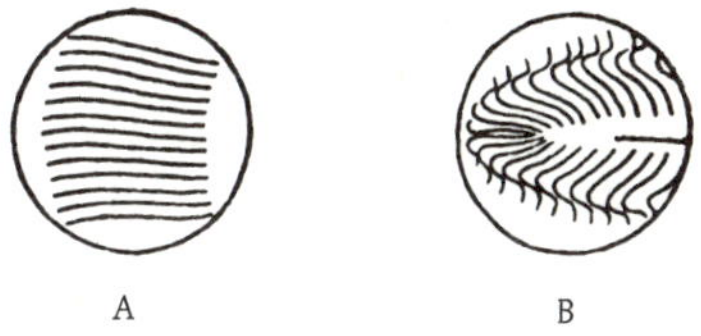

FIGURE 934. Plates of olfactory organ in Pleuronectes platessa (A) and Atherestes stomias (B) (Norman, 1934, fig. 27O and N).

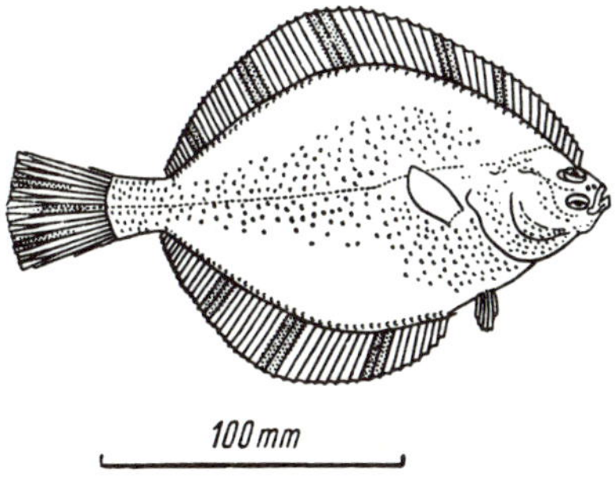

FIGURE 935. Pleuronectidae (Pleuronectinae) — Pleuronectes stellatus (Norman, 1934, fig. 275)

5 (6). Pectoral fins absent. Lateral line on blind side present, but indistinctly expressed; it runs along the base of the dorsal fin as far as the midlength of the body. (Figure 944) . . . . subfamily 461.3. Aseraggodinae

6 (5). Pectoral fins present on both sides. No lateral line on blind side running along the base of the dorsal fin.

7 (8). Anterior nares with a valve. Dermal processes on blind side of head in the form of folds. Bases of pectoral fins narrow, rays long, branched. (Figure 945) . . . . subfamily 461.4. Synapturinae

8 (7). Anterior nares without a valve. Dermal processes on blind side of head hairlike. Bases of pectoral fins on both sides wide, the rays not branched. (Figures 946, 947) . . . . subfamily 461.5. Soleinae

10 (9). Eyes on the left side . . . . 462. **Cynoglossidae**

2 subfamilies:

1 (2). One or more lateral lines always present on the seeing side of the body. (Figure 948) . . . subfamily 462.1. Cynoglossinae

2 (1). No lateral lines, either on the seeing or on the blind side of the body. (Figure 949) . . . . . . subfamily 462.2. Symphucinae

Order 54. ICOSTEIFORMES (theses 0—97, 156)

1 family: 463. **Icosteidae** (Figure 950).

Order 55. CHAUDHURIIFORMES (thesis 0—59)

1 family: 464. **Chaudhuriidae** (Figures 149, 951).

Order 56. MASTACEMBELIFORMES (thesis 0—58)

1 family: 465. **Mastacembelidae** (Figure 952).

Order 57. ECHENEIFORMES (thesis 0—65)

1 family: 466. **Echeneidae** (Figure 953).

54—57

FIGURE 936. Plates of olfactory organ in Poecilopsetta colorata (Norman, 1934, fig. 27 P)

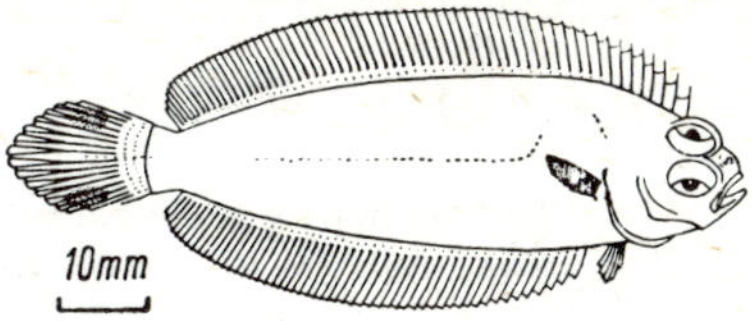

FIGURE 937. Pleuronectidae (Poecilopsettinae) – Poecilopsetta beani (Norman, 1934, fig. 277)

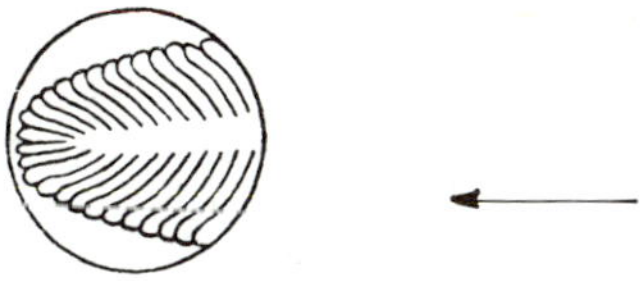

FIGURE 938. Plates of olfactory organ in Paralichthodes algoensis (Norman, 1934, fig. 27 Q)

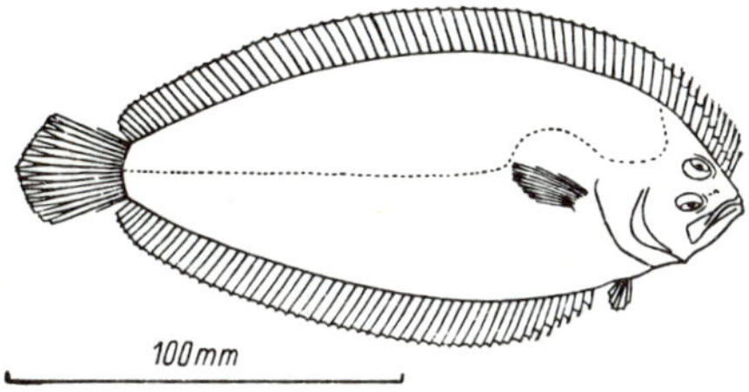

FIGURE 939. Pleuronectidae (Paralichthodinae) — Paralichthodes algoensis (Norman, 1934, fig. 288)

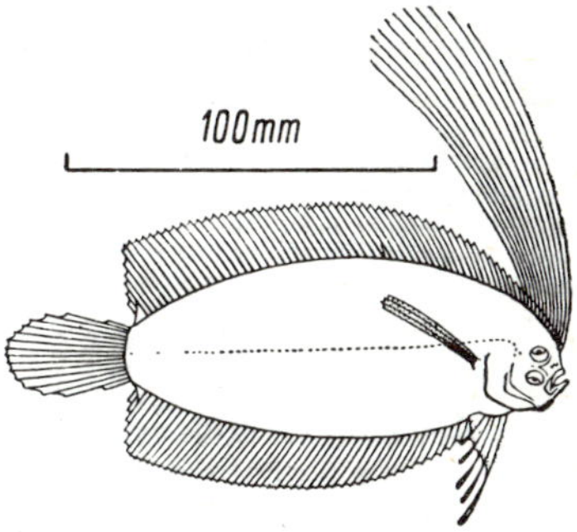

FIGURE 940. Pleuronectidae (Samarinae) — Samaris cristatus (Norman, 1934, fig. 291)

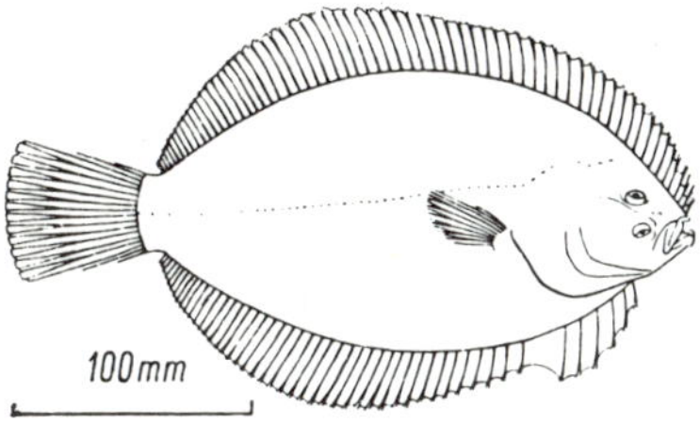

FIGURE 941. Pleuronectidae (Rhombosoleinae) — Rhombosolea retiaria (Norman, 1934, fig. 314)

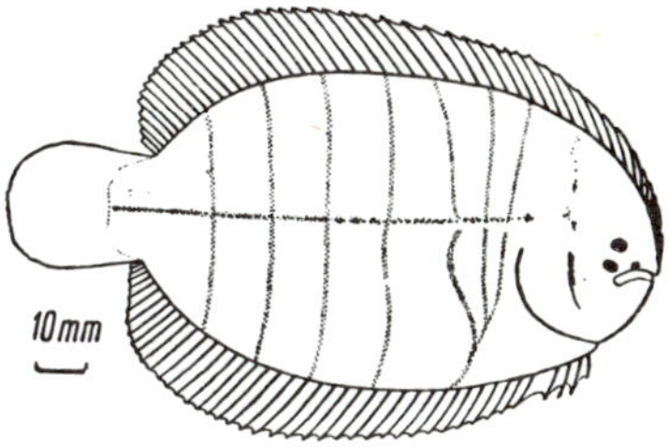

FIGURE 942. Soleidae (Achirinae) — Achirus fasciatus (J. and E., 1900, fig. 948, diagr.)

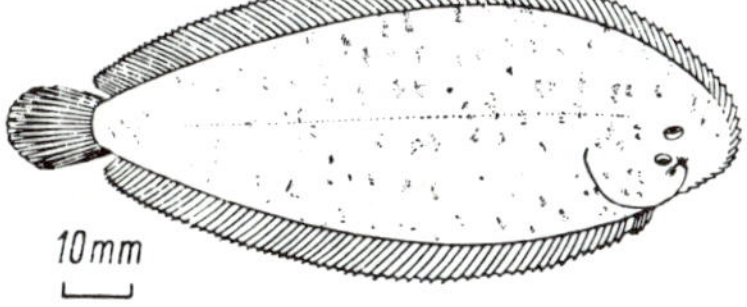

FIGURE 943. Soleidae (Heteromycterinae) — Heteromycterus japonicus (Chu et al., 1962, fig. 775)

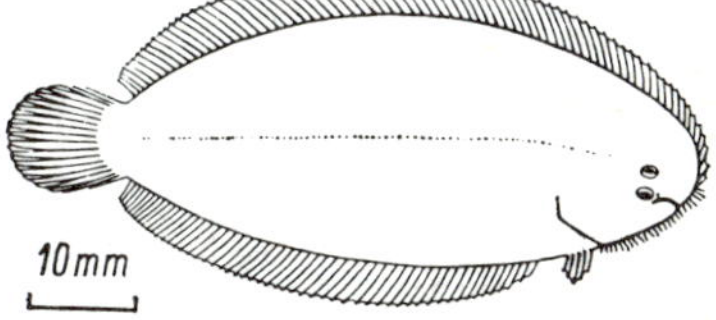

FIGURE 944. Soleidae (Aseraggodinae) — Aseraggodes kobensis (Chu et al., 1962, fig. 772, diagr.)

Order 58. TETRAODONTIFORMES (thesis 0—151)

4 suborders, 11 families (467—477):

1 (10). Pelvic bones developed; ventral fins with spiny rays, either a pair (one in each fin) or just one (in the fused fins). Spiny rays also present, as a rule, in the dorsal fin. Body laterally compressed. (Suborder 58.1. **Balistoidei.**[156])

2 (5). Left and right ventral fins each consisting of one spiny ray which is connected to the pelvic bone by means of a joint. Premaxillaries not grown together with the maxillaries and protrude freely. Scales round, not rhombic. Dorsal fin with 2—6 spiny rays. [Vertebrae 19—20.]

3 (4). Caudal peduncle short. Caudal fin generally round. Anterior pair of teeth on both jaws not having the form of a beak; all teeth small, conical, but if laterally flattened, not scalpriform. Spiny rays of dorsal fin large, gradually becoming shorter. (Figure 954) . . . . 468. **Triacanthodidae**

4 (3). Caudal peduncle long. Caudal fin with a deep notch. Anterior pair of teeth on both jaws in the form of a beak; teeth wide, laterally flattened, scalpriform. First spiny ray of dorsal fin very high, the 3—4 rays behind it small. (Figure 955) . . . . 467. **Triacanthidae**

5 (2). Left and right ventrals not expressed as independent fins; instead of them there is only one ray situated at the posterior end of the pelvic bone, or else ventral fins are absent altogether. Premaxillaries and maxillaries grown together. Scales of rhombic form.

6 (7). A long barbel on the chin. Gill openings situated in front of the vertical through the anterior margin of the eye. [Vertebrae 29—30] . . . . 471. **Psilocephalidae**

7 (6). No barbel on the chin. Gill openings situated behind the vertical through the anterior margin of the eye. [Fewer than 29 vertebrae.]

8 (9). First dorsal fin consisting of 3 spiny rays, rarely of 2; the first ray is considerably larger than the other(s). Scales comparatively large, coarse, arranged in a clear order and forming a kind of armor. Soft rays of fins branched. [Vertebrae 17—18.] Eight teeth in outer rows of both jaws; 6 teeth in the inner row of the upper jaw. (Figure 956) . . . . 469. **Balistidae**

9 (8). First dorsal fin consisting of one spiny ray; there is usually one small ray at its base. Scales small, weakly ossified, arranged haphazardly, often not touching each other, and creating a rough velutinous surface on the body. Soft rays of fins not branched. [Vertebrae 18—21.] Six teeth in outer rows of both jaws; 4 teeth in the inner row of the upper jaw. (Figure 957) . . . . 470. Aluteridae

[156] This suborder, with all its families except for family 474. Triodontidae, which has fused teeth and a beak, was referred by Le Danois (1955) to order 50. Perciformes. We cannot agree with this.

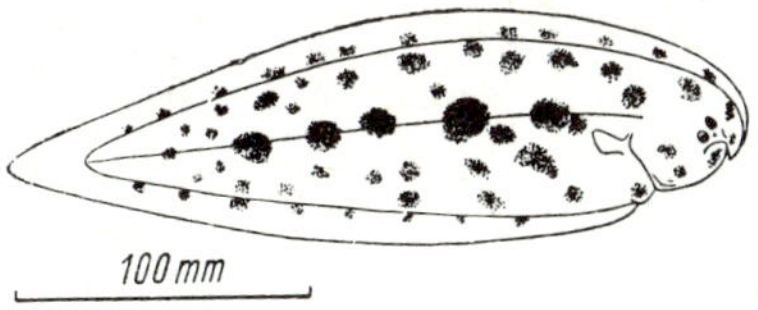

FIGURE 945. Soleidae (Synapturinae) — Synaptura punctatissima (Fowler, 1936, fig. 248, diagr.)

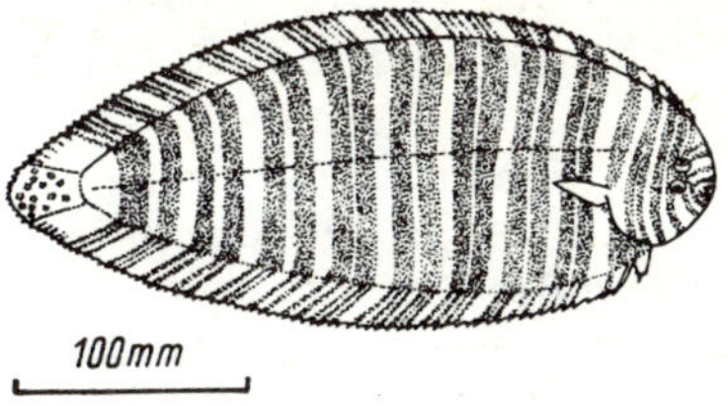

FIGURE 946. Soleidae (Soleinae) — Zebrias zebra (Okada, 1955, fig. 353, diagr.)

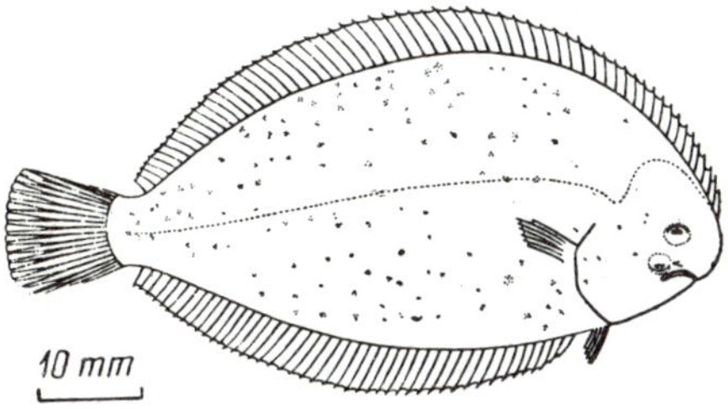

FIGURE 947. Soleidae (Soleinae) — Solea ovata (Chu et al., 1962, fig. 767, diagr.)

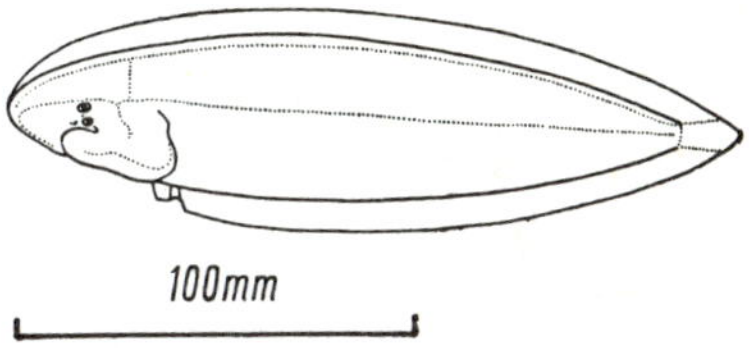

FIGURE 948. Cynoglossidae (Cynoglossinae) — Cynoglossus macrolepidotus (Fowler, 1937, fig. 194, diagr.)

FIGURE 949. Cynoglossidae (Symphurinae) — Symphurus marginatus (J. and E., 1900, fig. 949, diagr.)

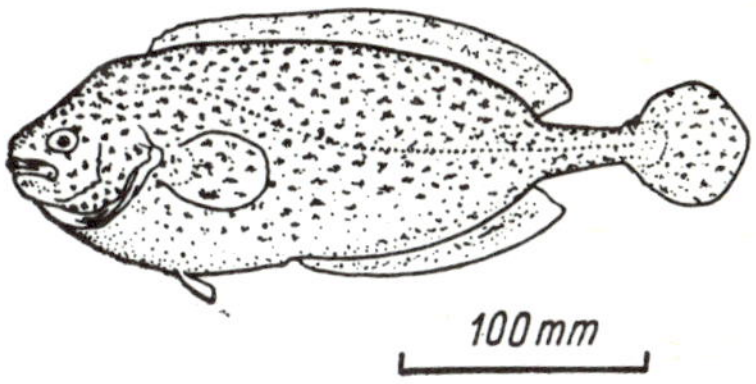

FIGURE 950. Icosteidae — Icosteus aenigmaticus, juv. (M., 1955, II, fig. 509, diagr.)

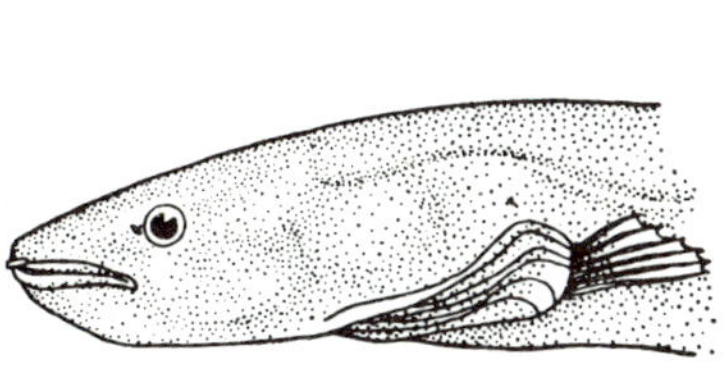

FIGURE 951. Chaudhuriidae — Chaudhuria caudata (M., 1955, II, fig. 510)

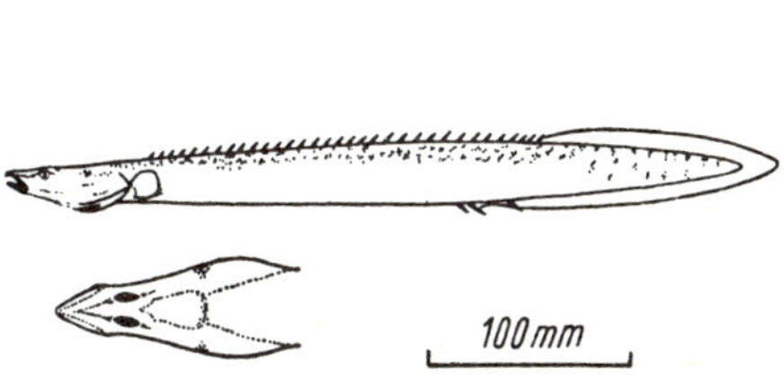

FIGURE 952. Mastacembelidae — Mastacembelus aculeatus (M., 1955, II, fig. 512)

10 (1). Pelvic bones absent; no ventral fins and no spiny rays replacing them. Dorsal fin also without spiny rays.
11 (14). Teeth not fused, clearly distinguishable, and not forming a beak. Body encased in an armor consisting of numerous polygonal bony plates. (Suborder 58.2. **Ostracoidei.**)
12 (11). Armor reaching only to the end of the base of the dorsal and anal fins. Abdominal ridge of armor more or less developed. [6 truncal vertebrae, 10 caudal.] (Figure 958) . . . . 473. **Aracanidae**
13 (12). Armor reaching beyond the end of the base of the dorsal and anal fins, or at least the end of the anal, but at any rate there is a small isolated plate behind the base of the dorsal. An abdominal ridge of armor is absent. [9—10 truncal vertebrae, 5—6 caudal.] (Figure 959). . . . . 472. **Ostraciontidae**
14 (11). Teeth fused and forming a beak. Body not encased in armor.
15 (20). Caudal peduncle present. Caudal fin well developed, of normal form. [Swim bladder present; capacity for inflation.] (Suborder 58.3. **Tetraodontoidei.**)
16 (19). Tooth plate of upper jaw, or else of both jaws, with a suture.
17 (18). Suture retained only on the upper tooth plate. The impression is of 3 teeth. Adominal part of body enlarged, laterally flattened, the skin on it wrinkled, with fanlike folds; it can be strongly inflated. (Figure 690) . . . . 474. **Triodontidae**
18 (17). Suture present both on upper and on lower tooth plate, giving the impression of 4 teeth . . . . 475. **Tetraodontidae**

2 subfamilies:

1 (2). Back broadly rounded. Body not, or very weakly, laterally compressed. Head wide. Nares usually clearly distinguishable. (Figure 961) . . . . subfamily 475.1. Tetraodontinae
2 (1). Back more or less sharply contoured. Body showing marked lateral compression. Head tapering, with a slightly elongate snout. Nares atrophied or very small and represented by a poorly discernible rim with a small aperture. (Figure 962) . . . . subfamily 475.2. Canthigasterinae

19 (18). Tooth plate of upper and lower jaw without a suture, so that the impression is of only 2 teeth. (Figure 963) . . . 476. **Diodontidae**
20 (17). Caudal peduncle absent, caudal fin with a very wide base. [No swim bladder, and no capacity for inflation.] (Suborder 58.4. **Moloidei.**) (Figure 964) . . . . 477. **Molidae**

Order 59. GOBIESOCIFORMES (thesis 0—41)

1 family: 478. **Gobiesocidae.**

8 subfamilies:

1 (8). Gills 3 $^1/_2$.
2 (5). Branchiostegal membranes free of the interbranchial space.

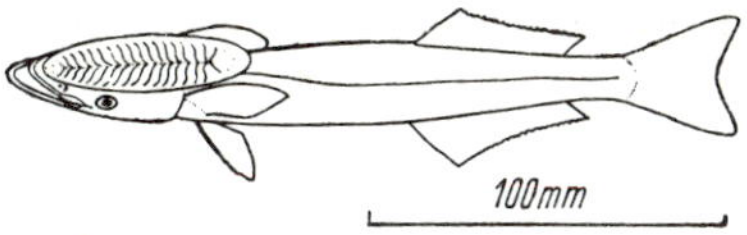

FIGURE 953. Echeneidae — *Remora remora* (Wang, 1958, fig. 590, diagr.)

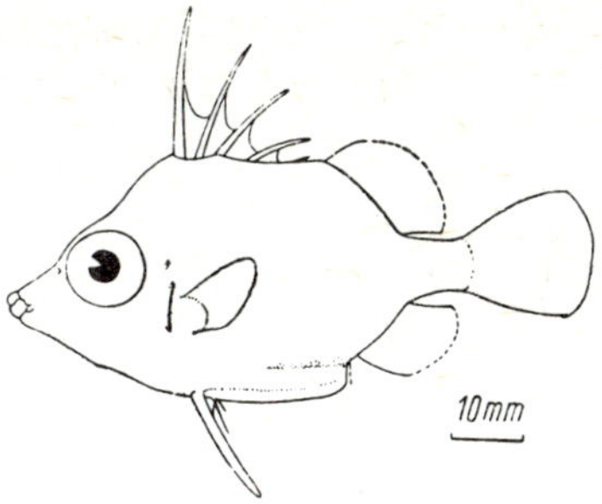

FIGURE 954. Triacanthodidae — *Triacanthodes anomalus* (M., 1955, III, fig. 350, diagr.)

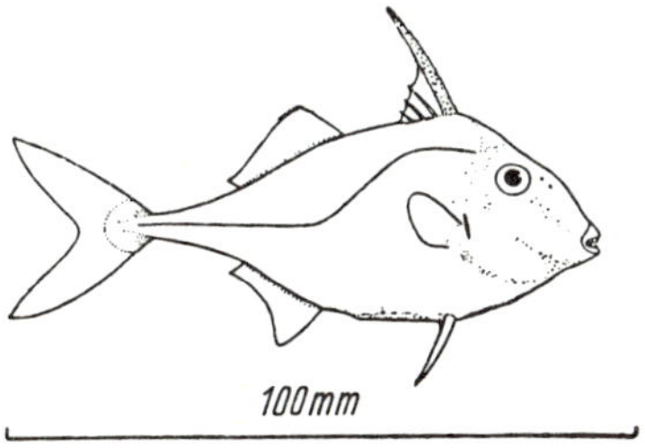

FIGURE 955. Triacanthidae — *Triacanthus brevirostris* (L. and L., 1965, fig. 36)

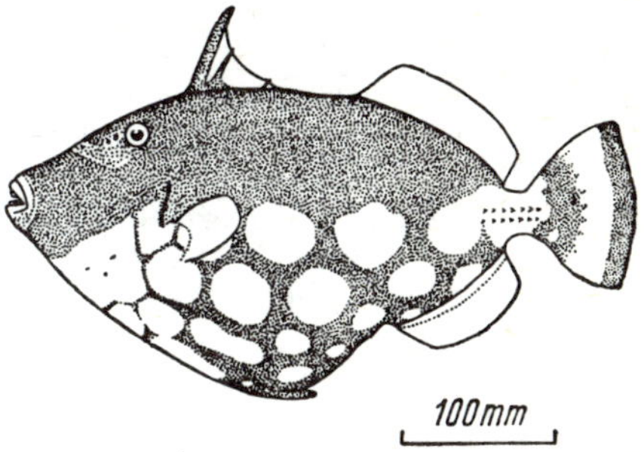

FIGURE 956. Balistidae — *Balistes conspicillum* (Smith, 1950, pl. 90, fig. 1161, diagr.)

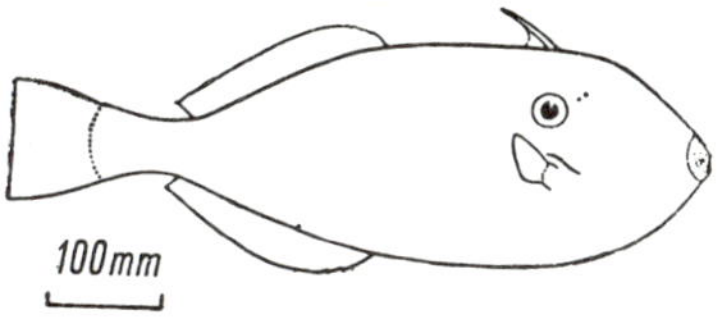

FIGURE 957. Aluteridae — *Aluterus monoceros* (Wang, 1958, fig. 608, diagr.)

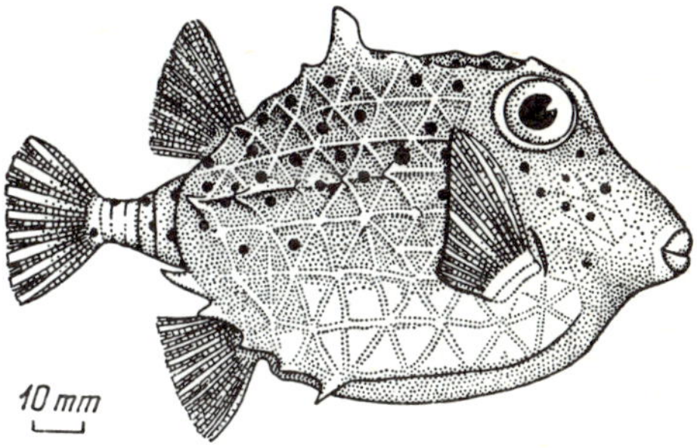

FIGURE 958. Aracanidae — *Kentrocapros aculeatus* (M., 1955, III, fig. 356)

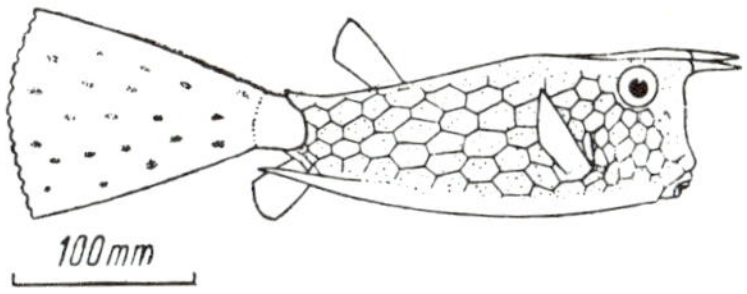

FIGURE 959. Ostraciontidae — *Lactoria cornutus* (Wang, 1958, fig. 611, diagr.)

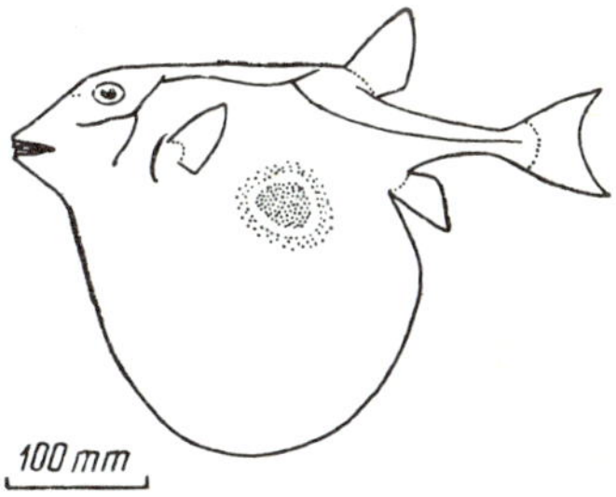

FIGURE 960. Triodontidae — *Triodon bursarius* (M., 1955, II, fig. 355, diagr.)

3 (4). Disk double. (Indian Ocean and western part of the Pacific north as far as Japan). . . . . .subfamily 478.1. Trachelochisminae

4 (3). Disk single. (New Zealand) . . . . subfamily 478.2. Haplocylicinae

5 (2). Branchiostegal membranes attached to the interbranchial space.

6 (7). Disk double. (All eastern Atlantic species and one from South Africa). . . . . subfamily 478.3. Lepadogasterinae

7 (6). Disk single. (South Africa) . . . . subfamily 478.8. Chorisochisminae

8 (1). Gills 3.

9 (12). Branchiostegal membranes free of the interbranchial space.

10 (11). Disk double. (South Africa, Indian Ocean, and western Pacific) subfamily 478.4. Diplocrepinae

11 (10). Disk single. (All species of the New World and one from South Africa). . . . . subfamily 478.5. Gobiesocinae

12 (9). Branchiostegal membranes attached to the interbranchial space.

13 (14). Disk double. (Indian Ocean and western Pacific north as far as Japan.) (Figure 965) . . . . . . subfamily 478.6. Aspasminae

14 (13). Disk single. (South Africa, Indian Ocean, and western Pacific). (Figure 966) . . . . subfamily 478.7. Diademichthyinae

Order 60. BATRACHOIDIFORMES (thesis 0—169)

1 family: 479. **Batrachoididae** (Figure 967).

Order 61. LOPHIIFORMES (thesis 0—67)

3 suborders, 15 families (480—494):

1 (10). Ventral fins present. [Infrapharyngeal bones generally well developed and bearing teeth.] Males not pygmies.

2 (3). Spiny dorsal fin with more than 3 rays. Apart from the first ray, the ilicium, there are another 3 separate rays and then 3 more rays which are joined by a membrane. Pseudobranchs present. Three pairs of gills, fully developed on gill arch I and absent on arch IV. Mouth almost terminal, slightly half-superior, very large, and opening into the wide pharynx. Body markedly flattened. (Suborder 61.1. **Lophioidei**.) (Figure 968) . . . . 480. **Lophiidae**

3 (2). Not more than 3 rays in the spiny dorsal fin. Pseudobranchs absent or rudimentary. Gills developed on arches II and III; gills absent on arches I and IV or reduced to hemibranchs. (Suborder 61.2. **Antennarioidei**.)

4 (7). Spiny dorsal fin with 3 spiny rays: the first, in the form of an ilicium, and 2 (sometimes represented externally as tubercles)

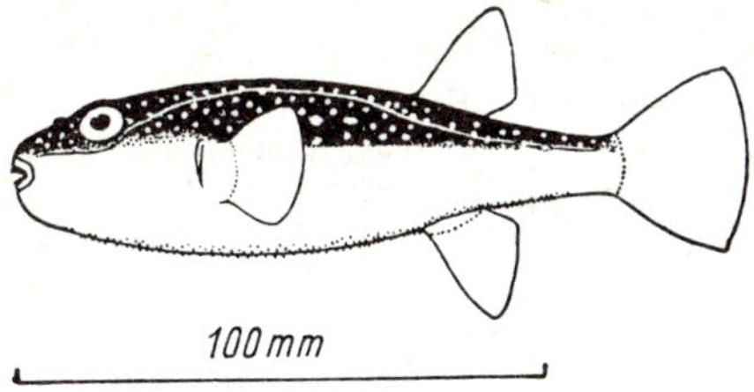

FIGURE 961. Tetraodontidae (Tetraodontinae) — Fugu niphobles (Okada, 1955, fig. 269, diagr.)

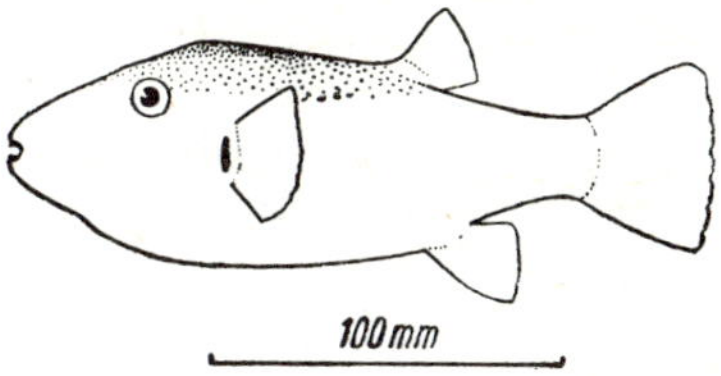

FIGURE 962. Tetraodontidae (Canthigasterinae) — Canthigaster rivulatus (Abe, 1958, fig. 41, B, diagr.)

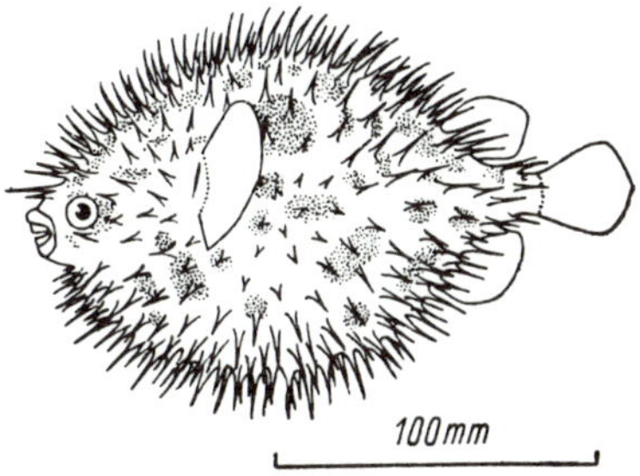

FIGURE 963. Diodontidae — Diodon holocanthus (Okada, 1955, fig. 275, diagr.)

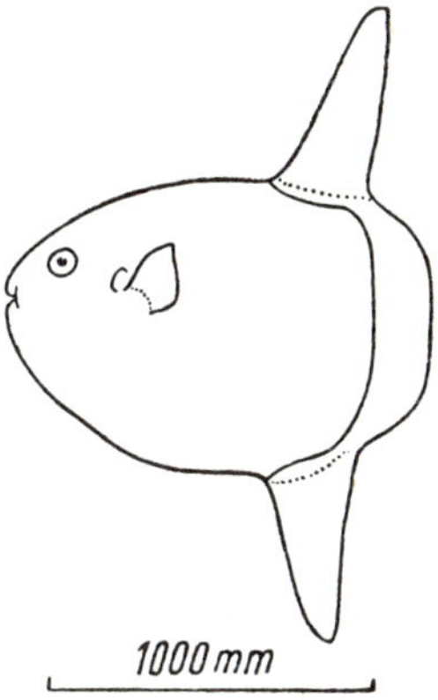

FIGURE 964. Molidae — Mola mola (Wang, 1958, fig. 622, diagr.)

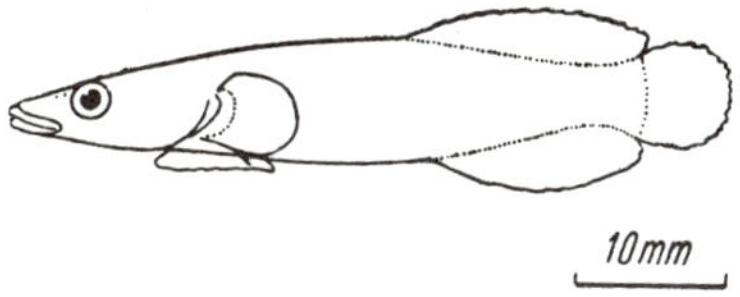

FIGURE 965. Gobiesocidae (Aspasminae) — Aspasma misakia (L. and L., 1965, fig. 8)

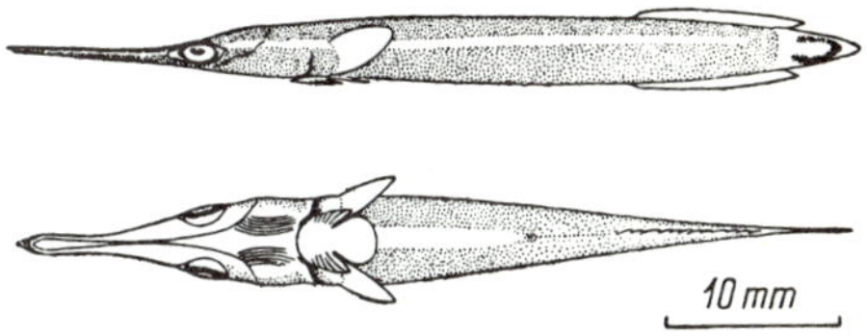

FIGURE 966. Gobiesocidae (Diademichthyinae) — Diademichthys lineatus (Briggs, 1955, fig. 114, diagr.)

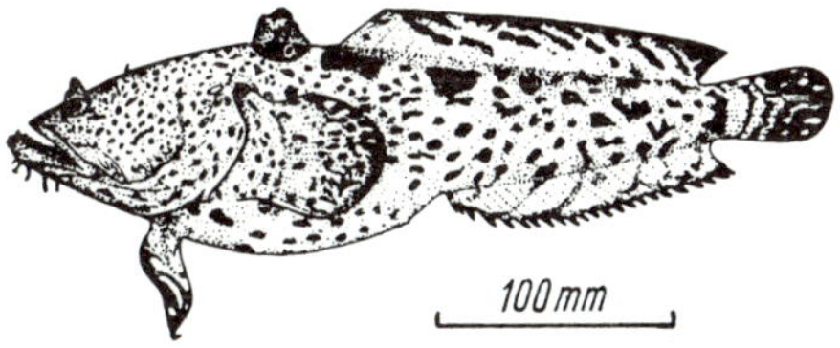

FIGURE 967. Batrachoididae — Opsanus pardus (Jordan, 1925, fig. 648)

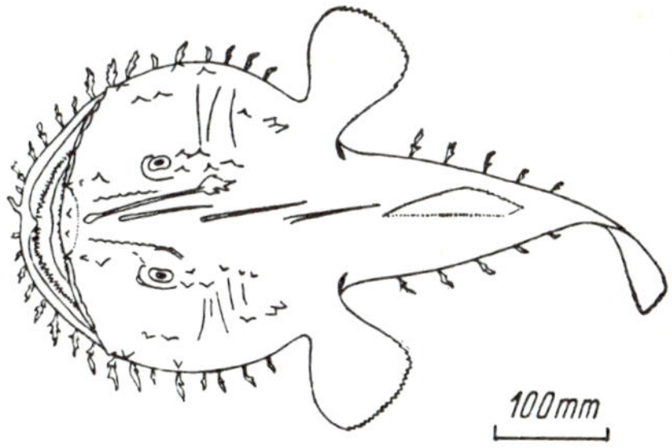

FIGURE 968. Lophiidae — Lophiomus setigerus (L. and L., 1965, fig. 16)

separated from each other or connected by a membrane. Mouth of moderate size, oblique, half-superior. Body more or less laterally compressed, not strongly vertically flattened.

5 (6). Second and third ray of spiny dorsal fin connected by a membrane along their whole height. Gill openings situated behind the base of the pectoral fins [in which there are 2 radials]. (Figure 969). . . . . 482. **Brachionichthyidae**

6 (5). Second and third ray of spiny dorsal fin sometimes expressed as tubercles that are separate or connected only at the base. Gill openings situated under the base of the pectoral fins [in which there are 3 radials] . . . . 481. **Antennariidae**

2 subfamilies:

1 (2). Body quite deep. Mouth of moderate size, vertical or oblique. Teeth well developed. Eyes situated on the sides of the head, not protruding from the orbits. Ventral fins not joined to pectorals by a membrane, free. (Figure 970) . . . . subfamily 481.1. Antennariinae

2 (1). Body slightly elongate. Mouth small, transverse, superior. Teeth weak. Eyes situated on top of the head, protruding from the orbits. Ventral fins joined by a membrane to the base of the pectorals . . . . subfamily 481.2. Tetrabrachiinae

7 (4). Spiny dorsal fin with only one ray, transformed into an ilicium.

8 (9). Mouth of moderate size, very oblique, superior. Gill openings situated behind the pectoral fins [in which there are 3 radials]. Ilicium under the snout. (Figure 971) . . . . . .483. **Chaunacidae**

9 (8). Mouth small, horizontal, subterminal or inferior. Gill openings situated above the pectoral fins [in which there are 2 radials]. Ilicium set in a depression on the anterior end of the snout. (Figure 972) . . . . 484. **Ogcocephalidae**

10 (1). Ventral fins absent. [Infrapharyngeal bones reduced, without teeth.] Males always pygmies, sometimes parasitize on females. No pseudobranchs. (Suborder 61.3. **Ceratioidei.**)

11 (12). No ilicium.[157] There are long, slightly curved, mobile teeth on the outsides of the jaws. II D 11—13, A 10—13. (Figure 973) . . . . 491. **Neoceratiidae**

12 (11). Ilicium present.

13 (14). There is no distinctly expressed club-shaped thickening with a luminescent organ on the tip of the ilicium. II D 14—22, A 13—19. (Figure 974) . . . . 493. **Caulophrynidae**

14 (13). There is a club-shaped thickening with a luminescent organ on the tip of the ilicium.

[157] A modified ray of the first dorsal fin, situated on the head, is absent also in Laevoceratias Parr, 1927, which was referred to a special family, Laevoceratiidae but placed by Bertelsen (1951 : 67) in family 486. Diceratiidae (see thesis 61—11, footnote); there are no long, mobile teeth in Laevoceratias, and there are no more than 6 rays in the dorsal and anal fins.

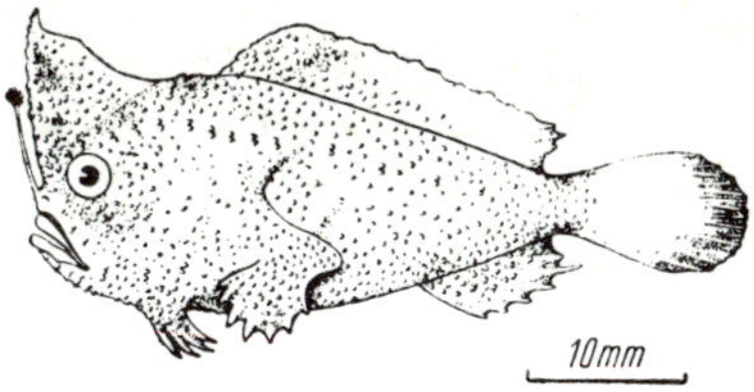

FIGURE 969. Brachionichthyidae – Sympetrichthys verrucosus (McCulloch and Waite, 1918, pl. 7, fig. 3, diagr.)

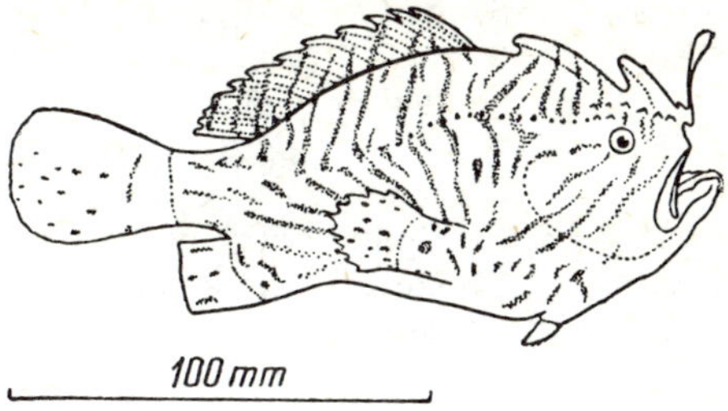

FIGURE 970. Antennariidae (Antennariinae) – Antennarius hispidus (Day, 1878, pl. 60, fig. 2, diagr.)

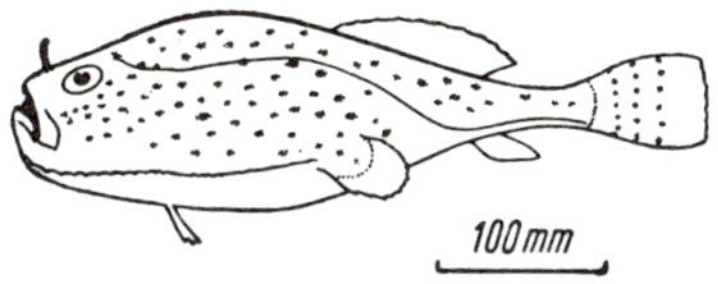

FIGURE 971. Chaunacidae – Chaunax fimbriatus (Okada, 1955, fig. 390, diagr.)

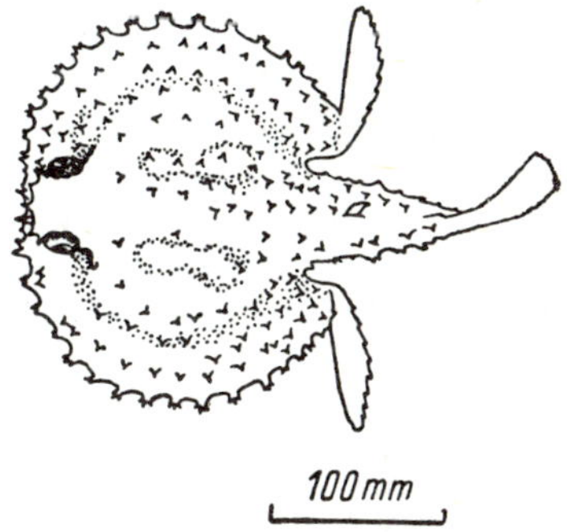

FIGURE 972. Ogcocephalidae – Halieutea stellata (Okada, 1955, fig. 391, diagr.)

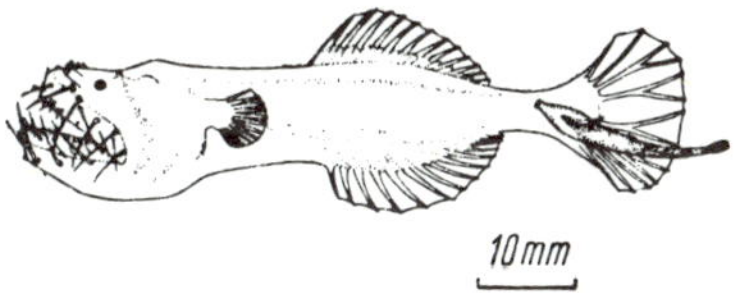

FIGURE 973. Neoceratiidae – Neoceratias spinifer (Bertelsen, 1951, fig. 106D)

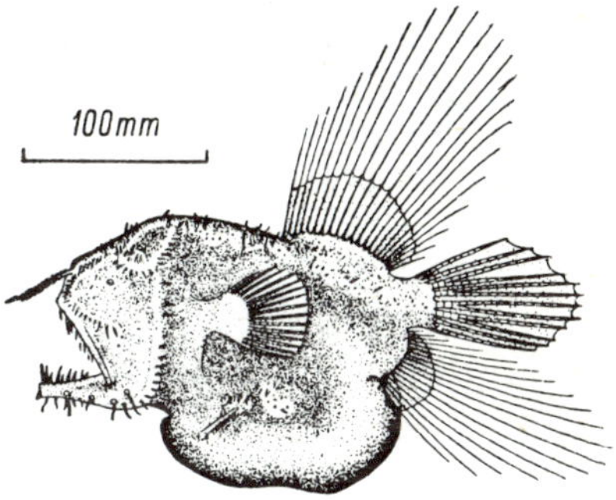

FIGURE 974. Caulophrynidae – Caulophryne jordani (Bertelsen, 1951, fig. 12)

FIGURE 975. Melanocetidae – Melanocetus murroyi (Günther, 1887, pl. 11, A, diagr.)

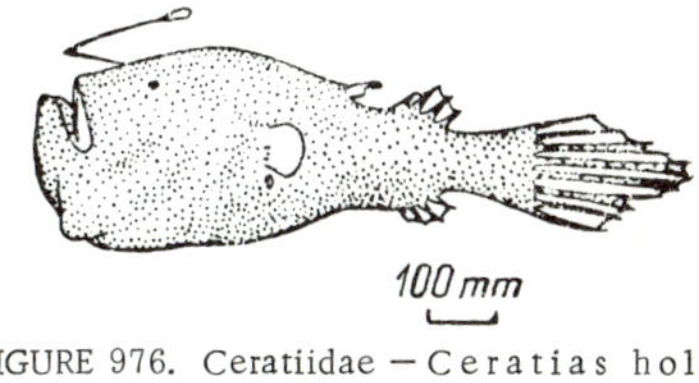

FIGURE 976. Ceratiidae – Ceratias holbolli (Gosline and Brock, 1960, fig. 25)

15 (16). Second dorsal fin with more than 11 rays. II D 12—17, A 3—4. (Figure 975) . . . . 485. **Melanocetidae**

16 (15). Second dorsal fin with fewer than 11 rays.

17 (18). Back bearing 2—3 small fleshy outgrowths. II D 3—5, A 3—5. (Figure 976) . . . . 492. **Ceratiidae**

18 (17). No fleshy outgrowths on the back.

19 (20). There is a second ilicium, but smaller. II D 4—6, A 4. (Figure 977) . . . . 486. **Diceratiidae**

20 (19). Second ilicium absent.

21 (22). Body slender, without thickenings or expansions in the region of the head. Ilicium filamentous, very long. (Figure 978) . . . . 490. **Gigantactinidae**

22 (21). Body markedly thickened or expanded in the anterior part. Ilicium small or of moderate length; thickening often with velutinous processes.

23 (28). Body covered with small spines.

24 (25). There is a small, papilla-like hyoid barbel. Skin covered with numerous small, close-packed spines. II D 5—7, A 5—6. (Figure 979) . . . . 489. **Centrophrynidae**

25 (24). No hyoid barbel. Spines distributed less densely, markedly scattered.

26 (27). Premaxillaries, armed with strong teeth, projecting markedly in front of the apex of the lower jaw; mouth subterminal. Spines small and thin, set directly in the skin. II D 4—6, A 4. (Figure 980) . . . . 488. **Oneirodidae**[158]

27 (26). Premaxillaries not protruding in front of lower jaw. Spines set in the center of plates scattered over the body. II D 5—6, A 4—5. (Figure 981) . . . . 487. **Himantolophidae**

28 (23). Body bare.

29 (30). Branchiostegal rays numbering 4—5. Second dorsal fin with not more than 4 rays. II D 2—4, A 2—4. (Figures 982, 983) . . . . 494. **Linophrynidae**

30 (29). Six branchiostegal rays. Second dorsal fin with more than 4 rays. II D [?]—8, A 4—7. (Figure 984) . . . 488. **Oneirodidae**

Order 62. PEGASIFORMES (thesis 0—39)

1 family: 495. **Pegasidae** (Figure 985).

[158] Two genera, *Thaumatichthys* Smith and Radcliffe, 1912 and *Amacrodon* Regan and Trewavas, 1932.

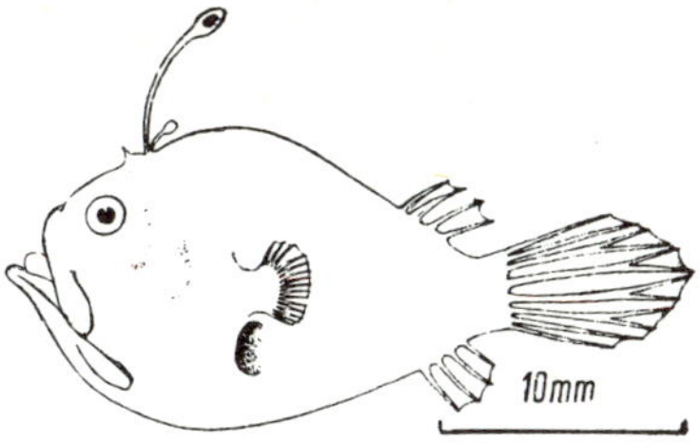

FIGURE 977. Diceratiidae — Diceratias glomerosus (Fowler, 1936, fig. 563)

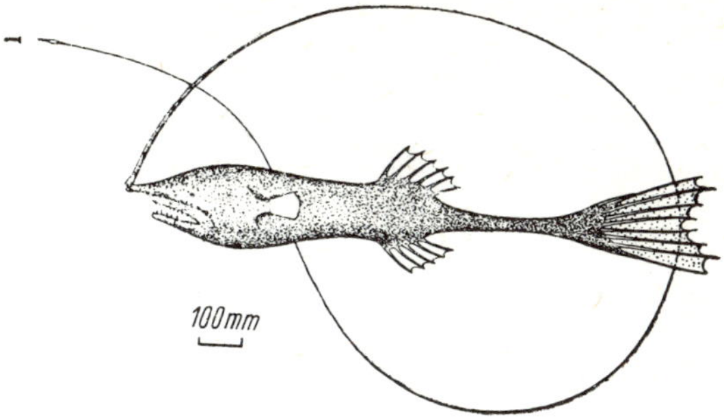

FIGURE 978. Gigantacinidae — Gigantactis macronema (Bertelsen, 1951, fig. 100)

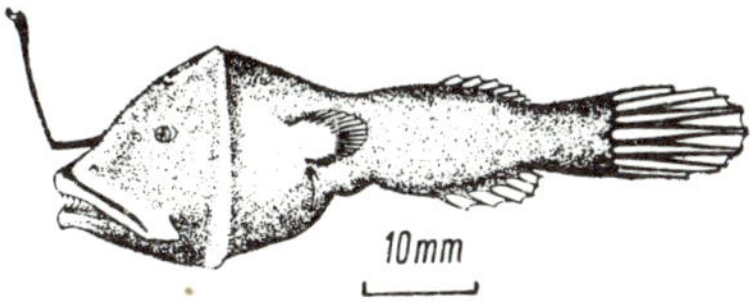

FIGURE 979. Centrophrynidae — Centrophryne spinulosa (Bertelsen, 1951, fig. 85, c)

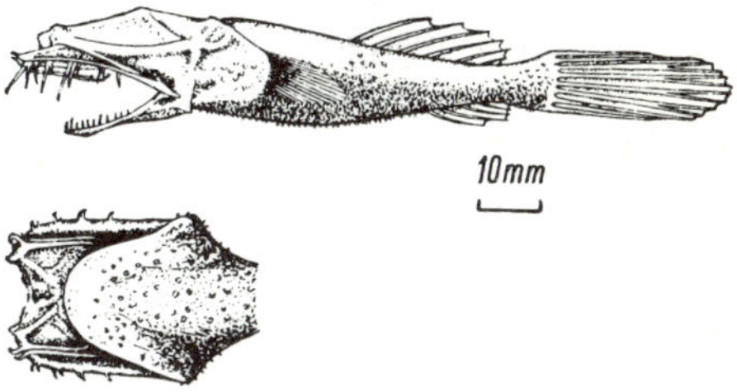

FIGURE 980. Oneirodidae — Thaumatichthys pagidostomus (Bertelsen, 1951, fig. 80, c,d)

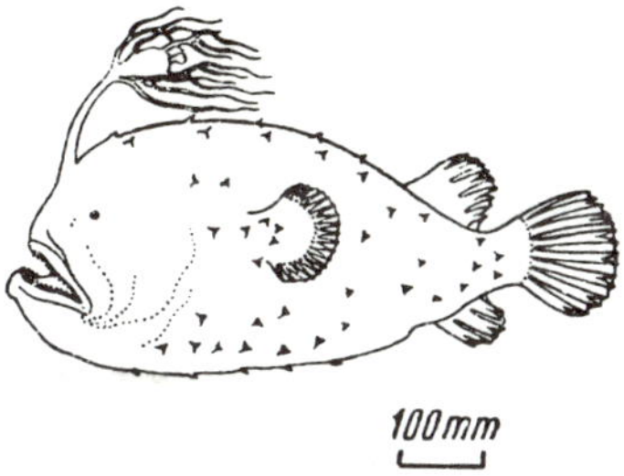

FIGURE 981. Himantolophidae — Himantolophus groenlandicus (Abe, 1958, fig. 3, diagr.)

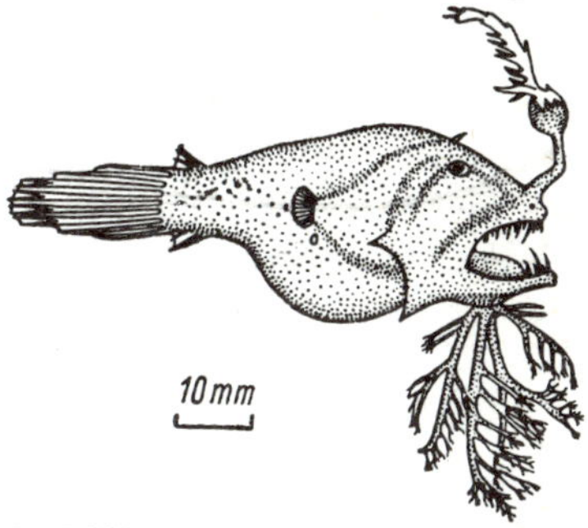

FIGURE 982. Linophrynidae — Linophryna arborifera (M., 1955, II, fig. 535, diagr.)

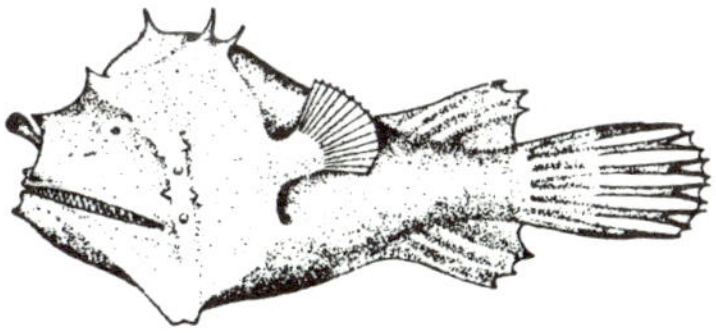

FIGURE 983. Linophrynidae — Photocorynus spiniceps (Bertelsen, 1951, fig. 109)

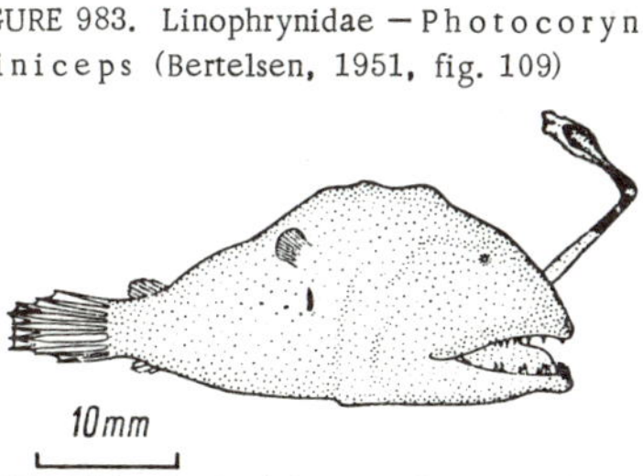

FIGURE 984. Oneirodidae — Chaenophryne parviconus (M., 1955, II, fig. 536)

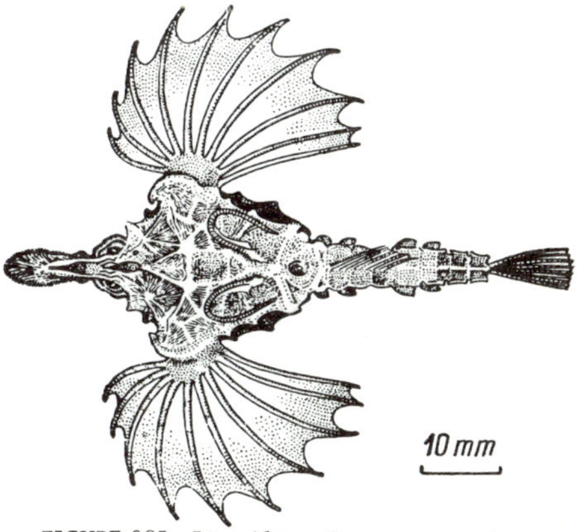

FIGURE 985. Pegasidae — Pegasus umitengu (Jordan, 1925, fig. 359)

CHECKLIST OF FAMILIES

This section contains a complete list of families from all over the world. Each family is given with:

its serial number

its name transcribed in accordance with the regulations of the XV International Zoological Congress

references to pp. I and II of Berg's "Classification of Fishes"

the thesis of the key

figure reference

Latin synonyms in parentheses

local names

published sources, arranged in chronological order

distribution

number of genera and species

commercial importance

The following notation and abbreviations have been used:

1 order (3)—number of orders in the class and their serial numbers (see Class 3. Myxini).

3 families (3—5)—number of families in the order and their serial numbers (see Order 3. Myxiniformes).

(37/41)—the serial numbers of the family in Berg's 1940 and 1955 works. The slashes signify that Berg gave a different spelling of the name of the family (see family 4. Eptatretidae).

(—/—)- means that the family is not mentioned in Berg (see family 21. Dalatiidae).

(86A/96)—the letter or number signifies that Berg mentions the name as a subfamily or as one not to be considered valid (see family 10. Rhinocodontidae).

The sign = placed in front of a name in parentheses indicates that it is a synonym.

The sign + designates a family which is not recognized as valid in the present work but has been attributed to the particular family (see family 16. Scyliorhinidae).

k'o and ka—endings of local national names of families, the first in Chinese and the second in Japanese.

Lit.—published sources.

J—Jordan, 1923; N—Norman, 1958; G—Golvan, 1962; GRWM—Greenwood, Rosen, Weitzman, and Myers, 1966; MA—McAllister, 1968.

A colon—in the references denotes the word page and is followed by the page numbers.

A dash after a colon means that the family is not mentioned in the given work.

Slashes signify that the name of the family on this page differs from the one adopted in the present work and is placed in the list of synonyms.

GRWM: 397, 417+family 212—means that these authors include family 212, recognized by us as a separate family, in the composition of the family mentioned in our work (see family 211. Macrouridae).

GRWM: (397) (family 211)—means that these authors do not recognize family 212 as valid and include it in family 211 (see family 212. Macrourodidae).

Commercial importance is assessed only for families of marine fishes that are included in world fishing statistics. The following expressions are used:

Extremely important—over 5,000,000 tons
Very important—from 1,000,000—to 5,000,000 tons
Important—500,000—1,000,000 tons
Fairly important—100,000—500,000 tons
Little important—10,000—100,000 tons
Unimportant—100—10,000 tons

Berg (Selected Works, IV, 1961 : 251) includes Sumatra, Java, and Borneo in Indonesia.

PHYLUM VERTEBRATA

Berg, 1940: 97. 2 subphyla.

Subphylum 1. ACRANIA

(Cephalocordata, Leptocardii, Myelozoa)

(Berg, 1940: 97, 1 class (1).

Class 1. *Amphioxi.* Berg, 1940: 98. 1 order (1).

Order 1. BRANCHIOSTOMATIFORMES (1/1), thesis 0—1. (Cirrostomi, Amphioxiformes.) Berg, 1940: 98. 1 family (1).

Family 1. **Branchiostomatidae** (1/1), thesis 1—0. Figure 176. (=Branchiostomidae=Amphioxidae,+Epigonichthyidae, +Asymmetrontidae,+Amphioxididae.) Lancelets, wench'ang yük'o, namekuji uo ka, lantsetnikovye.

Lit. J: (81); N: —; Berg, 1940: 98: Jordan and Snyder, 1901: 725—734; Hubbs, 1922: 1—16; Franz, 1922: 418; Nichols, 1929: 161—295; Pietschmann, 1933: 127—208, 209—336; Bigelow and Farfante, 1948: 1—28; Tortonese, 1956: 1—334; Lindberg and Legeza, 1959: 14—16.

Tropical, subtropical, and partly temperate seas. 3 subfamilies, 4 genera, more than 10 species. Fished locally.

Subphylum 2. CRANIATA
Berg, 1940: 98. 2 superclasses.

Superclass 1. AGNATHA.
(Cyclostomata). 2 classes (2, 3).

Class 2. *Petromyzones.* (Hyperoartii, Marsipobranchii ex parte, Cyclostomata ex parte, Cyclostomia ex parte.) Berg, 1940: 1906; Ogilby, 1896: 388—426; Berg, 1906: 173—188; Regan, 1911: 193—204; Holly, 1933: 1—62; Berg, 1937: 1277—1280; Bigelow and Schroeder, 1948: 29—58. 1 order (2).

Order 2. PETROMYZONIFORMES 6/7, thesis 0—4. Lampreys, lamproies, Neunaugen. Berg, 1940: 106. 1 family (2).

Family 2. **Petromyzonidae** 15/18, thesis 2—0. Figures 177, 178. (=Petromyzontidae, +Geotriidae=Mordaciidae). Lampreys, lamproies, Neunaugen, minogovye.

Lit. J: 83; N: 1; G: 7; Jordan and Snyder, 1901: 725—734; Berg, 1911: 1—337; Regan, 1911: 193—204; Creaser and Hubbs, 1922: 1—14; Berg, 1931: 87—116; Holly, 1933: 1—62; Drensky, 1935: 102—106; Hubbs and Trautman, 1937: 1—109; Bigelow and Schroeder, 1948: 43—58; Vladykov, 1949: 1—67; Berg, 1948—49: 25—26; Andriyashev, 1954: 25—28; Lindberg and Legeza, 1959: 16—21; Buen, 1959: 257—270; 1961: 101—124; Zanandrea, 1961: 523—534; Sterba, 1962: 263—344; Strahan, 1964: 334—336; Vladykov and Follet, 1967: 1067—1075; Potter and Strahan, 1968: 229—240, Add.— Potter et al. 1968: 533—546.

1,2

Freshwater and diadromous forms of temperate regions in both hemispheres. 2 subfamilies, 8 genera, more than 20 species. Little important.

Class 3. *Myxini* (Hyperotreti). Berg, 1940: 112. 1 order (3).

Order 3. MYXINIFORMES 15/17, thesis 0—5. (Myxinoidei, Hyperotreta.) Berg, 1940: 113; Berg, 1937: 1277—1280; Bigelow and Schroeder, 1948: 29—58 (31—42); Adam and Strahan, 1963: 1—8. 3 families (3—5).

Family 3. **Myxinidae** 38/42. thesis 3—1. Figure 179. Myxines, hagfishes, hags, mangman k'o, mekura unagi ka.

Lit. J: 82, N: 4; G: 7; Jordan and Snyder, 1901: 725—734; Regan, 1913: 395—398; Bigelow and Schroeder, 1948: 31—42; Nani and Gneri, 1951: 183—224; Richardson, 1953: 379—383; 1958: 283—287; Andriyashev, 1954: 29—31; Lindberg and Legeza, 1959: 21—26; Adam and Strahan, 1963: 1—8.

Atlantic and Pacific oceans; mainly temperate regions of both hemispheres; moderate depths. 4—5 genera, about 10 species.

Family 4. **Eptatretidae** (36/41), thesis 3—4. Figure 181. (=Bdellostomidae=Heptatretidae=Bdellostomatidae, Myxinidae ex parte.) Borers, bdellostomes, nien manman k'o, nuta unagi ka, piyavkorotye miksiny.

Lit. J: 82; N: (5); G: 7; Regan, 1912: 534—536; Strahan, 1962: 801—807. Temperate regions of seas in both hemispheres. 1 genus, about 10 species.

Family 5. **Paramyxinidae** 37/(41), thesis 3—3. Figure 180. (Myxinidae ex parte, Eptatretidae ex parte.) Fu manman k'o, kuro mekura unagi ka.

Lit. J: (82); N: (5); G: (7); Dean 1904: 1—23; Matsubara, 1937: 13—15; Strahan and Honma, 1961: 323—342; Strahan, 1962: 471—473.

Coasts of Japan. 1 genus and 1 species.

Superclass 2. GNATHOSTOMATA
Berg, 1940: 115. 4 classes (4—7).

Class 4. *Elasmobranchii* (Euselachii). Berg, 1940: 130; Jordan and Fowler 1903, : 593—674; Regan, 1906: 722—758; Berg, 1911: 1—337; Phillipps, 1924: 257—269; Ehrenbaum, 1927: 1—66; Fang and Wang. 1932: 213—283; Liu, 1932; 133—190; Wang, 1933: 87—177; Daniel, 1934: 1—331; Tang, 1934: 29—111; 1935: 165—173; White, 1936: 1—16; 1937: 25—138; Bigelow and Schroeder, 1948: 59—546; 1953: 1—514; 1954: 37—87; Tortonese, 1956: 1—334; Klausewitz, 1959: 43—50; Buen, 1960: 1—50; Chu, 1960: 1—225; Glikman, 1964: 89—107. 1 subclass.

Subclass *Selachii.* Sharks and skates. (Euselachii, Plagiostomi, Chondropterygii, Amacea; Chondrichthyes.) Berg, 1940: 133; Müller and Henle, 1903: 593—674; Pietschmann, 1908: 637—710; Engelhardt, 1913: 1—100; Garman, 1913: 1—528; Breder, 1928: 1—13; Phillipps, 1929: 98—107; Matsubara, 1936: 1—160; White, 1936: 1—16; 1937: 25—138; Bertin, 1939: 1—24; Bigelow and Schroeder, 1948: 59—546; 1953: 1—514; Poll, 1951: 1—154; Buen, 1960: 1—50; Krefft, 1961: 141—178; 1968: 33—76. 2 superorders, 7 orders (4—10).

Superorder A. *Selachoidei.* Sharks (Pleurotremata). Berg, 1940:133; Nichols and Murphy, 1916 : 1—34, Fowler, 1929 : 481—508; 1930 : 24—34, 79—88; Buen, 1931 : 8—23; Walford, 1935 : 1—66; Springer, 1938 : 1—66 (9—41); Whitley, 1940 :1—280; Beebe and Tee-Van, 1941 :1—34; Fowler, 1941 :1—879; Barnhart, 1944 :1—23; Müller and Mazet, 1946 :1—223; Phillipps, 1946 :1—20; Bigelow and Schroeder, 1948 : 59—546; Chen, 1948 :21—45; Roedel and Ripley, 1950 : 5—88; Poll. 1951 : 1—154; Misra, 1952; Bigelow and Schroeder, 1953 :1—64; Bott, 1953 :16—23; Scott, 1955 : 55—56; Lindberg and Legeza, 1959 : 1—208; Buen, 1959 : 171—201; 1960 : 3—50; Fourmanoir, 1961 : 3—81; Thompson and Springer, 1961 : 1—19; Chen, 1963 :1—102; Garrick and Schultz, 1963 : 3—60; Gilbert, 1963 :1—578; Abrey, 1964 : 1—95; McCormick and Young, 1964 :1—417; Glikman, 1964 :1—230; Gohar and Mazhar, 1964 :1—144; Stead, 1964 :1—211; Abrey, 1966 :161—255; Martisen, 1966 :1—31; Susumo et al., 1967; Maksimov, 1968 :1—26. Add.—Gilbert et al., 1967 :1—624; Kato et al., 1967 :1—47; Sadowsky, 1967 :71—88; Whitley, 1967 :173—188; Krefft, 1968 : 33—76. 5 orders (4—8). Sharks are of average importance in world marine fishing.

Order 4. HETERODONTIFORMES 36/40, thesis 0—12. (Cestraciontes, Heterodontoidea.), Berg, 1940 : 134. (Hexanchiformes, Heterodontoidei, Glikman, 1964 : 92, 93). 1 family (6).

Family 6. **Heterodontidae** 83/91, thesis 4—0. Figure 182. (=Cestraciontidae = Centraciontidae = Cestracionidae.) Rogatye akuly, bych'i akuly, horn sharks, bullhead sharks, requin de Port Jackson, husha k'o, neko zame ka.

Lit. J : 95; N : 24; G : 9; Regan, 1908 : 493—497; B. Smith, 1942 : 651—770; Bigelow and Schroeder, 1948 : 59—546 (95); Lindberg and Legeza, 1959 : 31—34; Glikman, 1964 : 93.

Indian and Pacific oceans. 1 genus, about 8 species.

Order 5. HEXANCHIFORMES 37/41, thesis 0—10. (Notidanoidei, Notidani + Chlamydoselachoidea. Selachophidichthyoidei, Hexanchoidea, Pteriodonta, Protoselachii, Diplospondyli.) Berg, 1940 : 136; Bigelow and Schroeder, 1948 : 77—92; Arambourg and Bertin, 1958 : 2025; Glikman, 1964 : 92. 2 families (7—8).

Family 7. **Hexanchidae** 85/93, thesis 5—2. Figure 184. (+ Heptranchidae = = Notidanidae = "Hexeptranchidae" Garman.) Grebnezubye akuly, cowsharks, griset, perlon, liu sai sha k'o, kagura zame ka.

Lit. J : 97; N : 7; G:9; Garman, 1884 : 3—15; Rivero, 1941 : 1—9; Bigelow and Schroeder, 1948 : 59—546 (77—93); Lindberg and Legeza, 1959 : 28—31; Glikman, 1964: 93.

Tropical and subtropical waters of oceans. 3 genera, several species.

Family 8. **Chlamydoselachidae** 84/92, thesis 5—1. Figure 183. (Chlamydoselachiformes Glikman.) Frilled sharks, requin-frangé, chousai sha k'o, rabuka ka, plashchenosnye akuly.

Lit. J : 97: N : 6; G : 9; Garman, 1884 : 3—15; Bigelow and Schroeder, 1948 : 59—546 (93—94); Lindberg and Legeza, 1959 : 31—32; Glikman, 1964 : 91.

Eastern Atlantic and western Pacific (Japan); moderate depths. 1 genus, 1 species.

Order 6. LAMNIFORMES 38/42, thesis 0—13. (Galeoidei, Galeiformes, Isuria, Lamnoidei, Scyllioidei, Euselachii, Carcharinoidei, Isuriformes.) (Squatiniformes ex parte, Carchariniformes, Odontaspidiformes Glikman.) Berg, 1940: 137; White, 1936: 1—16; 1937: 25—138. Bigelow and Schroeder, 1948: 59—546 (95—450); Arambourg and Bertin, 1958: 2029; Glikman, 1964: 93—106. 2 suborders, 11 families (9—19).

Suborder 1. Lamnoidei (Isuroidei). Berg, 1940: 137. 7 families (9—15).

Family 9. **Orectolobidae** 86/94, thesis 6—4. Figure 186. (+Hemiscylliidae, +Ginglymostomidae=Ginglystomidae.) (Squatiniformes, Ginglymostomatidae Glikman.) Carpet sharks, nurse sharks, requin-nourrice, requins-tapis, requins-zébrés, hsünsha k'o, tenjiku zame ka, kovrovye akuly.

Lit. J: 98; N: 11; G: 10, (12); Regan, 1908: 347—364; Ogilby and McCulloch, 1909: 264—299; Bigelow and Schroeder, 1948: 59—546 (178—187); Lindberg and Legeza, 1959: 37—42; Glikman, 1964: 96.

Tropical and subtropical, more rarely temperate regions of the Atlantic (Ginglymostoma) and Indian oceans and western Pacific. About 12 genera, a few species.

Family 10. **Rhincodontidae** (86A/96), thesis 6—2. Figure 185. (=Rhineodontidae). Whale sharks, requin-baleine, ching sha k'o jinbei zame ka, kitovye akuly.

Lit. J: (99): N: (10); G: (10); Bigelow and Schroeder, 1948: 187—194; McCann, 1954: 326—333; Lindberg and Legeza, 1959: 35—37.

Tropical, more rarely temperate, seas, pelagic zone. 1 genus, 1 species.

Family 11. **Odontaspidae** 87/95, thesis 6—19. Figure 197. (="Carchariidae" Garman et al.) (Odontaspidiformes ex parte Glikman.) Sand sharks, chuich'ih sha k'o, mizuwami ka, dlinnozubye akuly, peschanye akuly.

Lit. J: (99); N: 8; G: 10; Bigelow and Schroeder, 1948: 98—108; Lindberg and Legeza, 1959: 82—84; Glikman, 1964: 101.

Warm and temperate seas; near-bottom waters. 1 genus, about 6 species.

Family 12. **Scapanorhynchidae** 87A/95A, thesis 6—20. Figure 198. (=Mitsukurinidae, Odontaspidae ex parte.) (Odontaspidiformes, Scapanorhynchoidea Glikman.) Goblin sharks, chien wên sha k'o, mitsukuri zame ka, akuly domovye.

Lit. J: (99); N: (8, 9); G: (10), Jordan, 1898: 199—204; Bigelow and Schroeder, 1948: 109; Glikman, 1964: 191, 106.

Seas of Japan, Portugal, and possibly Australia. 1 genus, 1—2 species.

Family 13. **Lamnidae** (88/97), thesis 6—10. Figure 189. (Isuridae.) (Odontaspididae +Isuridae Glikman.) (Carcharodontidae.) Great white sharks, mackerel sharks, man-eaters, lamie, requin-bleu, taupe, porbeagle, Heringshai, sel'devye akuly, t'u sha k'o, nezumi zame ka.

Lit. J: (99): N: (9); G: 10; Bigelow and Schroeder, 1948: 109—145; Andriyashev, 1954: 33—37; Lindberg and Legeza, 1959: 50—57; Glikman, 1964: 101, 105; Garrick, 1967: 603—690.

Atlantic, Indian, and Pacific oceans. 3 genera, several species. Of commercial importance.

Family 13a. **Lamiostomatidae** (—/—), thesis 6—10, footnote. Figure 189A. (Odontaspidiformes, Isuroidea.)

Lit. J: —; N: —; G: —; Glikman, 1964: 105; 1964: 233, pl. 6; Garrick, 1967: 1967:663—690.

Pacific Ocean. 1 genus, 1 species.

Family 14. **Cetorhinidae** 88A/97A, thesis 6—11. Figure 190. (=Halsydridae, Lamnidae, ex parte) (Squatiniformes, Squaloidei Glikman.) Elephant sharks, basking sharks, pélerins, Riesenhai, lao sha k'o, uba zame ka, bol'shezhabernye akuly, gigantskie akuly.

Lit. J: 99; N: (10), G: 9: Bigelow and Schroeder 1948: 146—159; Siccardi, 1961: 61—101; Lindberg and Legeza, 1959: 57—58; Glikman, 1964: 64, 95.

Temperate latitudes of the Atlantic, Indian, and Pacific oceans; absent in tropical waters. 1 genus and 1 species.

Family 15. **Alopiidae** 88B/97B, thesis 6—15, Figure 192. (=Vulpeculidae, Lamnidae ex parte.) (Odontaspidiformes, Odontaspidoidea Glikman.) Fox sharks, whiptail sharks, thresher sharks, renards-de-mer, chienhai chang chienhai chang wei sha k'o, onaga zame ka, dlinnokhvostye akuly.

Lit. J: 99; N: (10); G: 9; Bigelow and Schroeder, 1948: 160—178; Lindberg and Legeza, 1959: 58—60; Glikman, 1964: 101.

Tropical and temperate latitudes of the Atlantic, Indian, and Pacific oceans. 1 genus, 4 species.

Suborder 2. S c y l i o r h i n o i d e i. (Carcharinidae) (Carchariniformes.) Berg, 1940: 137; White, 1936: 1—16; 1937: 25—138; Glikman, 1964: 98. 4 families (16—19).

Family 16. **Scyliorhinidae** 89/98, thesis 6—5. Figure 187. (=Scylliorhinidae = Scylliidae = Catulidae, + Halaeluridae, + Atelomycteridae, + Pentanchidae.) Cat sharks, roussettes, Katzenhai, mao sha k'o, torazame ka, koshach'i akuly.

Lit. J: (98): N: 13; G: (12); Regan, 1908: 453—465; Fowler (1933) 1934: 233—367 (237); Bigelow and Schroeder, 1948: 195—228; Andriyashev, 1954: 37—38; Lindberg and Legeza, 1959: 42—47; Glikman, 1964: 98; Svetovidov 1964: 22—25; Springer, 1966. 581—624.

Warm and temperate seas of both hemispheres; shallow and moderate depths. About 13 genera, considerable number of species.

Family 17. **Pseudotriakidae** 89A/98A, thesis 6—13. Figure 191. (Scyliorhinidae ex parte.) False cat sharks, lozhnokun'i akuly.

Lit. J: 98; N: (16); G: 10; Bigelow and Schroeder, 1948: 228—233.

Both shores of the northern part of the Atlantic. In the Pacific Ocean, off the coast of Japan. 1 genus, 2 species.

Family 18. **Carcharhinidae** 90/99, thesis 6 — 17. Figures 193—196. (=Carcharinidae=Carchariidae Regan=Eulamiidae, +Mustellidae, +Triakidae, +Galeorhinidae = Galeidae, Emissolidae.) Requiem sharks, gray sharks, chiens-de-mer, serye akuly, pilozubye akuly, kun'i akuly, chên sha k'o, mejiro zame ka.

Lit. J: (100); N: 16; G: 11; Bigelow and Schroeder, 1948: 233 — 407; Springer, 1950; 1—13; 1951:244; Andriyashev, 1954: 39 — 40; Rosenblatt and Baldwin, 1958: 137 — 160; Lindberg and Legeza, 1959: 60 — 82; Boeseman, 1960: 81—100; Springer, 1964: 559 — 632; Glikman, 1964: 98.

Tropical, subtropical, rarely temperate latitudes of all the oceans. Pelagic and littoral zones. About 25 genera, many species. Of commercial importance.

Family 19. **Sphyrnidae** 91/100, thesis 6—7. Figure 188. Akula molot, hammerhead sharks, requins-marteaux, shuang tza shak'o, shumoku zame ka.

Lit. J: 101; N: (20); G: 12; Bigelow and Schroeder, 1948: 407 — 450; Fraser-Brunner, 1950: 213 — 219; Tortonese, 1950: 37—75; Lindberg and Legeza, 1959: 47 — 50; Glikman, 1964: 98; Gilbert, 1967: 1—88.

Tropical and temperate seas. 2 genera, about 10 species.

Order 7. SQUALIFORMES 39/43, thesis 0 — 15. (Tectospondyli.) Berg, 1940: 138. (Squatiniformes ex parte Glikman.) 2 suborders, 4 families (20 — 23).

Suborder 1. Squaloidei. Berg, 1940: 138: Bigelow and Schroeder, 1957: 1—150; Garrick, 1960: 519 — 557; Glikman, 1964: 95; Webster, 1966: 1—263. 3 families (20 — 22).

Family 20. **Squalidae** 93/102, thesis 7—2. Figure 199. (+Spinacidae, +Oxynotidae.) Dogfish shark, dogfishes, requins épineux, requins chagrin, humantin, cochon-de-mer, lochon-de-mer, Dorhai, kolyuchie akuly, chiao sha k'o, tsuno zame ka.

Lit. J: 101; N: 26; G: 13; Regan, 1908: 39—57; Bigelow and Schroeder, 1948: 59 — 546: (450 — 499); Garrick, 1956: 555 — 571; 1960: 489 — 517. Garrick and Schultz. 1963: 3 — 60; Lindberg and Legeza, 1959: 85 — 93; Glikman, 1964: 95.

All the oceans, from the tropical to the temperate and high latitudes. About 10 genera, many species. Of commercial importance.

Family 21. **Dalatiidae** (—/—), thesis 7—4. Figure 200. (=Scymnorhinidae= =Scymnidae, +Somniosidae, Squalidae ex parte.) (Squaloidei Glikman.)

Sleeper sharks, requins-bouclés, dormeurs, kitefin sharks, spineless dogfishes, gurry sharks, pryamorotye akuly.

Lit. J: (102); N: (30); G: (13); Bigelow and Schroeder, 1948: 499 — 525; Andriyashev, 1954: 40 — 45; Lindberg and Legeza, 1959: 93 —94; Garrick and Schultz, 1963: 3—60; Glikman, 1964: 95; Svetovidov, 1964: 25 —32. Add. — Guitart, 1968: 1—61.

All the oceans in all latitudes. 6 genera, many species.

Family 22. **Echinorhinidae** 93A/102A, thesis 7–5. Figure 201. (Squalidae ex parte.) (Echinorhinoidei Glikman.) Bramble sharks, alligator dogfishes, shipovatye akuly.

Lit. J: (102); N: (27); G: (13); Bigelow and Schroeder, 1948: 526–532; Lindberg and Legeza, 1959: 94–95; Glikman, 1964: 95.

Tropical and temperate latitudes of all the oceans. 1 genus, 1 species.

Suborder 2. Squatinoidei (Squatiniformes). Berg 1940: 138. 1 family (23).

Family 23. **Squatinidae** 95/103, thesis 7–6. Figure 202. (="Rhinidae" Günther.) Angel sharks, anges-de-mer, morskie angely, pien sha k'o, kasu zame ka.

Lit. J: 102; N: 31; G: 14; Bigelow and Schroeder. 1948: 534–546; Lindberg and Legeza, 1959: 95–98; Glikman, 1964: 96.

Coastal regions of the Atlantic and Pacific oceans. 1 genus, a few species.

Order 8. PRISTIOPHORIFORMES 39A/44, thesis 0–16. (Pristiophoroidea.) Berg 1955: 70. (Squatiniformes, Pristiophoroidei Glikman, 1964: 96.) 1 family (24).

Family 24. **Pristiophoridae** 94/104, thesis 8–0. Figure 203. (+Pliotremidae.) Saw sharks, chü sha k'o, nokogiri zame ka, pilonosye akuly.

Lit. J: 101; N: 25; G: 14; Bigelow and Schroeder, 1948: 532–533; Lindberg and Legeza, 1959: 98–99; Glikman, 1964: 96.

Coastal regions of the Indian and Pacific oceans. 2 genera, 4 species.

Superorder B. ***Batoidei.*** Skates (Hypotremata). Berg, 1940: 139; Regan, 1906: 722–758; Annandale, 1909: 1–60; Garman, 1913: 1–528; Clark, 1922: 1–66; Bonde and Swart, 1924: 1–22; Clark, 1926: 1–36; Phillipps, 1929; 98–107; Fowler, 1930: 129–138; Walford, 1935: 1–66; Fang, 1936: 1–49; Whitley, 1940: 1–280; Beebe and Tee-Van, 1941: 245–280; Bigelow and Schroeder, 1948: 543–566; Chen, 1948: 23–50; Roedel and Ripley, 1950: 5–88; Bigelow and Schroeder, 1953: 1–514; Bott, 1953: 16–23; Scott, 1955: 55, 56; Buen, 1959: 171–201; 1960: 3–50; Lindberg and Legeza, 1959: 99–166; Thompson and Springer, 1961: 1–19; Bigelow and Schroeder, 1962: 161–244; Fourmanoir, 1963: 33–58; McCormick and Young, 1964: 1–417; Stead, 1964: 1–211; Bigelow and Schroeder, 1965: 443–477; Wahlquist, 1966: 1–20. 2 orders (9–10). Skates are of average importance in world marine fishing.

Order 9. RAJIFORMES* 40/45, thesis 0–18. (Sarcura, +Narciontes, + Masticura=Centrobates; +Rhinobatiformes, +Myliobatiformes; Rhinobatoidei, +Rajoidei, +Dasyatoidei.) Berg, 1940: 139. (Squatiniformes ex parte, Rhinobatoidei, Rajoidei Glikman, 1964: 96), 14 families (25–38).

Family 25. **Rhinobatidae** 96/105 thesis 9–6. Figure 206. (=Rhinobatoidae.) Guitarfishes, guitares-de-mer, morskie gitary, litou yao k'o, sakata zame ka.

* The new family, 25a, of skates off Chile was described by Buen (1959: 171–201) under the name Gurgesiellidae (genus *Gurgesiella*), but it has not been included in the key as Buen's work was not available to the author.

Lit. J : 103; N : 36; G : (14); Norman, 1926 : 941 — 982; Bigelow and Schroeder 1953 : 1—588 (46 — 80); Herre, 1955 : 381 —400; 1957 : 1957 : 1595 — 1620; Lindberg and Legeza, 1959 : 106 — 112.

Tropical and subtropical latitudes of the Atlantic, Indian, and Pacific oceans. 7 genera, many species.

Family 26. **Rhynchobatidae** 96A/105A, thesis 9 — 4. Figure 205. (+ Rhinidae nec Günther = Rhamphobatidae, Rhinobatidae ex parte.) Spotted guitarfishes, akulokhvostye skaty.

Lit. J : (102); N : (36); G : (14); Bigelow and Schroeder, 1953 : 44; Norman, 1926 : 941 — 982; Lindberg and Legeza, 1959 : 104 — 106.

Tropical and subtropical latitudes of the Atlantic, Indian, and Pacific oceans. 2 genera, a few species.

Family 27. **Pristidae** 97/106, thesis 9 — 1. Figure 204. Sawfishes, poissons-scie, pila ryba, chü yao k'o, nokogiri ou ka.

Lit. J : 102, N : 39 : G : 15; Bigelow and Schroeder, 1953 : 18 — 42; Lindberg and Legeza, 1959 : 103 — 104; Glikman, 1964 : 97.

Coastal regions of oceans and lower reaches of rivers in the tropical and subtropical latitudes. 1 genus, several species.

Family 28. **Platyrhinidae** (98/107), thesis 9—7. Figure 207. (=Discobatidae = Analithidae, + Zanobatidae, Rhinobatidae ex parte.) Thornback rays, t'uan shan yao ka, uchiwa zame ka, diskovye skaty.

Lit. J : 103; N : (38); G : 15; Bigelow and Schroeder, 1953 : 50; Glikman, 1964 : 97.

Tropical and subtropical latitudes of the Atlantic, Indian, and Pacific oceans. 3 genera, a few species.

Family 29. **Rajidae** 99/108; thesis 9 — 10. Figure 209. Skates, rays, raies, pocheteaux, roche, yao k'o, changi ei ka, skatovye.

Lit. J : 103, N : 39; G : 15; Steven, 1947 : 220 — 236; Bigelow and Schroeder, 1948 : 543 — 566; Ishiyama, 1950 : 30 — 36; 1952 : 1—34; Bigelow and Schroeder, 1953 : 1—588 (133 — 327); Roland, 1953 : 137 — 274; Andriyashev, 1954 : 46 — 66; Ishiyama, 1958 : 193 — 394; 1958; 1—24; 1967 : 1—82; Lindberg and Legeza, 1959 : 112 — 137; Glikman, 1964 : 97; Svetovidov, 1964 : 33 — 37; Ishiyama, 1967 : 1—82; Add. — Hubbs and Ishiyama; 1968 : 483 — 491.

All the seas and oceans; not reported for Micronesia, Polynesia, or the Hawaiian Islands. About 7 genera, many species.

Family 30. **Arhynchobatidae** (—/—), thesis 9—12. Figure 210. (Rajidae ex parte.) Odnoperye skaty.

Lit. J : (103); N : (41); G : 16; Waite, 1909 : 41 — 156; Bigelow and Schroeder, 1953 : 1—588 (133); Garrick, 1954 :119 — 132.

Coast of New Zealand. 1 genus, 1 species.

Family 31. **Anacanthobatidae** (—/—), thesis 9 — 14. Figure 211. (Rajidae ex parte, Dasyatidae ex parte.) Niterylye skaty.

Lit. J : —; N : (41); G : (16); Bigelow and Schroeder, 1953 ; 327 — 330.

Gulf of Guinea, coast of East Africa and Gulf of Mexico. 2 genera, 3 species.

Family 32. **Pseudorajidae** (—/—), thesis 9—15. Figure 212. (Rajidae ex parte.) Lozhnye skaty.

Lit. J : —; N : —; G : 15; Bigelow and Schroeder, 1954 : 1—16.

Gulf of Mexico. 1 genus, 1 species.

Family 33. **Dasyatidae** (100/109), thesis 9—21. Figure 215. (=Dasybatidae, =Trygonidae, =Brachiopteridae.) Stingrays, pastenagues, whiprays, roundrays, hung k'o, aka ei ka, morskie koty.

Lit. J: 104; N: 42; G: 16; Chen, 1948 : 1—14; Bigelow and Schroeder, 1951 : 110—113; 1953 : 335—395; Lindberg and Legeza, 1959 : 138—154; Glikman, 1964 : 98; Svetovidov, 1964 : 37—40.

Tropical, subtropical, more rarely temperate, latitudes of all the oceans; occasionally also in fresh waters in the lower reaches of rivers. 5 genera, many species.

Family 34. **Urolophidae** (—/—), thesis 9—17. Figure 214. (Dasyatidae ex parte.) Stingrays, tolstokhvostye skaty.

Lit. J: (104); N: (43); G: (16); Bigelow and Schroeder, 1953 : 416—432; Lindberg and Legeza, 1959 : 137—138.

Tropical species of the American coast of the Atlantic Ocean and both Pacific coasts. 3 genera, several species.

Family 35. **Gymnuridae** (—/—), thesis 9—23. Figure 217. (Dasyatidae ex parte.) Skaty babochki, yen hung k'o, tsubakuro ei ka.

Lit. J : (104); N : (43); G : (16); Bigelow and Schroeder, 1953 : 395—415; Lindberg and Legeza, 1959 : 154—157.

Tropical and subtropical latitudes of oceans; shores, estuaries, and mouths of rivers. 2 genera, a few species.

Family 36. **Potamotrygonidae** 101/110, thesis 9—22. Figure 216. River whiprays. (+ Paratrygonidae, + Elipesuridae.)

Lit. J. : 104; N : 45; G : 16; Bigelow and Schroeder, 1953 : 334; Castex, 1963 : 1—13.

Rivers of South America. 3 genera, several species.

Family 37. **Myliobatidae** 103/112, thesis 9—25. Figure 218. (+Aetobatidae, +Rhinopteridae.) Eaglerays, cownosed rays, aigles-de-mer, batrays, fen k'o, tobi ei ka, orlyakovye, skat orlyak.

Lit. J : 105; N : 46; G : (16); Bigelow and Schroeder, 1953 : 433—464+ +465—479; Lindberg and Legeza, 1959 : 157—160; Glikman. 1964 : 98.

Tropical and subtropical latitudes of oceans; near-bottom waters of the littoral and pelagic zones. 4 genera, several species.

Family 38. **Mobulidae** 104/113, thesis 9—26. Figure 219. (=Cephalopteridae, + Mantidae=Ceratopteridae.) Mantas, devilrays, diables-de-mer, raies-cornues, fufen k'o, itomaki ei ka, morskie d'yavoli, skat rogach.

Lit. J : 105; N : 47; G : 17; Bigelow and Schroeder, 1953 : 480—514; Lindberg and Legeza, 1959 : 160—162; Cadenat, 1960 : 1053—1084, Add.— Aguirre, 1965 : 171—256.

Tropical and subtropical latitudes of oceans; near-bottom waters of the littoral and pelagic zones. 4 genera, several species.

Order 10. TORPEDINIFORMES 41/46, thesis 0—19. (Narcobatoidei. Narcationtes, Narcaciontes, Torpedinoidea.) (Squatiniformes ex parte, Torpedinoidei Glikman.) Berg, 1940: 139; Glikman, 1964: 97. 3 families (39—41).

Family 39. **Torpedinidae** 105/114, thesis 10—1. Figure 220. (=Narcaciontidae = Narcationtidae = Narcobatidae.) Electric rays, torpedoes, torpilles, tien yao k'o, shibire ei ka, elektricheskie skaty.

Lit. J: 103; N: 32; G: 17; Whitley, 1940: 1—280; Bigelow and Schroeder, 1948: 543—566; 1953: 87—131; Takagi, 1951: 27—34; Lindberg and Legeza, 1959: 163—164; Glikman, 1964: 97.

Tropical and subtropical latitudes of the Atlantic, Indian, and Pacific oceans. 7—9 genera, many species.

Family 40. **Narkidae** (—/—), thesis 10—3. Figure 221. (Torpedinidae ex parte.) Numbrays, numbfishes.

Lit. J: (103); N: (34); G: (17); Takagi, 1951: 27—34; Bigelow and Schroeder, 1953: 86—87; Lindberg and Legeza, 1959: 164—166.

Tropical and subtropical latitudes of the Indian and Pacific oceans. 3 genera, a few species.

Family 41. **Temeridae** (—/—), thesis 10—4. No figure. (Torpedinidae ex parte.)

Lit. J: (104); N: (35); G: (17); Bigelow and Schroeder, 1953: 86—87.

Indo-Australian Archipelago. 1 genus, few species.

Class 5. *Holocephali* (Bradyodontia). Berg, 1940: 139; Bigelow and Schroeder, 1953: 515—562; Golvan, 1962: 18. 1 order (11).

Subclass *Chimaera.* Berg, 1940. 1 order (11).

Order 11. CHIMAERIFORMES 43/48, thesis 0—21. (Chimaeroidei, Chimaerea.) Berg, 1940: 142; Dean, 1906: 1—195; Garman, 1904: 245—272; 1911: 79—101; Matsubara, 1936: 1—70; Beebe and Tee-Van, 1941: 245—280; Fowler, 1941: 1—879; Poll, 1951: 1—154; Misra, 1952; Bigelow and Schroeder 1954: 37—87; Buen, 1960: 3—50; Thompson and Springer, 1961: 1—19. 3 families (42—44). Chimeras are of very little importance in world marine fishing.

Family 42. **Chimaeridae** 117/125, thesis 11—2. Figure 222. Chimeras, ratfishes, elephant fishes, chimères, Seeratte, yin chao k'o, gin zame ka.

Lit. J: 106; N: 50; G: 18. Bigelow and Schroeder, 1950: 385—408; 1953: 523—548; Andriyashev, 1954: 66— 69; Lindberg and Legeza, 1959: 166—173. Add.—Patterson, 1965: 101—219.

Deep waters of all the oceans. 2—3 genera, about 20 species.

Family 43. **Rhinochimaeridae** 118/126, thesis 11—3. Figure 223. (Chimaeridae ex parte.) Wên yin chiao k'o, tengu gin zame ka, nosatye khimery.

Lit. J: 107; N: (50); G: 18; Garman, 1904: 245—272; Bigelow and Schroeder, 1953: 548—558. Add.—Bullis and Carpenter, 1966: 443—450.

Atlantic and Indian oceans, Japan; deep waters. 3 genera, several species.

Family 44. **Callorhynchidae** 119/127, thesis 11—4. Figure 224. (Chimaeridae ex parte.) Plownosed chimeras, elephant fishes, zastuporyle khimery.
Lit. J: 107; N: (50); G: 18; Bigelow and Schroeder, 1953: 558—562.
Temperate waters of the southern hemisphere. 1 genus, small number of species.

Class 6. *Dipnoi* (Dipneusta, Dipteriformes, Sarcopterygii ex parte, Amphibioidei ex parte). Berg, 1940: 144; MA: 13; Holly, 1933: 1—30; Arambourg and Guibe, 1958: 2522—2540; Bouillon, 1961; 62—71. 1 superorder, 2 orders (12—13).

Superorder *Ceratodi*. Berg, 1940: 147; MA: 15 2 orders (12, 13).

Order 12. CERATODIFORMES 48/54, thesis 0—24, (Sirenoidei.) Berg, 1940: 148; MA: 15. 1 family (45).

Family 45. **Ceratodidae** 128/139, thesis 12—0. Figure 225. (=Ceratodontidae.) Barramundas, lungfishes, odnolegochnikovye, rogozub.
Lit. J: (110); N: (606): G: 173; MA: 15; Günther, 1871: 511—571; Arambourg and Guibe, 1958: 2522—2540; Grigg, 1965: 413—421.
Barnett and Mary rivers in Australia (Queensland). 1 genus, 1 species. Game fishes.

Order 13. LEPIDOSIRENIFORMES 49/55, thesis 0—25. Berg, 1940: 148; MA: 16. 2 families (46, 47).

Family 46. **Lepidosirenidae** 129/140, thesis 13—1. Figure 226. Lolach, mud sirens, sudamerikanishe Lugenfische, amerikanskie dvulegochnikovye.
Lit. J: 111: N: 605; G: 173; MA: 16; Peters, 1866: 12—14; Arambourg and Guibe, 1958: 2522—2540.
Rivers and swamps of tropical South America. 1 genus. Fished locally.

Family 47. **Protopteridae** 130/141, thesis 13—2. Figure 227. (Lepidosirenidae ex parte.) Afrikanische Lungenfische, protopterovye, mambovye.
Lit. J: 111; N: (605); G: 173; MA: 17; Vaillant, 1899: 219—222; Poll, 1961: 3—50.
Rivers and swamps of tropical Africa. 1 genus. Fished locally.

Class 7. *Teleostomi*. Higher fishes (Pisces, Osteichthyes). Berg, 1940: 149; MA: 1—239; Regan, 1904: 329—340; Boulenger, 1904: 161—190; Gregory, 1907: 437—508; Regan, 1912: 836—837; McAllister, 1968: 1—239. Nelson, 1968: 129—143; 888—889. 2 subclasses, 49 orders (14—62).

Subclass 1. *Crossopterygii* (Sarcopterygii ex parte, Choanichthyes ex parte, Amphibioidei ex parte.) Berg, 1939: 82; 1940: 149; MA: 11; 1 superorder.

Superorder *Coelacanthi*. Berg, 1940: 153. 1 order (14).

Order 14. COELACANTHIFORMES 54/59, thesis 0—27. (Actinistia, Coelacanthini.) Berg, 1940: 155; MA: 12. 1 family (48).

Suborder 14.1. Coelacanthoidei. Berg, 1940: 155; Smith J.; 1939: 1—106. 1 family (48).

Family 48. Latimeriidae 140a/152, thesis 14—0. Figure 228. (+Coelacanthidae.)

Lit. J—; N: (605); G: (174); MA: 13; Smith J., 1939: 455; 1939: 1—106; 1953: 279—281; 1956: 1—260; Lehman, 1952: 1—201; Millot, 1955: 58, 59.

Indian Ocean, off the coasts of South Africa and around the Seychelles in deep waters. 1 genus, 1 species.

Subclass 2 *Actinopterygii* (Actinopteri). Berg, 1940 : 159; MA : 18; Nybelin, 1963: 485—516. 48 orders (15—62).

(Chondrostei) Berg, 1940: 159—163; MA: 20; Eremeev, 1936: 35—66; Lehman, 1958: 2130—2172.

Order 15. POLYPTERIFORMES 55/60, thesis 0—29. (Cladistia, Brachiopterygii MA: 17.) Berg, 1940: 163; 1940: 727—740. 1 family (49).

Family 49. Polypteridae 142/154, thesis 15—0. Figure 229. (+Calamoichthyidae.) Bichir, poissons-roseau, Flösselhechte, bishirovye, mnogoperye.

Lit. J: 110; N: 52; G: 173; MA: 18, Poll, 1941: 141—179; 1942: 269—317; Daget, 1950: 1—178, 1958: 2501—2521. Add.—Poll, 1965: 553—569; Poll and Deswattines, 1967: 1—63.

The Nile and rivers of tropical Africa. 2 genera. Fished locally.

Order 16. ACIPENSERIFORMES 67/72, thesis 0—31. (Glaniostomi, Acipenseroidei, Chondrostei ex parte.) Berg, 1940: 194; MA: 26; Berg, 1911: 1—337; 1948: 7—57; Vladykov, 1963: 24—60; 1963: 24—58. 2 families Berg, 50, 51).

Family 50. Acipenseridae 166/179, thesis 16—1. Figures 230, 231. Osetrovye, sturgeons, esturgeons, Störe, hsün k'o, te zame ka.

Lit. J: 113; N: 53; G: 18; MA: 27; Berg, 1904: 665; Jordan and Snyder, 1906: 397—398; Soldatov, 1915: 95—415; Sowerby, 1923: 480—483; Mori, 1933: 6—10; Rauther, 1935: 49—64; Borzenko, 1942: 3—114; Babushkin, 1942: 115—131; Murgoci, 1942: 289—385; Rey, 1947: 1—839; Ting, 1949: 65—68; Berg, 1948: 57—109; Babushkin, and Borzenko, 1951: 1—67; Andriyashev, 1954: 69 — 73; Bailey and Cross, 1954: 169—208; Mead and Bradbury, 1963: 20—60; Ambroz, 1964: 287—347; 1966: 1—45; Svetovidov, 1964: 41—59; Lindberg and Legeza, 1965: 31—36.

Freshwater and diadromous fishes of the northern hemisphere. 4 genera, a few species. Valuable commercial forms.

Family 51. Polyodontidae 167/180, thesis 16—2. Figures 232, 233. (Selachostomi, Chondrostei ex parte.) Paddlefishes, spadefishes, bec-en-cuillère, pai hsün k'o, hera cho zame ka, veslonosye.

Lit. J: 113; N: 55; G: 19; MA: 27; Stockard, 1907: 753—766; Vladykov and Greeley, 1963: 24—58.

Rivers and lakes of the USA and China. 2 genera, a small number of species. Fished locally.

(Holostei), Berg, 1940 : 197; MA : 28.

Order 17. AMIIFORMES 68/73, thesis 0—34. (Cycloganoidei, Protospondyli ex parte, Halecomorphi ex parte. Semionotiformes ex parte.) Berg, 1940 : 197; MA : 29; Arambourg and Bertin, 1958 : 2173—2203. 1 family (52).

Family 52. **Amiidae** 173/186, thesis 17—0. Figure 234. (=Amiatidae.) Dogfishes, mud fishes, amies, bowfins, bowfishes Kahlhechte.

Lit. J : 116; N : 61; G : 19; MA : 29; Hay, 1898 : 341—349; Reighard, 1904 : 57—109; Arambourg and Bertin, 1958 : 2173—2203.

Rivers and lakes of North America. 1 genus. Not of commercial importance.

Order 18. LEPISOSTEIFORMES (72/77), thesis 0—35. (Ginglymodi, Rhomboganoidei, Semionotiformes ex parte, Lepisostei, Holostei ex parte, Lepidosteiformes.) Berg, 1940 : 211; MA : 30. (Amiiformes, Arambourg and Bertin, 1958 : 2181). 1 family (53).

Family 53. **Lepisosteidae** (180/193), thesis 18—0. Figure 235. (=Lepidosteidae.) Gars, brochets lances, garpikes, Knochenhechte, Kaimanfisches, kaimanovye ryby, pantsirnye shchuki.

Lit. J : 115; N : 61; G : 19; MA : 30; Hay, 1898 : 341—349; Regan, 1923 : 445—461; Arambourg and Bertin, 1958 : 2173—2203; Suttkus, 1963 : 61—86.

Fresh waters of the eastern part of North and Central America and Cuba. 1 genus, about 10 species. Game fishes.

(Teleostei) Berg, 1940 : 159, 197, 215; Boulenger, 1904 : 539—727; 1904 : 161—190; Regan, 1909 : 75—86; 1912 : 836—837; Boulenger, 1922 : 325—440; Starks, 1930 : 149—239; Tret'yakov, 1945 : 49—55; Hoedeman, 1954 : 50, 51; Poll, 1954 : 1—390; Bertin and Arambourg, 1958 : 2204—2500; Myers, 1958 : 27—30; Gosline, 1959 : 160—164; 1961 : 1—4; Mednikov, 1960 : 155—156; Hotta, 1961 : 1—155; Takahashi, 1962 : 1—75; Freihofer, 1963 : 80—189; Cadenat and Roux, 1964 : 81—102; Gosline, 1965 : 186—194; Greenwood, Rosen, Weitzman and Myers (GRWM), 1966 : 339—456; Greenwood and Myers, 1967 : 227—228; McAllister (MA), 1968 : 1—239 (33).

Order 19. CLUPEIFORMES 74/79, thesis 0—79. (Isospondyli, Malacopterygii s. str., Physostomi, Esociformes, Chanoiformes.), Berg, 1940 : 216; (Elopiformes GRWM : 393; Clupeiformes, Osteoglossiformes, Salmoniformes GRWM : 394; Ctenothrissiformes, Gonorynchiformes GRWM; 395.) (Clupeiformes + Galaxiiformes MA : 34); Jordan and Herre, 1906 : 613—645; Koefoed, 1910 : 1—12; Weber and Beaufort, 1913, 2 : 1—138; Kyle and Ehrenbaum, 1927 : 9—86; Breder, 1928 : 1—25; Fowler, 1931 : 1—14, 111—123, 198—208; Beebe, 1933 : 159—167; Roxas, 1934 : 231—295; Wang, 1935 : 1—65; Gregory and Conrad, 1936 : 21—36; Tchang, 1938 : 311—337; Matsubara, 1940—1941 : 314—319; Fowler, 1941 : 1—879; Rey, 1947 : 1—839; Maul, 1948 : 5—41; 1949 : 5—20; Misra, 1952 : 367—422; Poll, 1953 : 1—258;

Koefoed, 1956 : 1—21; 1960: 1—15; Gosline, 1960 : 327—365; Bigelow, 1963 : 89—104; Add.—Greenwood, Myers, et al., 1967 : 227—228; Hubbs, 1967 : 40—41; Myers, 1958 : 27—30; McAllister, 1968 : 1—239; Nelson, 1969 : 18—30. 15 suborders, 50 families (54—103).

Suborder 19.1. Clupeoidei, thesis 19—35. Berg, 1940 : 221; MA:37 (Elopiformes GRWM : 393; Clupeiformes, Clupeoidei ex parte GRWM : 394; Salmoniformes, Argentinoidei ex parte, GRWM : 394; Ctenothrissiformes GRWM: 395.) 4 superfamilies, 10 families (54—63).

Superfamily 19.1.1. Elopoidea (Elopoidei). Berg, 1940 : 221; (Elopiformes ex parte GRWM : 393.) (Elopoidei MA : 35); Gosline, 1960 : 327—365; 1961 : 1—42; Bigelow, 1963 : 107—110; Whitehead, 1965 : 227—281. 2 families (54 and 55).

Family 54. **Elopidae** 186/199, thesis 19—45. Figure 266. (Elopsidae ex parte.) Ladyfishes, ten-pounders, tarpons, hailien k'o, kara iwashi ka.

Lit. J : 117; N : 63; G : 19; GWRM : 393, 404; MA : 36; Regan, 1909 : 37—40; Hildebrand, 1963 : 111—131; Whitehead, 1962:321—329; 1965 : 225—281; 1966 ; 15—56; Lindberg and Legeza, 1965 : 40—41.

Tropical and subtropical latitudes of seas and oceans. 1 genus, about 7 species. Game fishes.

Family 55. **Megalopidae** 187/200, thesis 19—46. Figure 267. (Elopsidae ex parte.) Tarpons, grande-écailles, ta hailien k'o, isegon ka, tarponovye,

Lit. J : 118; N : (64); G : 19; GRWM : 393, 404; MA : 36; Hildebrand, 1963 : 111—131; Lindberg and Legeza, 1965 : 41—42.

Tropical and subtropical latitudes of seas and oceans. 1 genus, 2 species. Items of local and sport fishing.

Superfamily 19.1.2. Albuloidea. (Albuloidei MA : 36; Berg, 1940: 222.) (Elopiformes ex parte GRWM : 393.) 2 families (56, 57).

Family 56. **Albulidae** 188/202, thesis 19—49. Figure 268. Bonefishes, banane-de-mer; ladyfishes, peiso yü k'o, soto iwashi ka.

Lit. J : 118; N : 64; G : 19; GRWM:393: 404 + family 57; MA : 36; Ridewood 1904 : 35—81; Jordan and Herre, 1906 : 613—645; Hildebrand, 1963 : 132—145; Lindberg and Legeza, 1965 : 42—44.

Tropical and subtropical latitudes of seas and oceans. 2 genera, 3 species. Items of local and sport fishing.

Family 57. **Pterothrissidae** 189/203, thesis 19—50. Figure 269. (=Bathythrissidae, Albulidae ex parte.) Ch'ang pei yü k'o, gisu ka, gisovye.

Lit. J : 119; N : (65); G : 20; GRWM : (393) (family 56); MA : 36; Ridewood, 1904 : 35—81; Jordan and Herre, 1906 : 613—645; Lindberg and Legeza, 1965 : 44—45.

Tropical and subtropical latitudes of the Pacific and eastern part of the Atlantic Ocean; pelagial and bathypelagial. 1 genus, 2 species. A promising commercial item off the west coast of Africa.

Superfamily 19.1.3. **Clupeoidea** (Clupeoidei). Berg, 1940 : 223; MA : 40 (Clupeiformes, Clupeoidei ex parte GRWM : 394). Wang, 1934 : 33—49; Tchang, 1939 : 311—337; Campos, 1941 : 185—220; McHugh and Fitch, 1951 : 491—495; Nair, 1953 : 108—138; Buen, 1958 : 83—110; Bigelow, 1963 : 148—151; Whitehead, 1962 : 89—102; 1963 : 737—750; 1965 : 227—281; 1966 : 15—56; Add.—Whitehead, 1966 : 3—6; 1969 : 263—279. 2 families (58—59).

Family 58. **Clupeidae** 192/206, thesis 19—52. Figures 270—276. (=Clupidae, + 58a. Dorosomatidae MA : 41 = Dorosomidae, + Clupanodontidae, + Dussumieridae = 58b. Dussumieriidae MA : 40 = Dussumeriidae, + Congothrissidae MA : 42, + Pristigasteridae GRWM : 394.) Herrings, round-herrings, gizzard-shads, hareng, sardine, alose, Hering, fei k'o, nishin ka.

Lit. J : 120; N : 72; G : 21 (23); GRWM : 394. 406; MA : 40; Jordan and Herre, 1906 : 613—645; Schneider, 1908 : 66—120; Regan, 1916 : 1—19; 1917 : 198—207, : 226—229; : 297—316, : 377—395; Fage, 1920 : 1—140; Regan, 1922 : 587—590; Norman, 1923 : 1—22; Borcéa, 1936 : 306—344; Buen, 1937 : 317—419; Bertin, 1943 : 1—32; Chapman, 1944 : 6—21; 1948 : 25—41; Berg, 1948—49 : 110—168; Lozano-Rey, 1950 : 7—20; Miller, 1950 : 387—410; Rivas, 1950 : 275—309; Svetovidov, 1952 : 1—331; Andriyashev, 1954 : 73—85; Munro, 1955 : 1—350; Harder, 1958 : 367—388; Miller, 1960 : 371; Whitehead, 1962 : 89—102; 1962 : 511—512; Hildebrand, 1963 : 257—451; Miller, 1963 : 443—451; Whitehead, 1963 : 305—380; 1963 : 737—750; Poll, 1964 : 10; Svetovidov, 1964 : 60—126; Chan, 1965 : 1—26; Greenwood, 1965 : 337—338; Whitehead, 1965 : 225—281; 117—156; 1966 : 15—56; Lindberg and Legeza, 1965 : 45—66. Add.—Dutt, 1967 : 206—213; Whitehead, 1967 : 1—180.

From temperate to tropical latitudes in marine, brackish, and fresh waters. About 50 genera, many species. One of the three most important families in world fishing.

Family 59. **Engraulidae** 193/207, thesis 19—53. Figures 277, 278. (=Engraulididae + Stolephoridae, Clupeidae ex parte.) Anchovies, anchois, Anchovis, t'ik'o, katakuchi iwashi ka, anchousovye.

Lit. J : 122; N : (84); G : 24; GRWM : 394, 406; MA : 40; Ridewood, 1904 : 472—482; Jordan and Herre, 1906 : 613—645; Fage, 1920 : 1—140; Jordan and Seale, 1925 : 27—32; Jordan and Seale, 1926 : 355—418; Aleksandrov, 1927 : 37—92; Hardenberg, 1933 : 230—256; 1934 : 313—375; Puzanov, 1936 ; 1—64; Hildebrand, 1943 : 1—165; Chapman, 1944 : 6—21; Hildebrand and Carvalha, 1948 : 285—296; Lozano-Rey, 1950 : 7—20; Harder, 1958 : 367—388; Hildebrand, 1963 : 152—247; Svetovidov, 1964 : 126—142; Lindberg and Legeza, 1965 : 66—78. Add.—Whitehead. 1967 : 13—37.

Tropical, subtropical, and partly temperate latitudes of seas and oceans. About 15 genera, many species. One of the three most important families in world marine fishing.

Superfamily 19.1.4. **Alepocephaloidea**. Berg, 1940 : 225; MA : 38 (Salmoniformes, Alepocephaloidei, Argentinoidei GRWM : 394; Ctenothrissiformes GRWM : 395.) 4 families (60—63).

Family 60. **Alepocephalidae** 194/208, thesis 19—40. Figure 263. (+Platytroctidae = Platyproctidae, +60a. Leptochilichthyidae +60b. Bathyprionidae.) Slickheads, p'ing tou yü k'o, sekitori iwashi ka, gladkogolovye.

Lit. J : 122; N : 65; G : 20; GRWM : 394, 408 + family 61; MA : 38; Jordan and Herre, 1906 : 613—645; Roule, 1915 : 62—96; Beebe, 1933 : 1—147 (13—93); Parr, 1937 : 1—79; 1951 : 1—21; 1952 : 268—271; 1952 : 255—269; Tucker, 1954 : 163—214; Buen, 1961 : 1—90; Bigelow, 1963 : 250—252; Lindberg and Legeza, 1965 : 78—80; Marshall, 1968 : 1—10. Add.—1966 : 3—9; Gosline, 1969 : 185—218.

Deep oceanic waters. More than 20 genera, many species.

Family 61. **Searsiidae** (—/—), thesis 19—39. Figures 260—262. (=Searsidae.)

Lit. J : —; N : (69); G : (21); GRWM : (394) (family 60); MA : 38; Parr, 1951 : 1—21; Tucker, 1954 : 163—214; Maul, 1957 : 1—21; Parr, 1960 : 1—109; Bigelow, 1963 : 254, 255. Add.—Krefft, 1967 : 1—11.

Deep oceanic waters. 3 subfamilies, 15 genera, a few species.

Family 62. **Dolichopterygidae** 195/209, theses 19—37, 67, 74. Figures 259, 283, 287 (Alepocephalidae ex parte, Salmoniformes ex parte, Argentinoidei ex parte GRWM : 394.)

Lit. J : —; N : (71); G : (20); GRWM : (394) (family 91); MA : (57) (family 91); Grey, 1952 : 87—90; Cohen, 1958 : 47—52.

Deep oceanic waters. 1—2 genera, 4 species.

Family 63. **Macristiidae*** 196/210, thesis 19—42. Figure 264. (Ctenothrissiformes, GRWM : 395.) Shleifovye, shleifovaya rybka.

Lit. J : 123; N : 89; G : 21; GRWM : 395; 410; MA : 38; Regan, 1911 : 204—205; Marshall, 1961 : 353—370.

Region of the Azores in the Atlantic Ocean. 1 genus, 1 species.

Suborder 19.2. Chirocentroidei, thesis 19—22. Berg, 1940 : 227. (Clupeiformes, Clupeioidei ex parte, GRWM : 394; MA : 39.) (Chirocentroidea, MA : 39.) 1 family (64).

Family 64. **Chirocentridae** 198/212, thesis 19—22. Figure 248. Wolf herrings, dorab, pao tao yü k'o, oki iwashi ka, volkosel'devye.

Lit. J : 119; N : (72); G : 21; GRWM : 394, 406; MA : 39; Jordan and Herre, 1906 : 613—645; Hardenberg, 1930 : 51—56; Chevey, 1932 : 1—151; Lindberg and Legeza, 1965 : 80—81.

Indian and Pacific oceans north as far as Vladivostok. 1 genus, 1—2 species. Fished locally.

Suborder 19.3. Chanoidei, thesis 19—15. Berg, 1940 : 228; MA : 47 (Gonorynchiformes, Chanoidei ex parte, Chanoiformes GRWM : 395). 2 families (65, 66).

* Isolated into a new suborder, Macristioidei (McAllister, 1968 : 180).

Family 65. **Chanidae** 201/215, thesis 19—15. Figure 243. (Chanoidae.) Bangos, milkfishes, chêmu yü k'o, sabahi ka.

Lit. J: 119; N: 88; G: 21; GRWM: 395, 410; MA: 47; Jordan and Herre, 1906: 613—645; Lindberg and Legeza, 1965: 82.

Indian and Pacific oceans north as far as southern Japan, the Hawaiian Islands, and California. 1 genus, 1—2 species. Fished locally; sport fishing; pond maintenance.

Family 66. **Kneriidae** 202/216, thesis 19—18. Figure 244 (+Grasseichthyidae.)

Lit. J: 123; N: 88; G: 21; GRWM: 395, 410 + family 68; MA: 47; Gill, 1903: 338—339; Giltay, 1934: 1—22; Géry, 1964: 4805—4807; Poll, 1965: 1—29.

Fresh waters of tropical Africa. 2 genera, several species.

Suborder 19.4. Phractolaemoidei, thesis 19—19. Berg, 1940: 229 (Gonorynchiformes ex parte GRWM: 395; Chanoidei MA: 47). 1 family (67).

Family 67. **Phractolaemidae** 203/217, thesis 19—19. Figure 245.

Lit. J: 123; N: 88; G: 21; GRWM: 395, 410; MA: 47; Ridewood, 1905: 252—282; Pellegrin, 1925: 549—551; Poll, 1957: 1—191; Thys, 1961: 101—167.

Fresh waters of tropical Africa. 1 genus, 2 species.

Suborder 19.5. Cromerioidei, thesis 19—20. Berg, 1940: 230 (Gonorynchiformes, Chanoidei ex parte GRWM: 395); (Chanoidei MA: 47, 48). 1 family (68).

Family 68. **Cromeriidae** 204/218, thesis 19—20. Figure 246.

Lit. J: 123; N: 88; G: 24; GRWM: (395) (family 66); MA: 48; Pellegrin, 1935: 461—463; D'Aubenton, 1961: 131—164.

Fresh waters of Africa (Nile). 1 genus, 2 species.

Suborder 19.6. Salmonoidei, thesis 19—75. (Salmoniformes.) Berg, 1940: 231. (Salmoniformes, Salmonoidei, MA: 52 + family 107, Galaxioidei ex parte, GRWM: 394); (Salmonoidea); Chapman, 1942: 272—304; 1948: 1—22; Hubbs, 1953: 96, 97; Cohen, 1957: 1—294; Gosline, 1960: 327—365; Bigelow, 1963: 455, 456; Cohen, 1964: 1—70; Weitzman, 1967: 507—540. 7 families (69—75).

Family 69. **Salmonidae** 205/219, thesis 19—79. Figure 288. (+Coregonidae.) Salmons, trouts, Coregonus, lavarets, whitefishes, ciscoes, saumons, truites, Lachs, Maräne, Lachsartige, Forellenartige, sigovye, kuei k'o, sake ka.

Lit. J: 124; N: 102; G: 24 (25); GRWM: 394, 407 + family 70; MA: 53 + family 70; Steindachner and Kner, 1870: 421—446; Jordan and Snyder, 1902: 567—593; Berg, 1906: 395—398; 1907: 500—514; Regan, 1914: 405—408; Thieneman, 1921: 170—195; 1922: 415—471; Chernavin, 1923: 103—106; Berezovskii, 1924: 266—280; Pellegrin, 1924: 970—972; Karaman, 1926: 253—268; Kulmatycki, 1926: 275—336; 1927: 1—40; Fortunatov, 1927: 131; Järvi, 1928: 1—259; Koelz, 1929: 294—643; Fortunatova, 1929: 68; Perotti, 1930: 674—708; Koelz, 1931: 303—432; Friedenfelt, 1934: 49—163; Wagler, 1934: 1—48; Kendall, 1935: 3—166; Wagler, 1937: 345—446; Barach, 1938: 50—79; Karaman, 1938: 131—139; Oshima, 1938: 1821—1826; 1938: 1979—1936;

Dul'keit, 1939 : 40—46; Pravdin, 1941 : 1—62; Wagler, 1941 : 371—501; Blair, 1943 : 1-21; Dymond, 1943 : 171—231; Järvi, 1943 : 1—91; Pravdin, 1946 : 1—108; 1947 : 58—71; Berg, 1948 : 1—466 (168—421); Otterstrom, 1948 : 223—231; Pravdin, 1948 : 75—83, 1948 : 58—71; 1949 : 40—46; Svärdson, 1949 : 89—101; Dottrens, 1950 : 789—813; Miller, 1950 : 1—42; Steinmann, 1950 : 517—525; 1950 : 109—189; Wagler, 1950 : 3—62; Steinmann, 1951 : 54—155, 162—191; Dvinin, 1952 : 69—107; Järvi, 1953 : 1—33; Andriyashev, 1954 : 85—108; Mailyan, 1954 : 37—47; Pravdin, 1954 : 1—319; Vladykov, 1954 : 904—932; Vladimirskaya, 1956 : 136—148; Mailyan, 1957 : 137—195; Svärdson, 1957 : 267—356; Vlasova, 1959 : 89—100; Dottrens, 1959 : 1—66; Barsukov, 1960 : 3—17; Kulikova, 1960 : 111—114; Holt, 1960 : 192—300; McPhail, 1961 : 793—816; Norden, 1961 : 679—791; Bergeron, 1962 : 1—64; Hikita, 1962 : 1—97; Rounsefell, 1962 : 235—270; Stokell, 1962 : 181—190; Bigelow, 1963 : 547—551; 1963 : 553—598; Dymond, 1963 : 457—546; Vladykov, 1963 : 459—504; Bilton, 1964 : 1267—1288; Svetovidov, 1964 : 142—146; Behnke, 1965 : 1224; Lindberg and Legeza, 1965 : 84—96; Karaman, 1966 : 1—41; Dorofeeva, 1967 : 3—18, 1969 : 1—20; Shaposhnikova, 1968 : 207—256. Add.—idem, 1967 : 254—257; Lindsey and Woods, 1970 : 1—570.

Marine and fresh waters of the northern hemisphere; diadromous and freshwater fishes. About 10 genera. Of great importance in world marine fishing.

Family 70. **Thymallidae** 206/220, thesis 19—80. Figure 289. Graylings, ombre, huhei yü k'o, kawahime masu ka, khariusovye.

Lit. J : 125; N : (105); G : 25; GRWM : (394) (family 69); MA : (54) (family 69); Berg, 1907 : 500—514; Svetovidov, 1931 : 19—199; 1936 : 183—301; Berg, 1948—49 : 421—435; Andriyashev; 1954 : 108—110; Egorov and Il'yasova, 1958 : 84—102; Norden, 1961 : 679—791; Hadžišče, 1962 : 39—56.

Fresh waters of Europe, Northern Asia, and North America. 1 genus, 6 species. Fished locally; game fishes.

Family 71. **Plecoglossidae** 208/222, thesis 19—81. Figure 290. Ayunovye, ayus, sweetfishes, hsian yü k'o, ayu ka.

Lit. J : 124; N : (108); G : 25; GRWM, 394, 407; MA : 55; Jordan and Snyder, 1902 : 567—593; Chapman, 1941 : 425—455; Lindberg and Legeza, 1965 : 96, 97.

Coastal marine waters and rivers of Japan, Korea, and China; diadromous. 1 genus, 1 species.

Family 72. **Osmeridae** 209/223, thesis 19—83. Figure 291. Smelts, éperlans, prêtres, hugua yü k'o, kyuri uo ka, koryushkovye.

Lit. J : 125; N : 108; G : 25; GRWM : 394, 407; MA : 54; Hubbs, 1925 : 49—56; Petrov, 1925 : 87—108; Chapman, 1941 : 279—301; Hart and McHugh, 1944 : 1—27; Berg, 1948 : 1—468 (436—452); Andriyashev, 1954 : 110—119; Gosline, 1960 : 327—365; Bigelow, 1963 : 553—594; McAllister, 1963 : 1—53; 1966 : 227—238; Lindberg and Legeza, 1965 : 98—110; Klyukanov, 1966 : 990, 991. Add. Klyukanov, 1969 : 99—109; 1970 : 399—417.

Coastal marine, more rarely fresh, waters of the northern parts of the Atlantic and Pacific oceans. 2 subfamilies, about 6 genera, more than 10 species. Of little importance in world marine fishing.

Family 73. **Salangidae** 214/228, thesis 19—86. Figure 293. (Galaxioidei ex parte GRWM: 394.) Salangids, Chinese whitebaits, lapsha-ryby, yin yü k'o, shiro ya ka.

Lit. J: 125; N: 110; G: 25; GRWM: 394, 407; MA: 55; Regan, 1908: 444—446; Fang, 1934: 505—511; 1934: 231—268; Wakiya, 1936: 835—845; Wakiya and Takahasi, 1937: 265—296; Berg, 1948: 1—468 (452—454); Gosline, 1960: 327—365; Lindberg and Legeza, 1965: 115—125.

Littoral marine and brackish waters of eastern Asia from Indochina north to the Amur. 6 genera, a few species. Fished locally.

Family 74. **Retropinnidae** 215/229, thesis 19—87. Figure 294. (Galaxioidei ex parte GRWM: 394) (=Retropinnatidae.) New Zealand whitebaits.

Lit. J: 125; N: (110); G: 26; GRWM: 394, 407; MA: 55; Stokell, 1941: 361—372; Whitley, 1955: 110—119. Add.—Stokell, 1969: 379—381.

Fresh and brackish waters of Australia, Tasmania, and New Zealand. 2 genera, 4 species.

Family 75. **Aplochitonidae** (216/230), thesis 19—84. Figure 292. (Haplochitonidae, +Prototroctidae) (Galaxioidei ex parte, GRWM: 394.)

Lit. J: 125; N: 113; G: 26; GRWM: 394, 407; MA: 56; Regan, 1913: 229—292; Gosline, 1966: 327—365; Chapman, 1944: 149—165.

Freshwater, partly diadromous fishes of Australia, Tasmania, Chile, Pategonia, and the Falkland Islands. 3 genera, 5 species.

Suborder 19.7. Esocoidei, thesis 19—2. (Haplomi, Esociformes.) Berg, 1940: 242 (Salmoniformes ex parte, Esocoidei, GRWM: 394.) Regan, 1909: 75—86 ex parte; Berg, 1931: 461—462; MA: 57; Chapman, 1934: 371—404; Berg, 1936: 385—388; Gosline, 1960: 327—365. 3 superfamilies, 3 families (76—78).

Superfamily 19.7.1. Dallioidea. Berg, 1940: 243, MA: 59. 1 family (76).

Family 76. **Dalliidae** 217/231, thesis 19—5. Figure 237. (Xenomi.) Alaska blackfishes, chernye ryby, juan chien yü k'o.

Lit. J: 156; N: 121; G: 30; GRWM: (394) (family 77); MA: 59; Starks, 1904: 249—262; Chapman, 1934: 371—404; Berg, 1948: 454, 455. Shaposhnikova, 1960: 29—33.

Fresh waters of the Bering Sea basin. 1 genus, 1 species. Fished locally on a small scale.

Superfamily 19.7.2. Umbroidea. Berg, 1940: 243; MA: 58. 1 family (77).

Family 77. Umbridae 218/232, thesis 19—6. Figure 238. (+Novumbridae.) Mudminnows, poisson-chien, ombre, Hundfisches, evdoshkovye.

Lit. J: 157; N: 120; G: 30; GRWM: 394, 407+family 76; MA: 58; Schultz, 1929: 73—81; Chapman, 1934: 371—404; Berg, 1948: 455—457; Dineen and Stokely, 1954: 169—178. Add.—Kleijn, 1968: 35—40.

Fresh waters of Europe and North America. 2 subfamilies, 2 genera, 4 species.

Superfamily 19.7.3. Esocoidea. Berg, 1940: 246; McAllister 1968: 58. 1 family (78).

Family 78. **Esocidae** 220/234, thesis 19—3. Figure 236. (=Lyciidae). Shchukovye, pikes, brochets, Hechte, Muskellunge, pickerel, kou yü k'o, kawa kamasu ka.

Lit. J: 157; N: 120; G: 30; GRWM: 394, 407; MA: 58; Chapman, 1934: 371—404; Berg, 1948: 457—465; Andriyashev, 1954: 121—122; Crossman, 1960: 363—375; Dick, 1964: 550—560.

Fresh waters of Europe, western and northeastern Asia, and North America. 1 genus, 5 species. Fished locally. Game fishes.

Suborder 19.8. Stomiatoidei, thesis 19—88. Berg, 1940: 246 (Salmoniformes, Stomiatoidei, GRWM: 394, Stomiatoidea); Koefoed, 1910: 1—12; Regan, 1923: 612—614; Parr, 1927: 1—123; 1930: 136; Beebe, 1933: 160—175; Morrow, 1964: 71—77; Weitzman, 1967: 507—540. 3 superfamilies, 8 families (79—86).

Superfamily 19.8.1. Gonostomatoidea. (Heterophotodermi.) Berg, 1940: 247; MA: —; Parr, 1930: 136. 2 families (79, 80).

Family 79. **Gonostomatidae** (221/235), thesis 19—91. Figures 295, 296. (=Gonostomidae, + Maurolicidae.) Anglemouths, bristlemouths, tsuan kuan yü k'o, yoko eso ka.

Lit. J: (127); N: 90; G: 26 (27); GRWM: 394, 408, MA: 49; Norman, 1930: 261—374; 278—301; Bruun, 1931: 285—292; Parr, 1931: 1—53; Beebe, 1932: 47—107; Matsubara, 1943: 73—76; Poll, 1953: 1—258; Andriyashev, 1954: 122—123; Ahlstrom and Counts, 1958: 363—416; Grey, 1959: 167—184; 1960: 55—125; 1964: 78—240; Marshall, 1960: 1—121; Mukhcheva, 1964: 93—138; 1967: 182—199; Lindberg and Legeza. 1965: 126—129.

Deep oceanic waters. About 20 genera, more than 40 species.

Family 80. **Sternoptychidae** 222/236, thesis 19—92. Figure 297. (Sternoptychiidae.) Hatchetfishes, haches d'argent, silver hatchetfishes, hsin kuan yü k'o, mune eso ka, toporikovye.

Lit. J: 127; N: (93); G: 27; GRWM: 394, 408; MA: 49; Jespersen, 1915: 1—41; Jespersen and Tåning, 1919: 215—226; 1926: 1—59; Regan and Trewavas, 1930: 1—143; Sanzo, 1935: 121—182; Schultz, 1938: 135—155; Matsubara, 1950: 187—197; Fraser-Brunner, 1951; 39—44; Wilimovsky, 1951: 247—248; Misra, 1952: 367—422; Karlovac, 1953: 1—46; Andriyashev, 1954: 123—126; Schultz, 1961: 587—649; 1964: 241—273; Blache; 1964: 71—87. Add.—Bright and Pequegnat, 1969: 26—36.

Oceanic waters. 3—4 genera, several species.

Superfamily 19.8.2. Stomiatoidea. (Lepidophotodermi.) Berg, 1940: 247; MA: —; Koefoed, 1956: 1—21; 1958: 1—7; Morrow, 1964: 71—77; Weitzman, 1967: 507—540. 2 families (81, 82).

Family 81. **Stomiatidae** 223/237, thesis 19—95. Figure 299. Scaly dragonfishes, chükou yü k'o, wanitokage gisu ka.

Lit. J: 126; N: 96; G: 28; GRWM: 394, 408; MA: 49; Ege, 1918: 1—28; Regan, 1923: 612—614; Regan and Trewavas, 1930: 1—143; Parr, 1931: 1—53.

Ege, 1933 : 223 – 236; 1934 : 1–58; Matsubara, 1938 : 37 – 52; Karlovac, 1953 : 1–46; Maul, 1956 : 75 – 96; Gibbs, 1960 : 200 – 203; Morrow, 1964 : 290 – 310. Add. – Weitzman, 1967 : 507 – 540; Barnett and Gibbs, 1968 : 826 – 832; Gibbs, 1969 : 1–25.

Oceanic waters; bathypelagial. 2 genera, several species.

Family 82. **Chauliodontidae** 224/238, thesis 19 – 94. Figure 298. (=Chauliodidae.) Viperfishes, t'u chi yü k'o, horai eso ka.

Lit. J : 127; N : 95; G : (27); GRWM : 394, 408; MA : 50; Regan and Trewavas, 1929 : 1 – 39; Ege, 1948 : 1 – 148; Haffner, 1952 : 113 – 133; Morrow, 1961 : 249 – 294; Ege, 1962 : 1 – 148; Morrow, 1964 : 274 – 289.

Oceanic waters. 1 genus, 4 – 5 species.

Superfamily 19.8.3. **Astronesthoidea.** (Gymnophotodermi). Berg, 1940 : 247; MA : –; Parr, 1927 : 1–13; Koefoed, 1956 : 1–21. 4 families (83 – 86).

Family 83. **Astronesthidae** 225/239, thesis 19–98. Figure 300. Lomozubye, snaggletooths, hsinshan yü k'o, tokage hodako ka.

Lit. J : 127; N : 94; G : 27; GRWM : 394,408; MA : 50; Parr, 1927 : 1–123; Regan and Trewavas, 1929 : 1–39; Matsubara, 1943 : 76 – 81; Maul, 1956 : 75 – 96; Blache, 1964 : 17 – 31; Gibbs, 1964 : 311 – 350; Weitzman, 1967 : 1–56.

Oceanic waters. 6 genera, a few species.

Family 84. **Melanostomiatidae** 226/240, thesis 19–101. Figure 302. (Stomiatidae ex parte.) Scaleless dragonfishes, hei chü kou yü k'o, hotei eso ka, chernorotye.

Lit. J : (126); N : (100); G : (28); GRWM : 394, 408; MA : 50; Parr, 1927 : 1–123; Beebe and Crane, 1939 : 65 – 238; Chapman, 1939 : 501–542; Morrow and Gibbs, 1964 : 351 – 511.

Oceanic waters; bathyal. About 15 genera, many species.

Family 85. **Malacosteidae** 226A/240A, thesis 19 – 102. Figure 303. (Melanostomiatidae ex parte.) Loosejaws.

Lit. J : 155; N : 100; G : 31; GRWM : 394; 408; MA : 50; Regan and Trewavas, 1930 : 1–143; Maruyama, 1959 : 153 – 156; Günther and Deckart, 1959 : 1–54; Morrow, 1964 : 523 – 549.

Oceanic waters. 4 genera, several species.

Family 86. **Idiacanthidae** 227/241, thesis 19 – 99. Figure 301. (=Stylophthalmidae = Stylophthalmoidae.) Black dragons, ch'ichi k'o, mitsumata yariuo ka.

Lit. J : 127; N : (100); G : 27; GRWM : 394,408; MA : 51; Parr,1927 : 1–123; Beebe, 1933 : 390; 1934 : 129 – 241; Gibbs, 1964 : 512 – 522; Novikova, 1967 : 159 – 208.

Oceanic waters; bathyal. 1 genus, several species.

Suborder 19.9. Opisthoproctoidei, thesis 19—60. (Argentinoidea, Platygastrichthyes.) Berg, 1940: 248; (Salmoniformes ex parte, Argentinoidei GRWM: 394); (Salmonoidei, Argentinoidea, MA: 57); Trewavas, 1933: 601—614; Parr, 1937: 1—79; Cohen, 1964: 1—70. 6 families (87—92).

Family 87. **Argentinidae** 210/224, thesis 19—70. Figure 284. Deepsea smelts, argentines, Glasauge, argentins, shuichên yü k'o, nigisu ka.

Lit. J: 125; N: 106; G: 25; GRWM: 394, 407 + family 90; MA: 56 + families 89, 90; Regan, 1913: 229—292; Schmidt E., 1918: 1—40; Beebe, 1933: 1—147; Beaufort and Beebe, 1933—34: 1—245; Chapman, 1942: 104—117; 1943: 147—160; 1948: 1—22; Andriyashev, 1954: 119—121; Cohen, 1957: 1—294; 1958: 47—52; 1958: 93—172; Bertelsen, 1958: 1—10; Bertin and Arambourg, 1958: 2204—2500; Cohen, 1960: 1—5; McAllister, 1961: 39—43; Cohen, 1964: 1—70; Lindberg and Legeza, 1965: 111—115. Add.—Cohen and Atsaides, 1969: 13—36.

North Atlantic, southern coasts of Africa, North and South Pacific. 2 genera, several species. Of little importance in world marine fishing.

Family 88. **Bathylagidae** 211/225, thesis 19—73. Figure 286. Deepsea smelts, Shanghai kuei k'o, sono iwashi ka.

Lit. J: 125; N: (106); G: 26; GRWM: 394, 407 + family 89; MA: 56; Beebe, 1933: 1—147; Chapman, 1943: 147—160; Cohen, 1957: 1—294; 1964: 1—70; McAllister, 1961: 39—43; Rass and Kashkina, 1967: 209—221; Borodulina, 1968: 3—14.

Oceanic waters, bathyal. 2 genera, several species.

Family 89. **Microstomatidae** (212/226), thesis 19—71. Figure 285. (=Microstomidae.) Hsiao kou k'o, ginzaki iwashi ka.

Lit. J: (125); N: (107); G: (26); GRWM: (394) (family 88); MA: (56) (family 87); E. Schmidt, 1918: 1—40; Matsubara, 1943: 70—73; Chapman, 1948: 1—22; Cohen, 1964: 1—70.

Oceanic waters; bathyal. 2 genera, several species.

Family 90. **Xenophthalmichthyidae** 213/227, thesis 19—66. Figure 282A. (Microstomatidae ex parte, Prososcopidae Whitley, 1970: 245.)

Lit. J: —; N: (107); G: (26); GRWM: (394) (family 87); MA: (57) (family 87) Regan, 1925: 59—60; Bertelsen, 1958: 1—8; Rass, 1961: 1858; 1962: 1578—1579. Cohen, 1964: 1—70 (32).

Deep waters of the Caribbean Sea. 1 genus, 1 species.

Family 91. **Opisthoproctidae** 230/244, thesis 19—61. Figure 281. (+Winteridae = Winteriidae.)

Lit. J: 127; N: 107; G: 25; GRWM: 394; 407 + family 62, 92; MA: 57 + family 62, 92; E. Schmidt, 1918: 1—40; Chapman, 1942: 272—304; Whitley, 1943: 167—187; Cohen, 1957: 1—294; 1960: 1—5; 1960: 147—149; 1964: 1—70; Bekker, 1968: 241—246. Add.—Blache, 1963: 89—95.

Oceanic waters; bathyal. 4 genera, a small number of species.

Family 92. **Macropinnidae** (—/—), thesis 19—64. Figure 282. (Opisthoproctidae ex parte.) Barreleyes.

Lit. J: — ; N: (107); G: (25); GRWM: (394) (family 91); MA: (57) (family 91) Chapman, 1939: 501—542; 1942: 272—304.

Oceanic waters, 1 genus, 1 species.

Suborder 19.10. Gonorynchoidei, thesis 19—12. Berg, 1940: 250; MA: 45; (Gonorynchiformes, Gonorynchoidei ex parte, GRWM: 395). 1 family (93).

Family 93. **Gonorynchidae** (231/245), thesis 19—12. Figure 242. (=Gonorhynchidae.) Beaked salmon, sandfishes, shu hsi k'o, nezumi nisu ka.

Lit. J: (120); N: 119; G: (29); GRWM: 395, 410; MA: 46; Woodward, 1896: 500—504; Ridewood, 1905: 361—372; Jordan and Herre, 1906: 613—645; Lindberg and Legeza, 1965: 120.

Deep waters of the Indian and Pacific oceans north as far as southern Japan and the Hawaiian Islands. 1 genus, about 6 species.

Suborder 19.11. Notopteroidei, thesis 19—8. Berg, 1940: 251 (Osteoglossiformes ex parte, Notopteroidei GRWM: 394.) (Mormyriformes ex parte MA: 62, 65.) Notopteriformes Mednikov, 1962: 155, 156). 2 families (94, 95).

Family 94. **Hiodontidae** (232/246), thesis 19—10. Figure 241. (=Hyodontidae.) (Clupeiformes, Hiodontoidei MA: 44, 45). Moonfishes, mooneyes.

Lit. J: 120; N: 115; G: 20; GRWM: 395, 406; Ridewood, 1905: 188—217; Gosline, 1960: 327—365.

Rivers and lakes of North America. 2 genera, several species. Game fishes.

Family 95. **Notopteridae** 233/247, thesis 19—9. Figure 240. Spinoperye, Messerfische, featherbacks, peichi yü k'o, naginata namazu ka.

Lit. J: 123; N: 116; G: 20; GRWM: 394, 406; MA: 65; Ridewood, 1905: 188—217; Rahimullah and Das, 1936: 135—141; Poll, 1957: 1—191; Gosline, 1960: 327—365; Greenwood, 1963: 377—412.

Fresh waters of tropical Africa, India, and Indonesia. 2 genera, several species. Fished locally. Aquarium fishes.

Suborder 19.12. Osteoglossoidei, thesis 19—24. (Osteoglossoidea.) Berg, 1940: 252. (Osteoglossiformes ex parte, Osteoglossoidei. Clupeiformes ex parte, GRWM: 394); (Mormyriformes ex parte + Pantodontoidei MA: 62, 64); Ridewood, 1905: 252—282, Greenwood and Thompson, 1960: 283—301; Gosline, 1960: 327—365; 1965: 186—194; Greenwood, 1963: 379—412. Add.—idem, 1967: 581—597; Nelson, 1969: 1—37. 4 families (96—99).

Family 96. **Arapaimidae** 235/249, thesis 19—30. Figure 354. (=Arapamidae.) Vastrès.

Lit. J: 123; N: (115); G: 29; GRWM: (394) (family 97); MA: 64; Boulenger, 1901: 514, 515; Ridewood, 1905: 252—282; Gosline, 1965: 186—194.

Fresh waters of the Amazon and Guiana river basins in South America. 1 genus, 1 species. Fished locally; game fishes.

Family 97. **Osteoglossidae** 236/250, thesis 19—29. Figures 252, 253. Knochenzüngler, bonytongues, aravanovye, kosteyazychnye.

Lit. J: 123; N: 114; G: 29; GRWM: 394, 405 + families 96 and 98; MA: 64; Boulenger, 1901: 514—515; Ridewood, 1905: 252—282; Weber and Beaufort. 1913, 2: 12—14; Poll, 1957: 1—191.

Fresh waters of South America, Indonesia, Thailand, and Australia. 2 genera, 3 species. Fished locally; game fishes.

Family 98. **Heterotidae** 237/251, thesis 19—27. Figure 251. (=Clupisudidae.)

Lit. J: (123); N: (115); G: (29); GRWM: (394) (family 97); MA: 65; Boulenger, 1901: 514, 515; Ridewood, 1905: 252—282; Poll, 1957: 1—191.

Fresh waters of tropical Africa (Nile, Senegal, Gambia, Niger). 1 genus, 1 species. Fished locally.

Family 99. **Denticipitidae** (—/—), thesis 49—25. Figures 249, 250. (=Igborichthyidae.) (Clupeiformes, Denticipitoidei, GRWM 394.) (Clupeoidei MA: 42.) Shipikogolovye, zubchatogolovye.

Lit. J: —: N: —; G: 24; GRWM: 394, 405; MA: 42; Clausen, 1959: 141—156; Greenwood, 1968: 213—273.

Fresh waters of West Africa. 1 genus, 1 species.

Suborder 19.13. Pantodontoidei, thesis 19—32. Berg, 1940: 253; (Osteoglossiformes, ex parte GRWM: 394.) (Mormyriformes, Osteoglossoidei, MA: 64.) 1 family (100).

Family 100. **Pantodontidae** 238/252, thesis 19—32. Figure 255. Ryba motylek, poisson-papillon, Schmetterlingsfische.

Lit. J: 123; N: 115; G: 29; GRWM: 394, 405; Boulenger, 1901: 1—532, (120); Ridewood, 1905: 252—282; Greenwood and Thompson, 1960: 283—301; Whitehead, 1962: 103—137.

Fresh waters of tropical Africa. 1 genus, 1 species. Aquarium fish.

Suborder 19.14. Anotopteroidei, thesis 19—55. Berg, 1940: 253; (Salmoniformes, Myctophoidei ex parte, Cetomimiformes ex parte GRWM: 395); (Myctophiformes, Alepisauroidei ex parte, MA: 89, 95, 96). 2 families (101, 102).

Family 101. **Anotopteridae** 239/253, thesis 19—55; supp. 23—27. Figures 279, 310. (Salmoniformes, Myctophoidei ex parte GRWM: 395.) Daggertooths, javelin fishes, wupeich'i k'o, mizuo damashi ka, kinzhalozubye.

Lit. J: 127; N: —; G: 29; GRWM: 395, 409; MA: 96; Zugmayer, 1911: 138; Roule, 1935: 324—330; Nybelin, 1946: 1—16; Hubbs, Mead and Wilimovsky, 1953: 173—198; Marshall, 1955: 303—336; Bertelsen and Marshall, 1956: 1—34; Kobayashi and Ueno, 1956: 239—265; Rofen, 1966: 498—510.

Deep waters of the Atlantic Ocean. 1 genus, 1 species.

Family 102. **Rosauridae*** (—/—), thesis 19—57. Figure 280. (Cetomimiformes, Giganturoidei ex parte GRWM : 395); (Stomiatoidei ex parte MA : 52.)

Lit. J : —; N : —; G : 29; GRWM : 395, 410; MA : 52; Tucker, 1954 : 163—214.

Deep waters of the Atlantic Ocean and to the northeast of Brazil. 1 genus, 1 species.

Suborder 19.15. Bathylaconoidei, thesis 19—34. (Salmoniformes, Bathylaconoidei GRWM : 394.) MA : 43; Bigelow, 1964 : 561—565. 1 family (103).

Family 103. **Bathylaconidae** (—/—), thesis 19—34. Figure 256. (Synodidae ex parte.)

Lit. J : —; N : (126); G : (30); GRWM : 394, 408; MA : 43; Parr, 1948 : 48—54; Bertin and Arambourg, 1958 : 2204—2500; Bigelow, 1964 : 561—565. Add.—Nielsen and Larsen, 1968 : 221—238.

Atlantic and Pacific oceans; bathypelagial. 1 genus, 1 species.

Order 20. MIRIPINNIFORMES (—/—), thesis 0—45. (Miripinnati.) Bertelsen and Marshall, 1956 : 1—34; 1958 : 9—10; MA : 98; (Cetomimiformes, Miripinnatoidei GRWM : 395.) 4 families (104, 104a, 104b, 105).

Family 104. **Miripinnidae** (—/—), thesis 20—1. Figures 304, 305. (=Miripinnatidae.) Dvukhvostoperye.

Lit. J : —; N : —; G : 33; GRWM : 395, 409; MA : 99; Bertelsen and Marshall, 1956 : 1—34.

Temperate latitudes of the North Atlantic; bathypelagial. 1 genus, 1 species.

Family 104a. **Kasidoridae** (—/—), thesis 20—0, footnote. Figure 303A. (=Kasidoroidae.)

Lit. J : —; N : —; G : —; GRWM : 395; MA : 99; Hardy, 1965 : 9; Robins and Sylva, 1965 : 189—201; Robins, 1966 : 696—701. Add.—Thorp, 1969 : 61—70.

Western Atlantic. 1 genus, 1 species.

Family 104b. **Megalomycteridae** (—/—), theses 0—81, footnote, 20—0, footnote. Figure 35. (Megalomycteroidei.)

Lit. J : —; N : —; G : —; MA : 97; Myers and Freihofer, 1966 : 193—206.

North Atlantic. 4 genera, a small number of species.

Family 105. **Eutaeniophoridae** (—/—), thesis 20—2. Figures 306, 307. (=Taeniophoridae.) Lentokhvostye, nitekhvostye.

Lit. J : —; N : —; G : 33 GRWM : 395, 409; MA : 90; Bertelsen and Marshall, 1956 : 1—34; 1958 : 9, 10.

Tropical and subtropical waters of the Atlantic, Indian, and Pacific oceans; pelagial, bathypelagial. 2 genera, 3 species.

* GRWM (p.395) assume that the family Rosauridae was described from a young fish belonging to family 123. Giganturidae. It has been placed in the suborder Stomiatoidei (McAllister, 1968 : 48, 52).

Order 21. BATHYCLUPEIFORMES 75/80, thesis 0—78. Berg, 1940: 254 (Perciformes ex parte, Percoidei ex parte GRWM: 400; MA: 136.) Misra, 1952: 367—422. 1 family (106).

Family 106. **Bathyclupeidae** 240/254, thesis 21—0. Figure 308. Shenhai fei k'o, soko nishin ka.

Lit. J: 186; N: 259; G: 75; GRWM: 400, 427; MA: 138; Weber and Beaufort, 1931, 6: 1—448 (: 181—183); Misra, 1952: 367—422.

Deep waters of the Atlantic (Gulf of Mexico), Indian Ocean, and southwest Pacific. 1 genus, several species.

Order 22. GALAXIIFORMES 76/81, thesis 0—83. (Galaxiodei.) Berg, 1940: 254. (Salmoniformes, Galaxioidei GRWM: 394.) Clupeiformes, Salmonoidei, MA: 34; Chapman, 1944: 149—165; Misra, 1952: 367—422. 1 family (107).

Family 107. **Galaxiidae** 241/255, thesis 22—0. Figure 309. (=Galaxidae, +Paragalaxiidae.) Galaxids.

Lit. J: 125; N: 112; G: 26; GRWM: 394,407; MA: 55; Ogilby, 1896: 62—73; Regan, 1906: 363—384; 1913: 229—292; Scott, 1936: 83—112; 1938: 111—143; 1941: 55—69; Stokell, 1945: 124—137; 1949: 472—496; 1954: 411—418; Misra, 1952: 367—422; E. Scott, 1966: 244—258; Stokell, 1966: 73—80. Add.—Frankenberg, 1967: 225—228; McDonald, 1969: 796—824.

Fresh and marine waters of the southern hemisphere: New Zealand, Australia, South Africa, and South America. 6—7 genera, several species. Fished locally.

Order 23. MYCTOPHIFORMES 77/82, thesis 0—81. (Iniomi; Scopeliformes; Myctophoidei+Alepisauroidei.) Berg, 1940: 256; MA: 89; (Salmoniformes, Myctophoidei, GRWM: 395). Regan, 1911: 120—133; Weber and Beaufort, 1913, 2: 139—183; Parr, 1928: 1—193; 1929: 1—45; Gregory and Conrad, 1936: 21—36; Matsubara, 1940—41; 314—319; Parr, 1946: 260—262; Maul, 1946: 5—61; Misra, 1952: 367—422; Marshall, 1955: 303—336; 1960: 1—221; Bertelsen and Marshall, 1956: 1—34; Gosline, Marshall and Mead, 1966: 1—18; Fishes W. N. Atlantic, 1966: 1—647. 11 families (108—118).

Family 108. **Synodontidae** (242/256), theses 23—21, 23, supp. 23—6,7. Figures 320, 321. (=Synodidae, +Sauridae, +108b Bathysauridae, +108a Harpadontidae = Harpodontidae.) Lizardfishes, Bombay ducks, koumu yü k'o, eso ka, anoli de mer, yashcherogolovye.

Lit. J: 153; N: 124; G: (30), GRWM: 395, 408 + family 108a; MA: 92, 93 + family 108a; Fowler, 1932: 247—279; Norman, 1935: 99—135; Matsubara, 1938: 1—36; Matsubara and Iwai, 1951: 19—30; Lindberg and Legeza, 1965: 130—139; Anderson, Gehringer, and Berry, 1966: 30—102; Mead, 1966: 103—113.

Atlantic, Indian, and Pacific oceans. 6 genera, a few species. Of medium importance in world marine fishing.

Family 109. **Aulopodidae** (243/257), theses 23—17, supp. 23—1. Figure 318. (=Aulopidae MA: 90, +Scopelosauridae.) Threadsails, pi nü yü k'o, hime ka.

Lit. J: (153); N: (123); G: (30); GRWM: 395, 408, MA: 90; Mead, 1958: 188—191; 1966: 19—29; Lindberg and Legeza, 1965: 139—140.

Mediterranean Sea; Atlantic, Indian, and Pacific oceans north as far as Japan. 2—3 genera, a small number of species.

Family 110. **Scopelarchidae** 245/259, theses 23—24, supp. 23—30. Figure 322. (Evermannellidae ex parte.) Pearleyes, chuyen yü k'o, deme eso ka, zhemchuzhnoglazye.

Lit. J: (154); N: 126; G: 32; GRWM: 395, 409; MA: 95; Parr, 1928: 1—193; Chapman, 1939: 501—542; Mead and Böhlke, 1953: 241—245; Marshall, 1955: 303—336; Andriyashev, 1960: 563—566; Rofen, 1966: 566—602.

Oceanic waters. 5 genera, about 20 species.

Family 111. **Evermannellidae** 246/260, theses 23—12, supp. 23—29. Figure 316. (=Evermanellidae = Odontostomidae.) Sabertooth fishes.

Lit. J: (154); N: 126; G: (32); GRWM: 395, 409; MA: 95; E. Schmidt, 1918: 1—40; Parr, 1928: 1—193; Misra, 1952: 367—422; Rofen, 1966: 511—565.

Oceanic waters. 3 genera, 6 species.

Family 112. **Paralepididae** (247/261), theses 23—7, supp. 23—23. Figures 313, 314. (=Paralepidae, +Sudidae.) Barracudinas, Barrakudinovye, chingyen yü k'o, aome eso ka.

Lit. J: (154); N: (128); G: (31); GRWM: 395, 409; MA: 95; Parr, 1928: 1—193; 1929: 1—45; Ege, 1930: 1—201; 1931: 1—193; 1933: 223—236; Jensen, 1942: 3—28; Maul, 1945: 1—38; Harry, 1951: 17—35; Misra, 1952: 367—422; Tortonese, 1952: 1—12; Ege, 1953: 1—184; Harry, 1953: 219—249; 1953: 169—230; 1954: 219—249; Andriyashev, 1954: 126—128; Marshall, 1955: 303—336; Maul, 1956: 75—96; Ege, 1957: 1—101; Maul, 1962: 523—550; Rofen (Harry), 1963: 1—6; 1966: 205—461. Add.—Post, 1968: 139—146.

All the oceans, including the Antarctic, but excluding the Arctic Ocean; bathypelagial. 2 subfamilies, 11 genera, about 50 species.

Family 113. **Chlorophthalmidae** (247A/261A), theses 23—6, supp. 23—14. Figure 312. (Sudidae ex parte.) Greeneyes, zelenoglazye.

Lit. J: 154; N: (128); G: 31; GRWM: 395, 408; MA: 95; Misra, 1952: 367—422; Kamohara, 1953: 1—6; 1956: 1—8; Okada and Sano, 1960: 595—607; Lindberg and Legeza, 1965: 140—143; Mead, 1966: 162—189.

Oceanic waters. 3 genera, several species.

Family 114. **Bathypteroidae** (247B/261B), theses 23—25, 19; supp. 23—11, 12. Figures 323, 319. (Sudidae ex parte = Bathypteridae + Benthosauridae, +114a. Ipnopidae.) Spiderfishes, grid-eye fishes.

Lit. J: 154; N: (129); G: 32; GRWM: 395, 408 + family 114a; MA: 92 + family 114a; Mead, 1958: 362—373; 1959: 290—292; 1966: 114—146; : 147—161; Andersen, 1966: 77—90; Nielsen, 1966: 49—75.

Oceanic waters. 5 genera, several species.

Family 115. **Scopelosauridae** (—/—), theses 23—10, supp. 23—19. Figure 31! (+Notosudidae, Aulopidae ex parte, Sudidae ex parte.)

Lit. J: (153); N: (123); G: (31); GRWM: 395, 409; MA: 91; Kreft and Maul, 1955: 305—316; Marshall, 1966: 194—204.

In the southern hemisphere around Macquarie Island, in the North Atlantic off Madeira and around eastern Greenland. 1 genus, 3 species.

Family 116. **Omosudidae** 248/262, theses 23—13, supp. 23—24, Figure 317.

Lit. J: 155; N: 134; G: 33; GRWM: 395, 409; MA: 96; Parr, 1928: 1—193. Roule, 1931: 1255—1259; Ege, 1958: 1—20; Rofen, 1966: 462—481.

Atlantic and Indian oceans. 1 genus, 1 species.

Family 117. **Alepisauridae** 249/263, theses 23—3, supp. 23—26. Figure 311. (=Alepidosauridae = Plagyodontidae.) Handsaw fishes, lancetfishes, chichiang yü k'o, mizu uo ka, pilozubye.

Lit. J: (156); N: 134; G: 32; GRWM: 395, 409; MA: 96; Jensen, 1948: 1—182; Marshall, 1955: 303—336; Gibbs and Wilimovsky, 1966: 482—497.

Atlantic and Pacific oceans. 1 genus, a small number of species.

Family 118. **Myctophidae** (250/264), theses 23—27, 28: supp. 23—16, 17. Figures 324, 325. (=Scopelidae +118a. Neoscopelidae.) Myctophids, lanternfishes, poissons-lampes, skopelevye, svetyashchiesya anchousy, tenglung yü k'o, hadaka iwashi ka.

Lit. J: 155; N: 131; G: 31; GRWM: 395, 409 + 118a; MA: 93, 94 + family 118a; Gilbert, 1913: 67—107; Tåning, 1918: 1—154; 1928: 46—69; Parr. 1928: 1—193; 1929: 1—47; Norman, 1929: 510—515; Parr, 1931: 1—53; Tåning, 1932: 125—146; Parr. 1934: 41—53; 1934: 54—65; Bolin, 1939: 89—156; Matsubara, 1938: 52—60; 1943: 55—63; Beebe and Pyl. 1944: 59—95; Bolin, 1946: 137—152; Miller, 1947: 81—90; Fraser-Brunner, 1949: 1019—1106; Misra, 1952: 367—422; Karlovac, 1953: 1—46; Mead, 1953: 105—108; Andriyashev, 1954: 128—132; Sarenas, 1954: 375—427; Torchio, 1958: 1—6; Bolin, 1959: 1—45; Kulikova, 1960: 166—204; 1961: 5—39; Rass, 1960: 146—152; Ogawa, 1961: 81—89; Andriyashev, 1962: 216—294; Bekker, 1963: 15—28; : 145—163; : 164—191; Wisner, 1963: 24—28; Bekker, 1964: 11—75; 1965: 62—103; Lindberg and Legeza, 1965: 143—150; Bolin, 1966: 190—193; Bekker, 1967: 84—124; 145—181; Bekker and Borodulina, 1968: 779—798; Nafpaktitis, 1968: 1—131. Add.—Nafpaktitis et al., 1968: 1—29; 1969: 1—79.

All the oceans; pelagial, bathypelagial. More than 30 genera, many species. A promising commercial family.

Order 24. CETOMIMIFORMES* (—/—), thesis 0—81, footnote. (Cetunculi ex parte. Scopeliformes ex parte.) Berg, 1940: 257; MA: 97. (Cetomimiformes ex parte, Cetomimoidei, GRWM: 395; Stephanoberyciformes ex parte, see families 120 and 241) GRWM: 395): Rofen, 1957—59: 255—260. 3 families (119—121).

* McAllister (1968: 97) refers to this order family 104a. Megalomycteridae, which we place in order 20. Miripinniformes.

Family 119. **Cetomimidae** 252/266, thesis 24—1. Figure 326.

Lit. J : 156; N : 127; G : 89; GRWM : 395, 409; MA : 98; Goode and Bean, 1895 : 451—454; Parr, 1928 : 1—193; 1934 : 1—59; 1946 : 260—262; Harry, 1952 : 55—72; Koefoed, 1955 : 1—16; Rofen, 1957—59; 255—260.

Oceanic waters. 5 genera, 12 species.

Family 120.(241). **Rondeletiidae** 373/387, theses 24—4 and 43—5. Figure 328. Family 241, transferred from order 43. Stephanoberyciformes.

Lit. J : 156; N : 215; G : 89; GRWM : 395, 409; MA : 98; Goode and Bean, 1895 : 451—454; Parr. 1928 : 1—193; 1929 : 1—45 (: 39—44); Harry, 1952 : 55—72; Rofen; 1957—59; 255—260; Abe and Hotta, 1963 : 43—48.

Oceanic waters. 1 genus, 1 species.

Family 121. Barbourisiidae (—/—), thesis 24—3. Figure 327. (=Barbourisidae = Barburisidae.)

Lit. J : —; N : —; G : 33, 89; GRWM : 395, 409; MA : 98; Parr, 1945 : 127—129; 1946 : 260—262; Myers, 1946 : 41, 42; Rofen, 1957—59 : 255—260; Abe and Maruyama, 1963 : 49—50.

Oceanic waters. 1 genus, 1 species.

Order 25. ATELEOPODIFORMES 78/83, thesis 0—85. (Ateleopiformes, Ateleopoidei, Chondrobrachii, Chondrichthyes.) Berg, 1940 : 257; MA : 118; (Cetomimiformes ex parte, Ateleopodoidei GRWM : 395) : Regan, 1911 : 120—133; Smith and Radcliffe, 1912 : 105—140; Barnard, 1948 : 341—406; Misra, 1952 : 367—422. 1 family (122).

Family 122. Ateleopodidae (254/268), thesis 25—0. Figure 329. (=Ateleopidae = Podatelidae, +Guentheridae = Guentheriidae.) Pien yü k'o, shachiburi ka, lozhnodolgokhvostye.

Lit. J : 156; N : (134); G : (33); GRWM : 395, 409; MA : 119; Smith and Radcliffe, 1912 : 105—140; Rivero, 1935 : 91—106; Walters and Fitch, 1960 : 441—451; Cervigón, 1961 : 119—128; Palmer, 1961 : 335—351; Walters, 1963 : 455—457; Lindberg and Legeza, 1965 : 151—152.

Deep waters of the Atlantic, Indian, and Pacific oceans. 4 genera, a few species.

Order 26. GIGANTURIFORMES 79/84, thesis 0—47. Berg, 1940 : 258; MA : 87; (Cetomimiformes ex parte, Giganturoidei ex parte, GRWM : 395); Walters, 1964 : 566 — 577. 1 family (123).

Family 123. Giganturidae 255/269, thesis 26—0. Figure 330. Deep-sea giganturids, gigantokhvostye.

Lit. J : 166; N : 135; G : 87; GRWM : 395, 410; MA : 88; Regan, 1925 : 53—59; Walters, 1961 : 297—319; 1964 : 566—577.

Oceanic waters; bathypelagial. 2 genera, 4 species.

Order 27. SACCOPHARYNGIFORMES 80/85, thesis 0—63. (Lyomeri.) Berg, 1940 : 258; (Monognathiformes, MA : 88); (Anguilliformes ex parte, Saccopharyngoidei ex parte GRWM : 393); Regan, 1912 : 347—349; Bertin, 1934 : 1—56; Berg, 1948 : 1353—1355; Koefoed, 1955 : 1—16. Orton, 1963:6—15; Böhlke, 1966 : 603—609. 2 families (124, 125).

Family 124. **Saccopharyngidae** 256/270, thesis 27—1. Figure 333. Gulpers, meshkorotye.

Lit. J : 134; N : 136; G : 36; GRWM : 393, 405; MA : 88; Regan, 1912 : 347—349; Bertin, 1934 : 1—56; 1938 : 1—26; Böhlke, 1966 : 617 — 628.

Oceanic waters; bathypelagial. 1 genus, 4 species.

Family 125. **Eurypharyngidae** 257/271, thesis 27—2. Figure 334. (=Gastrostomidae.) Swallowers, gulpers, bol'sherotye.

Lit. J : 134; N : 136; G : 36; GRWM : 393, 405; MA : 89; Zugmayer, 1911 : 138; : 88 — 96; Bertin, 1934 : 26 —31; Berg, 1948 : 1353 — 1355; Böhlke, 1966 : 610 — 616.

Oceanic waters; bathypelagial. 1 genus, 2 species.

Order 28. MONOGNATHIFORMES (80A/85A), thesis 0 — 61. (Saccopharyngiformes ex parte MA : 88; Anguilliformes ex parte, Saccopharyngoidei ex parte GRWM : 393.) 1 family (126).

Family 126. **Monognathidae** 258/272, thesis 28 — 0. Figure 335.

Lit. J : —; N : 136; G : 36; GRWM : 393, 405; MA : 89; Bertin, 1937 : 353 —540; 1938 : 1—26; Bertin and Arambourg, 1958 : 2204 — 2500.

Deep oceanic waters. 1 genus, 3 species.

Order 29. MORMYRIFORMES 81—86, thesis 0 — 76. (Scyphophori.) Berg, 1940 : 260; GRWM : 394; MA : 62; Holly, 1927 : 115 — 150; Gosline, 1961 : 1—42. Add. — Taverne, 1969 : 1—85. 2 suborders, 2 families (127, 128).

Suborder 29.1. Gymnarchoidei. Berg, 1940 : 262. 1 family (127).

Family 127. **Gymnarchidae** 259/273, thesis 29 —1. Figure 336. Suyo.

Lit. J : 124; N : 119; G : 29; GRWM : 394, 406; MA : 66; Poll, 1957 : 1—191.

Fresh waters of tropical Africa and the Nile River. 1 genus, 1 species.

Suborder 29.2. Mormyroidei. Berg, 1940 : 262. MA : 66. 1 family (128). Fished locally.

Family 128. **Mormyridae** 230/274, thesis 29 —2. Figure 337. Nilhechte, klyuvorylye.

Lit. J : 124; N : 117; G : 29; GRWM : 394, 406; MA : 66; Boulenger, 1898 : 775 — 821; Ridewood, 1905 : 188 — 217; Boulenger, 1909 : 1—373 (29 — 144); 1916 : 152 — 170; Poll, 1945 : 36 — 77; 1957 : 1—191; Whitehead and Greenwood, 1959 : 283—295; Reizer, 1964 : 1—60. Add. — Blache, 1967 : 178—217; 695 —709; Taverne, 1968 : 1—91.

Fresh waters of tropical Africa and the Nile River. 11 genera, many species. Fished locally.

Order 30. CYPRINIFORMES 82/87, thesis 0—73. (Ostariophysi; Plectospondyli; Heterognathi, +Gymnonoti, +Eventognathi, +Nematognathi.) Berg, 1940 : 262; MA : 67; (Cypriniformes, Siluriformes, GRWM : 395, 396.) Bleeker, 1860 : 1—492; Fowler, 1906 : 431—483; Schlesinger, 1910 : 613—640; Regan 1911 : 13—32, 553 — 577; Berg, 1912 : 1—336; Weber and Beaufort, 1913,

2 : 184—375; 1916, 3: 1—239; Chranilov, 1927 : 501—597; 1929 : 323—462; Khranilov, 1929 : 47—59; Nichols, 1930 : 148—151; Wang, 1935 : 1—65; Uchida, 1939 : 1—458; Fowler, 1941 : 1—879.2 sections, 4 suborders, 46 families (129—174).

Section 1. Cyprini. Berg, 1940 : 263 (Cypriniformes GRWM : 395; Cyprinoidei MA : 68); Alexander, 1962 : 451—473; Weitzman, 1962 : 1—77. 3 suborders, 15 families (129—143).

Suborder 30.1. Characoidei, thesis 30—3, see 30—3, footnote. (Characinoidei, Heterognathi, Characoidei ex parte.) Berg, 1940 : 263. GRWM : 395; (Characoidea MA : 68); Regan, 1911 : 13—32; Holly, 1927 : 115—150; Norman, 1929 : 781—829; Weitzman, 1962 : 1—77; 1964 : 127—169. 6 families (129—134).

Family 129. **Characidae** (261)/275, thesis 30—3, footnote. Figures 338—342. (=Characinidae, +Crenuchidae, +Acestrorhynchidae, +Serrasalmidae, + Tetragonopteridae, +Creagrutidae, +Glandulocaudidae, +129a. Erythrinidae, +129b. Hepsetidae, + 129c. Cynodontidae, +129d. Lebiasinidae, +Nannostomidae, Cheirodontidae, Bivibranchiidae.) Salmler, tetras, characins, sal'mlerovye.

Lit. J : (134); N : —; G : 36; GRWM : 395, 410 +families 129a—d; MA : 68; Eigenmann, 1915 : 226—272; 1915 : 1—99; 1917—1929; 1—574; Gregory, 1937 : 319—360; Gregory and Conrad, 1937 : 319—360; Tortonese, 1941—42 : 11—76; Myers, 1942 : 89—114; Campos, 1943 : 285—288; Schultz, 1944 : 235—367; Alvarez, 1945 : 263—282; Amaral Campos, 1945 : 431—466; Poll, 1945 : 36—77; Travassos 1946 : 1—32; 1946 : 1—13; Stigchel, 1947 : 1—204; Myers, 1949 : 195—204; Fernandez-Yépez, 1949 : 353—355; 1950 : 169—181; Amaral Campos, 1950 : 137—143; Schultz, 1950 : 44—73; Gosline, 1951 :17—58; Hoedeman, 1951 : 1—8; Böhlke, 1953 : 658—664; 1954 : 97—104; Weitzman, 1954 : 213—263; Fernandez-Yépez, 1955 : 1—11; Travassos, 1957 : 73—101; Böhlke, 1958 : 1—121; Myers, 1960 : 206—211; Géry, 1960 : 15—39; 1963 : 502—503, 597—617; 1964 : 1—44, 1965 : 195—218; Weitzman, 1960 : 217—239; 1962 : 1—77; 1964 : 127—169; 1966 : 1—56; Nelson, 1964 : 59—152; Welters and Darder, 1964 : 1—114; Add.—Poll, 1967 : 1—153; Menezes, 1969 : 1—150; Roberts, 1969 : 391—500.

Fresh waters of Central and South America and Rio Grande del Norte in North America. More than 150 genera, very many species. Important commercial fishes. Many small forms are kept in aquariums.

Family 130. **Gasteropelecidae** 262/276, thesis 30—3, footnote. Figure 343. (=Gastropelecidae.) Beilbauchfische, klinobryukhie.

Lit. J : 137; N : —; G : 41; GRWM : 395, 410; MA : —; Pozzi, 1936 : 423—439; Fraser-Brunner, 1950 : 959—970; Weitzman, 1960 : 217—239; 1962 : 1—77.

Fresh waters of South America. 3 genera, several species.

Family 131. **Ctenoluciidae** (263/277), thesis 30—3, footnote. Figure 344. (=Xiphostomidae = Xiphostomatidae, +Hepsetidae ex parte.) Shchukosal'mlerovye, mecherotye.

Lit. J : (137); N : — ; G : (41); GRWM : 395; MA : —; Weitzman, 1962 : 1—77.

Fresh waters of South America. 2—3 genera, several species. Fished locally.

30

Family 132. **Anostomidae** 264/278, thesis 30–3, footnote. Figures 345–348. (=Anostomatidae, + 132a. Prochilodontidae, +132b. Curimantidae, +Anodontidae, +132c. Chilodontidae.) Malorotye sal'mlery, Engmaulsalmler.

Lit. J : 137; N : –; G : 41; GRWM : 395, 411 + 132a–c; ; MA : –; Fernandez-Yépez, 1948 : 1–79; Myers, 1950 : 184–198; Géry, 1961 : 93–112; Weitzman, 1962 : 1–77, Add. – idem, 1966 : 1–56.

Fresh waters of South America. About 40 genera, many species. Fished locally. Small forms kept in aquariums.

Family 133. **Hemiodontidae** 265/279, thesis 30–3, footnote. Figures 349–350. (=Hemiodidae, +Bivibranchiidae, +133a. Parodontidae.) Schlanksalmler, poluzubye sal'mlery.

Lit. J : 137; N : –; G : 42; GRWM : 395, 411 + family 133a : 410; MA : –; Hoedeman, 1950 : 11–27; Travassos, 1955 : 1–32; Weitzman, 1952 : 1–77.

Fresh waters of South America. More than 10 genera, a small number of species. Fished locally. Small forms kept in aquariums.

Family 134. **Citharinidae** 266/280, thesis 30–3, footnote. Figures 351–353. (+134a. Distichodontidae, +134b. Ichthyboridae = Ichthyoboridae.) Geradsalmler.

Lit. J : 138; N : –; G : 43; GRWM : 396, 411 + families, 134a, 134b: MA : –; Daget. 1962 : 81–106; 1966 : 376–386; Weitzman, 1962 : 1–77.

Fresh waters of Africa. About 20 genera, many species. Fished locally.

Suborder 30.2. Gymnotoidei, thesis 30–4. (Gymnonoti, Glanelcheli, Characoidei ex parte.) Berg, 1940 : 264; GRWM : 396. (Gymnotoidea MA : 69) Regan, 1911 : 13–32; Ellis, 1913–14 : 109–195; Travassos, 1960 : 1–34. 2 superfamilies, 4 families (135–138).

Superfamily 30.2.1. **Sternachoidea**. Berg, 1940 : 264; MA : –. 2 families (135, 136).

Family 135. **Rhamphichthyidae** 267/281, thesis 30–6. Figure 354. Amerikanische Messerfische.

Lit. J : 138; N : –; G : 43; GRWM : 396, 411; MA : (69) (family 137); Eigenmann and Allen, 1942 : 1–494; Travassos, 1960 : 1–34; Curra and Miranda Ribeiro, 1961 : 474–481.

Fresh waters of Central and South America. 2 genera, several species. Fished locally.

Family 136. **Apteronotidae** (268/282), thesis 30–7. Figure 355. (+Sternarchidae, +Sternopygidae.) Amerikanische Messerfische, sternarkhovye.

Lit. J : 138; N : –; G : (44); GRWM; 396, 411; MA (69) (family 137); Eigenmann and Allen, 1942 : 1–494; Curra, 1964 : 139–143.

Fresh waters of Central and South America. About 10 genera, a small number of species. Fished locally.

Superfamily 30.2.2. **Gymnotoidea**. Berg, 1940 : 264; MA : 69; 2 families (137 and 138).

Family 137. Gymnotidae 269/283, thesis 30—9. Figure 356. Gymnotes, Carapos, Amerikanische Messerfische.

Lit. J : 138; N : —; G : 43; GRWM : 396, 411; MA : 69 + family 135, 136; Eigenmann and Ward, 1905 : 159—188; Ellis,1913—1914 : 109—195; Eigenmann and Allen, 1942 : 1—494.

Fresh waters of Central America; from Guatemala to Rio de la Plata. 4 genera, several species. Fished locally. Small forms kept in aquariums.

Family 138. Electrophoridae 270/284, thesis 30—10. Figure 357. Elektricheskii ugor', electric eels, anguille électrique, elektrische Aale.

Lit. J : 138; N : —; G : 44; GRWM : 396, 411; MA : (69) (family 137); Eigenmann and Allen, 1942 : 1—494.

Fresh waters of the northeastern slope of South America; Orinoco and Amazon rivers. 1 genus, several species. Fished locally; game fishes.

Suborder 30.3. Cyprinoidei, thesis 30—11 (Eventognathi.) Berg, 1940 : 264; GRWM : 396; Cyprinoidea MA : 70; Berg, 1912 : 1—336; 1914 : 337—704; Weber and Beaufort, 1916, 3 : 1—239; Holly, 1927 : 115—150; Berg, 1933 : 705—846; Chu, 1935 : 1—225; Uchida, 1939 : 1—458; Ramaswami, 1952 : 125—150, 495—538; Tchang, 1959 : 1—130; 1960 : 1—67. 5 families (139—143).

Family 139. Catostomidae 271/285, thesis 30—14. Figures 359, 360. Chukuchanovye, suckers, buffalofishes, yangchi yü k'o.

Lit. J : 139; N : —; G : 44; GRWM : 396, 412; MA : 70; Hubbs, 1930 : 379—423; Legendre, 1943 : 227—233; Berg, 1948—49 : 477—479; Robins and Raney, 1957 : 291—318; G. Smith, 1966 : 1—132.

Fresh waters of Central and North America, northeastern Siberia (west to the Yana River), and the Yangtze River in China. About 13 genera, many species. Commercial fishes.

Family 140. Cyprinidae 272/286, thesis 30—15. Figures 362—375. (+Gobiobotidae, +Medidae, +140a. Psilorhynchidae.) Carps, minnows, chubbs, daces, carpes, vairons, poissons blancs, Karpfenartige, Karpfenfische, karpovye, li k'o, koi ka.

Lit. J : 139, N : —; G : 45; GRWM : 396, 412 +family 140a; MA : 70, Jordan and Fowler, 1903 : 811—862; Fowler, 1908 : 517—533; Berg, 1912 : 1—336; 1914 : 337—704; 1933 : 705—846; Hora, 1921 : 633—687; Tchang, 1930 : 1—159; 1931 : 1—171; Piton, 231 : 20—29; Lin, 1933 : 75—91, 197—215, 337—348, 489—505; Tchang, 1933 : 1—247; Lin, 1934 : 615—632; Hora and Mukerji, 1935 : 391—397; Lin, 1935 : 249—260; Fang, 1936 : 421—458; :686—712; Mukerji, 1936 : 323—359; Nichols, 1938 : 191—193; Taranets, 1938 : 453—472; H. Smith, 1945 : 1—622; Tret'yakov, 1946 : 149—156; Kryzhanovskii, 1947 : 53—64; Berg, 1948—49 : 479—847; Vasnetsov, 1950 : 2—84; Nikol'skii, 1950 : 59—68; Oliva, 1953 : 1—61; Spanovskaya, 1953 : 1—19; 259—270; Brittani, 1954 : 1—24; Menon, 1955 : 5—26; Lukash, 1956 : 13—38; Groenwald, 1958 : 263—230; Ladiges, 1960 : 105—150; Legendre, 1960 : 178—210; Miller and Hubbs, 1960 : 1—39; Bănărescu, 1961 : 318—346; 1962 : 38—64; Kafanova, 1961 : 9—18; Heuschmann, 1962 : 29—190; Bănărescu, 1963 : 457—463; 1964 : 87—98; Menon, 1964 : 173—260; Wu et al., 1964 : 1—228; Hopson, 1965 : 99—149; Lindberg and Legeza, 1965 : 153—157; Svetovidova, 1965 : 245—261; Bănărescu, 1968 : 628—636; Add.—Bănărescu and Nalbant, 1967 : 293—312.

: 341—355; Bănărescu, 1967 : 215—227, : 297—308; 1968 : 3—14, : 305—311; Lachner, 1967 : 557—580; Spillmann, 1967 : 127—133; Svetovidova, 1967 : 979—989; Shutov, 1969 : 1105—1107; Dashdorh et al., 1969 : 289—299.

Fresh waters of all parts of the world except South America, Australia, and Madagascar. Important commercial fishes. Small forms kept in aquariums. Several subfamilies, more than 200 genera, very many species.

Family 141. **Gyrinocheilidae** 273/287, thesis 30—19. Figure 380. (Cyprinidae ex parte.) Gyrinochelids.

Lit. J : (143): N : —; G : (55); GRWM : 396, 412; MA : 71; Berg, 1912 : 5; H. Smith, 1945 : 1—622; Jayaram, 1951 : 107—112; Bertin and Arambourg, 1958 : 2204—2500.

Fresh waters of Borneo and Indochina: Mekong River and rivers of Thailand and Cambodia. 1 genus, a small number of species.

Family 142. **Homalopteridae** 274/288, thesis 30—18. Figures 377—379. (+Lepidoglanidae, +142a. Gastromyzonidae MA : 71 =Gastromyzontidae.) Hillstream fishes, tsaiti wênmên ch'iu, ploskoperye.

Lit. J : 145 (149); N : —; G : 55; GRWM : 396, 412; MA : 71; Fang, 1930 : 25—42; Hora, 1920 : 195—215; 1931 : 67—69; 1932 : 263—330; Fang, 1933 : 39—50; Hora, 1941 : 221—232; : 44—64; Ramaswami, 1948 : 515—538; Chen and Liang, 1949 : 157—169; Hora and Jayaram, 1951 : 61—68; 1952 : 191—195; Jayaram, 1951 : 113—117; Silas, 1951 : 11—17; 1953 : 173—263; Alfred, 1961 : 32—37. Add.—Alfred, 1969 : 213—237.

Mountain streams of India, Indonesia, Indochina, Southern China, including Taiwan. About 30 genera, many species.

Family 143. Cobitidae 275/289, thesis 30—17. Figure 376. (=Acanthopsidae, +Adiposiidae.) Loaches, loches, Schmerlen Dorngrundeln. ch'iu k'o, dojo ka, v'yunovye.

Lit. J : 144; N : —; G : 54; GRWM : 396, 412; MA : 71; Jordan and Fowler, 1903 : 765—774; Berg, 1907 : 435—438; Hora, 1922 : 63—83; Drensky, 1928 : 156—181; Shaw and Tchang, 1931 : 63—84; Hora, 1936 : 299—321; Berg, 1938 : 314—318; Nichols, 1938 : 191—193; Okada and Ikeda, 1939 : 89—104; Hora, 1941 : 44—64; Rendahl, 1944 : 1—54; 1944 : 1—9; Berg, 1948—49 : 848—903; Martekhov, 1950 : 1—9; Tortonese, 1951—52 : 1—14; Sterba, 1958 : 201—234; Alfred, 1961 : 32—37; Băcescu, 1962 : 281—301; Bănărescu and Nalbant, 1963 : 159—201; Nalbant, 1963 : 343—379; Opalatenke, 1965 : 90—91; Add.—Zanandrea et al., 1965 : 233—259; Bănărescu and Nalbant, 1966 : 151—186; 1968 : 327—351; Bănărescu, 1968 : 353—356; Băcescu, 1967 : 357—370; Băcescu and Mayer, 1950 : 51—60.

Fresh waters of Europe and the whole of Asia (with Japan and Borneo), and part of Africa (Morocco and Ethiopia). More than 20 genera, many species. Some forms kept in aquariums.

Section 2. Siluri. Berg, 1940 : 271. (Siluriformes GRWM : 396.) (Siluroidei MA : 71.) 1 suborder, 31 families (144—174).

Suborder 30.4. Siluroidei, thesis 30—20. (Nematognathi, Siluroidiformes.) Berg, 1940 : 271; GRWM : 396; MA : 71; Bleeker, 1858 : 38—41; Eigenmann and Eigenmann, 1890 : 1—509; Regan, 1911 : 553—577; Ribeiro, 1912 : 1—504; Weber and Beaufort, 1913, 2 : 184—375; Herre, 1926 : 385—415;

Breder, 1928 : 1—25; Tchang and Shih, 1934 : 333 — 353; Tchang, 1936 : 33—56; Gosline, 1945 : 1—138; Schulz, 1945 : 173—338; Stigchel, 1947 : 1—204; Chaux and Fang, 1949 : 342—346; Lambert, 1958 : 39—56. Add. — Dmitrenko, 1968 : 65—83; 1969 : 39—43, 1968. 2 superfamilies, 31 families (144—174). Large catfishes are of great commercial importance.

Superfamily 30.4.1. **Diplomystoidea.** Berg, 1940 : 271; MA :—. 1 family (144).

Family 144. **Diplomystidae** 276/290, thesis 30—63. Figure 404.

Lit. J : 145; N : —; G : 56; GRWM : 396, 412; MA : 76; Fisher, 1917 : 405 — 422; Stigchel, 1947 : 1—204.

Fresh waters of Chile and Argentina. 1 genus, a small number of species.

Superfamily 30.4.2. **Siluroidea.** Berg, 1940 : 271; MA : —. 30 families (145 — 174).

Family 145. **Ariidae** 277/291, theses 30—43; 56, 60, 66. Figures 393, 400, 402, 405. (=Tachysuridae = Bagreidae.) Sea catfishes, ariid catfishes, morskie somy, hainien k'o, hama giki ka.

Lit. J : 145; N : —; G : 56; GRWM : 396, 413 + family 152; MA : 75; Chandy, 1953 : 1—18; Lindberg and Legeza, 1965 : 157 — 159.

Primarily marine waters of tropical and subtropical latitudes of the ocean; littoral zones, more rarely in the mouths of rivers, About 30 genera, many species. Of little importance in world marine fishing. Game fishes.

Family 146. **Doradidae** 278/292, thesis 30—83. Figure 416. Bokocheshuinikovye, Dornwelse, doradid catfishes.

Lit. J : 146; N : —; G : 57; GRWM : 396, 413; MA : 76 + family 147; Eigenmann, 1925 : 280 — 365. Add. — Fernandez, 1969 : 7 —72.

Fresh waters of the tropical latitudes of South America. About 50 genera, many species. Game and aquarium fishes.

Family 147. **Auchenipteridae** 279/293; thesis 30 — 74. Figure 409. (+Trachycorystidae, Doradidae ex parte.) Zatylkoperye somy.

Lit. J : (146); N : —; G : (57); GRWM : 396, 414; MA : (76) + (family 146); Schultz, 1945 : 173—338.

Fresh waters of the tropical latitudes of South America. 2 genera, a small number of species. Game fishes.

Family 148. **Ageneiosidae** (280/294), thesis 30 — 75. Figure 410. (=Ageniosidae, Doradidae ex parte.) Dantsellovye.

Lit. J : (146); N : — ; G : (57); GRWM : 396, 414; MA : 76, Schultz, 1945 : 173 — 338.

Fresh waters of the tropical latitudes of South America. 1 genus, a considerable number of species.

Family 149. **Plotosidae** 281/295, thesis 30—30. Figure 384. Stinging catfishes, plotosid marine catfishes, barbel eels, mannien k'o, gonzui ka, morskie kolyuchie somy, ugrekhvostye somy.

Lit. J : 147; N : —; G : 57; GRWM : 396. 414; MA : 75; Lindberg and Legeza, 1965 : 159 — 160. Add. — Jayaram et al., 1967 : 137 — 146.

Primarily marine waters of the tropical latitudes of the Indian and Pacific oceans north as far as Japan. More than 6 genera, a small number of species. Fished locally.

Family 150. **Siluridae** 282/296, thesis 30 — 25. Figure 381. Somovye, catfishes, glanes, sheatfishes, Welse, silurid catfishes, poissons-chats, silures, glanes, nien k'o, namazu ka.

Lit. J : 147; N : — ; G : 58; GRWM : 396, 412; MA : 73; Jordan and Fowler, 1903 : 897 — 911; Fisher, 1917 : 405 —422; Fowler, 1932 : 247 — 279; Hora, 1936 : 199 — 209; : 347 — 361; Myers, 1938 : 98; Hora and Gupta, 1941 : 12— 43; Berg, 1948 —1949 : 903 — 909; Nikol'skii and Soin, 1948 : 1357— 1360; Haig, 1950 : 59 — 116; Tomoda, 1961 : 347 — 354; Inger and Kong, 1962 : 1—268. Add. — Parameswaran et al., 1968 : 89 — 98.

Fresh waters of Europe and Asia. About 8 genera, many species. Fished locally; game fishes.

Family 151. **Bagridae** 283/297, theses 30 — 38, 57. Figures 389, 390, 401. (+ Porcidae, + Mystidae, + 151a. Cranoglanididae) Bagrid catfishes, ch'ang k'o, chiki ka, kasatkovye.

Lit. J : 148; N : — ; G : 58; GRWM : 396, 412 + family 151a, MA : 72 + families 151a + 162; Meyers, 1931 : 255 — 262; Hora and Gupta, 1941 : 12 — 43; Berg, 1948 — 49 : 909 — 919; Jayaram, 1955 : 120 — 128; 256 — 363; 1966 : 433 — 450; 1064 — 1139; Inger and Kong, 1962 : 1—268. Add. — Jayaram, 1968 : 287 — 386.

Fresh waters of Asia to the north as far as the Amur basin. More than 15 genera, many species. Fished locally. Small forms kept in aquariums.

Family 152. **Doiichthyidae** 284/298, thesis 30 — 33, footnote. Figure 387. (Ariidae ex parte.) Novogvineiskie somy.

Lit. J : (146); N : —; G : (56); GRWM : (396) (family 145); MA : 75; Weber and Beaufort, 1913, 2 : 333 — 335.

Brackish and fresh waters of the southern part of New Guinea. 1 genus, 1 species.

Family 153. **Ictaluridae** (285/299), thesis 30 — 61. Figure 403. (+Ameiuridae = Amiuridae.) Freshwater catfishes, horned pout, channel cats, Katzenwelse, north American catfishes, amerikanskii somik koshachii som.

Lit. J : (147); N : —; G : (59); GRWM : 396, 412; MA : 76; Hubbs and Bailey, 1947 : 1—15; Taylor, 1955 : 1—583. Add. — Taylor, 1969 : 1—315.

Fresh waters of South America, south as far as Guatemala. About 10 genera, quite a large number of species. Fished locally. Game fishes. Small forms kept in aquariums.

Family 154. **Amblycipitidae** (286)/300, thesis 30—36. Figure 388. (=Amblycepidae = Amblycepitidae.) Tolstokhvostye somy.

Lit. J: 148; N: —; G: 60; GRWM: 396, 413; MA: 73 + family 154; Hora, 1933: 607—621; Hora and Gupta, 1941: 12—43; H. Smith, 1945: 1—622.

Fresh waters of India, Burma, and Thailand. 3 genera, a few species.

Family 155. **Akysidae** 287/301, thesis 30—44. Figure 394. (Amblycipitidae ex parte.)

Lit. J: (148); N: —; G: (60); GRWM: 396, 413; MA: (73) (family 155); Weber and Beaufort, 1912, 2: 365—376; Hora, 1936: 199—209; Hora and Gupta, 1941: 12—43; H. Smith, 1945: 1—622.

Fresh waters of Southern Asia. 2 genera, several species.

Family 156. **Sisoridae** 288/302, thesis 30—42. Figure 392. (+ Bagariidae.) T'iao k'o, gornosomnikovye.

Lit. J: 148; N: —; G: 60; GRWM: 396, 413; MA: 74; Annandale, 1923: 573—577; Hora, 1925: 1—44; Mukerji, 1936: 323—359; Hora, 1938: 363—375; Hora and Gupta, 1941: 12—43; Berg, 1948—49: 920—925; Hora, 1950: 183—202; Silas, 1951: 367—370; Hora and Silas, 1952: 5—29; Steinitz, 1961: 105—115; Tilak, 1963: 281—320.

Fresh waters of Southern Asia. About 12 genera, many species. Game fishes.

Family 157. **Amphiliidae** 289/303, thesis 30—52. Figure 398. Afrikanskie myagkoperosomovye.

Lit. J: 149; N: —; G: 60; GRWM: 396, 413; MA: 74; Harry, 1953: 177—232.

Fresh waters of Africa. About 10 genera, a few species.

Family 158. **Chacidae** 290/304, thesis 30—31. Figure 385. Grosmaulwelse, lienwei t'iao k'o, bol'sherotye somy, khakovye.

Lit. J: 149; N: —; G: 60; GRWM: 396, 413; MA: 75; Hora and Gupta, 1941: 12—43; Jayaram and Majumdar, 1964: 177—181.

Fresh waters of India and Indonesia. 1 genus, a small number of species. Aquarium fishes.

Family 159. **Schilbeidae** 291/305, theses 30—33, 47. Figures 386, 395. (+ 159a. Pangastidae.) Pangazievye, Schilbeid catfishes.

Lit. J: 149; N: —; G: 60; GRWM: 396, 412 + family 459a; MA: 74 + family 159a; Myers, 1931: 255—262; Hora, 1937: 235—240; 1941: 97—115; Hora and Gupta, 1941: 12—43; Trewavas, 1943: 164—171; Kulkarni, 1952: 231—238; Inger and Kong, 1962: 1—268; Thys, 1964: 214—230.

Fresh waters of Africa, India, Indochina, and Indonesia. About 20 genera, many species. Fished locally. Small forms kept in aquariums.

Family 160. **Heteropneustidae** (292/306), thesis 30—26. Figure 382. (=Saccobranchidae, Clariidae ex parte.) Meshkozhabernye somy.

Lit. J: (149); N: —; G: (61); GRWM: 396, 413; MA: (73) (Family 161); Hora, 1936: 199—209; Munro, 1955: 50.

Fresh waters of India, Ceylon, and Indochina. 1 genus, 1 species. Fished locally.

Family 161. **Clariidae** 293/307, theses 30—27, 48. Figures 383, 396. Clarid catfishes, hutzŭ nien k'o, hire namazu ka.

Lit. J : 149; N : —; G : 61; GRWM : 396, 413; MA : 73 + family 160; Boulenger, 1907 : 1062 — 1097; David, 1935 : 77 — 147; Hora, 1936 : 347 — 361; 1941 : 97—115; Hora and Gupta, 1941 : 12 — 43; Menon, 1951 : 59 — 66; Greenwood, 1958 : 321—325; Jackson, 1959 : 109 — 128; Greenwood, 1961 : 215 — 241.

Fresh waters of Africa, western, eastern, and southern Asia. About 15 genera, quite a number of species. Of little importance in world marine fishing.

Family 162. **Olyridae** 294/308, thesis 30—39. Figure 391. (Bagridae ex parte.)

Lit. J : (148); N : —; G : (59); GRWM : 396, 413; MA (72) (family 151); Hora, 1936 : 199 — 209.

Fresh waters of India and Burma, Tenasserim River. 1 genus, a small number of species.

Family 163. **Mochokidae** (295/309), thesis 30—54. Figure 399. (Mochockidae = Mochochidae = Mochocidae = Synodontidae.) Fiederbartwelse, upside-down catfishes, bakhromchatousye somy.

Lit. J : 150; N : — ; G : (61); GRWM : 396, 413; MA : 74; Vaillant, 1895 : 233 — 284; 1896 : 87—178; Jordan and Herre, 1907 : 513 — 524; Whitehead, 1962 : 97 — 120. Add.—Jubb and Le Roux, 1969 : 13 — 23.

Fresh waters of Africa. About 10 genera, quite a number of species. Fished locally. Small forms kept in aquariums.

Family 164. **Malapteruridae** 296/310, thesis 30— 50. Figure 397. (=Malopteruridae = Torpedinidae.) Electric catfishes, elektricheskie somy.

Lit. J : 150; N : —; G : 62; GRWM : 396, 413; MA : 75; Sterba, 1959 : 314. Add.—Poll and Gosse, 1969; 1 — 12.

Fresh waters of tropical Africa and the Nile River. 1 genus, a small number of species. Fished locally. Aquarium fishes.

Family 165. **Pimelodidae** 297/311, thesis 30— 72. Figure 406. (+ Pseudopimelodidae.) Pimelodid catfishes, pimelodovye, ploskogolovye somy.

Lit. J : 150; N : —; G : 62; GRWM : 396, 414 + family 166; MA : 76; Gosline, 1941 : 83 — 88; Eigenmann and Allen, 1942 : 1 — 494; Schultz, (1944) 1945 : 173 — 388.

Fresh waters of Central and South America. About 60 genera, many species. Fished locally. Aquarium fishes.

Family 166. **Callophysidae** (—/—), thesis 30— 73. No figure. (Pimelodidae ex parte.)

Lit. J : —; N : —; G : (62); GRWM : 396) (family 165); MA : — ; Eigenmann and Allen, 1942 : 1—194; Schultz, (1944) 1945 : 173 — 388.

Fresh waters of Central and South America. 1 genus, a small number of species.

Family 167. **Helogeneidae** (298/312), thesis 30—72, footnote. Figure 407. (=Hologenidae = Helogenidae.)

Lit. J: (150); N: —; G: (62); GRWM: 396, 414; MA: 76; Regan, 1911: 573; Sterba, 1959: 310.

Fresh waters of tropical South America. 1 genus, 1 species. Aquarium fish.

Family 168. **Hypophthalmidae.** 299/313, thesis 30—72, footnote. Figure 408. Nizhneglazye somy.

Lit. J: 150; N: —; G: 62; GRWM: 396, 414; MA: 77; Regan, 1911: 573; Fisher, 1917: 405—422.

Fresh waters of tropical South America. 1 genus, 1 species.

Family 169. **Trichomycteridae** 300/314, thesis 30—80. Figures 413, 414. (=Pygidiidae, Pygiidae MA: 77, +Nemotogenyidae.) Schmerlenwelse, parasitic catfishes, vandellievye.

Lit. J: (151); N: —; G: (64); GRWM: 396, 414; MA: 77; Ribeiro, 1912: 1—31; Eigenmann, 1918: 259—398; Myers, 1944: 591—602; Tchernavin, 1944: 234—275; Schultz, (1944) 1945: 173—338; Miranda Ribeiro, 1951: 1—16; Ferreira and Soriano, 1960: 315—338; Myers and Weitzman, 1966: 277—287.

Fresh waters of South America. About 30 genera and 140 species. Aquarium fishes.

Family 170. **Cetopsidae** (300A/314A), thesis 30—79; Figure 412.

Lit. J: 152; N: —; G: 64; GRWM: 396, 414; MA: 77; Schultz, (1944) 1945: 173—338; Gosline, 1945: 54—55.

Fresh waters of South America. 4 genera, a few species.

Family 171. **Aspredinidae** (301/315), thesis 30—78. Figure 411. (+Bunocephalidae.) Bratpflannenwelse, banjo catfishes, bugorchatogolovye somy.

Lit. J: 151 (151); N: —; R: (63); GRWM: 396, 414; MA: 77; Myers, 1942: 89—114; Schultz, (1944) 1945: 173—338; Myers, 1960: 132—139.

Fresh waters of tropical South America. About 15 genera, quite a number of species. Aquarium fishes.

Family 172. **Callichthyidae** 302/316, thesis 30—82. Figure 415. Pantsernye somy, Panzerwelse, callichthyid catfishes, kallikhtovye.

Lit. J: 152; N: —; G: 65; GRWM: 396, 414; MA: 77; Ribeiro, 1912: 1—31; Gosline, 1940: 1—29; Schultz, (1944) 1945: 173—338; Rossi, 1951—1952: 1—10; Hoedeman, 1952: 1—11.

Fresh waters of South America. About 10 genera, quite a number of species. Aquarium fishes.

Family 173. **Loricariidae** 303/317, thesis 30—86. Figure 419. (+Hypostomidae.) Hornischwelse, loricariid catfishes, lorikarievye.

Lit. J: 152; N: —; G: 65; GRWM: 396, 414; MA: 78; Regan, 1904: 191—324; Ribeiro, 1912: 1—31; Giltay, 1936: 1—7; Eigenmann and Allen, 1942: 1—494; Schultz, (1944) 1945: 173—338; Gosline, 1947: 79—144. Add.—Schubart, 1964: 1—19; Tovar, 1967: 201—259; Boseman, 1968: 1—108.

Fresh waters of South America, partly Central America. About 50 genera, many species. Game and aquarium fishes.

Family 174. **Astroblepidae** 303A/317A, thesis 30—85. Figure 418. (=Argidae = Argiidae = Cyclopiidae = Cyclopidae, Loricariidae ex parte.)

Lit. J: (152); N: —; G: (64); GRWM: 396, 414; MA: 78; Schultz, (1944) 1945: 173—338; Gosline, 1947: 79—144.

Fresh waters of South America, partly Central America. 1 genus, quite a number of species.

Order 31. ANGUILLIFORMES 83/88, thesis 0—49. (Apodes.) Berg, 1940: 275; MA: 78; (Anguilliformes ex parte GRWM: 393); McClelland, (1844) 1845: 151—226; Kaup, 1856: 1—160; Jordan and Snyder, 1901: 837—890; Regan, 1912: 377—387; Weber and Beaufort, 1916, 3: 240—410; Herre, 1923: 123—236; Chen, 1929: 1—49 + 1—12; D'Ancona, 1932: 1—21; Breder, 1928: 1—25; Fowler, 1932: 46 63 + 126—144; Parr. 1932: 1—41; Rivero, 1932: 3—26; Trewavas, 1932: 639—659; Wang, 1934: 33—49; 1935: 1—65; Griffin, 1936: 12—26; Nair, 1948: 87—91; Bertin, 1951: 1—193; Ginsburg, 1951: 431—485; Koefoed, 1955: 1—16; Bertin, 1956: 1—192; Bal and Mohmed, 1957: 732—740; J. Smith, 1962: 421—444; 447—466; Asano, 1962: 1—143; Chang, 1964: 653—657; Blache, 1967: 1122—1187; Nelson, 1967: 562, 563. Add.—Chen and Weng, 1967: 1—86. 2 suborders, 24 families (175—198).

Suborder 31.1. Anguilloidei, thesis 31—8. (Carencheli, +Enchelycephali, + Colocephali; Anguilloidei, +Congroidei.) Berg, 1940: 276; MA: —; Anguilloidei, ex parte. GRWM: 393; Beebe, 1935: 1—23 (: 12, Figure 5), 18 families (175—192).

Family 175. **Derichthyidae** 307/321, thesis 31—10. Figure 427.

Lit. J: 129; N: 139; G: 66; GRWM: 393, 405; MA: 84; Trewavas, 1932: 639—659; Beebe, 1935: 1—23; Gosline, 1952: 130—135.

Deep waters of the Atlantic and Pacific. 3 genera, 3 species.

Family 176. **Anguillidae** 308/322, thesis 31—21. Figure 431. ("Muraenidae" Fowler.) Freshwater eels, true eels, anguilles, Aale, rechnye ugrevye, manli k'o, unagi ka.

Lit. J: 130; N: 138; G: 66; GRWM: 393, 404; MA: 81; E. Schmidt, 1914; J. Schmidt; 1928: 379—388; 1928: 179—210; Ege, 1939: 1—256; Berg, 1948—49: 937—940; Cairns, 1950: 43—52; Andriyashev, 1954: 132—133; Smith and Saunder, 1955: 238—269; Svetovidov, 1964: 147—150; Lindberg and Legeza, 1965: 162—166.

North Atlantic, Indian Ocean, and western Pacific. Marine and diadromous forms. 1 genus, several species. Of little importance in world marine fishing.

Family 177. **Simenchelyidae** 309/323, thesis 31—22. Figure 432. (=Simenchelidae.) Snubnosed eels, paraziticheskie ugrevye; parasitic snubnosed eels, slime eels, chishêng man k'o, kongo anago ka.

Lit. J: 130; N: (138); G: 66; GRWM: 393, 405; MA: 83; Trewavas, 1932: 639—659; Gosline, 1952: 130—135; Castle, 1961: 1—30.

Deep waters of the Atlantic and western Pacific off Japan. 2 genera, several species.

Family 178. **Xenocongridae** 310/324, thesis 31—15. Figure 429. (+Chlopsidae, Myridae ex parte.)

Lit. J : 130; N : 139; G : 66; GRWM : 393, 404 + family 188 ex parte; MA : 82 + family 82 ex parte); Regan, 1912 : 301—302; Böhlke, 1956 : 61 — 95; Gosline and Brock, 1960 : 1—372 (117); J. Smith, 1965 : 43 — 54; Böhlke and Smith, 1968 : 25 — 43.

Indian and Pacific oceans. 4 genera, a small number of species.

Family 179. **Myrocongridae** 311/325, thesis 31—19. No figure.

Lit. J : 130; N : 140; G : 66; GRWM : 393, 404; MA : 81; Trewavas, 1932 : 639 — 659; Nelson, 1967 : 562, 563.

Atlantic Ocean in the region of St. Helena Island. 1 genus, 1 species.

Family 180. **Muraenidae** 312/326, thesis 31—13. Figure 428. (+Echidnae, +Heteromyridae.) Morays, moray eels, murènes, haishan k'o, utsubo ka.

Lit. J : 133; N : 140; G : 66; GRWM : 393, 404; MA : 81; D'Ancona, 1928 : 1—146; Myers and Wade, 1941 : 65 — 110 (84 — 90); Buen, 1961 : 1 — 90; J. Smith; 1962 : 421 — 444; Lindberg and Legeza, 1965 : 166 — 170. Add. Blache, 1967 : 178 — 217; : 695 — 709; : 1122 — 1187.

Tropical and subtropical latitudes of oceans. More than 10 genera, many species. Game fishes.

Family 181. **Heterenchelyidae** 313/327, thesis 31—16. Figure 430. (=Heterenchelidae.)

Lit. J : 133, N : (144); G : 67; GRWM : 393, 404; MA : 82; Ben-Tuvia, 1956 : 401 — 408.

Atlantic Ocean. 2 genera, a small number of species.

Family 182. **Moringuidae** 314/328, thesis 31—23. Figure 433. (+Ratabouridae, +Stilbiscidae, +Anguillichthyidae.) Wormlike eels, thread eels, yinman k'o, gausen umihebi ka.

Lit. J : 133; N : 144; G : 67; GRWM : 393, 404; MA : 82; Trewavas, 1932 : 639 — 659; Deraniygala, 1952 : 1—149; Gordon, 1964 : 11 — 14; Gosline and Strasburg, 1956 : 9 — 18.

Indian and Pacific oceans. 3 genera, several species.

Family 183. **Muraenesocidae** 315/329, thesis 31—28. Figure 434, (+Sauromuraenesocidae.) Congerpikes, pike eels, false conger eels, haiman k'o, hamo ka, shchukorylye ugri.

Lit. J : 130; N : 148; G : 68; GRWM : 393, 404; MA : 84; Regan, 1912 : 377 — 387; Karayama and Takai, 1954 : 97 — 101; Jang, 1957 : 110 — 120; Lindberg and Legeza, 1965 : 170 — 174. Add. — Blache, 1968 : 690 — 736; Lane and Stewart, 1968 : 51 — 64.

Atlantic, Indian, and Pacific oceans. 3 genera, a considerable number of species. Of little importance in world marine fishing.

Family 184. **Neenchelyidae** 316/330, thesis 31—29. Figure 435. (=Neenchelidae.)

Lit. J : 133; N : (148); G : 68; GRWM : 393, 404; MA : 85; Trewavas, 1932 : 639 — 659; Nelson, 1967 : 562, 563.

Red Sea; Indo-Australian Archipelago. 1 genus, 1 species.

Family 185. **Nettastomatidae** (317/331), thesis 31—31. Figure 436. (=Nettastomidae.) Witch eels, duck-bill eels, sorcerers, ssŭ man k'o, kuzu anago ka, utkonosye ugri.

Lit. J: 131; N: (149); G: 68; GRWM: 393, 404; MA: 84; Trewavas, 1932: 639—659; Matsubara, 1955: 331, 341.

Deep waters of tropical and subtropical seas. About 10 genera, many species.

Family 186. **Nessorhamphidae** 318/332, thesis 31—32. Figure 437.

Lit. J: —; N: 150; G: 68; GRWM: 393; MA: 84; Trewavas, 1932: 639—659; Beebe, 1935—36: 25—51.

Oceanic waters. 1 genus, 1 species.

Family 187*. **Congridae** 319/333, thesis 31—34. Figure 438. (=Congeridae = Leptocephalidae, + Heterocongridae, + Colocongridae, + 187a. Todaridae.) Congers, conger eels, congres, Meeraal, kanji man k'o, anago ka.

Lit. J: 130; N: 150; G: 68; GRWM: 393; 405 + family 187a; MA: 93; Parr, 1932: 1—41 (19—35); Reid, 1934: 1—11; Myers and Wade, 1941: 65—110 (65—69); Wade, 1946: 181—214 (181—199); Böhlke, 1949: 218; 1957: 57—59; Kanazawa, 1958: 209—267; Asano, 1962: 1—143; Svetovidov, 1964: 150—152; Lindberg and Legeza, 1965: 174—193. Add.—Castle, 1967: 5—12; 1968: 685—726.

Atlantic, Indian, and Pacific oceans. More than 20 genera, many species. Of very little importance in world marine fishing.

Family 188. **Echelidae** 320/334, thesis 31—36. Figure 439. (+ Myridae, + Chilorhinidae, + Muraenichthyidae.) Worm eels, chervevidnye ugri, juan man k'o, medama anago ka.

Lit. J: 131; N: 157; G: 70; GRWM: (393) (ex parte family 173 and ex parte family 189); MA: (85) (family 189); Parr, 1930: 71—73; Myers and Wade, 1941: 65—110 (:70—74); Wade, 1946: 181—214; Schultz and Woods, 1949: 169—174; Gosline, 1950: 309—314; 1951: 195—202; 1952: 130—135 ex parte; Lindberg and Legeza, 1965: 193—194.

Atlantic, Indian, and Pacific oceans. More than 10 genera, a considerable number of species.

Family 189. **Ophichthidac** (321/335), thesis 31—37. Figure 440. (=Ophichthyidae, + Myrophidae, Myridae ex parte.) Snake eels, serpents-de-mer, shêman k'o, umi hebi ka, shilokhvostye ugri.

Lit. J: (132); N: (159); G: (70); GRWM: 393, 405 + family 188 ex parte; MA: 85 + families 188 and 197; Storey, 1939: 61—84; Myers and Wade, 1941: 65—100 (75—84); Gosline, 1951: 298—320; Cadenat, 1954: 238—244; Böhlke, 1956: 1—13; Tortonese, 1960: 233—247; Lindberg and Legeza, 1965: 195—202.

Seas and oceans, primarily tropical waters. More than 200 genera, many species.

* Family 187a. Todaridae (type genus *Todarus* Grassi and Calandrussio, 1896, syn. *Nettodarus* Whitley, 1952).

Family 190. **Ilyophidae** (322/336), thesis 31—40. Figure 441. (=Iliophiidae.)
Lit. J: 130; N: (164); G: 68; GRWM: (393) (family 192). MA: 93; Regan, 1912: 377—387; Trewavas, 1932: 639—659.
Deep Pacific waters. 1 genus, 1 species.

Family 191. **Dysommidae** 323/337, thesis 31—41. Figures 442, 443. (+191a. Dysomminidae = Dysominidae, Figure 443.) Mustard eels, chien-kang man k'o, mekura anago ka.
Lit. J: 130; N: 164; G: 68; GRWM: 393, 404 + family 191a; MA: 85, 82 + family 191a; Matsubara, 1936: 960 — 962; Böhlke, 1949: 33—39; 1951: 6; Böhlke and Hubbs, 1951: 7—10; Bertin and Arambourg, 1958: 2204—2500. Add. II—Robins, 1970: 293—335.
Deep waters of the Indian and Pacific oceans. 4 genera, several species.

Family 192. **Synaphobranchidae** 324/338, thesis 31—42. Figure 444. Deep-sea eels, longnose eels, hosai man k'o, hora anago ka, slitnozhabernye ugri, sinafobrankhovye.
Lit. J: 130; N: 165; G: 68; GRWM: 393, 405 + family 190; MA: 82; Bruun, 1937: 1—31; Matsubara, 1938: 60—66; Norman and Trewavas, 1939: 352—359; Matsubara and Ochiai, 1951: 251—259; Castle, 1961: 1—30; 1964: 29—42.
Deep waters of the Atlantic, Indian, and Pacific oceans. 2 genera, a few species.

Suborder 31.2. Nemichthyoidei, thesis 31—1. (Nemichthydiformes.) Berg, 1940: 270 (Anguilloidei ex parte GRWM: 393); MA: —; Roule and Bertin, 1929: 1—113. 6 families (193—198).

Family 193. **Serrivomeridae** 325/339, thesis 31—2. Figure 422. (+Gavialicipitidae = Gavalicipitidae, Nemichthyidae ex parte.) Deep-sea eels, pilososhnikovyi ugor'.
Lit. J: (132); N: 145; G: 72; GRWM: 393, 405; MA: 85; Roule and Bertin, 1929: 1—113 (: 58); Parr, 1932: 1—41; Trewavas, 1932: 639—659; Beebe and Crane, 1936: 54—102; 1937: 331—348; Bertin, 1941: 524—531; 1944: 101—108; Bauchot, 1959: 1—148; Castle, 1961: 1—30.
Warm and tropical seas. 2—3 genera, a few species.

Family 194. **Nemichthyidae** 326/340, thesis 31—6. Figure 424. (+Avocettinidae.) Thread eels, snipe eels, hsien man k'o, shigi unagi ka, bekasorylye ugri, nitekhvostye ugri.
Lit. J: 132; N: 146; G: 72; GRWM: 393,405 + family 196; MA: 86; Roule and Bertin, 1929: 1—113; Trewavas, 1932: 639—659; Beebe and Crane, 1937: 349—383; Castle, 1961: 1—30.
Deep waters of warm and tropical seas. More than 5 genera, a few species.

Family 195. **Cyemidae** 327/342, thesis 31—4. Figure 423. (=Cyematidae.)
Lit. J: 132; N: 147; G: 72; GRWM: 393, 405; MA: 86; Trewavas, 1933: 601—614; Bertin, 1937: 1—30.
Deep oceanic waters. 1 genus, 1 species.

Family 196. **Avocettinopsidae** 328/341, thesis 31—7. Figure 425. (Nemichthyidae ex parte.) Shiloklyuvye ugri.

Lit. J: (132); N: (149); G: 71; GRWM: (393) (family 194); MA: 86; Roule and Bertin, 1929: 1—113; Bertin, 1942: 101—111; Böhlke and Cliff, 1956: 95—99; Mead and Rubinoff, 1966: 1—6.

Oceanic waters. 1 genus, 1 species.

Family 197. **Macrocephenchelyidae** 329/343, thesis 31—0, footnote. Figure 420. (=Macrocephenchelidae, Macrocephanchelidae.) Bol'shegolovye ugri.

Lit. J: —; N: 166; G: 68; GRWM: 393, 405; MA: (85) (family 189); Fowler, (1933): 233—367; Myers and Wade, 1941: 65—110; Gosline, 1951: 298—320; 1952: 130—135.

Deep waters of Macassar Strait (between Borneo and Celebes). 1 genus, 1 species.

Family 198. **Aoteidae** 331/345, thesis 31—0, footnote. Figure 421 (=Aoteridae, Symbranchidae ex parte.)

Lit. J: —; N: —; G: (72); GRWM: 393, 405; MA: —; Phillipps, 1926: 529—357.

Marine waters of the New Zealand coast. 1 genus, 1 species.

Order 32. HALOSAURIFORMES 84/89, thesis 0—55. (Lyopomi.) Günther, 1887: 1—335 (: 235); Berg, 1940: 281. (Notacanthiformes ex parte GRWM: 393; MA: 59); Bertin and Arambourg, 1958: 2204—2500; Bailey, 1960: 1—21; Gosline, 1961: 1—42. 1 family (199).

Family 199. **Halosauridae** 332/346, thesis 32—0. Figure 445. Haihsi man k'o, tokage gisu ka.

Lit. J: 128; N: 166; G: 73; GRWM: 393; 405; MA: 60; Günther, 1887: 1—335; Goode and Bean, 1894: 455—470; Weber and Beaufort, 1922; 4: 1—6; Marshall, 1962, 249—270.

Deep oceanic waters. 2 genera, several species.

Order 33. NOTACANTHIFORMES 85/90, thesis 0— 56. (Heteromi.) Berg, 1940: 281 (Notacanthiformes ex parte GRWM: 393); MA: 59; D'Ancona, 1932: 280—306; Matsubara, 1936: 963—964; Bertin and Arambourg, 1958: 2204—2500; Bailey, 1960: 1—21; Gosline, 1961: 1—42; Marshall, 1962: 249—270. 2 families (200, 201).

Family 200. **Lipogenyidae** 333/347, thesis 33—1. Figure 446. (=Lipogenidae.)

Lit. J: 128; M: 167; G: 73; GRWM: 394, 405; MA: 61; Goode and Bean, 1894: 455—470; 1896: 1—553.

Deep Atlantic waters. 1 genus, 1 species.

Family 201. **Notacanthidae** 334/348, thesis 33—2. Figures 447, 448. Spiny eels, hsienchi yü ko, soko gisu ka, shipospinnye ugri.

Lit. J: 128; N: 167; G: 73; GRWM: 394, 405; MA: 61; Goode and Bean, 1894: 455—470; Tucker and Jones, 1951: 61—79; Maul, 1955: 5—19.

Deep oceanic waters. 3 genera, a few species.

Order 34. BELONIFORMES 86/91, thesis 0—101. (Pharyngognathi malacopterygii, Synentognathi Berg, 1940 : 282.) (Atheriniformes ex parte, Exocoetoidei GRWM : 397; MA : 125, 129); Gill, 1896 : 167—178; Jordan and Starks, 1903 : 525 — 544; Regan, 1911 : 327—335; Ogilby, 1916 : 127—177; Fowler, 1919 : 2—15; Weber and Beaufort, 1922; 4 : 115—194; Nichols and Breder, 1928 : 423 — 448; D'Ancona, 1931 : 157 — 177; 1932 : 94 — 225; Koefoed, 1953 : 1—39; Parin, 1967 : 43 — 66. 2 suborders (1—2), 5 families (202 —206).

Suborder 34.1. Scomberesocoidei. (Belonoidei.) (Exocoetoidei ex parte GRWM : 397.) (Scomberesocoidea MA : 129). 2 families (202 — 203).

Family 202. **Belonidae** 335/349, thesis 34 — 2. Figure 450. (=Esocidae= Esocesidae + Tylosuridae, + Petalichthyidae.) Needlefishes, garfishes, houndfishes, long toms, aiguillettes, orphies, Hornhechte, Halbhechte, êchen yü k'o, datsu ka, sarganovye.

Lit. J : 160; N : 168; G : 74; GRWM : 397; 418; MA : 129; Weber and Beaufort, 1922, 4 : 115 —194; Herre, 1928 : 215 — 232; Fowler, 1932 : 247 —279; Andriyashev, 1954 : 133—135; Berry and Rivas, 1962 : 152—160; Mees, 1962 : 1 — 96; 1964 : 311 — 326; Svetovidov, 1964 : 152 — 157; Lindberg and Legeza, 1965 : 205 — 208; Collette and Frederick, 1965 : 366 — 392; Collette, 1966 : 1—22; Parin, 1967 : 3—83.

Warm, partly temperate seas; pelagial; some forms enter rivers. 12 genera, a considerable number of species. Of very little importance in world marine fishing.

Family 203. **Scomberesocidae** 336/350, thesis 34—3. Figure 451. (=Scombresocidae.) Sauries, skippers, balaou, Makrelenhechte, skumbreshchukovye, makreleshchukovye, chuntao yü k'o, samma ka.

Lit. J : 161; N : 170; G : 74; GRWM : 397, 418; MA : 129; Fowler, 1932 : 247 — 279; Chapman, 1943 : 171—182; Andriyashev, 1954 : 135 —136; Lindberg and Legeza, 1965 : 209 — 210; Parin, 1968 : 275 — 190.

Warm and temperate seas. 2 genera, a few species. Of medium importance in world marine fishing.

Suborder 34.2. Exocoetoidei. (Exocoetoidei ex parte GRWM : 397.) (Exocoetoidea MA : 129.) 3 families (204 — 206).

Family 204. **Hemiramphidae** 337/351, thesis 34—5. Figure 453. (= Hemirhamphidae, +Evolantiidae.) Halfbeaks, demibecs, Halbschnabelhechte, alguilla, chên k'o, sayori ka, polurylye.

Lit. J : 161; N : 171; G : (74); GRWM : (397) (family 205); MA : 130; Weed, 1933 : 41—66; Fowler, (1933) 1934 : 233 — 367; Hiyama, 1934 : 401—410; Mohr, 1936 : 218—223; :34 — 64; Herre, 1944 : 41—80; Tortonese, 1951—52 : 1—8; Rosen, 1964 : 217 — 268; Collette, 1965 : 217—235; Lindberg and Legeza, 1965 : 210 — 215.

Tropical and subtropical seas of all the oceans; pelagial, more rarely rivers. 10 genera, a considerable number of species. Fished locally.

Family 205. **Exocoetidae** 338/352, thesis 34—8. Figure 457. Flyingfishes, poissons -volants, fei yü k'o, tobiuo ka, letuchie ryby.

Lit. J : 161; N : 174; G : 75; GRWM : 397, 418 + family 204, 206; MA : 130 + family 206; Fowler, 1932 : 247—279; Bruun, 1935 : 1—108; 1936 : 148; Breder,

1938 : 1—126; Imai, 1952 : 141—148; Mohr, 1954 : 1—55; Imai, 1956 : 91—102; Parin, 1960; 205—285; 1961 : 92—183; : 40—91; 1962 : 224—229; Evans and Sharma, 1963 : 53—59; Lindberg and Legeza, 1965 : 217—237; Parin and Besednov, 1965 : 104—117.

Tropical and subtropical latitudes of the open oceans; pelagial. 7 genera, a considerable number of species. Of little importance in world marine fishing.

Family 206. **Oxyporhamphidae** (338A/352A), thesis 34—7. Figure 456. (+ Evolantiidae, Exocoetidae ex parte; Hemiramphidae ex parte.) Smallwing flyingfishes, letuchii poluryl.

Lit. J : (161); N : (174); G : (75); GRWM : 397 (family 205); MA : (130) (family 205); Bruun, 1935 : 1—108 (: 84); Smith J. 1955 : 304—312; Abe, 1956 : 1120—1127; Parin, 1961 : 92—183; 1962 : 224—229; Parin and Besednov, 1965 : 104—117; Lindberg and Legeza, 1965 : 215—217.

Tropical latitudes of all the oceans. 1 genus, 2 species.

Order 35. GADIFORMES 87/92, thesis 0—159. (Anacanthini ex parte.) Berg, 1940 : 283. (Gadiformes ex parte; Muraenolepoidei, Gadoidei GRWM : 397; MA : 120); Regan, 1903 : 459—466; Smith and Radcliffe, 1912 : 105—140; Weber and Beaufort, 1929, 5 : 1—86; Svetovidov, 1937 : 1281—1288; 1939 : 583—585; 1948 : 1—221; Andrews, 1949 : 1—16; Koefoed, 1953 : 1—39; Gosline, 1961 : 1—42; 1963 : 1—38; Svetovidov, 1962 : 1—304. 2 suborders (1—2), 4 families (207—210).

Suborder 35.1. Muraenolepidoidei. Berg, 1940 : 284 (GRWM : 397; MA : 122). 1 family (207).

Family 207. **Muraenolepididae** (339/353), thesis 35—6. Figure 464. (=Muraenolepidae.) Parketnikovye.

Lit. J : (164); N : (206); G : (87); GRWM ; 397, 417; MA : 122; Svetovidov, 1939 : 583—585.

Antarctic and subantarctic seas. 1 genus, 4 species. Fished locally.

Suborder 35.2. Gadoidei. Berg, 1940 : 284. (GRWM : 397; MA : 121); Svetovidov, 1948 : 1—221; Hansen, 1961 : 113—161. 3 families (208—210).

Family 208. **Moridae** 340/354, thesis 35—2. Figure 459. (+Eretmophoridae, + Tripterophycidae, 208a. Melanonidae). Shênhai ssŭyeh k'o, chigo dara ka.

Lit. J : (163, 164); N : (203); G : 86; GRWM : 397, 417; MA : 121; Svetovidov, 1948 : 1—221; Böhlke and Mead, 1951 : 27—29; Maul, 1952 : 1—62; Koefoed, 1953 : 1—38; Rass, 1964 : 56—61; Lindberg and Legeza, 1965 : 238—244; Svetovidov, 1967 : 1684—1693; Templeman, 1968 : 877—901.

Deep waters of seas in all the oceans. 17 genera, many species.

Family 209. **Bregmacerotidae** 341/355, thesis 35—4. Figure 460. Hsi hsüeh k'o, sai uo ka.

Lit. J : 163; N : (203); G : 85; GRWM : 397, 417; MA : 121; Parr, 1931 : 1—53; Svetovidov, 1948 : 1—221; Munro, 1950 : 37—53; Maul, 1952 : 5—51; Maul,

1952 : 1—62; D'Ancona and Cavinato, 1965 : 1—92; Lindberg and Legeza, 1965 : 244 — 245.

Tropical oceanic waters; pelagial. 2 genera, several species. Of very little importance in world marine fishing.

Family 210. **Gadidae** 342/356, thesis 35 — 5. Figures 461—463. (+Gaidropsaridae, + Ranicipitidae, +210a. Merlucciidae =Merlangiidae.) Merluzovye, khekovye, codfishes, hakes, truecods, rocklings, morue, haddock, lieu, tacaud, motèles, mustèles, Kabeljau, Dorsch, Seehechte, hsüeh k'o, tara ka.

Lit. J : 163 (164); N : 198; G : 85; GRWM : 397, 417 +family 210a; MA : 121; Steindachner, 1870 : 421—446; Gill, 1891 : 235 — 238; Dietz, 1921 : 433—457; D'Ancona, 1932 : 280 —306; Fowler,1933 —35 : 156 —175; Norman, 1937 : 1—150; Svetovidov, 1948 : 1—221; Berg, 1948 — 49 : 942—963; Maul, 1951 : 5—55; 1952 : 5 — 51; : 1—62; Andriyashev, 1954 : 136 — 194; Svetovidov, 1956; 535—540; 1962 : 1—304; Gosline, 1963 : 1—38; Svetovidov, 1964 : 942—963; Marshall, 1964 : 86 — 93; 1966 : 275—280; Lindberg and Legeza, 1965 : 246—251; Mujib, 1967 : 1315 —1375; Nielsen and Jensen, 1967 : 1—28. Add. — Templeman, 1968 : 877—901; Sauskan, 1969 : 164 — 187.

Marine, partly fresh, waters of the temperate latitudes of both hemispheres. 22 genera, many species. One of the three most important families in world marine fishing.

Order 36. MACROURIFORMES 88/93, theses 0—160, 165. (Anacanthini ex p., Macruriformes.) Berg, 1940 : 286 (Gadiformes ex parte; Macrouroidei GRWM : 397; MA : 122); Svetovidov, 1948 : 1—222 (16); Marshall, 1965 : 299 — 322. 2 families (211, 212).

Family 211. **Macrouridae** (343/357), thesis 36 —1. Figures 465 — 467. (=Macruridae = Coryphaenoididae,+Lyconidae.) Grenadiers, rattails, Langschwanz, ch'ang wei hsüeh, soko dara ka, dolgokhvostye.

Lit. J : 162; N : (191); G : 84; GRWM : 397, 417 +family 212; MA : 122; Jordan and Gilbert, 1904 : 602 — 621; Gilbert and Hubbs, 1917 : 135 — 214, 1920 : 369 — 588; Farran, 1924 : 91—148; Weber and Beaufort, 1929, 5 : 12—86; Vinciguerra, 1932 : 1—13; Parr, 1946 : 1—99; Maul, 1951:5 — 55; Rass, 1963 : 212 —223; Andriyashev, 1954 : 194 — 197; Marshall, 1964 : 86 — 93; 1965 : 299 — 322; 1966 : 275 — 280; Lindberg and Legeza, 1965 : 251—258; Makushok, 1967 : 200 — 227. Add. II—Okamura, 1970 : 1—216.

Deep waters of all the oceans and seas. About 20 genera, many species. A promising commercial family.

Family 212. **Macrouroididae** 344/358, thesis 36 —2. Figure 468.

Lit. J : 162; N : (192); G : 84; GRWM : (397) (family 211); MA : 122; Radcliffe, 1913 : 105 — 140 (139); Gilbert and Hubbs, 1917 : 135 — 214; 1920 : 369 — 588; Grey, 1959 : 323 — 346.

Deep waters of the western Pacific off southern Japan and the Philippines. 2 genera, 2 species.

Order 37. GASTEROSTEIFORMES 89/94, thesis 0—108. (Thoracostei Regan, Hemibranchii ex parte, Scleroparei ex parte.) Berg, 1940 : 288; MA : 149; (Gasterosteiformes, Gasterosteoidei ex parte GRWM : 398); Jordan and Starks, 1902 : 57—73; Starks, 1902 : 619—634; Regan, 1909 : 75—86 (: 78); 1913 : 169—183; Kobayashi, 1932 : 145—153; Silva, 1956 : 35—45. 2 families (213—214).

Family 213. **Gasterosteidae** 345/359, thesis 37—1. Figure 469. (Sclerogenidae ex parte). Sticklebacks, épinoches, Stichlinge, t'zŭyŭ k'o, toge uo ka, kolyushkovye.

Lit. J : 173; N : —; G : 75; GRWM : 398, 421; MA : 149; Bertin, 1924 : 519—527; 1925 : 1—204; Kobayashi, 1932 : 145—153; Berg, 1948—49 : 965—976; Andriyashev, 1954 : 197—202; Svetovidov, 1964 : 172—177; Lindberg and Legeza, 1965 : 259—264.

Brackish and fresh waters of the northern hemisphere. 5 genera, a few species. Fished locally on a small scale. Aquarium fishes.

Family 214. **Aulorhynchidae** 346/360, thesis 37—2. Figure 470. Dlinnorylye kolyushki, kuangwên yü k'o, kudayagara ka.

Lit. J : 174; N : —; G : 76; GRWM : 398, 421; MA : 149; Jordan and Starks, 1902 : 57—73; Lindberg and Legeza, 1965 : 264—265.

Marine waters of the North Pacific off Korea, Japan, and California. 2 genera, a small number of species.

Order 38. SYNGNATHIFORMES 90/95, thesis 0—69. (Solenichthyes, Hemibranchii ex parte, Phthinobranchii ex parte; Lophobranchi + Aulostomi, Catosteomi ex parte, Aulostomiformes, Rhamphosiformes.) Berg, 1940 : 289; MA : 111; (Gasterosteiformes ex parte, Gasterosteoidei ex parte, Aulostomoidei, Syngnathoidei GRWM : 398); Kaup, 1856 : 1—80; Jordan and Snyder, 1901 : 1—20; Jordan and Starks, 1902 : 57—73; Starks, 1902 : 619—634; Jungerson, 1908 : 41—109; 1910 : 268—364; Waite and Hale, 1921 : 293—324; Weber and Beaufort, 1922, 4 : 7—114; Chen, 1935 : 1—22; Koefoed, 1953 : 1—39; Gosline, 1961 : 1—42; 1963 : 1—38. 2 suborders, 7 families (215—221).

Family 215.* **Indostomidae** 348/362, thesis 38—10. Figure 478. Inc. sedis. (Gasterosteiformes ex parte, MA : 150, inc. sedis Gasterosteoidei ex parte GRWM 398). Indostomids, Iglokolyushkovye.

Lit. J : —; N : 181; G : 76; GRWM : 398, 421; MA : 150; Prashad and Mukerji, 1929 : 219—222; Bolin, 1936 : 420—423.

A lake in Upper Burma. 1 genus, 1 species.

Suborder 38.1. A u l o s t o m o i d e i. Berg, 1940 : 291. (Gasterosteiformes ex parte, Aulostomoidei GRWM : 398) MA : —; 2 superfamilies, 4 families (216—219).

* GRWM (p. 398) and MA (p. 150) include family 215. Indostomidae in the suborder Gasterosteoidei (= Gasterosteiformes), to which Berg (1940 : 289) also hypothetically referred it, although he mentions a resemblance to the Syngnathidae.

Superfamily 38.1.1. Aulostomoidea. (Aulostomiformes.) Berg, 1940: 291; MA: —; 2 families (216, 217).

Family 216. **Aulostomidae** 349/363, thesis 38—3. Figure 473. (=Aulostomatidae). Trumpetfishes, painted flute-mouth, trompette-de-mer, kuankow yü k'o, hera yagara ka, fleitorylye, fleitovye.

Lit. J: 175; N: (178); G: 73; GRWM: 398, 421; MA: 113; Jungerson, 1910: 268—364; Mohr, 1937: 1—69; Wheeler, 1955: 613—623.

Tropical parts of the Atlantic, Indian, and Pacific oceans. 1 genus, 1 species.

Family 217. **Fistulariidae** 350/364, thesis 38—4. Figure 474, 475. (=Fistularidae.) Cornetfishes, hair-tailed flute-mouth, bouche-en-flute, yen kuan yü k'o, yagara ka, svistul'kovye.

Lit. J: 175; N: 178; G: 73; GRWM: 398, 421; MA: 113; Duncher and Mohr, 1925: 93—112; Lindberg and Legeza, 1965: 268—271.

Tropical parts of the Atlantic, Indian, and Pacific oceans. 1 genus, a few species.

Superfamily 38.1.2. Centriscoidea. (Solenichthyes.) Berg, 1940: 292; MA: —; 2 families (218, 219).

Family 218. **Macrorhamphosidae** 351/365, thesis 38—6. Figure 476. (=Macroramphosidae = Rhamphosidae.) Snipefishes, sniperfishes, chang-wên yü k'o, sagi fue ka, bekasovye.

Lit. J: 176; N: 179; G: 74; GRWM: 398, 421; MA: 112; Regan, 1914: 17—21; Weber and Beaufort, 1922, 4: 15—17; 1931: 183—187; Bruun, 1936: 148; Mohr, 1937: 1—69; Okada and Suzuki, 1951: 7—11; Lindberg and Legeza, 1965: 271—272.

Surface waters, more rarely at considerable depths, of tropical and temperate seas of both hemispheres. 3 genera, more than 10 species.

Family 219. **Centriscidae** 352/366, thesis 38—7. Figure 477. (=Amphisilidae = Amphisiliidae) Shrimpfishes, becasses-de-mer, razorfishes, po chia yü k'o, heko ayu ka, nozhebryushkovye.

Lit. J: 176; N: 180; G: 73; GRWM: 398, 421; MA: 113; Jungerson, 1908: 41—109; Oshima, 1922: 260—264; Mohr, 1937: 1—69; Kahsbauer, 1951: 118—121; Mohr, 1959: 1—73.

Tropical parts of the Indian and Pacific oceans; pelagial. 2 genera, 4 species.

Suborder 38.2. Syngnathoidei. Berg, 1940: 293. (Gasterosteiformes, Syngnathoidei GRWM: 398; MA: —). 2 families (220—221).

Family 220. **Solenostomidae** 353/367, thesis 38—11. Figure 479. (=Solenostomatidae = Solenostomatichthyidae = Solenichthyidae.) False pipefishes, ghost pipefishes, titao yü k'o, kamisori uo ka, truborylye.

Lit. J: 174; N: 181; G: 82; GRWM: 398, 421; MA: 112; Jungerson, 1910: 268—364; Weber and Beaufort, 1922, 4: 24—29; Matsubara, 1955: 419, 420.

Indian and Pacific oceans. 1 genus, several species.

Family 221. **Syngnathidae.** 354/368, thesis 38—12. Figures 480—485. (=Siphostomidae, +Hippocampidae). Pipefishes, Seenadels, hippocampes, seahorses, kon'kovye, morskoi konek, morskaya igla, hailung k'o, yoji uo ka.

Lit. J: 174; N: 181; G: 82; GRWM: 398, 421; MA: 114; Jungerson, 1910: 268—364; Duncker, 1912: 219—240; 1925: 9—120; Rauther, 1925: 1—366, D'Ancona, 1934: 3—77; Holly, 1936: 1—3; Ginsburg, 1937: 467—594; Dollfus, 1938: 496—506; Herald, 1940: 51—64; 1942: 125—132; Gaporiacco, 1948: 73—95; Berg, 1948—49: 977—986; Kahsbaur, 1949—1950: 263—272; Fiedler, 1954: 358—416; Andriyashev, 1954: 202—205; Whitley and Allan, 1958: 1—84; Svetovidov, 1964: 178—197; Lindberg and Legeza, 1965: 273—289.

Littoral and open waters of all the seas and oceans; occasionally river mouths. About 50 genera, many species.

Order 39. LAMPRIDIFORMES 91/96, thesis 0—93, 137. (Allotriognathi). Berg, 1940: 295. GRWM: 398; MA: 106; Regan, 1907: 634—643; Weber and Beaufort, 1929, 5:87—94; Matsubara, 1940—41: 314—319; Gosline, 1961: 1—42; 1963: 1—38; Patterson, 1964: 213—482. 4 suborders 6 families (222—227).

Suborder 39.1. Lampridoidei. (Selenichthyes.) Berg, 1940: 295, GRWM: 398; MA: 107; Frost, 1927: 439—445. 1 family (222).

Family 222. **Lampridae** 355/369, thesis 39—2. Figure 486. (=Lamprididae.) Opahs, moon-fishes, Gotteslashs, opakhovye, yüeh yü k'o, aka mambo ka.

Lit. J: 166; N: —; G: (87); GRWM: 398, 420; MA: 107; Gill, 1903: 915—924; Fowler, 1933—35: 156—175; Bell and Kask, 1936: 54—56; Andriyashev, 1954: 205—206; Lindberg and Legeza, 1965: 290—291.

Tropical and subtropical waters of all the oceans. 1 genus, 1 species.

Suborder 39.2. Veliferoidei. (Histichthyes.) Berg, 1940: 295; MA: 107; (Veliferoidei, Trachipteroidei ex parte GRWM: 398.) 2 families (223, 224).

Family 223. **Veliferidae** 356/370, thesis 39—3. Figure 487. Chiüheh yü k'o, kusa agi ka, ryba-veer, veerovye.

Lit. J: 165; N: —; G: 87; GRWM: 398, 420; MA: 107; Smith, 1951: 497—510; Walters, 1960: 245—247; Lindberg and Legeza, 1965: 291—293.

Indian and Pacific oceans. 1 genus, a small number of species.

Family 224. **Lophotidae** 357/371, thesis 39—7. Figure 490. (Trachipteroidei ex parte GRWM: 398.) Crestfishes, ssŭ yü k'o, aka namada ka.

Lit. J: 166; N: —; G: 87; GRWM: 398, 420; MA: 107; Matsubara, 1939: 193—199; Abe, 1954: 90—94; Lindberg and Legeza, 1965: 263—295.

Oceanic waters; pelagial. 2 genera, several species.

Suborder 39.3. Trachipteroidei. (Taeniosomi.) Berg, 1940: 295; MA: 107, (Trachipteroidei ex parte GRWM: 398.) 2 families (225, 226).

Family 225. **Regalecidae** 358/372, thesis 39—9. Figure 491. (+Agrostichthyidae, Taeniiformes.) Sel'dyanoi koral', oarfishes, sea-serpents, roides-harengs, fengkuan yü k'o, riuguno tsukai ka, korolevye.

Lit. J : 166; N : —; G : 87; GRWM : 398, 420; MA : 107; W. Phillipps, 1924; 539—540; Andriyashev, 1954 : 208—209; Lindberg and Legeza, 1965 : 295—296.

Oceanic waters, pelagial; 2 genera, several species.

Family 226. **Trachipteridae** (359/373), thesis 39—10. Figure 492. (=Trachypteridae = Trachipteriidae = Trachypteriidae, +Radiicephalidae.) Remen'-ryba, ribbonfishes, king of the herring, flambe, argentin, ruban-de-mer, shanwei yü k'o, furisode uo ka.

Lit. J : 166; N : —; G : 87; GRWM : 398, 420; MA : 107; Andriyashev, 1954 : 206—208; Walters and Fitch, 1960 : 441—451; Palmer 1961 : 335—351; Walters, 1963 : 455—457; Fitch, 1964 : 228—240; Lindberg and Legeza, 1965 : 297—300.

Oceanic waters; bathypelagial. 3 genera, several species.

Suborder 39.4. Stylephoroidei. (Stylophoroidei, Atelaxia.) Berg, 1940 : 296, GRWM : 398; MA : 108; Starks, 1908 : 17—22. 1 family (227).

Family 227. **Stylephoridae.** (360/374), thesis 39—5. Figures 488, 489. (=Stylophoridae.) Tube-eyes, palochkokhvostye.

Lit. J : 166; N : —; G : 87; GRWM : 398, 420; MA : 108; Regan, 1908 : 447—449; Starks, 1908 : 17—22; Regan, 1924 : 193—207; Norman, 1930 : 261—370; Matsubara, 1955 : 465.

Atlantic and Pacific oceans; bathypelagial. 1 genus, 1 species.

Order 40. CYPRINODONTIFORMES 92/97, theses 0—102, 157. (Microcyprini, Cyprinodontes + Amblyopsiformes.) Berg, 1940 : 296. (Percopsiformes ex parte, Amblyopsoidei ex parte; GRWM : 396; Atheriniformes ex parte, Cyprinodontoidei : GRWM : 397; MA : 125); Garman, 1895 : 5—179; Regan, 1911 : 320—327; Hubbs, 1924 : 1—31; 1926 : 1—86; Kulkarmi, 1948 : 65—119; Miller, 1948 : 1—155; Poll, 1952 : 292—305; Myers, 1955 : 7; Lambert, 1958 : 39—56; Sethi, 1960 : 1—274; Gosline, 1963 : 1—38; Rosen and Bailey, 1963 : 1—176. 2 suborders, 9 families (228—236).

Suborder 40.1. Amblyopsoidei (Amblyopsiformes), Berg, 1940 : 296. (Percopsiformes ex parte, Amblyopsoidei GRWM : 396; MA : 123, 125.) 1 family (228).

Family 228. **Amblyopsidae** 361/375, thesis 40—1. Figures 493, 494. (=Hypsocidae = Hypsaeidae.) Cavefishes, cave-blindfishes, springfishes, swampfishes, Nordamerikanische Höhlenfische, slepoglazkovye.

Lit. J : 160; N : —; G : 76; GRWM : 396, 415; MA : 125; Woods and Inger, 1957 : 282—256; Rosen, 1962 : 1—35.

Fresh waters of grottoes in the central and eastern parts of the USA. About 5 genera, several species. Aquarium fishes.

Suborder 40.2. Cyprinodontoidei (Poeciloidei). Berg, 1940: 296. (Atheriniformes ex parte, Cyprinodontoidei : GRWM: 397; MA: 127.) 2 superfamilies, 8 families (229—236).

Superfamily 40.2.1. **Cyprinodontoidea**, Berg, 1940: 297; MA: 127. 4 families (229—232).

Family 229. **Cyprinodontidae** 362/376, thesis 40—6, Figures 496—499. (+Orestiidae, +Empetrichthyidae, +Fundulidae, +229a. Oryziatidae, Adrianichthyoidea ex parte.) Killifishes, egglaying topminnows, tooth-carps, Körpflinge, Zahnkarpfen, zubatye karpy, karpozubye, chiang yü k'o, medaka ka.

Lit. J: 158; N—; G: 79; GRWM: 397, 418 +family 229a; MA: 127; Henn, 1916: 93—142; Ahl, 1928: 113—123; Myers, 1931: 1—14; Hubbs, 1932: 1—5; Myers, 1933: 180—185; 1935: 301—316; Schindler, 1935: 161—172; Myers, 1938: 136—143; Eigenmann and Allen, 1942: 1—494; Sozer, 1942: 307—316; Tchernavin, 1944: 140—293; Aksiray, 1948: 97—138; : 280—310; Trewavas, 1948: 408—415; Hubbs, 1950: 1—28; Tchernavin, 1955: 217, 218; Miller, 1956: 1—17; Brown, 1957: 69—77; Whitehead, 1962: 103—137; Rosen, 1964: 217—268; Hubbs and Miller, 1965: 1—104; Poll and Lambert, 1965: 615—631. Add.—Jubb, 1969: 1—11.

Fresh waters of North and South America, southern Europe, Africa, South and Southeast Asia, Indonesia. More than 50 genera, many species. Aquarium fishes.

Family 230. **Horaichthyidae** (—/—), thesis 40—8. Figure 500. (Cyprinodontidae ex parte.) (Adrianichthyoidei ex parte MA: 127)

Lit. J: —; N: —; G: (79); GRWM: 397—418; MA: 127; Kulkarni, 1940: 379—423; 1948: 65—119; Rosen, 1964: 217—268.

Fresh waters of Bombay Province, India. 1 genus, 1 species.

Family 231. **Tomeuridae** (—/—), thesis 40—9. Figures 501, 502. (=Tomeiuridae, Poeciliidae ex parte.)

Lit. J: (159); N: —; G: (81); GRWM: (397) (family 236); MA: (128) (family 236); Kulkarni, 1948: 65—119; Mohsen, 1962: 61—64; Rosen and Bailey, 1963: 1—176 (35—39).

Fresh waters of South America. 1 genus, 1 species.

Family 232. **Adrianichthyidae** 363/377, thesis 40—4. Figure 495. (Adrianichthyoidei ex parte MA: 127.) Adrianichthyids.

Lit. J: 160; N: —; G: 82; GRWM: 397, 418; MA: 127; Weber and Beaufort, 1922, 4: 376—381; Rosen, 1964: 217—268.

Lakes of Celebes. 1—2 genera and species.

Superfamily 40.2.2. **Poeciloidea**. Berg, 1940: 297. (Cyprinodontoidea MA: 127.) 4 families (233—236).

Family 233. **Goodeidae** 364/378, thesis 40—15. Figure 505. (+Characodontidae.) Goodeids.

Lit. J: 158; N: —; G: 80; GRWM: 397, 418; MA: 128; Hubbs and Turner, 1939: 1—80; 1946: 1—13; Mohsen, 1965: 1127.

Fresh waters of Mexico (Lerma River and adjacent territories). More than 18 genera, a considerable number of species. Aquarium fishes.

Family 234. **Jenynsiidae** 365/379, thesis 40—13. Figure 504. (=Fitzroyiidae = Fitzroyidae.) Jenynsiids.

Lit. J : (106); N :—; G : (81); GRWM : 397—418; MA : 128; Regan, 1913 : 232—234; Myers, 1931 : 1—14; Mohsen, 1963 : 1385—1387.

Fresh waters of the eastern part of South America (estuary of the Paraná River in Argentina—La Plata). 1 genus, 1 species.

Family 235. **Anablepidae** 366/380, thesis 40—11. Figure 503. (=Anablepsidae.) Four-eyed fishes, quatro ojos, chetyrekhglazkovye.

Lit. J : 160; N : —; G : 81; GRWM : 397—418; MA : 128; Garman, 1895 : 5—179; Jordan and Evermann, 1896 : 632; Jordan; 1925 : 413—416.

Fresh waters of Central and South America. 1 genus, several species.

Family 236. **Poeciliidae** 367/381, thesis 40—16. Figures 506, 507. (=Poecilidae.) Livebearers, viviparous topminnows, topminnows, gambuzievye, petsilievye, shih wên yü k'o, tappu minno ka.

Lit. J : (159); N : —; G : 80; GRWM : 307, 418 + family 231; MA : 128; Jordan and Snyder, 1906 : 287—290; Eigenmann, 1907 : 425—433; Regan, 1913 : 977—1018; Hubbs, 1924 : 1—31 (: 5—11); 1950 : 1—28; Rosen, 1952 : 151—156; Rivas, 1958 : 281—320; Rosen and Bailey, 1959 : 1—44; 1963 : 1—176; Rosen and Kollman, 1959 : 169—190. Add.—Zander, 1967 : 87—125.

Fresh and brackish waters of North and South America. About 20 genera, many species. Aquarium fishes.

Order 41. PHALLOSTETHIFORMES 93/98, thesis 0—43. Berg, 1940 : 297 (Atheriniformes, Atherinoidei ex parte GRWM : 297; MA : 125, 127); (Perciformes, Mugiloidei Gosline, 1968 : 9, 64); Myers, 1928 : 1—12; R. J. Bailey, 1936 : 453—483; Aurich, 1937 : 263—286; Te Winkel, 1939 : 59—69; Hubbs, 1944 : 60—79; Arbocco, 1956 : 51—60. 1 family (237).

Family 237. **Phallostethidae**. 369/383, thesis 41—0. Figures 508, 509. (+ 237a. Neostethidae, Berg, 368/382.)

Lit. J : 160; N : —; G : 76; GRWM : 398, 418 + family 237a; MA : 127; Regan, 1913 : 548—555; 1916 : 1—26; H. Smith, 1927 : 353—355; Villodolid and Manacop, 1934 : 193—220; Myers, 1935 : 5—6; 1937 : 137—143; R. J. Bailey, 1936 : 69—74; Herre, 1939 : 139—144; 1942 : 137—156; Hubbs, 1944 : 69—79; Gosline, 1962 : 207—217.

Fresh and brackish waters of Thailand, Malay Archipelago, Indonesia, and the Philippines. 10 genera, several species.

Order 42. PERCOPSIFORMES 94/99, theses 0—99, 104, 162. (Salmopercae.) Berg, 1940 : 300 (Percopsiformes ex parte GRWM : 396; MA : 123). Regan, 1911 : 294—296; Bailey, 1960 : 1—21; Gosline, 1961 : 1—42; 1963 : 1—38. 2 suborders, 2 families (238 and 239).

Suborder 42.1. Percopsidoidei. (Salmopercae.) Berg, 1940 : 300. (GRWM : 396.) (Percopsoidei MA : 125.) 1 family (238).

Family 238. **Percopsidae** 370/384, thesis 42—1. Figure 510. Trout perches, sand-rollers, perkopsovye, lososeokunevye.

Lit. J: 165; N: 177; G: 73; GRWM: 396, 415; MA: 125; Regan, 1911: 294—296; Hubbs and Lagler, 1949: 24, 79.

Fresh waters of North America. 2 genera and species. Small fishes.

Suborder 42.2. Aphredoderoidei. (Xenarchi.) Berg, 1940: 300. (GRWM: 396); MA: 124, 1 family (239).

Family 239. **Aphredoderidae**. 371/385, thesis 42—2. Figure 511. Pirate perch, Piratenbarsche, piratookunevye.

Lit. J: 165; N: 177; G: 73; GRWM: 396, 415; MA: 124; Regan, 1911: 294—296; Hubbs and Lagler, 1949: 24, 80.

Fresh waters of North America. 1 genus, 1 species. Small fishes.

Order 43. STEPHANOBERYCIFORMES 95/100, theses 0—95, 164. (Xenoberyces.) Berg, 1940: 300. (Beryciformes ex parte GRWM: 398; Stephanoberycoidei MA: 101, 106; Cetomimiformes ex parte GRWM: 395); Regan, 1911: 1—9; Parr, 1929: 1—45; Koefoed, 1953: 1—39. 5 families (240—244).

Family 240. **Stephanoberycidae**. 372/386, thesis 43—3. Figure 512. (Beryciformes, Stephanoberycoidei ex parte GRWM: 398.)

Lit. J: 171; N: 213; G: 89; GRWM: 398, 419; MA: 106; Regan, 1911: 1—9; Matsubara, 1955: 453.

Deep oceanic waters. 3 genera, a small number of species.

Family 241 (120). **Rondeletiidae** 373/387, theses 43—5 and 24—4. Figure 514. See family 120. Transferred to order 24. (Cetomimiformes ex parte, Cetomimoidei ex parte GRWM: 395.)

Family 242. **Anoplogasteridae** (381/395), thesis 43—7. Figure 515. (+Caulolepidae, Melamphaeidae ex parte), Beryciformes ex parte, Berycoidei ex parte GRWM: 398; MA: 104). Sablezubye.

Lit. J: (172); N: 215; G: (89); GRWM: 398, 419; MA: 104; Parr, 1933: 1—51; Maul, 1954 : 5—63.

Deep oceanic waters. 2 genera, a small number of species.

Family 243. **Korsogasteridae** 382/396, thesis 43—8. Figure 516. (Beryciformes, Berycoidei ex parte GRWM: 398.)

Lit. J: —; N: (209); G: 89; GRWM: 398, 419; MA: (104) (family 249); Parr 1933: 1—51 (9); Matsubara, 1955: 447.

Deep oceanic waters. 2 genera, a small number of species.

Family 244. **Melamphaeidae** (388/402), thesis 43—4. Figure 513. (=Melamphaidae = Melamphasidae) (Beryciformes, Stephanoberycoidei ex parte GRWM: 398.) Melamphids.

Lit. J: (172); N: (214); G: 89; GRWM: 398, 419; MA: 106; Norman, 1929: 163—168; Parr, 1931: 1—53; 1933: 1—51; Maruyama, 1957: 31—34; Ebeling, 1960: 1—373; 1962: 1—174; Moss, 1962: 1—10; Ebeling and Weed, 1963: 1—58.

Deep oceanic waters. 2 genera, a few species.

Order 44. BERYCIFORMES 96/101, theses 0—106, 126, 138,140, 142, 144, 147—149). (Berycomorphi, Berycoidei.) Berg, 1940 : 300. (Beryciformes ex parte, Polymixioidei, Berycoidei ex parte, MA : 101—104; Stephanoberycoidei ex parte, GRWM : 398; Perciformes, Percoidei ex parte GRWM : 400); Jordan and Fowler, 1902 : 1—21; Fowler, 1904 : 222—238; Starks, 1904 : 601—619; Regan, 1911 : 1—9; Frost, 1927 : 439—445; Mohr, 1927 : 85—140; Parr, 1929 : 1—45; Weber and Beaufort, 1929, 5 : 214—267; Koefoed, 1953 : 1—39; Maul, 1954 : 5—41; Qureshi, 1959 : 20—25; Gosline, 1961 : 1—42; 1963 : 1—38; Patterson, 1964 : 213—482. 11 families (245—255).

Family 245. **Polymixiidae.** 374/388, thesis 44—1. Figure 517. (Berycopsidae.) (Beryciformes, Polymixioidei GRWM : 398; MA : 102.) Beardfishes, barbudos, hsü tiao k'o, gimmeldaika, borodatkovye.

Lit. J : 172; N : 207; G : 88; GRWM : 398, 419; MA : 102; Fowler, 1933—1935; 156—175; Lachner, 1955 : 189—206; Patterson, 1964 : 213—482; Lindberg and Legeza, 1965 : 305.

Tropical latitudes of the Atlantic, Indian, and Pacific oceans. 1 genus, several species.

Family 246. **Berycidae.** 376/390, thesis 44—13. Figure 523. (Beryciformes, Berycoidei ex parte GRWM : 398.) Red snappers, alfonsinos, chinyen tiao k'o, kimme dai ka.

Lit. J : 172; N : 208; G : 88; GRWM : 398, 419; MA : 103; Regan, 1911 : 1—9; Maul, 1954 : 5—63; T. Scott, 1962 : 102; Lindberg and Legeza, 1965 : 306, 307; Yamame and Okamura, 1966 : 13—20.

Atlantic, Indian, and Pacific oceans. 2—3 genera, a small number of species. A promising marine item.

Family 247. **Diretmidae** 377/391, thesis 44—7, Figure 520. (Beryciformes, Berycoidei ex parte GRWM : 398.) (247a. Paradiretmidae Whitley, 1951, MA : 105. Figure 520A.) T'zuyinyang tiao k'o, nakamura gimme ka.

Lit. J : 172; N : 208; G : 88; GRWM : 398, 419; Maul, 1949 : 1—42; Whitley, 1951 : 61—68; Abe, 1953 : 39—47; Koefoed, 1953 : 1—38; Patterson, 1964 : 213—482.

North Atlantic and South Pacific. 4 genera, several species.

Family 248. **Caristiidae** 378/392, theses 44—16; 50.1.1—45. Figures 525, 624. (=Elephenoridae=Elephanoridae.) (Perciformes, Percoidei ex parte GRWM : 400.) Manefishes, ch'an yü k'o, yae niu ka.

Lit. J : 173; N : 208; G : 88; GRWM : 400, 426; MA : 105; Regan, 1912 : 637—638; Jordan, 1919 : 329—392; Maul, 1949 : 1—42; Koefoed, 1953 : 1—38; Mead and Maul, 1958 : 393—418.

Oceanic waters. 1 genus, 1 species.

Family 249. **Trachichthyidae** 379/393, thesis 44—12. Figure 522. (+Hoplopterygidae.) (Beryciformes, Berycoidei ex parte GRWM : 398.) Roughies, redfishes, slime heads, chouhsiung tiao k'o, hiuchi daika.

Lit. J : 173; N : 209; G : 88; GRWM : 398, 419 + family 254; MA : 104 + family 243; Regan, 1911 : 1—9; Weber and Beaufort, 1929, 5 : 215—218; Maul, 1954 : 5—63; T. Scott, 1962 : 102, 104.

Atlantic, Indian, and Pacific oceans. 5 genera, several species.

Family 250. **Monocentridae** 383/397, thesis 44—3. Figure 518. (Beryciformes, Berycoidei ex parte GRWM: 398.) Knightfishes, pinecone fishes, sung ch'iu yü k'o, matsukasa uo ka, ryba-shishka, shishkovye.

Lit. J: 172; N: 210; G: 88; GRWM: 398, 419; MA: 105; Starks, 1904: 601—619; Weber and Beaufort, 1929, 5: 222, 223; Fowler, 1933—35: 156—175; Lindberg and Legeza, 1965: 308—309.

Indian and Pacific oceans. 1—2 genera, a small number of species.

Family 251—252.* **Anomalopidae** 384/398, thesis 44—5. Figure 519. (Beryciformes, Berycoidei ex parte GRWM: 398.) Lantern eye fishes, ho ka anoma k'o, hikari kimme daika, fonareglazye.

Lit. J: 172; N: 210; G: 88; GRWM: 398, 419; MA: 105; Silvester and Fowler, 1926: 245—247; Weber and Beaufort, 1929, 5: 224—227; Bertin and Arambourg, 1958: 2204—2500.

Atlantic, Indian, and Pacific oceans; pelagial or among corals. 3 genera, a small number of species.

Family 253. **Holocentridae** 385/399, thesis 44—9. Figure 521. (=Holocenthridae,+Myripristidae.) (Beryciformes, Berycoidei ex parte GRWM: 398.) Soldierfishes, squirrelfishes, soldat-ryba, wei k'o, itto dai ka.

Lit. J: 173; N: 211; G: 88; GRWM: 398, 419; MA: 104; Montilla, 1938: 207—229; Woods, 1955: 91—119; Araga, 1964: 307—321; Patterson, 1964: 213—482; Lindberg and Legeza, 1965: 309—314; Greenfield, 1965: 229—247.

Atlantic, Indian, and Pacific oceans. 8 genera, a few species.

Family 254. **Sorosichthyidae** (—/—), thesis 44—9. No figure.

Lit. J: —; N: —; G: 89; GRWM: (398) (family 249); MA: 105; Whitley, 1945: 1—42; Patterson, 1964: 213—482.

Western Australia. 1 genus, 1 species.

Family 255. **Gibberichthyidae** 387/401, thesis 44—15, Figure 524. (Stephanoberycidae ex parte.) (Beryciformes, Stephanoberycoidei ex parte GRWM: 398.)

Lit. J: —; N: (213); G: 89; GRWM: 398, 419; MA: 106; Parr, 1933: 1—51; Matsubara, 1955: 447, 448.

Oceanic waters. 1 genus, 1 species.

Order 45. ZEIFORMES** 97/102, thesis 0—167. (Zeomorphi, Zeoidei.) Berg, 1940: 302. (Zeiformes ex parte GRWM: 398); MA: 108; Regan, 1910: 481—484; Jordan, 1925: 1—773; Frost, 1927: 439—445; Kamohara, 1936: 357—362; 1940: 1—79; Koefoed, 1952: 1—26; Myers, 1960: 89—98; Patterson, 1964: 213—482. 2 families (256—257).

* The family Trachyberycidae is included in family 296. Bramidae (Mead and Maul, 1958: 393—418).

** We transferred family 329. Caproidae (Antigoniidae) (391/405, thesis 50.1.1—37) to the order Perciformes because although it bears a close outward resemblance to family 257. Grammicolepidae (390/404, thesis 45—2), it differs in the small number of vertebrae (21—23), the presence of only 5 branched rays in the ventral fins, and other characters (see Jordan, 1926: 460, 609; Matsubara, 1955: 469, 928; Lindberg and Legeza, 1965: 314).

Family 256. **Zeidae*** 389/403, thesis 45–1. Figures 527–530. (+Cyttidae, +Cyttopsidae, –Zenidae, +256a. Parazenidae (Figure 528), +256b. Macrurocyttidae + Zeniontidae (Figure 529), +256c. Oreosomatidae (Figure 530), Dories, John-dories, Jean-doré, poule-de-mer, Saint-Pierre, Sonnenfische, haifang k'o, mato dai ka, zevsovye, solnechnikovye.

Lit. J: 171; N: –; G: 90; GRWM: 398, 420+families 256a, 256b and 256c; MA: 109, 110+families 256a, b, c; Starks, 1898: 469–476; Fowler, 1933–35: 156–175; Kamohara, 1934: 597–599; Abe, 1957: 225–233; Mead, 1957: 235–237; Myers, 1960: 89–98; Svetovidov, 1964: 200–203; Lindberg and Legeza, 1965: 315–321.

All warm seas; occasionally deep waters. About 10 genera, a considerable number of species. Possibly of commercial importance.

Family 257. **Grammicolepididae** 390/404, thesis 45–2. Figure 531. (=Grammicolepidae.) Hishi mato dai ka, rombocheshuinikovye.

Lit. J: (171); N: –; G: 90; GRWM: 398, 420; MA: 110; Myers, 1937: 146–156; J. Smith, 1960: 231–235.

Atlantic, Indian, and Pacific oceans. 2–3 genera, several species.

Order 46. MUGILIFORMES 98/103; thesis 0–128. (Percesoces.) Berg, 1940: 302. (Perciformes ex parte, Sphyraenoidei, Mugiloidei GRWM: 401; Atheriniformes ex parte GRWM: 397); (Perciformes, Mugiloidei MA: 136–141; Gosline, 1968: 9); Starks, (1899) 1900: 1–10; Jordan and Hubbs, 1919: 1–87 (7–9); Weber and Beaufort, 1922, 4: 195–311; Mohr, 1927: 174–201; Gosline, 1962: 207–217; Qureshi, 1964: 65–70. 2 suborders, 3 families (258–260).

Suborder 46.1. Sphyraenoidei. Berg, 1940: 302. (GRWM: 401.) MA (141) (Mugiloidei.) 1 family (258).

Family 258. **Sphyraenidae** 392/406, thesis 46–1. Figure 532. Barrakudovye, barrucudas, sea-pikes, brochets-de-mer, picudas, shu k'o, kamasu ka, sfirenovye, morskie shchuki.

Lit. J: 178; N: 513; G: 76; GRWM: 401–429; MA: 141; Weber and Beaufort, 1922, 4: 218–229; Fowler, 1933–35: 156–175; Smith J. 1956: 37–46; Williams, 1959: 92–128; Gosline, 1962: 207–217; Sylva, 1963: 1–179; Cadenat, 1964: 659–685; Svetovidov, 1964: 203–205; Lindberg and Legeza, 1965: 321–326.

All warm seas. 1 genus, several species. Of very little importance in world marine fishing.

Suborder 46.2. Mugiloidei. Berg, 1940: 303. (GRWM: 401; MA: 141+ Sphyraenoidei.) 2 families (259–260).

* Myers (1960) divided the family Zeidae into 4 families: 256. Zeidae, 256b. Macrurocyttidae, 256c. Oreosomatidae, Zeniodontidae. In 1966 the Zeniontidae were made a synonym of the Macrurocyttidae, but another family was recognized, 256a. Parazenidae (GRWM, 1957: 235–237; MA: 109).

Family 259. **Mugilidae** 393/407, thesis 46–3. Figures 533–535. Mullets, gray mullets, Meeräsche, tz'u k'o, bora ka, kefalevye.

Lit. J : 178; N : 513; G : 77; GRWM : 401, 429; MA : 141; Kner, 1868 : 1–433; Popov, 1920 : 47–115; Oshima, 1922 : 240–259; Popov, 1929 : 243–247; 1930 : 47–125; 1931 : 117–126; Fowler, 1933, 4, 2; Borcêa, 1934 : 247–286; Roxas, 1934 : 393–431; Smith J., 1935 : 587–644; Schultz, 1946 : 377–395; J. Smith, (1947), 1948 : 833–843; Berg, 1948–1949 : 990–1001; Ishiyama, 1951 : 238–250; Cadenat, 1954 : 584–591; Thomson, 1954 : 70–131; Ebeling, 1957 : 173–185; Gosline, 1962 : 207–217 ex parte; Pillay, 1962 : 254–269; 547–576; Thomson, 1964 : 1–127; Babayan,1965 : 1–131; Svetovidov, 1964 : 205–224; Lindberg and Legeza, 1965 : 326–334. Add.—Hoffa and Tun, 1966 : 62–66; De Angelis, 1968 : 5–36.

Warm and temperate seas. More than 10 genera, many species. Of medium importance in world marine fishing.

Family 260. **Atherinidae**. 394/408, thesis 46–4. Figures 536–538. (Atheriniformes ex parte, Atherinoidei GRWM : 397; MA : 125.) (+Bedotiidae, +Pseudomugilidae, +260a. Melanotaeniidae = Zanteclidae + Neoatherinidae (Figure 537), +260b, Isonidae (Figure 538).) Silversides, hardyheads, prêtres, pescados-del-rey, Peixerey, Aerenfische, yin han yü k'o, togoro iwashi ka.

Lit. J : 177; N : –; G : 77, (76); GRWM : 397, 418 + families 260a and b; MA : 126 +families 260a and b; Jordan and Starks, 1901 : 198–206; Jordan and Hubbs, 1919 : 1–87; Fowler, 1933–35 : 156–175 . . . Meshkov, 1941 : 400–406; Myers and Wade, 1942 : 113–149; Buen, 1945 : 475–532; Schultz, 1948 : 1–48; 1950 : 150; Berg, 1948–1949 : 1001–1004; Buen, 1953 : 3–80; Drapkin, 1961 : 143–145; Gosline, 1962 : 207–217; Rosen, 1964 : 217–268; Svetovidov,1964 : 224–232; J. Smith; 1965 : 601–632; Lindberg and Legeza, 1965 : 334–339; Alexander, 1967 : 233–255; Add.—Gilbert and Caldwell, 1967 : 1–16; Kiener and Spillmann, 1969 : 1–74.

Tropical, subtropical, partly temperate seas; coastal waters, more rarely mouths of rivers. More than 40 genera, very many species. Fished locally. Aquarium fishes.

Order 47. POLYNEMIFORMES. 99/104, thesis 0–71. (Polynemioidei, Rhegnopteri.) Berg, 1940 : 304 (Perciformes ex parte, Polynemoidei GRWM : 401; MA : 141); (Mugiloidei Gosline, 1968 : 9); Kamohara, 1940 : 1–79; Hubbs, 1942 : 31–33. 1 family (261).

Family 261. **Polynemidae** 395/409, thesis 47–0. Figure 539. Pal'tseperye, threadfins, bastard mullets, barbur, mayu k'o, tsubame konoshiro ka.

Lit. J : 178; N : 516; G : 78; GRWM : 401, 429; MA : 141; Myers, 1936 : 376–382; Qureshi, 1960 : 153–164; Lindberg and Legeza, 1965 : 339–343.

Sandy shores of all tropical seas, more rarely rivers. 7 genera, a considerable number of species. Of little importance in world marine fishing.

Order 48. CHANNIFORMES (100/105), thesis 0–88. (Labyrinthici ex parte. Ophicephaloidei. Ophiocephaliformes ex parte MA : 133 + suborders 50.13 and 50.14). Berg,1940 : 305 (GRWM : 398). Liem, 1963 : 1–149; Perciformes, Anabantoidei Gosline, 1968 : 9. 1 family (262).

Family 262. **Channidae** (396/410), thesis 48 — 0. Figure 540. (=Chanidae = Ophicephalidae = Ophiocephalidae = Parophiocephalidae). Snakeheads, murrel, Schlangenkopffische, li k'o, Taiwan doje ka, zmeegolovye.

Lit. J : (176); N : (512); G : (144); GRWM : 398, 421; MA : 136; Regan, (1909) 1910 : 767 — 787; Weber and Beaufort, 1922, 4 : 313 — 330; Myers and Shapovalov, 1931 — 32 : 33—37; Berg, 1948 — 1949 : 1004 — 1007; Blanc, 1963 : 70—77.

Fresh waters of tropical Africa, Indonesia, and eastern Asia north as far as the Amur inclusive. 1 genus, a considerable number of species. Fished locally.

Order 49. SYNBRANCHIFORMES 101/106, thesis 0 — 52. (Synbranchii, Symbranchii, Symbranchiformes, Alabiformes.) Berg, 1940 : 307 (GRWM : 398); MA : 158; Regan, 1912 : 387—390; Weber and Beaufort, 1916, 3 : 411—417. 2 suborders, 3 families (263— 265).

Suborder 49.1. Alabetoidei (Alabiformes). Berg, 1940 : 307 (GRWM : 398); MA : 158. 1 family (263).

Family 263. **Alabetidae** 397/411, thesis 49 —1. Figure 541. (=Alabidae = Cheilobranchidae = Chilobranchidae.)

Lit. J : (129); N : 602; G : (72); GRWM : 398, 421; MA : 158; Regan, 1912 : 387; T. Scott, 1962 : 73.

Fresh and brackish waters of Australia and Tasmania. 1 genus, 4 species. Fished locally.

Suborder 49.2. Synbranchoidei. (Symbranchoidei, Ichthyocephali + Holostomi). Berg, 1940 : 307 (GRWM : 398); MA : 159. 2 families (264 — 265).

Family 264. **Synbranchidae** (398/412), thesis 49 — 3. Figures 542, 543. (=Symbranchidae, +Flutidae = Monopteridae.) Swampeels, Kiemenschlitzaale, hosai k'o, ta unagi ka, sinbrankhovye, lozhnougrevye.

Lit. J : 129; N : 603; G : (72); GRWM : 399, 421; MA : 159; Regan, 1912 : 387; Weber and Beaufort, 1916, 3 : 411—417; Pellegrin, 1922, 884, 885; Chevey, 1932 : 1—155; Berg, 1948 — 49 : 1007—1008; T. Scott, 1962 : 73.

Fresh waters of the tropical parts of all continents, more rarely marine waters. 5 genera, a few species. Fished locally.

Family 265. **Amphipnoidae** 399/413, thesis 49 —4. Figure 544. (+ Cuchiidae, Norman, 1958, MA : 159.) Kuchievye.

Lit. J : 129; N : 604; G : 72; GRWM : 399, 421; MA : 159; Silas and Dawson, 1961 : 366 — 378.

Fresh and brackish waters of India, Burma, and Australia. 1 genus, 1 species. Fished locally.

Order 50. PERCIFORMES. 102/107, (104/109), theses 0—90, 129, 170. (Acanthopterygii, Thunniformes, Plecostei, Coryphaeniformes, Gadopseiformes.) Berg, 1940 : 308; MA : 136; (Zeiformes ex parte GRWM : 398; Gadiformes ex parte Zoarcoidei GRWM : 397); Boulenger, 1895 : 1—394; Regan, 1913 : 111—145; Mohr, 1927 : 85 — 140; Weber and Beaufort, 1929, 5 : 268 — 426; 1931, 6 : 1—408; 1936, 7 : 1—555; 1940, 8 : 1—472; 1951, 9 : 1—392;

Fowler, 1937–57 : 124–145 . . . ; Koefoed, 1952 : 1–26; Bauchot and Blanc, 1961 : 43–100; 1963 : 37–59; Gosline, 1961 : 265–270; 1968 : 1–78; C. Smith and Bailey, 1961 : 345–362; Patterson, 1964 : 213–482; Gosline, 1968 : 1–78; 16 suborders, 150 families (266–424).

Suborder 50.1. Percoidei, thesis 50.0–30. Berg,1940 : 308 (Perciformes ex parte, Percoidei, Labroidei, Trachinoidei, Notothenioidei, Gobioidei, GRWM : 399–402; Zeiformes ex parte GRWM : 398). Bauchot and Blanc, 1961 : 43–100; 1963 : 37–59; Bauchot, 1966 : 7–43; Gosline, 1966 : 409–418; 1968 : 15; McAllister, 1968 : 138; Lindberg and Krasyukova, 1969 : 26–33; Add.—Freihofer, 1969 : 858–861; Gosline, 1969 : 1–78; Bauchot, 1966 : 7–43; Gosline, 1966 : 409–418; 1968 : 15; McAllister, 1968 : 138; Lindberg and Krasyukova, 1969 : 26–33. 13 superfamilies, 108 families (266–373).

Superfamily 50.1.1. Percoidea, thesis 50.1.0–24. Berg, 1940 : 308. (Percoidei ex parte MA : 138). 71 families (266–336).

Family 266. **Centropomidae** 400/414, theses 50.1.1–85, 123. Figures 648, 675–677. (=Oxylabracidae, +Latidae, +Chandidae, +Ambassidae =Ambassiidae.). Robalos, snooks, ambassis, glassy perchlets, glassfishes, sea perches, cock-up, perche-du-Nil, Ketschr, Glassbarsche, t'zŭkai yü k'o, takasaga ishimochi ka, robalevye.

Lit. J : (189), 190 (191); N : 271; G : 95 (97); GRWM : 399, 424; MA : 138; Weber and Beaufort, 1929, 5 : 392–422; Fowler and Bean, 1930 : 1–334 (: 146–163); Fraser-Brunner, 1955 : 185–213. Add.—Holden, 1967 : 329–342.

Atlantic, Indian, and Pacific oceans, more rarely rivers of their basins. 9 genera, many species. Fished locally. Aquarium fishes.

Family 267. **Serranidae** 401/415, theses 50.1.1–148, 164. Figures 705, 706. (+Perciliidae = Percilidae, +Moronidae, +Oligoridae, +Niphonidae, +Epinephelidae, +Diploprionidae, +Rainfordiidae, +Hypoplectrodidae, +Chromileptidae, +Plectroplitidae, +Cephalopholidae, +Bostockiidae, +Plectropomidae, + Anthiidae, +Ostracoberycidae, +Paracentropristidae, +267a. Grammistidae + Rypticidae, +267b. Percichthyidae + Maccullochellidae, + Maquariidae.) Sea basses, groupers, garrupas, white basses, sea perches, rock cods, perches de-mer, barbiers, cerniers, mérous, bar, loup, loubine, babonne, vieille, Seebarsche, kamennye okuni, chih k'o, suzuki ka.

Lit. J : (191), 193, (195); N : 223; G : 91, (93), (94), (95), (99), (104); GRWM : 399, 424+family 267a; MA : 138+families 267a, b; Boulenger, 1895 : 1–394; Harris and Bean, 1905 : 1–238; Fowler, 1907 : 249–269; Jordan and Richardson, 1910 : 421–474; Ogilby, 1920 : 1–30; Fowler and Bean, 1930 : 1–334 (164–173); Weber and Beaufort, 1931, 6 : 1–138; Fowler, (1933); 1934 : 233–367 (351); Cadenat, 1935 : 377–422; Matsubara, 1939 : 121–128; Berg, 1948–49 : 1011–1018; Andriyashev, 1954 : 210–211; J. Smith, 1955 : 337–350; Franca, 1957 : 1–40; Katayama, 1959 : 103–180; Miller, 1959 : 35–68; Katayama, 1960 : 1–189; Gosline, 1960 : 28–38; McCully, 1961 : 1–4; Robins and Starck, 1961 : 259–314; Smith, 1961 : 359–369; Rivas, 1964 : 17–30; Svetovidov, 1964 : 233–241; C. Smith, 1965 : 1–20; Gosline, 1966 : 99–112;

Qureshi, 1965:172—186; Courtenay, 1967 : 241—293; Lindberg and Krasyukova, 1969 : 50—113; Add.—Cervigón and Velasquez, 1966 : 77—143; Rosenblatt and Zahuranec, 1967 : 228—245; Kotthaus, 1970 : 1—32.

Tropical and warm seas, more rarely fresh waters. About 100 genera, very many species. Of little importance in world marine fishing.

Family 268. **Pseudochromidae** (401A/415A), thesis 50.1.1—72. Figure 641. (Serranidae ex parte, Berg.) Dotty backs, lozhnokhromisovye.

Lit. J : 194; N : (246); G : 96; GRWM : 399, 424; MA : 138; Fowler, 1931 : 1—388; Aoyagi, 1941 : 41—54; Böhlke, 1960 : 1—11; Gosline, 1960 : 28—38; Qureshi, 1965 : 172—186; Lindberg and Krasyukova, 1969 : 113, 114.

Atlantic, Indian, and Pacific oceans. 2 genera, several species.

Family 269. Pseudogrammidae (—/—), thesis 50.1.1—74. Figure 642. (Serranidae ex parte Berg, + Rhegmatidae, Pseudochromidae ex parte.) Lozhnogramovye.

Lit. J : (194); N : (245); G : (96); GRWM : 399, 424; MA :—; J. Smith, 1953 : 548—560; Böhlke, 1960 : 1—11.

Warm waters of the Indian and Pacific oceans, including the coastal waters of the Panama isthmus. 3 genera, a few species. Game fishes.

Family 270. Grammidae (—/—), theses 50.1.1—63, 75. Figures 636, 643. (Serranidae ex parte Berg, Pseudochromidae ex parte, +Stigmatonotidae.) Gramovye.

Lit. J : (194); N : (245); G : (96); GRWM : 399, 424; MA : —; Böhlke, 1960 : 1—11; Böhlke and Randall, 1963 : 33—52.

Atlantic Ocean off the West Indies and Bahamas, Pacific Ocean around Australia, Japan, and the Hawaiian Islands. 6 genera, a few species.

Family 271. Glaucosomidae 402/416, thesis 50.1.1—153. Figure 699. Yeh tiao k'o, aoba, daika, zhemchuzhnotelye, zhemchuzhnye okuni.

Lit. J : 195; N : (271); G : 105; GRWM : 400, 424; MA : 138; Katayama, 1954 : 23—29; Lindberg and Krasyukova, 1969 : 115—116.

Southwest part of the Pacific off Japan, China, the Philippines, and Australia. 1 genus, about 6 species. Fished locally.

Family 272. **Theraponidae** 403/417, thesis 50.1.1—163. Figure 704. (=Teraponidae = Terapontidae, Tesapontidae.) Grunts, grunters, therapon-berch, tigerfishes, thornheads, la k'o, shima hisaki ka.

Lit. J : 197; N : 243; G : 108; GRWM : 400, 424; MA : 139; Ogilby, 1916 : 99—126; Fowler, 1931 : 1—388 (: 321—366); Weber and Beaufort, 1931, 6 : 139—167; Qureshi, 1965 : 172—186; Lindberg and Krasyukova, 1969 : 116—122.

Marine, partly fresh waters of the Indian and Pacific oceans. 3 genera, a small number of species. Fished locally. Aquarium fishes.

Family 273. Banjosidae 404/418, thesis 50.1.1—102. Figure 657. Shou yü k'o, tesen bakama ka, bandzhovye.

Lit. J : 197; N : (286); G : 110; GRWM : 400, 424; MA : (139) (family 309); Jordan and Thompson, 1912 : 521—601 (: 540); Fowler, 1933 : 1—465; Lindberg and Krasyukova, 1969 : 122—124.

Marine waters of Japan and China. 1 genus, 1 species.

Family 274. **Pseudoplesiopidae** 405/419, thesis 50.1.1—56. Figure 631. (Pseudochromidae ex parte). Ni tung k'o, lozhnopleziopsovye.

Lit. J : 194; N : (247); G : 96; GRWM : 399, 424; MA : 138; Weber and Beaufort, 1929, 5 : 379—381; J. Smith, 1954 : 195—208.

Marine waters of Indonesia and Australia. 1 genus, several species.

Family 275. **Anisochromidae** (—/—), thesis 50.1.1—57. Figure 632.

Lit. J : —; N : —; G : 93; GRWM : 399, 424; MA : —; J. Smith, 1954 : 298—302; Böhlke, 1960 : 1—11.

Atlantic Ocean off West Africa and the Bahamas. 1 genus, 1 species.

Family 276. **Plesiopidae** 406/420, theses 50.1.1—70, 161. Figures 640, 703 (=Pharopterycidae.) Roundheads, tun k'o, tanabata uo ka.

Lit. J : 194; N : 247; G : 96; GRWM : 399, 424; MA : 138; Ogilby, 1918 : 45—90; Weber and Beaufort, 1929, 5 : 372—378; J. Smith, 1952 : 139—151; Inger, 1955 : 259—276; Qureshi, 1965 : 172—186.

Indian Ocean and western part of the Pacific north as far as Southern Japan. 10 genera, a small number of species.

Family 277. **Acanthoclinidae** 407/421, thesis 50.1.1—6. Figure 595. Chikai yü k'o, toge tanabata uo ka.

Lit. J : 194; N : 248; G : 95; GRWM : 399, 424; MA : —; Chen and Liang, 1948 : 31—34; Böhlke, 1960 : 1—11.

Indian Ocean and western part of the Pacific north to Taiwan. 5 genera, a small number of species.

Family 278. **Kuhliidae** 408/422, thesis 50.1.1—159. Figure 702. (=Duleidae, +Nannatherinidae, +Nannopercidae.) Mountain bass, Sesele, Aholeholes, flagtails, t'ang li k'o, yugou ka.

Lit. J : 190; N : 249; G : 95; GRWM : 400, 424; MA : 138; Regan, 1913 : 374—381; Herre and Montalban, 1927 : 199—209; Weber and Beaufort, 1929, 5 : 268—274; Ikeda, 1939 : 131—158; Regan, 1940 : 173—175; Qureshi, 1965 : 172—186; Lindberg and Krasyukova, 1969 : 124—126.

Marine and fresh waters of the basins of the Indian Ocean and West Pacific from Australia north to Japan and the Hawaiian Islands. 3 genera, several species. Game fishes.

Family 279. **Centrarchidae** 409/423, thesis 50.1.1—157, Figure 701. Ushastyi okun'. (+Micropteridae = Cristidae = Grystidae, +Elassomatidae, = Elassomidae, +Eucentrarchidae.) Sunfishes, dwarf sunfishes, black basses, boers, pumpkinseeds, perche-soleil, Sonnenbarsche, Sonnenfische, chernye okuni, taiyang yü k'o, kuro masu ka.

Lit. J : 189 (190); N : —; G : 95,96; GRWM : 400, 425; MA : 138; Hubbs and Bailey, 1940 : 1—59; Berg, 1948—1949 : 1009—1011; Branson and Moore, 1952 : 1—108.

Fresh waters of North America. About 20 genera, quite a number of species. Game and aquarium fishes.

Family 280. **Priacanthidae** 410/424, theses 50.1.1—152, 155. Figures 698, 700. Bigeyes, catalufas, bullseyes, juif, chien tiao k'o, kitoki dai ka, bycheglazye okuni, katalufovye.

Lit. J : 194; N : 250; G : 97; GRWM : 400, 425; MA : 138; Weber and Beaufort, 1929, 5 : 382 — 391; Fowler, 1961 : 1—388 (64 — 80); Caldwell, 1962 : 417 — 424; Qureshi, 1965 : 172 — 186; Lindberg and Krasyukova, 1969 : 126 — 132.

Shallow depths of tropical and subtropical parts of the Atlantic and Indian oceans and of the West Pacific north to Vladivostok and the Hawaiian Islands. 2 genera, several species.

Family 281. **Apogonidae**. 411/425, thesis 50.1.1— 94. Figures 652, 653. (+Apogonichthyidae, +281a Henichthyidae = Henicichthyidae MA : 138, +Cheilodipteridae = Chilodipteridae, +"Amiidae", + Ostorhinchidae, +Gymnapogonidae, + Dinolestidae, +Epigonidae.) Kardinalovye, Cardinalfishes, tien chu tiao k'o, tenjiku dai ka.

Lit. J : 188, 203; N : (251); G : 98; GRWM : 400, 425; MA : 138 +family 281 a; Jordan and Snyder, 1901 : 891 — 913; Radcliffe, 1912 : 245 — 261; 1912 : 431 — 446; Tanaka, 1915 : 568; Weber and Beaufort, 1929, 5 : 275 — 371; Fowler and Bean, 1930 : 1—334; Regan, 1940 : 173 — 175; Schultz, 1940 : 403 — 423; Lachner, 1951 : 581— 610; J. Smith, 1954 : 775 — 795; Chang, 1959 : 359 — 362; Rass, 1961 : 1858; J. Smith, 1961 : 373 — 418; Garnaud, 1962 : 1—83; Jordan, 1963 : (203) 703; Mead and Falla, 1965 : 261 — 274; Qureshi, 1965 : 172 — 186; Böhlke and Randall, 1968 : 175 — 206; Lindberg and Krasyukova, 1969 : 132 — 144. Add. — Fourmanoir, 1967 : 265 — 266.

Warm waters of all the oceans; occasionally fresh waters. About 20 genera, many species. A promising item for local fishing.

Family 282. **Acropomatidae**. (412/426), thesis 50.1.1—90. Figure 650. (=Acropomidae.) Fakuang tiao k'o, hotaru daigako ka.

Lit. J : 189; N : (230); G : 97; GRWM : 400, 425; MA : (138) (family 267b); Matsubara, 1953 : 21—29; Lindberg and Krasyukova, 1969 : 144 — 145.

Deep waters of the Indian Ocean and West Pacific north to Japan. 1 genus, several species.

Family 283. **Percidae** 413/427, theses 50.1.1—95, 149. Figures 654, 697 (+ Etheostomatidae = Etheostomidae). Perches, darters, crawl-a-bottom, sandre, apron, gremille, walleyes, lu k'o, okunevye.

Lit. J : 186; N : —; G : 100; GRWM : 400, 425; MA : 138; Berg, 1948 — 1949 : 1018 — 1050; Disler, 1950 : 85 — 139; Bailey and Gosline, 1955 : 1— 44; Alverson and Westrheim, 1959 : 12—27; Gosline, 1961 : 265 — 270; Collette, 1962 : 115 — 121, 213 — 230; 1963 : 615 — 623; 1965 : 567 — 614; Collette and Verger, 1962 : 213 — 230; Svetovidov and Dorofeeva, 1963 : 625 — 651; Collette and Knapp, 1966 : 1—88; Gosline, 1966 : 409 — 418. Add. — Tsai Chu-fa, 1966 : 1— 396.

Fresh waters of the northern hemisphere. About 12 genera, many species. Fished locally. Game fishes.

Family 284. **Sillaginidae.** 414/428, theses 50.1.1—80, 146. Figures 646, 696. Sillagos, asohos, sand borers, whiting, hsi k'o, kisu ka, sillagovye.

Lit. J : 202; N : 258; G : 101; GRWM : 400, 425; MA : 139; Jordan and Snyder, 1902 : 461 — 497; Weber and Beaufort, 1931, 6 : 168 — 178; Fowler, 1933 : 1—465; Martin and Montalban, 1934 : 221 — 227; Qureshi, 1965 : 172 — 186; Lindberg and Krasyukova, 1969 : 145 — 150.

Indian Ocean and West Pacific north to Japan. 4 genera, several species. Fished locally. Game fishes.

Family 285. **Branchiostegidae** (415/429), theses 50.1.1—60, 144. Figures 634, 695. (=Latilidae.) Tilefishes, blanquillos, tailfishes, kafel'nikovye, blankillovye, fangtou yü k'o, ama daika.

Lit. J : 202; N : 257; G : (101); GRWM : 400, 425 + family 286; MA : 138; Ochiai, 1953 : 306 — 313; Lindberg and Krasyukova, 1969 : 150 — 154.

Marine waters of tropical and temperate latitudes. 6 genera, several species. Fished locally.

Family 286. **Malacanthidae** 416/430, thesis 50.1.1— 59. Figure 633. Malakantovye, matajuelos, false whiting, jochi k'o, kitsune ama dai ka.

Lit. J : 202; N : (258); G : 101; GRWM : (400) (family 285); MA : 138; Weber and Beaufort, 1936, 7 : 547 — 551; Berry, 1958 : 116 — 125; Qureshi, 1965 : 172 — 186.

Atlantic and Indian oceans and West Pacific north as far as Okinawa (Ryukyu) and the Hawaiian Islands. 1 genus, a small number of species.

Family 287. **Labracoglossidae** 417/431, thesis 50.1.1—141. Figure 694. Labrakoglossovye, takaba ka.

Lit. J: 203; N : 259; G : 142; GRWM : 400, 425; MA : 138; Lindberg and Krasyukova, 1969 : 154 — 156.

Western part of the Pacific from New Zealand northward to Japan. 3 genera, several species.

Family 288. **Lactariidae** 418/432, thesis 50.1.1—78. Figure 645. Laktarievye, milkfishes, whitefishes, juhsien yü k'o, akuta uo ka.

Lit. J : 186; N : 259; G : 102; GRWM : 400, 425; MA : 139; Weber and Beaufort, 1931, 6 : 306, 307; Woods and Inger, 1957 : 232 — 256; Qureshi, 1965 : 172 — 186.

Indian Ocean and West Pacific north to Taiwan; pelagial. 1 genus, several species. Of little importance in world marine fishing.

Family 289. **Pomatomidae** 419/433, thesis 50.1.1—82. Figure 647. Lufarevye, bluefishes, poissons-bleu, Tassergal.

Lit. J : 186; N : 260; G : 102; GRWM : 400, 425 + family 290; MA : 138; Weber and Beaufort, 1931, 6 : 304, 305; Svetovidov, 1964 : 244 — 248.

Most of the tropical seas. 1 genus, 1 species. Fished locally. Game fishes.

Family 290. **Scombropidae** 420/434, thesis 50.1.1—92. Figure 651. (=Scombropsidae, + Howellidae, + Sphyraenopsidae.) Lu k'o, mutsu ka, lozhnoskumbrievye.

Lit. J : 189; N : (260); G : 99; GRWM : (400) (family 289), MA : 138; Smith, 1950 : 210; Whitley, 1951 : 61 — 68; Lindberg and Krasyukova, 1969 : 156 —158.

Deep waters of the Atlantic (Caribbean Sea), Indian (South Africa), and West Pacific (Japan) oceans. About 6 genera, several species.

Family 291. **Rachycentridae** 421/435, thesis 50.1.1—11. Figure 598. (=Rhachycentridae = Elacatidae.) (Carangoidei ex parte MA : 140.) Kobievye, cobias, black kingfishes, sergent, sergeantfishes, chüntsao yü k'o, suga ka, chernaya ryba.

Lit. J : 186; N : 260; G : 102; GRWM : 400, 425; MA : 140; Weber and Beaufort, 1931, 6 : 301— 303; Lindberg and Krasyukova, 1969 : 158 — 160.

Most warm seas; pelagial. 1 genus, 1 species. Fished locally. Game fishes.

Family 292. **Carangidae** 422/436, thesis 50.1.1—13. Figures 600 — 604. (+ Seriolidae, + Juvenellidae), (Carangoidei ex parte MA : 140 + family 293). Stavridovye, jacks, scads, pompanos, hardtails, ranners, crevallas, trevallies, cavallos, sérioles, horsemackerel, queenfishes, darts, chinchards, fanfres, liches, Stöcker, shên k'o, adji ka.

Lit. J : 184; N : 261; G : 102; GRWM : 400, 425 + family 293; Ogilby, 1915 : 57 — 98; 1916 : 127 —177 ex parte; Wakiya, 1924 : 1—290 (139 — 244); Oshima, 1924 : 1571—1577; 1925 : 345 — 412; Mohr, 1927 : 85 — 140; Schnakenbeck, 1931 : 1—20; Weber and Beaufort, 1931, 6 : 189 — 300; Griffin, 1932 : 123 — 134; Norman, 1935 : 252; Roxas and Agco, 1941 : 1—82; Nichols, 1945 : 81 — 86; Bertin and Dollfus,1948 : 1—29; Tortonese, 1951 — 52 : 259 — 324; Ginsburg, 1952 : 43 — 117; Aleev, 1954 : 3— 12; Franca, 1956 : 99 — 150; Aleev, 1957 : 1— 137; Williams, 1958 : 369 — 430; Yokota and Mita,1958 : 1—59; J. Smith, 1959 : 255 — 261; Blanc and Bauchot, 1961 : 484 — 492; Suzuki, 1962 : 43—232; Wheeler, 1962 : 529 — 540; Fields, 1962 : 189 — 222; Svetovidov, 1964 : 249 — 265; Lindberg and Krasyukova, 1969 : 160 — 193; Nekrasov, 1969 : 211—220. Add. — J. Smith, 1967 — 1968 : 139 — 184. Nekrasov, 1970 : 89 — 138.

Almost all seas. More than 30 genera, many species. Of very great importance in world marine fishing.

Family 293. **Nematistiidae**,423/437, thesis 50.1.1—15. Figure 605. Peacockfishes, Poissons-paons, pavlinovye, dlinnoperye stavridy.

Lit. J : 185; N : —; G : 104; GRWM : (400) (family 292). MA : (140) (family 292); Jordan and Evermann, 1896 — 1900 : 894.

Northeastern Pacific from California to Panama. 1 genus, 1 species. Fished locally.

Family 294. **Formionidae** 424/438, thesis 50.1.1—40. Figure 621. (=Formiidae = Apolectidae.) (Carangoidei ex parte MA : 140.) Butterfishes, pomfrets, wu ch'ang k'o, kuro aji modoki ka, voronevye, formievye.

Lit. J : (184); N : (266); G : (102); GRWM : 400, 426. Lindberg and Krasyukova, 1969 : 193 — 195.

Indian Ocean and West Pacific from Australia to Japan; pelagial. 1 genus, 1 species.

Family 295. **Menidae** 425/439, thesis 50.1.1—43. Figure 623. (Carangoidei ex parte MA : 140.) Moofishes, yangching yü k'o, gin kagami ka.

Lit. J : 185; N : 268; G : 104; GRWM : 400, 426; MA : 140; Montilla, 1935 : 281 — 295. Lindberg and Krasyukova, 1969 : 195 — 197.

Indian Ocean and West Pacific north to Japan. 1 genus, 1 species.

Family 296. **Bramidae** 426/440, thesis 50.1.1—48. Figures 625, 626. (Bramiformes ex parte, + Steinegeriidae, + Trachyberycidae, + Lepidotidae, =Lepodidae.) (Scombroidei, MA : 139, 140.) Pomfrets, breams, seabreams, brèmes-de-mer, Costagnoles, morskie leshchi, wufang k'o, shima gatsuyu ka.

Lit. J : 181, (182); N : 269; G : 90; GRWM : 400, 426 + families 252 and 297; MA : 140 + family 297; J. Schmidt and Strasburg, 1918 : 1—15; Andriyashev, 1954 : 211—217; Mead, 1957 : 51 — 61; Buen, 1958 : 132 — 134; Mead and Maul, 1958 : 393 — 418; Parin, 1958 : 162 — 170; Abe, 1961 : 92 — 99; Mead and Haedrich, 1965 : 29 — 67; Lindberg and Krasyukova, 1969 : 197—208.

Most seas in the tropical and temperate latitudes; pelagial. 4 — 5 genera, several species. Fished locally.

Family 297. **Pteraclidae** (426A/440A), thesis 50.1.1—49. Figure 267. (=Pteraclididae.)

Lit. J : (182); N : (270); G : (91); GRWM : (400) (family 296). MA : (140) (family 296); Lindberg and Krasyukova, 1969 : 208 — 212.

Tropical and temperate latitudes of the oceans; pelagial. 3 genera, several species.

Family 298. **Coryphaenidae** 427/441, thesis 50.1.1—52. Figure 630. (Coryphaeniformes.) (Carangioidei ex parte MA : 140.) Dolphins, dorados, dolfinfishes, dauphins, grenadiers, deepsea rattails, doradovye, ryby del'-finy, ch'ich'iu k'o, shinra ka.

Lit. J : 181; N : 269; G : 91; GRWM : 400, 425; MA : 140; Weber and Beaufort, 1931, 6 : 183 — 185; Agco, 1940 : 313—315; Gibbs and Collette, 1958 : 117—152; Lindberg and Krasyukova, 1969 : 213—316.

Tropical and temperate latitudes of the oceans; pelagial. 1 genus, 2 species. Of little importance in world marine fishing. Game fishes.

Family 299. **Arripidae** 428/442, thesis 50.1.1—124. Figure 678. (=Arripididae.)

Lit. J : 195; N : (274); G : 105; GRWM : 400, 426; MA : 138; Jenyns, 1842 : 1—172; Fowler, 1933 : 1— 465.

South Pacific. 1 genus, 1 species. Fished locally. Game fishes.

Family 300. **Emmelichthyidae** 429/443, theses 50.1.1—87, 109. Figures 649, 662. (+ Erythrichthyidae, + Erytroclidae, + Inermiidae — Inermia, Poye, 1860, + Dipterygonotidae.) Rubyfishes, redbaits, hsieh yü k'o, chibaku ka, krasnoglazye okuni.

Lit. J : 200; N : 274; G : 104; GRWM : 400, 426 + families 301 and 314; MA : 138 + family 301; Chabanaud, 1924 : 248, 256; Weber and Beaufort, 1931, 6 : 178 — 180; Fowler, 1933 : 1— 465 (: 344 — 351); Schultz, 1945 : 132—136; Woods, 1958 : 249 — 252; Lindberg and Krasyukova, 1969 : 216 — 218.

Indian Ocean and the southern (Chile) and western parts of the Pacific north as far as Japan and the Hawaiian Islands. 7 genera, several species. Fished locally.

Family 301. **Inermiidae** 430/444, thesis 50.1.1—88. No figure. (Inermia Poye, 1861.)

Lit. J: 199; N: (275); G: (112); GRWM: (400) (family 300); MA: (138) (family 300).

Caribbean Sea. 1 genus, 1 species.

Family 302. **Lutjanidae** (431/445), thesis 50.1.1—128. Figures 679—681. (=Lutianidae = Luthianidae, + Etelidae, +Verilidae, +Hoplopagridae.) Snappers, hussars, basses, sea perches, vivaneaux, rifovye okuni, lut'yanovye, titiao k'o, fue dai ka, fue nai ka.

Lit. J: (195), (196); N: (276); G: 105; GRWM: 400, 426 + families 303 and 304; MA: 139; Jordan and Thompson, 1911: 435—471; Ogilby, 1918: 45—90; Fowler, 1931: 1—388; (81—198); Weber and Beaufort, 1936, 7: 232—457; Baughman, 1943: 212—215; Delais, 1952: 1214—1227; Kamohara, 1954: 107—117; J. Smith, 1954: 481—492; Talbot, 1957: 241—258; Lindberg and Krasyukova, 1969: 218—231. Add.—Shinohara, 1963: 1—147; Anderson, 1967: 1—14.

Warm waters of all the oceans. More than 20 genera, many species. Unimportant in world marine fishing but a promising item.

Family 303. Aphareidae (431A/445A) thesis 50.1.1—62. Figure 635.

Lit. J: 196; N: (282); G: 106; GRWM: (400) (family 302); MA: —; Jordan and Starks, 1901: 719—723; Matsubara, 1955: 588, 665, 666.

Tropical and subtropical waters of the Indian Ocean and the West Pacific north as far as Japan. 1 genus, 2—3 species.

Family 304. Caesionidae (—/—), thesis 50.1.1—138. Figure 689. (=Caesiodidae, Lutjanidae ex parte, Pomadasyidae ex parte.) Cesio, fusiliers.

Lit. J: (196); N: (279); G: (105); (107); GRWM: (400) (family 302); MA: —; Lindberg and Krasyukova, 1969: 231—234.

Indian and Pacific oceans, north to Japan. 1 genus, several species.

Family 305. **Nemipteridae** 432/446, thesis 50.1.1—130. Figure 683. (Denticidae ex parte, +Scolopsidae.) Besugos, bisugos, threadfin-breams, nemipterids, monocle bream, chinhsien yü k'o, itoyori dai ka, niteperye.

Lit. J: (198); N: 282; G: 106; GRWM: 400, 426; MA: 139; Ogilby, 1918: 45—90; J. Smith, 1941: 441—452; Lindberg and Krasyukova, 1969: 234—243.

Indian Ocean and West Pacific. 3 genera, several species. Fished locally.

Family 306. **Lobotidae** 433/447, theses 50.1.1—107, 132. Figures 661, 684. Trekhkhvostkovye, tripletails, flashers, sung tiao k'o, matsu dai ka.

Lit. J: 195; N: 283; G: 104; GRWM: 400, 426; MA: 138; Jordan and Thompson, 1911: 435—471; Fowler, 1931: 1—388 (43—44); Weber and Beaufort, 1936, 7: 457—464; Schultz, 1945: 132—136; Lindberg and Krasyukova, 1969: 243—245.

Tropical and subtropical latitudes of the Atlantic, Indian, and Pacific oceans; partly fresh waters. 2 genera, several species.

Family 307. **Leiognathidae** (434/448), thesis 50.1.1—111. Figure 663. (=Liognathidae = Equulidae.) Silver perches, jennies, slipmouth, ponyfish, sap-sap, fu k'o, hiiragi ka, srebrobryushkovye.

Lit. J : 186; N : 283; G : 106; GRWM : 400, 426; MA : 139 + family 308; Weber and Beaufort, 1931, 6 : 310 — 360; Lindberg and Krasyukova, 1969 : 245 — 253.

Marine, brackish, and fresh waters of the basins of the Mediterranean Sea, Indian Ocean, and West Pacific north as far as Japan. 2 genera, many species. Of little importance in world marine fishing.

Family 308. **Gerridae** 434A/448A, thesis 50.1.1—112. Figure 664. (Liognathidae ex parte = Xystaemidae, + Eucinostomidae.) Mojarras, silver perches, silver biddies, blanches, mokharrovye.

Lit. J : 200; N : (284); G : 109; GRWM : 400, 426; MA : (139) (family 307); Jordan, 1907 : 245 — 248; Fowler, 1933 : 1—465; Lindberg and Krasyukova, 1969 : 253 — 256.

Tropical and subtropical latitudes of all the oceans. More than 5 genera, many species. Unimportant in world marine fishing. Game fishes.

Family 309. **Pomadasyidae** 435/449, thesis 50.1.1—139. Figures 690—693. (=Pomadasidae, + Haemulidae = Haemulonidae, + Gaterinidae, + Pristipomidae = Pristipomatidae, + Plectorhynchidae, + Xenichthyidae.) Grunts, pomadasids, javelinfishes, grunters, sweetlips, ronco, shih lu k'o, isaki ka, vorchunovye.

Lit. J : (196); N : 286; G : 107; GRWM : 400, 426; MA : 139 + family 273; Fowler, 1931 : 1—388 (: 199 — 320); Matsubara, 1933 : 73 — 96; Arnov, 1952 : 414 — 437; J. Smith, 1952 : 711—716; Franca and Picciochi, 1958 : 143 — 195; Courtenay, 1961 : 66 — 149; Leccia, 1961 : 396 — 473; J. Smith, 1962 : 469 — 502; Lindberg and Krasyukova, 1969 : 256 — 269.

Warm waters of the Atlantic, Indian, and Pacific oceans. About 20 genera, many species. Fished locally. Game fishes.

Family 310. **Sciaenidae** 436/450, thesis 50.1.1—100. Figure 656. (+Otolithidae.) Drums, weakfishes, queenfishes, groundeurs, tambours, maigres, ombrines, corbs, croakers, roncadores, river kingfishes, Jewfishes, shihshou k'o, nibe ka, gorbylevye, stsienovye.

Lit. J : 201 (202); N : 291; G : 108; GRWM : 400, 427; MA : 139; Jordan and Thompson, 1911 : 241 — 261; Ogilby, 1918 : 45 — 90; Starks, 1919 : 1—88; Dieuzeide, 1929 : 131—161; Nichols, 1929 : 161—295; Fowler, 1933 : 1—465; Lin, 1935 : 1—30; Dharmarjan, 1936 : 1—72; Weber and Beaufort, 1936, 7 : 481 — 546; Matsubara, 1937 : 27 — 92; Lin, 1938 : 33 — 43; Scogsberg, 1939 : 1— 62; Lin, 1940 : 243 — 254; Campos, 1942 : 9 — 22; Jacob, 1948 : 118—124; Matsui and Takai, 1949 : 65 — 89; Franca, 1958 : 7 — 51; McPhail, 1958 : 1—20; Collingnon, 1959 : 1—10; 1960 : 55 — 84; Travassos and Paiva, 1959 : 139 — 169; Buen, 1961 : 1—90; Trewavas, 1961 : 2— 5; 1962 : 167 — 176; 1964 : 107 — 117; Wheeler, 1961 : 1—54; Longhurst, 1962 : 1 — 3; Shingu, 1962 : 65 —72; Chu, Lo and Wu, 1963 : 1—100; Svetovidov, 1964 : 265 —272; Lowe, 1966 : 20 — 57; Lindberg and Krasyukova, 1969 : 269 — 297. Add.—Lopez and Castello, 1968 : 14 — 27; Roux, 1968 : 261 — 264; Dutt and Thankam, 1969 : 335 — 347.

Most seas, occasionally fresh waters. About 40 genera, many species. Of average importance in world marine fishing.

Family 311. **Lethrinidae**. 437/451, thesis 50.1.1—134. Figure 686. (+ Neolethrinidae,+ Monotaxidae.) Scavengers, rudderfishes, pigface breams, sweetlips, barefaces, lochia tiao k'o, fue fuki daika.

Lit. J : 197; N : 300; G : 110 (111); GRWM : 400, 427; MA : 139; Ogilby, 1916 : 127—177; Fowler,1933 : 1—465; J. Smith, 1959 : 285—295; Wheeler, 1961 : 1—54; Silas and Toor, 1962 : 208—214. Lindberg and Krasyukova, 1969 : 297—304.

Eastern part of the Atlantic (West Africa), Indian Ocean, and West Pacific north to Japan. 3 genera, many species. Unimportant in world marine fishing.

Family 312. **Pentapodidae**. (—/—), thesis 50.1.1—136. Figures 687, 688. (Lethrinidae ex parte.) Large-eyed breams.

Lit. J : (197); N : (300); G : (110); GRWM : 400, 427; MA : 139; Akazaki, 1959 : 373—377; J. Smith, 1941 : 441—452; Lindberg and Krasyukova, 1969 : 304—305.

Indian Ocean and West Pacific north as far as Japan. 4 genera, several species.

Family 313. **Sparidae** 438/452, thesis 50.1.1—114. Figures 665—668. (Denticidae ex parte, Nemipteridae ex parte, Girellidae ex parte, +Pimelepteridae, + Paradicichthyidae = Paradichthyidae.) Porgies, pargos, sea breams, silver breams, dorades, sargues, borgues, pagres, pagels, dentés, brèmes-de-mer, Meerbrassen, morskie karasi, tiao k'o, tai ka.

Lit. J : 197; N : 301; G : 111; GRWM : 400, 427; MA : 139; Jordan and Fesler, 1893 : 421—544; Jordan and Thompson, 1912 : 521—601; Ogilby, 1916 : 127—177; Herre and Montalban, 1927 : 397—441; Oshimo, 1927 : 127—155; Fowler, 1933 : 1—465; Weber and Beaufort, 1936, 7 : 465—474; J. Smith, 1938 : 225—305; 1940 : 175—182; 1941 : 441—452; Tretjakoff, 1941 : 158—160; Campos, 1944 : 197—212; Berg, 1948—1949 : 1050—1051; Munro, 1949 : 182—224; Kubo and Onoe, 1952 : 321—324; Svetovidov, 1955 : 837—841; Caldwell, 1957 : 77—173; Akazaki, 1958 : 322—325; 1961 : 437—441; 1962 : 1—368; Svetovidov, 1964 : 272—291; Aloncle, 1966 : 55—66; Randall and Caldwell, 1966 : 1—47; Akazaki, 1952 : 328—368; Lindberg and Krasyukova, 1969 : 306—321. Add.—Yuner, 1969 : 20—22; Bonnet, 1969 : 97—116.

Marine waters, mainly of tropical and subtropical latitudes. More than 30 genera, very many species. Of average importance in world marine fishing.

Family 314. **Centracanthidae** (439/453), thesis 50.1.1—105. Figures 659, 660. (=Centracantidae, +Merolepidae, +Maenidae, + Spicaridae.) (Maenidae MA : 139.) Picarels, smaridovye.

Lit. J : (200); N : 309; G : (112); GRWM : (400) (family 300); MA : 139; Weber and Beaufort, 1931, 6 : 308, 309; Tretjakoff, 1941 : 158—160; Zei, 19 1941 : 135—190; Schultz, 1945 : 132—136; Berg, 1948—1949 : 1051, 1052; Svetovidov, 1964 : 291—301. Add.—Quintard-Dorques, 1966 : 79—88.

East Atlantic, Mediterranean Sea, and Indian Ocean. 5 genera, a few species.

Family 315. **Mullidae** 440/454, thesis 50.1.1—9. Figure 597. Goatfishes, surmullets, rougets, surmulets, Meerbarbe, redmullets, barabulevye, sultankovye, yang yü k'o, himeji ka.

Lit. J : 200; N : —; G : 110; GRWM : 400, 427; MA : 138; Snyder, 1907 : 87—102; Herre and Montalban, 1928 :95—137; Weber and Beaufort, 1931, 6 : 361—408; Fowler, 1933 : 1—465; Wang, 1936 : 1—18; Ebeling, 1957 : 173—185; Schultz, 1960 : 1—46; Svetovidov, 1964 : 301—309; Lindberg and Krasyukova, 1969 : 321—329; Lachner, 1954 : 497—532.

Marine waters of tropical, subtropical, and partly temperate latitudes. 5 genera, many species. Unimportant in world marine fishing.

Family 316. **Monodactylidae** (441/455), thesis 50.1.1—24. Figure 610. (=Psettidae, +Amphistiidae) (Chaetodontoidei ex parte,MA : 143.) Fingerfishes, batfishes, kitefishes, silver batfishes, Flossenblättler, monodactilids, chien ch'ang k'o, hime tsubame uo ka, monodaktilovye, odnopalye.

Lit. J : 205; N : 310; G : 112; GRWM : 400, 427; Fowler and Bean, 1929 : 1—352 (12—17); Weber and Beaufort, 1936, 7 : 206—209; Fowler, 1937—1953 : 1—77.

Marine, partly fresh, waters of the East Atlantic, Indian Ocean, and West Pacific. 3 genera, a small number of species. Small forms kept in aquariums.

Family 317. **Pempheridae** 442/456, thesis 50.1.1—50. Figures 628, 629. (+317a. Leptobramidae, Carangoidei MA : 140.) Sweepers, deep-water catalufas, tanchi yü k'o, hatampo ka, bol'sheglazy.

Lit. J : 194; N : 311; G : 98; GRWM : 400,427; MA : 138; Ogilby, 1913 : 60—80; Fowler, 1931 : 1—388 (45—64); Weber and Beaufort,1936, 7 : 210—220; Tominaga, 1963 : 269—290; 1965 : 33—56; 1968 : 43—95; Lindberg and Krasyukova, 1969 : 329—332. Add.—Tominaga, 1968 : 43—95.

Tropical and subtropical latitudes of the Atlantic, Indian, and Pacific oceans. 2 genera, several species.

Family 318. **Toxotidae** 443/457, thesis 50.1.1—17. Figure 606. (Toxotiformes.) (Chaetodontoidei MA : 143.) Archerfishes, blow-gun fishes, perche cracheuse, Schutzenfische, sheshui yü k'o, teppo uo ka, bryzgunovye.

Lit. J : 206; N : 312; G : 113; GRWM : 400—427; MA : 143; Fowler and Bean, 1929 : 1—352 (29—34); Weber and Beaufort, 1936, 7 : 194—205; Lüling, 1955 : 178—184.

Coastal marine waters and fresh waters of the basins of the Indian and West Pacific oceans north as far as the Philippines. 2 genera, several species. Small forms kept in aquariums.

Family 319. **Scorpididae** (444/458) thesis 50.1.1—129. Figure 682. (=Scorpidae, +Parascorpididae=Parascorpidae.) Halfmoons, halfmoon fishes, polulunnikovye, hsieh yü k'o, kagokagi dai ka.

Lit. J : (205); N : 312, 314; G : (112); GRWM : (400) (family 321); MA : 139; Fowler and Bean,1929 : 1—352; Smith, 1950 : 185; Lindberg and Krasyukova, 1969 : 332—334.

Indian and Pacific oceans. 7 genera, a few species.

Family 320. **Coracinidae** (445/459), thesis 50.1.1—119. Figure 672. (=Dichistiidae, Girellidae ex parte, = Corotinidae.)

Lit. J: (199); N: (315); G: (113); GRWM: 400, 427; MA: 138; J. Smith, 1935: 265–276; 1950: 248.

Coastal marine waters and fresh waters of Southeast Africa and Madagascar. 1 genus, several species.

Family 321. **Kyphosidae** (446/460), thesis 50.1.1–120. Figure 674. (=Cyphosidae.) Seachubbs, chopas, drummers, rudderfishes, pilotfishes, poissons-pilotes, poisson d'ail, to k'o, isuzumi ka, chopovye.

Lit. J: 199; N: 314; G: 113; GRWM: 400,427 + family 319 + 322; MA: 139 + + family 322; Herre and Montalban, 1927: 397–441; Fowler, 1933: 1–465; Weber and Beaufort, 1936, **7**: 221–231; Moore, 1962: 447–453; Lindberg and Krasyukova, 1969: 334–337.

Tropical and subtropical latitudes of the Atlantic, Indian, and Pacific oceans. 3 genera,several species. Fished locally. Game fishes.

Family 322. **Girellidae** 447/461, thesis 50.1.1–117. Figure 671. Nibblers, girelles, oblades, grisets, bogues, saupes, chi yü k'o, mejina ka, girellovye.

Lit. J: 199; N: 315; G: 113; GRWM: (400) (family 321); MA: (139) (family 321); Fowler, 1933: 1–465; Kobayashi and Igarashi,1961: 121–127; Nelson, 1967: 289–293; Lindberg and Krasyukova, 1969: 337–342.

Tropical and subtropical oceanic waters. About 7 genera, several species. Fished locally.

Family 323. **Ephippidae**, 448/462, theses 50.1.1–22, 32. Figures 609, 616. (+ Chaetodipteridae = Ilarchidae, Ephippiformes.) (Chaetodontoidei MA: 143.) Spadefishes, orbfishes, forgerons, pai ch'ang k'o, man'jü dai ka, pikovye, ryba tuz pik.

Lit. J: 205; N: (317); G: 113; GRWM: 400, 427 + family 325 + 326; MA: 143 + family 325; Fowler and Bean, 1929: 1–352 (24–27); J. Smith, 1936: 303–310; Matsubara, 1955: 925, 927.

Atlantic, Indian, and Pacific oceans. 2–3 genera, several species.

Family 324. **Rhinoprenidae** (–/–); thesis 50.1.1–32; footnote. Figure 616A.

Lit. J: –; N: –; G: –; GRWM: 400; MA: –; Munro, 1964: 141–186.

New Guinea. 1 genus, 1 species.

Family 325. **Platacidae** (448A/462A), thesis 50.1.1–25. Figure 612. (Ephippidae ex parte.) (Chaetodontoidei ex parte MA: 143.) Leaffishes, batfishes, sea bates.

Lit. J: 205; N: (317), 318; G: 112; GRWM: (400) (family 323); MA: (143) (family 323); Fowler and Bean, 1929: 1–352 (: 17–21); Lindberg and Krasyukova, 1969: 342–344.

Atlantic, Indian, and Pacific oceans. 1 genus, several species.

Family 326. **Drepanidae**, 449/463, thesis 50.1.1–34. Figure 617. (=Drepanichthyidae = Drepaneidae.) (Chaetodontoidei ex parte MA: 143.) Drepanes, spotted batfishes, sicklefishes, chilung ch'ang k'o, sudare dai ka.

Lit. J: 205; N: 318; G: (113); GRWM: (400) (family 323). MA: 143; Herre and Montalban, 1927: 1–133 (3); Matsubara,1955: 925, 927.

East Atlantic, Indian, and Pacific oceans. 1 genus, several species. Fished locally.

Family 327. **Scatophagidae**. 450/464, thesis 50.1.1—31. Figure 615. (Chaetodontiformes ex parte = Prenidae.) (Chaetodontoidei ex parte MA: 143.) Spadefishes, skats, butterfishes, Argusfische, agrusovye, skatofagovye, chinch'ang yü k'o, kurohoshi manju dai ka.

Lit. J: 206; N: 318; G: 114; GRWM: 400; 428; MA: 143; Gill, 1891: 355—360; Fowler and Bean, 1929: 1—352 (34—40); Myers, 1936: 83—86; Fraser-Brunner, 1938: 72—75; 1938: 76—80; Matsubara, 1955: 926, 946.

Marine and fresh waters of the basins of the Indian and Pacific oceans. 2 genera, several species. Small forms kept in aquariums.

Family 328. **Chaetodontidae** 451/465, theses 50.1.1—36, 98. Figures 618, 619,655. (Chaetodontiformes ex parte, + Pomacanthidae.) (Chaetodontoidei ex parte, MA: 143.) Butterflyfishes, coralfishes, angel fishes, papillons-de-mer, ryba babochka, korallovye ryby, huteh yü k'o, chocho no ka.

Lit. J: 206; N: 319; G: 114; GRWM: 400, 428; MA: 143; Jordan and Fowler, 1902: 513—563; Ahl, 1923: 1—205; Herre and Montalban, 1927: 1—113; Fowler and Bean, 1929: 1—352 (40—195); Fraser-Brunner, 1933: 543—599; Weber and Beaufort, 1936, 7: 1—194; Fowler, 1937—1957: 1—77; J. Smith, 1955: 377—384; Hubbs, 1963: 133—192; Kamohara, 1964: 1—6, Lindberg and Krasyukova, 1969: 345—352.

Tropical waters of all the oceans. About 20 genera, many species. Fished locally. Game fishes.

Family 329.* **Caproidae** 391/405, thesis 50.1.1—37. Figure 620. (Capriformes, + Antigoniidae = Caprophonidae, Zeiformes ex parte GRWM: 398; MA: 110; Ling tiao k'o, hishi dai ka.

Lit. J: 204; N: —; G: 90; GRWM: 398, 420; Starks, 1902: 565—572; Fowler and Bean, 1929: 1—352 (2—6); Weber and Beaufort, 1940, 5: 265—267; Fraser-Brunner, 1950: 721—724; Berry, 1959: 205—250.

Atlantic, Indian, and Pacific oceans. 2 genera, several species.

Family 330. **Enoplosidae** 452/466, thesis 50.1.1—21. Figure 608. Avstraliiskii kolyucheper.

Lit. J: 199; N: 324; G: 112; GRWM: 400, 428; MA: 138; Fowler, 1933: 1—465.

Southern part of the Pacific off Celebes and around southern and eastern Australia. 1 genus, 1 species.

Family 331. **Pentacerotidae** (453/467), thesis 50.1.1—28. Figure 613. (+ Histiopteridae MA: 138). Boarfishes, fanch'i yü k'o, kawa bisha ka, veprevye, kaban-ryba.

Lit. J: (199); N: (324); G: (115); GRWM: 400, 428; MA: 138; Jordan, 1907: 235—239; Follett and Dempster, 1963; 315—338; J. Smith, 1964: 87—91; Lindberg and Krasyukova, 1969: 353—358.

Indian and Pacific oceans. 6 genera, a few species. A promising item for world marine fishing.

* The family Caproidae was transferred by Matsubara from the order Zeiformes to the order Perciformes, suborder Chaetodontoidei, and we have followed this; in the system adopted by GRWM: 398 and MA: 110 it is included in the Zeiformes.

Family 332. **Pristolepididae** 454/468, thesis 50.1.1—67. Figure 638. (=Pristolepidae, +Nandidae ex parte.)

Lit. J: (202); N: —; G: (115); GRWM: (400) (family 333); MA: 138; Weber and Beaufort, 1936, 7: 475—480.

Fresh waters of India and Indonesia. 2 genera, several species.

Family 333. **Nandidae** 455/469, thesis 50.1.1—68. Figure 639. (333a and 417d. Badidae, Figure 848A). Nandids, leaffishes, Nanderbarsche.

Lit. J: 202; N: —; G: 115; GRWM: 400, 425 +family 332 and 334; MA: 138; Weber and Beaufort, 1936, 7: 475—480; Barlow, Liem, and Wickler, 1968: 425—447.

Fresh waters of West Africa, India, Indochina, Indonesia. 4 genera, several species. Aquarium fishes.

Family 334. **Polycentridae** 456/470, thesis 50.1.1—7. Figure 596. Südamerikanische Vielstachler, mnogoshipovye.

Lit. J: 202; N: —; G: 115; GRWM: (400) (family 333). MA: 138; Regan, 1913: 111—145; Sterba, 1959: 1—637 (486,488).

Fresh waters of the tropical part of South America and West Africa. 3 genera, a small number of species. Aquarium fishes.

Family 335. **Oplegnathidae** (457/471), thesis 50.1.1—3. Figures 593, 594. (=Hoplegnathidae.) (Ostorhinchidae MA: 138.) Rock beams, shih tiao k'o, ishi dai ka.

Lit. J: 200; N: 326; G: 110; GRWM: 400, 428; MA: 138; Jordan and Fowler, 1902: 75—78; Fowler, 1933: 1—465; Lindberg and Krasyukova, 1969: 358—360.

Marine waters of Japan, the Hawaiian Islands, Peru, Tasmania, West Australia, and South Africa. 1 genus, several species. Fished locally.

Family 336. **Cichlidae** 458/472, thesis 50.1.1—1. Figure 592. (=Chromidae, not from the Pomacentroidea, family 339.) (Pomacentroidei ex parte MA: 143.) Cichlids, perches des tropiques, Buntbarsche, tilyatsievye.

Lit. J: 219; N: —; G: 115; GRWM: 401, 428; MA: 144; Eigenmann and Kennedy, 1903: 497—537; Pellegrin, 1903: 41—399; 1904: 1—365; Ribeiro, 1918: 1—18; Regan, 1920: 33—53; 1922: 157—191; : 249—264; Worthington, 1932: 121—134; 1933: 34—52; Tee-Van, 1935: 281—300; Trewavas, 1935: 65—118; 1942: 526—536; Poll, 1952: 1—20, 1956: 1—619; Travassos and Pinto, 1959: 1—18; Blanc, 1962: 202—227; Greenwood, 1962: 139—214; Wickler, 1963: 83—96; Ypiranga, 1963: 45—48; Thys, 1964: 1—147; Schultz, 1967: 1—10. Add.—Greenwood, 1965: 315—357; 1967: 31—119; Fishelson, 1966: 571—656; Thys, 1966: 1—95; 1968: 349—391; 1968: 295—314; Rosemary and McConnell, 1969: 255—302.

Mainly fresh waters of tropical countries. Many genera, very many species. Game and aquarium fishes.

Superfamily 50.1.2. **Cepoloidea**, thesis 50.1.0—5. Berg, 1940: 312. (Percoidei ex parte MA: 138). 1 family (337).

Family 337. **Cepolidae.** 459/473, thesis 50.1.1—0. Figure 707. Bandfishes, lentotelye, chihtao yü k'o, aka chika.

Lit. J : 203; N : —; G : 118; GRWM : 401, 429; MA : 138; Jordan and Fowler, 1903 : 699 — 702; Herre, 1927 : 281 — 285; McCulloch, 1929 : 1—534 (: 255); Weber and Beaufort, 1936, 7 : 552—553; Okada and Sudzuki, 1956 : 185 — 194; Lindberg and Krasyukova, 1969 : 360 — 365.

Mediterranean Sea and northward as far as England, Indian Ocean and West Pacific from New Zealand to Japan. 2 genera, several species.

Superfamily 50.1.3. **Embiotocoidea.** Thesis 50.1.0 — 20. (Pharyngognathi ex parte; Holconoti.) Berg, 1940:312. Gosline, 1938 : 15 (Embiotocoidei MA : 143). 1 family (338).

Family 338. **Embiotocidae,** 460/474, thesis 50.1.3—0. Figure 708. (=Ambiotocidae, +Ditremidae, +Hysterocarpidae, +Holconotidae.) Surfperches, surffishes, viviparous perches, sea perches, ditremovye, hai chi k'o, umi tanago ka.

Lit. J : 217; N : —; G : 119; GRWM : 400, 428; MA : 143; Eigenmann, 1894 : 94 — 118; Eigenmann and Ulrey, 1894 : 382— 399; Jordan and Sindo, 1902 : 353 — 359; Hubbs, 1918 : 9 —14; Kamohara, 1940 : 1—79; Tarp, 1952 : 1—99; Carlisle, Scott and Abramson, 1960 : 3 — 79; Yamame, 1964 : 1—10; Nelson, 1967 : 289 — 293; Lindberg and Krasyukova, 1969 : 365 — 369.

North Pacific. 12 genera, many species. Fished locally.

Superfamily 50.1.4. **Pomacentroidea,** thesis 50.1.0—17. (Chromides, Amphiprioniformes, Pharyngognathi ex parte, Pomacentriformes.) Berg, 1940 : 312; Gosline, 1968 : 64; (Pomacentroidei, MA : 143). 1 family (339).

Family 339. **Pomacentridae** 461/475, thesis 50.1.4 — 0. Figures 709 — 712. (+Abudefdufidae =Glyphiodontidae, + Ctenolabridae, +Amphiprionidae, Chromidae ex parte, +Premnidae.) Damselfishes, anemonefishes, coralfishes, rock pilots, pomacentrids, pullers, demoiselles, bouteur, ch'ueh tiao k'o, suzume dai ka.

Lit. J : 218; N : 333; G : 119; GRWM : 401, 428; MA : 144; Steindachner, 1875 : 1—77; McCulloch, 1921 : 164 — 178; Fowler and Bean, 1928 : 1—525; Montalban, 1928 : 1—117; Whitley, 1929 : 207— 246; Fowler, 1937 — 1957 : 1— 110; 124 — 145 . . . Okada and Ikeda, 1937 : 67 — 95; 1939 : 159 — 206; Weber and Beaufort, 1940, 8 : 326 — 472; Aoyagi, 1941 : 157 — 279; Schultz, 1953 : 187 — 201; Fowler, 1954, 7 : 1— 110; Kamohara, 1960 : 1—10; Rivas, 1960 : 130 — 163; J. Smith, 1960 : 317 — 349; Svetovidov, 1964 : 309 — 311; Nelson, 1967 : 289 — 293; Lindberg and Krasyukova, 1969 : 309 — 380.

Marine, mainly tropical waters. More than 30 genera, very many species.

Superfamily 50.1.5. **Labroidea,** thesis 50.1.0 — 21. (Labroidei, Labriformes, Pharyngognathi ex parte.) Berg, 1940 : 313; Gosline, 1968 : 64. (Labroidei GRWM : 401; MA : 146); Lozano and Rey, 1952 : 387 — 703; Bauchot and Blanc, 1961 : 43 — 64, 3 families (340 — 342).

Family 340. **Labridae** 462/476, thesis 50.1.5—1. Figures 713—720. (=Cyclolabridae, +Coridae, +Neolabridae, +Bodianidae, +Harpidae.) Wrasses, slippery dicks, sublets, rasons, rainbow fishes, coquettes, vieilles, roucaous, Sublets, Lippfische, lungtou yü k'o, bera ka, gubanovye.

Lit. J : 221; N : 338; G : 121; GRWM : 401, 429; MA : 146; Jordan and Snyder, 1902 : 595—662; Caporiacco, 1921 : 49—101; Mohr, 1927 : 85—140; Fowler and Bean, 1928 : 1—525 (: 188 —372); Fowler, 1937—57 : 124—145. . . Weber and Beaufort, 1940, 8 : 16—255; Wang, 1941 : 87—119; Rhasis-Erasi, 1943 : 141—160; Schultz and Marshall, 1954 : 439—447; J. Smith, 1957 : 99—114; : 117—120; Kamohara, 1958 : 1—20; Randall, 1958 : 327—347; Blanc and Bauchot, 1960 : 88—96; Bauchot, 1961 : 84—97; : 43—100; Klausewitz, 1962 : 11—16; Masuda and Tanaka, 1962 : 1—98; Kamohara, 1963 : 1—9; Svetovidov, 1964 : 312—335; Randall, 1965 : 487—501; Randall and Böhlke, 1965 : 235—259; Quignard, 1966 : 1—247; Nelson, 1967 : 289—293; Lindberg and Krasyukova, 1969 : 381—410. Add.—Syad et al. 1967 : 418—434.

Marine, mainly tropical and subtropical waters. About 60 genera, very many species. Unimportant in world marine fishing.

Family 341. **Odacidae** 463/477, thesis 50.1.5—3. Figure 721. (+Siphonognathidae, +Neoodacidae = Neodaciidae.) Avstralogubanovye.

Lit. J : 223, N : 353; G : 124; GRWM : 401, 429; MA : 146; Graham, 1953 : 260, 261.

Marine waters, coasts of Australia and New Zealand. 6 genera, a considerable number of species.

Family 342. **Scaridae** 464/478, thesis 50.1.5—4. Figures 723—724. (=Callyodontidae, =Calliodontidae, +Sparisomidae, +Scarichthyidae.) Parrotfishes, perroquets-de-mer, popugaevye, popugai-ryba, yingtzui yü k'o, budai ka.

Lit. J : 223; N : 354; G : 123; GRWM : 401, 429; MA : 146; Fowler and Bean, 1928 : 1—525 (372—498); Fowler, 1937—57 : 124—145. . . Weber and Beaufort, 1940, 8 : 256—325; J. Smith, 1956 : 1—23; Schultz, 1958 : 1—143; J. Smith, 1959 : 265—282; Bauchot and Guibe, 1960 : 290—300; Masuda and Tanaka, 1962 : 1—98; Kamohara, 1963 : 1—24; Randall, 1963 : 225—234; Nelson, 1967 : 289—293; Lindberg and Krasyukova, 1969 : 410—414, Add.—Rosenblatt and Hobson, 1969 : 434—453; Schultz, 1969 : 1—50.

Tropical seas. 10 genera, many species, unimportant in world marine fishing.

Superfamily 50.1.6. G a d o p s o i d e a, thesis 50.1.0—3. (Gadopseiformes, Gadopsiformes.) Berg, 1940 : 313. (Ophidioidei ex parte Gosline, 1968 : 65; Percoidei ex parte MA : 138.) 1 family (343).

Family 343. **Gadopsidae** 465/479, thesis 50.1.6—0. Figure 725.

Lit. J : 204; N : 356; G : 112, GRWM : 401, 428; MA : 138; Ogilby, 1913 : 60—80.

Fresh waters of South Australia and Tasmania. 1 genus, several species.

Superfamily 50.1.7. **Cirrhitoidea**, thesis 50.1.0—13. (Cirrhitoidei.) Berg, 1940 : 313; (Percoidei ex parte, MA : 138) Gosline, 1968 : 64; Jordan and Herre,1907 : 157—167; Regan, 1911 : 259—262. 5 families (344—348).

Family 344. **Cirrhitidae** 466/480, thesis 50.1.7—2. Figure 726. Curlyfins, hawkfishes, wên k'o, gombei ka, kudreperye.

Lit. J : 203; N : 327; G : 118; GRWM : 401, 429; MA : 139; Fowler, 1937—57 : 124—145 . . . ; Weber and Beaufort, 1940, 8 : 1—15; Tee-Van, 1940 : 53—64; Schultz, 1950 : 547—552; J. Smith, 1951 : 625—652; Randall, 1963 : 389—451; Tortonese, 1964 : 1—8; Lindberg and Krasyukova, 1969 : 414—416.

Indian and Pacific oceans. 10 genera, a considerable number of species.

Family 345. **Chironemidae** 467/481, thesis 50.1.7—5. Figure 728. Avstraliiskie kudreperye.

Lit. J : 204; N : 329; G : 118; GRWM : 401,429; MA : 139; T. Scott, 1962 : 175, 207.

Marine waters of Australia and New Zealand. 2 genera, several species.

Family 346. **Aplodactylidae** (468/482), thesis 50.1.7—4, Figure 727. (=Haplodactylidae.) Yingpan tiao k'o, takano ha daika, mramornikovye.

Lit. J : 204; N : 329; G : 118; GRWM : 401, 429; MA : 139; Fowler, 1937—57 : 124—145; Lindberg and Krasyukova, 1969 : 416—421.

South Pacific. 3 genera, several species.

Family 347. **Cheilodactylidae** (469/483), thesis 50.1.7—7. Figures 729,730. (=Chilodactylidae, + 347a. Gregoryinidae*). Morvongovye.

Lit. J : 204; N : 330; G : 119; GRWM : 401, 429 + 347A : 400, 425; MA : 139; Waite, 1911 : 157—272; Fowler, 1928 : 223; Gosline and Brock, 1960 : 159; Scott, 1962 : 175, 208.

Indian and Pacific oceans, Atlantic Ocean around South America. About 7 genera, a considerable number of species. Fished locally.

Family 348. **Latridae** 470/484, thesis 50.1.7—8. Figure 731. (=Latrididae.)

Lit. J : 204; N : (331); G : 124; GRWM : 401, 429; MA : 139; T. Scott, 1962 : 175, 205.

Marine waters of Australia and New Zealand. 3 genera, a few species. Fished locally.

Superfamily 50.1.8. **Trichodontoidea**, thesis 50.1.0—9. (Trichodontiformes.) Berg, 1940 : 313, Gosline, 1968 : 64. (Trachinoidei ex parte, GRWM : 401.) (Percoidei, MA : 138.) 1 family (349).

Family 349. **Trichodontidae** 471/485, thesis 50.1.8—0. Figure 732. Sandfishes, ch'ang yü k'o, hata-hata ka, volosozubye.

Lit. J : 203; N : 357; G : 124; GRWM : 401, 429; MA : 138; Lindberg and Krasyukova, 1969 : 421—424.

North Pacific. 2 genera, a small number of species. Of little importance in world marine fishing.

* According to GRWM (p. 400), this family is based on some young specimens from the family Cheilodactylidae.

Superfamily 50.1.9. **Trachinoidea**, thesis 50.1.0—23. (Trachinoidei, Jugulares ex parte, Trachiniformes.) Berg, 1940 : 313 (Trachinoidei ex parte, MA : 141; Percoidei ex parte, GRWM : 401; Blennioidei ex parte Gosline, 1968, 38—64). Mohr, 1928 : 107—120; Schultz,1941 : 269—272. 14 families (350—363).

Family 350. **Opisthognathidae** 472/486, thesis 50.1.9—25. Figure 745. (Opistognathidae MA : 142.) Jawfishes, houho yü k'o, ago ama daika.

Lit. J : 230; N : —; G : 124; GRWM : 401, 430; MA : 142; Myers, 1935 : 1—5; Weber and Beaufort, 1951, 9 : 34—40; Böhlke, 1955 : 1—6; Mead, 1959 : 104—112; Lindberg and Krasyukova, 1969 : 424—426. Add.—McKay, 1969 : 1—2.

Tropical seas. More than 4 genera, a few species.

Family 351. **Owstoniidae** 473/487, thesis 50.1.9—24. Figure 744. (Percoidei ex parte, GRWM : 401.) Oushih yü k'o, soko ama dai ka.

Lit. J : 231; N : —; G : 126; GRWM : 401, 429; MA : 142; Kamohara, 1935 : 130—137; Myers, 1935 : 1—5; 1939 : 19—20; Okada and Suzuki, 1956 : 185—194.

Deep oceanic waters. 2 genera, a small number of species.

Family 352. **Bathymasteridae** 474/488, thesis 50.1.9—26. Figure 746. Ronquils, Shênhai wei yü k'o, medama uo ka.

Lit. J : 230; N : 360; G : 125; GRWM : 401, 430; MA : 142; Sato, 1940 : 95—98; Sato and Ueno, 1963 : 203—211; Lindberg and Krasyukova, 1969 : 426—427.

North Pacific. 3 genera, a small number of species.

Family 353. **Mugiloididae** 475/489, thesis 50.1.9—9. Figure 736. (=Pinguipedidae, +Parapercidae, MA : 142 +Parapercichthyidae.) Grubfishes, smelts, ni t'zŭ k'o, tora gisu ka, paraperkovye.

Lit. J : 229; N : (360); G : (124); GRWM : 401, 430; MA : 142; Martin and Montalban, 1935 : 215—225; Fowler, 1937—57 : 124—145. . . Weber and Beaufort, 1951, 9 : 11—29; Kamohara, 1960 : 1—14; Cantwell, 1964 : 239—280; Schultz, 1968 : 1—16; Lindberg and Krasyukova,1969 : 427—433.

Indian and Pacific oceans. Atlantic Ocean off South America. More than 4 genera, a few species.

Family 354. **Cheimarrhichthyidae** (476/490), thesis 50.1.9—13, Figure 738. (=Chimarrichthyidae, not Chimarrhichthys Siluroidei.) Papanokovye.

Lit. J : (229); N : 361; G : (125), GRWM : 401, 430; MA : 142; Heast, 1874 : 103; Lane, 1965 : 207—213.

Fresh waters of New Zealand. 1 genus, 1 species.

Family 355. **Trachinidae** 477/491, thesis 50.1.9—6, Figure 735. (+Callipterygidae.) Vives, weeverfishes, araignées-de-mer, Petermannchen, zmeika-ryba, drakonovye.

Lit. J : 228; N : 361; G : 125; GRWM : 401, 430; MA : 142; Boulenger, 1901 : 261—271; Regan, 1901 : 261—271; Weber and Beaufort, 1951, 9 : 34—40; Svetovidov, 1964 : 335—340.

Mediterranean Sea, eastern part of the Atlantic, Madeira, coast of Chile ? 1 genus, a small number of species. Fished locally.

Family 356. **Percophididae** (478/492), thesis 50.1.9—5. Figure 734. (=Percophidae = Percophiidae.) Flatheads.

Lit. J : 220; N : (362); G : (124); GRWM : 401, 430 + families 357, 358; MA : (142) (family 357); Quoy and Gaimard, 1824 : 1—712 (351); Ginsburg, 1955 : 623—639.

East coasts of South America. 2 genera, a small number of species.

Family 357. **Bembropsidae** (479—493), thesis 50.1.9—4. Figure 733. (=Bembropidae, +Pteropsaridae MA : 142.) Flatheads, smelt, kao chi shê t'zŭ k'o, honake tora gisu ka.

Lit. J : (229); N : 362; G : (125); GRWM : (401) (family 356); MA : 142 + family 356; Okada and Suzuki, 1952 : 485—516; Okamura and Kishida, 1963 : 45—48; Lindberg and Krasyukova, 1969 : 433—434.

Atlantic, Indian, and Pacific oceans. About 8 genera, a small number of species.

Family 358. **Hemerocoetidae** 480/494, thesis 50.1.9—10. Figure 737.

Lit. J : 229; N : 362; G : 125; GRWM : (401) (family 356); MA : 142; Weber and Beaufort, 1951, 9 : 31—33.

Pacific Ocean. 3—4 genera, a small number of species.

Family 359. **Trichonotidae** 481/495, thesis 50.1.9—15. Figure 739. Sand eels, sand divers, maopei yü k'o, bera gimpō ka, peskozhilye.

Lit. J : 230; N : 363; G : 125; GRWM : 401, 430; MA : 142 + family 362; Fowler, 1937—57 : 124—145. . . Weber and Beaufort, 1951, 9 : 29—30; Matsubara, 1952 : 89—92.

Indian Ocean, Pacific Ocean around the Hawaiian Islands, coast of Japan and shores of Australia. About 5 genera, several species.

Family 360. **Creediidae** 482/496, thesis 50.1.9—19. Figure 742.

Lit. J : 229; N : 364; G : 125; GRWM : 401, 430; MA : 142; Beaufort, 1948 : 475—478.

Shores of Australia. 3 genera,several species.

Family 361. **Kraemeriidae** 543/557, theses 50.1.9—16; 50.16—7. Figures 740, 862. (=Psammichthyidae, Trichonotidae ex parte Schultz, 1941.) (Perciformes ex parte, Gobioidei ex parte GRWM : 402.) Sandlances.

Lit. J : (230); N : 440; G : 152; GRWM : 402, 432; MA : 147; Fowler, 1928 : 1—540 (: 425); Whitley, 1935 : 215—255 (244); Schultz, 1941 : 269—272; Gosline, 1955 : 158—170; Matsubara and Iwai, 1959 : 27—32; Schultz et al., 1966 : 1—176 (4—8).

Indian and Pacific oceans. 1 genus, a small number of species.

Family 362. **Limnichthyidae** 483/497, thesis 50.1.9—18. Figure 741. (=Limnichthidae.)

Lit. J : 229; N : 364; G : 125; GRWM : 401, 430; MA : (142) (family 361); Gosline and Brock, 1960 : 241.

Shores of Australia and the Hawaiian Islands. 3—4 genera, a few species.

Family 363. **Oxudercidae** 484/498, thesis 50.1.9—21. Figure 743.
Lit. J: 230; N—; G: 125; GRWM: 401; MA: 142; Bleeker, 1873: 113—154 (129); Fowler, 1937—1957: 124—145.
China (Macao). 1 genus, 1 species.

Superfamily 50.1.10. Uranoscopoidea, thesis 50.1.0—1. Berg, 1940: 314; MA: 142; (Trachinoidei ex parte GRWM: 401); (Blennioidei, Trachinoidea Gosline, 1968, 66—78); Starks, 1923: 259—290. 3 families (364—366).

Family 364. **Leptoscopidae** 485/499, thesis 50.1.10—3. Figure 748. Avstraliiskie zvezdochetovye.
Lit. J: 231; N: 365; G: 125; GRWM: 401, 430; MA: 142; Günther, 1861: 85—90 (: 86).
Marine waters of eastern and South Australia and New Zealand. 2 genera, a few species.

Family 365. **Dactyloscopidae** 486/500, thesis 50.1.10—4. Figure 749. Sand stargazers, amerikanskie zvezdochetovye.
Lit.J: 231; N: —; G: 134; GRWM: 401,430; MA: 142; Myers and Wade, 1946: 151—178; Miller and Briggs, 1962: 1—11.
Atlantic and Pacific coasts of tropical America. About 7 genera, a few species.

Family 366. **Uranoscopidae** 487/501, thesis 50.1.10—2. Figure 747. (+Pleuroscopidae, +Astroscopidae.) Stargazers, electric stargazers, rat, tapecon, rascasses blanches, chan hsing yü k'o, mishima okoze ka, zvezdochetovye.
Lit. J: 231; N: —; G: 126; GRWM: 401,430; MA: 142; Stark, 1923: 259—290; Fowler, 1937—57: 124—145... Weber and Beaufort, 1951, 9: 40—49; Liang, 1955: 169—176; Mees, 1960: 46—58; Berry and Anderson, 1961: 563—586. Svetovidov, 1964: 340—343; Lindberg and Krasyukova, 1969: 434—442.
Atlantic, Indian, and Pacific oceans. About 10 genera, a considerable number of species.

Superfamily 50.1.11. Champsodontoidea, thesis 50.1.0—11. Berg, 1940: 315. Gosline, 1968: 64; (Trachinoidei ex parte, GRWM: 401; MA: 141, 142). 1 family (367).

Family 367. **Champsodontidae** 488/502, thesis 50.1.11—0. Figure 750. Êchih yü k'o, wani gisu ka.
Lit. J: 231; N: 358; G: 126, GRWM: 401, 430; MA: 142; Norman, 1929: 529—544; Fowler, 1937—57: 124—145... Weber and Beaufort, 1951, 9: 2—4; Matsubara, Ochiai, Amaoka and Nakamura, 1964: 1—20. Lindberg and Krasyukova, 1969: 442—444.
Indian and Pacific oceans. 1 genus, several species.

Superfamily 50.1.12. Chiasmodontoidea, thesis 50.1.0—8. Berg, 1940: 315; Gosline, 1968: 15, 64; (Trachinoidei ex parte GRWM: 401; MA: 141, 142). 1 family (368).

Family 368. **Chiasmodontidae** 489/503, thesis 50.1.12—0. Figure 751. Black swallowers, ch'ach'ih yü k'o, kuro bozu gisu ka.

Lit. J : 230; N : 366; G : 127; GRWM : 401, 430; MA : 142; Norman, 1929 : 529—544; Weber and Beaufort, 1951, 9 : 5—10. Lindberg and Krasyukova, 1969 : 444.

Oceanic waters. 5 genera, a few species.

Superfamily 50.1.13. **Notothenioidea**, thesis 50.1.0—16. (Nototheniiformes, Notothenioidei.) Berg, 1940 : 315 (Notothenioidei GRWM : 401; MA : 144); (Blennioidei Gosline, 1968 : 66—78); Regan, 1913 : 229—292; Norman, 1937 : 1—150; 1938 : 1—105 (8). 5 families (369—373).

Family 369. **Bovichthyidae** 490/504, thesis 50.1.13—1. Figure 752. (=Bovictidae = Bovichthidae = Bovichtidae, MA : 144, + Pseudaphritidae.) Rogoshchekovye.

Lit. J : (228); N : (368); G : (126); GRWM : 401, 430; MA : 144; Regan, 1913 : 229—292 (251—257); Norman, 1937 : 63—65; Graham, 1953 : 229—301.

Marine waters of the Antarctic, Subantarctic, and southern temperate belt. 4 genera, a few species.

Family 370. **Nototheniidae** 491/505, thesis 50.1.13—5. Figure 753. (+Gelididae.)

Lit. J : 228; N : 369; G : 126; GRWM : 401, 430 +family 371; MA : 144; Norman, 1938 : 8—43; Blanc and Hureau, 1962 : 339—342; Andriyashev, 1962 : 1048—1050. Add.—idem, 1967 : 389—412; De Witt, 1967 : 2541, 2542.

Marine waters of the Antarctic, Subantarctic, and temperate latitudes of the southern hemisphere. 5—6 genera, quite a large number of species. Of little importance in world marine fishing but a promising item.

Family 371. **Harpagiferidae** (491A/505A), thesis 50.1.13—6. Figure 754. (Nototheniidae ex parte.) Borodatkovye.

Lit. J : 228; N : 370; G : 126; GRWM : (401) (family 370); MA : 144; Regan, 1914 : 1—54; Norman, 1938 : 43—53; Add.—Andriyashev, 1967 : 389—412.

Marine waters of the Antarctic, Subantarctic, and temperate latitudes of the southern hemisphere. 5 genera, a few species.

Family 372. **Bathydraconidae** 492/506, thesis 50.1.13—7. Figure 755. Antarkticheskie ploskorylye.

Lit. J : 228; N : 371; G : 126; GRWM : 401, 431; MA : 144; Norman, 1938 : 53—68; De Witt, 1964 : 496—506.

Marine waters of Antarctica, Subantarctica, and temperate latitudes of the southern hemisphere. 8 genera, several species.

Family 373. **Channicthyidae** (493/507), thesis 50.1.13—8. Figure 756. (=Channichthyidae MA : 144 = Chaenichthyidae.) Icefishes, belokrovnye, belokrovnaya ryba.

Lit. J : (228); N : 373; G : (126); GRWM : 401, 431; MA : 144; Norman, 1938 : 69—81; Olsen, 1955 : 79—93.

Marine waters of the Antarctic, Subantarctic, and temperate latitudes of the southern hemisphere. 10 genera, a small number of species.

Suborder 50.2. Blennioidei, thesis 50.0—27. (Blennioidei, Jugulares ex parte, Blenniiformes + Zoarciformes.) Berg, 1940 : 315; MA : 145; (Blennioidei ex parte, Gosline, 1968 : 38—64, 66, 78); (Blennioidei, GRWM : 401. Schindlerioidei GRWM : 402; Gadiformes ex parte, Zoarcoidei GRWM: 397); Jordan and Snyder,1902 : 441—504; Regan, 1912 : 265—280; Hubbs, 1927 : 351—394; Duncker and Mohr, 1928 : 89—106; Herre, 1939 : 315—372; Fowler, 1958 : 147—339; : 67—97; Bauchot, 1966 : 63—91; Springer, 1968; 1—85, 111—122. 20 families (374—393).

Family 374. **Blenniidae** 494/508, thesis 50.2—14. Figures 769—771. (+Atopoclinidae, +Runulidae, +Salariidae, +Nemophididae, +Xiphastidae, +374a. Chaenopsidae, +Emblemariidae.) Combtooth blennies, blennies, cagnotte, mordacet, morde-au-see, baveuse, rock hoppers, pei k'o, ishi gimpō ka, sobachkovye, morskaya sobachka.

Lit. J : 232, 233, 235; N : 445; G : 127; GRWM : 401, 431 +family 374a : 431; MA : 145 +family 374a; Steindachner, 1870 : 421—446; Gilchrist and Thompson, 1908 : 97—143; Lindberg, 1938 : 499—514; Rhasis, 1941 : 118—127; Norman, 1943 : 793—812; Reid, 1943 : 373—384; Steinitz, 1949 : 129—152; : 170—197; 1950 : 60—87; Fraser—Brunner, 1951 : 213—220; Weber and Beaufort, 1951, 9 : 242—382, 446—448; Chapman and Schultz, 1952 : 507—528; Aoyagi, 1954 : 278—287; : 239—242; 1955 : 76—83; Böhlke, 1957 : 81—103; Svetovidov, 1958 : 584—593; J. Smith, 1958 : 123—129; 1959 : 229—252; Krejsa, 1960 : 322—336; Makushok, 1961 : 198—224; Springer, 1962 : 426—433; Stephens, 1963 : 1—165; Svetovidov, 1964 : 344—367; Springer, 1964 : 591—593; 1967 : 1—150; 1968 : 1—85; Randall, 1966 : 57—72. Add. —Springer, 1967 : 1—180; 1968 : 1—13.

Tropical, subtropical, and temperate seas. About 95 genera, many species.

Family 375. **Anarhichadidae** 495/509, thesis 50.2—1. Figure 762. (=Anarrhichadidae=Anarrhichthyidae.) Wolffishes, chat marin, loup marin, Katfisches, Wolffisches, lan yü k'o, okami uo ka, zubatkovye.

Lit. J : 235; N : 451a; G : 129; GRWM : 401, 431; MA : 145; Barsukov, 1953 : 1—15; 1959 : 1—171; Andriyashev, 1954 : 217—228.

Northern parts of the Atlantic and Pacific. 2 genera, 5 species. Fished locally.

Family 376. **Xenocephalidae** 496/510, theses 50.2—0, footnote; 50.0—27, footnote. No figure.

Lit. J : 235; N : (483); G : 132; GRWM : 401, 431, MA : 145.

Southern hemisphere, New Ireland. 1 genus, 1 species.

Family 377. **Congrogadidae** 497/511, thesis 50.2—27. Figure 792. Congrogadoidei Gosline, 1968 : 78.) Man wai k'o, sannin gaji ka, ugretreskovye.

Lit. J : 235; N : 452; G : 132; GRWM : 401, 431 + family 378; MA : 175 + family 378; Weber and Beaufort, 1951, 9 : 383—387; J. Smith, 1952 : 85—101 ex parte.

Sea coasts of East Africa and the West Pacific. 1 genus, several species.

Family 378. **Haliophidae** (—/—), thesis 50.2—21. Figure 789. (=Haliophiidae, +Halidesmidae, Congrogadidae ex parte.)

Lit. J: (235); N: (453); G: 132; GRWM: (401) (family 377); MA: (175) (family 377); J. Smith, 1952: 85—101.

Sea coasts of Southeast Africa, the Red Sea, and the southwestern part of the Pacific Ocean. 5 genera, a few species.

Family 379. **Notograptidae** 498/512, theses 50.2—0, footnote; 50.0—27; footnote. Figure 757. (+Stichariidae.)

Lit. J: 232; N: 453; G: 134; GRWM: 401, 431; MA: 145; Weber and Beaufort, 1951, 9: 388—389.

Australia. 1 genus, several species.

Family 380. **Peronedysidae** (499/513), theses 50.2—0, footnote; 50.0—27, footnote. Figure 758. (=Peronedyidae.) Ugresobachkovye.

Lit. J: (232); N: (463); G: (134), GRWM: 401, 431; MA: 145; T. Scott, 1962: 246, 248.

South Australia. 1 genus.

Family 381. **Ophiclinidae** (500/514), theses 50.2—0, footnote; 50.0—27, footnote. Figure 759. (=Ophioclinidae.) Zmeesobachkovye.

Lit. J: (232); N: (462), G: (134); GRWM: 401, 431; MA: 145 (family 382); Waite, 1906: 194—210.

Seas around Australia. 3 genera, several species.

Family 382. **Clinidae** 501/515, thesis 50.2—13. Figures 767, 768. (+Paraclinidae, +Xenopoclinidae.) Clinids, klipfishes, kelpfishes, scaled blennies, gonneles, papillons-de-mer, weedfishes, t'ai wei k'o, asahi gimpō ka, klinovye, cheshchuichatye sobachki.

Lit. J: 231; N: 453; G: 129; GRWM: 401, 431; MA: 145 + family 381; J. Smith, 1946: 535—546; Weber and Beaufort, 1951, 9: 389—398; Hubbs and Clark, 1952: 41—165; 1953: 11—23; : 113—136; Springer, 1954: 422—441; 1955: 66—80; Böhlke, 1957: 25—57; Springer, 1958: 417—492; Böhlke and Springer, 1961: 29—60; Rosenblatt, (1960) 1961: 1—23; J. Smith, 1961: 351—356; Buen, 1962: 53: 53—96. Add.—Milward, 1967: 1—9; Rosenblatt and Parr, 1969: 1—20.

Marine waters of temperate, subtropical, and tropical latitudes. More than 40 genera, many species.

Family 383. **Tripterygiidae** (—/—), thesis 50.2—11. Figure 766. (=Tripterygiontidae, Clinidae ex parte.) Troeperye.

Lit. J: (231); N: (460); G: (130); GRWM: 401, 431; MA: 145; Waite, 1913: 1—16; Hubbs, 1927: 380—388; Matsubara, 1955: 728—732; Svetovidov, 1964: 367—369.

Tropical and subtropical seas. 4 genera, several species.

Family 384. **Stichaeidae** 503/517, thesis 50.2—17. Figures 779—786. (+Lumpenidae 505/519, +Xiphisteridae 502/516 = Xiphidiontidae = Xiphiodontidae, +Chirolophidae, +Cebedichthyidae.) Pricklebacks, hsien wei k'o, taue gajika.

Lit. J : 234; N : 465; G : 131; GRWM : 401, 431 + family 385; MA : 145; Hubbs, 1927 : 368 — 380; Rass, 1936 : 395 — 463; Taranets, 1936 : 141 — 144; Andriyashev, 1954 : 228 — 250; Andriyashev and Makushov, 1955 : 50 — 53; Makushok, 1958 : 1—129; 1961 : 225 — 269; Peden, 1966 : 340 — 345.

Arctic seas, northern parts of the Atlantic and Pacific oceans. 30 genera, 54 species.

Family 385. **Cryptacanthodidae** 503A/517A, thesis 50.2 — 6. Figure 764. (Stichaeidae ex parte = Cryptacanthidae.) Wrymouth, krivorotye.

Lit. J : 235; N : (470); G : 131; GRWM : 401) (family 384); MA : 145; Hikita, 1950 : 140 — 144; Makushok, 1961 : 184 — 197.

Northern parts of the Atlantic and Pacific oceans. 1 genus, 4 species.

Family 386. **Pholididae** (504/518), thesis 50.2 — 16. Figures 776, 777. (=Pholidae, + Opisthocentridae.) Gunnels, papillons-de-mer, chin wei k'o, niji gimpō ka, maslyukovye.

Lit. J : (234); N : 470; G : (131); GRWM : 402, 431; MA : 145; Hubbs, 1927 : 388 — 393; Andriyashev, 1954 : 250 — 255; Makushok, 1958 : 1—129 (108).

Northern parts of the Atlantic and Pacific oceans. 4 genera, 13 species.

Family 387. **Ptilichthyidae** 507/521, thesis 50.2—3. Figure 763. Quillfishes.

Lit. J : 235; N : 473; G : 131; GRWM : 401, 431; MA : 145; Makushok, 1958 : 1— 129 (114); Kobayashi, 1961 : 5 — 8.

North Pacific. 1 genus, 1 species.

Family 388. **Zoarcidae** 508/522, thesis 50.2 — 28. Figure 793 — 804. (+ Lycodidae.) (Gadiformes ex parte, Zoarcoidei GRWM : 397) (Blennioidei, Zoarceoidea Gosline, 1968 :78) Eelpouts, loquette, Aalmutter, mien wei k'o, genge ka, bel'dyugovye.

Lit. J : 236; N : (474); G : 133; GRWM : 397, 417 + families 389, 390; MA : 145 + families 389, 390; Jensen, 1904 : 1—99; Knipowitsch, 1906 : 1—129; Regan, 1913 : 229 — 292 (241 — 249); Schmidt, 1936 : 97 — 100; Vladykov and Tremblay, 1936 : 1—45; Norman, 1937 : 1—150; Taranets, 1937 : 159 — 166; Andriyashev, 1939 : 1—187 (76); Zugmayer, 1940 : 209 — 211; Matsubara and Iwai, 1951 : 104 — 111; Jensen, 1952 : 1—28; Andriyashev, 1954 : 255 — 315; 1955 : 393— 400; : 349 — 384; 1958 : 171—180; 1960 : 349 — 384; Makushok, 1961 : 198 — 224; McAllister, 1964 : 85 — 110; Yarberry, 1965 : 442 — 462; Add.— Schultz, 1967 : 1—5. Add. II — Nielsen, 1968 : 225 — 250.*

The Arctic, Antarctica, and the northern parts of the Atlantic and Pacific oceans. 42 — 45 genera, many species. Fished locally on a small scale.

Family 389. **Lycodapodidae** 509/523, thesis 50.2 — 19. Figure 787. (=Lycodapidae.)

Lit. J : 236; N : (480); G : 134; GRWM : (397) (family 388), MA : (145) (family 388); J. Smith, 1955 : 545 — 550.

Pacific Ocean. Sakhalin. Straits of Magellan. 1 genus, 1 species.

* This author maintains that the genera Parabrotula Zugmayer, 1911 and Leucobrotula Koefoed, 1952 should be transferred from family 394. Brotulidae to family 388. Zoarcidae as a separate subfamily, Parabrotulinae, but according to Andriyashev, this subfamily should be considered an independent one, as should the family Melanostomatidae.

Family 390. **Derepodichthyidae** 510/524, thesis 50.2—25. Figure 791.
Lit. J: 236; N: (483); G: 134; GRWM: (397) (family 388); MA: (145) (family 388); Clemens and Wilby, 1961: 392, 393.
Pacific Ocean around British Columbia. 1 genus, 1 species.

Family 391. **Scytalinidae** 511/525, thesis 50.2—23. Figure 790. (Scytaliscidae) Graveldivers.
Lit. J: 235; N: 483; G: (133); GRWM: 402, 431; MA: 145; Clemens and Wilby, 1961: 384, 385.
Pacific shores of North America. 1 genus, 1 species.

Family 392. **Schindleriidae** 512/526, theses 50.2—0, footnote, 50.0—27, footnote. Figure 760. (Carapidae ex parte) (Perciformes, Schindleroidei GRWM: 402); MA: 145, 146; Gosline, 1968: 15, 66.
Lit. J:—; N:—; G: (136); GRWM: 402, 431; Giltay, 1934: 1—10; Bruun, 1940: 1—12; Gosline and Brock, 1960: 1—372; Gosline, 1959: 67—77; 1963: 90—101.
Coastal waters of the Hawaiian Islands and New Guinea. 1 genus, 1 species.

Family 393. **Zaproridae** 513/527, thesis 50.2—8. Figure 765. Prowfishes, bozu gimpō ka.
Lit. J: 230; N: 326; G: 125; GRWM: 402, 431; MA: 145; Chapman and Townsend, 1938: 89—117; Ueno, 1954: 79—82; McAllister and Krejsa, 1961: 1—4.
North Pacific. 1 genus, 1 species.

Suborder 50.3. Ophidioidei, thesis 50.0—23. Berg, 1940: 317; Gosline, 1968: 17—28, 65. (Gadiformes, Ophidioidei GRWM: 397) (Ophidiiformes MA: 114—117) Regan, 1912: 265—280; Matsubara and Iwai, 1951: 104—111; Gosline, 1961: 1—42; Freihofer, 1963: 80—189; Mead, Bertelsen and Cohen, 1964: 569—596. 2 superfamilies, 4 families (394—397).

Superfamily 50.3.1. Ophidioidea. Berg, 1940: 317. Ophidiiformes ex parte MA: 117. 2 families (394, 395).

Family 394. **Brotulidae** 514/528, thesis 50.3—2. Figures 805—808. (+Brotulophidae, +394a. Aphyonidae, see Add. II.) Brotulas, weaselfishes, hsü wei k'o, itachi uo ka.
Lit. J: 236; N: 484; G: 134; GRWM: (397) (family 395); MA: 117; Radcliffe, 1913: 135—176, Trotter, 1926: 29—33; Norman, 1939: 1—116 (: 79—92); Hubbs, 1944: 162—178; Weber and Beaufort, 1951, 9: 398—444; Koefoed, 1952: 1—26; Gosline, 1953: 215—225; Bougis and Ruivo, 1954: 155—209; Kamohara, 1954: 1—14; Smith, 1955: 545—560; Böhlke, 1957: 1—8; Nybelin and Poll, 1958: 1—7; Nielsen and Nybelin, 1963: 195—213. Add. II — Nielsen, 1968: 225—249; 1969: 1—90.
Coastal, more rarely deep, waters of all the seas. More than 60 genera, many species.

Family 395. **Ophidiidae** 515/529, thesis 50.3—3. Figures 809, 810. (Ophidiontidae.) Cusk-eels, donzelles, yü wei k'o, ashiro ka, oshibnevye.

Lit. J : 237; N : 499; G : 135; GRWM : 397, 417 + family 394; MA : 117; Jordan and Fowler, 1902 : 743—766; Weber and Beaufort, 1951, 9 : 445—446; Harry, 1951 : 17—35; Böhlke and Robins, 1959 : 37—52; Cohen, 1961 : 288—292; Robins, 1960 : 83—95; 1961 : 212—221; 1962 : 487 - 498; Coehn, 1964 : 1—22; 1966 : 183 - 204; Svetovidov, 1964 : 369—372; Fowler, 1958 : 67—97.

Tropical and temperate seas. About 7 genera, a considerable number of species. Fished locally.

Superfamily 50.3.2. Carapoidea, (Fierasferoidae, Carapieformes.) Berg, 1940 : 318. (Ophidiiformes ex parte MA : 114, 118. 2 families (396, 397).

Family 396. **Carapidae** (516/530), thesis 50.3—4. Figures 811, 813. (=Fierasferidae, + 396a. Pyramodontidae.) Aurins, kuang yü k'o, kakure uo ka, fierasferovye.

Lit. J : 238; N : 501; G : 136; GRAM : 397, 417 + families 396a, 397; MA : 118 + family 396a; C. Emeri; 1880 : 167—254; Radcliffe, 1913 : 135—176; Parr, 1930 : 1—148 (: 135); Padoa, 1947 : 102—121; Weber and Beaufort, 1951, 9 : 449—455; J. Smith, 1955 : 401—416; : 545—550; Arnold, 1956 : 245—307; Gosline, 1960 : 373—381; Cohen, 1964 : 1—22.

Atlantic, Indian, and Pacific oceans. 5 genera, several species.

Family 397. **Disparichthyidae** 516A/530A, thesis 50.3—4, footnote. Figure 812. (Carapidae ex parte.)

Lit. J : —; N : (502); G : (136); GRWM : (397) (family 396); MA : —; Herre, 1935 : 383—384; Fowler, 1938 : 1—349 (: 150); Schultz, 1939 : 473—496 (492).

Fresh waters of New Guinea and shores of Tahiti. 1 genus, 1 species.

Suborder 50.4. Ammodytoidei, thesis 50.0—25. (Ammodytiformes.) Berg, 1940 : 318; (GRWM : 402; MA : 144); (Percoidei, Ammodytoidea Gosline, 1968 : 64); Gill, 1904 : 159—163. 3 families (398—400).

Family 398. **Ammodytidae** 517/531, thesis 50.4—3. Figure 815. Sand lances, sand launces, sandeels, lançons, équilles, Sandspierling, Sandaal, yüchin yü k'o, ikanago ka, peschanikovye.

Lit. J : 230; N : 357; G : 136; GRWM : 402, 432 + family 399; MA : 144 + family 399; Gill, 1904 : 159—163; Jordan, 1906 : 715—719; Duncker and Mohr, 1935 : 216—220; Holly, 1937 : 1—19; Lindberg, 1937 : 85—93; Duncker and Mohr, 1939 : 1—31; Soleim, 1945 : 1—28; Corbin, 1949 : 287—313; 1950 : 83—89; Andriyashev, 1954 : 315—323; Ruivo and Monteiro, 1955 : 569—592; Kobayashi, 1961 : 111—120; Svetovidov, 1964 : 373—376.

Atlantic, Indian, and Pacific oceans. 3 genera, several species. Of average importance in world marine fishing.

Family 399. **Bleekeriidae** (517A/531A), thesis 50.4—2. Figure 814. (=Bleekeridae, Ammodytidae ex parte.) Yaponskie peschanki.

Lit. J : 230; N : —; G : 136; GRWM : (402) (family 398); MA : (144) (family 398); Matsubara, 1955 : 719, 720.

North Pacific. 2—3 genera, several species.

Family 400. **Hypoptychidae** (517B/531B), thesis 504—4. Figure 816. (Ammodytidae ex parte.) Korotkoperye peschanki.

Lit. J: 230; N: —; G: 136; GRWM: 402, 432; MA: 144; Gosline, 1963: 90—101.

Northern part of the Sea of Japan and southern part of the Sea of Okhotsk. 1 genus, 1 species.

Suborder 50.5. Callionymoidei, thesis 50.0—13. (Callionymiformes, Gosline, 1968: 15.) Berg, 1940: 319. (GRWM: 402, MA: 144); Regan, 1913: 111—145; Starks, 1923: 259—290 (267); 1926: 139—338. 2 families (401, 402).

Family 401. **Callionymidae** 518/532, thesis 50.5—2. Figure 818. Dragonets, dragonnets, doucets, chiqueurs, hsien k'o, nezuppo ka, lirovye.

Lit.: J: 229; N: 441; G: 127; GRWM: 402, 432 + family 402; MA: 145; Jordan and Fowler, 1903: 939—959; Okada and Ikeda, 1937: 67—95; Fowler, 1941: 1—31; Schultz and Woods, 1948: 419—420; Weber and Beaufort, 1951, 9: 50—81; Aoyagi, 1954: 238; Ochiai, Arago and Nakajima, 1955: 96—132; Drapkin, 1961: 146—151; 1967: 22—37; Svetovidov, 1964: 376—384, Add.—Suwardji, 1965: 303—323; Davis, 1966: 834—862.

Atlantic, Indian, and Pacific oceans. 10 genera, quite a number of species.

Family 402. **Draconettidae** 519/533, thesis 50.5—1. Figure 817. Pei hsien k'o, inaka numeri ka, drakonchikovye, drakonettovye.

Lit. J: 229; N: 443; G: 127; GRWM: (402) (family 401); MA: 145; Jordan and Fowler, 1903: 939—959; Briggs and Berry, 1959: 123—133.

Northern parts of the Atlantic and Pacific oceans. 2 genera, several species.

Suborder 50.6. Siganoidei, thesis 50.0—3. (Amphacanthi.), Berg, 1940: 319; MA: 147; (Acanthuroidei ex parte GRWM: 402). Gosline, 1968: 16, 65). 1 family (403).

Family 403. **Siganidae** 520/534, thesis 50.6—0. Figures 819. (=Theutyidae =Teuthidae, Teuthididae ex parte, MA: 147; = Amphacanthidae.) Rabbitfish, spinefeet, cordonnier, langtzŭ yü k'o, ango ka.

Lit. J: (206); N: (378); G: 137; GRWM: 402, 432; MA: 147; Günther, 1859—1870 (1961): 313; Starks, 1907: 211—218; Ogilby, 1916: 127—177; Starks, 1926: 139—338 (281); Herre and Montalban, 1928: 151—184; Fowler and Bean, 1929: 1—352 (288—332); Gregory, 1933: 75—481 (282); Weber and Beaufort, 1951, 9: 95—124; Bauchot, 1964: 570—577; 1966: 7—43.

Indian and Pacific oceans. 2 genera, several species.

Suborder 50.7. Acanthuroidei, thesis 50.0—29. (Teuthioidei.) Berg, 1940: 320 (Acanthuroidei ex parte GRWM: 402; Bauchot, 1966: 7—43; Gosline, 1968: 16, 65); (Chaetodontoidei MA: 143). 2 families (404—405).

Family 404. **Zanclidae** 521/535, thesis 50.7—2. Figure 821. (Zancliformes.) Moorish idols, trachoir, lien yü k'o, zunodashi ka.

Lit. J: 207; N: 375; G: 136; GRWM: (402) (family 405); MA: 143; Herre, 1927: 403—478; Fowler and Bean, 1929: 1—352 (195—196); Matsubara, 1955: 926, 947.

Indian and Pacific oceans; pelagial and coral reefs. 1 genus, several species.

Family 405. **Acanthuridae** 522/536, thesis 50.7—1. Figure 280. (=Teuthidae, Teuthididae ex parte, = Hepatidae, =Acronuridae, +Harpuridae, +Nasidae.) Surgeonfishes, unicornfishes, nosefishes, chirurgiens, licorne, lacefishes, t'zuwei yü k'o, niza dai ka, khirurgovye.

Lit. J : 207; N : 375; G : 136; GRWM : 402, 432 + family 404; MA : 143; Ogilby, 1916 : 127 — 177; Herre, 1927 : 403 — 478; Fowler and Bean, 1929 : 1— 352 (199 — 287); Kamohara, 1937 : 469 — 474; Weber and Beaufort, 1951, 9 : 125 — 186; Randall, 1955 : 149 — 166; : 396 — 412; : 350 — 367; J. Smith, 1955 : 169 — 174; Randall, 1956 : 159 — 235; 1961 : 215 — 272. Add. — J. Smith, 1966 : 635 — 682.

All warm seas, especially coral reefs. 12 genera, a considerable number of species. Unimportant in world marine fishing.

Suborder 50.8. T r i c h i u r o i d e i, thesis 50.0 — 19. Berg, 1940 : 320 (Scombroidei ex parte GRWM : 402; MA : 140) Gosline, 1968 : 31—38, 65; Regan, 1909 : 66 — 76; Starks, 1911 : 17—26. 3 families (406 — 408).

Family 406. **Gempylidae** 523/537, thesis 50.8 — 1. Figures 822, 822A. (=Acinaceidae = Lemnisomidae, +Ruvettidae) (+406a. Scombrolabracidae Gosline, 1968 : 31—38.) Snake mackerels, deep sea snakes, escolares, rouvets, tuan tai k'o, kurotachi komasu ka, zmeevidnye makreli.

Lit. J : 180; N : 379; G : 141; GRWM : 402, 432; MA : 140; Kamohara, 1938 : 45 — 50; Weber and Beaufort, 1951, 9 : 197 — 203; Matsubara and Iwai, 1952 : 193 — 212; 1958 : 23 — 54; Grey, 1953 : 135 — 141; 1960 : 210 — 215.

Oceanic waters; pelagial. About 20 genera, a considerable number of species. Fished locally. Game fishes.

Family 407. **Trichiuridae** 524/538, thesis 50.8 — 4. Figure 824. Cutlassfishes, hair-tails, jarretières; t'ai yü k'o, tachi uo ka, volosokhvostovye, sablya-ryba.

Lit. J : 180; N : 382; G : 141; GRWM : 402, 432 +family 408; MA : 140; J. Schmidt and Strasburg, 1918 : 1—15; Lin, 1936 : 1—16; Weber and Beaufort, 1951, 9 : 188 — 196; Tucker, 1953 : 171—187; 1955 : 1—26; 1956 : 73 — 130; Yian, 1960 : 75 — 81.

Indian and Pacific oceans. 8 genera, quite a number of species. Of little importance in world marine fishing.

Family 408. **Lepidopidae** (524A/538A), thesis 50.8 — 3. Figure 823. (Trichiuridae ex parte.)

Lit. J : (180); N : (382); G : (141); GRWM : (402) (family 407); MA : —; Tucker, 1956 : 73 — 130.

Deep oceanic waters. 1 genus, several species.

Suborder 50.9. S c o m b r o i d e i, thesis 50.0 — 18. (Plecostei, Thunniformes.) Berg, 1940 : 321, 333; GRWM : 402; MA : 139; Gosline, 1968 : 31— 38, 65; Regan, 1909 : 66 — 75; Starks, 1911 : 17 — 26; Kishinouye, 1923 : 293 — 475; Ehrenbaum, 1924 : 1—42; Takahasi, 1926 : 383 — 398; Mohr, 1927 : 85 — 140; Buen, 1930 : 1—22; Gregory, 1933 : 75 — 481 (312 — 314); Fowler, 1936 : 61 — 80; Kamohara, 1940 : 1—225; Baughman, 1941 : 14 — 26; Lozana and Rey, 1952 : 387 — 703; Buen, 1958 : 3 — 38; Bauchot and Blanc, 1961 : 369 — 379;

Blanc and Bauchot, 1964: 443—458; Merrett and Thorp, 1965: 367—384; Nakamura, 1965: 7—38; Parin, 1967: 88—127; Add.—Whitley, 1964: 221—253. 2 superfamilies, 3 families (409—411).

Superfamily 50.9.1. Scombroidea. (Scombriformes, Thunniformes.) Berg, 1940: 321, 333; MA: 140; (Scombroidei ex parte GRWM: 402).

Family 409. **Scombridae** 525/539, thesis 50.9—1. Figures 825—829. (=Scomberidae, +Cybiidae 526/540 = Cibiidae, +Thunnidae 565/579, +Katsuwonidae, +Scomberomoridae, +Sardidae, +Acanthocybiidae, +Gasterochismidae = Gasteroschismidae.) Mackerels, tunas, thons, germons, bonite, bonitou, albacores, tunnies, Spanish mackerel, maquereaux, péto, wahoo, mackrels, sier wahoo, Makrele, Thunfische, Thonine, chinchiang yü k'o, saba ka, p'a ka, sawara ka, maguro ka, tuntsovye, makrelevye.

Lit. J: 179 (179); N: 385; G: 139; GRWM: 402, 432; MA: 140; Starks, 1910: 77—99; Jordan and Evermann, 1926: 1—113; Takahasi, 1926: 383—398; Corwin, 1930: 1—103; Serventy, 1941: 1—48; Godsil and Byers, 1944: 1—131; Bellon and Bellon, 1949: 1—28; Fraser-Brunner, 1949: 622—627; 1950: 131—163; Godsil and Holmberg, 1950: 1—55; Weber and Beaufort, 1951, 9: 204—235; Nakamura, 1951: — ; Rivas, 1951: 209—230; Morice, 1953: 35—63; Andriyashev, 1954: 324—329; Godsil, 1954: 1—188; Sylva, 1955: 1—41; Lozano, 1958: 6—254; Manacop, 1958: 79—101; Caro, 1958: 1—254; Yokita and Mita, 1958: 1—59 ex parte; Jones and Silas, 1960: 369—393; Schultz, 1960: 1—438; Zharov, 1961: 17—30; Paiva, 1961: 1—100; Rivas, 1961: 126—148; Collette, 1962: 24; Jones and Silas, (1961) 1962: 189—206; Smith, 1962: 165—183; Talbot and Penrith, 1962: 558—559; Williams, 1962: 106—164; Mather, 1963: 1155—1157; : 1159—1161; Collette and Gibbs, 1963: 23—32; : 1—48; Watson, 1963: 1153, 1154. Svetovidov, 1964: 384—405. Zharov, Zherebenkov, Kadil'nikov et al., 1964: 1—182; Jones and Silas, 1964: 1—105; Osipov, 1964: 1—74; Rivas, 1964: 427, 428; J. Smith, 1964: 165—183; Talbot, 1964: 187—209; Iwai, Nakamura and Matsubara, 1965: 1—51; Merrett and Thorp, 1965: 367—384; Martinsen, Smyslov, and Tishin, 1965: 1—122; Collette, 1966: 362—375; Gibbs and Collette, 1966: 65—130; Matsui, 1967: 71—83; Zharov, 1967: 209—224.

All warm and some moderately warm seas. More than 12 genera, a considerable number of species. Very important in world marine fishing.

Superfamily 50.9.2. Xiphioidea. Berg, 1940: 322. (Xiphioidei, Gosline, 1968: 28—31, 65.)

Family 410. **Istiophoridae** (528/542), thesis 50.9—3. Figure 830. (=Histiophoridae, +Tetrapturidae, +Makairidae) Billfishes, marlins, sailfishes, spearfishes, spreadfishes, voiliers, poisson-pique, marlinovye, parusnikovye kol'tseperye, ch'i yü k'o, ma kajiki ka.

Lit. J: 181; N: 389; G: 140; GRWM: 402, 433; MA: 140; Jordan and Evermann, 1926: 1—113; Buen, 1928: 1—12; Gregory and Conrad, 1937: 1—25; La Monte and Marcy, 1941: 3—24; Farrington, 1949: 144—155; Weber and Beaufort, 1951, 9: 236—241; Deraniyagala, 1951: 137—142; Nakamura,

1951; La Monte, 1955 : 319 — 358; Rivas, 1956 : 59 — 73; J.Smith, 1956 : 25 — 34; Robins and Sylva, 1960 : 383 — 413; Talbot and Penrith, 1962 : 558 — 559; Morrow, 1964 : 429 — 440; Tinsley, 1964 : 1—216; Williams, 1964 : 107 — 164; Howard and Ueyanagi, 1965 : 1—134, 38 maps; Morrow and Harbo, 1969 : 34 — 44.

All the oceans; pelagial. 3 genera, a small number of species. Of average importance in world marine fishing.

Family 411. **Xiphiidae** 530/544, thesis 50.9 — 4. Figure 831. Swordfishes, espadons, gladiateurs, poisson-épée, chien yü k'o, me kajiki ka, mech-ryba, mecherylye.

Lit. J : 181; N : 390; G : 141; GRWM : 402, 433; MA : 140; Jordan and Evermann, 1926 : 1—113; Gregory and Conrad, 1937 : 1—25; La Monte and Marcy, 1941 : 3 — 24; Deraniyagala, 1951 : 137 — 142; Andriyashev, 1954 : 326 — 327; J. Smith, 1956 : 25 — 34; Royce, 1957 : 497 — 554; Postel, 1964 : 19 — 24; Svetovidov, 1964 : 405 — 408.

All the oceans; pelagial. 1 genus, several species. Of little importance in world marine fishing.

Suborder 50.10. Luvaroidei, thesis 50.0 — 16. (Luvariformes.) Berg, 1940 : 323 (Scombroidei ex parte GRWM : 402); MA : 140; (Xiphioidei Gosline, 1968 : 28 — 31, 65). 1 family (412).

Family 412. **Luvaridae** 532/546, thesis 50.10 — 0. Figure 832. (=Dianidae = Dionidae.) Louvars, louvaréou, luvarovye, ch'ich'ing k'o, amo shiiro ka.

Lit. J : 181, (182); N : 389; G : 142; GRWM : 402, 433; MA : 140; Regan, 1902 : 278 — 281; 1903 : 372 — 374; 1909 : 66 — 75. Gregory and Conrad, 1943 : 225 — 283; Abe, 1953 : 39 — 47; Buen, 1957 : 83 — 88.

Tropical and subtropical marine waters; pelagial, 1 genus, 1 species.

Suborder 50.11. Tetragonuroidei, thesis 50.0 — 9. Berg, 1940 : 323, (Stromateoidei ex parte GRWM : 402; MA : 143; Gosline, 1968 : 16, 65.) 1 family (413).

Family 413. **Tetragonuridae** 533/547, thesis 50.11 — 0, suppl. 50.12—5. Figure 833. Squaretails, fangwei yü k'o, uroko ibo dai ka, kubokhvostye.

Lit. J : 183; N : 507; G : 143; GRWM : 402, 433; MA : 143; Regan 1902 : 206 — 207; Fitch, 1951 : 55 — 60; Abe, 1953 : 39 — 47; J. Smith, 1953 : 51—66; Abe, 1954 : 192; 1954 : 255; Grey, 1955 : 1—75; Haedrich, 1967 : 31 — 139.

Mediterranean Sea, Atlantic and Pacific oceans. 1 genus, several species.

Suborder 50.12. Stromateoidei, thesis 50.0 — 11. (Stromateoidea, Stromateiformes.) Berg, 1940 : 323 (Stromateoidei ex parte GRWM : 402, MA : 142 + suborder 50.11; Gosline, 1968 : 16, 65; Haedrich, 1967 : 31 — 139. 3 families (414 — 416).

Family 414. **Stromateidae** 534/548, theses 50.12—2; suppl. 50.12 — 7, 8. Figures 837, 834. (+414a. Centrolophidae, + Icichthyidae, + Schedophilidae.) Butterfishes, fiatoles, pomfrets, Rudderfisches, ch'ang yü k'o, ibo dai ka.

Lit. J : 182 (182); N : 506; G : 142 (142); GRWM : 402, 433 + family 415 + family 414a; MA : 143 + families 414a, 415; Regan, 1902 : 115 — 131, 194 — 206;

Gilchrist, 1922 : 249 — 255; 1924 : 1—12; :1 — 24; Bühler, 1930 : 59 — 115; Bertin, 1939 : 378 — 382; J. Smith, 1949 : 839 — 851; Weber and Beaufort, 1951, 9 : 85 — 94; Apsangikar, 1953 : 41 — 50; Abe, 1954 : 170, 178, 192; : 222, 246, 255; Franca, 1958 : 7— 26; Parin, 1958 : 162 — 170; Le Danois, 1963 : 228 — 234; Ochiai and Mori, 1965 : 1—6; Ueno, 1965 : 1—12; Haedrich, 1967 : 31—139; 1969 : 1—14.

All the seas but primarily warm and tropical seas. 10 genera, a considerable number of species. Of little importance in world marine fishing.

Family 415. **Pampidae** (534A/548A), theses 50.12 — 4; suppl. 50.12 — 8. Figure 842. (Stromateidae ex parte) Harvestfishes, butterfishes, silvery pomfrets, zerkalovye.

Lit. J : 182; N : (507); G : 142; GRWM : (402) (family 414). MA : (143) (family 414); Haedrich, 1967 : 31—169.

Indian and Pacific oceans, north as far as Japan. 1 genus, several species.

Family 416. **Nomeidae** 535/549, theses 50.12 — 3, 4. Figure 838. (+Psenidae, +416a. Ariommidae, + 416b. Amarsipidae.) Black ruffs, man-of-warfishes, rudderfishes, shuang ch'i chang k'o, eboshi dai ka.

Lit. J : 183; N : 503; G : 143; GRWM : 402, 433; MA : 143 + family 416a; Sanz Echeverria, 1949 : 151 — 156; Abe, 1954 : 90 — 94; 1955 : 75 — 80; Ueno, 1954 : 240 — 247; Padoa, 1956 : 538 — 545; Parin, 1958 : 162 — 170; Abe, 1959 : 225 — 229; Tortonese, 1960 : 57 — 82; Le Danois, 1963 : 228 — 234; Haedrich, 1967 : 31—139; 1967 : 12; 1969 : 1—14.

Warm and tropical seas. About 4 genera, quite a number of species.

Suborder 50.13. Anabantoidei, thesis 50.0 — 6. (Labyrinthici ex parte.) Berg, 1940 : 324 (GRWM : 402); (Ophicephaliformes ex parte, MA : 134, 133); Regan, 1910 : 767 — 787 ex parte; Weber and Beaufort, 1922, 4 : 330 — 369; Torselius, 1957 : 93 — 597; Blanc, 1963 : 70 — 77; Liem, 1963 : 1—149; Gosline, 1968 : 9. 1 family (417).

Family 417. **Anabantidae** 536/550, theses 50.13 — 1, 3, 5, 6. Figures 845 — 848. (+417A. Belontiidae = Belontidae = Polyacanthidae, + 417b. Helostomatidae = Helostomidae, +417c. Osphronemidae = Osphromenidae = Labyrinthicidae +417d. Badidae.) Climbing perches, gouramis, colises, combattants, perches grimpeuses, Kletterfische, Paradise fishes, polzunovye, labirintovye, makropolovye, khelostomovye, guramievye, p'an lu k'o, kinobori uo ka.

Lit. J : 176 (176); N : 508; G : 143 (143), (144); GRWM : 402 — 433 + families 417a, b, c; MA : 134, 135 + families 417a, b, c; Regan, 1910 : 767 — 787; Deraniyagala, 1929 : 79 — 111; Shih, 1936 : 67 — 97; Liem, 1963 : 1—149; 1965 : 206 — 213; 1967 : 103 — 133; Barlow, Liem and Wickler, 1968 : 415 — 447.

Tropical and South Africa, Southern Asia, Indonesia. About 18 genera, many species. Fresh and brackish waters. Fished locally. Aquarium fishes.

Suborder 50.14. Luciocephaloidei, thesis 50.0 — 7. (Labyrinthici ex parte.) Berg, 1940 : 325 (GRWM : 402). (Ophicephaliformes ex parte MA : 134 (133)), (Anabantoidei, Gosline, 1968 : 9). 1 family (418).

Family 418. **Luciocephalidae** 537/551, thesis 50.14—0. Figure 849. Shchukogolovye.

Lit. J: 176; N: 512; G: 144; GRWM: 402, 433. MA: 134; Liem, 1967: 103—133.

Fresh waters of Indonesia. 1 genus, several species.

Suborder 50.15. Kurtoidei, thesis 50.0—1. (Kurtiformes.) Berg, 1940: 325. (GRWM: 402); MA: 141; Gosline, 1968: 15, 65. 1 family (419).

Family 419. **Kurtidae** 538/552, thesis 50.15—0. Figure 850. Hump heads, kou yü k'o.

Lit. J: 186; N: 379; G: 144; GRWM: 402, 432; MA: 141; Beaufort, 1914: 391—410; Weber and Beaufort, 1951, 9: 82—84; Le Danois, 1963: 228—234.

Indian and Pacific oceans. 1 genus, several species. Fished locally.

Suborder 50.16. Gobioidei, thesis 50.0—21. Berg, 1940: 323; (Gobioidei ex parte GRWM: 402); MA: 146; Gosline, 1968, 16, 66; Regan, 1911: 729—733; Iljin, 1930: 1—63; Berg, 1949: 1055—1125; Gosline, 1955: 158—170; Il'in, 1956: 185—192; Chen, 1964: 37—59. 2 superfamilies, 5 families (420—424).

Superfamily 50.16.1. Eleotrioidea. Berg, 1940: 327; (Gobioidei ex parte MA: 146); Aurich, 1938: 125—183; Koumans, 1940: 121—210 ex parte; Fowler, 1960—62: 91—161, 49—87, 203—250, 1—77; Schultz, Woods and Lachner, 1966: 1—13. 1 family (420).

Family 420. **Eleotridae** 540/554, thesis 50.16—3. Figures 852, 854. (+Gobiomoridae, + 420a. Rhyacichthidae, thesis 50.16—3.2. =Platypteridae.) Sleepers, loachgobies, Schläfergrundeln, gudgeons, t'angli yü k'o, kawa anago ka, goloveshkovye.

Lit. J: 224; N: 391; G: 144; GRWM: (402) (421) + family 420a; MA: 147 + family 420a; Regan, 1911: 729—733; Stokell, 1941: 265—276; Harry, 1948: 13—18; Berg, 1948—1949: 1055—1060; Weber and Beaufort, 1953, 10: 283—392; Herre, 1954: 345—373; Whitley, 1954: 23—30; J. Smith, 1958: 137—164; Böhlke, 1963: 1—10. Add.—Clark, 1968: 3—7.

Marine coastal and fresh waters of rivers and lakes of tropical, subtropical, and, more rarely, temperate latitudes. More than 60 genera, many species. Aquarium fishes.

Superfamily 50.16.2. Gobioidea. Berg, 1940: 327; (Gobioidei ex parte MA: 146). 4 families (421—424).

Family 421. **Gobiidae** 541/555, thesis 50.16—5. Figures 855—860, 863. (+Milyeringidae, +Doliichthyidae, +Benthophilidae, +Sicydiaphiidae, +Apocrypteidae = Apocryptidae, + 421a. Trypauchenidae, thesis 50.16—10). Gobies, Meergrundeln. hsiahu yü k'o, kumohajo ka, bychkovye, kolbnevye.

Lit. J: 224; N: 403; G: (144), 146; GRWM: 402, 432 +families 420, 423, 421a; MA: 147 +family 423; Jordan and Snyder, 1901: 33—132; Regan, 1911:

729—733; Buen, 1917 : 337—354; 1918 : 291—337, 1923 : 121—266; Hora, 1924 : 155—164; Berg, 1927 : 1885—1925; Herre, 1927 : 1—352; Il'in, 1927 : 128—143; : 1—18; Duncker, 1928 : 121—148; Buen, 1930 : 120—147; Iljin, 1930 : 1—63; Buen, 1931 : 1—76; 1931 : 120—147; Koumans, 1931 : 1—174; Ginsburg, 1932 : 3—51; Wang, 1932 : 253—268; Ginsburg, 1933 : 1—59; Pearse, 1933 : 173—178; Borcéa, 1934 : 1—231; Scott, 1934 (1935) : 47—62; Taranets, 1934 : 397—400; Tomiyama, 1936 : 37—112; Il'in, 1938 : 111—131; Ninni, 1938 : 1—169; Tchang, 1939 : 263—288; Buen, 1940 : 1—16; Herre, 1940 : 357—369; Koumans, 1940 : 121—210; 1941 : 205—329; Roxas and Ablan, 1940 : 301—311; Sözer, 1941 : 128—169; Herre, 1945 : 77—82; Whitley, 1945 : 1—42; Berg, 1948—49; 1060—1125; Il'in, 1949 : 16—30; Delais, 1951 : 343—370; Weber and Beaufort, 1953, 10 : 1—264; Gaibova, 1952 : 53—106; Il'in, 1956 : 185—192; Takagi, 1957 : 97—126; Inger, 1958 : 107—117; J. Smith, 1959 : 185—225; Böhlke and Robins, 1960 : 73—101; Klausewitz, 1960 : 149—162; J. Smith, 1960 : 299—314; Baimov, 1961 : 11—16; Miller, 1963 : 205—256; Svetovidov, 1964 : 409—466; Alizova, 1965 : 1—22; Pinchuk, 1965 : 729—732; : 1—14; Bil'ko, 1966 : 1—20; Dawson, 1966 : 379—409; Ragimov, 1966 : 1—20; Böhlke and Robins, 1968 : 45—174. Add.—Georgier, 1966 : 159—228; Ragimov, 1967 : 252—277; Zambriborshch, 1968 : 37—44; Pinchuk, 1969 : 31—38; Böhlke and Robins, 1969 : 1—24; Miller, 1969 : 831—855.

All the warm seas, more rarely rivers. More than 200 genera, very many species. Fished locally. Aquarium fishes.

Family 422. **Gobioididae** (541A/555A), thesis 50.16—11. Figure 864. (+Taenioidae MA : 147; = Taenioididae = Amblyopidae.) Eelgobies, ugrebychkovye, lentobychkovye.

Lit. J : (227); N : 437; G : 152; GRWM : 402, 432; MA : 147; Koumans, 1931 : 1—174; Roxas and Allan, 1938 : 261—265; Weber and Beaufort, 1953, 10 : 265—282.

Atlantic, Indian, and Pacific oceans. 8 genera, several species.

Family 423. **Periophthalmidae** 542/556, thesis 50.16—6. Figure 861. Jumping gobies, mudskippers, poissons-promeneurs, mudhoppers, papillon, t'anku yü k'o, tobi haze ka, prygunovye, ilistyi prygun.

Lit. J : 227; N : (436); G : 151; GRWM : (402) (family 421); MA : (147) (family 421); Eggert, 1935 : 29—116; J. Smith, 1959 : 185—225.

Tropical seas. 2 genera, a small number of species.

Family 424. **Microdesmidae** 506/520, theses 50.16—12; 50.0—21, footnote 50.2—0. Figures 761, 865. (+Cerdalidae, +Pholidichthyidae, +Gunnellichthyidae, +Paragobioididae.) Wormfishes.

Lit. J : (235); N : 473; G : 132; GRWM : 402, 432; MA : 147; Günther, 1864 : 23—27; Reid, 1936 : 55—72; Myers and Wade, 1946 : 151—178; Weber and Beaufort, 1951, 9 : 1—484 (446—448); Gosline, 1955 : 158—170; Robins and Manning, 1958 : 301—304. Add.—Dawson, 1967 : 73—82.

Both shores of Central America and the west coasts of Africa. 1 genus, several species.

Order 51. SCORPAENIFORMES (102A/107A), theses 0—111, 114, 116, 117, 119, 121, 123, 124, 133. (Cottoidei, Cottiformes, Cataphracti ex parte, Scleroparei ex parte, Pareioplitae, Loricati, Sclerogeni, Cottomorphi, Perciformes ex parte.) (GRWM: 399); (Perciformes, Cottoidei, MA: 148); Gill, 1888 (1889): 567—592; Berg, 1906: 30—32; 1907: 1—75; Allis, 1909: 1—219; Regan, 1913: 169—183; Duncker, 1927: 61—84; Gregory, 1933: 75—481 (: 321—343); Rendahl, 1933: 1—50; 1933: 1—106; Weber and Beaufort, 1962, 11: 1—177. 6 suborders, 31 families (425—455).

Suborder 51.1. Scorpaenoidei, theses 51—28, 51—43. (Scorpaenoidae.) Berg, 1940: 328 (GRWM: 399). (Cottoidei ex parte, MA: 148). 8 families (425—432).

Family 425. Scorpaenidae 544/558, theses 51—49, 55. Figures 916, 919. (Sclerogenidae ex parte, +Tetrarogidae), Scorpionfishes, rockfishes, rock cods, stingfishes, goblinfishes, firefishes, rascasses,yu k'o, fusa kasago ka.

Lit. J: 208; N: —; G: 154; GRWM: 399, 422; MA: 148; Eigenmann, 1894: 375—407; Cramer, 1895: 573—610; Jordan and Starks, 1904: 91—175; Allis, 1909: 1—219; Hubbs and Schultz, 1933: 15—44; Moiseev, 1935: 111—138; Matsubara, 1943: 1—486; Cadenat, 1944: 525—563; Alverson and Welander, 1952: 138—143; Herre, 1952: 381—482; Ginsburg, 1953: 1—103; Andriyashev, 1954: 329—340; Oshima, 1956: 236—238; Phillips, 1957: 5—158; J. Smith, 1957: 49—72; : 75—88; 1958: 167—181; Boutière, 1958: 1—84; Buen, 1961: 1—90; Phillips, 1961: 51—55; Weber and Beaufort, 1962, 11: 1—89; Palmer, 1963: 701—704; Barsukov, 1964: 233—266; Svetovidov, 1964: 467—474; Eschmeyer and Collette, 1966: 349—375; Eschmeyer, 1965: 84—164. Add.—Barsukov, 1968: 479—482.

All the warm and temperate seas. More than 70 genera, many species. Of great importance in world marine fishing.

Family 426. **Triglidae** 545/559, thesis 51—30. Figure 906. (Sclerogenidae ex parte, Craniomi, Trigliformes ex parte.) Searobins, grondins, gurnards, Knurrhahn, morskie petukhi, fangfu k'o, hobo ka.

Lit. J: 217; N: — ; G: 156; GRWM: 399, 422 + family 427; MA: 148; Jordan and Richardson, 1908: 629—670; Allis, 1909: 1—219; Matsubara and Hiyama, 1932: 1—67; J. Smith, 1934: 321—336; Svetovidov, 1936: 1—24; Kuronuma, 1939: 223—260; Ginsburg, 1950: 489—527; Shindo, 1951: 83—90; Teague, 1951: 1—59; 1952: 1—20; Andriyashev, 1954: 340—342; Weber and Beaufort, 1962, 11: 114—126; Asano and Okamura, 1963: 49—52. Svetovidov, 1964: 474—482; Richards, 1968: 77—114.

Coastal waters and the deep waters of warm and temperate seas. More than 10 genera, many species. Of little importance in world marine fishing.

Family 427. **Peristediidae** (545A/559A), thesis 51—31. Figure 907. (=Peristediontidae, Trigliformes ex parte, Triglidae ex parte). Armored searobins, malarmats, crocodilefishes, sea robins.

Lit. J: 216; N: —; G: 157; GRWM: (399) (family 426); MA: 148; Jordan and Richardson, 1908: 629—670; Kamohara, 1936: 436—441; 1952: 1—13; 1957: 1—6; Teague, 1961: 1—27. Weber and Beaufort, 1962, 11: 114—126.

Deep waters of warm and temperate seas. 5 genera, a considerable number of species.

Family 428. **Caracanthidae** 546/560, thesis 51—51. Figure 917. Velvetfishes, vel'vetovye.

Lit. J: 210; N: —; G: 157; GRWM: 399, 422; MA: 148; Kner, 1860: 531—546; 1868: 26—31; Fowler, 1900 (1901): 493—528 (515); J. Smith, 1958: 167—181; Weber and Beaufort, 1962, 11: 169—172.

Pacific Ocean, among coral reefs. 1 genus, a small number of species.

Family 429. **Aploactinidae*** (547/561), thesis 51—48. Figure 915. (=Aploactidae MA: 148, +Bathyaploactidae Beaufort, 1952.) Little velvetfishes, junp'i yü k'o, ibo okajo ka.

Lit. J: (209); N: —; G: (159); GRWM: 399, 422; MA: 148; Matsubara, 1943: 457—472; Beaufort, 1952: 44—45; Le Danois, 1963: 228—234.

Pacific Ocean. About 10 genera, a considerable number of species.

Family 430. **Synancejidae** (548/562), thesis 51—54. Figure 918. (=Synanceidae.) Stonefishes, goblinfishes, devilfishes, tu yü k'o, oni okoze ka, borodavchatkovye.

Lit. J: 210; N: —; G: 157; GRWM: 399, 422; MA: 148; Gill, 1905: 221—225; J. Smith, 1958: 167—181; Weber and Beaufort, 1962, 11: 93—114.

Indian and Pacific oceans. About 10 genera, many species.

Family 431. **Pataecidae** 549/563, thesis 51—45. Figure 914. Velvetfishes, avstraliiskie vel'vetki.

Lit. J: 210; N: —; G: 158; GRWM: 399, 422, family 432; MA: 148; T. Scott, 1962: 144—159.

Coastal waters of Australia. 2 genera, several species.

Family 432. **Gnathanacanthidae** (549A/563A), thesis 51—46. No figure. (=Gnathacanthidae, Pataecidae ex parte.)

Lit. J: 210; N: —; G: (158); GRWM: (399) (family 431); MA: 148; T. Scott, 1962: 145, 164.

Coastal waters of Australia. 1 genus, several species.

Suborder 51.2. Hexagrammoidei, thesis 51—56. (Hexagrammoidae, Hexagrammiformes.) Berg, 1940: 329 (GRWM: 399), (Cottoidei ex parte MA: 148). 2 families (433—434).

Family 433. **Hexagrammidae** 550/564, thesis 51—58. Figures 921—923. (+Ophiodontidae, +Oxylebiidae = Chiridae, + 433a. Zaniolepididae = Zaniolepidae.) Greenlings, combfishes, cultus cods, liu hsien yü k'o, ainame ka, terpugovye.

Lit. J: 211; N —; G: 158; GRWM: 399, 422 + family 433a; MA: 148; Rutenberg, 1950: 1—10; 1954: 151—155; 1955: 10—15; 1962: 1—100; Andriyashev, 1954: 342—346; Rass, 1962: 191—203; Klashtorin, 1962: 104—109; Quast, 1965: 563—600.

North Pacific. 7 genera, several species. Of average importance in world marine fishing. Game fishes.

* Matsubara (1955: 1093—1097) includes this family in family 439. Congiopodidae.

Family 434. **Anoplopomatidae** (551/565), thesis 51—57. Figure 920. (=Anoplopomidae = Anoplomidae, +Erilepidae.) Sablefishes, skilfishes, fat priests, coalfishes, ugol'nye ryby, yin hsuëh k'o, gin dare ka.

Lit. J: (210); N: —; G: 158; GRWM: 399, 422; MA: 148; Bell and Charrett, 1945: 94—103.

North Pacific. 2 genera, 2 species. A promising item of marine fishing.

Suborder 51.3. Platycephaloidei, thesis 51—34. (Platycephaloidae, Platycephaliformes.) Berg, 1940: 329. (GRWM: 399.) (Cottoidei ex parte MA: 148.) 3 families (435—437).

Family 435. **Platycephalidae** 552/566, thesis 51—38. Figure 910. Flatheadfishes, flatheads, t'ung k'o, kochi ka, ploskogolovye.

Lit. J: 211; N: —; G: 158; GRWM: 399, 423 + family 436, 437; MA: 148; Jordan and Richardson, 1908: 629—670; Matsubara and Ochiai, 1955: 1—109; 1955: 1102—1123; Weber and Beaufort, 1962, 11: 127—165.

Indian and Pacific oceans, eastern Atlantic. About 20 genera, quite a number of species. Fished locally. Game fishes.

Family 436. **Parabembridae** (—/—), thesis 51—35. Figure 908. (Platycephalidae ex parte.) Lozhnobembrovye.

Lit. J: (211); N: —; G: (159); GRWM: (399) family 435); MA: 148; Matsubara, 1955: 1049, 1101.

Seas of Southern Japan and China. 1 genus, several species.

Family 437. **Bembridae** (552A/566A), thesis 51—37. Figure 909, (=Bembradidae, Platycephalidae ex parte.)

Lit. J: (211); N: —; G: (158); GRWM: (399) (family 435); MA: 148; Jordan and Richardson, 1908: 629—670; Matsubara, 1955: 1049, 1101.

Seas of Japan, China, the Philippines, and the Hawaiian Islands. 4 genera, several species.

Suborder 51.4. Hoplichthyoidei, thesis 51—39. (Hoplichthyoidae.) Berg, 1940: 329; (GRWM: 399). (Cottoidei ex parte MA: 148.) 1 family (438).

Family 438. **Hoplichthyidae**, 553/567, thesis 51—39. Figure 911. (=Oplichthyidae.) chên t'ung k'o, hari gochi ka.

Lit. J: 211; N: —; G: 159; GRWM: 399, 423; MA: 148; Jordan and Richardson, 1908: 629—670; Matsubara, 1937: 264—265; Fowler, 1938: 31—135 (95); Matsubara and Ochiai, 1950: 73—88; 145—156. Weber and Beaufort, 1962, 11: 166, 167.

Indian and Pacific oceans. 1 genus, a small number of species.

Suborder 51.5. Congiopodoidei, thesis 51—41. (Congiopodoidae.) Berg, 1940: 330. (GRWM: 399.) (Cottoidei ex parte MA: 148.) 1 family (439).

Family 439. **Congiopodidae** 554/568, thesis 51—41. Figures 912, 913. (=Congiopidae = Agriopidae). Svinorylye.

Lit. J : 209; N :—; G: 159; GRWM: 399, 423; MA: 148; Matsubara, 1943: 627—456; Moreland, 1960: 241—246.

Indian Ocean and southern part of the Pacific, west and east coasts of the southern part of South America. About 8 genera, several species.

Suborder 51.6. Cottoidei, thesis 51—3. (Discoboli, Cottoidae.) Berg, 1940: 330, (GRWM: 399); (Cottoidei ex parte MA: 148). Garman, 1892: 1—96; Taranets, 1941: 427—448; Taliev, 1955: 3—603, 16 families (440—455).

Family 440. **Cottidae** 556/570, thesis 51—27. Figures 891—904. (Sclerogenidae ex parte,+Jordaniidae, +Neophrynichthyidae, +Icelidae 555/569, thesis 51—27, 24 + Cottocomephoridae 557/571, thesis 51—27, 1 +Abyssocottidae.) Sculpins, scaleless sculpins, chabots, sea scorpion, kerchakovye, pantsirnoshchekie bychki, tufu yü k'o, kajika ka.

Lit. J: 213; N:—; G: (160), 161; GRWM: 399, 423, +family 441—443, 446—448, families (555) + 444 and 445, family (557); MA: 148 +family 443; Berg, 1903: 99—114; Jordan and Starks, 1904: 231—335; Berg, 1906: 30—32; 1906; 906—911; 1907: 1—75; Gratzianow, 1907: 654—660; Hubbs, 1926: 1—16; 1—18; P. Schmidt, 1926: 359—369; 1927: 1—8; 25—32; : 1—10; 1929: 359—369; 405—426; : 503—506; 513—523; Berg, 1932: 17—20; Andriašev, 1935: 289—297; Svetovidov, 1935: 53—57; Taranets, 1935: 177—180; Shmidt, 1935: 413—418; Bolin, 1936: 25—38; 1936: 151—159; Matsubara, 1936: 97—114; Andriashev, 1937: 253—276; Bazikalova, Kalinnikova, Mikhin, and Taliev, 1937: 109—211; P. Schmidt, 1937: 279—281; 1940: 377—387; Nybelin, 1941: 215—224; Taranets, 1941: 427—435; Bolin, 1944: 1—135; 1947: 153—168; Andriyashev, 1949: 194—209; Berg, 1949: 1125—1174, 1329; Jensen and Valsöe, 1949: 1—26; Matsubara and Iwai, 1951: 86—93; Bolin, 1952: 431—441; Jensen, 1952: 1—21; Andriyashev, 1954: 346—415; Taliev, 1955: 3—603; Robins and Miller, 1957: 213—233; Watanabe, 1968: 1—461; 1960: 1—218; McAllister and Lindsey, 1959: 66—89; Andriyashev, 1961; 231—241; Cervigón, 1961: 119—128; McAllister, 1963: 50—59; Chu and Jin, 1965: 235—252; Vilimovskii, 1966: 89; McAllister, 1968: 58—69; Neelov, 1968: 99—103; Add.—Sandercock et al., 1968: 832—853.

Marine and fresh waters of the basins of the North Atlantic, North Pacific, and the arctic seas. 1 species off New Zealand. Fished locally. Promising for the feed meal industry. More than 70 genera, very many species.

Family 441. **Scorpaenichthyidae** (556A/570A), thesis 51—1. Figure 866. (Cottidae ex parte) Cabezones, lozhnoskorpenovye.

Lit. J: 212; N:—; G: 160; GRWM: (399) (family 440); MA:—; Starks, (1895) 1896: 410—412; Regan, 1913: 169—183; Taranets, 1941: 428; O'Connell, 1953: 7—76.

Northeastern part of the Pacific Ocean around North America. 1 genus, 1 species.

Family 442. **Synchiridae** (556B/570B), thesis 51—14. Figure 884. (Cottidae ex parte.)
Lit. J : 214; N :—; G : 162; GRWM : (393) (family 440); MA : —; Taranets, 1941 : 428; Clemens and Wilby, 1961 : 322, 323.
Northeastern part of the Pacific Ocean around Alaska and British Columbia. 1 genus, 1 species.

Family 443. **Rhamphocottidae** (556C/570C), thesis 51 — 16. Figure 885. (Cottidae ex parte). Shlemorogatkovye.
Lit. J:214; N:—; G :162; GRWM :(393) (family 440); MA : (148) (family 440).
Northeastern part of the Pacific Ocean around Alaska and British Columbia and off Japan. 1 genus, 1 species.

Family 444. **Ereuniidae** (555A/569A), thesis 51—19. Figure 886. (Icelidae ex parte.)
Lit. J : 214; N : —; G : 162; GRWM: (393) (family 440a); MA : —; Shmidt, 1928 : 319, 320; Matsubara, 1936 : 97—114; 1955 : 1132, 1133; Taranets, 1941 : 428; Clemens and Wilby, 1961 : 319 — 321.
Pacific coast of Japan. 1 genus, 1 species.

Family 445. **Marukawichthyidae** (555B/569B), thesis 51—20. Figure 887. (Icelidae ex parte.)
Lit. J :—; N :—; G : 164; GRWM : (393) (family 440a); MA : —; Sakamoto, 1931 : 53 — 56; Mukerji, 1932 : 441—444; Matsubara, 1936 : 97 — 114; 1955 : 1133; Taranets, 1941 : 428.
Sea of Japan and Pacific coast of Japan. 1 genus, 1 species.

Family 446. **Hemitripteridae** (556D/570D), thesis 51—23. Figure 888. (Cottidae ex parte.) Sea ravens, volosatye rogatki.
Lit. J : 214; N :—; G : 162; GRWM : (393) (family 440); MA : —; Taranets, 1941 : 428; Matsubara, 1955 : 1133, 1160.
North Pacific and North Atlantic. 2 genera, 3 species.

Family 447. **Blepsiidae** (556E/570E), thesis 51—24. Figure 889. (=Blepisiidae, Cottidae ex parte.) Silverspotted sculpins.
Lit. J : 212; N :—; G : (160); GRWM : (339) (family 440); MA : —; P. Schmidt, ; 1929 : 394 — 398; Taranets, 1941 : 428; Matsubara, 1955 : 1158 — 1160.
North Pacific. 1 genus, several species.

Family 448. **Aseelichthyidae**, 556F/570F, thesis 51—26. Figure 890. (Cottidae ex parte.) Rosylip sculpins.
Lit. J : 214; N : —; G : 162; GRWM : 399 (family 440); MA : —; Taranets, 1941 : 427; Clemens and Wilby, 1961 : 310, 311.
Pacific coast of North America. 1 genus, 1 species.

Family 449. **Comephoridae** 558/572, thesis 51—10. Figure 880. Baikalfishes, golomyankovye.
Lit. J : 215; N : —; G : 162; GRWM: 399, 423; MA : 148; Korotnev, 1905 : 1— 39; Berg, 1906 : 30 — 32; 906 — 911; 1907 : 1— 75; Vereshchagin, 1926 : 47— 50; Bazikalova, Kalinnikova, Mikhin and Taliev, 1937 : 109 — 211; Taranets, 1941 : 428; Berg, 1948 — 49 : 1175 — 1177; Taliev, 1955 : 9 — 603.
Lake Baikal. 1 genus, 2 species.

Family 450. **Normanichthyidae** 559/573, thesis 51—3, footnote. Figure 867.
Lit. J: —; N: —; G: 93; GRWM: 399, 423; MA: 148; Clark, 1937: 90—91; 1938: 29; Norman, 1938: 29—32.
Chile, Valparaiso Bay. 1 genus, 1 species.

Family 451. **Psychrolutidae** 561/575, thesis 51—52. Figures 881—883. (+Neophrynichthyidae, 451a. Cottunculidae, 560/574, thesis 51—126) Tadpolesculpins, kottunkulovye.
Lit. J: 214; N: —; G: 162; GRWM: 399, 423 + family 451a; MA: 148 + family 451a; Gill, 1888: 321—327; Taranets, 1941: 428, 435; Jensen, 1952: 1—21; Andriyashev, 1954: 415—421; Weber and Beaufort, 1962, 11: 167, 168.
North Pacific, coasts of South Africa, southeastern South America, and New Zealand. 11 genera, a small number of species.

Family 452. **Agonidae** 562/576, thesis 51—8. Figures 872—879. (+Aspidophoroididae = Aspidophoridae) Sea poachers, alligatorfishes, souris-de-mer, pa chiao yü k'o, toku bire ka, lisichkovye, morskaya lisichka.
Lit. J: 215; N: —; G: 162 (163); GRWM: 399, 423; MA: 148; Jordan and Starks, 1904: 575—599; Rendahl, 1933: 1—106; P. Schmidt, 1936: 58—59; Lindberg and Andriyashev, 1950: 293—302. Andriyashev, 1954: 421—437.
North Pacific, and also off the coasts of Chile, Uruguay, Brazil, North Atlantic, and Arctic Ocean. About 30 genera, about 50 species.

Family 453. **Cyclopteridae** 563/577, thesis 51—5. Figure 868. (+Liparopidae = Liparopsidae) (Perciformes, Cyclopteroidei MA: 148.) Lumpfishes, lumpsuckers, mollet, gros seigneur, lièvre-de-mer, Seehase, poules de mer, limaces de mer, lump, yüanchi k'o, dango uo ka, pinagorovye.
Lit. J: 215, (215); N: —; G: 163 (163); GRWM: 399, 423 + family 454, 455; Garman, 1892: 1—96; Jordan and Snyder, 1908: 343—351; Parr, 1926: 1—31; Popov, 1928: 47—63; 1930: 69—76; 1931: 85—99; Wu and Wang, 1933: 77—86; Perminov, 1936: 115—129; Ueno, 1954: 273—295; Andriyashev, 1954: 437—452; Lindberg and Legeza, 1955: 389—459; 1964: 1—75. Add.—Ueno, 1970: 1—233.
Northern parts of the Atlantic and Pacific oceans, Barents and Red seas, Straits of Magellan. 9 genera, about 30 species. Fished locally.

Family 454. **Liparidae** (563A/577A), thesis 51—6. Figure 869. (=Lipariidae = Cyclogasteridae, +Rhodichthyidae, Cyclopteridae ex parte.) (Perciformes, Cyclopteroidei, MA: 148.) Marmotte-de-mer, limace-de-mer, snailfishes, seasnails, liparovye, morskie slizni.
Lit. J: 216; N: —; G: 164, 135; GRWM: (399) (family 453); Garman, 1892: 1—96; Gilbert and Burke, 1912: 351—380; Burke, 1930: 1—204; Wu and Wang, 1933: 77—86; Andriyashev, 1954: 452—496; Matsubara and Iwai, 1954: 425—441; Cohen, 1960: 15—20. Add.—Cohen, 1968: 384—388.
Northern parts of the Atlantic and Pacific oceans. Arctic Ocean. 16 genera, quite a large number of species. A possible item for the feed meal industry.

Family 455. **Eutelichthyidae*** (—/—), thesis 51—6, footnote. Figure 870. (Perciformes, Cyclopteroidei MA : 148.)

Lit. J : —; N : —; G : 164; GRWM : (399) (family 453); Tortonese, 1960 : 226—232; Cohen, 1968 : 384—388.

Mediterranean Sea. 1 genus, 1 species.

Order 52. DACTYLOPTERIFORMES 103/108, thesis 0—132. (Craniomi ex parte, Dactylopteroidei.) Berg, 1940 : 331 (GRWM : 399); (Perciformes, Dactylopteroidei MA : 149); Allis, 1909 : 156—182; Regan, 1913 : 183; Fowler, 1933—35 : 156—175. 1 family (456).

Family 456. **Dactylopteridae** 564/578, thesis 52—0. Figure 924. (=Cephalacanthidae.) Flying gurnards, grondins volants, pao fangfu k'o, semi hobo ka, kryloperye.

Lit. J : 217; N : —; G : 164; GRWM : 399, 424; MA : 149; Gill, 1891 : 243—248; Jordan and Richardson, 1908 : 628—670; Weber and Beaufort, 1962, 11 : 173—176.

Tropical and subtropical seas. 2 genera, several species.

Order 53. PLEURONECTIFORMES 105/110, thesis 0—37. (Heterosomata.) Berg, 1940 : 335. (GRWM : 402); Regan, 1910 : 484—496; Hubbs, 1915 : 449—496; MA : 131; Regan, 1920 : 205—222; Bonde, 1922 : 1—29; Norman, 1926 : 219—308; 1927 : 7—48; Oshima, 1927 : 177—204; Norman, 1928 : 173—215; 1930 : 261—369; Weber and Beaufort, 1929, 5 : 95—213; P. Schmidt, 1931 : 313—320; Wu, 1932 : 1—179; Chabanaud, 1933 : 1—111; 1934 : 275—284; Wu and Wang, 1933 : 297—304; Hikita, 1934 : 10—15; 187—296; Norman, 1934 : 1—459; Breder, 1936 : 1—56; Chabanaud, 1936 : 223—297; 1937 : 1—121; 1938 : 59—139; 1939 : 1—31; Kuronumo, 1940 : 29—61; Nunes, 1941 : 23—62; Erazi, 1942 : 235—262; Chabanaud, 1949 : 3—102; McCully, 1949 : 11—13; Wimpenny, 1953 : 1—145; Silva, 1956 : 183—200; Nielsen, 1961 : 101—127; 1962 : 219—226; 1963 : 377—400; 1964 : 1—86; Abraham, 1963 : 57—80; Punpoka, 1964 : 1—86; Chen and Wang, 1965 : 1—65; Stauch and D'Aubenton, 1966 : 137—158. 2 suborders, 6 families (457—462).

Suborder 53.1. P s e t t o d o i d e i, thesis 53—1. Berg, 1940 : 335 (GRWM : 402); MA : 131. 1 family (457).

Family 457. **Psettodidae** 566/580, thesis 53—1. Figure 925. Spiny rayed flounders. Kolyuchoperye kambaly, chien k'o, bozu garei ka.

Lit. J : 167; N : 519; G : 165; GRWM : 402, 434; MA : 131; Norman, 1934 : 1—459; Franca, 1958 : 1—44; Monteiro, 1958 : 87—130; Stauch and Cadenat, 1965 : 19—30; Stauch and D'Aubenton, 1966 : 137—158. Add.—Amaoka, 1969 : 59—340.

Tropical waters of the Atlantic (off West Africa), Indian, and Pacific oceans. 1 genus, 1 species. Fished locally.

Suborder 53.2. P l e u r o n e c t o i d e i, thesis 53—2. Berg, 1940 : 335; MA : 132. (Pleuronectoidei, Soleoidei GRWM : 403). 2 superfamilies, 5 families, (458—462).

* See footnote to thesis 51—6.

Superfamily 53.2.1. **Pleuronectoidea**, thesis 53—3. Berg, 1940: 336; MA: 132; (Pleuronectoidei GRWM: 402). 3 families (458—460).

Family 458. **Bothidae** 568/582, thesis 53—6. Figures 928, 931, 932. (+Paralichthyidae, + 458a. Scophthalmidae, Figure 932.) Lefteye flounders, turbots, barbues, brills, Tarbutt, sanddobs, lefthand flounders, rombovye, kalkanovye, levoglazye kambaly, paralikhtovye, p'ing k'o, hirame ka.

Lit. J: 167, (168); N: 520; G: 165, (166); GRWM: 402, 434 + family 458a; MA: 132; Norman, 1934: 1—459; Chabanaud, 1950: 246—253; Ginsburg, 1952: 265—351; Aoyagi, 1954: 238; Andriyashev, 1954: 469—472; Franca, 1958: 1—44; Monteiro, 1958: 87—130; Torchio, 1959: 1—11; Buen, 1961: 1—90; Torchio, 1952: 667—678; Amaoka, 1963: 53—62; : 107—121; Svetovidov, 1964: 483—495; Günther, 1966: 445—479. Add.—Anderson, 1967: 892—913; Amaoka, 1969: 59—340.

Atlantic, Indian, and Pacific oceans. About 40 genera, many species. Of little importance in world marine fishing.

Family 459. **Citharidae** (—/—), thesis 53—4. Figures 926, 927. (Bothidae ex parte, +Brachypleuridae.) Bastard halibuts.

Lit. J: (167); N: (522); G: (165); GRWM: 402, 434; MA: 132; Hubbs, 1945: 1—38; Chabanaud, 1948: 18—23; Franca, 1958: 1—44; Monteiro, 1958: 87—130. Add.—Amaoka, 1969: 59—340.

Mediterranean Sea, Atlantic, Indian, and Pacific oceans. 5 genera, a small number of species. Fished locally.

Family 460. **Pleuronectidae** 569/583, thesis 53—7. Figures 935, 937, 939—941. (=Planidae, +Hippoglossidae, +Samaridae, +Rhombosoleidae, +Paralichthodidae.) Righteye flounders, flatfishes, halibuts, flétan, flet, plie, carrelet, limande, Scholle, Heilbutt, Flundern, right-hand flounders, kambalovye, pravoglazye kambaly, teh k'o, karei ka.

Lit. J: (168), 169; N: 351; G: 167 (167), (168); GRWM: 402, 434; MA: 132; Steindachner, 1870: 421—446; Jordan and Starks, 1906: 161—246; Starks and Thompson, 1910: 277—287; Ogilby, 1916: 127—177; Schmidt, 1929: 363—368; Chabanaud, 1931: 1—32; Hubbs, 1932: 1—9; Norman, 1933: 214—222; 1934: 1—459; Okhryamkin and Moiseev, 1936: 1—44; Vernidub, 1938: 182—199; Moiseev, 1946: 1—63; Berg, 1948—1949: 1178—1193; Rass, 1950: 855—857; Matsubara, 1951: 361—367; Andriyashev, 1954: 472—515; Ochiai and Amaoka, 1962: 83—91; Svetovidov, 1964: 495—500.

Atlantic, Indian, and Pacific oceans and the arctic seas. Very important in world marine fishing.

Superfamily 53.2.2. **Soleoidea**, thesis 53—8. Berg, 1940: 336; MA: 133; (Soleoidei GRWM: 403); Chabanaud, 1927: 1—67; 1955: 447—452; Nielsen, 1963: 7—36; Ochiai, 1963: 1—114; Cheng and Chang, 1965: 267—278. 2 families (461—462).

Family 461. **Soleidae** 570/584, thesis 53—9. Figures 942—947. (+Achiridae, +Synapturidae, +Trinectidae.) Saul, soles, Seezungen, pravostoronnie morskie yazyki, t'a k'o, sasaushino shita ka.

Lit. J: 169; N: 544; G: 168; GRWM: 403, 434; MA: 133; Jordan, 1923: 1—14; Chabanaud, 1928: 1—53; 1930: 1—21; Fowler, 1933—35: 156—175...

Chabanaud, 1935 : 212 — 224; : 1—24; 1940 : 13 — 31; Padoa, 1947 : 102 — 121; Ginsburg, 1951 : 185 — 201; Chabanaud, 1954 : 245 — 282; Ochiai, 1959 : 1—234; Dawson, 1964 : 646 — 665; Svetovidov, 1964 : 500 — 505; Chêng Pao-shan and Chang Yu-wei, 1965 : 267 — 278; Ochiai, 1966 : 1 — 97.

Warm waters of the Atlantic, Indian and Pacific oceans; some species enter rivers. More than 30 genera, many species. Of little importance in world marine fishing.

Family 462. **Cynoglossidae** 571/585, thesis 53 — 10. Figures 948, 949. Tonguefishes, soles, tongsoles, levostoronnie morskie yazyki, shêta k'o, ushino shita ka.

Lit. J : 171; N : 553; G : 169; GRWM : 403, 434; MA : 133; Fowler, 1933 — 35 : 156 — 175 . . . Chabanaud, 1940 : 1—182; 1949 : 60 — 66; : 202 — 209; : 347 — 353; : 516 — 521, 1955 : 43 — 45.

Atlantic, Indian, and Pacific oceans. About 10 genera, quite a number of species. Of little importance in world marine fishing.

Order 54. ICOSTEIFORMES 106/111, theses 0 — 97, 156. (Icosteoidei, Malacichthyes.) Berg, 1940 : 337; MA : 150; (Perciformes, Icosteoidei, GRWM : 402). 1 family (463).

Family 463. **Icosteidae** 572/586, thesis 54 — 0. Figure 950. (+ Acrotidae.) Ragfishes, lang yü k'o, irezumi konnyaku aji ka, tryapichnikovye, ikosteevye.

Lit. J : 183 (183); N : 578; G : 143 (143); GRWM : 402, 431; MA : 150; Regan, 1923 : 610 — 612; Bolin, 1940 : 287 — 289; Abe, 1954 : 90 — 94; Kobayashi and Ueno, 1956 : 239 — 265.

Moderate depths of the northeastern part of the Pacific Ocean off the coast of North America. 2 genera, several species.

Order 55. CHAUDHURIIFORMES 107/112, thesis 0 — 59. (Opisthomi ex parte.) Berg, 1940 : 337. (Perciformes, Mastacombeloidei ex parte GRWM : 402); (Mastacembeliformes ex parte MA : 156); Regan, 1912 : 217 — 219; 1919 : 198 — 199; Job, 1941 : 121—135; Bailey, 1960 : 121 — 135. 1 family (464).

Family 464. **Chaudhuriidae** 573/587, thesis 55 — 0. Figure 951. Mastacembeliformes ex parte.) K'eshih yü k'o, kaujuriya ka.

Lit. J : 129; N : 602; G : 170; GRWM : 402, 434; MA : 158; Annandale, 1918 : 33 — 64 (: 39 — 42); Annandale and Hora, 1923 : 327 — 333; Weber and Beaufort, 1962, 11 : 424 — 434).

Freshwater Lake Inle in Upper Burma. 1 genus, 1 species.

Order 56. MASTACEMBELIFORMES 108/113, thesis 0 — 58. (Opistomi ex parte, Mastacembeloidei.) Berg, 1940 : 338; MA : 156 + order 55. (Perciformes, Mastacembeloidei ex parte GRWM : 402); Regan, 1912 : 217 — 219 ex parte. 1 family (465).

Family 465. **Mastacembelidae** 574/588, thesis 56 — 0. Figure 952. (= Mastocembelidae, + Rhynchobdellidae.) Spiny eels, Stachelaale, t'zu yü k'o, toge unaji ka, khobotnorylye, kolyuchie ugri.

Lit. J : 129; N : 601; G : 170; GRWM : 402, 434; MA : 157; Job, 1941 : 121—135; Sufi, 1956 : 93 — 146; Weber and Beaufort, 1962, 11 : 424 — 434.

Fresh waters of tropical Africa, Asia, and the Malay Archipelago. 3 genera, several species. Aquarium fishes.

Order 57. ECHENEIFORMES 109/114, thesis 0 — 65. (Discocephali, Echeneioidei.) Berg, 1940 : 338; MA : 151. (Perciformes, Percoidei ex parte, GRWM : 400); Regan, 1912 : 634 — 637; Buen, 1934 : 397 — 412; Maul, 1956 : 5 — 75. 1 family (466).

Family 466. **Echeneidae** 576/590, thesis 57— 0. Figure 953. (=Echeneididae.) Remoras, shark pilots, sharksuckers, sucking fishes, sucets, yin k'o, koban zame ka, prilipalovye.

Lit. J : 227; N : (554); G : 154; GRWM : 400, 425; MA : 151; Regan, 1912 : 634—637; Gudger, 1926 : 1— 26; Norman, 1939 : 24 — 29; Szidat and Nani, 1951 : 385 — 417; Cadenat, 1953 : 672 — 683; Weber and Beaufort, 1962, 11 : 435 — 443); Strasburg, 1964 : 51—57.

Warm waters of seas and oceans. 5 genera, several species.

Order 58. TETRAODONTIFORMES (110/115), thesis 0 — 151. (Tetrodontiformes; Plectognathi, Diodontomorphi, Ostracioniformes.) Berg, 1940 : 338. (GRWM : 403); MA : 153; Regan, 1902 : 284 — 303; Annandale and Jenkins, 1910 : 1—21; Rosen, 1912 — 1916 : 1—23; 1—29; 1—14; 1—28; Kashkarov (1913), 1914 : 263 — 370; Herre, 1924 : 415 - 510; Gregory, 1933 : 75 — 481 (286 — 295); Fraser-Brunner, 1941 : 420 — 430; Breder and Clark, 1947 : 291 — 320; Clark, 1949 : 1—22; Koefoed, 1952 : 1—26; Clark and Gohar, 1953 : 1—80; Le Danois, 1955 : 1933 —1934; Tavani, 1955 : 177—200; Le Danois, 1959 : 1—274; 1961 : 207 — 338; Weber and Beaufort, 1962, 11 : 262 — 423; Tyler, 1963 : 203 — 206; Chu and Hsu, 1965 : 320 — 333. 4 suborders, 11 families (467 — 477).

Suborder 58.1. Balistoidei, thesis 58 — 1. (Sclerodermi.) Berg, 1940 : 339; MA : 154; (Balistoidei ex parte GRWM : 403); Fraser-Brunner, 1935 : 658 — 663; J. Smith, 1935 : 358 — 364; Kamohara, 1940 : 1—108; Bauchot, 1966 : 7 — 43. 5 families (467 — 471).

Family 467. **Triacanthidae** 579/593, thesis 58 — 4. Figure 955. Spikefishes, hornfishes, tripodfishes, santzŭ t'un k'o, gima ka, trekhshipye.

Lit. J : 239; N : 560; G : 138; GRWM : 403, 435 + family 468; MA : 154; Myers, 1934 : 1—12; Fraser-Brunner, 1941 : 420 — 430; Weber and Beaufort, 1962, 11 : 269 — 277. Add. — Tyler, 1968 : 1— 364.

Atlantic, Indian, and Pacific oceans. 4 genera, several species.

Family 468. **Triacanthodidae** (—/—), thesis 58 — 3. Figure 954. (Triacanthidae ex parte.)

Lit. J : (239); N : 557; G : 137; GRWM : (403) (family 467); MA : 154 + family 467; Myers, 1934 : 1—12; Kamohara, 1937 : 5 — 8; Fraser-Brunner, 1941 : 420 — 430; 1950 : 1—8; Weber and Beaufort, 1962, 11 : 263 — 268.

Indian and Pacific oceans. 9 genera, a few species.

Family 469. **Balistidae** 581/595, thesis 58—8. Figure 956. Filefishes, triggerfishes, arbalétriers, fanfrés, lin t'un k'o, mongara kawahagi ka, spinorogie.

Lit. J: 239; N: 561; G: 138; GRWM: 403, 433 + families 470 and 471; MA: 154; Kamohara, 1936: 1739—1745; Le Danois, 1955: 1933, 1934; Fraser-Brunner, 1935: 658—663; Weber and Beaufort, 1962, 11: 278—311; Svetovidov, 1964: 505—507; Berry and Boldwin, 1966: 429—474. Add.— Moore, 1967: 689—722.

Atlantic, Indian, and Pacific oceans. More than 10 genera, quite a number of species. Unimportant in world marine fishing.

Family 470. **Aluteridae** (581A/595A), thesis 58—9. Figure 957. (=Aleuteridae, + Monacanthidae, Balistidae ex parte.) Sandpaperfishes, leatherjackets, poissons-limes, edinorogie, kozhistye spinorogi, kurkovye.

Lit. J: (239); N: —; G: (138); GRWM: (403) (family 469); MA: 154; Jordan and Fowler, 1902: 251—286; Ogilby, 1918: 45—90; Fraser-Brunner, 1935: 658—663; 1940: 518—535; 1941: 176—199; Le Danois, 1955: 1933; 1934; Silva, 1959: 145—150; Weber and Beaufort, 1962, 11: 312—344; Randall, 1964: 331—361.

Atlantic, Indian, and Pacific oceans. More than 20 genera. Game fishes.

Family 471. **Psilocephalidae** (581B/595B), thesis 58—6. No figure. (=Anacanthidae, Balistidae ex parte.) Leather jackets, usatyi spinorog.

Lit. J: 240; N: —; G: 139; GRWM: (403) (family 469); MA: —; Jordan and Fowler, 1902: 251—286; J. Smith, 1925: 358—364; Fernandez Yépez, 1955: 137—139; Berry and Poll, 1961: 300—362; Berry and Vogele, 1961: 61—109.

Indian Ocean and West Pacific. 1 genus, several species.

Suborder 58.2. Ostracoidei, thesis 58—11. (Ostracodermi.) Berg, 1940: 340; MA: 155. (Balistoidei ex parte GRWM: 403). 2 families (472—473).

Family 472. **Ostraciontidae** (582/596), thesis 58—13. Figure 959. (Ostraciidae ex parte = Ostracionidae.) Trunkfishes, boxfishes, coffres, hsien t'un k'o, hako fugu ka, kuzovkovye.

Lit. J: (240); N: 565; G: (33); GRWM: 403, 435 + family 473; MA: 155 + family 473; Fraser-Brunner, 1935: 313—320; T. Scott, 1962: 302; Weber and Beaufort, 1962, 11: 345—360.

Tropical waters of the Atlantic, Indian, and Pacific oceans. 6 genera, a small number of species. Game fishes.

Family 473. **Aracanidae** (582A/596A), thesis 58—12. Figure 958. (Ostraciidae ex parte.)

Lit. J: (240); N: (565); G: 33; GRWM: (403) (family 472); MA: (155) (family 472); Jordan and Fowler, 1902: 251—286; Fraser-Brunner, 1935: 313—320; 1941: 306—313; Le Danois, 1961: 207—338.

Coasts of Australia and Japan. 7 genera, a small number of species.

Suborder 58.3. Tetraodontoidei, thesis 58—15. (Gymnodontes, Tetrodontoidei.) Berg, 1940: 340; MA: 155; (Tetraodontoidei ex parte, GRWM: 403); Jordan and Snyder, 1901: 229—264; Fraser-Brunner, 1943: 1—18; Tavani, 1955: 177—200. 3 families (474—476).

Family 474. **Triodontidae** 580/594, thesis 58—17. Figure 960. Trekhzubye (skladchatobryukhie), sanya t'un k'o, uchiwa fugu ka.

Lit. J: 240; N: 565; G: 34; GRWM: 403, 435; MA: 155; McCulloch and Waite, 1915: 477—493; Tyler, 1962: 793—801; Weber and Beaufort, 1962, 11: 361, 362.

Indian and Pacific oceans. 1 genus, several species.

Family 475. **Tetraodontidae** (583/597), thesis 58—18. Figures 961, 962. (=Tetrodontidae = Gymnodontidae, +Lagocephalidae, +Chonarhinidae, =Chonerhinidae = Xenopteridae, +Canthigasteridae = Tropidichthyidae, +Ovoididae, +Colomesidae, +Sphoeroididae.) Puffers, sharp-nosed puffers, swellfishes, globefishes, tobys, blowfishes, toadfishes, poissons-globes, Kugelfische, chetyrekhzubye, iglobryukhie, t'un k'o, fugu ka.

Lit. J: 240, (241); N: 571; G: (33), 34, (35); GRWM: 403, 435; MA: 155; Jordan and Snyder, 1901: 229—264; Parr, 1927: 245—269; Fraser-Brunner, 1943: 1—18; Kuronuma, 1943: 119—130; Abe, 1949: 89—140; 1952: 35—44, 93—97, 117—127; 1954: 121—128; 1960: 3—6; J. Smith, 1958: 156—160; Tyler, 1962: 793—801; Weber and Beaufort, 1962, 11: 363—409. Add.— Shipp and Yerger, 1969: 477—488.

Atlantic, Indian, and Pacific oceans; occasionally fresh waters. 19 genera, many species. Fished locally. Freshwater forms kept in aquariums.

Family 476. **Diodontidae** 584/598, thesis 58—19. Figure 963. Porcupinefishes, porcs-épics, dvuzubye, ezh-ryby, ts'ŭ t'un k'o, hari sambou ka.

Lit. J: 241; N: 575; G: 35; GRWM: 403, 435; MA: 155; Parr, 1927: 245—269; Fraser-Brunner, 1943: 1—18; Tyler, 1962: 793—801; Weber and Beaufort, 1962, 11: 410—416.

Atlantic, Indian, and Pacific oceans. 5 genera, a small number of species.

Suborder 58.4. Moloidei, thesis 58—20. Berg, 1940: 340; MA: 156; (Tetraodontoidei ex parte GRWM: 403). 1 family (477).

Family 477. **Molidae** 585/599, thesis 58—20. Figure 964. (=Orthagoriscidae = Triuridae), Molas, headfishes, ocean sunfishes, poissons-lunes, fanch'ê yü k'o, mambo ka, luna-ryba.

Lit. J: 241; N: 576; G: 36; GRWM: 403, 435; MA: 156; Gregory and Roven, 1934: 145—151; Fraser-Brunner, 1951: 89—121; Andriyashev, 1954: 515—517; Buen, 1957: 66—76; Tyler, 1962: 793—801; Weber and Beaufort, 1962, 11: 416—423.

All the tropical and subtropical and some temperate seas. 3 genera, a small number of species.

Order 59. GOBIESOCIFORMES 111/116, thesis 0—41. (Xenopteri, Xenopterygii, Gobiesocomorphi, Gobiesoxoidei.) Berg, 1940 : 341, (GRWM: 397); MA : 164; Regan, 1909 : 75—86; Briggs, 1955 : 1—224; Weber and Beaufort, 1962, 11 : 444—453; Freihofer, 1963 : 81—189. 1 family (478).

Family 478. **Gobiesocidae** 586/600, thesis 59—0. Figures 965, 966. (+Diademichthyidae.) Clingfishes, porte-écuelle, barbiers, ventouseurs, morskie utochki, prisoskoperye, hounan yü k'o, uba uo ka.

Lit. J : 238; N : 579; G : 153; GRWM : 397, 415; MA : 165; Jordan and Fowler, 1902 : 413—416; Wilby, 1936 : 116; Pfaff, 1942 : 413—422; Schultz, 1944 : 47—77; Briggs, 1951 : 57—108; Buen, 1960 : 69—82; Tortonese, 1960: 161—163; Briggs, 1962 : 445—453; Weber and Beaufort, 1962, 11 : 444—453; Murgoci, 1964 : 297—306; J. Smith, 1964 : 581—596; Svetovidov, 1964 : 507—514; Briggs, 1965 : 123—125. Add.—idem, 1969 : 464—466.

Atlantic, Indian, and Pacific oceans; fresh waters of Central America. 35 genera, many species.

Order 60. BATRACHOIDIFORMES 112/117, thesis 0—169. (Batrachoidei, Haplodoci, Jugulares ex parte, Pediculati ex parte.) Berg, 1940 : 342 (GRWM: 396); MA : 163; Regan, 1912 : 277—289. 1 family (479).

Family 479. **Batrachoididae** 587/601, thesis 60—0. Figure 967. (=Batrachidae.) Toadfishes, poissons-crapauds, poissons-chanteurs, ch'an yü k'o, batora koidesu ka, zhaba-ryba.

Lit. J : 238; N : 583; G : 152; GRWM : 396, 415; MA : 164; Ogilby, 1908 : 43—57; Bean and Weed, 1910 : 511—526; Schultz and Reid, 1937 : 211—212; Hubbs and Schultz, 1939 : 473—496; J. Smith, 1952 : 313—339; Señorans, 1958 : 275—285; Walters and Robins, 1961 : 1—24; Weber and Beaufort, 1962, 11 : 185—190; Menon, 1963 : 52—54; Collette, 1966 : 846—864. Add.—Gilbert, 1968 : 671—730.

Atlantic, Indian, and Pacific oceans. 20 genera, a considerable number of species.

Order 61. LOPHIIFORMES 113/118, thesis 0—67. (Pediculati ex parte.) Berg, 1940 : 343 (GRWM : 397); MA : 159; Jordan and Sindo, 1902 : 361—381; Annandale and Jenkins, 1910 : 1—21; Radcliffe, 1912 : 199—214; Regan, 1912 : 277—289; Parr, 1930 : 1—23; Gregory, 1933 : 75—481 (386—410); Breder, 1936 : 1—56; Gregory and Conrad, 1936 : 193—308; Barbour, 1941 : 7—14; Koefoed, 1944 : 1—18; Bertelsen, 1951 : 1—276; Monod, 1960 : 620—698; Weber and Beaufort, 1962, 10 : 184—261. Add.—Chen et al. 1968 : 173—195. 3 suborders, 15 families.

Suborder 61.1. Lophioidei, thesis 61—2. Berg, 1940 : 343 (GRWM: 397); MA : 160. 1 family (480).

Family 480. **Lophiidae*** 588/602, thesis 61—2. Figure 968. Goosefishes, anglers, fishing frogs, monkfishes, anglerfishes, baudroies, lotes-de-mer, Seeteufel; nogopery, morskie cherti, udil'shchikovye, ankang k'o, anko ka.

Lit. J: 242; N: 586; G: 170; GRWM: 397, 415; MA: 160; Regan, 1903: 277—285; Tåning, 1923: 1—30; Andriyashev, 1954: 517—519; Parrott, 1957: 1—76; Weber and Beaufort, 1962, 11: 191—195; Boeseman, 1964: 12—18. Svetovidov, 1964: 515—518.

Atlantic, Indian, and Pacific oceans. 5 genera, a few species.

Suborder 61.2. **Antennarioidei**, thesis 61—3. Berg, 1940: 343 (GRWM: 397); MA: 160. 2 superfamilies, 4 families (481—484).

Superfamily 61.2.1. **Antennarioidea**, thesis 61—3. Berg, 1940: 343. 3 families (481—483).

Family 481. **Antennariidae** 589/603, thesis 61—6. Figure 970. (+Saccariidae.) Frogfishes, fishing-frogs, pi yü k'o, izari uo ka, lyagushka-ryba.

Lit. J: 242; N: 588; G: 170; GRWM: 397, 415; MA: 160; Barbour, 1942: 21—40; Myers and Wade, 1946: 151—178; Delais, 1951: 145—150; Andriyashev, 1954: 519—521; Schultz, 1957: 47—105; Cadenat, 1959: 361—385; Weber and Beaufort, 1962, 11: 196—222; Le Danois, 1964: 1—162; Schultz, 1964: 171—182.

Tropical waters of the seas and oceans. About 13 genera, quite a number of species.

Family 482. **Brachionichthyidae** 590/604, thesis 61—5. Figure 969.

Lit. J: 242; N: 590; G: 171; GRWM: 397, 415; MA: 161; Regan, 1912: 277; Scott, 1962: 264, 268.

Seas around Australia. 1 genus, several species.

Family 483. **Chaunacidae** 591/605, thesis 61—8. Figure 971. Anglerfishes, tanchi pi yü k'o, fusa anko ka.

Lit. J: 242; N: 590; G: 171; GRWM: 397, 415; MA: 160; Fowler, 1946: 1—4; Weber and Beaufort, 1962, 11: 222, 223.

Atlantic, Indian, and Pacific oceans. 1 genus, several species.

Superfamily 61.2.2. **Ogcocephaloidea**, thesis 61—9. (Oncocephaloidae.) Berg, 1940: 343. 1 family (484).

Family 484. **Ogcocephalidae** (592/606), thesis 61—9. Figure 972. (=Oncocephalidae = Onchocephalidae, =Malthidae, =Malthcidae.) Batfishes, rattlefishes, handfishes, chauve-souris-de-mer, zvezdchatkovye, netopyrevye, p'an fu yü k'o, aka gutsu ka.

Lit. J: 242; N: 590; G: 171; GRWM: 397, 415; MA: 161; Kamohara, 1937: 11—14; Ochiai and Mitani, 1956: 271—285; Hubbs, 1958: 807—826; Weber

* Family 480a. **Galatheathaumatidae** (—/—), thesis —, no figure. Lit. J: —; N: —; G: —; GRWM: —; Add. Whitley, 1970: 246.

This family differs from the others of the order in that the barbel-like appendage is attached to the palate inside the oral cavity, and its luminescent tip is furcately split. The eyes are very small and are situated near the angles of the mouth. Length up to 47 cm.

and Beaufort, 1962, 11 : 224 — 241; Rees, 1963 : 1513 — 1517; Bradbury, 1963 : 440, 441; 1967 : 399 — 422; Chêng Pao-shan and Chang Yu-wei, 1964 : 155 — 160.

Atlantic, Indian, and Pacific oceans; at the bottom of moderate depths. 7 genera, a few species.

Suborder 61.3. Ceratioidei, thesis 61 — 10. (Ceratioidea.) Berg, 1940 : 344; (GRWM : 397); MA : 161; Jörgense, 1920 : 1—110; Regan, 1926 : 1 — 45; Parr, 1927 : 1— 34; 1930 : 1—23; 1930 : 129 — 135; Regan and Trewavas, 1932 : 1—113; Waterman, 1939; 65 — 81; Beebe and Crane, 1947 : 151 — 182; Bertelson, 1951 : 1—276. 10 families (485 — 494).

Family 485. **Melanocetidae** 593/607, thesis 61 — 15. Figure 975.

Lit. J : 243; N : 593; G : 171; GRWM : 397, 415; MA : 161; Regan, 1913 : 1096, 1097; Bertelsen, 1951 : 1—276; Maul, 1961 : 87 — 159; 1962 : 5 — 27; 33 — 46; Weber and Beaufort, 1962, 11 : 241 — 245.

Deep oceanic waters. 1 genus, several species.

Family 486. **Diceratiidae** 594/608, thesis 61 — 19. Figure 977. (+Laevoceratiidae 597/611, +Aeschynichthyidae, Himantolophidae ex parte.)

Lit. J : (243); N : 593; G : (173); GRWM : 397, 415; MA : 162; Bertelsen, 1951 : 1—276; Grey, 1959 : 225 — 228; Maul, 1962 : 5 — 27; Weber and Beaufort, 1962, 11 : 245, 246.

Deep oceanic waters. 3 genera, several species.

Family 487. **Himantolophidae** 595/609, thesis 61 — 27. Figure 981. Chochin anko ka.

Lit. J : 243; N : 594; G : 172; GRWM : 397, 415; MA : 161; Bertelsen, 1951 : 1 — 276; Maul, 1961 : 87 — 159; 1962 : 5 — 27; 33 — 46; Weber and Beaufort, 1962, 11 : 246 — 256.

Deep oceanic waters. 1 genus, several species.

Family 488. **Oneirodidae** 596/610, theses 61 — 26, 30. Figures 980, 984. (Himantolophidae ex parte.) Dreamers, rakuda anko ka.

Lit. J : (243); N : 595; G : 172; GRWM : 397, 416; MA : 162; Bertelsen, 1951 : 1—276; Grey, 1956 : 242 — 246; Maul, 1961 : 87 — 159; 1962 : 5 — 27; 33 — 46; Weber and Beaufort, 1962, 11 : 246 — 256.

Deep oceanic waters. More than 15 genera, quite a number of species.

Family 489. **Centrophrynidae** (—/—), thesis 61 — 24. Figure 979.

Lit. J : —; N : (596); G : —; GRWM : 397, 416; MA : 162; Bertelsen, 1951 : 1—276 (: 124).

Deep oceanic waters. 1 genus, several species.

Family 490. **Gigantactinidae** (598/612), thesis 61 — 21. Figure 978. (=Gigantactidae = Gigactinidae.) Dlinnoshchupye.

Lit. J : (243); N : 598; G : 172; GRWM : 397, 416; MA : 163; Waterman, 1948 : 81—149; Bertelsen, 1951 : 1— 276; Maul, 1962 : 33 — 46.

Deep oceanic waters. 2 genera, several species.

Family 491. **Neoceratiidae** 599/613, thesis 61—11. Figure 973. (Ceratiidae ex parte.)

Lit. J: (243); N: 598; G: 173; GRWM: 397, 416; MA: 163; Bertelsen, 1951: 1—276.

Deep oceanic waters. 1 genus, several species.

Family 492. **Ceratiidae** 600/614, thesis 61—17. Figure 976. Sea devils, mitsukuri enago chogin anko ka.

Lit. J: 243; N: 598; G: 172; GRWM: 397, 416; MA: 162; Jörgense, 1920: 1—110; Barbour, 1942: 77—86; Clarke, 1950: 1—32; Bertelsen, 1951: 1—276; Maul, 1962: 5—27; Weber and Beaufort, 1962, 11: 256—258.

Deep oceanic waters. 2 genera, a considerable number of species.

Family 493. **Caulophrynidae** 601/615, thesis 61—13. Figure 974.

Lit. J: 243; N: 599; G: 172; GRWM: 397, 416; MA: 161; Bertelsen, 1951: 1—276.

Deep oceanic waters. 1 genus, several species.

Family 494. **Linophrynidae** 603/617, thesis 61—29. Figures 982, 983. (+Aceratiidae, + Photocorhynidae 602/616, Himantolophidae ex parte.) Oni anko ka.

Lit. J: (243); N: 599; G: 173; GRWM: 397, 416; MA: 163; Bertelsen, 1951: 1—276; Maul, 1961: 87—151; 1962: 33—46; Weber and Beaufort, 1962, 11: 259—261.

Deep oceanic waters. 5 genera, a considerable number of species.

Order 62. PEGASIFORMES 114/119, thesis 0—39. (Pegasoidei, Hypostomides.) Berg, 1940: 344 (GRWM: 399); MA: 166; Jordan and Snyder, 1901: 1—20; Jungersen, 1915: 420—422; Weber and Beaufort, 1962, 11: 178—183. 1 family (495).

Family 495. **Pegasidae** 604/618, thesis 62—0. Figure 985. Pegasus-dragons, sea moths, seadragons, morskie moli, haie k'o, umi tengu ka.

Lit. J: 175; N: 518; G: 165; GRWM: 399, 424; MA: 168; Rendahl, 1930: 1—56; Weber and Beaufort, 1962, 11: 179—184.

Indian and Pacific oceans. 1 genus.

BIBLIOGRAPHY

For the convenience of the reader three separate lists of reference works are given.

1) The works on systematics are presented in an alphabetical list of publications mentioned in the sources given in the section "Checklist of Families." The works are given in chronological order for each author, first by himself and then in collaboration with others.

2) The general literature contains works not included in the other lists. They deal with the system and phylogeny of the fishes as a whole or of other larger systematic categories, and surveys of freshwater and marine aquarium fishes of the world. Various types of handbooks are also included.

3) The regional literature is a list of monographs, surveys, summaries, and catalogues on the fish faunas of different oceans, continents, seas, and countries.

The works on systematics comprise in the main literature published after 1917. The earlier publications included are those which are mentioned in the legends to the figures (Bleeker, Bloch, Day, Goode and Bean, Günther, Jordan and Evermann, Jordan, Tanaka and Snyder, Kner, Ogilby, Quoy and Gaimard, Richardson, Smith and Radcliffe, Waite) plus some works by eminent ichthyologists (Berg, Boulenger, Eigenmann, Garman, Gill, Jordan et al., Regan). In addition, works are presented by ichthyologists who have studied larger systematic categories higher than the family.

WORKS ON SYSTEMATICS

Abe, T. Taxonomic Studies on the Puffers (Tetraodontidae, Teleostei) from Japan and Adjacent Regions. V. Synopsis of the Puffers from Japan and Adjacent Regions. — Bull. Biogeogr. Soc. Japan, Nos. 14(13): 89—140. 1949. 11 pls.

Abe, T. Taxonomic Studies on the Puffers (Tetraodontidae, Teleostei) from Japan and Adjacent Regions. VII. Concluding Remarks, with the Introduction of Two New Genera, Fugu and Boesemanichthys. — Jap. J. Ichthyol., 2:35—54, 93—97, 117—127. 1952.

Abe, T. New, Rare or Uncommon Fishes from Japanese Waters. II. Records of Rare Fishes of the Families Diretmidae, Luvaridae, and Tetragonuridae, with an Appendix. — Ibid., 3:39—47, figs. 1—7, 543—549. 1953.

Abe, T. Taxonomic Studies on the Puffers from Japan and Adjacent Regions. Corrigenda and Addenda. Pt. 1. — Ibid., 3:121—128. 1954.

Abe, T. New, Rare or Uncommon Fishes from Japanese Waters. IV. Records of Rare Fishes of the Families Lophotidae, Nomeidae and Icosteidae. — Ibid., 3:90—94, figs. 1—3. 1954.

Abe, T. New, Rare or Uncommon Fishes from Japanese Waters. V. Notes on the Rare Fishes of the Suborders Stromateoidei and Tetragonuroidei (Berg). — Ibid., 3:170, 178, 192, 222, 246, 255. 1954.

Abe, T. Notes on the Adult of Cubiceps gracilis from the Western Pacific. — J. Oceanogr. Soc. Japan, 11, No. 2: 75—80. 1955.

Abe, T. Figures and Descriptions of the Fishes of Japan, 55: 1120—1127. 1956.

Abe, T. Notes on Fishes from the Stomachs of Whales in the Antarctic. I. Xenocyttus nemotoi, a New Genus and New Species of Zeomorph Fish of the Subfamily Oreosominae Goode et Bean, 1895. — Scient. Rep. Whales Res. Inst., Tokyo, 12:225—233. 1957. 2 pls.

Abe, T. On the Presence of at Least Two Species of Cubiceps (Nomeidae, Pisces) in the Path of the "Kuro-shiwo." — Rec. Oceanogr. Wks. Japan, No. 3: 225—229. 1959.

Abe, T. Taxonomic Studies on the Puffers from Japan and Adjacent Regions. Corrigenda and Addenda. II. Jap. J. Ichthyol., 8, No. 1:3—6, figs. 1—7. 1960.

Abe, T. Notes on Some Fishes of the Subfamily Braminae, with the Introduction of a New Genus Pseudotaractes. — Ibid., 8, Nos. 3—4:92—99. 1961. 13 figs; Nos. 5—6:101—110. 1961. 31 figs.

A b e, T. and H. Hotta. Description of a New Deep-sea Fish of the Genus Rondeletia from Japan.— Ibid., 10:43—48. 1963. 1 pl., 7 figs.

A b e, T. and K. Maruyama. A Record of Barbourisia rufa Parr from off the Kurile Islands.— Ibid., 10:49—50. 1963.

A b r a h a m, D. S. Bottom Fishes Collected by the Research Vessel "Conch" off the Kerala Coast during 1958—1963. Heterosomata.— Bull. Dept. Mar. Biol. Oceanogr. Univ. Kerala, 1:57—80. 1963. 3 figs.

A d a m, H. and R. Strahan. Systematics and Geographical Distribution of Myxynoids. The Biology of Myxine, pp. 1—8. Oslo. 1963.

A g c o, A. G. Philippine Coryphaenidae.— Philipp. J. Sci., 72:313—315. 1940. 1 pl.

A h l, E. Zur Kenntnis der Knochenfischfamilie Chaetodontidae insbesondere der Unterfamilie Chaetodontinae.— Arch. Naturgesch., 89, Abt. A, 5:1—205, pls. I, II. 1923.

A h l, E. Beitrage zur Systematik der afrikanischen Zahnkarpfen.— Zool. Anz., 79:113—123. 1928. 9 figs.

A h l s t r o m, E. H. and R. C. Counts. Development and Distribution of Vinciguerria lucetia and Related Species in the Eastern Pacific.— Fishery Bull. Fish Wildl. Serv. U. S., 58, No. 139:363—416. 1958.

A k a z a k i, M. Studies on the Orbital Bones of Sparoid Fishes.— Zool. Mag., Tokyo, 67:322—325. 1958. 1 fig. (English summary.)

A k a z a k i, M. Comparative Morphology of Pentapodid Fishes.— Ibid., 68:373—377. 1959. 2 figs.

A k a z a k i, M. Results of the Amami Islands Expedition. 4. On a New Sparoid Fish, Gymnocranius japonicus with Special Reference to its Taxonomic Status.— Copeia, 4:437—441. 1961. 2 figs.

A k a z a k i, M. Studies on the Spariform Fishes—Anatomy, Phylogeny, Ecology and Taxonomy.— Spec. Rep. Misaki Mar. Biol. Inst., Kyoto Univ., pp. 1—327 (in Japanese), pp. 328—368 (English summary). 1962. 58 figs.

A k s i r a y, F. Turkische Cyprinodontiden. I.— Revue Fac. Sci. Univer. d'Istanbul, 13B:97—138. 1948, 4 pls., 23 text-figs.

A k s i r a y, F. Über türkische Cyprinodontiden. II.— Ibid., 13B:280—310. 1948. 4 pls., 31 text-figs.

A l e e v, Yu. G. Horsemackerels (Trachurus) of the Seas of the USSR. Author's Summary of Candidate Thesis.— Zool. Inst. Acad. Sci., USSR (AN SSSR), pp. 3—12. Leningrad. 1954.

A l e e v, Yu. G. Horsemackerels (Trachurus) of the Seas of the USSR.— Trudy Sevastop. Biol. St., 9:1—137. 1957. ill.

A l e k s a n d r o v, A. I. Anchovies of the Azov-Black Sea Basin, their Origin, and Systematics.— Trudy Kerchensk. Nauch. Rybokhoz. Sta., 1, Nos. 2—3:37—92. 1927.

A l e x a n d e r, R. The Structure of the Weberian Apparatus in the Cyprini.— Proc. Zool. Soc. Lond., 139, No. 3:451—473. 1962. 1 pl., 9 text-figs.

A l e x a n d e r, R. Mechanisms of the Jaws of Some Atheriniform Fishes.— J. Zool. Res., 151:233—255. 1967. 10 figs.

A l f r e d, E. R. Notes on a Reexamination of Some Bleeker Type Specimens of Indo-Malayan Freshwater Fishes. Part 1. Cobitidae and Homalopteridae.— Bull. Natn. Mus. St. Singapore, 30:32—37. 1961.

A l i z o v a, N. A. Gobiidae of the Caspian Sea. Author's Summary of Candidate Thesis, pp. 1—22. Kaliningrad. 1965.

A l l i s, E. P. The Cranial Anatomy of the Mailcheeked Fishes.— Zoologica, Stuttg., 57:1—219. 1909. 8 pls.

A l o n c l e, H. Les sparides des côtes atlantiques du Maroc. 2.— Bull. Inst. Pêch. marit. Maroc., 14:55—66. 1966.

A l v a r e z, J. Revision del genero Anoptichthys con descripcion de una especie nueva (Pisces, Characidae).— An. Esc. nac. Cienc. biol., Mex., 4:263—282. 1945.

A l v e r s o n, D. L. and A. D. Welander. Notes on the Scorpaenid Fishes of Washington and Adjacent Areas with a Key for their Identification.— Copeia, 3:138—143. 1952. 2 text-figs.

A l v e r s o n, D. L. and L. J. Westrheim. A Review of the Taxonomy and Biology of the Pacific Ocean Perch and its Biology.— Intern. Comm. North. West. Atl. Fisher., Ser. 679, Contr. A-3, pp. 12—27. 1959.

A m a o k a, K. A Revision of the Flatfish Referable to the Genus Psettina Found in the Waters around Japan.— Bull. Misaki Mar. Biol. Inst., Kyoto Univ., 4:53—62. 1963. ill.

A m a o k a, K. A Revision of the Flatfishes Referable to the Genus Engyprosopon Found in the Waters around Japan.— Ibid., pp. 107—121.

A m a r a l Campos, A. Sobre os Caracidios do Rio Mogi-guacu (Estado de São Paulo).— Archos. Zool. Est. S Paulo, 4:431—466. 1945. 3pls.

Amaral Campos, A. Sobre a subfamilia Bryconinae especies existentes na coleçao de peixes do departamento de zoologia de São Paulo. — Papéis Dep. Zool. S Paulo, 9:137—143. 1950. 1 text-fig.

Ambroz, A.I. Acipenseridae of the Northwestern Part of the Black Sea. — Trudy Vses. Nauchno-Issled. Inst. Morsk. Ryb. Khoz. Okeanogr., 52:287—347. 1964. 12 figs.

Ambroz, A.I. Some Results of Investigations of Acipenseridae from the Black Sea, Dnieper River, Southern Bug and their Estuaries. — Reports of Thesis for the Degree of Doctor of Biological Sciences (according to a series of works), pp. 1—45. Kishinev. 1966.

Ancona, U. de. Murenoidi (Apodes) del Mar Rosso e del Golfo di Aden. — Memorie R. Com. talassogr. ital., 146:1—146. 1928. 5 pls.

Ancona, U. de. Ordine: Synentognathi. In uova, larve e stadi giovanili di Teleostei, Fauna e Flora del Golfo di Napoli. — Pubbl. Staz. zool. Napoli, 38:157—177, figs. 160—166, pls. 8—11. 1931.

Ancona, U. de. Heteromi, Apodes, Synentognathi et Gadidae. Fauna e Flora del Golfo di Napoli. — Ibid., pp. 1—21, 94—225, 280—306.

Ancona, U. de. Le specie mediterranee del genre Syngnathus. — Memorie R. Com. talassogr. ital., 210:3—77. 1934. 3 pls., 40 figs.

Ancona, U. de and G. Cavinato. The Fishes of the Family Bregmaceratidae. — Dana Rep., 64:1—92. 1965. ill.

Andersen, K. P. Classification of Ipnopidae by Means of Principal Components and Discriminant Functions. (Scient. results Danish deep-sea expedit. round the world 1950—1952.) — Galathea Rep., 8:77—90. 1966.

Anderson, W. W., J. W. Gehringer, and F. H. Berry. Family Synodontidae. — In: Fishes W. N. Atlantic. 5. Mem. Sears Found. Mar. Res., No. 1(5): 1—647, ex parte. 1966.

Andrews, A. C. The Codfishes of the Greeks and Romans. — J. Wash. Acad. Sci., 1, No. 39:1—16. 1949.

Andriašev, A. P. Übersicht der Gattung Stelgistrum Jordan et Gilbert (Pisces, Cottidae) nebst Beschreibung einer neuen Art aus dem Beringmeer. — Zool. Anz., 3, Nos. 11/12:289—297. 1935. ill.

Andriashev, A. P. Neue Angaben über die Systematik und geographische Verbreitung der zweihornigen pazifischen Icelus Arten. — Zool. Jber. Neapel, Seet. Syst. Ökol. und Geogr. der Tiere, 69, No. 4:253—276. 1937. ill.

Andriashev, A. P. Observations on the Eellike Lycodids (Lycenchelys Gill) (Pisces, Zoarcidae) and Related Forms in the Seas of the USSR and Neighbouring Waters. — Transl. Ser. Fish. Res. Bd. Canada, 278:1—4. 1960.

Andriyashev, A. P. Survey on the Zoogeography and Origin of the Fish Fauna of the Bering Sea and Adjacent Waters, pp. 1—187 (76). Leningrad State University (LGU). 1939.

Andriyashev, A. P. The Specific Composition and Distribution of Gobies of the Genus Triglops Reinh. in the Northern Seas. — Trudy Vses. Gidrobiol. Obshch., 1:194—209. 1949.

Andriyashev, A. P. A New Fish for the Fauna of the USSR, Erilepis zonifer (Lock.), Pisces, Anoplopomidae from Kamchatka Waters of the Pacific Ocean. — Vopr. Ikhtiol., 4:3—9. 1955.

Andriyashev, A. P. New and Rare Species of Eelpouts (Zoarcidae) from the Southeastern Shore of Kamchatka. — Ibid., 21:393—400. 1955.

Andriyashev, A. P. Supplement to the Survey of Lycenchelys Gill, with a Description of Three New Species from the Kurile-Kamchatka Trench. — Vopr. Ikhtiol., 11:171—180. 1958.

Andriyashev, A. P. New Families of Fish for the Antarctic. Communication 2. Pearleyes (Pisces, Scopelarchidae). — Zool. Zh., 39, No. 4:563—566. 1960.

Andriyashev, A. P. Survey of Hookear Sculpins of the Genus Artediellus Jord. (Pisces, Cottidae) of the Bering Sea. — Vopr. Ikhtiol., 1, No. 2(19):231—241. 1961. ill.

Andriyashev, A. P. Bathypelagic Fishes of the Antarctic. 1. Family Myctophidae. — Issled. Fauny Morei, 1(IX): 216—294. 1962. 36 figs.

Andriyashev, A. P. On the Systematic Position of the Giant Nototheniid (Pisces, Nototheniidae) from McMurdo Sound (Antarctica). — Zool. Zh., 41, No. 7:1048—1050. 1962.

Andriyashev, A. P. Fishes of the Northern Seas of the USSR, pp. 1—617. — Israel Prog. Sci. Transl., Jerusalem. 1964.

Andriyashev, A. P. A Survey of Fish of the Genus Pogonophryne Regan (Pisces, Harpagiferidae) with a Description of 5 New Species from the Eastern Antarctic and South Orkney Islands. — Issled. Fauny Morei, 12:389—419. 1967. ill.

Andriyashev, A. P. and V. M. Makushok. Azygopterus corallinus (Pisces, Blennioidei), a New Fish without Paired Fins. — Vopr. Ikhtiol., 3:50—53, figs. 1—2. 1955.

Annandale, N. Report on the Fishes Taken by the Bengal Fisheries Steamer "Golden Crown." 1. Batoidei. — Mem. Indian Mus., 2, No. 1:1—60, pls. 1—5. 1909.

Annandale, N. Fish and Fisheries of the Inle Lake. — Rec. Indian Mus., 14:33—64. 1918. 7 pls.

Annandale, N. The classification of the Siluroid Fishes Belonging to the Genus Glyptosternum and Allied Genera. — Ann. Mag. Nat. Hist., 9, No. 12:573—577. 1923. 4 figs.

Annandale, N. and S. L. Hora. The Systematic Position of the Burmese Fish Chaudhuria. — Ibid., 9, No. 11:327—333. 1923. 4 figs.

Annandale, N. and J. T. Jenkins. Report on the Fishes Taken by the Bengal Fisheries Steamer "Golden Crown." 3. Plectognathi and Pediculati. — Mem. Indian Mus., 3, No. 1:1—21, pls. 1—3. 1910.

Aoyagi, H. The Damsel Fishes Found in the Waters of Japan. — Proc. Biogeogr. Soc. Japan, 4, No. 1:157—279. 1941.

Aoyagi, H. The Fishes of the Family Pseudochromidae Found in the Waters of the Riu-Kiu Islands and the Palau Islands. — Annotnes zool. jap., 20, No. 1:41—54, figs. 1—5, pl. 4. 1941.

Aoyagi, H. Studies on the Coral Fishes of the Riu-Kiu Islands. VIII. Gobiesocidae, Limnichthidae, Callionymidae, Parapercidae, Brotulidae, Bothidae and Soleidae. — Zool. Mag., Tokyo, 63, No. 6:238. 1954.

Aoyagi, H. Additional Notes on the New and Rare Fishes of the Family Blenniidae from the Riu-Kiu Islands. — Ibid., pp. 239—242.

Aoyagi, H. Studies on the Coral Fishes of the Riu-Kiu Islands. IX. Blenniidae (1). — Ibid., 63, No. 7:278—287. 1954.

Aoyagi, H. Studies on the Coral Fishes of the Riu-Kiu Islands. X. Blenniidae. — Ibid., 64, No. 3:76—83. 1955. ill.

Apsangikar, D. K. The Systematic Position of Stromateus niger. — J. Univ. Bombay, n. ser. 21B, No. 5:41—50. 1953. 32 figs.

Araga, C. Soldier Fishes from Tanaba Bay and Adjacent Regions (Berycida, Holocentridae). — Publs. Seto Mar. Biol. Lab., 12, No. 4:307—321. 1964. ill.

Arambourg, C. A. and L. Bertin. Super-ordres des Holostéens et des Halécostomes. — Traité Zool., 13, No. 3:2173—2203, figs. 1536—1560. 1958.

Arambourg, C. and J. Guibé. Sous-classe des Dipneustes. — Ibid., 13, No. 2:2522—2540. 1958.

Arbocco, G. Morfologia, biologia e sistematica dei Phallostethiformes (Pisces). — Natura, Milano, 47:51—60. 1956. 3 figs.

Arnold, D. C. A Systematic Revision of the Teleost Family Carapidae (Percomorphi, Blennioidei) with Description of Two New Species. — Bull. Br. Mus. Nat. Hist., 4, No. 6:245—307. 1956. 20 figs.

Arnov, B. A Preliminary Review of the Western North Atlantic Fishes of the Genus Haemulon. — Bull. Mar. Sci. Gulf Caribb., 2, No. 2:414—437. 1952.

Asano, H. Studies on the Congrid Eels of Japan. — Bull. Misaki Mar. Biol. Inst., Kyoto Univ., 1:1—143, figs. 1—62. 1962.

Asano, H. and O. Okamura. A New Gurnard of the Genus Pterygotrigla from Tonking Bay. — Ibid., 4:49—52. 1963. 1 fig.

Auberton, S. C. Morphologie du crâne de Cromeria nilotica occidentalis Daget, 1954. — Bull. l'Inst. Afr. Noire, 23, Ser. A, 1:131—164. 1961. 14 figs.

Aubrey, J. D. de. Preliminary Guide to the Sharks off the East Coast of South Africa. — Invest. Rep. Oceanogr. Res. Inst., 8:1—95. 1964. 28 pls., 22 figs.

Aubrey, J. D. de. Preliminary Guide to the Sharks Found off the Coast of South Africa. — Intern. Ind. Ocean Exped., UNESCO. Collected Reprints, 3:161—255. 1966.

Aurich, H. Die Phallostethiden. — Int. Revue ges. Hydrobiol. Hydrogr., 36:263—286. 1937.

Aurich, H. J. Die Gobiiden (Ordnung Gobioidea). Mitteilung XXVIII der Wallacea-Expedition Woltereck. — Int. Revue ges. Hydrobiol. Hydrogr., 38:125—188. 1938. 28 text-figs.

Babayan, K. E. Mullets, pp. 1—131. Moscow. 1965.

Babushkin, N. Ya. Systematics of the Caspian Beluga. — Izv. Azerb. Nauchno-Issled. Rybokhoz. Sta., 7:115—131. 1942.

Babushkin, N. Ya. and M. P. Borzenko. Acipenseridae of the Caspian Sea, pp. 1—67. — Moscow, Pishchepromizdat. 1951.

Băčescu, M. C. Données nouvelles sur les loches (Cobitis) d'Europe avec des références spéciales, sur les Cagnettes de l'Italia de Nord. — Trav. Mus. hist. Nat. "Gr. Antipa," 3:281—301. 1962. 4 pls., 4 figs.

Bailey, R. J. The Relationships of the Phallostethid Fishes. — Proc. S. Dak. Acad. Sci., 16:69—74. 1936.

Bailey, R. J. The Osteology and Relationships of the Phallosthethid Fishes. — J. Morph., 59, No. 3:453—483. 1936.

Bailey, R.M. Forty-five Articles on Recent Fishes in Encyclop. Sci. Technol. McGraw-Hill Co., pp. 1-21. New York. 1960. ill.

Bailey, R.M. and F.B. Cross. River Sturgeons of the American Genus Scaphirhynchus: Characters, Distribution, and Synonymy. - Pap. Mich. Acad. Sci., 39:169-208. 1954.

Bailey, R.M. and W.A. Gosline. Variation and Systematic Significance of Vertebral Counts in the American Fishes of the Family Percidae. — Misc. Publs. Mus. Zool. Univ.Mich., 23:1—44. 1955. ill.

Baimov, U. The Species Composition and Population of Caspian Gobies in the Aral Sea. — Vestn. Karakalp. Fil. Akad. Nauk UzSSR, 3:11—16. 1961.

Bal, D.V. and K.H. Mohmed. A Systematic Account of the Eels of Bombay. — J. Bombay Nat. Hist. Soc., 54; No. 3:372—740. 1957. ill.

Bănărescu, P. Weitere systematische Studien über die Gattung Gobio (Pisces, Cyprinidae), insbesondere im Donaubecken. — Věst. čsl. Spol. zool., 25:318—346. 1961. 4 pls., 2 figs.

Bănărescu, P. Phylletische Beziehungen der Arten und Artbildung bei der Gattung Gobio (Pisces, Cyprinidae). — Ibid., 26:38—64. 1962.

Bănărescu, P. Révision du genre Toxabramis Günther (Pisces, Cyprinidae). — Bull. Mus. natn. Hist. nat., Paris, Ser. 2, 35, No. 5:457—463. 1963.

Bănărescu, P. Revizuirea genului Pseudolaubuca Bleeker, 1864, Parapelecus Günther, 1889 (Pisces, Cyprinidae). — Studii Cerc. Biol., Ser. Zool., 16, No. 2:87—98. 1889. ill.

Bănărescu, P. and T.T. Nalbant. Süsswasserfische der Türkei. Part 2. Cobitidae. — Mitt. Hamb. zool. Mus. Inst., 61:159—201. 1963. 4 pls. 2 maps.

Bănărescu, P. and T.T. Nalbant. Studies on the Systematics of Gobioinae (Pisces, Cyprinidae). — Revue roum. Biol., Ser. Zool., 10, No. 4:219—229, figs. 1—9. 1965.

Bănărescu, P. and T.T. Nalbant. Revision of Pseudogobio (Pisces, Cyprinidae) with Notes on Related Genera. — Ibid., 10, No. 5:301—308, figs. 1—4. 1965.

Bănărescu, P. and T.T. Nalbant. Revision of the Genus Microphysogobio (Pisces, Cyprinidae). — Věst. čsl. Spol. zool., 30, No. 3:194—209. 1966. ill.

Barach, G.P. Data on the Systematics of Trout from Transcaucasia. — Izv. Gruzinsk. Muzeya, 9A:50—79. Tbilisi. 1938.

Barbour, T. Notes on Pediculate Fishes. — Proc. New Engl. Zool. Club, 19:7—14. 1941. 6 figs.

Barbour, T. The Northwestern Atlantic Species of Frog Fishes. — Ibid., 19:21—40, pls. VIII—XVII. 1942.

Barbour, T. More Concerning Ceratioid Fishes. — Ibid., 21:77—86, pls. IX—XV. 1942.

Barlow, G.W., K.F. Liem, and W. Wickler. Badidae, a New Fish Family — Behavioral, Osteological, and Developmental Evidence. — J. Zool. Res., 156, No. 4:415—447. 1968. 17 figs., 2 pls.

Barnard, K.H. Further Notes on South African Marine Fishes. — Ann. S. Afr. Mus., 36, No. 5:341—406, figs. 1—17, pls. 9—13. 1948.

Barnhart, P.S. Pocket Natural History. Sharks of Southern California. — La Jolla, Cal.: 1—VI + 1—23. 1944.

Barsukov, V.V. A Survey of the Wolffishes (Family Anarhichadidae), pp. 1—15. Author's Summary of Candidate Thesis. Leningrad. 1953.

Barsukov, V.V. Fauna of the USSR. Fishes. 5.5. Family Anarhichadidae, pp. 1—171, figs. 1—42, pls. 1—XXII. — Moscow-Leningrad, Akad. Nauk SSSR. 1959.

Barsukov, V.V. Systematics of the Chukchi Chars of the Genus Salvelinus. — Vopr. Ikhtiol., 14:3—17, figs. 1—5. 1960.

Barsukov, V.V. Key to the Family Scorpaenidae. — Trudy Vses. Nauchno-Issled. Inst. Morsk. Ryb. Khoz. Okeanogr., 53:233—266. 1964.

Bauchot, M.L. Etude des larves léptocephales du groupe Leptocephalus lanceolatus Stromman et identification à la famille des Serrivomeridae. — Dana Rep., 48:1—148. 1959. 2 pls., 105 text-figs.

Bauchot, M.L. Catalogue critique des types de Poissons du Muséum National d'Histoire Naturelle. Famille des Siganidae (Poissons Téléostéens, Perciformes). — Bull. Mus. natn. Hist. nat., Paris, Sér. 2, 36, No. 5:570—577. 1964.

Bauchot, M.L. Poissons marins de l'Est Atlantique tropical. Téléostéens, Perciformes, Blennioidei. — Atlantide Rep., 9:63—91. 1966. ill.

Bauchot, M.L. Poissons marins de l'Est Atlantique tropical (Téléostéens, Perciformes). II. Percoidei (3-ème partie). III. Acanturoidei. IV. Balistoidei. (Scient. results Danish exped. coast of tropical West Africa 1945—1946.) — Ibid., pp. 7—43.

Bauchot, M.L. and M. Blanc. Poissons marins de l'Est Atlantique tropical. I. Labroidei; II. Percoidei (Téléostéens Perciformes) 1-ème partie. — Ibid., 6:43—100. 1961. 1 pl., 10 figs.

Bauchot, M.L. and M. Blanc. Catalogue des types de Scombroidei (Poissons, Téléostéens, Perciformes) des collections du Muséum d'Histoire Naturelle. — Bull. Mus. natn. Hist. nat., Paris, Ser. 2, 33, No. 4:369—379. 1961.

Bauchot, M.L. and M. Blanc. Poissons marins de l'Est Atlantique tropical. II. Percoidei (Téléostéens, Perciformes). 2-ème partie. — Atlantide Rep., 7:37—59. 1963.

Bauchot, M.L. and J. Guibé. Catalogue des types de poissons du Muséum National d'Histoire Naturelle. Famille des Scaridae. — Bull. Mus. natn. Hist. nat., Paris, Sér. 2, 32, No. 4:290—300. 1960.

Bauchot, M.L. and R. Les Crenilabres des côtes atlantiques françaises. (Téléostéens, Perciformes, Labridae). — Ibid., Ser. 2, 33: 84—97. 1961. 3 figs.

Baughman, J.Z. Scombriformes, New, Rare or Little Known in Texas Waters, with Notes on their Natural History or Distribution. — Trans. Tex. Acad. Sci., 24:14—26. 1941.

Baughman, J.Z. The Lutianid Fishes of Texas. — Copeia, 4:212–215. 1943.

Bazikalova, A.Ya., T.N. Kallinikova, V.S. Mikhin, and D.N. Taliev. Data for a Study of Gobies from Lake Baikal. — Trudy Baikal. Limnol. Sta., 7:109–211. 1037.

Bean, B.A. and A.C. Weed. A Review of Venomous Toadfishes. — Proc. U. S. Natn. Mus., 38:511—526. 1910. 4 pls., 8 figs.

Beaufort, L.F. de. Die Anatomie und systematische Stellung des Genus Kurtus Bloch. — Morph. Jb., 48:391—410, pl. 12, 1914. 3 text-figs.

Beaufort, L.F. de. — In: Weber, M. and L.F. de Beaufort. The Fishes of the Indo-Australian Archipelago. VIII. Percomorphi (continued): Cirrhitoidea, Labriformes, Pomacentriformes, pp. 1—508. 1940. 56 figs.

Beaufort, L.F. de. On a New Genus of Fishes of the Family Creediidae from South Africa with Remarks on its Geographical Distribution. — Trans. R. Soc. S. Afr., 31:475—478. 1948. 1 text-fig.

Beaufort, L.F. de. A New Generic Name for the Scleropareid Fish Cocotropus de Zwaani from the Indian Ocean. — Copeia, 3:44—45. 1952.

Beaufort, L.F. de and J.C. Briggs. — In: Weber, M. and L.F. de Beaufort. The Fishes of the Indo-Australian Archipelago. XI. Scleroparei, Hypostomides, Pediculati, Plectognathi, Opisthomi, Discocephali, Xenopterygii, pp. 1–481. 1962. 100 figs.

Beaufort, L.F. de and W.M. Chapman. — In: Weber, M. and L.F. de Beaufort. The Fishes of the Indo-Australian Archipelago. IX. Percomorphi (concluded), Blennioidei, pp. 1—484. 1951. 89 figs.

Beebe, W. Nineteen New Species and Four Post-larval Deep-sea Fish. — Zoologica, N. Y., 13:47—107, figs. 8—31. 1932.

Beebe, W. New Data on the Deep-sea Fish Stylophthalmus and Idiacanthus. — Science, N.Y., 78, No. 2026:390. 1933.

Beebe, W. Deep-sea Stomiatoid Fishes, One New Genus and Eight New Species. — Copeia, 4:160—175. 1933. 8 figs.

Beebe, W. Deep-sea Isospondylous Fishes. Two New Genera and Four New Species. — Zoologica, N. Y., 13:159—167, figs. 39—42. 1933.

Beebe, N.W. Deep-sea Fishes of the Bermuda Oceanographic Expeditions. 1. Family Alepocephalidae. 2. Argentinidae. — Ibid., 16:1—147. 1933. 46 figs.

Beebe, W. Deep-sea Fishes of the Bermuda Oceanographic Expeditions. Family Idiacanthidae. — Ibid., 16:149—241, figs. 47—81. 1934.

Beebe, W. Deep-sea Fishes of the Bermuda Oceanographic Expeditions. Family Derichthyidae. — Ibid., 20:1—23, figs. 1—9. 1935.

Beebe, W. Deep-sea Fishes of the Bermuda Oceanographic Expeditions. Family Nessorhamphidae.— Ibid., 20:25—51, figs. 10—22. 1935, 1936.

Beebe, W. and J. Crane. Deep-sea Fishes of the Bermuda Oceanographic Expeditions. Family Serrivomeridae, Part 1. Genus Serrivomer. — Ibid., 20: 54—102, figs. 23—42. 1936.

Beebe, W. and J. Crane. Deep-sea Fishes of the Bermuda Oceanographic Expeditions. Family Serrivomeridae. Part II. Genus Platuronides. — Ibid., 22:331—348. 1937. 14 text-figs.

Beebe, W. and J. Crane. Deep-sea Fishes of the Bermuda Oceanographic Expeditions. Family Nemichthyidae. — Ibid., 22:349—383. 1937. 22 figs.

Beebe, W. and J. Crane. Deep-sea Fishes of the Bermuda Oceanographic Expeditions. Family Malanostomiatidae. — Ibid., 24:65—238. 1939. 77 text-figs.

Beebe, W. and J. Crane. Eastern Pacific Expedition of the New York Zoological Society. 37. Deep-sea Ceratioid Fishes. — Ibid., 31:151—182. 1947. ill.

Beebe, W. and M.V. Pyl. Eastern Pacific Expeditions of the New York Zoological Society. XXXIII. Pacific Myctophidae (Fishes). — Ibid., 29:59—95, figs. 1—24. 1944.

Beebe, W. and J. Tee-Van. Eastern Pacific Expedition of the New York Zoological Society. XXV. Fishes from the Tropical Eastern Pacific from Cedros Island, Lower California, South to the Galapagos Islands and Northern Peru. Part 2. Sharks. — Ibid., 26:93—122, figs. 1—34, pls. 1—2. 1941.

Beebe, W. and J. Tee-Van. Eastern Pacific Expedition of the New York Zoological Society. XXVIII. Fishes from the Tropical Eastern Pacific, from Cedros Island, Lower California, South to the Galapagos Islands and Northern Peru. Part 3. Rays, Mantas and Chimaeras. — Ibid., 26:245—280, figs. 1—40, pls. 1—4. 1941.

Behnke, R.J. A Systematic Study of the Family Salmonidae with Special Reference to the Genus Salmo.— Diss. Abstr., 26:1224. 1965.

Bekker, V.E. New Data on the Lanternfishes Electrona and Protomyctophum (Pisces, Myctophidae) of the Southern Hemisphere. — Vopr. Ikhtiol., 3, No. 1 (26):15—28. 1963.

Bekker, V.E. Systematics and Distribution of Tarletonbeania crenularis (Myctophidae Pisces). Biological Investigations of the Sea (Fishes). — Trudy Inst. Okeanol., Akad. Nauk SSSR, 62:145—163. 1963. 2 figs.

Bekker, V.E. North Pacific Species of the Genus Protomyctophum (Myctophidae, Pisces). Biological Investigations of the Sea (Fishes). — Trudy Inst. Okeanol., Akad. Nauk SSSR, 62:164—191. 1963. 8 figs.

Bekker, V.E. Lanternfishes of the Genera Loweina, Tarletonbeania, Gonichthys, and Centrobranchus from the Pacific and Indian Oceans. — Ibid., 73:11—75. 1964.

Bekker, V.E. Fishes of the Indian Ocean and Southeastern Seas. Luminescent Pelagic Fishes of the Genus Hygophum (Myctophidae, Pisces). Systematics and Distribution. — Trudy Inst. Okeanol., Akad. Nauk SSSR, 80:62—103. 1965.

Bekker, V.E. Lanternfishes (Family Myctophidae). — In: Tikhii okean, biologiya, No. 3. Ryby otkrytykh vod, pp. 145—181. Moscow, "Nauka." 1967.

Bekker, V.E. Lanternfishes (Family Myctophidae) from the Collections of Three Atlantic Expeditions of the "Petr Lebedev" in 1961—1964. — Trudy Inst. Okeanol., Akad. Nauk SSSR, 84:84—124, figs. 1—13. 1967.

Bekker, V.E. New Data on Mesopelagic Fishes of the Genus Opisthoproctus Vaillant. — Vopr. Ikhtiol., 8, No. 2 (49): 241—246. 1968.

Bekker, V.E. and O.D. Borodulina. Lanternfishes of the Genus Ceratoscopelus Günther. Systematics and Distribution. — Vopr. Ikhtiol., 8, No. 5 (52):779—798. 1968. 5 figs.

Bell, F.H. and J.T. Charrett. The Pacific Coast Black Cod, Anoplopoma fimbria.— Copeia, 2:94—103, fig. 1. 1945.

Bell, F.H. and J.L. Kask. Lampris regius (Bonnaterre), the Opah or Moonfish from the North Pacific.— Ibid., 1:54—56. 1936.

Bellon, L. and E.B. Dellon. Algunos datos sobre los "Thunnidae" de Canarias. — Boln. Inst. esp. Oceanogr., 19:1—28. 1949. 1 text-fig. (French summary.)

Beneresku, P. and T. Nalbant. On the Systematics and Nomenclature of Gudgeons of the Subfamily Gobioninae (Pisces, Cyprinidae) in the Amur Basin.— Vopr. Ikhtiol., 8, No. 4 (51) :628—636. 1968.

Ben-Tuvia, A. Eels of the Family Heterenchelidae. — Ann. Mag. Nat. Hist., No. (12) 9: 401—408. 1956.

Berezovskii, A.I. On the Classification of the Coregonidae. — Russk. Gidrobiol. Zh., 3, Nos. 11—12: 266—280. Saratov. 1924.

Berg, L.S. Notes on the Systematics of the Baikal Cottidae. — Ezheg. Zool. Muz. Akad. Nauk, 8:99—114. 1903.

Berg, L.S. Zur Systematic der Acipenseriden. — Zool. Anz., 27:665—667. 1904.

Berg, L.S. Osteology of the Baikal Cataphracti. — Trudy S.-Peterb. Obshch. Estest., 37, No. 1:30—32. 1906.

Berg, L.S. Übersicht der Salmoniden vom Amur. — Zool. Anz., 30:395—398. 1906.

Berg, L.S. Übersicht der Cataphracti (Fam. Cottidae, Cottocomephoridae und Comephoridae) des Baikalsees. — Ibid., pp. 906—911.

Berg, L.S. Übersicht der Marsipobranchii des Russischen Reiches. — Izv. Akad. Nauk, 5, No. 24:173—188. 1906.

Berg, L.S. Die Cataphracti des Baikalsees. Beiträge zur Systematik. — Wiss. Ergebn. Zool. Exp. nach dem Baikalsee, 3. St. Petersburg und Berlin, pp. 1—75. 1907. 5 pls.

Berg, L.S. A Review of the Cobitoid Fishes of the Amur Basin. — Proc. U.S. Natn. Mus., 32:435—438. 1907.

Berg, L.S. Vorläufige Bemerkungen über die europäisch-asiatischen Salmoniden, insbesondere über die Gattung Thymallus. — Ezheg. Zool. Muz. Akad. Nauk, 12:500—514. 1907.

Berg, L.S. The Fauna of Russia. Fishes. 1. Marsipobranchii, Selachii and Chondrostei, pp. 1—337, figs. 1—18, 1 map. St. Petersburg. 1911.

Berg, L.S. The Fauna of Russia. Fishes. 3. Ostariophysi, 1:1—336, figs. 1—27, pls. 1—2. St. Petersburg. 1912.

Berg, L.S. The Fauna of Russia. Fishes. 3. Ostariophysi, 2:337—704, figs. 28—139, pls. 3—6. St. Petersburg. 1914.

Berg, L.S. Notes on the Caspian Forms of Benthophilus (Gobiidae). — Sbornik v chest' prof. N.M. Knipovicha, pp. 331—344. Moscow. 1927.

Berg, L.S. Classification of the Order Esociformes. — Izv. Akad. Nauk SSSR, Biol. Ser., 3:461—462. 1931.

Berg, L.S. A Review of the Lampreys of the Northern Hemisphere. — Ezheg. Zool. Muz. Akad. Nauk, 32, No. 1:87—116, pls. 1—8. 1931.

Berg, L.S. A Review of the Freshwater Cottoid Fishes of the Pacific Slope of Asia. — Copeia, 1:17—20. 1932. 4 figs.

Berg, L.S. The Fauna of Russia. Fishes. 3. Ostariophysi. 3:705—846, figs. 40—172. Leningrad. 1933.

Berg, L.S. The Suborder Esocoidei. — Izv. Biol. Nauchno-Issled. Inst. Biol. Sta. Perm. Gosud. Univ., 10:385—388. 1936.

Berg, L.S. A Classification of Fish-like Vertebrates. — Izv. Akad. Nauk SSSR, Biol. Ser., 4:1277–1280. 1937.

Berg, L. S. On Some South China Chars (Cobitidae, Pisces).— Byull. Mosk. Obshch. Ispyt. Prir., otd. biol., 47, Nos. 5–6:314–318. 1938.

Berg, L. S. Lungfishes, or Crossopterygii.— Priroda, 7:82. 1939.

Berg, L. S. Classification of Fishes Both Recent and Fossil.— Trudy Zool. Inst. Akad. Nauk SSSR, 5, No. 2:87–345, 346–500. 1940. (English text), pp. 501–517. (Index), pp. 1–190. 2nd edition, 20:1–286, figs. 1–263. 1955.

Berg, L. S. The Systematic Position of the Polypteridae.— Zool. Zh., 19, No.5:727–740. 1940.

Berg, L. S. The Systematic Position of the Acipenseriformes.—Trudy Zool. Inst. Akad. Nauk SSSR, 7, No.3:7–57. 1948.

Berg, L. S. The Systematic Position of the Saccopharyngiformes.— Dokl. Akad. Nauk SSSR, 59:1353–1355. 1948.

Berg, L. S. Freshwater Fishes of the USSR and Adjacent Countries. 4th edition. 1:1–468, figs. 1–287, Leningrad, Akad. Nauk SSSR. 1948; 2:469–925, figs. 288–674. 1949; 3:929–1382, figs. 675–946, 1 map. 1948, 1949.*

Bergeron, J. Bibliographie du saumon de l'Atlantique (Salmo salar L.).— Contr. Minist. Chasse Pêch., Québec, 88:1–64. 1962.

Berry, F. H. A New Species of Fish from the Western-North Atlantic, Dikellornynchus tropidolepis, and Relationships of the Genera Dikellorhynchus and Malacanthus.— Copeia, 2:116–125. 1958. 13 figs.

Berry, F. H. Boarfishes of the Genus Antigonia of the Western Atlantic.— Bull. Fla. St. Mus., Biol. Sci., 4, No. 7:205–250. 1959. 11 figs.

Berry, F. H. and W. W. Anderson. Stargazer Fishes from the Western-North Atlantic (Family Uranoscopidae). — Proc. U.S. Natn. Mus., 112: 563–586. 1961. 4 pls. 1 fig.

Berry, F. H. and W. J. Baldwin. Triggerfishes (Balistidae) of the Eastern Pacific.— Proc. Calif. Acad. Sci., 4th Ser., 34, No. 9:429–474. 1966.

Berry, F. H. and M. Poll. Synonymy of the Atlantic Ocean Filefish Alutera heudelotii Hollard.— Copeia, 3:360–362. 1961.

Berry, F. H. and L. R. Rivas. Data on Six Species of Needlefishes (Belonidae) from the Western Atlantic.— Copeia, 1:152–160. 1962. 3 figs.

Berry, F. H. and L. E. Vogele. Filefishes (Monacanthidae) of the Western-North Atlantic.— Fish. Bull. U.S., 61:61–109. 1961. 42 figs.

Bertelsen, E. The Ceratioid Fishes. Ontogeny, Taxonomy, Distribution and Biology.— Dana Rep., 39:1–276. 1951. 1 pl., 141 figs.

Bertelsen, E. The Argentinoid Fish Xenophthalmichthys danae.— Dana Rep., 45:1–8. 1958. 6 figs.

* [English translation by IPST, Vol. I, cat. No. 741. 1963. 602 pp.; Vol. II, cat. No. 742. 1964. 504 pp.; Vol. III, cat. No. 743. 1965. 520 pp., col. map.]

Bertelsen, E. and N.B. Marshall. The Miripinnati, a New Order of Teleost Fishes. — Dana Rep., 42: 1–34. 1956. 15 figs., 1 pl.

Bertelsen, E. and N.B. Marshall. Notes on Miripinnati (an Addendum to Dana Rep., No. 42). A Change of Name and Further Records. — Dana Rep., 42, Add. pp. 9–10. 1958. 1 fig.

Bertin, L. Classification, variabilité, distribution géographique des poissons de la famille des Epinoches.— C. r. Ass. fr. Avanc. Sci., 47:519–527. 1924. 5 figs.

Bertin, L. Recherches bionomiques, biométriques et systématiques sur les épinoches (Gastérostéidés). — Annls. Inst. oceanogr., Paris, 2, No. 1:1–204. 1925. 71 figs.

Bertin, L. Les poissons Apodes appartenant au sous-ordre des Lyomères. — Dana Rep., 3:1–56. 1934. 2 pls., 47 text-figs.

Bertin, L. Mise au point de la systématique des poissons abyssaux appartenant aux genres Saccopharynx et Eurypharynx. — Bull. Mus. natn. Hist. nat., Paris, (21), 6(1): 26–31. 1934.

Bertin, L. Un nouveau genre de poissons apodes caractérisé par l'absence de mâchoire supérieure.— Bull. Soc. zool. Fr., 61, No. 7:533–540, figs. 1–4. 1937.

Bertin, L. Les poissons abyssaux du genre Cyema Günther (anatomie, embryologie, bionomie).— Dana Rep., 10:1–30. 1937. 24 figs.

Bertin, L. Formes nouvelles et formes larvaires de poissons Apodes appartenant au sous-ordre des Lyomères. — Dana Rep., 15:1–26. 1938. 17 figs., 2 pls.

Bertin, L. Révision des Stomiatiformes (Téléostéens, Isospondyles) du Muséum. — Bull. Mus. natn. Hist. nat., Paris, Ser. 2, 11:378–382. 1939.

Bertin, L. Essai de classification et de nomenclature des poissons de la sous-classe des selaciens.— Bull. Inst. océanogr., Monaco, 775:1–24. 1939.

Bertin, L. Description anatomique du genre Stemonidium, type peu connu de serrivomérides, et définition de cette famille de poissons, Apodes. — Bull. Mus. natn. Hist. nat., Paris, Ser. 2, 13: 524–531. 1941.

Bertin, L. Ostéologie du genre Avocettinops (Apode abyssal) et révision du sous-ordre des Nemichthyiformes dont il fait partie. — Bull. Soc. zool. Fr., 67:101–111. 1942. 2 text-figs.

Bertin, L. Revue critique des Dussumieriidés actuels et fossiles. Description d'un genre nouveau.— Bull. Inst. océanogr. Monaco, 853:1–32. 1943. 8 text-figs.

Bertin, L. Synopsis ostéologique et synonymie des poissons de la famille Serrivomeridés (Apodes, Anguilliformes). — Bull. Mus. natn. Hist. nat., Paris, Ser. 2, 16:101–108. 1944. 2 text-figs.

Bertin, L. Les Anguilles. 2nd ed. Edit. Payot, pp. 1–193. Paris. 1951.

Bertin, L. Eels. A Biological Study, pp. 1–192. London. 1956. 8 pls., 55 figs.

Bertin, L. and C. Arambourg. Super-ordre des téléostéens. — In: Traité de zoologie, 42, No. 3: 2204–2500. 1958.

Bertin, L. and R.P. Dollfus. Révision des espèces du genre Decapterus (Téléostéens, Scombriformes). — Mém. Mus. natn. Hist. nat., Paris, n. ser., 26, No. 1:1–29. 1948.

Bigelow, H.B. Isospondyli; Elopoidea, Clupeoidea, Alepocephalidae, Searsiidae, Salmonoidea.— In: Fishes W.N. Atlantic, 3. Mem. Sears Found. Mar. Res., 1, No. 3:89–106, 107–110, 148–151, 250–253, 254–256, 455–456. 1963.

Bigelow, H.B. Coregonidae. — In: Fishes W.N. Atlantic. 3. Mem. Sears Found. Mar. Res., 1, No. 3: 547–551, fig. 130. 1963.

Bigelow, H.B. Bathylaconoidea. — Ibid., 1, No. 4:561–565. 1964.

Bigelow, H.B. and I.P. Farfante. Lancelets. — Ibid., 1, No. 1:1–28, figs. 1–3. 1948.

Bigelow, H.B. and W.C. Schroeder. Cyclostomes. — Ibid., pp. 29–58, figs. 4–5.

Bigelow, H.B. and W.C. Schreeder. Sharks. — Ibid., pp. 59–546 + 30, figs. 6–106.

Bigelow, H.B. and W.C. Schroeder. New Genera and Species of Batoid Fishes.— J. Mar. Res. Sears Found., 7, No. 3:543–566, figs. 1–9. 1948.

Bigelow, H.B. and W.C. Schroeder. New and Little Known Cartilaginous Fishes from the Atlantic.— Bull. Mus. Comp. Zool. Harv., 103:385–408. 1950. 7 pls.

Bigelow, H.B. and W.C. Schroeder. A New Genus and Species of Anacanthobatid Skate from the Gulf of Mexico.— J. Wash. Acad. Sci., 41:110–113. 1951. 1 fig.

Bigelow, H.B., W.C. Schroeder, and S. Springer. New and Little Known Sharks from the Atlantic and from the Gulf of Mexico. — Bull. Mus. Comp. Zool. Harv., pp. 1–64. 1953. ill.

Bigelow, H.B. and W.C. Schroeder. Sawfishes, Guitarfishes. Skates and Rays. — In: Fishes W.N. Atlantic. 2. Mem. Sears Found. Mar. Res., 1, No. 2:1–588, figs. 1–127. 1953.

Bigelow, H.B. and W.C. Schroeder. Deep-water Elasmobranchs and Chimaeroids from the Northwestern Atlantic Slope. — Bull. Mus. Comp. Zool. Harv., 112: 37—87. 1954.

Bigelow, H.B. and W.C. Schroeder. A New Family, a New Genus, and Two New Species of Batoid Fishes from the Gulf of Mexico. — Breviora, 24:1—16. 1954. 4 figs.

Bigelow, H.B. and W.C. Schroeder. A Study of the Sharks of the Suborder Squaloidea. — Bull. Mus. Comp. Zool. Harv., 117:1—150, pls. 1—4, figs. 1—16. 1957.

Bigelow, H.B. and W.C. Schroeder. New and Little Known Batoid Fishes from the Western Atlantic.— Ibid., 128:161—244. 1962. 1 pl.

Bigelow, H.B. and W.C. Schroeder. Osmeridae.— In: Fishes W.N. Atlantic. 3. Mem. Sears Found. Mar. Res., 1, No. 3:553—594, figs. 131—139. 1963.

Bigelow, H.B. and W.C. Schroeder. A Further Account of Batoid Fishes from the Western Atlantic.— Bull. Mus. Comp. Zool. Harv., 132, No. 5:443—477. 1965.

Bilton, H.T. et al. A Key to Five Species of Pacific Salmon (Genus Oncorhynchus) Based on Scale Characters.— J. Fish. Res. Bd. Can., 21:1267—1288. 1964. 7 figs., 10 tab.

Blache, J. Les genres Astronesthes et Borostomias dans l'Atlantique Tropical Oriental Sud (Pisces, Teleostomi, Clupeiformi, Stomiatoidei, Astronesthidae).— Cahiers O.R.S.T.O.M., Océanographie, 2, No. 1:17—31. 1964. ill.

Blache, J. Poissons bathypélagiques de la "Reine Pokou" et du "Gérard Treca" dans les eaux africaines de l'Atlantique tropical. — Cahiers O.R.S.T.O.M., Océanographie, 5:71—87. 1964.

Blache, J. Contribution à la connaissance des Poissons Anguilliformes de la côte occidentale d'Afrique, Muraenidae.— Bull. Inst. fr. Afr. noire, pp. 163—177; 2:178—216; 3:695—709; 4:1122—1187. 1967. 29 figs.

Blair, A.A. Atlantic Salmon of the East Coast of Newfoundland and Labrador, 1939. — Res. Bull. Dept. Fish. Res. Newfoundld., 13:1—21. 1943. 7 text-figs.

Blanc, M. Catalogue des types de Poissons de la famille des Cichlidae en collection au Muséum National d'Histoire Naturelle.— Bull. Mus. natn. Hist. nat., Paris, Ser. 2, 34, No. 3:202—227. 1962.

Blanc, M. Catalogue des types d'Anabantidae et d'Ophicephalidae (Poissons, Téléostéens, Perciformes) en collection au Muséum National d'Histoire Naturelle. — Ibid., 35, No. 1:70—77. 1963.

Blanc, M. and M.L. Bauchot. Révision des Thalassoma (Poissons, Téléostéens, Labridae) de l'Est Atlantique. — Ibid., 32:88—96. 1960. 5 figs.

Blanc, M. and M.L. Bauchot. Sur quatre genres de Carangidae (Téléostéens, Perciformes) de la côte occidental d'Afrique: Decapterus, Caranx, Trachurus, Sanureus. Affinités et rapports phylogéniques. — Ibid., 32:484—492. 1961. 10 figs.

Blanc, M. and M.L. Bauchot. Les Scombroidei (Poissons, Téléostéens, Perciformes) du Muséum National d'Histoire Naturelle de Paris. — Symp. Scombroid Fishes. Mar. Biol. Ass. India, (1), 1, pp.443—458. 1964.

Blanc, M. and J.C. Hureau. Catalogue des types de Poissons de la famille des Nototheniidae en collection au Museum National d'Histoire Naturelle. —Bull. Mus. natn. Hist. nat., Paris, Ser. 2, 34, No. 5:339—342. 1962.

Bleeker, P. De visschen van den Indischen Archipel. Siluri. — Act. Soc. Sci. Indo-Neerl., 4:38—41. 1858.

Bleeker, P. Ordo Cyprini, Karpers. — Act. Soc. Indo-Neerl., (n. ser. 2), 7:1—492. 1860.

Bleeker, P. Atlas ichthyologique des Indes Orientales Néêrlandoises, Amsterdam, 1862—1878. 9 vols., 420 pls.

Bleeker, P. Mémoire sur la faune ichthyologique de Chine. — Ned. Tijdschr. Dierk., 4:113—154. 1873.

Bloch, M.E. Ichthyologie ou histoire naturelle, générale et particulière des poissons. Berlin. 1785—1797. 12 vols., 432 pls.

Boeseman, M. A Tragedy of Errors: the Status of Carcharhinus Blainville, 1816; Galeolamna Owen, 1853; Eulamia Gill, 1861; and the Identity of Carcharhinus commersonii Blainville, 1825.— Zool. Meded., 37:81—100. 1960. 1—2 pls., 1 fig.

Boeseman, M. Notes on the Fishes of Western New Guinea. II. Lopichthys hoschmai, a New Genus and Species from Arafoera Sea. — Zool. Meded., 39:12—18. 1964. ill.

Böhlke, J. The Systematic Position of the Apodal Fish Genus Bathymyrus. — Copeia, 3:218. 1949.

Böhlke, J.E. Eels of the Genus Dysomma, with Additions to the Synonymy and Variation in Dysomma anguillare Barnard. — Proc. Calif. Zool. Club., 1, No. 7:33—39. 1949.

Böhlke, J. Meadia, a New Genus for the West Pacific Dysommid Eel, Dysomma abyssale Kamohara.— Stanford Ichthyol. Bull., 4, No. 1:6. 1951.

Böhlke, J. Studies on Fishes of the Family Characidae. 4. The South American Genus Prodontocharax.— Ann. Mag. Nat. Hist., (12) 6: 658—664. 1953.

Böhlke, J. Studies on Fishes of the Family Characidae. 6. A Synopsis of the Iguanodectinae.—Ibid., (12), 7: 97—104. 1954.

Böhlke, J. On the Bahaman Fishes of the Family Opisthognathidae.—Notulae Naturae, Acad. Sci. Nat. Sci. Philad., 281: 1—6. 1955. ill.

Böhlke, J. A Synopsis of the Eels of the Family Xenocongridae (Including the Chlopsidae and Chilorhinidae).— Proc. Acad. Nat. Sci. Philad., 108: 61—95. 1956.
1957. 3 pls., 3 figs.

Böhlke, J. On the Occurrence of Garden Eels in the Western Atlantic, with a Synopsis of the Heterocongrinae. — Ibid., pp. 59—79. 1 pl., 7 figs.

Böhlke, J. A Review of the Blenny Genus Chaenopsis, and the Description of a Related New Genus from the Bahamas. — Ibid., pp. 81—103. 2 pls., 3 figs.

Böhlke, J. A New Shallow-water Brotulid Fish from the Great Bahama Bank. — Notulae Naturae, Acad. Nat. Sci. Philad., 295:1—8. 1957. 1 fig.

Böhlke, J. Studies on Fishes of the Family Characidae. 14. A Report on Several Extensive Recent Collections from Ecuador. — Proc. Acad. Nat. Sci. Philad., 110:1—121. 1958.

Böhlke, J. E. Comments on Serranoid Fishes with Disjunct Lateral Lines, with the Description of a New One from the Bahamas. — Notulae Naturae, Acad. Nat. Sci. Philad., 330:1—11, fig.1. 1960.

Böhlke, J.E. The Species of the West Atlantic Gobioid Fish Genus Psilotris. — Ibid., 362:1—10. 1963. ill.

Böhlke, J.E. Lyomeri, Eurypharyngidae. — In: Fishes W.N. Atlantic. 5. Mem. Sears Found. Mar. Res., 1(5):603—628. 1966.

Böhlke, J. and F.S. Cliff. A Discussion of the Deep-sea Eel Genus Avocettinops, with Notes on a Newly Discovered Specimen. — Copeia, 2:95—99. 1956. 1 pl.

Böhlke, J. and C.L. Hubbs. Dysommina rugosa, an Apodal Fish from the North Atlantic, Representing a Distinct Family. — Stanford Ichthyol. Bull., 4, No. 1:7—10. 1951. 1 text-fig.

Böhlke, J.E. and G.W. Mead. Physiculus jordani, a New Gadoid Fish from Deep Water off Japan.— Ibid., pp. 27—29.

Böhlke, J.E. and J.E. Randall. The Fishes of the Western Atlantic Serranoid Genus Gramma.—Proc. Acad. Nat. Sci. Philad., 115, No. 2: 33—52. 1963. ill.

Böhlke, J.E. and J.E. Randall. A Key to the Shallow-waters West Atlantic Cardinal Fishes (Apogonidae), with Descriptions of Five New Species. — Ibid., 120, No. 4:175—206. 1968.

Böhlke, J.E. and C.R. Robins. Studies on Fishes of the Family Ophidiidae. 2. Three New Species from the Bahamas. — Ibid., 111:37—52. 1959.

Böhlke, J.E. and C.R. Robins. Western Atlantic Gobioid Fishes of the Genus Dythrypnus, with Notes on Quisquilius hipoliti and Garmannia pallens. — Ibid., 112, No. 4:73—101. 1960. ill.

Böhlke, J.E. and C.R. Robins. A Revision of the Gobioid Fish Genus Coryphopterus. — Ibid., 112, No. 5:103—128. 1960. 2 pls., 3 figs.

Böhlke, J.E. and C.R. Robins. Western Atlantic Seven-spined Gobies, with Descriptions of Ten New Species and a New Genus, and Comments on Pacific Relatives. — Ibid., 120, No. 3:45—174. 1968.

Böhlke, J.E. and D.G. Smith. A New Xenocongrid Eel from the Bahamas, with Notes on Other Species in the Family. — Ibid., 120, No. 2:25—43. 1968.

Böhlke, J.E. and V.G. Springer. A Review of the Atlantic Species of the Clinid Fish Genus Starksia.— Ibid., 113, No. 3:29—60. 1961.

Bolin, R.L. A Revision of the Genus Icelinus Jordan. — Copeia, 3:151—159, fig. 3. 1936.

Bolin, R.L. New Cottid Fishes from Japan and Bering Sea. — Proc. U. S. Natn. Mus., 84:25—38. 1936.

Bolin, R. The Systematic Position of Indostomus paradoxus Prashad and Mukerji, a Freshwater Fish from Burma. — J. Wash. Acad. Sci., 26, No. 10:420—423. 1936.

Bolin, R.L. A Review of the Myctophid Fishes of the Pacific Coast of the United States and of Lower California. — Stanford Ichthyol. Bull., 1:89—156. 1939. 29 text-figs.

Bolin, R.L. Brown Ragfish Taken at Monterey (Icosteidae). — Calif. Fish Game, 26, No. 3:287—289, fig. 110. 1940.

Bolin, R.L. A Review of the Marine Cottid Fishes of California. — Stanford Ichthyol. Bull., 1:1—135, figs. 1—40. 1944.

Bolin, R.L. Lantern Fishes from "Investigator" Station 670, Indian Ocean. — Nat. Hist. Mus. Stanford Univ., 3, No. 2:137—152. 1946.

Bolin, R.L. The Evolution of the Marine Cottidae of California with a Discussion of the Genus as a Systematic Category. — Ibid., 3, No. 3:153—168. 1947.

Bolin, R.L. Description of a New Genus and Species of Cottid Fish from the Tasman Sea, with a Discussion of its Derivation.— Vidensk. Meddr. dansk naturh. Foren., **114**:431—441. 1952. 2 figs.

Bolin, R. Iniomi Myctophidae from the "M. Sars" North Atlantic Deep-sea Expedition. 1910.— Rep. Scient. Results Michael Sars N. Atlant. Deep-sea Exped., 4, 2, No. 7:1—45. 1959. ill.

Bolin, R.L. Interim Account of the Family Myctophidae. — In: Fishes W.N. Atlantic. 5. Mem. Sears Found. Mar. Res., 1, No. 5:190—191. 1966.

Bonde, C. von. The Heterosomata (Flat Fishes) Collected by the S. S. "Pickle." — Rep. Fish. Mar. Biol. Surv. Un. S. Afr., Cape Town, 2, Spec. Rep. 1:1—29, pls. 1—6. 1922.

Bonde, C. von and D. B. Swart. The Platosomia (Skates and Rays) Collected by the S. S. "Pickle." — Ibid., 3, Spec. Rep., 5:1—22, pls. 20—23. 1924.

Borcéa, I. Révision systématique et distribution géographique des Gobiidés de la mer Noire et particulièrement des eaux roumaines. — Annls. scient. Univ. Jassy, 19:1—231. 1934. 91 figs.

Borcéa, I. Données pour servir à la systématique et à la biologie des Mugilidés. Formes de la mer Noire (Littoral roumain). — Ibid., pp. 247—286, 18 figs.

Borcéa, I. Les Clupéides de la région littorale roumaine de la mer Noire et des eaux intérieures. — Ibid., 22:306—344. 1936.

Bott, R. Haie und Rochen von der deutschen Nordseeküste. — Natur Volk, 83, No. 1:16—23. 1953. ill.

Bougis, P. and M. Ruivo. Recherches sur le poisson de profondeur Benthocometes robustus (Goode et Bean) (= Pteridium armatum Doederlein) (Brotulidae). — Vie et Milieu, Suppl., 3:155—209. 1954. figs. 1—33.

Bouillon, J. The Lungfish of Africa. — Natural History, 70, No. 3:62—71. 1961. ill.

Boulenger, G.A. Catalogue of the Perciform Fishes in the British Museum. 2nd edition. 1:1—394. 1895. 15 pls. 27 text-figs.

Boulenger, G.A. A Revision of the Genera and Species of Fishes of the Family Mormyridae. — Proc. Zool. Soc. Lond., pp. 775—821. 1898.

Boulenger, G.A. Les poissons du bassin du Congo, pp.1—62 + 1—532. (p. 120 — Pantodontidae). 1901. 25 pls., map, figs.

Boulenger, G.A. Notes on the Classification of Teleostean Fishes. 1. On the Trachinidae and their Allies. — Ann. Mag. Nat. Hist., (7). 8. **46**:261—271. 1901.

Boulenger, G.A. On the Genera of Osteoglossidae. — Ibid., pp. 514—515.

Boulenger, G.A. Fishes (Systematic Account of Teleostei). — In: Harmer, S.F. and A.E. Shipley (eds.). Cambridge Nat. Hist., 7:539—727. London. 1904.

Boulenger, G.A. A Synopsis of the Suborders and Families of Teleostean Fishes. — Ann. Mag. Nat. Hist., (7) 13, **75**:161—190. 1904.

Boulenger, G.A. A Revision of the African Silurid Fishes of the Subfamily Clariinae. — Proc. Zool. Soc. Lond., pp. 1062—1097. 1907.

Boulenger, G.A. Catalogue of the Freshwater Fishes of Africa in the British Museum. — Natural History, 1:1—373. 1909. 270 figs.

Boulenger, G.A. Catalogue of the Freshwater Fishes of Africa in the British Museum. — Ibid., 4:152—170. 1916.

Boulenger, G.A. Fishes (Systematic Account of Teleostei). — Cambridge Nat. Hist., 7:541—727. London, figs. 325—440. 1922.

Boutière, H. Les Scorpaenidés des eaux marocaines. — Trav. Inst. scient. chérif., 15:1—84. 1958. 5 pls.

Bradbury, M.G. Redefinitions of the Genera of the Fish Family Ogcocephalidae. — Diss. Abstr., 24:440—441. 1963.

Bradbury, M.G. The Genera of Batfishes (Family Ogcocephalidae). — Copeia, 2:399—422. 1967. ill.

Branson, B. A. and G. A. Moore. The Lateralis Components of the Acousticolateralis System in the Sunfish Family Centrarchidae. — Copeia, 1:1—108. 1962. 149 figs.

Breder, C.M. Jr. Elasmobranchii from Panama to Lower California. — Bull. Bingham Oceanogr. Coll., 2, No. 1:1—13. 1928. 12 figs.

Breder, C.M. Jr. Nematognathii, Apodes, Isospondyli, Synentognathi, and Thoracostraci from Panama to Lower California. — Ibid., 2, No. 2:1—25. 1928. ill.

Breder, C.M. Jr. Heterosomata to Pediculati from Panama to Lower California. — Ibid., 2, No. 3:1—56. 1936. figs. 1—19.

Breder, C.M. Jr. A Contribution to the Life Histories of Atlantic Ocean Flying-fishes. — Ibid., 6, No. 5: 1—126. 1938. 48 figs.

Breder, C.M. Jr. and E. Clark. A Contribution to the Visceral Anatomy, Development and Relationships of the Plectognathi. — Bull. Am. Mus. Nat. Hist., 88, No. 5:291—320. 1947. 8 figs., 4 pls.

Briggs, J.C. A Review of the Clingfishes (Gobiesocidae) of the Eastern Pacific with Descriptions of New Species. — Proc. Calif. Zool. Club, 1:57—108. 1951. 23 figs.

Briggs, J.C. A Monograph of the Clingfishes (Order Xenopterygii). — Stanford Ichthyol. Bull., 6:1—224, figs. 1—114. 1955.

Briggs, J.C. Order Xenopterygii. — In: Weber, M. and L.F. de Beaufort. The Fishes of the Indo-Australian Archipelago, 11:445—453. 1962.

Briggs, J.C. The Clingfishes (Gobiesocidae) of Guadalupe Island, Mexico. — Calif. Fish Game, 51, No.2: 123—125. 1965.

Briggs, J.C. and F.H. Berry. The Draconettidae — a Review of the Family with the Description of a New Species. — Copeia, 2:123—133. 1959. 7 figs.

Brittan, M.R. A Revision of the Indo-Malayan Freshwater Fish Genus Rasbora. — Monogr. Inst. Sci. Tech., 3:1—224. Manila. 1954.

Brown, L.J. A Key to the Species and Subspecies of the Cyprinodont Genus Fundulus in the United States and Canada East of the Continental Divide. — J. Wash. Acad. Sci., 47:69—77. 1957.

Bruun, A.F. On Some New Fishes of the Family Gonostomatidae. — Vidensk. Meddr. dansk naturh. Foren., 92:285—292, pl. 8. 1931.

Bruun, A.F. Flying-fishes (Exocoetidae) of the Atlantic. Systematic and Biological Studies. — Dana Rep., 6:1—108. 1935. 7 pls., 30 figs.

Bruun, A.F. Exococtidae, Macrorhamphosidae. — In: Faune Ichthyologique de l'Atlantique Nord, 16:148. Copenhague. 1936.

Bruun, A.F. Contributions to the Life Histories of the Deep Sea Eels; Synaphobranchidae. — Dana Rep., 9:1—31. 1937. 1 pl., 17 text-figs.

Bruun, A.F. A Study of a Collection of the Fish Schindleria from the South Pacific. — Ibid., 21:1—12, figs. 1—8. 1940.

Buen, F. de. Los Góbidos de la Peninsula Ibérica y Baleares. 1. El "Gobius Lesueurii" Risso.— Boln. Pescas, pp. 337—354. 1917. 5 figs.

Buen, F. de. Los Góbidos de la Peninsula Ibérica y Baleares. II. Catálogo sistemático y ensayo de distribución geográfica. — Ibid., pp. 291—337. 1918.

Buen, F. de. Gobius de la Peninsula Ibérica y Baleares. — Mems. Inst. esp. Oceanogr., 3:121—266. 1923.

Buen, F. de. Hallazgo del Makaira nigricans Lacépède en las costas españolas y consideraciones sobre los Xiphiiformes en general. — Notas Resúm. Inst. esp. Oceanogr., Ser. 2, 88:1—12. 1928. 6 figs.

Buen, F. de. Ichthiologia española. 1. Scombriformes y Thunniformes. — Boln. Oceanogr. Pesc., 2:1—22. 1930. ill.

Buen, F. de. Notas a la familia Gobiidae observaciones sobre algunos géneros y sinopsis de las especies ibéricas. — Notas y Res. Min. Marina, Madrid, Ser. 2, 54:1—76. 1931. 1 pl., 22 text-figs.

Buen, F. de. Sur une collection de Gobiinae provenant du Maroc. Essai de synopsis des espèces de l'Europe.— Bull. Soc. Sci. nat. Maroc, 10, Nos. 7—9:120—147. 1931. 12 figs.

Buen, F. de. Ictiologia española. II. Catálogo de los seláceos ibéricos. — Boln. Oceanogr. Pesc., 16:8—23. 1931.

Buen, F. de. Discocephali de España (Peces). — Boln. Soc. esp. Hist. Nat., 34, No. 7:397—412. 1934. 2 figs.

Buen, F. de. Clupéides et leur pêche (7-e Rapport). Cinquième note. — Rapp. Comm. Explor. Méditerranée, 10:317—419. 1937. 48 text-figs.

Buen, F. de. Les Gobiidae pélagiques ou vivant sur les fonds d'algues calcaires de l'Europe Occidentale. — Bull. Inst. océanogr. Monaco, 790:1—16. 1940. 2 text-figs.

Buen, F. de. Investigaciones sobre ictiologia Mexicana. 1. Atherinidae de aguas continentales de Mexico.– An. Inst. Biol. Univ. Méx., **16**:475–532. 1945. 2 text-figs.

Buen, F. de. Los pejerrey (familia Atherinidae) en la fauna Uruguaya, con descripcion de nuevas especies.– Bolm. Inst. Oceanogr., S.Paulo, **4**, Nos. 1–2:3–80. 1953. 45 figs.

Buen, F. de. Los peces de la familia Molidae. – Investnes zool. chil., **4**:66–76. 1957. 6 figs.

Buen, F. de. Suborden Luvaroidei neuevo para ña fauna Chilena. – Ibid., pp. 83–88, 2 figs.

Buen, F. de. La familia Lepidotidae en Chile. – Ibid., pp. 132–134. 1958.

Buen, F. de. Peces del suborden scombroidei en aguas de Chile. – Revta Biol. mar., **7**:3–38. 1958. 3 figs.

Buen, F. de. Peces de la superfamilia Clupeoidae en aguas de Chile. – Ibid., **8**:83–110. 1958. 1 fig.

Buen, F. de. Notas preliminares sobre la fauna marina preabissal de Chile, con descripcion de una familia de rayas, dos generos y siete especies nuevos. – Boln. Mus. nac. Hist. nat. Chile, **27**:171–201. 1959.

Buen, F. de. Lampres, tiburones, rayas y pices en la estacion de biologia marina de Montemar, Chile. – Revta. Biol. mar., **9**:257–270. 1959. 3 figs.

Buen, F. de. Tiburones, rayas y quimeras en la estacion de biologia marina de Montemar, Chile. – Ibid., **10**:3–50. 1960. 16 figs.

Buen, F. de. Los peje-sapos (familia Gobiesocidae) en Chile. – Ibid., pp. 69–82. 1 fig.

Buen, F. de. Las lampreas (Marsipobranchii o Ciclostomi) en aguas de Chile. – Investnes zool. chil., **7**:101–124. 1961. 10 figs.

Buen, F. de. Peces Chilenos. Familias Alepocephalidae, Muraenidae, Sciaenidae, Scorpaenidae, Liparidae y Bothidae, **1**:1–90. Montemar. 1961. 22 figs.

Buen, F. de. Fauna Chilena. Peces de la familia Clinidae, **2**:53–96. Montemar. 1962. 22 figs.

Bühler. Die Verdaungsorgane der Stromateidae. – Z. Morph. Ökol. Tiere, **19**:59–115. 1930.

Burke, V. Revision of the Fishes of the Family Liparidae. – Bull. U. S. Natn. Mus., **150**:1–204. 1930.

Bussing, W.A. and R.J. Lavenberg. A Classification of Bathypelagic Fishes. – Univ. South. California Antarctic Research Program. Rotoprint, pp. 1–11. 1964. ill.

Cadenat, J. Les serranidés de la côte occidentale d'Afrique (du Cap Spartel au Cap Vert). – Revue Trav. Inst. (scient. tech.) Pêch. marit., **8**:377–422. 1935. 30 text-figs.

Cadenat, J. Les Scorpaenidae de l'Atlantique et de la méditerranée. 1. Le genre Scorpaena. – Ibid., **13**: 525–563. 1944. 11 text-figs.

Cadenat, J. Notes d'Ichthyologie Ouestafricaine. Les Rémoras des côtes du Sénégal.– Bull. Inst. fr. Afr. noire, **15**, No. 2:672–683, figs. 1–12; **15**, No. 3:1051–1102. 43 figs. 1953.

Cadenat, J. Notes d'Ichthyologie Ouestafricaine. Sur quelques espèces d'Apodes du genre Caecula. – Ibid., **16**, No. 1:238–244. 1954. 2 figs.

Cadenat, J. Notes d'Ichthyologie Ouestafricaine. Sur les Nulets de la côte occidentale d'Afrique. – Ibid., Ser. A, **16**, No. 2:584–591. 1954.

Cadenat, J. Notes d'Ichthyologie Ouestafricaine. Les Antennarius. – Ibid., **21**, No. 1:361–385. 1959. 26 figs.

Cadenat, J. Notes d'Ichthyologie Ouestafricaine. – Les Mobulidae de la côte occidentale d'Afrique. – Ser. A, **22**:1053–1084. 1960. 24 pls.

Cadenat, J. Notes d'Ichthyologie Ouestafricaine. Les Sphyraenidae de la côte occidentale d'Afrique. – Ibid., **26**, No. 2:659–685. 1964. ill.

Cadenat, J. and C. Roux. Résultats scientifiques des campagnes de la "Calypso." Iles du Cap Vert. III. Poissons téléostéens. – Annls. Inst. océanogr., **41**:81–102. 1964. 3 figs.

Cairns, D. New Zealand Freshwater Eels. – Tuatara, Wellington, N. Z., **3**:43–52. 1950.

Caldwell, D.K. The Biology and Systematics of the Pin Fish, Lagodon rhomboides (Linnaeus). – Bull. Fla. St. Mus. Biol. Sci., **2**:77–173. 1957. 22 figs.

Caldwell, D.K. Western Atlantic Fishes of the Family Priacanthidae. – Copeia, **2**:417–424. 1962. 5 figs.

Campos, A.A. Contribução ao estudo dos Clupéoides das aguas Brasilieras.– Archos. Zool. Est. S Paulo, **3**:185–220. 1941. 9 pls.

Campos, A.A. Sciaenidae da água doce. Estudo das espécies que habitam os rios do Brasil. – Archos. Mus. parana., **2**:9–22, pls. II–V. 1942.

Campos, A.A. Algunas considerações sobre os generos da subfamilia Serrasalmoninae. – Papéis Dep. Zool. S Paulo, **3**:285–288. 1943.

Campos, A.A. Peixes da subfamilia Mylinae existentes na coleçado departamento de zoologia da Secretaria da Agricultura de São Paulo. – Ibid., **4**:197–212. 1944.

Cantwell, G.E. A Revision of the Genus Parapercis Family Mugiloididae. – Pacif. Sci., **18**, No.3: 239–280. 1964. 9 figs.

Caporiacco, L. di. Revisione delle specie mediterranee della famiglia Labridae. — Atti Soc. ital. Sci. nat., 60:49—101. 1921.

Caporiacco, L. di. Sygnathidae italiani. — Boll. Pesca Piscic. Idrobiol., 24:73—95. 1948.

Carlisle, J.G., J.W. Schott, and N.J. Abramson. The Barred Surf Perch (Amphistichus argenteus Agassiz) in Southern California (Embiotocidae). — Fish Bull. Calif., 109:3—79. 1960.

Caro, F.L. Los escómbrides de las aguas españolas y marroquies y su pesca. — Boln. Inst. esp. Océanogr., 25:1—254. 1958.

Casey, J.G. Anglers' Guide to Sharks of the Northeastern United States, Maine to Chesapeake Bay. — Fishery Bull. Fish Wildl. Serv. U.S., 179:1—32. 1964. ill.

Castex, M.N. Notas heuristicas sobre el genero Potamotrygon. — Mus. Argentino Cienc. Natur., 11:1—13. 1963.

Castle, P.H.J. Deepwater Eels from Cook Strait, New Zealand. — Zoology Publs. Vict. Univ. Wellington, 27:1—30. 1961.

Castle, P.H.J. Deep-sea Eels: Family Synaphobranchidae. — Galathea Rep., 7:29—42. 1964. ill.

Cervigón, F. Descripción de Anodontus mauritanicus nov. gen. nov. sp. (orden Ateleopiformes) y Cottunculus costaecanarie nov. sp. (fam. Cottidae) de las costas occidentales de Africa. — Investigación pesq., 19:119—128. 1961. ill.

Chabanaud, P. Remarques sur Dipterygonotus gruveli Chab. et sur la famille des Dipterygonotidae. — Bull. Soc. zool. Fr., 49: 248—256. 1924.

Chabanaud, P. Les Soles de l'Atlantique Oriental Nord et des mers Adjacentes. — Bull. Inst. océanogr. Monaco, 488:1—67. 1927.

Chabanaud, P. Révision des poissons hétérosomes de la sous-famille des Achirinae, d'après les types de Kaup, de Günther et de Steindachner. — Bull. Inst. océanogr. Monaco, 523:1—53. 1928.

Chabanuad, P. Les genres de poissons hétérosomates (Pisces, Heterosomata) appartenant à la sous-famille de Soleinae. — Ibid., 555:1—21. 1930. 2 text-figs.

Chabanaud, P. Les poissons Pleuronectes de la Méditerranée (Pisces, Heterosomata). — Riviera scient., Suppl., 2:1—32. 1931.

Chabanaud, P. Poissons hétérosomes recueillis par M. le Professor A. Gruvel et par M.M.R.-ph Dollfus et J. Liouvrille sur la côte atlantique du Maroc. — Mém. Soc. Sci. nat. phys. Maroc., 35:1—111, pls. 1—4, figs. 1—19. 1933.

Chabanaud, P. Hétérogenéité des téléostéens dyssymétriques. — Bull. Soc. zool. Fr., 59:275—284. 1934. 14 text-figs.

Chabanaud, P. Les Soleidae de la sous-famille des Heteromycterinae. — Ibid., 60:212—224. 1935. 6 figs.

Chabanaud, P. Achiridae nec Trinectidae. Caractères et synonymie de deux génotypes systématiques certains: Achirus achirus Linné 1758 et Trinectes maculatus (Bloch, M.S.) Schneider, 1801. — Bull. Inst. océanogr. Monaco, 661:1—24. 1935. 11 figs.

Chabanaud, P. Le neurocrane osseux des téléostéens dyssymétriques après la métamorphose. — Annls. Inst. océanogr., Paris, n. s., 16:223—297. 1936. 12 text-figs.

Chabanaud, P. Les téléostéens dyssymétriques du Mokattem inférieur de Tourah. — Mém. Prés. Inst., Egypte, 32:1—121. 1937. 4 pls., 19 text-figs.

Chabanaud, P. Contribution à la morphologie et la systématique des téléostéens dyssymétriques. — Archs. Mus. natn. Hist. nat., Paris, 6, No.15:59—139. 1938. 9 pls., 75 text-figs.

Chabanaud, P. Catalogue systématique et chorologique des téléostéens dyssymétriques du Globe. — Bull. Inst. océanogr. Monaco, 763:1—31. 1939.

Chabanaud, P. Contribution à la morphologie des Cynoglossidae (Teleostei, Pleuronectoidea, Soleiformes).— Bull. Mus. natn. Hist. nat., Paris, 2, No. 12:182—191. 1940. 6 text-figs.

Chabanaud, P. Sur les Achiridae (Pleuronectoidea, Soleiformes) totalement démunis d'écailles. — Bull. Soc. zool. Fr., 65:13—31. 1940. pl. 1, 5 text-figs.

Chabanaud, P. Contribution à la morphologie des Citharidae. — Ibid., 73:18—23. 1948. 4 text-figs.

Chabanaud, P. Révision des Cynoglossidae (s. str.) de l'Atlantique oriental. — Bull. Mus. natn. Hist. nat., Paris, 2, No. 21:60—66, 202—209, 347—353, figs. 1—7. 1949.

Chabanaud, P. Les Cynoglossus de l'Atlantique. — Ibid., 5:516—521. 1949.

Chabanaud, P. Résultats scientifiques des croisières du Navire école Belge "Mercator." 1. Téléostéens dyssymétriques (Heterosomata). — Mém. Inst. r. Sci. nat. Belg., 2, No. 33:3—102. 1949. 101 text-figs.

Chabanaud, P. Contribution à l'anatomie et à la systématique de la famille des Bothidae s. str. — Bull. Soc. zool. Fr., 74:246—253. 1950. 8 text-figs.

Chabanaud, P. Révision des Soleidés du genre Pegusa. Description d'une espèce inédite. — Bull. Inst. fr. Afr. noire, 16A:245—282, figs. 1—20. 1954.

Chabanaud, P. Rectifications afférentes à la nomenclature et à la systématique des Pleuronectiformes du sous-ordre des Soleoidei. — Bull. Mus. natn. Hist. nat., Paris, 27:447—452. 1955.

Chabanaud, P. Révision des Symphurus du Siboga. — Beaufortia, 5, No. 46: 43—45. 1955.

Chan, W.L. A Systematic Revision of the Indo-Pacific Clupeid Fishes of the Genus Sardinella (fam. Clupeidae). — Jap. J. Ichthyol., 12, Nos. 3—6: 104—118. 1965; 13, Nos. 1—3:1—26. 1965.

Chandy, M. A Key for the Identification of the Catfishes of the Genus Tachysurus Lacépède, with a Catalogue of the Specimens in the Collection of the Indian Museum (Zool. Surv.). — Rec. Indian Mus., 51:1—18. 1953. 3 pls.

Chang, Y. On the Structure of the Lateral Line Canal of Apodes and its Significance on Classification. — Acta zool. sin., 16:653—657 (English summary). 1964.

Chang Ch'un-lin and Chayu Yu-wei. Study of the Fish of the Genus Halieutaea (Onocephalidae) from China Waters. — Acta zool. sin., 16, No. 1:155—160. 1964.

Chapman, W.M. The Osteology of the Haplomous Fish, Novumbra, with Comparative Notes on Related Species. — J. Morph., 56:371—404. 1934.

Chapman, W.M. Eleven New Species and Three New Genera of Oceanic Fishes Collected by the International Fisheries Commission from the Northeastern Pacific. — Proc. U.S. Natn. Mus., 86:501—542. 1939.

Chapman, W.M. The Osteology and Relationships of the Isospondylous Fish Plecoglossus altivelis. — J. Morph., 68:425—455. 1941.

Chapman, W.M. The Osteology and Relationships of the Osmerid Fishes. — Ibid., 69: 279—301, figs. 1—15. 1941.

Chapman, W.M. The Osteology and Relationships of the Argentinidae, a Family of Oceanic Fishes. — J. Wash. Acad. Sci., 32, No. 4:104—117. 1942. 8 figs.

Chapman, W.M. The Osteology and Relationship of the Bathypelagic Fish Macropinna microstoma with Notes on its Visceral Anatomy. — Ann. Mag. Nat. Hist., (11), 9:272—304. 1942. 9 text-figs.

Chapman, W.M. Osteology of Cololabis. — Copeia, 3:171—182. 1943.

Chapman, W.M. The Osteology and Relationships of the Bathypelagic Fishes of the Genus Bathylagus Günther, with Notes on the Systematic Position of Leuroglossus stilbius Gilbert and Therobromus callorhinus Lucas. — J. Wash. Acad. Sci., 33: 147—160. 1943. 8 text-figs.

Chapman, W.M. The Comparative Osteology of the Herring-like Fishes (Clupeidae) of California. — Calif. Fish Game, 30, No. 1:6—21, figs. 2—19. 1944.

Chapman, W.M. On the Osteology and Relationships of the South American Fish Aplochiton. — J. Morph., 75: 149—165. 1944.

Chapman, W.M. The Osteology and Relationships of the Round Herring, Etrumeus microps Temminck et Schlegel.— Proc. Calif. Acad. Sci., Ser. 4, 26, No. 2: 25—41. 1948. 18 figs.

Chapman, W.M. The Osteology and Relationships of the Microstomidae, a Family of Oceanic Fishes. — Ibid., Ser. 4, 26:1—22, figs.1—12. 1948.

Chapman, W.M. Family Blenniidae (in Part). — In: Weber and Beaufort. The Fishes of the Indo-Australian Archipelago, 11: I—XI + 1—484. 1951.

Chapman, W.M. and L.P. Schultz. Review of the Fishes of the Blennoid Genus Ecsenius with Descriptions of Five New Species. — Proc. U.S. Natn. Mus., 102:507—528. 1952. 7 figs.

Chapman, W.M. and L.D. Townsend. The Osteology of Zaprora silenus Jordan. — Ann. Mag. Nat. Hist., (11), 2:89—117, figs.1—10. 1938.

Chaux, J. and P.W. Fang. Catalogue des Siluroidei d'Indochine de la collection du Labozatoire des pêches coloniales au Muséum, avec la description de six espèces nouvelles. — Bull. Mus. natn. Hist. nat., Paris, Ser. 2, 21, No. 3:342—346. 1949. ill.

Chen, J.T.F. A Review of the Apodal Fishes of Kwantung. — Bull. Biol. Dep. Coll. Sci. Sun Yat-Sen Univ., 1, No. 1:1—49 + 1—12, figs. 1—24, pls. 1—3. 1929.

Chen, J.T.F. A Preliminary Review of the Lophobranchiate Fishes of China. — Biol. Bull. Normal Coll., Canton, 1:1—22, pls. 1—4. 1935.

Chen, J.T.F. A Summary of the Chinese Sharks. — Q. Jl. Taiwan Mus., 1, No. 2:21—45. 1948. (In Chinese.)

Chen, J.T.F. Some Records of Platosomeae from Taiwan, with Description of a New Species of Dasyatis.— Ibid., 1, No. 3:1—14. 1948. ill.

Chen, J.T.F. A Synopsis of the Platosomeae of China. — Ibid., 1, No. 4:23—50. 1948.

Chen, J.T.F. A Review of the Sharks of Taiwan. — Biol. Bull. Normal Coll., Canton, Ichthyol. Ser.(1), 19:1—102. 1963.

Chen, J.T.F. and Y.S. Liang, A New Genus and Species of the Family Acanthoclinidae (Percoidei). — Q. Jl. Taiwan Mus., 1, No. 3:31—34. 1948. 1 text-fig.

Chen, J.T.F. and Y.S. Liang. Description of a New Homalopterid Fish, Pseudogastromyzon tungpeiensis, with a Synopsis of All the Known Chinese Homalopteridae. — Ibid., 2:157—169. 1949. 1 text-fig.

Chen, J.T.F. and H.T.C. Weng. A Review of the Flatfishes of Taiwan. — Biol. Bull. Normal Coll., Canton, 25 and 27. 1965.

Chen, T.R. A Review of Gobies Found in the Waters of Taiwan (Formosa) and Adjacent Seas. (1). — Q. Jl. Taiwan Mus., 17:37—59. 1964. 7 figs.

Cheng, P.S. and Y.W. Chang. Studies on the Chinese Soleoid Fishes of the Genus Zebrias, with Description of a New Species from the South China Sea. — Acta zootaxonom. sin., 2, No. 4: 267—278. 1965.

Ch'êng Ch'ing-t'ai. Taxonomy of Fish of the Family Apogonidae in China and New Species. — Dongwuwxue Zazhi, 3, No. 8:359—362. 1959. (In Chinese.)

Chêng Pao-shan and Chang Yu-wei. Study of the Chinese Pleuronectidae (Righteye Flounders, Flatfishes, Halibuts) of the Genus Zebrias with a Description of New Species from the South China Sea. — Acta zootaxonom. sin., 2, No. 4:267—278. 1965.

Chernavin, V.V. Experimental Attempt at a Systematic Classification of Some Salmonoidei, Based on Osteological Characters. — Izv. Gos. Inst. Opyt. Agron., 1:103—106. 1923.

Chevey, P. Les poissons de campagnes de "de Lanessan." — Trav. Inst. Océanogr. Indochine. 4-e Mém., pp. 1—155, pls. I — L. 1932.

Chevey, P. and Lemasson. Contribution à l'étude des poissons des eaux douces tonkinoises. — Ibid., 33:1—183. 1937. pls. 1—44.

Chranilov, N.S. Beiträge zur Kenntnis des Weber'schen Apparates der Ostariophysi. 1. Cypriniformes. — Zool. Jber. Neapel, Sec. Anat., 49:501—597. 1927.

Chranilov, N.S. Beiträge zur Kenntnis des Weber'schen Apparates der Ostariophysi. II. Siluroidea. — Ibid., 51:323—462. 1929.

Chu, Y.T. Comparative Studies on the Scales and on the Pharyngeals and their Teeth in Chinese Cyprinids, with Particular Reference to Taxonomy and Evolution. — Biol. Bull. St. John's Univ., Shanghai, 2, Nos.1—10:1—225. 1935. 30 pls.

Chu, Yu. T. et al. Fishes of the South China Sea, pp. 1—1184, figs. 1—860. 1962. (In Chinese.)

Chu, Yu. T. et al. Fishes of the East China Sea, pp. 1—642, figs. 1—442. 1963. (In Chinese.)

Chu, Y.T. and C. Hsu. The Geographical Distribution and Faunal Characteristics of Tetraodontiform Fishes of China. — Acta zool. sin., 17:320—333. 1965.

Chu, Y.T. and X.B. Jin. The Geographical Distribution and Faunal Characteristics of Cottoid Fishes of China. — Oceanologia Limnol. sin., 7, No. 3:235—252. 1965.

Chu, Y.T., L.Lo, and H.L. Wu. A Study on the Classification of the Sciaenoid Fishes of China, with Description of New Genera and Species. Monographs of Fishes of China. — Publ. Shanghai Fisch Inst., pp. 1—100, pls. 1—40. 1963. (In Chinese with English summary.)

Chu Yüan-ting. Species of Cartilaginous Fishes of China, pp. 1—225, figs. 1—203. Peking. 1960. (In Chinese.)

Clark, E. Notes on Some Hawaiian Plectognath Fishes, Including a Key to the Species. — Am. Mus. Novit., 1397:1—22. 1949. 9 text-figs.

Clark, E. and H.A.F. Gohar. The Fishes of the Red Sea. Order Plectognathi. — Publs. Mar. Biol. Stn. Ghardaqa, 8:1—80. 1953. 22 figs., 5 pls.

Clark, E. and K. Schmidt. Sharks of the Central Gulf Coast of Florida. — Bull. Mar. Sci. Gulf Caribb., 15:13—83. 1965. 18 figs.

Clark, H.W. New Fishes from the Temple-Crocker Expedition of 1935—1936. — Copeia, 2:90—91. 1937. 2 text-figs.

Clark, R.S. Rays and Skates. A Revision of the European Species. — Scient. Invest. Fishery Bd. Scotl., 1: 1—66. 1922.

Clark, R.S. Rays and Skates. A Revision of the European Species. — Ibid., Ser. 1, 66:1—36. 1926. 44 pls., ill.

Clarke, R. The Bathypelagic Angler Fish Ceratias holbölli Kröyer. – "Discovery" Rep., **26**:1–32. 1950. ill.

Clausen, H.S. Denticipitidae, a New Family of Primitive Isospondylous Teleosts from West African Fresh Water. – Vidensk. Meddr. dansk naturh. Foren, **121**:141–156. 1959. 2 pls., 1 fig.

Clemens, W.A. and G.V. Wilby. Fishes of the Pacific Coast of Canada. – Bull. Fish. Res. Bd. Can., pp. 1–443, figs. 1–281, pl. 1. 1961.

Cohen, D.M. Contribution to a Classification of the Fishes of the Suborder Opisthoproctoidei. Ph.D. Thesis, Stanford Univ., pp. 1–294. 1957. 6 figs.

Cohen, D.M. A Revision of the Fishes of the Subfamily Argentinidae. – Bull. Fla. St. Mus. Biol. Sci., **3**, No.3:93–172, figs. 1–9. 1958.

Cohen, D.M. Bathylychnops exilis, a New Genus and Species of Argentinoid Fish from the North Pacific. – Stanford Ichthyol. Bull., **7**:47–52, figs. 1–5. 1958.

Cohen, D.M. Notes on a Small Collection of Liparid Fishes from the Yellow Sea. – Proc. Biol. Soc. Wash., **73**:15–20. 1960. 1 fig.

Cohen, D.M. Isospondyli. 3. Argentinoidea (Argentinidae and Opisthoproctidae) from the "Michael Sars" North Atlantic Deep-sea Expedition. 1910. – Rep. Scient. Results Michael Sars N. Atlant. Deep Sea Exped., **4**, **2**, No. 9:1–5. 1960. 1 fig.

Cohen, D.M. New Records of the Opisthoproctid Genus Bathylychnops, with a Notice of Neoteny in the Related Genus Dolichopteryx. – Copeia, **2**:147–149. 1960. 3 figs.

Cohen, D.M. A New Genus and Species of Deepwater Ophidioid Fish from the Gulf of Mexico. – Ibid., **3**:288–292. 1961. 1 fig.

Cohen, D.M. A Review of the Ophidioid Fish Genus Oligopus with Description of a New Species from West Africa. – Proc. U.S. Natn. Mus., **116**:1–22. 1964.

Cohen, D.M. Argentinoidea. – In: Fishes W.N. Atlantic. 4. Mem. Sears Found. Mar. Res., **1**, No. 4:1–70, figs. 1–20. 1964.

Cohen, D.M. A New Tribe and a New Species of Ophidioid Fish. – Proc. Biol. Soc. Wash., **79**:183–204, figs. 1–5. 1966.

Collette, B.B. A Preliminary Review of the Tunas of the Genus Thunnus. – In: Pacific Tuna Biology Conference August 14–17, 1961. Honolulu, Hawaii. – Spec. Scient. Rep. U.S. Fish Wildl. Serv. Fisheries, **415**:24. 1962.

Collette, B.B. The Swamp Darters of the Subgenus Hololepis (Pisces, Percidae). – Tulane Stud. Zool., **9**, No. 4:115–211. 1962. ill.

Collette, B.B. The Subfamilies, Tribes and Genera of the Percidae (Teleostei). – Copeia, **4**:615–623. 1963.

Collette, B.B. Systematic Significance of Breeding Tubercles in Fishes of the Family Percidae. – Proc. U.S. Natn. Mus., **117**:567–614. 1965. ill.

Collette, B.B. Hemiramphidae (Pisces, Synentognathi) from Tropical West Africa. – Atlantide Rep., **8**:217–235. 1965.

Collette, B.B. Belonion, a New Genus of Freshwater Needlefishes from South America. – Am. Mus. Novit., **2274**:1–22. 1966.

Collette, B.B. A Review of the Venomous Toadfishes Subfamily Thalassophryninae. – Copeia, **4**:846–864. 1966. ill.

Collette, B.B. Revue critique des types de Scombridae des collections du Muséum National d'Histoire Naturelle de Paris. – Bull. Mus. natn. Hist. nat., Paris, Sér. 2, **384**:362–375. 1966.

Collette, B.B. and H.B. Frederick. Recent Studies of the Needlefishes (Belonidae). An Evaluation. – Copeia, **3**:366–392. 1965.

Collette, B.B. and R.H. Gibbs. Preliminary Field Guide to the Mackerel Tuna-like Fishes of the Indian Ocean (Scombridae). – Edit. U.S. Nat. Mus., **5**, Rotoprint, pp. 1–48. 1963. ill.

Collette, B.B. and R.H. Gibbs. A Preliminary Review of the Fishes of the Family Scombridae. – FAO Fisheries Rep., **6**, No. 1:23–32. 1963.

Collette, B.B. and L.W. Knapp. Catalog of Type Specimens of the Darters (Pisces, Percidae, Etheostomatini). – Proc. U.S. Natn. Mus., **119**, No. 3550:1–88. 1966. 5 figs.

Collette, B.B. and R.W. Verger. The American Percid Fishes of the Subgenus Villora. – Tulane Stud. Zool., **9**, No. 4:213–230. 1962. ill.

Collignon, J. La systématique des Sciaenidés de l'Atlantique oriental. – Bull. Inst. océanogr. Monaco, **1155**:1–10. 1959. 1 pl.

Collignon, J. Contribution à la connaissance des Otolithus des côtes d'Afrique Equatoriale. – Bull. Inst. Etud. centafr., Nos. 19–20:55–84. 1960. 44 figs.

Corbin, P.G. The Occurrence of the Smooth Sand-eel Gymnammodytes semisquamatus (Jourdain) in the Plymouth Area, with Notes on G. cicerelus (Rafinesque) and G. capensis (Barnard). – J. Mar. Biol. Ass. U.K., 29:83–89. 1950.

Corbin, P.G. and V. Vati. The Postlarval Sand-eels (Ammodytidae) of the Celtic Sea and Plymouth Area. – Ibid., 28:287–313. 1949. 2 pls., 6 text-figs.

Corwin, G. A Bibliography of the Tunas. – Fish Bull., Sacramento, Calif., 22:1–103. 1930.

Courtenay, W.R. Jr. Western Atlantic Fishes of the Genus Haemulon (Pomadasyidae): Systematic Status and Juvenile Pigmentation. – Bull. Mar. Sci. Gulf Caribb., 11:66–149. 1961. 17 figs.

Courtenay, W.R. Atlantic Fishes of the Genus Rypticus (Grammistidae). – Proc. Acad. Nat. Sci. Phila., 119:241–293. 1967.

Cramer, F. On the Cranial Characters of the Genus Sebastodes. – Proc. Calif. Acad. Sci., Ser. 2, 5:573–610. 1895.

Creaser, C.W. and C.L. Hubbs. A Revision of the Holarctic Lampreys. – Occ. Pap. Mus. Zool. Univ. Mich., 120:1–14. 1922. 1 pl.

Crossman, E.J. Variation in Number and Symmetry in Branchiostegal Rays in the Family Esocidae. – Can. J. Zool., 38:363–375. 1960. ill.

Curra, R.A. Notes on the Genera Apteronotus Lac., 1800 and Sternopygus Mueller et Troschel, 1848 with a Discussion on the Zoological Categories Apteronotoidea, nom. transl. Apteronotidae Berg, 1940 and Apteronotinae Berg, 1940, nom. transl. Eigenmann and Allen, 1942 (Cypriniformes, Gymnotoidei). – Bolm. Inst. Oceanogr. Univ. Oriente, 3, Nos. 1–2:139–143. 1964.

Curra, R.A. and P. Mirando Ribeiro. Notas sistematicas sobre Urumara rondoni Miranda Ribeiro, 1920 (Pisces, Gymnotoidei-Rhamplichthyidae). – Ibid., 1, No. 2:474–481. 1961. 2 figs.

Daget, J. Révision des affinités phylogénétiques des Polyptéridés. – Mém. Inst. fond. Afr. noire, 11:1–178. 1950. 57 figs.

Daget, J. Sous-classe des Brachioptérygiens (Brachiopterygii). – Traité de Zoologie, 13, No. 3:2501–2521. 1958.

Daget, J. Le genre Citharinus (Poissons, Characiformes). – Revue Zool. Bot. afr., 66:81–106. 1962. 12 figs.

Daget, J. Taxonomie numérique des Citharininae (Poissons, Characiformes). – Bull. Mus. natn. Hist. nat., Paris, Ser. 2, 38, No. 4:376–386. 1966. ill.

D'Ancona see – Ancona, de.

D'Auberton see – Auberton, de.

D'Aubrey see – Aubrey, de.

Daniel, J. The Elasmobranch Fishes. 3rd ed., pp. 1–331. Berkley, 1934.

David, L. Die Entwicklung der Clariiden und ihre Verbreitung. Eine anatomisch-systematische Untersuchung. – Revue Zool. Bot. afr., 28, No. 1:77–147. 1935. 24 figs., 5 tables.

Dawson, C.E. A Revision of the Western Atlantic Flatfishes Genus Gymnachirus (the Naked Soles). – Copeia, 4:646–665. 1964. ill.

Dawson, C.E. Studies on the Gobies (Pisces, Gobiidae) of Mississippi Sound and Adjacent Waters. 1. Gobiosoma, Notre Univ., Notre Dame Press, pp. 379–409. 1966.

Day, F. The Fishes of India: Being a Natural History of the Fishes Known to Inhabit the Seas and Fresh Waters of India, Burma and Ceylon, pp. 1–778. London. 1875–1878. 2 vols., pls. 1–195.

Day, F. Scientific Results of the 2nd Yarkand Mission. – Ichthyology, pp. 1–25, pls. 1–5, Calcutta. 1878.

Dean, B.D. Notes on Japanese Myxinoids. A New Genus Paramyxine and a New Species Homea okinoseanus. Reference also to their Eggs. – J. Coll. Sci. Imp. Univ. Tokyo, 19, No. 2:1–23. 1904. 4 figs.

Dean, B.D. Chimaeroid Fishes and their Development. – Publs. Carnegie Instn., Wash., 32:1–195. 1906. 144 figs.

Dean, B. A Bibliography of Fishes. – Am. Mus. Nat. Hist., 1:1–718; 2:1–702; 3:1–707. 1916–1923.

Delais, M. Notes d'ichthyologie Ouest-Africaine I. Note sur les Antennariidés en collection au laboratoire de biologie marine de l'I.F.A.N. à Gorée. – Bull. Inst. fr. Afr. noire, 13:145–150. 1951. 6 figs.

Delais, M. Notes d'ichthyologie Ouest-Africaine II. Les Gobiidae d'A.O.F. en collection au laboratoire de biologie marine de Gorée. – Ibid., pp. 343–370. 32 figs.

Delais, M. Notes d'ichthyologie Ouest-Africaine. III. Notes sur les Lutjanidae. – Ibid., **14**:1214–1227. 1952. 8 figs.

Deraniyagala, P.E.P. The Labyrinthici of Ceylon. – Ceylon J. Sci. Biol. Sci., **15**, No. 2:79–111, pls. 23–31. 1929.

Deraniyagala, P.E.P. Istiophoridae and Xiphiidae of Ceylon. – Spolia zeylon, **26**:137–142. 1951. 3 pls.

Deraniyagala, P.E.P. A Colored Atlas of Some Vertebrates from Ceylon. 1. Fishes. – Ceylon Nat. Mus. Publ., pp. 1–149, pls. 1–34, figs. 1–60. 1952.

De Witt, H.H. A Revision of the Antarctic Genus Racovitzia (Pisces, Bathydraconidae). – Copeia, **3**:496–506. 1964. ill.

Dharmarajan, M. The Anatomy of Otolithus rubes (Bloch et Schneider). 1. The Endoskeleton. – Jl. R. Asiat. Soc. Beng., Science, **2**:1–72. 1936.

Dick, M.M. Esocidae. – In: Fishes W.N. Atlantic. 4. Mem. Sears Found. Mar. Res., **1**, No. 4:550–560. 1964.

Dietz, P.A. Über die systematische Stellung der Gadidae. – Mitt. zool. Stn. Neapel, **22**:433–457. 1921.

Dieuzeide, R. Les Sciénides des côtes algériennes. – Bull. Stn. Agric. Pêche Castiglione, **1**:131–161. 1929.

Dineen, C.F. and P.S. Stokley. Osteology of the Central Mudminnow, Umbra limi. – Copeia, **3**:169–178. 1954.

Disler, N.N. Development of the Lateral Line Sense Organs in Perches and Rockfishes. – Trudy Inst. Morf. Zhivot. Akad. Nauk SSSR, **2**:85–139. 1950.

Disler, N.N. Sense Organs of the Lateral Line System and their Significance in Fish Behavior, pp. 1–309. – Moscow, Akad. Nauk SSSR. 1960. 57 figs.

Dollfus, R.P. Les Syngnathidae de la Mer Rouge. Liste des espèces avec la description d'une sous-espèce nouvelle. – Bull. Mus. natn. Hist. nat., Paris, Ser. 2, **10**, No. 5:496–506. 1938.

Dorofeeva, E.A. Comparative Morphology Principles of the Systematics of East European Salmons. – Vopr. Ikhtiol., **7**, No. 1(42):3–18. 1967.

Dorofeeva, E.A. Variability of Some Systematic Characters in the Evolution of Sevan Trout (Salmo ischchan Kessler). – Ibid., **8**, No. 1:45–53. 1968.

Dorofeeva, E.A. Morphological Principles of the Systematics of East European Salmons of the Genus Salmo. Author's Summary of Candidate Thesis. – Zool. Inst. Akad. Nauk SSSR, pp. 1–20. Leningrad. 1969.

Dottrens, E. Le Corégone actuel du Léman. – Revue suisse Zool., **57**:789–813. 1950. 6 figs., 3 tabs.

Dottrens, E. Systématique des Corégones de l'Europe occidentale basée sur une étude biométrique. – Ibid., **66**:1–66. 1959. 12 figs.

Drapkin, E.I. A Short Key to Sand Smelts (Pisces, Atherinidae) of the Black Sea and the Sea of Azov. – Trudy Novorossiisk. Biol. Sta., pp. 143–145. 1961. ill.

Drapkin, E.I. A Short Key to Frogfishes (Pisces, Callionymidae) of the Black and Mediterranean Seas. – Ibid., pp. 146–151.

Drapkin, E.I. Specific Composition and Some Problems of the Biology of Frogfishes (Pisces, Callionymidae) of the Black Sea. – Byull. Mosk. Obshch. Ispyt. Prir., otd. biol., **72**, No. 2:22–37. 1967.

Drensky, P. Die Fische der Familie Cobitidae in Bulgarien. – Bull. Inst. Roy. Hist. Nat., Sofia, **1**:156–181. 1928. 5 figs.

Drensky, P. Petromyzontiden (Pisces) aus dem Donaugebiet. – Sber. Ges. naturf. Freunde Berl., pp. 102–106. 1935. 2 figs.

Dul'keit, G.D. Whitefishes of the Upper and Central Reaches of the Ob River. – Trudy Biol. Nauchno-Issled. Inst. Tomsk. Gos. Univ., **6**:40–46. 1939.

Duncker, G. Die Gattungen der Syngnathidae. – Mitt. naturh. Mus. Ham., (Suppl. 2, Year Rep., Sci. Preparation), **29**:219–240. 1912.

Duncker, G. Revision der Syngnathidae. 1. – Ibid., **32**:9–120. 1915. 1 pl., 10 text-figs.

Duncker, G. II. Scleroparei (Physoclisti). – Tierwelt N. - u. Ostsee, **10**, No. 12:61–84. 1927.

Duncker, G. and E. Mohr. Die Fische der Südsee-Expedition der Hamburgischen Wissenschaftlichen Stiftung 1908–1909. – Mitt. zool. Mus. Hamb., **41**:93–112. 1925. pl. 11, 13 text-figs.

Duncker, G. and E. Mohr. 7. Bleniiformes. – Tierwelt N. – u. Ostsee, **12**, No. 3:89–106. 1928.

Duncker, G. and E. Mohr. Die nordeuropäischen Ammodytes-Arten des Hamburger Zoologischen Museums. – Zool. Anz., **110**:216–220. 1935.

Duncker, G. and E. Mohr. Revision der Ammodytidae. – Mitt. zool. Mus. Berl., **24**:1–31. 1939. 4 text-figs.

Dvinin, P.A. Salmons from Southern Sakhalin. – Izv. Tikhookean. Nauchno-Issled. Ryb. Khoz. Okeanogr., 37:69–107. 1952. 2 figs.

Dymond, J.R. The Coregonine Fishes of Northwestern Canada. – Trans. R. Can. Inst., 24, No. 2:171–231. 1943.

Dymond, J.R. Salmonidae. – In: Fishes W.N. Atlantic, 3. Mem. Sears Found. Mar. Res., 1, No. 3:457–546, figs. 118–129. 1963.

Ebeling, A.W. The Dentition of Eastern Pacific Mullets with Special Reference to Adaptation and Taxonomy. – Copeia, 3:173–185, figs. 1–6, pls. 1–3. 1957.

Ebeling, A.W. Systematics and Distribution of the Species in the Bathypelagic Fish Genus Melamphaes. Doctoral dissertation, Univ. Calif., Los Angeles, pp. 1–7 + 1–373, figs. 1–24. 1960.

Ebeling, A.W. Melamphaidae. I. Systematics and Zoogeography of the Species in the Bathypelagic Fish Genus Melamphaes Günther. – Dana Rep., 58:1–164, figs. 1–73. 1962.

Ebeling, A.W. and W.H. Weed. Melamphaidae. III. Systematics and Distribution of the Species in the Bathypelagic Fish Genus Scopelogadus Vaillant. – Ibid., 60:1–58, figs. 1–23. 1963.

Ege, V. Stomiatidae (Stomias). – Rep. Dan. Oceanogr. Exped. Mediterr., 1908–1910, 2, Biol., 1, No. 4:1–28. 1918. ill.

Ege, V. Contributions to the Knowledge of the North Atlantic and Mediterranean Species of the Genus Paralepis Cuv. A Systematic and Biological Investigation (Doctoral dissertation), 2A:1–201, figs. 1–37. Copenhagen. 1930.

Ege, V. Sulidae (Paralepis). – Rep. Dan. Oceanogr. Exped. Mediterr., 10; Rep. Dan. Biol. Stn., 2A, 13:1–193. 1931. 37 figs.

Ege, V. On Some New Fishes of the Families Sudidae and Stomiatidae. – Vidensk. Meddr. dansk naturh. Foren, 94:223–236. 1933.

Ege, V. The Genus Stomias, Taxonomy and Biogeography. – Dana Rep., 5:1–58. 1934. 12 figs.

Ege, V. A Revision of the Genus Anguilla Shaw. A Systematic Phylogenetic and Geographical Study.– Ibid., 16:1–256. 1939. 53 figs., 6 pls.

Ege, V. Chauliodus Schn., Bathypelagic Genus of Fishes. A Systematic, Phylogenetic and Geographic Study.– Ibid., 31:1–148. 1948. 9 figs., 2 pls.

Ege, V. Paralepididae. 1. (Paralepis and Lestidium). Taxonomy, Ontogeny, Phylogeny and Distribution. – Ibid., 40:1–184. 1953. 33 figs.

Ege, V. Paralepididae. 2. (Macroparalepis).– Ibid., 43:1–101. 1957. 24 figs.

Ege, V. Omosudis Günther, Bathypelagic Genus of Fish. – Ibid., 47:1–20, figs. 1–3. 1958.

Ege, V. Chauliodus Schn., Bathypelagic Genus of Fishes. A Systematic, Phylogenetic and Geographical Study. – Ibid., 31:1–148. 1962. 2 pls., 9 figs.

Eggert, B. Beitrag zur Systematik, Biologie und geographischen Verbreitung der Periophthalminae. – Zool. Jber. Jena, Sec. Syst., 67:29–116. 1935. 9 pls., 16 text-figs.

Egorov, A.G. and Z.Kh. Il'yasova. Systematics of Graylings from the Upper Reaches of the Angara River.– Izv. Biologo-Geogr. Nauchno-Issled. Inst. Irkutsk Univ., 17, Nos. 1–4:84–102. (1957) 1958.

Ehrenbaum, E. Scombriformes. – Rep. Dan. Oceanogr. Exped. Mediterr., 2, A, 11:1–42, figs. 1–10, etc. 1924.

Ehrenbaum, E. Elasmobranchii. – Tierwelt N.- u. Ostsee, 7, No. 12: 1–66. 1927.

Eigenmann, C.H. On the Viviparous Fishes of the Pacific Coast of North America. — Bull. U.S. Fish Commn., 12:281—378, pls. 94—118. 1894.

Eigenmann, C.H. The Poeciliid Fishes of Rio Grande do Sul and the La Plata Basin. — Proc. U.S. Natn. Mus., 32:425—433. 1907. ill.

Eigenmann, C.H. The Serrasalminae and Mylinae. — Ann. Carneg. Mus., 9:226-272. 1915. 15 pls.

Eigenmann, C.H. The Cheirodontinae, a Subfamily of Minute Characid Fishes of South America.— Mem. Carneg. Mus., 7:1—99, pls. 1—17. 1915.

Eigenmann, C.H. The Pygidiidae, a Family of South American Catfishes. — Ibid., 7, No. 5:259—398, pls. 36—66. 1918.

Eigenmann, C.H. The Fishes of Western South America. Part 1. The Freshwater Fishes of Northwestern South America, Including Colombia, Panama, and the Pacific Slopes of Ecuador and Peru, Together with an Appendix upon the Fishes of the Rio Meta in Colombia. — Ibid., 9, No. 1:1—350, pls. 1—38. 1922.

Eigenmann, C.H. A Review of the Doradiidae. — Trans. Am. Phil. Soc., 22:280—365. 1925. 27 pls.

Eigenmann, C.H. The Freshwater Fishes of Chile. — Mem. Natn. Acad. Sci., 22:1—80, pls. 2—16. 1928.

Eigenmann, C.H. and W.R. Allen. Fishes of Western South America. I. The Intercordilleran and Amazonian Lowlands of Peru. II. The High Pampas of Peru, Bolivia and Northern Chile — with a Revision of the Peruvian Gymnotidae, and of the Genus Orestias, pp. 1—494. Univ. of Kentucky, Lexington. 1942. 48 figs., 22 pls., 1 map.

Eigenmann, C.H. and C.H. Beeson. A Revision of the Fishes of the Subfamily Sebastinae of the Pacific Coast of America. — Proc. U.S. Natn. Mus., 17:375—407. 1894.

Eigenmann, C.H. and R.S. Eigenmann. A Revision of the South American Nematognathi or Catfishes. — Occ. Pap. Calif. Acad. Sci., 1:1—509. 1890. figs.and map.

Eigenmann, C.H. and C. Kennedy. On a Collection of Fishes from Paraguay, with a Synopsis of the American Genera of Cichlids. — Proc. Acad. Nat. Sci. Philad., 55, No. 2:497—537. 1903.

Eigenmann, C.H. and G.S. Myers. The American Characidae. — Mem. Mus. Comp. Zool. Harv., **43**, 5 parts:1—574. 101 pls.; 1:1—102; 2:103—208; 3:209—310; 4:311—428; 5:429—574. 1917—1929.

Eigenmann, C.H. and A.B. Ulrey. A Review of the Embiotocidae. — Bull. U.S. Fish Commn., **12**: 382—399, pl. (1892) 1894.

Eigenmann, C.H. and D.P. Ward. The Gymnotidae. — Proc. Wash. Acad. Sci., **7**:159—188. 1905. 4 pls.

Ellis, M.M. The Gymnotid Eels of Tropical America. — Mem. Carneg. Mus., **6**, No. 3:109—195. pls.15—23. 1913—1914.

Emery, C. Fierasfer. Studi interno alla sistematica, l'anatomia e la biologia delle specie meditorranee di questo genero. — Atti Accad. naz. Lincei (Sc. Fis.), **3**, No. 7:167—254. 1880.

Engelhardt, R. Monographie der Selachier. — Abh. bayer. Akad. Wiss., 4, Suppl., **3**:1—100. 1913.

Erazi, R.A.R. Bogaziçi, Haliç ve Marmara Denizinin Heterosomat türleri. The Heterosomata of the Bosphorus, the Golden Horn and the Sea of Marmara. — Revue Fac. Sci. Univ. Istanbul, **7B**:235—262. 1942. 21 text-figs.

Eremeev, V.F. Bibliography on the Acipenseridae. — Rab. Zool. Inst. Moskov. Univ., **3**:35—66. 1936.

Eschmeyer, W.N. Western Atlantic Scorpionfishes of the Genus Scorpaena Including Four New Species. Univ. Miami Press, Coral Gables, Florida, USA. — Bull. Mar. Sci., **15**, No. 1:84—164. 1965.

Eschmeyer, W.N. and B.B. Collette. The Scorpionfish Subfamily Setarchinae, Including the Genus Ectreposebastes. — Ibid., **16**, No. 2:349—375. 1966.

Evans, F. and R.E. Sharma. The Exocoetidae of the Petula Transatlantic Expedition. — J. Linn. Soc., **45**, No. 303:53—59. 1963.

Fage, L. Engraulidae, Clupeidae. — Rep. Dan. Oceanogr. Exped. Mediterr., 1908—1910, 2, Biol., **A9**:1—140. 1920.

Fang, P.W. New Homalopterid Loaches from Kwangsi, China. With Supplementary Notes on Basipterygia and Ribs. — Sinensia, Shanghai, **1**:25—42. 1930. 2 pls., 1 text-fig.

Fang, P.W. Notes on Some Chinese Homalopterid Loaches. — Ibid., **4**, No.1:39—50. 1933. 2 figs.

Fang, P.W. Study on the Fishes Referring to Salangidae of China. — Ibid., **4**, No. 9:231—268. 1934. 10 figs.

Fang, P.W. Supplementary Notes on the Fishes Referring to Salangidae of China. — Ibid., **5**, Nos. 5—6: 505—511. 1934.

Fang, P.W. Study on the Batoid Fishes of China. — Ibid., **7**, No. 1:1—49. 1936. 6 text-figs.

Fang, P.W. On Some Schizothoracid Fishes from Western China Preserved in the National Research Institute of Biology. Academia Sinica. — Ibid., **7**, No.4:421—458. 1936. 13 text-figs.

Fang, P.W. Chinese Freshwater Fishes Referring to Cyprininae (sen. str.). — Ibid., **7**, Nos. 5—6: 686—712. 1936. 11 text-figs.

Fang, P.W. and K.F. Wang. The Elasmobranchiate Fishes of Shangtung Coast. — Contr. Biol. Lab. Sci. Soc. China, Zool. Ser. 8, **8**:213—283, figs. 1—29. 1932.

Farran, G.P. Seventh Report on the Fishes of the Irish Atlantic Slope. The Macrurid Fishes (Coryphaenoididae). — Proc. R. Ir. Acad., Sec.B, **36**:91—148. 1924. pls. 6—7, 11 figs.

Farrington, S.K. Jr. Spearfish of the World. — In: Vesey-Fitzgerald, B. and F. La Monte. Game Fish of the World, pp. 144—145. N.Y. 1949.

Fernandez-Yepez, A. Los Curimatidos (Peced fluviales de Sud America). Catalogo descriptivo con nuevas adiciones genericas y especificas. — Boln. taxon. Lab. Pesq. Caiguire, **1**:1—79. 1948. 37 text-figs.

Fernandez-Yepez, A. Contribucion al estudio de la familia Bivibranchitidae.—Mem.Soc.Cienc.Nat. La Salle, Caracas, **9**:353—355. 1949. 6 figs.

Fernandez--Yepez, A. A Revision of the South American Characid Fishes of the Genus Carnegiella. — Stanford Ichthyol. Bull., **3**:169—181. 1950. 5 figs., 1 map.

Fernandez-Yepez, A. Los peces neotropicales de la familia Acestrorhynchidae.—Revta Fac. Agric. Univ. Cent. Venez., 1, No.4:1—11.1955. 8 figs.

Fernandez-Yepez, A. Monacanthidae, una nueva familia de peces para Venezuela.— Mem. Soc. Cienc. Nat., La Salle, Caracas, 15:137—139. 1955. 2 figs.

Ferreira, R. and B.S. Soriano. Dos Trichomycteridae.— Revta Fac. Hum. Cienc. Univ. Repub. Urug., 18: 315—338. 1960. 3 pls.

Fiedler, K. Vergleichende Verhaltensstudien an Seenadeln, Schlangennadeln und Seepferdchen (Syngnathidae).— Z. Tierpsychol., 11:358—416. 1954. 35 figs.

Fields, H.M. Pompanos (Trachinotus sp.) of South Atlantic Coast of United States.— Fishery Bull. Fish Wildl. Serv. U.S., 62, No.207:189—222. 1962. 23 figs.

Fisher, H.G. A List of the Hypophthalmidae, the Diplomystidae, and of Some Unrecorded Species of Siluridae in the Collections of the Carnegie Museum.— Ann. Carneg. Mus., 11:405—422. 1917. ill.

Fitch, J.E. Notes on the Squaretail, Tetragonurus cuvieri.— Calif. Fish Game, 37, No.1:55—60 figs. 36—37. 1951.

Fitch, J.E. The Ribbon Fishes (Fam. Trachipteridae) of the Eastern Pacific Ocean with a Description of a New Species.— Ibid., 50, No.4:228—240. 1964. 5 figs.

Follett, W.I. and L.J. Dempster. Relationships of the Percoid Fish Pentaceros richardsoni Smith, with Description of a Specimen from the Coast of California.— Proc. Calif. Acad. Sci., 4, No.32: 315—338. 1963. 4 figs.

Forselius, S. Studies of Anabantid Fishes. 1—111.— Zool. Bidr. Upps., 32:93—527. (1957). 18 pls., 78 figs.

Fortunatov, M.A. Trouts from Lake Sevan. Conspecies Salmo ischchan Kessler. Systematics.— Trudy Sevan. Ozer. Sta., 1, No.2:1—131. 1927.

Fortunatova, K.R. Trouts from Lake Gek-gel.—2, Ibid., No.2:1—68. 1929.

Fourmanoir, P. Requins de la côte ouest de Madagascar.— Mem. Inst. scient. Madagascar, Série F. Oceanographie, 4: 3—81. 1961. 18 pls., 42 figs.

Fourmanoir, P. Raies et requins-scie de la côte ouest de Madagascar (Ordre des Batoidei).—Cah. O.R.S.T.O. oceanogr., 6: 33—58. 1963. ill.

Fowler, H.W. Contribution to the Ichthyology of the Tropical Pacific.— Proc. Acad. Nat. Sci. Philad., 52, No.3:493—528, pls. 18—20. (1900) 1901.

Fowler, H.W. New, Little Known and Typical Berycoid Fishes.— Ibid., 56, No.1:222—238. 1904. ill.

Fowler, H.W. Further Knowledge of Some Heterognathous Fishes. 1—2.— Ibid., 58, No.2:293—351; No.3:431—483. 1906. ill.

Fowler, H.W. Notes on Serranidae.— Ibid., 59, No.2:249—269. 1907.

Fowler, H.W. Notes on Synentognathous Fishes.— Ibid., 71, No.1:2—15, figs. 1—4. 1919.

Fowler, H.W. The Fishes of Oceania.— Mem. Bernice P. Bishop Mus., 10:1—540, pls. 1—49, text-figs. 1—82. 1928.

Fowler, H.W. A List of the Sharks and Rays of the Pacific Ocean.— Proc. 4th Pacific Congr., pp.481—508. 1929.

Fowler, H.W. A Synopsis of the Fishes of China. Part 1. The Sharks, Rays and Related Fishes.— Hong Kong Nat., 1:24—34, 79—88, 129—138, 177—189. 1930.

Fowler, H.W. A Synopsis of the Fishes of China. Part 2. The Herrings and Related Fishes.— Ibid., 2:1— 14, 111—123, 198—208. 1931.

Fowler, H.W. The Fishes of the Families Pseudochromidae, Lobotidae, Pempheridae, Priacanthidae, Lutjanidae, Pomadasyidae, and Teraponidae, Collected by the United States Bureau of Fisheries Steamer "Albatross" Chiefly in Philippine Seas and Adjacent Waters.— Bull. U.S. Natn. Mus., 100, No.11:1—388, figs. 1—29. 1931.

Fowler, H.W. A Synopsis of the Fishes of China. Part 3. The Eels.— Hong Kong Nat., 3:46—63, 126—144. 1932.

Fowler, H.W. A Synopsis of the Fishes of China. Part 4. The Cats, Lizard Fishes, Green Gars, Half Beaks and Flying Fishes.— Ibid., 3: 247—279, figs. 1—22. 1932.

Fowler, H.W. The Fishes of the Families Banjosidae, Lethrinidae, Sparidae, Girellidae, Kyphosidae, Oplegnathidae, Gerridae, Mullidae, Emmelichthyidae, Sciaenidae, Sillaginidae, Arripidae and Enoplosidae Collected by the United States Bureau of Fisheries Steamer "Albatross" Chiefly in Philippine Seas and Adjacent Waters.— Bull. U.S. Natn. Mus., 100, No. 12: 1—465. 1933.

Fowler, H.W. Descriptions of New Fishes Obtained 1907 — 1910, Chiefly in the Philippine Islands and Adjacent Seas.— Proc. Acad. Nat. Sci. Philad., 85, No. 2: 233—367. (1933) 1934. 117 figs.

Fowler, H.W. A Synopsis of the Fishes of China. Part 5. The Cods, Opahs, Flounders, Soles, John Dories, Berycoids, Pipefishes, Silversides, Mullets, Barracudas and Threadfishes.— Hong Kong Nat., 4, No.2: 156—175. 1933; 5, No.1:54—67. 1934; 5, No.2:146—155. 1934; 5, No.3:210—225. 1934; 5, No.4: 304—319. 1934; 6, No.1:62—77. 1935; 6, No.2:132—147. 1935; 6, Nos.3—4:276—284. 1935. 284. 1935.

Fowler,H.W. Zoological Results of the Third de Schauensee Siamese Expedition. Part VI—Fishes Obtained in 1934.— Proc. Acad. Nat. Sci. Philad., 87, No.1:89—163, figs. 1—132. 1935.

Fowler,H.W. A Synopsis of the Fishes of China. Part 6. The Mackerels and Related Fishes.— Hong Kong Nat., 7, No.1:61—80; 7, No.2:186—202; 7, Nos. 3—4:271—315. 1936.

Fowler,H.W. Zoological Results of the Third de Schauensee Siamese Expedition. Part VIII — Fishes Obtained in 1936.— Proc. Acad. Nat. Sci. Philad., 89, No.1:125—264, figs. 1—300. 1937.

Fowler,H.W. A Synopsis of the Fishes of China. Part 7. The Perch-like Fishes.— Hong Kong Nat., 8:124—145. 1937; 8, Nos. 3—4:249—289. 1937; 9, Nos. 1—2: 58—86. 1938; 9, No.3:141—164. 1938; 10, No.1:39—62. 1940; 10, No.2:109—121. 1940; 10, Nos. 3—4:205—222. 1941. J. Hong Kong Fish., Res. Stn., 2, No.1:3—65. 1949; Q.Jl. Taiwan Mus., 6, No.1:1—77. 1953; 7, Nos.1—2: 1—110. 1954; 9, Nos. 3—4:161—354. (1956). 1957.

Fowler,H.W. The Fishes of the George Vanderbilt South Pacific Expedition, 1937.— Monogr. Acad. Nat. Sci. Philad., 2:1—349, figs. 1—31. 1938.

Fowler,H.W. Descriptions of New Fishes Obtained by United States Bureau of Fisheries Steamer "Albatross" Chiefly in the Philippine Islands and Adjacent Waters.— Proc. U.S. Natn. Mus., 85, No.1;31—135, figs. 6—61. 1938.

Fowler,H.W. Zoological Results of the Second Bolivian Expedition. 1. The Fishes.— Proc. Acad. Nat. Sci. Philad., 92:43—103. 1940. 52 figs.

Fowler,H.W. New Fishes of the Family Callionymidae, Mostly Philippine Obtained by the United States Bureau of Fisheries Steamer "Albatross".—Proc.U.S.Natn. Mus., 90, No.1:1—31, figs.1—16. 1941.

Fowler,H.W. The Fishes of the Groups Elasmobranchii, Holocephali; Isospondyli and Ostariophysi Obtained by the United States Steamer "Albatross" in 1907 to 1910, Chiefly in the Philippine Islands and Adjacent Seas.— Bull. U.S. Natn. Mus., 100, No.13: 1—879, figs. 1—30. 1941.

Fowler, H.W. Description of a New Deep-water Angler (Chaunacidae) from off New Jersey.— Notulae Naturae Acad. Nat. Sci. Philad., 180: 1—4, figs. 1—6. 1946.

Fowler,H.W. A synopsis of the Fishes of China. Part 8. The Blennioid and Related Fishes.— Q. Jl. Taiwan Mus., 11:147—339; 12:67—97. 1958.

Fowler,H.W. A Synopsis of the Fishes of China. Part 9. The Gobioid Fishes.— Ibid., 13:91—161. 1960; 14:49—87, 203—250. 1961; 15:1—77. 1962.

Fowler,H.W. and B.A.Bean. The Fishes of the Families Pomacentridae, Labridae, and Callyodontidae, Collected by the United States Bureau of Fisheries Steamer "Albatross," Chiefly in Philippine Seas and Adjacent Waters.— Bull. U.S. Natn. Mus., 100, No.7:1—525, pls. 1—49. 1928.

Fowler,H.W. and B.A.Bean. The Fishes of the Series Capriformes, Ephippiformes and Squamipennes, Collected by the United States Bureau of Fisheries Steamer "Albatross," Chiefly in Philippine Seas and Adjacent Waters — Ibid., 100, No.8:1—352, figs. 1—25. 1929.

Fowler,H.W. and B.A.Bean. The Fishes of the Families Amiidae, Chandidae, Duleidae and Serranidae, Obtained by the United States Bureau of Fisheries Steamer "Albatross".— Ibid., 100, No.10:i + ix + 1—334, figs. 1— 27. 1930.

Franca,P. da. Contribuicão para o conhecimento dos Carangédeos (Carangidae, Pomatomidae e Coryphaenidae) de Angola.— Anais Jta. Invest. Ultramar, 9, No.2:99—150. 1956. 6 pls.

Franca, P. da. Contribuicão para o conhecimento dos Serranidae de Angola.— Ibid., 10, No.2. 1957. 40 pp. 4 pls.

Franca, P. da. Contribuicão para o connecimento dos Stromateidae de Angola.— Ibid., 11, No.2:7—26. 1958. 2 pls., 1 fig.

Franca,P. da. Heterosomata de Angola. 1. Contribuicão para o estudo des familias Psettodidae, Citharidae, Paralichthyidae e Bothidae.— Ibid., 12, No.2:1—44. 1958. 26 figs.

Franca, P.da. Contribuicão para o conhecimento dos Sciaenidae de Angola.— Mems. Ita. Invest. Ultramar, 2, No.4:7—52. 1958. 11 figs.

Franca, P. da, and P.Picciochi. Contribuicão para o conhecimento dos Pomadasyidae de Angola.— Ibid., pp. 143—195. 7 figs.

Franz,V. Die japanischen Knochenfische der Sammlungen Haberer und Doflein.— Abh. bayer. Akad. Wiss., Math.— Phys. Kl., Suppl. 4, 1:1—135. 1910. 7 figs. pls. 1—11.

Franz,V. Systematische Revision der Akranier.— Jena. Z.Naturw., 58:418. 1922.

Fraser-Brunner,A. A Revision of the Chaetodont Fishes of the Subfamily Pomacanthinae.— Proc. Zool. Soc. Lond., pp.543—599. 1933. 1 pl., 29 text-figs.

Fraser- Brunner,A. Notes on the Plectognath Fishes. 1. A Synopsis of the Genera of the Family Balistidae.— Ann. Mag. Nat. Hist., (10), 15:658—663. 1935. 2 figs.

Fraser-Brunner, A. Notes on the Plectognath Fishes. 2. A Synopsis of the Genera of the Family Ostraciontidae.— Ibid. (10), 16:313—320. 1935. 6 figs.

Fraser-Brunner, A. A New Fish of the Genus Selenotoca.— Ibid., No.2:76—80. 1938.

Fraser-Brunner, A. Notes on the Scatophagid Fishes, with Description of a Species New to Science.— Aquarist Pondkpr., 8, No.3:72—75. 1938. 3 text-figs.

Fraser-Brunner, A. Notes on the Plectognath Fishes. 3. On Monacanthus setifer Bennett and Related Species, with a Key to the Genus Stephanolepis and Descriptions of Four New Species.— Ann. Mag. Nat. Hist., (11), 5:518—535. 1940. 7 figs.

Fraser-Brunner, A. Notes on the Plectognath Fishes. 5. The Families of Triacanthiform Fishes, with a Synopsis of the Genera and Description of a New Species.— Ibid. (11) 7:420—430. 1941. 4 text-figs.

Fraser-Brunner, A. Notes on the Plectognath Fishes. 7. A Synopsis of the Genera of the Family Aluteridae, and Descriptions of Seven New Species.— Ibid. (11) **8**: 176 — 199. 1941. 9 text-figs.

Fraser-Brunner, A. Notes on the Plectognath Fishes. 7. Aracanidae, a Distinct Family of Ostraciontoid Fishes, with Descriptions of Two New Species.— Ibid., pp. 306 — 313, figs. 1, 2.

Fraser-Brunner, A. Notes on the Plectognath Fishes. 8. The Classification of the Suborder Tetraodontoidea, with a Synopsis of the Genera.— Ibid. (11) 10: 1 — 18, text-figs. 1—4. 1943.

Fraser-Brunner, A. On the Fishes of the Genus Euthynnus.— Ibid. (12) **2**: 622 — 627. 1949. 2 text-figs.

Fraser-Brunner, A. A Classification of the Fishes of the Family Myctophidae.— Proc. Zool. Soc. Lond., **118**, No. 4: 1019 — 1106. 1949, figs., 1 pl.

Fraser-Brunner, A. Studies in Plectognath Fishes from the Celebes Sea.— Dana Rep., **35**: 1—8. 1950. 5 text-figs.

Fraser-Brunner, A. A Synopsis of the Hammerhead Sharks (Sphyrna), with Description of a New Species.— Rec. Aust. Mus., **22**, No. 3: 213 — 219, fig. 1—3. 1950.

Fraser-Brunner, A. The Fishes of the Family Scombridae.— Ann. Mag. Nat. Hist., (12) 3: 131 — 163, figs. 1 — 35. 1950.

Fraser-Brunner, A. Note on the Fishes of the Genus Antigonia (Caproidae). Ibid., pp. 721 — 724.

Fraser-Brunner, A. A Revision of the Fishes of the Family Gasteropelecidae.— Ibid., pp. **3**: 956 — 970. 5 figs.

Fraser-Brunner, A. The Hatchetfishes.— Aquarium, Philad., **20**: 39 — 44. 1951. 10 text-figs.

Fraser-Brunner, A. The Ocean Sunfishes (Fam. Molidae).— Bull. Br. Mus. Nat. Hist., Zoology, 1, No. 6: 89 — 121, figs. 1—18. 1951.

Fraser-Brunner, A. Some New Blennioid Fishes, with a Key to the Genus Antennablennius.— Ann. Mag. Nat. Hist., (12) **4**: 213 — 220. 1951. 6 text-figs.

Fraser-Brunner, A. A Synopsis of the Centropomid Fishes of the Subfamily Chandinae, with Descriptions of a New Genus and Two New Species.— Bull. Raffles Mus., **25**: 185 — 213, figs. 1—4. 1955.

Freihofer, W.C. Patterns of the Ramus Lateralis Accessorius and their Systematic Significance in Teleostean Fishes.— Stanford Ichthyol. Bull., **8**, No. 2: 80 — 189. 1963.

Freidenfelt, T. Untersuchungen über die Coregonen des Wenersees.— Int. Revue ges. Hydrobiol. Hydrogr., **30**, Nos. 1—2: 49 — 163. 1934. 1 map, 36 figs., 3 text-figs.

Frost, G.A. A Comparative Study of the Neopterygian Fishes (Continued). Orders Allotriognathi, Berycomorphi, Zeomorphi.— Ann. Mag. Nat. Hist., **9**, No. 19: 439 — 445. 1927.

Gaibova, R.A. Gobiidae of the Shikhovo-Karadag Region of the Caspian Sea.— Trudy Zool. Inst., Baku, **15**: 53 — 106. 1952. 4 figs.

Galkin, G. G. Atlas of the Scale Cover of Freshwater Teleost Fishes.— Izv. Vses. Nauchno-Issled. Inst. Ozern. Rechn. Ryb. Khoz., **46**: 1 — 105, figs. 1— 155. 1958.

Garman, S.W. New Sharks: Chlamydoselachus anguineus and Heptranchias pectorosus.— Bull. Essex Inst., **16**: 3 — 15. 1884.

Garman, S.W. The Discoboli, Cyclopteridae, Liparopsidae and Liparidae.— Mem. Mus. Comp. Zool. Harv., 14, No. 2: 1—96, pls. 1— 13. 1892.

Garman, S.W. The Cyprinodonts.— Ibid., 19, No. 1: 5 — 179, pls. 1—12. 1895.

Garman, S.W. The Chimaeroids, Especially Rhinochimera and its Allies.— Bull. Mus. Comp. Zool. Harv., **41**, No. 2: 145 — 272. 1904. 15 pls.

Garman, S.W. The Chismopnea (Chimaeroids).— Mem. Mus. Comp. Zool. Harv., **40**, No. 3: 79 — 101. 1911.

Garman, S.W. The Plagiostomia (Sharks, Skates, and Rays).— Ibid., **36**: 1— 528. 1913. 77 pls.

Garnaud, J. Monographie de l'Apogon méditerraneen, Apogon imberbis (Linné, 1758).— Bull. Inst. océanogr. Monaco, **1248**: 1—83. 1962. ill.

Garrick, J.A.F. Studies on New Zealand Elasmobranchii. Part I. Two Further Specimens of Arhynchobatis asperrimus Waite (Batoidei) with an Account of the Skeleton and a Discussion on the Systematic Position of the Species.– Trans. R.Soc. N.Z., **82**, No. 1: 119 – 132, text-figs. 1–3. 1954.

Garrick, J.A.F. Studies on New Zealand Elasmobranchii. Part V. Scymnodalatias n.g. Based on Scymnodon sherwoodi Archev, 1921 (Selachii).– Ibid., **83**: 555 – 571. 1956. 2 figs.

Garrick, J.A.F. Studies on New Zealand Elasmobranchii, Part XI. Squaloids of the Genera Deania, Etmopterus, Oxynotus and Dalatias in New Zealand Waters.– Ibid., **88**, No. 3: 489 – 517. 1960.

Garrick, J.A.F. Studies on New Zealand Elasmobranchii. Part XII. The Species of Squalus from New Zealand and Australia; and a General Account and Key to the New Zealand Squaloidea.– Ibid., pp. 519 – 557. 6 figs.

Garrick, J.A.F. Revision of Sharks of Genus Isurus with Description of a New Species (Galeoidea, Lamnidae).– Proc. U.S.Natn. Mus., **118**, No. 3537: 663 – 690. 1967. 9 figs., 4 pls.

Garrick, J.A.F. and L.P.Schultz. Sharks and Survival. Chapter 1. A Guide to the Kinds of Potentially Dangerous Sharks.– In: Sharks and Survival (ed. Gilbert). Smithson. Inst. Wash., D.C., pp. 3 – 60, figs. 1 – 33. 1963.

Géry, J. New Cheirodontidae from French Guiana (Characoid Fishes Study, 6).– Senckenberg. biol., **41**, Nos. 1 – 2: 15 – 39. 1960.

Géry, J. Contributions à l'étude des poissons Characoides. 13. Structures et évolution des Anostominae.– Bull. Aquat. Biol., **2**: 93 – 112. 1961. 24 figs.

Géry, J. Contributions à l'étude des poissons Characoides. 27. Sistématique et évolution de quelques Piranhas (Serrasalmus). – Vie Milieu, **14**, No. 3: 597 – 617. 1963.

Géry, J. Paired Frontal Foramina in Living Teleosts: Definition of a New Family of Characoid Fishes, the Crenuchidae.– Nature, **198**: 502 – 503. 1963. 2 figs.

Géry, J. Une nouvelle famille des poissons dulcaquicoles africains: les Grasseichthyidae.– C.r.hébd. Séanc. Acad. Sci., Paris, **259**, No. 25: 4805 – 4807. 1964.

Géry, J. Poissons characoides de l'Amazonie péruvienne. Characoid Fishes Study. 37.– Beitr. neotrop. Fauna, **1**, No. 1: 1–44. 1964.

Géry, J. Poissons characoides sud-américains du Senckenberg Museum. 2. Characidae et Crenuchidae de l'Igarapé Peto (Haute Amazonie).–Senckenberg. biol., **46**:11–45. 1965. 4 pls., 4 figs.; **46**, No. 3: 195–218. 1965. 2 pls., 8 figs.

Gibbs, R.H. The Stomiatoid Fish Genera Eustomias and Melanostomias in the Pacific, with Descriptions of Two New Species.– Copeia, **3**: 200 – 203. 1960.

Gibbs, R.H. Astronesthidae.– In: Fishes of the W.N.Atlantic. 4. Mem. Sears. Found. Mar. Res., **1**, No. 4: 311 – 350, figs. 77 – 91. 1964.

Gibbs, R.H. Idiacanthidae.– Ibid., pp. 512 – 522, figs. 137 – 140.

Gibbs, R.H. and B.B.Collette. On the Identification, Distribution, and Biology of the Dolphins Coryphaena hippurus and C. equisetis.– Bull. Mar. Sci. Gulf Caribb., **9**, No. 2: 117 – 152, figs. 1–18 (1958) 1959.

Gibbs, R.H. and B.B.Collette. Comparative Anatomy and Systematics of the Tunas, Genus Thunnus.– Fish. Bull., **66**, No. 1: 65 – 130. 1966.

Gibbs, R.H. and N.J.Wilimovsky. Alepisauridae.– In Fishes W.N.Atlantic, 5, Mem. Sears Found. Mar. Res., **1**, No. 5: 482 – 497. 1966.

Gilbert, C.H. The Lantern-fishes of Japan.– Mem. Carneg. Mus., **6**, No. 2: 67 – 107, pls. 11–14. 1913.

Gilbert, C.H. and C.V.Burke. New Cyclogasterid Fishes from Japan.– Proc. U.S. Natn. Mus., **42**: 351 –380, pls. 41 – 48. (1910) 1912.

Gilbert, C.H. and C.L.Hubbs. Report on the Japanese Macrouroid Fishes Collected by the United States Fisheries Steamer "Albatross" in 1906, with a Synopsis of the Genera.– Ibid., **51**: 135 – 214, pls. 8 – 11. (1916) 1917.

Gilbert, C.H. and C.L.Hubbs. The Macrouroid Fishes of the Philippine Islands and East Indies.– Bull. U.S.Natn. Mus., **100**, Nos. 1, 7: 369 – 588. 1920. 40 text-figs.

Gilbert, C.R. A Revision of the Hammerhead Sharks (Fam. Sphyrnidae).– Proc. U.S. Natn. Mus., 119: 1–88. 1967. 22 figs., 10 pls.

Gilbert, P.W. (ed.). Sharks and Survival. D.C. Heath a. Co., Boston: 1–XIV, 1–578. 1963.

Gilchrist, J.D.F. Note on the Oesophageal Teeth of Stromateidae.– Ann. Mag. Nat. Hist., (9) 10: 249–255, figs. 1–2. 1922.

Gilchrist, J.D.F. and C. von Bonde. The Stromateidae (Butter Fishes) Collected by the S.S. "Pickle." – Fisheries and Mar. Biol. Surv. S. Afr. Rep. 3. 1922. Spec. Rep., 4: 1–12, pls. 17–19; 1924; Spec. Rep., 7: 1–24. 1924. 6 pls.

Gilchrist, J.D.F. and W. Thompson. The Blenniidae of South Africa.– Ann. S. Afr. Mus., 6: 97–143. 1908.

Gill, T. On the Psychrolutidae of Günther.– Proc. U.S. Natn. Mus., 11: 321–327. (1888) 1889. ill.

Gill, T. On the Classification of the Mail-cheeked Fishes.– Ibid., pp. 567–592.

Gill, T. On the Family Ranicipitidae.– Ibid., 13: 235–238, pl. 18, figs. 1–4. (1890) 1891.

Gill, T. The Characteristics of the Dactylopteroidea.– Ibid., pp. 243–248.

Gill, T. The Characteristics of the Family of Scatophagoid Fishes.– Ibid., pp. 355–360.

Gill, T. The Families of Synentognathous Fishes and their Nomenclature.– Ibid., 18: 167–178 (1895) 1896.

Gill, T. On the Relations of the Fishes of the Family Lamprididae or Opahs.– Ibid., 26: 915–924. 1903.

Gill, T. The Fishes of the African Family Kneriidae.– Science, N.Y., 2 Ser., 18: 338–339. 1903.

Gill, T. On the Systematic Relations of the Ammodytoid Fishes.– Ibid., 28: 159–163. 1904.

Gill, T. Note on the Genera of Synanceine and Pelorine Fishes.– Ibid., pp. 221–225.

Giltay, L. Notes ichthyologiques. 8. Les larves de Schindler sont-elles des Hemirhamphidae.– Bull. Mus. r. Hist. nat. Belg., 10, No. 13: 1–10. 1934. 4 figs.

Giltay, L. Notes ichthyologiques. 9. Contribution à l'étude du genre Xenopomatichthys (Kneriidae).– Ibid., 10, No. 44: 1–22. 1934. 14 figs.

Giltay, L. Notes ichthyologiques. 11. Révision du genre Hemipsilichthys (Loricariidae).– Ibid., 12, No. 14: 1–7. 1936.

Ginsburg, I. A Revision of the Genus Gobionellus (Family Gobiidae).– Bull. Bingham Oceanogr. Coll., 4: 3–51. 1932. 7 figs.

Ginsburg, I. A Revision of the Genus Gobiosoma (Family Gobiidae) with an Account of the Genus Garmannia.– Bull. Bingham Oceanogr. Coll., 4, No. 5: 1–59. 1933.

Ginsburg, I. Review of the Seahorses (Hippocampus) Found on the Coasts of the American Continents and of Europe.– Proc. U.S. Natn. Mus., 83: 497–494, text-figs. 54–71. 1937.

Ginsburg, I. Review of the Western Atlantic Triglidae (Fishes).– Text. J. Sci., 2: 489–527. 1950. tabs.

Ginsburg, I. Western Atlatnic Tonguefishes with Descriptions of Six New Species.– Zoologica, N.Y., 36: 185–201. 1951. 3 pls., 6 tabls.

Ginsburg, I. The Eels of the Northern Gulf Coast of the United States and Some Related Species.– Tex. J. Sci., 3: 431–485. 1951. 16 figs.

Ginsburg, I. Fishes of the Family Carangidae of the Northern Gulf of Mexico and Three Related Species.– Publ. Inst. Mar. Sci., Univ. Texas, 2, No. 2: 43–117. 1952. 7 pls.

Ginsburg, I. Flounders of the Genus Paralichthys and Related Genera in American Waters.– Fish. Bull. U.S., 52: 265–351. 1952. 15 pls.

Ginsburg, I. Western Atlantic Scorpionfishes.– Smithson. Misc. Collns., 121, No. 8: 1–103. 1953. 6 figs.

Ginsburg, I. Fishes of the Family Percophididae from the Coasts of Eastern United States and the West Indies with Descriptions of Four New Species.– Proc. U.S. Natn. Mus., 104: 623–639, fig. 3. 1955.

Glikman, L.S. Sharks of the Paleogene and their Stratigraphic Importance, pp. 1–230.– Moscow – Leningrad, "Nauka." 1964. 76 figs., 32 pls.

Glikman, L.S. Subclass Elasmobranchii, Sharks and Rays.– In: Osnovy paleontologii. Beschelyustnye. Ryby, pp. 196–237. Moscow, "Nauka." 1964. 39 figs., 6 pls.

Godsil, H.C. A Descriptive Study of Certain Tunalike Fishes.– Calif. Fish Game, Fish. Bull., 97: 188. 1954.

Godsil, H.C. and R.D. Byers. A Systematic Study of the Pacific Tunas.– Fish. Bull. Calif., 60: 1–131. 1944. 1 pl., 74 text-figs.

Godsil, H.C. and E.K. Holmberg. A Comparison of the Bluefin Tunas, Genus Thunnus, from New England, Australia and California.– Calif. Fish Game, Fish. Bull., 77: 1–55, figs. 1–15. 1950.

Gohar, H.A. and F.M. Mazhar. The Elasmobranchs of the Northwestern Red Sea. — Publs. Mar. Biol. Stn. Ghardaga, **13**:1—144. 1964. 16 pls., 81 figs., 2 maps.

Goode, G.B. and T.H. Bean. A Revision of the Order Heteromi, Deep-sea Fishes, with a Description of the New Generic Types Macdonaldia and Lipogenys. — Proc. U.S. Natn. Mus., **18**:455—470, pl. 18. 1894.

Goode, G.B. and T.H. Bean. On Cetomimidae and Rondeletiidae, Two New Families of Bathybial Fishes from the Northwestern Atlantic. — Ibid., **17**:451—454, pl. 17. 1895.

Goode, G.B. and T.H. Bean. Oceanic Ichthyology. — Mem. Mus. Comp. Zool. Harv., **22**:1—553, pls. 1—124, 27 text-figs. (1895) 1896; Bull. U.S. Natn. Mus., **35**:1—529, pls. 1—123. 1895.

Goodrich, E.S. Cyclostomes and Fishes. — In: Lancaster, R. (ed.) A Treatise on Zoology, 9:1—518, London. 1909.

Gordon, M.S. The Eels of the Genus Stilbiscus. — Copeia, **1**:11—14. 1954.

Gosline, W.A. A Revision of the Neotropical Catfishes of the Family Callichthyidae. — Stanford Ichthyol. Bull., **2**, No. 1:1—29. 1940. 3 figs.

Gosline, W.A. Synopsis of the Genera of Pimelodid Catfishes without a Free Orbital Rim. — Ibid., **2**:83—88. 1941.

Gosline, W.A. Catalogo dos Nematognatos de aqua-doce da America do sul e central. — Bolm. Mus. nac. Rio de J., n.s. Zool., **33**:1—138. 1945.

Gosline, W.A. Contributions to the Classification of the Loricariid Catfishes. — Archos. Mus. nac., Rio de J., **41**:79—144. 1947. 9 pls.

Gosline, W.A. The Osteology and Relationships of the Echelid Eel, Kaupichthys diodontus. — Pacif. Sci., **4**:309—314. 1950. ill.

Gosline, W.A. Notes on the Characid Fishes of the Subfamily Serrasalminae. — Proc. Calif. Acad. Sci., **4**, No. 27:17—58. 1951. 2 pls., 6 figs.

Gosline, W.A. Chilorhinus brocki, a New Echelid Eel, with Notes on the Classification of the Order Anguillida. — Copeia, **3**:195—202. 1951.

Gosline, W.A. The Osteology and Classification of the Ophichthid Eels of the Hawaiian Islands. — Pacif. Sci., **5**, No. 4:298—320, figs. 1—18. 1951.

Gosline, W.A. Notes on the Systematic States of Four Eel Families. — J. Wash. Acad. Sci., **42**, No. 4: 130—135. 1952. 2 figs.

Gosline, W.A. Hawaiian Shallow-water Fishes of the Family Brotulidae, with the Description of a New Genus and Notes on Brotulid Anatomy. — Copeia, **4**:215—225. 1953. 5 figs.

Gosline, W.A. The Osteology and Relationships of Certain Gobioid Fishes, with Particular Reference to the Genera "Kraemeria" and "Microdesmus." — Pacif. Sci., **9**, No. 2:158—170. 1955.

Gosline, W.A. Mode of Life, Functional Morphology and the Classification of Modern Teleostean Fishes. — Syst. Zool., **8**, No. 3:160—164. 1959.

Gosline, W.A. Four New Species, a New Genus, and a New Suborder of Hawaiian Fishes. — Pacif. Sci., **13**:67—77. 1959. 6 figs.

Gosline, W.A. Hawaiian Lava-flow Fishes. IV. Snyderidia canina Gilbert, with Notes on the Osteology of Ophidioid Families.— Ibid., 14:373-381. 1960. 4 figs.

Gosline, W.A. A New Hawaiian Percoid Fish, Suttonia lineata, with a Discussion of its Relationships and a Definition of the Family Grammistidae. — Ibid., pp. 28—38.

Gosline, W.A. Contributions toward a Classification of Modern Isospondylous Fishes. — Bull. Br. Mus. Nat. Hist., Zoology, **6**, No. 6:327—365, figs. 1—15. 1960.

Gosline, W.A. Some Osteological Features of Modern Lower Teleostean Fishes. — Smithson. Misc. Collns., **142**, No. 3:1—42. 1961.

Gosline, W.A. The Perciform Caudal Skeleton. — Copeia, **3**:265—270. 1961. ill.

Gosline, W.A. Systematic Position and Relationships of the Percesocine Fishes. — Pacif. Sci., **16**, No. 2: 207—217. 1962. 3 figs.

Gosline, W.A. Considerations Regarding the Relationship of the Percopsiform, Cyprinodontiform, and Gadiform Fishes. — Occ. Pap. Mus. Zool. Univ. Mich., **629**:1—38. 1963. ill.

Gosline, W.A. Notes on the Osteology and Systematic Position of Hypoptychus dubowskii Steindachner and Other Perciform Fishes. — Pacif. Sci., **17**, No. 1:90—101. 1963.

Gosline, W.A. Teleostean Phylogeny. — Copeia, **2**:186—194. 1965.

Gosline, W. A. Comments on the Classification of the Percoid Fishes. — Pacif. Sci., **20**, No. 4:409—418. 1966. 2 figs.

Gosline, W. A. The Limits of the Fish Family Serranidae, with Notes on Other Lower Percoids. — Proc. Calif. Acad. Sci., **33**, No. 6:99—112. 1966. 10 figs., 1 table.

Gosline, W. A. The Suborders of Perciform Fishes. — Proc. U. S. Natn. Mus., **124**, No. 3647:1—78. 1968. 12 figs.

Gosline, W. A. and V. E. Brock. Handbook of Hawaiian Fishes, pp. 1—372, figs. 1—277. Honolulu. 1960.

Gosline, W. A., N. B. Marshall, and G. W. Mead. Order Iniomi. Characters and Synopsis of Families. — In: Fishes W. N. Atlantic. 5. Mem. Sears Found. Mar. Res., **1**, No. 5:1—18, figs. 1—6. 1966.

Gosline, W. A. and D. W. Strasburg. The Hawaiian Fishes of the Family Moringuidae: Another Eel Problem. — Copeia, **1**:9—18. 1956. 3 figs.

Graham, D. H. A Treasury of New Zealand Fishes, pp. 1—404. Wellington. 1953. ill.

Gratzianow, V. Übersicht der Süsswasser-Cottiden des russischen Reiches. — Zool. Anz., **31**, Nos. 21/22: 654—660. 1907.

Greenfield, D. W. Systematics and Zoogeography of Myripristis in the Eastern Tropical Pacific. — Calif. Fish Game, **51**:229—247. 1965. 6 figs.

Greenwood, P. H. A New Genus and Species of Catfish (Pisces, Clariidae) from the Deeper Waters of Lake Victoria. — Ann. Mag. Nat. Hist., **13**, No. 1:321—325. 1958. 1 fig.

Greenwood, P. H. A Revision of the Genus Dinotopterus (Pisces, Clariidae) with Notes on the Comparative Anatomy of the Suprabranchiae Organs in the Clariidae. — Bull. Br. Mus. Nat. Hist., Zoology, **7**, No. 4:215—241. 1961. ill.

Greenwood, P. H. A Revision of the Lake Victoria Haplochromis Species (Pisces, Cichlidae). 5. — Ibid., **9**, No. 4:139—214. 1962. ill.

Greenwood, P. H. The Swimbladder in African Notopteridae (Pisces) and its Bearing on the Taxonomy of the Family. — Ibid., **11**, No. 5:377—412. 1963.

Greenwood, P. H. The Status of Acanthothrissa Gras., 1961 (Pisces, Clupeidae). — Ann. Mag. Nat. Hist., Ser. B., **7**:337—338. 1965.

Greenwood, P. H. The Osteology and Relationships of the Denticipitidae: a Family of Clupeomorph Fishes. — Bull. Br. Mus. Nat. Hist., Zoology, **16**, No. 6:213—273. 1968. ill.

Greenwood, P. H., G. S. Myers, D. E. Rosen, and S. H. Weitzman. Named Main Divisions of Teleostean Fishes. — Proc. Biol. Soc. Wash., **80**:227—228. 1967.

Greenwood, P. H., D. E. Rosen, S. H. Weitzman, and G. S. Myers. Phyletic Studies of Teleostean Fishes with a Provisional Classification of Living Forms. — Bull. Am. Mus. Nat. Hist., **131**, No. 4:339—456. 1966.

Greenwood, P. H. and K. S. Thompson. The Pectoral Anatomy of Pantodon buchholzi Peters (a Freshwater Flying Fish) and the Related Osteoglossidae. — Proc. Zool. Soc. Lond., **135**:283—301. 1960. 9 figs.

Gregory, W. K. The Orders of Teleostomous Fishes. — Ann. N. Y. Acad. Sci., **17**:437—508, pls. 29—30. 1907.

Gregory, W. K. Fish Skulls. — Trans. Am. Phil. Soc., **23**:75—481, figs. 1—302. 1933.

Gregory, W. K. and G. M. Conrad. Pictorial Phylogenies of Deep Sea Isospondyli and Iniomi. — Copeia, **1**:21—36. 1936.

Gregory, W. K. and G. M. Conrad. The Evolution of the Pediculate Fishes. — Am. Nat., **70**:193—308, figs. 1—5. 1936.

Gregory, W. K. and G. M. Conrad. The Phylogeny of the Characin Fishes. — Zoologica, N. Y., **23**:319—360. 1937. 37 text-figs.

Gregory, W. K. and G. M. Conrad. The Comparative Osteology of the Swordfish (Xiphias) and the Sailfish (Istiophorus). — Am. Mus. Novit., **952**:1—25. 1937. 12 figs.

Gregory, W. K. and G. M. Conrad. The Osteology of Luvarus imperialis, a Scombroid Fish: a Study in Adaptive Evolution. — Bull. Am. Mus. Nat. Hist., **81**:225—283. 1943. 38 figs.

Gregory, W. K., C. L. Hubbs, and G. S. Myers. Zoological Names. A list of Phyla, Classes and Orders. Prepared for Section F. — Am. Ass. Adv. Sci., pp. 1—24. 1949.

Gregory, W. K. and H. C. Roven. Notes on the Anatomy and Relationships of the Ocean Sunfish (Mola mola). — Copeia, **4**:145—151, pl. 1934.

Grey, M. First Record of the Deep Sea Fish Dolichopteryx longipes from the Pacific with Notes on Ophthalmopelton macropus. — Ibid., **2**:87—90. 1952. 1 fig.

Grey, M. Fishes of the Family Gempylidae, with Records of Nesiarchus and Epinnula from the Western Atlantic and Descriptions of Two New Subspecies of Epinnula orientalis.– Ibid., 3:135–141. 1953.

Grey, M. The Fishes of the Genus Tetragonurus Risso.– Dana Rep., 41:1–75. 1955. 16 figs.

Grey, M. New Records of Deep-sea Fishes, Including a New Species Oneiroides bradburyce, from the Gulf of Mexico.– Copeia, 4:242–246. 1956.

Grey, M. Deep-sea Fishes from the Gulf of Mexico with the Description of a New Species Squalogadus intermedius (Macrouroididae). – Fieldiana, Zool., 39, No.29:323–346, figs.54–57. 1959.

Grey, M. Three New Genera and One New Species of the Family Gonostomatidae. – Bull. Mus. Comp. Zool. Harv., 121, No.4:167–184, figs.1–3. 1959.

Grey, M. Description of Newly Discovered Western Atlantic Specimens of Diceratias bispinosus Günther and Paroneirodes wedli (Pietschmann). – Copeia, 3:225–228, fig.1. 1959.

Grey, M. Description of a Western Atlantic Specimen of Scombrolabrax heterolepis Roul and Notes on Fishes of the Fam. Gempylidae.– Copeia, 3:210–215. 1960. 3 figs.

Grey, M. A Preliminary Review of the Family Gonostomatidae, with a Key to the Genera and the Description of a New Species from the Tropical Pacific. – Bull. Mus. Comp. Zool. Harv., 122, No.2:55–125. 1960. 3 figs.

Grey, M. Gonostomatidae. – In: Fishes of the W.N. Atlantic. 4. Mem. Sears Found. Mar. Res., 1, No.4:78–240, figs.21–61. 1964.

Griffin, L.T. A Revision of the Carangid and Seriolid Fishes of New Zealand. – Rec. Auckland Inst. Mus., 1:123–134, pls. XVIII–XXIV. 1932.

Griffin, L.T. Revision of the Eels of New Zealand. – Trans. R. Soc. N.Z., 66:12–26, pls.5, 6, text-figs.1–6. 1936.

Grigg, G.C. Studies on the Queensland Lungfish Neoceratodus forsteri (Kreff), 1, 2, 3.– Aust. J. Zool., 13:243–253. 1 pl., 2 figs., pp.407–411. 1 fig; pp.413–421. 3 figs. 1965.

Groenwald, A.A. and J. A Revision of the Genera Barbus and Varicorhinus (Pisces, Cyprinidae) in Transvaal. – Ann. Transv. Mus., 23:263–330. 1958. 12 pls., 3 figs.

Gudger, E.W. A Study of the Smallest Sharksuckers (Echeneididae) on Record, with Special Reference to Metamorphosis. – Am. Mus. Novit., 234:1–26. 1926.

Günther, A. Catalogue of the Acantopterygian Fishes in the Collection of the British Museum. 1859–1870. 1961. 8 vols.

Günther, A. On Three New Trachinoid Fishes. – Ann. Mag. Nat. Hist., 3, No.7:85–90. pl.10, fig.2. 1861.

Günther, A. On Some New Species of Central-American Fishes. – Proc. Zool. Soc. Lond., pp.23–27. pls.3, 4. 1864.

Günther, A. Description of Ceratodus. – Phil. Trans. R. Soc., 161:511–571. 1871. 13 pls.

Günther, A. Report on the Deep-sea Fishes Collected by H.M.S. Challenger during the Years 1873–1876. – Rep. Sci. Res. Voyage of Challenger, Zool., 22:1–335. 1887. 73 pls.

Günther, K. and K.Deckert. Morphologie und Funktion des Kiefer- und Kiemen-apparates von Tiefseefischen der Gattungen Malacosteus und Photostomias (Teleostei, Isospondyli, Stomiatoidei, Malacosteidae). – Dana Rep., 9, No.49:1–54. 1959. 33 figs.

Guntherz, E.J. Revision of the Flounder Genus Ancylopsetta (Heterosomata, Bothidae) with Descriptions of Two New Species from the Antilles and the Caribbean Sea. – Bull. Mar. Sci., 16, No.3:445–479. 1966.

Haast, J. On Cheimarrichthys fosteri, a New Genus Belonging to the New Zealand Fishes. – Trans. and Proc. New Zealand Inst., 6:103. 1873, pl.18, fig.38a. 1874.

Hadzišče, S. Zur Kenntnis der Gattung Salmothymus Berg zugleich ein Beitrag zur Systematik der Familie der Salmoniden (Pisces), 3, No.2:39–56. 1962.

Haedrich, R.L. The Stromateoid Fishes: Systematics and a Classification. – Bull. Mus. Comp. Zool. Harv., 135, No.2:31–139. 1967. 56 figs.

Haedrich, R.L. A New Family of Aberrant Stromateoid Fishes from the Equatorial Pacific. – Am. Soc. Ichth. Herp., 47th Ann. Meeting Abstr. Ichth., p.12. 1967.

Haedrich, R.L. A New Family of Aberrant Stromateoid Fishes from the Equatorial Indo-Pacific. – Dana Rep., 76:1–14. 1969. 10 figs.

Haffner, R.E. Zoogeography of the Bathypelagic Fish, Chauliodus. – Syst. Zool., 1:113–133. 1952.

Haig, J. Studies on the Classification of the Catfishes of the Oriental and Palaearctic Family Siluridae. – Rec. Indian Mus., 48:59–116. 1950. 1 fig.

Hansen, P.M. et al. Gadoid Fish. – Anls. Biol., Copenh., 16:113–161. 1961. 38 figs.

Hardenberg, J.D.F. Some Remarks on the Genus Chirocentrus (Cuv.). – Treubia, Buitenzorg, 12, No.1:51–56. 1930.

Hardenberg, J.D.F. Notes on Some Genera of the Engraulidae.– Natuurk. Tijdschr. Ned.-Indië, 93:230–256. 1933.

Hardenberg, J.D.F. Some Remarks on the Genus Stolephorus Lacépède in the Indo-Australian Archipelago. – Treubia, Buitenzorg, 14:313–375. 1934. 11 figs.

Harder, W. The Intestine as a Diagnostic Character in Identifying Certain Clupeioids (Engraulididae, Clupeidae, Dussumieriidae) and as a Morphometric Character for Comparing Anchovetta (Cetengraulis mysticetus) Populations. – Bull. Inter-Amer. Tuna Comm., 2:267–388. 1958. 6 figs.

Hardy, E. A New Fish in the Atlantic. – Fishg. News, **2714**, No.9. 1965.

Harris, W.C. and T.H. Bean. The Basses, Freshwater and Marine, pp.1–238, New York. 1905. ill.

Harry, R.R. The Gobies of the Indo-Malayan Eleotrid Genus Bunaka. – Proc. Calif. Zool. Club, 1, No.3:13–18. 1948. ill.

Harry, R.R. Deep-sea Fishes of the Bermuda Oceanographic Expeditions. Family Paralepididae. –Zoologica, N.Y., **36**, No.1:17–35. 1951. 9 figs.

Harry, R.R. Deep-sea Fishes of the Bermuda Oceanographic Expeditions. Families Cetomimidae and Rondeletiidae. – Ibid., **37**, No.1:55–72, fig.4, pl.1. 1952.

Harry, R.R. A Contribution to the Classification of the African Catfishes of the Family Amphiliidae, with Description of Collections from Cameroon. – Revue Zool. Bot. afr., **47**, Nos.1–2, 3–4:177–232. 1953. 11 figs.

Harry, R.R. Studies on the Bathypelagic Fishes of the Family Paralepididae (Order Iniomi). 2. A Revision of the North Pacific Species. – Proc. Acad. Nat. Sci. Philad., **105**:169–230. 1953. 28 figs.

Harry, R.R. Studies on the Bathypelagic Fishes of the Family Paralepididae. 1. Survey of the Genera. – Pacif. Sci., **7**, No.2:219–249. 1953. 22 figs.

Hart, J.L. and J.L. Mchugh. The Smelts (Osmeridae) of British Columbia. – Bull. Fish. Res. Bd. Can., **64**:1–27. 1944. 18 text-figs.

Hay, O.P. Classification of the Amioid and Lepidosteoid Fishes. – Am. Nat., **32**:341–349. 1898. 8 figs.

Henn, A.W. On Various South American Poecilid Fishes. – Ann. Carneg. Mus., **10**, Nos.1–2:93–142. 1916. 4 pls., 17 figs.

Herald, E.S. A Key to the Pipefishes of the Pacific American Coasts with Descriptions of New Genera and Species. – Rep. Allan Hancock Pacif. Exped. 1932–1938, 951:64. 1940.

Herald, E.S. Three New Pipefishes from the Atlantic Coasts of North and South America, with a Key to the Atlantic American Species. – Stanford Ichthyol. Bull., **2**, No.4:125–132. 1942.

Herre, A.W. A Review of the Eels of the Philippine Archipelago. – Philipp. J. Sci., 23, No.2:123–263, figs.1–14, pls.1–11. 1923.

Herre, A.W. Poisonous and Worthless Fishes. An Account of the Philippine Plectognaths. – Philipp., J. Sci., 1, **25**:415–510. 1924. 2 pls.

Herre, A.W. A Summary of the Philippine Catfishes, Order Nematognathi. –Ibid., 31, No.3:385–413, pl.1. 1926.

Herre, A.W. Gobies of the Philippines and the China Sea. – Manila Monograph., 23:1–352. pls.1–30, text-figs.1–6. 1927.

Herre, A.W. The Philippine Bandfishes.– Philipp. J. Sci., 34, No.3:281–285, pl.1. 1927.

Herre, A.W. Philippine Surgeonfishes and Moorish Idols. – Ibid., 34, No.4:403–478. pls.1–16. 1927.

Herre, A.W. The Philippine Gars or Needlefishes.– Ibid., 36:215–232. 1928. 4 pls.

Herre, A.W. New Fishes Obtained by the Crane Pacific Expedition. – Field Mus. Publ. (Zool.), Chicago, **18**, No.12:383–384, figs.31–33. 1935.

Herre, A.W. The Philippine Blennies. – Philipp. J. Sci., **70**:315–372. 1939. 5 pls.

Herre, A.W. The Genera of Phallostethidae. – Proc. Biol. Soc. Wash., 52:139–144. 1939.

Herre, A.W. Notes on Fishes in the Zoological Museum of Stanford University. VII. New and Rare Philippine Gobies from the Herre 1936–1937 Oriental Expedition and in the Collections of the Bureau of Science. – Philipp. J. Sci., 72:357–369. 1940. 6 pls.

Herre, A.W. New and Little Known Phallostethids, with Key to the Genera and Philippine Species. – Stanford Ichthyol. Bull., 2:137–156. 1942. 1 text-fig.

Herre, A.W. A Review of the Halfbeaks or Hemiramphide of the Philippines and Adjacent Waters. – Stanford Univ. Publs., Ser. Biol. Sci., 9, No.2:41–80. 1944. 1 chart.

Herre, A.W. Notes on Fishes in the Zoological Museum of Stanford University. XIX. The New Philippine Gobies with Key to the Genera of Gobies with Vomerine Teeth. – Proc. Biol. Soc. Wash., **58**:77–82. 1945.

Herre, A.W. A Review of the Scorpaenoid Fishes of the Philippines and Adjacent Seas. – Philipp. J. Sci., **80**:381–482. 1952.

Herre, A.W. The Eleotrid Gobies of the Philippines and Adjacent Regions. – Ibid., **82**, No.4:345–373. 1954.

Herre, A.W. The Guitarfishes, Family Rhinobatidae, of the Philippines and Adjacent Seas. – Ibid., **83**, No.4:381–400, pls.1–3. (1954) 1955.

Herre, A.W. The Guitarfishes, Family Rhinobatidae, of the Philippines and Adjacent Seas. – Proc. 8th Pac. Sci. Congr. **3A**:1595–1620. 1957. 7 pls.

Herre, A.W. and H.R. Montalban. The Philippine Species of Kuhliidae. – Philipp. J. Sci., **33**, No.2: 199–209, pl.1. 1927.

Herre, A.W. and H.R. Montalban. Philippine Sparoid and Rudder Fishes. – Ibid., **33**, No.4:397–441, pls.1–9. 1927.

Herre, A.W. and H.R. Montalban. The Philippine Butterfly Fishes and their Allies. – Ibid., **34**:1–113, pls.1–24. 1927.

Herre, A.W. and H.R. Montalban. The Philippine Siganids. – Ibid., **35**:151–184. 1928. 6 pls.

Herre, A.W. and H.R. Montalban. The Goatfishes or Mullidae of the Philippines. – Ibid., **36**, No.1: 95–137, pls.1–6. 1928.

Heuschmann, O. Weissfische (Cyprinidae). – Handb. Binnenfisch. Mitteleur., **3B**:23–190. 1962. ill.

Hikita, T. Flatfishes Found in Northern Japan. – Bull. Sch. Fish. Hokkaido Imp. Univ., **4**:10–15, 187–296. 1934.

Hikita, T. and T. On a Wrymouth Fish Found in Japan. – Jap. J. Ichthyol., **1**:140–144. 1950. 2 text-figs.

Hikita, T. Ecological and Morphological Studies of the Genus Oncorhynchus (Salmonidae) with Particular Consideration on Phylogeny. – Scient. Rep. Hokkaido Salm. Hatch., **17**:1–97. 1962. 30 pls., 9 text-figs.

Hildebrand, S.F. A Review of the American Anchovies (Family Engraulidae). – Bull. Bingham Oceanogr. Coll., **8**, No.2:1–165. 1943. 72 text-figs.

Hildebrand, S.F. Elopidae, Albulidae. – In: Fishes W.N. Atlantic, 3. Mem. Sears Found. Mar. Res., **1**, No. 3:111–145. 1963.

Hildebrand, S.F. Engraulidae. Ibid., pp.152–247.

Hildebrand, S.F. Clupeidae. – Ibid., pp.257–451, figs.62–117.

Hildebrand, S.F. and I. de Paiva Carvalha. Notes on Some Brazilian Anchovies (Fam. Engraulidae) with Description of Four New Species. – Copeia, **4**:285–296. 1948. ill.

Hiyama, Y.A. Preliminary Note on Fishes of Hemirhamphidae of Japan. – Zool. Mag., Tokyo, **46**:401–410. 1934. 9 text-figs. (In Japanese.)

Hoedeman, J.J. Rediagnosis of the Characid-Nannostomine Fish Genera Nannostomus and Poecilobrycon. – Amst. Nat., **1**:11–27. 1950. 2 pls., 5 text-figs.

Hoedeman, J.J. Studies on African Characid Fishes. I. The Tribe Alestidi. – Beaufortia, **3**:1–8. 1951.

Hoedeman, J.J. Notes on the Ichthyology of Surinam (Dutch Guiana). The Catfish Genera Hoplosternum and Callichthys, with Key to the Genera and Groups of the Family Callichthyidae. – Ibid., **12**:1–11. 1952.

Hoedeman, J.J. Remarks on the Classification and Phylogeny of Teleostean Fishes. – Bull. Aquat. Biol., **2**, No.15:50–51. 1954.

Holly, M. Mormyriden, Characiniden und Cypriniden aus Kameroon. – Sber. Akad. Wiss. Wien, **136**, No.1:115–160. 1926. 9 figs.

Holly, M. Cyclostomata. – Tierreich, **59**:1–62. 1933. 57 figs.

Holly, M. Dipnoi. – Tierreich, **61**, Pisces, No.2:1–30. 1933. ill.

Holly, M. Die Syngnathiden der belgischen Küstengewässer. – Bull. Mus. r. Hist. nat. Belg., **12**, No.7:1–3. 1936.

Holly, M. Die Ammodytesarten der Küste des Königreiches Belgien. – Ibid., **12**, No.5:1–19. 1937.

Holt, R.D. Comparative Morphometry of the Mountain Whitefish Prosopium williamsoni. – Copeia, 3:192–300. 1960. 1 fig.

Hopson, A. Barbus (Pisces, Cyprinidae) of the Volta Region. – Bull. Br. Mus. Nat. Hist., Zool., **13**, No.4:99–149. 1965. ill.

Hora, S.L. Revision of the Indian Homalopteridae and of the Genus Psilorhynchus (Cyprinidae). — Rec. Indian Mus., 19:195–215, pls. X–XI. 1920.

Hora, S.L. Indian Cyprinoid Fishes Belonging to the Genus Garra with Notes on Related Species from Other Countries. — Ibid., 22:633–687, 5 figs., pls. 24–26. 1921.

Hora, S.L. Notes on Fish in the Indian Museum. III. On Fishes Belonging to the Family Cobitidae from High Altitudes in Central Asia. — Ibid., 24:63–83. 1922. 5 figs.

Hora, S.L. Notes on Fishes in the Indian Museum. V. On the Composite Genus Glyptosternon McClelland. — Ibid., 25:1–44, pls. I–IV. 1923.

Hora, S.L. Notes on Fishes in the Indian Museum. 6. On a New Genus of Gobioid Fishes (Subfamily Trypaucheninae) with Notes on Related Forms. — Ibid., 26:155–164. 1924. 4 text-figs.

Hora, S.L. Classification of the Homalopterid Fishes. — Ibid., 33:67–69. 1931.

Hora, S.L. Classification, Bionomics and Evolution of Homalopterid Fishes. — Mem. Indian Mus., 12, No. 2:263–330. 1932. 3 pls.

Hora, S.L. Siluroid Fishes of India, Burma and Ceylon. I. Loachlike Fishes of the Genus Amblyceps Blyth. — Rec. Indian Mus., 35:607–621. 1933. 7 figs.

Hora, S.L. On a Collection of Fish from Afghanistan. — J. Bombay Nat. Hist. Soc., 37, No. 4:784–802. 1935. ill.

Hora, S.L. Siluroid Fishes of India, Burma and Ceylon. II. Fishes of the Genus Akysis Bleeker. III. Fishes of the Genus Olyra McClelland. IV. On the Use of the Generic Name Wallago Bleeker. V. Fishes of the Genus Heteropneustes Muller. — Ibid., 38:199–209. 1936. 4 text-figs.

Hora, S.L. Siluroid Fishes of India, Burma and Ceylon. VI. Fishes of the Genus Clarias Gronovius. VII. Fishes of the Genus Silurus Linnaeus. VIII. Fishes of the Genus Callichrous Hamilton. — Ibid., pp. 347–361. 6 text-figs.

Hora, S.L. Report on Fishes. Part 1. Cobitidae. — Mem. Conn. Acad. Arts Sci., 10:299–321, pl. 12, 9 text-figs. 1936.

Hora, S.L. Catfishes of the Genus Helicophagus Bleeker. — Rec. Indian Mus., 39, No. 3:235–240. 1937.

Hora, S.L. Notes on Fishes in the Indian Museum. XXXVIII. On the Systematic Position of Bagrus lonah Sykes, with Descriptions of and Remarks on Other Glyptosternoid Fishes from the Deccan. — Ibid., 40:363–375, pl. 7. 1938.

Hora, S.L. Siluroid Fishes of India, Burma and Ceylon. XI. Fishes of the Schilbeid Genera Silonopangasius Hora, Pseudotropius Bleeker, Proeutropiichthys Hora and Ailia Gray. XII. A Further Note on Fishes of the Genus Clarias Gronovius. — Ibid., 43:97–115. 1941. 6 text-figs.

Hora, S.L. Homalopterid Fishes from Peninsular India. — Ibid., pp. 221–232, pl. 8.

Hora, S.L. Notes on Malayan Fishes in the Collection of the Raffles Museum, Singapore, 2 and 3. Loaches of the Families Cobitidae and Homalopteridae. — Bull. Raffles Mus., 17:44–64. 1941.

Hora, S.L. Siluroid Fishes of India, Burma and Ceylon. XIII. Fishes of the Genera Erethistes Müller et Troschel, Hara Blyth and of Two New Allied Genera. — Rec. Indian Mus., 47:183–202. 1950. 2 pls., 5 figs.

Hora, S.L. and J.C. Gupta. Notes on Malayan Fishes in the Collection of the Raffles Museum, Singapore. 1. Catfishes of the Families Siluridae, Bagridae, Amblycepidae, Akysidae, Sisoridae, Schilbeidae, and Clariidae. — Bull. Raffles Mus., 17:12–43. 1941.

Hora, S.L. and K.C. Jayaram. A Note on the Systematic Position of the Two Castromyzonid Genera Protomyzon Hora and Paraprotomyzon Pellegrin and Fang (Fishes: Cyprinoidea). — Rec. Indian Mus., 48:61–68. 1951. 4 figs.

Hora, S.L. and K.C. Jayaram. On Two New Gastromyzonid Fishes from Borneo. — Ibid., 49:191–195. 1952. 2 figs.

Hora, S.L. and D.D. Mukerji, Fish of the Naga Hills, Assam. — Ibid., 37, No. 3:381–406. 1935. ill.

Hora, S.L. and D.D. Mukerji. Table (Key) for the Identification of Indian Freshwater Fishes with Descriptions of Certain Families and Observations on the Relative Utility of the Probable Larvivorous Fishes of India. — Hlth. Bull. Malar. Inst. India, 4:1–47. 1938.

Hora, S.L. and E.G. Silas. Revision of the Glyptosternoid Fishes of the Family Sisoridae with Descriptions of New Genera and Species. — Rec. Indian Mus., 49:5–19. 1952. 1 pl., 2 figs.

Hotta, H. Comparative Study of the Axial Skeleton of Japanese Teleostei. — Tohoku Reg. Fisher. Res. Lab., 5, No. 2:1–155. 1961. 79 pls.

Howard, J.K. and S. Ueyanagi. Distribution and Relative Abundance of Billfishes (Istiophoridae) of the Pacific Ocean. — Stud. Trop. Oceanogr., Miami, 2:1–134. 1965. 38 maps.

Hubbs, C.L. Flounders and Soles from Japan Collected by the U. S. Bureau of Fisheries Steamer "Albatross" in 1906. — Proc. U.S. Natn. Mus., 48:449–496, pls.25–27. 1915.

Hubbs, C.L. A Revision of the Viviparous Perches. — Proc. Biol. Soc. Wash., 31:9–14. 1918.

Hubbs, C.L. A List of the Lancelets of the World, with Diagnoses of Five New Species of Branchiostoma. — Occ. Pap. Mus. Zool. Univ. Mich., 105:1–16. 1922.

Hubbs, C.L. Studies of the Fishes of the Order Cyprinodontes. 1. A Classification of the Fishes of the Order Cyprinodontes. — Misc. Publs. Mus. Zool. Univ. Mich., 13:1–31. 1924.

Hubbs, C.L. A Revision of the Osmerid Fishes of the North Pacific. — Proc. Biol. Soc. Wash., 38:49–56. 1925.

Hubbs, C.L. Descriptions of New Genera of Cottoid Fishes Related to Artedius. — Occ. Pap. Mus. Zool. Univ. Mich., 170:1–16. 1926.

Hubbs, C.L. A Revision of the Fishes of the Subfamily Oligocottinae. — Ibid., 171:1–18. 1926.

Hubbs, C.L. Studies of the Fishes of the Order Cyprinodontes. VI. — Misc. Publs. Mus. Zool. Univ. Mich., 16:1–86. 1926. 4 pls.

Hubbs, C.L. Notes on the Blennioid Fishes of Western North America. — Pap. Mich. Acad. Sci., Arts Letters, 7:351–394. 1927.

Hubbs, C.L. Materials for a Revision of the Catostomid Fishes of Eastern North America. — Misc. Publs. Mus. Zool. Univ. Mich., 20:379–423. 1930.

Hubbs, C.L. Studies of the Fishes of the Order Cyprinodontes. XII. A New Genus Related to Empetrichthys. — Occ. Pap. Mus. Zool. Univ. Mich., 252:1–5. 1932.

Hubbs, C.L. The Japanese Flounders of the Genera Tanakius, Microstomus and Glyptocephalus.— Ibid., 249:1–9. 1932.

Hubbs, C.L. Limits and Status of the Fish Group Rhegnopteri. — Copeia, 1:31–33. 1942.

Hubbs, C.L. Fin Structure and Relationships of the Phallostethid Fishes. — Ibid., 2:69–79. 1944

Hubbs, C.L. Species of the Circumtropical Fish Genus Brotula. — Ibid., 3:162–178. 1944. ill.

Hubbs, C.L. Phylogenetic Position of the Citharidae, a Family of Flatfishes. — Misc. Publs. Mus. Zool. Univ. Mich., 63:1–38. 1945. 1 fig.

Hubbs, C.L. Studies of Cyprinodont Fishes. XX. A New Subfamily from Guatemala, with Ctenoid Scales and a Unilateral Pectoral Clasper. — Ibid., 78:1–28, pls.1–4. 1950.

Hubbs, C.L. Synonymy of the Bathypelagic Fish Genus Rhynchohyalus, Referred to the Expanded Family Argentinidae. — Copeia, 2:96–97. 1953.

Hubbs, C.L. Ogcocephalus darwini, a New Batfish Endemic of the Galapagos Islands. — Contr. Scripps Instn. Oceanogr., 1045:807–826. 1958. ill.

Hubbs, C.L. Chaetodon aya and Related Deep-living Butterflyfishes: their Variation, Distribution and Synonymy. — Bull. Mar. Sci. Gulf Caribb., 13, No.1:133–192. 1963. 14 figs.

Hubbs, Clark. A Contribution to the Classification of the Blennioid Fishes of the Family Clinidae, with a Partial Revision of the Eastern Pacific Forms. — Stanford Ichthyol. Bull., 4, No.2:41–165, figs.1–64. 1952.

Hubbs, Clark. Revision of the Eastern Pacific Fishes of the Clinid Genus Labrisomus. — Zoologica, N.Y., 38, No.3(9):113–136. 1953. 9 figs.

Hubbs, Clark. Revision and Systematic Position of the Blenniid Fishes of the Genus Neoclinus. — Copeia, 1:11–23. 1953. 16 figs.

Hubbs, C.L. and R.M.Bailey. A Revision of the Black Basses (Micropterus and Huro) with Descriptions of Four New Forms. — Misc. Publs. Mus. Zool. Univ. Mich., 48:1–59, pls.1–6, maps 1–2. 1940.

Hubbs, C.L. and R.M.Bailey. Blind Catfishes from Artesian Waters of Texas. — Occ. Pap. Mus. Zool. Univ. Mich., 499:1–15. 1947. 1 pl.

Hubbs, C.L. and K.F.Lagler. Fishes of the Great Lakes Region. — Bull. Cranbrook Inst. Sci., 26:1–186, figs.1–251. 1949.

Hubbs, C.L., G.W.Mead, and N.Wilimovsky. The Widespread Probably Antitropical Distribution and the Relationships of the Bathypelagic Iniomous Fish Anotopterus pharao. — Bull Scripps Instn. Oceanogr., 6, No.5:173–198, pls.2–6, 1 fig. 1953.

Hubbs, C.L. and R.R.Miller. Studies of Cyprinodont Fishes. XXII. Variation in Lucania parva, its Establishment in Western United States, and Description of a New Species from an Interior Basin in Coahuila, Mexico. — Misc. Publs. Mus. Zool. Univ. Mich., 127:1–104. 1965. 3 pls.

Hubbs, C.L. and L.P.Schultz. Descriptions of Two New American Species Referable to the Rockfish Genus Sebastodes with Notes on Related Species. — Univ. Wash. Publs. Biol., 2, No.2:15–44. 1933.

Hubbs, C.L. and L.P. Schultz. A Revision of the Toadfishes Referred to Porichthys and Related Genera. — Proc. U. S. Natn. Mus., 86:473—496, fig.57. 1939.

Hubbs, C.L. and M.B. Trautman. A Revision of the Lamprey Genus Ichthyomyzon. — Misc. Publs. Mus. Zool. Univ. Mich., 35:1—109, figs.1—5, pls.1—2. 1937.

Hubbs, C.L. and C.L. Turner. Studies of the Fishes of the Order Cyprinodontes. XVI. A Revision of the Goodeidae. — Ibid., 42:1—80. 1939. 5 pls.

Ikeda, H. Notes on the Fishes of the Riu-Kiu Islands. III. A Biometric Study on the Species of Kuhlidae in the Riu-Kiu Islands. — Biogeographica, Trans. Biogeogr. Soc. Japan, 3, No. 2:131—158. 1939. 8 figs.

Il'in, B.S. A Key to Gobies (Fam. Gobiidae) of the Sea of Azov and the Black Sea. — Trudy Azov.-Chernomorsk. Nauchno-Prom. Eksped., 2:128—143. 1927. ill., 1 pl.

Il'in, B.S. Gobies of the Northwestern Region of the Black Sea Basin. — Trudy Gos. Ikhtiol. Opyt. Sta., 3, No.1:1—18. 1927.

Il'in, B.S. Gobiidae, from Material of the Expedition by the Academy of Sciences of the USSR to the Mertvyi Kultuk and Kaidak. — Trudy Komis. po kompleks. izuch. kaspiisk. morya Akad. nauk (KASP) i Sovet po izuch. proizvod. sil (SOPS), 2 : 111 — 131. 1938. ill.

Il'in, B.S. A Brief Survey of Black Sea Gobies. — Byull. Mosk. Obshch. Ispyt. Prir., otd. biol., 65, No.3: 16—30. 1949.

Il'in, B.S. Observations and Amendments to the Suborder Gobioidei in the Book by L.S.Berg "Freshwater Fishes of the USSR and Adjacent Countries, 4th edition, 1948—1949, pp. 1055—1125. — Vopr. Ikhtiol., 7:185—192. 1956.

Iljin, B. S. Le système des Gobiides. — Trab. Inst. esp. Océanogr., 2:1—63. 1930.

Imai, S. On a Japanese Flying Fish and its Juvenile of the Genus Prognichthys Breder. — Mem. Fac. Fish. Kagoshima Univ., 2:141—148. 1952. 1 pl., 1 fig.

Imai, S. The Characteristics and Keys for the Determination of the Species of Flyingfishes Obtained in Japan. I. Key to Adult Specimens. II. Key to Young Specimens. — Ibid., 5:91—102. 1956. (In Japanese.)

Inger, R.F. A Revision of the Fishes of the Genus Plesiops Cuvier. — Pacif. Sci., 9:259—276. 1955. 4 figs.

Inger, R.F. Notes on Fishes of the Genus Brachygobius (Gobiidae). — Fieldiana, Zool., 39:107—117. 1958. 20 figs.

Inger, R.F. and C.P. Kong. The Freshwater Fish of North Borneo. — Ibid., 45:1—268. 120 figs.

IIshikawa, C. On a New Species of Maurolicus, M. japonicus. — J. Coll. Agric. Imp. Univ. Tokyo, 6, No.2:183-191, pls.12-13. 1915.

Ishiyama, R. Studies on the Rays and Skates Belonging to the Family Rajidae, Found in Japan and Adjacent Regions. - Jap. J. Ichthyol., 1:30-36. 1950. 2 text-figs. (In Japanese, English summary.)

Ishiyama, R. Revision of the Japanese Mugilid-fishes, Especially Based upon the Osteological Characters of the Cranium. - Ibid., 1, No.4:238-250, fig.5. 1951.

Ishiyama, R. Studies on the Rays and Skates Belonging to the Family Rajidae, Found in Japan and Adjacent Regions. 4. A Revision of Three Genera of Japanese Rajids with Descriptions of One New Genus and Four New Species Mostly Occurring in Northern Japan. - J. Shimonoseki Coll. Fish., 2:1-34. 1952. 4 pls., 7 figs.

Ishiyama, R. Observations on the Egg-capsules of Skates of the Family Rajidae Found in Japan and its Adjacent Waters. - Bull. Mus. Comp. Zool. Harv., 118, No.1:1-24, figs.1-10. 1958.

Ishiyama, R. Studies on the Rajid Fishes (Rajidae) Found in the Waters around Japan. - J. Shimonoseki Coll. Fish., 7, Nos.2-3:193-394. 1958. 3 pls., 86 figs.

Ishiyama, R. Rajidae. - Fauna Japonica, pp.1-82, pls.1-32. Tokyo. 1967.

Iwai, T., I. Nakamura, and K. Matsubara. Taxonomic Study of the Tunas. - Misaki Mar. Biol. Inst., Kyoto Univ., Spec. Rep., 2:1-51. 1965. figs.

Jackson, P.B.N. Revision of the Clariid Catfishes of Nyasaland with a Description of a New Genus and Seven New Species. - Proc. Zool. Soc. Lond., 132:109-128. 1959. 7 figs.

Jacob, P.K. Sciaenids of the West Coast of Madras Province. - J. Bombay Nat. Hist. Soc., 48:118-124. 1948. 1 pl., 1 text-fig.

Jang Chyi-Yeong. Studies on the Skeleton of Muraenesox cinereus (Forskål). - Acta zool. sin., 9, No.2:110-120, pls.1-5, figs.1-17. 1957.

Järvi, T.H. Über die Arten und Formen des Coregonus s.str. in Finnland. - Finl. Fisk., 10, and Acta zool. fenn., 5:1-259. 1928. 48 tab.

Järvi, T.H. Zur Kenntnis der Coregonen Formen Nord-Finnlands, insbesondere des Kuusamo-Gebietes. - Acta zool. fenn., 40:1-91. 1943. 28 pls.

Järvi, T.H. Über die Coregonen s. str. im Päijänne und in einigen anderen Gewässern Mittelfinnlands. – Ibid., 75:1–33. 1953. 7 pls.

Jayaram, K.C. Respiratory and Other Adaptive Modifications in the Genus Gyrinocheilus Vaillant and their Significance in Constituting the Family Gyrinocheilidae Hora. – Rec. Indian Mus., 48:107–112. 1951. 2 figs.

Jayaram, K.C. Notes on Two Homalopterid Fishes from Szechuan, China. – Ibid., pp.113–117. 2 figs.

Jayaram, K.C. A Preliminary Review of the Genera of the Family Bagridae (Pisces: Siluroidea). – Proc. Natn. Inst. Sci. India, Ser.B, 21:120–128. 1955.

Jayaram, K.C. Taxonomic Status of the Chinese Catfish Family Cranoglanididae Myers, 1931. – Ibid., pp.256–363. 1 pl., 3 figs.

Jayaram, K.C. Contributions to the Study of Bagrid Fishes (Siluroidea: Bagridae). 1. A Systematic Account of the Genera Rita Bleeker, Rama Bleeker, Mystus Scopoli, and Horabagrus Jayaram. – Int. Revue ges. Hydrobiol. Hydrogr., 51, No.3:433–450. 1966. ill.

Jayaram, K.C. Contribution to the Study of the Fishes of the Family Bagridae. 2. A Systematic Account of the African Genera with a New Classification of the Family. – Bull. Inst. fr. Afr. noire, Ser.A, 28, No.3:1064–1139. 1966. ill.

Jayaram, K.C. and N. Majumbar. Siluroid Fishes of India, Burma and Ceylon. 15. Fishes of the Genus Chaca Gray. 1831. – Proc. Zool. Soc., India, 17, No.2:177–181. 1964.

Jensen, A.S. The North European and Greenland Lycodinae. – Dan. Ingolf-Exped., 2, No.4:1–99. 1904. ill.

Jensen, A.S. Contributions to the Ichthyofauna of Greenland. I. The Northern Species of the Genus Paralepis (Teleostomi, Iniomi – Sudidae). – Spolia zool. Mus. haun. (Skrift Univ. Zool. Mus. København), 2:3–28, figs.1–8, pl.1. 1942.

Jensen, A.S. Contributions to the Ichthyofauna of Greenland. – Ibid., 9:1–182. 1948.

Jensen, A.S. On the Greenland Species of the Genera Artediellus, Cottunculus, and Gymnocanthus (Teleostei, Scleroparei, Cottidae). – Meddr. Grønland, 142, No.7:1–21. 1952. 1 pl.

Jensen, A.S. Recent Finds of Lycodinae in Greenland Waters. – Ibid., pp.1–28. 2 pls.

Jensen, A.S. and H. Valsöe. A Revision of the Genus Icelus (Cottidae) with Remarks on the Structure of its Urogenital Papilla. – Denske Vidensk Selsck. Biol. Meddel. Köbenh., XXI, 6:1–26. 1949,

Jenyns, L. The Zoology of the Voyage of H.M.S. Beagle under the Command of Captain Fitzroy, R.N. during the Years 1832–1836. Part IV. Fish., pp.1–172, pls.1–29. London. 1842.

Jespersen, P. Sternoptychidae (Argyropelecus and Sternoptyx). – Rep. Dan. Oceanogr. Exped. Mediterr., 2 (Biol.) 3, A, 2:1–41. 1915.

Jespersen, P. and A.V. Täning. Some Mediterranean and Atlantic Sternoptychidae. – Nath. Medd. Kjöbenhavn, 70:215–226, pl.XVII. 1919.

Jespersen, P. and A.V. Tåning. Mediterranean Sternoptychidae. – Rep. Dan. Oceanogr. Exped. Mediterr., 2, A, 12:1–59, figs.1–30. 1926.

Job, T.J. Life History and Bionomics of the Spiny Eel, Mastacembelus pancalus (Hamilton), with Notes on the Systematics of the Mastacembelidae. – Rec. Indian Mus., 43:121–135. 1941. 6 text-figs.

Jones, S. and E.G. Silas. Indian Tunas. A Preliminary Review, with a Key for their Identification. – Indian J. Fish., 7:369–393. 1960. 15 figs.

Jones, S. and E.G. Silas. On the Fishes of the Subfamily Scomberomorinae (Family Scombridae) from Indian Waters. – Ibid., 8:189–206 (1961) 1962. 9 figs.

Jones, S. and E.G. Silas. A Systematic Review of the Scombroid Fishes of India. – Symposium on Scombroid Fishes. 1. Mar. Biol. Assoc. India, Mandapan Camp., S. India, pp.1–105. 1964. 15 figs., 9 pls.

Jordan, D.S. Description of a Species of Fish (Mitsukurina owstoni) from Japan, the Type of a Distinct Family of Lamnoid Sharks. – Proc. Calif. Acad. Sci., 3 Ser., Zool., 1:199–204, pls.11–12. 1898.

Jordan, D.S. A Review of the Sand Lances or Ammodytidae of the Waters of Japan. – Proc. U.S. Natn. Mus., 30:715–719. 1906.

Jordan, D.S. A Review of the Fishes of the Family Histiopteridae, Found in the Waters of Japan, with a Note on Tephritis Gnth. – Ibid., 32:235–239. 1907.

Jordan, D.S. A Review of the Fishes of the Family Gerridae Found in the Waters of Japan. – Ibid., pp.245–248. 2 figs.

Jordan, D.S. On Elephenor, a New Genus of Fishes from Japan. – Ann. Carneg. Mus., 12:329–392. 1919.

Jordan, D.S. On the Family of Achiridae or Broad-soles, with Description of a New Species Achirus barnharti from California. – Univ. Calif. Publs. Zool., 26:1–14, pl.i. 1923.

Jordan, D.S. Fishes, pp.1–773, figs.1–673. New York. 1925.

Jordan, D.S. The Genera of Fishes and a Classification of Fishes, Reprinted with a Foreword by G.S.Myers and a Comprehensive Index by H.M.Smith and L.P.Schultz, pp.1–800.

Jordan, D.S. and B.W.Evermann. The Fishes of North and Middle America. – Bull. U.S. Natn. Mus., 47. Nos.1–4: I–CCXIV+1–3313, pls.1–392. 1896–1900.

Jordan, D.S. and B.W.Evermann. The Aquatic Resources of the Hawaiian Islands. I. The Shore Fishes. – Bull. U.S. Fish Commn., 23, No.1:I–XXVIII, 1–574 (1903) 1905. 229 figs.

Jordan, D.S. and B.W.Evermann. A Review of the Giant Mackerel-like Fishes, Tunnies, Spearfishes and Swordfishes. – Occ. Pap. Calif. Acad. Sci., 12:1–113. 1926. 20 pls.

Jordan, D.S. and B.Fesler. A Review of the Sparoid Fishes of America and Europe. – Rep. U.S. Fish Commn., 17:421–544, pls.28–62. 1893.

Jordan, D.S. and H.W.Fowler. A Review of the Oplegnathoid Fishes of Japan. – Procl U.S. Natn. Mus., 25:75–78. 1902.

Jordan, D.S. and H.W.Fowler. A Review of the Trigger-fishes, File-fishes, and Trunk-fishes of Japan. – Ibid., pp.251–286, figs.1–6.

Jordan, D.S. and H.W.Fowler. A Review of the Cling-fishes (Gobiesocidae) of the Waters of Japan. – Ibid , pp.413–416.

Jordan, D.S. and H.W.Fowler. A Review of the Chaetodontidae and Related Families of Fishes Found in the Waters of Japan. – Ibid., pp.513–563, figs.1–6.

Jordan, D.S. and H.W.Fowler. A Review of the Ophidioid Fishes of Japan. – Ibid., pp.743–766, figs.1–5.

Jordan, D.S. and H.W.Fowler. A Review of the Berycoid Fishes of Japan. – Ibid., 26:1–21, figs.1–4. 1902.

Jordan, D.S. and H.W.Fowler. A Review of the Elasmobranchiate Fishes of Japan. – Ibid., 26:593–674, figs.1–10. 1903.

Jordan, D.S. and H.W.Fowler. A Review of the Cepolidae or Band Fishes of Japan. – Ibid., pp.699–702, 1 pl.

Jordan, D.S. and H.W.Fowler. A Review of the Cobitidae or Loaches of the Rivers of Japan. – Ibid., pp.765–774.

Jordan, D.S. and H.W.Fowler. A Review of the Cyprinoid Fishes of Japan. – Ibid., pp.811–862, figs.1–8.

Jordan, D.S. and H.W.Fowler. A Review of the Siluroid Fishes of Japan. – Ibid., pp.897–911.

Jordan, D.S. and H.M.Fowler. A Review of the Dragonets (Callionymidae) and Related Fishes of Japan. – Ibid., pp.939–959.

Jordan, D.S. and C.H.Gilbert. Macrouridae. – In: Jordan, D.S. and E.C.Starks. List of Fishes Dredged by the Steamer "Albatross" off the Coast of Japan. – Bull. U.S. Fish Commn., 22:602–621 (1902) 1904. pls.

Jordan, D.S. and A.C.Herre. A Review of the Herring-like Fishes of Japan. – Proc. U.S.Natn. Mus., 31:613–645. 1906. figs.1–5.

Jordan, D.S. and A.C.Herre. A Review of the Cirrhitoid Fishes of Japan. – Ibid., 32:157–167. 1907.

Jordan, D.S. and A.C.Herre. A Review of the Lizard-fishes or Synodontidae of the Waters of Japan. – Ibid., pp.513–524. 2 figs.

Jordan, D.S. and C.L.Hubbs. A Monographic Review of the Family of Atherinidae or Silversides. – Stanford Univ. Ser., Stud. Ichthyol., pp.1–87, pls.1–12. 1919.

Jordan, D.S. and R.E.Richardson. A Review of the Flat-heads, Gurnards and Other Mail-cheeked Fishes of the Waters of Japan. – Proc. U.S. Natn. Mus., 33:629–670. 1908.

Jordan, D.S. and R.E.Richardson. A Review of the Serranidae or Sea Bass of Japan. – Ibid., 37:421–474. 1910. 16 figs.

Jordan, D.S. and A.Seale. List of Fishes Collected in 1882–83 by Pierre Louis Jouy at Shanghai and Hongkong, China. – Proc. U.S. Natn. Mus., 29:517–529, figs.1–6. 1905.

Jordan, D.S. and A.Seale. Analysis of the Genera of Anchovies or Engraulidae. – Copeia, 141:27–32. 1925.

Jordan, D.S. and A.Seale. A Review of the Engraulidae, with Description of New and Rare Species. – Bull. Mus. Comp. Zool. Harv., 67:355–418. 1926.

Jordan, D.S. and M.Sindo. A Review of the Japanese Species of Surf-fishes or Embiotocidae. – Proc. U.S. Natn. Mus., 24:353–359, figs.1–2. 1902.

Jordan, D.S. and M.Sindo. A Review of the Pediculate Fishes or Anglers of Japan. – Ibid., pp.361–381, figs.1–7.

Jordan, D.S. and J.O.Snyder. A Review of the Lancelets, Hagfishes and Lampreys of Japan, with a Description of Two New Species. – Ibid., 23:725–734, pl.30. 1901.

Jordan, D.S. and J.O.Snyder. A Review of the Apodal Fishes or Eels of Japan, with Descriptions of Nineteen New Species. – Ibid., pp.837–890. 21 figs.

Jordan, D.S. and J.O.Snyder. A Review of the Cardinal Fishes of Japan. – Ibid., pp.891–913, pls.43–44.

Jordan, D.S. and J.O.Snyder. A Review of the Hypostomide and Lophobranchiate Fishes of Japan. – Ibid., 24:1–20, pls.1–12. 1901.

Jordan, D.S. and J.O.Snyder. A Review of the Gobioid Fishes of Japan, with Descriptions of Twenty-One New Species. – Ibid., pp.33–132.

Jordan, D.S. and J.O. Snyder. A Review of the Gymnodont Fishes of Japan. – Ibid., pp.229–264.

Jordan, D.S. and J.O. Snyder. Discobolous Fishes of Japan. – Ibid., 24:343–451. 1902.

Jordan, D.S. and J.O. Snyder. A Review of the Trachinoid Fishes and their Supposed Allies Found in the Waters of Japan (Sillaginidae). – Ibid., pp.461–497.

Jordan, D.S. and J.O. Snyder. A Review of the Salmonoid Fishes of Japan. – Ibid., pp.567–593, figs.1–5.

Jordan, D.S. and J.O. Snyder. A Review of the Labroid Fishes and Related Forms Found in the Waters of Japan. – Ibid., 595–662.

Jordan, D.S. and J.O. Snyder. A Review of the Blennioid Fishes of Japan. – Ibid., 25:441–504. 1902.

Jordan, D.S. and J.O. Snyder. A Synopsis of the Sturgeons (Acipenseridae) of Japan. – Ibid., 30:397–398. 1906.

Jordan, D.S. and J.O. Snyder. A Review of the Poeciliidae or Killifishes of Japan. – Ibid., 31:287–290. 1906. 1 fig.

Jordan, D.S. and E.C. Starks. On the Relationships of the Lutianoid Fish, *Aphareus furcatus*. – Ibid., 23:719–723, pl.28. 1901.

Jordan, D.S. and E.C. Starks. A Review of the Atherine Fishes of Japan. – Ibid., 24:198–206. 1901. 4 figs.

Jordan, D.S. and E.C. Starks. A Review of the Hemibranchiate Fishes of Japan. – Ibid., 26:57–73. 1902. 3 figs.

Jordan, D.S. and E.C. Starks. A Review of the Synentognathous Fishes of Japan. – Ibid., 26:525–544. 1903. 3 figs.

Jordan, D.S. and E.C. Starks. A Review of the Scorpaenoid Fishes of Japan. – Ibid., 27:91–175. 1904. 2 pls.

Jordan, D.S. and E.C. Starks. A Review of the Cottidae or Sculpins Found in the Waters of Japan. – Ibid., pp.231–335. 43 figs.

Jordan, D.S. and E.C. Starks. A Review of the Japanese Fishes of the Family of Agonidae. – Ibid., pp.575–599.

Jordan, D.S. and C.E. Starks. A Review of the Flounders and Soles of Japan. – Ibid., 31:161–246. 1906. 27 figs.

Jordan, D.S., S. Tanaka, and J.O. Snyder. A Catalogue of the Fishes of Japan. – J. Coll. Sci. Imp. Univ. Tokyo, 33, No.1:1–497. 1913. 396 figs.

Jordan, D.S. and W.F. Thompson. A Review of the Sciaenoid Fishes of Japan. – Proc. U.S. Natn. Mus., 39:241–261. 1911. 4 figs.

Jordan, D.S. and W.F. Thompson. A Review of the Fishes of the Families Laboridae and Lutianidae Found in the Waters of Japan. – Ibid., pp.435–477. 8 figs.

Jordan, D.S. and W.F. Thompson. A Review of the Sparidae and Related Families of Perch-like Fishes Found in the Waters of Japan. – Ibid., 41:521–601. 1912. 15 figs.

Jörgense, E. Mediterranean Ceratia. – Rep. Dan. Oceanogr. Exped. Mediterr., 1903–1910, 2, Biol., No.1:1–110. 1920. 94 figs.

Jungersen, H. Some Facts Regarding the Anatomy of the Genus *Pegasus*. – Rep. 84th Meeting British Assoc. Adv. Sci., 1914, pp.420–422. London. 1915.

Jungerson, H.F.E. Ichthyological Contributions I. The Structure of the Genera *Amphisile* and *Centriscus*. – Danske Vid. Selsk. Skr., (7), 6:41–109. 1908. 2 pls., 35 text-figs.

Jungerson, H.F.E. Ichthyological Contributions. II. The Structure of the Aulostomidae, Syngnathidae and Solenostomidae. – Ibid., 8:268–364. 1910. 7 pls., 1 text-fig.

Kafanova, V.V. On the Systematics of the "Altai Osmans" of the Genus *Oreoleuciscus* Warpachowski.– Vopr. Ikhtiol, 1, No.1 (18):9–18. 1961.

Kähsbauer, P. Beitrag zur Systematik des Syngnathiden (Pisces). – Annln. naturh. Mus. Wien, 57:163–272. 1949–1950.

Kähsbauer, P. Beitrag zur Systematik der Centriscidae (Pisces). – Ibid., 58:118–121. 1951.

Kamohara, T. On a New Fish, *Zenion japonicum* from Japan. – Proc. Imp. Acad. Japan, 10, No. 9:597–599. 1934. ill.

Kamohara, T. On the Owstoniidae of Japan. – Ann. Zool. Jap., 15, No.1:130–137, figs.1–4. 1935.

Kamohara, T. A Review of the Peristedioid Fishes Found in the Waters of Japan. – Ibid., 15, No.4:436–441, pls.29, 30. 1936.

Kamohara, T. On the Zeomorphi of Japan. – Botany Zool., Tokyo, 4:357–362. 1936. 5 text-figs. (In Japanese.)

Kamohara, T. On the Fishes of the Family Balistidae of Prov. Tosa, Japan. – Ibid., pp.1739–1745. 5 text-figs. (In Japanese and English.)

Kamohara, T. On the Fishes of the Family Hepatidae from Prov. Tosa, Japan. – Ibid., 5:469–474. 1937. 3 text-figs. (In Japanese.)

Kamohara, T. A Review of the Triacanthodid Fishes Found in the Waters of Japan. – Ann. Zool. Jap., **16**, No.1:5–8, pl.1. 1937.

Kamohara, T. Fishes of the Family Oncocephalidae Obtained by Trawlers off Prov. Tosa, Japan. – Ibid., pp.11–14, pl.2.

Kamohara, T. Gempylidae of Japan. – Ibid., **17**, No.1:45–50, pl.3. 1938.

Kamohara, T. Sclerodermi. – Fauna Nipponica, 15–2 (3):1–108, figs.1–56. 1940. (In Japanese.)

Kamohara, T. Zeoidei. Rhegnopteri. Holconoti. – Ibid., 15–2 (4):1–79. 1940. 26 figs. (In Japanese.)

Kamohara, T. Scombroidei (Exclusive of Carangiformes). – Ibid., 15–2 (5):1–225, figs.1–102. 1940.

Kamohara, T. Studies on the Family Peristediidae Found in Japan. – Jap. J. Ichthyol., 2:1–13. 1952. 5 text-figs. (In Japanese, English summary.)

Kamohara, T. A Review of the Fishes of the Family Chlorophthalmidae Found in the Waters of Japan. – Ibid., 3:1–6. 1953. 4 figs.

Kamohara, T. On the Fishes of the Genus Lutianus (Lutianidae) from Prov. Tosa, Japan. – Ibid., 3:107–117. 1954. 2 figs. (In Japanese, English summary.)

Kamohara, T. A Review of the Family Brotulidae Found in the Waters of Prov. Tosa, Japan. – Rep. Usa Mar. Biol. Stn. Kochi Univ., **1** (2):1–14. 1954.

Kamohara, T. On the Fishes of the Family Chlorophthalmidae. – Res. Rep. Kochi Univ., **5**, No.15:1–8, pls.1–3. 1956.

Kamohara, T. Notes on Twenty Additions to the Marine Fish Fauna of Prov. Tosa, Japan, Including One New Genus (Family Peristediidae). – Ibid., **6**, No.5:1–6. 1957. 1 fig.

Kamohara, T. A Review of the Labrid Fishes Found in the Waters of Kochi Prefecture, Japan. – Rep. Usa Mar. Biol. Stn. Kochi Univ., **5**, No.2:1–20, pls.1–8. 1958.

Kamohara, T. On the Fishes of the Genus Chromis (Fam. Amphiprionidae, Chromides, Pisces) Found in the Waters of Japan. – Ibid., **7**, No.1:1–10. 1960. 2 figs.

Kamohara, T. A Review of the Fishes of the Family Parapercidae Found in the Waters of Japan. – Ibid., **7**, No.2:1–14. 1960. figs.

Kamohara, T. On the Fishes of the Family Scaridae of Japan, Including the Riu-Kiu Islands. – Ibid., **10**, No.1:1–24, pls.1–6. 1963.

Kamohara, T. On the Labrid Fishes Collected from Okinawa, Miyakojima and Ishigakijima. – Ibid., **10**, No.2:1–9, pls.1–3. 1963.

Kamohara, T. On the Fishes of the Family Chaetodontidae Obtained in the Okinawa and the Yaeyama Islands. – Ibid., **11**, No.2:1–6. 1964. pls.1–3.

Kanazawa, R.H. A Revision of the Eels of the Genus Conger with Descriptions of Four New Species. – Proc. U.S. Natn. Mus., **108**:209–267. 1958. 7 figs., 4 pls.

Karaman, S. Salmonidae of the Balkans. – Glasn. skops. nauč. Društ., Nos.1–2:253–268. 1926.

Karaman, S. Beitrag zur Kenntnis der Süsswasserfische Jugoslaviens. Salmoniden, Part 1. – Bull. Soc. Sci. Skopje, 18:131–139. 1938. 3 text-figs.

Karaman, S. Beitrag zur Kenntnis der Salmoniden Südeuropas. – Hydrobiologia, **28**:1–41. 1966. 2 figs.

Karlovac, J. Sternoptychidae, Stomiatidae and Scopelidae in the Adriatic Sea. – Rep. Inst. Oceanogr., Split, **5**, No.2B:1–46. 1953. 5 maps.

Katayama, M. Systematic Position of the Genus Glaucosoma. – Bull. Fac. Educ. Yamaguchi Univ., **4**, No.1:23–28. 1954. 2 figs.

Katayama, M. Studies on the Serranid Fishes of Japan. I. – Ibid., **8**, No.2:103–180, figs.1–39. 1959.

Katayama, M. Serranidae. Fauna Japonica (Pisces). – Biogeogr. Soc., Japan, pp.1–189. 1960. 86 pls.

Katayama, M. and T. Takai. A New Conger-like Eel Muraenesox yamaguchiensis from the Inland Sea of Japan. – Jap. J. Ichthyol., 3, Nos.3–4–5:97–101, figs.1,2. 1954.

Kaup, J.J. Catalogue of Lophobranchiate Fish in the Collection of the British Museum, pp.1–80, pls.1–4. London. 1856.

Kaup, J.J. Catalogue of Apodal Fish in the Collection of the British Museum, pp.1–160, figs.1–11, pls.1–19. London, 1856.

Kendall, W.C. Monographs on the Natural History of New England. The Fishes of New England. The Salmon Family. Part 2. The Salmons. – Mem. Boston Soc. Nat. Hist., 9:1–166, 1–11. 1935. 1 fig.

Khranilov, N.S. The Weberian Apparatus in Serrasalmo piraya. – Trudy Leningr. Obshch. Estest., 59, No.1:47–59. 1929.

Kishinonye, K. Contributions to the Comparative Study of the So-called Scombroid Fishes. – J. Coll. Sci. Imp. Univ. Tokyo, 8:293–475, pls.13–34. 26 text-figs. 1923.

Klashterin, L.R. Study of the Greenlings (Hexagrammidae Pisces) from the Kurile Islands. – Trudy Inst. Okeanol., Akad. Nauk SSSR, 59:104–109. 1962.

Klausewitz, W. Fische aus dem Roten Meer. I. Knorpelfische (Elasmobranchii). – Senckenberg. biol., 40, Nos.1–2:43–50. 1950. ill.

Klausewitz, W. Fische aus dem Roten Meer. IV. Einige systematische und ökologisch bemerkenswerte Meergrundeln (Pisces, Gobiidae). – Ibid., 44, Nos.3–4:149–162. 1960.

Klausewitz, W. Taxonomische Untersuchungen an der Gattung Comphosus (Pisces, Percomorphi, Labridae). – Ibid., 43, No.1:11–16. 1962. ill.

Klyukanov, V.A. New Data on the Distribution of Silver Smelts in Soviet Waters. – Dokl. Akad. Nauk SSSR, 166, No.4:990–991. 1966.

Kner, R. Über einige noch unbeschriebene Fische. – Sber. Akad. Wiss. Wien, 39:531–546, pl., figs.1–5. 1860.

Kner, R. Fische. – In: Reise Novara Exped., 1:1–433, pls.1–16. 1868.

Kner, R. Über neue Fische. – Sber. Akad. Wiss. Wien, 58:26–31, pl.3, figs.8. 1868.

Knipowitsch, N. Ichthyologische Untersuchungen im Eismeer. 1. Lycodes und Lycenchelys. – Zap. Akad. Nauk, Peterburg, Ser.8, 19, No.1:1–129. 1906.

Kobayashi, J. General Observations of Japanese Gasterosteid Fishes. – J. Sci. Hiroshima Univ. (Zool.), No.1:145–153. 1932. 2 pls.

Kobayashi, K. Larvae and Young of the Quilt-fish Ptilichthys goodei Bean from the Okhotsk Sea. – Bull. Fac. Fish. Hokkaido Univ., 12:5–8. 1961. 4 figs. (English abstract.)

Kobayashi, K. Larvae and Young of the Sandlance Ammodytes hexapterus Pallas from the North Pacific. – Ibid., pp.111–120, figs.2.

Kobayashi, K. and M. Igarashi. Larvae and Young of Girella punctata Gray from Hakodate Bay in Southern Hokkaido. – Ibid., pp.121–127. 3 pls. (English abstract.)

Kobayashi, K. and T. Ueno. Fishes from the Northern Pacific and from Bristol Bay. – Ibid., 6, No.4:239–265. 1956.

Koefoed, E. Isospondyli. 2. Heterophotodermi. 3. From the "Michael Sars" North Atlantic Deep-sea Expedition 1910. – Rep. Scient. Results Michael Sars N. Atlant. Deep Sea Exped., 4, 2, No.10:1–12. 1910. 2 pls., 2 figs.

Koefoed, E. Pediculati from the "Michael Sars" North Atlantic Deep-sea Expedition 1910. – Ibid., 4, 2, No.1:1–18, pls.1–3, 2 text-figs. 1944.

Koefoed, E. Zeomorphi, Percomorphi, Plectognathi from the "Michael Sars" North Atlantic Deep-sea Expedition 1910. – Ibid., 4, 2, No.2:1–26, figs.1–3, pls.1–3. 1952.

Koefoed, E. Synentognathi, Solenichthyes, Anacanthini, Berycomorphi, Xenoberyces from the "Michael Sars" North Atlantic Deep-sea Expedition 1910. – Ibid., 4, 2, No.3:1–39, figs.1–6, pls.1–4. 1953.

Koefoed, E. Iniomi (Myctophidae Exclusive), Lyomeri, Apodes from the "Michael Sars" North Atlantic Deep-sea Expedition 1910. – Ibid., 4, 2, No.4:1–16. 1955. 2 pls.

Koefoed, E. Isospondyli. 1. Gymnophotodermi and Lepitophotodermi. – Ibid., 4, 2, No.5:1–21. 1956. 3 pls.

Koefoed, E. Isospondyli. 2. Heterophotodermi from the "Michael Sars" North Atlantic Deep-sea Expedition 1910 (with addenda and corrigenda to Isospondyli. 1). – Ibid., 4, 2, No.6:1–7. 1958. 1 pl., 1 fig.

Koefoed, E. Isospondyli. – Ibid., 4, 2, No.8:1–15. 1960.

Koelz, W. Coregonid Fishes of the Great Lakes. – Bull. Bur. Fish, Wash., 43, No.2:294–643. 1929. 30 figs.

Koelz, W. The Coregonid Fishes of North-Eastern America. – Pap. Mich. Acad. Sci., 13:303–432, pl.39. 1931.

Korotnev, A. Comephoridae of Lake Baikal. – Zool. Issled. Oz. Baikal, No.2:1–39, Kiev. 1905. 3 pls.

Koshkarov, D.N. Comparative Study of the Systematics of Plectognathi. – Byull. Mosk. Obshch. Ispyt. Prir., otd. biol., 27:263–370. (1913) 1914.

Koumans, F.P. A Preliminary Revision of the Genera of the Gobioid Fishes with United Ventral Fins. – Proefschrift, Lisse, pp.1–174. 1931.

Koumans, F.P. Results of a Reexamination of the Types and Specimens of Gobioid Fishes, with Notes on the Fish Fauna of the Surroundings of Batavia. – Zool. Meded., Leiden, 22:121–210. 1940.

Koumans, F.P. Gobioid Fishes of India. – Mem. Indian Mus., 13:205–329. 1941.

Koumans, F.P. – In: Weber, M. and L.F. de Beaufort. The Fishes of the Indo-Australian Archipelago. X. Gobioidae, pp.1–392, 1953, 95 figs.

Krefft, G. Knorpelfische (Chondrichthyes), gesammelt von der Deutschen Indien-Expedition 1955–1958. – Mitt. hamb. zool. Mus. Inst., 59:141–178. 1961. 2 pls., 9 figs.

Krefft, G. Knorpelfische (Chondrichthyes) aus dem tropischen Ostatlantik. – Atlantide Rep., 10:33–76. 1968. 4 pls.

Krefft, G. and G.E. Maul. Notosudis lepida n.sp. (Iniomi, Notosudidae), eine neue Fischart aus dem östlichen Nord-Atlantik. – Arch. FischWiss., 6:305–316. 1955. 4 figs.

Krejsa, R.J. The Eastern, Tropical Pacific Fishes of the Genus Blenniolus, Including a New Island Endemic. – Copeia, 3:322–336. 1960. 10 figs.

Kryzhanovskii, S.G. The System of the Family Cyprinidae. – Zool. Zh., 26, No.1:53–64. 1947. 4 figs.

Kubo, I. and J. Onoe. A Population Study of the Fish Taius tumifrons of the Tosa Bay. – J. Tokyo Univ. Fish., 38:321–334. 1952. 4 figs.

Kulikova, E.B. Whitefishes of Yamal. – Trudy Inst. Okeanol., Akad. Nauk SSSR, 31:111–144. 1960.

Kulikova, E.B. Fishes of the Genus Lampanyctus of the Far Eastern Seas and Northwest Pacific (Pisces, Scopelidae). – Ibid., pp.166–204, figs.1–19.

Kulikova, E.B. Data on Luminescent Pelagic Fishes of the Genus Diaphus (Family Scopelidae) from the West Pacific. – Ibid., 43:5–39, figs.1–27. 1961.

Kulkarni, C.V. On the Systematic Position, Structural Modifications, Bionomics and Development of a Remarkable New Family of Cyprinodont Fishes from the Province of Bombay. – Rec. Indian Mus., 42:379–423. 1940. 20 text-figs.

Kulkarni, C.V. The Osteology of Indian Cyprinodonts. I. Comparative Study of the Head Skeleton of Aplocheilus, Oryzias and Horaichthys. – Proc. Natn. Inst. Sci. India, 14:65-119. 1948. 23 text-figs.

Kulkarni, C.V. A New Genus of Schibeid Catfishes from the Deccan (India). – Rec. Indian Mus., 49:231–238. 1952. 2 figs.

Kulmatycki, W.J. Studien an Coregonen Polens. – Arch. Hydrobiol. Ichthyol., Suwałki, 1, No.4:275–336. 1926. 1 fig.

Kulmatycki, W.J. Studien an Coregonen Polens. – Ibid., 2, Nos.1–2:1–40. 1927. 2 maps.

Kuronoma, K. A Study on the Triglidae of Japan. – Bull. Biogeogr. Soc. Japan, 9, No.14:223–260, figs.1–10. 1939.

Kuronuma, K. The Heterosomate Fishes Collected in Deep Waters of Japan. I. – Ibid., 10, No.3:29–61. 1940.

Kuronuma, K. Osteological Study on Japanese Fish. I. Comparative Osteology, Especially of Cranial Characteristics in Tetraodontid Genera Liosaccus, Lagocephalus and Sphoeroides. – J. Shigenkagaku Kenkyosyo, 1, No.2:119–130, pl.VII, 2 figs. 1943.

Kyle, H.M. and E. Ehrenbaum. Teleostei Physostomi. – Tierwelt N. -u. Ostsee (Part XII f.), No.9:9–86. 1927.

Lachner, E.A. Studies of Certain Apogonid Fishes from the Indo-Pacific with Descriptions of Three New Species. – Proc. U.S. Natn. Mus., 101:581–610, pls.17–19. text-fig.105. 1951.

Lachner, E.A. A Revision of the Goatfish Genus Upeneus with Descriptions of Two New Species. – Ibid., 103:497–532. 1954.

Lachner, E.A. Populations of the Berycoid Fish Family Polymixiidae. – Ibid., 105:189–206. 1955. 1 pl., 5 tables.

Ladiges, W. Süsswasserfische der Türkei. Part I., Cyprinidae. – Mitt. hamb. zool. Mus. Inst., 58:105–150. 1960. 14 figs., map.

Lambert, J.G. Poissons Siluriformes Cyprinodontiformes récoltés en Guinée Française, avec la description d'une nouvelle espèce de Microsynodontis. – Revue Zool. Bot. afr., 57:39–56. 1958. 7 figs.

La Monte, F.R. A Review and Revision of the Marlins, Genus Makaira. – Bull. Am. Mus. Nat. Hist., 107, No.3:319–358. 1955. 9 pls.

La Monte, F. and D.E. Marcy. Swordfish, Sailfish, Marlin, and Spearfish. – Ichthyol. Contrib. Intern. Game Fish Assoc., N.Y., Nos.1 (2):3–24. 1941. ill.

Lane, E.D. The Osteology of Cheimarrichthys fosteri Haast. – Trans. R. Soc. N.Z., 6, No.20:207–312. 1965. 10 figs.

Lebedev, V.D., V.D. Spanovskaya, K.A. Savvaitova, L.I. Sokolov, and E.Z. Tsepkin. Fishes of the USSR, pp.1–448. – Moscow, "Mysl'". 1969. 243 figs., 24 col. pls.

Leccia, F.M. Osteologia comparada en ocho especies de Pomadasyidae (Pisces, Perciformes) del Golfo de Cariaco, Venezuela y areas adyacantes. – Bolm. Inst. Oceanogr. Univ. Oriente, 1, No.2:396–473. 1961. ill.

Le Danois, Y. Sur le remaniement du sous-ordre des Poissons Plectognathes et la définition d'un nouveau sous-ordre: les Orbiculates. – C. r. hebd. Séanc. Acad. Sci., Paris, 240, No.19:1933–1934. 1955.

Le Danois, Y. Etude ostéologique, myologique et systématique des poissons du sous-ordre des Orbiculates. – Annls. Inst. océanogr., Monaco, n. s., 36:1–274, figs.1–221. 1959.

Le Danois, Y. Remarques sur les poissons orbiculates du sous-ordre des Ostracioniformes. – Mém. Mus. natn. Hist. nat., Paris, n.s. A, Zool., 19, No.2:207–338. 1961. 57 figs.

Le Danois, Y. Catalogue des types de Poissons du Muséum National d'Histoire naturelle (Nomeidae, Stromateidae, Aploactidae, Kurtidae). – Bull. Mus. natn. Hist. nat., Paris, 35, No.3:228–234. 1963.

Le Danois, Y. Etude anatomique et systématique des Antennaires de l'ordre des Pédiculates. – Mém. Mus. natn. Hist. nat., Paris, n. s. A, Zool., 31, No.1:1–162. 1964. ill.

Legendre, V. Un nouveau poisson pour la province de Québec.– Revue can. Biol., No.2:105–107. 1943.

Legendre, V. Les poissons d'eau douce. 2. Clef des Cyprinides ou Ménés du Québec. – Jeune Naturaliste, 10, Nos.9–10:178–210. 1960. ill.

Lehman, J.P. Etude complémentaire des poissons de l'eotrias de Madagascar. – K. svenska Vetensk-Akad. Handl., 2, No.6-1–201. 1952. 48 pls., 129 text-figs.

Lehman, J.P. Super-ordre des Chondrostéens. Traité de Zoologie, 13, No.3: 2130–2172. 1958. 30 figs.

Liang, Y. Notes on the Fishes of the Family Uranoscopidae from Taiwan (Formosa). – Q. Jl. Taiwan Mus., 8:169–176. 1955. 5 figs.

Liem, K.F. The Comparative Osteology and Phylogeny of the Anabantoidei (Teleostei, Pisces). – Illinois Biol. Monogr., 30:1–149, figs.1–104. 1963.

Liem, K.F. The Status of Anabantoid Fish Genera Ctenopus and Trichopsis. – Copeia, No.2:206–213. 1965. ill.

Liem, K.F. A Morphological Study of Luciocephalus pulcher, with Notes on Gular Elements in Other Recent Teleosts. – J. Morph., 121:103–133. 1967. 23 figs.

Lin, Fan-Hsuen. The Elasmobranchiate Fishes of North China. – Sci. Rep. Natn. Tsing Hua Univ., Ser.B, 1, No.5:133–190, pl.6, fig.15. 1932.

Lin, S.Y. Contribution to a Study of Cyprinidae of Kwantung and Adjacent Provinces. – Lingnan Sci. J., 12, No.1:75–91; 12, No.2:197–215; 12, No.3:337–348; 12, No.4:489–505. 1933; 13, No.2:231–238. 2 figs.; 13, No.4:615–632. 1934; 14, No.2:149–260; 14, No.3:403–414; 14, No.4:651–663. 1935.

Lin, S.Y. Notes on Some Important Sciaenids of China. – Bull. Chekiang Prov. Fish. Exp. Stn., 1, No.1:1–30. 1935.

Lin, S.Y. Notes on Hair-tails and Eels of China. – Ibid., 2, No.5:1–16. 1936.

Lin, S.Y. Further Notes on Sciaenid Fishes of China. – Lingnan Sci. J., 17, No.1:33–43; No.2:161–173; No.3:367–381; No.4:539–550. 1938.

Lin, S.Y. Croakers of the South China Sea. – J. Hongkong Fish. Res. Stn., 1, No.2:243–254. 1940. 6 figs.

Lindberg, G.U. The Systematics and Distribution of Sand Lances of the Genus Ammodytes (Pisces). – Vest. Dal'nevost. Fil. Akad. Nauk SSSR, 27:85–93. 1937.

Lindberg, G.U. On the Genera and Species of Fishes of the Family Blenniidae (Pisces) Related to the Genus Anoplarchus. – Trudy Gidrobiol. Eksped. Zool. Muz. Akad. Nauk SSSR. 1934 na Yaponskoe More, No.1:499–514. Moscow–Leningrad, Akad. Nauk SSSR. 1938.

Lindberg, G.U. and A.P.Andriyashev. A Survey of the Genus Sarritor (Agonidae) from Far Eastern Seas. – Issled. Dal'nevost. Morei SSSR, No.2:293–302. Leningrad, Akad. Nauk SSSR. 1950.

Lindberg, G.U. and Z.V.Krasyukova. Fishes of the Sea of Japan and Adjacent Parts of the Okhotsk and Yellow Seas. 3. Teleostomi. XXIX. Perciformes, 1. Percoidei (XC Fam. Serranidae – CXLIV Fam. Champsodontidae), pp.1–480. – Leningrad, "Nauka." 1968. 431 figs.

Lindberg, G.U. and M.I.Legeza. Fishes of the Sea of Japan and Adjacent Parts of the Okhotsk and Yellow Seas. 1. Amphioxi, Petromyzones, Myxini, Elasmobranchii, Holocephali, pp.1–208. – Akad. Nauk SSSR. 1959. 108 figs.

Lindberg, G.U. and M.I.Legeza. Review of Genera and Species of Fishes of the Subfamily Cyclopterinae (Pisces). – English Translation U.S. Dept. Interior with Nat. Sci. Found. by Israel Prog. Sci. Transl., 617:1–75. (1955) 1964.

Lindberg, G.U. and M.I.Legeza. Fishes of the Sea of Japan and Adjacent Parts of the Okhotsk and Yellow Seas. 2. Teleostomi. XII. Acipenseriformes – XXVIII Polynemiformes, pp.1–391. – Moscow–Leningrad, "Nauka." 1965. 324 figs.

Lindberg, G.U., T.K.T'ai, Ch.Shu-ning, K.M.Su, and A.Dashidorzhi (editors). Illustrated Glossary of Names of Commercial Fishes from the West Pacific, pp.1–601. Peking. 1964. ill.

Longhurst, A.R. Notes on Nomenclature of West African Sciaenid Fishes, Lagos. 1962. – Federal Fisher. Service, Nigeria, Occas. Pap., 5:1–3. 1962. 2 tables.

Lowe (McConnell), R.H. The Sciaenoid Fishes of British Guiana. – Bull. Mar. Sci. Gulf Caribb., 16:20–57. 1966. 6 figs.

Lozano, C.F. Los Escombridos de Las Aguas Españolas y Marroquies y su Pesca. I. – Trab. Inst. esp. Oceanogr., 25:6–254. 1958. 187 figs.

Lozano-Rey, L. Etude systématique des Clupéidés et des Engraulidés de l'Espagne, du Maroc et du Sahara Espagnols. – Rapp. P.-v. Réun. Commn. int. Explor. Scient. Mer Méditerr., 126:7–20. 1950. ill.

Lozano-Rey, L. Peces fiscoclistos. Labridiformes y escombriformes. – Mems. R. Acad. Cienc. Exact. fis. nat. Madr., 14:1–703. 1952.

Lukash, B.S. Data on the Phylogeny of the Family Cyprinidae. – Trudy Karel. Fil. Akad. Nauk SSSR, 5:13–38. 1956.

Lüling, H. Schützenfische (Toxotidae). – Aquar.- u. Terrar. – Z., 8:178–184. 1955. 3 figs.

McAllister, D.E. A Collection of Oceanic Fishes from off British Columbia with a Discussion of the Evolution of Black Peritoneum. – Bull. Natn. Mus. Can., Zool., 172:39–43. 1961.

McAllister, D.E. Systematic Notes on the Sculpin Genera Artediellus, Icelus, and Triglopos on Arctic and Atlantic Coasts of Canada. – Ibid., 185:50–59. 1963. ill.

McAllister, D.E. A Revision of the Smelt Family Osmeridae. – Ibid., 191:1–53. 1963. 14 figs.

McAllister, D.E. Numerical Taxonomy and the Smelt Family Osmeridae. – Can. Fld., Nat., 80, No.4:227–238. 1966.

McAllister, D.E. Evolution of Branchiostegals and Classification of Teleostome Fishes. – Bull. Natn. Mus. Can. Biol., 221:1–239. 1968. 3 figs., 21 pls.

McAllister, D.E. Mandibular Pore Pattern in the Sculpin Family Cottidae. – Ibid., 223:58–69. 1968.

McAllister, D.E. and R.J.Krejsa. Placement of the Prowfishes, Zaproridae, in the Superfamily Stichaeoidae. – Nat. Hist. Pap. Natn. Mus. Can., 11:1–4. 1961.

McAllister, D.E. and C.C.Lindsey. Systematics of the Freshwater Sculpins (Cottus) of British Columbia. – Bull. Natn. Mus. Can., Zool., 172:66–89. 1959. 5 figs.

McAllister, D.E. and E.I.S.Rees. A Revision of the Eelpout Genus Melanostigma with a New Genus and with Comments on Maynea. – Ibid., 199:85–110. 1963, 1964. 9 figs.

McCann, C. The Whale Shark, Rhineodon typus (Smith). – J. Bombay Nat. Hist. Soc., 53:326–333. 1954. 2 pls.

McClelland, J. Apodal Fishes of Bengal Calcutta. – J. Nat. Hist., 5, No.18:151–266, pls.V–XIV. (1844) 1845.

McCormick, H.W. and W.E.Young. Shadows in the Sea. The Sharks, Skates and Rays, pp.1–417. London. 1964. ill.

McCulloch, A.R. Notes and Illustrations of Queensland Fishes. 2. – Mem. Qd. Mus., 7:164–178, pls.8–11. 1921.

McCulloch, A.R. A Checklist of the Fishes Recorded from Australia. – Mem. Aust. Mus., 1:1–144; 2:145–329; 3:329–436; 4:437–534. 1929–1930.

McCulloch, A.R. and E.R.Waite. A Revision of the Genus Aracana and its Allies. – Trans. Proc. R. Soc. S. Aust., 39:477–493, pls.16–25. 1915.

McCulloch, A.R. and E.R.Waite. Some New and Little-known Fishes from South Australia. – Rec. S. Aust. Mus., 1:1–78, pls.2–7. 1918.

McCully, H. A New Type of Field Key Applied to Flatfishes of California. – Calif. Fish Game, 35, No.1:11–13. 1949.

McCully, H.H. The Comparative Anatomy of the Serranid Fishes. – Dissertation Abstracts, 22, No.5:1–4. 1961.

McHugh, J.L. and J.E.Fitch. An Annotated List of the Clupeoid Fishes of the Pacific Coast from Alaska to Cape San Lucas, Baja California. – Calif. Fish Game, 37:491–495. 1951.

McPhail, J.D. Key to the Croakers (Sciaenidae) of the Eastern Pacific. – Inst. Fish. Univ. Brit. Col. Mus. Contr., 2:1–20. 1958. 4 figs.

McPhail, J.D. A Systematic Study of the Salvelinus alpinus Complex in North America. – J. Fish. Res. Bd. Can., 18, No.5:793–816. 1961.

Mailyan, R.A. The Systematics of Sevan Whitefishes. – Izv. Akad. Nauk Arm.SSR, Biol., 7, No.9:37–47. 1954.

Mailyan, R.A. Whitefishes of Lake Sevan. – Trudy Sevan. Gidrobiol. Sta., Akad. Nauk Arm.SSR, 15:137–195. 1957.

Maksimov, V. Sharks of the Atlantic, pp.1–26. – Moscow, Vses. Nauchno-Issled. Inst. Morsk. Ryb. Khoz. Okeanogr. (VNIRO). 1968.

Makushok, V.M. Morphological Principles of the System of Stichaeidae and Related Families (Stichaeoidae, Blennioidae, Pisces). – Trudy Zool. Inst. Akad. Nauk SSSR, 25:1–129. 1958. 83 figs.

Makushok, V.M. Additional Data on the Morphology and Systematics of Wrymouths (Cryptacanthodidae, Blennioidei, Pisces). – Trudy Inst. Okeanol. Akad. Naul SSSR, 43:184–197. 1961.

Makushok, V.M. The Systematic Position of the Neozoarcinae (Zoarcidae, Blennioidei, Pisces). – Ibid., pp.198–224.

Makushok, V.M. Some Structural Features of the Seismosensory System in Northern Blennies (Stichaeoidea). – Ibid., pp.225–269. 9 figs.

Makushok, V.M. Grenadiers (Fam. Macrouridae or Coryphaenoididae auct.). – In: Tikhii okean, biol., No.3. Ryby otkrytykh vod, 200–227. Moscow, "Nauka." 1967.

Manacop, P.R. A Preliminary Systematic Study of the Philippine Chub Mackerels, Family Scombridae, Genera Pneumatophorus and Rastrelliger. – Philipp. J. Fish., 4, No.2:79–101. 1958.

Marshall, N.B. Studies of Alepsisauroid Fishes. – "Discovery" Rep., 27:303–336. 1955. 1 pl., 9 figs.

Marshall, N.B. Swimbladder Structure of Deep-sea Fishes in Relation to their Systematics and Biology. – Ibid., 31:1–121. 1960. 3 pls., 47 figs.

Marshall, N.B. A Young Macristium and the Ctenothrissid Fishes. London. – Bull. Br. Mus. Nat. Hist., Zool., 7, No.8:353–370. 1961.

Marshall, N.B. Observations on the Heteromi, an Order of Teleost Fishes. London. – Ibid., 9, No.6:249–270. 1962.

Marshall, N.B. Bathypelagic Macrourid Fishes. – Copeia, 1:86–93. 1964. ill.

Marshall, N.B. Systematic and Biological Studies of the Macrourid Fishes (Anacanthini – Teleostei). – Deep Sea Res., 12, No.3:299–322. 1965. ill.

Marshall, N.B. The Relationships of the Anacanthine Fishes, Macruronus, Lyconus and Steindachneria. – Copeia, 2:275–280. 1966. ill.

Marshall, N.B. Scopelosauridae. – In: Fishes W.N.Atlantic, 5. Mem. Sears Found. Mar. Res., 1, No.5:1–647 ex parte. 1966.

Marshall, N.B. Bathyprion danae, a New Genus and Species of Alepocephaliform Fishes. – Dana Rep., 68:1–10. 1968. 3 figs.

Martekhov, P.F. Loaches from the Ili River Basin and their Biocenotic and Commercial Importance. Author's Summary of Candidate Thesis, pp.1–9. Alma-Ata. 1950.

Martin, C. and H.R. Montalban. Philippine Sillaginidae. – Philipp. J. Sci., 55:221–227. 1934. 1 pl.

Martin, C. and H.R. Montalban. Philippine Parapercidae. – Ibid., 56, No.2:215–225. 1935. pls.1–3.

Martinsen, G.V. Sharks of the World Ocean, pp.1–31. – Moscow, VNIRO. 1966. 21 figs.

Martinson, G.V., I.G. Smyslov, and V.E. Tishin. Tunas, their Biology, Fishing and Processing (Survey), pp.1–122, figs.1–50. – Moscow, Vses. Nauchno-Issled. Inst. Morsk. Ryb. Khoz. Okeanogr. (VNIRO). 1965.

Maruyama, K. Rare Deep-water Fishes off Tohoku and Adjacent Regions. II. Record of a Rare Species of the Genus Melamphaes (Family Melamphaidae). – Jap. J. Ichthyol., 6, Nos.1–2:31–34, fig.1. 1957. (In Japanese.)

Maruyama, K. Rare Deep-water Fishes from off Tohoku and Adjacent Regions. IV. Record of a Rare Species Photostomias guernei Collett of the Family Malacosteidae. – Ibid., 7, Nos.5–6:153–156, figs.1–2. 1959. (In Japanese.)

Masuda, T. and K. Tanaka. Young of Labroid and Scaroid Fishes from the Central Pacific Coasts of Japan. – J. Tokyo Univ. Fish., 48:1–98. 1962. 41 figs.

Mather, F.J. Tunas (Genus Thunnus) of the Western North Atlantic. II. Description, Comparison and Identification of Species of Thunnus Based on External Characters. – F.A.O. Fish Rep., 3, No.6:1155–1157. 1963.

Mather, F.J. Tunas (Genus Thunnus) of the Western North Atlantic. III. Distribution and Behavior of Thunnus Species. – Ibid., pp.1159–1161.

Matsubara, K. A Review of Hapalogenys, a Genus of Perch-like Fishes from Japan and Adjacent Regions. – J. Imp. Fish. Inst., Tokyo, 28, No.2:73–96. 1933.

Matsubara, K. Order Plagiostomi. I. (Sharks). – Fauna Nipponica, 15, No.2 (1):1–160, figs.1–93. 1936. (In Japanese.)

Matsubara, K. Order Plagiostomi. II. (Rays). Order Holocephali. – Ibid., 15, No.2(2):1–70, figs.1–40. 1936. (In Japanese.)

Matsubara, K. Studies on the Deep-sea Fishes of Japan. I. On a New Apodal Fish Dysomma japonicus, with an Emendation of the Genus Dysomma. – Zool. Mag., Tokyo, 48:960;962. 1936. 1 text-fig.

Matsubara, K. Studies on Deep-sea Fishes of Japan. II. On a New Fish Belonging to Heretomi. – Ibid., pp.963–964. 1 text-fig.

Matsubara, K. A Review of Two Genera of Japanese Sculpins Ereunias and Marukawichthys. – J. Imp. Fish. Inst., Tokyo, 31, No.2:97–114. 1936.

Matsubara, K. Studies on the Deep-sea Fishes of Japan. III. On Some Remarkable Variations Found in Paramyxine atami Dean with Special Reference to its Taxonomy. – Ibid., 32, No.1:13–15, figs. 1–3, pl. 1.

Matsubara, K. Sciaenoid Fishes Found in Japan and its Adjacent Waters. – Ibid., 32, No.2:27–92. 1937. 28 figs.

Matsubara, K. Studies on the Deep-sea Fishes of Japan. IV. A New Mail-cheeked Fish, Hoplichthys fasciatus, Belonging to Hoplichthyidae. – Zool. Mag., Tokyo, 49:264–265. 1937. 1 text-fig.

Matsubara, K. A Review of the Lizard-fishes of the Genus Synodus Found in Japan. – J. Imp. Fish. Inst., Tokyo, 33:1–36. 1938.

Matsubara, K. Studies on the Deep-sea Fishes of Japan. VI. On Some Stomiadoid Fishes from Kumano-Nada.– Ibid., 33, No.1:37–52, figs.1–8. 1938.

Matsubara, K. Studies on the Deep-sea Fishes of Japan. VII. On Some Rare or Imperfectly-known Lantern Fishes Found in Kumano-Nada. – Ibid., 33:52–60, figs.9–12, tab.1. 1938.

Matsubara, K. Studies on the Deep-sea Fishes of Japan. VIII. On the Individual Variations Found in an Apodal Fish Synaphobranchus pinnatus (Gronow), with Special Reference to its Taxonomy. – Ibid., 33, Nos.1–2:60–66, fig.13. 1938.

Matsubara, K. Studies in the Deep-sea Fishes of Japan. XI. On an Imperfectly-known Ribbonfish, Eumethichthys fiski (Günther), with a Supplement to the Genus Eumethichthys. – Bull. Biogeogr. Soc. Japan, 9, No.11-193–199. 1939.

Matsubara, K. Studies on the Deep-sea Fishes of Japan. XII. On Two New Berycoid Fishes Belonging to Ostracoberycidae from Suruga Bay. – Bull. Jap. Soc. Scient. Fish., 8:121–128. 1939. 2 text-figs.

Matsubara, K. Studies on the Deep-sea Fishes of Japan. XIII. On prof. Nakazawa's Collection of Fishes Referable to Isospondyli, Iniomi and Allotriognathi. (1–3). – Suisan Kenkiu-shi, (1), 35, No.12:314–319. 1940; (2), 36, No.1:1–10. 1941. fig.1; (3) 36, No.2:34–41. 1941.

Matsubara, K. Ichthyological Annotations from the Depth of the Sea of Japan. III. A Review of the Scopelid Fish, Referable to the Genus Neoscopelus. – J. Sigenkogaku Kenkyusyo, Tokyo, 1, No.1:55–63, figs.11–15. 1943.

Matsubara, K. Ichthyological Annotations from the Depth of the Sea of Japan. V. On a New Microstomid Fish, Leuroglossus lineatus, with an Emendation of the Family Microstomidae. – Ibid., pp.70–73, figs.20–21.

Matsubara, K. Ichthyological Annotations from the Depth of the Sea of Japan. VI. A New Stomiatiid Fish, Yarrella surugaensis, Belonging to Gonostomatidae. – Ibid., pp.73–76, fig.22.

Matsubara, K. Ichthyological Annotations from the Depth of the Sea of Japan. VII. On Two Rare Stomiatoid Fishes Belonging to Astronesthidae. – Ibid., pp.76–81, figs.23–24.

Matsubara, K. Studies on the Scorpaenoid Fishes of Japan. I and II. – Trans. Sigenkagaku Kenkyusyo, Tokyo, Nos.1–2:1–486. 1943. 4 pls., 156 text-figs.

Matsubara, K. Studies on the Fishes of the Genus Polyipnus Found in Japan. – Jap. J. Ichthyol., 1, No.3:187–197. 1950. 6 figs.

Matsubara, K. A Species of the Fishes of the Family Trichonotidae New to the Fauna of Japanese Waters. – Ibid., 2, No.2:89–92. 1952. 2 text-figs. (In Japanese, English summary.)

Matsubara, K. Revision of Japanese Serranid Fish, Referable to the Genus Acropoma. – Men. Coll. Agric. Kyoto Univ., 66:21–29, fig.3. 1953.

Matsubara, K. Fish Morphology and Hierarchy, pp.1–1605, text-figs.1–536, pls.1–135, figs.1–461. Tokyo. 1955. (In Japanese.)

Matsubara, K. and Y. Hiyama. A Review of Triglidae, a Family of Mail-cheeked Fishes Found in the Waters around Japan. – J. Imp. Fish. Inst., Tokyo, 28, No.1:1–67. 1932. 22 figs.

Matsubara, K. and T. Iwai. On an Ophidioid Fish, Petroschmidtia toyamensis Katayama with Some Remarks on the Genus Petroschmidtia. – Bull. Jap. Soc. Scient. Fish., 16, No.12:104–111. 1951. 5 figs.

Matsubara, R. and T. Iwai. A New Cottid Fish Found in Toyama Bay. – Misc. Rep. Res. Inst. Nat. Resour., Tokyo, 19–21:86–93. 1951. 3 figs.

Matsubara, K. and T. Iwai. Comparative Study of the Lizard-fishes Referred to the Genus Saurida Found in the Waters of Japan and China. – Mem. Coll. Agric. Kyoto Univ., 59:19–30. 1951. 6 figs.

Matsubara, K. and T. Iwai. Studies on Some Japanese Fishes of the Family Gempylidae. – Pacif. Sci., 6, No.3:193–212. 1952. 12 figs.

Matsubara, K. and T. Iwai. Some Remarks on the Family Liparidae, with Descriptions of Three New Species and Two Interesting Ones of the Genus Liparis. – Rep. Fac. Fish. Prefect. Univ. Mie, 1, No.3:425–441, figs.1–11. 1954.

Matsubara, K. and T. Iwai. Anatomy and Relationships of the Japanese Fishes of the Fam. Gempylidae. – Mem. Coll. Agric. Kyoto Univ., Spec. Number, pp.23–54. 1958. 14 figs.

Matsubara, K. and T. Iwai. Descriptions of a New Sandfish, Kraemeria sexradiata, from Japan, with Special Reference to its Osteology. – J. Wash. Acad. Sci., 1:27–32, figs.1–3. 1959.

Matsubara, K. and A. Ochiai. Studies on Hoplichthyidae, a Family of Mail-cheeked Fishes, Found in Japan and its Adjacent Waters. I. Jap. J. Ichthyol., 1, No.2:73–88. 2 figs.; III. 1, No.3:145–156. 3 figs. 1950.

Matsubara, K. and A. Ochiai. Notes on the Eels of the Genus Synaphobranchus Found in Japanese Waters. – Ibid., 1, No.4:351–259. 1951. 4 text-figs. (In Japanese, English summary.)

Matsubara, K. and A. Ochiai. A Revision of the Japanese Fishes of the Family Platycephalidae (the Flatheads). – Mem. Coll. Agric. Kyoto Univ., 68:1–109, figs.1–33, pls.1–3. 1955.

Matsubara, K., A. Ochiai, K. Amaoka, and I. Nakamura. Revisional Study of the Trachinoid Fishes of the Family Champsodontidae from the Waters around Japan and Tonking Bay. – Bull. Misaki Mar. Biol. Inst., Kyoto Univ., 6:1–20. 1964. 3 pls., 6 figs.

Matsubara, K. and H. Takamuki. The Japanese Flatfishes of the Genus Samariscus. – Jap. J. Ichthyol., 1, No.6:361–367. 1951. 4 text-figs.

Matsui, T. Review of the Mackerel Genera Scomber and Rastrelliger with Description of a New Species of Rastrelliger. – Copeia, No.1:71–83. 1967. 7 figs.

Matsui, I and T. Takai. Ecological Studies on the Important Fishes in East China and Yellow Sea. I. Ecological Studies on a Croaker, Pseudosciaena manchurica (J. et T.). – J. Shimonoseki Coll. Fish., 1:65–89. 1949. 20 tables, 10 figs. (In Japanese, English summary.)

Maul, G.E. Monografia dos peixes do Museu Municipal do Funchal. Famila Sudidae. – Bolm. Mus. munic. Funchal, 1, No.1–38, figs.1–10. 1945.

Maul, G.E. Monografia dos peixes do Museu Municipal do Funchal. Ordem Iniomi. – Ibid., 2, No.2:5–61, figs.1–22. 1946.

Maul, G.E. Monografia dos peixes do Museu Municipal do Funchal. Ordem Isospondyli. – Ibid., 3, No.5:5–41, figs.1–16. 1948.

Maul, G.E. Monografia dos peixes do Museu Municipal do Funchal. Ordem Isospondyli (Conclusão). – Ibid., 4, No.9/11:5–42. 1949. 15 text-figs.

Maul, G.E. Monografia deo peixes do Museu Municipal do Funchal, Familia Macrouridae e Merlucciidae. – Ibid., 5, No.12:5–55. 1951. 12 figs.

Maul, G.E. Monografia dos peixes do Museu Municipal do Funchal, Familia Gadidae e Bregmacerotidae. – Ibid., 6, No.15:5–51, figs.1–12. 1952.

Maul, G.E. Monografia dos peixes do Museo Municipal do Funchal, Familia Gadidae e Bregmacerotidae. Additions to Previously Revised Families. – Ibid., 6, Nos.15–16:1–62. 1952. 17 figs.

Maul, G.E. Monografia dos peixes do Museu Municipal do Funchal, Ordem Berycomorphi. – Ibid., 7, No.17:5–63. 1954. 21 figs.

Maul, G.E. Monografia dos peixes do Museu Municipal do Funchal, Ordem Heteromi. – Ibid., 8, No.2:5–19. 1955. 2 text-figs.

Maul, G.E. Additions to the Previously Revised Orders of Families of Fishes of the Museu Municipal do Funchal (Stomiatidae, Astronesthidae, Paralepididae). – Ibid., 9, No.24:76–96, figs.6–18.

Maul, G.E. Monografia dos peixes do Museu Municipal do Funchal, Ordem Discocephali. – Ibid., 9, No.25:5–75. 1956.

Maul, G.E. Further Additions to the Previously Revised Family Searsidae. – Ibid., 10, No.25:1–21. 1957.

Maul, G.E. The Ceratioid Fishes in the Collection of the Museu Municipal do Funchal (Melanocetidae, Himantolophidae, Oneirodidae, Linophrynidae). – Ibid., 14, Nos.42–50:87–159. 1961. 32 figs.

Maul, G.E. On a Small Collection of Ceratioid Fishes from off Dakar and Two Recently Acquired Specimens from Stomachs of Aphanopus carbo Taken in Madeira (Melanocetidae, Himantolophidae, Diceratiidae, Oneirodidae, Ceratiidae). – Ibid., 1, No.16:5–27. 1962. 10 figs.

Maul, G.E. Report on the Fishes Taken in Madeiran and Canarian Waters during the Summer-Autumn Cruises of the "Discovery II" 1959–1961. I. The Ceratioid Fishes (Melanocetidae, Himantolophidae, Oneirodidae, Gigantactinidae, Linophrynidae). – Ibid., 16:33–46. 1962. 6 figs.

Maul, G.E. On Four Rare Paralepidids from off Dakar, with a Discussion on Two Type Specimens of Omosudis elongatus Brauer from the Atlantic Ocean. – Bull. Inst. fr. Afr. noire, 24A:523–550. 1962. 9 figs.

Mead, G.W. Tarletonbeania taylori, a New Lantern Fish from the Western North Pacific. – Scient. Contr. N.Y. Zool. Soc., 38:105–108. 1953.

Mead, G.W. An Atlantic Record of the Zeoid Fish Parazen pacificus. – Copeia, 3:235–237. 1957.

Mead, G.W. On the Bramid Fishes of the Gulf of Mexico. – Zoologica, N.Y., 42, No.2:51–61. 1957. 3 pls.

Mead, G.W. A New Species of Inimous Fish from the Gulf of Mexico. – J. Wash. Acad. Sci., 48, No.6:188–191. 1958. 1 fig.

Mead, G.W. Three New Species of Archibenthic Inimous Fishes from the Western North Atlantic. – Ibid., 48, No.11:362–373. 1958. 4 figs.

Mead, G.W. Bathypterois pectinatus, a New Bathyal Inimous Fish from the Eastern Pacific. – Ibid., 49, No.8:290–292. 1959. 1 fig.

Mead, G.W. The Western Atlantic Jawfishes of the Opisthognathid Genus Lonchopisthus. – Stud. Fauna Suriname, 2:104–112, figs.41–42. 1959.

Mead, G.W. Aulopidae. – In: Fishes W.N. Atlantic. 5. Mem. Sears Found. Mar. Res., 1, No.5:19–20, fig.7. 1966.

Mead, G.W. Bathysauridae. – Ibid., pp.103–113, figs.36–37.

Mead, G.W. Bathypteroidae. – Ibid., pp.114–146, figs.38–41.

Mead, G.W. Ipnopidae. – Ibid., pp.147–161, figs.42–43.

Mead, G.W. Chlorophthalmidae. – Ibid., pp.162–189, figs.44–47.

Mead, G.W., E.Bertelsen, and D.M.Cohen. Reproduction among Deep-sea Fishes. – Deep Sea Res., 11:569–506. 1964.

Mead, G.W. and J.Böhlke. Scopelarchus linguidens, a New Bathypelagic Fish from off Northern Japan. – Jap. J. Ichthyol., 2, No.6:241–245, fig. 1. 1953.

Mead, G.W. and M.G.Bradbury. Acipenseridae. – In: Fishes W.N. Atlantic. 3. Mem. Sears Found. Mar. Res., 1, No.3:20–60. 1963.

Mead, G.W. and J.E. de Falla. New Oceanic Cheilodipterid Fishes from the Indian Ocean. – Bull. Mus. Comp. Zool. Harv., 134, No.7:261–274. 1965. 3 figs.

Mead, G.W. and R.L.Haedrich. The Distribution of the Oceanic Fish Brama brama. Ibid., 134, No.12:29–67. 1965. 8 maps.

Mead, G.W. and G.E.Maul. Taractes asper and the Systematic Relationships of the Steinegeriidae and Trachybericidae. – Ibid., 119, No.6:393–418. 1958. 7 figs.

Mead, G.W. and I.Rubinoff. Avocettinops yanoi, a New Nemichthyid Eel from the Southern Indian Ocean. – Breviora, 241:1–6. 1966. 1 fig.

Mednikov, B.M. Some Aspects of the Systematics and Phylogeny of the Lower Teleostei. – Byull. Mosk. Obshch. Ispyt. Prir., otd. biol., 67, No.1:155–156. 1962.

Mees, G.F. The Uranoscopidae of Western Australia (Pisces, Perciformes). – J. Proc. R. Soc. West. Aust., 43:46–58. 1960. 9 figs.

Mees, G.F. A Preliminary Revision of the Belonidae. – Zool. Verh., Leiden, 54:1–96, pl.1, fig.11. 1962.

Mees, G.F. Further Revisional Notes on the Belonidae. – Zoöl. Meded., Leiden, 39:311–326, fig.1. 1964.

Menon, A.G.K. On a Remarkable Blind Siluroid Fish of the Family Clariidae from Kerala (India). – Rec. Ind. Mus., 48:59–66. 1951. 1 pl., 3 text-figs.

Menon, A.G.K. Notes on Malayan Fishes in the Collection of the Raffles Museum, Singapore, 4. The Cyprinid Fishes. – Bull. Raffles Mus., 25:5–26. 1955. 9 figs.

Menon, A.G.K. Taxonomy of the Indian Frogfishes (Fam. Batrachoididae). Labdev. – J. Sci. Technol., 1, No.12:52–53. 1963.

Menon, A.G.K. Monograph of the Cyprinid Fishes of the Genus Garra Hamilton. – Mem. Indian Mus., 14:173–260. 1964. 2 pls., 29 figs.

Merrett, N.R. and C.H.Thorp. A Revised Key to the Scombroid Fishes of East Africa with New Observations on their Biology. – Ann. Mag. Nat. Hist., 13, No.8:367–384. 1965.

Meshkov, M.M. On the Systematics of the Family Atherinidae in the Black and Caspian Seas. – Izv. Akad. Nauk SSSR, Biol. Ser., pp.400–406. 1941.

Miller, R.J. Taxonomy and Biology of the Genus Lebetus (Teleostei – Gobioidea). – Bull. Br. Mus. Nat. Hist. Zool., 10, No.3:205–256. 1963. ill.

Miller, R.J. A Review of the Seabasses of the Genus Centropristes (Serranidae). – Tulane Stud. Zool., 7:35–68. 1959. 30 figs.

Miller, R.R. A New Genus and Species of Deep-sea Fish of the Family Myctophidae from the Philippine Islands. - Proc. U.S. Natn. Mus., 97:81–90. 1947.

Miller, R.R. The Cyprinodont Fishes of the Death Valley System of Eastern California and Southwestern Nevada. - Misc. Publs. Mus. Zool. Univ. Mich., 68:1–155. 1948. 15 pls., 5 text-figs.

Miller, R.R. A Review of the American Clupeid Fishes of the Genus Dorosoma. - Proc. U.S. Natn. Mus., 100:387–410. 1950.

Miller, R.R. Notes on the Cutthroat and Rainbow Trouts with the Descriptions of a New Species from Gila River, New Mexico. - Occ. Pap. Mus. Zool. Univ. Mich., 529:1–42, pl.1. 1950.

Miller, R.R. A New Genus and Species of Cyprinodontid Fish from San Luis Potosi, Mexico, with Remarks on the Subfamily Cyprinodontinae. - Ibid., 581:1–17, pls.1–2. 1956.

Miller, R.R. Systematics and Biology of the Gizzard Shad (Dorosoma cepedianum and Related Fishes.- Fishery Bull. Fish Wildl. Serv. U.S., 60, No.173:371. 1960. 4 figs.

Miller, R.R. Genus Dorosoma. - In: Fishes W.N. Atlantic. 3. Mem. Sears Found. Mar. Res., 1, No.3:443–451, figs.116, 117. 1963.

Miller, R.R. and J.C. Briggs. Dactyloscopus amnis, a New Sand Stargazer from Rivers of the Pacific Slope of Southern Mexico. - Occ. Pap. Mus. Zool. Univ. Mich., 627:1–11. 1962. 3 figs.

Miller, R.R. and C.L. Hubbs. The Spinyrayed Cyprinid Fishes (Plagopterini) of the Colorado River System. - Misc. Publs. Mus. Zool. Univ. Mich., 115:1–39, figs.1, 2, pls.I–III. 1960.

Millot, J. Unité spécifique des Coelacanthes actuels. - Nature, Paris, 3238:58–59. 1955. 2 figs.

Mina, M.V. Data on the Ecology and Taxonomy of Lake Trouts of the Genus Salvelinus from the Lena River Delta. - Vopr. Ikhtiol., 2, No.23:230–241. 1962.

Miranda Ribeiro, P. Notes para o estudo dos Pygidiidae Brasileiros. - Bolm. Mus. nac. Rio de J., 106:1–16. 1951. 3 pls.

Misra, K.S. An Aid to the Identification of the Fishes of India, Burma and Ceylon. 1. Elasmobranchii and Holocephali. - Rec. Indian Mus., 49, No.1. 1952.

Misra, K.S. An Aid to the Identification of the Fishes of India, Burma and Ceylon. 2. Clupeiformes, Bathyclupeiformes. Galaxiiformes. Scopeliformes and Ateleopiformes. - Ibid., 50, Nos.3–4:367–422. 1952. ill.

Mohr, E.W. Mugiliden-Studien. - Zool. Iber. Neapel, Sect. Syst., 54:174–204. 1927.

Mohr, E.W. Teleostei physoclisti. 12–15. Labriformes, Carangiformes, Beryciformes, Perciformes, Scombriformes. - Tierwelt N.- u. Ostsee, No.12:85–140. 1927. ill.

Mohr, E.W. Teleostei physoclisti. 8. Trachiniformes. - Ibid., No.12:107–120. 1928. 11 figs.

Mohr, E.W. Hemirhamphiden-Studien, 7–9. - Zool. Anz., 116:218–223. 1936. 2 figs.

Mohr, E.W. Hemirhamphiden-Studien. - Mitt. zool. Mus., 21:34–64. 1936.

Mohr, E.W. Revision der Centriscidae. - Dana Rep., 13:1–69. 1937. 2 pls., 33 text-figs.

Mohr, E.W. Fliegende Fische. Wittenburg-Lutherstadt (Ziemsen), pp.1–55. 1954. 50 figs.

Mohr, E. Revision der Centriscidae (Acanthopterygii, Centrisciformes). - Dana Rep., 2, No.13:1–73. 1959. ill.

Mohsen, T. Sur le dimorphisme sexuel au niveau de la nageoire anale et de son système suspensorial chez le Cypronodonte ovipare Tomeurus gracilis Eigenmann. - Bull. Aquat. Biol., 3, No.27:61–64. 1962. ill.

Mohsen, T. Sur le système génital mâle chez Jenynsia lineata (Cyprinodontiformes, Jenynsiidae) et les affinités phylogénétiques de cette espèce avec les familles voisines. - C. r. hebd. Séanc. Acad. Sci., Paris, 256, No.6:1385–1387. 1963. ill.

Mohsen, T. A New Key Character in Males of the Family Goodeidae (Cyprinodontiformes). — Nature, 4976:1127. 1965.

Moiseev, P.A. Study of the Family Scorpaenidae of the Far Eastern Seas. - Issled. Morei SSSR, 23:113–138. 1935.

Moiseev, P.A. Commercial Flounders of the Far East, pp.1–63. Vladivostok, Primizdat. 1946. ill.

Montalban, H.R. Pomacentridae of the Philippine Islands. - Phil. Bur. Sci. Monogr., 24:1–117, pls.1–19. (1927) 1928.

Monteiro, R. Heterosomata de Angola. 1. Contribução para o estudo das familias Psettodidae, Citharidae, Paralichthyidae e Bothidae. - Trabhs. Miss. Biol. marit.; Anais Jta. Invest. Ultramar, 12, No.2:87–130. 1958. 26 figs.

Montilla, J.R. A Review of Philippine Menidae and Gerridae. - Philipp. J. Sci., 58:281–295. 1935. 3 pls.

Montilla, J.R. A Review of Philippine Holocentridae. – Ibid., 67:207–229. 1938. 5 pls.
Moore, D. Development, Distribution, and Comparison of Rudder Fishes Kyphosus sectatrix (L.) and K. incisor in the Western North Atlantic. – Fishery Bull. Fish. Wildl. Serv. U.S., 61:447–453. 1962.
Moreland, J. A New Genus and Species of Congiopodid Fish from Southern New Zealand. – Rec. Dom. Mus., Wellington, 3, No.3:241–246. 1960. 7 figs.
Mori, T. On Acipenseridae from Korea (Japanese). – J. Chosen Nat. Hist. Soc., 16:6–10. 1933. 1 fig.
Morice, J. Essai systématique sur les familles des Cybiidae, Thunnidae et Katsuwonidae, poissons Scombroides. – Revue Trav. Off. (scient. tech.) Pêch. marit., 18, No.1:35–63. 1953. 10 figs.
Morrow, J.E. Taxonomy of the Deep-sea Fishes of the Genus Chauliodus. – Bull. Mus. Comp. Zool. Harv., 125:249–294. 1961. 10 figs.
Morrow, J.E. Marlins, Sailfish and Spearfish of the Indian Ocean. – Proc. Symp. Scombroid Fish. Mandapam, India, 1:429–440. 1964.
Morrow, J.E. Stomiatoidea. General Discussion and Key to Families. – In: Fishes W.N. Atlantic. 4. Mem. Sears Found. Mar. Res., 1, No.4:71–77. 1964.
Morrow, J.E. Chauliodontidae. – Ibid., pp.274–289.
Morrow, J.E. Stomiatidae. – Ibid., pp.290–310.
Morrow, J.E. Malacosteidae. – Ibid., pp.550–560.
Morrow, J.E. and R.H. Gibbs. Melanostomiatidae. – Ibid., 351–511, figs.92–136.
Morrow, J.E. and S.J. Harbo. Revision of the Sailfish Genus Istiophorus. – Copeia, 1:34–44, figs.1–15. 1969.
Moss, S.A. Melamphaidae. II. A New Melamphaid Genus Sio with a Redescription of Sio nordenskjoldii (Lönnberg). – Dana Rep., 56:1–10. 1962.
Mujib, K.A. The Cranial Osteology of the Gadidae. – J. Fish. Res. Bd. Can., 24, No.6:1315–1375. 1967.
Mukerji, D.D. Systematic Position of the Japanese Sculpins Marukawichthys and Ereunias. – Annotnes. Zool. Jap., 13, No.5:441–444. 1932.
Mukerji, D.D. Report of Fishes. II. Sisoridae and Cyprinidae. – Mem. Conn. Acad. Arts Sci., 10:323–359. 1936. 20 text-figs.
Mukhacheva, V.A. The Specific Composition of the Genus Cyclothone (Pisces, Gonostomidae) in the Pacific. Biology and Distribution of Fish from the Pacific and Indian Oceans. – Trudy Inst. Okeanol., Akad. Nauk SSSR, 73:93–138. 1964. 17 figs.
Mukhacheva, V.A. The Genus Cyclothone (Fam. Gonostomidae). – In: Tikhii okean, Biol., No.3.. Ryby otkrytykh vod, pp.182–199. Moscow, "Nauka." 1967.
Müller, C.G. and H.S. Mazet. Tigers of the Sea, pp.1–223. Philadelphia. 1946. ill.
Müller, J. and J. Henle. Systematische Beschreibung d. Plagiostomen, pp.1–200, pls.1–59. Berlin. 1841.
Munro, I.S.R. Revision of Australian Silver Breams Mylio and Rhadbosargus. – Mem. Qd. Mus., 12, No.4:182–224, figs.1–5, pls.16–23. 1949.
Munro, I.S.R. Revision of Bregmaceros with Descriptions of Larval Stages from Australia.— Proc.R.Soc. Qd., 61, No.5:37—53. 1950. 10 figs.
Munro, I.S.R. The Marine and Freshwater Fishes of Ceylon. – Dep. External Affairs, Canberra, pp.1–351. 1955. ill.
Munro, I.S.R. Additions to the Fish Fauna of New Guinea. – Papua New Guin. Agric. J., 16, No.4:141–186, figs.1–22. 1964.
Murgoci, A. Contributions à l'étude des Acepensérides de Roumanie. – Annls. scient. Univ. Jassy, 28:289–385. 1942.
Murgoci, A. Contribution à la connaissance des Gobiésocides (ordre des Xenopterygii) de la mer Noire. – Journ. Rev. Roum. Biol., Ser. Zool., 9, No.5:297–306. 1964. ill.
Myers, G.S. The Systematic Position of the Phallostethid Fishes. – Am. Mus. Novit., 295:1–12. 1928.
Myers, G.S. On the Fishes Described by Koller from the Hainan in 1926 and 1927. – Lingnan Sci. J., 10:255–262. 1931.
Myers, G.S. The Primary Groups of Oviparous Cyprinodont Fishes. – Stanford Univ. Publs., Biol. Sci., 6, No.3:1–14. 1931.
Myers, G.S. The Genera of Indo-Malayan and African Cyprinodont Fishes Related to Panchax and Nothobranchius. – Copeia, 4:180–195. 1933.
Myers, G.S. Reports on the Collections Obtained by the First Johnson-Smithsonian Deep-sea Expedition to the Puerto Rican Deep. Three New Deep-water Fishes from the West Indies. – Smithson. Misc. Collns., 91, No.9:1–12. 1934. 1 pl., 2 text-figs.

Myers, G.S. An Annotated List of the Cyprinodont Fishes of Hispaniola, with Descriptions of Two New Species. – Zoologica, N.Y., **10**:301–316, figs.273–279. 1935.

Myers, G.S. A New Phallostethid Fish from Palawan. – Proc.Biol. Soc. Wash., **48**:5–6. 1935.

Myers, G.S. A New Genus of Opisthognathid Fishes. – Smithson. Misc. Collns., **91**, No.23:1–5. 1935. 1 fig.

Myers, G.S. A New Polynemid Fish Collected in the Sadong River, Sarawak, by Dr. William T.Hornaday, with Notes on the Genera of Polynemidae. – J. Wash. Acad. Sci., 26:376–382. 1936. 1 text-fig.

Myers, G.S. On the Indo-Australian Fishes of the Genus *Scatophagus*, with Description of a New Genus, *Selenotoca*. – Proc. Biol. Soc. Wash., 49:83–86. 1936.

Myers, G.S. Notes on Phallostethid Fishes. – Proc. U.S. Natn. Mus., **84**:137–143. 1937.

Myers, G.S. The Deep-sea Zeomorph Fishes of the Family Grammicolepidae. – Ibid., pp.145–156, pls.5–7.

Myers, G.S. Notes on *Ansorgia*, *Clarisilurus*, *Wallago*, and *Ceratoglanis*, Four Genera of African and Indo-Malayan Cat-fishes. – Copeia, 2:98. 1938.

Myers, G.S. Studies on the Genera of Cyprinodont Fishes. XIV. *Aplocheilichthys* and its Relatives in Africa. – Ibid., 3:136–143. 1938.

Myers, G.S. A New Owstoniid Fish from Deep Water off the Philippines. – Proc. Biol. Soc. Wash., 52:19–20. 1939.

Myers, G.S. Studies on South American Freshwater Fishes. I. – Stanford Ichthyol. Bull., **2**:89–114. 1942. 19 text-figs.

Myers, G.S. Two Extraordinary New Blind Nematognath Fishes from the Rio Negro, Representing a New Subfamily of Pygidiidae, with a Rearrangement of the Genera of the Family and Illustrations of Some Previously Described Genera and Species from Venezuela and Brazil. – Proc. Calif. Acad. Sci., 4, No.23:591–602, pls.52–56. 1 text-fig. 1944.

Myers, G.S. On a Recently Proposed New Family of Deep-sea Fishes (Barbourisiidae Parr, 1845). – Copeia, **1**:41–42. 1946.

Myers, G.S. The Family Name of the Characid Fishes. – Copeia, 3:195–204. 1949.

Myers, G.S. Studies on South American Freshwater Fishes. II. The Genera of Anostomine Characids. – Stanford Ichthyol. Bull., **3**:184–198. 1950. 3 figs.

Myers, G.S. Notes on the Classification and Names of Cyprinodont Fishes. – Trop. Fish Mag., **7**, March 1955.

Myers, G.S. Trends in the Evolution of Teleostean Fishes. – Stanford Ichthyol. Bull., **7**:27–30. 1958.

Myers, G.S. A New Zeomorph Fish of the Family Oreosomatidae from the Coast of California, with Notes on the Family. – Ibid., pp.89–98. 1960. 1 fig.

Myers, G.S. The Genera and Ecological Geography of the South American Banjo Catfishes, Family Aspredinidae. – Ibid., pp.132–139.

Myers, G.S. The South American Characid Genera *Exodon*, *Gnathoplax* and *Roeboexodon* with Notes on the Ecology and Taxonomy of Characid Fishes. – Ibid., pp.206–211.

Myers, G.S. and W.C.Freihofer. Megalomycteridae. A Previously Unrecognized Family of Deep-sea Cetomimiformes Fishes, Based on Two New Genera from North Atlantic. – Ibid., **8**:193–206, figs.1–5. 1966.

Myers, G.S. and L.Shapovalov. On the Identity of *Ophicephalus* and *Channa*, Two Genera of Labyrinth Fishes. – Peking Nat. Hist. Bull., **6**, No.2:33–37. 1931–1932.

Myers, G.S. and C.B.Wade. Four New Genera and Ten New Species of Eels from the Pacific Coast of Tropical America. – Allan Hancock Pacif. Exped. 1932–1940, **9**, No.4:65–110, pls.7–16. 1941.

Myers, G.S. and C.B.Wade. The Pacific American Atherinid Fishes of the Genera *Eurystole*, *Nectarges*, *Coleotropis* and *Melanorhinus*. – Ibid., **9**, No.5:113–149, pls.17–19. 1942.

Myers, G.S. and C.B.Wade. New Fishes of the Families Dactyloscopidae, Microdesmidae, and Antennariidae from the West Coast of Mexico and the Galapagos Islands. – Ibid., **9**, No.6:151–178. 1946. 4 pls.

Myers, G.S. and S.H.Weitzman. Two Remarkable New Trichomycterid Catfishes from the Amazon Basin in Brazil and Colombia. – J. Zool. Res., **149**:277–287. 1966. 4 figs.

Nafpaktitis, B.G. Taxonomy and Distribution of the Lantern Fishes, Genera *Lobianchia* and *Diaphus*, in the North Atlantic. – Dana Rep., **73**:1–131. 1968. 69 figs., 2 pls.

Nair, R.V. Leptocephali of the Gulf of Manaar. – Proc. Indian Acad. Sci., 27**B**:87–91. 1948. 2 text-figs.

Nair, R.V. Key for the Field Identification of the Common Clupeoid Fishes of India. – J. Zool. Soc. India, 5, No.1:108–138, figs.1–18. 1953.

Nakamura, H. Tunas and Spearfishes. - Spec. Scient. Rep. U.S. Fish Wildl. Serv. Fisheries, 48, 1951.
Nakamura, I. Relationships of Fishes Referable to the Subfamily Thunnidae on the Basis of the Axial Skeleton. - Bull. Misaki Mar. Biol Inst., Kyoto Univ., 8:7–38. 1965. ill.
Nalbant, T. A Study of the Genera of Botiinae and Cobitinae (Pisces, Ostariophysi, Cobitidae). - Trav. Mus. Hist. nat. Gr. Antipa, 4:343–379. 1963.
Nani, A. and F. Gneri. Introduccion al estudio de los Mixinoideos Sudamericanos. 1. Un nuevo genero de "Bahosa de mar," "Notomyxine" (Classe Myxini, familia Myxinidae). - Revta Inst. nac. Invest. Cienc. nat. Mus. argent. Cienc. nat., Zool., 2, No.4:183–224, pl.3, fig.6. 1951.
Neelov, A.V. The Systematic Position of Hookear Sculpins (Cottidae) of the Genus Artediellus Jordan and Related Genera. - Zool. Zh., 47, No.1:99–103. 1968.
Nekrasov, V.V. Revision of Species of the Genus Decapterus (Family Carangidae, Order Perciformes) from the Indian Ocean. - Vopr. Ikhtiol., 9, Nos.2(55):211–220. 1968. 5 figs.
Nelson, G.J. Notes on the Systematic Status of the Eels Neenchelys and Myroconger. - Pacif. Sci., 21, No.4:562–563. 1967.
Nelson, G.J. Gill Arches of Some Teleostean Fishes of the Families Girellidae, Pomacentridae, Embiotocidae, Labridae and Scaridae. - J. Nat. Hist., 1:289–293. 1967.
Nelson, G.J. Gill-arch Structure in Acanthodes. Nobel Symposium, 4. Current Problems of Lower Vertebrate Phylogeny, pp.129–143. N.Y., London, Sydney. 1968. 6 figs.
Nelson, G.J. Evolution of Branchiostegals and Classification of Teleostome Fishes, by D.E.McAllister, 1968. - Copeia, 4:888, 889. 1968.
Nelson, G.J. Gill Arches of Teleostean Fishes of the Division Osteoglossomorpha. - J. Linn. Soc., Zool., 47, No.312:261–277. 1968. 11 figs.
Nelson, G.J. Gill Arches and the Phylogeny of Fishes, with Notes on the Classification of Vertebrates. - Bull. Am. Nat. Hist., 141, No.4:475–552, figs.1–26. 1969.
Nelson, K. Behavior and Morphology in the Glandulocaudinae Fishes (Ostariophysi, Characidae). - Univ. Calif. Publs. Zool., 75, No.2:59–152. 1964.
Nichols, J.T. The Fishes of Porto Rico and the Virgin Islands, Branchiostomidae and Sciaenidae. - Scient. Surv. P. Rico, 10:161–295. 1929. 174 figs.
Nichols, J.T. Speculation on the History of the Ostariophysi. - Copeia, 4:148–151. 1930.
Nichols, J.T. Classification of Carp-like Fishes. - Zoologica, N.Y., 23, Nos.2, 6:191–193. 1938.
Nichols, J.T. The Freshwater Fishes of China. - Am. Mus. Nat. Hist., Nat Hist. Central Asia, 9:I–XXXVI, 1–322. 1943. 10 pls., 143 figs.
Nichols, J.T. Fishes of the Subfamily Caranginae Listed from China. - Lingnan Sci. J., 21, Nos.1–4:81–86. 1945.
Nichols, J.T. and C.M. Breder. An Annotated List of Synentognathi with Remarks on their Development and Relationships. - Zoologica, N.Y., 8, No.7:423–498, figs.156–176. 1928.
Nichols, J.T. and R.C. Murphy. Long Island Fauna. IV. The Sharks (Order Selachii).— Brooklyn Mus. Sci. Bull., 3, No.1:1–34. 1916. ill.
Nielsen, J. Psettodoidea and Pleuronectoidea (Pisces, Heterosomata). - Atlantide Rep., 6:101–127. 1961. 1 pl., 8 figs.
Nielsen, J. Heterosomata (Pisces). - Galathea Rep., 4:219–226. 1962. ill.
Nielsen, J.G. Soleoidea (Pisces, Heterosomata). - Atlantide Rep., 7:7–36. 1963. ill.
Nielsen, J.G. Notes on Some Heterosomata (Pisces) from N.W. South America with the Description of a New Genus and Species and a New Subspecies of Paralichthyinae. - Vidensk. Meddr. dansk naturh. Foren, 125:377–400, figs.1–8, pls.13–15. 1963.
Nielsen, J.G. Synopsis of the Ipnopidae (Pisces, Iniomi) with Description of Two New Abyssal Species. - Galathea Rep., 8:49–75, pls.15–17. 1966.
Nielsen, J.G. and J.M. Jensen. Revision of the Arctic Cod Genus Arctogadus (Pisces, Gadidae). - Meddr. Grønland, 184, No.2:1–28. 1967. pl.
Nielsen, J.G. and O. Nybelin. Brotulidae (Pisces, Percomorphi) from Tropical West Africa. - Atlantide Rep., 7:195–213. 1963. ill.
Nikol'skii, G.V. Data on the Systematics of the Genus Gobio from the Amur Basin. - Byull. Mosk. Obshch. Ispyt. Prir., otd. biol. 51, No.5:59–68. 1950. ill.
Nikol'skii, G.V. Specialized Ichthyology, pp.1–458, figs.1–312. - Moscow, "Sovetskaya Kniga." 1954.

Nikol'skii, G.V. and S.G.Soin. On Catfishes (Family Siluridae) in the Amur Basin. – Dokl. Akad. Nauk SSSR, 59, No.7:1357–1360. 1948.

Ninni, E.I. Gobius dei mari e delle aeque interne d'Italia. – R. Comitato Talassografico Italiano, Venezia, 242:1–169. 1938. 19 pls.

Norden, C.R. Comparative Osteology of Representative Salmonid Fishes, with Particular Reference to the Grayling (Thymallus arcticus) and its Phylogeny. – J. Fish. Res. Bd., Can., 18, No.5:679–791. 1961. 16 pls., 2 text-figs.

Norman, J.R. A Revision of the Clupeid Fishes of the Genus Ilisha and Allied Genera. – Ann. Mag. Nat. Hist., 9, No.11:1–22. 1923.

Norman, J.R. A Synopsis of the Rays of the Family Rhinobatidae, with a Revision of the Genus Rhinobatus.– Proc. Zool. Soc. Lond., pp.941–982. 1926. 30 figs.

Norman, J.R. A Report on the Flatfishes (Heterosomata) Collected by the F.I.S. Endeavour, with a Synopsis of the Flatfishes of Australia and a Revision of the Subfamily Rhombosoleinae. – Zool. (Biol.) Results Fish.Exp. "Endeavour." 1909–1914, 5:219–308. 1926. 15 figs.

Norman, J.R. The Flatfishes (Heterosomata) of India, with a List of the Specimens in the Indian Museum, Paris, I, II. – Rec. Indian Mus., 29:7–48. pls.2–7, 12 text-figs.; 30:173–215. 30 figs. (1927) 1928.

Norman, J.R. The South American Characid Fishes of the Subfamily Serrasalmoninae, with a Revision of the Genus Serrasalmus Lacépède. – Proc. Zool. Soc. Lond., pp.781–829. (1928) 1929. 1 pl., 20 figs.

Norman, J.R. The Teleostean Fishes of the Family Chiasmodontidae. – Ann. Mag. Nat. Hist., 10, No.3:529–544. 1929. 11 text-figs.

Norman, J.R. A Preliminary Revision of the Berycoid Fishes of the Genus Melamphaes. – Ibid., 10, No.4:153–168. 1929.

Norman, J.R. Notes on the Myctophid Fishes of the Genera Diaphus and Myctophum in the British Museum (Natur. Hist.). – Ibid., pp.510–515. ill.

Norman, J.R. Oceanic Fishes and Flatfishes Collected in 1925–1927. – "Discovery" Rep., 2:261–370, pl.II, text-figs.1–47. 1930.

Norman, J.R. Notes on Flatfishes (Heterosomata) IV. A Synopsis of the Genera of the Subfamily Pleuronectinae. – Ann. Mag. Nat. Hist., 10, No.11:214–222. 1933.

Norman, J.R. A Systematic Monograph of the Flatfishes (Heterosomata). 1. Psettodidae, Bothidae, Pleuronectidae. London (Brit. Mus.), pp.1–459. 1934. 317 figs.

Norman, J.R. The Carangid Fishes of the Genus Decapterus Bleeker. – Ann. Mag. Nat. Hist., 10, No.16:252. 1935.

Norman, J.R. A Revision of the Lizard-fishes of the Genera Synodus, Trachinocephalus and Saurida. – Proc. Zool. Soc. Lond., pp.99–135. 1935. 18 figs.

Norman, J.R. Coast Fishes. II. The Patagonian Region. – "Discovery" Rep., 16:1–150. 1937. 5 pls., 76 text-figs.

Norman, J.R. On the Affinities of the Chilean Fish, Normanichthys crockeri Clark. – Copeia, 1:29–32. figs.1–3. 1938.

Norman, J.R. Coast Fishes. III. The Antarctic Zone. – "Discovery" Rep., 18:1–105. 1938. 1 pl., 62 text-figs.

Norman, J.R. The Remoras or Sharksuckers (Echeneidae). – Proc. Linn. Soc. Lond., Sess.151, 1938–1939, 1:24–29. 1939. ill.

Norman, J.R. Fishes. – Scient. Rep. John Murray Exped., 1933–1934, 7:1–116. 1939. 41 text-figs.

Norman, J.R. Notes on the Blennioid Fishes. I. A Provisional Synopsis of the Genera of the Family Blenniidae. – Ann. Mag. Nat. Hist., 11, No.10:793–812. 1943.

Norman, J.R. A Draft Synopsis of the Orders, Families and Genera of Recent Fishes and Fish-like Vertebrates. – Bull. Br. Mus. Nat. Hist., pp.1–649. 1958.

Norman, J.R. and E.Trewavas. Notes on the Eels of the Family Synaphobranchidae. – Ann. Mag. Nat. Hist., 11, No.3:352–359. 1939. 2 figs.

Novikova, N.S. The Black Dragons (Pisces, Idiacanthidae) from the Indian and Pacific Oceans. – Trudy Inst. Okeanol., Akad. Nauk SSSR, 84:159–208. 1967.

Nunes, A.A. Contribuicões para o conhecimento dos Peixes "Heterosomata," I and II. – Archos. Mus. Bocage, 12:23–62. 1941. 2 pls., 1 text-fig.

Nybelin, O. Cottiden-Studien. – Zool. Anz., 133:215–224. 1941. 2 text-figs.

Nybelin, O. Sur quelques espèces du genre Anotopterus et sur la position systématique de la famille des Anotopteridae. – Meddn. Göteborgs Mus. Zool., (B), 5:1–16. 1946.

Nybelin, O. Zur Morphologie und Terminologie des Schwanzskelettes der Actinopterygier. – Ark. Zool., Ser.2, 15:485–516. 1963. 22 figs.

Nybelin, O. and M.Poll. Brotulidae des côtes africaines de l'Atlantique sud avec description d'une espèce nouvelle de Lamprogrammus. – Bull. Inst. r. Sci. nat. Belg., 34, No.19:1–7. 1958. 1 fig.

Ochiai, A. Comparative Studies of Branquillos of the Genus Branchiostegus Found in the Waters of Japan and China. – Zool. Mag., Tokyo, 62:306–313. 1953. (In Japanese, English summary.)

Ochiai, A. Morphology, Taxonomy and Ecology of the Soleoid Fishes Found in Japan, pp.1–234, figs.1–70. 1959.

Ochiai, A. Fauna Japonica, Soleina (Pisces). – Biogeographica, pp.1–114. 1963. 24 pls., 54 text-figs.

Ochiai, A. Studies on the Comparative Morphology and Ecology of the Japanese Soles. – Spec. Rep. Misaki Mar. Biol. Inst., Kyoto Univ., 3:1–97, figs.1–39, 2 pls. 1966.

Ochiai, A. and K.Amaoka. Review of the Japanese Flatfishes of the Genus Samariscus, with the Description of a New Species from Tonking Bay. – Ann. Mag. Nat. Hist., 13, No.5:83–91. 1962.

Ochiai, A., Ch.Araga, and M.Nakajima. A Revision of the Dragonets Referable to the Genus Callionymus Found in the Waters of Japan. – Publs. Seto Mar. Biol. Lab., V, 1:96–132. 1955. 19 figs.

Ochiai, A. and F.Mitani. A Revision of the Pediculate Fishes of the Genus Malthopsis Found in the Waters of Japan (Family Ogcocephalidae). – Pacif. Sci., 10, No.3:271–285. 1956.

Ochiai, A. and K.Mori. Studies on the Japanese Butterfish Referable to the Genus Psenopsis. – Bull. Misaki Mar. Biol. Inst., Kyoto Univ., 8:1–6. 1965. fig.

O'Connell, Ch.P. The Life History of the Cabezon Scorpaenichthys marmoratus (Ayres). – Dep. Fish and Game Mar. Fisher. Branch., Fish. Bull., 93:7–76, pls.1–10, figs.1–40. 1953.

Ogawa, T. Study on the Fishes of the Family Myctophidae in the Northeastern Sea Area along the Pacific Coast of Japan. I. Species and Distribution. – Bull Tohoku Reg. Fish. Res. Lab., 19:81–89. 1961. ill.

Ogilby, J.D. Edible Fishes and Crustaceans of New South Wales, pp.1–212, pls.1–51. Sydney. 1893.

Ogilby, J.D. On a Galaxias from Mount Kosciusko. – Proc. Linn. Soc., N.S. Wales, 21:62–73. 1896.

Ogilby, J.D. A Monograph of the Australian Marsipobranchii. – Proc. Linn. Soc., N.S. Wales, 21:388–426. 1896.

Ogilby, J.D. Revision of the Batrachoididae. – Ann. Qd. Mus., 9:43–57. 1908.

Ogilby, J.D. Edible Fishes of Queensland. Part I – Family Pempheridae. Part II – The Gadopseiform Percoids. – Mem. Qd. Mus., 2:60–80, pls.18–20. 1913.

Ogilby, J.D. Edible Fishes of Queensland. Part III – Carangidae (No.1). – Ibid., 3:57–98. 1915. 10 pls.

Ogilby, J.D. A Revision of the Australian Therapons with Notes on Some Papuan Species. – Ibid., 5:99–126, pls.10–13, 1 text-fig. 1916.

Ogilby, J.D. Edible Fishes of Queensland. Part IV – Synentognathi (No.1). Part V – Heterosomata (No.1). Part VI (misprinted III) – Carangidae (No.2). Part VII – Lethrinidae (No.1). Part VIII – Sparidae (No.1). Part IX – Teuthidoidea (No.1). – Ibid., pp.127–177, pls.14–23. 1916.

Ogilby, J.D. Edible Fishes of Queensland. Part X – Plesiopidae (No.1). Part XI – Lutianidae (No.1). Part XII – Nemipteridae (No.1). Part XIII – Sciaenidae (No.1). Part XIV – Balistidae (No.1). – Ibid., 6:45–90, pls.16–26. 1918.

Ogilby, J.D. Edible Fishes of Queensland. Part XV – Serranidae (No.1). – Ibid., 7, No.1:1–30, pls.1–3. 1920.

Ogilby, J.D. and A.K.McCulloch. A Revision of the Australian Orectolobiae. – Proc. R. Soc. N.S. Wales, 42:264–299. (1908) 1909. 2 pls., 1 text-fig.

Okada, Y. Fishes of Japan. Illustrations and Distributions of Fishes of Japan, pp.1–432, figs.1–391. Tokyo, Maruzen Co. 1955.

Okada, Y. and H.Ikeda. Notes on the Fishes of the Riu-Kiu Islands. II. Pomacentridae and Callionymidae. – Bull. Biogeogr. Soc. Japan, 7, No.7:67–95, figs.1–5, pls.4–6. 1937.

Okada, Y. and H.Ikeda. Notes on the Fishes of the Riu-Kiu Islands. IV. The Damsel Fish, Pomacentridae, Collected in 1938. – Trans. Biogeogr. Soc. Japan, 3, No.2:159–206, pl.6, 30 figs. 1939.

Okada, Y. and H.Ikeda. A Revision of the Japanese Striped-loaches, Referred to the Genus Cobitis. – Sci. Rep. Tokyo Bunrika Daig., 4 B, 69:89–104. 1939. 3 text-figs.

Okada, Y. and K.Matsubara. Keys to the Fishes and Fish-like Animals of Japan, pp.1–584, pls.1–113. Tokyo and Osaka. 1938.

Okada, Y. and R. Sano. Taxonomical Consideration on the Fishes Referable to the Genus Chlorophthalmus. – Rep. Fac. Fish. Prefect. Univ. Mie, 3, No.3:595–607, text-figs.1–7, tables 1–4. 1960.

Okada, Y. and K.A. Suzuki. A Review on the Macroorhamphosus Fishes of Japan. – Ibid., 1, No.1:7–11. 1951. 5 figs.

Okada, Y. and K. Suzuki. On Two New Bembroid Fishes. – Ibid., 1, No.2:67–74. 1952.

Okada, Y. and K. Suzuki. On the Similarity of the Osteological Characters Found between Owstoniidae and Cepolidae. – Ibid., 2, No.2:185–194. 1956. 3 figs.

Okamura, O. and S. Kishida. A New Genus and Species of the Bembroid Fish Collected from the Bungo Channel, Japan. – Bull. Misaki Mar. Biol. Inst., Kyoto Univ., 4:43–48. 1963.

Okhryamkin, D.I., P.A. Moiseev, and A.Ya. Taranets. Commercial Flounders of the Maritime Territory, pp.1–44. Vladivostok. 1936. figs.

Oliva, O. A Revision of the Cyprinoid Fishes of Czechoslovakia with Regard to their Secondary Sexual Characters. – Bull. int. Acad. tchéque Sci., 53:1–61, pls.1–2. 1953.

Olsen, S. A Contribution to Systematics and Biology of Chaenichthyid Fishes from South Georgia. – Nytt Mag. Zool., 3:79–93. 1955. 3 figs., 6 tables.

Ogalatenko, L.K. The Family Cobitidae in the Upper Dniester. – In: Flora, fauna Ukrayyins'kykh Karpat, pp.90–91. Uzhgorod. 1965.

Orton, G.L. Notes on Larval Anatomy of Fishes of the Order Lyomeri. – Copeia, 1:6–15. 1963. 4 figs.

Oshima, M. A Review of the Fishes of the Family Mugilidae Found in the Waters of Formosa. – Ann. Carneg.. Mus., 13:240–259, pls.XI–XIII. 1922.

Oshima, M. A Review of the Fishes of the Family Centriscidae Found in the Waters of Formosa. – Ibid., pp.260–264, pl.13.

Oshima, M. A List of the Carangoid Fishes from the Waters of Formosa. – Proc. Pan-Pacif. Sci. Congr., 2:1571–1577. 1924.

Oshima, M. A Review of the Carangoid Fishes Found in the Waters of Formosa. – Philipp. J. Sci., 26, No.3:345–412. 1925.

Oshima, M. A Review of the Sparoid Fishes Found in the Waters of Formosa. – Jap. J. Zool., 1B, 5:127–155, figs.1–4. 1927.

Oshima, M. List of Flounders and Soles Found in the Waters of Formosa, with Descriptions of Hitherto Unrecorded Species. – Ibid., 1:177–204. 1927.

Oshima, M. Review of the Charrs Found in Japanese Waters, with Description of One New Species. III. – Botany Zool., Tokyo, 6:1821–1826. 1938. 4 figs. (In Japanese.)

Oshima, M. Review of the Charrs Found in Japanese Waters, with Description of One New Species. – Ibid., pp.1979–1986. 1 pl.

Oshima, M. Description of a New Species of Scorpaenoid Fishes from Shibushi, Osumi, Kagoshima Prefecture. – Zool. Mag., Tokyo, 65:236–238. 1956. (In Japanese, English summary.)

Osipov, V.G., I.V. Kizevetter, and A.V. Zhuravlev. Tunas and Swordfishes of the Pacific and Indian Oceans, pp.1–74. Moscow, "Pishchevaya promyshlennost'." 1964. ill.

Otterstrom, C.V. Baltic Salmon and Trout. Guide to Determination. – J. Cons. perm. int. Explor. Mer., 15:223–231. 1948. 22 text-figs.

Padoa, E. Note di ittiologia Mediterranea. Nota IV. Soleidae Italiani. Nota V. Forme post-larvali e giovanili di Carapus (sin. Fierasfer). – Publ. Staz. zool. Napoli, 20:102–121. 1947. 1 pl., 1 text-fig.

Padoa, E. Centrolophidae, Nomeidae. – In: Fauna e Flora Golfo di Napoli, Monogr., Part 3, 38:538–545. 1956.

Paiva, M.P. Cartas do posca para os atuns e afins do Atlântico Tropical. – Arg. Est. Biol. Mar. Univ. Ceará, Fortaleza, 1, No.2:1–100. 1961. 96 figs.

Pallas, P. Zoographia Rosso-Asiatica. 3. pp.1–428. Petropoli. 1811.

Palmer, G. The Dealfishes (Trachipteridae) of the Mediterranean and Northeast Atlantic. – Bull. Br. Mus. Nat. Hist. Zool., 7, No.7:335–351, pl.62, fig.1. 1961.

Palmer, G. The Scorpaenid Fishes of the Genera Rhinopias Gill and Peloropsis Gilbert. – Ann. Mag. Nat. Hist., (13), 6, No.71:701–704. 1963. ill.

Parin, N.V. Rare Pelagic Fishes of the Northwestern Pacific. Taractes steindachneri, Palinurichthys japonicus and Centrolophus lockingtoni. – Vopr. Ikhtiol., 11:162–170. 1958. 3 figs.

Parin, N.V. Flying Fishes (Exocoetidae) of the Northwestern Pacific.—Trudy Inst. Okeanol. Akad. Nauk SSSR, 31:205–285. 1960.

Parin, N.V. On the Fauna of Flying Fishes of the (Family Exocoetidae) of the Pacific and Indian Oceans. – Ibid., 42:40–91. figs.1–19. 1961.

Parin, N.V. Fundamentals of the System of Flying Fishes of the (Families Oxyporhamphidae and Exocoetidae). – Ibid., 43:92–183. 1961. 45 figs.

Parin, N.V. Flying Fishes (Exocoetidae, Oxyporhamphidae) of the Sea of Japan and Adjacent Waters. – Vopr. Ikhtiol., 2, Nos.2 (23):224–229. 1962.

Parin, N.V. A Survey of Garfishes and Needlefishes of the Pacific and Indian Oceans. – Trudy Inst. Okeanol., Akad. Nauk SSSR, 84:3–83. 1967. 25 figs.

Parin, N.V. Belonidae from the Open Ocean. – In: Tikhii okean, Biol., No.3. Ryby otkrytykh vod, pp.43–66. Moscow, "Nauka." 1967.

Parin, N.V. Scombridae of the Open Ocean. – In: Tikhii okean, Biol., No.3. Ryby otkrytykh vod, pp.88–127. Moscow, "Nauka." 1967.

Parin, N.V. Scomberosocidae (Pisces, Synentognathi) of the Eastern Atlantic Ocean. – Atlantide Rep., 10:275–290. 1968. figs.

Parin, N.V. and C.N. Besednov. Flying Fishes (Oxyporhamphidae and Exocoetidae) of the Gulf of Tonkin. – Trudy Inst. Okeanol., Akad. Nauk SSSR, 80:104–117, figs.1–3. 1965.

Parr, A.E. Investigations on the Cyclopterini. – Bergens Mus. Årb., 1924–1925, No.2; Naturvid. raekke, Bergen, 7:1–31, pl.I, fig.6. 1926.

Parr, A.E. On the Functions and Morphology of the Postclavicular Apparatus in *Spheroides* and *Chilomycterus*. – Zoologica, N.Y., 9:245–269. 1927.

Parr, A.E. Scientific Results of the Third Oceanographic Expedition of the "Pawnee" 1927. Ceratioidea. – Bull. Bingham Oceanogr. Coll., 3, No.1:1–34, figs.1–13. 1927.

Parr, A.E. The Stomiatoid Fishes of the Suborder Gymnophotodermi (Astronesthidae, Melanostomiatidae, Idiacanthidae). – Ibid., 3, No.2:1–123. 1927.

Parr, A.E. Deep-sea Fishes of the Order Iniomi from the Waters around the Bahama and Bermuda Islands with Annotated Keys to Sudidae, Myctophidae, Scopelarchidae, Evermannelidae, Omosudidae, Cetomimidae and Rondeletiidae of the World. – Ibid., 3, No.5:1–193. 1928. 45 figs.

Parr, A.E. Notes on the Species of Myctophine Fishes Represented by Type Specimens in the United States National Museum. – Proc. U.S. Natn. Mus., 76:1–47, figs.1–21. 1929.

Parr, A.E. A Contribution to the Osteology and Classification of the Orders Iniomi and Xenoberyces. – Occ. Pap. Bingham Oceanogr. Colln., 2:1–45. 1929. 19 text-figs.

Parr, A.E. Jugostegalia, an Accessory Skeleton in the Gill Cover of the Eels of the Genus *Myrophis*. – Copeia, 3:71–73, fig.2. 1930.

Parr, A.E. On the Probable Identity, Life History and Anatomy of the Free-living and Attached Males of the Ceratioid Fishes. – Ibid., 4:129–135. 1930.

Parr, A.E. A Note on the Classification of the Stomiatoid Fishes. – Ibid., p.136.

Parr, A.E. Teleostean Shore and Shallow Water Fishes from the Bahamas and Turk Island. – Bull. Bingham Oceanogr. Coll., 3, No.4:1–148. 1930. 38 figs.

Parr, A.E. On the Osteology and Classification of the Pediculate Fishes of the Genera *Aceratias*, *Rhynchocerarias* ..... – Occ. Pap. Bingham Oceanogr. Colln., 3:1–23. 1930. ill.

Parr, A.E. Deep-sea Fishes from off the Western Coast of North and Central America. With Keys to the Genera *Stomias*, *Diplophos*, *Melamphaes* and *Bregmaceros* and a Revision of the Macropterus Group of the Genus *Lampanyctus*. – Bull. Bingham Oceanogr. Coll., 2, No.4:1–53. 1931. 18 figs.

Parr, A.E. Deep-sea Eels, Exclusive of Larval Forms. – Ibid., 3, No.5:1–41. 1932. 15 figs.

Parr, A.E. Deep-sea Berycomorphi and Percomorphi from the Waters around the Bahama and Bermuda Islands. – Ibid., 3, No.6:1–51. 1933. 22 figs.

Parr, A.E. Report on Experimental Use of a Triangular Trawl for Bathypelagic Collecting. With an Account of the Fishes Obtained and a Revision of the Family Cetomimidae. – Ibid., 4, No.6:1–59. 1934. 21 figs.

Parr, A.E. Studies of Myctophinae in the Museum of Comparative Zoology. I. Revision of Type Specimens. – Bull. Mus. Comp. Zool. Harv., 77, No.2:41–53, figs.1–5. 1934.

Parr, A.E. Studies of Myctophinae in the Museum of Comparative Zoology. II. Myctophinae Collected by C.O.D. Iselin in the North Atlantic in 1928. – Ibid., pp.54–65, figs.6–7.

Parr, A.E. Concluding Report on Fishes. – Bull. Bingham Oceanogr. Coll., 3:1–79. 1937.

Parr, A.E. Barbourisidae, a New Family of Deep-sea Fishes. – Copeia, 3:127–129, pl.1. 1945.

Parr, A.E. On Taxonomic Questions Related to the Classification of Barbourisia, the Cetomimidae and the Iniomi. – Ibid., 4:260–262. 1946.

Parr, A.E. The Macrouridae of the Western North Atlantic and Central American Seas. – Bull. Bingham Oceanogr. Coll., 10, No.1:1–99. 1946. 1 pl., 28 figs.

Parr, A.E. The Classification of the Fishes of the Genera Bathylaco and Macromastax, Possible Intermediates between the Isospondyli and the Iniomi. – Copeia, 1:48–54. 1948. 2 figs.

Parr, A.E. Preliminary Revision of the Alepocephalidae, with the Introduction of a New Family Searsidae. – Am. Mus. Novit., 1531:1–21. 1951.

Parr, A.E. Revision of the Genus Talismania, with Description of a New Species from the Gulf of Mexico. – J. Wash. Acad. Sci., 42:268–271. 1952. 1 fig.

Parr, A.E. Revision of the Species Currently Referred to Alepocephalus, Halisauriceps, Bathytractes and Bajacalifornia with Introduction of Two New Genera. – Bull. Mus. Comp. Zool. Harv., 107, No.4:255–269. 1952.

Parr, A.E. The Fishes of the Family Searsidae. – Dana Rep., 51:1–109, figs.1–73. 1960.

Parrott, A.W. Sea Anglers, Fishes of New Zealand, pp.1–176. – London, Hodder and Stoughton. 1957. 9 pls., ill.

Patterson. A Review of Mesozoic Acanthopterygian Fishes, with Special Reference to Those of the English Chalk. – Phil. Trans. R. Soc., Ser.3. Biol. Sci., 247:213–482. 1964. 103 figs.

Pearse, A.S. The Gobies at Paknam. – J. Siam. Soc., 9, No.2:173–178. 1933.

Peden, A.E. Reexamination of Two Species in the Stichaeid Genus Anoplarchus. – Copeia, 2:340–345. 1966. ill.

Pellegrin, J. Contribution à l'étude anatomique, biologique et taxonomique des poissons de la famille des Cichlidés. – Mém. Soc. zool. Fr., 16:41–402. 7 pls., 42 figs. 1904.

Pellegrin, J. Sur un nouveau poisson aveugle des eaux douces de l'Afrique occidentale. – C. r. hebd. Séanc. Acad. Sci., Paris, 174:884–887. 1922. 1 fig.

Pellegrin, J. Les Salmonides du Maroc. – Ibid., 178:970–972. 1924.

Pellegrin, J. Sur les poissons africains de la famille des Phractolaemides. – Ibid., 180:549–551. 1925.

Pellegrin, J. Les poissons africains de la famille des Cromeriidées et leurs affinités. – Archs. Mus. natn. Hist. nat., Paris (6), 12:461–463. 1935.

Perminov, G.N. A Survey of Species of the Genus Eumicrotremus. – Vest. Dal'nevost. Fil. Akad. Nauk SSSR, 19:115–129. 1936.

Perotti, P. L'accrescimento dei Coregoni nei laghi italiani. – Riv. Biol., Milano, 11:674–708. 1930. 4 pls., 9 figs.

Peters, W. Über die systematische Stellung der Lepidosirenes. – Mber. dt. Akad. Wiss. Berl., pp.12–14. 1866.

Petrov, V.V. On the Systematics of Russian Smelts. – Izv. Ord. Prikl. Ikhtiol. Nauchno-Promysl. Issled., 3, No.1:87–108. 1925.

Pfaff, J.R. Papers from Dr. Th. Mortensen's Pacific Expedition 1914–1916. LXXI. On a New Genus and Species of the Family Gobiesocidae from the Indian Ocean, with Observations on Sexual Dimorphism in the Gobiesocidae, and on the Connection of Certain Gobiesocids with Echinids. – Vidensk. Meddr. dansk naturh. Foren, 105:413–422, pl.3. 1942.

Phillips, J.B. A Review of the Rockfishes of California (Family Scorpaenidae). – Fish Bull. Calif., 104:5–158. 1957. 66 figs.

Phillips, J.B. Problems in the Identification of Fishes with a Comparison between Shallow-water and Deep-water Species of Sebastodes (Scorpaenidae). – Rapp. P.-v. Réun. Commn. int. Explor. scient. Mer Méditerr., 150:51–55. 1961. ill.

Phillips, W.J. A Review of the Elasmobranch Fishes of New Zealand. I. – N.Z. Jl. Sci. Technol., 6:257–269. 1924. 14 figs.

Phillips, W.J. Agrotichthys, a New Genus of Ribbonfishes. – Proc. Zool. Soc. Lond., 1:539–540. 1924.

Phillips, W.J. New or Rare Fishes of New Zealand. – Trans. Proc. N.Z. Inst., 56:529–537, pls.87–92. 1926.

Phillips, W.J. Elasmobranch Fishes of New Zealand. 3. Skates and Rays. – N.Z. Jl. Sci. Technol., 11:98–107. 1929. 8 figs.

Phillips, W.J. Sharks of New Zealand. – Rec. Dom. Mus., Wellington, 1, No.2:1–20. 1946. ill.

Pietschmann, V. Japanische Plagiostomen. – Sber. Akad. Wiss. Wien, Mathematisch-naturwiss. Klasse, 117, No.1:637–710, figs.1–14, tabs.1–2. 1908.

Pietschmann, V. Acrania (Cephalochorda) = Cyclostoma Ichthya. Kükenthal and Krumbach. – Handb. Zool., 6, 1 Halfs. Supp. 2–3:127–208, 209–336. 1933. figs.

Pillay, S.R. A Revision of Indian Mugilidae. Parts 1, 2. – J. Bombay Nat. Hist. Soc., 59, No.1:254–269. 1962. ill; 2:547–576. 1962. 1 pl., ill.

Pinchuk, V.I. Gobies of the Group Ponticola (Iljin) and Some Aspects of the Process of Morphogenesis in Fish. Author's Summary of Candidate Theses. Odessa. 1965. 14 pp.

Pinchik, V.I. Remarks on the Family Gobiidae in the Book by A.N.Svetovidov "Fishes of the Black Sea." – Vopr. Ikhtiol., 5, No.4:729–732. 1965.

Pinchuk, V.I. A Key to Sharks, pp.1–44. – Moscow, Vses. Nauchno-issled. inst. ryb. khoz. i okeanogr. 1968.

Piton, L. Faune de l'Auvergne. Poissons: Famille des Cyprinides. – Bull. Soc. Hist. nat. Auvergne, 17:20–29. 1931. 1 pl.

Poll, M. Contribution à l'étude systématique des Polypteridae (Pisces). – Revue Zool. Bot. afr., 35:141–179, figs.1–12. 1941.

Poll, M. Contribution à l'étude systématique des Polypteridae (Pisces). – Ibid., 35:269–317, text-figs.13–26. 1942.

Poll, M. Descriptions de Mormyridae et de Characidae nouveaux du Congo belge avec une étude du genre Stomatorhinus et des genres de Characidae nains africains. – Ibid., 39:36–77. 1945. 9 text-figs.

Poll, M. Poissons. I. Généralités. II. Selaciens et Chimères. – Rés. Sci. Exped. Océanogr. Belg. Eaux Côt. Afr. Atlant. Sud (1948–1949), 4, No.1:1–154. 1951. 13 pls., 67 text-figs.

Poll, M. Notes sur les Cyprinodontidae du Musée du Congo Belge. II. Les Aplocheilichthyini et les Lamprichthyini. – Revue Zool. Bot. afr., 45:292–305. 1952.

Poll, M. Quatrième série de Cichlidae nouveaux recueillis par la mission hydrobiologique belge au lac Tanganyika (1946–1947). – Bull. Mus. r. Hist. nat. Belg., 28, No.49:1–20. 1952. 7 figs.

Poll, M. Poissons. III. Téléostéens Malacoptérygiens. – Rés. Sci. Exped. Océanogr. Belg. Eaux Côt. Afr. Atlant. Sud (1948–1949), 4, No.2:1–258. 1953. 8 pls., 104 figs.

Poll, M. Poissons. IV. Téléostéens Acanthoptérygiens. 1-e partie. – Ibid., 4, No. 3A:1–390. 1954. 9 pls., 107 figs.

Poll, M. Poissons Cichlidae. – Explor. Hydrobiol. Lac Tanganyika (1946–1947), 3, No.5B:1–619. 1956. 10 pls., 131 figs.

Poll, M. Les Genres des Poissons d'eau douce de l'Afrique. – Annls. Mus. r. Congo belge, Sciences zoologiques, 54:1–191. 1957. 425 figs.

Poll, M. Révision systématique et raciation géographique des Protopteridae de l'Afrique centrale. – Annls. Mus. r. Afr. cent., Ser. 8, 103:3–50. 1961. ill.

Poll, M. Une famille dulcicole nouvelle de poissons africains: des Congothrissidae. – Acad. Roy Sci. D'outre-Mer, N.S., 15, No.2:1–40. 1964. 8 pls., 7 figs.

Poll, M. Contribution à l'étude des Kneriidae et description d'un nouveau genre, le genre Parakneria (Pisces, Kneriidae). – Acad. Roy Belg. Cl. Sci., Mem., 36, No.4:29. 1965. ill.

Poll, M. and J. Lambert. Contribution à l'étude systématique et zoogéographique des Procatopodinae de l'Afrique centrale (Pisces, Cyprinodontidae). — Bull. Séanc. Inst. Roy Sci. D'outre-Mer, pp. 615–631. 1965. 1 pl., 1 fig.

Popov, A.M. On the Systematics of the Genus Eumicrotremus. – Izv. Tikhookean. Nauchno-Issled. Sta., 1:47–63. 1928. 2 figs.

Popov, A.M. Preliminary Survey of Russian Mullets (Pisces, Mugilidae). – Dokl. Akad. Nauk SSSR, pp.243–247. 1929.

Popov, A.M. A Preliminary Revision of the Russian Mullets (Pisces, Mugilidae). – C. r. Acad. Sci. USSR, pp.243–247. 1929. 2 figs.

Popov, A.M. Mullets (Mugilidae) of Europe with a Description of a New Species from Pacific Waters of the USSR. – Trudy Sevastopol. Biol. Sta. Akad. Nauk SSSR, 2:47–125, figs.1–6. 1930.

Popov, A.M. A Short Review of the Fishes of the Family Cyclopteridae. – Ann. Mag. Nat. Hist., 10, No.6:69–76. 1930.

Popov, A.M. Cyclopteridae (Pisces) from the Sea of Okhotsk according to the Collections of the Hydrographic Expedition to the Eastern Ocean. – Izv. Akad. Nauk SSSR, Biol., 1:85–99. 1931.

Popov, A.M. Some Remarks on the Genera of the Family Mugilidae (Pisces). – Annls. Mus. Zool. Acad., Leningrad, 32, No.1:117–126. 1931.

Postel, E. Les Xiphiiformes ou poissons porte-épeé de la Région ibéro-marocaine. – Bull. Inst. Pêch. marit. Maroc., 11:19–24. 1964.

Pozzi, A.J. Las especies Argentinas de la subfamila Gasteropelecinae. – An. Mus. nac. Hist. nat. B. Aires, 38:423–439, pl.33, 3 text-figs. 1936.

Prashad, B. and D.D. Mukerji. The Fish of the Indawgyi Lake and the Streams of the Myitkyima District (Upper Burma). – Rec. Indian Mus., 31:219–222, pl.10, figs.1–3. 1929.

Pravdin, I.F. Whitefishes from Water Bodies in the Leningrad Region and Measures Necessary for Intensifying Fishing, pp.1–62. – Leningrad, Vses. nauchno-issl. inst. ozern. i rechn. ryb. khoz. 1941.

Pravdin, I.F. Whitefishes of Water Bodies in the Karelo-Finnish SSR, pp.1–108. Petrozavodsk. 1946.

Pravdin, I.F. Whitefishes of Lake Vyg. – Uch. Zap. Karelo-Finsk. Univ., Biol., 2, No.3:58–71. 1947. 3 figs.

Pravdin, I.F. Morphological Classification and Genesis of Whitefishes of the (Genus Coregonus s. str.) of Lake Ladoga. – Izv. Karelo-Finsk. Bazy Akad. Nauk SSSR, Nos.1–2:75–83. Petrozavodsk. (1947) 1948.

Pravdin, I.F. Morphological and Biological Classification and Genesis of Whitefishes (Genus Coregonus s. str.) of Lake Onega and its Basin. – Ibid., No.1:40–46. Petrozavodsk. 1949.

Pravdin, I.F. Whitefishes of Water Bodies in the Karelo-Finnish SSR, pp.1–319, figs.1–65. – Akad. Nauk SSSR, Karelo-Finsk.Fil. 1954.

Punpoka, S. A Review of the Flatfishes (Pleuronectiformes = Heterosomata) of the Gulf of Thailand and its Tributaries in Thailand. – Bangkok, Kasetsart Univ., Fishery Res. Bull., 1:1–86. 1964. ill.

Puzanov, I.I. Anchovy: Attempts at a Scientific and Commercial Monograph. – Uch. Zap. Gor'kovsk. Gos. Univ., 5:1–64. 1936. ill.

Quast, J.C. Osteological Characteristics and Affinities of the Hexagrammid Fishes, with a Synopsis. – Proc. Calif. Acad. Sci., 4, 31, No.21:563–600. 1965.

Quignard, J.P. Recherches sur les Labridae (Poissons, Téléostéens, Perciformes) des côtes européennes. Systém. et biologie. These. Doc. Sci. Natur. Fac. Sci. Montpellier, pp.1–247. 1966. ill.

Quoy, J.R. and P. Gaimard. —In: Freycinet, L. de. Voyage autour du monde – éxécuté sur les corvettes de S.M. "L'Uranie" et "La Physicienne" pendant les années 1817–1820. Zoology. Pillet Aîné, Paris, Poissons, pp.192–401, folio atlas, pls.43–65. 1824.

Qureshi, M.R. A Field-key for the Identification of Fishes (Order Beryciformes). – Scientist, Karachi, 3, Nos.2–3:20–25, fig.9. 1959.

Qureshi, M.R. A Field-key to the Identification of Fishes (Order Polynemiformes – Family Polynemidae). – Agriculture Pakist., 11, No.1:153–164. 1960.

Qureshi, M.R. A Field-key to the Identification of Fishes (Order Mugiliformes). – Scientist, Karachi, 4: 65–70. 1961. 5 figs.

Qureshi, M.R. A Field-key to the Identification of Fishes. (Order Perciformes. II. Families: Pseudochromidae, Diploprionidae, Theraponidae, Plesiopidae, Kuhliidae, Priacanthidae, Apogonidae, Sillaginidae, Malacanthidae, and Lactariidae).– Ibid., 7:172–186. 1965.

Radcliffe, L. Notes on Some Fishes of the Genus Amia, Family of Cheilodipteridae, with Descriptions of Four New Species from the Philippine Islands. – Proc. U.S. Natn. Mus., 41:245–261. 1912. 6 pls., 3 figs.

Radcliffe, L. Descriptions of Fifteen New Species of the Family Cheilodipteridae from the Philippine Islands and Contiguous Waters. – Ibid., pp.431–446. 5 pls.

Radcliffe, L. New Pediculate Fishes from the Philippine Islands and Contiguous Waters. – Ibid., 42:199–214. 1912. 12 pls., 3 figs.

Radcliffe, L. Description of a New Family, Two New Genera and Twenty-nine New Species of Anacanthine Fishes from the Philippine Islands and Contiguous Waters. – Ibid., 43:105–140, pls.22–31, 11 text-figs. (1912) 1913.

Radcliffe, L. Descriptions of Seven New Genera and Thirty-one New Species of Fishes of the Families Brotulidae and Carapidae from the Philippine Islands and the Dutch East Indies. – Ibid., 44:135–176, pls.7–17. 1913.

Ragimov, D.B. Specific Composition, Biology and Stocks of Sculpins (Gobiidae) off the West Coast of the Central and Southern Caspian. Author's Summary of Candidate Thesis, pp.1–20. Baku. 1966.

Rahimullah, M. and B.K. Das. Remarks on Certain Hitherto Unknown Characters in the Family Notopteridae (Fauna of the Hyderbad State, Deccan). – Bull. Soc. port. Sci. nat., 12, No.18:135–141, pl.23. 1936.

Rakov, V.S. Keys to the Higher Systematic Groups (Including Family) of the Cyclostomata and Fish Fauna of the USSR, pp.180. – Mosk. Gos. Univ. 1962.

Ramaswami, L.S. The Homalopterid Skull. – Proc. Zool. Soc. Lond., 118:515–538. 1948.

Ramaswami, L.S. Skeleton of Cyprinoid Fishes in Relation to Phylogenetic Studies. – Proc. Natn. Inst. Sci. India, Pts.1–2, 18, No.2:125–150. 1952; Pts.3–4, 18, No.6:495–538. 1952.

Randall, J.E. A Revision of the Surgeon Fish Genus Ctenochaetus, Family Acanthuridae, with Descriptions of Five New Species. – Zoologica, N.Y., 40:149–166. 1955. 2 pls., 3 figs.

Randall, J.E. An Analysis of the Genera of Surgeon Fishes (Fam. Acanthuridae). – Pacif. Sci., 9, No.3:359–367. 1955.

Randall, J.E. A Revision of the Surgeon Fish Genera Zebrasoma and Paracanthurus. – Ibid., pp.396–412. 8 figs.

Randall, J.E. A Revision of the Surgeon Fish Genus Acanthurus. – Ibid., 10, No.2:159–235. 1956. 23 figs., 3 pls.

Randall, J.E. A Review of the Labrid Fish Genus Labroides, with Descriptions of Two New Species and Notes on Ecology. – Ibid., 12:327–347. 1958. 1 pl., 6 figs.

Randall, J.E. A Contribution to the Biology of the Convict Surgeonfish of the Hawaiian Islands, Acanthurus triostegus sandvicensis. – Ibid., 15:215–272. 1961.

Randall, J.E. Review of the Hawkfishes (Family Cirrhitidae). – Proc. U.S. Natn. Mus., 114:389–451, pls.1–16. 1963.

Randall, J.E. Notes on the Systematics of Parrotfishes (Scaridae), with Emphasis on Sexual Dichromatism. – Copeia, 2:225–237. 1963. 4 figs., 3 pls.

Randall, J.E. A Revision of the Filefish Genera Amanses and Cantherhines. – Ibid., 2:331–361. 1964. ill.

Randall, J.E. A Review of the Razorfish Genus Hemipteronotus (Labridae) of the Atlantic Ocean. – Ibid., 4:487–501. 1965.

Randall, J.E. The West Indian Blenniid Fishes of the Genus Hypleurochilus, with the Description of a New Species. – Proc. Biol. Soc. Wash., 79:57–72. 1966.

Randall, J.E. and J.E.Böhlke. Review of the Atlantic Labrid Fishes of the Genus Halichoeres. – Proc. Acad. Nat. Sci. Philad., 117, No.7:235–259. 1965. 11 figs.

Randall, J.E. and D.K.Caldwell. A Review of the Sparid Fish Genus Calamus, with Descriptions of Four New Species. – Bull. Los Angeles County Museum Natur. Hist. Sci., 2:1–47. 1966. ill.

Rass, T.S. Systematisch-morphologische Studien über zwei nahe-verwandte Arten: Lumpenus fabricii (C.V.) und Lumpenus medius Reinh. – Acta zool., Stockh., 17:395–463, pls.1–16. 1936.

Rass, T.S. The "Long" Flounders of the Far Eastern Seas of the USSR: Microstomus, Glyptocephalus, Tanakius (Pleuronectidae). – Dokl. Akad. Nauk SSSR, 74, No.4:855–857. 1950.

Rass, T.S. Study of the Pacific Moridae (Pisces, Gadiformes). – Trudy Inst. Okeanol., Akad. Nauk SSSR, 11:56–61. 1954.

Rass, T.S. Geographical Distribution of Fish of the Family Myctophidae in the Pacific. – Trudy Inst. Okeanol., Akad. Nauk SSSR, 41:146;152. 1960.

Rass, T.S. A New Deepwater Fish, Proscopa stilbia Rass g.n., sp.n. from the Indian Ocean. – Zool. Zh., 40, No.12:1858;1861, fig. 1961.

Rass, T.S. The Family of Greenlings (Hexagrammidae, Pisces) and their Acclimation in the Northern Seas of the European USSR. – Trudy Inst. Okeanol., Akad. Nauk SSSR, 59:191–203. 1962. 2 figs.

Rass, T.S. Protoscopa stilbia Rass, 1961 Identical with Xenophthalmichthys danae Regan, 1925 (Xenophthalmichthyidae). – Zool. Zh., 41, No.10:1578–1579. 1961.

Rass, T.S. Deepwater Fishes – Grenadiers (Pisces, Macruridae) of the Sea of Okhotsk. – Trudy Inst. Okeanol., Akad. Nauk SSSR, 62:212–223, fig.1–4. 1963.

Rass, T.S. and A.A.Kashkina. Deepwater Smelts (Pisces, Bathylagidae) of the North Pacific. – Ibid., 84:209–221. 1967. 8 figs.

Rauther, M. Die Syngnathiden des Golfes von Neapel. – Fauna Flora Golfo Napoli, 36 A:1–366. 1925. 24 pls., 62 figs.

Rauther, M. Zur Kenntnis von Psephurus Gthr. (Pisces, Chondrostei). – Zool. Anz., 109:49–64. 1935. 12 figs.

Regan, Notes on the Classification of Teleostean Fishes. I. On the Trachinidae and their Allies. – Ann. Mag. Nat. Hist., 7, No.8:261–271. 1901.

Regan, C.T. On the Classification of the Fishes of the Suborder Plectognathi. – Proc. Zool. Soc. Lond., 2: 284–303. 1902. 2 pls., 4 figs.

Regan, C.T. A Revision of the Fishes of the Family Stromateidae. – Ann. Mag. Nat. Hist., 7, No.10:115–131, 194–206. 1902.

Regan, C.T. A Revision of the Fishes of the Family Tetragonuridae. – Ibid., pp.206–207.

Regan, C.T. On the Systematic Position of Luvarus imperialis. – Ibid., pp.278–281.

Regan, C.T. A Revision of the Fishes of the Family Lophiidae. – Ibid., 7, No.11:277–285. 1903.

Regan, C.T. On the Skeleton and Systematic Position of Luvaris imperialis. – Ibid., pp.372–374. fig.

Regan, C.T. On the Systematic Position and Classification of the Gadoid or Anacanthine Fishes. – Ibid., pp.459–466.

Regan, C.T. The Phylogeny of the Teleostomi. – Ibid., 7, No.13:329–349, pl.7. 1904.

Regan, C.T. A Monograph of the Fishes of the Family Loricariidae. – Trans. Zool. Soc. Lond., 17, Nos.3, 1:191–324, pls.9–21. 1904.

Regan, C.T. A Revision of the Fishes of the Family Galaxiidae. – Proc. Zool. Soc. Lond., pp.363–384, pls.10–13. (1905) 1906.

Regan, C.T. A Classification of the Selachian Fishes. – Ibid., pp.722–758. 10 figs.

Regan, C.T. On the Anatomy, Classification and Systematic Position of the Teleostean Fishes of the Suborder Allotriognathi. – Ibid., pp.634–643. 1907. 6 figs.

Regan, C.T. The Systematic Position of Stylophorus. – Ann. Mag. Nat. Hist., 8, No.1:447–449. 1908.

Regan, C.T. A Synopsis of the Sharks of the Family Scyliorhinidae. – Ibid., pp.453–465.

Regan, C.T. A Synopsis of the Sharks of the Family Cestraciontidae. – Ibid., pp.493–497. 1908.

Regan, C.T. A Synopsis of the Sharks of the Family Squalidae. – Ibid., 8, No.2:39–57. 1908.

Regan, C.T. A Synopsis of the Fishes of the Subfamily Salanginae. – Ibid., pp.444–446.

Regan, C.T. A Revision of the Sharks of the Family Orectolobidae. – Proc. Zool. Soc. Lond., pp.347–364, pls.11–13. 1908.

Regan, C.T. A Revision of Fishes of the Genus Elops. – Ann. Mag. Nat. Hist., 8, No.3:37–40. 1909.

Regan, C.T. On the Anatomy and Classification of the Scombroid Fishes. – Ibid., pp.66–75. 4 text-figs.

Regan, C.T. The Classification of Teleostean Fishes. – Ibid., pp.75–86.

Regan, C.T. The Asiatic Fishes of the Family Anabantidae. – Proc. Zool. Soc. Lond., pp.767–787, pls.77–79. (1909) 1910.

Regan, C.T. The Anatomy and Classification of the Teleostean Fishes of the Order Zeomorphi. – Ann. Mag. Nat. Hist., 8, No.6:481–484. 1910.

Regan, C.T. The Origin and Evolution of the Teleostean Fishes of the Order Heterosomata. – Ibid., pp.484–496. 3 text-figs.

Regan, C.T. The Anatomy and Classification of the Teleostean Fishes of the Orders Berycomorphi and Xenoberyces. – Ibid., 8, No.7:1–9, pl.1, 2 text-figs. 1911.

Regan, C.T. The Anatomy and Classification of the Teleostean Fishes of the Order Iniomi. – Ibid., pp.120–133. 7 figs.

Regan, C.T. A Synopsis of the Marsipobranchs of the Order Hyperoartii. – Ibid., pp.193–204.

Regan, C.T. On the Systematic Position of Macristium chavesi. – Ibid., pp.204–205. ill.

Regan, C.T. On the Cirrhitiform Percoids. – Ibid., pp.259–262.

Regan, C.T. The Osteology and Classification of Teleostean Fishes of the Order Microcyprini. – Ibid., pp.320–327.

Regan, C.T. The Classification of the Teleostean Fishes of the Order Synentognathi. – Ibid., pp.327–335, pl.9, 4 text-figs.

Regan, C.T. The Classification of the Teleostean Fishes of the Order Ostariophysi. 1. Cyprinoidea. – Ibid., 8, No.8:13–32. 1911.

Regan, C.T. The Anatomy and Classification of the Teleostean Fishes of the Order Salmopercae. – Ibid., pp.294–296.

Regan, C.T. The Classification of the Teleostean Fishes of the Order Ostariophysi. 2. Siluroidea. – Ibid., pp.553–577.

Regan, C.T. The Osteology and Classification of the Gobioid Fishes. – Ibid., pp.729–733. 2 text-figs.

Regan, C.T. The Osteology of the Teleostean Fishes of the Order Opisthomi. – Ibid., 8, No.9:217–219. 1912.

Regan, C.T. The Classification of the Teleostean Fishes of the Order Pediculati. – Ibid., pp.277–289. 6 figs.

Regan, C.T. The Anatomy and Classification of the Symbranchoid Eels. – Ibid., pp.387–390, pl.9.

Regan, C.T. A Synopsis of the Myxinoids of the Genus Heptatretus or Bdellostoma. – Ibid., 534–536.

Regan, C.T. The Classification of the Blennioid Fishes. – Ibid., 8, No.10:265–280. 1912. 4 text-figs.

Regan, C.T. The Anatomy and Classification of the Teleostean Fishes of the Order Lyomeri. – Ibid., pp.347–349. 1 fig.

Regan, C.T. The Osteology and Classification of the Teleostean Fishes of the Order Apodes. – Ibid., pp.377–387. 2 figs.

Regan, C.T. The Anatomy and Classification of the Teleostean Fishes of the Order Discocephali. – Ibid., 634–637. 2 figs.

Regan, C.T. The Caristiidae, a Family of Berycomorphous Fishes. – Ibid., pp.637–638.

Regan, C.T. New Fishes from Aldabra. – Trans. Linn. Soc. Lond. (2), 15, No.2:301–302. 1912.

Regan, C.T. Notes on the Classification of the Teleostean Fishes. – Proc. 7th Int. Zool. Congr. (Cambridge, Mass.), pp.836–837. 1912.

Regan, C.T. The Osteology and Classification of the Teleostean Fishes of the Order Scleroparei. – Ann. Mag. Nat. Hist., 8, No.11:169–183. 1913. 5 figs.

Regan, C.T. The Poeciliid Fishes of the Genus Jenynsia. – Ibid., pp.232–234.

Regan, C.T. A Revision of the Myxinoids of the Genus Myxine. – Ibid., pp.395–398.

Regan, C.T. The Classification of the Percoid Fishes. – Ibid., 8, No.12:111–145. 1913.

Regan, C.T. Phallostethus dunckeri a Remarkable New Cyprinodont Fish from Johore. – Ibid., pp.548–555.

Regan, C.T. A Revision of the Fishes of the Genus Kuhlia. – Proc. Zool. Soc. Lond., pp.374–381. 1913.

Regan, C.T. A Revision of the Cyprinodont Fishes of the Subfamily Poeciliinae. – Ibid., pp.977–1018.

Regan, C.T. A Deep Sea Angler Fish Melanocetus johnsoni. – Ibid., pp.1096, 1097.

Regan, C.T. The Antarctic Fishes of the Scottish National Antarctic Expedition. – Trans. R. Soc. Edinb., 49, II, No.2:229–292. 1913. 11 pls., 6 text-figs.

Regan, C.T. A Synopsis of the Fishes of the Family Macrorhamphosidae. – Ann. Mag. Nat. Hist., 8, No.13:17–21. 1914.

Regan, C.T. The Systematic Arrangement of the Fishes of the Family Salmonidae. – Ibid., pp.405–408. 3 figs.

Regan, C.T. British Antarctic ("Terra Nova") Expedition 1910. Fishes. – Br. Antarct. Exped. Nat. Hist., Rep. Zool., London, 1, No.1:1–54. 1914. 13 pls., 8 figs.

Regan, C.T. The British Fishes of the Subfamily Clupeinae and Related Species in Other Seas. – Ann. Mag. Nat. Hist., 8, No.18:1–19, pls.1–3. 1916.

Regan, C.T. The Morphology of the Cyprinodont Fishes of the Subfamily Phallostethidae. – Proc. Zool. Soc. Lond., pp.1–26. 1916. 4 pls.

Regan, C.T. A Revision of the Clupeoid Fishes of the Genus Pellonula and of Related Genera in the Rivers of Africa. – Ann. Mag. Nat. Hist., 8, No.19:198–207. 1917.

Regan, C.T. The Fishes of the Genus Clupea. – Ibid., pp.226–229.

Regan, C.T. A Revision of the Clupeoid Fishes of the Genera Pomolobus, Brevoortia and Dorosoma, and their Allies. – Ibid., pp.297–316.

Regan, C.T. A Revision of the Clupeoid Fishes of the Genera Sardinella, Harengula, etc. – Ibid., pp.377–395.

Regan, C.T. Note on Chaudhuria, a Teleostean Fish of the Order Opisthomi. – Ibid., 9, No.3:198–199. 1919.

Regan, C.T. The Classification of the Fishes of the Family Cichlidae. I. Tanganyika Genera. – Ibid., 9, No.5:33–53. 1920.

Regan, C.T. A Revision of the Flatfishes (Heterosomata) of Natal. – Ann. Durban Mus., 2:205–222. 1920.

Regan, C.T. The Classification of the Fishes of the Family Cichlidae. II. On African and Syrian Genera not Restricted to the Great Lakes. – Ann. Mag. Nat. Hist., 9, No.10:249–264. 1922.

Regan, C.T. Fishes of the Clupeoid Genera Clupeoides and Potamalosa, and Allied Genera. – Ibid., pp.587–590.

Regan, C.T. The Cichlid Fishes of Lake Victoria. – Proc. Zool. Soc. Lond., pp.157–191, pls.I–IV, 14 text-figs. 1922.

Regan, C.T. The Fishes of the Family Icosteidae. – Ann. Mag. Nat. Hist., 9, No.11:610–612. 1923. 2 figs.

Regan, C.T. The Classification of the Stomiatoid Fishes. – Ibid., pp.612–614.

Regan, C.T. The Skeleton of Lepidosteus with Remarks on the Origin and Evolution of the Lower Neopterygian Fishes. – Proc. Zool. Soc. Lond., pp.445–461. 1923. 8 figs.

Regan, C.T. The Morphology of Rare Oceanic Fish, Stylophorus chordatus Shaw. – Proc. R. Soc., B, 96:193–207. 1924.

Regan, C.T. The Fishes of the Genus Gigantura A. Brauer Based on Specimens Collected in the Atlantic by the "Dana" Expedition, 1920–1922. – Ann. Mag.Nat. Hist., 9, No.15:53–59. 1925. 4 figs.

Regan, C.T. Description of a New Salmonoid Fish from the Caribbean Sea, Obtained by the "Dana" Expeditions 1920–1922. – Ibid., pp.59–60.

Regan, C.T. The Pediculate Fishes of the Suborder Ceratioidea. – Oceanogr. Rep. "Dana" Exped., 1920–1922, 2:1–45. 1926. 13 pls., 27 text-figs.

Regan, C.T. Articles on Fishes. – "Fishes". Encyclopaedia Britannica, 14th ed., pp.305–328, figs.1–4, pls.1–2. 1929.

Regan, C.T. The Perciform Genera Gymnapogon and Nannatherina. – Copeia, 3:173–175. 1940.

Regan, C.T. and E. Trewavas. The Fishes of the Families Astronesthidae and Chauliodontidae. – Oceanogr. Rep. "Dana" Exped., 1920–1922, 5:1–39. 1929. 7 pls., 25 text-figs.

Regan, C.T. and E. Trewavas. The Fishes of the Families Stomiatidae and Malacosteidae. – Ibid., 6:1–143. 1930. 14 pls., 138 text-figs.

Regan, C.T. and E. Trewavas. Deep-sea Angler-fishes (Ceratioidea). – Oceanogr. Rep. "Dana" Exped., 1928–1930, 2:1–113. 1932. 10 pls., 172 text-figs.

Rees, E. The Batfish, Dibranchus atlanticus Peters, on the Canadian Atlantic Slopes. – J. Fish. Res. Bd. Can., 20, No.6:1513–1517. 1963. ill.

Reid, E.D. Two New Congrid Eels and a New Flatfish. – Smithson. Misc. Collns., 91, No.15:1–11. 1934. 1 pl., 2 text-figs.

Reid, E.D. Revision of the Fishes of the Family Microdesmidae, with Description of a New Species. – Proc. U.S. Natn. Mus., 84:55–72, pl.2, text-figs.9–12. 1936.

Reid, E.D. Review of the Genera of Blennioid Fishes Related to Ophioblennius. – J. Wash. Acad. Sci., 33, No.12:373–384. 1943. 4 text-figs.

Reighard, J.E. The Natural History of Amia calva Linnaeus. – In: Mark Anniversary, N.Y., 4:57–109. 1904. pl., figs.

Reizer, C. Révision systématique et raciation des Mormyrus de l'Afrique Centrale. – Annls. Mus. r. Afr. cent., Sér. Zoologie, 133:1–60. 1964. ill.

Rendahl, H. Pegasiden-Studien. – Ark.Zool., 21A, No.27:1–56. 1930. 15 figs.

Rendahl, H. Zur Osteologie und Myologie des Schultergürtels und der Brustflosse einiger Scleroparei. – Ibid., 26A, No.12:1–50. 1933. 21 figs.

Rendahl, H. Studien über die Scleroparei. 1. Zur Kenntnis der kranialen Anatomie der Agoniden. – Ibid., 26A, No.13:1–106. 1933. figs.

Rendahl, H. Über das Vorkommen des Misgurnus anguillicaudatus (Cantor) in Birma. – Ibid., 35A, No.4:1–9. 1944. 2 text-figs.

Rendahl, H. Einige Cobitiden von Annam und Tonkin. — Göteborgs K.Vetensk. – o. VitterhSamh. Handl., 6, 3B:1–54. 1944. 22 text-figs.

Rey, D.L.L. Peces Ganoideos y Fisostomos. – Mems. R. Acad. Cienc. Mads., 11:1–839. 1947. 20 pls.

Rhasis Erazi, R.A. Les Blenniidés du Bosphore et de la Mer de Marmara. – Revue Fac. Sci. Univ. d'Istanbul, 6B, Nos.1–2:118–127. 1941. 3 text-figs.

Rhasis Erazi, R.A. The Labridae (Wrasses) of the Bosphorus and of the Sea of Marmara. – Ibid., 8B:141–160. 1943. 17 txet-figs.

Ribeiro, A.M. Peixes. IV. A. Eleutherobranchios Aspirophoros (Scleracanthi). – Archos. Mus. nac., Rio de Janeiro, 16:1–504. (1911) 1912. 54 pls., 144 figs.

Ribeiro, A.M. Loricariidae, Callichthyidae, Doradidae i Trichomycteridae. – Commissao de Linhas Telegraphicas Estrategicas de Matto-Grosso ao Amasonas, Rio de Janeiro, 5:1–31. 1912.

Ribeiro, A.M. Cichlidae. - Ibid., 41:1–18, pls. I–XVI, 1918.

Richards, W.J. Eastern Atlantic Triglidae (Pisces, Scorpaeniformes). - Atlantide Rep., 10:77–114. 1968.

Richardson, J. The Zoology of the Voyage of H.M.S. "Sulphur" under the Command of Captain Sir Edward Belcher, during the Years 1836–1842. - Ichthyology, 1:51–150. Smith Elder Co., London. 1844. 30 pls.

Richardson, J. and J.E. Gray. The Zoology of the Voyage of H.M.S. "Erebus and Terror," under the Command of Capt. Sir. J.C.Ross etc. Edward Newman. - Ibid., 2:i–viii, 1–139. 1844–1848. 60 pls.

Richardson, L.R. Neomyxine n.g. (Cyclostomata) Based on Myxine biniplicata Richardson and Jowett, 1951, and Further Data on the Species. - Trans. R. Soc. N.Z., 81:379–383. 1953. 2 figs.

Richardson, L.R. A New Genus and Species of Myxinidae (Cyclostomata). - Ibid., 85:283–287. 1958. 1 fig.

Ridewood, W. On the Cranial Osteology of the Fishes of the Families Elopidae and Albulidae. - Proc. Zool. Soc. Lond., 2:35–81, 453–482. 1904.

Ridewood, W. On the Cranial Osteology of the Families Mormyridae, Notopteridae and Hyodontidae. - J. Linn. Soc., 29:188–217, pls.24, 25. 1904.

Ridewood, W. On the Skull of Gonorhynchus greyi. - Ann. Mag. Nat. Hist., 7, No.15:361–372, pl.16. 1905.

Ridewood, W. On the Cranial Osteology of the Families Osteoglossidae, Pantodontidae and Phractolemidae. - J. Linn. Soc., 29:252–282, pls.30–32. 1905.

Rivas, L.R. A Revision of the American Clupeid Fishes of the Genus Harengula, with Descriptions of Four New Subspecies. - Proc. U.S. Natn. Mus., 100:275–309. 1950. 3 pls., 41 text-figs.

Rivas, L.R. A Preliminary Review of the Western North Atlantic Fishes of the Family Scombridae. - Bull. Mar. Sci. Gulf Caribb., 1, No.3:209–230. 1951.

Rivas, L.R. The Occurrence and Taxonomic Relationships of the Blue Marlin (Makaira ampla Poey) in the Pacific Ocean. - Bull. Mar. Sci. Gulf Caribb., 6, No.1:59–73, figs.1–2. 1956.

Rivas, L.R. The Origin, Evolution, Dispersal and Geographical Distribution of the Cuban Poeciliid Fishes of the Tribe Girardinini. - Proc. Am. Phil. Soc., 102:281–320. 1958. 13 figs.

Rivas, L.R. The Fishes of the Genus Pomacentrus in Florida and the Western Bahamas. - Q. Jl. Fla. Acad. Sci., 23:130–163. 1960. 8 figs.

Rivas, L.R. A Review of the Tuna Fishes of the Subgenera Parathunnus and Neothunnus (Genus Thunnus). - Annali Mus. civ. Stor. nat. Giacomo Doria, 72:126–148. 1961.

Rivas, L.R. Western Atlantic Serranid Fishes (Groupers) of the Genus Epinephelus. - Q. Jl. Fla. Acad. Sci., 27, No.1:17–30. 1964.

Rivas, L.R. Key to the Atlantic Ocean Tuna Fishes of the Genus Thunnus. - Proc. Symp. Scombroid Fishes, Mar. Biol. Ass. India, Ser.1, 1:427–428. 1964.

Rivero, L.H. The Apodal Fishes of Cuba. —Proc. New Engl. Zool. Club, 13:3–26. 1932.

Rivero, L.H. The Family Ateleopidae and its West Indian Form. - Mems. Soc. cub. Hist. nat., 9:91–106, pl.8, 3 text-figs. 1935.

Rivero, L.H. Un nuevo tiburon para la fauna cubana de la familia Heptranchidae. - Torreia, 9:1–9. 1941. 4 pls.

Robins, C.R. Studies on Fishes of the Family Ophidiidae. - Bull. Mar. Sci. Gulf Caribb., 10:83–95. 1960. 2 figs.

Robins, C.R. Studies on the Fishes of the Family Ophidiidae. VI. Two New Genera and a New Species from American Waters. - Copeia, 2:212–221. 1961. 6 figs.

Robins, C.R. Studies on Fishes of the Family Ophidiidae. VII. The Pacific Species of Lepophidium. - Ibid., 3:487–498. 1962. 4 figs.

Robins, C.R. Additional Comments on the Structure and Relationships of the Mirapinniform Fish Family Kasidoridae. - Bull. Mar. Sci., 16:696–701. 1966. 3 figs.

Robins, C.R. and R.R. Miller. Classification, Variation, and Distribution of the Sculpins, Genus Cottus, Inhabiting Pacific Slope Waters in California and Southern Oregon, with a Key to the Species. - Calif. Fish Game, 43:213–233. 1957.

Robins, C.R. and R.B. Manning. The Status and Distribution of the Fishes of the Family Microdesmidae in the Western Atlantic. - J. Wash. Acad. Sci., 48:301–304. 1958.

Robins, C.R. and E.C. Raney. The Systematic Status of the Suckers of the Genus Moxostoma from Texas, New Mexico and Mexico. - Tulane Stud. Zool., 5:291–318. 1957. 12 figs.

Robins, C.R. and W.A.Starck. Materials for a Revision of Serranus and Related Fish Genera. – Proc. Acad. Nat. Sci. Philad., 113:259–314. 1961. 8 figs.

Robins, C.R. and D.P. de Sylva. Description and Relationships of the Longbill Spearfish, Tetrapturus belone, Based on Western North Atlantic Specimens. – Bull. Mar. Sci. Gulf Caribb., 10, No.4:383–413, figs.1–5. 1960.

Robins, C.R. and D.P. de Sylva. The Kasidoridae, a New Family of Mirapinniform Fishes from the Western Atlantic Ocean. – Bull. Mar. Sci., 15, No.1:189–210. 1965.

Roedel, P.M. and W.W.E.Ripley. California Sharks and Rays. – Fish. Bull. Calif., 75:5–88, figs.1–65. 1950.

Rofen, R.R. (formerly Harry, R.R.). The Whale-fishes: Families Cetomimidae, Barbourisiidae and Rondeletiidae (Order Cetunculi). – Galathea Rep., 1:255–260. 1957–1959. 4 figs.

Rofen, R.R. (formerly Harry, R.R.). Diagnoses of New Genera and Species of Alepisauroid of the Family Paralepididae. – Aquatica, 2:1–6, fig.1. 1963.

Rofen, R.R. Family Paralepididae. – In: Fishes W N. Atlantic. 5. Mem. Sears Found. Mar. Res., 1, No.5:205–461. 1966.

Rofen, R.R. Families Omosudidae, Anotopteridae. – Ibid., pp.462–510.

Rofen, R.R. Family Evermannellidae. – Ibid., pp.511–565.

Rofen, R.R. Family Scopelarchidae. – Ibid., pp.566–602.

Roland, J. Diagnoses de quelques Raies des côtes algériennes. – Bull. Sta. Aquic. Pêche Castiglione, N.S., 4:137–274. 1953. 32 figs.

Rosen, D.E. A Revision of the Fishes of the Subfamily Alfarinae in the Family Poeciliidae. – Zoologica, N.Y., 37, No.3:151–156. 1952. 10 figs.

Rosen, D.E. Comments on the Relationships of the North American Cave Fishes of the Family Amblyopsidae.– Am. Mus. Novit., 2109:1–35. 1962.

Rosen, D.E. Relationships and Taxonomic Position of the Halfbeaks, Killifishes, Silversides, and their Relatives. – Bull. Am. Mus. Nat. Hist., 127, No.5:217–268. 1964. 23 figs.

Rosen, D.E. and R.M.Bailey. Middle American Poeciliid Fishes of the Genera Carlhubbsia and Phallichthys, with Descriptions of Two New Species. – Zoologica, N.Y., 44, No.1–44, pls.1–6, figs.1–10. 1959.

Rosen, D.E. and R.M.Bailey. The Poeciliid Fishes (Cyprinodontiformes), their Structure, Zoogeography, and Systematics. – Bull. Am. Mus. Nat. Hist., 126, No.1:1–176. 1963. 62 figs.

Rosen, D.E. and K.D.Kollman. Development and Evolution of Skeletal Deletions in a Family of Viviparous Fishes (Cyprinodontiformes, Poeciliidae). – Q. Jl. Fla. Acad. Sci., 22:169–190. 1959. 9 figs.

Rosen, N. Studies on the Plectognaths. – Ark. Zool., 7, No.25:1–24. 1912; 7, No.30:1–23. 1912; 8, No.10:1–29. 1913; 8, No.18:1–14. 1913; 10, No.8:1–28. 1916.

Rosenblatt, R.H. The Atlantic Species of the Blennioid Fish Genus Enneanectes. – Proc. Acad. Nat. Sci. Philad., 112:1–23, fig.2. (1960) 1961.

Rosenblatt, R.H. and W.J.Baldwin. A Review of the Eastern Pacific Sharks of the Genus Carcharhinus with a Redescription of C. malpeloensis (Fowler) and Californian Records of C. remotus (Dumeril). – Calif. Fish Game, 44, No.2:137–160, figs.1–19. 1958.

Rossi, L. Revisione del Callichthyidae (Pisces, Nematognathi) del Museo di Torino. – Bull. Ist. Mus. Zool. Univ. Torino, 3, No.11:1–10. 1951–1952. 2 pls.

Roule, L. Considérations sur les genres Xenodermichthys Günther et Aleposomus Gill dans la famille de Alepocephalidae. – Bull. Mus. natn. Hist. nat., Paris, 21:02 9C. 1915.

Roule, L. Notice sur la révision des genres de poissons abyssaux appartenant à la famille des Omosudidés. – Archo. zool. ital., 16:1255–1259. 1931.

Roule, L. Nouvelles observations sur un poisson abyssal (Anotopterus pharao Zugm.). – Bull. Soc. Zool. Fr., 60:324–330. 1935.

Roule, L. and L.Bertin. Les poissons Apodes appartenant au sous-ordre des Nemichthydiformes. – Oceanogr. Rep. "Dana" Exped., 1920–1922, 4:1–113. 1929. 57 text-figs., pls. I–IX.

Rounsefell, G.A. Relationships among North American Salmonidae. – Fishery Bull. Fish Wildl. Serv. U.S., 62, No.209:235–270. 1962. 19 figs.

Roxas, H.A. A Review of Philippine Mugilidae. – Philipp. J. Sci., 54, No.3:393–431. 1934.

Roxas, H.A. A Review of Philippine Isospondylous Fishes. – Ibid., 55, No.3:231–295. 1934.

Roxas, H.A. and G.L.Ablan. A New Taenioid Fish from Occidental Negros. – Ibid., 66, No.3:261–265. 1938. 2 pls.

Roxas, H.A. and G.L.Ablan. New Philippine Gobioid Fishes. – Ibid., 73, No.3:301–311. 1940. 8 pls.
Roxas, H.A. and A.G.Agco. A Review of the Philippine Carangidae. – Ibid., 74, No.1:1–82. 1941. 12 pls.
Royce, W.F. Observations of the Spearfishes of the Central Pacific. – Fishery Bull. Fish Wildl. Serv. U.S., 57, No.124:497–554, figs.1–27. 1957.
Ruivo, M. and R.Monteiro. Contributions à l'étude de la famille Ammodytidae, Gymnammodytes cicerellus (Raf.) de la region de Banyuls. – Vie Milieu, 5, No.4:569–592, figs.1–16. 1955.
Rutenberg, E.P. A Survey of Greenlings (Hexagrammidae). Author's Summary of Candidate Thesis. – Zool. Inst. Akad. Nauk SSSR, pp.1–10. Leningrad. 1950.
Rutenberg, E.P. System of Fishes of the Family Hexagrammidae. – Vopr. Ikhtiol., 2:151–155. 1954.
Rutenberg, E.P. The Systematic Position of the Genus Pleurogrammus Gill (Pisces, Hexagrammidae). – Ibid., 4:10–15, figs.1–2. 1955.
Rutenberg, E.P. A Survey of Fishes of the Family Hexagrammidae. — Trudy Inst. Okeanol., Akad. Nauk SSSR, 59:1–100, figs.1–29. 1962.
Sakamoto, K. Type of a New Family of Mail-cheeked Fish from the Japan Sea, Marukawichthys ambulator, n.g., n.sp. – J. Imp. Fish Inst., Tokyo, 26, No.2:53–56, fig.1. 1931.
Sanz-Echeverria, J. Identificatión de los peces de la familia Centrolophidae de España por medio de los otolitos. – Roy. Soc. esp. Hist. Nat., Tomo Extraord., 1946, pp.151–156. 1949. 1 pl.
Sanzo, L. Sternoptychidae. 3. Maurolicus pennanti (Walb.). – Roy Comitato Talossografico Italiana. II. Monogr. Venezia, pp.121–182, figs.13–15, pls.10–12. 1935.
Sarenas, A.M. A Revision of the Philippine Myctophidae. – Philipp. J. Sci., 82:375–427. 1954. 2 pls., 12 figs.
Sato, S. Note on the Fishes of Family Bathymasteridae in Northern Japan. – J. Fac. Sci. Hokkaido Univ., Ser. 6, Zool., 7, No.2:95–98, figs.1, 2. 1940.
Sato, S. and T.Ueno. On a Rare Fish, Bathymaster signatus Cope, Taken from Northern Pacific, and Notes on Allied Species. – Bull. Fac. Fish. Hokkaido Univ., 4, No.3:203–211, figs.1–6. 1953.
Schindler, O. Cyprinodontiden aus Costa-Rica. – Zool. Anz., 109:161–172. 1935. 5 figs.
Schlesinger, G. Die Gymnonoten. Eine phylogenetisch ethologische Studie. – Zool. Jber. Neapel, Syst., 29, No.6:613–640. 1910. ill.
Schmidt, E.J. On the Classification of the Freshwater Eels (Anguilla). – Meddr. Danm. Fisk. – og Havunders, 4, No.7:19. 1914.
Schmidt, E.J. Argentinidae, Microstomidae, Opisthoproctidae, Mediterranean Odontostomidae. – Rep. Dan. Oceanogr. Exped. Mediterr., 1908–1910, 4, Nos.2 (A 5):1:1–40, figs. 1–23. charts 1–4. 1918.
Schmidt, J. The Freshwater Eels of Australia. With Some Remarks on the Short-finned Species of Anguilla. – Rec. S. Aust. Mus., 16:179–210. 1928. 14 figs.
Schmidt, J. The Freshwater Eels of New Zealand. – Trans. Proc. N.Z. Inst., 58:379–388. 1928.
Schmidt, J. and A.C.Strusberg. Mediterranean Bramidae and Trichiuridae. – Rep. Dan. Oceanogr. Exped. Mediterr., 1908–1910, 4, Nos.2 (A 6):1–15. 1918.
Schmidt, P. A Revision of the Genus Hemilepidotus Cuvier (Pisces, Cottidae) and of the Allied Genera. – Annls. Mus. Zool. l'Acad. Sci. l'URSS, pp.359–369. 1926.
Schmidt, P. A Review of the Cottoid Fishes of the Genus Artediellus. – Proc. U.S. Natn. Mus., 71:1–10. 1927.
Schmidt, P. A Revision of the Genus Icelus Kröyer (Pisces, Cottidae) with the Description of a New Species from the Sea of Okhotsk. – Annls. Mus. Zool. l'Acad. Sci. l'URSS, pp.1–8. 1927.
Schmidt, P. A Revision of the Genus Gymnocanthus Swainson (Pisces, Cottidae). – Ibid., pp.25–32.
Schmidt, P. On a Rare Japanese Deep-sea Fish Ereunias grallator Jordan and Snyder. – C. r. Acad. Sci. URSS, pp.319–320. 1928.
Schmidt, P. On the Pacific Species of the Genera Microstomus and Glyptocephalus Gottsche (Pisces, Pleuronectidae). Ibid., pp.363–368. 1929.
Schmidt, P. A Revision of the Genus Hemilepidotus Cuvier (Pisces, Cottidae) and of the Allied Genera. – Annls. Mus. Zool. l'Acad. Sci. l'URSS, pp.359–369. 1929.
Schmidt, P. On the Subfamily Blepsiinae (Pisces, Cottidae) of the Pacific. – C. r. Acad. Sci. URSS, pp.394–398. 1929.
Schmidt, P. A Revision of the Genus Myoxocephalus Tilesius (Pisces, Cottidae) and of Some Allied Genera of the Pacific. – Annls. Mus. Zool. l'Acad. Sci. l'URSS, pp.405–426, figs.1–5. 1929.
Schmidt, P. A Revision of the Genus Crossias Jordan et Starks (Pisces, Cottidae). – Ibid., pp.503–506.

Schmidt, P. A Revision of the Genus Triglops Reinhardt (Pisces, Cottidae). – Ibid., pp.513–523, figs.1, 2.

Schmidt, P. On a Collection of Flatfishes from Fusan (Korea). – C. r. Acad. Sci. URSS, pp.313–320. Leningrad. 1931. 1 fig.

Schmidt, P. On the Genera Davidojordania Popov and Bilabria n. g. (Pisces, Zoarcidae). – C. r. Acad. Sci., Moscow, N.S., pp. 97–100. 1936. 1 text-fig.

Schmidt, P. On the Systematics and Distribution of the Genus Agonus Bloch et Schneider. – Copeia, 1:58–59. 1936.

Schmidt, P. On the Pacific Genera Porocottus Gill and Crossias Jordan et Starks (Pisces, Cottidae). – Bull. Acad. Sci. URSS, Ser. Biol., pp.377–387. 1940.

Schnakenbeck, W. Carangidae. – Rep. Dan. Oceanogr. Exped. Mediterr., 1908–1910, 2, Biol., A, 14:1–20. 1931.

Schnakenbeck, W. Acrania (Cephalochorda) – Cyclostoma – Pisces. – Handb. Zool., 6, 1 half, Part 1. Suppl. 2:1001–1115. 1962.

Schneider, G. Die Clupeiden der Ostsee. – Rapp. P.-v. Réun. Cons. perm. int. Explor.Mer., 9:66–120. 1908.

Schultz, L.P. Description of a New Type of Mud-minnow from Western Washington, with Notes on Related Species. – Univ. Wash. Publs. Fish., 11, No.6:73–81. 1929. 2 pls.

Schultz, L.P. Review of the Fishes of the Genera Polyipnus and Argyropelecus (Family Sternoptichidae) with Descriptions of Three New Species. – Proc. U.S. Natn. Mus., 86:135–155, text-figs.42–45. 1938.

Schultz, L.P. A Revision of the Toadfishes Referred to Porichthys and Related Genera. – Ibid., 86:473–496. 1939.

Schultz, L.P. Two New Genera and Three New Species of Cheilodipterid Fishes, with Notes on the Other Genera of the Family. – Ibid., 88:403–423, figs. 19, 20. 1940.

Schultz, L.P. Kraemeria bryani, a New Species of Trichonotid Fish from the Hawaiian Islands. – J. Wash. Acad. Sci., 31, No.6:269–272, fig.1. 1941.

Schultz, L.P. The Catfishes of Venezuela, with Descriptions of Thirty-eight New Forms. – Proc. U.S. Natn. Mus., 94:173–338. (1944) 1945.

Schultz, L.P. The Fishes of the Family Characinidae from Venezuela, with Description of Seventeen New Forms. – Ibid., 95:235–367, Figs.30–56. 1944.

Schultz, L.P. A Revision of the American Clingfishes, Family Gobiesocidae, with Descriptions of New Genera and Forms. – Ibid., 96:47–77. 1944. 1 pl.

Schultz, L.P. Emmelichthyops atlanticus, a New Genus and Species of Fish (Family Emmelichthyidae) from the Bahamas, with a Key to Related Genera. – J. Wash. Acad. Sci., 35, No.4:132–136. 1945.

Schultz, L.P. A Revision of the Genera of Mullets, Fishes of the Family Mugilidae, with Descriptions of Three New Genera. – Proc. U.S. Natn. Mus., 96:377–395, figs.28–32. 1946.

Schultz, L.P. A Revision of Six Subfamilies of Atherine Fishes with Descriptions of New Genera and Species. – Ibid., 98:1–48, figs.1–9, pls.1–2. 1948.

Schultz, L.P. Corrections for "A Revision of Six Subfamilies of the Atherine Fishes." – Copeia, 2:150. 1950.

Schultz, L.P. Review of Thirteen Genera of South American Fishes in the Subfamilies Cynodontinae, Hepsetinae and Characinae, with the Description of a New Cyrtocharax. Studies Honoring Trevor Kincaid, ed. by M.H.Hatch, Seattle, Univ. Washington Press, pp.44–73. 1950.

Schultz, L.P. Three New Species of Fishes of the Genus Cirrhitus (Family Cirrhitidae) from the Indo-Pacific. – Proc. U.S. Natn. Mus., 100:547–552, pl. 13. 1950.

Schultz, L.P. Review of the Indo-Pacific Anemone Fishes Genus Amphiprion, with Descriptions of Two New Species. – Ibid., 103:187–201. 1953. 2 pls.

Schultz, L.P. The Frogfishes of the Family Antennariidae. – Ibid., 107:47–105. 1957. 8 figs., 14 pls.

Schultz, L.P. Review of the Parrotfishes. Family Scaridae. – Bull. U.S. Natn. Mus., 214:1–143. 1958. 26 pls., 31 figs.

Schultz, L.P. Scombrina. – In: Fishes of the Marshall and Marianas Islands. – Ibid., 202, No.2:1–9, 1–438. 1960.

Schultz, L.P. Revision of the Marine Silver Hatchetfishes (Fam. Sternoptychidae). – Proc. U.S. Natn. Mus., 112:587–649, figs.1–26. 1961.

Schultz, L.P. Sternoptychidae. – In: Fishes W.N. Atlantic. 4. Mem. Sears Found. Mar. Res., 1, No.4:241–273, figs.62–72. 1964.

Schultz, L.P. Three New Species of Frogfishes from the Indian and Pacific Oceans with Notes on Other Species (Family Antennariidae). – Proc. U.S. Natn. Mus., 116:171–182. 1964. 3 figs.

Schultz, L.P. Review of South American Freshwater Angelfishes – Genus Pterophyllum. – Ibid., 120, No.3555:1–10. 1967. 4 pls.

Schultz, L.P. Four New Species of the Genus Parapercis with Notes on Other Species from the Indo-Pacific Area (Fam. Mugiloididae). – Ibid., 124, No.3636:1–16, pls.1–4. 1968.

Schultz, L.P. and N.B. Marshall. A Review of the Labrid Fish Genus Wetmorella with Descriptions of New Forms from the Tropical Indo-Pacific. – Ibid., 103:439–447. 1954. 1 pl., 3 figs.

Schultz, L.P. and E.D. Reid. The American Atlantic Toadfishes of the Genus Opsanus. – Copeia, 4:211–212. 1937.

Schultz, L.P. and L.P. Woods. A New Name for Synchiropus altivelis Regan with a Key to the Genera of the Fish Family Callionymidae. – J. Wash. Acad. Sci., 38, No.12:419–420. 1948.

Schultz, L.P. and L.P. Woods. Keys to the Genera of Echelid Eels and the Species of Muraenichthys of the Pacific, with Two New Species. – Ibid., 39, No.5:169–174, figs.1–2. 1949.

Schultz, L.P., L.P. Woods, and E.A. Lachner. Fishes of the Marshall and Marianas Islands.— Bull. U.S. Natn. Mus., 202, No.3:1–176, pls.124–148, figs.133–156. 1966.

Scogsberg. The Fishes of the Family Sciaenidae (Croakers) of California. – Fish. Bull. Divis. Fish Game Calif., 54:1–62. 1939. 15 figs.

Scott, E.O.G. Notes on the Gobies Recorded from Tasmania, with Description of a New Genus. – Pap. Proc. R. Soc. Tasm., pp.47–62, pl. IV, 2 text-figs. 1935.

Scott, E.O.G. Observations of Fishes of the Family Galaxiidae. I–III. – Proc. R. Soc. Tasm., I, pp.85–112. 1936. 4 figs.; II, pp.111–143, pls.18–27. (1937) 1938; III, pp.55–69, pl.9, map. 1941.

Scott, E.O.G. The Genera of the Galaxiidae. – Aust. Zool. 13, No.3:244–258. 1966.

Scott, T.D. The Sharks and Rays of South Australia, with Keys to the Species. – S. Aust. Nat., 29, No.4:55–56. 1955. ill.

Scott, T.D. The Marine and Freshwater Fishes of South Australia, pp.1–338. – Adelaide, Govt. Printer. 1962. Many text-figs.

Señorans, J.S. Notas sobre los Batrachoidiformes del Uruguay. – Revta Fac. Hum. Cienc. Univ. Repub. Urug., 16:275–285. 1958. 1 fig.

Serventy, D.L. The Australian Tunas. – Rep. Div. Fish. Oceanogr. C.S.I.R.O. Aust., 4:1–48, pls.1–4. 1941. 9 figs.

Sethi, R.P. Osteology and Phylogeny of Oviparous Cyprinodont Fishes (order Cyprinodontiformes). Ph.D. Thesis, Univ. Florida, pp.1–274. 1960. 59 figs.

Shaposhnikova, G.Kh. Some Data on Dallia pectoralis Bean. from the Chukchi Peninsula. – Vopr. Ikhtiol., 14:29–33. 1960. 2 figs.

Shaposhnikova, G.Kh. Comparative Morphological Analysis of Whitefishes of the Soviet Union. – In: Morfologiya nizshikh pozvonochnykh zhivotnykh; Trudy Zool. Inst. Akad. Nauk SSSR, 46:207–256. 1968. 26 figs.

Shaw, T.H. and T.L. Tchang. A Review of the Cobitoid Fishes of Hopei Province and Adjacent Territories. – Bull. Fan. Meml. Inst. Biol., Peking, 2, No.5:63–84. 1931.

Shih, H.J. Notes on the Labyrinth Fishes of China. – Bull. Fan. Meml. Inst. Biol., Peking, Zool., 7, No.2:67–97. 1936.

Shindo, S. Studies on the Stock of Lepidotrigla of the Eastern Sea. (1). On the Specific Characteristics. – Bull. Jap. Soc. Scient. Fish., 17:83–90. 1951. 1 pl., 4 figs.

Shingu, C. On the Maturity and the Spawning of White Croaker, Argyrosomus argentatus (Houttuyn), and Yellow Croaker, Pseudosciaena manchurica (Jordan et Thompson). – Rec. Oceanogr. Wks. Japan, No.6:65–72. 1962. 1 pl., 6 figs.

Shmidt, P.Yu. On the Genus Icelus (Cottidae). – Izv. Akad. Nauk SSSR, pp.413–418. 1935.

Shmidt, P.Yu. On the Pacific Genera Eurymen Gilbert et Burke and Gilbertidia C.Berg. – Dokl. Akad. Nauk SSSR, 15, No.5:279–281. 1937.

Shmidt, P.Yu. Fishes of the Sea of Okhotsk, pp.1–370. – Moscow–Leningrad, Akad. Nauk SSSR. 1950. 51 figs., 20 pls.

Siccardi, E.M. Cetorhinus en el Atlantico Sud (Elasmobranchii: Cetorhinidae). – Revta Mus. argent. Cienc. nat. Bernardino Revadavia Inst. nac. Invest. Cienc. nat., Zool., 6, No.2:61–101. 1961. 6 pls.

Silas, E.G. Notes on Fishes of the Genus Glyptothorax Blyth from Peninsular India, with Description of a New Species. – J. Bombay Nat. Hist. Soc., 50:367–370. 1951.

Silas, E.G. Notes on Two Homalopterid Fishes. – J. Zool. Soc. India, 3:11–17. 1951. 2 figs.

Silas, E.G. Classification, Zoogeography and Evolution of the Fishes of the Cyprinoid Families Homalopteridae and Gastromyzonidae. – Rec. Indian Mus., 50:173–263. (1952) 1953. 1 pl., 6 figs.

Silas, E.G. and E.Dawson. Amphipnous indicus, a New Synbranchoid Eel from India, with a Redefinition of the Genus and a Synopsis to the Species of Amphipnous Müller. – J. Bombay Nat. Hist. Soc., 56:366–378. 1961. 2 pls., 2 figs.

Silas, E.G. and H.S.Toor. On Some New Records of Pigface Breams (Family Lethrinidae; Pisces) from the Andaman Sea. – J. Mar. Biol. Ass. India, 3:208–214. 1962. 1 pl., 1 fig.

Silva, P.H.D.H. de. The Flatfishes (Heterosomata) of Ceylon with a List of the Specimens in the Colombo Museum. – Ceylon J. Sci., C, 7, No.2:183–200. 1956. 2 pls.

Silva, P.H.D.H. de. The Order Thoracostei off Ceylon, with a List of the Specimens in the Colombo Museum. – Spolia zeylan., 28, No.1:35–45. 1956. ill.

Silva, P.H.D.H. de. The Monacanthid Genera Pervagor and Paramonacanthus and the Diodontid Genera Chilomycterus and Diodon off Ceylon. – Ibid., 28, No.2:145–150. 1959. ill.

Silvester, C.F. and H.W.Fowler. A New Genus and Species of Phosphorescent Fish, Kryptophanaron alfredi. – Proc. Acad. Nat. Sci. Philad., 78:245–247. 1926. 2 pls.

Slastenenko, E.P. Les Goujons de l'Ukraine. – Bull. Soc. zool. Fr., 59:346–362. 1934.

Smith, B.G. The Heterodontid Sharks: their Natural History and External Development of Heterodontus japonicus Based on Notes and Drawings by Bashford Dean. – Bash. Dean Mem., 8:651–770, col.pls.1–7, text-figs.1–69. 1942.

Smith, C.L. The Patterns of Sexuality and the Classification of Serranid Fishes. – Am. Mus. Novit., 2207:1–20. 1965.

Smith, C.L. and R.M.Bailey. Evolution of the Dorsal Fin Supports of Percoid Fishes. – Pap. Michigan Acad. Sci., 46:345–362. 1961. 1 pl.

Smith, C.L. and R.M.Bailey. The Subocular Shelf of Fishes. – J. Morph., 110, No.1:1–18. 1962.

Smith, G.R. Distribution and Evolution of the North American Catostomid Fishes of the Subgenus Pantosteus, Genus Catostomus. – Misc. Publs. Mus. Zool. Univ. Mich., 129:1–132. 1966. ill.

Smith, H.M. The Fish Neostethus in Siam. – Science, N.S., 65:353–355. 1927.

Smith, H.M. The Freshwater Fishes of Siam, or Thailand. – Bull. U.S.Natn. Mus., 188:1–622, figs.1–107, pls.1–9. 1945.

Smith, H.M. and L.Radcliffe. Description of a New Family, Two Genera and Twenty-nine New Species of Anacanthini Fishes from the Philippine Islands and Contiguous Waters. – Proc. U.S. Natn. Mus., 42:105–140. 1912.

Smith, J. The South African Species of the Family Aluteridae. – Rec. Albany Mus., 4, No.2:358–364. 1935. 3 pls.

Smith, J.L.B. The Triglidae of South Africa. – Trans. R. Soc. S. Afr., 22:321–336, pls.16–23. 1934. 1 text-fig.

Smith, J.L.B. The Fishes of the Family Mugilidae in South Africa. – Ann. S. Afr. Mus., 30:587–644, pls.XV–XXII. 1935. 17 text-figs.

Smith, J.L.B. The "Galjoen" Fishes of South Africa. – Trans. R. Soc. S. Afr., 23:265–276, pls.13–17. 1935.

Smith, J.L.B. The Genus Tripterodon Playfair.– Ibid., 23:303–310. 1936.

Smith, J.L.B. The South African Fishes of the Families Sparidae and Denticidae. – Ibid., 26:225–305, pls.18–29. 1938. 25 text-figs.

Smith, J.L.B. A Living Fish of Mesozoic Type. – Nature, 18:455. March. 1939. fig.

Smith, J.L.B. A Living Coelacanthid Fish from South Africa. – Trans. R. Soc. S. Afr., 28:1–106, pls.1–44. 1939. 20 text-figs.

Smith, J.L.B. Sparid Fishes from Portuguese East Africa with a Note on the Genus Gymnocranius Klunzinger. – Ibid., 28:175–182, pl.1. 1940. 3 text-figs.

Smith, J.L.B. The Genus Gymnocranius Klunzinger, with Notes on Certain Rare Fishes from Portuguese East Africa. – Ibid., 28:441–452, pl.58. 1941.

Smith, J.L.B. The Fishes of the Family Clinidae in South Africa. – Ann. Mag. Nat. Hist., 11, No.12: 535–546. 1946. 4 text-figs.

Smith, J.L.B. A Generic Revision of the Mugilid Fishes of South Africa.— Ibid., 11, No.14:833–843, figs.1–15. (1947) 1948.

Smith, J.L.B. The Stromateid Fishes of South Africa. – Ibid., 12, No.2:839–851. 1949.

Smith, J.L.B. The Sea Fishes of Southern Africa. 2nd ed. Central News Agency, Cape Town, S.Africa, pp.i–xvi, 1–550. 1950. 105 pls., 1232 figs.

Smith, J.L.B. The Fishes of the Family Veliferidae from South-East Africa. – Ann. Mag. Nat. Hist., 12, No.4:497–510. 1951. 3 pls., 2 figs.

Smith, J.L.B. The Fishes of the Family Cirrhitidae. – Ibid., pp.625–652. 3 figs.

Smith, J.L.B. The Fishes of the Family Haliophidae. – Ibid., 12, No.5:85–101. 1952. 5 figs.

Smith, J.L.B. Plesiopid Fishes from South and East Africa. – Ibid., pp.139–151. 2 pls., 2 figs.

Smith, J.L.B. The Fishes of the Family Batrachoididae from South and East Africa. – Ibid., pp.313–339. 3 figs.

Smith, J.L.B. Preliminary Notes on Fishes of the Family Plectorhynchidae from South and East Africa, with Descriptions of Two New Species. – Ibid., pp.711–716. 1 pl.

Smith, J.L.B. The Genus Tetragonurus Risso, 1810. – Ibid., 12, No.6:51–66. 1953. 1 pl., 3 figs.

Smith, J.L.B. The Fishes of the Family Pseudogrammidae from East Africa. – Ibid., pp.548–560. 3 figs.

Smith, J.L.B. Problems of the Coelacanth. – S. Afr. J. Sci., 49:279–281. 1953.

Smith, J.L.B. Pseudoplesiopsine Fishes from South and East Africa. – Ann. Mag. Nat. Hist., 12, No.7:195–208. 1954. 3 figs.

Smith, J.L.B. The Anisochromidae, a New Family of Fishes from East Africa. – Ibid., pp.298–302. 1 fig., 1 pl.

Smith, J.L.B. Fishes New to Africa Obtained by Deep Line Fishing in Kenya Waters, with a Revision of the East African Species of the Genus Pristipomoides Bleeker, 1852. – Ibid., pp.481–492. 2 pls.

Smith, J.L.B. Apogonid Fishes of the Subfamily Pseudamiinae from Southeast Africa. – Ibid., pp.775–795. 1 pl.

Smith, J.L.B. Evolantiidae f.n. (Beloniformes). The Fishes of Aldabra. Part 1. – Ibid., 12, No.8:304–312. 1955. 1 pl.

Smith, J.L.B. The Fishes of the Family Anthiidae of the Western Indian Ocean. – Ibid., pp.337–350, figs.1–4.

Smith, J.L.B. The Fishes of the Family Pomacanthidae in the Western Indian Ocean. – Ibid., pp.377–384.

Smith, J.L.B. The Fishes of the Family Carapidae in the Western Indian Ocean. – Ibid., pp.401–416. 8 figs.

Smith, J.L.B. The Genus Pyramodon Smith et Radcliffe. – Ibid., pp.545–550, figs.1, 2.

Smith, J.L.B. East African Unicorn Fishes from Mozambique. – S. Afr. J. Sci., 51:169–174. 1955. 2 pls.

Smith, J.L.B. The Parrot Fishes of the Family Callyodontidae of the Western Indian Ocean. – Ichthyol. Bull. Rhodes Univ., 1:1–23, pls.41–45. 1956.

Smith, J.L.B. Swordfish, Marlin and Sailfish in South and East Africa. – Ibid., 2:25–34, pls. I, II, text-figs.1, 2. 1956.

Smith, J.L.B. The Fishes of the Family Sphyraenidae in the Western Indian Ocean. – Ibid., 3:37–46, pls.1–2, text-fig.1. 1956.

Smith, J.L.B. Old Fourlegs. The Story of the Coelacanth, pp.1–260. – London, Longmans, Green and Co. 1956. 7 photos, 7 figs.

Smith, J.L.B. The Fishes of the Family Scorpaenidae in the Western Indian Ocean. – Ichthyol. Bull. Rhodes Univ., 4:49–72, pls. I–IV, text-figs.1–5. 1957.

Smith, J.L.B. The Fishes of the Family Scorpaenidae in the Western Indian Ocean. Part 2. The Subfamilies Pteroinae, Apistinae, Setarchinae and Sebastinae. – Ibid., 5:75–88, pls. V–VI, text-figs.6–9. 1957.

Smith, J.L.B. List of the Fishes of the Family Labridae in the Western Indian Ocean with New Records and Five New Species. – Ibid., 7:99–114. 1957. 4 figs., 2 pls.

Smith, J.L.B. The Labrid Fishes of the Subgenus Julis Cuvier, 1814 (in Coris Lacépède, 1802) from South and East Africa. – Ibid., 8:117–120. 1957. 2 pls., 1 fig.

Smith, J.L.B. The Gunnelichthid Fishes with Description of Two New Species from East Africa and of Gunnellichthys (Clarkichthys) bilineatus (Clark). 1936. – Ibid., 9:123–129. 1958. 2 figs.

Smith, J.L.B. The Fishes of the Family Eleotridae in the Western Indian Ocean. – Ibid., 11:137–164, pls.1–3, text-figs.1–17. 1958.

Smith, J.L.B. Fishes of the Families Tetrarogidae, Caracanthidae, and Synanciidae, from the Western Indian Ocean. – Ibid., 12:167–181, pls. VII–VIII. 1958.

Smith, J.L.B. Tetraodont Fishes from South and East Africa. – Ann. Mag. Nat. Hist., 13, No.1:156–160. 1958. 1 pl.

Smith, J.L.B. Gobioid Fishes of the Families Gobiidae, Periophthalmidae, Trypauchenidae, Taenioididae, and Kraemeriidae of the Western Indian Ocean. - Ichthyol. Bull. Rhodes Univ., 13:185-225, pls.9-13, figs.1-42. 1959.

Smith, J.L.B. Fishes of the Families Blenniidae and Salariidae of the Western Indian Ocean. -Ibid., 14:229-252, pls.15-19, text-figs.1-16. 1959.

Smith, J.L.B. Serioline Fishes (Yellowtails, Amberjacks) from the Western Indian Ocean. - Ibid., 15:225-261. 1959. 6 figs.

Smith, J.L.B. The Identity of Scarus gibbus Rüppell, 1928 and of Other Parrot Fishes of the Family Callyodontidae from the Red Sea and the Western Indian Ocean. - Ibid., 16:265-282. 1959. 5 pls., 10 figs.

Smith, J.L.B. Fishes of the Family Lethrinidae from the Western Indian Ocean. - Ibid., 17:285-295, pls.20-25. 1959.

Smith, J.L.B. Fishes of the Family Gobiidae in South Africa. - Ibid., 18:299-314. 1960. 13 figs.

Smith, J.L.B. Coral Fishes of the Family Pomacentridae from the Western Indian Ocean and the Red Sea. - Ibid., 19:317-349. 1960. 8 pls., 6 figs.

Smith, J.L.B. A New Grammicolepid Fish from South Africa. - Ann. Mag. Nat. Hist., 13, No.3:231-235. 1960. 2 pls.

Smith, J.L.B. Fishes of the Family Xenopoclinidae. - Ichthyol. Bull Rhodes Univ., 20:351-356. 1961. 4 figs.

Smith, J.L.B. Fishes of the Family Anthiidae. - Ibid., 21:359-369. 1961. 2 pls., 5 figs.

Smith, J.L.B. Fishes of the Family Apogonidae of the Western Indian Ocean and the Red Sea. - Ibid., 22:373-418, pls.46-52, text-figs.1-11. 1961.

Smith, J.L.B. The Moray Eels of the Western Indian Ocean and the Red Sea. - Ibid., 23:421-444. 1962. 9 pls., 6 figs.

Smith, J.L.B. Sand-dwelling Eels of the Western Indian Ocean and the Red Sea. - Ibid., 24:447-466. 1962. 4 pls., 10 figs.

Smith, J.L.B. Fishes of the Family Gaterinidae of the Western Indian Ocean and the Red Sea, with a Resume of All Known Indo-Pacific Species. - Ibid., 25:469-502. 1962. 4 pls., 22 figs.

Smith, J.L.B. Scombroid Fishes of South Africa. - Proc. Symp. Scombroid Fishes Mar. Biol. Ass. India, 1:165-183. 1962.

Smith, J.L.B. Fishes of the Family Pentacerotidae. - Ichthyol. Bull. Rhodes Univ., 29:567-578 and Addendum, pls.87-91, text-figs.1, 2. 1964.

Smith, J.L.B. The Clingfishes of the Western Indian Ocean and the Red Sea. - Ibid., 30:581-596. 1964. 6 pls., 1 fig.

Smith, J.L.B. Scombroid Fishes of South Africa. - Proc. Symp. Socmbroid Fishes. Mar. Biol. Ass. India, Ser.1, 1:165-183. 1964. 10 pls., 1 fig.

Smith, J.L.B. Fishes of the Family Atherinidae of the Red Sea and the Western Indian Ocean with a New Freshwater Genus and Species from Madagascar. - Ibid., 31:601-632. 1965. 5 pls., 7 figs.

Smith, J.L.B. Kaupichthys diodontus Schultz in the Western Indian Ocean. A Problem in Systematics. - Dep. Ichthyol. Univ. Occas. Pap., 5:43-54, pl.12. 1965.

Smith, M.W. and J.W. Saunders. The American Eel in Certain Fresh Waters of the Maritime Provinces of Canada. - J. Fish. Res. Bd. Can., 12, No.2:238-269. 1955. ill.

Snyder, J.O. A Review of the Mullidae Surmullets, or Goatfishes of the Shores of Japan. - Proc. U.S. Natn. Mus., 32:87-102. 1907. 3 figs.

Soldatov, V.K. A Survey of Acipenseridae from the Amur River. - Mater. Russk. Ryb., 3, No.12:95-415. 1915. figs.

Soldatov, V.K. and G.U. Lindberg. A Survey of Fishes of the Far Eastern Seas. - Izv. Tikhookean. Nauchno-Issled. Inst. Ryb. Khoz. Okeanogr., 5:1-576, figs.1-76. 1930.

Soleim, P.A. A Contribution to the Knowledge of the Lesser Sandeel (Ammodytes lancea) in North European Waters. - Rep. Norw. Fishery Mar. Invest., 8:1-28. 1945.

Sowerby, A. de. The Chinese Sturgeon. - China J. Sci. Arts, 1:480-483. 1923. 2 figs.

Sözer, F. Türkiye Gobiidleri. Les Gobiides de la Turquie. - Revue Fac. Sci. Univ. Istanbul, 6B:128-169. 1941.

Sözer, F. Türkiye Cyprinodontid'leri hakkinda. Contributions à la connaissance des Cyprinodontides de la Turquie. - Ibid., 7B, No.4:307-316. 1942. 2 text-figs.

Spanovskaya, V.D. Fishes of the Subfamily Gobionini from the Amur Basin. (Taxonomy, Biology, Importance in the Life of the Amur Ichthyofauna). Author's Summary of Candidate Thesis, pp.1–19. Moscow. 1953.

Spanovskaya, V.D. Systematics of the Pacific Gudgeons. – Zool. Zh., 32, No.2:259–270, figs.1–8. 1953.

Springer, S. Notes on the Sharks of Florida. – Proc. Fla. Acad. Sci., 3:9–41. 1938. 23 figs.

Springer, S. A Revision of North American Sharks Allied to the Genus Carcharhinus. – Am. Mus. Novit., 1451:1–13. 1950.

Springer, S. Correction for "A Revision of North American Sharks Allied to the Genus Carcharhinus." – Copeia, 3:244. 1951.

Springer, V.G. Western Atlantic Fishes of the Genus Paraclinus. – Tex. J. Sci., 6:422–441. 1954. 1 fig.

Springer, V.G. The Taxonomic Status of the Fishes of the Genus Stathmonotus, Including a Review of the Atlantic Species. – Bull. Mar. Sci. Gulf Caribb., 5:66–80. 1955. figs.

Springer, V.G. Systematics and Zoogeography of the Clinid Fishes of the Subtribe Labrisomini Hubbs. – Publs. Inst. Mar. Sci. Univ. Tex., 5:417–492. 1958. 4 figs., 7 pls.

Springer, V.G. A Review of the Blenniid Fishes of the Genus Ophioblennius Gill. – Copeia, 2:426–433. 1962. 4 figs.

Springer, V.G. A Revision of the Carcharinid Shark Genera Scoliodon, Loxodon and Rhizoprionodon. – Proc. U.S. Natn. Mus., 115:559–632. 1964. 14 figs.

Springer, V.G. Review of "A Revised Classification of the Blennioid Fishes of the Family Chaenopsidae" by J.S.Stephens. – Copeia, 3:591–593. 1964.

Springer, V.G. A Review of Western Atlantic Cat Sharks Scyliorhininae, with Descriptions of a New Genus and Five New Species. – Fishery Bull. Fish. Wildl. Serv. U.S., 65, No.3:581–624. 1966. ill.

Springer, V.G. Revision of the Circumtropical Shorefish Genus Entomacrodus (Blenniidae: Salariinae). – Proc. U.S. Natn. Mus., 122, No.3582:1–150. 1967.

Springer, V.G. Osteology and Classification of the Fishes of the Family Blenniidae. – Bull. U.S. Natn. Mus., 284:1–85. 1968. 16 figs., 11 pls.

Springer, V.G. The Indo Pacific Blenniid Fish Genus Stanulus, with Description of a New Species from the Great Barrier Reef (Blenniidae, Blenniinae, Salarini). – Proc. Biol. Soc. Wash., 81:111–122. 1968.

Starks, E.C. Description of a New Genus and Species of Cottoid from Puget Sound. – Bull. Stanford Univ. Publ., Biol. Sci., 6, No.2:410–412. (1895) 1896.

Starks, E.C. The Osteology and Relationships of the Family Zeidae. – Proc. U.S. Natn. Mus., 21:469–476, pls.33–38. 1898.

Starks, E.C. The Osteological Characters of the Fishes of the Suborder Percesoces. – Ibid., 22:1–10. (1899) 1900. 3 pls.

Starks, E.C. The Relationship and Osteology of the Caproid Fishes or Antigoniidae. – Ibid., 25:565–572. 1902. ill.

Starks, E.C. The Shoulder Girdle and Characteristic Osteology of the Hemibranchiate Fishes. – Ibid., pp.619–634.

Starks, E.C. The Osteology of Dallia pectoralis. – Zool. Jber. Neapel, Sect. Syst., 21:249–262. 1904.

Starks, E.C. The Osteology of Some Berycoid Fishes. – Proc. U.S.Natn. Mus., 27:601–619. 1904.

Starks, E.C. On the Relationship of the Fishes of the Family Siganidae. – Biol. Bull. Mar. Biol. Lab., Woods Hole, 13:211–218. 1907. ill.

Starks, E.C. The Characters of Atelaxia, a New Suborder of Fishes. – Bull. Mus. Comp. Zool. Harv., 52:17–22. 1908. 5 pls.

Starks, E.C. The Osteology and Mutual Relationships of the Fishes Belonging to the Family Scombridae. – J. Morph., 21:77–99, figs.1–2. 1910. 3 pls.

Starks, E.C. The Osteological Characters of the Scombroid Fishes of the Families Gempylidae, Lepidopidae, and Trichiuridae. – Stanford Univ. Publs., Univ. Ser. 5:17–26. 1911. 2 pls.

Starks, E.C. The Fishes of the Croaker Family (Sciaenidae) of California. – Calif. Fish Game, 5, No.1:1–88. 1919.

Starks, E.C. The Osteology and Relationships of the Uranoscopoid Fishes. – Stanford Univ. Publs., Ser. Biol. Sci., 3, No.3:259–290. 1923.

Starks, E.C. Bones of the Ethmoid Region of the Fish Skull. – Ibid., 4, No.3:139–338. 1926.

Starks, E.C. The Primary Shoulder Girdle of Bony Fishes. – Ibid., 6, No.2:149–239. 1930. 38 figs.

Starks, E.C. and W.F. Thompson. A Review of the Flounders Belonging to the Genus Pleuronichthys. – Proc. U.S. Natn. Mus., 38:277–287. 1910.

Stauch, A. and J. Cadenat. Révision du genre Psettodes Bennett, 1831 (Pisces, Teleostei, Heterosomata). – Cahier O.R.S.T.O.M., Océanogr., 4:19–30. 1965. 11 figs.

Stauch, A. and F. D'Aubenton. Poissons Pleuronectiformes du Cambodge. – Ibid., 4, No.1:137–158. 1966.

Stead, D.G. Sharks and Rays of Australian Seas, pp.1–211. London. 1964. ill.

Steindachner, F. Beiträge zur Kenntnis der Chromiden des Amazonenstromes. – Sber. Akad. Wiss. Wien, Mathematisch-naturwissenschaftliche Klasse, 71, No.1:1–77. 1875. ill.

Steindachner, F. and R. Kner. Über einige Pleuronectiden, Salmoniden, Gadoiden und Blenniiden aus der Decastris-Bay und von Viti-Levu. – Ibid., 61, No.1:421–446. 1870. 1 pl.

Steinitz, H. Contributions to the Knowledge of the Blenniidae of the Eastern Mediterranean. – Revue Fac. Sci. Univ. Istanbul, I, B14:129–152. 1949. 4 text-figs.; II, pp.170–197. 1949. 8 figs.; III, B15:60–87. 1950. 7 figs.

Steinitz, H. Notes on Some Glyptosternoid Fishes (Sisoridae, Siluroidea). – Mitt. hamb. zool. Mus. Inst., 59:105–115. 1961. 11 figs.

Steinmann, P. Ein neues System der mitteleuropäischen Coregonen. – Revue suisse Zool., 57:517–525. 1950. 2 figs.

Steinmann, P. Monographie der Schweizerischen Koregonen. Beitrag zum Problem der Entstehung neuer Arten. – Schweiz. Z. Hydrol., 12:109–189. 25 figs., and pp.340–491. 39 figs. 1950; 13:54–155 and 162–191. 1951. 14 pls., 4 figs.

Stephens, J.S. A Revised Classification of the Blennioid Fishes of the American Family Chaenopsidae. – Univ. Calif. Publs. Zool., 68:1–165. Berkeley–Los Angeles, Univ. Calif. Press. 1963. ill.

Sterba, G. Die Schmerlenartigen (Cobitidae). – In: Demoll and Maier, Handb. Binnenfisch. Mitteleur., 3, No.9:201–234. 1958. 28 figs.

Sterba, G. Süsswasserfische aus aller Welt, pp.1–637, figs.1–1193. – Leipzig, "Urania." 1959.

Sterba, G. Neunaugen (Petromyzonidae). – Ibid., 3B:263–344. 1962. ill.

Steven, G.A. The British Raiidae. – Sci. Prog., Lond., 35:220–236. 1947. 4 text-figs.

Stigchel, J.W. van der. The South American Nematognathi of the Museums at Leiden. – Zool. Meded., Leiden, 27:1–204. 1947. 2 tables.

Stockard, C.R. Observations on the Natural History of Polyodon spathula. – Am. Nat., 41:753–766. 1907. 3 figs.

Stokell, G. A Revision of the Genus Retropinna. – Rec. Canterbury Mus., 4:361–372, pls.55–57. 1941.

Stokell, G. A Revision of the Genus Gobiomorphus. – Trans. Proc. R. Soc. N.Z., 70:265–276, pls.25, 26. 1941.

Stokell, G. The Systematic Arrangement of the New Zealand Galaxiidae. I. Generic and Subgeneric Classification. – Ibid., 75:124–137, pls.8–12. 1945.

Stokell, G. The Systematic Arrangement of the New Zealand Galaxiidae. II. Specific Classification. – Ibid., 77:472–496. 1949. 12 text-figs.

Stokell, G. Contributions to Galaxiid Taxonomy. – Trans. R. Soc. N.Z., 82, No.2:411–418. 1954. 1 pl.

Stokell, G. Pacific Salmon in New Zealand. – Trans. R. Soc. N.Z., Zool., 2:181–190. 1962. 1 pl.

Stokell, G. A Preliminary Investigation of the Systematics of Some Tasmanian Galaxiidae. – Pap. Proc. R. Soc. Tasm., 100:73–80. 1966.

Storey, M.H. Contributions towards a Revision of the Ophichthyid Eels. I. The Genera Callechelys and Bascanichthys, with Descriptions of New Species and Notes on Myrichthys. – Stanford Ichthyol. Bull., 1:61–84. 1939. 6 text-figs.

Strahan, R. Survival of the Hag, Paramyxine atami Dean, in Diluted Sea Water. – Copeia, 2:471–473. 1962.

Strahan, R. Variation in Eptatretus burgeri (Family Myxinidae), with a Further Description of the Species. – Copeia, 4:801–807. 1962. 1 fig.

Strahan, R. Lampreys in Australia. – Aust. Nat. Hist., 14, No.10:334–336. 1964.

Strahan, R. and Y. Honma. Variation in Paramyxine, with a Redescription of P. atami Dean and P. springeri Bigelow and Schroeder. – Bull. Mus. Comp. Zool. Harv., 125, No.11:323–342. 1961.

Strasburg, D.W. Further Notes on the Identification and Biology of Echeneid Fishes. – Pacif. Sci., 18:51–57. 1964. 2 figs.

Sufi, S.M.K. Revision of the Oriental Fishes of the Family Mastacembelidae. – Bull. Raffles Mus., 27:93–146. 1956. 12 pls.

Susumo Kato, S. Springer, and M. Wagner. Field Guide to Eastern Pacific and Hawaiian Sharks. - U.S.Dep. Interior, Circ., p.271. 1967.

Suttkus, R.D. Lepisostei. - In: Fishes W.N. Atlantic. 3. Mem. Sears Found. Mar. Res., 4, No.3:61-86, figs.11-17. 1963.

Suvorov, E.K. Principles of Ichthyology, pp.1-580. Moscow. 1948.

Suzuki, K. Anatomical and Taxonomical Studies on the Carangid Fishes of Japan. - Rep. Fac. Fish. Prefect. Univ. Mie, 4:43-232. 1962. 61 figs.

Svärdson, G. The Coregonid Problem. I. Some General Aspects of the Problem. - Rep. Inst. Freshwat.. Res. Drottningholm, 1948, pp.89-101. 1949. 1 fig.

Svärdson, G. The Coregonid Problem. 6. The Palearctic Species and their Intergrades. - Ibid., 38:267-356. 1957.

Svetovidov, A.N. Data on the Taxonomy and Biology of Graylings from Lake Baikal. - Trudy Baikal. Limnol. Sta., 1:19-199, pls.1-4. 1931.

Svetovidov, A.N. On the Systematics of the Genus Cottocomephorus Pellegrin (Pisces, Cottocomephoridae). - Ibid., 6:53-57. 1935.

Svetovidov, A.N. Family Triglidae. - In: Fauna SSSR, Ryby, 6, No.9:1-24, pls.1-3. Leningrad. 1936.

Svetovidov, A.N. European-Asian Graylings (Genus Thymallus Cuvier). - Trudy Zool. Inst. Akad. Nauk SSSR, 3:183-301. 1936.

Svetovidov, A.N. Über die Klassifikation der Gadiformes oder Anacanthini (Vorläufige Mitteilung). - Bull. Acad. URSS, Biol., pp.1281-1288. 1937. 3 text-figs.

Svetovidov, A.N. Comparative-Anatomical Data on the Genus Muraenolepis from the Gadiformes. - Dokl. Akad. Nauk, 23, No.6:583-585. 1939.

Svetovidov, A.N. Clupeidae. - In: Fauna SSSR, Ryby, 2, No.1:1-331, figs.1-54, pls.1-53. 1952.

Svetovidov, A.N. Connection between the Swim Bladder and the Auditory Capsules in Fishes of the Family Sparidae and its Significance for the System. - Zool. Zh., 34, No.4:837-841. 1955.

Svetovidov, A.N. Morphological Principles of the Classification of the Gadidae. - In: XIV Intern. Congr. Zool., Copenhagen, pp.535-540. 1956.

Svetovidov, A.N. Specific Composition of the Family Blenniidae in the Black Sea. - Zool. Zh., 37, No.4:584-593. 1958.

Svetovidov, A.N. Gadiformes, pp.1-304. ill. (Translated from Russian by Israel Progr. Sci. Transl. 1962.)

Svetovidov, A.N. Fishes of the Black Sea, pp.1-552, figs.1-191. - Moscow-Leningrad, "Nauka." 1964.

Svetovidov, A.N. Contribution to the Study of the Family Moridae (Pisces, Gadiformes). - Zool. Zh., 46, No.11:1684-1693. 1967.

Svetovidov, A.N. and E.A. Dorofeeva. Taxonomic Relationships, Origin and the History of Distribution of European, Asian and North American Perches and Pike-perches (Genera Perca, Lucioperca and Stizostedion). - Vopr. Ikhtiol., 3, No.4(29):625-651. 1963.

Svetovidova, A.A. A Revision of the Genus of Altai Osmans Oreoleuciscus Warp. (Pisces, Cyprinidae). - Ibid., 5, No.2:245-261. 1965.

Swainson, W. On the Natural History of Fishes, Amphibians, and Reptiles, London, I:299. Cypsilurus. 1838; II:187, 296. Cypsilurus. 1839.

Sylva, D.P. de. The Osteology and Phylogenetic Relationships of the Blackfin Tuna, Thunnus atlanticus (Lesson). - Bull. Mar. Sci. Gulf Caribb., 5:1-41. 1955. 61 figs.

Sylva, D.P. de. Systematics and Life History of the Great Barracuda, Sphyraena barracuda (Walbaum). - Stud. Trop. Oceanogr. Miami, 1:i-viii, 1-179. 1963. 36 figs.

Szidat, L. and A. Nani. Las Remoras del Atlantico Austral con un estudio de su nutricion natural y de suo parasitos (Pisces, Echeneidae).— Revta Mus. argent. Cienc. nat. Bernardino Rivadavia Inst. nac. Invest. Cienc. nat., Zool., 6:385-417. 1951. 14 figs.

Takagi, K. Sur la nouvelle raie Torpille Crassinarke dormitor gen. et sp. nov. appartenant à la sous-famille narkinée. - J. Tokyo Univ. Fish., 38, No.1:27-34. 1951. 1 pl.

Takagi, K. Description of Some New Gobioid Fishes of Japan, with a Proposition on the Sensory Line System as a Taxonomic Character. - Ibid., 43, No.1:97-126. 1957. 8 figs.

Takahachi, N. On the Plecostei, an Order of the Teleostomi, Established by Prof. Kishinouye. - J. Coll. Agric. Imp. Univ. Tokyo, 7, No.4:383-398, pl.26. 1926.

Takahashi, J. Study for Identification of Species Based on the Vertebral Column of Teleostei in Inland Sea and its Adjacent Waters. - Bull. Naikai Reg. Fish. Res. Lab., 16:1-75, pls.1-122. 1962. (In Japanese.)

Talbot, F.H. The Fishes of the Genus Lutianus of the East African Coast. – Ann. Mag. Nat. Hist., 12, No.10:241–258. 1957. 9 pls.

Talbot, F.H. The South African Tunas. Symposium on Scombroid Fishes. 1. – Mar. Nat. Biol. Assoc. India, Mandapan Camp. S.India, pp.187–209. 1964. 7 figs.

Talbot, F.H. and M.J. Penrith. Tunnies and Marlins of South Africa. – Nature, 193:558, 559. 1962.

Taliev, D.N. Bullheads and Sculpins (Cottoidei) from Lake Baikal, pp.3–603, figs.9–179. – Moscow-Leningrad, Akad. Nauk SSSR. 1955.

Tanaka, S. Henicichythyidae. – Zool. Mag., Tokyo, 27, No.325:568. Nov.15. 1915; In: Jordan, D.S. A Classification of Fishes, p.203. 1923. (Translated from Japanese.)

Tang, D.S. The Elasmobranchiate Fishes of Amoy. – Nat. Sci. Bull. Univ., Amoy, 1:29–111. 1934. 22 text-figs.

Tang, D.S. An Annotated List of the Elasmobranchs of Kwantung Province. – Ibid., 1, No.2:165–173. 1935.

Tåning, A.V. Mediterranean Scopelidae (Saurus, Aulopus, Chlorophthalmus and Myctophum). – Rep. Dan. Oceanogr. Exped. Mediterr., 1908–1910, 5, No.2 (A7):1–154, figs.1–49. 1918.

Tåning, A.V. Lophius. – Rep. Dan. Oceanogr. Exped. Mediterr., Biol., 2, No.A10:1–30. 1923. 22 figs.

Tåning, A.V. Synopsis of the Scopelids in the North Atlantic. – Vidensk. Meddr. dansk. naturh. Foren, 86:49–69, figs.1–2. 1928.

Tåning, A.V. Notes on Scopelids from the Dana Expedition. 1. – Ibid., 94:125–146. 1932.

Taranets, A.Ya. A Brief Survey of Fishes of the Genus Gymnogobius, with a Description of One Species and Notes on Some Allied Genera. – Dokl. Akad. Nauk SSSR, 3, No.5:397–400. 1934.

Taranets, A.Ya. A Brief Survey of Species of the Genus Porocottus. – Vest. Dal'nevost. Fil. Akad. Nauk SSSR, 14:177–180. 1935.

Taranets, A.Ya. A Brief Survey of the Genera of the Family Blenniidae Allied to Stichaeus from the Bering Sea, the Sea of Okhotsk, and the Sea of Japan. – Dokl. Akad. Nauk SSSR, Nos.1 (10), 3 (80):141–144. 1936.

Taranets, A. Ya. A Short Key to Fishes of the Soviet Far East and Adjacent Waters. – Izv. Tikhookean. Nauchno-Issled. Inst. Ryb. Khoz. Okeanogr., 11:1–140. 1937.

Taranets, A.Ya. On the Relations and Origin of Gudgeons from the Amur Basin. – Zool. Zh., 17, No.3:453–472. 1938.

Taranets, A.Ya. Contribution to the Classification and Origin of Gobies of the Family Cottidae. – Izv. Akad. Nauk SSSR, Biol., 3:427–447. 1941.

Tarp, F.H. A Revision of the Family Embiotocidae. – Fish Bull. Calif. Fish Game Commn., 88:1–99, figs.1–32. 1952.

Tavani, G. Osservazioni su alcuni Plectognathi (Gymnodonti). – Memorie Soc. tosc. Sci. nat., 62A, No.1:177–200. 1955. 2 pls.

Taylor, W.R. Revision of the Genus Noturus with a Contribution to the Classifications of the North American Catfishes. Ph.D. Thesis. Univ. Michigan. 1955. 583 pp., 13 maps, 17 pls. Unpubl. (from McAllister, 1968.)

Tchang, T.L. Contributions à l'étude morphologique, biologique et taxonomique des Cyprinidés du Bassin du Yangtze. – Thès. Fac. Sci. Univ. Paris, Ser.A, 209, No.233:1–159. 1930. 4 pls., 11 figs.

Tchang, T.L. Cyprinidés du bassin du Yangtze. – Contrib. étude morphol. biolog. et taxonomique, pp.1–171. Paris. 1931.

Tchang, T.L. The Study of Chinese Cyprinoid Fishes. 1. – Zoologica sinica, Peking, Ser.B., 2, No.1:1–247. 1933. 5 pls., 115 text-figs.

Tchang, T.L. Study of Some Chinese Catfishes. – Bull. Fan. Meml. Inst. Biol. Peking, 7:33–56. 1936. 5 text-figs.

Tchang, T.L. Some Chinese Clupeoid Fishes. – Ibid., Zool. Ser., 8, No.4:311–337, figs.1–11. 1938.

Tchang, T.L. The Gobies of China. – Ibid., 9:263–288. 1939.

Tchang, T.L. The Cyprinoid Fishes of China, pp.1–130, figs.1–108. 1959. (In Chinese.)

Tchang, T.L. The Cyprinoid Fishes of China, pp.1–67, figs.1–42. 1960. (In Chinese.)

Tchang, T.L. and C.Y. Shih. Notes on Some Chinese Catfishes. – Sci. Q. Natn. Univ. Peking, 4:333–353. 1934.

Tchernavin, V.V. A Revision of the Subfamily Orestiinae. – Proc. Zool. Soc. Lond., 114:140–233. 1944. 27 text-figs.

Tchernavin, V.V. A Revision of Some Trichomycterinae Based on Material Preserved in the British Museum (Natural History). – Ibid., pp.234–275.

Tchernavin, V.V. A Revision of the Subfamily Orestiinae. - Trans. Linn. Soc. Lond., Ser.3, 1, No.3:217, 218. 1955.

Teague, G.W. The Sea-robins of America. A Revision of the Triglid Fishes of the Genus Prionotus. - Comm. Zool. Mus. Hist. Nat., Montevideo, 3, No.61:1–59, pls. I–V. 1951.

Teague, G.W. The "Mercator" Sea-robins. A Revision of the Triglid Fishes of the Genus Prionotus. - Bull. Inst. r. Sci. nat. Belg., 28, No.59:1–20. 1952. ill.

Teague, G.W. The Armored Sea-robins of America. A Revision of the Family Peristediidae. - An. Mus. Hist. nat., Montevideo, Ser.2, 7, No.2:1–27. 1961.

Tee-Van, J. Cichlid Fishes in the West Indies with Special Reference to Haiti, Including the Description of a New Species of Cichlasoma. - Zoologica, N.Y., 10:281–300, figs.269–272. 1935.

Tee-Van, J. Eastern Pacific Expedition of New York Zoological Society. XVII. A Review of the American Fishes of the Family Cirrhitidae. - Ibid., 25, No.1:53–64, figs.1–4. 1940.

Temminck, C.J. and H.Schlegel. Poissons. - In: P.F.Siebold. Fauna japonica, Leiden, pp.1–323, pls.1–160. 1942–1950.

Templeman, W. A Review of the Morid Fish Genus Halargyreus with First Records from the Western North Atlantic. - J. Fish. Res. Bd. Can., 25, No.5:877–901. 1968. ill.

Te Winkel, L.E. The Internal Anatomy of Two Phallostethid Fishes. - Biol. Bull. Mar. Biol. Lab., Woods Hole, 76:59–69. 1939. 3 text-figs.

Thienemann, A. Über einige Schwedische Coregonen mit Bemerkungen über die Systematik der Gattung Coregonus und die Wege und Ziele der künftigen Coregonenforschung. - Arch.Naturgesch., Sec.A, 87, No.2:170–195. 1921.

Thienemann, A. Weitere Untersuchungen an Coregonen. - Arch. Hydrobiol., 13:415–471, pls.5–8. 1922.

Thompson, J.M. The Mugilidae of Australia and Adjacent Seas. - Aust. J. Mar. Freshwat. Res., 5:70–131. 1954. 2 pls., 16 figs.

Thompson, J.M. A Bibliography of Systematic References to the Grey Mullets (Mugilidae). - Tech. Pap. Div. Fish. Oceanogr., C.S.I.R.O. Aust., 16:1–127. 1964.

Thompson, J.R. and S.Springer. Sharks, Skates, Rays and Chimaeras. - Fishery Bull. Fish Wildl. Serv. U.S., 119:1–19. 1961. ill.

Thys van den Audenaerde, D.F.E. L'anatomie de Phractolaemus ansorgei Blgr. et la position systématique des Phractolaemidae. - Annls. Mus. r. Afr. cent., Sér. Zoologie, 8, 103:101–167. 1961.

Thys van den Audenaerde, D.F.E. Revision systématique des espèces congolaises du genre Tilapia (Pisces, Cichlidae). -Ibid., 124:1–147. 1964. 10 pls., 24 figs.

Thys van den Audenaerde, D.F.E. Revision of the Genus Eutropiellus Nichols et Lamonte (Pisces, Schilbeidae) with a Description of a New Species from Lower Nigeria Eutropiellus vanderweyeri sp.n. - Revue Zool. Bot. afr., 69:214–230. 1964. 3 figs.

Tilak, R. The Osteocranium and the Weberian Apparatus of the Fishes of the Family Sisoridae (Siluroidea): A Study in Adaptation and Taxonomy. - Z. wiss. Zool., 168, Nos.3–4:281–320. 1963.

Ting Han-po. Notes on a Sturgeon from the Min River, China. - Copeia, 1:65–68. 1949.

Tinsley, J.B. The Sailfish, Swashbuckler of the Open Sea. - Gainesville, Univ. Florida Press. 1964. 216 pp.

Tominaga, Y. A Revision of the Fishes of the Family Pempheridae of Japan. - J. Fac. Sci. Tokyo Univ., Sec.4, 10, No.1:269–290. 1963. 13 figs.

Tominaga, Y. The Internal Morphology and Systematic Position of Leptobrama mülleri, Formerly Included in the Family Pempheridae. - Jap. J. Ichthyol., 12, Nos.3–6:33–56. 1965. 10 figs.

Tominaga, Y. Internal Morphology, Mutual Relationships and Systematic Position of the Family Pempheridae. - Ibid., 15, No.2:43–95, figs.1–17. 1968.

Tomiyama, I. Gobiidae of Japan. - Jap. J. Zool., 7, No.1:37–112, figs.1–44. 1936.

Tomiyama, I. and T.Abe. Figures and Descriptions of the Fishes of Japan (A Contribution of Dr. S.Tanaka's Work, XLIX-LVIII:961–1219, pls.191–235.) 1953–1958.

Tomiyama, I. and T.Abe. Encyclopedia Illustrated in Colour. 2. Fishes, pp.1–306, figs.1–912. Tokyo. 1958. (In Japanese.)

Tomoda, Y. Two New Catfishes of the Genus Parasilurus Found in Lake Biwa-Ko. - Mem. Coll. Sci. Kyoto Univ., 28B:347–354. 1961. 2 figs.

Torchio, M. I.Myctophidae (Pisces) presenti nel Mar Ligure. - Doriana, 2, No.91:1–6. 1958.

Torchio, M. Revisione degli Arnoglossus (Pisces, Pleuronectiformes) del mar Ligure. - Doriana, Suppl. agli Annali del Museo Civico di storia naturale "C.Doria," 3, 102, Res. Ligusticae, 117:1–11. 1959. ill.

Torchio, M. Osservazioni sui Bothidae delle acque italiane (Pisces, Pleuronectiformes). - Boll. Zool., 29:667-678. 1962.

Tortonese, E. Ricerche ed osservazioni sui Caracidi delle sottofamiglie Tetragonopterinae, Glandulocaudinae a Stethaprioninae (Teleostei, Plectospondyli). - Boll. Musei Zool. Anat. comp. R. Univ. Torino, 49:11-76, pls.1-5. 1941-1942. 8 text-figs.

Tortonese, E. Studi sui Plagiostomi. II - Evoluzione, corologia e sistematica della famiglia Sphyrinidae (Pesci Martello). - Boll. Ist. Mus. Zool. Univ. Torino, 2, No.2:37-75. 1950. 11 figs.

Tortonese, E. Gli Hemirhamphidae del Mediterraneo (Pisces, Synentognathi). - Ibid., 3, No.3:1-8. 1951-1952.

Tortonese, E. Ricerche sistematico-faunistiche sui Pesci d'acqua dolce dell'Anatolia. I. Ibid., 3, No.8:1-14. 1951-1952. 5 figs.

Tortonese, E. Monografia dei Carangini viventi nel Mediterraneo. - Annali Mus. civ. Stor. nat. Giacomo Doria, 65:259-324. 1951-1952. 19 figs.

Tortonese, E. Revisione delle specie Mediterranee della subfam. Sudinae (Pisces, Iniomi). - Boll. Pesca Piscic. Idrobiol., 6, No.2:1-12, figs.1-3. 1952.

Tortonese, E. Leptocardia, Cyclostomata, Selachii. - Fauna Ital., 2:1-334, 1-163. 1956. figs.

Tortonese, E. Revisione dei Centrolophidae (Pisces, Perciformes) del Mare Ligure (1). - Annali Mus. civ. Stor. nat. Giacomo Doria, 71:57-82. 1960. 5 figs.

Tortonese, E. Un nuovo Pesce mediterraneo di profondita: Eutelichthys leptochirus n.gen. et n.sp. (Fam. Eutelichthyidae, nov.). - Ibid., pp.226-232. ill.

Tortonese, E. Contributo allo studio degli Ophichthyidae del Mediterraneo (Pisces, Anguilliformes). - Ibid., pp.233-247. ill.

Tortonese, E. Révision des Gobiesocidae du golfe de Gênes. - Rapp. Comm. Int. Mer. Medit., 15, No.2:161-163. 1960.

Tortonese, E. Contributo allo studio dei Cirrhitidae (Pisces, Perciformes). - Doriana, Suppl. agli Ann. Mus. Stor. Natur. "G.Doria," 3, No.148:1-8. 1964. ill.

Traité de zoologie. ed. P.Grasse, 13:1813-2758. Paris. 1958. ill.

Travassos, H. Contribuicaõ ao estudo da familia Characidae Gill., 1893, II, III. - Summa bras. Biol., 1, No.5:1-32. 4 pls.; 1, No.9:1-13. 1946.

Travassos, H. Ictiofauna de Pirassununga. I. Subfamilia Parodontinae Eigenmann, 1910 (Cypriniformes). - Bolm. Mus. nac. Rio de J., n.s., Zool., pp.1-32. 1955. ill.

Travassos, H. Sôbre o gênero Deuterodon Eigenmann, 1907 (Characoidei - Tetragonopteridae). - Anais Acad. bras. Cienc., 29:73-101. 1957. 25 figs.

Travassos, H. Ictiofauna de Pirassununga. IV. Subordem Gymnotoidêi Berg, 1940. - Bolm. Mus. nac. Rio de J., Zool., 217:1-34. 1960. 22 figs.

Travassos, H. and M.P.Paiva. Lista dos sciaenidae marinhos brasi beiros, contendo chave de identificaçaõ e proposta de "nomes vulgares oficiais." - Bolm. Inst. Oceanogr., S Paulo, 8, Nos.1-2:139-169. 1959. 25 figs.

Travassos, H. and S.Y.Pinto. Estudos sôbre a familia Cichlidae. III. - Bolm. Mus. para "Emilio Goeldi," Ser. Zoologia, 23:1-18. 1959.

Tretjakoff, D.K. Morphologische Ähnlichkeit der Maenidae und der Sparidae. - C. r. Acad. Sci. URSS, Moscow N.S., pp.158-160. 1941.

Tret'yakov, D.K. Notes on the Phylogeny of Fish, pp.1-176. - Kiev, Akad. Nauk UkrSSR. 1944. (Translated into Russian from Ukrainian.)

Tret'yakov, D.K. Classification of Primitive Teleostei. - Izv. Akad. Nauk SSSR, Biol., 1:49-55. 1945. 2 figs.

Tret'yakov, D.K. Taxonomic Groups in Cyprinidae. - Zool. Zh., 25, No.2:149-156. 1946. 1 fig.

Tret'yakov, D.K. Fishes and Cyclostomata. Their Life and Importance. - Moscow-Leningrad, Akad. Nauk SSSR. 1949. 420 pp., ill.

Trewavas, E. A Contribution to the Classification of the Fishes of the Order Apodes, Based on the Osteology of Some Rare Eels. - Proc. Zool. Soc. Lond., pp.639-659. 1932. 4 pls., 9 text-figs.

Trewavas, E. On the Structure of Two Oceanic Fishes, Cyema atrum Günther and Opisthoproctus soleatus. - Ibid., pp.601-614, pl.2. 1933.

Trewavas, E. A Synopsis of the Cichlid Fishes of Lake Nyasa. - Ann. Mag. Nat. Hist., 10, No.16:65-118. 1935. 14 figs.

Trewavas, E. The Cichlid Fishes of Syria and Palestine. – Ibid., 11, No.9:526–536. 1942. 1 fig.

Trewavas, E. New Schilbeid Fishes from the Gold Coast, with a Synopsis of the African Genera. – Proc. Zool. Soc. Lond., 113B:164–171. 1943. 1 text-fig.

Trewavas, E. Cyprinodont Fishes of San Domingo, Island of Haiti. – Ibid., 118:408–415. 1948. 1 pl., 5 text-figs.

Trewavas, E. The Sciaenidae of West Africa: Synonyms in Four Works on West African Fishes and Key to the Genera of Sciaenidae in West African Waters. – C.C.T.A./C.S.A. West Coast, 60, No.8:2–5. (1960) 1961.

Trewavas, E. A Basis for Classifying the Sciaenid Fishes of Tropical West Africa. – Ann. Mag. Nat. Hist., 13, No.5, 51:167–176. 1962. ill.

Trewavas, E. The Sciaenid Fishes with a Single Mental Barbel. – Coepia, 1:107–117. 1964.

Trotter, E.S. Brotulid Fishes from the Arcturus Oceanographic Expedition. – Zoologica, N.Y., 8:107–125, pl.C, text-figs.29–33. 1926.

Tucker, D.W. The Fishes of the Genus Benthodesmus (Family Trichiuridae). – Proc. Zool. Soc. Lond., 123, No.1:171–187. 1953. 3 pls., 5 figs.

Tucker, D.W. Report "On the Fishes Collected by 'Rosaura' in the North and Central Atlantic, 1937–1938." Pt.1. Families Carcharhinidae, Torpedinidae, Rosauridae (nov.), Salmonidae, Alepocephalidae, Searsidae, Clupeidae. – Bull. Br. Mus. Nat. Hist., Zoology, 2:163–214. 1954. 2 pls., 19 figs.

Tucker, D.W. Studies on the Trichiuroid Fishes. (2). Benthodesmus tenuis (Günther) Collected by the Expédition océanographique Bele dans les eaux côtières de l'Atlantique sud (1948–1949), with Additional Notes on the Genus Benthodesmus. – Bull. Inst. r. Sci. nat. Belg., 31, No.64:1–26. 1955.

Tucker, D.W. Studies on the Trichiuroid Fishes. (3). A Preliminary Revision of the Family Trichiuridae. – Bull. Br. Mus. Nat. Hist., Zoology, 4, No.3:73–130, text-figs.1–23, pl.10. 1956.

Tucker, D.W. and J.W.Jones. On a Rare Deep-sea Fish Notacanthus phasaganorus Goode (Heteromi, Notacanthidae) from the Arctic Bear Isle Fishing Grounds. – Ibid., 1, No.5:69–79. 1951. 9 pls.

Turner, C.L. A Contribution to the Taxonomy and Zoogeography of the Goodeid Fishes. – Occ. Pap. Mus. Zool. Univ. Mich., 495:1–13. 1946. 1 pl.

Tyler, J.C. Triodon bursarius, a Plectognath Fish Connecting the Sclerodermi and Gymnodontes. – Copeia, 4:793–801. 1962. 1 fig.

Tyler, J.C. A Critique of Y. Le Danois' Work on the Classification of the Fishes of the Order Plectognathi. – Ibid., 1:203–206. 1963.

Uchida, K. The Fishes of Korea, Part 1. Nematognathi. – Bull. Fishery Exp. Stn. Pusan Fusan, pp.1–458. 1939. (In Japanese.)

Ueno, T. Studies on the Cyclopterid Fishes from Northern Japan and Adjacent Regions. 1. Remarks on Two Genera, Cyclolumpus and Eumicrotremus. – Bull. Fac. Fish. Hokkaido Univ., 4, No.4:273–295. 1954. 12 figs.

Ueno, T. First Record of a Strange Bathypelagic Species Referable to the Genus Centrolophus (Centrolophidae, Stromateiformes) from Japanese Waters with Remarks on the Specific Differentiation. – Ibid., 5, No.2:240–247, figs.1–4. 1954.

Ueno, T. Studies on the Deep-water Fishes from off Hokkaido and Adjacent Regions. I. On a Rare Fish, Zaprora silenus Jordan, Found off Kushiro, Hokkaido.– Jap. J. Ichthyol., 3, No.2:79–82. 1954.

Ueno, T. The Stromateid Fishes (Suborder Stromateoidei) Captured from the Waters of Hokkaido. – Scient. Rep. Hokkaido Fish Exp. Sta., 4:1–12. 1965. 6 figs. (In Japanese.)

Vaillant, L.L. Essai monographique sur les Silures du genre Synodontis. – Nouv. Archs. Mus. natn. Hist. nat., Paris, Ser.3, 7:233–284. 1895. 6 pls.

Vaillant, L.L. Essai monographique sur les Silures du genre Synodontis. – Ibid., Ser.3, 8:87–178. 1896.

Vaillant, L.L. Protopterus retropinnis et Epiceratodus foae, espèces nouvelles de l'Afrique équatoriale. – Bull. Mus. natn. Hist. nat., Paris, 5:219–222. 1899.

Van der Stigchel, J.W.B. The South American Nematognathi of the Museums at Leiden and Amsterdam.– Zool. Meded., Leiden, 27:1–204. 1947. 2 text-figs.

Vasnetsov, V.V. Phylogeny of the Schizothoracinae. – Trudy Inst. Morf. Zhivot. Akad. Nauk SSSR, 2:2–84. 1950. 20 figs.

Vereshchagin, G.Yu. Systematics and Biology of the Comephoridae. – Dokl. Akad. Nauk SSSR, A, pp.47–50. 1926.

Vernidub, M.F. Arrow-toothed Halibuts of the Far Eastern Sea. – Trudy Petergof. Biol. Inst., 16:182–199. 1938. ill.

Vilimovskii, N.D. Evolution and Distribution of Sculpins of the Family Cottidae. – Synopses of Reports, 2nd Inter. Oceanogr. Congr., 30 May – 9 June 1966, p.89. Moscow. 1966.

Villadolid, D. and P. Manacop. The Philippine Phallostethidae. – Philipp. J. Sci., 55:193–220. 1934. 5 pls.

Vinciguerra, D. Res Ligusticae. LXII. Del genere Hymenocephalus (Pesci, Macruridi) e particolarmente della specie Mediterranea (H. italicus Gigl.). – Annali Mus. civ. Stor. nat. Giacomo Doria, 56:1–13, pl.1. 1932.

Valdimirskaya, M.I. Whitefishes of Lake Imandra Basin. – Vopr. Ikhtiol., 6:136–148. 1956.

Vladykov, V.D. Quebec Lampreys (Petromyzonidae) 1. List of Species and their Economic Importance. – Contr. Dép. Pêch., Québ., 26:1–67. 1949. 21 text-figs.

Vladykov, V.D. Taxonomic Characters of the Eastern North America Chars (Salvelinus and Cristivomer). – J. Fish. Res. Bd. Can., 11, No.6:904–932. 1954. 12 figs.

Vladykov, V.D. A Review of Salmonid Genera and their Broad Geographical Distribution. – Trans. R. Soc. Can., 4, No.1:459–504, figs.1–17. 1963.

Vladykov, V.D. and W.I. Follett. The Teeth of Lampreys (Petromyzonidae): their Terminology and Use in a Key to the Holarctic Genera. – J. Fish. Res. Bd. Can., 24, No.5:1067–1075. 1967.

Vladykov, V.D. and J.R. Greeley. Order Acipenseroidei. – Contr. Dép. Pêch., Québ., 53:24–60. 1963. ill.

Vladykov, V.D. and J.R. Greeley. Acipenseroidei. – In: Fishes W.N.Atlantic. 3. Mem. Sears Found. Mar. Res., 1, No.3:24–58, figs.7–10. 1963.

Vladykov, V.D. and J.L. Tremblay. Nouvelles espèces de Lycodes (Pisces, Zoarcidae) du Saint-Laurent et révision de toutes les espèces du même genre de l'Atlantique occidental. – Fauna Flora laurent., 1:1–45. 1936. 17 figs.

Vlasova, E.K. Salmonoidei of the Transcarpathian Rivers. – Nauch. Zap. Uzhgorod. Gos. Univ., 40:89–100. 1959.

Wade, C.B. Two New Genera and Five New Species of Apodal Fishes from the Eastern Pacific. – Allan Hancock Pacif. Exped., 9, Nos.7, 8:181–214, pls.24–28. 1946.

Wagler, E. Die Coregonen in den Seen des Voralpengebietes. – Int. Revue Hydrobiol. Hydrogr., 30, Nos.1–2:1–48. 1934. 2 pls., 8 figs.

Wagler, E. Die Coregonen in den Seen des Voralpengebietes. IX. Die Systematik der Voralpencoregonen. – Ibid., 35:345–446. 1937. 7 pls., 5 figs.

Wagler, E. Die Lachsartigen (Salmonidae). II Teil. Coregonen. Demoll und Maier. – Handb. Binnenfisch. Mitteleur., 3:371–501. 1941. 109 figs.

Wagler, E. Die Coregonen in den Seen des Voralpengebietes. – Veröff. zool. StSamml., Münch., 1:3–62. 1950. 8 pls., 6 figs.

Wahlquist, H. A Field Key to the Batoid Fishes (Sawfishes, Guitarfishes, Skates and Rays) of Florida and Adjacent Waters. – Tech. Ser. Fla. St. Bd. Conserv., 50, No.6:1–20. 1966. ill.

Waite, E.R. Descriptions and Notes on Some Australian and Tasmanian Fishes. – Rec. Aust. Mus., 6, No.3:194–210, pls.34–36. 1906.

Waite, E.R. Scientific Results of the New Zealand Government Trawling Expedition, 1907. I. – Rec. Canterbury Mus., 1, No.2:41–156, pls.13–23. 1909.

Waite, E.R. Scientific Results of the New Zealand Government Trawling Expedition, 1907. II. – Ibid., 1, No.3:157–272, pls.24–57. 1911.

Waite, E.R. Fishes of the Genus Tripterygion and Related Genera in New Zealand. – Ibid., 2:1–16. 1913. 5 pls.

Waite, E.R. Illustrated Catalogue of the Fishes of South Australia. – Rec. S. Aust. Mus., 2, No.1:1–208. 1921. 293 figs., 1 pl.

Waite, E.R. and H.M. Hale. Review of the Lophobranchiate Fishes (Pipe-fishes and Sea-horses) of South Australia. – Ibid., 1:293–324. 1921.

Wakiya, Y. The Carangoid Fishes of Japan. – Ann. Carneg. Mus., 15, Nos.2–3:1–290, pls.15–38. 1924.

Wakiya, Y. A Review of Salangidae. – Zool. Mag., Tokyo, 48:835–845. 1936. 2 text-figs. (In Japanese, English summary, p.835.)

Wakiya, Y. and N. Takahasi. Study on Fishes of the Family Salangidae. – J. Coll. Agric. Imp. Univ. Tokyo, 14, No.4:265–296, pls.16–21. 1937.

Walford, L.A. The Sharks and Rays of California. – Fish. Bull. Divis. Fish Game Calif., 45:1–66. 1935. 57 figs.

Walters, V. Synopsis of the Lampridiform Suborder Veliferoidei. – Copeia, 3:245–247. 1960.

Walters, V. A Contribution to the Biology of the Giganturidae, with Description of a New Genus and Species. – Bull. Mus. Comp. Zool. Harv., 125:297–319. 1961. 7 figs.

Walters, V. On Two Hitherto Overlooked Teleost Families Guentheridae (Ateleopodiformes) and Radiicephalidae (Lampridiformes). – Copeia, 2:455–457. 1963.

Walters, V. Order Giganturoidei. – In: Fishes W.N. Atlantic. 4. Mem. Sears Found. Mar. Res., 1, No.4:566–577. 1964.

Walters, V. and J.E. Fitch. The Families and Genera of the Lampridiformes (Allotriognathi, Suborder Trachipteroidei). – Fish. Bull. Divis. Fish Game Calif., 46, No.4:441–451. 1960.

Walters, V. and C.R. Robins. A New Toadfish (Batrachoididae) Considered to Be a Glacial Relict in the West Indies. – Am. Mus. Novit., **2047**:1–21. 1961. 3 figs.

Wang, K.F. Preliminary Notes on Some Chinese Gobioid Fishes. – Sci. Q. Natn. Univ. Peking, 3, No.4:253–268. 1932.

Wang, K.F. Preliminary Notes on the Fishes of Chekiang (Elasmobranches). – Contr. Biol. Lab. Sci. Soc. China, Zool., Ser.9, 3:87–117. 1933. 12 figs.

Wang, K.F. A Synopsis of the Herring and Apodal Fishes of Fukien. – Rep. Mar. Biol. Ass. China, 3:33–49. 1934.

Wang, K.F. Preliminary Notes on the Fishes of Chekiang (Isospondyli, Apodes and Plectospondyli). – Contr. Biol. Lab. Sci. Soc. China, Zool. Ser.11, 1:1–65. 1935.

Wang, K.F. Notes on Mulloid Fishes from Hainan. – Ibid., Ser.12, 1:1–18. 1936.

Wang, K.F. The Labroid Fishes of Hainan. – Ibid., Ser.15:87–119. 1941.

Wang-I-K'ang. Classification of Fishes. Shanghai. 1958. 597 pp., 630 figs. (In Chinese.)

Watanabe, M. Studies on the Cottid Fishes of Japan. Tokyo. 1958. 461 pp., 222 figs., 124 pls. (In Japanese.)

Watanabe, M. Fauna japonica. Cottidae (Pisces). – Proc. Biogeogr. Soc. Japan, pp.1–218. 1960. 40 pls., 74 text-figs.

Waterman, T.H. Studies on Deep-sea Anglerfishes (Ceratioidea). I. An Historical Survey of Our Present State of Knowledge. – Bull. Mus. Comp. Zool. Harv., 85, No.3:65–81. 1939.

Waterman, T.H. Studies on Deep-sea Anglerfishes (Ceratioidea). III. The Comparative Anatomy of Gigantactis longicirra Waterman. – J. Morph., **82**:81–149. 1948. 10 text-figs.

Watson, M.E. Tunas (Genus Thunnus) of the Western North Atlantic. I. Key to the Species of Thunnus Based on Skeletal and Visceral Anatomy. – F.A.O. Fish Repts., 3, No.6:1153–1154. 1963.

Weber, M. and L.F. de Beaufort. The Fishes of the Indo-Australian Archipelago. II. Malacopterygii, Myctophoidea, Ostariophysi: I. Siluroidea. Leiden. 1913. 104 pp., 151 figs.

Weber, M. and L.F. de Beaufort. The Fishes of the Indo-Australian Archipelago. III. Ostariophysi: II. Cyprinoidea, Apodes, Synbranchii. 1916. 455 pp., 213 figs.

Weber, M. and L.F. de Beaufort. The Fishes of the Indo-Australian Archipelago. IV. Heteromi, Solenichthyes, Synentognathi, Percesoces, Labirinthici, Microcyprini. 1922. 410 pp., 103 figs.

Weber, M. and L.F. de Beaufort. The Fishes of the Indo-Australian Archipelago. V. Anacanthini, Allotriognathi, Heterosomata, Berycomorphi, Percomorphi: Kuhliidae, Apogonidae, Plesiopidae, Pseudoplesiopidae, Priacanthidae, Centropomidae. 1929. 458 pp., 98 figs.

Weber, M. and L.F. de Beaufort. The Fishes of the Indo-Australian Archipelago. VI. Perciformes (Continued): Serranidae, Theraponidae, Sillaginidae, Emmelichthyidae, Bathyclupeidae, Coryphaenidae, Carangidae, Rachycentridae, Pomatomidae, Lactariidae, Menidae, Leiognathidae, Mullidae. 1931. 448 pp., 81 figs.

Weber, M. and L.F. de Beaufort. The Fishes of the Indo-Australian Archipelago. VII. Perciformes (Continued): Chaetodontidae, Toxotidae, Monodactylidae, Pempheridae, Kyphosidae, Lutjanidae, Lobotidae, Sparidae, Nandidae, Sciaenidae, Malacanthidae, Cepolidae. 1936. 607 pp., 106 figs.

Weber, M. and L.F de Beaufort. The Fishes of the Indo-Australian Archipelago. VIII. Beaufort, L.F. de. Percomorphi (Continued): Cirrhitoidea, Labriformes, Pomacentriformes. 1940. 508 pp., 56 figs.

Weber, M. and L.F. de Beaufort. The Fishes of the Indo-Australian Archipelago. IX. Beaufort, L.F. de and W.M. Chapman. Percomorphi (Continued): Blennioidei. 1951. 484 pp., 89 figs.

Weber, M. and L.F. de Beaufort. The Fishes of the Indo-Australian Archipelago. X. Koumans, F.P. Gobioidea. 1953. 392 pp., 95 figs.

Weber, M. and L.F. de Beaufort. The Fishes of the Indo-Australian Archipelago. XI. Beaufort, L.F. de and J.C.Briggs. Scleroparei, Hypostomides, Pediculati, Plectognathi, Opistomi, Discocephali, Xenopterygii. 1962. 481 pp., 100 figs.

Webster, D.K. Myth and Maneater; the Story of the Shark. — Norton. 1963. 223 pp., pls.

Weed, A.C. Notes on Fishes of the Family Hemirhamphidae. – Zool. Ser. Field Mus. Nat. Hist., 20:41–66. 1933. 2 figs.

Weitzman, S.H. The Osteology and the Relationships of the South American Characid Fishes of the Subfamily Gasteropelecinae. – Stanford Ichthyol. Bull., 4:213–263. 1954. 18 figs.

Weitzman, S.H. Further Notes on the Relationships and Classification of the South American Characid Fishes of the Subfamily Gasteropelecinae. Ibid., 7:217–239. 1960. 8 figs.

Weitzman, S.H. The Osteology of Brycon meeki, a Generalized Characid Fish, with an Osteological Definition of the Family. – Ibid., 8, No.1:1–77. 1962.

Weitzman, S.H. Osteology and Relationships of South American Characid Fishes of Subfamilies Lebiasininae and Erythrininae, with Special Reference to Subtribe Nannostomina. – Proc. U.S. Natn. Mus., 116:127–169. 1964.

Weitzman, S.H. Review of South American Characid Fishes of Subtribe Nannostomina. – Ibid., 119, No.3538:1–56. 1966. 12 figs.

Weitzman, S.H. The Osteology and Relationships of the Astronesthidae, a Family of Oceanic Fishes. – Dana Rep., 71:1–56. 1967. 31 figs.

Weitzman, S.H. The Origin of the Stomiatoid Fishes with Comments on the Classification of Salmoniform Fishes. –Copeia, 3:507–540. 1967.

Welters, O. and M. Darder. Los Peces tropicales (Characidae), No.2:1–114. Barcelona, ed. Corona. Madrid. 1964. ill.

Wheeler, A.C. A Preliminary Revision of the Fishes of the Genus Aulostomus. – Ann. Mag. Nat. Hist., 12, No.8:613–623. 1955.

Wheeler, A.C. The Nomenclature of the European Fishes of the Subfamily Trachinotinae. – Ibid., 13, Nos.5, 57:529–540. 1962. ill.

Wheeler, J.F.G. The Genus Lethrinus in the Western Indian Ocean. – Fishery Publs., Colon. Off., 15:1–54. 1961. ill.

White, E.G. A Classification and Phylogeny of the Elasmobranch Fishes. – Am. Mus. Novit., 837:1–16. 1936.

White, E.G. Interrelationships of the Elasmobranchs, with a Key to the Order Galea. – Bull. Am. Mus. Nat. Hist., 74:25–138. 1937. 51 pls., 66 text-figs., 11 tables.

Whitehead, P.J.P. A New Species of Synodontis (Pisces, Mochocidae) and Notes on a Mormyrid Fish from the Eastern Rivers of Kenya. – Revue Zool. Bot. afr., 65:97–120. 1962. 7 figs.

Whitehead, P.J.P. The Species of Elops (Pisces, Elopidae). – Ann. Mag. Nat. Hist., 13, No.5:321–329. 1962.

Whitehead, P.J.P. A Review of the Indo-Pacific Gizzard Shad Genera Nematolosa, Clupanodon and Konosirus. – Bull. Br. Mus. Nat. Hist., Zool., 9, No.2:89–102. 1962. 4 figs.

Whitehead, P.J.P. The Pantanodontinae Edentulous Toothcarps from East Africa. – Ibid., 9, No.3:103–137. 1962. 19 figs.

Whitehead, P.J.P. Abdominal Scutes in the Round-herrings (Dussumieriidae).— Nature, Lond., 195:511–512. 1962. 3 figs.

Whitehead, P.J.P. A Contribution to the Classification of Clupeoid Fishes. – Ann. Mag. Nat. Hist., 13, No.5:737–750. 1963.

Whitehead, P.J.P. A Revision of the Recent Round-herrings (Pisces, Dussumieriidae). – Bull. Br. Mus. Nat. Hist., Zool., 10, No.6:305–380. 1963. 33 figs.

Whitehead, P.J.P. A Preliminary Revision of the Indo-Pacific Alosinae (Pisces, Clupeidae). – Ibid., 12:117–156. 1965. 13 figs.

Whitehead, P.J.P. A Review of the Elopoid and Clupeoid Fishes of the Red Sea and Adjacent Regions. – Ibid., pp.227–281. 4 figs.

Whitehead, P.J.P. A Review of the Elopoid and Clupeoid Fishes of the Red Sea and Adjacent Regions. – Ibid., 12, No.7:225–281. 1965.

Whitehead, P.J.P. The Elopoid and Clupeoid Fishes in Richardson's, 1846: "Ichthyology of the Seas of China and Japan." - Ibid., 14, No.2:15-56. 1966. ill.

Whitehead, P.J.P. and P.H. Greenwood. Mormyrid Fishes of the Genus Petrocephalus fliroides (Vinc.). - Revue Zool. Bot. afr., 60:283-295. 1959.

Whitley, G.P. Some Fishes of the Order Amphiprioniformes. - Mem. Qd. Mus., 9:207-246, pls.27-28. 1929. 4 text-figs.

Whitley, G.P. Studies in Ichthyology. 9. - Rec. Aust. Mus., 19, No.4:215-250, pl.18, figs.1-11. 1935.

Whitley, G.P. The Fishes of Australia. I. The Sharks, Rays, Devil-fish, and Other Primitive Fishes of Australia and New Zealand. 1940. 280 pp., 299 figs.

Whitley, G.P. New Sharks and Fishes from Western Australia. Pt.2. - Aust. Zool., 11:1-42, pl.1. 1945. 15 text-figs.

Whitley, G.P. Studies in Ichthyology. 15. - Rec. Aust. Mus., 22:389-408. 1951. 14 figs.

Whitley, G.P. New Fish Names and Records. - Proc. R. Zool. Soc. N.S.Wales for 1949-1950, pp.61-68, figs.8-10. 1951.

Whitley, G.P. New Locality Records for Some Australian Fishes. - Proc. R. Zool. Soc. N.S. Wales for 1952 - 1953, pp.23-30. 1954. 5 figs.

Whitley, G.P. Sidelights on New Zealand Ichthyology. - Aust. Zool., 12:110-119. 1955.

Whitley, G.P. and J. Allan. The Sea Horse and its Relatives. Melbourne. 1958. 84 pp., 24 figs.

Wickler, W. Zur Klassifikation der Cichlidae, am Beispiel der Gattungen Tropheus, Petrochromis, Haplochromis und Hemihaplochromis n.gen. (Pisces, Perciformes). - Senckenberg. biol., 44, No.2:83-96. 1963.

Wilby, G.V. On the Gobiesocid Genus Rimicola. - Copeia, 2:116. 1936.

Wilimovsky, N.J. The Correct Generic and Family Name of the Deepsea Hatchetfishes (Sternoptyx and Sternoptychidae). - Ibid., 3:247-248. 1951.

Williams, F. Fishes of the Family Carangidae in British East African Waters. - Ann. Mag. Nat. Hist., 13, No.1:369-430, pls.6-16. 1958.

Williams, F. The Barracudas (Genus Sphyraena) in British East African Waters. - Ibid., 13, No.2:92-128. 1959. 2 pls.

Williams, F. The Scombroid Fishes of East Africa. - Proc. Symp. Scombroid Fishes. Mar. Biol. Ass. India, Ser.1, 1:107-164. 1964. 8 figs.

Wimpenny, R.S. The Plaice. Being the Buckland Lectures for 1949. London. 1953. 145 pp., 27 figs.

Wisner, R.L. A New Genus and Species of Myctophid Fish from the South Central Pacific Ocean, with Notes on Related Genera and Designation of a New Tribe. - Copeia, 1:24-28. 1963.

Woods, L.P. Western Atlantic Species of the Genus Holocentrus. - Fieldiana, Zool., 37:91-119, figs.14-18. 1955.

Woods, L.P. A New Genus and Species of Fish from the Gulf of Mexico (Family Emmelichthyidae). - Ibid., 39:249-252. 1958. 1 fig.

Woods, L.P. and R.F. Inger. The Cave, Spring and Swamp Fishes of the Family Amblyopsidae of Central and Eastern United States. - Am. Midl. Nat., 58:232-256. 1957. 11 figs.

Woodward, A.S. On Some Extinct Fishes of the Teleostean Family Gonorhynchidae. - Proc. Zool. Soc. Lond., pp.500-504. 1896. ill.

Worthington, E.B. Scientific Results of the Cambridge Expedition to the East African Lakes, 1930-1931. 2. Fishes Other than Cichlidae. - J. Linn. Soc., 38:121-134. 1932. 5 figs.

Worthington, E.B. The Fishes (Other than Cichlidae) of Lake Bangweulu and Adjoining Regions, Including Descriptions of Three New Species. - Ann. Mag. Nat. Hist., 10, No.12:34-52. 1933. 1 fig.

Wu, H.W. Contribution à l'étude morphologique, biologique et systématique des Poissons Hétérosomes de la Chine. - Theses Univ., Paris, 244:1-179, figs.1-26. 1932.

Wu, H.W. and K.F. Wang. A Review of the Discobolous Fishes on the Chinese Coast (Cyclopteridae, Liparidae). - Contr. Biol. Lab. Sci. Soc. China, 9, No.2:77-86. 1933. 7 figs.

Wu, H.W. and K.F. Wang. Supplementary Notes on the Fishes of Heterosomata of China. - Ibid., 9, No.7:297-304, fig.1. 1933.

Wu, H.W. et al. The Cyprinid Fishes of China, pp.1-228. Shanghai. 1964. (In Chinese.)

Yamane, S. 1. A Revisional Study of the Surffishes Referable to the Genus Ditrema. - Bull. Misaki Mar. Biol., Inst. Kyoto Univ., 5:1-10. 1964.

Yamane, S. and O. Okamura. A Review of the Pacific Species of the Berycoid Fish Belonging to the Genus Polymixia. - Ibid., 9:13-20. 1966. ill.

Yarberry, E.L. Osteology of the Zoarcid Fish Melanostigma pammelas. – Copeia, 4:442–462. 1965. ill.

Yian, Y. Studies on Ribbon Fish (Trichiurus) and their Juveniles. – Q. Jl. Taiwan Mus., 13:75–81. 1960.

Yokita, T. and N. Mita. Introduction to Studies on the Carangoid and Sombroid Fishes in the Southern Regions of the Pacific Coast of Japan. – Rep. Nankai Reg. Fish. Res. Lab., 9:1–59. 1958. ill.

Ypiranga, P.S. Estudos sôbre e familia Cichlidae. V. (Actinopterygii, Perciformes). – Revta. bras. Biol., 23, No.1:45–48. 1963.

Zanandrea, G.S.J. Studies on European Lampreys. – Evolution, 15, No.4:523–534. 1961.

Zharov, V.L. Tunas from the Tropical Atlantic. – Trudy Balt. Nauchno-Issled. Inst. Morsk. Ryb. Khoz. Okeanogr. (BaltNIRO), 7:17–30. 1961.

Zharov, V.L. The System of Scombroid Fishes (Suborder Scombroidei, Order Perciformes). – Vopr. Ikhtiol., 7, No.2 (43):209–224. 1967.

Zharov, V.L., Yu. Zherebenkov, Yu. Kadil'nikov, et al. Tunas and their Fishing in the Atlantic Ocean. Kaliningrad. 1964. 182 pp., ill.

Zugmayer, E. Résultats des campagnes scientifiques accomplies sur son yacht Prince Albert I, 35:138, pl.4, fig.4. Monaco. 1911.

Zugmayer, E. Poissons provenant des campagnes du yacht Princesse Alice (Eurypharyngidae), pp.88–96, pl.IV, fig.3. Monaco. 1911.

Zugmayer, E. Diagnoses de quelques poissons nouveaux provenant des campagnes du yacht Hirondelle. II. (1911–1913). – Res. Camp. Sci. Monaco, 103:209–211. 1940.

GENERAL LITERATURE

Abe, T. Illustrative Key of Fishes. Tokyo. 1963. 358 pp.

Allyn, R.R. A Dictionary of Fishes. 9th edition. Florida, Great Outdoors Assoc. (1901). 1965. 140 pp., ill.

Angel, F. Petit atlas des poissons. 4. Poissons des eaux douces, espèces exotiques et d'ornement. 1946. 12 pls., 41 figs.

Angel, F. Atlas des poissons. 4. Poissons des eaux douces, espèces exotiques et d'ornement, aquariophilie. 4-e éd. et augment. N, Boubée et Cie, Paris. 1967. 195 pp.

Aoyagi, H. Coral Fishes. Tokyo, Maruzen Co. 1943. 224 pp., 37 pls.

Arnold, J.P. and E. Ahl. Fremdländische Süsswasserfische. Braunschweig. 1936. 592 pp., 7 pls.

Axelrod, H.R. Tropical Fish as a Hobby. N.Y. 1952. 264 pp., ill.

Axelrod, H.R. and L.P. Schultz. Handbook of Tropical Aquarium Fishes. N.Y., McGraw-Hill. 1955. 718 pp., ill. (col.).

Axelrod, H.R. and W. Vorderwinkler. Encyclopedia of Tropical Fishes, with Special Emphasis on Techniques of Breeding. N.Y., Sterling Publ. Co. 1957. 733 pp., ill. (some col.).

Axelrod, H.R. and W. Vorderwinkler. Salt Water Aquarium Fishes. New Jersey, USA, T.F.H. Publ. 1966. 335 figs.

Axelrod, H.R. et al. Exotic Tropical Fishes. N.Y. 1963. 884 pp., 850 figs.

Bailey, R.M. Forty-five Articles on Recent Fishes. – In: McGraw-Hill Encyclopedia of Science and Technology, pp.1–21. N.Y. 1960. ill.

Berg, L.S. A Classification of Fish-like Vertebrates. – Izv. Akad. Nauk SSSR, Biol. Ser., 4:1277–1280. 1936.

Berg, L.S. Classification of Fishes Both Recent and Fossil. – Trudy Zool. Inst. Akad. Nauk SSSR, 5, No.2:87–517. 1940. 190 figs. (In Russian.)

Berg, L.S. Classification of Fishes Both Recent and Fossil. – Trav. Inst. Zool. Acad. Sci., USSR, 5:517. 1947. Reprint, Edwards Brothers, Ann Arbor, Mich. (In English.)

Berg, L.S. System der rezenten und fossilen Fischartigen und Fische. – Deutsche Verh. Wissensch., pp.1–310. (Translated from the 2nd Russian edition.)

Berg, L.S. Classification of Fish-like Vertebrates and Fishes. – Trudy Zool. Inst. Akad. Nauk SSSR, 2nd edition, 20:1–286, figs.1–263. 1955. (In Russian.)

Berg, L.S. Classification of Fish-like Vertebrates and Fishes. 2nd edition, pp.1–283, figs.1–263. Peking. 1959. (In Chinese.)

Berg, L.S., T.S.Rass et al. (eds.). Commercial Fishes of the USSR. – Moscow, Pishchepromizdat. 1949. 787 pp., ill. and atlas, 230 pls.

Bougis, P. Atlas des poissons. Poissons des eaux douces, espèces françaises, 3. Espèces exotiques et d'aquarium, 4. Paris. 1948–1954. 348 pp., 144 figs., 36 pls.

Bougis, P. Atlas des poissons. Poissons marins. Fasc.I, 1:1–200. Paris. 1959; Fasc.II, 2:1–234. 1959. ill.

Briggs, J.C. Fishes of Worldwide (Circumtropical) Distribution. – Copeia, 3:171–180. 1960.

Briggs, J.C. Emendated Generic Names in Berg's Classification of Fishes. – Ibid., 2:161–166. 1961.

Buen, F. de. Las familias de peces de importancia económica. – F.A.O., pp.1–311. 1952. 256 figs.

Bussing, W.A. Studies of the Midwater Fishes of the Peru-Chile Trench. – Biol. Antarct. Seas. II. Antarct. Res. Ser.5, pp.185–227. 1965. 16 figs.

Bussing, W.A. and R.J.Lavenberg. A Classification of Bathypelagic Fishes. – Univ. S. California. Antarctic Research Program, pp.1–11. Rotoprint. 1964. 18 figs.

Coates, C.W. and J.W.Atz. Fishes of the World. – In: Drimmer. The Animal Kingdom, Garden City, N.Y., pp.1393–1640. 1954. ill.

Daniel, R.J. A Guide to Marketable Fish. – Proc. Trans. Lpool. Biol. Soc., App.1, 57:1–68. 1950. 12 figs.

Dean, B. A Bibliography of Fishes. – Am. Mus. Nat. Hist., 1:1–718. 1916; 2:1–702. 1917; 3:1–707. 1929.

Demidov, K.N. Freshwater Aquarium Fishes. 3rd edition. Rostov-on-Don. 1960. 176 pp.

Dutta, R. Tropical Fish Encyclopaedia, London, Pelham. 1966. 102 pp., ill.

Fitzgerald, B.V. and F.Lamonte. Game Fish of the World. London–Brussels, Nicholson and Watson. 1949. pp.i–xvii, 446 frontis col., 80 pls. (col.).

Frey, H. Illustrated Dictionary of Tropical Fish. – T.F.H. Publ., New Jersey, USA. 1966. 1000 photographs.

Gabrielson, I.N. and F.R. La Monte. The Fisherman's Encyclopedia, N.Y. 1950. 698 pp., ill.

Galkin, G.G. Atlas of the Scale Cover of Freshwater Teleosts. – Izv. Vses. Nauchno-Issled. Inst. Ozern. Rechn. Ryb. Khoz., 46:1–106. 1958. 155 figs.

Gilbert, P.W. (ed.). Sharks and Survival, pp.i–xiv+1–578. Boston, Heath and Co. 1963.

Golvan, Y.J. Catalogue systématique des noms de genres de poissons actuels. – Annls. Parasitol. Humaine et Co., 6bis:1–227. 1962.

Gosline, W.A. The Names of the Higher Categories of Fishes. – Copeia, 4:242–246. 1949.

Gosline, W.A. Teleostean Phylogeny. – Ibid., 2:186–194. 1961.

Gosline, W.A. The Suborders of Perciform Fishes. – Proc. U.S. Natn. Mus., 124, No.3647:1–78. 1968. 12 figs.

Grassé, P.P. (ed.). Agnathes et poissons. Anatomie, éthologie, systématique.–In: Traité de zoologie, 13, No.3:1813–2758. Paris. 1958.

Gregory, W.K. Fish Skulls: a Study of the Evolution of Natural Mechanism. – Trans. Am. Phil. Soc., (n.s.), 23, No.2:i–vii+75–481. 1933. 382 figs.

Gregory, W.K., C.L.Hubbs, and G.S.Myers. Zoological Names. A List of Phyla, Classes, and Orders. Prepared for Section F. – Am. Ass. Adv. Sci. Durham, North Carolina (Part of Fishes). 1949. 24 pp.

Gregory, W.K. and F.La Monte. The World of Fishes. – Am. Mus. Nat. Hist., 122:1–96. 1947. ill.

Günther, K. and K.Deckert. Creatures of the Deep Sea. London, George Allen and Unwin Ltd. 1956. 222 pp., 140 figs.

Günther, S. Freshwater Fishes of the World. 1962. 878 pp., 192 pls.

Hennig, W. Phylogenetic Systematics. Urbana. 1966. 263 pp., 69 figs.

Herald, E.S. Living Fishes of the World. London, Hamish Hamilton. 1961. 304 pp., 80 pls. (col.).

Herald, E.S. Les poissons vivants du monde. – Trad. Paris, Hachette. 1965. 326 pp., ill.

Hervey, G.F. and J.Hems. Freshwater Tropical Aquarium Fishes. An Encyclopedic Survey. London, Butterworths Press. 1952. pp.i–xiv+1–425. 32 pls. (8 col.), 87 figs.

Hiyama, Y. Poisonous Fishes of the South Sea. – Spec. Scient. Rep. U.S.Fish. Wildl. Serv. Fisheries, 25:1–188. 1950.

Hoedeman, J.J. Aquariumvissen-encyclopaedie. – Uitgeverij de Bezige bij. Amsterdam. 1959. 728 pp., 477 figs.

Howard, G.V. and E.Godfrey. A Summary of Information on the Fish and Fisheries of Latin America. – Fisheries Division, F.A.O. Washington, D.C. 1951. 262 pp.

Hubbs, C.L. A Fresh Look at Teleost Evolution. – Q. Rev. Biol., 42, No.1:40–41. 1967.

Hvass, H. Fishes of the World in Color. – N.Y., Dullon and Co., Inc. 1965. 156 pp.

Il'in, M.N. Breeding Fish in the Aquarium. – Moscow, Gos. Univ. 1965. 320 pp., ill.

Innes, W.T. Exotic Aquarium Fishes, a Work of General Reference. 19th ed. Edited by G.S.Myers. Philadelphia, Inners Publ. Co. 1957. 541 pp., ill.

Innes, W.T. Exotic Aquarium Fishes. – New Jersey, T.F.H. Publications, Inc. USA. Newest edition, with 70 new color photographs.

International Code of Zoological Nomenclature Adopted by the XV International Congress of Zoology 1961. – Intern. Commiss. Zool. Nomenclature (Br. Mus. Nat. Hist. London), pp.i–xviii+1–176. 1961.

Jordan, D.S. The Genera of Fishes (1833–1858). – Stanford Univ., 2:163–284. 1919.

Jordan, D.S. The Genera of Fishes (1859–1880). Ibid., 3:285–410. 1919.

Jordan, D.S. The Genera of Fishes (1881–1920). – Ibid., 4:411–576. 1920.

Jordan, D.S. A Classification of Fishes Including Families and Genera as Far as Known. – Biol. Sci. Stanford Univ., 3, No.2:77–243. 1923.

Jordan, D.S. Fishes. N.Y.-London. 1925. 773 pp., 673 figs.

Jordan, D.S. The Genera of Fishes and a Classification of Fishes. Reprinted with a New Foreword by George S.Myers and a Comprehensive Index by Hugh M.Smith and Leonard P.Schultz, Stanford, California. 1963. 800 pp.

Jordan, D.S. and B.W.Evermann. The Genera of Fishes (1758–1833). – Stanford Univ., 1:1–162. 1917.

Kennedy, M. The Sea Angler's Fishes. London. 1954. 524 pp., ill.

Klausewitz, W. and J.G.Nielsen. On Forskål's Collection of Fishes in the Zoological Museum of Copenhagen. – Spolia zool. Mus. Laun., 22:1–29. 1965. 38 pls., 3 figs.

Kumada, T. Illustrations of Edible Aquatic Fauna of the South Seas. 2nd ed. pp.i–vii+1–47, Kumada, Tokyo. 1949. 130 pls.

Ladiges, W. Tropical Fishes. Hamburg. 1934. 228 pp., ill.

Ladiges, W. Tropische Meeresfische, Arten, Lebensweise und Haltung. Kernen, Stuttgart. 1956. 122 pp.

La Monte, F. Marine Game Fishes of the World. N.Y. 1952. 190 pp., 69 pls., ill.

Le Danois, E. et al. Fishes of the World. London. 1957. 190 pp., 15 pls., ill.

Lindberg, G.U. An Attempt to Emend Generic Names in Berg's "Classification of Fishes." – Zool. Zh., 42, No.7:1105–1107. 1963.

McAllister, D.E. Evolution of Branchiostegals and Classification of Teleostome Fishes. – Bull. Natn. Mus. Can., 221:1–239. 1968. 3 figs., 21 pls.

McCormick, H.W. et al. Shadows in the Sea. London, Sudgwick and Jackson. 1964. 415 pp., ill.

McInerny, D. and A.G.Gerard. All About Tropical Fish. New ed. rev. Harrap, London, 1963. 408 pp., ill.

Mager, H.H. and S.K.Mager. A Guide to Tropical Fish. N.Y.-Washington. 1960. 277 pp., ill.

Marshall, N.B. Tiefseebiologie. Jena, Gustav Fischer. 1957. 334 pp., 5 pls. (col.), 103 figs.

Matsubara, K. Animal Systematic Taxonomy, 9, No.2, Vertebrates (Ib), Fishes, pp.197–531, figs.195–657. Tokyo. 1963. (In Japanese.).

Mayr, E., E.G.Linsley, and R.L.Usinger. Methods and Principles of Systematic Zoology. N.Y. McGraw-Hill. 1953. 328 pp.

Mednikov, B.M. On the Taxonomy and Phylogeny of Terrestrial Teleostei. – Byull. Mosk. Obshch. Ispyt. Prir. otd. biol., 67, No.1:155–156. 1962.

Migdalski, E.C. Angler's Guide to the Salt Water Game Fishes – Atlantic and Pacific. N.Y., Ronald Press. 1958. 506 pp.

Morgan, A. Tropical Fishes and Home Aquaria. – London, Rich and Cowan, 1936. pp.i–xvi+1–254, ill.

Morgan, R. World Sea Fisheries. – London, Methuen. 1956. 307 pp., 16 pls., 61 figs.

Multilingual Dictionary of Fish and Fish Products. – Fishg. News (Books). London. 1968. 448 pp.

Myers, G.S. Report of the Committee of Fish Classification. – Copeia, 4:326–327. 1950.

Myers, G.S. Trends in the Evolution of Teleostean Fishes. – Stanford Ichthyol. Bull., 7, No.3:27–30. 1958.

Myers, G.S. Nomenclator of Certain Terms Used for Higher Categories of Fishes. – Ibid., pp.31–42.

Neave, S.A. Nomenclator zoologicus. A List of the Names of Genera and Subgenera in Zoology from the 10th edition of Linnaeus 1758 to the End of 1945. London. 1939–1941. I. A–C, pp.i–xiv+1–957. 1939; II. D–L, pp.1–1025. 1939; III M–P, pp.1–1065. 1940; IV. Q–Z, pp.1–758. 1940; V, pp.1–308. 1936–1945.

Nielsen, J.G. Fishes from Depths Exceeding 6000 Meters. – Galathea Rep., 7:113–124. 1964. 8 figs.

Norman, J.R. Fishes Sci. Rep. John Murray Exped. 1933–1934, 7, No.1:1–116. 1939. 41 text-figs.

Norman, J.R. A Draft Synopsis of the Orders, Families and Genera of Recent Fishes and Fish-like Vertebrates. – Bull. Br. Mus. Nat. Hist. 1957. 649 pp.

Norman, J.R. and F.C.Fraser. Giant Fishes, Whales and Dolphins. London. 1937. 1372 pp., ill.
Norman, J.R. and F.C.Fraser. Giant Fishes, Whales and Dolphins. N.Y., Norton and Co., 1938. pp.1–13+1–361, 97 figs., 9 pls. (col.).
Nybelin, O. Deep-sea Bottom-fishes. – Rep. Swed. Deep Sea Exped., Zool., 20:250–345. 1957. 7 pls., 50 figs.
Parin, N.V. Ichthyofauna of the Ocean Epipelagic. – Moscow, "Nauka." 1968. 186 pp., 56 figs.
Parr, A.E. Concluding Report on Fishes with Species Index for Articles 1–7 (Fishes of the Third Oceanographic Expedition of the "Pawnee"). – Bull. Bingham Oceanogr. Coll., 3, No.7:1–79, figs.1–22. 1937.
Phillips, V.T. and M.E. Writings of Henry Weed Fowler, Published from 1897 to 1965. – Proc. Acad. Nat. Sci. Philad., 117:173–212. 1965.
Prosvirov, E. Poisonous and Dangerous Fishes. Kaliningrad. 1963. 80 pp., 34 figs.
Ray, C. and E.Clampi. The Underwater Guide to ... Marine Life. London. 1958. 338 pp., 194 figs.
Ricker, W.E. (ed.). Methods for Assessment of Fish Production in Fresh Waters. – Intern. Biol. Progr. Handbook, 3:1–314. London. 1968. ill.
Ricketts, E.F. et al. Between Pacific Tides. 3rd ed. revised. California, Stanford Univ. Press. 1964. pp.i–xiii+1–516, 46 pls., 135 figs.
Roule, L. Les poissons et le monde vivant des eaux. Paris. 1926–1937. 10 vols.
Roule, L. and F.Angel. Poissons provenant des campagnes du "Prince Albert I" de Monaco. – Rés. Camp. Sci. Monaco, 86:1–115. 1933, 4 pls.
Schneider, E. and L.F.Whitney. The Complete Guide to Tropical Fishes. N.Y. 1957. 549 pp.
Schultz, L.P. Results of a Preliminary Survey of Group Endings in Zoological Classifications above the Category of Genus. – Science, 113, No.2945:655–657. 1951.
Schultz, L.P. and E.M.Stern. The Ways of Fishes. Appendix – Classification of Fishes. – N.Y., Nordstrand Co. 1948. pp.i–xii+1–264, 80 figs.
Severtsov, A.N. Origin and Evolution of the Lower Vertebrates. – Moscow, Akad. Nauk SSSR. 1948. 397 pp., ill.
Smith, C.L. and R.M.Bailey. The Subocular Shelf of Fishes. – J. Morph., 110, No.1:1–18. 1962.
Spillman, Ch.J. Poissons d'eau douce. Ed. P.Lechevalier, Paris. 1961. 304 pp., ill.
Sterba, G. Süsswasserfische aus aller Welt. Leipzig, Urania. 1961. 637 pp., 1193 figs.
Sterba, G. Freshwater Fishes of the World. London. 1962. 878 pp., 1193 figs. Translated from German and Revised by D.W.Tucker, Vista Books.
Thinès, G. Les poissons aveugles. I. Origine, taxonomie, répartition géographique, comportement. – Annls. Soc. r. zool. Belg., 86:1–128. 1955. 36 figs.
Traité de zoologie. 1958. 13, No.3:1813–2758. Ed. p. Grassé. Paris. 1958.
Tret'yakov, D.K. Notes on the Phylogeny of Fishes. – Kiev, Akad. Nauk UkrSSR. 1948. 176 pp., 60 figs. (Translated into Russian from Ukrainian.)
Valenti, R.J. The Salt Water Aquarium Manuel. N.Y. 1968. 162 pp.
Wang-I-K'ang. Classification of Fishes. Shanghai. 1958. 597 pp., 630 figs. (In Chinese.)
Weber, M. and L.F.de Beaufort. The Fishes of the Indo-Australian Archipelago. I. Index of the Ichthyological Papers of P.Bleeker, Leiden. 1911. 410 pp.

REGIONAL LITERATURE
(Works on Individual Seas and Countries)

1 – Arctic
111 – basin of the Arctic seas
111a – fresh waters

Arshinov, N. Fishes of the Lakes of the Taiga Zone of Western Siberia. Author's Summary of Candidate Thesis. Tomsk University. 1964. 18 pp.
Belykh, F.I. Lake Lama and its Fishery. – Trudy Inst. Polyarn. Zemled., Ser. "Prom. Khoz.", 11:73–100. 1940.
Belyaeva, K.I. Fishes from Lake Keret. – Trudy Karelo-Fin Otd. Vses. Nauchno-Issled. Inst. Ozern. Rechn. Ryb. Khoz., 2:255–289. 1946. map.

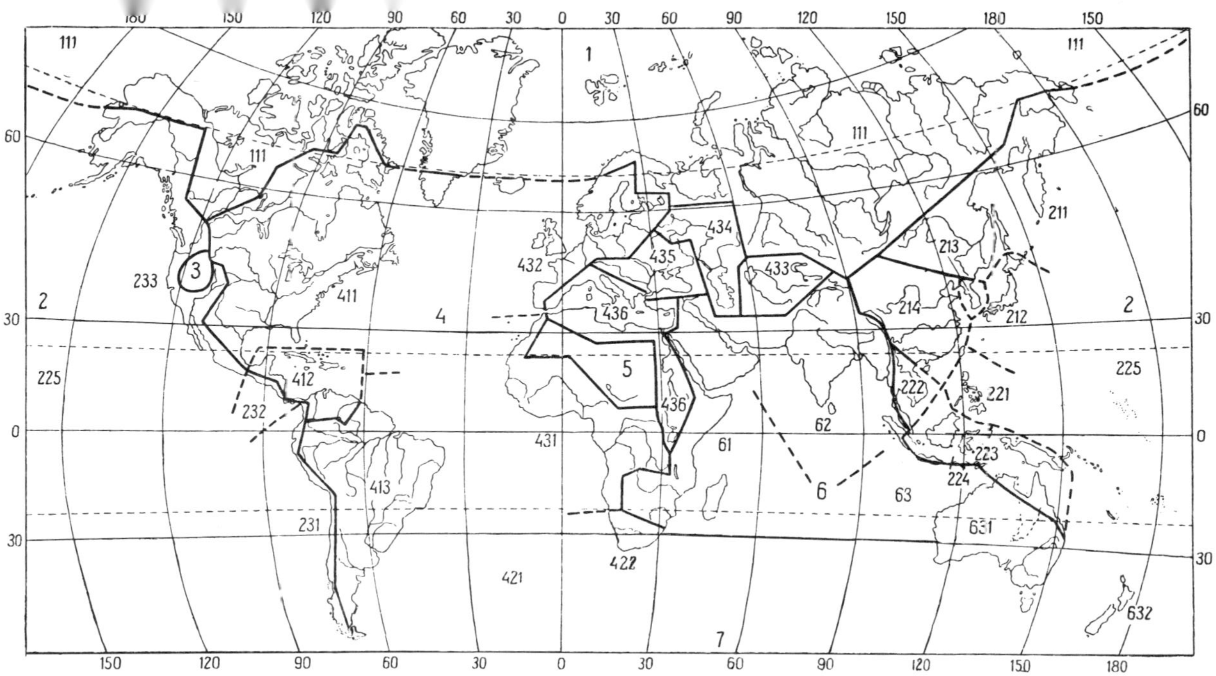

FIGURE 986. Scheme showing the distribution of works on individual seas and countries

1 – Arctic.
111 – basin of the Arctic seas.
2 – Pacific Ocean,
21 – western part:
211 – basin of the Far Eastern seas,
212 – Japan and Ryukyu Islands,
213 – Korea,
214 – basin of the China seas;
22 – southern part:
221 – Philippines,
222 – Indochina,
223 – Sunda Islands and New Guinea,
224 – Indo-Australian Archipelago,
225 – Oceania;
23 – eastern part:
231 – South America,
232 – Central America,
233 – North America.
3 – North America (as a whole).
4 – Atlantic Ocean,
41 – western part:
411 – North America,
412 – Central America and Caribbean islands,
413 – South America;
42 – southern part:
421 – Tristan da Cunha Islands;
422 – South Africa;
43 – eastern part:
431 – Africa,
432 – Europe,
433 – Northern Asia,
434 – basin of the Caspian Sea,
435 – basin of the Black Sea,
436 – basin of the Mediterranean Sea.
5 – Africa (as a whole)
6 – Indian Ocean,
61 – western part:
62 – northern part;
63 – eastern part;
631 – Australia,
632 – New Zealand.
7 – Antarctica.

Berg, L.S. Fishes from the Khatanga River Basin. – Mater. Kom. Izuch. Yakut. Respubl., pp.1–22. 1926. ill.

Berg, L.S. Freshwater Fishes of the USSR. 4th edition, Leningrad–Moscow. 1:1–466. 1948; 2:467–926. 1949; 3:927–1382. 1949. 943 figs.

Berg, L.S. and I.F. Pravdin. Fishes of the Kola Peninsula. – Izv. Vses. Nauchno-Issled. Inst. Ozern Rechn. Ryb. Khoz., 26, No.2:3–24. 1948.

Berezovskii, A.I. Ichthyofauna of the Lakes of the Minusinsk and Achinsk Districts of Yenisei Province. – Trudy Sib. Ikhtiol. Lab., 2, No.1:11–76. 1924.

Bogan, F.E. Ichthyofauna of the Ilmen Reservation and Some Lakes of the Adjacent Regions. – Trudy Il'men. Zapoved., 7:33–68. 1959.

Borisov, P.G. Fishes of the Lena River. – Trudy Yakutsk Kom. Akad. Nauk SSSR, 9:1–181. 1928. 6 pls.

Chaban, A.P. Fishes from the Mouth of the Kamennogorsk Reservoir and Biological Principles of Fishery. Author's Summary of Candidate Thesis. Tomsk University. 1965. 19 pp.

Chao K'en-t'ang and E. Ku-la. New Data on the Distribution of Freshwater Fishes in Inland Waters of Mongolia. – Tun Wuhsüeh Tsachin, 6:216–220. Ulan Bator. 1964. (In Mongolian.)

Danilenko, L.A. Ichthyofauna of the Volonga River in the Arkhangel'sk Region. – Vopr. Ikhtiol., 4, No.2(31):382–384. 1964.

Dmitriev, V.I. Fishes and Fishery in the Lower Reaches of the Yenisei. – Trudy Inst. Polyarn. Zemled., Ser. "Prom. Khoz.", 16:7–36. 1941.

Dorogostaiskii, V.Ch. A Key to the Fishes from the Basin of Lake Baikal and the Angara River. Irkutsk. 1926.

Dryagin, P.A. Fishery Resources of Yakutia. – "Yakutskaya ASSR," No.5:1–94, figs.1–4. Leningrad, Akad. Nauk SSSR. 1933. 2 pls.

Dryagin, P.A. Commercial Fishes of the Ob-Irtysh Basin. – Izv. Vses. Nauchno-Issled. Inst. Ozern. Rechn. Ryb. Khoz., 25, No.2:3–104. 1948.

Dryagin, P.A. New Data on the Geography of Fishes from the Continental Waters of Siberia. – In: Proc. 2nd All-Union Geographical Congress, pp.215–220. Moscow. 1949.

Dul'keit, G.D. Ichthyofauna of Lake Teletskoe and the Bii River. – In: Zametki po faune i flore Sibiri, 8:9–12. Tomsk. 1949.

Fishes and Fishery in Eastern Siberia. – Izv. Vses. Nauchno-Issled. Ozern. Rechn. Ryb. Khoz., 35:1–84. 1955.

Fishes of the Murmansk Region. Habitat Conditions, Life and Fishery. Murmansk. 1968. 336 pp.

Galkin, G.G. and A.N. Komoshev. Fishes from Lakes of the Murmansk Region. – In: Synopses of Reports 9th Sci. conf. on Studying Water Bodies of the Baltic Region 14–16 September 1961, pp.46–49. Riga. 1961.

Gundrizer, A.N. Ichthyological and Geographical Zonation of West Mongolia and Adjacent Regions of Siberia. – Dokl. Zool. soveshch. posvyashchennogo 100-letiyu so dnya rozhdeniya M.D.Ruzskogo, pp.123–125. Tomsk. 1964.

Ioganzen, B.G. Fishes from the Ob River Basin. Tomsk. 1948. 62 pp., ill.

Ioganzen, B.G., A.N. Gundrizer, V.V. Kafanova, and G.M. Krivoshchekov. Lake Teletskoe (Fishes, 66–88). Barnaul. 1963. 102 pp., ill.

Ivanova, Z.A. Fishes of the Steppe Zone of the Altai Territory. Barnaul. 1962. 152 pp., ill.

Ivanova, Z.A. Fishes of the Steppe Zone of the Altai Territory. Author's Summary of Candidate Thesis. Tomsk University. 1963. 18 pp.

Karantonis, F.E., F.N. Kirillov, and F.B. Mukhomediyarov. Fishes of the Central Reaches of the Lena River. (On the Problem of Fishery in the Basin). – Trudy Inst. Biol. Yakutsk. Fil. Akad. Nauk SSSR, 2:3–144. 1956.

Karasev, G.L. The Specific Composition of Fishes in the Ivano-Arakhleiskie Lakes (Transbaikalia). – Izv. Zabaikal. Otd. Geogr. Obshch. SSSR, 1, No.1:104–105. 1965.

Kartushin, A.I. Run-of-the-Mill Fishes of the Floodplain System of Lake Baikal. Author's Summary of Candidate Thesis. Irkutsk University. 1966. 24 pp.

Kirillov, F.N. Fishes of the Indigirka River and their Fishery. Author's Summary of Candidate Thesis. – Yakutsk Fil. Akad. Nauk SSSR. 1953. 14 pp.

Kirillov, F.N. Fishes from the Indigirka River. – Izv. Vses. Nauchno-Issled. Inst. Ozern. Rechn. Ryb. Khoz., 35:141–167, fig.2. 1955.

Kirillov, F.N. Water Bodies of Yakutia and their Fishes. Yakutsk. 1955. 48 pp.

Kirillov, F.N. (ed.). Fauna of Fishes and Invertebrates of the Vilyui River. – Yakutsk. Fil. Sib. Otd. Akad. Nauk SSSR. 1962. 161 pp.

Kirillov, F.N. Fishes of the Vilyui River Basin. – Trudy Inst. Biol., Yakutsk. Fil. Sib. Otd. Akad. Nauk SSSR, 8:5–71. 1964. 14 figs.

Kornilova, V.P. Ichthyofauna of the Lake of Golodnaya Bay in the Pechora Delta. – In: Mater. rybokhoz. issled. Sevanskogo basseina, 9:32–41. 1967.

Kozhevnikov, G.P. Fishery Resources of the Lakes of the Vilyui Lowlands. – Izv. Vses. Nauchno-Issled. Inst. Ozern. Rechn. Ryb. Khoz., 35:168–183. 1955.

Kozhov, M.M. Composition and Distribution of the Fauna of Eastern Siberia. Yakutsk. 1926. 40 pp.

Kozhov, M.M. Lake Baikal and its Life. – Monographiae biol., 1:1–360. 1963. 111 figs., 3 pls. (col.).

Kuchina, E.S. Features of the Ichthyofauna of the Pechora River within the Ust-Usa Region. – Trudy Komi Fil. Akad. Nauk SSSR, 4:142–155. 1956.

Kuchina, E.S. New Data on the Ichthyofauna of the Pechora River Basin. – Izv. Komi Fil. Vses. Geogr. Obshch., 5:184–187. 1959.

Lindsey, C.C. Distribution and Taxonomy of Fishes in the Mackenzie Drainage of British Columbia. – J. Fish Res. Bd. Can., 13:759–789. 1956.

Logashov, M.V. Lake Melkoe and its Fishery. – Trudy Inst. Polyarn. Zemled. Ser. "Prom. Khoz.," 11:1–72. 1940.

Lukash, B.S. Fishes from the Vychegda River. – In: Sever, pp.163–176. Vologda. 1923.

Materials on the Ichthyofauna of the North Ob Area. – Trudy Salekhardsk. Statsionara. Ural'sk Fil. Akad. Nauk SSSR, 3:1–31. Sverdlovsk. 1963. ill.

Mel'yantsev, V.G. Fishes of Pyaozero. Petrozavodsk. 1954. 120 pp.

Men'shikov, M.I. On the Ichthyofauna of Lake Marka-Kul. – Uchen. Zap. Perm. Gos. Univ., 3, No.2:119–144. 1939.

Men'shikov, M.I. Fishes from the Ob River Basin. Author's Summary of Doctoral Thesis, Leningrad University. 1949. 9 pp.

Mikhin, V.S. Fishes and Fishery of the Khatanga River and Khatanga Bay. – Trudy Inst. Polyarn. Zemled., Ser. "Prom. Khoz.," 16:37–72. 1941.

Mikhin, V.S. Fishes from Lake Taimyr and Taimyr Bay. – Izv. Vses. Nauchno-Issled. Inst. Ozern. Rechn. Ryb. Khoz., 35:5–44, fig.21, pl.31. 1955.

Mitrofanov, V.P. Fishes from Lake Marka-Kul. – Trudy Konf. ryb. Khoz. respubl. Sred. Azii i Kazakhstana, pp.51–61. Frunze. 1958.

Mitrofanov, V.P. Fishes from Lake Marka-Kul. Author's Summary of Candidate Thesis. – Frunze, Akad. Nauk KirgSSR. 1961. 20 pp.

Moskalenko, B.K. Whitefishes from the Ob River Basin. – Prom. Biol. Ocherk. Tyumen'. 1955. 108 pp.

Nikol'skii, G.V., G.I. Morozova, N.L. Gromchevskaya, and V.A. Pikuleva. Fishes of the Upper Pechora Basin. Contribution to the Study of the Fauna and Flora of the USSR. – Byull. Mosk. Obshch. Ispyt. Prir., New Ser. Otd. Zool., 6, No.21:1–223, figs.1–10. 1947.

Novikov, A.S. Fishes of the Kolyma River. – Moscow, "Nauka." 1966. 135 pp., ill.

Novikov, A.S. Fishes of the Kolyma River. Author's Summary of Candidate Thesis. Irkutsk University. 1967. 20 pp.

Novikov, P.I. Fishes from the Water Bodies of the Arkhangel'sk Region and their Commercial Importance. Arkhangel'sk. 1964. 143 pp., ill.

Ol'shanskaya, O.L. A Survey of the Ichthyofauna of the Pyasina River. – Vopr. Ikhtiol., 5, No.2(35):262–278. 1965.

Ostroumov, N.A. Fishes and Fishery of the Pyasina River. – Trudy Polgar. Kom., 30:7–114. 1937.

Ostroumov, N.A. Fishes from the Middle and Lower Reaches of the Pechora River. – Dokl. Akad. Nauk SSSR, 59, No.8:1497–1500. 1948.

Ostroumov, N.A. Data on the Fishes of the Pechora River. – Trudy Karelo-Fin. Otd. Vses. Nauchno-Issled. Inst. Ozern. Rechn. Ryb. Khoz., 3:307–320. 1951.

Ostroumov, N.A. Fishes of the Mezen River. – Izv. Komi Fil. Vses. Geogr. Obshch., 2:33–41. 1954.

Pallon, L.O. Fishes and Fishery of Segozero. – Trudy Olonets. Nauch. Eksped., 8, No.3:3–34. 1929.

Petrov, V.V. Ichthyofauna of Lakes of the Monche and Vol'chya Tundras. – Trudy Otd. Gidrol. Len. Obl. Gidrometeorol. Upr. Mater. Monchezerskoi Limnol. Eksped., pp.133–168. 1933.

Pirozhnikov, P.L. The Pyasina River and its Fishery Resources. – In: Za industrializatsiyu sovetskogo Vostoka, 3:166–209. 1933.

Podlesnyi, A.V. Fishes of the Yenisei River, Life Conditions and Fishery. – Izv. Vses. Nauchno-Issled. Inst. Ozern. Rechn. Ryb Khoz., 44:97–178. 1958.

Podlesnyi, A.V. and A.A.Lobovikova. Fishes of Lake Taimyr. – Vopr. Geogr. Sib., 2:269–291. Tomsk. 1951.

Probatov, A.N. Fishery Research Material on Kara Bay and the Kara River. – Moscow, Vses. nauchno-issled. inst. ryb. khoz. okeanogr. 1934. 140 pp. (col.).

Rawson, D.S. Studies on the Fish of Great Slave Lake. – J. Fish Res. Bd. Can., 8:207–240. 1951. 14 figs., 9 tables.

Rodionova, T. Zur Ichthyologie des Baikalseesystems. – Zool. Anz., 69:11–12. 1927.

Ruzskii, M.D. Fishes of the Tom River. – Izv. Inst. Issled. Sibiri; Trudy Estest.-Istor. Otd., 1:29–41. Tomsk. 1920.

Scott, W.B. A Checklist of the Freshwater Fishes of Canada and Alaska. – Roy. Ontario Mus., Ottawa, Div. Zool. a. Paleontol. Rotoprint. 1958. 30 pp.

Smirnov, A. Fishes of Segozero and Means of Increasing their Productivity. Author's Summary of Candidate Thesis. Petrozavodsk. 1953. 15 pp.

Soldatov, V.K. Fishes from the Pechora River. – Trudy Sev. Nauchno-Prom. Eksped., 17:1–73. 1924.

Solovkina, L.N. Data on the Ichthyofauna of the Usa River. – Trudy Komi Fil. Akad. Nauk SSSR, 4:132–141. 1956.

Solovkina, L.N. Fishes of the Middle and Lower Reaches of the Usa River. – In: Ryby basseina reki Usy i ikh kormovye resursy; Trudy Komi Fil. Akad. Nauk SSSR, pp.88–135. 1962.

Starikov, P.S. Fishes of the Butyar-Mongol SSR. Ulan-Ude. 1965. 33 pp., ill.

Tatarnikova, E.A. Fishes from the Vasyugan River Basin. Author's Summary of Candidate Thesis. Tomsk University. 1968. 17 pp.

Tolchanev, V.S. Fishes of Lake Bol'shoi Kisyagach (Il'men Reservation). – Trudy Perm. Univ., 10, No.2:139–152. 1948.

Tsepkin, E.A. Ichthyofauna of the Ingoda and Shilka Rivers and Some of its Biological Characteristics. – Nauch. Dokl. Vyssh. Shk., Biol., 2:40–43. 1962.

Veber, D.G. and V.F.Titova. Fishes of Lakes Mikkeli and Kroshnozero (and their Commercial Importance). – Trudy Karelo-Fin. Fil. Akad. Nauk SSSR, 2:12–31. 1956.

Walters, V. Fishes of Western Arctic America and Eastern Arctic Siberia. Taxonomy and Zoogeography. – Bull. Am. Mus. Nat. Hist., 106, No.5:259–368. 1955. 3 maps.

Zhinkin, L.N. On Fishes from Lakes of the Katun Alps. – In: Issledovaniya ozer SSSR, 8:293–297. 1935.

Zvereva, O.S., E.S.Kuchina, and N.A.Ostroumov. Fishes and Fishery of the Middle and Lower Reaches of the Pechora River. – Komi Fil. Akad. Nauk SSSR, pp.3–239. 1953. (col.).

111b – marine waters

Altukhov, K.A., A.A.Mikhailovskaya, F.B.Mukhomediyarov et al. Fishes of the White Sea. Petrozavodsk. 1958. 162 pp., ill.

Andriashev, A.P. A Contribution to the Knowledge of the Fishes from the Bering and Chukchi Seas.— Spec. Scient. Rep. U.S. Fish. Wildl. Serv. Fisheries, 145:1–81. 1955. ill.

Andriashev, A.P. Fishes of the Northern Seas of the USSR. – Israel Progr. Sci. Transl. Jerusalem. 1964. 617 pp., 297 figs.

Andriyashev, A.P. Contribution to the Study of Fishes of the Laptev Sea. – Trudy Zool. Inst. Akad. Nauk SSSR, 7:76–100. 1948.

Andriyashev, A.P. Fishes of the Chukchi Sea and Bering Strait. – In: Krainii severo-vostok Soyuza SSR, 2:311–322. Moscow–Leningrad. 1952.

Andriyashev, A.P. Fishes of the Northern Seas of the USSR. – Moscow–Leningrad, Akad. Nauk SSSR. 1954. 566 pp., 300 figs.

Andriyashev, A.P. A List of Fishes Collected by the Expedition on the Icebreaker "F.Litke" (1955) to the North of Franz Josef Land and Spitsbergen. – Trudy Arkt. Antarkt. Inst., 259:373–377. 1964.

Burmakin, E.V. Composition of the Ichthyofauna in the Basin of Gyda Bay. – Problemy Arktiki, 3:93–97. 1938.

Burmakin, E.V. Fishes from Ob Bay. – Trudy Inst. Polyarn. Zemled., Ser. "Prom. Khoz.," 10:33–47. 1940.

Burmakin, E.V. Fishes from the Soviet Arctic Archipelago. – Trudy Arktich. Inst., 205:127–151. 1957.

Chumaevskaya-Svetovidova, E.V. Specific Composition of Fishes in the Region of the Murmansk Biological Station. – Trudy Murman. Biol. Sta., 2:5–11. 1955.

Commercial Fishes of the Barents and White Seas. – Polyar. nauch.-issled. inst. morsk. ryb. khoz. i okeanogr., pp.1–238, figs.1–59. 1952.

Deryugin, K.M. Fauna of the White Sea and its Life Conditions. – Issled. Morei SSSR, Nos.7–8:1–511. Leningrad. 1928.

Esipov, V.K. Fishes Collected by the Expedition to Franz Josef Land in Summer 1929.– Trudy Inst. Izuch. Severa, 49:156–165. 1931.

Esipov, V.K. Fishes Collected by the 1930 Expedition on the Icebreaker "G.Sedov" to Franz Josef Land and Severnaya Zemlya.– Trudy Arktich. Inst., 8:93–100. 1933.

Esipov, V.K. Index to the Literature on the Fisheries of the European North of the USSR (1917–1933), pp.3–145. – Leningrad, Arktich. Inst. 1935.

Esipov, V.K. Fishes from the Polar Basin and Adjacent Depths. – Problemy Arktiki, 4:85–97. 1937.

Esipov, V.K. Commercial Fishes of the Barents Sea. Leningrad–Moscow. 1937. 109 pp., ill.

Esipov, V.K. Fishes Collected by the Expedition on the Icebreaker "Sadko" in 1935. – Zool. Zh., 18, No.5:877–887. 1939.

Esipov, V.K. Fishes of the Laptev Sea. – Ibid., 19, No.1:139–142. 1940.

Esipov, V.K. Fishes of the Kara Sea. – Leningrad, Akad. Nauk SSSR. 1952. 147 pp.

Hansen, P.M. and F.Hermann. Fisken og havet ved Grønland. – Skr. Kommn. Havunders., Kbh., 5:1–128. 1953. 61 figs.

Hognestad, P.T. Contributions to the Fish Fauna of Spitsbergen. 1. The Fish Fauna of Isfjorden. 1961. – Norway, Tromsø Museum, pp.1–37. 1962. ill; Acta boreal., A, 18:1–36. 1962. ill.

Jensen, A.S. Researches on the Distribution, Biology, and Systematics of the Greenland Fishes. – Vidensk. Meddr. dansk. naturh. Foren, 74:89–109. 1922. 2 figs.

Jensen, A.S. Investigations of the "Dana" in West Greenland Waters, 1925. Appendix (List of the Fishes of Greenland). – Rapp. P.-v. Réun. Commn. int. Explor. scient. Mer Méditerr., 39:85–102. 1926.

Jensen, A.S. Contribution to the Ichthyofauna of Greenland. – Spolia zool. Mus. haun., pp.1–44. 1942; pp.1–60. 1944; pp.1–182. 1948. 20 pls., ill.

Kirillov, F.N. Fishes of Tiksi Bay. – Uchen. Zap. Tomsk. Univ., 15:155–162. 1950.

Knipovich, N.M. Keys to Marine and Anadromous Fish from the European Arctic Ocean and White and Kara Seas. – Trudy Sevan. Nauch. Prom. Eksped., 2:1–20. 1920.

Knipovich, N.M. A Key to Fishes from the Barents, White and Kara Seas. – Trudy Inst. Izuch. Severa, 27:1–183. 1926. 126 figs.

Knipovich, N.M. Keys to Marine and Anadromous Fish from the European Arctic Ocean and White and Kara Seas. 2nd edition. – Ibid., 31:1–36. 1926.

McAllister, D.E. Keys to the Marine Fishes of Arctic Canada. – Nat. Hist. Pap. Natn. Mus. Can., 5:1–21. 1960. ill.

McAllister, D.E. Revised Keys to the Marine Fishes of Arctic Canada. Rotoprint. 1961. 17 pp.

McAllister, D.E. Bibliography of the Marine Fishes of Arctic Canada. – Inst. Fisher. Univ. Brit. Columbia, Vancouver, Canada Mus. Contribution, 8:1–16. 1966.

Maslov, N.A. et al. Commercial Bottom Fishes of the Barents Sea. – Trudy Polyar. Inst. Ryb. Khoz. Okeanogr., 8:1–428. 1944.

Mukhomediyarov, F.B. Ichthyofauna of Chupa Bay. – In: Mater. kompleksn. izuch. Belogo morya, 2:90–99. – Moscow–Leningrad, Akad. Nauk SSSR. 1963.

Nikolaev, A.P. Specific Composition of Fishes from the "Pomorskoe" and Karelian Shores of the White Sea. – Izv. Karelo-Fin. Fil. Akad. Nauk SSSR, 3:93–99. 1951.

Pietschmann, V. Ichthyologische Ergebnisse einer Fischdampferreise nach Grönland. – Meddr. Grønland, 92, No.3:1–59. 1952. 23 figs.

Pirozhnikov, P.L. New Data on Fishes of the Laptev Sea. – Dokl. Akad. Nauk SSSR, 56, No.4:441–443. 1947.

Popov, A.M. On Fishes of the Kara Sea and Adjacent Regions of the Barents Sea. – Trudy Leningr. Obshch. Estestvoisp., 6, No.1:27–58. 1926.

Popov, A.M. On the Fishes of the Siberian Sea. – Arktika, 1:157–167. 1933. 1 pl., figs. (In English, Russian summary.)

Popov, A.M. The Fauna of Avacha Bay and its Distribution into Communities. – C. r. Acad. Sci. URSS, 4(9), Nos.8–9(77):373–376. 1935.

Rass, T.S. A Survey of Fishes Collected by the Murmansk Biological Station in Summer 1926. – Rab. Murman. Biol. Sta., 3:1–30. Aleksandrovsk na Murmane. 1930.

Rass, T.S. Composition of the Ichthyofauna of the Barents Sea and Taxonomic Characters of the Eggs and Larvae of Fishes from This Water Body. – Trudy Vses. Nauchno-Issled. Inst. Morsk. Ryb. Khoz. Okeanogr., 17:7–65. 1949.

Rendahl, H. Fische aus dem östlichen Sibirischen Eismeer und dem Nordpazifik. – Ark. Zool., 22A, No.10:1–82. 1931.

Soldatov, V.K. Data on Fishes from the Kara Sea and Eastern Part of the Barents Sea from the Collections by the Institute's Expedition of 1921. With an Appendix of a List of Fishes Collected by Zoologist I.D.Strel'nikov in the Kara Sea in 1921. – Trudy Plovuch. Morsk. Nauch. Inst., 3:1–80. 1923.

Suvorov, E.K. On the Fishes of the Chesha Bay. – Trudy Inst. Izuch. Severa, 43:101–131. 1929.

Walters, V. The Fishes Collected by the Canadian Arctic Expedition, 1923 – 1918. With Additional Notes on the Ichthyofauna of Western Arctic Canada. – Bull. Nat. Mus. Canada, 128:257–274. 1953. ill.

Yessipov, W.K. Brief Review of the Ichthyofauna of the Kara Sea. – Arctica, 1:169–185. 1933.

Zborovskaya, M.B. A List of Fishes from Gridin Bay of the White Sea. – Trudy Karelo-Fin. Otd. Vses. Nauchno-Issled. Inst. Ozern. Rechn. Ryb. Khoz., 3:197–210. 1951.

2 – Pacific Ocean
21 – western part
211 – basin of the Far Eastern seas
211a – fresh waters

Berezantsev, Yu.A. Fishes from the Upper Reaches of the Tym River on Sakhalin. – Vopr. Geogr. Dal'. Vostoka, 2:111–119. 1955.

Berg, L.S. Fishes from the Sungara River. – Ezheg. Zool. Muz. Akad. Nauk SSSR, 32, No.2:211–225. 1931. ill.

Berg, L.S. Freshwater Fishes of the USSR. 4th edition. Leningrad-Moscow. I, pp.1–466. 1948; 2:467–926. 1949; 3:927–1382. 1949. 943 figs.

Dashi-Dorzhi, A. Fishes from the Rivers and Lakes of Eastern Mongolia. – Shinzhlekh ukhaan, 2:56–59. 1954. (In Mongolian.)

Dashi-Dorzhi, A. Contribution to the Study of Water Bodies and Aquatic Fauna of Eastern and Northern Mongolia. Author's Summary of Candidate Thesis, Irkutsk University. 1955. 20 pp.

Dashi-Dorzhi, A. Data on the Ichthyofauna from the Upper Reaches of the Selenga and Amur Rivers within Mongolia. – Zool. Zh., 34, No.3:570–577. 1955.

Dul'keit, G.D. A List of Fishes from the Suifun River Basin. – Izv. Tomsk. Univ., 75:68–72. 1925.

Dul'keit, G.D. On the Freshwater Fish Fauna of the Southern Sikhote-Alin Range. – Ezheg. Zool. Muz. Akad. Nauk SSSR, pp.9–24. 1927.

Grigor'ev, V.I. (editor). Lakes of Southern Sakhalin and their Ichthyofauna, pp.3–265. Mosk. Univ. 1964.

Karedin, E.P. Ichthyofauna of Lake Khasan. – Ryb. Khoz., 1:26, 27. 1966.

Klimakhin, F.S. Fishes of the Amur Region. – Uchen. Zap. Blagoveshch. Ped. Uchitel'sk. Inst., 5:79–117. 1953.

Klyuchareva, O.A. Data on Fishes and Fishery in the Lakes of Southern Sakhalin. – In: Ozera Yuzhnogo Sakhalina i ikh ikhtiofauna, pp.223–266. Mosk. Univ. 1964.

Krasheninnikov, S.P. A Description of Kamchatka. Summary of the Original edited by N.V.Dumitrashko and L.K.Kamanin. – Moscow, Geografgiz. 1948. 196 pp., ill., maps.

Krasheninnikov, S.P. A Description of Kamchatka. With an Appendix of Reports, Notes and Other Unpublished Material. – Moscow–Leningrad, Glavsevmorput'. 1949. 842 pp., ill., maps.

Lindberg, G.U. A List of Fishes Collected by A.A.Emel'yanov in the Botchi and Kopi Rivers, Which Empty into the Sea of Japan, with a Description of a New Species of the Genus Cottus (C. emeljanovi). – Trudy Dal'nevost. Gos. Univ., Ser.8, 2:1–9. Vladivostok. 1927. 1 pl.

Lindberg, G.U. A Note on Fishes Collected by G.N.Gassovskii in the Basin of the Urkan and Gilyui Rivers (The System of the Seya River, Amur Region). – In: Proizvod. sily Dal' Vostoka, No.4:571–573. Khabarovsk-Vladivostok, "Zhivotnyi mir," "Knizhnoe delo." 1927.

Lindberg, G.U. Data on the Fishes of the Maritime Territory. – Trudy Zool. Inst. Akad. Nauk SSSR, 3:393–407, figs.1–10. 1936.

Mina, M.V. On the Ichthyofauna of the Zeya River. – Nauch. Dokl. Vyssh. Shk., Biol. Sci., 4:33–37. 1962.

Nikol'skii, G.V. The Amur River and its Freshwater Fishes. – Moscow, Mosk. obshch. ispyt. prir. 1948. 95 pp.

Nikol'skii, G.V. The Amur River and its Fishes. Khabarovsk. 1953. 99 pp., ill.

Nikol'skii, G.V. Fishes from the Amur River Basin. – Moscow, Akad. Nauk SSSR. 1956. 554 pp., 60 figs.

Nikol'skii, G.V. and A.Ya. Taranets. Some New Data on Fishes from the Sungara and Yalu Rivers. – Sb. Trud. Gos. Zool. Muz. pri Mosk. Gos. Univ., 5:151–154. Moscow. 1939.

Polutov, I.A., I.I. Lagunov, P.G. Nikulin et al. Commercial Fishes of Kamchatka. Fishery Administration. Petropavlovsk-Kamchatskii. 1966. 125 pp., ill., map.

Postnikov, V.M. Raw Material, Resources of the Principal Lakes of Chukchi.–Izv. Tikhookean. Nauchno-Issled. Inst. Ryb. Khoz. Okeanogr., 59:227–245. 1965.

Probatov, A.N. Run-of-the-Mill Fishes of the Amur River. – Izv. Biol. Nauchno-Issled. Inst. Biol. Sta. Perm. Gosud. Univ., 10, Nos.1–2:53–64. 1935.

Rendahl, H. Ichthyologische Ergebnisse der Schwedischen Kamtchatka-Expedition 1920–1922. – Ark. Zool., 22A, No.18:1–76. 1931.

Rozov, V.E. A List of Species of the Lake Khauka Ichthyofauna. – Rub. Khoz. D. Vostoka, Nos.1–2:79–84. 1934.

Rozov, V.E. The Fauna and Flora of the Tuguro-Chumikan Region. – Vest. Dal'nevost. Fil. Akad. Nauk SSSR, 32:127–138. 1938.

Taranets, A.Ya. Fishes Collected in the Pos'et District (Vladivostok Region) in Summer 1928. – Rab. Kruzhka Yunykh Kreevedov. Vladivost. Otd. Russk. Geograf. Obshch., 3:27–53. 1929.

Taranets, A.Ya. Freshwater Fishes of the Basin of the Northwestern Sea of Japan. – Trudy Zool. Inst. Akad. Nauk SSSR, 4:483–540. 1936.

Taranets, A.Ya. Contribution to the Study of the Soviet Sakhalin Ichthyofauna. – Vest Dal'nevost. Fil. Akad. Nauk SSSR, 12:5–44. 1937.

Taranets, A.Ya. A Short Survey of the Fishes of the Middle Amur Basin. – Izv. Tikhookean. Nauchno-Issled. Inst. Ryb. Khoz. Okeanogr., 12:51–66. 1937.

Taranets, A.Ya. Fishes and Fishery in the Nor-Selemdzha District. – Ibid., pp.71–77.

Tsepkin, E.A. Ichthyofauna of the Ingoda and Shilka Rivers and Some of its Biological Characteristics. – Nauch. Dokl. Vyssh. Shk., Biol.Sci., 2:40–43. 1962.

211b – marine waters

Agapov, I.D. Fishes and Fishing in the Anadyr Liman. – In: Ryby i rybnye promysly v nizov'yakh reki Eniseya, v reke Khatange i v Anadyrskom limane; Trudy Inst. Polyarn. Zemled., Ser. "Prom. Khoz.," 16:73–114. 1941.

Andriyashev, A.P. On the Ichthyofauna of the Bering and Chukchi Seas.– Issled. Morei SSSR, 25:292–335. Leningrad, Gidrometeoizdat. 1937.

Andriyashev, A.P. Fishes of the Bering Sea and Adjacent Waters (A Survey of Zoogeography and the Origin of the Fish Fauna). Author's Summary of Candidate Thesis. Leningrad University. 1937. 3 pp.

Andriyashev, A.P. A Survey of Zoogeography and the Origin of the Fish Fauna of the Bering Sea and Adjacent Waters. Leningrad University. 1939. 187 pp.

Barsukov, V.V. Fishes from Provideniya Bay and Adjacent Waters of the Chukchi Peninsula.– Trudy Zool. Inst. Akad. Nauk SSSR, 25:130–176. 1958. 11 figs.

Commercial Fishes of Kamchatka. Petropavlovsk-Kamchatskii. 1966. 125 pp. ill.

Fadeev, N.S. Flounders from the Southeastern Bering Sea. Yuzhno-Sakhalinsk. 1968. 47 pp.

Federov, V.V. Oceanic-deepwater Ichthyofauna of the Bering Sea. – In: Konferentsiya molodykh uchenykh Dal'nego Vostoka, Sekts. Biol. p.166. Vladivostok. 1965.

Klyuchareva, O.A. Fishes from the Lagoon Lakes of Kunashir Island (Kuriles). – Zool. Zh., 46, No.3:384–392. 1967.

Kulikov, M.Yu. New Data on the Fish Fauna of the Komandorski Islands. – Izv. Tikhookean. Nauchno-Issled. Inst. Ryb. Khoz. Okeanogr., 55:249–250. 1964.

Lindberg, G.U. Fish Fauna of the Sea of Japan and the History of its Origin (Report and Discussions at the Conference of the Biological Group of the Academy of Sciences on Zoological Problems). – Izv. Akad. Nauk SSSR, Ser. Biol. 4:1225–1245. 1937.

Lindberg, G.U. Preliminary List of Fishes from the Sea of Japan. – Izv. Tikhookean. Nauchno-Issled. Inst. Ryb. Khoz. Okeanogr., 25:125–206. 1947.

Lindberg, G.U. and G.D.Dul'keit. Data on Fishes from the Shantar Sea. – Izv. Tikhookean. Nauchno-Promysl. Sta., 3, No.1:1–140. Vladivostok. 1929. ill., map.

Lindberg, G.U. and Z.V.Krasyukova. Fishes of the Sea of Japan and Adjacent Areas of the Sea of Okhotsk and the Yellow Sea. Part III. Perciformes, Percoidei. – Leningrad, "Nauka." 1969. 480 pp., 431 figs.

Lindberg, G.U. and M.I.Legeza. Fishes of the Sea of Japan and Adjacent Areas of the Sea of Okhotsk and the Yellow Sea. 1. Amphioxi, Petromyzones, Myxini, Elasmobranchii, Holocephali. – Israel Program Sci. Transl., Jerusalem. (1959) 1967. 198 pp., 108 figs.

Lindberg, G.U. and M.I.Legeza. Fishes of the Sea of Japan and Adjacent Areas of the Sea of Okhotsk and the Yellow Sea. 2. Teleostomi. XII. Acipenseriformes – XXVIII. Polynemiformes. – Israel Program Sci. Transl., Jerusalem. (1965) 1969. 389 pp., 324 figs.

Lindberg, G.U. et al. A List of the Fauna of Southern Sakhalin and the Southern Kurile Islands.– Issled. Dal'nevost. Morei SSSR, 6:173–256. 1959.

Moiseev, P.A. Cod and Flounder of the Far Eastern Seas. – Izv. Tikhookean. Nauchno-Issled. Inst. Ryb. Khoz. Okeanogr. (TINRO), 40:1–288. Vladivostok. 1953. ill.

Okada, S. and K.Kobayashi. Colored Illustrations of Pelagic and Bottom Fishes in the Bering Sea. – Hokuyu-Gyorui-zusetsu. 1968. 180 pp. (In Japanese.)

Okhryamkin, D.I. Marine Fishes of the Far East. Moscow–Khabarovsk. 1931. 50 pp.

Polutov, I.A. and V.I.Tikhonov. Commercial Fishes of the Bering Sea. – Kanuch. Sovnarkhoz. Tekhn. Ekonom. Byull., Nos.5–6:16–22. 1959.

Popov, A.M. Study of the Fish Fauna in the Sea of Okhotsk. – Issled. Morei SSSR, 14:121–154. Leningrad. 1931.

Popov, A.M. On the Ichthyofauna of the Sea of Japan. – Issled. Morei SSSR, 19:139–155, pl.1, figs.1–5. Leningrad. 1933.

Popov, A.M. Fishes of Avatcha Bay on the Southern Coast of Kamchatka. – Copeia, 2:59–67. 1933.

Rass, T.S. Deep-sea Fishes of the Far Eastern Seas. – Priroda, 2:107–109, figs.1–3. 1953.

Rass, T.S. Deep-sea Fishes of the Far Eastern Seas of the USSR. – Zool. Zh., 33, No.6:1312–1324. 1954.

Rass, T.S. Deep-sea Fishes of the Kurile-Kamchatka Trench. – Trudy Inst. Okeanol. Akad. Nauk SSSR, 12:328–339, figs.1–5. 1955.

Rass, T.S. Deep-sea Fishes of the Northern Pacific and Far Eastern Seas. – XVth Intern. Congress of Zoology, Sec.III, Pap. 34. 1958.

Romanov, N.S. Index of Literature on Fisheries in the Far East for 1923–1956. – Moscow, Akad. Nauk SSSR. 1959. 292 pp.

Sato, S.I. A Check-list of the Freshwater Fishes of Saghalien Island. – Trans. Sapporo Hist. Soc.,Soc., 17, No.2:102–112. 1942.

Shmidt, P.Yu. The Sea of Okhotsk and its Fish Fauna. – Vestn. Akad. Nauk SSSR, 5:29–40. 1935.

Shmidt, P.Yu. Fishes of the Pacific Ocean. – Moscow, Pishchepromizdat. 1948. 124 pp.

Shmidt, P.Yu. Fishes of the Sea of Okhotsk. – Israel Progr. Sci. Transl., Jerusalem. 1963. 392 pp., 20 pls., 51 figs.

Shuntov, V.P. Distribution of the Ichthyofauna in the Southeastern Bering Sea. – Zool. Zh., 42, No.5:704–715. 1963.

Skalkin, V.A. Otoliths of Some Fishes of the Far Eastern Seas. – Izv. Tikhookean. Nauchno-Issled. Inst. Ryb. Khoz. Okeanogr., 49:159–199. 1963.

Soldatov, V.K. and G.U.Lindberg. A Survey of Fishes of the Far Eastern Seas. – Ibid., 5:47–576, figs.1–76. 1930. pls.

Taranets, A.Ya. New Data on the Ichthyofauna of the Bering Sea. – Vest. Dal'nevost. Fil. Akad. Nauk SSSR, Nos.1–3:67–77. 1933.

Taranets, A.Ya. A Short Key to Fishes of the Soviet Far East and Adjacent Waters. – Izv. Tikhookean. Nauchno-Issled. Inst. Ryb. Khoz. Okeanogr., 11:1–200. 1937. 103 figs., 1 map.

Taranets, A.Ya. Marine and Freshwater Commercial Resources of the Far Eastern Territory. – Vest. Dal'-nevost. Fil. Akad. Nauk SSSR, 30, No.3:143–188. 1938.

Vedenskii, A.P. Notes on Fishes and Fisheries on the Southern Kurile Islands. – Ryb. Khoz., 7:32–39. 1949.

212 – Japanese and Ryukyu islands

Aoyagi, H. Note on the Fishes of the Ryukyu Islands. V. The Marine Fishes of Miyako Island. – Biogeographica, Trans. Biogeogr. Soc. Japan, 3, No.3:287–301, figs.1–5, pl.19. 1941.

Aoyagi, H. General Notes on the Freshwater Fishes of the Japanese Archipelago. – Taishukan, Tokyo, pp.1–272, 1–17, 1–20. 1957. 212 figs. (In Japanese.)

Boeseman, M. Revision of the Fishes Collected by Burger and von Siebold in Japan. – Zoöl. Meded., Leiden, 28:1–242. 1947. 5 pls.

Fowler, H.W. A Collection of Fishes Obtained in the Riu-Kiu Islands by Captain Ernest R.Tinkham A.U.S. – Proc. Acad. Nat. Sci. Philad., 98:123–218, figs.1–76. 1946.

Hiyama, Y. Systematic List of Fishes of the Ryu-Kyu Islands. – G.H.Q. Allied Powers Nat. Res. Sec. Rep., 150:1–47. 1951.

Honma, Y. A List of the Fishes Collected in the Province of Echigo, Including Sado Island. – Jap. J. Ichthyol., Nos.2–9. 1952–1962.

Honma, Y. Fish-Fauna (Agnatha, Chondrichthyes, Osteichthyes) of Sado Island, Sea of Japan. – Publ. Sado Mus., 5:12–32. 1963.

Honma, Y. and T.Kitami. A List of the Fishes Found in the Vicinity of Sado Marine Biological Station. IV. – J. Fac. Sci. Niigata Univ., Ser.D. (Biology), 4:59–74. 1967.

Japanese Fishes. – Uchida Rokakuho, Tokyo; 1968. 1–156+i–xxxix pp., 210 pls.

Jordan, D.S., S.Tanaka, and J.O.Snyder. A Catalogue of the Fishes of Japan. – J. Coll. Sci. Imp. Univ. Tokyo, 33, No.1:1–497. 1913. 396 figs.

Jordan, D.S. and C.L.Hubbs. Record of Fishes Obtained by D.S.Jordan in Japan, 1922. – Mem. Carneg. Mus., 10, No.2:93–346, fig.1, pls.5–12. 1925.

Kamohara, T. On the Offshore Bottom Fishes of Province Tosa, Shikoku, Japan. – Kochi Koto Gakko. 1938. 86 pp., 43 figs.

Kamohara, T. Description of the Fishes from the Provinces of Tosa and Kishu, Japan. – Bunkyu Kyokai, 1950. 287 pp., 220 figs. (In Japanese.)

Kamohara, T. Revised Descriptions of the Offshore Bottom Fishes of Province Tosa, Shikoku. – Japan Rep. Kochi Univ. Nat. Sci., Japan, 3:1–122. 1952. 100 figs.

Kamohara, T. A List of Fishes from the Tokara Islands, Kagoshima Prefecture, Japan. – Publs. Seto Mar. Biol. Lab., 3:165–299. 1954. 17 figs.

Kamohara, T. Coloured Illustrations of the Fishes of Japan. – Osaka (Hoikusha). 1955. 136 pp., 64 pls., col. (In Japanese.)

Kamohara, T. A List of Fishes from Amami-Oshima and Adjacent Regions, Kagoshima Prefecture, Japan. – Rep. Usa Mar. Biol. Stn. Kochi Univ., 4, No.1:1–65, figs.1–38. 1957.

Kamohara, T. A Catalogue of Fishes of Kochi Prefecture (Province Tosa), Japan. – Ibid., 5, No.1:1–76. 1958.

Kamohara, T. Coloured Illustrations of the Fishes of Japan (II). Osaka. 1961. 1–288+5+48+27 pp., 220 figs.

Kamohara, T. Revised Catalogue of Fishes of Kochi Prefecture, Japan. 1964. 99 pp., 63 figs.

Kamohara, T. Coloured Illustrations of the Fishes of Japan. (I). Osaka, pp.1–158, figs.1–93. 1964.

Kamohara, T. and Yamakawa. Fishes from Amami-Oshima and Adjacent Regions. – Rep. Usa Mar. Biol. Stn. Kochi Univ., 12, No.2:1–27. 1965. 10 figs.

Katayama, M. A Catalogue of the Fishes of Toyama Bay. – Toyama Hakabutsugaku-Koishi, 3:1–28. 1940.

Kuroda, N. A Catalogue of the Fishes of Shizuura, Suruga, Japan. – Amoeba, Tokyo, 3, Nos.1–2:85–127. 1934.

Kuroda, N. A Nominal List with Distribution of the Fishes of Suruga Bay, Inclusive of the Freshwater Species Found near the Coast. – Jap. J. Ichthyol., 1, No.5:314–338. 1951. 1 fig.

Kuroda, N. Fishes of Lake Biwa, with their Distribution Records. – Ibid., 2, No.6:271–284. 1953.

Kuroda, N. A New List of the Fishes of Lake Suwa. – Ibid., 8, Nos.1–2:35–46. 1960. 7 figs.

Lindberg, G.U. and M.I.Legeza. Fishes of the Sea of Japan and the Adjacent Areas of the Sea of Okhotsk and the Yellow Sea. 1. Amphioxi, Petromyzones, Myxini, Elasmobranchii, Holocephali. – Israel Progr. Sci. Trans., Jerusalem. (1959) 1967. 198 pp., 108 figs.

Lindberg, G.U. and M.I.Legeza. Fishes of the Sea of Japan and Adjacent Areas of the Sea of Okhotsk and the Yellow Sea. 2. Teleostomi. XII. Acipenseriformes – XXVIII. Polynemiformes. – Israel Prog. Sci. Transl., Jerusalem. (1965) 1969. 389 pp., 324 figs.

Makino, S. Coloured Illustrations of Exotic Aquarium Fishes. Revised by I.Amamiya. Flora and Fauna of Japan. – Osaka (Hoikusha), 10:1–130. 1956. 72 pls.

Matsubara, K. Fish Morphology and Hierarchy. Tokyo. 1955. 1605 pp., 267 text-figs., 135 pls., 461 figs. (In Japanese.)

Matsubara, K. Pisces. – In: T.Uchida (ed.). Systematic Zoology. Nakagama Shoten, Tokyo, 9, No.2:197–531. 1963.

Mead, G.W. and F.H.C.Taylor. A Collection of Oceanic Fishes from off Northeastern Japan. – J. Fish. Res. Bd. Can., 10, No.8:560–582. 1953. 8 figs.

Mori, T. Fishes of Sanin District, Including Oki Islands and its Adjacent Waters (Southern Japan Sea). – Mem. Hyogo Univ. Agric., 2, No.3:1–62. 1956.

Nakamura, M. Keys to the Freshwater Fishes of Japan. Fully Illustrated in Color. – Hokuryukan. 1963. 258 pp.

Okada, Y. A Catalogue of Vertebrates of Japan. Tokyo. 1938. 412 pp. (Cyclostomes and Fishes, pp.115–275).

Okada, Y. Fishes of Japan. Illustrations and Descriptions of Fishes of Japan. – Tokyo, Maruzen Co. Ltd. 1955. 432 pp., 391 figs.

Okada, Y. Studies on the Freshwater Fishes of Japan. – J. Fac. Fish Pref. Univ. Mie-Tsu, Sool. Analys., pp.251–265. 1959–1960.

Okada, Y. Fishes of Japan. 2nd revised ed. 1965. 470 pp., 26 figs.

Okada, Y. Fishes of Japan. Illustrations and Descriptions of Fishes of Japan. Revised ed. – Tokyo, Uno Shoten Co. Ltd. 1966. 474 pp., ill.

Okada, Y. and H.Ikeda. Contribution to the Study of the Freshwater Fish Fauna of Hokkaido, Japan. – Tokyo Zool. Inst. 1938. 162 pp., 6 ill.

Okada, Y. and K.Matsubara. Keys to the Fishes and Fish-like Animals of Japan. Tokyo–Osaka. 1938. 584 pp., 113 pls.

Okada, Y. and K.Matsubara. Bibliography of Fishes in Japan (1912–1950). – Univ. of Mie. 1953. 228 pp.

Okada, Y., K.Uchida, and K.Matsubara. Iconography of Japanese Fishes. Tokyo–Osaka. 1935. 1–425+46 pp., 166 pls. (In Japanese.)

Oshima, M. List of the Freshwater Fishes Obtained in the Southeastern Kiushu. – Jap. J.Ichthyol., 6, Nos.1–2:9–13. 1957.

Schmidt, P.J. Fishes of the Riu-Kiu Islands. – Trans. Pacif. Comm. Acad. Sci., USSR, 1:19–156. 1930. 6 pls.

Schmidt, P.J. Fishes of Japan Collected in 1901. – Ibid., 2:1–176. 1931. 30 figs.

Tanaka, S. Figures and Descriptions of the Fishes of Japan, Including Riu-Kiu Islands, Bonin Island, Formosa, Kurile Islands, Korea and Southern Sakhalin. 1911–1930. 47 vols., 960 pp., CXC pls., ill.

Tanaka, S. Japanese Fishes in Life Colors. 60+203 pp., 355 figs. (In Japanese.)

Tanaka, S. On the Distribution of Fishes in Japanese Waters. – J. Fac. Sci. Tokyo Univ., 4, Zool., 3, No.1:1–90. 1931.

Tanaka, S. Fishes of Japan. Tokyo. 1935. 557 pp., ill.

Tomiyama, I. and T.Abe. Figures and Descriptions of the Fishes of Japan. (A Continuation of Dr.Shigeho Tanaka's Work), 48–58:961–1219, figs.523–593. Tokyo. 1953–1958.

Tomiyama, I. and T.Abe. Encyclopedia Zoologica Illustrated in Colour, Fishes, 2:1–306, figs.1–912. Tokyo. 1958. (In Japanese.)

Uchida, K. and H.Tsukahara. The Fish Fauna of Ariake Sound. – Bull. Biogeogr. Soc. Japan, Nos.16–19:292–302. 1955.

Uchida, K. and H.Yabe. The Fish Fauna of Saisyu to (Quelpart Island) and its Adjacent Waters. – J. Chosen Nat. Hist. Soc., 25:3–16. 1939.

Ui, H. Monograph of Fishes of Kishu, Wakayama Prefecture, 3rd ed. Kindaibungeisha Book Co. 1932. 1–45+282+10 pp. – Osaka. (In Japanese.)

Yamai, T. Fishes of Sanin District. – Zool. Mag., Tokyo, 59, No.1:17–22. 1950. (In Japanese.)

Yoshida, H. and T.Ito. Fish Fauna of the Japan Sea. – J. Shimonoseki Coll. Fish., 6:261–270. 1957.

213 – Korea

Chir Zya Gyun. Fishes from Kyongen Bay. – Senmul'khak, 6, No.2:15–22. 1967. (In Korean.)

Chyung, M.K. Illustrated Encyclopedia: the Fauna of Korea. 2. Fishes. Ministry of Education. Korea. Seoul. 1961. i–iv+1–861 pp., 322 pls. (72 col.), ill. (In Korean, English summary). The aspects of the Korean seas and the distribution of marine life therein.

Kil Che Gyun. Ichthyofauna of the Renkhyngan, Dektigan and Senmul' Rivers. – Zh. Biol. Nauki, 2, No.1:27–33. 1963. (In Korean.)

Kim Li Tkhe. Freshwater Fishes of Korea. – Choson susan, 8:45–48. 1963. (In Korean.)

Kim Li Tkhe. Freshwater Fishes of Korea. – Ibid., 9:36–39. 1963. (In Korean.)

Mori, T. A Catalogue of the Fishes of Korea. – J. Pan-Pacif. Res. Instn., 3, No.3:3–8. 1928.

Mori, T. Checklist of the Fishes of Korea. – Mem. Hyogo Univ. Agric., 1, No.3:1–228. 1952. map.

Tsoi, E. and Gu. Fishes from the Tendongan River. – Choson minchuchui inmin konkhvaguk kvakhakvon Tkhonbo; Vest. Akad. Nauk KNRD, 1:18, 19. 1960. (In Korean.)

Tsoi, E. and Gu. Fishes of Korea, Pkhen'yan (Pyongyang). 1964. 1–375+35 pp., 439 figs. (In Korean.)

Uchida, K. The Fishes of Työsen (Korea). – Bull. Fish. Exp. Stn. of the Government General of Työsen. Husan. Part 1. – Nematognathi, Eventognathi. 1939. 458 pp., 46 figs.

214 – basin of the China seas

Alfred, E.R. The Freshwater Fishes of Singapore. – Zool. Verh., Leiden, 78:1–68. 1966. ill.

Besednov, L.N. Ichthyofauna of the Gulf of Tonkin. – Uchen. Zap. Dal'nevost. Univ., 15, No.2:47–85. 1968.

Besednov, L.N. Brief Description of the Ichthyofauna in the Gulf of Tonkin (North Vietnam). – Vopr. Ikhtiol., 3, No.2(27):222–234. 1963.

Chang, H.W. Notes on the Fishes of Western Szechwan and Eastern Sikang. – Sinensia, 15, Nos.1–6:27–60. 1944. ill.

Chang-Chun-lin. Report of Investigation into the Fish of Huagan Po Hai. Peking. 1955. 353 pp., 206 figs.

Chang-Chun-lin, Ch'ên Ch'ing-t'ai, Chêng Pao-shan, Li Ssu-chung, Chêng Wên-lien, and Wang Wên-pin. Investigation of Fishes from Pohai Strait of the Yellow Sea. Peking. 1956. 353 pp., 206 figs. (In Chinese.)

Chang-Chun-lin et al. Fishes from Pohai Strait (Yellow Sea), 2nd edition. 1957. 360 pp., 206 figs. (In Chinese.)

Chen, T. Taiwan Gyorui-shi (Monograph of the Fishes of Taiwan). – Q. Jl. Taiwan Mus., 4:110–163. 1951. (In Chinese.)

Chen, J.T.F. Checklist of the Species of Fishes Known from Taiwan (Formosa). – Ibid., 4:181–210. 1951; 5:305–341. 1952; 6:102–140. 1953.

Ch'ên Ch'ing-t'ai and Wang Ts'un-hsing. Preliminary Study of Fishes of Hsisha Island (China).- Oceanologia Limnol. sin., 8, No.1:29–36. 1966. (In Chinese, English summary.)

Cheng, T.H. A Revised Checklist of Fishes Heretofore Recorded from Fukien Province. – Lingnan Sci. J., Canton, 16:219–236, 415–433. 1937.

Cheng, T.H. List of Common Vertebrates of Fukien. – Biol. Bull. Fukien Christ. Univ., 3:111–142 (Fishes, pp.112–120). 1947. (In Chinese, English summary.)

Cheung, F. A List of Marine Fishes of Tsingtao. – J. Sci. Nat. Univ., Shantung, 1, No.2:486–502. 1934. (In Chinese.) (English summary in Lingnan Sci. J., 13, No.3:544.)

Chu, Y.T. Bibliography of Chinese Fishes. – Bull. Soc. Nat. Hist., 4, No.4:45–65. Peking. 1930.

Chu, Y.T. Index piscium sinensium. – Biol. Bull. St Johns Univ., Shanghai, 1:292. 1931.

Chu, Y.T. Fishes of the West Lake Museum, Hangchow, Chekiang. 1932. 58 pp., 39 figs.

Chu, Y.T. et al. Fishes of the South China Sea. 1962. 1184 pp., 860 figs. (In Chinese.)

Chu, Y.T. et al. Fishes of the East China Sea. 1963. 462 pp., 442 figs. (In Chinese.)

Fowler, H.W. A Synopsis of the Fishes of China. Hong Kong Naturalist. Part 1. The Sharks, Rays and Related Fishes, 1:24–34, 79–88, 129–138, 177–189. 1930; Part 2. The Herrings and Related Fishes, 2:1–14, 111–123, 198–208. 1931; Part 3. The Eels, 3:46–63, 126–144. 1932; Part 4. The Cats, Lizard Fishes, Green Gars, Half Beaks and Flying Fishes, 3:247–279. 1932; Part 5. The Cods, Opahs, Flounders, Soles, John Dories, Berycoids, Pine Fishes, Silversides, Mullets, Barracudas and Thread Fishes, 4:156–175. 1933; 5:54–67, 146–155, 210–225, 304–319. 1934; 6:62–77, 132–147, 276–284. 1935; Part 6. The Mackerels and Related Fishes, 7:61–80, 186–202, 271–315. 1936; Part 7. The Perch-like Fishes, 8:124–145, 249–289. 1937; 9:58–86, 141–164. 1938; 10:39–62, 109–121. 1940; 10:205–222. 1941. J.Hong Kong Fish. Res. Stn., 2:3–65. 1949; Q.Jl. Taiwan Mus., 6:1–77. 1953; 7:1–100. 1953; 9:161–354. 1957; Part 8. The Blennioid and Related Fishes. 11:147–339. 1958; 12:67–97. 1958; Part 9. The Gobioid Fishes, 13:91–161. 1960; 14:49–87, 203–250. 1961; 15:1–77. 1962. 1930–1962. ill.

Fowler, H.W. and B.A. Bean. Fishes from Formosa and the Philippine Islands. – Proc. U.S. Natn. Mus., 62:1–73, figs.1–4. 1922.

Fu, T.S. Study of the Fishes of Pai-Chuan. – Bull. Honan Mus., Nat. Hist., 1, No.2:47–120, figs.1–38. 1934.

Harada, I. Monograph of Freshwater Fishes in Hainan. Kainan Kaigun Tokumubu. 1943. 114 pp., 28 pls.

Herklots, G.A. and S.Y.Lin. Common Marine Food-fishes of Hong-Kong. Hong Kong. 1938. 75 pp., 41 text-figs.

Herre, A.W.C.T. and S.Y.Lin. The Freshwater Fishes of Chusan Island. – Lingnan Sci. J., Canton, 17, No.1:1–8. 1938.

Kimura, S. Descriptions of the Fishes Collected from the Yangtze-Kiang, China, by the Late Dr. Kishinouye and his Party in 1927–1929. – J. Shanghai Sci. Inst., 3, No.1:11–247, pls.1–6. 1934. 1 map.

Kimura, S. Freshwater Fishes of the Tsung-Ming Island, China. – Ibid., 3, No.4:99–120. 1935. 1 fig.

Koo, K. The Fishes of Chefoo. – Contr. Inst. Zool. Natn. Acad. Peiping, 1, No.3:111–235, pls.1–35. 1933.

Kwang-Chung, K. The Fishes of Chefoo. – Ibid., pp.1–235, pls.1–35. 1933.

Liang, S.Y. Notes on a Collection of Fishes from Pescadores Islands, Taiwan. – Q. Jl. Taiwan Mus., 1, No.2:1–20. 1948.

Liang, Y. A Checklist of the Fish Specimens in the Taiwan Fisheries Research Institute. – Rep. Taiwan Fish. Res. Inst., 3:1–35. 1951.

Liang, Y.S., P.W.Yan, and H.C.Yang. Common Food Fishes of Taiwan. Taipei. 1962. 90 pp.

Lieh Min-w'ên. Commercial Fishes of the Gulf of Tonkin. – Vopr. Ikhtiol., 8, No.5(52):817–833. 1968.

Lin, S.Y. Freshwater Fishes of Hong Kong. – J.Hong Kong Fish. Res. Stn., 2, No.1:75–101. 1949. 17 text-figs.

Lin, T.T. A Review of the Fishes of Nanking. – Contr. Biol. Lab. Sci. Soc. China, 4, No.4:1–41. 1928. 48 figs.

Miao, C.P. Notes on the Freshwater Fishes of the Southern Part of Kiangsu I., Chinkiang. – Ibid., Zool. Ser., 10:111–244. 1934. 54 figs.

Miyadi, D. Freshwater Fishes of Manchoukuo. – Rep. Limnolog. Survey of Kwantung and Manchoukuo, pp.22–88. 1928. 120 figs. (In Japanese.)

Mori, T. The Freshwater Fishes of Jehol. – Rep. First Sci. Exped. Manchoukuo, Sec.V, 1:1–61. Tokyo. 1934. 21 pls.

Nichols, J.T. A Provisional Check-list of the Freshwater Fishes of China. – Bull. Am. Mus. Nat. Hist., 58, No.1:1–62. 1928.

Nichols, J.T. The Freshwater Fishes of China. – Bull. Am. Mus. Nat. Hist., Nat. Hist. Central Asia, 9:i–xxxvi+1–322. 1943. 10 pls., 143 figs.

Nichols, J.T. and C.H.Pope. The Fishes of Hainan. – Bull. Am. Mus. Nat. Hist., 54, No.2:321–394, pl.26. 1927. 51 figs.

Oshima, M. Contributions to the Study of Freshwater Fishes of the Island of Formosa. – Ann. Carneg. Mus., 12, Nos.2–4:169–328, pls.48–53. 1919.

Read, B.E. Common Food Fishes of Shanghai. – Publ. North China Branch Roy. Asiatic Soc. 1939. 52 pp., 33 figs.

Reeves, C.D. A Catalogue of the Fishes of Northeastern China and Korea. – J. Pan-Pacif. Res. Instn., 2, No.3:3–16. 1927.

Reeves, C.D. Manual of the Vertebrate Animals of Northeastern and Central China Exclusive of Birds. – Shanghai, Chung Hwa Book Co. 1933. 1–31+1–806 pp., 169 figs.

Rendahl, H. Beiträge zur Kenntnis der marinen Ichthyologie von China. – Ark. Zool., 16A, No.2:1–37. 1924.

Rendahl, H. Beiträge zur Kenntnis der chinesischen Süsswasserfische. – Ibid., 20A, No.1:1–194. 1928.

Rendahl, H. Die Fischfauna der chinesischen Provinz Szetschwan. – Ibid., 24A, No.16:1–134. 1932.

Rendahl, H. Studien über innerasiatische Fische. – Ibid., 25A, No.11:1–51. 1933.

Shaw, T.H. Fishes of Soochow. – Bull. Fan Meml. Inst. Biol. Peking, 1:165–205. 1930. ill.

Shen, S.C. A List of the Fishes from Hong Kong. Part 1. – Q. Jl. Taiwan Mus., 17:193–208. 1964.

Shih, H.J. List of the Fishes of Szechuan. – Sci. Q. Natn. Univ. Peking, 5:425–436. 1935.

Sowerby, A. de C. The Fish of the Manchurian Seas. – In: The Naturalist in Manchuria, 4:43–286. Tientsin. 1930.

Tchang, T.L. List of Fishes from Ho-nan. – Peking Nat. Hist. Bull., 16:79–84. 1941.

Tchang, T.L. List of Fishes from Kiangsi. – Ibid., 18:7–10. 1949.

Tchang, T.L. A List of the Fishes and a New Species from Hsi-Shuan-Pan-Ma, Yunnan. – Acta zool. sinica, 14:95–98. 1962. (In Chinese, English summary.)

Wang, K.F. Study on the Teleost Fishes of the Coastal Region of Shangtung. – Contr. Biol. Lab. Sci. Soc. China, Zool. Ser., I, 9, No.1:1–76, figs.1–39. 1933; II, 10, No.9:393–481, figs.1–51. 1935.

Wang, K.F. and S.C. Wang. Study of the Teleost Fishes of the Coastal Region of Shangtung. III. - Contr. Biol. Lab. Sci. Soc. China, Zool. Ser., 11, No.6:165-237, figs.1-52. 1936.

Whitehead, P.J.P. and K.A.Joysey. The Vacheli Collection of Chinese Fishes in Cambridge. - Bull. Br. Mus. Nat. Hist., Zool., 15, No.3:123-166. 1967.

Wu, H.W. Study of the Fishes of Amoy. 1. - Contr. Biol. Lab. Sci. Soc. China, Zool. Ser., 5, No.4:1-90, figs.1-70. 1929.

Wu, H.W. Liste des poissons d'eau douce du Tchekiang (China). Descriptions de deux especes nouvelles de la famille des Cyprinidés. - Bull. Mus. Hist. Nat. Paris, 2, No.3:433-439. 1931.

22 - South Pacific

221 - Philippines

Ayery, A.C. Fish Processing Handbook for the Philippines. - Res. Rep. U.S. Fish. Wildl. Serv., 26:1-149. 1950.

Blanco, G.J. and H.R.Montalban. A Bibliography of Philippine Fishes and Fisheries. - Philipp. J. Fish., 1:107-130. 1956.

Fowler, H.W. Description and Figures of New Fishes Obtained in Philippine Seas and Adjacent Waters by U.S.Bur. Fish. Steamer "Albatross." Contrib. to the Biology of the Philippine Archipelago and Adjacent Waters. - Bull. U.S. Natn. Mus., 100, 14P, No.1:53-91, figs.4-25. 1943.

Herre, A.W. Distribution of the True Freshwater Fishes in the Philippine Islands. - Philipp. J. Sci., No.3:249-306. 1924. 2 pls.

Herre, A.W. A Checklist of Fishes from Dumaguete, Oriental Negros, P.I. and its Immediate Vicinity. - J. Pan-Pacif. Res. Instn., 8, No.4:6-11. 1933.

Herre, A.W. The Fishes of the Herre Philippine Expedition of 1931. Hong Kong. 1934. 106 pp.

Herre, A.W. Checklist of Philippine Fishes. - Res. Rep. U.S.Fish. Wildl. Serv., 20:1-977. 1953.

Herre, A.W. and W.S.Herald. Noteworthy Additions to the Philippine Fish Fauna with Descriptions of a New Genus and Species. - Philipp. J. Sci., 79, No.3:309-340, figs.1-12. 1951.

Roxas, H.A. and C.Martin. A Checklist of Phillippine Fishes. Commonwealth of the Philippines Department of Agriculture and Commerce, Manila, Technical Bull., 6:1-314. 1937.

Umali, A.F. Edible Fishes of Manila. - Ibid., Popular Bull., 6:1-192, figs.1-145, pls.1-8. 1936.

Umali, A.F. Key to the Families of Common Commercial Fishes in the Philippines. - Res. Rep. U.S. Wildl. Serv., 21:1-47. 1950. ill.

222 - Indochina

Alfred, E.R. Singapore Freshwater Fishes. - Malay. Nat. J., 15:1-19. 1961. 4 pls.

Alfred, E.R. The Freshwater Food Fishes of Malaya. - Fedn. Mus. J., 9:80-83. (1964) 1965.

Alfred, E.R. The Freshwater Fishes of Singapore. - Brill, 78:1-68, pls.1-8. Leiden. 1966.

Berry, A.J. The Natural History of the Shore Fauna of North Penang. - Malay. Nat. J., 118:81-103. 1964. 6 figs.

Blanc, M. and P.Fourmanoir. Etude préliminaire des poissons de la côte cambodgienne. - Cahiers Pacifiques, 6:33-46. 1964.

Bourret, R. La faune de l'Indochine. Vertébrés. Hanoi. Fishes, pp.267-427. 1927. 7 figs.

Bui Huu Cui. Liste des Poissons d'Indochine. - Inst. Océanograph. Indochine. 1952.

Chabanaud, P. Inventaire de la faune ichthyologique de l'Indochine.. Première liste, 1-ière Note. - Inst. Océanogr. Indochine, pp.1-26. 1926.

Chevey, P. Les poissons de campagnes de "de Lanessan." - Trav. Inst. Océanogr. Indochine, 4-ième Mém. 1932. 155 pp., 50 pls.

Chevey, P. Inventaire de la faune ichthyologique de l'Indochine. Deuxième liste. 19-ième Note. - Inst. Océanogr. Indochine, pp.1-31. 1932.

Chevey, P. Révision synonymique de l'oeuvre ichthyologique de G.Tirant. Notes Stn. marit. Cauda, 7:1-291. 1934.

Chevey, P. Faune ichthyologique de quelques lacs volcaniques de l'Annam et de la Chine du Sud. - Verh. Int. Verein. theor. angew. Limnol., 8, No.2:1-87. 1937. figs.

Chevey, P. and Lemasson. Contribution à l'étude des poissons des eaux douces tonkinoises. – Trav. Inst. Océanogr. Indochine, pp.1–183, pls.1–44. 1937.
Chevey, P. and F. Le Poulain. La pêche des eaux douces du Cambodge. – Mem. Inst. Océanogr. Indoch., 5:1–193. 1940. 68 pls, 7 charts, 119 text-figs.
First Guide to the Literature of the Aquatic Sciences and Fisheries in Bangkok. – Thailand Bull. Kasetsart Univ. Fish. Res., 2:1–46. 1965.
Fowler, H.W. Zoological Results of the Third de Schauensee Siamese Expedition. Part I. Fishes. – Proc. Acad. Nat. Sci. Philad., 86:67–163, figs.1–129, pl.12. 1934.
Fowler, H.W. Zoological Results of the Third de Schauensee Siamese Expedition. Part VI. Fishes Obtained in 1934. – Ibid., 87:89–163, figs.1–132. 1935.
Fowler, H.W. Zoological Results of the Third de Schauensee Siamese Expedition. Part VIII. Fishes Obtained in 1936. – Ibid., 89:125–264, figs.1–300. 1937.
Fowler, H.W. A List of the Fishes Known from Malaya. – Proc. Acad. Nat. Sci. Philad., Bull. Fish. Singapore, 1:1–268+1–56. 1938.
Fowler, H.W. Zoological Results of the Third de Schauensee Siamese Expedition. Part IX. Additional Fishes Obtained in 1936. – Proc. Acad. Nat. Sci. Philad., 91:39–76. 1938–1939.
Herre, A.W. Addition to the Fish Fauna of Malaya and Notes on Rare or Little Known Malayan and Bornean Fishes. – Bull. Raffles Mus., 16:27–61. 1940.
Herre, A.W.C.T. and G.S. Myers. A Contribution to the Ichthyology of the Malay Peninsula. – Ibid., 13:5–75, pls.I–VII. 1937.
Hora, S.L. On a Collection of Fish from Siam. – J. Natn. Hist. Soc. Siam, Bangkok, 6:143–184, pls.X–XII. 1923.
Hora, S.L. Fish of the Talé Sap. Peninsular Siam. – Mem. Asiat. Soc. Bengal, Calcutta, 6:463–501. 1924. 10 figs.
Hora, S.L. Notes on Malayan Fishes in the Collection of the Raffles Museum, Singapore. Parts 2 and 3. – Bull. Raffles Mus., 17:44–64, pls. V, VI. 1941. 6 text-figs.
Kuronuma, K. A Checklist of Fishes of Vietnam. – Div. Agric. Nat. Res. U.S. Oper. Mission to Vietnam. Saigon. 1961. 66 pp.
Maxwell, C.N. Malayan Fishes. – J. Straits Asiat. Soc., Singapore, 84:181–280, 72. 1921.
Rofen, R.R. et al. Handbook of the Food Fishes of the Gulf of Thailand. – Aquat. Res. Inst. Spec. Rep., I–II:1–236. 1963.
Scott, J.S. An Introduction to the Fishes of Malaga. – Minist. Agr., Federation of Malaya. Kuala Lumpur. 1959. 180 pp., 152 figs.
Smith, H.M. Contribution to the Ichthyology of Siam. – J. Siam. Soc., 9, No.3:287–325. 1934. 5 pls., 1 fig.
Smith, H.M. The Freshwater Fishes of Siam or Thailand. – Bull. U.S. Natn. Mus., 188:1–622. 1945. 9 pls., 107 figs.
Suvatti, C. Index to Fishes of Siam. – Bureau of Fisheries; Bangkok. 1936. 226 pp.
Suvatti, C. Fauna of Thailand. – Bangkok (Dep. of Fisheries), pp.1–1100 (Fishes:180–446). 1959.
Tirant, A. 6-ième Note. Oeuvre ichthyologique de G.Tirant (Service océanographique des pêches de l'Indochine. – Notes Stn. marit. Cauda; Province de Thaivang (Côte Ann.). Gouvernement Général de l'Indoch., Saigon. 1929. 175 pp.

223 – Sunda Islands and New Guinea

Beaufort, L.F. de. A List of the Freshwater Fishes Occurring in Java. – Treubia, 11:71–75. 1929.
Boeseman, M. Notes on the Fishes of Western New Guinea. – Zoöl. Meded., Leiden, 38, No.14:221–242. 1963.
Daget, J. and A. Iltis. Poissons de Côte d'Ivoire (eaux douces et saumâtres). – Mém. Inst. fond. Afr. noire, 74:1–385. 1965. 4 pls.
Delsman, H.C. Dierenleven in Indonesii. – Gravenhage-Bandung. "De vissen," pp.254–323. 1951.
Fowler, H.W. Zoological Results of the George Vanderbilt Sumatran Expedition 1936–1939. Part II. – Proc. Acad. Nat. Sci. Philad., 91:369–398. (1939) 1940. 11 text-figs.
Giltay, L. Résultats scientifiques. Voyage Indes Néerlandaises. Poissons. – Mem. Mus. r. Hist. nat. Belg. (n.s.), 5, No.3:1–129. 1933.

Hardenberg, J.D.F. On a Collection of Fishes from the Estuary and the Lower and Middle Course of the River Kapuaas (W. Borneo). – Treubia, 15:225–254. 1936.

Hardenberg, J.D.F. Fishes of New Guinea. – Ibid., 18:217-231. 1941. 4 text-figs.

Herre, A.W. A Checklist of Fishes from Madang, New Guinea. – J. Pan-Pacif. Res. Instn., 8, No.4:1–12. 1933.

Herre, A.W. A Checklist of Fishes from Sandakan, British North Borneo. – Ibid., pp.2–5.

Inger, R.F. Report on a Collection of Marine Fishes from North Borneo. – Fieldiana, Zool., 36, No.3:341–405. 1957. 2 figs.

Inger, R.F. and C.P.Kong. The Freshwater Fishes of North Borneo. – Ibid., 45:1–268. 1962. 120 figs.

Klausewitz, W. See- und Süsswasserfische von Sumatra und Java. – Senckenberg. biol., 36:309–323. 1955. 7 figs.

Munro, I.S.R. The Fishes of the New Guinea Region. A Check List. – Papua New Guin. Agric. J., 10, No.4:97–369. (1956) 1958. 1 fig., 3 maps.

Munro, I.S.R. Additions to the Fish Fauna of New Guinea. – Ibid., 16, No.4:141–186, figs.1–22. 1964.

Munro, I.S.R. The Fishes of New Guinea. – Dep. Agricult., Stock and Fish., Port Moresby. 1967. 651 pp., 6 col. pls., 78 pls.; 1968. 729 pp., ill.

Thiemmedh, J. Fishes of Thailand. Their English, Scientific and Thai Names. – Kasetsart Univ. Fish. Bull., 4:1–212. 1966. 160 text-figs., col. front.

Vinciguerra, D. Catalogo dei pesci raccolti a Borneo. Genoa. 1926. 97 pp., ill.

Volz, W. Catalogue of the Fishes of Sumatra. – Natuurw. Tijdschr. Ned. – Indië, 66:35–250. 1907.

224 – Indo-Australian Archipelago

Weber, M. and L.F. de Beaufort. The Fishes of the Indo-Australian Archipelago. II. Malacopterygii, Myctophoidea, Ostariophysi: I. Siluroidea. 1913. 404 pp., 151 figs.

Weber, M. and L.F. de Beaufort. The Fishes of the Indo-Australian Archipelago. III. Ostariophysi: II. Cyprinoidea, Apodes, Synbranchii. 1916. 455 pp., 213 figs.

Weber, M. and L.F. de Beaufort. The Fishes of the Indo-Australian Archipelago. IV. Heteromi, Solenichthyes, Synentognathi, Percesoces, Labyrinthici, Micrycyprini. 1922. 410 pp., 103 figs.

Weber, M. and L.F. de Beaufort. The Fishes of the Indo-Australian Archipelago. V. Anacanthini, Allotriognathi, Heterosomata, Berycomorphi, Percomorphi: Kuhliidae, Apogonidae, Plesiopidae, Pseudoplesiopidae, Priacanthidae, Centropomidae. 1929. 458 pp., 98 figs.

Weber, M. and L.F. de Beaufort. The Fishes of the Indo-Australian Archipelago. Perciformes (continued): Serranidae, Theraponidae, Sillaginidae, Emmelichthyidae, Bathyclupeidae, Coryphaenidae, Carangidae, Rachycentridae, Pomatomidae, Lactariidae, Menidae, Leiognathidae, Mullidae. 1931. 448 pp., 81 figs.

Weber, M. and L.F. de Beaufort. The Fishes of the Indo-Australian Archipelago. VII. Perciformes (continued): Chaetodontidae, Toxotidae, Monodactylidae, Pempheridae, Kyphosidae, Lutjanidae, Lobotidae, Sparidae, Nandidae, Sciaenidae, Malacanthidae, Cepolidae. 1936. 607 pp., 106 figs.

Weber, M. and L.F. de Beaufort. The Fishes of the Indo-Australian Archipelago. VIII. Beaufort, L.F. de. Percomorphi (continued): Cirrhitoidea, Labriformes, Pomacentriformes. 1940. 508 pp., 56 figs.

Weber, M. and L.F. de Beaufort. The Fishes of the Indo-Australian Archipelago. IX. Beaufort, L.F. de. and W.M.Chapman. Percomorphi (concluded): Blennioidei. 1951. 484 pp., 89 figs.

Weber, M. and L.F. de Beaufort. The Fishes of the Indo-Australian Archipelago. X. Koumans, F.P. Gobioidea. 1953. 392 pp., 95 figs.

Weber, M. and L.F. de Beaufort. The Fishes of the Indo-Australian Archipelago. XI. Beaufort, L.F. de and J.C.Briggs. Scleroparei, Hypostomides, Pediculati, Plectognathi, Opisthomi, Discocephali, Xenopterygii. 1962, 481 pp., 100 figs.

225 – Oceania

Abe, T. A List of the Fishes of the Palao Islands. – Palao Tropical Station Studies, 4:523–584. 1939.

Adam, G. La faune ichthyologique de l'Ile de Pâques. – Bull. Mus. natn. Hist. nat., Paris, (2), 17, No.5:381–394. 1945.

Brock, V.E. Keys to Hawaiian Fishes. – Div. Fish Game Territory Hawaii, Spec. Bull., 4:1–191. 1950.

Bruun, A.F. and J.Nielsen. The Freshwater Fishes of Rennell Island. – Nat. Hist. Rennell Island, 1:221–226, fig.1. 1958.

Buen, F. de. Los Pesces de la Isla de Pascua. – Boln. Soc. Biol. Santiago Chile, 15, No.4 [1960–1961]:3–80. 1963.

Fowler, H.W. The Fishes of Oceania. – Mem. Bernice P.Bishop Mus., 10:1–540, figs.1–82, pls.1–49. 1928.

Fowler, H.W. The Fishes of Oceania. Suppl. 1. – Ibid., 11, No.5:311–381. 1931. ill.

Fowler, H.W. The Fishes of Oceania. Suppl. 2. – Ibid., 11, No.6:383–466. 1934.

Fowler, H.W. The Fishes of the George Vanderbilt South Pacific Expedition, 1937. – Proc. Acad. Nat. Sci. Philad., Monographs, 2:1–349, pls.I–XII. 1938.

Fowler, H.W. Zoological Results of the Denison-Crockett South Pacific Expedition for the Academy of Natural Sciences of Philadelphia, 1937–1938. Part III. The Fishes. – Proc. Acad. Nat. Sci. Philad., 91:77–96. (1938) 1939. 1 text-fig.

Fowler, H.W. Fishes Obtained in the New Hebrides by Dr.Edward L.Jackson. – Ibid., 96:155–199, figs.1–35. 1944.

Fowler, H.W. The Fishes of Oceania. Suppl.3. – Mem. Bernice. P.Bishop Mus., 12, No.2:1–186. 1949.

Fowler, H.W. Fishes of Fiji, pp.1–670, figs.1–243+1–3 (bis) (Suva. Publ. by Govt. Fiji). 1959.

Gosline, W.A. The Inshore Fish Fauna of Johnston Island, a Central Pacific Atoll. – Pacific Sci., 9:442–480. 1955. 4 figs.

Gosline, W.A. The Nature and Evolution of the Hawaiian Inshore Fish Fauna. – Proc. 8th Pacific Sci. Congr., 3:347–356. 1957.

Gosline, W.A. and V.E.Brock. Handbook of Hawaiian Fishes. – Honolulu, Univ. Hawaii Press. 1960. 372 pp., 277 figs.

Harry, R.R. Ichthyological Field Data of Raroia Atoll. Tuamotu Archipelago. – Atoll. Res. Bull. Wash., Nat. Acad. Sci., 18:1–190, figs.1–7. 1953.

Herre, A.W. A Checklist of Fishes from the Solomon Islands. – J. Pan-Pacif. Res. Instn., 6, No.4:4–9. 1931.

Herre, A.W. A List of Fishes Collected at Moorea, One of the Society Islands, Being the First Record from This Island. – Ibid., pp.1–10.

Herre, A.W. A Checklist of the Fishes Recorded from the New Hebrides. – Ibid., pp.11–14.

Herre, A.W. A Checklist of Fishes Recorded from Tahiti. – Ibid., 7, No.1:2–11. 1932.

Herre, A.W. A Checklist of the Fishes of the Pelew Islands. – Mid-Pacif. Mag., pp.163–166. 1935.

Herre, A.W. New Fishes Obtained by the Crane Pacific Expedition. – Field Museum of Nat. Hist., Zool. Ser., Chicago, 18, No.12:383–438. 1935.

Herre, A.W. Fishes of the Crane Pacific Expedition. – Ibid., 21:1–472, figs.1–50. 1936.

Jordan, D.S. and E.K.Jordan. A List of the Fishes of Hawaii, with Notes and Descriptions of New Species. – Mem. Carneg. Mus., 10, No.1:1–92. 1922.

Legand, M. Première liste de poissons collectés en Nouvelle-Calédonie. – Bull. Soc. zool. Fr., 75, Nos.5–6:206, 207. 1951.

Nichols, J.T. and P.Bartsch. Fishes and Shells of the Pacific World. New York. Section on Fishes, pp.3–118. 1946. 83 text-figs.

Pietschmann, V. Remarks on Pacific Fishes. – Bull. Bernice P.Bishop Mus., 73:1–144. 1930.

Randall, J.E. Fishes of the Gilbert Islands. – Atoll Res. Bull. Wash., 47:i–xi+1–243. 1955. 2 figs. (Mimeographed, unpublished manuscript.)

Rofcn, R.R. The Marine Fishes of Rennell Island. – Nat. Hist. of Rennell Island British Solomon Islands, Copenhagen, 1, No.10:149–218. 1958. 11 pls.

Schmidt, J. Nomenclature des poissons d'eau douce de Papeari (Tahiti). – Bull. Soc. Etud. océanien., 17:176–179. 1927.

Schultz, L.P. Fishes of the Phoenix and Samoan Islands Collected in 1939 during the Expedition of the U.S.S. "Bushnell." – Bull. U.S. Natn. Mus., 180:1–316, figs.1–27. 1943.

Schultz, L.P., E.S.Herald, E.A.Lachner, A.D.Welander, and L.P.Woods. Fishes of the Marshall and Marianas Islands, Vol.1. Families from Asymmetrontidae through Siganidae. – Bull. U.S.Natn. Mus., 202, No.1:i–xxxii+1–685, text-figs.1–90, pls.1–74. 1953.

Schultz, L.P., W.B.Chapman, E.A.Lachner, and L.P.Woods. Fishes of the Marshall and Marianas Islands, Vol.2. Families from Mullidae through Stromateidae. – Ibid., 202, No.2:1–438, text-figs.91–132, pls.75–123. 1960.

Schultz, L.P., L.P.Woods, and E.A.Lachner. Fishes of the Marshall and Marianas Islands, Vol.3. Families Kraemeriidae through Antennariidae. – Ibid., 202, No.3:1–176, figs.133–156, pls.124–148. 1966.

Tinker, S.W. Hawaiian Fishes. A Handbook of the Fishes Found among the Islands of the Central Pacific Ocean. Honolulu, Hawaii, 1944. 404 pp., ill.

Whitley, G.P. A Checklist of Fishes Recorded from Fijian Waters. – J. Pan-Pacif. Res. Instn., 2, No.1:3–8. (1926) 1927.

Whitley, G.P. and A.N.Colefax. Fishes from Nauru, Gilbert Islands, Oceania. – Proc. Linn. Soc. N.S.W., 63:282–304, pl.14. 1938. 3 text-figs.

Wilhelm, O.E. and A.L.Hulot. Pesca y peces di la Isla de Pascua. (Notas ictiológicas de Chile). – Boln. Soc. Biol. Concepción, 32:139–152. 1957. 4 figs.

23 – Eastern Pacific

231 – South America

231a – fresh waters

Buen, F. de. Los peces exoticos en las aguas dulces de Chile. – Investnes. zool. chil., 5:103–137. 1959. 2 figs.

Chirichigno, F.N. Estudio de la fauna ictiológica de los esteros y parte bajo de los rios del Departamento de Tumbes (Perú). – Divalgación Cientifica, Servicio Pesqueria Perú, Lima, 22:1–87. 1963.

Dahl, G. New Freshwater Fishes from Western Colombia. – Caldasia, 8, No.39:451–484. 1960. ill.

Diaz, E.L. Bibliographic Material on the Fishes of Colombia and Northwestern South America. – Fish. Tech. Pap. F.A.O., 53:1–72. 1965.

Eigenmann, C.H. The Fishes of Western South America. Part 1. The Freshwater Fishes of Northwestern South America, Including Colombia, Panama, and the Pacific Slopes of Ecuador and Peru. – Mem. Carneg. Mus., 9:1–246. 1922.

Eigenmann, C.H. The Freshwater Fishes of Chile. – Mem. Natn. Acad. Sci. Wash., 22:1–80, pls.2–16. 1928.

Fowler, H.W. A Collection of Fishes Obtained by Mr.William C.Morrow in the Ucayali River Basin, Peru. – Proc. Acad. Nat. Sci. Philad., 91:219–289. (1939) 1940. 64 text-figs.

Fowler, H.W. Los peces del Perú; catálogo sistemático de los peces que habitan en aguas peruanas. – Mus. Hist. Nat. "Javier Prado" Univ. Nac. Mayor de San Marcos, Lima. 1945. 298 pp., 92 figs.

Hildebrand, S.F. and O.Barton. A Collection of Fishes from Talara, Peru. – Smithson. Misc. Collns., 111, No.10:1–36. 1949. 9 text-figs.

Ovchynnyk, M.M. Annotated List of the Freshwater Fish of Ecuador. – Zool. Anz., 181, Nos.3–4:237–268. 1968.

Rendahl, H. The Fishes of the Juan Fernandez Islands. – In: The Natural History of Juan Fernandez and Easter Islands, ed. by C.Scottsberg, Uppsala, 3, No.1:49–58. 1921.

Rendahl, H. Fische aus dem pazifischen Abflussgebiet Kolumbiens. – Ark. Zool., 33A, No.4:1–15. 1941. 3 text-figs.

231b – marine waters

Bini, G. Osservazioni sulla fauna marina delle coste del Chile e del Perú con speciale riguardo alle specie ittiche in generale ed ai tonni in particolare. – Boll. Pesca Piscicolt., Idrobiol., 28:11–60. 1952. 27 figs.

Bini, G. and E.Tortonese. Missione sperimentale di pesca nel Chile e nel Peru. Pesci marini peruviani. – Boll. Piscicolt. e Idrobiol., 2:151–185. 1954. ill.

Buen, F. de. Notes sobre Ichtiologia Chilena, con descripcion de dos especies nuevas. – Revta Biol. mar., 9:257–296. 1959.

Buen, F. de. Lampreas, tiburones, rayas y peces en la Estacion de Biologia Marina de Montemar, Chile. – Ibid., pp.3–200. 17 figs.

Bussing, W.A. Studies of the Midwater Fishes of the Peru-Chile Trench. – Am. Geophys. Union, Antarctic Res., Ser.5, pp.185–227. 1965.

Fischer, W. Die Fische des Brackwassergebietes Legna bis Concepcion (Chile). – Int. Revue ges. Hydrobiol. Hydrogr., 48, No.3:419–511. 1963.

Fowler, H.W. Fishes of Chile. Systematic Catalog. – Revta. chil. Hist. nat., años 45–47 (1941–1943), 45:1–36. 1941; 46:37–97. 1942; 47:103–171. 1943. numerous figs.

Fowler, H.W. Los peces del Perú. – Boletin Mus. Hist. Nat. "Javier Prado," Lima, años 5–8, pp.218–236, 363–391, 466–487, figs.1–34. 1941; pp.71–91, 206–222, 352–381, figs.35–50. 1942; pp.96–124, 275–293, figs.51–75. 1943; pp.89–126, figs.76–84. 1944.

Fowler, H.W. Fishes of Chile. Systematic catalog. – Revta. chil. Hist. nat., años 45–47 (1941–1943), pp.1–172. 1945. ill.

Fowler, H.W. Analysis of the Fishes of Chile. – Ibid., años 51–53 (1947–1949), pp.263–326. 1951. 50 text-figs.

Hildebrand, S.F. A Descriptive Catalog of the Shore Fishes of Peru. – Bull. U.S. Natn. Mus., 189:1–530. 1946. 95 figs.

Koepcke, H.W. Lista de los peces marinos conocidos del Perú. Condatos de su distribución geografica. – Biota, 3, No.29:1–17. 1962; 4, No.32:145–154. 1962; 4, No.34:237–258. 1963; 5, No.40:141–181. 1964.

Mann, G. Peces de Chile. Clave de determinacion de las especies importantes. Santiago de Chile (Min. Agricult.). 1950. 48 pp., ill.

Mann, G. La vida de los peces en aguas chelinas. Santiago de Chile (Min. Agricult.). 1954. 342 pp., 1 map, col. ill.

Morrow, J.E. Shore and Pelagic Fishes from Peru, with New Records and the Description of a New Species of Sphoeroides. – Bull. Bingham Oceanogr. Coll., 16, No.2:5–55. 1957. 12 figs.

Nichols, J.T. and R.C. Murphy. On a Collection of Marine Fishes from Peru. – Bull. Am. Mus. Nat. Hist., 46:501–516, pls.25–26. 1922. 2 text-figs.

Oliver, S.C. Catálogo de los peces marinos del litoral de Concepción, 17:75–126. 1943.

Orces, G. Contribuciones al conocimiento de los peces marinos del Ecuador, 88:107–160. 1959.

Orces, G. Peces marinos del Ecuador que se conservan en las colecciones de Quito. – Cienc. y Nat. Quito, 2:72–91. 1959. 2 figs., map.

Pearson, N.E. The Fishes of the Atlantic and Pacific Slopes near Cajamarca, Peru. – Proc. Calif. Acad. Sci., 4, No.23:87–98, pls.12, 13. 1937. 1 text-fig.

Rendahl, H. The Fishes of Easter Island. – In: The Nat. Hist. of Juan Fernandez and Easter Island, ed. by C.Skottsberg, Uppsala, 3, No.1:49–68. 1921.

Yánez, A.P. Peces útiles de la costa chilena. – Revta. Biol. mar., 6, Nos.1–3:29–81. 1955.

232 – Central America

Breder, C.M. Scientific Results of the Second Oceanographic Expedition of the "Pawnee," 1926. Nematognathi, Apodes, Isospondyli, Synentognathi, and Thorocostraci from Panama to Lower California, with a Generic Analysis of the Exocoetidae. – Bull. Bingham. Oceanogr. Coll.; Peabody Mus. Nat. Hist., Yale Univ., 2, No.2:1–25, figs.1–10. 1928.

Breder, C.M. Scientific Results of the Second Oceanographic Expedition of the "Pawnee," 1926. Heterosomata to Pediculati from Panama to Lower California. – Ibid., 2, No.3:1–56. 1936.

Meek, S.E. and S.F. Hildebrand. The Marine Fishes of Panama. Part III. – Field Mus. Publ., Zool. Ser., Chicago, 15, No.226:709–1045. 1928. ill.

Miller, R.R. Geographical Distribution of Central American Freshwater Fishes. – Copeia, 4:773–802. 1966.

Nichols, J.T. and R.C. Murphy. A Collection of Fishes from the Panama Bight, Pacific Ocean. – Bull. Am. Mus. Nat. Hist., 83, No.4:221–260, pls.15–18. 1944. 6 figs.

233 – North America
233a – fresh waters

Behre, E.H. A List of the Fresh Water Fishes of Western Panama between 81°45'W. – Ann. Carneg. Mus., 18:305–328. 1928. 1 pl.

Bond, C.E. Keys to Oregon Freshwater Fishes. – Bull. Agric. Exp. Stn., Oregon State Univ. Tech., 58:1–42. 1961. 10 figs.

Clifford, C.G., W.A.Clemens, and C.C.Lindsey. The Freshwater Fishes of British Columbia. – Br. Col. Prov. Mus. Dep. Educ., 5:1–132. 1948.

Clifford, C.G., W.A.Clemens, and C.C. Lindsey. The Freshwater Fishes of British Columbia. – Ibid., 3rd ed., 5:1–192. 1959.

Kimsey, J.B. and L.O.Fisk. Keys to the Freshwater and Anadromous Fishes of California. – Calif. Fish Game, 46:453–479. 1960.

Kimsey, J.B. and L.O.Fisk. Freshwater Nongame Fishes of California. – Calif. Fish Game, pp.1–54. 1964.

Schultz, L.P. Checklist of the Freshwater Fishes of Oregon and Washington. – Univ. Wash. Publs. Fish., 2:45–50. 1929.

Shapovalov, L. and W.A.Dill. A Checklist of the Freshwater and Anadromous Fishes of California. Fish Game, 36, No.4:382–391. 1950.

Shapovalov, L. et al. A Revised Checklist of the Freshwater and Anadromous Fishes of California. – Ibid., 45, No.3:159–180. 1959.

Sigler, W.E. and R.R.Miller. Fishes of Utah. – Salt Lake Min. Rev. 1963. 204 pp., ill.

233b – marine waters

Alverson, D.L., A.T.Pruter, and L.L.Rontolt. – In: MacMillan, H.R. Lectures in Fisheries. A Study of Demersal Fisches and Fisheries of the Northeastern Pacific Ocean. – Inst. of Fisheries, Univ. Br. Columbia. 1964. 190 pp., 72 figs.

Barnhart, P.S. Marine Fishes of Southern California, Univ. Calif. Press. 1936. 209 pp., 290 figs.

Baxter, J.L. Inshore Fishes of California. – Calif. Fish Game. 1960. 84 pp., ill.

Berdegue, A. Peces de importancia comercial en la costa Nor–occidental de Mexico. 1956. 376 pp., 206 figs.

Berry, F.H. and H.C.Perkins. Survey of Pelagic Fishes of the California Current Area. – Fishery Bull. Fish Wildl. Serv. U.S., 65:625–682. 1966.

Briggs, J.C. California Fish Families with Suggested References for Identification of Species. – Circ. Dir. Syst, Biol. Stanford Univ., 9:1–13. 1962.

Chapman, W.M. Oceanic Fishes from the North East Pacific Ocean. – Occ. Pap. Br. Columb. Prov. Mus., 2:1–44. 1940. Rotoprint.

Clemens, W.A. and G.V.Wilby. Fishes of the Pacific Coast of Canada. – Bull. Fish. Res. Bd. Canada, 68:1–386, figs.2–253, pl.1. 1946.

Clemens, W.A. and G.V.Wilby. Fishes of the Pacific Coast of Canada. Revised edition. – Ibid., pp.1–443, figs.1–281, pl.1. 1961.

Clothier, C.R. A Key to Some Southern California Fishes Based on Vertebral Characters. – Fish. Bull., 79:1–83, pls.1–23. 1950.

De Lacy, A.C. et al. Fishes of the Puget Sound Region. – Contr. Univ. Wash. College (Sch.) Fish., 147:32. 1963.

Fitch, J.E. Offshore Fishes of California. – Calif. Fish Game. 1958. 80 pp.

Fitch, J.E. and R.J.Lavenberg. Deepwater Teleostean Fishes of California. – Univ. Calif. Press. Calif. Nat. Hist. Guides, 25:1–155. 1968. 74 figs.

Follett, W.I. Annotated List of Fishes Obtained by the California Academy of Sciences during Six Cruises of the U.S.S. Mulberry Conducted by the United States Navy off Central California in 1949 and 1950. – Proc. Calif. Acad. Sci., 27, No.16:399–432, pls.21–26. 1952.

Hikita, T. A Preliminary List of Fishes from the Northern Pacific Ocean. – J. Fac. Sci. Hokkaido Univ. (Zool.), 13:46–48. 1957. 1 fig.

Hubbs, C.L. A Checklist of the Marine Fishes of Oregon and Washington. – J. Pan-Pacif. Res. Instn., 3, No.3:9–16. 1928.

Hubbs, C.L. and L.P.Schultz. Contribution on the Ichthyology of Alaska with Descriptions of Two New Fishes. – Occ. Pap. Mus. Zool. Univ. Mich., 431:1–31. 1941.

Kobayashi, K. and T.Ueno. Fishes from the Northern Pacific and from Bristol Bay. – Bull. Fac. Fish. Hokkaido Univ., 6, No.4:239–265, figs.1–9. 1956.

Kumada, T. and Y.Hiyama. Marine Fishes of the Pacific Coast of Mexico. – Nissan Fisheries Institute, Odawara, Japan. 1937. 75 pp., 102 pls.

Lavenberg, R.J. and J.E.Fitch. Annotated List of Fishes Collected by Midwater Trawl in the Gulf of California, III–IV 1964. – Calif. Fish Game, 52, No.2:92–110. 1966.

Macphee, C. and W.A.Clemens. Fishes of the San Juan Island Archipelago, Washington. – Northwest Sci., 36, No.2:27–138. 1962. 1 fig.

Miller, D.J. A Field Guide to Some Common Ocean Sport Fishes of California. – Calif. Fish Game. 1959. 41 pp., figs.

Parr, A.E. Deepsea Fishes from the Western Coast of North and Central America. – Bull. Bingham. Oceanogr. Coll., 2, No.4:1–53. 1931.

Rhode, C.J. and W.Barker. Alaska's Fish and Wildlife. – Circ. Fish Wildl. Serv., Wash., 17:1–60. 1953. ill.

Ricker, K.E. Mexican Shore and Pelagic Fishes Collected from Acapulco to Cape San Lucas during the 1957 Cruise of the "Marijean." – Inst. Fish. Univ. Brit. Columbia Mus., Contr., 3:1–18. 1959.

Roedel, P.M. Common Marine Fishes of California. – Fish. Bull., 62:1–150. 1948.

Roedel, P.M. Common Ocean Fishes of the California Coast. – Fish. Bull. Calif. Fish Game, 91:1–184. 1953. 175 figs.

Schultz, L.P. Keys to the Fishes of Washington, Oregon and Closely Adjoining Regions. – Univ. Wash. Publs. Zool, 2, No.4:103–228. 1936. figs.1–49.

Schultz, L.P. and A.C.De-Lacy. Fishes of the American Northwest. A Catalogue of the Fishes of Washington and Oregon. – Mid-Pacif. Mag.; J. Pan-Pacif. Res. Instn., 10, No.4:365–380. 1935; pp.63–78, 127–142, 211–226, 275–290. 1936.

Thomas, G.C., Jr. and W.G.C.Thomas. Game Fish of the Pacific, Southern Californian and Mexican. – Philadelphia, J.B.Lippincott Co. 1930. 293 pp.

Ulrey, A.B. A Checklist of the Fishes of Southern California and Lower California. – J. Pan-Pacif. Res. Instn., 4, No.4:2–11. 1929.

Ulrey, A.B. and P.O.Greeley. A List of the Marine Fishes (Teleostei) of Southern California with their Distribution. – Bull. S. Calif. Acad. Sci., 27:1–53. 1928.

Walford, L.A. Handbook of Common Commercial and Game Fishes of California. – Fish. Bull. Calif. Fish Game, 28:1–183, figs.1–137. 1931.

Walford, A.L. Marine Game Fishes of the Pacific Coast from Alaska to the Equator. – Berkeley, Univ. Calif. Press. 1937. i–xxix+1–205 pp., 69 pls.

Walker, B.W. The Distribution and Affinities of the Marine Fish Fauna of the Gulf of California. – Syst. Zool., 9, Nos.3–4:123–133. 1960.

Wilimovsky, N.J. List of Fishes of Alaska. – Stanford Ichthyol. Bull., 4, No.5:279–294. 1954.

Wilimovsky, N.J. Provisional Keys to the Fishes of Alaska. – Fish. Res. Lab., Fish Wildl. Serv. U.S. 1958. 113 pp.

Wilimovsky, N.J. Inshore Fish Fauna of the Aleutean Archipelago. – Sci. Alaska, College Alaska Div. Amer. Assoc. Advancement Sci., pp.172–190. (1963) 1964.

3 – North America (as a whole)
3a – inland waters (drainless)

Fowler, H.W. A Study of the Fishes of the Southern Piedmont and Coastal Plain. – Proc. Acad. Nat. Sci. Philad., Monogr., 7:1–408, figs.1–313. 1945.

Rivers, I.L. and T.J.Trelease. An Annotated Checklist of the Fishes of Nevada. – Calif. Fish Game, 38, No.2:113–123. 1952.

3ab – fresh and marine waters of the Pacific and Atlantic basins

Buen, F. de. Lista de peces de agua dulce de México. En preparación de su catálogo. – Trab. Estac. limnol. Patzcuaro, 2:1–66. 1940. (Processed, in 4 parts.)

Buen, F. de. Investigaciones sobre ictiologia mexicana. I. Catalogo de los peces de la region neartica en suelo mexicano. - An. Inst. Biol. Univ. Méx., 18, No.1:257-348. 1947.

Eddy, S. How to Know the Freshwater Fishes. - Dubuque, Iowa, W.C.Brown Co. 1957. 253 pp., 615 figs.

Gunter, G. A List of the Fishes of the Mainland of North and Middle America Recorded from Both Freshwater and Sea Water. - Am. Midl. Nat., 28:305-326. 1942.

Jordan, D.S. and B.W.Evermann. American Food and Game Fishes. A Popular Account of All the Species Found in America, North of the Equator, with Keys for Ready Identification, Life Histories and Methods of Capture. - N.Y., Doubleday, Page and Co. 1920. I-L+1-572 pp., ill.

Jordan, D.S., B.W.Evermann, and H.W.Clark. Checklist of the Fishes and Fish-like Vertebrates of North and Middle America North of the Northern Boundary of Venezuela and Colombia. - Rep. U.S. Fish Commn., 2:1-670. 1930.

La Monte, F. North American Game Fishes. - N.Y., Doubleday, Doran and Co. 1945. 202 pp.

McAllister, D.E. List of the Marine Fishes of Canada. - Bull. Natn. Mus. Can., 168:1-76. 1960.

Moore, G.A., in Blair, W.F. et al. Vertebrates of the United States, Fishes, pp.31-210. - N.Y., McGraw-Hill. 1957. 111 figs.

Nichols, J.T. Representative North American Freshwater Fishes. - N.Y., MacMillan. 1942. 128 pp., ill.

Ommanney, D. Los peces. México Ed. Offset Multicolor, S.A. 1964. 192 pp., ill.

Rostlund. Freshwater Fish and Fishing in Native North America. - Univ. Calif. Publs. Geogr., 9:1-313. 1952. 47 maps.

Schrenkeisen, R. Field Book of Freshwater Fishes of North America, North of Mexico. - N.Y., Putnam's Sons. 1938. pp.i-xii+1-312, ill.

Slastenenko, E.P. The Freshwater Fishes of Canada. Toronto. 1958. 388 pp.

Wolden, H.T. Familiar Freshwater Fishes of America. - N.Y.-London, Harper and Row. 1964. 324 pp.

Zim, H.S. and H.H.Shoemaker. Fishes - a Guide to Fresh- and Saltwater Species. - N.Y., Golden Nature Guide, Simon and Schuster. 1954. 160 pp., ill.

4 - Atlantic Ocean
41 - western part
411 - North America
411a - fresh waters

Alvarez, J. Claves para la determinación de especies en los peces de las aquas continentales Méxicanas. - Méx. Secretaria de Marina. 1950. 144 pp., 16 figs.

Anderson, W.D. Fishes of Some South Carolina Coastal Plain Streams. - Q. Jl. Fla. Acad. Sci., 27, No.1:31-54. 1964.

Bailey, J.R. and J.A.Oliver. The Fishes of the Connecticut Watershed. - Surv. Rep. New Hamps. Fish Game Dep., 4:150-189, figs.59-80. 1939.

Bailey, R.M. The Fishes of the Merrimack Watershed. - Ibid., 3:149-185. 1938.

Bailey, R.M. A Checklist of the Fishes of Iowa with Keys for Identification. - Iowa Fish and Fishing, pp.187-238. 1951. ill.

Bailey, R.M. A Revised List of the Fishes of Iowa with Keys for Identification. - Des Moines, Iowa (Iowa State Conserv. Comm.,), pp.327-377. 1956. ill.

Bailey, R.M. and M.O.Allum. Fishes of South Dakota. - Misc. Publs. Mus. Zool. Univ. Mich., 119:1-131. 1962. 7 figs.

Bailey, R.M., H.E.Wimm, and Smith. Fishes from the Escambia River, Alabama and Florida, with Ecologic and Taxonomic Notes. - Proc. Acad. Nat. Sci. Philad., 56:109-164. 1954.

Behnke, R.J. and R.M.Wetzel. A Preliminary List of the Fishes Found in the Fresh Waters of Connecticut. - Copeia, 2:141-143. 1960.

Blatchley, W.S. The Fishes of Indiana. - Indianapolis, The Nature Publ. Co. 1938. 121 pp., 38 figs.

Boschung, H.J. An Annotated List of Fishes of the Coosa River System in Alabama. - Am. Midl. Nat., 66:257-285. 1961. 1 fig.

Bousfield, E.L. and A.H.Leim. The Fauna of Minas Basin and Minas Channel. - Bull. Natn. Mus. Can., 166:1-30. 1960. 3 figs.

Brown, C.J.D. A Preliminary List of Montana Fishes. – Proc. Mont. Acad. Sci., 22:21–26. (1962) 1963.

Carr, A.F. A Key to the Freshwater Fishes of Florida. – Proc. Fla. Acad. Sci., 1:72–86. 1937.

Carson, L.C. Fishes of the Middle West. – U.S. Dep., Int. Conserv. Bull., 34:1–44. 1943. 25 text-figs.

Cook, F.A. Freshwater Fishes in Mississippi. – Miss. Game Fish Commission Jackson Hederman Bros. Printers. 1959. 239 pp.

Cross, F.B. Handbook of Fishes of Kansas. – Univ. Kans. Publs. Mus. Nat. Hist. 1967. 357 pp., ill.

Darnell, R.M. Fishes of the Rio Tamesi and Related Coastal Lagoons in East-Central Mexico. – Publs. Inst. Mar. Sci. Univ. Tex., 8:299–365. 1962. 2 figs.

Dickinson, W.E. Handbook of Wisconsin Fishes. – Pop. Sci. Handb. Ser. Milwaukee Publ. Mus., 8:1–83. 1960. 167 figs.

Dymond, J.R. The Fishes of Lake Nipigon. – Univ. Toronto Stud. Biol. Ser., 27:1–108. 1926. 11 pls.

Dymond, J.R. The Fishes of the Ottawa Region. – Contr. Region. – Contr. R. Ont. Mus. Zool. Palaeont., 15:1–43. 1939.

Dymond, J.R. A List of the Freshwater Fishes of Canada East of the Rocky Mountains, with Keys. – Misc. Publs. R. Ont. Mus. Zool., 1:1–36. 1947.

Dymond, J.R., J.L.Hart, and A.L.Pritchard. The Fishes of the Canadian Waters of Lake Ontario. – Univ. Toronto Stud. Biol. Ser., 33:1–35. 1929.

Eddy, S. and T.Surber. Northern Fishes with Special Reference to the Upper Mississippi Valley. 1943. 1–11+1–252 pp., 3 diags., 57 figs., 2 pls. Revised ed. 1947. 1–12+1–276 pp.

Fisher, H.J. Some Fishes of the Lower Missouri River. – Am. Midl. Nat., 68, No.2:424–429. 1962.

Fowler, H.W. Fishes from the Middle Atlantic States and Virginia. – Occ. Pap. Mus. Zool. Univ. Mich., 56:1–19, pls.I–II. 1918.

Fowler, H.W. A List of the Fishes of Pennsylvania. – Proc. Biol. Soc. Wash., 32:49–74. 1919.

Francis, Ph. Florida Fish and Fishing. – N.Y., MacMillan. 1956. 230 pp., ill.

Friedrich, G.W. A Catalog of the Fishes of Central Minnesota. – Copeia, 1:27–30. 1933.

Gerking, S.D. The Distribution of the Fishes of Indiana. – Invest. Indiana Lakes Streams, 3:1–137. 1945. ill.

Gerking, S.D. Key to the Fishes of Indiana. – Ibid., 4:49–86. 1955.

Gordon, M. The Fishes of Eastern New Hampshire. – Surv. Rep. New Hamps. Fish Game Dep., 2:1–101. 1937. 118 figs.

Harlan, J.R. and E.B.Speaker. Iowa Fish and Fishing. – State Printer, Des Moines. 1951. 237 pp., 22 pls.

Hinks, D. The Fishes of Manitoba. Winnipeg. 1944. 102 pp., ill.

Hubbs, C.L. A Checklist of Texas Freshwater Fishes. – Tex. Game Fish, Comm., Ser. 1F, 3:1–14. 1957.

Hubbs, C.L. and C.W.Greene. Further Notes on the Fishes of the Great Lakes and Tributary Waters. – Pap. Mich. Acad. Sci., 8:371–392. 1928.

Hubbs, C.L., R.A.Kuehne, and J.C.Ball. The Fishes of the Upper Guadalupe River, Texas. – Tex. J. Sci., 5:216–244. 1953. 34 figs.

Hubbs, C.L. and K.F.Lagler. Guide to the Fishes of the Great Lakes and Tributary Waters. – Bull.213. 1958. Cranbrock Inst. Sci., 18:1–100, figs.1–118. 1941.

Hubbs, C.L. and K.F.Lagler. Annotated List of the Fishes of Foots Pond, Gibson County, Indiana. – Invest. Indiana Lakes Streams, 2:73–83. (1942) 1944.

Hubbs, C.L. and K.F.Lagler. Fishes of the Great Lakes Region. – Bull. Cranbrook Inst. Sci., 26:i–ix+1–186. 1947. frontis col., 18 pls.; 26:1–186. 1949; 26:1–213. 1958.

Hubbs, C.L. and K.F.Lagler. Fishes of Isle Royale, Lake Superior, Michigan. – Pap. Mich. Acad. Sci., 33:73–133. 1949. 2 pls.

Juchereau-Duchesnay, E. Les poissons du Québec. Montréal, Ed. Home. 1964. 47 pp., ill.

Knapp, F.T. Fishes Found in the Fresh Waters of Texas. – Brunswick, Georgia, Ragland Studio and Litho Printing Co. 1953. i–vii+1–166 pp., 190 figs.

Koster, W.J. Guide to the Fishes of New Mexico. – Univ. New Mex. Publs. Biol. 1957. 116 pp.

Kuhne, E.R. A Guide to the Fishes of Tennessee and the Mid-South. – Div. Fish and Game, Tenn. Dep. Cons., Nashville. 1939. 124 pp., 81 figs.

Legendre, V. The Freshwater Fishes, Vol.1. Key to Game and Commercial Fishes of the Province of Quebec. – Société Canadienne D'Ecologie. 1954. 180 pp., 80 figs.

Livingstone, D.A. The Freshwater Fishes of Nova Scotia. – Proc. Trans. Nova Scotian Inst. Sci., 23, No.1:1–90. 1953. 36 figs.

Magnin, E. Premier inventaire de la faune ichthyologique du lac et la rivière Waswanipi. – Naturaliste can., 91, No.11:273–308. 1959.

McKenzie, R.A. Marine and Freshwater Fishes of the Miramichi River and Estuary, New Brunswick. – J. Fish. Res. Bd. Can., 16, No.6:807–833. 1959.

Metcalf, A.L. Fishes of Chautauqua, Cowley and Elk Counties. – Univ. Kans. Publs. Mus. Nat. Hist., 11, No.6:347–400. 1959. ill.

Metcalf, A.L. Fishes of the Kansas River System in Relation to Zoogeography of the Great Plains. – Ibid., 17, No.3:23–189. 1966. ill.

Miller, R.R. and C.H.Lowe. An Annotated Checklist of the Fishes of Arizona. The Vertebrates of Arizona. Annot. Checklist of Vert. of the State: The Species and Where They Live. C.H.Lowe (ed.), Part II, pp.133–151. – Univ. Arizona Press. 1964. 1 fig.

Minckley, W.L. Fishes of the Big Blue River Basin, Kansas. – Univ. Kans. Publs. Nat. Hist., 11, No.7:403–442. 1959.

Norden, C.R. Fishes of the Little River Drainage in Louisiana. – Proc. Louisiana Acad. Sci., 28:96–104. 1965. 1 fig.

O'Donnell, D.J. Annotated List of the Fishes of Illinois. – Bull. Ill. St. Nat. Hist. Surv., 20:473–500. 1935. 4 figs.

Osburn, R.C., E.L.Wickliff, and M.B.Trautman. A Revised List of the Fishes of Ohio. – Ohio J.Sci., 30:169–176. 1930.

Parker, J.C. An Annotated Checklist of the Fishes of the Galveston Bay System, Texas. – Publs. Inst. Mar. Sci., 10:201–220. 1965.

Riggs, C.D. and E.W.Bonn. An Annotated List of the Fishes of Lake Texoma, Oklahoma and Texas. – S West. Nat., 4:157–168. 1959. map.

Ryder, R.A., W.B.Scott, and E.J.Crossman. Fishes of Northern Ontario, North of the Albany River. – Contr. R. Ont. Mus. Zool., 60:1–30. 1964. ill.

Scott, T.D. Freshwater Fishes of Eastern Canada, Toronto.–Univ. Toronto Press. 1954. i–xiv+1–128 pp., ill.

Scott, W.B. and E.J.Crossman. The Freshwater Fishes of New Brunswick: a Checklist with Distributional Notes. – Contr. R. Ont. Mus. Zool., 51:1–37. 1959. ill.

Scott, W.B. and E.J.Crossman. Fishes Occurring in the Fresh Waters of Insular Newfoundland. – Ibid., 58:1–123. 1964. 18 figs.

Simon, J.R. and F. Checklist and Keys of the Fishes of Wyoming. – Union Wyoming Publs., 6:47–62. 1939.

Smith, P.W. A Preliminary Annotated List of the Lampreys and Fishes of Illinois. – Biol. Notes Nat. Hist. Surv. Div., St. Ill., 54:1–12. 1965. 3 figs.

Surber, T. A Preliminary Catalogue of the Fishes and Fishlike Vertebrates of Minnesota. – App. Bien. Rept. Minn. St. Game and Fish Comm. Period Ending June, 30:1–92. 1920. 62 figs.

Trautman, M.B. The Fishes of Ohio with Illustrated Keys. – (Columbus), Ohio St. Univ. Press. 1957. 1–18+1–683 pp., 7 col. pls., 172 figs., 172 maps.

Tubb, R.A., F.A.Copes, and C.Johnston. Fishes of the Sheyenne River of North Dakota. – Proc. N. Dak. Acad. Sci., 19:120–128. 1965.

411b – marine waters

Ackerman, B. Handbook of Fishes of the Atlantic Seaboard. – Am. Publs. Comp. Wash. 1951. 144 pp., ill.

Backus, R.H. The Fishes of Labrador. – Bull. Am. Mus. Nat. Hist., 113, No.4:279–337, tables 273–332. 1957. 2 pls., 2 figs.

Beebe, W. Preliminary List of Bermuda Deepsea Fish. – Zoologica, N.Y., 22:197–208. 1937.

Beebe, W. and J.Tee-Van. Field Book of the Shore Fishes of Bermuda. – N.Y.–London, Putnam's Sons. 1933. 337 pp., 343 figs., 4 col. pls.

Bergeron, J. Liste des poissons marins de l'estuaire et du Golfe St.-Laurent. – Contr. Dép. Pêch., Québ., 80:1–27. 1960.

Bigelow, H.W. and W.C.Schroeder. Fishes of the Gulf of Maine. – Fishery Bull. Fish Wildl. Serv. U.S., 74, No.53:1–577. 1953. 288 figs.

Bigelow, H.B. and W.W.Welsh. Fishes of the Gulf of Maine. – Bull. Bur. Fish., Wash., 40, Part 1:1–567. 1925. 278 figs.

Borodin, N.A. Atlantic Deepsea Fishes. – Bull. Mus. Comp. Zool. Harv., 72, No.3:55–89, fig.1, pls.1–5. 1931.

Breder, C.M. Field Book of Marine Fishes of the Atlantic Coast from Labrador to Texas. – N.Y.-London, Putnam's Sons. 1929. 332 pp., 2nd ed. 1948. 1–37+1–331 pp.

Briggs, J.C. A List of Florida Fishes and their Distribution. – Bull. Fla. St. Mus. Biol. Sci., 2, No.8:223–318. 1958. 3 figs.

Carson, R.L. and K.L.Howe. Fish and Shellfish of the Middle Atlantic Coast, South Atlantic and Gulf Coast. – Bull. U.S.Dep. Interior, Conservation, 37:1–32; 38:1–45. 1945.

Domanevskii, L.N. and V.A.Rikhter. Key to the Main Commercial Fish of the Northwestern Atlantic. Kaliningrad. 39 pp., figs.; – In: Rybolovstvo v severo-zapadnoi Atlantike, pp.402–447. 1967.

Dunbar, M.I. and H.H.Hildebrand. Contribution to the Study of the Fishes of Ungawa Bay. – J. Fish. Res. Bd. Can., 9, No.2:83–128. 1952. ill.

Edwards, R.L. The Fishes of Richmond Gulf, Ungawa, Canada. – Proc. Am. Phil. Soc., 105, No.2:196–205. 1961.

Fowler, H.W. A List of the Fishes of New Jersey. – Proc. Biol. Soc. Wash., 33:139–170. 1920.

Fowler, H.W. A List of the Fishes of New Jersey, with Off-shore Species. – Proc. Acad. Nat. Sci. Philad., 104:89–151. 1952. 1 fig.

Gordon, B.L. The Marine Fishes of Rhode Island. A Guide Book. – Watch Hill, R.I., Book and Tackle Shop. 1960. 136 pp., 77 pls.

Grey, M. Notes on a Collection of Bermuda Deepsea Fishes. – Fieldiana, Zool., 37:265–302. 1955. 12 figs.

Gunter, G. Studies on Marine Fishes of Texas. – Publs. Inst. Mar. Sci. Univ. Tex., 1:1–190. 1945. 11 text-figs.

Hildebrand, S.F. An Annotated List of the Fishes Collected on the Several Expeditions to Greenland, the Fox Basin Region, and the Coast of Labrador by Captain R.A.Bartlett, from 1925 to 1935. – Meddr. Grønland, 125, No.1:1–12. 1939.

Hildebrand, S.F. and W.C.Schroeder. Fishes of Chesapeake Bay. – Bull. Bur. Fish., Wash., 43, No.1:1–366, figs.1–211. 1928.

Hoese, H.D. A Partially Annotated Checklist of the Marine Fishes of Texas. – Publs. Inst. Mar. Sci. Univ. Tex., 5:312–352. 1958. 1 fig.

Huntsman, A.G. The Fishes of the Bay of Fundy. – Contr. Can. Biol. Fish. (1921) 1922. 24 pp.

Kanazawa, R.H. More New Species and New Records of Fishes from Bermuda. – Fieldiana, Zool., 34:71–100. 1952. 5 figs.

Kilby, J.D. and D.K.Caldwell. A List of Fishes from the Southern Tip of the Florida Peninsula. – Q. Jl. Fla. Acad. Sci., 18:195–206. 1955. 1 fig.

Kincaid, T. An Annotated List of Puget Sound Fishes. – Dept. Fisher., Seattle. 1919. 51 pp.

Koefoed, E. Fishes from the Sea-bottom. – Rep. Scient. Results Michael Sars N. Atlant. Deep Sea Exped. 1910, IV, No.1:1–147, figs.1–55, pls. I–VI. 1932.

Leim, A.H. and W.B.Scott. Fishes of the Atlantic Coast of Canada. – Bull. Fish. Res. Bd. Can., 155:436–459. 1966. ill.

Longley, W.H. and S.F.Hildebrand. Systematic Catalogue of the Fishes of Tortugas, Florida, with Observations on Color, Habits, and Local Distribution. – Publs. Carnegie Instn., 535, Pap. Tortugas Lab., 34: I–XIII, 1–331, pls.1–34. 1941.

Mélançon, C. Les poissons de nos eaux. 2nd ed. – Montréal, Granger Frères. 1946. 254 pp., 110 figs., 1 pl.

Newfoundland Fishery Research Commission Laboratory. 1932–1935. First List of Fishes in the Newfoundland Fishing Area. – Ann. Rept. Newfoundland Fish. Res. Comm. for 1931, 1, 4, app.D, pp.107–110. 1932; Second . . . l.c. for 1932, 2, 1, app.D, pp.125–127. 1933; Third . . . l.c. for 1933, 2, 2, app.D, pp.115–117. 1934; Fourth . . . l.c. for 1934, 2, 3, app.D, p.79. 1935.

Nichols, J.T. and C.M.Breder. The Marine Fishes of New York and Southern New England. – Zoologica, N.Y., 9, No.1:1–192. 1927.

Perlmutter, A. Guide to the Marine Fishes. Atlantic Coast of the USA (A New Method for Identification of Marine Fishes). – N.Y., Univ. Press. 1961. 431 pp., ill.

Richards, S.W. The Demersal Fish Population of Long Island Sound. – Bull. Bingham Oceanogr. Coll., 18:1–101. 1963. 11 figs.

Richmond, E.A. The Fauna and Flora of Horn Island, Mississippi. – Gulf Res. Rep., 1, No.2:1–106. 1962. 27 figs.

Rivas, L.R. Florida Game and Commercial Marine Fishes. – Mar. Lab. Univ. of Miami, Educ. Ser., 4:1–39. 1949.

Robins, C.R. Florida Game and Commercial Marine Fishes. – Ibid., 12:1–46. 1958.
Scott, W.B. and M.G. A Check-list of Canadian Atlantic Fishes with Keys for Identification. – Contr. R. Ont. Mus. Zool., 66:1–106. 1965. ill.
Taylor, H.F. et al. Survey of the Marine Fisheries of North Carolina. – Univ. North Carolina Press, Chapel Hill. 1951. 555 pp.
Truitt, R.V., B.A.Bean, and H.W.Fowler. The Fishes of Maryland. – Md. St. Cons. Dep. Cons. Bull., 3:1–120, figs. 1–62. 1929.
Vladykov, V.D. and D.E.McAllister. Preliminary List of Marine Fishes of Quebec. – Naturaliste can., 88, No.3:53–78. 1961.
Vladykov, V.D. and R.A.MacKenzie. The Marine Fishes of Nova Scotia. – Proc. Trans. Nova Scotian Inst. Sci., 19, No.1:17–113. 1935. 131 figs.

412 – Central America and islands of the Caribbean Sea
412a – fresh waters

Bauchot, M.L. La faune ichthyologique des eaux douces antillaises. – C. r. somm. Séanc. Soc. Biogéogr., 36, No.311:7–26. 1959. 7 figs.
Boeseman, M. The Freshwater Fishes of the Island of Trinidad. Studies on the Fauna of Curaçao and Other CaribbeanIslands, 10. – Uitg. natuurw. Stud.-Kring Suriname, 21:72–153, figs.36–37. 1960.
Boeseman, M. The Freshwater Fishes of the Island of Trinidad: addenda, errata et corrigenda. – Stud. Fauna Curaçao, 82, No.20:52–57. 1964.
Breder, C.M. The Fishes of the Rio Chucunaque Drainage, Eastern Panama. – Bull. Am. Mus. Nat. Hist., 57, No.3:91–176. 1927. ill.
Breder, C.M. An Annotated List of Fishes from Lake Forsyth, Andros Island, Bahamas, with the Descriptions of Three New Forms. – Am. Mus. Novit., 551:1–8. 1932. 3 figs.
Carr, A.F. and L.Giovannoli. The Fishes of the Choluteca Drainage of Southern Honduras. – Occ. Pap. Mus. Zool. Univ. Mich., 523:1–38. 1950. ill.
Eigenmann, C.H. The Freshwater Fishes of Panama, East of Longitude 80°W. – Univ. Stud. Indiana, 7:1–19. 1920.
Hildebrand, S.F. A New Catalogue of the Freshwater Fishes of Panama. – Field Mus. Publs. Chicago, Zool. Ser., 22, No.4:219–359. 1938.
Hildebrand, S.F. A List of Freshwater Fishes from San José Island, Pearl Islands, Panama. – Smithson. Misc. Collns., 106, No.3:1–3. 1946.
Norman, J.R. Zoological Results of the Cambridge Expedition to the Suez Canal, 1924. Report on the Fishes. – Trans. Zool. Soc. Lond., 22:375–390. 1927. 2 figs., 4 tables.

412b – marine waters

Beebe, W. and J.Tee-Van. The Fishes of Port-au-Prince Bay, Haiti, with a Summary of the Known Species of Marine Fishes of the Island of Haiti and Santo Domingo. – Zoologica, N.Y., 10, No.1:1–279. 1928.
Betancourt, A.N. Cordel y anzuela. Identificación, morfolóca y habitas de los pesces de interés de neustra mares, con comentarios sobre su aporte a la economia nacional. – Depart. Divers. Agric. Sec. Asuntas Pesq, Banco Fomento. Agric. Indus. Cuba. 1956. 252 pp.
Butsch, R.S. A List of Barbadian Fishes. – J. Barbados Mus., 7, No.1:17–31. 1939.
Caldwell, D.C. and M.C. Fishes from the Southern Caribbean Collected by Velero III in 1939. – Allan Hancock Pacif. Exped., 10:1–61. 1964. ill.
Cervigón, F. Lista de los peces marinos de Venezuela. – Lagena, 5:8–71. 1965.
Erdman, D.S. Recent Fish Records from Puerto Rico. – Bull. Mar. Sci. Gulf Caribb., 6:315–340. 1957.
Meek, S.E. and S.F.Hildebrand. The Marine Fishes of Panama. – Field Mus. Nat. Hist. Publs., Zool. Ser., Chicago, 15, 226. Part I, pp.1–330, pls.1–24. 1923; Part II, pp.331–707, pls.25–71. 1925; Part III, pp.709–1045. 1928. ill.

Nichols, J.T. The Fishes of Porto Rico and the Virgin Islands. Pomacentridae to Ogcocephalidae. - Scient. Surv. P.Rico, 10:299-399. 1930. 139 figs.

Smith, V. The Reef Fish Fairyland of Jamaica. Pts.I-III. - Nat. Hist. Notes Jamaica, 45:185-191. 1950. 11 text-figs.; 46:199-205. 1950. 10 text-figs.; 47:221-227. 1951. 15 text-figs.

412 ab - fresh and marine waters

Buesa, R. J. Las Pesquerias Cubanas. - Contrnes. Cent. Invest. pesq. Habano, 20:1-93. 1964. 7 figs.

Caiñas, F. Historia Natural: Zoologia, en Cuba en la Mano, Ucar Garcia y Cia., Habana, pp.476-564. 1940. ill.

Caldwell, D.K. Marine and Freshwater Fishes from the West Coast of Jamaica. - Sci. Ser., 17:1-120. 1966.

Caldwell, D.K., L.H.Orgen, and L.Giovannoli. Systematic and Ecological Notes on Some Fishes Collected in the Vicinity of Tortuguero, Caribbean Coast of Costa Rica. - Revta Biol. trop., 7, No.1:7-33. 1959. 2 figs.

Diaz, E.L. Bibliographic Material on the Fishes of Colombia and Northwestern South America. - Fish Tech. Pap. F.A.O., 53:1-72. 1965.

Duarte-Bello, P.P. Catalogo de peces Cubanos Univ. Villanueva. - Lab. Biol. Mar., Monogr., 6:1-208. 1959.

Fowler, H.W. Results of the Fifth George Vanderbilt Expedition, 1941 (Bahamas, Caribbean Sea, Panama, Galapagos Archipelago and Mexican Pacific Islands). The Fishes. - Monogr. Acad. Nat. Sci. Philad., 6:57-530. figs.1-264, pls.1-20. 1944.

Fowler, H.W. The Fishes of Hispaniola. - Mems. Soc. cub. Hist. nat. "Felipe Poey," 21, No.1:83-122. 1952. 7 pls.

Hildebrand, S.F. Fishes of the Republic of El Salvador, Central America. - Bull. Bur. Fish., Wash., 41:237-287. 1926. 20 figs.

Hubbs, C.L. Fishes of the Yucatan Peninsula. - Publs. Carnegie Instn., 457:157-287. 1936. 1 text-fig., 15 pls.

Longley, W.N. and S.F.Hildebrand. Systematic Catalogue of the Fishes of Tortugas. - Pap. Tortugas Lab., 34:1-331. 1941. 34 pls.

Poey, F. La monumental obra de Don Felipe Poey y Aloy. Ictiologia Cubana. Transcripta y comentada por . . . M. Sánchez Roig, . . . con la colaboracion de F.Gómez de la Maza etc. Vol.I. - Publ. Com. Encarg. Recop. Hist. Nat. Cuba, 1:1-372. 1955. 5 pls.

Poey, F. Ictiologia Cubana. Habana. 1962. 106 pp., 87 pls.

Rivero, L.H.Y. List of the Fishes, Types of Poey, in the Museum of Comparative Zoology. - Bull. Mus. Comp. Zool. Harv., 82:169-227. 1938.

Röhl, E. Fauna descriptiva de Venezuela. - Boln. Acad. Cienc. Caracas, 12, Nos.36-37:i-xxxvi+1-495. 1949. 246 figs.

Sánchez, R.M. and F.Gómez de La Maza. La Pesca en Cuba. - Min. de Agric. 1952. 272 pp., ill.

413 - South America

413a - fresh waters

Boeseman, M. A Preliminary List of Surinam Fishes not Included in Eigenmann's Enumeration of 1912. - Zool. Meded., Leiden, 31:179-200. 1952.

Boeseman, M. The Freshwater Fishes of the Island of Trinidad. Studies on the Fauna of Curacao and Other Caribbean Islands. - Uitg. natuurw. Stud.-Kring Suriname, 21:72-153, figs.36, 37. 1960.

Devincenzi, G.J. and G.W.Teague. Ictiofauna del Rio Uruguay Medio. - An. Mus. nac. Montevideo, Ser.2, 5, No.4:1-104. 1942. 6 pls.

Eigenmann, C.H. The Fishes of Lake Valencia, Caracas and of the Rio Tuy at el Concejo, Venezuela. - Univ. Stud. Indiana, 7:1-13, pls.1-3. 1920.

Eigenmann, C.H. and W.R. Allen. Fishes of Western South America. I. The Intercordilleran and Amazonian Lowlands of Peru. II. The High Pampas of Peru, Bolivia, and Northern Chile. Lexington, Kentucky. 1942. i–xv+1–494 pp., 22 pls., 48 text-figs.

Fowler, H.W. Zoological Results of the Second Bolivian Expedition for the Academy of Natural Sciences of Philadelphia, 1936–1937. Part I. Fishes. – Proc. Acad. Nat. Sci. Philad., 92:43–103. 1940. 52 figs.

Fowler, H.W. A Collection of Freshwater Fishes Obtained in Eastern Brazil by Dr. Rodolpho von Ihering. – Ibid., 93:123–199, figs.1–104. 1941.

Fowler, H.W. Os peixes de áqua doce do Brasil. – Archos Zool. Est S Paulo, Part 1, 6:1–204, figs.1–237. 1948; Part 2, 6:205–404, figs.238–447. (1950) 1951; Part 3, 6:405–628, figs.448–589. 1951; Part 4, 9:1–400, figs.590–905. 1954.

López, R.B. Peces demersales del sur del Brasil, Uruguay y Norte de la Argentina. Distribution geografica. – Anais. cong. Lat.-Am., Zool., 2:155–185. 1965.

Luengo, J.A. La fauna ictiologica del lago de Valencia (Venezuela) y algunas consideraciones sobre las demas hoyas del pais y Trinidad. – Acta biol. venez., 3, No.22:321–339. 1963.

MacDonagh, E.J. Los peces de las aguas termales de Barreto. – Revta. Mus. La Plata, n. s., Zool., 1:45–87. 1938. 2 pls.

MacDonagh, E.J. Contribución a la sistemática y etologiá de los peces fluviatiles Argentinos. – Ibid., pp.119–208. 5 pls.

Mago Leccia, F. Contribución a la sistemática y ecologiá de los peces de la Laguna de Unare, Venezuela. – Bull. Mar. Sci. Gulf Caribb., 15:274–330. 1965. 14 figs.

Miles, C. Los Peces del Rio Magdalena. 1947. 214 pp., 134 text-figs.

Myers, G.S. Descriptions of New South American Freshwater Fishes Collected by Dr. Carl Ternetz. – Bull. Mus. Comp. Zool. Harv., 68:107–135. 1927.

Myers, G.S. Fishes from the Upper Rio Meta Basin, Colombia. – Proc. Biol. Soc. Wash., 43:65–72. 1930.

Myers, G.S. Studies on South American Freshwater Fishes. I. – Stanford Ichthyol. Bull., 2:89–114. 1942. 19 text-figs.

Pearse, A.S. The Fishes of Lake Valencia, Venezuela. – Univ. Wis. Stud. Sci., 1:1–51. 1920.

Pearson, N.E. The Fishes of the Eastern Slope of the Andes. I. The Fishes of the Rio Beni Basin, Bolivia, Collected by the Mulford Expedition. – Indiana Univ. Stud., 11, No.64:1–83. 1924. 12 pls. 4 figs.

Pearson, N.E. The Fishes of the Beni-Mamoré and Paraguay Basins, and a Discussion of the Origin of the Paraguayan Fauna. – Proc. Calif. Acad. Sci., 4, No.23:99–114. 1937.

Pozzi, A.J. Sistematica y distribucion de los peces de agua dulce de la Republica Argentina. – Gaea, Buenos Aires, 7:239–292. 1945.

Rendahl, H. Einige Fische aus Ecuador und Bolivia. – Ark. Zool. 29A, No.11:1–11. 1937. 3 text-figs.

Ribeiro, P. de Miranda. Catalogo dos peixes do Museo Nacional. – Publções. avuls. Mus. nac., Rio de J., Parts I–XI. 1954–1962.

Ringuelet, R.A. and R.H. Aramburu. Peces argentinos de dulce. Clave de reconocimiento y caracterización de familias y subfamilias, con glosario explicativo. – Argo, 3, No.7:1–98. 1961. 9 figs.

Schneider, C.O. Catálogo de los peces fluviales de la provinciá de Concepçión. – Boln. Soc. Biol. Concepçión., 24:51–60. 1949.

413b – marine waters

Ameghino, F. Notes sur les poissons du Patagonien. Notas sobre los peces de Patagonico. – Obras completas y correspondencia cientifica de Florentino Ameghino, La Plata, 17:383–421. 1934. 2 text-figs.

Barcellos, B.N. Ictiofauna marinha do Rio Grande do Sul. – Boln. I. C.N. 17:1–16. 2 figs.; 18:1–40. 9 figs. 1963.

Buen, F. de. El Mar de Solis y su fauna de peces. – Publnes. cient. Serv. oceanogr. Pesca, Montev., 1:1–43. 15 text-figs.; 2:45–144. 1949, 1950. ill.

Carvalho, J. de P. Nota preliminar sôbre a fauna ictiologica do litoral sul do Estado de São Paulo. – Bolm. Ind. anim., n. s., 4, Nos.3–4:27–81. 1941.

Carvalho, J. de P. Resultados cientificos do cruzeiro do "Baependi" e do "Vega" á i. da Trinidade. Peixes. – Bolm. Inst. Oceanogr., S Paulo, 1, No.1:97–133. 1950. 4 figs. (English abstract.)

Cervigón, F. Lista de los peces marinos de Venezuela. – Lagena, 5:8–71. 1965.

Cervigón, M.F. Los peces marinos de Venezuela. 2. – Fund. La Salle Cien. Nat., Monogr., 12:441–951, figs.182–385. 1966.

Dahl, G. Los peces cartilaginosus de la bahia de Cispata y del estuario del Rio Sinu. – Revta. Colomb. cienc. exact., fis. y natur., 12, No.46:175–195. 1964.

Devincenzi, G.J. Peces del Uruguay. – An. Mus. nac. Montevideo, Ser.3, 4:97–138, pls.9–12. 1920; II, 5:139–290, pls.13–23. 1924.

Devincenzi, G.J. El primer ensayo sobre ictiológica del Uruguay. – Ibid., 6:295–323. 1925.

Devincenzi, G.J. Peces del Uruguay. Notas complementarias. II. – Ibid., 4, No.3:1–11. 1933. 1 pl., 1 fig.

Devincenzi, G.J. Notas ictiológicas sobre peces de la región Patagónica. Análisis de la obra de J.R.Norman: Coast Fishes. II. The Patagonian Region. – Discovery Rep., Vol.16. 1937; An. Mus. nac. Montevideo, Ser.2, 4, No.14:1–21. 1939. 1 text-fig.

Devincenzi, G.J. Peces del Uruguay. Notas complementarias. III. – An. Mus. nac. Montevideo, Ser.2, 4, No.13:1–39. 1939. ill.

Devincenzi, G.J. and D.Legrand. Album Ictiológico del Uruguay. – Ibid., Ser.3, pls.XXV–XXXVI. 1936.

Fowler, H.W. A List of the Fishes Known from the Coast of Brazil. – Archos. Zool. Est. S Paulo, 3:115–184. (1941) 1942.

Fowler, H.W. Notes and Descriptions of New or Little-known Fishes from Uruguay. – Proc. Acad. Nat. Sci. Philad., 95:311–334, figs.1–25. 1943.

Fowler, H.W. The Brazilian and Patagonian Fishes of the Wilkes Expedition, 1838–1842. – Bolm. Inst. Oceanogr., S Paulo, 2, No.1:3–39. 1952.

Fowler, H.W. The Shore Fishes of the Colombian Caribbean. – Caldasia, 6:43–73. 1953. 3 text-figs.

Grey, M. Descriptions of Abyssal Benthic Fishes from the Gulf of Mexico. – Fieldiana, Zool., 39:149–183. 1958.

Koepcke, H.W. Lista de los peces marinos conocidos del Peru. – Biota, 4, No.36:325–352. 1963.

Lopez, R.B. La pesca en la Republica Argentina. – Revta. Mus. munic. Cienc. nat. Mar. del Plata, 1, No.2:26–49. 1954.

Lowe, R.H. The Fishes of the British Guiana Continental Shelf, Atlantic Coast of South America, with Notes on their Natural History. – J. Linn. Soc. Lond., Zool., 44:669, 700. 1962.

McConnell, R.H. Introduction on the Fish Fauna of British Guiana. – Timehri, 37:25–35. 1958. 3 figs.

MacDonagh, E.J. and M.R.Covas. Peces patagónicos y fueguinos coleccionados por el doctor Federico G.Lynch. – Notas Mus. La Plata, 9, Zool. 76:229–241. 1944. ill.

Martin, S.F. Ictiologia del archipelago de los Roques. – In: Mendez, A. et al. El archipelago de les Roques y la Orchila. Soc. Cien. Nat. La Salbe, Caracas, pp.87–144. 1958. 16 pls.

Mendez, A.A. and S.F.Martin. Actividades pesquoras. – In: El archipelago de Los Roques y la Orchila, Caracas, pp.224–251, figs.1–13. 1956. 4 pls.

Norman, J.R. Coast Fishes. Part II. The Patagonian Region. – Discovery, Rep., 16:1–150. 1937. 5 pls., 76 text-figs.

Pozzi, A.T. and L.F.Bordale. Cuadro sistematice de los peces marinos de la República Argentina. – An. Soc. cient. argent., 120:145–189. 1935. 1 map.

Puyo, J. Contribution à l'étude ichthyologique de la Guyane Française. – Bull. Soc. Hist. nat. Toulouse, 70:1–258. 1936.

Puyo, J. Poissons de la Guyane française. – Faune emp. fr., 12:1–280. 1949. 139 text-figs.

Ringuelet, R. and R.H.Aramburu. Peces marinos de la republica Argentina. Clave para el reconocimiento de familias y generos. Catalogo critico abreviado. – Argo, 2, No.5:1–141. 1960. 72 figs.

Roth, V. Fish Life in British Guiana. Georgetown. 1947. 282 pp.

Santos, E. Nossos peixes marinhos. Rio de Janeiro. 1952. 265 pp.

Schultz, L.P. A Further Contribution to the Ichthyology of Venezuela. – Proc. U.S. Natn. Mus., 99:1–211. 1949.

Schweigger, E. El litora peruano. Lima. 1947. 262 pp.

Springer, S. and H.R.Bullis. Collections by the Oregon in the Gulf of Mexico. – Spec. Scient. Rep. U.S. Fish Wildl. Serv. Fisheries. 1956. 134 pp.

Travassos, H. Catálogo dos peixes do Vale do Rio São Francisco. – Bolm. Soc. cearense Agron., 1:1–66. 1960.

Weibezahn, F. H. Lista de los Peces de las costas de Venezuela. – Boln. Mus. Cienc. nat., 1, Nos.3–4:225–257. 1959.

42 – South Atlantic

421 – Tristan da Cunha Islands

Sivertsen, E. Fishes of Tristan da Cunha, with Remarks on Age and Growth Based on Scale Readings. – Res. Norw. Sci. Exped. to Tristan da Cunha, 1937–1938, Oslo, 12:1–44. 1945. 8 pls., 17 text-figs.

422 – South Africa

422 ab – marine and fresh waters

Barnard, K.H. A Monograph of the Marine Fishes of South Africa. 1–2. London. – Ann. S. Afr. Mus., 21:1–1065. 1925–1927. 37 pls.

Barnard, K.H. Revision of the Indigenous Freshwater Fishes of the S.W. Cape Region. – Ann. S. Afr. Mus., 36:101–262. 1943. 33 text-figs.

Barnard, K.H. A Pictorial Guide to South African Fishes (Marine and Freshwater). Cape Town. 1947. 226 pp., 25 pls.

Barnard, K.H. Further Notes on South African Marine Fishes. – Ann. S. Afr. Mus., 36, No.5:341–406, pls. IX–XIII. 1948. 17 text-figs.

Barnard, K.H. South African Shore Life. – Cape Town, Maskew Miller. 1954. 135 pp., 25 pls.

Fowler, H.W. Fishes from Natal, Zululand, and Portuguese East Africa. – Proc. Acad. Nat. Sci. Philad., 77:187–268, figs.1–4. 1925.

Jubb, R.A. A Revised List of the Freshwater Fishes of Southern Africa. – Ann. Cape Prov. Mus., 3:5–39. 1963.

Jubb, R.A. Fishes of the Cape Province. – Ibid., 4:1–72. 1965.

Jubb, R.A. Freshwater Fishes of Southern Africa. – Cape Town, Amsterdam, A. Balkema. 1967. 248 pp.

Jubb, R.A. and F.L. Farquharson. The Freshwater Fishes of the Orange River Drainage Basin. – S. Afr. J. Sci., 61, No.3:118–125. 1965.

Marchand, J.M. The South African Marine Fishes of Commercial and Angling Importance. – Fish. Bull. Un. S. Afr., 2:1–160. 1935. 115 text-figs.

Smith, J.L.B. Sea Fishes of Southern Africa. Johannesburg. 1953. 580 pp.

Smith, J.L.B. The Sea Fishes of Southern Africa (Cape Town). – Central News Agency. 1961. 580 pp., 103 col. pls., ill.

Smith, J.L.B. and M.M. Smith. Fishes of the Tsitsikama Coastal National Park. Johannesburg. 1967. 161 pp., col. figs.

43 East Atlantic

431 – Africa

431a – fresh waters

Blache, J.A. et al. Les poissons du Bassin du Tchad et du Bassin adjacent du Mayo-Kebbi. – Off. Rech. Sci. Tech. Outre-Mer. Paris. 1964. 483 pp.

Blanc, M. and J. Daget. Les eaux et les poissons de Haute-Volta. Mém. Inst. fr. Afr. noire, 36:1–391. 1957.

Boeseman, M. On a Collection of Fishes from Stanley Pool (Belgian Congo). – Zoöl. Meded., Leiden, 35, No.11:139–151. 1957. ill.

Boeseman, M. An Annotated List of Fishes from the Niger Delta, 61:1–48. 1963. ill.

Boulenger, G.A. A List of the Freshwater Fishes of Sierra Leone. – Ann. Mag. Nat. Hist., 9, No.4:34–36. 1919.

Boulenger, G.A. Poissons recueillis au Congo Belge par l'expédition du Dr. C. Christy. – Annls. Mus. r. Congo belge, Zool. Sér., Matériaux pour la faune du Congo, 2, No.4:1–38. 1920. ill.

Coulter, G.W. Research Results, Lake Tanganyika. – N. Rhodesia, Joint Fish. Res. Org. Rept., 10:7–30, pls.1–8. (1960) 1962. 11 figs.

Daget, J. Les Poissons du Niger supérieur. – Mém. Inst. fr. Afr. noire, 36:1–391, figs.1–141. 1954.

Daget, J. Deuxième Partie. Les Poissons in Blanc, M. and J. Daget. Les eaux et les poissons de Haute-Volta.– Ibid., 50:95–169 (Poissons, pp.113–169, figs.10–30). 1957.

Daget, J. Mémoire sur la Biologie des poissons du Niger Moyen. – Bull. Inst. fr. Afr. noire, Ser.A, 19, No.1:1–391. 1957. 141 figs.

Daget, J. Les poissons du Niger supérieur (1-ière note complémentaire). – Ibid., 21, No.2:664–688. 1959. 8 figs.

Daget, J. La faune ichthyologique du bassin de la Gambie. – Ibid., 22, No.2:610–619. 1960.

Daget, J. Contribution à la connaissance de la faune du fleuve Sénégal; poissons du Baoulé et du Bakoy. – Bull. Mus. natn. Hist. nat., Paris, 32, No.6:506–512. (1960) 1961:

Daget, J. and A. Iltis. Poissons de côte d'Ivoire (eaux douces et saumâtres). – Mém. Inst. fr. Afr. noire, 74:1–385. 1965. 212 figs., 4 pls.

Damas, H. Les poissons des lacs africains. – Tribune CEBEDEAU, 16, No.240:503–508. 1963,

David, L. Contribution à l'étude de la faune ichthyologique du lac Tanganyjka. – Revue Zool. Bot. afr., 28:149–160. 1936. 5 text-figs.

David, L. and M. Poll. Contribution à la faune ichthyologique du Congo Belge. – Annls. Mus. r. Congo belge, Sér., 1, No.3:189–294. 1937. 31 text-figs. 12 pls.

Dollfus, R.P. Première contribution à l'établissement d'un fichier ichthyologique du Maroc atlantique de Tanger. Direction publique au Maroc. – Trav. Inst. scient. chérif., Sér. Zool., 6:1–227. 1955.

Johnels, A.G. Notes on Fishes from the Gambia River. – Ark. Zool., Sér.2, 6, No.17:327–411. 1954. 19 figs.

Kähsbauer, P. Beitrag zur Kenntnis der Fischfauna von Nigeria. – Annln. naturh. Mus. Wien, 65:139–165. 1962. ill.

Ladiges, W. and J. Voelker. Untersuchungen über die Fischfauna in Gebirgsgewässern des Wasserscheiden-hochlands in Angola. – Mitt. hamb. zool. Mus. Inst., 59:117–140. 1961. ill.

Lambert, J. Contribution à l'étude des poissons de forêt de la cuvette congolaise. – Annls. Mus. r. Afr. cent. Sér. Zoologie, 93:1–40. 1961. ill.

Lockley, G.J. The Families of Freshwater Fishes of Tanganyika Territory, with a Key to their Identification.– E. Afr. Agric. J., 14:212–218. 1949. 2 text-figs.

Matagne, F. La pêche au Katanga. – C. r. Congr. Sci., Elisabethville, 4:420–435. (1950) 1951. 2 pls.

Matthes, H. Les poissons du lac Tumba et de la région d'Ikeda, étude systématique, écologique et zoogéographique des poissons dulcaquicoles africains (Doctoral Thesis, Univ. Amsterdam). 1964. 1–13+201+32 pp., 3 maps, 6 pls.

Monod, T. Notes d'ichthyologie ouest-africaine. – Bull. Inst. fr. Afr. noire, Sér.A, 12:1–71. 1950. 110 text-figs.

Pellegrin, J. Les poissons des eaux douces de l'Afrique occidentale (du Sénégal au Niger). – Publs. Com. Etud. hist. scient. Afr. occid. fr. 1923. 373 pp., 76 figs.

Poll, M. Contribution à la faune ichthyologique du Katanga. – Annls. Mus. r. Congo belge Sér. Zool., 1, 3, No.3:101–152. 1933. 15 figs.

Poll, M. Contribution à la Faune ichthyologique du Congo Belge: Collections du Dr. H. Schouteden (1924–1926) et d'autres récolteurs. – Ibid., 1, 3, No.5:189–294, pl. XII. 1937. 31 figs.

Poll, M. Poissons du Katanga (bassin du Congo) récoltés par le professeur Paul Brien. – Revue Zool. Bot. afr., 30:389–423. 1938. 15 text-figs.

Poll, M. Les poissons du Stanley Pool. – Annls. Mus. r. Congo belge, Sér. Zool., 1, 4, No.1:1–60. 1939. 36 figs.

Poll, M. Les poissons du Lac Tumba, Congo Belge. – Bull. Mus. r. Hist. nat. Belg., 18, No.36:1–25. 1942. 6 text-figs.

Poll, M. La Pêche en eau douce au Congo Belge. – Bull. agric. Congo belge, 34, Nos.1–2:111–162. 1943. 31 figs.

Poll, M. Révision de la faune ichthyologique du Lac Tanganika. – Annls. Mus. r. Congo belge, Sér. Zool., Poissons, Reptiles Amphibies, Sér.1, 4, No.3:141–364. figs.1–87, pls.1–3. 1946.

Poll, M. Poissons recueillis au Katanga par H.J. Bredo. – Bull. Mus. r. Hist. nat. Belg., 24, No.21:1–24. 1948. ill.

Poll, M. Poissons non Cichlidae. – Résult. scient. Explor. hydrobiol. Lac Tanganika, (1946–1947). 3, No.5A:1–251. 1953. 11 pls., 34 figs.

Poll, M. Résultats Scientifiques des Missions Zoologiques au Stanley Pool subsidiées par le Cemubac (Université Libre de Bruxelles) et le Musée Royal du Congo (1957–1958). III. Recherches sur la faune ichthyologique de la région du Stanley Pool. – Annls. Mus. r. Congo belge, (8), 71:75–174. 1959. 15 pls.

Ricardo, C.K. The Fishes of the Bangweulu Region. – J. Linn. Soc., Zool., 41:183–217. 1940. 2 figs.

Roman, B. Les poissons des Haut-Bassins de la Volta. – Annls. Mus. r. Afr. cent. Sér. 8a, 150:1–191. 1966. 7 pls.

Sandon, H. An Illustrated Guide to the Freshwater Fishes of the Sudan. – Sudan Notes Rec., pp.1–61. 1950. 14 pls.

Schultz, L.P. The Freshwater Fishes of Liberia. – Proc. U.S. Natn. Mus., 92:301–348, pls.35–36. 1942.

Svensson, G.S.O. Freshwater Fishes from the Gambia River (British West Africa). Results of the Swedish Expedition, 1931. – K. svenska VetensAkad. Handl., 12, No.3:1–102. 1933. 8 pls., 28 text-figs.

Thys van den Audenaerde, D. F. E. List of the Freshwater Fishes Presently Known from the Island of Fernando Poo. – Bonn zool. Beitr., 16, Nos.3–4:316–317. (1965) 1966.

Trewavas, E. and F.R. Irvine. Freshwater Fishes (pp.221–282). – In: The Fish and Fisheries of the Gold Coast by F.R.Irvine. Crown Agents, London. 1947. 352 pp.

Worthington, E.B. and C.K. Ricardo. The Fish of Lake Tanganyika (Other than Cichlidae). – Proc. Zool. Soc., Lond., 4:1061–1112. (1936) 1937. 12 figs.

431b – marine waters

Bassindale, R. On the Marine Fauna of Ghana. – Proc. Zool. Soc., Lond., 137:481–510. 1961. 5 figs.

Belloc, G. Catalogue des poissons comestibles du Maroc et de la côte occidentale d'Afrique (du Cap Spartel au Cap Vert). – Revue Trav. Inst. Pêch. marit., 7:117–194. 1934. 38 figs.

Cadenat, J. Recherches systématiques sur les poissons littoraux de la côte occidentale d'Afrique. – Ibid., 10:425–562. 1937.

Cadenat, J. Poissons de Mer du Sénégal. – Bull. Inst. fr. Afr. noire. (1950) 1951. 345 pp., 241 figs.

Cadenat, J. Notes d'Ichthyologie Ouest-Africain. VI. Poissons des Campagnes du "Gérard Tréca." – Bull. Inst. fr. Afr. noire, Sér.A, 15, No.3:1051–1102, figs.1–43. 1953.

Cadenat, J. Notes d'Ichthyologie Ouest-Africaine. XXX. Poissons de mer ouest-africans observés du Sénégal au Cameroun et plus spécialement au large des côtes de Sierra Leone et du Ghana. – Ibid., 22, No.4:1358–1420, pls.1–3. 1960.

Cadenat, J. Principales espèces de poissons de mer des eaux sénégalaises. – Notes Afric., 103:91–95. 1964.

Cadenat, J. and E. Marchal. Résultats des campagnes océanographiques de la Reine-Pokou aux îles Sainte-Hélène et Ascension. Poissons. –Bull. Inst. fr. Afr. noire, Sér.A, 25, No.4:1235–1315. 1963. 48 figs.

Cervigón, F. Peces recogidos en el cursa de las campañas realizadas a bordo del "Costa Canaria" desde cabo Bojarod Portuguesa (Africa occidental) y consideraciones sobre su distribución. – Investigation Pesq., 17:33–107. 1960. ill.

Chabanaud, P. and T. Monod. Les poissons de Port-Etienne. Contribution à la faune ichthyologique de la région du Cap Blanc (Mauritanie Française). – Bull. Com. Etud. hist. scient. Afr. occid. fr., pp.225–287, figs.1–33, pls.I–III. 1926.

Copley, H. The Game Fishes of Africa. London. 1952. 276 pp.

Correira da Costa. Estudos de pescas em S. Tomé e Principe. – Mems. Ita Invest. Ultramar, 2, No.8:215–271. 1959. 5 maps.

Daget, J. Les poissons du Fouta-Dialon et de la basse Guinée. – Mém. Inst. fr. Afr. noire. Sér.A, 65:1–210. 1962. 13 pls., 61 figs.

Dieuzeide, R., M. Novella, and J. Roland. Catalogue des poissons des côtes algériennes. – Bull. Stn. Agric. Pêche Castiglione, 4:1–135. 1953. ill; 5:1–258. 1953; pp.1–384. 1955; Atlas. 1956.

Dieuzeide, R. and J. Roland. Complément au catalogue des poissons des côtes Algériennes. – Ibid., 8-87–106. 1957. 4 pls.

Dollfus, R.P. Première contribution à l'établissement d'un fichier ichthyologique du Maroc Atlantique de Tanger à l'embouchure de l'Oued Dra. – Trav. Inst. scient. chérif., Sér. Zool., 6:1–229. 1955. ill.

Dollfus, R.P. Exposé sommaire des récents progrès dans la connaissance ichthyologique du Maroc atlantique. – Bull. Soc. Sci. nat. phys. Maroc, 39, No.2:91–116. 1959.

Fowler, H.W. The Marine Fishes of West Africa. – Bull. Am. Mus. Nat. Hist., 70, Nos.1–2:1–1493, figs.1–567. 1936.

Furnestin, J. et al. Données nouvelles sur les poissons du Maroc atlantique. – Revue Trav. Off. (scient. tech.) Pêch. marit., 22:381–487. 1958. 75 figs.

Hornell, J. The Principal Fishes of Economic Value in Sierra Leone. – Sierra Leone Stud., 14:1–9. 1929.

Irvine, F.R., A.P. Brown, J.R. Norman, and E. Trewavas. The Fishes and Fisheries of the Gold Coast. 1947. 352 pp., 217 figs.

Maul, G.E. Peixes. – In: Noronha and Sarmento. Vertebrados da Madeira. Junta Geral. Distrito Autónoma do Funchal, 2:1–181. 1948.

Monod, T. Contribution à la faune du Cameroun. Pisces. I. Pisces marini. – Faune Colon. fr., 1:643–742. 1927. 35 figs.

Norman, J.R. and F.R.Irvine. The Fishes and Fisheries of the Gold Coast. – Marine Fishes, pp.81–220, figs.17–134. 1947.

Nunes, A.A. Peixes da Madeiro, Funchal, Ilha da Madeira. 1954. 1–274+A–L pp., 25 col. pls.

Pellegrin, J. Les poissons des eaux de l'Afrique du Nord française. – Mém. Soc. Sci. nat. phys. Maroc, 1:1–202. 1921.

Poll, M. Poissons en Expédition océanographique Belge dans les eaux côtières Africaines de l'Atlantique sud (1948–1949). – Bull. Inst. r. Sci. nat. Belg., 4, No.1. 1951. I. Généralités: 1–14, figs.1–67; II. Sélaciens et Chimères:15–154, pls. I–XIII, figs.1–104; 4, No.2. 1953. III. Téléostéens Malacoptérygiens:1–258, pls. I–VIII, figs.1–107; 4, No.3 A. 1954. IV, V. Téléostéens Acanthoptérygiens, I:1–390, pls. I–IX, figs.1–127; 4, No.3 B. 1959. II:1–417, pls. I–VII.

Postel, E. Pêche sur les côtes d'Afrique Occidentale. II. Poissons de surface. – Rapport et note sur quelques poissons de surface, Gov. Gen. de l'Afr. Occ. Franc. Insp. Gén.del'Elevage. Dakar. 1950. 77 pp.

Prosvirov, E.S., V.I.Skornyakov, and K.Ya.Batal'yants. Commercial and Some Noncommercial Fishes off the West African Coast (from Levrier Bay to the Gulf of Guinea). Textbook for Fishermen. Kaliningrad. 1961. 176 pp., ill.

Radakov, D.V. Distribution of the Marine Ichthyofauna off the Shores of the Republic of Guinea. – Vopr. Ikhtiol., 6:98–207. 1966. 2 figs.

Roule, L. Description de poissons abyssaux provenant de l'île Modère et des parages du Maroc. – Bull. Inst. océanogr., Monaco, 546:1–18. 1929. 3 figs.

Roux, C. Poissons marins. – In: Collignon, J., M.Rossignol, and C.Roux. Mollusques, Crustacés et Poissons marins des côtes d'A.E.F. en collection au Centre d'Océanographie de l'Institut d'Etudes Centrafricaines de Pointe-Noire. – Office de la Recherche Scientifique et Technique Outre-Mer, pp.137–368, figs.1–121. 1957. 1 pl.

Seurat, L.G. Poissons de l'Algérie. – Exploration Zoologique de l'Algérie, 1830–1930, pp.217–251. Paris. 1930. 3 pls., 7 figs.

432 – Europe
432a – fresh waters

Aleksandrov, B.M. et al. Lakes of Karelia, Nature, Fishes, and Fishery. Handbook. Petrozavodsk. 1959. 619 pp., ill.

Angel, A.F. Atlas des Poissons. III. Poissons des eaux douces. Espèces françaises. Paris. 1943. 55 pp., XII pls., 13 text-figs.

Athanassopoulas, G. Particularités de la distribution de l'ichthyofaune des eaux douces en Grèce. – In: Verhandlungen der Internationalen Vereinigung für theoretische und angewandte Limnologie, 7, No.1:117–121. 1935.

Bagdazhyus, B. Fishes and Fishery Prospects for Some Lakes of Lithuania. Author's Summary of Candidate Thesis. Vilnius. 1961. 8 pp.

Balon, E.K. A Preliminary List of the Slovakian Lampreys and Fishes (Petromyzones and Teleostomi). – Biológia, Bratislava, 19:343–358. 1964. 1 fig. (In Czechoslovakian, English summary.)

Bauch, G. Die einheimischen Süsswasserfische. 3rd edition. Berlin. 1955. 201 pp., ill.

Bauch, G. Die einheimischen Süsswasserfische. 4th edition. Radebeul-Berlin. 1963. 200 pp., ill.

Berg, L.S. Übersicht der Verbreitung der Süsswasserfische Europas. – Zoogeografica, 1, No.2:107–208, figs.1–16. 1932.

Berg, L.S. A Survey of Fishes Inhabiting Small Lakes of the Leningrad Region. – Izv. Vses. Nauchno-Issled. Inst. Ozern. Rechn. Ryb. Khoz., 22:7–13. 1939.

Berg, L.S. Freshwater Fishes of the USSR. 4th edition, Leningrad–Moscow, 1, No.1:1–466. 1948; 2:467–926. 1949; 3:927–1382. 1949. ill.

Berg, L.S. Freshwater Fishes of the USSR and Adjacent Countries. – Israel Program for Scientific Translations. Jerusalem, 1:1–504. 1962; 2:1–496. 1964; 3:1–510. 1965. ill.

Buen, F. de. Notas sobre la fauna ictiológica de nuestras aguas dulces. – Boln. Oceanogr. Pesc., 15:450–512. 1930. 71 figs.

Chernov, V.K. Data on the Fishes of Lakes in the Region of the Borodino Freshwater Biological Station. - Trudy Borodin. Biol. Presnovod. Sta., 5:1–14. 1927.

Domrachev, P.F. and I.F. Pravdin. Fishes of Lake Ilmen and the Volkhov River and their Commercial Importance. - Mater. Issled. r. Volkhova i ego Basseina, 10, No.1:1–290. 1926.

Drensky, P. Ochrida-See und seine Fischfauna. - Trav. Soc. Bulg. Sci. Nat., 9:103–112. Sofia. 1921.

Drensky, P. Zur Kenntnis der Süsswasserfischfauna Bulgariens. - Zool. Jber., Jena (Syst.), 59:663–680. 1930.

Gasowskiej, M. (editor) Krąglouste i ryby. - In: Klucze do oznaczania kręgowców Polski, Part 1, pp.1–240. 1962.

Hartley, P.H.T. The Coarse Fishes of Britain. - Scient. Publs. Freshwat. Biol. Ass., 12:1–40. 1947. 4 text-figs.

Hodgson, N.B. Freshwater Fishes of the British Isles, 2nd ed. London. 1949. 59 pp., ill.

Ivanauskas, T. et al. Leituvos geluju vandenu zuvys. Freshwater Fishes of Latvia. Vilnius. 1956. 238 pp., 3 pls., 80 figs.

Jaskowski, J. Materialien zur Kenntnis der Fischfauna der Warta und ihrer Nebenflüsse. - Fragm. faun., Warszawa, 9:449–499. 1962.

Karaman, S.L. Die Fische der Strumica (Struma-System). - Acta Mus. maced. Sci. nat., 3, No.7:181–208. 1955. 7 figs., map.

Kux, Z. and T. Weisz. Ichthyofauna jižni časti Slovenského Záhoří. - Čas. morav. Mus., Věda Přír., 46:187–202. 1961. ill.

Ladiges, W. and D. Vogt. Die Süsswasserfische Europas bis zum Ural und Kaspischen Meer. - Hamburg-Berlin, Paul Parey. 1965. 250 pp.

Lehman, J.P. Les poissons du Downtonian de la Scanie (Suède) Rennes. - Mém. Pres. Fac. Sci. Univ. Paris. 1937. 98 pp., VIII pls.

Lozano, C.F. Los peces de las aquas continentales españolas. - Min. Aguc. Madrid. 1964. 307 pp., ill.

MacMahon, A.F.M. British Freshwater Fishes. Middlesex, England. 1946. 208 pp., ill.

Manyukas, I. Study of the Ichthyofauna of the Nyamunas River. - Gidrobiol. Issled., Tallinn, 3:206–213. 1962.

Margalef, R. Contribucion al estudio de la fauna de las aguas dulces del noroeste de España. - Publnes. Inst. Biol. apl., Barcelona, 21:137–171. 1955. 14 figs. (English summary.)

Michailova, L. Untersuchungen über die Fischfauna des Struma-Flusses. - Izv. Zool. Inst., Sofia, 19:55–71. 1965.

Mihályi, F. Revision der Süsswasserfische von Ungarn und der angrenzenden Gebiete in der Sammlung des Ungarischen Naturwissenschaftlichen Museums. - Annls. hist.-nat. Mus. natn. hung., n. s., 5:433–456. 1954.

Nikolaev, I.I. Specific Composition of the Fishes of the Latvian SSSR. - Trudy Latv. Otd. Vses. Nauchno-Issled. Inst. Morsk. Ryb. Khoz. Okeanogr., 1:27. 1953.

Odenwall, E. Fiskfaunan i Lappajärvi sjö. - Acta Soc. Fauna Flora fenn., 56, No.13:1–48. 1927. ill.

Parenzan, P. I pesci del bacino del lago Regina Margherita nell Galla e Sidama. - Boll. Pesca Piscic. Idrobiol., 15:146–167. 1939. 9 text-figs.

Peczalska, A. Ryby użytkowe Bałtyku. Ser.2. - Warszawa, Państw. Zakł. Wydawn. Szkoln. 1955. 85 pp., ill., map.

Peshev, I. A Survey of the Ichthyofauna of the Elishnitsa River. - Izv. Narod. Muzei, Varna, 2:179–191. 1966.

Pokrovskii, V.V. Commercial Fishes of the Northeastern Region of Lake Onega. - Ryb. Khoz. Karelii, 3:41–90. 1936.

Poljakov, G.D., N. Filipi, and K. Basho. Peshqit ë Shqipërise. - Univ. Shtetëror i Tiranës. 1958. 185 pp., ill.

Pravdin, I.F. Commercial Fishes of the Neva River. - Izv. Vses. Nauchno-Issled. Inst. Ozern. Rechn. Ryb. Khoz., 22:38–49. 1939.

Pravdin, I.F. Fishes from the Water Bodies of the Karelian Isthmus. - Uchen. Zap. Karelo-Fin. Univ., Biol. Sci., 3, No.3:126–162. 1948.

Pravdin, I.F. Specific Composition of the Fishes of Lake Ladoga and the Surrounding Area. - Izv. Vses. Nauchno-Issled. Inst. Ozern. Rechn. Ryb. Khoz., 38:12–30. 1956.

Prieditis, A.R. Freshwater Fishes of the Latvian SSR, their Distribution and Migration Routes. Author's Summary of Candidate Thesis. Riga. 1950. 26 pp.

Rey, L.L. Los peces fluviales de España. - Mems. R. Acad. Cienc. exact. fis. nat. Madr., 5:1–390. 1935. 28 pls., 25 figs.

Ribaut, J.P. Les poissons du canton de Vaud (Suisse). I. Poissons des cours d'eau. – Mém. Soc. vaud. Sci. nat., 14, No.3:69–128. 1966.

Roule, L. Les poissons des eaux douces de la France. Paris. 1925. i–xv+1–228. ill.

Sauerzopf, F. Beitrag zur Fischfauna des Burgenlandes. – Wiss. Arb. Burgenld., 32:142–146. (1963–1964). 1965.

Scheffelt, E. and W. Schweizer. Fische und Fischerei im Bodensee. – Stuttgart, F.Enke. 1926. i–viii+1–172 pp.

Schindler, O. Unsere Süsswasserfische. Stuttgart. (1953) 1959. 222 pp.

Schindler, O. Freshwater Fishes. Translated and edited by P.A.Orkin. – London, Thames and Hudson. 1957. 243 pp.

Shaposhnikova, G.Kh. Data on the Ichthyofauna of the Venta River. – Trudy Inst. Biol. Akad. Nauk LatvSSR, 7:313–322. 1958.

Sloka, Ya.Ya. Fish Fauna and Production of Lake Reznas. Author's Summary of Candidate Thesis. Riga. 1960. 14 pp.

Spillmann, C.J. Faune de France. 65. Poissons d'eau douce. – Paris, Eds. Paul Lechevalier. 1961. 303 pp., ill.

Staff, F. Ryby słodkowodne Polski i krajów ościennych. Warszawa. 1950. 286 pp., ill.

Stanković, S. Die Fauna des Ohridsees und ihre Herkunft. – Arch. Hydrobiol., 23:557–617. 1932. 1 pl.

Stanković, S. The Balkan Lake Ohrid and its Living World. – Monogr. Biol., 9:1–357. 1960. 1 pl., 100 figs.

Steinmann, P. Die Fische der Schweiz. Aarau. 1936. 154 pp.

Streseman, E. et al. Excursionsfauna von Deutschland.. Wirbeltiere. – Berlin (Volk u. Wissen Volkseigener Verlag). 1955. i–xii+1–340 pp., 46 pls., 255 figs.

Taler, Z. List of Freshwater Fishes of Yugoslavia. – Glas. Muz. srp. Zeml., Biološke Nauk, Ser.B, Nos.5–6. 1953.

Varley, M.E. British Freshwater Fishes: Factors Affecting their Distribution. – Fishg. News, pp.1–148. 1967. ill.

Vladykov, V. Fishes of Ruthenia and Principal Methods of Fishery, pp.3–147. Uzhgorod. 1926.

Voronin, F.N. Fishes of the Belorussian SSR. Minsk. 1957. 83 pp.

Yankovskaya, L.A. Fishes of the Neva River, their Biology and Commercial Importance. Author's Summary of Candidate Thesis. Leningrad. 1955. 17 pp.

Zernova, A.I. Ichthyofauna of the Luga River Basin. Author's Summary of Candidate Thesis. Leningrad. 1953. 16 pp.

Zhukau, P.I. Specific Composition of Fishes from the Neman River in the Belorussian SSR. – Izv. Akad. Nauk BelorussSSR, Ser. Biol., 1:97–107. 1956. (In Ukrainian.)

Zhukau, P.I. Specific Composition of Fishes of the Western Dvina River Basin in the Belorussian SSR. – Ibid., 2:82–90. 1959. (In Ukrainian.)

Zhukov, P.I. Key to the Fishes of the Belorussian SSR. – Minsk, Akad. Nauk BelorussSSR. 1960. 123 pp.

Zhukov, P.I. Fishes of Belorussia. – Ibid. 1965. 415 pp.

Zhukov, P.I. Fishes of the Neman River Basin and their Commercial Importance. Author's Summary of Thesis. Beloruss. Univ. 1967. 16 pp.

Zykov, P.V. Fishes of Lake Chimol'sk. – Izv. Karelo-Fin. Fil. Akad. Nauk SSSR, 3:75–81. 1951.

432ab – fresh and marine waters

Albuquerque, R.M. Peixes de Portugal e ilhas adjacentes chaves para a sua determinaçao. – Acta biol. Lisbon, 5B: i–xvi+1–1167. 1956. 445 figs.

Angelis, R. de. La pesca in Albania. – Boll. Pesca Piscic. Idrobiol., 16:213–228. 1940. 8 text-figs.

Berg, L.S. Fishes of the Gulf of Finland. – Izv. Vses. Nauchno-Issled. Inst. Ozern. Rechn. Ryb. Khoz., 23, No.2:3–46. 1940.

Buen, F. de. Lista de peces. – Boln. Pescas, Madrid, pp.153–161. 1920. 2 figs.

Buen, F. de. Fauna ichthyologia. Catalogo de los peces Ibéricos; de la plánicie continental, aguas dulces, pelágicos y de los abismos proximos. Part 2. Notas y resumenes. – Trab. Inst. esp. Oceanogr., (2), 89:91–149. 1935; Part 3, (2), 94:151–173. 1936.

Duncker, G. Die Fische der Nordmark. – Abh. Verh. naturw. Ver. Hamburg, 2 Suppl. – Hamburg, Cram de Gruyter und Co.in Komm. 1960. 432 pp., ill.

Halme, E.S. Pohjolan kalat varikuvina. Suomeksi toimitt. Halme Erkki s.l. WSOY. Fishes of Scandinavia in Coloured Plates. – Suomen kirjakauppalenti, 67, No.20:1–574. 1964.

Helling, H. Tabela dicotómica dos ciclostomos e dos peixes de Portugal. – Mem. Mus. Zool. Univ. Coimbra, Ser.1, 114:1-67. 1940. 20 text-figs.

Helling, H. Novo catalogo dos peixes de Portugal em colecção no museu de zoologia da Universidade de Coimbra. – Ibid., 149:1–110. 1943.

Ionescu, V. Vertebratele din România. Ed. Acad. Rep. Soc. România, pp.1–500, figs.1–766, Fishes, pp.21–130, figs.11–171. 1968.

Jenkins, J.T. The Fishes of the British Isles Both Freshwater and Salt. London. 1925. i–vii+1–376 pp., 143 pls.

Jenkins, J.T. The Fishes of the British Isles Both Freshwater and Salt, 2nd ed. Reprinted. – London, F.Warne and Co. 1950. 408 pp.

Joubin, L. and E.Le Danois. Catalogue illustré des animaux marins comestibles des côtes de France et des mers limitrophes avec leurs noms communs français et étrangers. – Mém. Off. scient. tech. Pêch. marit., sér. spéc. 1. Poissons osseux, pp.1–220; 2. Poissons cartilagineux, mollusques, etc., pp.1–77. 1924. ill.

Lozano-Rey, L. Fauna Ibérica. Pisces. – Mems. R. Acad. Cienc. exact. fis. nat. Madr., 1:i–xi+1–692. 20 pls.; 2:i–xv+1–839. 20 pls.; 3:i–xv+1–703. 51 pls. 1928.

Lozano-Rey, L. Los principales peces marinos y fluviales de España. 3rd ed., revised. – Subsecretaria Marina Mercante, Madrid, 8:1–134. 1964. ill.

Manyukas, I.L. Fishes from the Courland Lagoon and the Baltic Sea off the Shore of Lithuania. – In: Synopses of Reports of the 9th Scientific Conference on the Water Bodies of the Baltic Area, 14–16 September 1961, Riga, pp.110–111. 1961.

Nikolaev, I.I. Specific Composition of the Fishes of Latvia. – Trudy Latv. Otd. Vses. Nauchno-Issled. Inst. Morsk. Ryb. Khoz. Okeanogr., 1:5–27. 1953.

Nikolaev, I.I. Russian Literature on Biology and Fisheries of the Baltic Sea. – Trudy Balt. Fil. Vses. Nauchno-Issled. Inst. Morsk. Ryb. Khoz. Okeanogr., 1:125–133. 1955.

Norman, J.R. List of British Vertebrates (Fishes, pp.40–66). London. 1935.

Perrier, R. La faune de France en tableaux synoptiques illustrés. Fasc. 10. Vertébrés, Poissons. Paris. 1924. i–vii+1–212 pp.

Rey, L.L. Fauna Ibérica. Peces, 1(2), 3:1–691, figs.1–197, pls.I–XX. 1928.

Stanković, S. Die Fauna des Ohridsees und ihre Herkunft. – Arch. Hydrobiol., 23:557–617. 1932. 1 pl.

Stanković, S. The Balkan Lake Ohrid and its Living World. – Monogr. Biol., 9:1–357. 1960. 1 pl., 100 figs.

Strublerg, A.C. and N.Norvil. Danske fisk. Vore saltvands og ferskvandsfisk. 2nd ed. – København, Gad. 1953. 128 pp., ill.

Tambs-Lyukhe, Kh. Commercial Fishes of Norway. – Moscow, Min. rybn. prom. SSSR. 1956. 158 pp.

Vinciguerra, D. Pesci di Albania. Raccolti dae Dr. Pietro Parenzan nel 1930. – Ann. Mus. Stor. Nat. Genova, 56:303–310. 1933.

Wolleback, A. Norges fisker. Kristiania. 1924. 239 pp., 256 figs.

432b – marine waters

Anon. Inventaire de la faune marine de Roscoff. Poissons. – Trav. Stn. biol. Roscoff, n.s., Suppl.8, 7, No.34:1–67. 1956.

Bassindale, R. and J.H.Barrett. The Dale Fort Marine Fauna. – Proc. Bristol. Nat. Soc., 29:227–328. 1957. 3 figs.

Blegvad, H. (editor). La faune ichthyologique de l'Atlantique Nord. – Conseil Permanent International pour l'Exploration de la Mer. – Copenhagen, A.F.Host. 1929–1938. 418 pls.

Bougis, P. Atlas des poissons. Poissons marins, 1:1–200, 2:201–435. Paris. 1959. 102 figs., 56 pls.

Casier, E. La faune ichthyologique de l'Yprésien de la Belgique. – Mém. Mus. r. Hist. nat. Belg., 104:1–267. 1946. 6 pls., 19 text-figs.

Collins, B.L. Lista de peixes dos mares dos Açores. – Açoreana, 5, No.2:1–40. 1954.

Curry-Lindahl, K. Fiskarna i Färg. – Stockholm, Almquist and Wiksell. 1953. 189 pp., 64 col. pls.
Demel, K. Ryby Bałtyku Polskiego. Książnica-Atlas. – Bibljoteka Przyrody i Techniki, 11:1–48. Lwów–Warszawa. 1924.
Demel, K. Spis ryb Bałtyku Naszego (Liste des poissons de la Baltique polonaise). – Archwm. Ryb. pol., 1:50–54. 1925.
Demel, K. Note complémentaire à la liste des invertébrés et des poissons des eaux polonaises de la Baltique. – Archwm. Hydrobiol. Ryb., 10:197–204. 1937. (In Polish, French summary.)
De Noronha, A.C. Vertebrados da Madeira, 2 (Peixes). – Junta Geral do Distrito Autónomo do Funchal. 1926. 181 pp.
Dons, C. Notes on Fishes. IV. List of Marine Fishes from the Trondheimsfjord and the Adjacent Waters. – K. norske Vidensk. Selsk. Skr., 11:165–168. 1939.
Duncker, G. Die Fische der Nordmark. – Beih. Schr. Naturw. Ver. Schleswig-Holstein, Nos.1–5:1–224. Kiel. 1935–1939.
Duncker, G. Die Fische der Nordmark. – Abh. Verh. naturw. Ver. Hamburg, Suppl., 3:1–432, figs.1–145. 1960. map.
Ehrenbaum, E. Naturgeschichte und wirtschaftliche Bedeutung der Seefische Nordeuropas. Lübert u. Ehrenbaum. – Handb. Seefisch. Nordeur., 2:1–337. 1936. 26 pls., 276 text-figs.
Fridriksson, A. and P.Hannesson. The Fishes of Iceland and the Icelandic Fishery. – Danskislandsk Samfunds Smaaskrifter, 14:1–56. Kjöbenhavn. 1925. (In Danish.)
Gąsowskiej, M. (editor). Krągłouste – Cyclostomi. Ryby – Pisces. – Warszawa–Kraków, Polska Akad. Nauk. 1962. 240 pp., ill.
Holdgate, M.W. The Fauna of the Mid-Atlantic Islands. – Proc. R. Soc. Lond., Ser.B, 152:550–567. 1960. 5 figs.
Joubin, L. Faune Ichthyologique de l'Atlantique Nord. – Conseil Permanent International pour l'Exploration de la Mer, Fasc.1–18. Copenhague. 1929–1938.
Joubin, L. and E. le Danois. Catalogue illustré des animaux marins comestibles des côtes de France et des mers limitrophes avec leurs noms communs français et étrangers. 1. Poissons osseux. – Mem. Off. scient. tech. Pêch. marit., spéc. sér., 1:1–220. 1924. figs.
Joubin, L. and E.le Danois. Catalogue illustré des animaux marins comestibles des côtes de France et des mers limitrophes avec leurs noms communs français et étrangers. 2. Poissons cartilagineux, Mollusques, Crustacés, etc. – Ibid., 2:1–77. 1925. figs.
Legendre, R. La faune pelagique de l'Atlantique, au large du golfe de Gascogne, recueillie dans des estomacs de Germons. – Annls. Inst. océanogr., 14:253–418. 1934; 16:1–99. 1936; 20:127–310. 1940. 1934–1940.
Leriche, M. Les poissons famenniens de la Belgique. – Mém. Acad. r. Belg. Cl. Sci., 10:1–72. 1931. 8 pls., 7 figs.
Lloyd, A.J. The Marine Fish Fauna of the Southern Shores of the Bristol Channel. – Proc. Bristol Nat. Soc., 4, No.9:202–230. 1941.
Lozano, R.L. Fauna Ibérica: Pisces. – Mems. R. Acad. Cienc. exact. fis. nat. Madr., No.1:i–xi+1–692. 20 pls.; No.2:i–xv+1–839. 20 pls.; No.3:i–xv+1–703. 51 pls. 1928.
Mannsfeld, W. Verbreitung der Meerfische an der Küste Lettlands. – KorrespBl. NaturVer. Riga, 62:83–86. 1937. 4 figs.
Nielsen, J.G. Marine Fishes New or Rare to the Danish Fauna from the Period 1937–1961. – Vidensk. Meddr. dansk. naturh. Foren, 125:147–165. 1963.
Nobre, A. Fauna Marinha de Portugal. Vertebrados (Mamiferos, Reptis e Peixes). Porto. III. Peixes. 1935. 574 pp., ill.
Nybelin, O. Fishes Collected by the "Skagerrak" Expedition in the Eastern Atlantic, 1946. – Göteborgs K. Vetensk. – O.Vitterh. Samh. Handl. (B), 5, No.16:1–95. 1948. 6 pls., 9 figs.
Otterstrøm, C.V. Bidrag til Bornholms Fiskefauna. – Flora Fauna, Silkeborg, 3:73–94. 1927.
Paes da Franca, M.L. and M.S.Vasconcelos. Peixes do Arquipélago de Cabo Verde. – Notas mimeogr. Cent. Biol. pisc., 28:1–86. 1962.
Peczalska, A. Ryby użytkowe Bałtyku, Ser.2. – Warszawa, Panstw. Zakł. Wydawn. Szkol. 1955. 85 pp.
Poll, M. Poissons marins. Faune de Belgique. – Mém. Mus. r. Hist. nat. Belg. 1947. 452 pp., 267 figs., 3 maps.

Postel, E. Liste commentée des poissons signalés dans l'Atlantique tropico-oriental nord, du Cap Spartel au Cap Roxo, suivie d'un bref aperçu sur leur répartition bathymétrique et géographique. 1. – Bull. Soc. scient. Bretagne, 34, No.1:129–170. 1 fig.; No.2:241–281. 1959, 1960.

Redeke, H.C. Fauna van Nederland, Pisces, 10:1–331. Leiden. 1941. ill.

Rey, L.L. Peces ganoideos y fisostomos. – Mems. R. Acad. Cienc. exact. fis. nat. Madr., 11:1–839. 1947. 20 pls.

Saemundsson, B. Synopsis of the Fishes of Iceland. Reykjavik. 1927. 68 pp.

Saemundsson, B. Marine Pisces. – In: The Zoology of Iceland, 4, No.72: 1–150. 1949.

433 – Central Asia

Abylkosymova, T.A. Noncommercial Fishes of Lake Issyk-Kul. Author's Summary of Candidate Thesis. Frunze, Kirgizia University. 1966. 17 pp.

Aliev, D. Ichthyofauna of Freshwater Lakes of the Western Uzboi. Author's Summary of Candidate Thesis, pp.2–7. Moscow University. 1951.

Amanov, A.A. Fishes in the Water Bodies of the Surkhan Darya River Basin. Author's Summary of Candidate Thesis. Frunze, Kirgizia University. 1963. 16 pp.

Bazatov, Sh. On Fishes from the Kazatag and Khanaka Rivers (Tadzhikistan). – Izv. Akad. Nauk TadzhSSR, otd. biol., 3, No.17+79–85. 1964.

Berg, L.S. Notes on Fishes from the Lower Reaches of the Zeravshan. – Ezheg. Zool. Muz., 30:249–250. 1929.

Berg, L.S. Juvenile Fishes from the Lower Reaches of the Amu Darya. – Izv. Otd. Prikl. Ikhtiol. Nauchno-Promysl. Issled., 9, No.2:225–230. 1929.

Berg, L.S. Fishes. – Trudy Pamir. Eksp. Akad. Nauk SSSR, 8:23–28. 1931. 5 pls.

Berg, L.S. Die Fische des Issykulsees. – Zool. Anz., 96, Nos.11–12:311–316. 1931.

Berg, L.S. Fishes from the Artek Basin. – Trudy Sov. Izuch. Proizv. Sib., Ser. Turkmen., 6:239–251. 1934.

Berg, L.S. Fingerlings from the Dyushambinka River Basin (Basin of the Amu Darya, Tadzhikistan). – Tadzhik. Kompl. Eksp., 10:255–260. Tadzhikistan, Akad. Nauk SSSR. 1935.

Berg, L.S. Freshwater Fishes of the USSR. 4th edition. Leningrad–Moscow, 1:1–466. 1948; 2:467–926. 1949; 3:927–1382. 1949. ill.

Bulgakov, G.P. On the Ichthyofauna of Turkestan. – Trudy Turkest. Nauch. Obshch., 1:225–238. 1923. 2 figs.

Bulgakov, G.P. and G.B. Sokurov. A Study of the Ichthyofauna from Lake Yashil-Kul. – Trudy Sred.-Aziat. Gos. Univ., Ser. 8a, Zool., 25:1–19. 1936.

Dement'ev, P.P. Preliminary List of the Fishes of Kirgizia. – Sb. Trud. Gos. Zool. Muz. pri Mosk. Gos. Univ., 2:75–78. 1935.

Dryagin, P.A. Fishes of the Chu River and their Commercial Exploitation. – Trudy Kirgiz. Kompl. Ekst., 3, No.1:49–87, figs.1–16. 1936.

Ereshchenko, V.I. Fishes from the Sary-Su River Basin. Author's Summary of Candidate Thesis. – Inst. Zool. Akad. Nauk Kazakh SSR. Alma-Ata. 1955. 14 pp.

Ivanova-Berg, M.M. Index to the Literature on the Fauna of Turkestan (Fauna, Agricultural Pests, Fishery, Hunting and Animal Husbandry). – Akad. Nauk SSSR. 1927. 236 pp.

Kamilov, G. Fishes from the Reservoirs of the Zeravshan River Basin. Author's Summary of Candidate Thesis. Tashkent University. 1960. 22 pp.

Kamilov, G. Specific Composition of Fishes from Water Bodies in Uzbekistan. – Nauch Trudy Tashkent. Univ., Biol. Sci., 241, No.44:138–156. 1964.

Kasimova, Z.Ya. Fishes from Reservoirs of the Angren River Basin (Akhan-Garan). Author's Summary of Candidate Thesis. Tashkent University. 1967. 25 pp.

Lindberg, G.U. Larva-Eating Fishes of Central Asia. – Leningrad, Akad. Nauk SSSR. 1947. 56 pp.

Maksunov, V.A. On the Morphological and Biological Characteristics of Fishes in the Farkhad Reservoirs. – Trudy Inst. Zool. Parazitol. Akad. Nauk Tadzhik SSR, 23:1–159. 1962.

Maksunov, V.A. Fishes of Northern Tadzhikistan and their Commercial Value. Dushaube. 1964. 44 pp., ill.

Men'shikov, M.I. On the Ichthyofauna of Lake Marka-Kul. – Uchen. Zap. Perm. Gos. Univ., 3, No.2:119–142. 1939.

Nekrashevich, N.G. Fishes of the Ala-Kul Lakes. – Vopr. Geogr. Kazakhstana, 12:236–268. Alma-Ata, "Nauka." 1965.

Nikol'skii, G.V. Fishes of the Middle and Lower Reaches of the Chu River. – Ezheg. Zool. Muz., 32:227–268. 1931.

Nikol'skii, G.V. Fishes of Tadzhikistan. – Trudy Tadzhik. Bazy Akad. Nauk SSSR, 7:9–217. 1938. 62 figs.

Nikol'skii, G.V. Fishes of the Aral Sea. – Mater. Pozn. Fauny Flory SSSR. Mosk. obshch. ispyt. prir., nov. ser., otd. zool., 1, No.16:7–215, figs.1–39. 1940.

Nikol'skii, G.V. and N.A. Evtyukhov. Fishes from the Plainland Course of the Ili River. Part II. Cobitidae and Percidae. – Byull. Mosk. Obshch. Ispyt. Prir., otd. biol., 49, Nos.5–6:57–70. 1940.

Nikol'skii, G.V. and F.F. Tsentilovich. Fishes from the Murgab River Basin (Turkmenia). – Sb. Trud. Zool. Muz. Mosk. Univ., 6:105–112. 1951.

Nikolskij, G.W. Zur Kenntnis der Ichthyofauna Kasakstans (Kirgisenland). Die Fische des Mittel- und Unterlaufs des Flusses Tschu. – Zool. Anz., 89, Nos.3–4:113–120. 1930.

Pertseva-Ostroumova, T.A. Fishes from the Lakes of the Lower Reaches of the Vakhsh River and Ways of Replenishing the Fauna. – Trudy Akad. Nauk TadzhikSSSR, 115:171–177. 1959.

Shaposhnikova, G.Kh. Fishes of the Amu Darya. – Trudy Zool. Inst. Akad. Nauk SSSR, 9, No.1:16–54. 1950.

Starostin, I.V. Ichthyofauna of the Streams Flowing down the Northern Slope of Kopet Dagh. – Byull. Turkm. Zool. Sta., 1:77–97. 1936.

Starostin, I.V. A Key to the Vertebrates of Turkmenia. I. Fishes, pp.5–72. Ashkhabad. 1937.

Svetovidov, A.N. Material on the Ichthyofauna of the Amu Darya System within Southern Tadzhikistan. – Trudy Zool. Inst. Akad. Nauk SSSR, 10:118–130. 1952.

Turdakov, F.A. Ichthyofauna of the Middle Reaches of the Zeravshan River and Mountain Sai. – Trudy Uzbek. Univ., 7:167–195. 1936.

Turdakov, F.A. On the Ichthyofauna of Central Asian Rivers. – Sb. Trud. Zool. Muz. Mosk. Univ., 6:215–223. 1941.

Turdakov, F.A. Fishes of the At-Bashi River. – Trudy Biol. Inst. Kirgiz. Fil. Akad. Nauk SSSR, 2:157–158. 1947.

Turdakov, F.A. Fishes of the Chon-Alai Valley. – Uchen. Zap. Biol.-Pochv. Fak. Kirgiz. Univ., 3:54–59. 1952.

Turdakov, F.A. Fishes of Kirgizia, pp.3–170, figs.1–56. – Frunze, Kirgiz. fil. Akad. nauk SSSR. 1952.

Turdakov, F.A. Data on the Ichthyofauna of the Rers (Assa) and Talas Rivers. – Trudy Inst. Zool. Parazitol. Kirgiz. Fil. Akad. Nauk SSSR, 1:113–122. 1954.

Turdakov, F.A. Fishes of Kirgizia, pp.5–283, figs.1–39. – Frunze, Akad. nauk KirgizSSR. 1963.

Zanin, A.P. Material on the Natural, Historical and Fishery Characteristics of the Talas Basin. – Trudy Kirgiz. Kompl. Eksp., 3, No.1:89–115. 1936.

434 – Caspian Basin
434ab – fresh and marine waters

Abbasov, N.S., Z.M. Guliev, and A.E. Agadzharova. Study of the Ichthyofauna of the Dzheiranbatan Reservoir. – Izv. Akad. Nauk AzerbSSR, Biol. and Med. Ser., 1:63–65. 1961. (In Azerbaidzhanian.)

Abdurakhmanov, Yu.A. Data on Fishes from the Alazan River. – Trudy Inst. Zool. Akad. Nauk AzerbSSR, 14:5–28. 1950.

Abdurakhmanov, Yu.A. Ichthyofauna of the Soyukhbulag River. – Ibid., 15:107–153. 1952. pls.

Abdurakhmanov, Yu.A. Fishes of Azerbaidzhan. – Baku, Akad. nauk AzerbSSR. 1955. 148 pp., 80 figs. (In Azerbaidzhanian.)

Abdurakhmanov, Yu.A. On the Geographical Distribution of Fishes in Fresh Waters of Azerbaidzhan. – Izv. Akad. Nauk AzerbSSR, Biol. and Agric. Ser., 6:63–72. 1958.

Abdurakhmanov, Yu.A. Freshwater Fishes of Azerbaidzhan. – Baku, Akad. nauk AzerbSSR. 1962. 407 pp., ill., map.

Abdurakhmanov, Yu.A., R.A. Gaibova, and G.S. Abbasov. Fishes of Azerbaidzhan. Baku. 1966. 80 pp., col. ill. (In Azerbaidzhanian.)

Aliev, D. Ichthyofauna of the Freshwater Lakes of Western Uzboi. Author's Summary of Candidate Thesis. Moscow. 1951. 8 pp.

Barach, G.P. Fishes of Armenia. – Trudy Sevan. Gidrobiol. Sta., 6:5–70. 1940.

Barach, G.P. Freshwater Fishes. Fauna of Georgia. I. – Tbilisi, Akad. nauk GruzSSR. 1941. 287 pp., 51 figs.
Belogurov, A.Ya. The Lake Seliger System. Fishes and Fishery Characteristics. – Uchen. Zap. Mosk. Univ., Biol., 8:65–97. 1936.
Berg, L.S. Freshwater Fishes of the USSR. 4th edition. Leningrad-Moscow, 1:1–466. 1948; 2:467–926. 1949; 3:927–1382. 1949. ill.
Bisk, D.I. Fishes and Fishery in the Moscow Sea. – Byull. Mosk. Obshch. Ispyt. Prir., otd. biol., 43, No.4. 1939.
Demetrashvili, M.G. Fishes of the Khram Reservoir and the Rivers Emptying into It (the Khram and Agrichai Rivers). – Trudy Inst. Zool. Akad. Nauk GruzSSR, 13:133–178. 1954.
Demin, D.Z. Semi-anadromous Fishes of the Terek Delta. – Vopr. Ikhtiol., 2, No.1:90–99. 1962.
Derzhavin, A.N. Fishes from the Kara-Su River. – Izv. Bakin Ikhtiol. Lab., 2, No.1:161–182. 1926.
Derzhavin, A.N. Notes on Fishes from the Karaj River (Northern Iran). – Ibid., 2, No.2:69–79, figs.1–3. 1929.
Derzhavin, A.N. Freshwater Fishes off the Southern Shore of the Caspian. – Trudy Azerb. Otd. Zakavk. Fil. Akad. Nauk SSSR (Zool.), 7:91–126. 1934.
Derzhavin, A.N. Catalogue of Freshwater Fishes of Azerbaidzhan. – Baku, Akad. nauk AzerbSSR. 1949. 47 pp.
Dryagin, P.A. The Letka River, its Fishes and Fishery. – In: Vyatskovetluzhskii krai, Nos.5–6:1–10. 1927.
Dryagin, P.A. Ichthyofauna of the Vyatka River Basin from the City of Vyatka to the Letka River. – Vyatskoe Khozyaistvo, 3:10–106. 1930.
Dushin, A.I. Data on the Fishes of the Moksha River. – Uchen. Zap. Mordovsk. Univ., 54:171–199. 1966.
Elanidze, R.F. Data for a Study of the Ktsiya-Khrami River. – Trudy Zool. Inst. Akad. Nauk GruzSSR, 7:171–198. 1947. (In Georgian, Russian summary.)
Elanidze, R.F. Material on the Ichthyofauna of the Iora River. – Ibid., 11:25–61. 1953. pls.
Elanidze, R.F. Material on the Ichthyofauna of the Kura River (within Georgia). – Ibid., 12:49–53. 1953. pls.
Fortunatov, M.A. Fishes and Fishery in Lake Sevan. – Izv. Otd. Prikl. Ikhtiol.Nauchno-Promysl. Issled., 4, No.2:240–246. 1926.
Kazancheev, E.N. Fishes of the Caspian Sea (a Key and a Brief Description). – Astrakhan, "Volga." 1956. 113 pp., ill.
Kazancheev, E.N. Fishes of the Caspian Sea. Moscow. 1963. 180 pp.
Kiparisov, G.N., V.I.Kozlov, and I.I.Puzanov. Animals, Birds, Reptiles and Fish of the Gorki Region, pp.3–452. Gorki.
Kiselevich, K.A. Keys to Fishes Occurring in the Volga-Caspian Region. – Ikhtiol. Lab., Astrakhan. 1922. 27 pp.
Knipovich, N.M. The Caspian Sea and its Fisheries. Berlin. 1923. 87 pp.
Kostarev, G.F. Specific Composition of the Ichthyofauna of the Chu River. – Uchen. Zap. Perm. Univ., 125:23–33. 1965.
Kozhin, N.I. Data on the Ichthyofauna of the Iranian Coast of the Caspian. – Vopr. Ikhtiol., 8:8–18. 1957.
Koz'min, Yu.A. Fishes from the Middle Kama River and Kama Reservoir. Paper for the Degree of Candidate of Sciences. 1962.
Kulaev, S.I. and G.V.Ermolina. Description of the Fish Population of the Klyazma River. – Zap. Bolshevskoi Biol. Sta., 10:75–85. 1937.
Kuz'min, A.G. Fishes of Lake Seliger. Composition (16 Species) and Distribution of the Ichthyofauna according to Data of Observations by the Author in 1928. – Mater. Obshch. Izuch. Tver. Kraya, 7:64–67. 1930.
Ladiges, W. and D.Vogt. Die Süsswasserfische Europas bis zum Ural und Kaspischen Meer. – Hamburg und Berlin, Paul Parey. 1965. 250 pp.
Lukash, B.S. Fishes of the Vyatka River Basin above the Town of Slobodsk. – Trudy Vyatsk Nauchno-Issled. Inst. Kraev., 1:1–50. 1925.
Lukash, B.S. Fishes from the Upper Reaches of the Kama River. – Ibid., 5:1–36. 1929.
Lukash, B.S. Fishes from the Lower Reaches of the Vyatka River. – Ibid., 6:5–10. 1933.
Lukash, B.S. Fishes of the Kirov Region. Kirov. 1940. 71 pp.
Matyukhin, V.P. Ichthyofauna of the Iriklinskii Reservoir and Principal Features of its Formation. Author's Summary of Candidate Thesis. Sverdlovsk. 1967. 23 pp.
Men'shikov, M.I. Fishes from the Kama River and its Valley in the Vicinity of Perm. – Izv. Biol. Inst. Perm. Univ., 6, No.8:377–407. 1929.

Men'shikov, M.I. and A.I. Bukirev. Fishes and Fishery in the Upper Reaches of the Kama River. – Trudy Biol. Nauchno-Issled. Inst. Perm. Gos. Univ., 6, Nos.1–2:1–99. 1934.
Modestov, V.M. Fishes of the Moscow River and Prospects for their Commercial Utilization. – Sb. Nauch. Rab. Stud., Biol., 6:85–102. Moscow. 1939.
Monastyrskii, G.N. et al. Fishes of the Caspian Sea. – Trudy Vses. Nauchno-Issled. Inst. Ryb. Khoz. Okeanogr., 18:1–256. 1951.
Paramonov, G.V. Fishes in the Water Bodies of the Bashkir Reservation (Notes on Distribution and Mode of Life). – Trudy Bashkir. Zapov., 2:115–126. 1963.
Pavliashvili, G. Study of the Ichthyofauna of the Engura River. – Trudy Tbilis. Univ., 82:247–254. 1962.
Pervukhin, M.A. Lake Pereslavl. Data for a Monograph. – Trudy Pereslavl-Zalessk. Istor.-Khodozh. Kraev. Muz., 2:26–82; 3:3–93. 1927.
Probatov, A.N. Fishes from the Kuma River. – Dokl. Akad. Nauk SSSR, 58, No.6:1211–1214. 1947.
Rass, T.S. Notes on the Fishes Collected in Mertvyi Kultuk and Kaidak Bays (Caspian Sea). – Byull. Mosk. Obshch. Ispyt. Prir., otd. biol., 48, Nos.2–3:93–97. 1939. map.
Rass, T.S. Ichthyofauna of the Caspian Sea and Some Aspects of its History. – Trudy Inst. Okeanol. Akad. Nauk SSSR, 6:105–116. 1951.
Rymashevskii, V.K. Fishes of the Tambov Region. – In: Nash krai, I, pp.54–59. –Voronezh-Tambov, Tsentr-chernozemn. izd. 1964.
Seleznev, V.V. Fishes from Water Bodies of the Oka Reservation. – Trudy Oksk. Zapoved., 5:5–26. 1963.
Shaposhnikova, G.Kh. Biology and Distribution of Fishes in Rivers of the Ural Type. – Moscow, "Nauka." 1964. 176 pp.
Shmidtov, A.I. Specific Composition and Population of Fishes in the Kuibyshev Reservoir. – Uchen. Zap. Kazan Univ., 116, No.1:221–226. 1956.
Solov'ev, N.S. and T.V. Dubova. Data on the Systematics and Commercial and Biological Characteristics of Fishes in the Kama Reservoir. – Izv. Estestv.-Nauch. Inst. pri Perm. Univ., 14, No.6:75–85. 1963.
Svetovidov, A.N. Fishes from Komsomolets (Mertvyi Kultuk) and Kaidak Bays of the Caspian Sea. Commission for an All-round Study of the Caspian (KASP) and Council for the Study of Productive Resources (SOPS). – Trudy Komis. Kompl. Izuch. Kasp. Morya, 1, No.1:184–212, pls.1–3, figs.1–7. 1936.
Tanasiichuk, N.P. Commercial Fishes of the Volga-Caspian Rivers. Moscow, Pishchepromizdat. 1951. 88 pp.
Tikhii, M.I. Fishes and Fishery of the Water Bodies of Kelif Uzboi. – Trudy Inst. Zool. Parazitol., Akad. Nauk TurkmSSR, 6:100–110. 1960.
Tkeshelashvili, V.G. Material for a Study of the Iora River. – Trudy Tbilis. Univ., 42:73–78. 1951. (In Georgian, Russian summary.)
Tsentilovich, F.F. Fauna of the Mordvinian State Reservation (Fishes, pp.112–136). Moscow. 1938.

435 – Black Sea Basin
435a – fresh waters

Aleksandrov, A.I. Material on the Fishes of the Kuban River Basin. – Trudy Kerchensk. Nauch. Rybokhoz. Sta., 1, Nos.2–3:151–176. 1927.
Ambroz, A.I. Fishes of the Dnieper and Southern Bug Rivers and the Dniepropetrovsk-Bug Liman. – Kiev, Akad. nauk UkrSSR. 1956. 214 pp., 58 figs.
Antonescu, C.S. Peştii din apele Rep. Pop. Romîne. Bucharest. 1957. 216 pp., ill.
Balabai, P.P. Study of the Ichthyofauna of the Upper Dniester River Basin. – Naukovi Zap. Pryrodoznavchoho Muz. Inst. Ahrobiol., Akad. Nauk URSR, 11:3–26. 1952. pls. (In Ukrainian.)
Balon, E.K. Vývoj ichtyofauny Dunaja. Bratislava. 1967. 176 pp.
Balon, E.K. Ryby Slovenska. Bratislava. 1967. 418 pp.
Bănărescu, P. Les poissons des environs de Timişoara. – Notat. biol., Buc., 4:135–165, pls.I, II. 1946.
Bănărescu, P. Fauna Republicii Populare Romîne, Pisces – Osteichthyes (Peşti Ganoizi şi osoşi.). – Acad. Republ. Popul. Romîne, 13:1–959, figs.1–402. 1964.

Bănărescu, P. Fauna Republicii Socialiste România. Cyclostomata şi Chondrichthyes. XII. 1. – Ed. Acad. Republ. Soc. România. 1969. 104 pp., 50 figs.

Barach, G.P. Freshwater Fishes of Abkhazia. Material on the Fauna of Abkhazia, pp.45–114. – Tbilisi, Gruzin. fil. Akad. nauk SSSR. 1939.

Beling, D. Beiträge zur Kenntnis der Fauna des Dnjeprbassins. – Zap. Fiz.-Mat. Otd. Vseukr. Akad. Nauk, 2:25–28. 1923.

Beling, D.E. Material on the Hydrofauna and Ichthyofauna of the Lower Reaches of the Dnieper River. – Trudy Cherno-Azovsk. Nauchno-Prom. Opyt. Sta., 1:1–72 (Fishes, pp.55–65). 1925.

Beling, D.E. Material on the Ichthyofauna of the Southern Bug River. – Zbirn. Prats' Dniprov. Biol. Sta., 2:333–356. 1927. (In Ukrainian.)

Beling, D.E. Notes on the Ichthyofauna of the Ukrainian SSR. Some Data on the Fishes of the Teterev and Ros Rivers. – Trudy Gidrobiol Sta., Akad. nauk UkrSSR, 15:175–183. 1937. (In Ukrainian.)

Belyaev, L.D. Ichthyofauna of the Lower Reaches of Tributaries of the Middle Dnieper. – Vest. Dnepropetr. Nauchno-Issled. Inst. Gidrobiol., 12:209–226. 1960.

Belyaev, L.D. Ichthyofauna of the Accessory System of the Dnieper Middle Reaches. Author's Summary of Candidate Thesis. Dnepropetrovsk. 1967. 18 pp.

Berg, L.S. Freshwater Fishes of the USSR, 4th edition. Leningrad–Moscow, 1:1–466. 1948; 2:467–926. 1949; 3:927–1382. 1949. ill.

Bezrukova, E.A. Ichthyofauna of Water Bodies of the Usman Forest Massif. – Byull. Obshch. Estestv. Voronezh. Gos. Univ., 5:46–53. 1949.

Buşniţă, T. and I. Alexandrescu. Atlasul Peştilor din apele R.P.R.Bucureşti (Editura Ştiinţifică). 1963. 172 pp., col. pls.

Buşniţă, T., D. Bogatus, and V. Stănciulescu. Contribuţii la studiul ihtiofauna rîului Siret in sectorul Cozmeşti-Galaţi. – Hidrobiologia Acad. RSR, 7:29–54. 1966.

Chichkoff, G. Sur la faune ichthyologique de la Kamtchia. – Ann. Univ. Sofia, Fac. Sci., 30, No.3:131–184. 1934. 2 pls. (In Bulgarian.)

Chichkoff, G. Poissons nouveaux et peu connus des eaux douces de la Bulgarie. – Ann. Univ. Sofia, Fac. Phys.-Math., 35, No.3:91–199. 1939. 4 pls. (In Bulgarian, French summary.)

Chizhik, A.K. Ichthyofauna of the Karlovka Reservoir. Author's Summary of Candidate Thesis. 1956. 13 pp.

Danko, I.A. Ichthyofauna of the Water Bodies of the Transcarpathian Region. – In: Vyizna sesiya viddilu biolohichnykh nauk po problemi vyvchennya flory i fauny Karpat, pp.57–60. Kiev. 1956. (In Ukrainian.)

Danko, I.A. Notes on the Systematics of Fishes of the Transcarpathian Region. – Dokl. Soobshch. Uzhgor. Univ., Biol. Ser., 1:45–47. 1957.

Delyamure, S.L. Study of the Fishes of the Streams on the Southern Crimean Coast. – Trudy Krym. Med. Inst., 7:301–304. 1940. ill.

Delyamure, S.L. Freshwater Fishes of Water Bodies. Two editions. – Simferopol; "Krym." 1964, 1966. 70 pp.

Drenski, P. Fish of Bulgaria. Fauna of Bulgaria, 2. – Zool. Inst. Bulgarian Acad. Sci., Sofia. 1951. 270 pp., 172 figs.

Drensky, P. Zur Kenntnis der Süsswasserfischfauna Bulgariens. – Zool. Jber., Jena (Syst.), 59:663–680. 1930.

Dushin, A.I. Fishes of the Mordvinian ASSR. Saransk. 1967. 143 pp., ill.

Dyk, V. Das heutige Vorkommen der Fische im Flusse Moravice. – Sb. Přír. Spol. Mor. Ostravě, 13, Nos.3–4:1–24, pls. 1–10. 1952.

Dyk, V. Naše ryby. No.143. 1956. 344 pp., 48 col. pls.

Elanidze, R.F. Material for a Study of the Ichthyofauna of the Supsa River. – Trudy Inst. Zool. Akad. Nauk GruzSSR, 13:197–214. 1954.

Elanidze, R.F. Ichthyofauna of the Riona River. – Ibid., 15:111–168. 1956.

Elanidze, R.F. Ichthyofauna of the Kodora River. – Ibid., 18:53–72. 1961.

Esipov, V. Fishes of the Kuban Delta and their Fishery. – Trudy Azov.-Chernomorsk Nauch. Rybokhoz. Sta., 7:37–67. 1930.

Fedii. S.P. and L.D. Belyaev. On the Fish Fauna of the Vorskla River. – Vest. Dnepropetr. Nauchno-Issled. Inst. Gidrobiol., 12:227–240. 1960.

Fedorov, A.V. A Brief Survey of the Ichthyofauna of the Voronezh Region. – Byull. Obshch. Estestvoisp. Voronezh.Univ., 10:83–95. 1956.

Fedorov, A.V. Ichthyofauna of the Don River Basin in the Voronezh Region. – In: Ryby i rybnoe khozyaistvo Voronezhskoi oblasti, pp.149–247. Voronezh University. 1960.

Gal'tsova, M.E. and V.S. Penyaz'. Data on the Fishes of Rivers of the Belorussian Polesye. – Trudy Kompleks. Eksped. Izuch. Vodoemov Poles'ya, pp.239–246. Minsk University. 1956.

Gladkov, N.A. Fishes from the Svapa and Seim River Basins in the Former Lgov District. – Izv. Kursk Obshch. Kraev., III, Nos.3–6 (15–18):45–52. (1929) 1930.

Hochman, L. Ichthyologische Untersuchungen des Flusses Moravice. – Acta Univ. Agric. silv., Brünn, A, **1**:83–117. 1957. 4 pls.

Karaman, S. Pisces Macedonia. Split. 1924. 90 pp.

Kastsyuchanka, A.A. Specific Composition of Fishes from the Dnieper River Basin within the Belorussian SSR. – Vestsi Akad. Nauk BSSR, 1:87–94. 1962. (In Ukrainian.)

Kheladze, P. Study of the Ichthyofauna of the Dzirula River. – Trudy Tbilis. Univ., **109**:153–159. 1965.

Korotkii, I.I. Ichthyofauna of the Dnieper Rapids and the Changes Caused by the Dnieper Hydroelectric Dam. – Visn. Dnipropetr. Hidrobiol. Sta., 2:133–141. 1937. (In Ukrainian.)

Kostyuchenko, A.A. Fishes of the Dnieper River (within the Belorussian SSR). Author's Summary of Candidate Thesis. – Beloruss. University. 1963. 21 pp.

Kryzhanovskii, S.G. and S.K. Troitskii. Material on the Ichthyofauna of the Rivers of the Black Sea Coast (within the Krasnodar Territory). – Vopr. Ikhtiol., 2:144–150. 1954.

Kux, Z. Příspěvek k ichtyofauně dolní Moravy a Dunaje. – Čas. morav. zemsk. Mus., 41:92–112. 1956.

Ladiges, W. Süsswasserfische der Türkei. Part 3. Restliche Gruppen. – Mitt. hamb. zool. Mus. Inst., 61:203–220. 1964.

Ladiges, W. and D. Vogt. Die Süsswasserfische Europas bis zum Ural und Kaspischen Meer. – Hamburg-Berlin, Paul Parey. 1965. 250 pp., ill.

Loshakov, A.S. Fishes of the Berd and Obitochnaya Rivers. – Vopr. Ikhtiol., 5, No.2 (27):235–242. 1963.

Magnitskii, A.N. A Short Essay on the Distribution of Fishes in the Penza Province. – Trudy Penz. Obshch. Lyub. Estest. Kraev., 12:1–26. 1928.

Markevich, O.P. and I.I. Korotkii. Key to Freshwater Fishes of the Ukrainian SSR. – Kiev, "Radyans'ka Shkola." 1954. 208 pp., 137 figs (In Ukrainian.)

Maslovskii, A.D. Composition of the Fish Population of the Oskol River. – Trudy Nauchno-Issled. Inst. Biol. i Biol Fak. Kharkov Univ., **23**:259–268. 1956.

Meskhidze, D.Kh. Study of the Ichthyofauna from the Choloka River. – Trudy Batum. Ped. Inst., **10**:161–184. (1963) 1964. (In Georgian, Russian summary.)

Nikol'skii, G.V. Study of the Ichthyofauna of the Kuban River. – Byull. Mosk. Obshch. Ispyt. Prir., otd. biol., **64**; No.2:121–125. 1937.

Nosal', P.D. Fishes of the Floodplain Water Bodies in the Region of the Middle Dnieper Reservation. – Zbirn. Prats Seredn'odnipr. Zapoved., **1**:69–132. 1937. (In Ukrainian.)

Oleinikov, N.S., L.I. Shirokova, and N.N. Pavlova. Material on the Fauna and Biology of Fishes from Lakes Abran and Limanchik. – Uchen. Zap. Rostovsk.-na-Don. Univ., 7, No.1:75–97. 1957. 7 pls.

Oliva, O. Seznam ryb středního Polabí. – Věst čsl. Spol. zool., 25, No.4:366–368. 1961.

Opalatenko, L.K. Ichthyofauna of the Upper Dniester River Basin. Author's Summary of Candidate Thesis. Kishinev. 1967. 26 pp.

Panshin, I. On the Ichthyofauna of the Dnepropetrovsk Region from Dnepropetrovsk to Nikopol'. – Izv. Akad. Nauk UkrSSR, pp.111–139. 1931.

Parfenik, A.N. Systematic Survey and Biological Characteristics of Fishes of the Family Cyprinidae from the Kabardino-Balkar ASSR. – Uchen. Zap. Kabardino-Balkar. Univ., **10**:147–160. 1961.

Penyaz', V.S. Fishes from the Priper River and their Commercial Value. Author's Summary of Candidate Thesis. Minsk University. 1955. 17 pp.

Penyaz', V.S. Composition of the Ichthyofauna and Growth Rate of Commercial Fishes of the Belorussian Polesye. – Trudy Kompleks. Eksped. Izuch. Vodoemov Poles'ya, pp.205–230. Minsk. 1956. ill.

Popa, L.L. Distribution of the Ichthyofauna of the Prut River by Sectors. – Uchen. Zap. Kishinev Univ., **62**; No.1:101–115. 1962.

Rodionova, T.V. Ichthyofauna of the Dnieper River Basin. Fishes from the Seim River. – Trudy Obshch. Naturalist., 53:111–115. Kharkov. 1930. (In Ukrainian.)

Romanov, N.S. Index of Literature on Fisheries in the Southern Basins of the USSR for 1918–1953. – Moscow, Akad. nauk SSSR. 1955. 296 pp.

Rymashevskii, V.K. Fishes of the Tambov Region. – In: Nash krai, I, pp.54–59. – Voronezh-Tambov, Tsentr.-chernozema. izd. 1964.

Sattarov, K. Fishes and Fishery in the Lower Reaches of the Pripet River. Author's Summary of Candidate Thesis. 1967. 16 pp.

Shaposhnikova, G.Kh. Ichthyofauna of the Tshchiksk Reservoir in the Krasnodar Territory. – Trudy Zool. Inst. Akad. Nauk SSSR, 26:375–413. 1959.

Shcherbukha, A.Ya. Commercial Fishes of the Lower Reaches of the Southern Bug River. Author's Summary of Candidate Thesis. – Dnepropetrovsk University. 1965. 28 pp.

Shmidt, E.A. Water Bodies, Fishes and Fisheries in the Smolensk Region. Smolensk. 1949. 96 pp.

Shnarevich, I.D. Fishes of Soviet Bukovina. – In: Zhivotnyi mir Sovetskoi Bukoviny, pp.206–263. Chernovtsy. 1959.

Slastenenko, E. The Fishes of the Black Sea Basin. Istanbul. 1956. 1–711+1–XLIX pp., 142 figs. (In Turkish.)

Slastenenko, Yu.P. Material for a Study of the Ichthyofauna of the Upper and Middle Reaches of the Southern Bug River. – Zbirn. Prats Dnipr. Biol. Sta., 6:75–92. Kiev. 1932. (In Ukrainian.)

Solodovnikov, S.V. Study of Fishes of the Donets River. – Priroda i Okhota na Ukraine, Nos.1–2:1–14. Kharkov. 1924.

Tomnatik, E.N., M.Z.Vladimirov, and V.L.Oleinikova. On the Fauna of Small Rivers in Moldavia. – In: Biol. resursy vodoemov Moldavii, pp.40–49. Kishinev. 1962.

Tret'yakov, D.K. A Key to Cyclostomata and Fishes of the Ukrainian SSR. – Kiev, Akad. nauk URSR. 1947. 111 pp. (In Ukrainian.)

Troitskii, S.K. Fishes. – In: Priroda Rostovskoi oblasti, pp.225–248. Krasnodar. 1940.

Troitskii, S.K. Fishes of the Krasnodar Territory. Krasnodar. 1948. 80 pp.

Tseeb, Ya.Ya. Preliminary Results of an Investigation into Ichthyofauna of Small Rivers in the Crimea. – Trudy Krymsk. Nauchno-Issled. Inst., 2, No.2:113–123. 1929.

Vainshtein, A.S. Fishes from Water Bodies of the Upper Dniester Basin and their Commercial Importance. – Author's Summary of Candidate Thesis. Kiev. 1961. 19 pp.

Valkanov, A. Katalog unserer Schwarzmeerfauna. – Trud. Norsk Biol. Sta. Varna, Sofia, 19:1–62. 1957. (In Bulgarian, German summary.)

Vasiliu, G.D. Revizuire sistematică a faunei ichtyologice din România şi provinciile învecinate din ne şi est cu consideraţiuni speciale de răspândire geografica. – Notat. biol., Buc., 4, Nos.1–3:204–300. 1948.

Vasiliu, G.D. Peştii apelor noastre. Bucharest. 1959. 404 pp.

Velikokhat'ko, F. Fishes of the Belaya Tserkov Region. – Bilotserkiv. Kraeznav. Tovarystvo, 2, No.3:1–28. Bila-Tserkva. 1929. (In Ukrainian.)

Vladykov, V. Poissons de la Russie sous-carpathique (Tchécoslovaquie). – Mém. Soc. zool. Fr., 29:217–374. 1931. 29 figs.

Vlasova, E.K. Data on the Ichthyofauna of the Transcarpathian Region. – Nauch. Zap. Uzhgorod. Univ., 16:3–38. 1956.

Vorontsev, E.M. Composition of the Ichthyofauna of Water Bodies in the Western Region of Belorussia and a Description of the Ichthyofauna of the Upper Dnieper River Basin. – In: Fauna i ekologiya, 3:59–85. Smolensk. 1937.

435b – marine waters

Borcêa, I. Données, sommaires la faune de la Mer Noire (Littoral de Roumanie). – Annls. scient. Univ. Jassy, 14, No.3–4:536–581. 1927.

Chepurnov, V.S., S.Burnashev, and V.N.Dolgii. Material for a Study of the Fish Fauna of the Northwestern Black Sea. – Uchen. Zap. Kishinev. Univ., 13:3–16. 1954.

Devedjian, K. Pêche et pêcheries en Turquie. Constantinople. 1926. 1–480+196 pp.

Drapkin, E.I. On the Changes in the Fish Fauna of Novorossiisk Bay. – Nauch. Dokl. Vyssh. Shk., Biol. Sci., 3:54–58. 1959.

Knipovich, N.M. Key to Fishes from the Black Sea and the Sea of Azov. Moscow. 1923. 130 pp., 87 figs.

Koloshev, I.I. A Short Key to Fishes from the Transcarpathian Region. 1949. 33 pp., 43 pls.

Kovachev, V.T. Freshwater Fishes of Bulgaria. – Arkhiv na Min. na zeml., Sofia, 3:1–165. 1922. (In Bulgarian.)

Kubrak, I.F. and N.I. Dorokhova. Ichthyofauna of the Sasyk Liman. – In: Synopses of Reports of Scientific Conference, Kishinev University. pp.142–143. 1956.

Malyatskii, S.M. Note on the Ichthyofauna of Novorossiisk Bay. – Trudy Novoross. Biol. Sta., 2, No.2:31–41. 1938.

Nalbant, F. Considerații zoogeografice asupra faunei ihtiologice a Mării Negre. – Bull. Inst. cercetări proiect. piscic., 21, No.3:73–84. 1962.

Nikitina, V.R. A List of References on the Ichthyology of the Black Sea and the Sea of Azov. – Trudy Nauch. Rybokhoz. Biol. Sta. Gruzii, 1, No.1:237–280. 1934.

Nikitina, V.R. A List of References on the Ichthyology of the Black Sea and the Sea of Azov (Suppl.). – Ibid., 2:173–195. 1939.

Popov, A.M. On the Ichthyofauna of the Caucasian Coast of the Black Sea. – Trudy Leningr. Obshch. Estestvoisp., pp.29–56. 1930.

Schmidt, P. and A. Popov. List of the Fishes of the Black Sea Collected by Prof. S.A.Zernov in 1908–1912. – Trudy Sevastop. Biol. Sta. Akad. Nauk SSSR, 3:11–26. 1932.

Slastenenko, E.P. Revue de la faune ichthyologique de la Mer Noire. – Annls. scient. Univ. Jassy. 22, Nos.1–4:280–296. 1936.

Slastenenko, E.P. Fishes of the Mediterranean, Black Sea and the Sea of Azov. – Sb. Trud. Gos. Zool. Muz. pri Mosk. Gos. Univ., 4:63–100. 1937.

Slastenenko, E.P. Les poissons de la Mer Noire et de la mer d'Azov. – Annls. scient. Univ. Jassy, 25, 2, No.1:1–196. 1939.

Stoyanov, S. Composition and Characteristics of the Fish Fauna of the Bulgarian Part of the Black Sea. – Izv. Tsentr. Nauchno-Issled. Inst. Rybov'dstvo Rybolov., 3:79–101. 1963. (In Bulgarian.)

Stoyanov, S. et al. Fishes of the Black Sea (Bulgarian Coast). Varna. 1963. 247 pp., ill.

Tikhonov, V.N. Fishes of the Black Sea (Scientific-Popular Survey). – Simpferopol', Krymizdat. 1951. 79 pp.

Valkanov, A. Katalog unserer Schwarzmeerfauna. – Trud. Norsk. Biol. Sta. Varna, Sofia, 19:1–62. 1957. (In Bulgarian, German summary.)

Vinogradov, K.A. Data on Fishes in the Region of the Karadag Biological Station (Black Sea). – Trudy Karadag. Biol. St., 4:137–143. 1931.

Vinogradov, K.A. List of Black Sea Fishes in the Region of the Karadag Biological Station, with Remarks on their Biology and Ecology. – Trudy Karadag. Biol. St. Akad. nauk UkrSSR, 7:76–106. 1949.

Vinogradov, K.O. Ichthyofauna of the Northwestern Black Sea. – Izd. Akad. nauk UkrSSR, Kiev. 1960. 116 pp. (In Ukrainian.)

436 – Mediterranean Basin
436a – fresh waters of Asia Minor and North Africa

Bănărescu, P. and T. Nalbant. Süsswasserfische der Türkei. 2. Cobitidae. – Mitt. hamb. zool. Mus. Inst., 61:159–201. 1964.

Battalgil, F. Türkiyenin tatli su baliklari. Les poissons des eaux douces de la Turquie (Collection de l'Institut de Turquie, Collection de l'Institut de Zoologie de l'Université d'Istanbul). – Revue Fac. Sci. Univ. d'Istanbul, 6B:170–186. 1941.

Battalgil, F. Türkiye tatli su baliklari Hakkinda. Contribution à la connaissance des poissons des eaux douces de la Turquie. – Ibid., 7B:287–306. 1943. 9 text-figs.

Beckman, W.C. The Freshwater Fishes of Syria and their General Biology and Management. – Fish. Biol. Tech. Paper F.A.O., Rome, 8:1–297. 1962.

Bodenheimer, F.S. Prodromus faune Palestinae.– Mém. Inst. égypt., 33:1–286. 1937.

Fowler, H.W. and H. Steinitz. Fishes from Cyprus, Iran, Israel and Oman. – Bull. Res. Coun. Israel, 5B:260–292. 1956. 33 figs.

Girgis, S. A List of Common Fish of the Upper Nile with their Shilluk Dinka and Nuer Names. – Sudan Notes, 29:120–125. 1948.

Greenwood, P.H. The Fishes of Uganda. – Uganda J., I, 19, No.2:137–155. 1955; II, 20, No.2:129–165. 1956. 28 figs.; III, 21 No.1:47–80. 1957. 22 figs.; IV, 21, No.2:191–219. 1957. 11 figs.

Greenwood, P.H. The Fishes of Uganda. – Uganda Soc., Kampala. 1958. 124 pp., 61 figs.
Greenwood, P.H. The Fishes of Uganda. – Ibid., 2nd ed., revised. 1966. 131 pp., 61 figs.
Gruvel, A. Les états de Syrie. Richesses marines et fluviales, pp.1–453 (Poissons, pp.289–309). Paris. 1931.
Hankó, B. Fische aus Klein-Asien. – Annal. Mus. Nat. Hungarici, Budapest, 21:137–158. 1924. ill.
Holly, M. Synopsis der Süsswasserfische Kameruns. – Sber. Akad. Wiss. Wien, Sec.1, 139:195–281. 1930. 2 pls. 5 figs.
Kosswig, C. and F. Battalgil. Beiträge zur türkischen Faunengeschichte. I. Süsswasserfische. – C. r. annuel et Arch. Soc. turque Sci. Phys. Nat., 8:18–63. 1942.
Ladiges, W. Süsswasserfische der Türkei. Part 3. Restliche Gruppen. – Mitt. hamb. zool. Mus. Wien, 61:203–220. 1964.
Pellegrin, J. Les poissons des eaux douces d'Asie Mineure. – Voyage Zool. Gadeau de Kerville en Asie-Mineure, Paris, 2:1–134. 1928. 2 pls., 32 text-figs.
Poll, M. Exploration du Parc National Albert. Mission G.F. de Witte (1933–1935). Poissons. – Inst. Parcs Nat. Congo Belge, 24:1–81. 1939. 29 figs., 11 pls.
Poll, M. Exploration du Parc National Albert. Mission H.Damas (1935–1936). Poissons. – Ibid., 6:1–73. 1939. 42 figs., 9 pls.
Steinitz, H. The Freshwater Fishes of Palestine. An Annotated List. – Bull. Res. Coun. Israel, 3:207–227. 1953.
Suyehiro, Y. Fishes of Egypt (U.A.R.). – Jap. J. Ichthyol., 9:117–126. 1962.
Tortonese, E. Pesci e Cetacei del mar Ligure. – Geneva, Mario Bozzi. 1965. 216 pp., 8 pls., ill.
Whitehead, P.J. The Anadromous Fishes of Lake Victoria. – Revue Zool. Bot. afr., 59:329–363. 1959. 4 figs.

436b – marine waters

Ancona, U.D. and A. Razzauti. Pesci e pesca nelle acque dell' Archipelago Toscano. – Rapp. Comm. Explor. Méditerranée Paris, 11:129–144. 1938. 1 chart.
Ben-Tuvia, A. Mediterranean Fishes of Israel. – Bull. Sea Res. Stn. Israel, 8:1–40. 1953. 20 figs.
Borodin, N.A. Scientific Results of the Yacht "Alva" Mediterranean Cruise, 1933, in Command of William K.Vanderbilt. – Fish. Bull. Vanderbilt Marine Mus., 1:103–124. 1934. 2 pls.
Brunelli, G., G. Bullo, E, Ninni, and E. Bellems. Le pesca nelle Laguna. – La Laguna di Venezia, 3, 6, No.11:1–332, pls.1–108. 1940.
Brunelli, G. Notizie e caratteristiche della pesca nel litorale Dalmato. – Boll. Pesca Piscic. Idrobiol., 2:261–281. 1941.
Buen, F. de. Catalogo Ictiologico del Mediterraneo Español y de Marruecos. – Trab. Inst. esp. Oceanogr., 2:1–221. 1926.
Dieuzeide, R. Rapport sur les travaux récents d'ichthyologie Méditerranéenne. – Rapp. Comm. int. Mer Médit., 14:297–309. 1958; 15:377–387. 1960.
Fage, L. Shore-fishes. – Rep. Dan. Oceanogr. Exped. Mediterr. 1908–1910, Ser.2. Biol., A, 3:1–154. 1918.
Konsuloff, S. and P. Drensky. Die Fischfauna der Aegaeis. – Ann. Univ. Sofia Fac. Phys.-Math., 39, No.3:293–308. 1943. (In Bulgarian, German summary.)
Lanfranco, G.G. A Complete Guide to the Fishes of Malta. Malta. 1958. 74 pp., 11 pls.
Luther, W. and K. Fiedler. Die Unterwasserfauna der Mittelmeerküsten. Ein Taschenbuch für Biologen und Naturfreunde. – Hamburg–Berlin, Verlag P.Parey. 1961. 253 pp., 16 pls., (32 col.)
Matta, F. La pesca a strascico nell'arcipelago Toscano.– Boll. Pesca Piscic. Idrobiol., 34 (N.F.13):23–371. 1958. 182 figs.
Oliver, M. Carta de Pesca de las Baleares. I. Este y sur de Menorca. – Trab. Inst. esp. Oceanogr., 26:1–20. 1959. 2 maps.
Palombi, A. and M. Santarelli. Gli animali commestibili dei mari d'Italia. Descrizione enomi italiani, dialettalie stranieri dei pesci, tunicati, echinodermi, molluschi, crostacei. – Milano, Ulrico Hoepli. 1953. 349 pp., 2 col. pls., 261 figs.; 2nd ed., 11:1–437. 1961. ill.
Parenzan, P. Pesci abissali e preabissali del golfo di Taranto (con considerazioni sulla pianificazione ambientale e sulla nomenclatura). – Thalassia jonica, 3:3–68. 1960. 17 figs.
Rhasis Erazi, R.A. Marine Fishes Found in the Sea of Marmara and in the Bosphorus. – Revue Fac. Sci. Univ. Istanbul, 7B, Nos.1–2; 103–115. 1942.

Riedl, R. Fauna und Flora der Adria. Vertebrata, Pisces, pp.496–565. 1963.
Slastenenko, E.P. Fishes from the Sea of Marmara. – Trudy Novoross. Biol. Sta., 2, No.2:177–181. 1938.
Šoljan, T. Ribe Jadrana (Fishes of the Adriatic). – Zagreb, Nakl. Zav. Hovatsch. 1948. 437 pp., ill.
Šoljan, T. Fishes of the Adriatic (Ribe Jadrana), 1:1–428. – Inst. Ocean. Ribar. FNR Jugoslavije. 1963.
Steinitz, H. Notes on Fishes from Cyprus. – Bull. Inst. océanogr., Monaco, 1004:1–12. 1952.
Torchio, M. Contributo alla conoscenza di talune forme ittiche del Mar Ligure. 2. – Atti. Soc. ital. Sci. nat., 100, No.3:225–256. 1961.
Tortonese, E. Fauna d'Italia: Leptocardia, Cyclostomata, Selachii, 2. – Bologna, Ed. Calderini. 1956. 334 pp.
Tortonese, E. Elenco dei pesci teleostei viventi nel Mediterraneo. – Fauna Flora Golfo Napoli, Monogr. 38. 1956.
Tortonese, E. Elenco dei Leptocardi, Ciclostomi, Pesci cartilaginei ed ossei del Mare Mediterraneo. – Atti. Soc. ital. Sci. nat., 97, No.4:307–345. 1958.
Tortonese, E. and L. Trotti. Catalogo del pesci del Mare Ligure. – Atti . Accad. ligure, 6, No.1:1–118. 1949; 6, No.1:49–164. 1950.
Zolezzi, G. La Pesca in Istria. – Archo. Oceanogr. Limnol., 4, Nos.1–3:85–125. 1948.
Zei, M. Cyclostomata, Chondrichthyes, Osteichthyes. – In: Riedl, R. Fauna und Flora der Adria, pp.496–565. Hamburg-Berlin. 1963.

5 – Africa

5a – inland waters

Ricardo, C.K. The Fishes of Lake Rukwa (Rhodesia). – J. Linn. Soc., Lond., 40:625–656. 1939.
Worthington, E.B. and C.K. Ricardo. Scientific Results of the Cambridge Expedition to the East African Lakes 1930-1931. 15. The Fish of Lake Rudolf and Lake Baringo. – J. Linn. Soc., Zool., 39:353–389. 1936. 2 figs.

5ab – fresh and marine waters of the Atlantic and Indian Ocean basins

Boulenger, G.A. Catalogue of the Freshwater Fishes of Africa. London. 1909–1915. 3 vols. Reprinted. 1964.
Copley, H. The Game Fishes of Africa. London. 1952. 276 pp.
Fowler, H.W. Zoological Results of the George Vanderbilt African Expedition of 1934. III. The Freshwater Fishes. – Proc. Acad. Nat. Sci. Philad., 88:243–335, figs.1–152. 1939.
Poll, M. Les genres des poissons d'eau douce de l'Afrique. – Annls. Mus. r. Congo belge, 54:1–191. 1957. 49 pls.

6 – Indian Ocean

61 – western part

61a – fresh waters

Arnoult, J. Poissons des eaux douces. – Faune Madagascar, 10:1–163. 1959. 2 figs., 23 pls.
Barnard, K.H. Report on a Collection of Fishes from the Okovango River, with Notes on Zambezi Fishes. – Ann. S. Afr. Mus., 36:407–458. 1948. 9 text-figs.
Bertram, C.K.R., H.J.H. Borley, and E. Trewavas. Report on the Fish and Fisheries of Lake Nyasa. Crown Agents for the Colonies, London. 1942. 181 pp., 1 map, 12 pls.
Borodin, N.A. On a Collection of Freshwater Fishes from Lakes Nyasa, Tanganyika and Victoria in Central Africa. – Zool. Jber., Jena (Syst.), 68:1–34 p.1. 1936.
Copley, H. Common Freshwater Fishes of East Africa. London. 1958. 172 pp., 4 pls., 89 figs.
Crass, R.S. Notes on the Freshwater Fishes of Natal with Descriptions of Four New Species. – Ann. Natal Mus., 14, No.3:405–458. 1960. ill.

Fowler, H.W. Scientific Results of the Vernay-Lang Kalahari Expedition, March to September 1930. Freshwater Fishes. – Ann. Transv. Mus., 16:251–293. 1935. 4 pls., 18 figs.

Jackson, P.B.N. Kariba Studies. Ichthyology. The Fish of the Middle Zambesi. – Manchester University Press. 1961. 36 pp., 4 pls., ill.

Jackson, P.B.N. The Fishes of Northern Rhodesia. A Checklist of Indigenous Species. – Rep. Game Fish. Nth. Rhod. 1961. 140 pp.

Jackson, P.B.N. Checklist of the Fishes of Nyasaland. – Occ. Pap. Natn. Mus. S.Rhod., 3:535–621. 1961.

Jackson, P.B.N. Ichthyology: the Fish of the Middle Zambezi. – Manchester University Press. 1961. 40 pp., ill.

Jubb, O. An Illustrated Guide to the Freshwater Fishes of the Zambezi River, Lake Kariba, Pungwe, Sabi, Lundi and Limpopo Rivers. – Bulawayo, Stuart Manning. 1961. 171 pp., ill.

Määr, A. Introductory Checklist of Fish of the Zambezi Subregion of the Ethiopian Region. – Proc. 1st Fed. Sci. Congr., Salisbury. 1960. 8 pp.

Pellegrin, J. Les poissons des eaux douces de Madagascar et des îles voisines (Comores, Seychelles, Mascareignes). – Mém. Acad. malgache, 14:1–222. 1933. 3 pls., 105 text-figs.

Worthington, E.B. The Fishes of Lake Nyasa (Other than Cichlidae). – Proc. Zool. Soc. Lond., 2:285–316. 1933. 10 figs.

61b – marine waters

Arnoult, J. et al. Les poissons de l'île Aldabra. Campagne océanographique de la Calypso (1954). – Annls. Inst. océanogr., Paris, N.S., 34:47–90. 1958. 3 figs.

Baisac, J. de B. Contribution à l'étude des poissons de l'île Maurice. – Proc. Roy. Soc. Mauritius, IV, 1:123–152. 1951. 6 figs.; V, 1:185–240. 1953; VI, 1:319–365. 1956; VII, 2:1–37. 1960; VIII, 2:162–189. 1962.

Bonde, C. von. A Collection of Marine Fishes from Zanzibar. – Ann. Natal. Mus., 7:435–458, pl.23. 1934.

Fourmanoir, P. Ichthyologie et pêche aux Comores. – Mém. Inst. scient. Madagascar, 9A:187–239. 1955. 19 figs.

Fourmanoir, P. Poissons Téléostéens des eaux malgaches du Canal de Mozambique. – Ibid., Ser.F., 1:1–316. 1957. 195 figs., 17 pls.

Fourmanoir, P. Liste complémentaire des poissons du Canal de Mozambique. – Ibid., 4:83–107. 1961. 19 figs.

Fourmanoir, P. and A. Crosnier. Deuxième liste complémentaire des poissons du Canal de Mozambique. – Cahiers O.R.S.T.O.M. – Océanographie, 6. 1963.

Gonçalves, S.J. Panorama das pescas em Moçambique. – Notas mimeogr. Cent. Biol. pisc., 8:5. 1960.

Smith, J.L.B. Os piexes apanhados no canal de Moçambique pelo Sr. Mussoline P.Fajardo. – Mem. Mus. de Castro, 2:3–20. 1953. 1 pl., 2 figs.

Smith, J.L.B. The Fishes of Aldabra. – Ann. Mag. Nat. Hist. (12), I, No.8:304–312. 1955. ill.; II, No.8:689–697. 1955. ill.; III, No.8:886–896. 1955. ill.; IV, No.8:928–937. 1955. ill.; V, No.9:686–688. 1956 (1957). 1 fig.; No.9:721–729. 1956 (1957). ill.; VI, No.9:817–829. 1956 (1957). 5 figs.; VII, No.9:888–892. 1956 (1957). 1 fig.; VIII, No.10:395–400. 1957 (1958), 2 pls., 1 fig.; IX, No.10:833–842. 1957 (1958). 2 figs.; (13), X, No.1:57–63. 1958. 1 pl.

Smith, J. and M. Smith. The Fishes of Seychelles. Grahamst. 1963. 215 pp.

Williams, F. Preliminary Survey of the Pelagic Fishes of East Africa. – Fishery Publs. Colon. Off., 8:1–68. 1956. 15 pls.

62 – northern Indian Ocean

62ab – marine and fresh waters

Ahmad, N. Fishes of Lahore. – Bull. Dep. Zool. Panjab Univ., 1. Fauna of Lahore, 5:253–374. 1943. ill.

Ahmad, N. Fish Fauna of East Pakistan. – Pakist. J. Scient. Res., 5:18–24. 1953.

Allouse, B.E. A Bibliography of the Vertebrate Fauna of Iraq and Neighbouring Countries. IV. Fishes. – Iraq Nat. Hist. Mus. Publs., 7:1–32. 1955.

Annandale, N. and S.L.Hora. The Fish of Seistan. - Rec. Indian Mus., 18, No.4:151-203. 1920.
Annandale, N. and S.L.Hora. The Freshwater Fish from the Andaman Islands. - Ibid., 27, No.2:33-41. 1925.
Berg, L.S. Freshwater Fishes of Iran and Adjacent Countries. - Trudy Zool. Inst. Akad. Nauk SSSR, 8:783-858. 1949. ill.
Bhimachar, B.S. and A.S.Rau. The Fishes of Mysore State. I. Fishes of Kadur District. - Half-yearly J. Mysore Univ., N.S., 1B:141-153, pls. IV, V. 1941. 1 chart.
Bhuiyan, A.L. Fishes of Dacca. - Publs. Asiatic Soc. Pakistan, 13:1-148. 1964. ill.
Blegvad, H. and B. Løppenthin. Fishes of the Iranian Gulf. - Dan. Scient. Invest. Iran, 3:1-247, pls. I-XI. 1944. 135 text-figs.
Chang Chung-lin and Wang Wêng-pin. Preliminary Communication on the Fishes of Tibet. - Acta zool. sin., 14, No.4:529-536. 1962.
Chaudhuri, B.L. Fauna of the Chilka Lake. Fish. IV. - Mem. Indian Mus., 5:711-736. 1923.
Chauhan, B.S. and G.Ramakrishna. Fauna of the Balangir District (Formerly Patna State), Orissa. Fishes. - Rec. Indian Mus., 51:395-416. 1954. 4 pls.
Clark, E. and H.A.F.Gohar. The Fishes of the Red Sea. - Publs. Mar. Biol. Stn. Ghardaqa, 8:1-80. 1953. 22 figs., 5 pls.
D'Abreu, E.A. A List of Fish Obtained in the Seran District, Bahar, Chiefly from the Ghogra River near the Town of Chapra and in its Vicinity. - J. Bombay Nat. Hist. Soc., 30:707-711. 1925.
Day, F. The Fishes of India; Being a Natural History of the Fishes Known to Inhabit the Seas and Fresh Waters of India, Burma and Ceylon (1878 ed., facsimile). - London, Wm.Dawson's Sons. 1958. 2 vols.
Deraniyagala, P.E.P. A Colored Atlas of Some Vertebrates from Ceylon. I. Fishes. - Ceylon Nat. Mus. Publ., Colombo: i-xii, 1-149. 1952. 35 pls.
De Witt, H.H. A Contribution to the Ichthyology of Nepal. - Stanford Ichthyol. Bull., 7, No.4:63-88. 1960. ill.
Fowler, H.W. Fishes of the Red Sea and Southern Arabia. I. Branchiostomida to Polynemida. - Jerusalem, Weizmann Science Press of Israel. 1956. 240 pp., 117 figs.
Fowler, H.W. and H.Steinitz. Fishes from Cyprus, Iran, Israel and Oman. - Bull. Res. Coun. Israel, 5B:260-292. 1956. 33 figs.
Hardenberg, J.D.F. The Fishfauna of the Rokan Mouth. - Treubia, 13, No.1:81-168. 1931. 1 chart.
Hardenberg, J.D.F. Additional Notes to my Paper "The Fishfauna of the Rokan Mouth." - Ibid., 14, No.3:299-312. 1934.
Herre, A.W. On a Collection of Littoral and Freshwater Fishes from the Andaman Islands. - Rec. Indian Mus., 41, No.4:327-372. 1939.
Herre, A.W. A List of the Fishes Known from the Andaman Islands. - Mem. Indian Mus., 13:331-403. 1941.
Hora, S.L. Fish and Fisheries of Manipur with Some Observations on Those of the Naga Hills. - Rec. Indian Mus., 22:165-214, pls.9-12. 1921.
Hora, S.L. Fish of the Salt Range, Punjab. - Ibid., 25:377-386, pl.8. 1923. 3 text-figs.
Hora S.L. Fish of Afganistan. - J. Bombay Nat. Hist. Soc., 36:688-706. 1933. ill.
Hora, S.L. The Fish of Chitral. - Rec. Indian Mus., 36, No.2:279-319. 1934. 3 pls., ill.
Hora, S.L. On a Collection of Fish from Afganistan. - J. Bombay Nat. Hist. Soc., 37, No.4:784-802. 1935. ill.
Hora, S.L. A List of Fishes of the Mysore State and of the Neighbouring Hill Ranges of the Nilgiris, Wynaad and Coorg. - Rec. Indian Mus., 44:193-200. 1942.
Hora, S.L. and D.D.Mukerji. Fish of the Naga Hills, Assam. - Ibid., 37:381-406. 1935. ill.
Hora, S.L. and D.D.Mukerji. Pisces. Wissenschaftliche Ergebnisse der Niederländischen Expeditionen in den Karakorum und die angrenzenden Gebiete 1922, 1925 und 1929/1930. - Zoologie, pp.425-446. Leipzig. 1935. ill.
Hora, S.L. and D.D.Mukerji. Table (Key) for the Identification of Indian Freshwater Fishes with Descriptions of Certain Families and Observations on the Relative Utility of the Probable Larvivorous Fishes of India. - Health Bull., 12, Malaria Bureau, 4:1-47. Delhi. 1938.
Hora, S.L. and K.S.Misra. On a Small Collection of Fish from Iraq. - J.Asiat. Soc. Beng., Sci., 9, No.1:1-15. 1943. 7 text-figs.
John, C.C. Fish and Fisheries of the Cape Comorin Bank. - Bull. Res. Inst., Univ. Kerala, Ser.C, 7, No.1:65-145. 1959.

Kähsbauer, P. Zur Kenntnis der Ichthyofauna von Iran. – Annln. naturh. Mus. Wien, 66:317–355. 1963; Part 2, 67:453–475. 1964.

Khalaf, K.T. Fishes of Iraq. Baghdad. 1961. 92 pp.

Khalaf, K.T. The Marine and Freshwater Fishes of Iraq. Baghdad. 1961. 164 pp.

Klausewitz, W. Die Erforschung der Ichthyofauna des Roten Meeres (Introd. to Reprint of C.B.Klunzinger. Synopsis der Fische des Roten Meeres). – Wheldon and Wesley, Codicote, Herts: V–XXXVI. 1964. 4 vols.

Kotthaus, A. Fische des Indischen Ozeans. Ergebnisse der ichthyologischen Untersuchungen während der Expedition des Forschungsschiffes "Meteor" in den Indischen Ozean, Oktober 1964 bis Mai 1965. – "Meteor" Forschungsergebnisse Reihe D, 1:1–84. 1967. 96 pls.

Malaviya, R.B. A List of Fishes from Jabalpur, M.B., India. – Proc. Natn. Acad. Sci., India, 32B:349–354. 1962.

Mandi, N. Fishes of Iraq. Baghdad. (The Author) (post 1959). 1961. 82 pp., ill.

Marine Fishes of Karachi and the Coasts of Sind and Makran. Karachi. 1955. 80 pp., 113 figs.

Marshall, N.B. Fishes from the Cocos-Keeling Islands. – Bull. Raffles Mus., 22:100–205. 1950. 2 pls.

Marshall, N.B. The "Manihine" Expedition to the Gulf of Aqaba 1948–1949. IX. Fishes. – Bull. Br. Mus. Nat. Hist., 1, No.8:221–252, figs.1–3. 1952.

Mendis, A.S. Fishes of Ceylon (a Catalogue, Key and Bibliographies). – Bull. Fish. Res. Stn. Ceylon, 2:1–222. 1954.

Mendis, A.S. and C.H.Fernando. A Guide to the Freshwater Fauna of Ceylon. – Ibid., pp.1–160. Pisces, pp.101–125. 1962. ill.

Menon, A.G.K. A Distributional List of Fishes of the Himalayas. – J. Zool. Soc. India, 14, Nos.1–2:23–32. 1962.

Menon, M.A.S. On a Third Collection of Fish from Iraq. – Rec. Indian Mus., 54, Nos.3–4:139–158. (1956) 1960.

Menon, M.A. On a Collection of Fish from Lake Chilka, Orissa. – Ibid., 59, Nos.1–2:41–69. (1961) 1963.

Misra, K.S. A Checklist of the Fishes of India, Burma and Ceylon. – Ibid., I, 45:1–46. 1947; II, 45:377–431. 1949.

Misra K.S. An Aid to the Identification of the Common Commercial Fishes of India and Pakistan. – Ibid., 57, Nos.1–4:1–320. 1962. ill.

Mukerji, D.D. On a Collection of Fish from Lower Burma. – Ibid., 34:281–286. 1932. 3 figs.

Mukerji, D.D. Report on Burmese Fishes Collected by Lt.-Col. R.W.Burton from the Tributary Streams of the Mali Hka of the Myitkyina District (Upper Burma). – J. Bombay Nat. Hist. Soc., 36:813–831. 1933. 3 pls., 3 figs; 37, No.1:38–80. 1934. 14 figs.

Mukerji, D.D. Notes on Some Rare and Interesting Fishes from the Andaman Islands, with Descriptions of Two New Freshwater Gobies. – Rec. Indian Mus., 37:259–277, pl. VI. 1935. 2 text-figs.

Munro, I.S.R. The Marine and Freshwater Fishes of Ceylon. Canberra. 1955. 351 pp., 19 figs., 56 pls.

Pellegrin, J. Etude sur les poissons rapportés par M. Henri Gadeau de Kerville de son voyage zoologique en Syrie (avril–juin, 1908). – Voyage zool. H.Gadeau de Kerville en Syrie, Paris, 4:1–37. 1923. 5 pls.

Pillay, R.S.N. A List of Fishes Taken in Travancore from 1901–1915. – J. Bombay Nat. Hist. Soc., 33:347–379. 1929.

Qureshi, M.R. Fishes of Mekran Coast. – Agriculture Pakist., 3:237–256. 1952. 28 figs.

Ranade, M.R. A Checklist of Fishes Occurring in the Fresh Waters of Baroda. – J. Bombay Nat. Hist. Soc., 51:472–474. 1953.

Rao, C.R.N. and B.R.Seshachar. Notes on the Freshwater Fish of Mysore. – Half-yearly J. Mysore Univ., 1:115–143. 1927.

Rass, T.S. Commercial Ichthyofauna and Fishery Resources of the Indian Ocean. – Trudy Inst. Okeanol. Akad. Nauk SSSR, 80:3–31, figs.1–4. 1965.

Roux-Esteve, R and P.Fourmanoir. Résultats scientifiques des campagnes de la Calypso. Poissons capturés par la Mission de la "Calypso" en Mer Rouge. – Annls. Inst. océanogr., Monaco, 30:198–203. 1955.

Spence, R. and S.H.Prater. Game Fishes of Bombay, the Deccan and the Neighbouring Districts of the Bombay Presidency. – J. Bombay Nat. Hist. Soc., 36:29–66. 1933. 19 pls.

Steinitz, H. and A.Ben-Tuvia. Fishes from Eylath (Gulf of Aqaba), Red Sea. – Bull. Sea Fish. Res. Stn. Israel, 11:1–15. 1955.

Svetovidov, A.N. Fishes of Iran, from Data Collected by Academician E.N.Pavlovskii. – Trudy Zool. Inst. Akad. Nauk SSSR, 8:859–869. 1949.

Tandon, K.K. and S.S.Thind. The Fish Fauna of the Black Bein. – Res. Bull. Panjab Univ. Sci., 14, Nos.1–2:161–165. 1963.

Varma, N.S. et al. Fishes of Kanpur District. – Proc. Natn. Acad. Sci. India, 32B:213–232. 1962.

Vasiliu, G.D. Beschreibung der Ceylon-Fische aus der Sammlung Plate. – Jena. Z. Naturw., 65:319–360. 1931. 4 pls.

Witt, H.H. de. A Contribution to the Ichthyology of Nepal. – Stanford Ichthyol. Bull., 7:63–88. 1960. 3 figs.

63 – eastern Indian Ocean

631 – Australia

Bleakley, M.C. and E.M.Grant. Key to the Common Freshwater Fishes of Southern Queensland. – Qd. Nat., 15, Nos.1–2:21–26. 1954. 1 fig.

D'Ombrain, A. Game Fishing off the Australian Coast. – Sydney, Angus and Robertson. 1957. 1–18+1–230 pp.

Gillett, K. and F.McNeill. The Great Barrier Reef and Adjacent Isles. – Sydney, Coral Press Pty. Ltd. 1959. 1–194 pp., ill.

Hiley, T.A. Know your Fishes. An Illustrated Guide to the Principal Commercial Fishes and Crustaceans of Queensland. Dep. of Harbours and Marine, Brisbane. 1959. 126 pp.

Lord, C. A List of the Fishes of Tasmania. – Pap. Proc. R. Soc. Tasm., pp.60–73. 1923.

Lord, C. A List of the Fishes of Tasmania. – J. Pan-Pacif. Res. Instn., **2**, No.4:11–14. 1927.

McCulloch, A.R. Checklist of the Fish and Fish-like Animals of New South Wales. – Aust. Zool., Pts.1, 2, 1, No.2:1–58, pls.16–18. 1920; Pt.3, 2:86–130, pls.25–43. 1922.

McCulloch, A.R. A Checklist of the Fishes Recorded from Australia. – Mem. Aust. Mus., 5:1–534. 1929–1930.

McCulloch, A.R. The Fishes and Fish-like Animals of New South Wales. 3rd ed. – Roy. Zool. Soc. N.S.Wales. 1934. 1–26+1–104 pp. 43 pls.

Marshall, T.C. et al. Know your Fishes. An Illustrated Guide to the Principal Commercial Fishes and Crustaceans of Queensland. Dep. of Harbours and Marine, Brisbane. 1959. 137 pp., 2 col. pls., ill.

Marshall, T.C. Fishes of the Great Barrier Reef and Coastal Waters of Queensland. – London, Angus and Robertson. 1964. 566 pp., 72 col. pls., 497 figs., 12 text-figs.

Mees, G.F. Additions to the Fish Fauna of Western Australia, 4. – Bull. W. Aust., 9:31–55. 1964.

Munro, I.S.R. Handbook of Australian Fishes, 31–36. – Fishg. News, 19:125–148. 1960. figs.

Ogilby, J.D. Edible Fishes of Queensland. – Mem. Qd. Mus., 6:45–90, pls.XVI–XXVI. 1918; 7:1–30, pls.I–III. 1920.

Ogilby, J.D. (revised and illustrated by M.C.Marshall). The Commercial Fishes and Fisheries of Queensland. – Fisher. Br. Dep. Harb. Mar., Brisbane. 1954. 122 pp., 122 figs., 1 pl.

Okada, S., K.Kobayashi, and H.Omi. List of Fishes Collected with Trawl Net and Tuna Long-line Fishing by "Oshoro Maru" in 1963. – Record of Oceanographic Observations and Exploratory Fishing, Fac. Fish. Hokkaido Univ., 8:190–198, pls.1–27, figs.1–171. 1964.

Osipov, V. Atlas of Marine Fishes of Australia. – Vladivostok, Dal'ryba. 88 pp., 82 figs.

Paradise, W.E.J. and G.P.Whitley. Northern Territory Fishes. – Mem. Qd. Mus., 9:76–106, pls.XI–XV. 1927. 3 text-figs.

Rendahl, H. Results of Dr.E.Mjöberg's Swedish Scientific Expeditions to Australia, 1910–1913. XXVIII. – K. svenska Vetensk. Akad. Handl., 61; No.9:1–24. 1921.

Rendahl, H. A Contribution to the Ichthyology of North-West Australia. – Nytt. Mag. Naturvid., Kristiania (Medd. Zool. Mus., 5), 60:163–197. 1922. 6 figs.

Roughley, T.C. Fish and Fisheries of Australia. Sydney–London. 1951. 343 pp., 76 pls., 10 figs.

Roughley, T.C. Fish and Fisheries of Australia. 3rd ed., revised. – Sydney, Angus and Robertson. 1955. 328 pp., 59 col. pls., 29 pls., 11 figs.

Scott, T.D. The Sharks and Rays of South Australia with Keys to the Species. – S. Aust. Nat., 29:55–66. 1955.

Scott, T.D. The Marine and Freshwater Fishes of South Australia. – Govt. Printer, Adelaide. 1962. 338 pp., ill.

Taylor, W.R. Fishes of Arnhem Land (N. Australia). – Rec. Am. Aust. Sci. Exped. to Arnhem Land, 4, No.3:45–307. 1964. 68 figs.

Waite, E.R. Illustrated Catalogue of the Fishes of South Australia. – Rec. S. Aust. Mus., 2, No.1:1–208. 1921. 293 figs., 1 pl.

Waite, E.R. The Fishes of South Australia. – Handbooks Flora and Fauna S. Australia. 1923. 243 pp., figs.

Waite, E.R. Supplement to the Catalogue of the Fishes of South Australia. – Rec. S. Aust. Mus., 3:223–234, pl.13. 1927.

Waite, E. Checklist of the Marine Fishes of South Australia. – J. Pan-Pacif. Res. Instn., 3:3–10. 1928.

Whitley, G.P. The Fishes of Australia. Part 1. The Sharks, Rays, Devil-fish and Other Primitive Fishes of Australia and New Zealand. – Sydney Roy. Zool. Soc. N.S.Wales, Austral. Handb. 1940. 280 pp., 303 figs.

Whitley, G.P. A List of the Fishes of Western Australia. – W. Aust. Fish Dep. Bull., 2:1–35. 1948.

Whitley, G.P. Native Freshwater Fishes of Australia. – Brisbane, Jacaranda Press. 1960. 128 pp.

Whitley, G.P. Marine Fishes of Australia, 1:1–144; 2:145–288. Brisbane, Jacaranda Press. 1962. ill.

Whitley, G.P. Presidential Address. A Survey of Australian Ichthyology. – Proc. Linn. Soc. N.S. Wales. 89, No.1:11–127. 1964.

Whitley, G.P. Fishes from the Coral Sea and the Swain Reefs. – Rec. S. Aust. Mus., 26, No.5:145–195. 1964. ill.

Woodland, D.J. and R.J. Slack-Smith. Fishes of Heron Island, Capricorn Group, Great Barrier Reef. – Pap. Dep. Zool. Univ., Qd., 2, No.2:13–69. 1963.

Woods, C. Native and Introduced Freshwater Fishes. – Reed, Wellington–Auckland. 1963. 64 pp.

632 – New Zealand

Allen, K.R. Freshwater Fish. – New Zealand Marine Dep. Fish. Lab. Publs., 34:1–12. 1957.

Bassett, D. A Bibliography of the Freshwater Fishes of New Zealand. – Wellington Library School, Nat. Library Serv., Bibliogr. Ser., 5:1–46. 1961.

Graham, D.H. A Treasury of New Zealand Fishes, 1st ed. 1953. 404 pp., ill.; 2nd ed. 1956. 424 pp., ill.

Griffin, L.T. Addition to the Fish Fauna of New Zealand. – Trans. N.Z. Inst., 58:136–150. 1927.

McDowall, R.M. A Bibliography of the Indigenous Freshwater Fishes of New Zealand. – Trans. R. Soc. N.Z. (Zool.), 5:1–38. 1964.

McDowall, R.M. A Guide to the Identification of New Zealand Freshwater Fishes. – Tuatara, 14, No.2:89–104. 1966.

Morehead, J.M. Marine Fishes of New Zealand. Wellington. 1968. 56 pp.

Moreland, J. Nature in New Zealand. Native Sea Fishes. Reed, Wellington. 1936. 64 pp., ill.

Moreland, J. Game Fish of New Zealand. – In: Fighting Fins. Big Game Fishing in New Zealand Waters, pp.59–90. 1961.

Parrott, A.W. Studies in New Zealand Fishes. – Rec. Canterbury (N.Z.) Mus., 5:137–160, pls. XXX, XXXI. 1948.

Parrott, A.W. Sea Anglers of New Zealand. – London, Hadder and Stoughton. 1957. 176 pp.

Parrott, A.W. Big Game Fishes and Sharks of New Zealand. London. 1958. 127 pp.

Parrott, A.W. Fishes from the Auckland and Campbell Islands. – Rec. Dom. Mus. Wellington, 3, No.2:109–119. 1958.

Parrott, A.W. The Queer and Rare Fishes of New Zealand. London. 1960. 192 pp.

Phillipps, W.J. A Checklist of the Fishes of New Zealand. – J. Pan-Pacif. Res. Instn., 2, No.1:9–15. 1927.

Phillipps, W.J. Bibliography and Index of New Zealand Fishes. – New Zealand Marine Dep. Wellington. Fish Bull., 1:1–68. 1927.

Rendahl, H. Papers from Dr. Th. Mortensen's Pacific Expedition, 1914–1916. XXX. Fishes from New Zealand and the Auckland-Campbell Islands. – Vidensk. Meddr. dansk. naturh. Foren, 81:1–14. 1926. 6 figs.

Stokell, G. Freshwater Fishes of New Zealand. – Christchurch, Smith and Williams. 1955. 145 pp.

Whitley, G.P. A Checklist of the Fishes Recorded from the New Zealand Region. – Aust. Zool., 15, No.1:1–102. 1968.

7 – Antarctica

Andriashev, A.P. A General Review of the Antarctic Fish Fauna. – In: Biogeography and Ecology in Antarctica. Ed. by P.van Oye and J.van Mieghem. –Monogr. Biol., 15:491–550, figs.1–18. 1965.

Andriyashev, A.P. A Survey of the Fish Fauna of the Antarctic. – Issled. Fauny Morei, 2, No.10:335–386. 1964. 18 figs.

Andriyashev, A.P. A Field Key to the off Shore Species of Fish from Eastern Antarctica. – Inf. Byull. Sov. Antarkt. Eksped., 53:31–37. 1965. ill.

Beddings, L.G. Notas sobre ictiologia Antarctica. Investigaciones efectuadas en la tercera Expedicion Antarctica en 1949. – Boln. soc. Biol. Concepción, 24:91–99. 1949. 5 text-figs.

Bellisio, N.B. Peces Antarticos, del sector Argentino, 1:1–90. 1964; 2:1–78. 1965; 3:1–94. 1966. ill.

Blanc, M. Les poissons des Terres australes et antarctiques françaises. – Mém. Inst. scient. Madagascar, F., 4:109–159. 1961. 51 figs.

De Witt, H.H. Antarctic Ichthyology. – Bioscience, 15:290–293. 1965. 3 figs.

De Witt, H.H. and J.C. Tyler. Fishes of the Stanford Antarctic Biological Research Program, 1958–1959. – Stanford Ichthyol. Bull., 7, No.4:162–199. 1960. ill.

Gosse, J.P. Poissons antarctiques récoltés par l'expédition belge "Iris." 1961. Bruxelles. – Bull. Inst. r. Sci. nat. Belg., 37, No.29:1–10. 1961.

Hureau, J.C. Poissons antarctiques récoltés au cours de la onzième expédition française en Terre Adélie (1960–1962). – Bull. Mus. natn. Hist. nat., Paris, 2, 34:228–240. 1962. 6 figs.

Korotkevich, V.S. Fishes from Alasheev Bight and Leningradskii Bay. – Inf. Byull. Sov. Antarkt. Eksped., 66:44–47. 1964. ill.

Matsubara, K. and T. Iwai. Fishes. – Spec. Pap. Seto Mar. Biol. Lab. Biol. Results of the Japanese Antarctic Expedition, 9:1–8. 1959. ill.

Norman, J.R. Coast Fishes. I. The South Atlantic. – Discovery Rep., 12:1–58. 1935. 15 figs.

Norman, J.R. Fishes. – Rep. B.A.N.Z. Antarct. Res. Exp., Ser. B, 1, No.2:50–88. 1937. 11 figs.

Norman, J.R. Coast Fishes. III. The Antarctic Zone. – Discovery Rep., 18:1–105. 1938. 1 pl., 62 figs.

Nybelin, O. Antarctic Fishes. – Scient. Results Norw. Antarct. Exped., 1927–1928, 2, No.26:1–76. 1947. 6 pls., 2 text-figs.

Nybelin, O. Subantarctic and Antarctic Fishes. – Scient. Results Brategg Exped., 1947–1948, 2. Publ. Christensens Hvalfanstum, 18:1–32. 1951. 3 figs.

Nybelin, O. Fishes Collected during the Norwegian-British-Swedish Antarctic Expedition 1949–1952. – Göteborgs K. Vetensk. – o Vitterh.Samh. Handl., Sjätte fölyd., Ser.B, 6, No.7:1–13. 1952. 4 figs.

Permitin, Yu.E. New Data on the Specific Composition and Distribution of Fish in the Scotia Sea, Antarctica. – Vopr. Ikhtiol., 6, No.3(40):424–431. 1966.

Permitin, Yu.E. New Data on the Specific Composition and Distribution of Fish in the Scotia Sea, Antarctica. – Ibid., 9, No.2(55):221–239. 1969.

Slack-Smith, R.J. A Small Collection of Fish from Macquarie Island. – Mem. Natn. Mus. Vict., 25:13–16. 1962.

Tortonese, E. Pesci del mar Rosso. – Boll. Musei Zool. Anat. comp. R. Univ. Torino, Ser.3, 45, No.63:153–218. 1935–1936. ill.

Whitley, G.P. A Checklist of the Fishes Recorded from the New Zealand Region. – Aust. Zool., 15, No.1:1–102. 1968.

ADDITIONAL LITERATURE ON SYSTEMATICS (ADD.)

Aguirre, J.L.C. Peces sierra, rayas, mantas y especies afines de México. – An. Inst. Nac. Invest. Biol. Pesq. México, 1:171–256. 1965. 34 pls., 16 figs.

Alfred, E.R. The Malayan Cyprinoid Fishes of the Family Homalopteridae. – Zool. Meded., Leiden, 43, No.18:213–237. 1969.

Amaoka, K. Studies on the Sinistral Flounders Found in the Waters around Japan. Taxonomy, Anatomy and Phylogeny. – J. Shimonoseki Coll. Fish., 18, No.2:59–340. 1969. 131 figs.

Anderson, W.D. Field Guide to the Snappers (Lutjanidae) of the Western Atlantic. – Circ. Fish Wildl. Serv., Wash., 252:1–14. 1967. 29 figs.

Anderson, W.W. and E.J. Guntherz. Revision of the Flatfish Genus Trichopsetta (Bothidae) with Descriptions of Three New Species. – Bull. Mar. Sci., 17, No.4:892–913. 1967.

Andriyashev, A.P. A Survey of Fishes of the Genus Pogonophryne Regan (Pisces, Harpagiferidae) with a Description of Five New Species from the Eastern Antarctic and South Orkney Islands. – Issled. Fauny Morei, 4:389–412. 1967. figs.

Băcescu, M. Contribution to the Study of the Genus Noemacheilus (Pisces – Cobitidae). – Trav. Mus. Hist. nat. Gr. Antipa, 7:357–370. 1967.

Bănărescu, P. Notes on the Genus Erythroculter Berg (Pisces, Cyprinidae), with Description of a New Subspecies. – Revue roum. Biol. Ser. Zool., 12, No.4:215–227. 1967.

Bănărescu, P. Studies on the Systematics of Cultrinae (Pisces, Cyprinidae) with Description of a New Genus. – Ibid., 12, No.5:297–308. 1967.

Bănărescu, P. Süsswasserfische der Türkei. Ergänzende Angaben zu Teil 2: Cobitidae. – Mitt. hamb. biol. Mus. Inst., 65:353–356. 1968.

Bănărescu, P. Revision of the Genera Zacco and Opsariichthys (Pisces, Cyprinidae). – Věst. čsl. Spol. zool., 32, No.4:305–311. 1968.

Bănărescu, P. Revision of the Indo-Burmanese Genus Salmostoma Swainson (Pisces, Cyprinidae) with Description of a New Subspecies. – Revue roum. Biol., Ser. Zool., 13, No.1:3–14. 1968.

Bănărescu, P. and T.T. Nalbant. The 3rd Danish Expedition to Central Asia. Zoological Results. 34. Cobitidae (Pisces) from Afghanistan and Iran. – Vidensk. Meddr. dansk. naturh. Foren, 129:151–186. 1966. 17 figs., 3 pls.

Bănărescu, P. and T.T. Nalbant. Revision of the Genus Sarcocheilichthys (Pisces, Cyprinidae). – Věst. čsl. Spol. zool., 31:293–312. 1967. 8 figs., 4 pls.

Bănărescu, P. and T.T. Nalbant. Revision of the Genus Gnathopogon Bleeker, 1859 (Pisces, Cyprinidae). – Trav. Mus. Hist. nat. Gr. Antipa, 7:341–355. 1967. 11 figs.

Bănărescu, P. and T.T. Nalbant. Cobitidae (Pisces, Cypriniformes) Collected by the German India Expedition. – Mitt. hamb. zool. Mus. Inst., 65:327–351. 1968.

Barlow, G., K.F. Liem, and W. Wickler. Badidae, a New Fish Family – Behavioural, Osteological and Developmental Evidence. – J. Zool., Lond., 156:415–447, pls.1–2. 1968. 13 figs.

Barnett, M.A. and R.H. Gibbs. Four New Stomiatoid Fishes of the Genus Bathophilus with a Revised Key to Species of Bathophilus. – Copeia, 4:826–832. 1968.

Barsukov, V.V. On the Systematic Relationships of Rockfishes of the Genus Sebastes of the Northwest Atlantic. – Dokl. Akad. Nauk SSSR, 183, No.2:479–482. 1968.

Bechesku [Băcescu], M. and R. Maier. On the Study of Spiny Loaches (Cobitis) from the Don and Volga Rivers. – Vopr. Ikhtiol., 9, No.1:51–60. 1969.

Blache, J. Poissons bathypélagiques rares ou peu connus provenant des eaux de l'Atlantique oriental tropical. 1. Note. Famille des Opisthoproctidae. – Cahiers O.R.S.T.O.M., Océanographie, 5:89–95. 1963. 4 figs.

Blache, J. Contribution à la connaissance des poissons Anguilliformes de la côte occidentale d'Afrique. – Bull. Inst. fr. Afr. noire, 29A. 1967: 2. Le genre Muraena (Artedi) Linné, 1758 (Muraenidae), 1:178–217. 19 figs.; 3. Le genre Echidna Forster, 1788 (Muraenidae), 2:695–709. 7 figs.; 4. Le genre Lycodontis McClelland, 1845, 3:1122–1187. 29 figs.; 5. Le genre Gymnothorax Bloch, 1795, l.c., 4:1695–1705. 5 figs.; 6 Les genres Anarchias, Uropterygius et Channomuraena (Muraenidae), l.c., 4:1706–1731. 14 figs.; 7. La famille des Muraenesocidae, 30A, 1968: 2:690–736. 31 figs.

Boeseman, M. The Genus Hypostomus Lacépède, 1803, and its Surinam Representatives (Siluriformes, Loricariidae). – Zool. Verh., Leiden, 99:1–108. 1968. ill.

Böhlke, J.E. and C.R. Robins. Western Atlantic Sponge-dwelling Gobies of the Genus Evermannichthys, their Taxonomy, Habits and Relationships. – Proc. Acad. Nat. Sci. Philad., 121, No.1:1–24. 1969. ill.

Bonnet, M. Les sparidés des côtes nord-ouest africaines. – Revue Trav. Inst. Pêch. marit., 33, No.1:97–116. 1969. 11 figs.

Briggs, J.C. A New Species of Lepadichthys (Gobioesocidae) from Seychelles, Indian Ocean. – Copeia, 3:464–466. 1969.

Bright, T.J. and W.E. Pequegnat. Deep Sea Hatchet Fishes of the Gulf of Mexico. – Q. Jl. Fla. Acad. Sci., 32, No.1:26–36. 1969.

Bullis, H.R. and J.S. Carpenter. Neoharriotta carri – a New Species of Rhinochimaeridae from the Southern Caribbean Sea. – Copeia, 3:443–450. 1966. 4 figs.

Castle, P.H.J. Heterocongrine Eels in the Southwest Pacific. – Rec. Dom. Mus. Wellington, 6:5–12. 1967. 1 fig.

Castle, P.H.J. The Congrid Eels of the Western Indian Ocean and the Red Sea. – Ichthyol. Bull. Rhodes Univ., 33:685–726, pl.108. 1968.

Cervigon, F. and E.Velasquez. Las especies del genero Mycteroperca de la costas de Venezuela (Pisces – Serranidae). – Mems. Soc. Cienc. nat. "La Salle," 26, No.74:77–143. 1966. 29 figs.

Chen, J.T.F., Liu Mo-chao, and Lee Sin-che. A Review of the Pediculate Fishes of Taiwan. – Tunghai J., 9, No.1:173–195. 1968.

Chen, J.T.F. and H.T.Weng. A Review of the Apodal Fishes of Taiwan. – Biol. Bull. Tunghai Univ. (Ichthyol. Ser., 6), 32:1–86. 1967. 64 figs.

Clark, E. Eleotrid Gobies Collected during the Israel South Red Sea Expedition (1962), with a Key to Red Sea Species. – Sea Fish Research Station Haifa, Israel Bull., 49:3–7. 1968.

Cohen, D.M. The Cyclopterid Genus Paraliparis, a Senior Synonym of Gymnolycodes and Eutelichthys, with the Description of a New Species from the Gulf of Mexico. – Copeia, 2:384–388. 1968.

Cohen, D.M. and S.P.Atsaides. Additions to a Revision of Argentinine Fishes. – Fishery Bull. Fish Wildl. Serv. U.S., 68, No.1:13–36. 1969. 14 figs.

Dashdorh, A., A.Dulmaa, and K.Pivnička. Contribution to the Systematics of the Genus Oreoleuciscus Warpachowski. 1889 (Cyprinidae). – Věst. čsl. Spol. zool., 33, No.4:289–299. 1969.

Davis, W.P. A Review of the Dragonets (Pisces, Callionymidae) of the Western Atlantic. – Bull. Mar. Sci., 16:834–862. 1966. 10 figs.

Dawson, C.E. Paragunnellichthys seychellensis, a New Genus and Species of Gobioid Fish (Microdesmidae) from the Western Indian Ocean. – Proc. Biol. Soc. Wash., 80:73–82. 1967.

De Angelis, C.M. Osservazioni sulle specie del genere Mugil segnalate lungo le coste del Mediterranéo.– Boll. Pesca Piscic. Idrobiol., 22, No.1:5–36. (1967) 1968.

De Witt, H.H. A Revision of the Antarctic and Southern Notothenia (Pisces, Nototheniidae). – Diss. Abstr., 27B:2541–2542. 1967.

Dmitrenko, E.M. Catfishes of the Northwestern Indian Ocean. Communications I and II. – Vest. Zool., 6:65–83. 1968; 2:39–43. 1969.

Dutt, S. Fishes of the Genus Ilisha Richardson, 1846, from Visakhapatnam. – Proc. Indian Acad., B66, No.5:206–213. 1967.

Dutt, S. and V.Thankam. The Sciaenidae of the Coastal Waters of Visakhapatnam. – J. Bombay Nat. Hist. Soc., 65, No.2:335–347. 1969.

Fernández, Y.A. Contribución al conocimiento de la familia Doradidae en Venezuela. – Bolm. Inst. Oceanogr. Univ. Oriente, 7, No.1:7–72. (1968) 1969.

Fishelson, V.L. Untersuchungen zur vergleichenden Entwicklungsgeschichte der Gattung Tilapia (Cichlidae, Teleostei). – Zool. Jber. Neapel, Anat., 83:571—656. 1966. 67 figs.

Fourmanoir, P. Nouvelle détermination proposée pour un Apogonidae de Mer Rouge et de l'Océan Indien. – Bull. Mus. natn. Hist. nat., Paris, 2, No.39-265–266. 1967. 1 fig.

Frankenberg, R.S. The Vertebrate Fauna of the Bass Strait Islands: III. The Galaxiid Fishes of Flinders and King Islands. – Proc. Soc. Victoria, 80, No.2:225–228. 1967.

Freihofer, W.C. The Suborders of Perciform Fishes by W.A.Gosline. – Copeia, 4:858–861. 1969.

Georgier, J.M. Composition d'espèce et caractéristique des Gobiidés, Pisces, en Bulgarie. – Izv. Nauchnoizsl. Inst. Rib. Stop. Okeanogr., Varna, 7:159–228. 1966. 57 figs., tables.

Gibbs, R.H. Taxonomy, Sexual Dimorphism, Vertical Distribution, and Evolutionary Zoogeography of the Bathypelagic Fish Genus Stomias (Stomiatidae). – Smithsonian Contrib. to Zool., 31:1–25. 1969. 6 figs.

Gilbert, C.R. Western Atlantic Batrachoidid Fishes of the Genus Porichthys, Including Three New Species. – Bull. Mar. Sci., 18, No.3:671–730. 1968.

Gilbert, C.R. and D.K.Caldwell. The American Atherinid Fishes of the Genus Coleotropis. – Contr. Sci. Los Angeles County Mus., 125:1–16. 1967. ill.

Gilbert, P.W., R.F.Matthewson, and D.P.Rall (editors). Sharks, Skates and Rays. – Baltimore, J.Hopkins Press. 1967. i–xv, 1–624 pp., ill.

Gosline, W.A. The Morphology and Systematic Position of the Alepocephaloid Fishes. – Bull. Br. Mus. Nat. Hist., Zool., 18, No.6:185–218. 1969. 14 figs.

Gosline, W.A. The Suborders of Perciform Fishes. – Proc. U.S. Natn. Mus., 124 (3647):1–78. 1969. 12 figs., 3 tables.

Greenwood, P.H. The Cichlid Fishes of the Lake Nabugabo, Uganda. – Bull. Br. Mus. Nat. Hist., Zool., 12, No.9:315–357. 1965. 12 figs.

Greenwood, P.H. The Caudal Fin Skeleton in Osteoglossoid Fishes. – Ann. Mag. Nat. Hist., 9 (106–108): 581–597. 1967.

Greenwood, P.H. A Revision of the Lake Victoria Haplochromis Species (Pisces, Cichlidae). Part VI.– Bull. Br. Mus. Nat. Hist., Zool., 15, No.2:31–119. 1967. 24 figs.

Greenwood, P.H., G.S. Myers, D.E. Rosen, and S.H. Weitzman. Named Main Divisions of Teleostean Fishes. – Proc. Biol. Soc. Wash., 80:227–228. 1967.

Guitart, M.D. Guia para los tiburones de aguas cubanas. – Acad. cienc. Cuba, Oceanol., 1:1–61. 1968.

Holden, M.J. The Systematics of the Genus Lates (Teleostei: Centropomidae) in Lake Albert, East Africa. – J. Zool., Lond., 151:329–342. 1967. 3 figs.

Hotta Hideyuki and Tung-I-sü. Determination of Fishes of the Family Mugilidae according to the Number of Pyloric Caeca and the Position of the First Interneuralia of the Dorsal Fin. – Jap. J. Ichthyol., 14, Nos1, 2, 3:62–66. 1966.

Hubbs, C.L. A Fresh Look at Teleost Evolution. – Q. Rev. Biol., 42, No.1:40–41. 1967.

Hubbs, C.L. and R. Ishiyama. Methods for the Taxonomic Study and Description of Skates (Rajidae). – Copeia, 3:483–491. 1968. 1 fig.

Jayaram, K.C. Contribution to the Study of Bagrid Fishes (Siluroidea: Bagridae). 3. A Systematic Account of the Japanese, Chinese, Malayan and Indonesian Genera. – Treubia, 27, Nos.2–3:287–386. 1968.

Jayaram, K.C. and N. Majumdar. Siluroid Fishes of India, Burma and Ceylon. 16. Fishes of the Genus Plotosus Lacépède. – Proc. Zool. Soc., 20, No.2:137–146. 1967.

Jubb, R.A. The Nothobranchius (Pisces, Cyprinodontidae) of Southern Africa and a New Species from Lake Chilwa, Malawi, Part 1. – Ann. Cape Prov. Mus. Nat. Hist., 8, No.1:1–11. 1969. ill.

Jubb, R.A. and P. Le Roux. Revision of the Chiloglanis (Pisces, Mochokidae) of Southern Africa and Descriptions of Two New Species. Part 1. Limpopo, Incomati and Pongola Rivers. – Ibid., 8, No.2:13–23. 1969.

Kato, S., S. Springer, and M.H. Wagner. Field Guide to Eastern Pacific and Hawaiian Sharks. – Circ. Fish. Wildl. Serv., Wash., 271:1–47. 1967.

Kiener, A. and C.J. Spillmann. Contributions à l'étude systématique et écologique des athérines des côtes françaises. – Mém. Mus. natn. Hist. nat., A60, No.2:1–74. 1969. ill., 8 pls.

Kleijn, L.J.K. Identificatie van de in Nederland voorkomende soort van het genus Umbra Walbaum, 1792 (Hondsvissen). – Natuurh. Maandbl., 57, No.3:35–40. 1968.

Klyukanov, V.A. Morphological Principles of the Systematics of Smelts of the Genus Osmerus (Osmeridae). – Zool. Zh., 48, No.1:99–109. 1969.

Klyukanov, V.A. Classification of Smelts (Osmeridae) in Relation to the Features of the Skeletal Structure of the Genus Thaleichthys. – Ibid., 49, No.3:399–417. 1970. 10 figs.

Kotthaus, A. Flagelloserranus, a New Genus of Serranid Fishes with the Descriptions of Two New Species (Pisces, Percomorphi). – Dana Rep., 78:1–32. 1970. 25 figs.

Krefft, G. Paraholtbyrnia cyanocephala gen. nov., spec. nov. (Pisces, Salmoniformes, Alepocephaloidei), ein neuer Searside aus dem tropischen Atlantik. – Arch. FischWiss., 18, No.1:1–11. 1967.

Krefft, G. Knorpelfische (Chondrichthyes) aus dem tropischen Ostatlantik.– Atlant. Rep., 10:33–76. 1968.

Lachner, E.A. and R.E. Jenkins. Systematics, Distribution and Evolution of the Chub Genus Nocomis (Cyprinidae) in the Southwestern Ohio River Basin, with the Description of a New Species. – Copeia, 3:557–580. 1967. 7 figs.

Lane, E.D. and K.W. Steward. A Revision of the Genus Hoplunnis Kaup (Apodes, Muraenesocidae), with the Description of a New Species. – Contr. Mar. Sci., 13:51–64. 1968.

Lindsey, C.C. and C.S. Woods (editors). Biology of Coregonid Fishes. – Canada, Univ. Manitoba Press. 1970. 29 papers: 570 pp., 208 figs., 114 tables.

López, R.B. and J.P. Castello. Corvinas del Rio de la Plata (Pisces, Sciaenidae). – Boln. Serv. hidrog. naval, 5, No.1:14–27. 1968.

McAllister, D.E. Evolution of Branchiostegals and Classification of Teleostome Fishes. – Bull. Natn. Mus. Can., 221:1–239. 1968. 21 pls.

McDowall, R.M. Relationships of Galaxioioid Fishes with a Further Discussion of Salmoniform Classification. – Copeia, 4:796–824. 1969.

McKay, R.J. The Genus Tandya in Western Australia, with a Description of a New Opisthognathid Fish, Tandya reticulata sp. nov. – J. Proc. R. Soc. N.S.W., 52, No.1:1–2. 1969.

Marshall, N.B. Bathyprion dana. A New Genus and Species of Alepocephaliform Fishes. – Dana Rep., 68:3–9. 1966.

Menezes, N.A. Systematics and Evolution of the Tribe Acestrorhynchini (Pisces, Characidae). – Archos. Zool. Est. S Paulo, 18, Nos.1–2:1–150. 1969.

Miller, P.J. Systematics and Biology of the Leopard-spotted Goby, Gobius ephippiatus (Teleostei: Gobiidae), with Description of a New Genus and Notes on the Identity of G. macrolepis Kolombatovic. – J. Mar. Biol. Ass. U.K., 49:831–855. 1969. 7 figs., 1 pl.

Milward, N.E. The Clinidae of Western Australia (Teleostei, Blennioidea). – J. Proc. R. Soc. N.S.W., 50, No.1:1–9. 1967.

Moore, D. Triggerfishes (Balistidae) of the Western Atlantic. – Bull. Mar. Sci., 17, No.3:689–722. 1967.

Myers, G.S. Trends in the Evolution of Teleostean Fishes. – Stanford Ichthyol. Bull., 7:27–30. 1958.

Nafpaktitis, B.G. Taxonomy and Distribution of the Lanternfishes, Genera Lobianchia and Diaphus in the North Atlantic. – Dana Rep., 73:1–131. 1968. 69 figs., 2 pls.

Nafpaktitis, B.G. and M. Nafpaktitis. Lanternfishes (Family Myctophidae) Collected during Cruises 3 and 6 of the R/V Anton Bruun in the Indian Ocean. – Bull. Los Angeles County Mus. Nat. Hist. Sci., 5:1–79. 1969. 82 figs.

Nafpaktitis, B.G. and J.R. Paxton. Review of the Lanternfish Genus Lampadena with a Description of a New Species. – Contr. Sci. Los Angeles County Mus., 138:1–29. 1968.

Nekrasov, V.V. Horsemackerels (Family Carangidae) of the Eastern Coast of Africa. – Trudy Azov-Chernomorsk. Nauchno-Issled. Inst. Morsk. Ryb. Khoz. Okeanogr., 29:89–133. 1970.

Nelson, G.J. Infraorbital Bones and their Bearing on the Phylogeny and Geography of Osteoglossomorph Fishes. – Am. Mus. Novit., 2394:1–37, figs.1–22. 1969.

Nelson, G.J. Origin and Diversification of Teleostean Fishes. – Ann. New-York Acad. Sci., 167, No.1:18–30. 1969. 3 figs.

Nielsen, J.G. and V. Larsen. Synopsis of the Bathylaconidae (Pisces, Isospondyli), with a New Eastern Pacific Species. – Galathea Rep., 9:221–238, pls.13–15. 1968. 10 figs.

Parameswaran, S., C Selvaraj, and S. Radhakrishnan. A Review of the Indian Freshwater Fishes of the Genus Ompok Lacépède. – J. Zool. Soc. India, 19, Nos.1–2:89–98. (1967) 1968.

Patterson, C. The Phylogeny of the Chimaeroids. – Phil. Trans. R. Soc., 249, No.747:101–219. 1965. 7 pls., 44 figs.

Pinchuk, V.I. On the Gobies (Family Gobiidae) from the Caucasian Rivers of the Black Sea Basin. – Vest. Zool., 2:31–38. 1964.

Poll, M. Anatomie et systématique des Polypterus. – Bull. Acad. r. Belg. Cl. Sci., 51, No.5:553–569. 1965.

Poll, M. Révision des Characidae nains Africains. – Annls. Mus. r. Afr. cent., Ser. Zool., 162:1–153, figs.1–32. 1967.

Poll, M. and C. Deswattines. Etude systématique des appareils respiratoire et circulatoire des Polypteridae. – Annls. Mus. r. Afr. cent., 158:1–63. 1967. 35 figs.

Poll, M. and J.P. Gosse. Révision des Malapteruridae (Pisces, Siluriformes) et description d'une deuxième espèce de silure électrique: Malapterurus microstoma sp. n. – Bull. Inst. r. Sci. nat. Belg., 45, No.38:1–12. 1969. ill.

Post, A. Die Paralepididae (Pisces) der 15. Forschungsfahrt des FFS "Walther Herwig." – Zool. Anz., 180, Nos.1–2:139–146. 1968.

Potter, J.C., W.J. Lanzing, and R. Strahan. Morphometric and Meristic Studies on Populations of Australian Lampreys of the Genus Mordacia. – J. Linn. Soc., Lond. (Zool.), 47, No.313:533–546. 1968.

Quintard-Dorques, B. Contribution à l'étude des poissons de la famille des Centracanthidae genre Spicara de la région de Sete. – Ass. reg. Etude Rech. Sci. Reims, 4, No.2:79–88. 1966.

Ragimov, D.B. On the Systematics of Fishes Belonging to the Genus Gobius in the Caspian Sea. – In: Biologicheskaya produktivnost' Kurinsko-Kaspiiskogo rybopromyslovogo raiona, pp.252–277. Baku. 1967. 3 figs., 10 pls.

Roberts, T. Osteology and Relationships of Characoid Fishes, Particularly the Genera Hepsetus, Salminus, Hoplias, Ctenolucius and Acestrorhynchus. – Proc. Calif. Acad. Sci., 36, No.15:391–500. 1969. ill.

Rosemary, H.L. and F.L.S. McConnell. The Cichlid Fishes of Guyana, South America, with Notes on their Ecology and Breeding Behavior. – Zool. Linn. Soc., 48:255–302. 1969. 3 figs.

Rosenblatt, R.H. and E.S. Hobson. Parrotfishes (Scaridae) of the Eastern Pacific, with a Generic Rearrangement of the Scarinae. – Copeia, 3:434–453. 1969.

Rosenblatt, R.H. and T.D. Parr. The Pacific Species of the Clinid Fish Genus Paraclinus. – Copeia, 1:1–20. 1969.

Rosenblatt, R.H. and B.J. Zahuranec. The Eastern Pacific Groupers of the Genus Mycteroperca, Including a New Species. – Calif. Fish Game, 53, No.4:228–245. 1967.

Roux, C. A propos des poissons du genre Umbrina (Sciaenides) des côtes atlantiques d'Amérique du Sud. – Bull. Mus. natn. Hist. nat., 40, No.2:261–264. 1968.

Sadowsky, V. Selachier aus dem litoral von São Paulo, Brasilien. – Beitr. neotrop. Fauna, 5:71–88. 1967. 1 fig., 5 pls.

Sandercock, F.K. and N.J. Wilimovsky. Revision of the Genus Enophrys. – Copeia, 4:832–853. 1968. 10 figs.

Sauskan, V.I. Morphology and Systematics of the Atlantic Hakes. – Trudy Atlant. Nauchno-Issled. Inst. Rub. Khoz. Okeanogr., 22:164–187. 1969.

Schubart, O. Sôbre algumas Loricariidae da bacia do Rio Mogi Guaçu (Pisces, Nemathognatha). – Bolm. Mus. nac. Rio de J., n.s. Zool., 251:1–19. 1964. 6 figs.

Schultz, L.P. A New Genus and New Species of Zoarcid Fish from the North Pacific Ocean. – Proc. U.S. Natn. Mus., 122, No.3598:1–5. 1967.

Schultz, L.P. The Taxonomic Status of the Controversial Genera and Species of Parrotfishes with a Descriptive List (Family Scaridae). – Smithsonian Contrib. to Zoology, 17:1–50, figs.1, 2. pls.1–8. 1969.

Shinohara, S. Studies of the Family Lutjanidae of Ryukyu Islands. Morphology, Taxonomy and Zoogeography. Mimeographed. 1963. 147 pp., 56 figs. (In Japanese.)

Shipp, R.L. and R.W. Verger. A New Puffer Fish Sphoeroides parvus from the Western Gulf of Mexico, with a Key to Species of Sphoeroides from the Atlantic and Gulf Coasts of the United States. – Proc. Biol. Soc. Wash., 82:477–488. 1969.

Shutov, V.A. Revision of the Genus Blicca and Some Indexes of Phyletic Relations between the Representatives of the Genus Abramis (Pisces, Cyprinidae). – Zool. Zh., 48, No.7:1105–1107. 1969.

Smith, J.L.B. Fishes of the Subfamily Nasinae with a Synopsis of the Prionurinae. – Ichthyol. Bull. Rhodes Univ., 32:635–682, figs.1–13, pl.104. 1966.

Smith, J.L.B. Studies in Carangid Fishes, 1, 2, 3. 1967; 4. 1968. – Ichthyol. Bull. Rhodes Univ., Occas. Papers, 12, 13, 14. 1967; 15. 1968, pp.139–184.

Spillman, J. Etude comparative de poissons téléostéens des genres Leucaspius et Phoxinellus (Pararhodeus) récoltés dans les eaux douces françaises et grecques.– Bull. Mus. natn. Hist. nat., 39, No.1:127–133. 1967.

Springer, V.G. Revision of the Circumtropical Shorefish Genus Entomacrodus (Blenniidae: Salariinae).– Proc. U.S.Natn. Mus., 122, No.3582:1–180. 1967. ill.

Springer, V.G. and W.F. Smith-Vaniz. Systematics and Distribution of the Monotypic Indo-Pacific Blenniid Fish Genus Atrosalarias. – Proc. U.S. Natn. Mus., 124, No.3643:1–13. 1968. ill.

Stokell, G. New Zealand Retropinnidae. – Rec. Canterbury Mus., 8, No.4:379–381. 1969.

Suwardji. Notes on the Genus Callionymus (Pisces, Callionymidae) Mostly from Indonesian Waters with the Description of Three New Species and a New Subspecies (Papers from Dr. Th. Mortensen's Pacific Expedition 1914–1916, 82). – Vidensk. Meddr. dansk naturh. Foren., 128:303–323. 1965.

Svetovidova, A.A. Systematics of the Central Asia Daces of the Genus Leuciscus (Cyprinidae, Pisces).– Vopr. Ikhtiol., 7, No.6:979–989. 1967.

Syad, Sabihul Hasan Zaidi, and M.Rahimullah Qureshi. Fishes of the Family Labridae Found in Pakistan Waters. – Sci. and Ind. (Pakistan), 5, No.3:418–434. 1967.

Taverne, L. Ostéologie du genre Gnathonemus Gill sensu stricto (Gnathonemus petersii (Gthr.) et espèces voisines) (Pisces, Mormyriformes). – Annls. Mus. r. Afr. cent., 170:1–91. 1968. 44 figs., 4 pls.

Taverne, L. Etude ostéologique des genres Boulengeromyrus Taverne et Géry, Genyomyrus Boulenger, Petrocephalus Marcusen (Pisces, Mormyriformes). – Ibid., Ser. Zool., 174:1–85. 1969. 2 pls., 46 figs.

T a y l o r, W.R. A Revision of the Catfish Genus N o t u r u s Rafinesque with an Analysis of Higher Groups in the Ictaluridae. - Bull. Smithsonian Inst. U.S. Nat. Mus., Wash. 1969. 315 pp., 21 pls.

T e m p l e m a n, W. A Review of the Morid Fish Genus H a l a r g y r e u s with First Records from the Western North Atlantic. - J. Fish Res. Bd. Can., 25, No.5:877-901. 1968.

T h o r n, C.H. A New Species of Mirapinniform Fish (Family Kasidoroidae) from the Western Indian Ocean. - J. Nat. Hist., Lond., 3, No.1:61-70. 1969.

T h y s van den A u d e n a e r d e, D.F.E. Les T i l a p i a (Pisces, Cichlidae) du sud-Cameroun et du Gabon. Etude systématique. - Annls. Mus. r. Afr. cent., Ser. Zool., 153:1-95, pl.11. 1966.

T h y s van den A u d e n a e r d e, D.F.E. Preliminary Contribution to a Systematic Revision of the Genus P e l m a t o c h r o m i s Hubrecht sensu lato (Pisces, Cichlidae). - Revue Zool. Bot. afr., 77 Nos.3-4:349-391. 1968

T h y s van den A u d e n a e r d e, D.F.E. Le statut taxonomique des espèces de Tilapie décrites par Aug. Duméril en 1959. - Ibid., 78, Nos.3-4:295-314. 1968.

T o m i n a g a, Y. Internal Morphology, Mutual Relationships and Systematic Position of the Fishes Belonging to the Family Pempheridae. - Jap. J. Ichthyol., 15, No.2:43-95. 1968.

T s a i C h u - fa. A Study of the Systematics of E t h e o s t o m a z o n a l e (Cope) and its Relatives, and the Phylogeny of Subgenus E t h e o s t o m a Rafinesque (Percidae, Teleostei). Thesis, Cornell University. 1966. 396 pp.

T o v a r - S e r p a, A. Peces del Oriente Peruano. Algunas especies de Loricariidae con referencia especial de la carachama P t e r y g o p l i c h t h y s m u l t i r a d i a t u s (Hancock). Ecologia y utilidad. - Biota, 6, No.50:201-259. 1967. 9 pls., 4 figs.

T y l e r, C.C. A Monograph on Plectognath Fishes of the Superfamily Triacanthoidea. - Monograph. Acad. Nat. Sci. Philad., 16:1-364. 1968. 209 figs.

W e i t z m a n, S.H. Review of South American Characid Fishes of Subtribe Nannostomina. - Proc. U.S. Natn. Mus., 119 (3538):1-56. 1966. 12 figs.

W e i t z m a n, S.H. The Origin of the Stomiatoid Fishes with Comments on the Classification of Salmoniform Fishes. - Copeia, 3:507-540. 1967.

W h i t e h e a d, P.J.P. Notes on the Herring-like Fishes of the Israel South Red Sea Expedition, 1962 (and Some Earlier Collections). - Sea Fish. Res. Stn. Israel. Haifa Bull., 41:3-6. 1966. 1 fig.

W h i t e h e a d, P.J.P. The Clupeoid Fishes Described by Lacépède and Cuvier and Valenciennes. - Bull. Br. Mus. Nat. Hist., Zool., Suppl., 2:1-180. 1967. 11 pls., 15 figs.

W h i t e h e a d, P.J.P. Indian Ocean Anchovies Collected by the Anton Bruun and Te Vega 1963-1964. -J. J. Mar. Biol. Ass. India, 9:13-37. 1967. 4 figs.

W h i t e h e a d, P.J.P. The Clupeoid Fishes Described by Bloch and Schneider. - Bull. Br. Mus. Nat. Hist., Zool., 17, No.7:263-279. 1969. 3 pls., 3 figs.

W h i t l e y, G.P. Scombroid Fishes of Australia and New Zealand. - Proc. Symp. Scombroid Fishes, Mar. Biol. Ass. India, 1:221-253. 1964.

W h i t l e y, G.P. Sharks of the Australian Region. - Aust. Zool., 14, No.2:173-188. 1967. 2 figs.

W h i t l e y, G.P. Ichthyological Oddities. — Ibid., 15, No.3:242—247, pl.12. 1970. 2 figs.

Y u n e r. Sea Breams (P a g r u s) in Turkish Waters. - Balyk ve balykkilek, 17, No.2:20-22. 1969. (In Turkish.)

Z a m b r i b o r s h c h, F.S. On the Systematics of Gobies from the Black Sea and the Sea of Azov. - Vest. Zool., 1:37-44. 1968.

Z a n a n d r e a, G., G. C a v i c c h i o l i, and P. G u a r n i e r i. Sui Cobitidi italiani. Richerche sistematiche e faunistiche. - Archo. zool. ital., 50:233-259. 1965. 1 pl., 11 figs.

Z a n d e r, C.D. Ökologische und morphologische Beiträge zur Systematik und geographischen Verbreitung der Gattung X i p h o p h o r u s (Pisces). - Mitt. hamb. zool. Mus. Inst., 64:87-125. 1967. 40 figs.

ADDITIONAL REGIONAL LITERATURE

0

B l a c k w e l d e r, R.E. Taxonomy: a Text and Reference Book. N.Y., London, Sydney, 1967.. 968 pp., ill.

Current Bibliography for Aquatic Sciences and Fisheries. - FAO, 13:1-409. London. 1969.

E d d y, S. How to Know the Freshwater Fishes. Iowa. 1969. 586 pp.

Nelson, G.J. Gill Arches and Phylogeny of Fishes with Notes on the Classification of Vertebrates. – Bull. Am. Mus. Nat. Hist., 141, No.4:479–552, pls.79–92. 1969.

Norman, J.R. A Draft Synopsis of the Orders, Families and Genera of Recent Fishes and Fishlike Vertebrates.– Bull. Br. Mus. Nat. Hist. 1966. 649 pp.

Smith, M. (ed.). J.L.B.Smith Ichthyological Papers 1931–1943, I:1–300; II:301–576. – Grahamstown, Rhodes University. 1969.

Tominaga, S. Anatomical Sketches of 500 Fishes. – Kadokawa Shoten, 1:1–191 (ill.), 1–274 (text). 1965; 2:1–204 (ill.), 1–312 (text); suppl. vol.:1–432. 1967.

Whitehead, P.J.P. The Reeves Collection of Chinese Fish Drawings. – Bull. Br. Mus. Nat. Hist., Hist. Ser., 3, No.7:193–233. 1969. 23 pls.

111

Berg, L.S. Freshwater Fishes of the USSR and Adjacent Countries. – Israel Program for Scientific Translations, 1. 1963, 602 pp.; 2. 1964, 504 pp.; 3. 1965, 520 pp., col. map.

Gundrizer, A.N. A Study of the Fishes of Tuva. – Uchen. Zap. Tomsk. Univ., 53:67–78. 1967.

Khokhlova, L.V. Fishes of the Selenga River. – In: Ryby i kormovye resursy basseinov rek i vodokhranilishch vost. Sibiri, pp.291–324. Krasnoyarsk. 1967.

Luk'yanchikov, F.V. Fishes of the Khatanga River System. – Ibid., pp.1–213 (11–93).

Strelkov, O.E. Study of the Ichthyofauna of the Tym River. – Uchen. Zap. Tomsk. Ped. Inst., 27:100–106. 1969.

211

Klyuchareva, O.A. Ichthyofauna of the Lagoon Lakes of Kunashir (Kurile Islands). – Zool. Zh., 46:348–392. 1967. 2 pls.

212

Kamohara, T. Fishes of Japan in Colour. Hoikusha, Osaka. 1967. I–XI, 1–135 pp., 64 pls., figs., map.

Mori, S. List of Animal and Plant Species, Living in or on Lake Biwa. – Mem. Fac. Sci. Kyoto Univ., Ser. Biol., 3:22–46. 1970.

Shibata, Y. A List of the Fresh- and Brackishwater Fishes of Tsushima, Preserved in the Osaka Museum of Natural History. – Bull. Osaka Mus. Nat. Hist., 21:19–29, figs.1–2. 1968.

213

Soulier, A. Preliminary Bibliography of Fish and Fisheries for the Republic of Korea. – Occ. Pap. Indo-Pacif. Fish Coun., 65, No.6:1–68. 1965.

222

Besednov, L.N. Ichthyofauna of the Gulf of Tonkin. – Uchen. Zap. Dal'nevost. Univ., 15, No.2:47–85. 1968.

Besednov, L.N. Fishes from the Gulf of Tonkin. – Izv. Tikhookean. Nauchno-Issled. Inst. Ryb. Khoz. Okeanogr. (TINRO), 66:1–138. 1969. 110 figs.

Johnson, D.S. Distributional Patterns of Malayan Freshwater Fish. – Ecology, 48:722–730. 1967. 1 fig.

223

Tortonese, E. Contributo allo studio sistematico e biogeographico. Study of the Fishes of New Guinea. – Ann. Mus. Civ. Stor. Nat. Giacomo Doria, 75:13–98. 1965.

225

Quiguer, J.P. Poissons des récifs coralliens de Nouvelle-Calédonie (Collection B. Salvat – premiere liste).– Cah. Pacif., 10:79–83. 1967.

231

Sanchez, R.J.F. Peces comunes de la costa Peruana. – Ser. Divulg. Cient. Peru, 2nd ed. (1st, 1955), 6:1–121. 1966. ill.

Walker, B.W. The Origin and Affinities of the Galapagos Shorefishes. – Proc. Symp. Galapagos Intern. Sci. Project, 7–16 January 1964, pp.172–174. Berkeley, Calif. Univ. Press. 1966.

232

Bussing, W.A. New Species and New Records of Costa Rican Freshwater Fishes; a Tentative List of Species.– Revta Biol. trop., 14, No.2:205–249. 1966.

Bussing, W.A. Familias de peces marinos costa-ricenses y de aguas contiguas. – Publs. Univ. Costa Rica, Ser. cienc. Natur., 6:1–39. 1969. ill.

Gosse, J.P. Poissons d'eau douce du versant pacifique du Costa Rica et de Panama récoltés par sa Majesté le roi Léopold de Belgique. – Bull. Inst. r. Sci. nat. Belg., 42, No.28:1–24. 1966. 1 fig.

233

Clifford, C.G. Some Common Marine Fishes of British Columbia. – Br. Columbia Provin. Mus. Dep. Recreation and Conservation. Handbook, 23:7–47. 1964. figs.

Contreras, B.S. Lista de peces de del estado de Nuevo Leon. – Cuad. Invest. Inv. cient. Univ. Nuevo Leon, Monterrey, 11:1–12. 1967.

Hernandez, E.R. and J.A. Martinez. Investigaciones ictiologicas en las costas de Baja California. 1. Lista de peces marinos de Baja California colectados en el periodo 1961–1965. – An. Inst. nac. Invest. Biol-Pesq. Mexico, 1:297–324. 1965. 1 map.

Romero, H. Catálogo sistemático de los peces de Alto Lerma con descripción de una nueva especie. – An. Esc. nac. Cienc. biol., Méx., 14, Nos.1/4:47–77. 1967.

Taylor, F.H.C. Unusual Fishes Taken by Midwater Trawl off the Queen Charlotte Islands, British Columbia. – J. Fish. Res. Bd. Can., 24, No.10:2101–2115, figs.1–4. 1967.

411

Becker, G.C. Fishes of Southwestern Wisconsin. – Trans. Wis. Acad. Sci. Arts Lett., 55:87–117. 1966. 1 fig.

Böhlke, J.E. and Ch.C.G. Chaplin. Fishes of the Bahamas and Adjacent Tropical Waters. Philadelphia. 1968. I–XXIII, 1–771 pp., 223 figs., 36 pls., 511 unnumbered figs.

Branson, B.A. Fishes of the Neosho River System in Oklahoma. – Am. Midl. Nat., 78, No.1:126–154. 1967.

Bullis, H.B. and J.R. Thompson. Collections by the Exploratory Fishing Vessels Oregon, Silver Bay, Combat and Pelican Made during 1956–1960 in the Southwestern North Atlantic. – Spec. Scient. Rep. U.S. Fish Wildl. Serv. Fisheries, 510:1–130. 1965.

Hernández, E.R. and J.P. Barrera. Investigaciones ictiologicas en las costas de Guerrero. 1. Lista de peces marinos de Guerrero colectados en el periodo 1961–1965. – An. Inst. nac. Invest. Biol-pesq. Mexico, 1:329–358. 1965. 1 map.

Perlmutter, A. Handbook for Identification of Marine Fishes (of the Atlantic Shore, U.S.A). – Moscow, "Pishchevaya promyshlennost'." 1970. 248 pp., ill.

Radakov, D.V. and N.E. Sal'nikov. Composition and Distribution of the Ichthyofauna in the Gulf of Mexico. – In: Sovet.-Kubinsk. rybokhoz. issled., 2:99–106. Moscow, "Pishchevaya promyshlennost'." 1967.

Scott, W.B. Freshwater Fishes of Eastern Canada. 2nd ed. – Univ. Toronto Press. 1967. 137 pp.

Scott, W.B. and E.J. Crossman. Checklist of Canadian Freshwater Fishes with Keys for Identification. – Life Sciences Miscellaneous Publs. Roy. Ontario Mus., Toronto. 1969. 104 pp., ill.

Summerfelt, R.C. Fishes of the Smoky Hill River, Kansas. – Trans. Kans. Acad. Sci., 70:102–139. 1967.

Tagatz, M.E. Fishes of the Johns River, Florida. – Q. Jl. Fla. Acad. Sci., 30, No.1:25–50. 1967.

Underhill, J.C. and J.B. Moyle. The Fishes of Minnesota's Lake Superior Region. – Conserv. Volunt., 31, No.177:29–53. 1968.

Whitworth, W.R., P.L. Berriena, and W.T. Keller. Freshwater Fishes of Connecticut. – Bull. St. Geol. Nat. Hist. Surv. Conn., 101:1–134. 1968.

412

Barriga, E. et al. La Isla de San Andrés. – Bogota: 1–52; Pisces: 78–98. 1969. ill.

Bussing, W.A. New Species and New Records of Costa Rican Freshwater Fishes; a Tentative List of Species. – Revta Biol. trop., 14, No.2:205–249. 1966.

Bussing, W.A. Familias de peces marinos, costa-ricensis y de aguas contiguas. – Publ. Univ. Costa Rica, Ser. Cienc. Natur., 6:1–39. 1969. ill.

Randall, J.E. Caribbean Reef Fishes. Jersey City. 1968. 318 pp., 224 figs. (col.)

413

Ringuelet, R.A. et al. Los peces argentinos de agua dulce. La Plata. 1967. 602 pp., 10 pls., 37 figs.

421

Penrith, M.J. The Fishes of Tristan da Cunha Gough Island and the Vema Seamount. – Ann. S. Afr. Mus., 48:523–548. 1967. 1 pl., 2 figs.

431

Blanc, M., J. Cadenat, and A. Stauch. Contribution à l'étude de l'ichthyofaune de l'île Annobon. – Bull. Inst. fr. Afr. noire, A30, No.1:238–256. 1968.

Massuti, M. Los fondos de pesca en la plataforma continental de Marruecos, Sáhara español Mauritania, Senegal, República de Guinea, Ensenada di Biafra y Archipiélago de Cabo Verde. – Trab. Inst. esp. Oceanogr., Madrid, 34:7–97. 1967. 105 figs.

Navarro, F. de et al. La pesca de arrastre los fondos del Cabo blanco y del banco Arguin (Africa sahariana). – Ibid., 18:1–225, pls.1–38. 1943.

Sanches, J.G. Peixes de Angola (Teleósteos). – Notas mimeogr. Cent. Biol. pisc., 46:1–227. 1966. 200 figs.

Thys van den Audenaerde, D.F.E. The Freshwater Fishes of Fernando Poo. – Verh. K. vlaam. Acad. Wet. Klasse der wetenschappen, Ser.A, 29, No.100:1–167, fig.47. 1967.

Thys van den Audenaerde, D.F.E. Addendum to the "Freshwater Fishes of Fernando Poo." On Some Fishes Collected by Col. J.J. Scheel. – Revue Zool. Bot. afr., 78, Nos.1–2:123–128. 1968.

432

Casier, E. Le Landénien de Dormaal (Brabant) et sa faune ichthyologique. – Mém. Inst. r. Sci. nat. Belge, 156:1–66. 1967. 8 pls., 10 figs., 2 tables.

Grimås, U. On the Fauna in the Lower Reaches of the River Viskan, Southern Sweden. – Rep. Inst. Freshwat. Res. Drottningholm, 47:87–97. 1967. 7 tables, 1 map.

Maitland, P.S. The Fauna of the River Endrick. – In: Studies on Loch Lomond. 2. – Univ. Glasgow and Blackie, London. 1966. 194 pp., 30 figs.

Muus, B.J. The Fauna of Danish Estuaries and Lagoons. – Meddr. Danm. Fisk.- og Havunders, 5:1–316. 1967. 119 figs., 60 tables.

Peronaci, A. La fauna delle acque interne e del mare. – Florence, Edit. Olimpia. 1966. 537 pp.

Rudnicki, A. Ryby wód polskich (Atlas wyd. 2). – Warsaw, Państw. wydawn. szkol. 1968. 103 pp.

Titenkov, I.S. Fishes and Fisheries of Lake Ladoga (Laboratory of Lake Fishery of the State Scientific Research Institute of Lake and River Fisheries (GosNIORKh)).— In: Biol. resursy Ladozhsk. ozera (Zool.), pp.130–173. Leningrad, "Nauka." 1968.

Vibritskas, Yu., A. Astrauskas, and P.V. Sinyavichyus. Ichthyofauna of Lake Zhuvintas. – In: Zapovednik Zhuvintas, pp.301–313. Vilnius. 1968.

Wheeler, A. The Fishes of the British Isles and North-West Europe. – London, Macmillan. 1969. 613 pp., 177+392 figs.

435

Bănărescu, P. Lista revizuită a peştilor din România. – Bull. Inst. Cerc. Proiectări pisc., 27, No.3:53–62. 1968.

Buşniţă, T. Die Ichthyofauna des Donauflusses. – Limnol. Donau, 3:198–224. 1967. 4 figs.

Cottiglia, M. La distribuzione della ittiofauna dulciacquicola in Sardegna. – Riv. idrobiol., 7, Nos.1–2:63–116. 1968.

Dorko, J. Die Ichthyofauna in der Tief-Ebene Blatská nížina. – Acta Fac. Rerum nat. Univ. comen., Bratisl. (Zool.), 12:183–191. 1967. (English summary.)

Dudich, E. Systematisches Verzeichnis der Tierwelt der Donau mit einer zusammenfassenden Erläuterung. – Limnol. Donau, 3:4–69. 1967.

436

Ben-Tuvia, A. Red Sea Fishes Recently Found in the Mediterranean. – Copeia, 2:254–275. 1966.

Dieuzeide, R. and M. Novella (collab. J. Roland). Catalogue des poissons des côtes algériennes. – Alger., I:1–135. 1953. 73 figs. (Trav. Stat. Aquicult. et Pêche de Castiglione, n.s. No.4. 1952 (1953)); II:1–258. 1954. 135 figs. (ibid., No.5. 1953 (1954)); III:1–384. 1955. 202 figs. (ibid., No.6. 1954 (1955)).

Dieuzeide, R. and J. Roland. Complément au Catalogue des poissons des côtes algériennes. – Trav. Stat. Aquicult. et Pêche de Castiglione. Alger., n.s. No.8:83–106. figs.1–8. 1956 (1957); No.9:103–132, figs.1–12. 1958 (1959); No.10:21–59. 1958–1959 (1960). 12 figs.

Massuti, M. Carta de pesca de la region surmediterranea española (desde Estepona a Adra). – Trab. Inst. esp. Oceanogr., 33:4–24. 1967. 6 figs., 4 maps.

Michailova, L. Über die Ichthyofauna Thrakiens. – Fauna Trakiya, Sofia, 2:265–289. 1965. 8 figs. (In Bulgarian, German summary.)

Rini, G. Atlante dei pesci delle coste italiane. 1. Leptocardi – Ciclostomi – Selaci. – Milan, Mondo Sommerso Editrice. 1967. 206 pp.

Tortonese, E. Pesci e Cetacei del Mar Ligure con particolare riguando alle specie economicamente importanti. Genoa. 1965. 216 pp., 150 figs.

5

Blache, J. et al. Première contribution à la connaissance de la pêche dans le bassin hydrographique Logove-Chari – Lac Tchad. – Off. Rech. Sci. Tech. Outre-Mer. Paris. 1962 (1963). 143 pp., 61 pls., 10 figs.

6

Kotthaus, A. Fische des Indischen Ozeans. Ergebnisse der ichthyologischen Untersuchungen während der Expedition des Forschungsschiffes "Meteor" in den Indischen Ozean. Oktober 1964 bis Mai 1965. A. Systematischer Teil III. Ostariophysi und Apodes. – Meteor. Forschungsergebn., D, 3:14–56. 1968.

61

Ben-Tuvia, A. Report on the Fisheries, Investigations of the Israel South Red Sea Expedition, 1962. – Bull. Sea Fish Res. Stn. Israel, 52:21–55, figs.1–6. 1968.

Fourmanoir, P. and P. Guézé. Poissons nouveaux ou peu connus provenant de la Réunion et de Madagascar. – Cah. O.R.S.T.O.M. Océanogr., 5, No.1:47–58. 1967.

Pienaar Uys de Villiers. The Freshwater Fishes of the Kruger National Park. – Pretoria, Nat. Parks Board, II:1–1196. 1968. ill.

Tortonese, E. Fishes from Eilat (Red Sea). – Bull. Sea Fish. Res. Stat. Ministry Agric., Israel, 51:6–30. 1968.

631

McKay, R.J. Additions to the Fauna of Western Australia. – West. Aust. Nat., 10:92–95. 1967. 1 fig.

632

Mooreland, J.M. Marine Fishes of New Zealand. Wellington. 1968. 56 pp.

Skrzynski, W. Freshwater Fishes of the Catcham Islands. – N.Z.J. Mar. Freshwat. Res., 1:89–98. 1967. 1 fig.

Whitley, G.P. A Checklist of the Fishes Recorded from the New Zealand Region. – Aust. Zool., 15, No.1:1–102. 1968.

7

Andriashev, A.P. Biogeography and Ecology in Antarctica. 25. A General Review of the Antarctic Fish Fauna. – Monographiae Biol., 15:491–550. 1965. 18 figs.

Bellisio, N.B. Peces antarticos del sector argentino. V. – Publ. serv. hidrogr. naval, 905:1–45. 1967 (1968). ill.

Everson, I. Inshore Fishes from the South Orkney and South Shetland Islands. The Antarctic Peninsula and South Georgia. – Bull. Br. Antarct. Surv., 19:89–96. 1969.

Gosse, J.P. Poissons récoltés par l'expédition Antarctique Belge Iris, 1965. – Bull. Inst. r. Sci. nat. Belge, 42, No.24:1–16. 1966.

Permitin, Yu.E. New Data on the Specific Composition and Distribution of Fishes of the Scotia Sea in the Antarctic (Communication 2). – Vopr. Ikhtiol., 9, No.2:221–239. 1969.

ADDITIONAL LITERATURE (ADD. II)

Cohen, D.M. How Many Recent Fishes Are There? – Proc. Calif. Acad. Sci., 38, No.17:341–346. 1970. 1 fig.

Nielsen, J.G. Redescription and Reassignment of *Parabrotula* and *Leucobrotula* (Pisces, Zoarcidae). – Vidensk. Meddr. dansk. naturh. Foren, 131:225–249. 1968.*

* See families 388 and 394.

Nielsen, J.G. Systematics and Biology of the Aphyonidae (Pisces, Ophidioidea). – Galathea Rep., **10**:1–90. 1969. 57 figs., 4 pls.*

Okamura, O. Macrourina (Pisces). – Fauna japonica. 1970. 216 pp., 87 figs., 44 pls.

Rass, T.S. (ed.) The Life of Animals. Fishes, 4, No.1:1–655. – Moscow, "Prosveshchenie." 1971. 221 figs., 54 pls.

Robins, C.H. and C.R.Robins. The Eel Family Dysommidae (Including the Dyssominidae and Nettodaridae), its Osteology and Composition, Including a New Genus and Species. – Proc. Acad. Nat. Sci. Philad., 122, No.6:293–335. 1970. ill.**

* See family 394. Family 394a. Aphyonidae differs in the number of precaudal vertebrae: 34–48, instead of the 9–23 in other families of the suborder, and in the absence of scales, pyloric caeca, and spines on the operculum.

** See families 191, 191a, 187, footnote.

INDEXES OF NAMES OF FAMILIES

The names of orders and families accepted in this work are printed in bold face.

The reference is not to the page number, but to the **number** of the order, family, etc.

An italicized number of a family means that the systematic group of a rank higher than the family (superfamily, order, subclass, class) is placed before the indicated number of the family in the section "check-list of families."

For families and orders recognized as valid in this work, besides the number are also given the number of the thesis in the key and the number of the appropriate figure, accompanied by an asterisk.

Order of references: number of family, thesis, figure(s), and additional data (with the abbreviations fn. =footnote, supp. = supplement), e.g.

Acipenseridae 50; 16—1; 230*, 231*
Acipenseriformes *50*; 0—31; 21*, 22*
Aulopodidae 109; 23—17; 318*; supp. 23—1

*INDEX OF LATIN NAMES**

* [Reproduced from the Russian original.]

*INDEX OF NAMES IN VARIOUS WESTERN LANGUAGES**

* [Reproduced photographically from the Russian original.]

*INDEX OF RUSSIAN NAMES**

* [This index does not include names which are direct transcriptions of the Latin names of fishes.]

INDEX OF CHINESE AND JAPANESE NAMES IN LATIN TRANSCRIPTION